G.K.'S WEEKLY

A Sampler

G.K.CHESTERTON

G.K.'S WEEKLY

A Sampler

Edited with an Introduction by
Lyle W. Dorsett

LOYOLA UNIVERSITY PRESS
Chicago

Loyola University Press
3441 North Ashland Avenue
Chicago, Illinois 60657

Library of Congress Cataloging-in-Publication Data
GK's weekly, a sampler.
Thirty issues of the journal published by
G.K. Chesterton from 1925 to 1936.
Includes index.
1. Chesterton, G. K. (Gilbert Keith), 1874-1936—
Political and social views. 2. Great Britain—
Politics and government—1910-1936—Sources.
3. Great Britain—Intellectual life—20th century—
Sources. I. Chesterton, G. K. (Gilbert Keith),
1874-1936. II. Dorsett, Lyle W. III. G.K.'s weekly.
PR4453.C4Z6474 1986   828'91209   86-10319
ISBN O-8294-0531-3

Design by C.L. Tornatore

I dedicate this volume, with love,
to my nieces and nephews:
The Dorris children
Edie, Currey, Marah, Duncan, Carolina, Henry

CONTENTS

PREFACE

IT IS COMMONLY said that there is nothing so out of date as yesterday's newspaper. This conviction causes most people to use dated periodicals for wrapping garbage or kindling the fireplace. Folks with a conservationist nature might collect newspapers for recycling, feeling solace in the knowledge that their stacks of yesterday's news will become the pages of tomorrow's books. But few people gather old news journals for republication a generation later.

My involvement in gathering thirty issues of a half-century-old periodical for reprinting requires an explanation. One impetus springs from my historian's commitment to finding, preserving, and making available to a thoughtful public the records of a bygone era. *GK's Weekly* is scarce. Few complete sets of this periodical published from March 1925 through December 1936 are still preserved. There is also something fascinating about reading old periodicals. Perusing the classifieds, reading the advertisements, and dipping into front-page news of yesteryear touches the antiquarian nature that lurks inside so many of us. Furthermore, for those who know and love the writings of Gilbert Keith Chesterton, this weekly that bears his initials contains some of his scarcest prose, making the reprinting of this weekly paper a service to people who appreciate the late Englishman's

work. Finally, the thirty unabridged and unedited weeklies bound here are reprinted because the Reverend Daniel L. Flaherty, S.J., Director of Loyola University Press in Chicago, enthusiastically shared my vision for promulgating the story of G.K. Chesterton. Father Flaherty agrees with my desire to introduce Chesterton and his writings to those who are unfamiliar with the man and his works, and he joins me in wanting to make some rare Chestertoniana available to the sizable group of avid Chesterton readers.

A few words need to be said about my particular choice of thirty issues of *GK's Weekly*. There is no magic in thirty. Nevertheless, I decided this was a large enough sample to give the reader more than a superficial glimpse of the paper, yet not so bulky as to make the book impossible to hold in one's lap while reading. The specific issues reprinted here are representative of the life cycle of the paper. The first four numbers demonstrate the paper's beginnings, and they show how the editors defined their objectives. The last two issues in this book encompass Chesterton's final contribution, as well as the memorials written by his friends and colleagues at the time of his death. The other two dozen selections are representative samples from each year between 1925 and 1936. In selecting these I have attempted to give an overview of the era, with an eye to including representative subjects that Chesterton and the staff cared about. I likewise tried to present news and commentary focusing on some of the major events that took place in Britain and the rest of the world during those tumultuous years.

I am indebted to Father Flaherty for putting his distinguished press behind this venture. Without him there would be no book. My obligations also extend to Father Brocard Sewell and Mr. Gregory Macdonald, both of whom worked at the *Weekly* and knew Chesterton. They each welcomed me and openly shared their reminiscences and understanding. I am also grateful to Father Ian Boyd, Professor of English Literature at St. Thomas More College in Saskatchewan and editor of *The Chesterton Review,* for critically reading the Introduction. These four men neither bear responsibility for errors in the introduction, nor necessarily endorse my interpretations. Their devotion to truth, scholarship, and ideas, however, have enhanced this project. My wife, Mary Hayes Dorsett, and my colleagues at the Marion E. Wade Collection, Wheaton College—Evelyn Brace, Ruth Cording, P.A. Hargis, Marjorie Mead, Susan Sanders, and Thad Voss—have all been extremely supportive and helpful.

LYLE W. DORSETT

Wheaton, Illinois

INTRODUCTION

I

THIRTY issues of *GK's Weekly*, unabridged and unedited, are reprinted in their original 8½" x 11" format in this volume to give the modern reader a taste of the rich fare served to British readers between mid-March 1925 and the close of 1936. For over ten years, this unique weekly periodical came out of Little Essex Street, Strand, in London. Printed on cheap wood pulp paper that is now yellowed and crumbling, this journal of opinion presented a non-conventional view of world economic, political, and social issues.

During the years *GK's Weekly* was published, people in Great Britain experienced shock waves from some of the most potent upheavals that ever touched a nation. Underlying most of the changes were the twin forces of industrialization and urbanization. Britain developed an urban-industrial economy before other European countries, and it did so with intensity. For better or worse, by the eve of World War I Britain had seven standard metropolitan areas or "conurbations," while no other European nation boasted more than two. Over eighty percent of the total population was urban—a higher percentage than any other European nation. Older cities such as London, Liverpool, and Manchester grew larger, and new cities like Middlesbrough sprung up as if by magic.

Great population shifts accompanied urban growth in the 19th and early 20th centuries. Every year, thousands of people deserted farms and rural villages for employment opportunities in the cities. English, Scottish, and Welsh newcomers were joined by thousands of Irish urbanites who had fled the Emerald Isle for Britain's factories during and after the famine. The polyglot nature of the cities was even more marked by the time of World War I, because Great Britain's urban areas absorbed large numbers of the East European Jews who had been driven from the Continent by the savage "rural depopulation" persecutions.

In the wake of massive immigration and farm-to-city migration came problems unprecedented in world history. Factories, warehouses, and railroad yards disrupted neighborhoods; the air was filled with noise and smoke. Housing shortages led to make-shift dwellings that were neither safe nor

1

sightly; facilities for health care and education seldom equalled the need. Streets required paving, sewage systems were outmoded or nonexistent, and police and fire protection failed to keep pace with demand.

Because Great Britain was the first nation to experience massive urbanization and industrialization, there were no models to imitate in solving problems. Nevertheless, a variety of reforms were offered at the local and national levels. Panaceas were presented by politicians, journalists, educators, and religious leaders, as well as those who suffered the brunt of the pain. But each measure of reform was costly, imperfect, and controversial.

Although World War I drew attention away from the nation's ills, the respite was short lived. Temporarily inflated farm prices dropped, overseas markets were disrupted, and a monstrous national debt led to boisterous calls for economy despite the need for reforms. Outbursts of labor unrest plagued the British Isles in the 1920s, with growing trade unionism and militant agitation culminating in the General Strike of 1926. This event paralyzed and injured the economy, but its effects were not as devastating as the eruptions of nationalism that permanently split and tore the fabric of the nation. Displays of nationalism in Scotland and Wales were disconcerting, but they were minor compared to the civil war that exploded in Ireland. Indeed, a temporary cessation to the bloodletting came only after January 1922, when the 26 southern counties of Ireland were allowed to form the Irish Free State, leaving the six Protestant counties in Ulster as the only remnant of Ireland in the United Kingdom.

Disillusionment with the war, the economy, and the political system spilled over into discontent and even disdain for the traditional arbiters of moral standards. Nowhere was this more evident than in religion. A.J.P. Taylor noted in his survey

history of the period that there was widespread rejection of the dogmas of revealed religion during the 1920s. This development he maintained, "was as great a happening as any in English history since the conversion of the Anglo-Saxons to Christianity."[1] The Book of Common Prayer was revised, and membership and attendance fell off in the Church of England. The chapels in Scotland and Wales suffered membership loss as well. The Roman Catholic Church was less obviously affected, but this was due more to its sizable Irish membership than to influence among the people. Many of those people who gave up faith in God placed it in themselves or in material well-being. Others drifted into agnosticism, while thousands sought meaning in Eastern religions or modernist "New Religions."

Traditional views of the family, as well as religion, were questioned. Feminism grew and spread during this time. Women not only won the right to vote (partially in 1918 and conclusively in 1928), but they also rebelled against the double standard of sexual taboos for women, unveiled less modest clothing that Victorians thought scandalous, and insisted on their right to consume alcohol and smoke cigarettes in public. Women demanded and won a few victories against discriminatory practices in education and the marketplace. They battled, too, for at least an equal voice with men in family planning and birth control.

Intellectual trends both reflected and inspired the revolt against 19th century mores and folkways. Sigmund Freud was widely discussed, even if few people actually read his books. Indeed, those who disliked the new face of Great Britain blamed it on the analyst and the automobile, both of which symbolized the new independence. Freud, however, was only one spokesman for the post-war culture. Socialism was celebrated by leaders such as playwright George Bernard Shaw and the novelist H.G.

Wells. Victorian idealism was thunderously ridiculed by philosophers Bertrand Russell and G.E. Moore. The avant-garde "Bloomsbury Group" of intellectuals and artists, which included such lights as Virginia Woolf, played a significant role in the erosion of commitment to conventional ways of viewing life.

Decadence, nihilism, and a full spectrum of liberated cultural self-expression was manifested in more than the arts; it was lived out in free love, homosexuality, and revolts against all forms of established authority. New "isms," movements, clubs, and cults found fertile ground in the soil of post-war urban and industrialized Britain. Though these voices of change battered the bulwarks of tradition, the scaffolding of Victorian life and thought did not entirely crumble. Indeed, in the face of increasingly vocal and powerful opposition, the guardians of convention built surprisingly powerful defense works. Combatants from the left and right armed themselves and did battle for two decades, until Adolf Hitler's Third Reich turned the eyes of Great Britain away from itself and its problems, and towards the old enemy across the English Channel.

II

IT WAS DURING this exciting and tumultuous time between the wars that *GK's Weekly* was published. Gilbert Keith Chesterton, the already famous and controversial journalist whose initials adorn this publication, was determined to make a difference for good in his world beset by problems. Born into a prosperous, upwardly mobile, middle-class family in West London, G.K. was the oldest of three children. From the outset he was a remarkable lad. Noted for his apparent backwardness in early life, the youngster did not learn to talk until he was three, and he was unable to read until age eight. Assumed to be dull by his teachers, he appeared absent-minded as well as a slow learner. Besides his somewhat sluggish mental powers, he grew up faster than his peers. Attaining six feet in height by his teens, he was always taller and lankier than his school friends. Furthermore, he exhibited all the awkwardness that frequently accompanies rapid growth.[2]

The gangly boy had a brother five years his junior named Cecil. The two would be close friends until the latter died from wounds he received battling for Britain in World War I. There was an older sister, too, but she died when Gilbert was young. His father's steadfast refusal to discuss either her existence or her death later caused his son much pain.[3]

Despite that dark secret in the boy's world, he was inherently pleasant and endowed with a warm sense of humor. His childhood and adolescent years were filled with family companionship and love, as well as books—some of which were read to him and others which he later on read to himself. Literature opened up his imagination and, early on, he communicated his fantasies in poems, stories, and drawings. By the time Gilbert reached the end of his teens, thoughtful observers knew he was brilliant rather than dull. Indeed, although one doctor labeled him either "a genius or an idiot," the High Master at his school assured his mother that he was "six foot of genius."[4]

While most of his fellow students were packing off to Oxford, Cambridge, or the less-celebrated universities, G.K. Chesterton remained in London and attended art school. From 1892 until 1895 he studied at the Slade School of Art, and during that period he sometimes listened to lectures in English Literature at University College. In love with literature and art, the young student grappled with a tangle of agnosticism (his parents were vaguely Unitarian if not agnostics) and fashionable new religions promulgated by literary esthetes and artists who either dipped into those stylish faiths or tended to be atheists. Essentially, Chesterton longed for something to believe in and a medium of thought with which to express it.

While he was studying art and weighing his ability to earn a living with sketches, he found modest success as a writer. Through publishing poetry and reviews in the early 1890s while still a student, he gradually discerned that his future lay primarily with words rather than drawings. By 1895 Chesterton left the Slade School and took a position with a publisher. Soon thereafter he was on his own as a free-lance writer.

Greybeards at Play and *The Wild Knight and Other Poems* established his reputation as a poet of promise by 1900. Then his first major prose work, *The Defendant* (1901), underscored his versatility and some of the themes he would champion the rest of his life. In this book published half a dozen years after he left art school, the aspiring writer defended patriotism, humility, detective stories, and the "Man [who] was rejected of men" at Calvary.[5]

Gilbert Chesterton was gifted with a fine mind, complemented by a keen sense of imaginative vision. He could see depths and angles others missed, and he had a sharp and clear writing style that enabled him to describe what he saw. By the early 20th century he observed the shallowness of the established scepticism of the educated class. It puzzled him that these people embraced values, and yet denied all basis for their value system. He was equally unimpressed by a growing class of spiritual seekers— especially those who claimed to search for truth but vilified anyone who claimed to have found it. The spread of Socialism likewise failed to impress him. The problems of urban industrialism convinced him that mere transfer of ownership from private investors to the State was no solution for a fundamental problem that was disturbing the very moorings of the nation he was beginning to love.

During his years of searching for truth and meaning, a number of people impressed him as being extraordinarily sensible. One of these was an Anglican assistant curate named Conrad Noel, and the other was a woman who, as he described her, "actually practised a religion." He noted that "any number of people proclaimed religions, chiefly oriental religions, analyzed or argued about them; but that anybody who could regard religion as a practical thing like gardening was something quite new to me and, to her neighbors, new and incomprehensible." To "all that agnostic and mystic world" that Chesterton lived in, "practising a religion was much more puzzling than professing it."[6]

Chesterton was never a slave to the dictates of consensus. He began to question the conventional wisdom of his peers in journalism, education, the arts, and the professions. Much of what had passed for schools of thought were really nothing more than gropings, negation, and curiosity. He had a vision of what it all meant. "There was no Theistic Church; there was no Theosophical Brotherhood; there were no Ethical Societies; there were no New Religions," he wrote in his *Autobiography*, "but I saw Israel scattered on the hills as sheep that have not a shepherd; and I saw a large number of sheep run about bleating eagerly in whatever neighborhood it was supposed that a shepherd might be found." In his *Autobiography* also, Chesterton recalled that in these years immediately after the turn of the century, he began "to piece together the fragments of the old religious scheme." The more he observed human nature, the more he grew convinced that it was unfortunate that the scheme had been cast aside. To be sure, many of the spokesmen for the post-Christian society were noble, and they held "noble and necessary truths in the social and secular area." But, he continued, "even these they held less firmly than they might have done, if there had been anything like a fundamental principle of morals and metaphysics to support them."[7] Finally, Chesterton said, "I began to examine more exactly the general Christian theology which many execrated and few examined. I soon found that it did in fact correspond to many of [my] experiences of life.... The old theological theory seemed more or less to fit into the experience, while the new and negative theories did not fit into anything, least of all each other."[8]

During these years of moving toward at least a nominally Christian stance, Chesterton was building a reputation as an able essayist, critic, and novelist. Between 1902 and 1906 he published eight books, including the popular little volumes on *Robert Browning, G.F. Watts,* and *Charles Dickens.* His well-received novel, *The Napoleon of Notting Hill,* came out during this period, but nothing attracted more attention than *Heretics*. This book, which included previously published and reworked newspaper articles attacking modernist philosophy, drew criticism because he tore into fashionable assumptions without offering anything in their place.

Two years later, Chesterton answered this criticism. He committed himself to paper and the public. *Orthodoxy* was unveiled in 1908, making the already controversial journalist even more embattled. In this important book, still in print nearly eight decades later, G.K. Chesterton took his stand as one of those rare intellectuals who accepts the Apostle's Creed because it is true, and because it is "the best root of energy, and sound ethics."⁹

Orthodoxy put Chesterton, at the age of 34, squarely into the small and besieged camp of early 20th-century Christian apologists. Here he would stand until his death in 1936, adding such classics to his list of publications as *St. Francis of Assisi* (1923), *The Everlasting Man* (1925), and *St. Thomas Aquinas* (1933). Although the great defender of the faith is celebrated for these books, many other works such as *The Man Who Was Thursday* (1908), *What's Wrong With the World* (1910), *The Ballad of the White Horse* (1911), *The Victorian Age in Literature* (1913), *Robert Louis Stevenson* (1927), *The Return of Don Quixote* (1927), and his Father Brown detective stories have established him as one of the most versatile and original writers in the first half of this century.

To understand Chesterton and the mass of writing he produced, it is necessary to grasp his strongest convictions. He was markedly influenced by the writings of St. Thomas Aquinas and the late 19th-century revival of the Thomist tradition. Chesterton eventually came to embrace natural law, popular sovereignty, and the inherent right to overthrow governments that interfere with

these concepts. In the same vein the prolific author distrusted riches, and he maintained sincere concerns for the poor. Indeed, he was stirred by Pope Leo XIII's 1891 encyclical, *Rerum Novarum,* which advocated sympathy for the working class and a more equitable distribution of property.¹⁰

Because Chesterton became a Roman Catholic in 1922 (and some say he would have become one years before if it had not been for his Anglo-Catholic wife), it is often argued that nearly everything he wrote emanated from that perspective. This is not true.¹¹ To be sure, after 1922 Chesterton spoke as a Catholic, and he took Catholic philosophy and ethics to the common people. But he was always open to other viewpoints, never requiring that one be a Catholic to find a forum in *GK's Weekly.*¹² Margaret Canovan in *G.K. Chesterton: Radical Populist,* presents evidence to show that "Chesterton did not derive his political views from the authority of the Church." Actually, "as he articulated his views and became fully aware of them, he became convinced both that they were intrinsically dependent upon Christianity, and that the salient doctrines of Christianity were best represented within the Roman Catholic Church."¹³

Certainly Chesterton's ideas—at least those he had firmly established by 1925 and the launching of the *Weekly*—flowed naturally from his faith. But to say these ideas were Catholic is to oversimplify the teachings of the Church and distort the views of those who embraced Catholicism. Catholics in Britain as elsewhere united around Catholicism and little else. To say that they shared common views on domestic politics, foreign policy, economics, or the arts is absurd. What Chesterton came to believe, because of a complex combination of intelligent friends, a Victorian upbringing, his middle class environment, a stable and loving home life, and an education that included neither public schools nor Oxford or

Cambridge, was not particularly Catholic or original.

In his *Autobiography* he put it this way: "I saw our industrial civilization as rooted in injustice, long before it became so common a comment as it is today." Early in his life he possessed an "instinct about justice, about liberty and equality, [a position] somewhat different from that current in our age; and from all the tendencies towards concentration and generalization. It was my instinct to defend liberty in small nations and poor families; that is, to defend the rights of man as including the rights of property; especially the property of the poor." He maintained that he hoped all people could possess something, even if it was no more than their own body. He found that many "authorities" stood opposed to his condemnation of collectivism—either by capitalist or socialist means. Though the world stood against him, he said at the end of his last book, "I have found one authority on my side." His authority, of course, was Jesus Christ. It was through Him, said Chesterton, that we find the key to everything else.[14]

Chesterton's understanding of God's will was that all people should worship their Creator, delight in Him, and enjoy all creation—including one another. These assumptions forced Chesterton to question society's acceptance of technological progress when there was no commitment to moral values. To him, people were freest to relate to God when they were close to nature, in family units, and within small communities. This necessitated decentralization, cottage industries, equitable distribution of property among all people, and a return to an agriculturally based economy. Chesterton's vision required an end to imperialism as well as large scale urban-industrialism. In brief, it

called for values and attitudes closer to those of the Middle Ages than to those of modern Europe in the 20th century.

His critics often called him a dreamer, a fanciful escapist, or a living anachronism. But these labels missed his point. He was not trying to turn the clock back several hundred years. Instead he was raising the question, "What is a good life?"[15] Confident that he knew the answer, he could not stand by and say that all is right with the world. On the contrary, this world as he saw it was a mess. People were not free; they were enslaved to an economic order that had impoverished them and stripped them of dignity. The advocates for Britain's new order controlled the political parties whose differences were superficial; and the major newspapers on Fleet Street toadied to the politicians and the bankrupt philosophy of progress.

Chesterton did not suffer from megalomania or a messianic complex. He was no different from numerous people of his era in believing he saw a way to make Britain a better place to live. It is just that he eschewed the elitism implicit in each major pillar of Britain's political framework. The Tories wanted to preserve traditional privilege. The Liberals called for equality of opportunity, but only through the vision of an educated elite. The Fabian Socialists were concerned for social welfare, but skilled administrators and state ownership were the tools required for their scheme of reconstruction. In brief, all three positions were elitist—they overlooked the common people. As Chesterton wrote in *The Common Man,* "If you ask me whether I think the populace, especially the poor, should be recognized as citizens who can rule the state, I answer in a voice of thunder, 'Yes'."[16]

III

ONE OF CHESTERTON'S critics, Samuel Hynes, said this of him: "The sense of the world as a moral battlefield is the center of Chesterton's thought. . . . It made it possible for him to live in a world of anarchies and negations and yet preserve that moral energy that he called optimism."[17] This optimism convinced Chesterton that he could help make Great Britain a better place to live, and it was to that end that he devoted most of his energy during the last two decades of his life. His friend and literary associate, Hilaire Belloc, put it this way: "The whole meaning of his *life* was the discovery, the appreciation, of reality. But his *work* was made up of bequeathing to others the treasure of knowledge and certitude upon which he had come."[18] Belloc might have added that as a thinker, writer, and lecturer himself, he joined Chesterton in this crusade. And so did Cecil Chesterton, G. K.'s younger brother.

A significant effort in this direction was *GK's Weekly.* This paper gave Chesterton and his like-minded associates a platform from which to attack the ills of society, and to offer something positive and substantial instead. The program Chesterton embraced was called Distributism. Ian Boyd, editor of *The Chesterton Review,* has an excellent chapter on this socio-political philosophy in his book, *The Novels of G.K. Chesterton: A Study in Art and Propaganda.* Fr. Boyd correctly notes that although "Chesterton never gave a systematic account of what he meant by Distributism anywhere in his writing, . . . the outline . . . is clear to anyone who is familiar with his work and that of the circle of writers to which he belonged."[19] Underlying the movement, says Boyd, is the

assumption that "property should be distributed in the widest possible way."[20]

Aidan Mackey, a Distributist himself and a student of this movement which was started over a generation ago, defines Distributism "in its practical aspect, [as] a social system which encourages *small-scale* private *productive* ownership, based on the family unit and primarily, though not necessarily, on the land: the small farm, the small shop, the small factory, the small professional practice, formed into small communities widely distributed over what is now a largely depopulated countryside, and each centered on church and school and living together in warm Christian neighborliness." The other side of Distributism, according to Mackey, is that "it involves disengagement from all manifestations of the existing practice of usurious finance, expressed for so many people in processes of house mortgage, hire purchase, and substitution of thrifty independence by the false 'norm' of urban life."[21]

The social and political ideas that were eventually systematized into Distributism were foreshadowed by Chesterton in his weekly columns for the Liberal London *Daily News.* One can detect part of the emerging pattern for Distributism in these readable and popular articles, produced between 1901 and 1913. Chesterton, however, grew disillusioned with Liberalism, and he was forced to seek a platform elsewhere. At about the same time, Cecil Chesterton and Hilaire Belloc published *The Party System* in 1911, adding more planks in the platform of Distributism. The following year Belloc brought out *The Servile State.* It was this latter book that became, as

Fr. Boyd phrased it, "the text-book of the movement."[22] If *The Servile State* was the Distributist text, two newspapers that preceded *GK's Weekly* became the journalistic organs. Hilaire Belloc and the two Chesterton brothers were involved, as were several other men. *Eye-Witness,* published between June 22, 1911, and October 31, 1912, was edited by Belloc for one year and then headed by Cecil Chesterton when the latter man's father bought it for him.[23] This paper was primarily dedicated to the "Clean Government Movement," but it promulgated the essential ideas that became Distributism. Although lack of finances plagued the newspaper from the beginning, the editors remained committed. When bankruptcy ruined *Eye-Witness* in autumn 1912, Cecil Chesterton launched *New Witness* the following week. This paper was directed by Cecil until he joined the Army in 1916. At that time, G.K., whose health kept him from service, took over the *New Witness,* because he shared his brother's concern about the overall deplorable state of journalism in England. To their minds, the "Yellow Press" that dominated Fleet Street worshiped violence and success. As a consequence the people were given distorted reporting, and editorials were inspired by destructive assumptions.[24]

Cecil Chesterton never resumed his editorial duties at *New Witness.* Like thousands of other young men, the younger Chesterton became a casualty of the first World War, dying in a French hospital in December 1918. The bereaved brother carried on the work at *New Witness* for another four and a half years, partly out of loyalty to Cecil and partly because he was dedicated to the ideas of Distributism. These motives notwithstanding, lack of money hit the little Fleet Street venture once again. In May 1923, Chesterton and his colleagues ceased publishing of *New Witness.*

The little paper once edited by Cecil Chesterton never saw another edition, but the people and ideas behind the journal were still alive. The *New Witness* office was not closed with the cessation of publication, and a skeletal staff continued to meet and plot the paper's revival. G. K. Chesterton paid the salaries—as meager as they were—and he paid the rent. He, too, hoped to find a way to revitalize *New Witness,* for, as he put it, "there was *no* journalistic organ in all England dedicated to defending this plain principle" that "private property is good for Man."[25]

Dedication to this principle eventually led to the publication of *GK's Weekly.* A pilot issue was printed on November 8, 1924, and the first regular issue came off the press March 25, 1925. The revived paper bore the initials of G.K. Chesterton, and he assumed the editorship of the new periodical. The use of his initials, and his appointment as editor, were not efforts on his part to extol himself or take control of the enterprise for selfish ends. Indeed, he said, "I could see nobody else who could at the moment do it." Cecil "could have done it a thousand times better; but he was dead." Belloc, too, "would have done it a thousand times better; but he was occupied with the sort of studies that really consume a man's time." In brief, according to Chesterton, "I was not the best person to do it . . . I was the only person."[26] Chesterton's humility notwithstanding, he might have added that he loved newspapers too. At heart a journalist, he craved a pulpit from which to preach the good news of Distributism, as well as the social and political doctrines he had come to believe. The "jolly journalist" was no longer welcome to promulgate his political and economic views from the major dailies that were dependent upon political party support and advertising from financiers and industrialists. To be sure, he wrote books and gave public lectures, but this dedicated man who was a journalist at heart desired the wider audience and greater liberty his own paper provided.

By 1925, then, the decision was final.

Another Distributist paper was to be published. Chesterton wanted it, and so did a number of his bright, energetic, and well-informed associates. They knew from previous experience that little advertising income would be forthcoming. One could not, after all, sell promotional space to the people one was verbally assaulting. These dedicated early Distibutists were undaunted however. Agreeing to work for low wages in primitive conditions, they trusted that Chesterton's name would sell papers, and that small contributors and a few wealthy people might help the venture.

Chesterton agreed to use his personal income to finance the paper as necessary, despite his wife Frances' doubts about the entire enterprise. And while the paper cost the Chestertons hundreds of pounds per year right up until his death, it by no means bankrupted the family. Indeed, when G.K. died in 1936 he left his wife a substantial legacy of nearly 30,000 pounds (about 300,000 by today's standards) at a time when the pound was considerably stronger than it is now. Furthermore he left Frances the royalty income from his books. In fact, it could be reasonably argued that Mr. Chesterton's subvention of *GK's Weekly* was a good investment. The paper, it was claimed, reached a circulation of eight thousand by 1926. No one knows how many people actually read the little weekly periodical, but it is safe to assume that more than the subscribers picked it up and consumed the fare.[27] Members of Parliament were known to devour the news analyses, as were other journalists along Fleet Street. The witty if controversial newspaper kept G.K. Chesterton continually before the public eye, and this certainly enhanced his reputation. Although it is impossible to quantify the paper's influence, it most certainly helped sell Chesterton's books and promote his public lectures.

Chesterton also underwrote some of the costs because Alderman Cedric Chivers, one

of only a handful of donors who provided sizable support, died soon after *GK's Weekly* was on its feet. Other money came mostly from a limited number of advertisers, scores of supporters who contributed a few pounds when they could, and subscriptions. The unsung support, however, came from the loyal staff who worked effectively for long hours and paltry wages. They contributed their time and their substantial talent, and they reaped no returns from books they published or lectures they gave. G.K. Chesterton was the editor of the *Weekly*, but the bulk of the work always fell on the shoulders of his assistant editors and the small staff.

George Tyke was the first business manager, but he was soon followed by Van Norman Lucas. Miss Eleanor "Bunny" Dunham did the typing and answered the telephone. There was usually a young man about who ran errands and did chores that did not require journalistic skills. The heaviest responsibility was left to the assistant editor. W.R. Titterton filled this place in the beginning, but he was replaced two years later by Edward Macdonald, who labored at that post until *GK's Weekly* was put to rest in December 1936.

Father Brocard Sewell, who as a young man worked at the weekly as an office assistant, was on staff between 1928 and 1931. Paid only three pounds per week, he remembers that the headquarters of *GK's Weekly* was on the top floor of a rickety old building on Little Essex Street. The *Weekly* staff occupied a single room, and immediately next door was the office of the Distributist League with George C. Hesseltine at the command post. Sewell remembers that the offices were separate but the work in each place overlapped. Sewell himself began work at nine in the morning, and he worked until five with a break between one and two for lunch. Staff members frequently ate the mid-day meal across the street at the new Cheshire Cheese, where they were sought out by an interesting array of journalists, writers, and remarkable characters from the offices nearby.

Sewell began his day opening the mail for both Hesseltine and Lucas. Then he spent his remaining hours "being useful" or preparing the paper for delivery. On Wednesdays he collected the papers from the train station—they were printed at Nuneaton in Warwickshire. Then Thursdays were a whirl of putting on name labels so that subscriptions sent by mail could be out in a day.

Some of his fondest memories were of visits by G.K. Chesterton. The editor only came to the office about once a month, in the afternoon, because most of the plans for the paper were done by telephone with Edward Macdonald or W.R. Titterton. Chesterton faithfully mailed in a lead editorial, or leader as it was known, as well as a few notes or material for the columns "Top and Tail" or "Straws in the Wind."[28] When the big man with feet and a voice that seemed much too small for his immense body did make an appearance, he usually sat in the assistant editor's swivel chair and drew cartoons on his omnipresent paper pads, all the while he engaged them in conversation about the paper. Chesterton usually smoked a cigar, and he sipped a glass of sherry during the hour he was there.

W.R. Titterton remembered his visits this way:

> I am sitting in the editorial chair, when the door opens, and discloses Chesterton, floppy hat in one hand, sprouting cigarillo and sword-stick in the other. Of course, his pince-nez hangs sideways on his nose. A beaming smile, half of surprise, half of joy, is on his face as if, on a long and hazardous voyage of discovery, most unexpectedly he'd found *us*!
>
> The next few moments are taken up with his depositing his impedimenta carefully anywhere and his apologies for disturbing us. And then he is seated in the editorial chair, happy and at ease.
>
> Usually he feels in an inside pocket and takes out some manuscripts done in that marvelous Gothic handwriting. He hands the articles to me, and probably his work in town is finished. But now and then he'd say to the secretary, "Oh, Miss Dunham, would you mind taking down this for me?" And he'd stride up and down the small office, hands behind his back, while Bunny Dunham typed his conversation.
>
> Every now and then would come a chuckle, ending in a roar and a squeak. When his talk had ended, and he'd quickly read it through, he'd chat for a while and then with infinite reluctance vanish. Afterwards I have (but not often) seen him in a dim corner of a Fleet Street tavern, or in El Vino's wineshop, blissfully contemplating the universe.
>
> But the paper was "made-up" over the phone. G.K.C. would say: "I thought of doing the leader on Gas-and-Gaiters"—or whatever it was. "And I could do three or four notes on so-and-so. Will you do the rest? And have you thought about a second leader?" And so on. But much was the stuff he did each week, such as Top-and-Tail, and his current series, such as The Outline of Sanity, or Straws in the Wind. I said I supposed that Straws in the Hair would do, and he burbled and said it was too near the truth.[29]

Gilbert Keith Chesterton wrote and mailed in most of the leaders, but sometimes these were done by Edward J. Macdonald (or Titterton in the earlier issues). All members of the staff were drafted to write for Notes, and even young Sewell was allowed to try his hand from time to time. A larger pool of supporters contributed book reviews. Indeed, Sewell and a few other neophytes unveiled their writing careers by doing critiques of new books for *GK's Weekly.*

Chesterton and Edward Macdonald assembled an army of contributors rather quickly. It was these able people who kept the paper alive. Contributors were knowledgeable and talented, but equally important to this down-at-the-heel paper was their willingness to write for no fee. Frances Chesterton occasionally contributed pieces, as did J.K. Prothro (Mrs. Cecil Chesterton). Added to their jottings were the manuscripts of other dedicated and generous writers. The reputation of the paper was enhanced by contributions from such lights as Msgr. Ronald A. Knox, J.B. Morton, Walter De la Mare, and Patrick Cahill. Chesterton's good friends G.B. Shaw, Maurice Baring, and Hilaire Belloc lent prestige to the weekly, as did pieces submitted by popular figures such as Eric Gill, H.D.C. Pepler, J. Desmond Gleeson, and Father Vincent McNabb, O.P.

One of the most astute writers for *GK's Weekly* was Gregory Macdonald, the brother of the paper's assistant editor. Gregory Macdonald was a foreign-affairs specialist with expert knowledge on central and east Europe. American-born but English-educated, this journalist became the BBC's Polish editor during World War II. He eventually became head of news services relating to central and east Europe for the BBC. Gregory Macdonald's analyses and predictions about Poland, Germany, and other European trouble spots in the late 1920s and 1930s for *GK's*

Weekly were so insightful and prophetic that his articles were carefully read and discussed by politicians and competing newspaper men.[30]

Articles by Gregory Macdonald were popular and informative, but they were also controversial. Not everyone embraced this Oxford man's distrust of Germany and the Soviet Union, and his predictions of a German-Soviet alliance in July 1932, before Hitler came to power, was novel to be sure. Macdonald's pro-Polish stance was disputed, but no more so than W.R. Titterton's positions on the Scots and the Irish.[31] The paper's pro-Italian position—Macdonald said they were anti-Leftist rather than pro-Fascist —was debated, but so was the generally anti-American and anti-Scottish tone of some articles.[32]

Articles in *GK's Weekly* attacked the political parties, supported the General Strike of 1926, and launched verbal barrages against Bolshevism, socialism, and capitalistic monopolies. On a more positive note, the causes of paupers, workers, small farmers, and craftsmen were supported with zeal. Today some proponents of the paper are embarrassed by the mild strains of anti-Semitism that seeped into the *Weekly* from time to time, but they are equally proud that, long before anyone else much cared, they turned out articles against divorce, sterilization, and industrial pollution.[33]

IV

IT has now been a half century since the last issue of *GK's Weekly* was put to press. The perspective of five decades enables the historian to make some judgments. Mrs. Chesterton had worried that the little periodical would drain her husband's energy, health, and purse. But this was apparently not the case. Although some historians have concluded that these things did happen, the evidence shows that G.K. Chesterton was financially well-off when he died. Furthermore, the cause of his death was not overwork. His immoderate use of food, beverages, and tobacco probably shortened his years more than anything; and if he died sooner than he should have from overwork, it was not work on *GK's Weekly* that killed him. Indeed most of the burden for the paper was left to others rather than Chesterton. The truth is that he immensely enjoyed his work with the Distributist journal. It gave him a platform for his views, and it most certainly stimulated sales of his books.[34]

It has been argued that the *Weekly* and the Distributist League had little impact on their times because they were dominated by quarrelous men who could not get along with one another, and who likewise wasted their energies attempting to turn the clock back to the Middle Ages. The truth is that the men and women who wrote for the paper, as well as the men who met at the meetings of the League, had no more disagreements than one would find in any organization or institution. To be sure, the weekly meetings in the Devereux, the public house where the Distributists gathered once a week for dinner, lectures, and discussion, were frequently lively with debate. The Distributists included a wide range of people who represented the entire spectrum of politics,

from the extreme left to the far right. But it was generally a jolly time of intellectual stimulation and vibrant disputation. Like the politically electrified saloons in American cities during the late 19th and early 20th centuries, London's Devereux was a generating point for ideas of social and political reform. Pubs all over Great Britain were centers of polemical debate. The Devereux was unique only in its political persuasion.[35]

That these people had minimal impact on their times because they were hopelessly anachronistic is an erroneous assessment. There is no way to measure with precision the impact of the Distributist movement and its organ, *GK's Weekly.* Suffice it to say that the effect of Distributism can be seen all the way from the English Dominicans and their *Blackfriars* journal, on across the Atlantic to Peter Maurin and Dorothy Day's Catholic Worker movement in New York. On both sides of the ocean, numerous lives were touched and people left the industrial cities to return to the land. The impact of Chesterton and his ideas can be traced to America's *Commonweal* magazine, and, in the United Kingdom, A.R. Orage's *New Age* shows indisputable signs of Chesterton's impact on that man's attitudes toward state socialism, the idea of progress, and original sin.[36]

Finally, if the ideas of the Distributists left a modest imprint on Britain between the wars, these ideas hold a growing attraction for our times. Increasingly, citizens of the urbanized and industrialized nations of the western world are questioning the benefits of unbridled growth. There is a back-to-the-land movement today of unprecedented proportions. The phrase "small is beautiful" is heard more frequently. Choosing to want less rather than need more is not necessarily fashionable in the English-speaking world, but those who voice it are a growing and articulate minority.

G.K. Chesterton believed he could make an impact on his world for good. That he touched countless lives and brought a little light to dark places no one can deny. He is certainly taken more seriously today than he was in his own lifetime. But that is not an unusual fate for God's prophets.[37]

NOTES

1 A.J.P. Taylor, *English History, 1914-1945* (New York, 1965), p. 147.

2 Maisie Ward, *Gilbert Keith Chesterton* (London, 1945), chapters 2 and 3.

3 G.K. Chesterton, *Autobiography* (London, 1937), pp. 35-36.

4 Ward, *Chesterton,* pp. 42-43.

5 Karl G. Schmude, *The Man Who Was Chesterton* (Melbourne, 1974), pp. 5-6.

6 Chesterton, *Autobiography,* pp. 152-153.

7 *Ibid.,* pp. 175-176.

8 *Ibid.,* pp. 176, 177.

9 G.K. Chesterton, *Orthodoxy,* (London, 1908), p. 18.

10 Margaret Canovan, *G.K. Chesterton: Radical Populist* (New York, 1977), p. 118.

11 Ian Boyd, *The Novels of G.K. Chesterton: A Study in Art and Propaganda* (London, 1975) presents impressive evidence that shows how Maisie Ward in *Gilbert Keith Chesterton* overemphasizes this impetus in Chesterton's work. Especially valuable on this is Boyd's Chapter 4. Peter Hunt, "Chesterton and Industrialism: A Last Word to Margaret Canovan" (*Chesterton Review,* Vol. 8, No. 1, Feb. 1982), sees G. K. Chesterton as "inseparable from his orthodox Catholic vision . . ." p. 67.

12 Mr. Gregory Macdonald maintained this thesis to me in a personal interview I had with him in Wimbledon, July 19, 1985. See also Mother Mary Malachy Loughran, S.H.C.J., "Catholics in England Between 1918 and 1945," Ph.D. dissertation, University of Pennsylvania, 1954, pp. 168, 184.

13 Canovan, *Radical Populist,* p. 118.

14 Chesterton, *Autobiography,* pp. 342-343.

15 Przemyslaw Mroczkowski, *The Medievalism of G.K. Chesterton: A Critical Enquiry* (Warsaw, 1976), Vol. 2, p. 111.

16 G.K. Chesterton, *The Common Man* (London, 1950), p. 38. See also Canovan, *Radical Populist,* Chapter I.

17 Quoted in Edmund Fuller, "A Witty Optimist on the Moral Battlefield," *Wall Street Journal,* January 27, 1983.

18 Quoted in Loughran, "Catholics in England," p. 185.

19 Boyd, *Novels,* p. 77.

20 *Ibid.*

21 Aidan Mackey, "A Distributist Colony: 'Tis Forty Years Since," *The Chesterton Review,* Vol. III, No. 1, Fall-Winter 1976-77, p. 163.

22 Boyd, *Novels,* p. 77.

23 Personal interview with Father Brocard Sewell, April 25, 1985, Charlton Kings, England. Transcript on file at The Marion E. Wade Collection, Wheaton College, Wheaton, Illinois.

24 Ward, *G.K. Chesterton,* p. 275; John Coates, *Chesterton and the Edwardian Cultural Crisis* (Hull, 1984), pp. 53-55; Boyd, *Novels, pp. 209-210.*

25 *GK's: A Miscellany of the First 500 Issues of G.K.'s Weekly* (London, 1934), pp. 15-16.

26 *Ibid.,* p. 27.

27 In a personal interview with Father Brocard Sewell, April 25, 1985, Charlton Kings, England, he told me that he first read the paper when it was passed on to him by one of his teachers who was a subscriber.

28 *Ibid.*

29 W.R. Titterton, "Bigger Puppets," *Columbia,* January 1960, p. 28. See also Titterton's *G.K. Chesterton: A Portrait* (New York, 1973).

30 From an interview with Gregory Macdonald, July 19, 1985, Wimbledon, England. Transcript on file at the Marion E. Wade Collection, Wheaton College, Wheaton, Illinois. See also photocopies of Mr.

Macdonald's reminiscences of his years with *GK's Weekly,* also on file at the Wade Collection.

31 See, for example, *GK's Weekly,* April 26, 1934.

32 See, for example, *GK's Weekly,* January 3, 10, 17, 1931.

33 Although the magazine ridicules racist ideas, *GKs Weekly,* Vol. I, No. 3, p. 40 and No. 4, p. 63 contain mild examples of anti-Semitism. Articles on divorce are in Vol. I, No. 3, and material on sterilization and pollutants can be found in these issues: August 1, 1931; January 25, 1934; February 1, 1934; February 8, 1934; March 1, 1934.

34 For the debates among historians about *GK's Weekly,* see *The Chesterton Review,* Volumes I, No. 2; II, Nos. 1, 2; III, Nos. 1, 2; VIII, No. 3. See also transcripts of interviews with Fr. Brocard Sewell and Gregory Macdonald cited above.

35 See the Macdonald file at the Wade Collection, especially his debates with Alzina Stone Dale, *The Outline of Sanity: A Life of G.K. Chesterton* (Grand Rapids, 1982) and Dudley Barker, *G.K. Chesterton: A Biography* (New York, 1975).

36. See Coates, *Chesterton and the Edwardian Cultural Crisis,* Chapter XI; Bernard McCabe's review of A.N. Wilson's biography of H. Belloc in *New York Review of Books,* No. 7, 1985, p. 39. It should be noted that Cecil Chesterton worked as Orage's assistant editor at *The New Age.* See Brocard Sewell, *Cecil Chesterton* (Faversham, Kent, 1975).

37 The "Chesterton as prophet" concept can be found in Maurice B. Reckitt, *G.K. Chesterton: A Christian Prophet For England Today* (London: 1950), and Ian Boyd, C.S.B., "G.K. Chesterton: A Christian Prophet for Today," Eleventh Annual Marion E. Wade Lecture, November 8, 1985, Wheaton College, Wheaton, Illinois.

Week ending March 21, 1925.

G.K.'s Weekly

EDITED BY G.K. Chesterton

Nº 1

WILL OWEN

Price 6ᵈ

G.K.'s Weekly

No. 1.—Vol. I. Week ending Saturday, March 21, 1925.

PRICE SIXPENCE.
YEARLY (52 ISSUES)
£1 10 4.

Telephone No. City 1978. *Offices, 20 & 21, Essex Street, Strand, W.C.*

CONTENTS:

THE FIRST PRINCIPLE.

THIS single adventure in weekly journalism cannot compete with our wealthy and world-wide press in resources and reports. In the case of Russia our modest distinction is only this; that we are really concerned with the abuses of Bolshevism and not only with the abuse of it. When the Trade Union Report on the experiment in Eastern Europe came out and was considered in the press, the result was very interesting indeed; its very dullness was interesting. We think it highly probable that the Trade Union delegates did not understand the conditions in Russia. But we are sure they understood them a great deal better than their English critics understand the conditions in England. It is all very well to repeat distractedly, " What are we coming to, with all this Bolshevism? " It is as relevant to add, " What are we coming to, even without Bolshevism? " The answer is : Monopoly. It is certainly not " private enterprise." The American Trust is not private enterprise. It would be truer to call the Spanish Inquisition private judgment. Monopoly is neither private nor enterprising. It exists to prevent private enterprise. And that is the present goal of our progress, if there were not a Bolshevist in the world. This paper exists to demand that we fight Bolshevism with something better than plutocracy. But anyhow we must get something better than silence about plutocracy. Compared with these evasions, the Trade Union Report is really a very philosophical document. It suffers of course from the faults of an age of very superficial philosophy. It is amusing to note the rather dazed solemnity with which the writers report the position of Woman in the new Russia. But in the same connection there was another reference that was not superficial but fundamental. In describing the marriage laws, which seem to be chiefly directed against marriage, the writers say that in this general divorce and dissolution it would certainly be hard for anyone to found a great family. That is precisely true and profoundly important. It marks again the narrowness of mere industrialism like our own, that the writer cannot really imagine any rooted family except a great family. But he is right about what made the family great. Aristocracy became powerful, much too powerful, because it did not consist of individuals, but had a name like a nation. Democracy will never become powerful unless every family is a great family. Perhaps it would have been better if the French Revolution had extended and not extinguished heraldry; if all the stormers of the Bastille, having undoubtedly borne arms, had borne armorial bearings. Anyhow, the State will always defeat the individual; if the citizen is to rule he must be more than an individual. But do we want him

21

to rule? Bolshevism does not; and Bolshevism is not alone in that. It is absolutely certain that democracy will not be democratic unless it is domestic. But the Bolshevist does not want it to be domestic, because he does not want it to be democratic. That is the vital distinction between the two kinds of revolution. The old phrase Home Rule was really applicable to the revolt of a people who believe in homes. It is more doubtful if the *Daily Herald* will ever call itself the *Family Herald*.

The thing behind Bolshevism and many other modern things is a new doubt. It is not merely a doubt about God; it is rather specially a doubt about Man. The old morality, the Christian religion, the Catholic Church, differed from all this new mentality because it really believed in the rights of men. That is, it believed that ordinary men were clothed with powers and privileges and a kind of authority. Thus the ordinary man had a right to deal with dead matter, up to a given point; that is the right of property. Thus the ordinary man had a right to rule the other animals within reason; that is the objection to vegetarianism and many other things. The ordinary man had a right to judge about his own health, and what risks he would take with the ordinary things of his environment; that is the objection to Prohibition and many other things. The ordinary man had a right to judge of his children's health, and generally to bring up children to the best of his ability; that is the objection to many interpretations of modern State education. Now in these primary things in which the old religion trusted a man, the new philosophy utterly distrusts a man. It insists that he must be a very rare sort of man to have any rights in these matters; and when he is the rare sort, he has the right to rule others even more than himself. It is this profound scepticism about the common man that is the common point in the most contradictory elements of modern thought. That is why Mr. Bernard Shaw wants to evolve a new animal that shall live longer and grow wiser than man. That is why Mr. Sidney Webb wants to herd the men that exist like sheep, or animals much more foolish than man. They are not rebelling against an abnormal tyranny; they are rebelling against what they think is a normal tyranny; the tyranny of the normal. They are not in revolt against the king. They are in revolt against the citizen. The old revolutionist, when he stood on the roof (like the revolutionist in *The Dynamiter*) and looked over the city, used to say to himself, " Think how the princes and nobles revel in their palaces; think how the captains and cohorts ride the streets and trample on the people." But the new revolutionist is not brooding on that. He is saying, " Think of all those stupid men in vulgar villas or ignorant slums. Think how badly they teach

their children; think how they do the wrong thing to the dog and offend the feelings of the parrot." In short, these sages, rightly or wrongly, cannot trust the normal man to rule in the home; and most certainly do not want him to rule in the State. They do not really want to give him any political power. They are willing to give him a vote; because they have long discovered that it need not give him any power. They are not willing to give him a house, or a wife, or a child, or a dog, or a cow, or a piece of land; because these things really do give him power.

Now we wish it to be understood at the start that our policy is to give him power by giving him these things. We wish to insist that this is the real moral division underlying all our disputes, and perhaps the only one really worth disputing. We are far from denying, especially at this stage, that there is much to be said on the other side. We would rather insist that nearly everything that is said is said on the other side. We alone, perhaps, are likely to insist in the full sense that the average respectable citizen ought to have something to rule. We alone, to the same extent and for the same reason, have the right to call ourselves democratic. A republic used to be called a nation of kings; and in our republic the kings really have kingdoms. All modern governments, Prussian or Russian, all modern movements, Capitalist or Socialist, are taking away that kingdom from that king. Because they dislike the independence of that kingdom, they are against property. Because they dislike the loyalty of that kingdom, they are against marriage.

In this our first leading article we are most concerned to lay down that proposition; more concerned even than to prove it. That is what we think; and Bolshevism and Capitalism are absolutely at one in thinking the opposite. We shall answer in due course the arguments based on the weakness and vulgarity of the average citizen; we merely point out here that the arguments are based on that and nothing else. Both use the same argument against us; that a human life has now become impossible to humanity. We do not agree; we hold the old mystical dogma, that what a man has done man can do. They hold a rather more mysterious dogma; that man cannot do a thing because he has done it. But anyhow, it is a strange conclusion of the modern scientific advance that it leaves us with a choice between the impossible and the intolerable. For if we cannot go back, it hardly seems worth while to go forward. There is nothing in front but a flat wilderness of standardisation either by Bolshevism or Big Business. And it is strange that we at least have seen sanity, if only in a vision, while they go forward chained eternally to enlargement without liberty and progress without hope.

NOTES OF THE WEEK.

WE dislike saying that we have something serious to say. For in current journalese something serious means something solemn, and something solemn means something frivolous. But we have something urgent and sincere to say to those who are busy on a new bargain for guaranteeing peace between England, France and Germany, at the price of some "rectifications" in eastern Europe, which we can comfort our consciences by leaving a little vague. These people are very fond of talking about international considerations and the evil of narrowing our outlook to ourselves or our nearest and dearest. What they are doing is taking advantage of this natural narrowness: and sacrificing more remote people simply because they are remote. They want to patch up our civilisation in the West at the expense of its heroic outpost in the East; which defeated Bolshevism in battle while we were raving at it in the papers and bargaining with it at the bank. It is very kind of Germany to be ready to guarantee Belgium. It seems to have become quite a habit. But we do not think that the Prussian's well-known habit of observing his guarantee to Belgium is sufficient reason for our breaking our guarantee to Poland. The Prussian, to quote his own pretty profanity, would doubtless still like to partake of the sacramental body of Poland. But we see no reason why we should eat and drink to our damnation, by assisting at his Black Mass.

* * * *

ON two recent occasions Mr. Baldwin has shown his sense, or perhaps only his sanity. One was the trivial matter of Mr. Kirkwood's suspension; which is only interesting as part of a study of the Parliamentary language and how to translate it into the English language. The stuff in the more snobbish newspapers may be neglected; but when a Chairman of Committees writes to the Prime Minister to say that he still thinks under the circumstances his own action was justified, it is not difficult to infer that a good many other people (by no means "Bolshevists") think it was quite unjustifiable. The other was the more real business of the Levy; and there the Prime Minister showed a good deal of real wisdom and right feeling. There are a hundred reasons why a Prime Minister should not thus attack Trade Unionism; but one so staring as to be staggering. Political subscriptions may well be a delicate matter with the older parties. The Labour Party has at least adopted from the first the principle of publishing its accounts. But in the older parties the secret fund has not ceased to be a secret fund; though its secrecy is no longer a secret. In the abstract a Party Whip might still be receiving money from anybody, from the Kaiser to the King of the Cannibal Islands. Until they have brought the Party up to the standard of any twopenny workman's club, the less they say the better about workmen's funds.

* * * *

MR. BALDWIN says very truly that this is no longer the time of the small family business; it is the time of the big business combinations covering vast areas. It is also the time of the influenza, which covers exceedingly vast areas. But this does not reconcile all of us to encouraging the influenza, and has even maddened some medical enthusiasts here and there into an attempt to cure the influenza. It is the time of big business; it is also the time of big bankruptcy, of big debts, of big bodies of unemployed, of a big shortage of houses, and a big blank in the minds of politicians. Ours is the time of all these things; and a high old time we are having. But we are not bound to submit to the big ideas of big business, any more than Mr. Baldwin is bound to submit to the big ideas of Bolshevism. We can entertain the hope of altering these things, or at least make the attempt to do so; and the only question is to what shape or image they shall be altered. Anyhow, we altogether decline to accept the foggy fatalism of the phrase "This is the Age of . . ." as it seems to be generally accepted by those who use it. We refuse as Alfred would have refused to surrender because it was the Age of Barbarian Invasions; as Jenner would have refused to surrender because it was the Age of Smallpox. And that is the real spiritual difference behind all the solemn assurances that this is the age of this or the age of that. This is the age of yielding to the age: and that is the one element in it to which we must not yield.

* * * *

IN any case, Mr. Baldwin is right in point of fact when he says that two great combinations oppose each other; they are in fact the Trust and the Trade Union. But when he talks as if they were to be treated in the same way, to be criticised or tolerated in the same way, he goes much too fast. He goes too fast by the standard which should be his standard, if parties still had any standards; the standard of conservatism or tradition. He goes too fast, that is, by the very standard that is meant to prevent people from going too fast. It is history, it is memory, it is the mighty past and the real wisdom of our fathers, that should specially emphasise the real difference between a Trade Union and a Trust. It is simply that our fathers called the first a guild and called the second a crime. The Trade Union has indeed been a blind, unconscious and illogical sort of guild, as the Trust has been an equally blind, unconscious and illogical sort of crime. But to the common conscience of Christendom, by which we live, the former is a social institution and the latter an anti-social action. One was a community for which a man might get a charter or a patron saint: the other was a conspiracy for which a man might go to the pillory or the gallows. We shall go deeper into the darkness, unless we see these things as simply as they were seen in simpler times. To organise all the woodcutters so that they shall all receive the same pay is in its nature a neighbourly act. To buy up all the wood yourself so that you can sell it to shivering people at your own price, is in its nature an unneighbourly act. It makes no difference that both are called great modern organisations; that the Woodcutters' Guild is called the Woodcutters' Union, and the crime of forestalling is called the Cosmic Cosmopolitan Timber Trading Syndicate.

* * * *

MEANWHILE, of course, everybody agrees that we cannot go back to the paternal principle in business described by Mr. Baldwin. In our existing political conditions, when everybody agrees about something, it is generally untrue. But it is even more remarkable that even when people agree on something that is true, they do not understand how true it is. This remark about the paternal business is true in a special sense and for a special reason. The ordinary phrase that we cannot go back to an old principle or an old system is not true at all. It is quite false to say that we cannot paint ourselves blue like Ancient Britons. If " we " are the whole people, we can do it to-morrow if we like. It is quite false to say that we cannot return to the feudal system; we can do it whenever we want to; only we don't want to. But there is here a distinction which is rather notable, and is never noted. It is always possible to return to the principles of the past; but it is in a special sense more difficult to return to the compromises of the past. For the compromises were the individual, indefinable arrangements by which some people for some reason were allowed to evade the principle. We can tell all British subjects to paint themselves blue; but we cannot reproduce the exceptional examples of some who were allowed to be a certain fine shade of violet or peacock green because it suited their complexions. We can recreate a real feudalism; but we could not easily recreate an unreal feudalism; the understanding by which a man was really a sovereign though he was supposed to have a suzerain. Englishmen could all become Catholics or Calvinists; but they could hardly return to the transition stage when the conventicles were beginning to be tolerated or the Penal Laws were beginning to be ignored.

* * * *

NOW the reason why the principle of Mr. Baldwin's family business can hardly be restored is because the principle was not a principle. It would really be difficult to return to that system, simply because the system was not a system. It is what we call an understanding; but might more correctly call a personal satisfaction with something you never try to understand. These compromises were always praised as practical. But nobody noticed that in one respect they are exceedingly unpractical. And that is the fact that when once they are broken they can never be mended. They have no plan or formula for reconstruction; they depended on a mood and died with a mood. That was the truth about the sort of business that was just big enough to have something of the discipline of a ship, but not too big to have something of the geniality of a household. We do not say that the conditions creating that mood might not appear here and there, in that variety that would be essential to a fresh and healthy society. But we cannot build a fresh society on that formula; because there is no formula to build on. But the moral is not that we cannot go back; but must go on to a tyranny of Trusts which will simply be Socialism without social justice. The moral is that we must go much further back; to a time before capitalism had appeared in its smaller and milder form. The old clerk might be attached to his master with something of the loyalty of a vassal. But the old apprentice could look forward to being himself a master and a free man.

* * * *

IN the discussion about St. Paul's Cathedral, and the dangerous condition of its dome, there is one point of view which we are surprised not to see more boldly set forth. In all debates about the insecurity of the sacred building, it is still apparently taken for granted that we wish to make a sacred building secure. Everywhere there is the old assumption that it must be made out of permanent materials; that the religious edifice may remain

what it is. Now we are told in the newspapers every morning that our religion can never remain what it is. All the publicists and popular preachers assure us in a chorus that religion is in a state of eternal transition from what it was to what it will be—or, if the thinkers are very German, from what it might have been to what it can never altogether utterly become. Why should not St. Paul's be built of some similar substance? None of the thinkers are more German, in this and many other respects, than the brilliant gentleman who has to preach these things in St. Paul's Cathedral. Dean Inge said some little time ago that our northern (we beg pardon, nordic) and national religion was to be congratulated on having become flexible. In that case, would not some material such as gutta-percha seem to be indicated, instead of the stubborn and static materials of stone and marble? We are told that our creeds are elastic; might not our churches be literally elastic; so that the long-drawn aisle might be drawn out yet longer to accommodate those huge crowds of the populace that are sure to surge from the slums to hear a Hegelian version of Relativity? Indiarubber churches are much more advanced than tin houses; and, like other advanced ideals, would please the millionaires who have their money in Rubber.

* * * *

BUT at least, if we must build in a definite form, we need not build in a final form. The Catholics who built old St. Paul's, the Protestants who built the existing St. Paul's, were under the delusion that their religion was final, or in other words that it was true. But if there is to be no permanence in faith, it is absurd to aim at this permanence in form. It is being in the very worst sense ritualists and idolators. What we obviously want is a series of light and temporary structures, perhaps made of painted wood or even paste-board in the style of stage scenery; that could be rapidly run up or taken down so as to keep pace if possible with our changes of fundamental philosophy. It is agreed that modern art must mirror the modern mood. There has been considerable artistic sympathy of late with the serene agnosticism in the poets and philosophers of China. When in that Confucian mood we should naturally expect to look up and see a pagoda on the top of Ludgate Hill. There is the modern and highly mysterious taste for being the reincarnation of an Egyptian princess; for the whole population of ancient Egypt appears to have consisted of princesses. The typist walking up Ludgate Hill with this obsession will naturally expect to look up and see a pyramid. But it would never do to build as carefully as the Chinese built pagodas or the Egyptians pyramids. That would require a Great Fire whenever we changed our religion. Besides, another dreadful doubt crosses our minds. Is it really progressive that St. Paul's should stand still? If a cathedral were a caravan, wandered about, appearing now on Ludgate Hill, now on Primrose Hill, now on the peaks of Upper Tooting . . . .

* * * *

NOTHING could be more grimly amusing than the grumbling in the English papers against the possibilities of Irish action against divorce. The theory seems to be that Ireland ought to be free to manage her domestic affairs, so long as she does not want to be domestic. The Irish do not like divorce; they are attached to another and alternative institution called marriage. What is still more extraordinary, they are not in any way moved by the movement that is so fashionable elsewhere, in spite of its being recommended to them by persons of undoubted fashion. They see aristocrat after aristocrat, of the great houses that have governed England and misgoverned Ireland, going into the witness-box, each of them explaining that his grandmother was re-married on the day his mother was divorced; that his mother's stepdaughter by her third marriage has bolted with the ex-co-respondent of his own second *decree nisi;* that it was at the house of his second wife that he made a collusive arrangement to be temporarily re-married to his first wife, while his third wife was waiting for a divorce from his elder brother; or in some similar fashion propounding the general problem that fathers and mothers has he none, but his only offspring is somebody else's son. They see all this; and their dreamy unpractical minds grow tired of following the intricate pattern; they are so blind as not to see how all this increases the dignity and stability of a superior race. Their preversity annoys our newspaper proprietors, with their prodigious propaganda against marriage. And many of them are disposed to insist that, though the Irish may be allowed to have Irish institutions, they must be forbidden to have Christian institutions.

*   *   *   *

WE doubt whether anything will follow on that protest. The English have very sensibly and cheerfully abandoned what they once professed to be an attempt to impose their virtues on Ireland. It would be amusing if they tried now to impose their vices on Ireland. But the English have still their national sense of humour; and the notion of a crusade on behalf of conjugal infidelity would be a little too much for it. But indeed the idea of disputing autonomy in such a case is quite as irrational as it is ridiculous. Self-government would not be self-government at all, if it did not permit the self-governing body to be stricter on some points as well as more lax on others. It is as if we said that a Protectionist policy in Canada denied to some of the King's subjects their divine right to Free Trade. It would be amusing if the Empire, which does not guarantee Free Trade to the colonists, were practically to impose Free Love on the Free State. The point can be made plain by supposing any moral matter on which we have not become entirely lax and vague, if such can be found. If fools insist on pitting Trusts against Trades Unions, it is not impossible that we may really have Communism; and that with the English temperament it may be a kindly but rather chaotic Communism. Certainly the English might have Communism long before the Irish. Would the Irish then become tyrants or rebels because they continue to recognise property as they now continue to recognise marriage? Would it become an intolerable privilege that the cow was owned in Ireland that was shared in England; or that the English Bolshevist was punished for expropriating Irish spoons?

*   *   *   *

OUR large scale journalism, like most of our large business, is a curious mixture of weariness and haste. It is elliptical not through energy but through exhaustion. Thus its most casual terms have a queer look; and it is producing monstrosities without knowing it. We read a moment ago, under the picture of a monster of the deep, the quiet inscription: "The largest octopus ever found in Yorkshire." That seems a curious way of putting it. We are assured that no larger octopus was ever found wandering on the moors between Wharfedale and Keighley Gate. It is larger than all the octopi that throng the streets even of Leeds and Bradford. Yorkshire is a large place; but it may be assumed that the active journalist has searched every lonely hamlet and humble home to see that no larger octopus was concealed on the premises. The truth is that the active journalist was not really active but very inactive. He had a confused idea of compression, but it was mixed with a great deal of mere idleness. In a thousand little things like that, which anybody can see by skimming a newspaper, we can see that there is something very loose in the joints of journalism. Big journalism, like all big business, has incurred the nemesis of ca'canny.

*   *   *   *

THE craze for Cross-Word Puzzles, which seems to have eclipsed that of Acrostics, is in one way at least a change for the worse. The Acrostic is much more suited to the English genius, which is elusive and atmospheric. A riddle goes round and round; and talks about a thing rather than of it. Over the signature of R. A. Knox, the Acrostic became a string of literary and historical allusions and a sort of witty commentary. For we are a nation of poets, if only of minor poets. But we are not a nation of logicians and possibly not even of grammarians. And this present cross-word system really requires equivalents shortly expressed; things that at least partake of the nature of definitions or synonyms. And it is at once apparent that the journalist, who can produce an acrostic that is in its way as perfect as a sonnet, has not even a notion of a short equivalent. A cross-word puzzle recently described the word " stare " as " observe closely "; which is not in the least what it means. A man might observe a thing closely with his eyes half-closed; indeed, some short-sighted people generally do.

*   *   *   *

WHEN it says in the romance " The Count was scowling, apparently at the cigarette between his claw-like fingers, but I was sure that he observed us closely," it does not mean that he stared. When it says in the newspaper " The Prime Minister assured the honourable member that the Government were observing closely the design of the Little Puddleton Red Sunday School to destroy the British Empire," it does not mean that the Ministers stood out in the road staring at the little tin chapel, from which the Bolshevists of Little Puddleton are shaking the world with revolution. Elsewhere, once again, we find by the same casual inspection that the word " wonder " is treated as parallel to " awe." Of course they are not in the least parallel. If we saw Lord Curzon playing leap-frog in the Strand in yellow pyjamas, it might well be an occasion for wonder; but not necessarily for awe. On the other hand, when our dependence on banks and big businesses, our trusting to trusts and the nominees of trusts, our confidence in commercial genius and success, have finally and for ever wrecked our foreign policy, ruined our home market and brought us to defeat in battle and starvation in the streets—in that dreadful hour the destruction of a great and noble nation will assuredly be a matter for awe; but not in the least a matter for wonder.

FROM G.K.'s WEEKLY A HUNDRED YEARS AGO.

[So many papers have printed with legitimate pride an extract from their issue of the previous century that we cannot consent to begin publication without equipping ourselves with so normal a feature of journalism; and our first issue seems the most appropriate moment for this slightly sentimental retrospect. After all, everybody seems to have a centenary in these days without any particular difficulty. We are all centenarians now.]

March 21, 1825.—Nearly ten years have passed since that glorious afternoon in summer, when Wellington and Blücher met and cemented an eternal peace between Prussia and England. Hopes of such a permanent peace, held out by the Holy Alliance, have not been contradicted by any great convulsion; and it seems probable that the conflict that ended at Waterloo may prove to be, in the witty phrase of an aged Russian diplomatist at the Council of Vienna, " the war that will end war." The anxious considerations that now weigh down a patriotic heart relate to the conditions of the country itself, so often forgotten in the glow of patriotism. That ingenious person, Mr. Bentham, delights to demonstrate that men only pursue their own interest in supporting an ordered society; in which case there would seem to be something highly and dangerously disinterested about the conduct of the landlords who set man-traps and the tenants who burn hay-ricks. We have never joined in the universal invective against Mr. Cobbett, many of whose strictures seem to us to reflect credit on his head as well as his heart; but we cannot but think him guilty of an exaggeration sometimes degenerating into enthusiasm (like that of the Methodists whom he loves to castigate) when he attributes so much of the evil to the prevalence of paper money. We allow for his rhetorical figures and highly coloured style; but there are conceits that appear incredible even when treated as tropes; and sometimes, in reading Mr. Cobbett, one would really imagine that a hundred years hence such a thing as a gold piece would never be seen in England; and that anyone dealing in some modest sum like ten shillings would solemnly present his neighbour with a piece of paper! The best students of political economy assure us that free competition, unhampered by any State interference, will soon find for every man the work for which he is most suited. But even the assurance of the whole population, in the year 1925, being in regular employment under merchants whose businesses will show a continually increasing security and prosperity, does not altogether reconcile us to the disappearance of the English yeoman and the systematic destruction of commons and rights of way. We are sorry to have nothing to oppose to predictions so solid and authoritative, except these sentimental regrets and these formless forebodings.

WHY WEMBLEY WAS WOBBLY.

THE immediate causes of the comparative failure at Wembley are pretty sure to be generally discussed. They will divide themselves into two classes; those that are too trivial to be investigated and those that are too important to be investigated. The former are familiar enough; everybody knows the man who is sure the thing would be a success if the palings were painted pink or if stilts were provided that shorter people might see the show; everybody knows the man who complains that when he went there he slipped on a banana-skin or was not allowed to pay his entrance fee in half-penny stamps. But the other conception is at the very root of all our real politics; if anybody did cheat on a large scale in connection with the imperial show, he will not be punished; for cheating on a large scale is supposed to have something about it imperial and therefore impeccable. A Labour Member was speaking quite correctly when he said the other day that our Commissions of Inquiry are practically always whitewashing Commissions, from the Jameson Raid downwards. We have never punished a big profiteer; a fact that would have astounded our ancestors and may astound our descendants. But the very mention of the Jameson Raid reminds us that there are causes much more radical which will seem to many much more remote. The Wembley Exhibition was noisy with every new invention and pushing enterprise; but its weakness was that it was out of date. The sort of imperial sentiment it appealed to was the sentiment of thirty years ago, when a Kruger loomed larger than a Kaiser, when we did not know what dreadful thing was really meant by painting the map red; when the Cape to Cairo continent seemed really bestridden by the Colossus of Rhodes.

Now the English are of all men the most moody. The fact is disguised merely because their gesture happens to be heavier or slower than that of Latins or Americans. The Englishman thinks that the Frenchman is always gesticulating or the American always hustling. But that very fact ought to show him that the American or the Frenchman is always the same. But the Englishman is not always the same. He has numberless and nameless moods; that do not appear very much in the trivial English talk, though they do appear in the very elemental English poetry. One disadvantage is that these moods which are not often described, and never defined, can seldom be recovered. In our judgment the mood of 1914 was a very noble mood. In our judgment the mood of Mafeking Night was a very ignoble one. But neither the noble nor the ignoble mood can be exactly recovered; and the ignoble mood is fortunately much further away. If our mood is no longer in the last poems of Rupert Brooke, it is not likely to be in the first poems of Rudyard Kipling.

That was the real weakness of Wembley; that it so completely mistook the English temperament as to appeal to a stale mood. It appealed to a stale mood of success; when we need to appeal to a new and more noble mood of failure, or at least of peril. The English did not understand being asked to boast of a Burmese house when they were houseless, or admire the works of Colonial genius when they were out of work. But we believe they would understand being told that, homeless and workless, they were still English, and that England herself was being driven out of house and home. They no longer care to be told of an Empire on which the sun never sets. Tell them the sun is setting, and they will fight though the battle go against them to the going down of the sun: if they do not stay it, like Joshua.

There are two reasons to be given when we are rallying men round a flag; first that it is victorious and second that it is defeated; or at least in danger of being defeated. But you cannot rally people to something that is already defeated, and continues to deny even the danger of defeat. A man can call upon his friends because things are all right or because things are all wrong. But he cannot attract them to things merely because they are all wrong, while he continues to declare they are all right. It is vulgarly said that a man appealing for help must either be in rags and realistically starving, or else dressed expensively and even extravagantly in the very latest fashion. But he cannot impress anybody by being dressed extravagantly in what is no longer the latest fashion. He cannot impress anybody by being at once dressy and dowdy. And that is the effect now produced by England plastering herself with the diamonds of the Diamond Jubilee or the gold of the South African War. The parallel is not perfect; for fortunately the world is not perfectly practical and businesslike yet. The really efficient man of business would no doubt sack his own father as inefficient, unless he dressed up to the nines and dyed his hair to avoid being too old at forty. But his attitude towards his father would hardly be our attitude towards our fatherland. We should not judge England our mother by so rapid and resolute a test; she would, let us hope, be sufficiently sacred to us if she did appear in rags and starving; as desolate as Poland sitting among her ruins; as bent and withered as the little old woman whom the Irish call Kathleen-na-Hulahan. But, anyhow, we should regret much more her appearing in clothes that were flashy without being fashionable; something that was fast and yet left far behind. There is no advantage in looking worldly in what is no longer the way of the world; in appealing to practical things that are no longer really in practice. And that is the impression produced just now by the British talking about the British Empire or counting the Colonies like jewels in its crown. They are the old Kimberley diamonds; and the style of the setting is no longer admired. This does not mean that we need no longer love things that are old-fashioned; but it does mean that we can no longer praise them as fashionable, or push them as fashionable. In other words, we come back to the other view of our power in the past and to the other reason for rallying to it. It must be one or the other; and as things stand, we ourselves believe that it must be the other.

Now no nations have ever been loved and served like the unhappy nations. The moment the nation is admittedly unlucky, men will always stake their lives and fortunes for her. Ten thousand swords will leap from their scabbards, as if misfortune were a magnet attracting steel. The amount of energy and suffering put into the long effort of Poland or Ireland, to shift one dead-weight of a stone, would seem enough to have steered a planet. But to have this devotion a nation must need it; a nation must ask for it. England does need it; but she does not ask for it. It is assumed that she must go on making a failure of an attempt to look like a success; instead of possibly making a success of the forlorn hope that can retrieve failure. The Englishman must continue to swagger as a capitalist with no capital; and go on being purse-proud with an empty purse. He must boast that he has a big

Empire, even at the moment that he is driven to have a small Navy. He must swagger about the Colonies he has made, though it be as a bankrupt squire swaggering over the land he has mortgaged. He must be hated by the poor for a wealth that he has not got; and still disliked by the foreigner for a superiority he can no longer feel. This is what our Americanised press recommends to us as "Optimism": it is making the worst of all possible worlds.

We seriously propose that England should take her stand among the unhappy nations; it is too dismal a fate to go on being one of the happy ones. We must be as proud as Spain and Poland and Serbia; nations made more dear to their lovers by their disasters. Our disasters have begun; but they do not seem to have endeared us to anybody in particular. Our sorrow has come; but we gain no extra loyalty by it. The time has come to claim our crown of thorns; or at least not to cover it any longer with such exceedingly faded flowers.

ANSWERS TO THE POETS.

The Skylark Replies to Wordsworth

(As it might have appeared to Byron.)

EPHEMERAL minstrel, staring at the sky,
    Dost thou despise the earth where wrongs abound
    Or, eyeing me, hast thou the other eye
Still on the Court, with pay-day coming round,
That pension that could bring thee down at will
Those rebel wings composed, that protest still?

Past the last trace of meaning and beyond
Mount, daring babbler, that pay-prompted strain
Twixt thee and Kings a never-failing bond
Swells not the less their carnage o'er the plain.
Type of the wise, who drill but never fight,
True to the kindred points of Might and Right.

The Sea Replies to Byron.

(As it might have appeared to Wordsworth.)

STROLL on, thou dark not deep "blue" dandy, stroll
    Ten thousand duns call after thee in vain
    The tailor's marked with ruin; his control
Stops with my shore; beyond he doth retain
No shadow of a chance of what's his own
But sinks above his bills with bubbling groan
"Absconded; gone; abroad; address unknown."

Thy songs are speeches, void of all save Thee
Childe Harold, Lara, Manfred, what care I?
My water washed them down—you got it free
And many a wine-cup since, when you were dry
Till nature blows the man-hater sky-high
Howling against his gods in stark D.T.
And dashes him against the Truth. There let him *lie*.

DON'T SAY IT.

WE beg officially to announce, in the exercise of the prophetical office, that somebody will shortly utter a loud scream, somebody will be strangled, stabbed, or otherwise murdered, the town will be blown up with dynamite, the end of the world will come, or something else will happen to indicate that the last limit of human endurance has been reached, if anybody anywhere says only once more any one of the following things.

"We are only at the beginning of the wonders of the wireless telegraphy."

This misses the point to the point of falsehood. The truth is quite the other way. The *first* whisper of such things really is wonderful. The rest is merely application; it is doubtful if the applications are any more wonderful; and it is certain that we do not go on wondering. The first man in London to use a telephone and talk to an hotel-keeper in Brighton probably did feel that the far-off voice was a miracle. But it is simply not true to say that we go on for ever saying " I can talk to the hotel-keeper; but surely not to the tobacconist! Surely, surely, not to the tailor! Do not tell me it is possible to talk also to the hatter! Wonder of wonders, the principle actually applies to the greengrocer ! " Hearing a human voice over the hills and far away is marvellous; but hearing everybody in the directory is not any more marvellous; and nobody ever marvels at it. The principle is of some spiritual importance. Without it science becomes a scheme for creating wonders and destroying wonder. It is perpetually kicking down the starry ladder by which it scales the sky. The real lesson of such marvels is not in merely going forward to fresh things that instantly become stale things. Rather it is in going backward to make the stale things fresh. It is marvellous to fly if it reminds us that it is marvellous to move; and therefore marvellous to walk. So it is matter of admiration that we should hear without wires; but also most admirable that we should hear with wires; and most admirable of all that we should hear with ears. " He that hath ears to hear, let him hear."

"We are beginning to recognise that religion must accept the conclusions of science."

When we read this in the leading article every morning, we never seem to have sufficient scepticism or liveliness in us to ask the obvious question about it. That religion may accept the conclusions of science, it is necessary that science should conclude. And science never does conclude. It is the whole claim and boast of science that she never does conclude. To conclude means to shut up; and the very last thing the man of science is likely to do is to shut up. When we say " You must accept the conclusions of the Court of Chancery " we mean something by it. We mean that even a Chancery suit does come to an end at last. When we say that we must accept the conclusions of the Home Secretary, we mean something very practical indeed. We mean that a particular man will be hanged on a particular morning, not having sufficient social influence to get his insanity accepted as one of the conclusions of science. We mean that when he has been hanged, it becomes a delicate matter to offer him an apology. But it is the whole point of science never to be in this sense final or irrevocable. Of course,

this does not mean that we shall not work more wisely if we work in the light of the suggestions of science, or take note of the general tendencies of science. It only means that the people who use these words ten thousand times a year have not taken note of what they are saying. As a matter of fact, if men had altered their doctrines to suit discoveries, they would often have had to alter them back again, when the discoveries were, so to speak, undiscovered again. Religion was asked to accept the conclusions of science, when science no longer accepted the conclusions of science. But the main point is not a particular one of science but a general one of reason. If science had concluded, it would mean almost literally that science had shut up shop.

"America has the faults of a young nation " or sometimes " one of the new nations."

As a matter of fact, this is not the case. America has the faults (and the virtues) of a nation in many ways very backward and old-fashioned; in which many things remain that Europe has left behind. Where else in the world would people be alarmed at the sudden appearance of Mr. Charles Darwin, that rising young biologist? Where else would he still be giving shocks to Puritans who take for granted that absolutely materialistic version of the Hebrew Scriptures, which St. Augustine said was too childish to be considered? With us Darwin is a venerable Victorian memory that is defended like a religion; with them he is still a revolution. With us he is riddled by the rising generation; with them he is still being frowned down by the older one. Where else in the world do people still really and truly believe in the story of the Industrious Apprentice as narrated by Hogarth? Where else can they persuade themselves that if all the apprentices were industrious, they would all be mayors—or millionaires? Where else do men still hold the views of the Manchester School, which have long disappeared from Manchester? They have not disappeared from Massachussets. Where else is Socialism a secret of juvenile dynamiters, instead of being, as with us, an affectation of aged dons? In some ways there is splendid activity in the United States. But there is not in that sense much intellectual activity among the Americans, or among the people who talk in that way about America.

(To be continued indefinitely, as there are any number more.)

The New Fiction.

(" *Leave them alone,*" we seem to hear Mr. Galsworthy say of his young people.—With apologies to **Mr.** Bettany.)

LITTLE Blue-Fits has lost his wits,
     And doesn't know where to find them;
     Leave them alone and they'll come home,
And leave their tales behind them.

The remarkable tales, with remarkable sales,
     And Bonnets and Bees in disorder;
For the Bonnets we view are exceedingly Blue,
     And decidedly over the Border.

THE BAG.
A Moral Tale in Defence of Property.

ONCE there was a very rich man who had a great deal of gold which he kept in a large leather bag. It gave him great pleasure to consider this bag and its contents. He kept it beside his chair and stroked it continually. In this attitude he was found by a man who had come in to play the prophet, and who said to him in a distracted, fiery manner:

" Sir! you are accursed! That gold which you cherish was wrung from the widow and the orphan. Your fortune reposes upon the torture of the innocent. The tears of the oppressed call to heaven for vengeance."

" Oh! what a lie! " answered the owner of the gold, startled by such rudeness. " I inherited this bag from my Cousin Arthur, who was killed out hunting, and I'm sure he was as good a man as ever breathed! "

" The vengeance of heaven . . ." began the visitor, with his voice raised to a shriek. But the rich man would have no more of this: so he rang a little bell and two strong serfs, beautifully apparelled, threw the prophet out into the street, where he fell prone, and staggered off calling loudly upon God, and covered with mud.

To him succeeded a second visitor, who would speak with the rich man, and what he said was this:—

" Your wealth grinds the faces of the people. They sweat and toil for you while you live here in luxury, idle. Such evils cannot endure. Your judgment is approaching. The gods have woollen feet."

At this last sentence the rich man was very much perplexed and also interested.

" I do not see," he said, " how the gods can have woollen feet. I could understand their having woollen *boots*: I knew a radical once who dressed like that, damn him, and he may have been one of the gods for all I know. But woollen feet? absurd! Why, sheep don't go as far as that! An' as to this dear bag of mine being wicked," and here he patted the leathern bag, " why, it's 'bsurd. It's you're wild an' woolly. My dear ol' bag's done no harm at all. None. It just sots there doing nothing and being a darling; keeps me company, ye know, while I'm thinking what I'll do with it all. Now see here, if I use that dough to pay men for ploughin' new land in Australia, what harm's that going to do anyone, eh? Won't it be better for everyone all round? "

" If you will read this book," said the second man, bringing out an enormous volume in small type, " translated from the German . . . ."

" I'll do nothing o' the sort," said the rich man pettishly. " I'm done with readin'. I only go to plays now. You go away." And the second visitor was not thrown out, but went out of his own accord, looking oh! so highbrow, and the beautifully apparelled servants bowed to him as he went through the door. Then came a third visitor who addressed the rich man soberly and beautifully, with no anger but with a deep compassion in his voice.

" Your wealth," said he, " is a mill-stone round the neck of your soul! It weighs you down and robs you of all power to rise to higher things. How can you taste the purer joys when you are clogged and held back by the dross of this world? Have you not heard that it is easier for a rich man . . . ."

" Yes, yes," said his host impatiently. " I have heard it a hundred times, and it isn't true. O' course *you* don't know it, 'cause you've never had any money yourself, but ye'll never have real, what ye may call *spiritual* enjoyment till ye're easy! Now take me. 'Fore I inherited this jolly leather bag, what was I? Why, moody, an' discontented, and, eh? what? Pullin' the devil by the tail, as th' sayin' goes, an' borrowin' from Peter to pay Paul, lyin' awake and wonderin' how I'd meet next morning. An' look at me now! All serene, all joyful, spiritual. I'm more kindly, and more humorous—oh! much—an' I've a better judgment, as you may say. I tell you—you may think it odd—but I'm more humble. Yes, I am, I've lost all bitterness,"—and once again he stroked the leather bag until it almost smiled.

The moralist looked at him in a deep, most melancholy way, sighed, or rather groaned, and mournfully took his leave, shaking his head as over a brother who was lost.

Then came in a fourth, who spoke more briskly and who said:—

" You know as well as I do that it makes no difference whether you are rich or poor. Men soon get used to whatever they have got, whether it's much or little or none. The first day or two after you got all this you felt pleased, didn't you? And no doubt the first day or two after you lost it you'd feel miserable. But in a week after either you'd be where you've always been. The whole thing's an illusion, and cherishing it a folly. I don't say get rid of it. What I do say is, take your mind off it. Don't make it more important than it is."

" I've heard that kind of talk before," said the rich man rather wearily. " I've even heard it—yes, I have— from people who ought to know better, an' all I can say is, it's folk who talk like that are deaf, dumb an' blind. Else they're lyin'. Anyhow, I'm not one of 'em. What, all this? " and here he patted the bag, " all this makes no difference? Chase me! You might just as well say while you're about it that—well!—it's beyond me. Poverty! Why, my dear sir—my dear sir, poverty's worse 'n the tooth-ache. I know what I'm talkin' about. I've been through it."

And with that he put the tips of his fingers together and hummed a little air.

The fourth visitor shrugged his shoulders and said that it really didn't matter whether he learned commonsense or not, for he would be just as happy or unhappy either way; and with that he went his way.

Then came yet another visitor, who approached the rich man with a bland directness which amused him. He said: " You have more there than you know what to do with. Give me part of it. It is not for me to order you about; I don't say give me half, or even a quarter; I leave that for you to judge. But give me a good lump. You won't feel it, and it will make a lot of difference to me."

" I am sure it would make a lot of difference to you," answered the rich man, kindly. " And I'm sure I'd like to do it at once." The fifth visitor smiled. " But there's this, ye' know, and I can't get away from it. If I gave *you* part of what lies here," and here he leant forward with an earnest look, " there'd be less for *me*."

Then he leant back and added: " Ye' know, the thought of that, I tell ye' frankly, it's quite intolerable. I am sorry. You must go and try it on somebody else. Somebody soft. There's plenty about." And he laughed genially.

The fifth visitor smiled, nodded, thanked him, and disappeared.

Then there was a little lull, which was very grateful to the rich man, for he was getting tired of seeing so many people, and all of them quite wrong; when there came in to see him a last caller, of a very different sort from the others. He had what is called a military demeanour; he was dressed in a light grey suit and each leg of his trousers had a crease so prominent that you might almost have called it a ridge. His boots shone. He had a heavy watch chain. He had well-groomed iron-grey hair. He carried his handsome face high, and well; and if there was one slightly displeasing thing about him, it was a very large cigar whch he wore oddly in the corner of his mouth. There entered with him a humble attendant, pushing a neat little truck on wheels.

He said that he had come to talk business. The rich man, with a sigh of relief, attuned his mind to something new and worth hearing. The visitor put down his hat, which was of the old pre-war kind and polished to eight reflections. He leaned his gold-headed stick against the table, crossed his legs, took the cigar from his mouth, puffed a large cloud of smoke into his host's face, after the fashion of a man of the world, and came down to brass tacks. His talk was of shares, options, and contracts; of maturing—even of combines; nor were there absent from it " debentures," " splitting," " reconstruction," " ground-floor," and " getting in early "; and " cutting up the pie," " packet," also—all the phrases of the great world. As his last visitor spoke the rich man was enlarged and enlarged until he felt himself a god, and he nodded and nodded, and he took his visitor to his heart.

So at last, the rich man, with the best will in the world, hoisted his leather bag upon the truck with his own hands, and his visitor, with many a hearty handshake, left him, his attendant trundling the truck away; and the rich man was left alone in the seventh heaven of happiness, contemplating future things.

But meanwhile this last visitor had gone all the way back to his own home, where he dumped the bag down into his own cellar, and there it was secured by process of law and a guard set over it; and the rich man never saw it again.

H. BELLOC.

True Sensibility.

(" *A Russian woman would be quite offended if a man opened a door for her.*")

THE Bolshevist lady is no less refined
   Than Victorian misses, but more.
      They shrank if a man might be under the bed;
   She shrieks if he opens the door.

Though shirt-sleeves might shock them, the Bolshevist
      maid
   Is far more fastidious than that.
They frowned at a man if he took off his coat;
   She faints when he takes off his hat.

She blushes at anything all the day long,
   Which is why it is commonly said
That while other young ladies are normally pink,
   She is now irretrievably Red.

FOUND WANDERING.

BY G. K. CHESTERTON.

HOW I TRIED TO BOOM THIS PAPER.

I HAVE often told elsewhere the horrid tale of how this paper came to have its horrid title. It is enough to say here that I certainly never contemplated the title when I conceived the paper. I had always thought that there ought to be a paper expressing a certain serious body of opinion that has no other organ. But it were expressing mildly to state I am not a business man; and I had and still have to consult friends who are much more businesslike. When they answered my question by saying earnestly that the only way it could be worked would be as a personal organ with my initials on the front page, I naturally thought it was a joke. It has taken me two years to realise and be reconciled to the cold and blood-curdling fact that they really are practical men; and it is a practical joke. That practical joke is now in operation. The reader has seen the booby-trap at work; though I have disquieting doubts about who is the booby. I was too much exhausted with my hopeless struggle against business efficiency to resist the further outrage of my portrait being put on the outer cover of the first number. I am told that this also is a part of efficiency; though I have not the least idea of what it is supposed to effect. Perhaps it has something to do with the principle by which a dubious character is expected to put his photograph on his passport. In that case, perhaps it would be even better to have a large finger-print or an even larger foot-print.

And with these brighter thoughts my mood changed; and I began to see my duty in a clearer and more cheerful fashion. If I must sell the paper in order to spread the opinions, and perform these mysterious antics in order to sell the paper, I will cut my capers heartily and in a more varied and vigorous fashion. It is evidently no time to be hampered by my middle-class traditions. I must abandon all this affectation of the fine and fastidious self-respect of a Bohemian journalist of Fleet Street. I must be rolled in the mud just as if I were a great nobleman, a great Minister of State, the ruler of a historic nation or the bearer of a historic name. I must remember the washing baskets full of dirty linen that pass from the great houses to the law courts; I must remember the general change in the manners of the great. I have seen a fashionable lady, after a public dinner, set out a sort of dressing-table on the dinner-table and proceed to paint herself all the colours of the rainbow. I have often wondered what she would think if I took out a tooth-brush and a tube of tooth-paste and began to clean my teeth in the same public fashion; which would seem a much more normal and necessary proceeding after a meal. I have seen at the top of a column announcing the chief news of the day, in a great newspaper, several paragraphs devoted to describing how Mr. Winston Churchill insisted on having two or three more bathrooms in his private residence and personally supervised their erection, lest there should be too few of them. I do not know how the journalist could carry a trivial indignity much further, except by one of those triple snap-shots, showing the unfortunate politician taking three baths at once, and wearing a different sort of hat in each. I am capable of overflowing far more bathrooms than Mr. Churchill; but I will not pursue the parallel, beyond saying that I am quite willing that a picture of my hat should be substituted for a picture of my head. I am quite ready for anything, in the reckless reaction of my mood; and I only wish to find relief by flinging myself with enthusiasm into the efficient side of the business. I wish to be a bustling business man; a hustler; a live wire. But it is my melancholy duty to report that when I came back to my business advisers, bursting with brilliant suggestions for selling the paper like hot cakes, their reception of my hot cakes was decidedly cold.

For instance, I pointed out that to put my name, my initials and my portrait on the same page was as monotonous as the pattern of a wallpaper. It was to use vain repetitions, as the Gentiles do. There was no zip, no pep, none of the bright business qualities that I felt boiling within me at the moment. Now if there could only be a portrait of somebody else, with my name printed underneath it, the combination might possibly attract remark. Suppose a portrait of Mr. Compton Mackenzie, for instance, who was to have written the principal article in the number but has been obliged to postpone it to a later one: the reader's attention might really be arrested by noting his much more distinguished appearance, his pointed beard and his strenuous elegance; and then reading underneath the simple words "Mr. G. K. Chesterton." I should like to pursue the policy for several numbers; varying the portrait with the same unvarying title; so that the faces of Lord Carson, Lord Beaverbrook, Sir Squire Bancroft, Mr. Amery and Sir Alfred Mond should successively look forth from the front page to adorn and illustrate the name of G. K. Chesterton. That might really arouse a certain stir of interest. That might really cause the simple to exclaim: "I never knew he looked like that" and the obliging to send a snowstorm of letters into the correspondence column to correct the little error. The circulation among the people who like writing to correct a little error would alone be enormous. But when I urged this on my practical friends, who are so keen on publicity and advertisement, they said they could not conscientiously advise it. They have no true enterprise; no real fire. I admitted that there might be some danger of libel in calling a person G. K. Chesterton. It is not a thing to be said lightly of any man. I offered as an alternative to draw, myself, a series of symbolical portraits of myself; refined gentlemen with bald heads and black whiskers, far more likely to obtain the confidence of the business public; beautiful youths with Greek profiles, far more likely to give an air of hope and promise to the enterprise. All my inspirations fell back blunted from the deplorable conservatism of the business world. I was not even allowed to do what any little boy can do with the portrait of his sainted grandmother, and add large, bushy whiskers, horns, or other appendages; anything that would avoid the stale redundancy of the name and the portrait referring to the same man. One might almost use it as a threat or a form of blackmail: "Buy this paper or I will grow these whiskers." I remember that when Mr. Max Beerbohm grew a moustache (which I cannot but regard as a headlong fall from those high terraces of the eighteenth century, on which he moved with the combined graces of Beau Nash and Voltaire) I dreamed that some desperate measures might perhaps be taken to arrest the growth. I began to draw dreadful pictures on pieces of paper; showing what would have been the appearance of the most historic and famous clean-shaven persons if they had grown moustaches. Mr. Gladstone with a waxed moustache. Cardinal Manning with a curly moustache. Shelley with a heavy cavalry moustache. I do not know whether it would have turned back Mr. Max Beerbohm from the crime which he rushed away to hide in Italy; if indeed the terrible transformation did not take place in that land of magic and crime. Whiskers or a chin-beard might have been used perhaps with equally menacing effect in many cases; but hardly in mine, as I have no such eighteenth century outline to spoil. The only eighteenth century association I can boast is that somebody in a moment of madness compared me to Dr. Johnson, which is enough to make that great man turn in his grave. Anyhow, I have often taken a walk down Fleet Street; but my attempt to rush madly down Fleet Street, in the capacity of an excited newsboy, was evidently not regarded as a success.

I had many other ideas of the same smart and commercial sort. Owing to the printers requiring the copy much earlier than had been expected, contributions from several distinguished writers have unfortunately been rather late for this issue. I had a wild temptation to write all their contributions myself and sign them with their names; to see whether I could write a poem by Mr. de la Mare, a story by Mr. Compton Mackenzie, a criticism by Mr. Maurice Baring, or what not. If I were Mr. J. C. Squire, I could forge a whole magazine complete from start to finish and nobody would ever know the difference; because the writers would want the credit of having imitated themselves so well. He could produce that little-known poem of Mr. de la Mare, so little known that it is as yet unknown to its author, which is called "Mare's Nests by Moonshine," and begins with an old man in a white hat finding the marks of horse-hoofs running straight up the grey-green trunk of a tree. He would be able to write the last chapter in the brilliant biography of Mr. Mackenzie's clergyman; the magnificent pageant of white and gold when the reverend gentleman is made Pope. He could imagine the next imaginary conversation of Mr. Maurice Baring; that cheery little chat between Goethe and Catullus and the world-famous Russian poet Muffsky, about the complete misunderstanding in England of the Slavonic system of punctuation. Best of all, if I were Mr. J. C. Squire, I could write a perfect imitation of Mr. J. C. Squire; and that is the author whom I like him best to imitate. Only if I were Mr. J. C. Squire, I should have an admirably conducted magazine of my own already; and this would not be G.K.'s WEEKLY, but *The Mercury;* and such inconsequent balderdash as this article would be very promptly and properly returned with thanks. Since, however, I have touched on that topic in a personal sense, I will add a word more upon the personal side of it. My colleagues in the more practical department will not resent the levity with which I have written here; for they have long learned to tolerate a levity which they probably associate with lunacy. But at least I have not taken liberties with their names as I have with those of poets and politicians; or compromised their business prospects and reputations for sanity by associating with myself and my scheme. But if there is one of my most practical advisers whom I may be allowed to name, it is one whom I have named already; a man without whose sympathy and good nature this number might never have been in print. And as a new book often recommends itself by inscription to a familiar name, I should like to dedicate this first number of the first volume of this weekly paper to Jack Collings Squire, a man active and adroit in so many fields, whose creative work creates and whose criticism criticises; an original poet but a traditional judge; who is critical of all the thousand things in art and letters which it is his duty to criticise; critical of his criticisms; and, fortunately for some of us, not too critical of his friends.

The World State.

OH how I love Humanity
  With love so pure and pringlish:
  And how I hate the horrid French
Who never will be English.

The International Idea,
The largest and the clearest,
Draws me to all the nations now
Except the one that's nearest.

This compromise has long been known,
This scheme of partial pardons,
In Ethical Societies
And small suburban gardens.

The villas and the chapels where
I learned with little labour
The way to love my fellow-man
And hate by next-door neighbour.

PARLIAMENT FROM WITHIN.
THE PROBLEM STATED.

By Sir Henry Slesser, K.C., M.P.

IF the progress of a battle is to be understood it is an advantage if the onlooker has some knowledge of the disposition and nature of the contending forces. For this reason I propose here to describe the various political elements which make up the House of Commons to-day. To look at the Order Paper and Proceedings of that venerable House one would imagine that Party was unknown at Westminster, and that each Member was of equal importance; one would gather, on the other hand, from the newspapers that our politicians were divided into three camps: Conservative, Labour and Liberal, but it is the proud aim of G.K.'s WEEKLY that it seeks to find realities behind the formalism of the past or the superficiality of the present, and to the Realist, observing the interplay of political forces at close range, it soon becomes evident that neither the artificial unity of the constitutional lawyer nor the irreconcilable trinity of the Party Whips accounts adequately for the situation.

While it is true that there are only two Division Lobbies in the House and three Parties to pass through them, one soon finds when in actual contact with Members of Parliament that their views, uncurtailed by considerations of Party loyalty and discipline, tend to collect round principles unknown to organisers and often unheard in debate, and that the number of such congeries of opinion is considerably more than the historic three. Thus, to take the Governmental side of the House first, there are quite clearly three distinct Parties at present at Westminster all of which answer to the name of Conservative. There is, first of all, the monied Party, which should most certainly be given priority in so far as it is the most active and influential. It is fairly well represented in the Industrial Group who were responsible for the Trade Union Levy Bill, and are promoting the protection of all industries except that of Agriculture, with which enterprise they appear to have no concern. They also favour the legal recognition of great Trusts and Combines, such as the Electric Companies which are to be set up by Statute all over England.

The second Group, which is erroneously confused with the plutocrats under the name of Die-Hard, whose opinions on most subjects are entirely divergent, is even larger than that of the Commercial Group in numbers, but somewhat lacking in intellectual equipment. It is composed, for the most part, of retired Army and Naval officers of various ages together with a certain number of country squires. It is more strongly represented in this Parliament than it was in the Lloyd George time, and combines a nationalistic idealism with a curious incapacity to realise that its political bedfellows, the plutocrats, are menacing the integrity and honour of the Empire which this Group defend.

The third and smallest group of all is that which has inherited the production of Young England and is concerned with specific social reform. It shares with the second or Nationalistic Group a dislike to Pacifism, Bolshevism and the International Outlook, but realises, as the second group do not, the perils by which their own ideals are beset by the Plutocrats.

I pass next to the Federation known as the Official Opposition or Labour Party. I cannot pretend to be entirely impartial as to the welfare of this Party or as to its success or failure, but endeavouring to view it *ab extra*, it also appears to contain three classes of opinion. In the first place, there is the Party of the Socialists of the School, as they would be called abroad, mostly members of the Independent Labour Party. This Group have certainly given the public the impression from their activity and eloquence that they constitute the whole and orthodox opinion of the Labour Party as a whole. Their views derive very largely from the early work of the Fabian Society, but recently they have so far mitigated the true doctrine of collectivism as to admit that it is desirable that the workers should have some share of control in their industries. They are, for the most part, indifferent as to the emotions of the nationalists, and favour Pacifism in international affairs. It is this group who were responsible for a Motion to reduce the Air Force to a few thousand men, and they received in the Lobby the support of twenty-five members of the Labour Party out of a total of 150.

The second group, which is the largest, the most widely representative of working-class opinion, and the least articulate, is the Trade Union Group. I do not think that this group, apart from such members of it as are associated with the Independent Labour Party, are definitely collectivist or likely to become so. That is, while they certainly would look upon our present monopoly by Trusts of industry as highly dangerous and in the loose but useful phrase so often employed, are " opposed to the Capitalist System," the views which are held by the Editor of this paper would be at least as satisfactory to them in theory as the views of Mr. Sidney Webb, and indeed, I have little doubt that were capitalism in its present form to be ended, no one would be more concerned that the people should retain their fair share of private property than this great group which numbers over one hundred of the one-hundred and fifty members of the Labour Party.

The third, smallest, and most interesting class is that commonly called the Clyde. They, more than any other element in the House of Commons, constitute a real protest against existing industrial conditions at their worst. They are not concerned with the pacifism of the Independent Labour Party, and, as one of them recently stated in the House in the debate on the air estimates, they only supported the amendment for the reduction of the Air Force to nothing because they thought that the money could better be employed in Clydebank, and not, as he was particular to say, for sentimental reasons. In economics I do not believe that, strictly speaking, they are socialist at all. At any rate if that much vexed word is to be used in the sense of sympathy with State control and State ownership I think they are far more concerned to obtain property for those whom they represent than to see it vested in the public authority. But this part of their view is not dominant, nor, I think, in their opinion, important, at the moment. The interesting thing about them is that they are vital and practical, and are supremely, nay inconveniently, honest, not only in their dealings with others, but with themselves. They are the least Parliamentarian of all the Members at Westminster.

Finally, to speak of last things, we come to the Liberal Party. Here again division may be observed, partly real and partly artificial. There is a real division between the small Radical Group headed by Runciman and the rest of this Party. There is an artificial division between the centre as represented by Sir John Simon, and the followers of Lloyd George. The latter division being purely Parliamentary will not interest the readers of G.K.'s WEEKLY, but the Radical Group are important in that small though they are, they represent from the middle-class angle an insistent demand for the consideration of the individual. They can be relied upon vehemently to criticise legislation by Government Department and political collectivism, but they are carelessly blind to the fact that liberty is as much menaced by the Trust and the Bank as by any Government official.

To sum up, therefore, there are at least eight political parties at Westminster. Certain artificial divisions have been produced, but what is emerging more and more clearly is that there exists a fundamental cleavage between those who accept modern plutocracy and think it capable of improvement, and those who would repudiate it as based on avarice and ruinous to the just State.

This question dominates Debate, whatever nominally may be the question for consideration; it has brought reality once more into the House of Commons—but a refusal to consider the principles upon which condemnation of capitalism should be based or to suggest what order of social conditions should be substituted for it has so far robbed its exponents of much driving force. Nevertheless, I am of the opinion that the domination of the State collectivist mind over the opponents of Plutocracy is passing away, though we have yet to see what political philosophy will take its place.

House of Commons, March, 1925.

The Old Gentleman in the Park.

BEYOND the trees like iron trees
   The painted lamp-posts stand.
      The old red road runs like the rust
Upon this iron land.

Cars flat as fish and fleet as birds,
Low-bodied and high speeded,
Go on their belly like the Snake
And eat the dust as he did.

But down the red dust never more
Her happy horse-hoofs go.
O what a road of rust indeed!
O what a Rotten Row!

THE THIEF.

BY WALTER DE LA MARE.

ONCE upon a time there lived in a mansion in the Great City of London a Thief. There never was a thief of so much pomp and riches. He had coaches and carriages—apple-green, cardinal, scarlet, canary and maroon. He had stabling for forty horses—bay, cream, roan, and piebald; he had coachmen and footmen, linkboys and outriders, white, yellow and black.

There were so many servants indeed to do his bidding that he never even attempted to remember their names. He just clapped his hands, and they came; clapped his hands and they went.

His rooms bulged with furniture of the utmost magnificence. Gilt was nothing to him. Not only were his plates and dishes, jugs and basins of solid gold, but so were his chair-castors and bell-pulls; while his warming pans were of purest Thracian silver. There was velvet on his floors; and tapestries of Arras and Gobelin and Bayeaux with the date in the corner of 999 on the walls. Silken mats from Persia and India, Bangkok and Samarkand beflowered his marble and alabaster stair-cases. As for his Pictures—he had a Siege of Athens fourteen yards by six in his privy parlour, with frame to match. His cellars were full of wine, and his attics crammed—boards to rafters—with sacks of moidores, doubloons, diamonds, rubies, Orient pearls, and Pieces of Eight. There never was such a Thief since the world began, and he lived in his mansion all alone.

He had a fine constitution, too. He was a square burly man with a large head and a slight squint in his little green eyes, and he dressed in a velvet doublet and rose-silk hose, like Henry VIII. And being now come to be about sixty years of age, and having stolen everything he thought worth stealing, his one desire was to marry and settle down. He desired to be safe and comfortable and respectable and beloved. What is more, he lusted and longed in good time to be able to share his ill-gotten gains among his children—ten at least: five strapping sons, and five golden daughters.

And then perhaps in full season, when he was ninety-nine or a hundred and so, he would die and be buried in an enormous tomb made of a hundred kinds of marble inlaid with sardonyx and chalcedony. And he hoped by that time no one would feel inclined to remember where his wicked wealth had come from, he being so much beloved. And multitudes upon multitudes of mourners—men, women and children—in deepest black would attend him to his grave. And they would cut out upon his tomb in gold-filled lettering:—

> Here lies, in our belief
> Of honourable men the Chief.
> He died respected of us all
> After a Splendid Funeral.

Just like Enoch Arden, who had never stolen a sixpence or even a yam.

But this was only a hope and a dream in this Thief's head. For after all, there was one thing he really wanted to do before he died—much more important than tombstones and funerals—and that was to be happy. But it was difficult for such a Thief as he even to be contented. It was difficult for such a Thief as he to be contented because it was impossible for him even to be at ease. He hadn't a real Friend to his name, and more enemies than he could count. He could not even stir out of his house except after dark, or in a thick fog, in case he should be recognised in the Streets by someone whom he had robbed. He was therefore compelled to keep within doors all day. His only chance, that is, against being found out was always to remain *in*.

Even at night he would sit shivering in his coach on his way to a Ball or a Rout or a Banquet or a Ceremony or a Function, with the gold-laced blinds tightly drawn, and his piebald horses heavily caparisoned in ear-nets and flowered velvet, and silver tassels, so that nobody should notice their tell-tale spots. And as likely as not he put on a false beard and whiskers.

All this was second nature to him, but the one thing he could not understand when he was safe at home sitting by himself looking at a beautiful book he had not yet learned to read, or playing over a tune with one finger on his American organ, or biting his nails and looking out of the window at the people walking in the streets, every one of whom was twenty-thousand times at least poorer than his chief footman—there was one thing he could not understand. Which was why he was not happy.

At first he thought it was because he had not yet managed to marry a wife. But then for a Thief as rich as he only a very few wives could be fine enough. It must be a Great Lady. He had asked all such of these as he could, but not a single one would at last say, Yes.

First there was the Duchess of Anjou and Angelette. She was a duchess absolutely in her own right, with finer manners than a queen, and a nose so aristocratic that it rose up between her eyes like the Duke of Wellington's, or like the wing of a seraph in full flight. The Thief sent her a most polite little note, copied out of a Guide to Letter Writing, and inscribed in the most beautiful Italian handwriting by his Writing-Master, Signor Babbinotti. At first the Duchess had said Yes—though not in such few words as that.

But when her High Chamberlain came to look over the Thief's mansion, and to count his sacks of diamonds and doubloons, and taste the wine in his cellar, he began to have suspicions. There were bureaux of ivory and ebony there and coffers of cedar-wood and crysopras that he seemed to remember to have seen in the Palace of the King of Portugal. And there was a necklet of black duck's egg pearls that he knew in his heart had once dangled round the neck of the fair Duchess of Anjou and Angelette herself. And as soon as he had returned home and had refreshed himself with a little sleep after his visit to the Thief's cellars, the Duchess addressed in the third person another little letter to the Thief, which said not Yes, but a most emphatic No.

So, too, with the Countess Couterau de Côtelette with the three golden plaits, one of whose ancestors had been King of Troy before Helen was born. *Her* first faint Yes was also followed by an emphatic No.

(To be continued.)

[*When I was contemplating the crime of pretending to be Mr. de la Mare, as described elsewhere, his charming fairytale arrived in time to appear in this issue, but unfortunately not in its entirety. It will be continued next week.*—G.K.C.]

THE DRAMA.

Spring Cleaning—and Brinsley Sheridan.

SPRING cleaning from a sufferer's point of view is a groaning penance. We are told—and unwillingly believe—that the time of the singing of birds calls for the upheaval of the home and the tidying of our comfort out of existence. True it is that the grime of winter may be removed or covered over with new paint, but to the uninitiated the onslaught of vacuum cleaners, whitewashers and dustmen seems hardly justified. The aspect of things in general remains the same.

Something of this was in my thoughts at the performance of Mr. Frederick Lonsdale's brightly-written comedy at St. Martin's Theatre. We hear so much of the moral dirt of Mr. Richard Sones's house; we are warned so gravely as to the decadence behind the cornice, the degeneration under the mat; we are so often and so violently informed that, at all costs, Mr. Sones intends to clean his residence that when, at last, the house is garnished we wonder if, after all, it is so very different.

There is a mode at the moment for the exploitation of degeneracy upon the stage with its due concomitant of reprobation. Degeneracy is eternally the same; it is in the matter of denunciation that the dramatist gets a new angle. Mr. Noel Coward's modern handling of a Shakespearean situation between mother and son is a case in point. Mr. Frederick Lonsdale does the same thing from another direction.

In "Spring Cleaning" we have a bad-mannered husband in love with his wife and knowing that he is in love. We have a pretty and vain wife, in love with her husband but not knowing it. These are the central figures. Margaret, bored by Richard—his novels and his rudeness—surrounds herself with a collection of idle and amusing people who go about with each other's husbands, drink cocktails, and make pets of ladylike young men instead of rabbits.

They are all established types, moving in a regular and tiny orbit, outside which they are not seen. The most prominent, Ernest Steele, is not ladylike. He is thoroughly unmoral, makes love with the art and assiduity of the Regency, and Margaret very nearly succumbs to his daily gift of flowers and his telephone inquiries.

It is all very witty, most intimate, and admirably suited to a small theatre where the audience are continually seeing a stage likeness to their acquaintance. Richard demands that Margaret shall get rid of all the dear farmyard creatures and, on her refusal, like a post-war Petruchio, determines to bring her to her knees. He calls it "saving her from herself." Of course he means saving her from Steele, but it comes to the same thing.

The method which he adopts is the *clou* of the whole play. Margaret is giving a dinner to the menagerie and Richard suddenly appears at the table with a prostitute. The thrill that vibrated through the audience when Miss Cathleen Nesbitt appeared in a state of pitiful bedragglement was perceptible. What a situation! How *piquante!* How naughty! The women—at least eighty-five per cent. of the house—hugged themselves in anticipation.

And here again I thought of the denunciator on the hearth when, armed with brooms and brushes, she sweeps up your papers. There is a special kind of broom which scratches your nerves. I wonder if it is more efficacious than the milder variety or used merely to scarify.

Mona of the streets creates as great a disturbance in the Sones's dining room as in the theatre. The guests run into the corners screaming "how dreadful," the women clutch their skirts; the men study their boots and look very unhappy. Margaret's friends would not have done so. They would have crowded round Mona crying "how quaint," "isn't she divine?" and have addressed searching inquiries as to the details of her calling and where she bought her hat.

Such an attitude of eagerness would have been equally barbarous as the other extreme, but when we are told that a certain set of people are utterly degenerate they should behave as such. The production of Mona emphasises the tendency we find in all these essays in decadence. The study of cruelty on the stage is as legitimate as the study of any moral quality. But to me there is an offence against human dignity in pillorising a prostitute in order to annoy your wife.

The first two acts are set with a dead seriousness, except for the degenerates; the last act is light comedy, full of sparkling lines and much the best of the show. Steele "explains" woman to Sones at length, but the inevitable ending is mercifully short. Margaret falls into her husband's arms, and we feel certain that her future friends will be very dull and most respectable.

The acting is good. Mr. Ronald Squire as Ernest Steele is persuasive, and his sly humour never fails in the most trying passage. Miss Cicely Byrne is admirably cast as Margaret and makes a most attractive young matron. Miss Edna Best's attempts to be degenerate are a little pathetic. Her garments are authentic and her hair is shingled to the latest angle, but though her eyeglass is freakish her voice remains as young and eager as a March morning. She is still the agreeable flapper, no matter what she wears. Miss Cathleen Nesbitt suggests a nursery governess of the less instructed type; the wildest imaginings cannot see in her a lady of the streets. Her dress is wrong and her hat impossible.

The suburbs—so far as the theatre is concerned—no longer can be used as a term of reproach. The West End gives us Frederick Lonsdale; Hammersmith produces "The Rivals." Sheridan's play is staged with the zest and freshness that characterised Mr. Nigel Playfair's previous productions. He has the spirit of the period and his company act as though it were the first time the dialogue has been spoken. The setting is delicious in its gracious austerity, a couch for Lydia Languish, a dressing table that Bob Acres may admire himself.

Mr. Playfair gives Bob Acres the right quality of vain simplicity. He is by no means an oaf, and suggests that in time to come he may yet ruffle it in Tunbridge Wells if not in Bath. Miss Isabel Jeans is adorable as Lydia Languish, though she suffers a little from the chilliness of Mrs. Malaprop. Miss Dorothy Green has not the ripeness necessary for the character. Her speech is mincing where it should be a rolling tide, and she shows no joy in her parts of speech. But this is but a small criticism on a fine revival, and it is a joy to know that the Lyric Theatre is continuously full.   J. K. PROTHERO.

REVIEWS.

THE WHITE MONKEY *

SOME of us think the " Forsyte Saga " the nearest approach to a masterpiece that any living English novelist has given us since the Hardy era As we study the architecture of the cycle and note the breadth of its design and the consistency of its detail, as we walk round the pile or make our way through its long gallery of pictures, as we watch in this elaborate history of a Victorian family the process by which its hero is converted from an ogre who jars our nerves into a thing of pathos to whom we must extend our sympathy, we feel that Mr. Galsworthy, contemplating his amazingly uniform trilogy, might use the words of a greater Creator and hail the world of his shaping as good. But just because it is so good we were bound to look with a suspicious eye on any story of his which might claim to be or might be taken for a sequel, any further chapter of Forsyte adventures. After all, there was symmetry and there was completeness about the original plan; it was rounded off; the old sin of that modern Helen of Troy, Irene, had worked out its Nemesis in thwarting the happiness of young love; we were content to leave Mr. Galsworthy's characters, much as we liked them, where he had left them and bid them good-bye. To revisit them might be delightful but would involve risks. Might not a new and modern wing mar the harmony of the old scheme; might not a re-touching of cherished portraits spoil their appeal? When all was said, Soames Forsyte and his daughter, Fleur, were public property and almost classic figures. What if Fleur lost her charm and individuality! What—to mention a more melancholy possibility—if Soames should suffer a sea-change of the sort that brings a Falstaff debased into the company of the " Merry Wives of Windsor "!

So " The White Monkey " must have been opened by many of Mr. Galsworthy's worshippers with fear and trembling and just at starting point they must have found some warrant for their concern. For not only does the novelist's method of telling his tale seem for a while to show the influence of the modernity he is seeking to describe, so that it copies, perhaps unconsciously, the jerkiness of our young jazz-writers of to-day, but Fleur, as we first meet her again, appears type rather than living, breathing woman. Oh, yes, she is true enough to type! Don't we know her, this newly married girl, with no child but with a dog she over-pets, this social climber who collects celebrities of art and music and letters, as other folk collect curios, though without their discrimination and preferences, merely fixing on this or that man of the hour because he is in the fashion, because she is so afraid of making a mistake and being out of the movement, really but half-educated for all her flair and sensibility, much less of a judge than the husband who puzzles her and lacks her love? She is representative enough of large numbers of the new generation—that is to say of the froth that it throws on the top—but for a time she is too typical to take on life, to reveal more to us than that side of herself which she shows to the world. Even when she is in some danger at the hands of her poet-lover, Wilfred Desert, whom she merely likes but does not want to relinquish, even when she meditates for a moment about " going over the deep end " with him " just once." She is but the mimic of the jargon and sentiments of her set. But gradually as we see her alone with the father who adores the ground she treads or watch her relentings, her gushes of pity, her little tendernesses towards the unselfish and sunny-hearted husband, Michael Mont, whose misfortune it is to have caught her on the rebound, the old Fleur comes back to us—restless, adventurous, self-

centred but warm of heart and loyal at the core. Long before she becomes a mother and is made quite safe, Mr. Galsworthy has done the trick again and made the young wife of Michael as fascinating a reality as the girl sweetheart of Jon.

As for Soames—the other object of our concern—he has so mellowed under his inventor's re-handling that whereas we hated him in " A Man of Property," tolerated him in " In Chancery," and grew sorry for him in " To Let," we like him and admire him, for all his grimness, in " The White Monkey." The old Adam, of course, is still permitted to remain. Once more this lawyer among the Forsytes is in at the death-bed of a relative, the sardonic George, who once dubbed his cousin an " undertaker," and recalling this insult, we catch Soames reflecting to himself: " Well! One by one those who had injured or gibed at him—Irene, Bosinney, old and young Jolyon, and now George, had met their fates. Dead, dying, or in British Columbia." It is a perfect touch, as rich in its humour as it is true to character, Soames's old character, though one can imagine a reader who comes fresh to " The White Monkey " with no knowledge of " The Forsyte Saga," asking himself with dismay: " Who was Irene or this Bosinney? What on earth has British Columbia to do with this story? " For Mr. Galsworthy does not rehearse the family history of the Forsytes in this book as he did in the two sequels to " The Man of Property," so that it was possible to read each of them independently. If the student of " The White Monkey " is to grasp all its allusions he will need to turn to the " Saga " for enlightenment, and only if he does so will he understand the transformation that has come over Soames and appreciate its piquancy. Has the novelist learnt to understand this old Victorian better, the more he has lived with him? At all events, here is the once sinister, grasping, " mousing " Soames, who treated his wife as if he had bought her body and soul, exuding kindliness at every pore. This Soames keeps up his passion for buying good pictures, watches carefully after his money, but he is to be seen tipping a poor hawker in the street, arranging that a man who has lost his job in the cause of honesty gets new employment. This Soames has learnt patience with the slang and seeming flippancy of his son-in-law, and even loses his director's fees sooner than countenance the possibility of the shareholders of a company in which he is concerned having their prosperity menaced. He is a hero of finance who gets all the kicks and none of the halfpence for doing the decent thing. He haunts his beloved daughter's house, this Soames, keeps unloading his fortune on her and when he thinks he may lose his wealth, actually says: " As for himself—what did he care? A room at his club near Fleur—he would be just as happy, perhaps happier ! " Does it require age to understand old age?

In between whiles, need it be repeated? Mr. Galsworthy is giving us a picture of that disillusioned, unrestful, unanchored section of our youth of to-day, whom we are apt to style at its own valuation as the " new generation," though he is careful to show that the phrase in that sense does not cover more than a fraction of our community. He shows us the " pan-joys " and the " new faithfuls," and with them a big group of " thinking " young people on whom the war and its aftermath has brought disaster of soul, carefully leavening his lump, however, with such studies as those of his Bickets—man and wife with old-fashioned instincts of self-sacrifice and propriety. It is this minority of our world at whom the title of his new book glances. " The White Monkey " is a picture in which the small beast is to be seen tearing at an orange and scattering its rind while it stares

---

* " The White Monkey." By John Galsworthy. Heinemann 7/6 net.

at the spectator with almost human, inquiring eyes. That is meant to typify the "new generation," with its eager quest for sensation, its resolve to suck life dry, its indifference to the shards of belief, and its pathetic inquiry as to the drift of all going on around. Mr. Galsworthy has caught its types, its lingo, its manifestations in art and literature, its bankruptcy in principles and faith. But if his book has any moral it is that the social phenomena on which he expends his irony and his acute observation are but flotsam on the tide of our race which holds on firmly to its inheritance from the past. "Pan-joys" may show up in the limelight, but it is the Bickets, one of whom thieves to keep his partner alive, while the other shamefacedly sits for the "altogether" to give him his chance, that are a constant quantity in our history. The differences between the generations are skin-deep, he would seem to say. A Michael Mont may murder the King's English, but his motto of "Play the game" is but a variant on that of his father-in-law, and his practice is vastly better than his creed. A Fleur may look over the edge, but when once her heart is stilled and her child is coming, her one simple desire is that her son shall be as good and cheerful as his father and escape the modern unrest. "Leave them alone," we seem to hear Mr. Galsworthy say of his young people, "and they will find their way back, through fever, through fret, to the things their fathers reverenced." Meantime, his art remains as beautifully objective and fair and restrained as in any of his work from "The Country House" onwards.

F. G. BETTANY.

NOVELS OF THE DAY.

IT was wise of Mr. Sinclair Lewis to devise a house for himself in England. I understand that the Americans have forgiven him "Main Street" and "Babbitt" but it is more than doubtful if they will pardon him for his most serious book, "Martin Arrowsmith." This novel is what "Red Lewis" himself would call "fierce." There is a great searching for the truth in it, a tremendous irritation against all forms of medical humbug, but "Martin Arrow-smith" is written in a vernacular that seems to exclude literature, though it may mirror, in a magnifying way, all the crudities of American life, with its "boost," its "pep," its "bunk" and its flapdoodle.

As long as Martin Arrowsmith is a medical student among medical students one can follow the rough slang with equanimity, but when Martin becomes a scientist, a bacteriologist, moving amongst adult people, one feels plunged into the society of naive barbarians. Mr. George Bernard Shaw has been almost merciful to doctors in comparison with Mr. Sinclair Lewis. This may be partly due to the fact that in the United States doctors are allowed to advertise, but there is a certain reticence even amongst English charlatans which saves them from figuring as intellectual hooligans.

The hero of Mr. Sinclair's fierce book is credited with a genuine love for science, but his own bacteriological experiments savour somehow of quackery. The characters are plunged in pools of serum and anti-toxin and there is a test-tube in every page. Towards the end, after long, clumsy endeavour, Martin succeeds in brewing a "bacteriophage," thereafter called "phage" which cures bubonic plague in the West Indies; but one is not sure of the "phage" all the same.

Story there is none in particular. Two persons only emerge from the laboratories whom one loves and pities as human beings—the cranky Martin, who is a hobo throughout, and his wife, Leora, who is the acme of hearty vulgarity. Martin has an earlier love affair and a second marriage, but Leora remains, an indelible memory of a splendid little soul who loves her man through thick and thin, bad temper and good.

There are dozens of appalling doctors in the book, and a

couple of honest professors. Our old poetic friend, Chum Frith, immortalises one of them in a boosting stanza :—

> Zenith welcomes with high hurraw
> A friend in Almus Pickerbaugh,
> The two-fisted fighting poet doc
> Who stands for health like Gibraltar's rock.
> He's jammed with figgers and facts and fun,
> The plucky old, lucky old, son-of-a-gun.

In Zenith we get the faintest glimpse of George F. Babbitt, but Mr. Lewis is evidently tired of him.

While Martin is curing plague in the West Indies, the little wisp of an uneducated hospital nurse he married contracts it and dies of it. This is one of the few passages in which Mr. Lewis falls back on the English language :—

All day, all night as her throat cracked with thirst, she lay longing for someone to help her. Once she crawled to the kitchen for water. The floor of the bedroom was an endless heaving sea, the hall a writhing dimness, and by the kitchen door she dropped and lay for an hour whimpering. . . . She was bewildered; she was lonely; she dared not start on her long journey without his hand to comfort her. She listened for him—listened—tense with listening. . . . Then she slipped on into the kindly coma. There was no more pain, and all the shadowy house was quiet, but for her hoarse and struggling breath.

By all our standards of learning and culture, " Martin Arrowsmith "* is a coarse book written in a crude dialect— but it comes very near greatness.

In completest contrast to Mr. Sinclair Lewis's sheerly American performance is Mrs. Beatrice Kean Seymour's completely English, " The Romantic Tradition,"† faultlessly written, about the psychological complexes of middle-class people of the Intelligensia variety. Sinclair Lewis is mainly concerned with false doctoring. Mrs. Seymour's book is a protest against the divagations of sex. It is written in the first person by a novelist, Miss Adela Stokes, about Kennedy Armfield and his blameless wife, Enid. The art of this novel is that although we are told nothing about " Stokey," as Enid's children call her, we know exactly what she is like and what her dry passion for Armfield is.

Enid is opposed to war, will not eat meat, has a grudge against sentiment, and considers that the idea that all women should be mothers is a pernicious one. She appears to have no religious beliefs whatever, but has a high and dry ethical standard. The only thoroughly feminine person in the novel is Sophie Birch, who is deficient in morals. Adela shares the view of her Feminist set about the so-called Romantic Tradition.

She states the case very well for a variety of interests in life beyond the mating and child-bearing interests; but the curious thing about her and Enid and Kennedy and their friends is that sex appears to occupy their thoughts to a quite remarkable extent.

It is good of Enid to bear Kennedy healthy twins. It is unreasonable of her to blame her husband for an accident to another child at birth. It is generous of her to have no jealousy of her husband with Sophie; but it is quite foolish of her to throw him into Sophie's arms from the beginning and to deny him any fine feeling because he had desires to remain her (Enid's) husband. It is hard lines on Kennedy that he should not only have to suffer tortures from his wife's celibate disdain, but that he should be killed by poor little Sophie, who was obviously not the type of girl who could have handled a gun with any effectiveness.

Finely as the book is written, one turns with relief to the humanity of Mr. Donn Byrne.

The short story is returning as a part of literature, and apart from the stereotyped merchandise of the fiction magazine. Donn Byrne, who takes his roots from the North of Ireland, and is only widely known in America, presents a volume of quite extraordinary excellence in " Changeling and Other Stories."‡ Byrne has the pictured imagination of a poet, but fortunately he does not write prose with a false gallop of rhythm in it. He made his name with " Messer Marco Polo," a jewel of a book, but a jewel somewhat too flamboyantly set. In " Changeling " he has changed for the better, as he uses reticences at times when he could use ecstasies.

" A Story Against Women " tells of a shabby old Irish gentleman, who makes his living by the almost incredible means of taking his money from bookmakers by the backing of successful horses. O'Connor Mellon, a tubby man with a grey-straiked red beard, an unbrushed frock-coat, and a bulging umbrella, came from Royal Meath where, under the peat of Allen, lie buried the Irish elk and the Irish boar, the Irish wolf and the wolf-dog who hunted him, and the invaders of old time, the brown Phoenicians and the red Danes. And yet Mellon was a professional backer.

From women he recoiled, as the young man in Scripture should have recoiled, from the lady whose feet were not in her own house. " Of course," as Mr. Byrne suggests, " he might have married an Irish colleen, but to get one of these he would have had to go to New York or Chicago and raid a musical comedy, Irish colleens not being, and never having been, indigenous to Ireland."

But old Mellon gallantly succumbs to a deceptive woman, and, so doing, fails to lodge a bet that would have won him £100,000, and have enabled him to nail the skin of his enemy, Regan, the bookmaker, on a wall. And poor old Mellon is left lamenting. There is fierce humour and blasting irony in this story.

In entirely different vein is Donn Byrne's " The Parliament of Thebes," in which the elephant, the lion, the tiger, the crocodile, the polar bear, the horse, the dog and others come before Michael John, an Irish angel, and tell him of the wrongs done to them by man. They all object to be exterminated, but they object also to the Fall of Man under civilisation :—

" I know nothing of painted Pharaohs," said the great white bear, " Nor anything of Indian queens. In the North are neither kings nor masons, but day and night and ice and a little people. . . . And the swarthy little people were happy then. In the long nights they sang, and they bowed to the gods in boulder and stream, and set out in the little kayaks on the Arctic Seas to hunt the great walrus, or they set off in sledges through the pathless wastes. They were a brave people, a healthy people. And came the boats hunting our sister the whale, and the strangers taught the little swarthy people progress, and everywhere now they are cunning and degraded and crusted with sin, and a great plague makes them spit blood, and waste to nothingness and die."

Michael John does his best to reconcile the scheme of creation to the dumb beasts, and more out of pity for him than anything else, they shuff-shuff-shuff over the sand on their way east, west, north and south, but the horse remains and nudges Michael John with his mouth, and the dog puts a cold nose into his hand, and Michael John groans of the departed ones, including the crocodile, " Och, me darlings."

Louis J. McQuilland.

---

* " Martin Arrowsmith." By Sinclair Lewis. Jonathan Cape, 7s. 6d.

† " The Romantic Tradition." By Beatrice Kean Seymour. Chapman & Hall, 7s. 6d.

‡ " Changeling and Other Stories." By Donn Byrne. Sampson, Low, Marston & Co., 7s. 6d.

LIBRARY LIST.

A NAVAL SCRAP-BOOK. By Admiral Sir Reginald Bacon. Hutchinson & Co. 24s.

Sir Reginald begins his naval log in 1877 before wood had vanished as a material for ships and wind had ceased to be used as a motive power. The old three-decker had become a thing of the past, but the best battleships were still rigged with masts, yards and sails as well as being provided with engines. The Silent Service was a fairly leisurely one. Sir Reginald recalls an old boatswain, whose Biblical knowledge was more colloquial than accurate, apostrophising the fo'c'sle men in this wise : "You're a blooming Portuguese army, you are, all blessed centurions. I say to one of you beggars, go, and he comes, and to another, do this, and he sees me damned first." The last quarter of the nineteenth century was the closing chapter in the history of the Old Navy. In a future volume Sir Reginald has promised to tell us all he remembers of the New. This should be noteworthy, as he started the submarine boats in the Navy, was assistant to Lord Fisher when he initiated his drastic naval reforms, and held command at Dover during the Great War.

SOME CONTEMPORARY DRAMATISTS. By Graham Sutton. Leonard Parsons. 6s.

The enthusiast generally communicates some of his ardency to his readers. Mr. Graham Sutton is so visibly exalted by the existence of the theatre and the importance of playwrights that one almost agrees with him that these are the most important considerations in life. There is one piece of striking originality in the book—Mr. Shaw is excluded—either on the grounds that he is behind contemporaneity or before it. Mr. Sutton is right in saying that "The Conquering Hero" is immensely bigger than anything Mr. A. N. Monkhouse has done as a playwright, but he is too serious about the seriousness of Monkhouse. There is shrewd observation of the influence of Synge in Eugene O'Neill's "Anna Christie" as being quite the weakest part of the play. The Irishman in "Anna Christie" has even less probability of character than Kipling's Mulvaney. Mr. Granville Barker is in danger of being forgotten as a playwright. It is pleasant to see that Mr. Sutton gives prominence to the author of "The Voysey Inheritance." It is a pity, though, that he gives any prominence to Barker's worst play, "The Madras House." However, Sutton's book is all good reading. The mere fact that it at once challenges a friendly critic is a sure sign that it has sound stuff in it.

THE SHINING PYRAMID. By Arthur Machen. Secker. 7s. 6d.

Within the last few years an American admirer of Mr. Machen's work has issued two pirate volumes of stories and essays. Only in self defence has Mr. Machen gone through the two volumes, rejecting a great many of the fragments, and the result is "The Shining Pyramid," which requires no apology whatsoever. The story that gives the book its name has that element of dread which should always accompany the evilly supernatural. "The Martyr" is a delicious satire on one, Charles Hexton, the editor and director of *The Materialist*, who, writing a confutation of the Christian religion and an impeachment of the Sacraments as things worse than useless, had the illuminating thought that food and drink were mere idle superstitions, and so, dogmatically thinking, died of starvation. The treasure of the book is an essay as full of learning as of charm on "The Secret of the Sangraal."

CUBWOOD. By W. R. Sunderland Lewis. The Bodley Head. 7s. 6d.

A most unusual and convincing book about children, which recovers the thoughts, hopes, fears and appetites of youth. "Cubwood" is not a jolly book; its characters have no gaiety; they are oppressed with curious terrors. The book cannot, therefore, be recommended to parents for the purpose of presentation to their small boys and girls; but the parents themselves may spend some fascinated hours reading about the morbid boys who saw a dead man in a tree and of the little girl, Hilda, who was on such contemptuous terms with her very mad relative. "Cubwood" is a terribly atmospheric book; and Hilda, with her courage and her caprice, is one bright figure in it. Almost it deserves Mr. Walter de la Mare's preface of high praise in which he declares : "The reading of ' Cubwood ' then, is not only an arresting and refreshing, but an unusual piece of experience. It is a visit into a country of uncontaminated delight and loveliness and freedom, not unknown, but more or less forgotten. And fresh and sweet are its airs and scenes, its dreams and solemn absurdities, its perennial nonsense and enthusiasm." It must not be forgotten that Mr. Walter de la Mare is enormously fascinated by the sinister.

THE MONKEY-PUZZLE. By J. D. Beresford. Collins. 7s. 6d.

Should normal, nice people sacrifice themselves to artists who have no morals or manners in order that masterpieces may come? It is very doubtful, and the coming of the masterpiece is still more doubtful. However, we will grant Mr. Beresford his long query. Tristram Wing and his wife are an attractive couple, and Tristram, for a village squire, is marvellously magnanimous in permitting his Brenda to compromise herself thoroughly with Abby Mattocks, the drinking and drugging artist. Perhaps it is rather an insult to the men than a reproach to Brenda that she figures in this deftly written book as a monkey-puzzle. The book's only fault in expression is its continued incursions into psycho-analysis, a bogus science of our day, which has temporarily harmed some of our best novelists.

Messrs. LONGMANS' LIST

THE NIGHTINGALE.

A Life of Chopin.　　By MARJORIE STRACHEY.

With Frontispiece. Crown 8vo. **7s. 6d.** net.

The book is an attempt to give reality to the Life of Chopin by treating it as if it were fiction. Much of the detail is invented, but there is authority for nearly every incident, and often what Chopin is made to say occurs in one of his letters or is reported of him by a friend.

A New Novel by a New Writer.

THE AXE IS LAID.

By JOHN MACKWORTH.　Crown 8vo.　**7s. 6d.** net.

This novel tells the story of the discovery and frustrating of a Revolutionary plot against England.

THE WONDER OF LOURDES.

What It Is and What It Means.

By JOHN OXENHAM.　　With 16 Illustrations.
Fcap. 8vo. Paper Covers, **1s. 6d.** ; Cloth, **2s. 6d.**

AIR POWER AND WAR RIGHTS.

By J. M. SPAIGHT, Author of " War Rights on Land " and " Aircraft in War."　　8vo. **25s.** net.

" A remarkable book."—*Evening Standard.*
" Thumbnail sketches of exciting adventures and episodes."
Sheffield Telegraph.
" A brilliant contribution to a subject of universal interest."
Army Quarterly.

THE HISTORY OF MUNITIONS SUPPLY IN CANADA, 1914-1918.

By DAVID CARNEGIE, C.B.E., M.Inst.C.E.
With a Preface by Sir Joseph Flavelle, Bart., and a Foreword by the Right Hon. David Lloyd George, M.P. With numerous Portraits and Illustrations. 8vo. **18s.** net.

TUDOR STUDIES.

Presented by the Board of Studies in History in the University of London to **Professor A. F. POLLARD,** being the work of twelve of his Colleagues and Pupils. Edited by **R. W. SETON-WATSON.** Royal 8vo. **15s.** net.

CHEMISTRY IN THE SERVICE OF MAN.

By ALEXANDER FINDLAY, M.A., Ph.D., D.Sc., F.I.C.
New Edition. With Illustrations. Crown 8vo. **6s.** net.

" No volume of similar dimensions that we are acquainted with gives the reader anything like the same insight into the debt that we owe to the scientists, who are not only continually preparing the way for new and important industries, but are ministering to the comfort and convenience of mankind in thousands of ways that the beneficiaries have no knowledge of."—*Belfast Northern Whig.*

THE CHRISTIAN OUTLOOK.

Being the Sermons of an Economist.

By Sir WILLIAM J. ASHLEY, M.A., Ph.D.
Crown 8vo. **4s. 6d.** net.

THE ANGLICAN REVIVAL.

Studies in the Oxford Movement.

By the Rev. YNGVE BRILIOTH, D.Phil., Lecturer in Church History in the University of Uppsala. With a Preface by the Right Rev. the Lord Bishop of Gloucester. 8vo. **16s.** net.

THE TWO CITIES.

Or Statecraft and Idealism.

By M. D. PETRE.　　Crown 8vo. **4s. 6d.** net.

LONGMANS, GREEN & CO.
39, Paternoster Row, London, E.C. 4

George Allen & Unwin Ltd.

Memoirs of a Napoleonic Officer

Edited by MAURICE BARRES. Translated by BERNARD MIALL.　　**12s. 6d.**

" A modest record splashed with vivid and unforgettable incidents."—*Sunday Times.*

Green Islands in Glittering Seas

By W. LAVALLIN PUXLEY, author of " Wanderings in the Queensland Bush." *Profusely Illustrated.* **12s. 6d.**

" An alluring travel book. Full of curious matters that are none the less solid, stolid facts. . . . One of the most readable and reliable books about the South Sea Islands which we have had for a long time."—*Morning Post.*

The Long White Cloud : Ao-Tea-Roa

By the HON. W. PEMBER REEVES, Ph.D. *New Revised Edition. Illustrated.* **16s.**

" A fascinating book, as informative as the severest work of reference, as interesting as a first-class novel, and delightfully written."—*British Australian and New Zealander.*

The Shadow of the Gloomy East

By Prof. FERDINAND A. OSSENDOWSKI, author of " Beasts, Men and Gods."　　**7s. 6d.**

" A squalid truth is at last asserting itself, and this book may do something to speed up that salutary process."—*Truth.*

Outlines of Polish History

By ROMAN DYBOSKI, Ph.D. *With a Map.* **7s. 6d.**

" This excellent work which certainly forms the best account of Polish history which has yet appeared in English."—*Times.*

Waterside Creatures

By FRANCIS PITT, author of " Woodland Creatures," " Shetland Pirates," etc. *Illustrated.* **12s. 6d.**

Intimate accounts from personal observation. The author's aim is to set forth facts to throw light on the mind, behaviour, and intelligence of these creatures.

Studies in Victorian Literature

By STANLEY T. WILLIAMS.　　**12s. 6d.**

" Vigorous, lucid and sympathetic criticism."—*Times.*

The Psychology of the Poet Shelley

By EDWARD CARPENTER and GEORGE BARNEFIELD.　　**4s. 6d.**

" A slim, though in a measure dynamic, book."—*The Times.*

Industry and Civilisation

By C. DELISLE BURNS, author of " Government and Industry," " A short History of International Intercourse," etc.　　**10s. 6d.**

This is a study of the psychological and moral factors underlying the " economic " characteristics of modern industry.

The World's Industrial Parliament

By E. M. OLIVER. With an Introduction by the Rt. Hon. Viscount Burnham.　　**2s.**

A short popular account of the work of the International Labour Office.

40, Museum Street, London, W.C.1

Published by the Proprietors, G.K.'s WEEKLY, LTD., at their offices, 20 & 21 Essex Street, Strand, London, W.C.2 (incorporating THE NEW WITNESS). Telephone No. City 1978. Printed by THE ALLIED PRESS, LTD., 19 Clerkenwell Close, London, E.C.1. Sole agents for Australasia : Gordon & Gotch (Australasia), Ltd. Sole Agents for South Africa : Central News Agency, Ltd.

Week ending March 28, 1925.

G.K.'s Weekly

EDITED BY GKChesterton

Nº 2

WILL·OWEN

Price 6ᵈ

G.K.'s Weekly

No. 2.—Vol. I.　　　Week ending Saturday, March 28, 1925.　　　PRICE SIXPENCE.
YEARLY (52 ISSUES)
£1　10　4.

Telephone No. City 1978.　　　CONTENTS :　　　*Offices, 20 & 21, Essex Street, Strand, W.C.*

THE REAL BOLSHEVIST PERIL

THE other day a daily paper, returning to the agreeable alliteration of the great days of the *Morning Advertiser*, headed a column in huge letters, " Russian Reds Rattle the Soviet Sabre." It then proceeded to ask the nature and purpose of the demonstration. In fact it asked, in the precise formula of Peter Piper : " If Russian Reds Rattle Soviet Sabre, What's the Soviet Sabre that Russian Reds Rattle?" Incidentally, it may be worth remarking that it is not a Soviet sabre. It is vividly typical of our public information that it has seized on the one perfectly human and harmless thing in the Russian system, and held it up as the one inhuman and horrible thing in that system. People say " Soviet " which is the Russian for " assembly " just as they used to say " knout " which is the Russian for " whip." There is nothing particularly bad about Soviets; there is nothing particularly Bolshevist about Soviets; there is nothing even particularly Socialist about them. A foreign word is simply used as a bogey; and Bolshevism is much too serious a thing to be fought with bogies. The sabre could not be in the hands of the Soviet, even under the most democratic government in the world; certainly it is not in the most despotic government of the world. And the real case against Bolshevism is that it is, not as a matter of silly abuse but of scientific logic, the most despotic government in the world. A Socialist government is one which in its nature does not tolerate even a temporary opposition. For there the government provides everything; and it is absurd to ask a government to *provide* an opposition.

You cannot go to the Sultan and say reproach-fully, " You have made no arrangements for your brother dethroning you and seizing the Caliphate." You cannot demand indignantly why he has not stirred up a mutiny among his own janissaries; or why he does not keep a special slave in the Divan officially paid to poison him. Nor can you reproach a government which professes to set up everything, that it has not set up anything to pull down all it has set up. The tradition of a true opposition is part of the tradition of property and liberty; it is a tradition of the West. It can only be tolerated where other rights are allowed to strike root besides the royal or senatorial power. Those rights must be protected by a morality which even a strong central government will hesitate to defy. In other words, there can only be criticism where there are sub-units of property and sub-loyalties of the family and the guild. There can only be a critic of the state where a religious sense of right protects his claim to his own pen or his own printing-press. It is absurd to suppose that he could borrow the royal pen to advocate regicide or use the government printing-presses to expose the government. The whole point of Socialism, the whole case for Socialism, is that the State is directly responsible for everything. Everything is staked on the State's justice; it is putting all the eggs in one basket. Many of them will be rotten eggs; but you will not even be allowed to use them at political elections.

It is desirable to get this point clear; that it is necessarily nearer the truth to say the sabre is in the hands of a Sultan than of a Soviet. With this clearly understood, we can go back to the question asked in the newspaper; against what is the sabre likely to be drawn? It may be drawn sooner or later against anything or anybody that represents the opposite idea of an opposition. Any place where our own culture (corrupted by gross vices which we have to cure) does still in some ways stand for the idea of liberty and criticism, of sub-units in the state that can resist the state, may be in collision with the new theory of concentration. The newspaper which we have quoted says, " There is, for instance, the quarrel with Roumania over the possession of Bessarabia. Besides there is always Poland." The last remark is of a somewhat sinister simplicity. It might figure in one of those old fables in which a man uttered an omen, that was all the more ominous because he himself did not understand it. Blindly, and without purpose, this augur has pointed to the White Eagle and said of it " Esto Perpetua." Certainly that nation has proved itself perpetual under conditions when it was thought that anything would have perished. And if indeed we come to a chaos in which it seems that everything has perished, if this Semitic sophistry does link up the Teutons with the Slavonic hordes, if there returns that welter of barbarism which Europe has often seen, many who do not now understand may find themselves saying, if only under their breath: " There is always Poland."

Darwin said, " You cannot observe without a theory," a single sentence of considerably more monumental and enduring value than the vanishing hypothesis of Natural Selection. Nobody makes much sense of the present position in Europe, because people will not clarify and summarise their own general impression, apart from the question of whether it agrees with somebody else's. We are well aware that there are a number of intelligent modern people, perhaps the greater number of intelligent modern people, who do not agree even with our fundamental theories of liberty and ownership. We are well aware that, even among those who do agree on these matters, there are many who would not follow us in our application of them to international relations. But it is essential that they and we and everybody else should state clearly what are the general principles on which they conduct their observations. Then we shall all know what each other think, and not merely what each other say; and have some chance of learning, as the judge said, if not from our own mistakes at least from each other's. There are people who believe that Germany is a thing exactly like France; that India is a thing exactly like Germany; that Thibet and the Antarctic Circle are nations in exactly the same solid and separate sense as Poland. There are others who believe, at least as reasonably we think, that there are no nations at all; and that flags and frontiers are but an artificial advertisement of the interests of certain capitalistic groups. Anyhow, it is only by understanding these assumptions that we can argue with these people; it is only by understanding ours that anybody can argue

with us. Even with many of our supporters there might be an argument; there might, though we think it unlikely, be a quarrel; but at least there would not be a misunderstanding.

Now we think that liberty and citizenship and fair ownership and full and conscious nationality have, as an historical fact, largely crystallised in the old Christendom of the south and west. There lies to the north and east something that is not quite the same; that may have many good qualities and many worthy visions, but which is in fact vaguer and less strictly national. Among the visions, in some ways worthy but in many ways vague, which are possible to that world is Bolshevism. Bolshevism is very much abused in our press; but is not really very much resisted in our politics. That is, it is not resisted in the field where it might too easily become irresistible. It is not resisted in our international policy towards the worlds less affected by national sentiment. Our scaremongers are always looking for it in Manchester; but they are not looking at it in Moscow. They are always offering to show where it hides itself; but we might almost say that they always hide from it where it shows itself. They are more interested in a man waving a Red Flag than in a man leading a Red Army.

Now we say, quite without panic, and indeed not without sympathy, that the real Bolshevism in those vast and vague territories may be a real danger. It is a danger rather like that of the great days of Islam; which it would be quite possible to recognise with considerable sympathy for Islam. Islam welded numberless tribes together; partly by preaching a real brotherhood, but partly also because the tribes were not exactly nations. And just as we would rather have resisted than reviled Islam, so we would rather resist than revile Bolshevism.

The two have one point in common; and that is a certain oneness. They are insane simplifications. Just as the one said, " There is no God but God," so the other really says, " There is no man but Man." Both sound like truisms and both are most dehumanising and devastating heresies. " There is no God but God " really means that there is no God made man, no sacramental quality in love or localised things. " There is no man but Man " really means that there is no Man except collective Man, Man abstract and communal; that there is no individual; in a word that there is no citizen but only a city. We talk of the Simple Life; we hardly realise the mystery that might be called the Simple Death. In that sea of simplification and destruction there is one island that serves as a breakwater. It is not an infallible nation or a faultless nation, but it is a nation; and in our sense a normal nation. It is Christendom in a sea that is like the sea of Islam. If Poland is weakened it will be War; and we shall be left to trust in Trusts : and defend ourselves with indefensible things.

NOTES OF THE WEEK

A GREAT deal of mystery is made about Mr. Austen Chamberlain and the position of our Foreign Policy, and some discretion about it is reasonable enough. The clamour against secret diplomacy resulted in practice in creating the most secret diplomacy of all, the diplomacy of winks and digs in the ribs that accompany tips given among shady financiers. Compared with these our Foreign Office is a very decent thing, and Mr. Austen Chamberlain has a certain dignity. A vast amount of trouble would be saved if everybody understood that politicians have for a long time past been servants of a certain cause, which is in practice the cause of the cosmopolitan banker. But there are servants and servants. There is a great deal of difference between a respectable Scotch gardener or game-keeper and an eavesdropping and venal valet. Among our Parliamentarians there are both these types, though both may be called the servants of plutocracy. Some of them are even completely honest in this sense; that they not only believe in plutocracy, but cannot imagine anything else except plutocracy. To know the difference between the one type and the other is about the only thing that now deserves to be called practical politics. And one of the most honourable of these conventional public men is Mr. Austen Chamberlain, and it is the more significant that he has failed completely to change the French policy.

*   *   *   *

A PROMINENT Prohibitionist started once more, in a recent speech, the suggestion that the opposition to this piece of coercion and negation is due to the corrupt conspiracy of the Drink Traffic. This was made to apply generally to all that position which has been called true temperance, but obviously need only be called temperance. Obviously a Prohibitionist cannot possibly be temperate, even if he is right. A missionary denouncing cannibalism is right; but we do not call him a temperate cannibal. Nobody can be temperate in a thing he does not do at all. However, the point is here that the Prohibitionist in question fell back on the suggestion that those who prefer temperance to teetotalism must be relying on the support of what is called the Trade. We have no reason to defend what is called the Trade. We have every reason to denounce it, in so far as it tends rather to be called the Trust. But the time has come when such nonsense as that of the particular Prohibitionist taunt should be disposed of for good. To begin with, even if the teetotaller is right, he is a reformer introducing a new view of right and wrong. He is attacking what we have always felt to be normal and native. That, for instance, is where all parallels with drugs break down at the beginning. A man establishing the parallel would have to show as many references to cocaine as there are to wine in the literature and legend of Christendom. He would have to show that Christ turned the water into tincture of laudanum. He would have to show that the Holy Grail was a hypodermic syringe. He would have to show that the Greek Symposium means a doping party; that Horace asked his friends to eat hashish at the Sabine farm; or that the Mermaid and the Tabard were drugging dens in the Chinese quarter.

*   *   *   *

V ERY well; their view may be an improvement, but it is an innovation. In the face of that simple fact, the whole argument about the backing by the Trade becomes too ludicrous to be looked at. A new sect rises in the middle of an old society and chooses to say that it is wicked to wear boots; as one sect in America does say that it is wicked to wear buttons. Some urge the social devastation done by boots; as that it is with boots that the coster jumps on his mother or kicks his wife; and even the milder husband tortures long-suffering womanhood by leaving mud in the drawing room. Others take higher ground of spiritual ideals; saying that we should always have our boots off, since on God's green earth the place on which we stand is always holy ground. Anyhow they say this; and many sects say many sillier things. But they need not be quite so silly as to say that every man who goes on wearing boots must be bribed by a bootmaker. They need not say that, merely because we are all shod like our fathers before us, therefore we are all conspirators connected by underground passages with the Boot Trade of Northampton. To all our fathers, to most of ourselves, beer was as normal as boots. Indeed, beer is much older and more universal than boots. They have a right to do the extraordinary things: but no right to allege extraordinary reasons for our doing the ordinary thing. These people are already applying what they call their argument to the case of tobacco; in America the coercionist campaign has begun. And when the police arrest the editor of *G.K.'s Weekly* for being in the act of smoking (as at this moment), no doubt his horrid habit will be explained by his lifelong commercial connection with Salmon and Gluckstein.

*   *   *   *

D R. MARIE STOPES has let the cat out of the bag. At least not everybody knew that what was supposed to be the little black bag of the medical profession contained a wild cat of religious or sectarian hatred. She is reported as saying: " I am out for a much greater thing than birth control. I am out to smash the tradition of organised Christianity, and to enthrone Christ's own tradition of wholesome, healthy, natural love towards sex life." It is interesting to learn that the tradition of organised Christianity, having survived the power of Nero, the prestige of Julian, the genius of Voltaire, and the apocalypse of the French Revolution, is now to be smashed; and if we knew where this ceremony is appointed to take place, we should like to go and see it. But meanwhile, we fear that neither Julian nor Voltaire would be much impressed with the mental quality of the lady's remarks. She says she wants to enthrone Christ's own tradition (very secretly handed down) of " natural love towards sex life." It is not what may be called brilliantly clear what this means; but at least everybody knows what birth-control means. It means love towards sex that is *not* towards life. Now to some of us a baby appears to be a natural thing; and a product of purely natural causes, as Aurelian M'Goggin would say. If you are professedly not going to allow those natural causes to operate, why in the world should you worship them because they are natural? Why are you bound to think natural feelings good, when you yourself are thwarting their natural fruition as something bad? If nature has bad products, why not bad passions? With or without organised religion, the lady would be none the worse for a little organised thinking.

*   *   *   *

BARONESS ORCZY has delighted us all by committing a vast number of murders, of a vicarious and visionary sort, of course, in the shape of very inventive and ingenious detective stories. She has also put us all in her debt by creating one of those permanent and picturesque figures of romance, like Robin Hood or Sherlock Holmes, which the English greatly prefer to history. It is with friendly acknowledgment to the Scarlet Pimpernel and the Old Man in the Corner that we venture to criticise a political parenthesis. We do not think that Baroness Orczy need go out of her way to confirm a contempt only too common in commercial countries like England for peasant countries like Italy. In one of her excellent short stories, she recently described an Italian peasant orphaned and beggared by an earthquake; and added gratuitously that nobody helped him because Italy is not like England where " the much-abused capitalist " helps the poor. If this were said in Italy by an Englishman defending England, it would be very defensible; said in England it merely prolongs the agony of the defence of the indefensible. We quite accept the parable of the earthquake; if it means that the capitalist needs an earthquake to make him charitable. But the ordinary uninterrupted operation of capitalism in England, through the eighteenth and nineteenth centuries, was to dispossess thousands who might have been English peasants. Italy was fortunate in starting later in the industrial movement and not losing all her small owners. After that, it is cold comfort to be told that an English capitalist was kind to an Italian peasant. His effect on his own countrymen still demands an explanation; but perhaps this is the explanation. There are no earthquakes in England.

*   *   *   *

WE think of having a column in this paper consisting entirely of extracts without comments; extracts about which our feelings are too great for words. A statement was made in the newspaper the other day which it seems a pity to have to spoil with any sort of remark; not even a gasp or a groan should be allowed to break the tremendous silence that follows such an announcement. It was stated that an American millionaire had made his infant child a present of a sky-scraper. This, it was explained, was intended to teach him to have high ideals; and also to reflect that he was the only little boy in the world who owned a sky-scraper. Let us hope so, at any rate; but it is not so certain, unfortunately, that the civilisation which produced one such half-witted monster might not go through some

unnatural convulsive effort and manage to produce one more. Psychologists tell us that much may be learned by studying the ways of lunatics; indeed, many of our modern philosophies and religions are evidently based on such a study and suited to such a society. And it is perfectly true that there are certain influences, immense and impalpable and intermingled with the whole life of America and even of England, which can hardly be understood by any sane man so well as by simply studying that story. If anybody wants to seize some unthinkable confusion of thought between idealism and success, between success and size, between childishness and the dreams of avarice, let him consider that parable; of the child on Christmas morning searching his stocking for the Eiffel Tower or the Woolworth Building.

*   *   *   *

THE conflagration at Madame Tussaud's, not being fortunately in the realistic sense a human tragedy, can be contemplated by the artistic sense with an irony that is curiously dehumanised. There is not only always something terrible about fire, but there is always something ghastly about wax-works. The combination of these two terrors has about it something very unnerving; the conception of those great glaring dolls burning away like gigantic wax candles. But there is another notion that may occur to many; a notion that has also an agreeable touch of nightmare. We all know that these are days in which any sort of credulity or superstition may safely be encouraged, so long as it is not tainted with Christianity. Surely the fashionable world must be full of people, by this time, who believe in and practise the good old experiment in psychic influence which consisted in melting the waxen image of somebody who appeared socially *de trop*. It would be interesting to inquire which politician would be burnt in effigy, by which newspaper proprietor, and *vice versa*, and what leading society figures are copied and consumed in the private furnaces of the leading society hostesses. But in Madame Tussaud's on fire we have one vast holocaust of witches' images wasting in the flame. Would it be indelicate to inquire whether the leading persons whose images suffered felt any slight indisposition during the process? Might we hope that some of them would actually waste away as the fire increased?

*   *   *   *

WE do not remember very well the arrangements at Madame Tussaud's; nor have we studied in detail the scope of the destruction. We are glad to hear that several things were rescued from the Chamber of Horrors; but for some reason or other the leaders of the political and social world are not in the Chamber of Horrors. It seems a just nemesis that the accident of a fire should have made it certain for once that all of them should inhabit a very vivid sort of Chamber of Horrors. But so far the title has never been officially transferred to the Chamber of Peers or the Chamber of Commons. The point that intrigues us is whether the ancient ceremony of the black art, conducted on a scale far beyond the modest resources of Sister Helen, had any appreciable effect that would be of interest to the Psychical Research Society. Might one hope that a leading statesman leaping to his feet to lead the Liberal Party, or at least to prevent somebody else from doing it, may have begun to droop and eventually to melt all over the floor of the House? Is it possible to suppose that some solid and prosperous financial magnate walking down Threadneedle Street, whose philanthropic activities have given him a place among the wax-works, might vanish and leave only a large pool? All this opens an interesting vista for imaginative writers; but we will not pursue it. It might encourage arson in Baker Street.

*   *   *   *

THE great increase of grumbling about the Dole, in those organs that exist for the suburban culture and the small clerical income, is not very magnanimous in its expression, but is natural enough in its essence. Indeed, nothing that the clerk who is Knight Harbinger of the Primrose League of Putney can possibly say against the Dole could be stronger than what was said against it by Mr. George Lansbury, whom the clerk has probably been taught to regard as the cut-throat Commissar of the Red Revolution that will lay Putney in ruins. It is characteristic of the unreal world of journalism in which he lives that when he hears of Mr. George Lansbury, he probably does connect that almost saintly but highly gullible old gentleman with some such desperate deeds of slaughter. But though Mr. Lansbury tends by nature to be only too vague, on this matter his remarks were perfectly sharp and clear and sensible. He realised as well as any reactionary that the Dole is an unnatural thing. The summary of all our strange position is that what is not natural has become necessary. Now this is a point upon which we are much concerned to insist. Patriotism for an Englishman must now consist in realising that all that is most national is no longer natural; in the sense that it cannot come naturally. He must realise that his country has already suffered an abnormal accident or calamity. We said in another connection that there are no earthquakes in England; but in this sense all England is one vast earthquake.

*   *   *   *

THE best the patriot can give is a true picture of a false position. What most of the papers and politicians give is a false picture of a true or trustworthy position. If we go on insisting that the British Empire bestrides the earth with beneficent energy, then the Dole will appear to the malcontents a mere meaningless sentimentalism of being beneficent to those who are not being energetic. They will be able to give a description in which a State seems merely to be infested with parasites, as if it were infested with pickpockets. If we are always saying that Britannia rules the waves, it will be extraordinary that we should throw men shillings without asking them to build ships. If we are always repeating that Britons never shall be slaves, people will ask why they should be kept when they are not working, just as if they were slaves. The answer is that these exceptional things are always done after a great disaster; but we really want to deny the disaster and yet do the things. Relief in the Russian famine is thought natural, because the breakdown of Russia was admitted as a great catastrophe. The Serbian Relief Fund was thought natural, because the Serbian retreat was admitted to be

a great catastrophe. But people will not admit that the collapse of the old capitalism was a great catastrophe; because they do not want to admit that the old capitalism has collapsed. The Dole is simply the Famine Fund raised after industrial England was ruined, as imperial Russia was ruined. It was simply the Relief Fund after the retreat of the whole nineteenth century progress, like the retreat of the Serbian army.

*   *   *   *

IN other words, when there is what is approximately to be called a state of famine, there is what was legally called a state of siege. A sort of temporary communism is established; food is handed out to the starving lest their despair should be dangerous to the besieged city. But it would be very foolish of the city magistrates to begin conducting their communism in the market-place while flatly denying that the enemy was without the wall. It would be very foolish of them to boast of being at peace, when they might claim all the excuses of war. And it is most foolish of all, it is pushing folly to the point of frenzy, to go on boasting of the old system and its success, when the only possible argument for their own actions is the argument of its failure. Yet the Capitalists are still solemnly arguing with the Socialists (both sides using the terms of forty years ago) and are actually basing their case on the argument that capitalism makes England great, proud, prosperous, comfortable, and so on. The truth is that capitalism would have already made England a hell of howling anarchy if we had not had enough English commonsense to use the desperate expedient of the Dole, which is contrary to all the principles of capitalism. The shorthand of it is to say that the Dole has saved us from Bolshevism; historically it is even more true to say that it has saved us from capitalism.

*   *   *   *

THE course of action demanded is not that we should begin blaming each other, or even that we should occupy the whole time in blaming ourselves. As a matter of fact, it is rather a comfortable and convenient fact that all parties are equally to blame. The Tory squires, by insisting on mere landlordism and refusing to permit even the beginnings of a free peasantry, kept the stiff framework of oligarchy on which the whole modern machine of industrial capitalism was erected. The Liberal merchants, by preaching a coarse and heartless competition, gave the rich man all the advantage of his long start, instead of having the humanity or even the sportsmanship to organise a handicap. And then, when the rich man had grown so outrageously rich that he was not only an employer but a ruler, a Member of Parliament and a Minister of State, the philosophical Socialist proposed that all forms of property should pass, bit by bit, into his control. That is the best foundation for that union of all parties of which politicians talk so much. We cannot be all right; but we might embrace with the beatific conviction that we are all wrong. Meanwhile, what really matters is that the magistrates giving corn in the market-place should not talk like luxurious Roman emperors tossing people *panem et circenses*, but like great guildsmen of a medieval city sharing the food because the foeman is at the gate.

FROM G.K.'s WEEKLY A HUNDRED YEARS HENCE

March 28, 2025.—

. . . Professor Chew is already famous among the Higher Critics for his reconstruction of the history of St. Joan or Joanna, to whom he has assigned a date much later than that of the orthodox tradition; such documents as have survived the Great Change indicating that the canonisation following on her rehabilitation can definitely be fixed in the twentieth century. Moreover it is clear that the most enlightened classes knew nothing of her until her cause was championed by Bernhardi Shaw, the famous German propagandist. Her surname seems to have been Southcott, though she was sometimes called " of the Ark " in reference to the sacred box that contained her scriptures. The Church is much criticised for still stubbornly refusing to accept these results of research; especially since Professor Chew's final discovery about the oil-fields of Champagne. He points out that the affair obviously happened under the dynasty of the Oil Kings, which preceded our present royal house of Rubber Kings; since there is definite reference to Joanna making a king at Rheims through the power of oil.

His new work is concerned with his old thesis that our present system is much older than is commonly supposed; and that the alleged period of anarchy, in which economic and sexual actions were left to the caprice of individuals, was altogether legendary. He points out that there is no official record of the alleged " love-making " and personal proposals of marriage in any of the State papers or government reports; and that these individual adventures are only recorded in the " novels " or narratives of the period, which are full of improbable events. " To ask us to believe," he concludes, " That a man felt a personal attraction to a woman at the same time as the woman to the man, and that this occurred continually throughout society, is to ask us to believe that society was founded on a coincidence." He points out, moreover, that as men are not equal in attractive power, any more than in money making, all the attractive men would have had enormous harems and all the unattractive have remained celibate. In this there is probably some exaggeration: the professor hardly allows for a readiness for such reciprocation in normal psychology. We suspect that in the Victorian time polygamy in a legalised sense was the exception rather than the rule . .

FRANCE AND ANTI-CLERICALISM

THE natural man is sometimes tempted to wish that the French were not such a religious people. It seems intolerable that the most important public questions should be suddenly upset by the only question that matters. It is like the universe taking an unfair advantage. Just when we suppose that this strange people has settled down to consider whether it ought to charge foreign invaders for ravaging its country, at the risk of foreign financiers ruining its currency, just when everybody is talking about its cynicism and materialism and love of money, somebody starts to his feet and asks the question that all politicians try to forget: " Is there indeed a God, and has He spoken to mankind? "

The French, who made the Crusades and the Counter-Reformation, and even the Calvinistic heresy, always disturb us in this way, because they ask the question not as a rhetorical question but as a real question. It is that unreasonable sort of question that expects an answer. It even expects to be answered with yes or no. German philosophies do not matter; for they are attempts, conducted in a quiet lunatic asylum, at the reconciliation of yes and no. It is as if the philosopher were to say, in a deep, meditative voice, " Yo." English compromises do not so much matter; for they are an attempt to find a middle point between yes and no, which is fortunately better achieved by the philosopher saying nothing at all. In Germany the most wild speculation has always gone along with the most tame behaviour. Goethe could be a courtier and a sceptic; because just as religion was and was not true, so royalty was and was not tolerable. Even Faust could say of God: " Who dare say I believe or I do not believe? " Either Calvin or Diderot could have told him which a man might dare to say. Therefore both Calvin and Diderot created revolutions; they were a nuisance, as Frenchmen are so often a nuisance, by answering yes or no. The English have had healthier instincts than the Germans; they have not gone in for crazy contradictions but for comfortable compromises. In recent centuries, at least, we might almost say they have

kept all the virtues except the love of truth. They have not so much believed in God, as believed in believing in God. But the French, being neither transcendentalists nor pragmatists, are always disturbing both. They are always saying "If there is no God, let us behave as if there were no God. If there is a God, let us behave as if there were." The alternative is appalling.

That intellectual passion is at the back of the belated burst of secular policy in France. But it is belated; and by this time the real intellectual passions are on the other side. France is a deeply religious country; and therefore the few people who really dislike religion dislike it furiously; they lie awake at night thinking about it. It is not that they do not believe; but that they cannot bear to think of anybody else believing. Unfortunately this small and unrepresentative body of unbelievers largely corresponds to the small and unrepresentative body of politicians. Here we are faced, of course, with the paradox of Parliamentarism. It almost amounts to this; that aristocracy often meant being governed by a popular minority; while democracy now means being governed by an unpopular minority. The truth is, of course, that the democracy is not democracy but plutocracy. But this minority that has ruled modern France will not easily give up its privilege; and the appeal to anti-clericalism is one of its gestures or attitudes of bravado. Even the mean and mercenary French politician has one thing in which he resembles a Frenchman. He is irritating; and he means to be. He is in the most exact sense of the word exasperating; he means to exasperate his enemies; to taunt and defy them. He has that much of the national military tradition that attack is the best defence. And he never attacks so aggressively as when he is indefensible. That much of virtue he has; and it is like a fantastic shadow of the insolent feather of Cyrano de Bergerac. That is where men like Clemenceau and even Briand have something in them that is not in our Nonconformist atheists. And that is why they can even fling in the faces of their enemies so dirty a thing as Caillaux.

TWO EXAMINATION PAPERS

I.

[Three hours are allowed for this paper. Not more than three questions should be attempted. Full marks can be obtained with two questions alone. Write on one side of the paper only: Name and Christian name should be in Block Letters on the space reserved for them on the cover.]

1.—Give in general terms any one of the twenty-two points in the recent Manifest of the French Bishops in defence of the Christian religion, and say what arguments have been brought against it in the *Times* newspaper. Analyse same and give reasons for your answer.

2.—Give the names of any *two* of the following:—

The Controller of the Nickel Trust; the Controller of the Base Metal Trust; the Controller of the Wireless Trust; the Controller of the London Transport Trust; the principal Controller of the Bank Rate.

3.—Give the fortune of the wealthiest Labour Leader in the House of Commons (to thousands only), and outline *very briefly* how it was acquired.

4.—"The Honourable Gentleman proceeded to say that he yielded to none in his devotion to the principles of Unionism." (Loud cheers.) Describe briefly but accurately the exact meaning of this phrase, and give grounds for the cheering.

5.—"Modern thought can no longer admit the Johannine authorship of the Fourth Gospel." (DEAN INGE.)

State briefly:—

(a) What modern thought is and its title to final authority in the matter.

(b) Why modern thought has arrived at this conclusion.

(c) Why the term "Fourth Gospel" is more intellectual than the term "According to St. John."

(d) Whether any educated man has anywhere at any time presumed to differ with Dean Inge, and if so where, when and why.

6.—"Primitive speech took the form of a few simple sounds, indicative of hunger and pain." (Text book of Anthropology: Standard G.) Comment in relation to this on the speech of (a) cats; (b) dogs. Is it admissible to say that a small dog says "Pen-an'-ink" when it is whipped?

7.—"A hundred years hence we shall look upon war as we now look upon duelling." (Charlie Blake.) Supposing Mr. Blake to be now fifty-three years of age and four months (as stated in the books of reference), what will be his age on the consummation to which he bears witness and his faculties for appreciating the same?

8.—"There is no need to abandon the conception of an intelligent and even volitional Deity on account of electrons." (Principal Bolney.)

(a) Does this apply to vitamines? If not why not? Illustrate by diagram if possible.

(b) What is an electron and where may they be seen on exhibition in London? *

* Candidates in provincial towns may take as an alternative to the last section the question "and why are they so very small?"

II.

1. Were there any good points in the characters of the following?

(1) Napoleon Bonaparte.

(2) Thomas à Becket.

(3) Louis XIV.

(4) James II. of England.

(5) George IV.

(6) Any member of the House of Hohenzollern except Frederick the Great.

(7) Mussolini.

(8) Torquemada.

2.—What blemishes, if any, in any *one* of the following:—

(1) Hengist and Horsa.

(2) Alfred of England.

(3) St. Francis Xavier.

(4) Lord Tennyson (the first peer).

(5) Lord William Russell.

(6) Frederick the Great.

(7) Queen Victoria.

(8) Garibaldi.

(9) The First Duke of Wellington.

3.—Account briefly for the fact that whereas some nations are invariably defeated in battle and others uniformly successful, neither appear to suffer or enjoy any lasting advantage or disadvantage therefrom.

4.—Give the name of the modern author of whom the following is characteristic in style:—

"Flossie wondered how he would be like when she might meet with him although she had been virtually told that literally the whole family differed from the general conception of them."

5.—Which is the greater poem:—

The Lord of Burleigh,

The Charge of the Six Hundred, or

We are Seven?

Why has Wordsworth been called "The Mind of God speaking through an Englishman"?

6.—"Lady Beryl Catchem was looking wonderful in *Oeuf-de-Crocodile*. She is, of course, the daughter of the Duke of Thanet."

    (*a*) Describe approximately the colour of *Oeuf-de-Crocodile*.

    (*b*) Why " of course " in the second sentence?

7.—Write a *brief* essay on any *one* of the following subjects:—

    (*a*) The Elephant.
    (*b*) The Lord Chancellorship.
    (*c*) The advantage of a University Education.

8.—Account for the superiority of northern races over their southern neighbours and contrast the Esquimo with the Lapp.

[*The results will be put up on the left-hand board of the entrance lobby on April* 1.]   H. BELLOC.

ANSWERS TO THE POETS

Dolores Replies to Swinburne

COLD passions and perfectly cruel
    Long odes that go on for an hour.
With a most economical jewel
And a quite metaphorical flower—
I implore you to stop it and stow it,
I adjure you relent and refrain
O pagan Priapian poet,
      You give me a pain.

I am sorry, old dear, if I hurt you
No doubt it is all very nice,
With the lilies and languors of virtue
And the raptures and roses of vice,
But the notion impels me to anger
That vice is all rapture for me,
And if you think virtue is languor,
      Just try it and see.

We shall know what the critics discover,
If your poems were shallow or deep,
Who read you from cover to cover
Will know if they sleep not or sleep.
But you say I've been living for ages
(Which is rude) as Our Lady of Pain,
You have said it for several pages,
      So say it again.

REFUTATION OF THE ONLY TOO PREVALENT SLANDER THAT PARLIAMENTARY LEADERS ARE INDIFFERENT TO THE STRICT FULFILMENT OF THEIR PROMISES AND THE PRESERVATION OF THEIR REPUTATION FOR VERACITY.

THEY said (when they had dined at Ciro's)
    The land would soon be fit for heroes;
And now they've managed to ensure it,
For only heroes could endure it.

FOUND WANDERING

By G. K. CHESTERTON.

HOW I GOT INSIDE THIS PAPER

I HAVE given to the most personal and informal of my contributions to this paper the general title of " Found Wandering," because I believe that is the official description often given of persons of weak intellect when found by the police, into whose arms I shall probably eventually wander. Then I suppose I shall be examined, perhaps with all the new apparatus of criminology. The police will play a sort of parlour game with me, which apparently consists of saying disconnected words and leaving it to somebody else to connect them with something. The policeman will say, in a bright intelligent way, " fork." Then if I join in the game and say " spoon " he will know I am the man who is wanted for the burglary up at Vanderbilt Villas; where the silver was successfully stolen while the whole family were Listening In. If, on the other hand, he says " fork " and I say " knife," then he will know it was I who killed and cut up my third wife on Wimbledon Common and was seen escaping in a bright green car. Whatever I answer, in short, the wide range of police information will be able to refer my case to its proper heading; and the march of criminology will go on. They will put a pulsimeter on my wrist, to see whether I show any agitation on realising that my life depends on whether I am agitated. Or perhaps it is more likely that they will merely class me as mentally deficient, as heaven knows I am, in all sorts of ways; though not quite so mentally deficient as the men who make up scientific tests for crime or deficiency. These men will be ready beforehand with the usual instruments of torture. They will produce diagrams, of the sort that might well be the relaxations of a student of the Higher Mathematics, but are supposed to commend themselves immediately to all eyes but those of the hopelessly insane. Or they would ask me, as they do the schoolchildren, how I should set about looking for a lost cricket-ball in a large field; and if I replied that I shouldn't, I should be committed for contempt of court. And very justly committed; for I am guilty of a very complete contempt for that sort of court. But even if I were pressed for a practical answer about what I should probably do in the field, the result would be no more happy. For as a matter of fact, I should do what every other actual living human being (as distinct from gentlemen who live in two dimensions and whose names are A and B) invariably does do when he has lost anything. I should be Found Wandering.

But until that fate befalls me, and I find my last haven in the embrace of some scientific policeman, I shall continue to wander, making no more moral boast than that I also continue to wonder. I wonder unceasingly at any number of things, from the grass to the Great Pyramid, and from the pelican in the wilderness to the patience of the poor in the streets. This permanent astonishment is no doubt also noted down in the text-books as one of the signs of a weak mind. But of all the marvels the thing at which I wonder most is that I am editor of this paper; or perhaps that I am editor of it, and yet it has come out. Yet I enjoy editing it; and that for one reason I should like to make clear. In criticising the plutocracy we must criticise the plutocratic press; and in doing that we may be accused of a superior tone towards the ordinary pressman, who is far from plutocratic. But it is not the tenant of Bohemia that we contemn, but the absentee landlord in Belgravia.

In truth nothing is more notable than the superiority of journalists to journalism. The inside of Fleet Street is far larger than the outside. Most of us have known men of really large minds perpetually engaged in the production of small things; minds that were almost like mountains in labour to produce this one little scurrying and squeaking mouse. For the hustling press is very like a mouse in this; that it is only rapid because it is timid. Anyhow, the intelligence that comes out is often quite out of proportion to the intelligence that goes in. That is the truth behind the old joke about the grizzled veteran of the taverns (of the sort described in the famous misprint as a bottle-scarred veteran) who writes the column that is signed "Doris" or "Lady Gwen." I have resisted the temptation, which was at first strong, to call myself Doris or Lady Gwen in writing this personal page; because I rather wish it to be, in another way, a protest against what is so often the true tragedy of the bottle-scarred veteran. The truth in that joke or legend, about the identity of Lady Gwen, is that it is generally a very small and unrepresentative part of each man that gets into the paper he writes for. It is not himself, or any large portion of himself. He is playing a part; generally a small part; and not often the part he would have chosen. The old man in the tavern, the old talker and toper, whose journalistic job it is to give advice to imaginary flappers on imaginary love-affairs, has perhaps in his time given advice to great editors and newspaper-proprietors in some crisis that has affected the whole world; has assisted in some great public work, such as the blackmailing of a Prime Minister, the buying up of a dangerously truthful journal or the hurried departure of some distinguished person to South America. Get him to talk about these things and he is worth hearing; in the sense that nothing that he ever writes will ever be worth reading. And what is true of this particular journalistic type, is true of journalism as a whole. In one sense it is a machine for multiplying and magnifying one small thing indefinitely. But in another sense it does not magnify but diminish. It does not multiply but rather sub-divide. It uses only a very little of the mental and moral material at its disposal. It was said that the Chicago pork-machine used every part of a pig except the squeal. It might be said that the Fleet Street press-machine uses only the squeal. When I compare the journalist to a pig I mean it, of course, as a compliment and I include myself in the compliment. Pork is a truly traditional symbol of Christian morals and peasant civilisation; and it is true to say that by the present process of elimination all such inherited and substantial things have vanished. We have lost a pig and have nothing left but a pig's whisper. We have lost the substance, the experience, the real humour and knowledge of the world of the jolly old journalist; and have nothing left but some small separate thing squeezed out of his necessity or his fear. That is what many solemn scientific asses have called the "Division of Labour." It means that a man must always be divided from the labour he could really do. It means producing nothing except a by-product.

In short, nobody reading the newspapers could form the faintest notion of how intelligent we newspaper people are. The whole machine is made to chop up each mind into meaningless fragments and waste the vast mass even of those. Such a thing as one complete human being appearing in the press is almost unknown; and when an attempt is made at it, it necessarily has a certain air of eccentric egotism. That is a risk which I am obliged to run, everywhere in this paper and especially on this page. As I have said, the whole business of actually putting a paper together is a new game for me to play, to amuse my second childhood; and it combines some of the characters of a jig-saw and a cross-word puzzle. But at least I am called upon to do a great many different sorts of things; and am not tied down to that trivial specialism of the proletarian press. When blank spaces yawn in the paper at the last moment, I can fill them up with anything I like; and I do, remorselessly, ruthlessly, without shame or pity. I can put in rhymes or songs of my own private manufacture; not likely, I daresay, to add to my public reputation; but

at least giving me the sensation of putting myself into the paper and not merely sending little bits of myself by post, in the ordinary journalistic style. I shall be told that my rhymes are too silly for a paper, as I shall be told that my religion is too serious for a paper. But since I have reluctantly accepted the description of this paper as mine, it shall not at least be narrower than I am. It shall not treat all mankind as something having less sense of fun, or less seriousness of faith, than the only man I know.

And this personal page will be useful for another purpose which I think important. I have often pointed out that in our time it is the really public things that are kept private, while it is only the really private things that are made public. A revelation can always be scandalous so long as it is also trivial. On the other hand, we have far too little reply from responsible people about the reasons of their public action. In my small way I should like to reverse this. We have no concern with the triviality of scandal. Readers who want revelations about a novelist by his own wife before them a stretch of barren reading without any such refreshment. Those who want Don Juan re-written in prose without the wit must look elsewhere for the new fiction. But I do want to have an opportunity of explaining to the reader, if necessary, why I do this or that in my responsible editorial capacity. I have said this is the first time I have been trusted with this sort of scrap-book; it is impossible that there should not be errors, small or great. I know not if it was a misprint or a momentary madness that put " Council of Vienna " instead of " Congress of Vienna "; or wrote " by " instead of " my " in the verses on the World State, as if the poet had a cold in his nose. But apart from mistakes there must be difficulties and differences of opinion; and within reason I shall always be ready to discuss them here.

I would discuss them with the reader, because they really are both my business and his. By the modern fashion the same public man, who has answered a public question by saying he has nothing to add to what the Leader of the House said on the accession of George the Fourth, will then go away and write for a Sunday paper a psycho-analytic account of his own infant impulse to bite his grandmother. I should like a little less of the latter form of egotism and more of the former. But it is inevitable that I should seem to indulge egotism in many forms. Even to meet practical problems of space I have to write far more of the paper myself than I had expected. But over and above that, I have resolved to put the whole of myself into this paper; and if there is too much of me, it is a joke to which I am accustomed.

SONG

THERE'S a sound of the flutes and the lutes
      to-night
         In the island of Nevercometrue;
In a fire-lit isle in the seas of night
   Black with the depth of blue:
And the man that might have been I shall dance
   With the woman that might have been you:
Under the world where a man remembers
   More than he ever knew.

There's a noise of songs in the gongs to-night,
   In the garden of Nevercometrue:
Under the trees of the terrible flowers
   That bloom when the moon is blue:
And the man that never was I is wed
   To the woman that never was you—
O nothing nearer than all that is,
   In Nevercometrue come true.

AT THE BACK OF METHUSELAH
No. 1.—From our Series of Modified Modern Dramas

ACT I.—The Garden of Eden. Eve is still arranging flowers on the table, but ADAM has already sat down before a foaming tankard and a big cheese.

ADAM (*saying grace*): God be thanked for thirst and hunger. One never gets tired of bread and cheese and beer; they are always the same.

EVE: And what about the wife who milked the cow and brewed the ale?

ADAM: One never gets tired of her; she is always different.

EVE: Somebody told me the other day that we ought to live a more simple life.

ADAM: Well, what could be simpler than bread and cheese and beer?

EVE: He said—at least he may have been a lady—I mean she may have been a gentleman. Anyhow It was kind enough to explain that It combined in Itself the attractions of both sexes.

ADAM: How horrible! But what did It want us to do?

EVE: It suggested a light fruitarian diet consisting of one apple carefully masticated at a regular hour. It said that an apple a day keeps the devil away.

(*Enter the* SERPENT, *a being of ambiguous sex, with art draperies instead of arms and legs.*)

SERPENT: I particularly recommend the nutritive properties of the apple of the *Arbor Scientiæ*, vulgarly called the tree of knowledge, which I perceive just behind you.

ADAM (*gruffly*): I'm on my honour about that.

SERPENT (*producing a pamphlet*): If you will kindly read this little work on Totemism, Trial by Battle, Tribal Taboos, the Duel, the Herd Instinct, Human Sacrifice and other matters, you will find that you have quite outgrown the Honour concept.

ADAM: All right. (*Reads and outgrows it. He begins to slowly climb the tree. The Serpent coils itself round the roots and breaks off the lower branches so that he cannot get down again.*)

ADAM: I seem to be rather up a tree.

SERPENT: You are now arboreal. Nothing can be done till one has been arboreal. But you will soon get tired of it.

ADAM: I can quite believe it. Well, one must do something. (*Eats the apple.*)

EVE (*mystically*): Do you feel a thrill and hear thunder?

ADAM: On the contrary, I feel as if I should never have a thrill again. What a bore!

SERPENT: It is the beginning of all Progress. At last you are bored!

EVE: What can you see up there?

ADAM: I can see nothing but rows and rows of other little gardens all exactly alike. Rather like the pattern on a wall-paper.

SERPENT: It is Balmoral Avenue, Upper Tooting, where you reside. By-and-by you will see rows and rows of other worlds all exactly alike. It is the Cosmic Vision.

EVE (*with fine feminine inconsistency, to the Serpent*): You silly old fool, what do you want to come meddling here for? We were perfectly happy till you came butting in!

SERPENT (*producing another pamphlet*): If you will cast your eye over this little work, a lady of your strong independent intellect will soon outgrow the Happiness concept.

EVE (*casting her eye over it*): Oh yes, I feel ever so much more independent and intellectual now. I feel quite sure I shall never be happy again.

SERPENT: Those who eat the fruit of knowledge grow tired of happiness. You will go forth from this place. . . .

EVE: Do you mean to say I must leave my garden?

SERPENT: You will get tired of it. Progress entirely consists of getting tired of things. But there are plenty of other things for you to get tired of. Fresh fields of fatigue lie before you; infinite oceans of boredom await your coming; undreamed of novelties in the way of disappointment and disillusion and general dullness will always be ready to begin the same business all over again. You have no notion of what a number of different ways there are of never getting anything you want; and you will never get to the end of them. It is enough that there is always a beyond.

ADAM: Well, it's beyond me.

EVE (*stamping with exasperation*): Oh, it's beyond everything!

ACT II.—A large prehistoric farm, with large prehistoric agricultural engines and machinery, only a little more advanced than those of to-day, showing in fantastic outlines against the morning sky.

Enter Cain and the Serpent.

CAIN: Yes, if there is one thing I pride myself on it is being a strict vegetarian.

SERPENT (*tolerantly*): Yes. you are evolving . . . you are advancing; though, of course, there are even higher planes for you to reach. I myself, for instance, have already outgrown vegetarianism. I find it far more hygienic to consume directly the chemical constituents of matter, the molecules that go to make up the ordinary geological deposits of the soil. To those capable of rising to this height in defiance of vulgar ridicule, it will be found that these chemicals are most sustaining when consumed in a horizontal posture; which puts less strain upon the system during the process of digestion.

CAIN : Why, that must be the origin of that funny legend; that God said to you " On thy belly shalt thou go and the dust shalt thou eat."

SERPENT (*very stiffly*) : I cannot imagine to what you refer. (*Changing the subject*) I hope there are none of the old carnivora troubling you now?

CAIN : Some of the old flocks and herds still drifting about are troubled, I am sorry to say, by one of the larger parasites. The creature commonly consumes the milk of the cattle, but the oxen occasionally die.

SERPENT : Obviously it would be better for the parasite to die.

(*Enter* ABEL, *very ragged and shaggy, driving sheep and goats*).

SERPENT : Surely, this is the unfortunate creature.

ABEL : Marnin, zur; mubbe I might be milkin' my goat here.

CAIN : Of course, one would kill the creature as humanely as possible.

(*Kills* ABEL *as humanely as possible*).

ABEL (*with his dying breath*) : You be a vine zort of brother. (*Dies.*)

CAIN (*firmly*) : I am sorry, but I am a Humanitarian on principle.

ACT III.—The scene is at first completely dark except for something like a red star, which as it gradually lightens reveals itself as a fiery sign on the forehead of a great dark figure seated on a high throne. It is the brand of Cain. On the stairways leading up to the throne are surging and rebellious crowds waving weapons or shaking their fists at the sky.

FIRST VOICE : The world is weary of his conquests. It is time to conquer the conqueror !

SECOND VOICE : Down with the tyrant !

THIRD VOICE : He has taken our land !

FIRST VOICE : He has taken our cattle !

SECOND VOICE : Our children go barefoot that he may be shod with gold !

ALL THE VOICES : Down with the tyrant !

(*As the crowd sweeps up the steps with a rush, the* SERPENT *suddenly rises behind* CAIN *like a dark column from the top of which his voice cries like a trumpet.*)

SERPENT : Stay ye and hearken to the prophet, for I am the prophet of the Lord, even of Bel the

Lord; and it is given to me to see visions, and the things that shall come upon the earth. And I say unto you that in those days ye shall all be as gods; and live longer than the trees. And you shall have no cattle and need none, for you shall live on the holy herbs. And you shall have no children and need none, for you shall be born mighty and wise. And you shall have no shoes, and need none, for you shall not walk but fly or go everywhere with wheels and not feet.

(*While he is speaking the twilight scene changes and turns to a lecture theatre with a high platform, the same great figure occupying the chair. The* SERPENT *continues without a pause, but his voice has become the clear and carefully trained voice of a modern public speaker.*)

. . . And the suggestion of Mr. Bernard Shaw is of particular sociological importance in the light of the recent revival of the discredited demand for what has been called Three Acres and a Cow. It will be very unwise to tie posterity to such limitations if the tendency of the higher evolution is to outgrow them. Now Shaw has taught us to hope that in a higher evolution there will be no such thing as a cow. Similarly we have learnt from Einstein that it is equally doubtful whether, when his system is understood, there will be any such thing as an acre.

Again, the inspired Ibsen has expressed a doubt about whether two and two always make four, which would seem to apply equally to the question of whether two and one always make three. If then we take the whole formula, " three acres and a cow," we shall find that each of its terms will tend in turn to be superseded in the. . . .

FIRST VOICE : The children are starving !

SERPENT : My honourable friend says that the children are starving. Well, gentlemen, I think this is a subject on which we should take not only a broad view, but a long view. (Cheers.) It is by no means certain that starvation is not merely a transition stage. The scientific authority I have already quoted is of the opinion that in a later and higher stage of social development we shall have no bodies at all. In my judgment, it would be very grave responsibility for the Government to expend large sums of public money on storing food that may never be needed. (Cheers.) To begin with, if it be true, as Mr. Shaw has taught us, that in a fully evolved society there will be no children, but only more or less gigantic adults, the question becomes one of common prudence and economy. It has been said that these children are going barefoot and are without proper clothing. Sir, I can imagine no more scandalous and indefensible waste of the national wealth than to set our factories to work making many thousands of small shoes or shirts for a generation that will take a most unprecedented outsize. (Cheers.) But even apart from this evolutionary consideration, it may well be doubted whether the child is a social symptom to be encouraged. The most moderate of reformers are now agreed that the fewer the children anybody has the better; so that this illogical and transitional type which we call the child, which was once perhaps legitimately regarded as a thing of the future, will in its turn become a thing of the past. Mr. President, I beg to move the motion standing in my name.

THE PRESIDENT: (*speaking with breathless rapidity to a staring and stupified assembly*): The motion before the committee is that this committee ratifies the fifteen recommendations made by the Anti-Population Commission, and especially the necessity of co-ordinated effort for anasthetic asphyxiation to the problem of domestic economy in families receiving less than the income specified in the schedule of the Compulsory Amputation Act of 1932. Any objections? The motion is carried unanimously.

(*The scene darkens gradually; the distant voice of the secretary is heard talking down a telephone. Then all is black, except the red glow of the brand of* CAIN *which remains, burning in the darkness.*)

ACT IV.—The inside of a cavern, with the entrance partly blocked by a rock. Through the aperture can be seen from time to time the fantastic outlines of deformed or formless creatures of great size, peering in or attempting to enter. They appear, however, to be somewhat alarmed at a large fire burning on the floor of the cave; over which a large pot is suspended: ADAM sitting on the one side and EVE on the other.

EVE: This is quite like old times.

ADAM: Yes; when I had left off being an Arboreal Anthropoid I was told the next step in progress was to be a Cave-man.

EVE: In other words, after finding yourself up a tree, you went on and found yourself in a hole.

ADAM: Well, the hole might have been worse. Some natural tears we shed, but wiped them soon. I had great fun drawing pictures on the wall of the wild creatures outside.

EVE: Yes, it kept you quiet.

ADAM: Things weren't always quiet; and I had to fight them as well as draw them. Do you remember those huge things with horns and tusks and those other slimy dragons from the sea and the river? I remember the Serpent used to give them very long names and say they were my ancestors. I do believe there's one of them outside now.

(*A monster with long fingers like tentacles shakes and tries to shift the rock in the doorway.*)

EVE: Oh, no; he doesn't say those are your ancestors. He says those are your descendants.

ADAM: My descendants!

EVE: Yes, I believe that outside is what is called the Rising Generation knocking at the door.

ADAM: I never knew the rising generation was so polite as to knock. Indeed its way of poking its head in strikes me as pretty bad form.

EVE: The rising generation is supposed to be a higher form.

ADAM: Well, the form I see out there is uncommonly like the form I used to draw on the wall (surveying the walls of the cave), and according to that view, I suppose they were a gallery of family portraits.

EVE: Well, I'm glad the form skipped our generation.

ADAM: (*suddenly*): Eve! Suppose it's all nonsense!

EVE: Suppose what is?

ADAM: Suppose we never did have any such ancestors and never need have any such descendants. Suppose it's just you and me after all, to tame the wild world and replenish the earth and subdue it. Suppose it's all as nonsensical as all the nonsense it has led us to? What has it ever done except pretend there was something better than justice whenever we were trying to be just? What has it done except cut off a man's legs with the promise of turning them into wheels, or cut off his arms with the pretence of giving him wings, and all because the old liar himself crawls about without legs or arms.

(*Enter the* SERPENT, *gliding through the crack in the rocks.*)

EVE: Well, of course it's all nonsense. I always knew it was all nonsense even when I did it.

ADAM: Eve, suppose we really are the image of God?

SERPENT (*very angry*): You—you miserable amputated monkey! You needn't be quite so proud of having no tail.

ADAM: And you needn't be quite so proud of having nothing else.

SERPENT: I hope I am too much of a gentleman to make a scene.

ADAM (*in a voice of thunder*): Get thee behind me, Satan. I know you will always be behind me. I know you will always be my tail; and the only tail I ever had. I know you will always pursue me with whispers and appeals. But never again shall you go before me, to lead me on with your lies, further and further into the wilderness of wild nonsense that you perpetually tell me is the promised land. Go back in the name of God.

(*The* SERPENT *recoils with a sudden and convulsive movement.*)

EVE (*cheerfully*): So that's all right. And now we'll begin again.

THE THIEF

(Continued from last week.)

BY WALTER DE LA MARE.

INDEED, the Thief grew more and more dejected and more and more anxious and miserable and angry. One after the other, these noble ladies: next a widowed Marchioness with a wig, and next a dowager Baroness without, and next the step-daughter of a Baronet, and next the aunt by marriage of a Knight, and so on and on and on—they one and all refused with disdain at last to accept his proffered hand. And it was by no means ever because he squinted or dressed like Henry VIII.: but simply because he was no honest man but a Thief.

After a whole year of arduous letter-writing (Signor Babbinotti, poor creature, having been meanwhile reduced almost to a skeleton), the Thief was just as much a bachelor as ever and ten times more unhappy. Indeed news had long since got abroad of his vain endeavours to find a bride. His neighbours less and less often left their cards: many of them left the neighbourhood. And now, oftentimes, strangers from foreign parts, and peculiar-looking men like pirates and bandits might be seen standing and gazing up at his windows from the deserted street, who as like as not would turn away with a frown of the most truculent contempt or a grimace.

And the Thief peering down and out on them from behind his damask curtains, would tremble in his shoes, partly in rage and partly in fear. Yes, he began to be afraid of what might now befall him—what mishap. And he even bought twenty more red Morocco leather buckets to be filled with water and hung in rows by the front door in case an enemy should set his house on fire. Moreover, he had three heavy chains hung upon the door itself, and new locks fitted to all the windows. Why? To keep out Thieves!

Not only this, but his mind began to be gnawed by remorse. And now and then, especially at Christmastide and on St. Valentine's Day, a great van would draw up to the house and would carry away a sack or two of money, and cabinets, and carpets, and pictures and such like, for gifts as often as not to people the Thief had never seen. He would not even put his name and address on the packages—in case. They were anonymous. But at last he even wearied of copying out with the help of Signor Babbinotti the names and addresses of new strangers to send gifts to. And one night a happy thought came to him. With chisel, hammer, and jemmy, he cut away the bars of some of the lower windows and left them wide open to the empty dark in the dead of night.

And one such dark night, as he sat muffled up listening in an Arabian shawl, three strangers in masks and list slippers came creeping in through the open windows and began to put treasures into their sacks.

The Thief rubbed his hands together with a gentle sigh. But alas, in a little while he heard the first thief say to the second thief, " Silas, what have we here?"

And the third thief said to the first thief, " And this, too?"

And presently, leaving their bulging sacks behind them, the three thieves crept out once more through the open window and were swallowed up in the darkness. And *the* Thief, with his little green squinting eyes, muffled up in his Arabian shawl, knew that these not wholly dishonest men had been ashamed to meddle with such a bad man's goods. And for the first time in his wicked life he blushed up to his eyes.

And so—and so—he grew more and more unhappy, and more and more suspicious and sullen and sly and stupid. He never even went out at night now, and his horses grew so fat over their mangers of wheat and oats and barley that they could scarcely stir in their stables. And at last he sold them one and all—bay and cream, roan and piebald; and he sold his coaches and carriages— apple-green, cardinal, scarlet, canary and maroon. And he dismissed his grooms and coachmen and outriders and linkboys, and his butler and cup-bearer, his three valets and all his servants. And in a few days there was nobody left in that vast mansion but himself. He was alone.

But *still* he did not know where to turn or what to do, to be at peace or in comfort; while the street and the complete neighbourhood grew emptier and emptier, and there was scarcely a sound to be heard but the saw-saw-sawing of moths gnawing at his tapestries, the mice at his cedar-wood, and the rats at his butts. His doublet hung looser and looser on his stooping shoulders, his rose-silk hose sagged in folds on his shanks. He hiccoughed whenever he ate or drank. He was a creature almost without hope.

And one late afternoon, as he sat on his striped marble staircase going down to the door, there came a tap. Tap, tap, tap. With his damascened silver-mounted blunderbuss in his left hand, the Thief opened the door on its chain and peered through the crevice.

" Who's there? " he said.

And a voice said, " Pity the blind."

" I didn't make your eyes," muttered the Thief peering through and clutching tighter his blunderbuss.

" Pity the blind," repeated the voice. " I starve."

And there was a slip of moon standing over the house-tops by whose light the Thief could see the thin, white trembling eyelids of the blind man and his fallen cheeks. He stared at him a while.

" Wait there," he said.

So, ascending into his empty banqueting hall, he carried down from the table at which he had been sitting and looking at the pictures in the book of Jeremiah—he carried down to the blind man a manchet of white bread and a cup of water. And he thrust the manchet through the crevice of the door into the beggar's one hand; and the cup of water into the other.

Whereupon, having drained the cup of water, the blind beggar, shaking there with palsy in the moonlight, inquired if there was anything he could do for the Thief in return for his charity. And the Thief shook his heavy head.

And the blind beggar, lifting his face in the moonlight, sniffed softly, and cried in a low, still voice, " Nay, but I smell the Magic Egg."

" What is that? " cried the Thief sharply.

" Hatched," was the reply, " it brings happiness! " And with that the blind beggar turned himself about, and clutching his loaf groped his way down from out of the Thief's marble porch.

(To be continued.)

UTOPIAS UNLIMITED
1.—The Paradise of Human Fishes

MR. PETER PAUL SMITH had just put on a new suit of clothes; but he did not strike any special attitudes of vanity over it. His face was more or less masked with a sort of goggles, even larger than those which perfect the personal beauty of the American dude; but he was not going motoring. His trousers were as roomy and shapeless as plus fours; but he was not going golfing. His costume was in a sense a uniform, for he was an official; but it was not a uniform such as tradition associates with the ambition to fascinate the fair. It was even in a sense a bathing-suit; but not one which the most sensitive town councillor would forbid as being of a seductive indelicacy. It was in fact the costume of a deep-sea diver, with the helmet like the head of a huge owl, the four limbs like the legs of an elephant and a long pipe protruding from the back of the head like a monkey's tail in the wrong place. The town councillor might well consider the compulsory enforcement of this costume at all our watering-places, since it would at once quiet his moral alarms about mixed bathing, and extend the educational range for the innocent and scientific study of the wonders of the deep. Some such reform is bound to come sooner or later, for we live in an age of re-organised efficiency; as nobody knew better than Mr. Smith himself, who was re-organising something or other in connection with contraband; which had necessitated his going with his friend, Dr. Robinson, and a staff of assistants, who were now cautiously lowering him into the sea.

He got on much better than he had expected. Only once in the course of the first half hour's groping did he feel anything like a hitch, an instantaneous strangling sensation as if his communications were cut or caught somewhere; but it passed away; and he must have acted automatically even during the seizure, for he recovered to find himself walking stolidly on the great grey slime under the sea. At first it seemed as dark as a cavern; but he began to be conscious that the darkness itself was less and less impenetrable. The profiles of fishes seemed to be drawn in faint lines of light; as extravagant as caricatures of politicians. It was as if devils as well as angels could have halos. But the halo came from a faintly increasing light which turned the twilight at last into a transparency unnatural in colour but luminous enough as a medium for movement. Smith thought of a great green sunrise. It suggested some grand savage myth about the sun being drowned in the sea. He was surprised, however, to find how soon he grew accustomed to the green daylight. Something in the elemental transition had acted like the transit of time; he felt as if he had been walking on that slimy floor for a hundred years. The smooth and serpentine columns of titanic seaweed seemed to him quite as natural as trees; tall trees round which the birds dart and wheel. For an instant he almost expected the birds to sing; when he remembered that they were fishes; the dumb birds of those buried skies.

He stood still and stared at something in front of him. The shapeless slime rose into the shape of a sharp ridge with an opening cut through it, cut sharply and squarely as by the hand of man. Through this opening gleamed stripes and patches of all the colours of sunset, as when one looks through a gate into a garden. It was a garden; and none the less a garden because a glimpse of hundreds of writhing tentacles or twiddling fingers showed that it was made of sea anemones instead of flowers. They were arranged in mathematical patterns following their variegated colours, as nature does not arrange them. At the end of the straight path between the coloured plots was the low dome of a building, dark against the light of whatever mysterious dayspring illumined those springs of the sea. Grey gleams clinging to it here and there

suggested some metal like lead or pewter. It might have been a giant diver's helmet; and coming towards him down the path surmounted by the dark streak of his pipe of communication was another diver. But as the man came nearer, he saw that the helmet was of another shape than his own, moulded into other metal features, like those of a mask. He had a momentary thrill at the thought that the head inside the helmet might also be of a strange shape; that the thing looking at him out of its windows was not a man.

On this, however, he was soon reassured. The stranger unhooked some apparatus resembling a telephone and clapped it against Smith's helmet; he immediately felt a new electric throbbing, and then the unmistakeable voice of the United States speaking very distinctly in his ear.

"See here," said the voice, "has the City Inspector seen you?"

"What Inspector? What City?" asked Smith.

"Why, our City, of course. Gubbins City," answered the native.

"Good heavens," cried Smith, "You don't mean to tell me that men actually *live* down here."

"Only seventy-five thousand of them at present," admitted the other man, "but we're an expansive burg. You must be about the only guy that don't know how Old Man Gubbins bought all the bottom of the Atlantic dirt cheap, because all the other boobs thought it was only dirt with nothing to it. He's planted his factories here; and I tell you, Sir, this is going to be the new civilisation. Folks used to put paradise above the sky, but I guess the real paradise is going to be under the sea."

"It's got a garden like paradise anyhow," said Smith. "a garden of sea-anemones for flowers. You'll be telling me next you have a dogfish chained up instead of a dog."

"Why, as to that," answered the other, "these private fancies aren't exactly encouraged by the old man, and he says the gardens have got to go. Of course in our situation we have to do pretty much as we're told by the headquarters on land; and the old man likes to keep his finger on the string— I guess we're all on a string; and if we did have a dog, it would be on a chain."

"And I think you're on a chain yourself," said Smith. "What an awful life—to live and die breathing air that is only pumped down to you by the favour of somebody miles away."

"Where do you live?" asked the American abruptly.

"Brompton," replied Smith; he found the conversation had become quite easy, easier than an ordinary telephone.

"Are there many brooks in Brompton?" asked his companion, "or have you a well in your front garden, or do you go out and drink the rain? No, you have all your water pumped to you by the favour of somebody miles away. I don't see there's much difference between us. You are surrounded by air and have water pumped to you. We are surrounded by water and have air pumped to us. But we should both die if anything went wrong."

"You must have great confidence in Mr. Gubbins and the people who sent you down," said Smith. "Suppose he sold the plant to somebody else; suppose he went mad; suppose there was a strike or a revolution. Who are these gods who sit above you in the heights and give you the very breath of life in your underworld?"

"Let's see," said the other, with an air of abstraction, "I forget the names of the Water Board that supplies Brompton."

"My God," cried Smith, "and I never knew them either!"

Then he was silent and stared away into the distance beyond the dome. He saw something that looked at first like a forest of very thin trees of almost infinite height; then he saw it was a bunch or fringe formed of countless filaments like the filament he had seen attached to the distant figure of the other diver. It seemed to waver in a rhythmic manner and then gradually recede.

"Men falling in for work," said his informant briefly.

"It's horrible," cried Smith suddenly; "They are like marionettes."

"I fancy you people are hung on wires, too; telephone wires; telegraph wires; all sorts of wires. But it's odd you should mention marionettes; for there really is a proposal for something of the sort. Some of them up there think the work could be better checked if wires were really attached to the arms and legs of the operatives, so that—what are you doing?"

"I'm going back!" cried Smith, "I'm going back where I can get a breath of fresh air."

"No," said the other, and his voice rang sad and hollow in his helmet, "That is the one thing you can never do. You cannot go back. You cannot go back to the peasant owning his own well. You cannot go back to the primitive man drinking of the river. This is the way the whole world is going; if you did return to your own cities, you would soon find them so thick with chemical vapours that air will have to be pumped into them from the country outside. But you will never go."

He lurched forward and caught the other diver by his vital part, which is the pipe above him, only to be caught by the other in the same fashion. They hung there in a deadlock, each in a new fashion with his grip on the other's wind-pipe. Then Smith felt everything blacken about him, and awoke very slowly to find Dr. Robinson administering first aid on the pier.

"You're all right," he was saying, reassuringly. "you weren't down ten minutes when the thing caught somehow for a jiffy—here, you needn't be so energetic as that yet. Where do you think you're going?"

"Brompton," replied Smith, rising on wavering legs, "I want to see if anything—if anything more's happened there."

The Logic of Progress

[" *Some people still object to bobbed hair; there are always people who object to progress; but progress will go on.*" *From a Lady Correspondent's letter in the daily press.*]

CAN Progress pause? We know from this prediction
　　Girls will be shaved like convicts from conviction
　　Or holy faith, when every happy hoyden
Shares a monastic tonsure with Miss Royden.

To rest even here were retrograde and dull:
Baldness will crawl over the female skull,
Till save for one faint streak the scalp is bare
And Beauty draws us with a single hair.

On Professor Freud

THE ignorant pronounce it Frood,
　　To cavil or applaud.
　　　The well-informed pronounce it Froyd.
But I pronounce it Fraud.

The Class War

IT was the day of the General Strike. At the command of the Supreme Socialist Council of the United Solar System, the Class War between all employers and all employees was to begin. Every kind of worker was to throw down his tools. As the tools mostly consisted of huge complicated engines as big as a house, it was often difficult to hurl them away with any sudden fury, to toss them away with any gay gesture of contempt. But the principle applied also to agricultural labourers; and among others to an agricultural labourer named Simon Smale. It was noted in official documents that this proletarian worked for a landed capitalist; and he was duly advised that if he ceased work at the given hour, he would force the capitalist to assent to his terms; which he did. Meanwhile the capitalist, whose name was duly recorded at headquarters as Smale, Simon, was directed to surrender all his private property to the proletarian as the representative of the International Proletariat; which he did. The employer and the employee continued to figure in the books of bureaucracy and the science of economics; and Mr. Simon Smale continued to potter about in his own funny little kitchen-garden. During the interregnum of the Servile State, he had paternally supported himself, on condition of never striking against himself. But with the Dictatorship of the Proletariat these relations had been reversed; and it was as a proletarian that he ruled himself and as a capitalist that he went on working. The vegetables are doing well.

A Hard Case

SIR,—I am aware that you maintain the principle of private property; and that many seek to confront you with what they consider the problems of private property. Most of them seem to me easy of solution; anybody can feel there is a difference between owning a field and owning a road, even if it is a rail-road. I have a really fascinating problem of casuistry to propound; soon, I hope, to be the subject of a long and expensive law-suit. Is an Echo private property? Who owns it; the man who makes the noise or the man who owns the reverberating surface? A remarkable echo is produced by the barking of my dog on my neighbour's wall. Its acoustic quality is so entirely new to science, so melodious to some, so hideous to others, that the place has become a goal of pilgrimage like a haunted house; vast crowds of trippers arrive in waggonettes; and though they can hear the echo a mile off, I need not say that, being holiday-makers, they are willing to pay a shilling each to examine the wall. My neighbour, being a man of business, has seized the commercial opportunity and is rapidly becoming a millionaire. I remain a comparatively poor man, though it is entirely through my labour, or rather my dog's labour, that he is growing rich. Is not this exploitation? And why cannot those to whom private property seems an odd idea think of a few really difficult cases like that?—Yours,

EXPLOITED.

"G.K.'s WEEKLY"

Every Thursday.　　　　　Price Sixpence.

NOTICES.

Tel. No.: City 1978.　　　Annual Subscription Rate (52 Issues) £1 10 4. Cheques and Postal Orders should be made payable to G.K.'s Weekly, Ltd., and crossed a/c payee Westminster Bank, Ltd. MSS. submitted to the Editor must be accompanied by a stamped addressed envelope. Copies of "G.K.'s Weekly" can be obtained from, or subscriptions placed with, any News dealer or News Company in the United States or Canada, or direct from *The International News Co.*, 83-85, Duane Street, New York; *The American News Co., Ltd.*, at Toronto, Winnipeg, Vancouver, Montreal, Ottawa, St. John, Halifax and Hamilton. Sole agents for Australasia: Gordon & Gotch (Australasia), Ltd. Sole Agents for South Africa: Central News Agency, Ltd.

Offices: **20 & 21, Essex Street, Strand, London, W.C.2.**

THE WIRES AND THE WIRELESS

THE British Broadcasting Company has been granted a monopoly. To this fortunate Company has been given the sole right to tax the ether. Others may transmit messages through the ether, but only the B.B.C. can compel payment for doing so. Payment, that is, from any person who is equipped to receive messages!

The B.B.C. have a programme. You may find it dull, or worse. You may desire to communicate only with Jones of Balham, who has views on postage-stamps. All the same, if you have a receiving set, you must pay the B.B.C. This is to be the only broadcasting company, and theirs will be the only entertainment telegraphed each day by wireless into the Englishman's home.

From the start, then, the granting of this monopoly was a serious invasion of our liberties. The daily newspapers lie, but we can choose our brand of liar, and we may now and then find a newspaper which, by accident or design, lets out a bit of the truth. Many of the theatres are run by combines whose only interest in the stage *is* one of interest—on capital. Yet, since there is competition, even the big firms do sometimes stage good plays; and there are individual managements which are all for adventure. But imagine what it would mean if only one firm of proprietors was allowed to sell copies of its paper or papers, if only one firm of theatre-financiers was allowed to stage plays! Imagine what it means to us now that this one company has already the monopoly of "Wireless entertainment." Let me make the songs, and who will shall make the laws. The B.B.C., or companies like them, have for a long time made our laws; if now they make our songs, God help us!

There is something comic in the tragedy. For I do not suppose that the B.B.C., or the Ministers or Government officials responsible for the granting of the monopoly, have any desire to sing a certain sort of song to the English people. They are, I mean the company are, only out to make money, the songs just happen—inspired from the atmosphere of the offices and the board-room of the B.B.C. But it is not unusual for tyranny to start as a bad joke.

But how were the B.B.C. to collect the fees for their concerts and chatty talks? Obviously by charging for admission. And since you cannot limit your wireless current to subscribers it was natural that the Company should regard a receiving set as the ticket of admission and seek powers to tax it. Of course, they got their powers; of course, the plea that a man might have a receiving set and yet not want to listen to the blissful snip-bits of the B.B.C. was disregarded.

At least, I think it is not certain that under the present Act they have those powers; it has merely been assumed that they have them. Hundreds of thousands of people have paid up meekly; but there have been very many pirates; perhaps as many pirates as licence-holders; but nobody knows. To establish the right—in law—to tax the possessor of a receiving set, and to find out who has one are the main purposes of the new Bill.

The parties in opposition may oppose the Bill. If they do, it will be for the wrong reasons. Their real reason will be that it is a Government measure, and the reason publicly announced will be either the very idiotic one that the Bill goes too far, or the frivolous one that it interferes with the work of private experimenters. A few newspapers, while acknowledging the need to suppress pirates, have asked plaintively, or jocularly, if the Englishman's home is not his castle. Certainly nobody has said that the Bill, in its intention, and in its every detail, is an outrage, is a barefaced attack upon our freedom—or, rather, is a cynical declaration that we are no longer free.

As you know, the Bill provides that the possessor of a receiving set, as well as the possessor of a transmitting set, shall hold a licence; it gives the police the right to search premises if they "suspect" there is an unlicensed receiving set upon them; and it provides as penalties for the possession of an unlicensed set the infliction of heavy fines or heavy terms of imprisonment.

I grant you that this may be the only way of preventing me listening to the B.B.C.'s entertainment (which I never do) without paying for the privilege. If it is, so much the worse for the B.B.C., not so much the worse for our freedom! It may be that the makers of wireless-sets and parts thereof would find it worth their while to subsidise the B.B.C. In any case, it is none of my concern. But it is my concern that, should this infamous measure become law, my house may be forcibly entered, as if I were a criminal, on suspicion that I owe a debt which I have never acknowledged for something which I never asked for and which I may never have received. It is my concern that I may be sent to prison should I refuse to acknowledge this purely fictitious indebtedness, which would only be a civil indebtedness, if it were real. It is my concern that my Government is prepared to make itself the tool of a private monopoly. Mr. Winston Churchill is a member of the present Government. He has said much about the tyranny of State monopolies; what has he to say to this?

The authorities inform us that the new measure is no more than an extension of powers which already exist. That is untrue. The right of search where the possession of a transmitter was suspected is quite another affair; it was a war-time precaution intended to stop the sending of messages to the enemy. I know that other war-time precautions, some justifiable, some not, have been maintained until now, to serve as a goad to the temper of decent citizens. But nothing which has been done, no, not the stupid limiting of the hours for the sale of strong drink, can serve as a precedent for this tremendous jump from the defence of the realm against alien enemies to the defence of the British Broadcasting Company against the English public. Let this thing happen, and it will spread; and then we shall soon be made to realise that our Government and its magistracy are the servants of the B.B.C. and kindred monopolies, and that we are their slaves.

I do not regard the new measure as a unique phenomenon. Never before has an English Government shown itself so whole-heartedly on the side of a private monopoly, for in the Marconi case there were excuses, evasions, denials, and, finally, there was silence. But for long we have been sliding down hill towards the Servile State, and perhaps we should thank the authorities for giving us this striking foretaste of what awaits us in the mud at the bottom.

W. R. TITTERTON.

THE DRAMA

" The Painted Swan " and " The Irish Players "

THERE are several kinds of Painted Swans. The author of the play at Everyman Theatre tells us about the Swan that decorates the car of a roundabout. There is, however, a more familiar variety—a tin swan covered with paint which tempts children to sickness and needs a daily immersion in the bath for cleansing purposes.

Hampstead is not the most favourable jumping off place for Princess Bibesco's play. The nonconformist austerity of the theatre seems to emphasise the vacuity of the dialogue which impedes the action. Witty lines are frequent in the dramatist's short stories; they only occur by accident in her attempt at drama.

The first act is a dreary business; the characters sit round in a sewing circle and laboriously churn out faded epigrams concerning Lady Candover, whose maiden name was Ann Cathcart. She is not so much discussed as labelled until what character she has is snowed under by insistent phrasing. She is wonderful; she is good; she is fascinating; all men are in love with her; she loves no man.

On the top of a wave of ponderous adulation the heroine enters and Miss Edith Evans having arrived we hope at long last that the play is going to begin. Not a bit of it. The family circle, having disappeared, the floor is taken by Timothy Carstairs, an infatuated adorer of Ann, who chants the litany of calf love to his lady recumbent on the sofa. Miss Edith Evans listens to his outpourings with a matronly calm that shows more than a trace of self sufficiency.

Timothy is followed by Philip Jordan, a he-man, a politician, and Ann's lover. The intensity of Ann's emotion alarms him. He has no use for a grand passion and laboriously explains that love affairs of this sort must end sometime. There is, however, an unexpected simplicity about Lady Candover. " Love is enough," she cries, and finally induces the he-man to kiss her.

In the second act we make the acquaintance of Ninian, Lord Candover, in the ancestral drawing room of the London house. Into this Victorian atmosphere comes Jordan to explain again that the affair is getting more than he can tackle. Ann, however, is all for love and everything well lost and sends him smiling on his way. His departure is the signal for the return of the sewing circle.

Lord William Cathcart, admirably played by Felix Aylmer, is well observed and fairly true to type. Amiably cynical, he preserves an amusing pose in refreshing contrast to the rest of the male characters. Selina, his daughter, supposed to be ultra modern, is merely provincial. Miss Margaret Carter infuses Lady Margaret with life, but Mr. Clifford Mollison can do little with Mr. Molyneux. None of these people—except Lord William—suggest the slightest acquaintance with that strata of life known as society. They might quite easily live at Streatham.

Having exhausted Ann as a subject of conversation, they go on to consider Philip Jordan, Ninian joining in. Lord William explains that the politician is done. He should have been present at a division the previous evening, but instead of turning up at the House he went off with a woman of the streets. Ann gets perturbed not to say excited and insists that he was with her.

The family refuse to believe it. Why should an M.P. call on her at 2 a.m.? Ann counters this by the statement that he is her lover. And here I must pause to express my surprise that so accomplished an artist as Miss Edith Evans should make such a confession in so mild a manner. Having said " He is my lover," she sits back in her chair folding a scarf about her shoulders. It is impossible to credit that even Ann would have remembered her scarf !

For an instant one hopes for some dramatic sequence. But nothing happens. Thus in the third act we find Ninian asserting his marital authority. Ann's confession has awakened his love. If she wants cave methods she shall have them. Mr. Frank Cellier is entirely adequate at this moment and one feels that Ann, at long last, may be battered into sense. But sense is the last thing to be discovered in this study of Streatham life. Lord William, like a mild oracle, states that Philip Jordan was seen going into the flat of the strange woman, whereat Ninian realises that his cave methods have availed him nothing. His wife is virtuous after all; he humbly begs her pardon, and re-dusts her pedestal.

The production of the play is uniquely bad. To begin with, all the women are wrongly dressed. Selina, replete with eyeglass, Eton crop and Fair Isle sweater, might be credible. In the undistinctive garments that she wears, each hit is a miss. The same can be said of Mrs. Martineau and Lady Emily, their clothes are worthy, all of them, and one suspects, woolly also. The settings are as wrong as the dresses and the drama-like stillness of the sewing circle in the first act, is a powerful depressent.

I have a great admiration for Miss Edith Evans and shall always remember her Millament with delight. Ann, I realise, must be a great trial to her temperament but even so she should, I think, suggest a little more vitality. She is matronly in her manner, cooing in her speech and the combination of mother and child is not effective. A dull play with all the irrelevances and none of the humour of Mr. F.'s aunt. One is painfully conscious of the milestones.

There is all the Fun of the Fair—without the roundabout— at the Little Theatre where the Irish Players appear in " Persevering Pat." Mr. Lynn Doyle has not attempted drama, but is content to portray a phase of Irish life, and though the action is at times somewhat long drawn out, the humour is so spontaneous that there is little of the play that we would spare. Matchmaking is still a popular game among the Irish peasantry, and the efforts of Pat Murphy to get Peter O'Hare married, give Mr. Arthur Sinclair and Mr. Fred O'Donovan fine scope for their art.

Peter O'Hare has a farm and a balance at the bank which leaps from six to sixteen hundred in the twinkling of an eye. He is what English novelists call an " omadhun " with a sheepish eye and a sly smile. He proposes to Mary O'Connor, the daughter of the local publican, but sets light to his trousers at the critical moment and is laughed out of court. Rose Dorrian is the next on the list but the announcement of the engagement piques Mary who intrigues a second offer. Meanwhile the widow Dougherty has entered the field and carries off the prize while the others are quarrelling.

But Peter is not done yet. He slips off to America, leaving his farm and his troubles behind. A simple story but so full of raciness and humour that it fills the stage. To see the Irish Players is to enjoy a rare example of ensemble. They respond to each other with the quickness and perception of the Russian ballet, so often quoted as the perfection of team work. Miss Maire O'Neill gives us the life history of the widow in her creamy smile. Miss Kathleen O'Regan is a delicious Mary and Miss Ethel O'Shea gives a fine performance as the bedraggled Rose.

I sincerely hope that this is but the beginning of a long season, and that the Irish Players at the Little Theatre have come to stay.

J. K. PROTHERO.

REVIEWS

FRITTO MISTO *

THE very title of the last book of Mr. Haynes expresses the idea of variety, and variety is really one of the virtues that spring out of his favourite cult of liberty. He is not only interested in a great many very different things, but (what is perhaps less common) in a great many really different people; people very different from himself or from his friends. In some cases he is perhaps more tolerant than I might be; though perhaps I should find it easier to enter into the sort of sympathy he has for Horatio Bottomley than into the sort of sympathy he has for Lord Birkenhead. Yet here again it is possible that he is right; that he is being charitable to men where I am being hostile, not indeed merely to name, but possibly merely to symbols. The truth is, that Mr. Haynes has, along with a great deal of a very English eccentricity, a curiously fair mind. He has an all-round love of liberty; and though he extends the idea of liberty to things to which I should no more apply it than to murder or forgery, he never gives the impression of that quite irrational impatience and pressure of passion that come from a bad motive. One has about him what is really a very unique and even paradoxical impression; that if one could convince him, he would be convinced. He would not cling to error with the mere sulks of self-indulgence. There are necessarily many things in this book about which I disagree with him; and some about which he actually has occasion to disagree with me. In his only too generous note on my American sketches, he complains of several things that I should still be disposed to defend. For instance, I remarked that the humanitarian ideal in my generation and the last had suffered chiefly from the inroads of science; much more than from the remains of superstition. If I may be so flippant, human equality was safer when some men could be segregated as monks than when some men could be exterminated as monkeys. To this Mr. Haynes replies by going back to the Roman Stoics, and saying that their humanitarian ideal was indeed taken over by the Church, but rendered ineffectual so that it could not be really revived until the eighteenth century. But if it comes to ineffectualness, what about the Stoics? It would be hard to show, I think, that the Church was not more practical even for purposes of charity than the last dawdling sophists of the decline of pagan culture. Christians have indeed fallen far below their mission; and unless they know it they are not Christians at all. But I doubt whether their inadequacy can offer any more complete picture of impotence than that of Marcus Aurelius sitting unmoved above the amphitheatre or Seneca justifying the power of Nero. After all, there are hospitals and humane institutions still working with the names of remote medieval saints. I doubt if many would in any case have lingered so long with the names of pagan sages. It is highly characteristic of Mr. Haynes (and perhaps of me) that I set out to compliment him and have begun at once to controvert with him; but indeed the controversy is a compliment. It is in a special sense a compliment; because in several controversies which I have had with him, on very delicate and deadly points of faith and morals, I have always found him a very just controversialist. And it is interesting to note that in his criticism of the religious sentiment of Mr. H. G. Wells, Mr. Haynes says almost exactly the same thing as Mr. Belloc; except that one would insist that revelation and religion must be rejected together and the other that they must be accepted together. But it would give quite a false impression of this collection of essays to dwell exclusively on controversies, especially theological or moral controversies. A great deal of it is concerned with that sort of gossip which is only possible to really intelligent people. I like especially the study of the fascinating family of Huxley, beginning with that really rather grand old man, who was the most virile of the Victorians. Some have said that there was only one Christian who died on the cross. It might be said with similar exaggeration that there was only one agnostic, who invented the name and was the only person who understood it. There is a great deal in the suggestion that Huxley showed all the more vigorously his natural literary talent because he was not professionally a literary man; and there may be something in the suggestion that Mr. Aldous Huxley incarnates the sportive side of his grandfather. But I rather suspect that the dancing of the moderns is more melancholy than the marching of the Victorians.

G. K. C.

NOVELS OF THE DAY.

THIS is an age of realism and cynicism on Irish fiction and on the Irish stage. The movement, on the whole, is a healthy one as a reaction against false idealisms, but the Irish people, at large, do not care for the scathing novels of Mr. Brinsley MacNamara and Mr. Liam O'Flaherty, and the cynical plays of Mr. Sean O'Casey with their biting invective against hero-worship and lush sentimentalism. Anything, however, is better than national self-complacency built upon crumbling foundations. No nation to-day is compact of saints and scholars, of fighting gods and singing archangels. Ireland has become wearied of many illusions. If to-day her most representative writers can only perceive her faults, such an over-severe examination of conscience can do no harm and will make in the end for a sounder national self-respect.

Mr. Shaw Desmond is at heart a romanticist, but his brain tells him that realities—most unpleasant realities—must be faced now that Ireland has come to stock-taking after a destructive war against England, and a still more destructive civil war in which many fine things of love and chivalry and good citizenship have gone by the wall. In "The Isle of Ghosts "* he has written a strong book, weakened somewhat by too poetic a diction for everyday folk. The novel will be fiercely attacked by many Irish at home and in Great Britain. Desmond will probably be denounced as a traitor and a West Briton because he has not used the gold of the missal-painter but the acid of the etcher in his depiction of national character. He can say with considerable truth that he is a more sincere lover of the real Ireland than some of his opponents.

" The Isle of Ghosts " is a story of treachery and weakness, of ambition and brutality, of courage and constancy, of ideals and renunciations—of all the virtues and all the vices of a country in travail and disillusionment. Its two main characters are a possible saint, who becomes an apostate in Jasper Moriarty of the pale Christ-like face, and Sergeant MacGuire, the well-favoured and full-blooded R.I.C. man who serves Dublin Castle ruthlessly and is base and heartless in his appetites and his betrayals. The duel is one to the death. The end of MacGuire described in detail in the chapter called " The Lime-Kiln " surpasses anything in Grand Guignol in its revolting horror. Moriarty, living like Judas, dies like him. He is goaded to that death by a woman who loved him, but loved her country better.

The women in " The Isle of Ghosts " have no mercy on their men-folk when they find them, as they think, wavering. Mr. Desmond states that the characters in his book are

---

* FRITTO MISTO. By E. S. P. Haynes. The Cayme Press. 7s. 6d.

* " THE ISLE OF GHOSTS." By Shaw Desmond. Duckworth. 7s. 6d.

entirely fictitious, but they are mostly true to life in the years of blood—and the merciless women are especially true.

It is a pity that the author has written a kind of Synge-and-Lady-Gregory prose, because it gives the book an air of unreality a little damaging to its true psychology. There is a whole panorama of tragedy in this book of many characters.

I also will be called a West Briton in concurring with Desmond's estimates of certain weakness of Irish character—notably intolerance and jealousy and a cruel contempt for fallen leaders. Desmond makes his own apologies in the words of crazed Maggie McCann, who wrote doggerel about Ireland, but talked like a Sibyl:

"She has killed her dearest and best, but Ireland will rise again, rise through death and love to save herself from herself and maybe to save the world."

No greater contrast could be found between the Irish and English temperament than Mr. Shaw Desmond's " The Isle of Ghosts " and Miss Margaret Rivers Larminie's " Soames Green "† the quietest of annals of a quiet family in a sleepy English country-town. But Miss Larminie has only a surface quietude. In the hearts of her characters, old and young, there are deep under-currents. Middle-aged men will be grateful to Miss Larminie for making Peter Celian, with grown-up son and daughter, the book's real hero. In spite of his cold and small blue eyes and his pedantic speech, Celian is the most lovable character in a fine gallery of genuine portraits. After him one places Lena Corry, his wife's niece: Lena of the curved white forehead and hollowed eyes, the faintly haggard cheeks and secret red lips. We see her externally as a flirt, almost heartless, certainly a little cruel. She seems a pariah beside Celian's daughter, Phoebe, with her pitying love for Martin Holme, married to a wife who drinks and makes scenes; but long before the end of the book one realises that Lena has a sensitivity entirely alien to Phoebe and her brother, Roger. Miss Larminie has one great quality as a writer, tolerance. Her handling of Flora, Martin's pretty little querulous jealous wife, is a triumph of understanding tenderness. The other girl in the book, Cicely, is obvious young English womanhood at its best. Brave and attractive is her approach to Peter Celian, with her flushed request: " I want your permission to propose to your son." Roger Celian is poor and sensitive and feels the loss of an arm as an unpardonable mutilation; so Cicely has to coerce him into happiness. " Soames Green " will count as one of the books of the year as well as of the day.

I do not know anything of Mr. Struthers Burt except that he is an American, and has developed to admiration the American art of the short story. His work is equal to the best of Willa Cather's, and has much more of the stuff of life in it. In " The Scarlet Hunter "‡ and other stories, he succeeds not only as a teller of tales, but as a searcher of souls. " Each in His Generation " is a detailed and exquisite study of the impatience of the young against the old. Mr. Burt, with almost malicious counsel, well-nigh succeeds in persuading us that old Henry McCain, with his beautiful manners, his fine hospitality and his chivalry to Mrs. Denby, is merely a hedonist, whose sole motive in life is to safeguard himself as an epicure in living. One almost sympathises with his nephew, Adrian, and Adrian's wife, Cecil, in feeling that McCain is only a cumberer of the earth. And then, when Adrian has his last dinner with the old man, and the old man telephones to the nurse of dying Mrs. Denby that he cannot intrude on account of his weak heart, we realise as Adrian does that Henry McCain is not at all contemptible. Adrian does not realise it just at once. His first angry thought is: " And yet, what possible difference could it make should his uncle die suddenly in Mrs. Denby's house? Fall dead across

† " SOAMES GREEN." By Margaret Rivers Larminie. Chatto & Windus. 7s. 6d.
‡ " THE SCARLET HUNTER." By Struthers Burt. Hodder & Stoughton. 7s. 6d.

her bed, or die kneeling beside it? Poor twisted old fool, afraid even at the end that death might catch him out; afraid of a final undignified gesture."

The quietly named "A Cup of Tea" has touches of farce which do not prevent it being the tensest of tragedies. It is Burnaby who is telling the story, Burnaby, the wanderer, whose life has been a series of travels and shipwrecks, is recounting to a dinner-party, especially to Sir John Masters, the English Semite, and his rose-and-grey wife, how he once entertained in the wilds a squaw and a squaw man to tea, and how the squaw man very clearly said: "By Jove, that's the first decent cup of tea I've had in ten years." Then Sir John Masters talks of a man called Morton and a man called Bewsher, who were school friends and friends in after life, and of how Morton owed his social advancement to Bewsher and how Bewsher allowed Morton to make him wealthy, and, again, of how Morton, with some reason on his side, broke Bewsher and married the girl who cared for him. The squaw man of the dirty teepee was Geoffrey Boisseleir Bewsher, and Morton was Sir John Masters. Why did Sir John go over a past which discredited him so much? Because he had a contempt for the ordinary compromising human being, because his wife in the shadow has given an unmistakeable sign of the passion of the long ago past.

Burnaby understood the wolf-man as well is the squaw man. Of Israelitish Sir John he comments, when that gentleman has left the house of Mrs. Malcolm: "Can you see him now in his motor? He'll have turned the lights out, and she—his wife—will be looking out of the windows at the snow? All you can see of him would be his nose and his beard and the glow of his cigar—except his smile."

Mr. Struthers would not have us think of Sir John as a villain. In grain he was really a better man than the declassed Bewsher, but he believed in no compromise in such a hard game as life.

It is perhaps hardly justice to the author to attempt any synopsis of his stories. They are so constructed that no word is unnecessary and are infinitely better than any suggestion I have been able to make of them. Mr. Struthers is only betrayed as an American by two provincialisms—"back of" and "in years."   LOUIS J. McQUILLAND.

LIBRARY LIST

THE OLD FLAME. By A. P. Herbert. Methuen. 3s. 6d.
One of the most gifted of "Punch's" young men, Mr. Herbert, wrote a very tragic war novel, "The Secret Battle," which was so true, and so inconveniently true, that it did not meet with the wide recognition it deserved. "The Old Flame" is in Herbert's lightest vein, and though skittish in the extreme might safely be read in Low Church rectories. Robin Moon is very happily married to his Angela, but there are times when trouble arises. At such a crisis, which generally arrives once in two years, they decide to separate for a month, each going their own way. This is easy for Angela who has been an actress, but Robin finds his club cheerless. The cause of the present misunderstanding is Robin's admiration for Phyllis Fair (who is as nice as her name) and Angela's appreciation of the attentions of Major Bim Trevor (who is quite like his middle name). The friends of the four parties concerned pretend to be scandalised, but the flirtations are not of such a nature to entail an appearance before Mr. Justice MacCardie. "The Old Flame" is an ideal book to read by the fire on a customarily Arctic English spring evening.

THE CATHOLIC REACTION IN FRANCE. By Denis Gwynn. MacMillan. 7s. 6d.
There is a touch of diplomacy about Mr. Gwynn's title. People who regard the Vatican with distrust will be disappointed that the Reaction is a Reformation. Mr. Gwynn has made a very careful study of the condition of the Church in France since the war years, and his conclusion is that the anti-clericals are being beaten all along the line. It is the fifth chapter that contains the clue to the name of the book. In it Mr. Gwynn, a very able Irish journalist who spent some years in France contributing to the Press there, tries to explain how far it is true that the Catholics of France have allowed themselves to become identified with Conservative or reactionary politics. In this chapter he deals also with the education question. The author does not claim complete knowledge of all the *nuances* of French politics, but he has devoted much study to salient questions like the Catholic Press and Catholic trade unions.

THE COMPLETE POEMS OF MELEAGER OF GADARA. Translated from the Greek by F. A. Wright. Birch. 3s.
Meleager's Egeria was Heliodora, and his best love poems are written in her honour. Mr. Wright has got the right lyric note into his renderings. If anything he is almost too free and easy as in the song which he calls with easy modernity, "The Irish Rose," which trippingly runs :—

> I've said it before
> And they'll say it again,
> My love's lips the sweetest
> You ever have seen.
> You'd perhaps like to know,
> Heiydora's her name,
> She's a fairy who puts
> E'en the fairies to shame.

Palpably one of the Irish Healys.

CHAPTERS FROM RICHARD BAXTER'S CHRISTIAN DIRECTORY (1673). Selected by Jeanette Tawney with a Preface by The Rt. Rev. Charles Gore, D.D. G. Bell & Son. 6s.
It was an excellent idea to republish a book of casuistry by the most humane and sympathetic of the seventeenth century Puritans with a preface by the most humane and sympathetic of the modern High Churchman. Being humane and sympathetic, Richard Baxter naturally found himself in conflict with that fast rising tide of commercial materialism which was largely coincident with the great religious change; and being humane and sympathetic, Dr. Gore naturally selects the most striking passages of this kind as they bear on the modern social problems. It is of some special interest to us that Baxter had already to contend against the loss of a social sense in the matter of corners and combines. But we think it a little unfair for Dr. Gore to begin by saying of Catholic Casuistry, criticised by Pascal, that it referred to "the need to get numbers of men and women absolved who had no intention of keeping the law of God." All Catholic casuists would at least agree that people who had no such intentions could get no absolution, or it would not be valid if given by the Pope.

THE FIGHT FOR MAN. By the Rev. Prebendary A. W. Gough, M.A., F.R.S.L. The Boswell Printing and Publishing Co. 3s. 6d.
There is much in Prebendary Gough's reflections upon pacifism and socialism with which we necessarily agree; but it must be said that we agree more often negatively than positively. He has indeed the sort of persuasiveness that always belonged to the statement of conviction, or even prejudices, that a man holds as part of himself and without any complex sophistry. But if he is right in a sense in setting Christianity against Socialism, the reader is more disposed to agree with him about Socialism than about Christianity. He falls into one very hopeless hole, always gaping for the man who makes this attempt. He suggests that the richer man must be accepted, not because it is necessary for social order or the way of this wicked world, but because he has "probably worked harder, used more skill and thrift." Now the truth is that the Christian tradition sometimes urged peace for the sake of order, and sometimes declared war for the sake of justice, but *never* argued that the man who was stronger or richer was probably better. Such nonsense was never talked at all till Christianity was weakened.

SHADOWED. Anon. Melrose. 2s. 6d.
All literature is imitative, but the literature of illness is peculiarly so, with the exception, perhaps, of the dying records of "Barbellion." Many books of suffering derive from "Michael Fairless's" "The Road Mender," and "At the White Gate." In all these records of the last half century, or less, there is a constant cry arising from the weakness of self-pity, that subtly disintegrating emotional weakness. The author of "Shadowed" is very sorry for herself, and, perhaps, with deep and bitter cause. Her book may possibly help other sufferers to see something fine and beautiful in a world from whose activities they may have been barred. The volume is written in good English and reveals one who has something of the poet and something of the painter in her composition. There is also, alas! a good deal of commonplace spiritual thinking in "Shadowed."

THE HAPPY WANDERER. From the writings of the late Charles Godfrey Turner. Edited by Ethel M. Richardson Rice. Literary Year Book Press. 10s. 6d.
Turner was a New Zealand journalist, an extensive traveller and a trained observer. At the beginning of the Great War he took to soldiering. Before he began his writing records of what England meant to a Colonial, he had experiences as a camper-out, a rancher, a gold-miner, and what not. In England "The Happy Wanderer" had a happy time, as the volume testifies cheerily; but London was always the goal of his desire, and, coming to it, at the last, to face an English winter against doctor's orders, the English climate killed him. He probably jested about it before dying. Turner died too soon. This collection of his scattered writings is something better than good journalism. Portion of it has the lasting quality of literature. He was fascinated always by London streets. In Rupert Street on a Saturday night, in the flare of naphtha lamps, he saw Fagin the Jew buy bananas and the Marchioness salvage orange peel, and a girl straight from a Phil May drawing swept his face with her flamboyant feather hat. White-faced women staggered beneath bundles, and Carmen, red-lipped, wide-hipped, swayed through the throng as though she walked to music. Pity such a London-lover should be out of the glare of the light of her magic streets.

Prepaid Classified Advertisements

RATES.

Minimum 20 Words (Two Lines) ... ... **Four Shillings.**
Every Additional 10 Words (One Line) ... ... **Two Shillings.**
Less than 10 Words charged as a line.
Heading and each additional line set in capital letters charged as two lines.
Instructions should be addressed to—
PREPAID CLASSIFIED ADVERTISEMENTS DEPARTMENT,
G.K.'s WEEKLY, 20-21 Essex Street, Strand,
London, W.C.2, by first post on Saturday of each week.

For Sale and To Let.

NOKE RECTORY, OXFORDSHIRE.—FOR SALE.

Delightful country residence, 5 miles from Oxford, 1½ from Islip station. Well-built in charming village. 4 reception, 9 bedrooms, 2 dressing-rooms, bathroom (h. and c.), conservatory, stables, garage and usual offices, all in good order.
With 4 acres of garden, orchard and pasture. Well-known hunting district. With educational advantages at Oxford. Freehold and tithe-free. Price 2,200. Possession April. Has been the residence of the Rectors of Noke for over 100 years.
Apply RECTOR OF ISLIP, Oxford.

Appointments, &c., Vacant and Wanted.

UNIVERSITY OF BIRMINGHAM.
FACULTY OF COMMERCE.

PROFESSORSHIP OF COMMERCE.

The Council of the University invites applications for the Professorship of Commerce.
Annual stipend £950. The Professor will be required to take up his duties on October 1, 1925.
Twenty copies of applications (accompanied by testimonials) should be received on or before May 1.
Full particulars may be obtained from the undersigned.
C. G. BURTON, Secretary.

UNIVERSITY OF BRISTOL.

The University invites applications for the following non-professional appointments :—
HEAD OF THE DEPARTMENT OF GERMAN.
HEAD OF THE DEPARTMENT OF ECONOMICS.
Stipend in each case £500 per annum.
The status and title of the persons appointed will depend on qualifications. Duties to commence on October 1, 1925.
Applications should be lodged on or before April 20, 1925, with the REGISTRAR of the University, from whom further particulars may be obtained.

THE Board of Inland Revenue invite applications for permanent appointments to the position of Examiner in the Estate Duty Office, London, of the Inland Revenue Department, on the scale £150—£15—£500.
The higher posts of the Office are graded as follows :—

Controller of Death Duties	... ...	£1,200.
Assistant Controllers of Death Duties	...	£850—£25—£1,000.
Principal Clerks	... ...	£750—£25—£850.
Assistant Principal Clerks	... ...	£550—£20—£700.

In addition to salary cost of living bonus is payable at the rates applicable to the Civil Service generally. At the present time this addition results in a scale of £244—£19—£696 for Examiners.
Applicants must be qualified Solicitors or Articled Clerks who have passed their Final Examination, and must be between 21 and 25 years of age on April 1, 1925; in reckoning age for this purpose a candidate may deduct from his age time served in His Majesty's Forces between August 4, 1914, and December 31, 1919. Preference will be given to ex-Service candidates and in particular to eligible ex-Service men, if any, with temporary service in Government Departments.
In special circumstances an initial salary of £165 or £180 (exclusive of bonus) may be given, provided that the candidate is over 22 or 23 years of age respectively.
Candidates selected for appointment will be referred to the Civil Service Commissioners for the usual medical and other enquiries, subject to which they will be admitted to serve on strict probation for a period of two years. Upon satisfactory completion of probation they will be finally certificated for establishment. They will not be allowed to practise as Solicitors or to take out Certificates entitling them so to practise, or to accept any fee or reward whatsoever for professional or official services.
Forms of application may be obtained from the Director of Establishments, Inland Revenue, Somerset House, London, W.C.2. The last date for making application will be April 18, 1925.

UNIVERSITY OF BIRMINGHAM.

EDUCATION DEPARTMENT.

A LECTURER (Man or Woman) will be required on the Method of Modern Language Teaching and for the supervision of Language Teaching in the Schools, together with some work in the French Department of the University. A high honours degree and school teaching experience essential. Duties to begin September 1, 1925.
Stipend beginning at £300 per annum.
Applications, with copies of four testimonials, should be sent in not later than May 14, 1925, to the undersigned, from whom further particulars may be obtained.
C. G. BURTON, Secretary.

CORNWALL EDUCATION COMMITTEE.

PENZANCE COUNTY SCHOOL FOR BOYS.

Wanted, to begin duty on April 30, 1925, an ASSISTANT MASTER with good Honours Degree to teach French in Upper Forms.
Scale—£198—£385.
Forms of application may be obtained (on receipt of a stamped addressed foolscap envelope) from the HEAD-MASTER, County School for Boys, Penzance.
Education Department,
County Hall, Truro.
March 16, 1925.

Lectures, Scholarships, &c.

STRATHEARN COLLEGE, EDINBURGH.—Post scholastic trainings in Cookery. All Domestic Arts. Gardening and Poultry (residential). Diplomas awarded. Extensive grounds. Motoring, Dancing. Summer Travel Tours arranged. Illustrated Prospectus from PRINCIPAL.

ANSTEY PHYSICAL TRAINING COLLEGE, - Erdington, Birmingham (Ling's Swedish System) offers complete Teacher's Training (Women) in Swedish Educational Gymnastics, Medical Gymnastics and Massage, Dancing, Hockey, Lacroses, Cricket, Tennis, Netball, Swimming, Anatomy, Hygiene, Physiology, etc. Three Years' Course. Prospectus on application.

Girls' Schools and Colleges.

MISS IRONSIDE'S BUREAU.
JOURNALISTIC AND SECRETARIAL TRAINING.
Prospectus on application. 73 Gower Street, W.C.1.

OVERDALE SCHOOL, FARLEY HALL, near Oakamoor, N. Staffs.
Good all-round education for limited number of Girls in charming country residence, 650 ft. above sea level. Principals : Miss PICKARD, M.A. (Newnham College), and Miss KITTS.

WYCOMBE ABBEY SCHOOL, BUCKS.—Not less than Six Scholarships of the nominal value of £10 a year will be offered by the Council on the result of an Examination to be held in May, 1925, to GIRLS Under Fourteen on May 1. The Council are prepared to give, if necessary, additional grants varying from £30 to £90 a year to scholars. All entry forms must be received before March 31, 1925. For further particulars apply to the HEAD-MISTRESS.

HARROGATE COLLEGE FOR GIRLS, YORKSHIRE.
Chairman :—The Right Hon. LORD GISBOROUGH.
Entrance Scholarship Examination will be held on May 20, 21 and 22, for the award of Five Scholarships varying in value, according to merit, from £30 to £100 a year, and open to girls under 14 years of age on May 1. Entry Forms must be returned before May 6, 1925, to the HEAD-MISTRESS.

Boys' Schools and Colleges.

ALDENHAM SCHOOL.—Six or seven Entrance Scholarships of the value of £50 each will be offered early in June.—Particulars from the HEAD-MASTER, Aldenham School, Elstree, Herts.

KING EDWARD VI. SCHOOL, BURY ST. EDMUND'S.
Two House-Scholarships of £9 per ann., open to boys under 13. One Exhibition of £20 per ann., restricted to sons of officers deceased on active service. Examination June 9, 1925.
Further particulars from HEAD-MASTER.

DALHOUSIE CASTLE. NEAR BONNYRIGG, MIDLOTHIAN.)
K. M. MYLNE, M.A., Oxon,
having resigned the Head-Mastership of Merchiston Castle Preparatory School as from July next, will open Dalhousie Castle as a Boys' Preparatory School in September.
For preliminary prospectus and all particulars application should be made to K. M. MYLNE, Merchiston House, Edinburgh, until the end of July, and thereafter at Dalhousie Castle.

Published by the Proprietors, G.K.'s WEEKLY, LTD., at their offices, 20 & 21 Essex Street, Strand, London, W.C.2 (incorporating THE NEW WITNESS). Telephone No. City 1978. Printed by THE ALLIED PRESS, LTD., 19 Clerkenwell Close, London, E.C.1. Sole agents for Australasia : Gordon & Gotch (Australasia), Ltd. Sole Agents for South Africa : Central News Agency, Ltd.

G.K.'s Weekly

EDITED BY G. K. CHESTERTON.

No. 3.—Vol. I.   Week ending Saturday, April 4, 1925.   PRICE SIXPENCE.
YEARLY (52 ISSUES)
£1 10 4.

Telephone No. City 1978.   *Offices, 20 & 21, Essex Street, Strand, W.C.*

CONTENTS:

A DEBATE ON DEGENERACY

WHEN we are for a moment satisfied, or sated, with reading the latest news of the loftiest social circles, or the most exact records of the most responsible courts of justice, we naturally turn to the serial story, called " Poisoned by Her Mother " or " The Mystery of the Crimson Wedding Ring " in search of something calmer and more quietly convincing, more restful, more domestic and more like real life. But as we turn over the pages in passing from the incredible fact to the comparatively credible fiction, we are very likely to encounter a particular phrase on the general subject of social degeneracy. It is one of a number of phrases that seem to be kept in solid blocks in the printing-offices of newspapers. Like most of these solid statements, it is of a soothing character. It is like the headline of " Hopes of a Settlement," by which we learn that things are unsettled; or that topic of the " Revival of Trade," which it is part of the journalistic trade periodically to revive. The sentence to which we refer is to this effect; that the fears about social degeneracy need not disturb us, because such fears have been expressed in every age; and there are always romantic and retrospective persons, poets and such riff-raff, who look back to imaginary " good old times."

It is the mark of such statements that they seem to satisfy the mind; in other words it is the mark of such thoughts that they stop us from thinking. The man who has thus praised progress does not think it necessary to progress any further. The man who has dismissed a complaint, as being old, does not himself think it necessary to say anything new. He is content to repeat this apology for existing things; and seems unable to offer any more thoughts on the subject. Now, as a matter of fact, there are a number of further thoughts that might be suggested by the subject. Of course, it is quite true that this notion of the decline of a state has been suggested in many periods, by many persons, some of them unfortunately poets. Thus, for instance, Byron, notoriously so moody and melodramatic, had somehow or other got it into his head that the Isles of Greece were less glorious in arts and arms in the last days of Turkish rule than in the days of the Battle of Salamis or the Republic of Plato. So again Wordsworth, in an equally sentimental fashion, seems to insinuate that the Republic of Venice was not quite so powerful when Napoleon trod it out like a dying ember as when its commerce and art filled the seas of the world with a conflagration of colour. So many writers in the eighteenth and nineteenth centuries have even gone so far as to suggest that modern Spain played a less predominant part than Spain in the days of the discovery of America or the victory of Lepanto. Some, even more lacking in that Optimism which is the soul of commerce, have made an equally perverse comparison between the earlier and the later conditions of the commercial aristocracy of Holland. Some have even maintained that Tyre and Sidon are not quite so fashionable as they used to be; and somebody once said something about " the ruins of Carthage."

In somewhat simpler language, we may say that all this argument has a very big and obvious hole in it. When a man says " People were as pessimistic as you are in societies which were not declining, but were even advancing," it is permissible to reply, " Yes, and people were probably as optimistic as you are in societies which really declined." For after all, there were societies which really declined. It is true that Horace said that every generation was worse than the last, and implied that Rome was going to the dogs, at the very moment when all the external world was being brought under the eagles. But it is quite likely that the last forgotten court poet, praising the last forgotten Augustulus at the stiff court of Byzantium, contradicted the seditious rumours of social decline by saying that, after all, Horace had said the same thing. In other words, we have to consider every such case of moral degeneracy, or the allegation of moral degeneracy, on its own merits. It is no answer to say that people have sometimes thought there was degeneracy when there was not; since it is equally true that they have sometimes thought there was no degeneracy when there was a great deal. It is no answer to say, what is, of course, perfectly true, that some people are naturally prone to such pessimism. We are not judging them, but the situation which they judged or misjudged. We may say that schoolboys have always disliked having to go to school. But there is such a thing as a bad school. We may say that farmers always grumble at the weather. But there is such a thing as a bad harvest. And we have to consider as a question of the facts, and not of the farmer's feelings, whether the moral world of modern England is likely to have a bad harvest.

In considering this, of course, any sensible person will allow a great deal for the considerations with which the optimists console themselves; for the vividness of present as compared with past evil; for the very rich often being the rottenest part of any society; for the paradox of all legal interference; by which the law necessarily turns the limelight upon the darkest corner rather than the most outstanding object. We cannot expect to see all the innocent people in the dock; or even to see all the normal people in the newspapers. We cannot expect to see headlines in large letters, " Man Fond of His Wife in Cricklewood," or " Wandsworth Wife Has Never Poisoned Husband." We cannot expect to hear newsboys shouting down the street that Mr. Jones is not yet murdered, or even that Mr. Smith is still married. In this sense it is perfectly true that most ordinary people are healthy enough in Cricklewood; and in this sense it is probable that most people were healthy enough in Byzantium. In this sense doubtless the normal woman is still very womanly in Wandsworth; and in this sense the normal man is still exceedingly manly in Spain.

It is a question of proportion; but there is a proportion that amounts to a peril. In the present case we believe there really is a peril. It is not so much in the actions as in the assumptions. It is not so much in the sins for which individual sinners are pilloried, as in the sins for which they are not pilloried; the sins that seem to be no longer regarded as sins at all. It is in the things taken for granted; the things passed over; even the things forgotten, that the glaring change appears. It is involved in the very words used to whitewash it. People say, " There were blackguards like that a hundred years ago and in every age." The answer is " Yes; there were blackguards like that a hundred years ago. But there were not respectable people like that a hundred years ago. Society did not assume a convention of sin, which only became unconventional when it actually turned into crime. It is not that more people have broken the law; it is that the law is broken; broken in the sense of having broken down." It is not a mere question of divorce, as it was understood by its more moderate advocates in the last generation, who respected marriage as a social contract though not as a sacrament. They regarded divorce as the exception; as the exception existing only for very exceptional cases. The importance of the recent revelations is not that they have revealed the almost fantastic figures of queer scoundrels and " vamps " who have existed in all ages. It is that they have given glimpses of whole tracts or sections of society in which this abnormal dissolution has become normal. In short, we all knew the sort of story that ended in the divorce-court. But this sort of story began in the divorce-court.

We might note many other of these really important alterations; alterations in the assumptions. For instance, there is the abjectly helpless part played by the husband. It is all very well to mock the individual for his weakness; but our modern moralists really cannot have it both ways. If the man had defended the dignity of his house, he would have been told by the same lawyers and journalists that he was a pre-historic ruffian treating his wife as a chattel. We have to deal with a change in the ideals even of idealistic people. And for these people there is no longer even the shadow of the notion that has seemed so normal to mankind; the notion that was expressed by the two terms of honour and the home.

Now we ourselves do not want to sentimentalise about those terms; we want to use them. Without the preservation of those ideas, there is not the shadow of a hope of the recovery of liberty and property. In an individual capacity, we have, of course, more serious reasons for holding them sacred; but the point here is strictly practical. As certainly as a brick house is made of bricks, a free state is made of families. People may prefer to live in a steel house built by a steel trust; they may prefer to live in a large hotel made of iron and sham marble with a labyrinth of more or less communal bedrooms; they may prefer to wander into the wilderness of all the cranks and sleep in one vast canvas tent. But if they want to keep the idea of a house, they must defend it like a castle. For there is no right so real as the right to open and shut a door; and the roof-tree is the tree of liberty.

NOTES OF THE WEEK

THE armed guard surrounding Lord Balfour on his visit to Palestine was a grim commentary on the conception that he went there as the deliverer of a people or the founder of a nation. We are well aware, as every parliamentary voice would hasten to remind us, that the phrase used was not " nation " but " national home." That is the sort of distinction upon which the destinies of civilisations are made to depend. So it was said that England and France had not an alliance but an understanding; and some would only allow us to say " understanding " if we said it in French. If it will soothe such people's feelings, we are quite prepared to say " national " in Yiddish and " home " in Arabic. We leave it to the logician to decide what is gained by the longer expression. We leave him to decide how a thing can be national if there is no nation; or how you make it less of a nation by calling it a home. The truth is that the best of the Zionist Jews regard it as a nation given to them to rule; the worst of the Zionist Jews regard it as a conquered province given to them to rob; and the whole of the Arab population, Moslem and Christian, regard it as quite as outrageous to be ruled by Jews as to be robbed by them. Indeed, the phrase " national home " might have been invented to express the irony. Palestine may or may not be the Arab's nation, but it was certainly his home. Zionism, as it stands, consists in taking away his home in order to pretend that it is somebody else's nation. We have always believed, for instance, in Irish nationality; but this is as if we were to allow the Irish to have a national home somewhere in India.

* * * *

THE middle course is often the very worst course; for the middle course introduced the middleman. This business of Zionism is a very good example of such falling between two stools into the mud of mere commercialism. There was some good in the idea of Zionism; but Zionism does not include that good. There might have been a purpose in the policy; but the policy does not serve the purpose. The only real object of making a Jewish nation (not a national home) would be to make it on a sufficiently large scale and of a sufficiently consistent substance, to relieve the pressure of the Jewish problem on all the other nations; to drain the Jewish element that lies everywhere in lakes or puddles, or wanders everywhere in streams or sewers, into that central sea of a real spiritual unity; the kingdom of Israel. That would be thoroughly well worth doing, if it could be done. It would be so worth doing that it is still worth while to consider whether it could be done. It is very doubtful whether it could be done in Palestine. But what we have done is the very opposite. Instead of diminishing the areas on which the Jewish problem presses, we have added another area upon which it can press. Instead of giving the Jew a commonwealth of which he can really be a citizen, we have given him yet another country in which he can be an interloper and a nuisance. The Jew is in Jerusalem as he is in Johannesburg; and he is as ready to call himself a Palestinian as to call himself a Parisian or a Peruvian. But he is not at home there; for he cannot rest. And he probably does not really regard it as his own country; for he develops it like all the others.

* * * *

PEOPLE continue to talk about the prospects of Prohibition being adopted by Liberal politicians as the last hope of the Liberal Party. If it is the last hope, the party must be pretty hopeless. The most amusing fact, too familiar to be commonly noticed, is that nobody thinks of considering whether the Liberal politicians, who would welcome it as a law they must enforce, would also welcome it as a law they must obey. We humble citizens, when we are considering whether we agree with the proposal to take away tobacco, cannot entirely exclude the ego-eccentric calculation of whether we should like tobacco taken away. Politicians have no such deplorable selfishness of outlook. It never seems to cross their minds that their social habits would ever be altered; for the very simple reason that they would not. The part of the governing class that calls itself Liberal drinks wine in the same way as the part that calls itself Conservative; again for the very simple reason that they all drink the same wine at the same dinner-tables. There will certainly be the same wine on the same dinner-tables whatever Bills are put on the table of the House. There is, perhaps, rather less to go round because there is less money to pay for it; but there is no more for Tories than for Radicals. The one thing we really know about Prohibition is that this sort of fashionable drinking is never prohibited. In plain words, these Liberal leaders would like us to become teetotallers that they may become bootleggers.

* * * *

WE believe, however, that their calculations about reviving the Liberal Party is a mistake, even from their own dreary and cynical point of view. It is largely the notion that they can effect one of those great Nonconformist rallies that were really possible some little time ago; and which were organised with a considerable mixture of excitement and efficiency. It was really true, until a little while ago, that while what are called the Free Churches were supposed to protest against authority, there was no class of things that had so much uniformity. While Anglicans thought about wine or war as individuals, while a Catholic could be every sort of aristocrat or democrat, every chapel and every minister said exactly the same thing about the cause of temperance or the curse of militarism. This was true; but it is less true every day. The blunder of the politicians comes from their extraordinary ignorance of the world of thought; and especially of religious thought. There is no rising generation of Puritans that would to-day support W. T. Stead against the horse-racing of Rosebery or the love-making of Parnell. The sons of the Puritans are wandering about everywhere—to Agnosticism, to Anglo-Catholicism, to Rome or occasionally to ruin. The politicians probably have another calculation which may be more correct; that the female vote will prove Puritan upon this point. Even about that we think that, both for good and evil, the trend of the time is against them. The rising generation of girls is almost as likely to know too much about cocktails as too little. But this possibility doubtless increases the anxiety of those who dread the increase of the female vote, by the granting of the franchise to girls before they are twenty-five.   *   *   *   *

FOR our part, we incline to think that people ought to have the Vote *until* they are twenty-five, and not afterwards. Afterwards they have found it out. Youth is the time when a fiery and plastic power of fiction can really make it seem that the small-featured lawyer standing in the Liberal interest is a statute of Liberty, and the well-fed colonial cad standing in the Conservative interest is a monument of England, and the greasy chapel sidesman on the make, standing in the Labour interest, is the rugged giant of Labour risen from the red earth like Adam. It is youth that can fill these very empty vessels with coloured liquid like the bowls in Miss Edgworth's story. Think of all the suffragettes, many of them mere children, for whom a short time ago the Vote shone in the air like the Holy Grail. They have all got the Grail now; yet somehow the glow of their glorious joy and peace does not seem to be filling all society. Voting ought to be one of the sports of youth; like aviation and the Russian ballet, it should be a game from which the players are forced to retire very early. Youth is the time of comradeship; and comradeship is the only virtue of party politics. And it is unnecessary to point out how much more healthily and harmlessly the young might be employed, in electing people who will never rule and pledging them to bills that will never pass, than if the same young people indulged in things that have a result, such as seduction, murder, delirium tremens and suicide.   *   *   *

IT is true that our reform would involve even the granting of the vote to infants, in the popular as well as the legal sense. We do not shrink from the logical consequences of our own principle. A child has exactly the right view of a machine; he regards it as a toy. And just as the child would have an innocent pleasure in a sewing-machine or a sausage-machine, so he might have the same pleasure in the Party-machine. The whole business of an election, as at present conducted, seems exactly fitted to be a nursery game. The two sides are distinguishable only by the use of two very bright primary colours; and the child exults in pointing out so many blues and so many reds in the street. Nothing would please the littler toddler more than to toddle down a street, knocking at each of the doors and bringing out an indignant workman in his shirt-sleeves to say "Yes" or "No"; and this is all that is ever done by canvassers. The child would also rejoice in the rides in richer people's motor-cars, which are the chief appeals to democratic citizenship to-day. He would be enormously gratified if he were allowed to sit up late on the night of the poll and see the votes counted. The child, being near to God, would not be bored even by that. And there is always just the chance that the child would do what the youth will never do; see the truth and tell it. We might be saved by the Terrible Child who saw that the Emperor had no clothes.   *   *   *   *

SPIRITUALISM is being boomed in certain sections of the very commercial press and mostly in connection with highly commercial names. In short, if we want to find spiritualism, we must now look for it in the world of materialism. But we doubt whether spiritualists like Sir Oliver Lodge will be very much gratified at the display of their new religion made by spiritualists like Mr. Hannen Swaffer. We do not quite know why the capacity to see a ghost should entail the incapacity to see a joke. But unless it has done so, it would really seem that the "proofs" in the *Sunday Express* would be enough to kill the most vigorous new religion. It is not easy to make death a laughing matter; but Mr. Swaffer has really succeeded. The very names of the people involved are an entertainment in themselves; Mr. Dennis Bradley and a film actor seem to be the chief priests and prophets interpreting between mortals and immortality. There is a great deal of music in the programme, mostly in the way of exceedingly sentimental hymns; but the actual instrument of revelation is apparently a trumpet. All this harmony does not prevent a certain sense of discord, when we come to the strange collection of human beings chosen to search out super-human things. There is too much occasional verse in this paper; but we are tempted to write a fine Shakespearean sonnet beginning "Music to hear, why hearest thou Dennis Bradley?"

        *   *   *   *

THE description of the seance given by Mr. Hannen Swaffer in the *Sunday Express* contains, among other memorable things, the following passage. "Miss Collier's mother spoke through the trumpet the next time. She did so, using it with anxious affection. The trumpet stroked Constance's arms, body, head and knees." We have read the more gruesome works of Poe; a few trifles about vampires and cannibalism; we are not unacquainted with poetry like that of Miss Petowker, who recited "The Blood-Drinker's Burial"; but for the purely artistic creation of a creepy and repulsive sensation we can imagine few things worse than sitting in the dark and being stroked all over by a live trumpet. We do not know whether this is what is meant by using the trumpet with anxious affection. On the face of it, we should have been a little puzzled about how one could use a trumpet with anxious affection. We should be disposed to quote the text which says that if the trumpet be used with anxious affection, who shall prepare himself for the battle? Anyhow, our own little toy trumpet will give no uncertain sound about how we are to prepare ourselves for religious experiences of this sort. And we do not recommend any lady to join a religion, during the services of which she may find herself suddenly being embraced by a trombone or forced to repulse the too affectionate gestures of the big drum. Mr. Bradley and the other gentlemen do not seem to have been caressed by the trumpet. Each of them could be trusted to bring his own.

        *   *   *   *

ALL this nonsense began with the Northcliffe manifestation, which was alone a sufficient manifestation of the mean and snobbish standard involved. It revealed something about the living, if not about the dead. It revealed people under the extraordinary impression that Alfred Harmsworth was a person of some importance, even in this life; let alone the more inconceivable inference that he must be a person of importance in another life. Heaven is a large hotel, at which the arrival of a millionaire naturally creates something of a stir. It would be nearer the truth to say of poor Harms-worth, in another sense than that of the poet, that we might hope eventually to look for him in the nurseries of heaven. The best thing that can be said for him is that he never had a notion of the real truth about this world; that he lived on rumours and reputations; just as his own reputation was never anything but a rumour. He passed his life trying to pull down anything he had himself set up; because he never looked to see if there was a solid pedestal on which to set it up. He first swallowed a legend of Kitchener exactly in the manner of a schoolgirl at sixteen. Then he revenged himself on the reality for not being like the legend, with the doll-destroying frenzy of a child of six. Having thus played idolator and iconoclast to a Kitchener he never knew, he went on to play idolator and iconoclast to a Lloyd George he never knew. It was on this side of the Styx that he lived among shadows.

* * * *

THE lady known as Jane Burr was once famous for walking about the world in masculine costume; which, to do her justice, would probably now appear much more decorous than a good deal of feminine costume. She is a lady of kindly but cloudy ideals, like so many true-born children of the United States. It seems that the other day, at some social function of the sort common in New York and other new cities (divorcing a husband, we fancy, or some such festivity), she said she suffered in the same way as "every intellectual woman" of her acquaintance. "Not one of them has married a he-man." Translated into the English language (with the assistance of an interpreter employed on one of the Atlantic liners) this means that they complain of a man for not being sufficiently masculine. But if intellectual women may worthily complain of a man being like a woman, why was it considered unworthy of intellectual men to complain of a woman dressing up as a man? Or if feminism has discovered its own instincts in the end, what was there so very wrong in the mas-culinism that followed its own instincts from the beginning? The truth is that masculinism was too masculine to make the really logical retort. There were a great many novels and plays, mostly silly, about the man regaining his position by being a bully; or a mythical being called a "cave-man." But the logical retort would be for the man to put flowers in his hair and paint his face and powder his nose. It would be much too dis-gusting even for the most realistic play. But it would be intelligible, even to the most intellectual woman.

* * * *

WE gather from the press that clergymen of various denominations are discussing, in a somewhat disturbed manner, a great film of the Life of Christ, which some of them think "would reform the world." It might be suggested that this rather implies that the film version of the events would do more than the events themselves; for which it was only claimed that they would reform anybody who wanted to be reformed. But apart from that question, a debate seems to have arisen upon the representation as a mere question of taste, or even of art. And as a question of art a rather interesting point is really raised. As a matter of morals, it cannot be more wrong to put Christ on a film than on a stage or in a picture. But as a matter of art there is a difference, of some importance in aesthetics. A profound instinct in all popular tradition made the representation of really sacred things not hazy but rather hard and clear. They were quite stiff because they were quite symbolic. It does not seem false when an old picture shows us God with a grey beard and a gold crown, sitting on a solid seat in some quiet corner of His heavenly garden. The moment He is represented on the stage as a light, a vapour, a voice or some other vague evasion, the effect is suddenly materialistic. The cinematic effect would be often inappropriate, not so much because photography is realistic as because it is impressionist. It could not have the absolute character of real religious art.

* * * *

WE have no intention of being drawn into a discus-sion about the Australian artist whose paganism is being so much discussed in the papers; but we are glad to have a somewhat parallel problem con-sidered in this issue by Mr. Bernard Gilbert; because Mr. Bernard Gilbert, over and above his claim as a pioneer of rural reconstruction, seems to be almost the only man we have come across anywhere, who is capable of dis-cussing this point of art and morals and seeing that they are two different things. The ordinary argument is endless and useless; one man saying "This is immoral," the other replying hotly "It is not immoral; it is a masterpiece"; the first rejoining indignantly "You call that a masterpiece which degrades and defiles, etc., etc.," and so on for ever. This is exactly as if a man were to see the Vicar of his parish on the top of the church spire inspecting the weather-cock, and were to shoot the reverend gentleman very neatly in a vital spot. A judge of shooting would say "That is a good shot"; somebody else would reply "How can you call that a good shot which deprives us of our dear Vicar? etc., etc." Of course it is a good shot, but not a good action. Where the artists get muddled is in not seeing that we *act* on the moral and not the artistic judgment. We say "Let us hang this marksman." Few but Mr. Bernard Gilbert have the moral courage to say "Let us burn this master-piece."

NOTE.

Some delay in the arrangements for the section to be called the Cock-pit, or controversial arena, has been caused by the pressure of material kindly provided by correspondents. We apologise for the difficulties of selection, and hope to have the first sample ready for the next number. In this matter, if not in others, we suffer from the embarrassment of riches.　　　　EDITOR.

THE MYSTERY OF G.K.'s WEEKLY

(From Notes and Queries of the later twentieth century.)

THE question of the meaning of the letters "G.K." on this rare and quaint old broadsheet have been much disputed. "Curious" will find the question discussed at length in Pillington's "The Alphabet in Industrial England." The view that the two initials stood for the "German Kaiser" is now generally abandoned; though Higgs points out that the German sovereign in question was an amateur in many of the arts, and was quite likely to have edited a literary paper all by himself; and that the contents of the paper show traces of the mental disturbance or weakness that is said to have been hereditary in his house. It is now generally agreed that the monogram probably stands for the statement "God Knows," which was a ritual or religious reply common in the England of that time to a variety of questions affecting public life and private welfare. It can be ascertained from contemporary documents that questions such as "What will happen next?"—"What is a Protocol?"—"Where shall we get a house?"—"Why was Jinks knighted?"—"Who is playing with the bank rate?"—"What has become of the Navy?"—"What does this picture mean?"—"Who are the Slovenes?"—"Where will the income tax stop?"—"What on earth is to become of us?" and even "Is there a God?" were all answered by this devout and dignified reply of "God Knows." It is itself a sufficient proof of the passionate devotion to dogmatic theology that was a mark of the time, and a refutation of the idea that it was infected with scepticism. Various other theories, as that G.K. stood for Getting Kicked, Golfing Knickers, Going to the Kinema, General Kissing and Gratuitous Killing may be dismissed as most improbable. But a case may perhaps be made out for the theory recently advanced by Professor Pooter, that the Gin King, the celebrated bootlegger who became the richest man in the world by providing all the Prohibitionist countries with their chief article of consumption, conducted this organ in the interests of his immense business. This, as the learned scholar truly remarks, would account both for the formal concealment of a formally illegal thing under initials, and for the actual ostentation and even vulgarity with which the initials are displayed. It has all the character of a brazen and accepted legal fiction. As to the notion that the personal initials of some obscure individual journalist, now forgotten, could ever have been counted sufficiently important for such a place, it is too absurd for discussion.

A GLASS OF CHAMPAGNE

IT is a solemn and awful fact that the following paragraph, with large headlines, appeared lately in a great newspaper called *The Daily News*, founded by Charles Dickens and devoted by him and his successors to the defence of Liberal ideas.

"The Directors of the Livingstone Film are receiving protests from Prohibitionists in the Scottish Churches against the scene representing Livingstone and Stanley celebrating their meeting over a glass of champagne. The reply of the film directors is naturally that their picture is true to the facts. The incident is confirmed by missionary authorities. Whether Livingstone was aware of the nature of the liquor may be a question open to enquiry."

Was Livingstone really as drunk as all that? Might we ask the missionary authorities, who apparently represent the new principle of authority in religion, whether the great traveller was really in such a state that he could not be trusted with a glass of champagne? We think it worth while, however, to commemorate this paragraph; as a small sample of the quality or level of dignity, sanity, culture, common-sense, knowledge of the world, appreciation of the conditions of travel, imagination in the contemplation of distant and barbaric scenes, historical information about a previous generation, lucidity of thought, charity of sentiment, love of liberty and sense of humour, which we may expect to find prevalent if our civilisation accepts Prohibition. Indeed it is so precious and subtle a sample, that we think it worth while to break up the rich complexity into a few of its constituent parts.

(1) It will be noted that Prohibitionists not only prohibit people from drinking wine but prohibit them from seeing a picture of anybody else drinking wine. Henceforth we are to accept the principle that anything which is wrong to do is equally wrong to depict. A picture of a pirate ship is as much a crime as piracy on the high seas; to draw a picture of a pickpocket is tantamount to picking pockets. Apply this principle to the pictures in the Family Bible, not to mention any possible performance of Shakespeare's plays.

(2) It is impossible to admire any historical character, who lived before the time of Prohibition, unless we can pretend that he was a Prohibitionist. Everybody who knows the elements of the real religious history of Protestantism knows that the old Puritan generation never was teetotal. If Livingstone had been even more of a Puritan, he might possibly not have been a Prohibitionist. Apply this principle to Oliver Cromwell, the Brewer and other Puritan heroes.

(3) It is implied that Livingstone had lived so domestic and secluded a life, never stirring from his pious mother's home, that he had never heard of champagne and did not know it when he saw it. Nor does it occur to the writers that travellers can reach a point of exhaustion when champagne is a recognised medicine. Nor do they know that a rescue is often regarded as an occasion of rejoicing, when champagne is a recognised social symbol. Evidently they at least wish to imitate the untravelled innocence and parochial immobility characteristic of Livingstone.

(4) It is interesting to know that Scottish Ministers of the Gospel have nothing better to do than to discuss how historical facts can be concealed from people at a cinema theatre, when the moral problems of their nation and their age have begun to sound in our ears with a name that has already the noise and roar of a great river: the Clyde.

PARLIAMENT FROM WITHIN
"SUPPLY"

By Sir Henry Slesser, K.C., M.P.

THE process of Supply, which is very mysterious to the uninitiated, has been employing the attention of Parliament for the greater part of the last fortnight. In theory it consists of the sanctioning by the House of Commons of every penny which is to be spent on the Army, the Navy, and the Civil Service, apart from such sums as have been deliberately taken out of the control of Parliament and put upon the Consolidated Fund. The Estimates are in constant course of preparation by the Departments—like the painting of the Forth Bridge, no sooner is one set disposed of than another Estimate is in preparation—and are bound up in large yellow volumes, and they contain a most meticulous account of the money claimed and the purposes for which it is to be spent. This wealth of detail, however, does not disguise from the Parliamentarian the fact that the credit and expense of a Government is involved in the passage of every penny; so that although an outsider might think that Parliament was really exercising a financial control over the expenditure of monies, in fact, the supporters of the Government are obliged uncritically to support each item and the opponents of the Government are similarly bound to oppose the Estimates in some form or another. This tournament, in which no bones are broken, has been continuing in a desultory form for the last fortnight. Someone proposes to reduce a vote by £100 and raises a discussion on his own pet topic. The Minister reveals just so much of what is in his mind as he deems expedient and, in the end, the Estimate is duly passed and the Amendment defeated. It would be quite easy for an official to insert the most immense sums to be spent on the most ludicrous objects with very little prospect of the joke being discovered, if it were only sufficiently buried away in the mass of figures which Parliament gratuitously prints and presents to its members. At any rate, we are now in the happy position of again being assured an Army and a Navy, an Air Force and a Civil Service if we can find the money in the Budget to maintain them.

By far the most interesting debate took place last Friday on a proposal to facilitate the acquisition of allotments. Like most interesting debates it originated in a Private Member's Motion, and at least one member of the Labour Party who is not hostile to the Chestertonian economics, definitely claimed that it was essential that every citizen should possess a piece of land in order that he might be independent of economic exploitation. This view was apparently accepted by the bulk of the Trade Unionists present, but one Labour member, Mr. Montague, took the view that the notion that men should own land individually was retrograde. He said that such an organisation of agriculture was unscientific and if consistent should only be upheld by those who followed Belloc and Chesterton in advocating the medieval state and the craft industry. He condemned small farming and small shopkeeping alike in a speech worthy, I think, of quotation. He said :—

I do not support the principle upon which the Bill is based. I listened with great interest to the speech of the ex-Solicitor-General. He said that getting people back to the land by supporting the provision of financial aid for allotments would lead to a larger and fuller life in the country. There are different kinds of contentment, and I imagine the contentment which Liberal and Conservative members believe in for the common people is what is known as the bovine kind. I do not want that kind of contentment, and I do not think it is desirable that the spare time of the working folk of this country should be spent in cultivating little patches of ground some miles from where they live and work. I do not think that is a progressive policy. It is entirely and flagrantly a reactionary policy. The hon. and learned member for South-East Leeds (Sir H. Slesser) said this would be a part solution of the poverty problem and the unemployment. For the life of me I cannot understand how the fact of urban industrial workers who are carrying out their ordinary occupational function in life for eight or more hours every day, going on to the land in their spare time to cultivate it, to grow foodstuffs, and, presumably, to market them, is going to help the solution of these problems. I do not believe that providing two jobs for one man is the way to solve the unemployment problem, and so far as the general problem of poverty is concerned, you will have to do a great deal more in the way of reorganisation and scientific adjustment before you even approach a solution of that problem.

Why should the question of agriculture be considered in a different aspect from that in which we consider questions of industrial production? If I spoke for that school of thought which Mr. G. K. Chesterton represents—the medieval school—and preached the idea of getting back to earlier forms of handicraft; if I were to suggest it would be economically advantageous to this country, instead of depending upon coal and electric power and machine production, to go back to the period when the Lancashire weaver worked in his own home, with the aid of his own family, produced his cloth upon a primitive machine, and went out into the market himself to sell his product—that doctrine would be recognised at once as economically reactionary. I suggest that the idea of solving the agricultural problem by the niggling method of getting people to work hard in their spare time on little plots of ground is equivalent to the proposal that we should go back to the conditions of the domestic industries period in the 16th and 17th centuries. That is not the way in which the problem can be solved. I know that the industrial system is top-heavy. We want more organisation of agriculture, we want more agricultural production, and, in view of diminishing foreign markets, it would be a great thing if we could bring back into cultivation the land which has gone out of cultivation and make ourselves to a larger extent—as we could—self-sufficing and independent of the fluctuations of foreign trade.

If working people are pleased to cultivate gardens as a hobby, that is another matter, but to consider the idea of getting working people to use their spare time in this way as an economic proposition, as something which will solve the agricultural, the unemployment, and the poverty problems is wide of the mark. It may be true that small cultivation in present circumstances will pay. It pays just in the same way as does the venture of a poor devil of a workman who manages to save a few pounds and buys a decrepit kind of business in a side street in a slum and opens a small shop where everything is sold from toffee apples to mouse-traps. I know the kind of life such people live when they become what is called "independent and self-respecting," and it is simply a dog's life. I know from practical experience what it means, and it is precisely on a par with the idea that people should spend their spare time on allotments in order to make themselves independent, self-respecting, and contented. I do not want anything of the kind, and though I am probably the only member who will express these ideas, in view of the general support which has been given to this Bill, I think they are ideas which call for expression on this occasion. We want scientific organisation of agriculture in this country and mass production on the highest scientific principles, and only in that way shall we be able to restore agriculture to its old pre-eminence.

My own view is that there is a considerable amount of logic in this argument; but he and others who denounce such proposals as "putting the clock back" evidently favour a completely industrialised community and seem to differ primarily on the question of the distribution of wealth in that community, rather than in the nature of the Society itself.

Towards the end of the week Foreign Affairs have been debated in connection with Singapore and the Protocol. Various views were expressed as to the competing sovereignty of the Nations and the League of Nations. A somewhat merciless analysis of the constitution of the League of Nations in reality—four of five Nations were, in fact, the real power over the other forty—was delivered by Mr. Duff-Cooper, who is one of the ablest debaters on the Conservative side of the House. He declared that the League of Nations was not founded on a rock, with which sentiment some of us were inclined to agree; but any reference to that medieval League of Nations, the Holy Roman Empire, was completely absent from the debate.

The argument against the Singapore Base, that it would become another Gibraltar and must inevitably be regarded by the Japanese as an hostile act, seemed to me to be unanswerable. The Australians, who are more frank perhaps in this matter than we are, definitely welcome the Singapore as a defence against the Japanese, and Mr. MacDonald, I think, was right when he said that the ultimate political consequences of the construction of that Base are far more important in the growing feeling between East and West than, say, the mere strategic considerations.

—*House of Commons*, *April*, 1925.

THE CANNIBAL RESTAURANT

CONSIDERABLE interest continues to be aroused in the neighbourhood by the opening of the Cannibal Restaurant in the artistic quarter of Chelsea, where so many unconventional departures have aroused curiosity and comment. The proprietor informed our representative that he had to answer a continual stream of inquiries from many influential persons. He is emphatic in his assertion that there is no kind of cruelty in the operations involved; as they deal only with the completely or nearly dead; and the question of eating those who only indicate in a general way that they are tired of life has not yet come up for final discussion. "Its economic advantages are enormous," he added, "the problem of producing enough meat for these islands could easily be solved without any further trouble or fuss."

Professor Yegg, the famous biologist, said that science as such had an open mind on the matter. "There is no doubt," he remarked, "that in many matters we are coming to regard the distinction between man and the other animals as one of degree rather than kind." On the other hand, the Bishop of Buffington, who belongs to the old school, frankly expressed himself as very doubtful in the matter. "We must go slowly," he said, "and these young people want to go too fast. For my own part, I am not ready to be eaten yet." Our representative made further inquiries in the neighbourhood, where comparatively little anxiety seems to be aroused by the new project.

Our correspondent has provided us with the above facts; but we hesitate to accept them; not that there is anything in the idea inconsistent with modern progress and modern ideas, but rather because the whole story seems curiously parallel to that of a recent experiment in another primitive idea: that of teaching children to go without clothes, which aroused similar comments.

THE RELIGION FOR BUSINESS MEN

[*It has been remarked that Spiritualism has proved especially attractive to business men both in America and in this country; and a recent seance, consisting of communications from the dead with a great deal of incidental music, has suggested to these organising minds the desirability of arranging a regular concert programme. We have pleasure in printing below the items of the programme as selected.*]

Programme

Overture: Selections from "The Golden Legend."

Reading from St. Chrysostom, The Mouth of Gold: by a dark-robed Sybil standing against a rich gold background of designs of American dentistry.

THE GHOST OF SHAKESPEARE, who has kindly consented to recite a poem descriptive of the commercial conditions of the Empire, beginning: "Come the three Corners of the world in arms." Mr. Shakespeare will kindly oblige with an encore if called upon: "Absent thee from publicity awhile."

Song: "I once had a dear Little Dollar."

THE GHOST OF SHELLEY, recently returned from his visit to the American seances, will recite a slightly improved version of his "Ode to a Skylark," entitled "Ode to a Skyscraper."

Song: "I know a Bank."

MR. WALT WHITMAN, recently risen from the dead, will recite "Profiteers, O Profiteers."

The proceedings will conclude with the Ghost of Mr. Rupert Brooke, now engaged in commerce, intoning the lines "In Manchester, in Manchester."

The late Lord Tennyson, who suffers from uncertain temper, is unable at the last moment to recite his great poem of the future: "TRUST me not at all, or all in all."

MRS. MARKHAM'S HISTORY OF ENGLAND
(continued).

TOMMY: You promised, dear Mamma, to tell us about the way in which we were governed.

MAMMA: So I did, my dear, and I will be very happy to do so to-day. You must know then . . .

MARY: Oh, Mamma, you also promised to tell us about kangaroos!

TOMMY (*angrily*): A murrain on you, Mary.

MAMMA (*severely*): How often have I told you, Tommy, not to use the word "murrain." It is exceedingly vulgar! And you, Mary, never dare to interrupt me when I am speaking! Well, then, you must know that we live in England in what we call a Democracy.

TOMMY: Oh, Mamma, how delightful that sounds! Pray what is the meaning of this interesting word?

MAMMA: You do well to ask, my dear Tommy. A Democracy is a kind of government in which everyone governs themselves because they love freedom too much to allow others to govern them. There was once a wicked King called Charles 1st, who tried to govern us instead of letting us govern ourselves, but we cut off his head, and from that moment no-one has dared interfere with us.

MARY: Is that the one of whom there is a statue in Charing Cross, Mamma?

MAMMA: Yes, my dear, it was put up as a warning against anyone doing such a thing again.

TOMMY: Then, Mamma, we can all do what we like— I shall begin to-morrow after breakfast.

MAMMA: No, my dear, this is not true of children, who have to do what they are told. It is only for grown-up people.

MARY: Then when I am grown up I shall make a law that I am to have a large box of chocolates every day.

MAMMA (*smiling indulgently*): I am afraid, Mary, you hardly understand the difficulty we should be in if everybody went on in that way! No; the only way in which people can govern themselves, when there are very many of them, is for them to vote who shall be what is called "their representatives" and make laws for them according to the orders they shall have received from us.

TOMMY (*in tones of horror*): What! like that bald old man with the long white beard who shook hands with Papa at the Flower Show?

MAMMA (*solemnly*): My dear, you must not laugh at Lord Harold Howk, our Member: for though he does not represent our Party in Parliament he is deservedly respected.

MARY (*puzzled*): But, Mamma, if he does not represent us, how can he be our representative?

MAMMA: I will explain. In every part of the country two or even three gentlemen come forward and ask to be made Members of Parliament. Then we vote, and the one who gets most votes is successful and becomes a Member. Thus, though you may vote for one of these three, yet another becomes your Member of Parliament. Indeed, this is often the case.

TOMMY: Thank you, dear Mamma, it is now all perfectly clear. And pray what do these Members of Parliament do when they are chosen?

MAMMA: They go to a place called the House of Commons which is at Westminster and very beautifully decorated, and then some of them say "I was sent here to make such and such a law" and others say "Well, I was sent to make a different law."

TOMMY: Well, then, if they cannot agree there is nothing left I suppose but to fight it out.

MAMMA: Why that does indeed happen in less advanced Nations: but we have a better way. The Members do not fight but *vote*, and whichever proposal gets the most votes is successful . . . .

MARY: What! Again?

MAMMA (*continuing*): . . . and is ready to become a law. You will see what a good way this is, for it means that nothing is ever done in England if only a few people want it. Nothing is done unless most people want it, and that is why we are all so happy and contented, unlike a pack of quarrelling foreigners. Then it goes to some people called Lords, who look at it.

TOMMY: Yes, Mamma, you were kind enough to tell us all about these Lords long ago.

MAMMA (*continuing*): And then it is signed by the King and becomes a true law at last, which we are all happy to obey.

TOMMY: Can you give us an example, Mamma, of some laws made like this?

MAMMA (*cheerfully*): Indeed I can, my dear. There is a law which prevents working men from drinking before mid-day or in the middle of the afternoon, or after ten o'clock at night: and there is another law saying that if a man is working very hard he must pay a quarter or a third of what he earns and give it to the bankers and certain other rich men. If these laws had been made by outsiders we should be very angry, no doubt, but as we know that they have been made by ourselves we are quite pleased with them. You see first all the people talked about it thoroughly for a long time. Some were for preventing poor people drinking at all.

MARY: Would not that have been a very good thing, Mamma?

MAMMA: Well, my dear, *I* think so, but we must bow to the majority. Now after we had all discussed it for a long time, we sent our Members of Parliament to vote in favour of these hours, which shows that most of the English people wanted them. Even the people who make the beer obeyed the law because they knew that the English people wanted it.

TOMMY: That was indeed noble of them, Mamma!

MAMMA: Yes, my dear, you would not have found this self-sacrifice in any other country. But note what followed! It turned out that people drank more than ever, and so these good men became much richer; and that shows us that a good deed is never thrown away.

MARY (*anxiously*): And was it the same about people having to pay that money, Mamma?

MAMMA: Yes, my dear, just the same. We all talked it over a great deal together. Some were for taking away all the money everybody had, others for taking more, and others again less, and then we all voted and it turned out that what we wanted was for people to have about a quarter or a third taken away and given to the bankers.

TOMMY: Were not the bankers very pleased, Mamma, when this law was made?

MAMMA: Yes, my dear, and in their gratitude they put

up very fine buildings all over London, some of which are still in process of erection; and they would have done more had it not been for the wicked working men, who will not put up buildings for more than eight hours at a time and even then quite slowly.

MARY: Thank you, dear Mamma, for telling us all this. I was so interested I quite forgot about kangaroos.

TOMMY: Next time, dear Mamma, will you not talk to us about lawyers and policemen? It must be a most fascinating subject!

MAMMA: Certainly, my dear Tommy; we will talk about these people next time, and I will show you how it is that they have become so good and kind, and why everybody is so fond of them.

H. BELLOC.

The Experimentalist

[*Personality does not survive death.*"—Mr. Edison.]

TRUTH'S test is in experiment:
    And with empiric care
    He went into the other world
And found he wasn't there.

We must believe, if this by rule
    Of science may be read,
That he has died while still alive
    And lives to say he's dead.

But till that last discovery
    His dogma stands disputed:
Nor need we be electrified
    Till he's been electrocuted.

Everest.

THERE were the pillared peaks took hold on heaven,
    The hammer-headed eagles flashed and fell,
    Glared the abyss through gaping rocks and riven,
Like fallen heavens, inhospitable as hell.

And still he found, who thought to find the cone,
    Colossal corner-stones of starrier towers,
Till trifles swelled, grotesque and overgrown,
    And momentary thoughts dragged on for hours.

The madness of the mountains over-ruled him,
    The hell that hides high up in light and air,
Till words were wheels within his head and fooled him
    With thoughts that danced in circles of despair.

Though the peak shone that none should see and live
    Only remained in him to trick and tease,
A worry of words, a split infinitive,
    Above those splintering split infinitives.

Throbbed through his brain one brainless barren jest,
    He was too dull to fancy dull or clever;
There is no way for man to Everest,
    To ever rest until he rest for ever.

Finance

THE Mouse that helped the Lion
    Is no fable, we're aware;
      Who know how much the guinea-pig
Can help the Bull and Bear?

FOUND WANDERING
By G. K. CHESTERTON.
HOW I SHALL DEFACE THIS PAPER

IN this the third and last of these merely egotistical and editorial explanations, I bring my preliminary sketch of this personal experiment to an end. I shall still be found wandering all over this page; but in my subsequent wanderings I shall have left myself at home. I shall survey the landscape of the world in a more impersonal fashion. If I am found wandering by the police, it will be as that really happy wanderer who has lost his own address and forgotten his own name. There will be no name for me to miss when I become known merely as a number, in the penal or mentally curative establishment. But for these three articles I have claimed a license to talk about myself, if only to talk about my paper.

In the first of these three articles I merely described a few of the ways of advertising this paper, which would commend themselves to me as being really funny. I have discovered, alas, that advertisement has to be vulgar without being funny. I say a few of the ways of advertising; for I should not like anyone to suppose my mind to be so lacking in fertility as to limit itself to those few. The very first and most obvious idea, that of a fat man standing on his head on a poster placarded all over London, was regarded by the fastidious as lacking in dignity; though it states with a dignified simplicity the substance of a great many criticisms on my whole philosophical position. Well, I have no particular objection to a man standing on his head. I only want a world in which every man will stand on his own head, instead of sitting on somebody else's head. But this heraldic blazon of a fat man inverted gules had also to be abandoned. Mr. Will Owen and I, feeling ourselves to be artists left alone together in a wilderness of efficiency, made several other suggestions of which the world was not worthy. He drew an admirable portrait of the back of my head; which might have opened a new era in portrait painting A new school of art; called the Dorsal School or what not, might persuade everybody that it was a very vulgar and sentimental sort of representational art to draw anything so obvious as the human face; that the face was like the fan of a peacock or a pigeon, a mere terminal flourish and meritricious anterior adornment; and that strong artists all look for a man's soul in the back of his head. It might create a new school of psychology; the function of Cerebellation to supersede the effete habit of Cerebration. It might lead to a new fashion in manners; with gentlemen walking backwards down the street. It might lead to many things—but hardly perhaps to the subject in hand.

In the second article I attempted to indicate, in an equally wandering fashion, that the reader would probably have to put up, for the present especially, with my writing a good many different things in this paper; and that the things might really be rather different. This necessity is partly due to pure accidents connected with the printing trade, which have delayed the arrival of my reinforcements from other writers. but partly also to a deliberate policy of doing as many different sorts of things as I can. This paper exists to insist on the rights of man; on possessions that are of much more political importance than the principle of one man one vote. I am in favour of one man one house, one man one field; nay I have even advanced the paradox of one man one wife. But I am almost tempted to add the more ideal fancy of one man one magazine. I am almost tempted to say that every citizen ought to have a weekly paper of this sort to splash about in; that every grown man ought to have this kind of scrapbook to keep him quiet. I am not sure exactly how it would work, if we all lived by taking in each other's washing, or rather each other's writing. But I am sure it would add very much to the universality and human range of each human being. I am sorry if the reader is ruthlessly sacrificed to my editorial education. I shall not carry my experiments to an extreme. It is unlikely at present that I shall figure as a financial expert; or tell people how to do a financial flutter, except perhaps by telling them not to. It is far from probable that I shall write any hints upon housekeeping, upon the cutting out of garments or the serving of light luncheons; and I resolutely decline to be Aunt Maisie and make myself responsible for other people's love-affairs. I shall draw the line at the Higher Mathematics and be silent when there is music. But outside these limits, there is no saying what I may not try to do; and it is well to utter a general warning and apology beforehand.

In this third article I should like to explain that such a journalistic jigsaw puzzle has more plan about it than may appear at first sight. When I was very young, and first thinking of going in for journalism, I was always told by all the venerable advisers of the young journalist, that the great point was to adapt oneself to the tone of the paper. The young journalist must make sure that he is sportive enough for the *Sporting Times* or academic enough for the *Academy*. I take, of course, the names of papers that were then existent and effective. He must set himself to echo the *Echo* and write up to the standard of the *Standard*. When I was first faintly hoping for a journalistic position, that was what I was always told to do. When I did in some mysterious fashion fall into some sort of journalistic position, I believe it was almost entirely through doing the opposite. When I happen to look back on the sort of things I used to write, I am interested and intrigued by the mystery of why they ever were accepted or noticed at all. But I am inclined to think that they were only noticed because they were so extremely unsuitable to the papers in which they appeared. I have always professed a complete incapacity to give advice to young journalists, arising out of a complete incapacity to explain my own emergence as a young journalist. But if I were absolutely driven and goaded into giving advice, I really think this is the advice I should give. I should recommend him to write his two articles, exactly suited to the tone of his two papers; the one exquisitely fitted for the *Church Times*, the other tinted to the exact roseate shade of the Pink 'Un. Let him fold up these two contributions carefully and put them in the wrong envelopes. The result may be a reputation for paradox and ultimately the editorship of a paper, with a ruthless picture of himself outside the first number. Allowing for some slight exaggeration, there is something in it. The article will stand out from its setting; and yet at the same time do credit to its setting. Reading the acute and even cutting disquisition on modern morals in the middle of the sporting paper, the reader will slap the table and cry " Hang it all, they have some rattling good stylists on the sporting rags! " Reading the playful and even skittish article in the Church paper, he will say with hearty wonder and admiration " How the Church is waking up! How human it is, and how much once more in the main stream of human life! " Both these conclusions will be quite true, though the impression of truth may have been reached by an incidental error. Now it is that sort of contrast and that sort of combination that I am going to aim at in this paper. I cannot for the life of me see why an organ of opinion should not be as convinced as a religious paper and as amusing as a sporting paper. I cannot see why convictions should look dull or why jokes should be insincere. I should like a man to pick up this paper for amusement and find himself involved in an argument. I should like him to pursue it purely for the sake of argument and find himself pulled up short by a joke, neither better nor worse than a joke in a comic paper. I should like a man not always to find what he would expect; but sometimes to be agreeably disappointed.

In other words, I do not want everything in this paper to be suited to the style of this paper. It is possible that some may think the style of this paper not suited to the paper at all. For in weekly journalism, as a whole, it is not unfair to say that most of the work done is divided into two styles; the serious and the popular; or what their critics would call the highbrow and the vulgar. I do not want the thing to be either vulgar or highbrow; but I never can see why a thing should not be both popular and serious; that is, in the sense of being both popular and sincere. Sincerity is a question of whether you mean what you say; popularity seems to be largely a question of whether you say it plainly. Even if it is a question of saying it in large letters or short paragraphs, there cannot possibly be anything essentially evil about saying it plainly. What is the matter with the vulgar press is that it has nothing to say. What is wrong with that sort of journalism is that it always uses the largest letters for the smallest things. On the other hand, the weekly papers that are written for intellectuals are quite needlessly afraid of this air of challenge and popular appeal. Many of the writers think they are telling the truth; but they seem almost afraid of telling it plainly. It is almost as if it would not look quite so true in large letters. Rather in the same way, their refinement shrinks instinctively from the breaking up of a page into different items or short paragraphs. They are reminded (with a slight shudder) of the clauses of a creed.

Now I do not see why, merely because a thing happens to be intelligent, it should be its duty to look dull. I do not see, for instance, why it should have such pompous polysyllabic titles as are generally adopted in serious reviews and periodicals. To take an example which I happened to mention lately, I was once asked to take part in a scheme to Brighten London. I told the people that I did not want to Brighten London in the way that they and their sort wanted to Londonise Brighton. The form of this remark was foolish and was meant to be; but the substance of it was perfectly sincere. And I would rather put a silly remark like that in large letters at the head of a column than make the whole column look unreadable by calling it, in the fashion of a social reformer's leaflet, " The Prospects of Municipal Development in the London Area."

ANSWERS TO THE POETS

From the Spanish Cloister

GRRRR !—what's that? A dog? A poet?
    Uttering his damnations thus
      If hate killed things, Brother Browning,
God's Word, would not hate kill us?

If we'd ever met together
   Salve tibi! I might hear
How you know poor monks are really
   So much worse than they appear.

There's a great text in Corinthians
   Hinting that our faith entails
Something else, that never faileth,
   Yet in you, perhaps, it fails. . . .

But if *plena gratia* chokes you
   You, at least, can teach us how
To converse in wordless noises
   Hy, zi; hullo !—Grrrr—Bow-wow !

THE TRAGEDY OF JAMES JOYCE

By Bernard Gilbert.

GILBERT: My dear Rosser: what's the matter?

PAUL ROSSER: ! ! ! ! !

GILBERT: I daresay: but what?

ROSSER: One of my nieces, in Boston, asked me to take back a book that she couldn't get in the States, because it was somewhat progressive. Presently, I got a copy sent over from Paris.

GILBERT: What's the book?

ROSSER: " Ulysses."

GILBERT: I see! You've been reading it!

ROSSER: I read it from cover to cover and then ripped it up. Never, Gilbert, did I dream that such books could be written.

GILBERT: Hasn't Rabelais reached your States yet?

ROSSER: He's a classic; besides . . . he's dull. But this book isn't dull. Where it isn't crazy or blasphemous, it's just filthy. There aren't words! I'd sooner see my niece in her grave than reading that last section, where a woman says things ! ! !

GILBERT: Never mind! Doubtless your Customs will continue to protect your shores and your niece; though, mind you, Ulysses isn't crazy. It's lots of queer things; but if read with intelligent care, it's quite straightforward.

ROSSER: I managed to follow some of it after the practice I'd had with your Bly Market; but a lot of Ulysses is the meandering of a lunatic.

GILBERT: Joyce parodies many styles, and in certain sections he carries out advanced experiments in literary presentation, which it would take too long to go into——

ROSSER: God forbid!

GILBERT: But his threads may be unravelled and his pattern followed. I read it three times——

ROSSER: ! ! !

GILBERT: You see, I, too, had done experiments in literary presentation and was interested from that angle. But it *is* a work of genius.

ROSSER: A filthy genius: a crazy genius! Anyway, I don't agree. Where's the genius?

GILBERT: Where it always is . . . in the creator. If you ask me to define genius, I can only say it's vision, and after that you drive me into the sea; but I can point to the results of genius, quickly enough.

ROSSER: Santanya says—what's wrong? What's the matter with Santanya? He's a great man, and has vision. If you side with Mencken and Pound and those cranks, I'm done.

GILBERT: Mencken I only know by hearsay, and Pound doesn't matter. But, I repeat, Ulysses is a work of genius.

ROSSER: And I repeat that it's a farrago of crazy filth.

GILBERT: Which leaves us where we were. Let us then look at it for a moment.

ROSSER: No, thanks!

GILBERT: It is a masterpiece which will do a great mischief in our disrupted world. Your police—and ours—are right in trying to keep it away, although such efforts are useless. You can't suppress a genius, and Joyce is one of the greatest living disruptive artists in England—or America. He is an evil force. He will have an enormous influence on rising writers. He is a tragic figure.

ROSSER: Why tragic? I don't see that.

GILBERT: His two books: Portrait of the Artist, and Ulysses, disclose his tragedy. The tragedy of disruption.

ROSSER: Young Tyrell says you're cracked on disruptive art and uprooted communities.

GILBERT: Having grasped the key of our age, everything falls into place, accordingly.

ROSSER: Young Tyrell admires Ulysses enormously. We quarrelled.

GILBERT: That was a pity.

ROSSER: He thinks nobody appreciates Ulysses except you and he; and says you are wrong-headed about it. All the reviews, he believes, were silly.

GILBERT: How can a reviewer cope with a book like that? It would take an artist as great as Joyce to deal with it adequately, and that dealing would occupy a volume of the same size. It's unreasonable to expect anything of the sort. Our reviewers are neither better nor worse than their papers, and their public.

ROSSER: You're a bit like the fox who couldn't get the grapes. You made your mind up, at the start of Old England, that you wouldn't ever get any money out of the volumes, and so you stand aloof and pretend to be superior. I notice the *Times* Supplement thinks you small beer.

GILBERT: I don't mind that. It is always painstaking and thorough—as far as it goes—which is as far as its public wants and will allow. It does represent our best reading public.

ROSSER: That's how you get out of it, is it?

GILBERT: In England, my dear Rosser, the *serious* artist—the writer with something vital to put forth—can hope for no recognition under thirty years. Having grasped that essential fact, I don't worry over the opposition of the *Times*; or any other opposition.

ROSSER: All the same, I'm sorry . . . for my sake as well as yours. In the States the Supplement has more influence than all your other reviews put together.

GILBERT: I discussed that once with Clutton Brock when I was visiting him at Godalming. He wrote for the Supplement, you remember. He advised me to put forward my side of the case and leave it there.

ROSSER: Much good that will do!

GILBERT: I'm not trying to alter England. I accept it. We have no first-rate reviewing in our Press. The nature of the case forbids that.

ROSSER: In the States we look on your reviewers as Old Masters.

GILBERT: Our literary criticism is almost entirely done by log-rollers and sentimental noodles.

ROSSER: You've glided away from the beastliness of Joyce. I'm waiting to hear you defend that.

GILBERT: I don't. Joyce saw it in his native Dublin and set it forth. I'm only thankful I wasn't born in a city. My lot was cast in a rooted community whose people are frank about sex; but neither repressed, furtive, nor beastly. I was therefore able to set them forth without demur; and, although to keep my publishers free from the police I had to leave a few expressions blank, they are very few. Now the beastliness of Ulysses is the beastliness of the modern city.

ROSSER: Not our cities. They are clean.

GILBERT: I doubt that. Even so, it doesn't affect the way in which Joyce saw Dublin.

ROSSER: Then you do defend him!

GILBERT: I *accept* him exactly as I accept snakes, hornets, poisons, tigers, and Communists; as a part of the cosmos.

ROSSER: You destroy snakes and tigers. You keep poisons and hornets well in hand.

GILBERT: I would destroy the Communist and the Disruptive Artist.

ROSSER: Oh, would you! We shall see you over in the States! That talk would go down well, there.

GILBERT: Old England's enough for one lifetime, even if I didn't hate travelling. The measures your people take in weeding out disruptive elements seem admirable. The instinct is fundamentally sound, for a community that fails to defend itself from disruption is like a body that yields to cancer.

ROSSER: You know, Gilbert, I alternately agree and disagree with you, when you talk. Where *are* you?

GILBERT: Right here. Maybe you are in the air?

ROSSER: I'm just where you placed me, out in the States, ready to receive those long letters from Hugo Thorpe that you are drafting for your next volume—or is it the next but one. Let us confine ourselves to Ulysses.

GILBERT: Ulysses *is* Joyce. I enjoy his art just

as I enjoy the work of other disruptive artists, like Dostoievsky, Anatole France, Richard Strauss or Thomas Hardy; just—let us say—as I enjoy the colouring of a tropical snake and the striped liveliness of a hornet. We kill the hornet, without malice—

ROSSER: If he hasn't stung us!

GILBERT: —— as a danger to our being. That is my attitude to the disruptive artist.

ROSSER: But you can't kill Joyce, nor stop the spread of his work; so what's the tragedy you speak of? I hear he has made money from his Ulysses. He is world-famous . . . or infamous. Thanks to the embargo, I am told that copies of Ulysses fetch two hundred dollars in the States; and no doubt he is as happy as any king.

GILBERT: He is unhappy as any king.

ROSSER: Do you know him, personally?

GILBERT: I spoke to him, once, in Paris; but I know nothing of him beyond that which lies open to all, in his work.

ROSSER: Then I don't understand you.

GILBERT: I wish you had read Janko Lavrin's critical books, where he deals with the four great writers of the 19th century: Tolstoy, Ibsen, Nietzsche, and Dostoievsky. None of those could accept the world they lived in. They had no fixed values, and, having broken their roots, were lost in the Void. Lavrin calls them God-Strugglers, which is a good term. They were searching in agony for some God, and couldn't find one; and being unable to exist without, they perished. That struggle drove Nietzsche mad; it destroyed Dostoievsky; the end of Tolstoy is known to all, whilst as for Ibsen. . . .

ROSSER: Ibsen never went mad.

GILBERT: Ibsen was the most finished artist of the four, but I shouldn't have classed him with the other three. But if you look up your Harper's Magazine you will find what befell the repressed Scandinavian in his old age.

ROSSER: Like Canon Makepeace?

GILBERT: It was hushed up, and only came out in his last plays. Ibsen himself was repressed and smothered like your Mark Twain.

ROSSER: That picture of Mrs. Clemens sitting on the verandah and striking out every phrase that might offend the neighbours is too piteous to have been invented.

GILBERT: It was his own affair, and it doesn't matter, does it, for he wasn't even fourth-rate. Indeed, you have never produced one of the first rank.

ROSSER: Indeed! Indeed!

GILBERT: Where is your candidate to sit with the Great Ones on Parnassus?

ROSSER: Well, you must give us time.

GILBERT: All the time you want! Though time isn't a factor. You have two admirable specimens in the second rank : one rooted, the other uprooted : Whitman and Melville.

ROSSER : Whitman's been blown on lately, but Meby Dick is a vast book.

GILBERT : Nobody admires or enjoys it more than I. It is a revelation of the struggles of——

ROSSER : Captain Ahab—the White Whale !

GILBERT : —of the tortured soul of Herman Melville. He was a God-Struggler and a tragic figure, which brings me again to Joyce. One learns from his books that he was trained by the Jesuits as a priest. Being hurled from home, he lost, at one stroke, his religion, his country, and his foothold in the universe.

ROSSER : Hurled, was he?   Did he get into trouble?

GILBERT : My dear Rosser ! What a question ! What drives any artist from his community? Joyce drove forth Joyce, and his roots once severed, the wind carried him to . . . Trieste, I believe, for he dates Ulysses from there   The wind has borne him hither and thither, and no man knows his direction. There is no harbour for the lost soul.

ROSSER : No rest for the wicked?

GILBERT : It is not a joke, but a tragedy. Having lost all that holds a man secure to the earth, James Joyce, whirled by the tempest, alighted on alien soil and produced his masterpiece.   With incredible artistry, he laboured for seven years to exhibit a wonderful picture of—himself !

ROSSER : I thought you said of Dublin.

GILBERT : What is Dublin or London or Bly, but the observer?   There are idealised, sentimental Dublins (and Blys), but as Joyce is a greater artist than the others, his Dublin overshadows them all.

ROSSER : Do you think, then, that a man must be uprooted and storm-tossed in order to become a great artist.

GILBERT : Certainly not. Though that, too, depends on the age. If we have no more Bachs in their nests, it is because of the passing of the nest. With the possible exception of Landor, you might say it has been true in England for over a century.

ROSSER : One might almost fancy you despised modern art !

GILBERT : Perhaps I do . . . and the artists. The members of a harmonious community need no Art, in the modern sense—but that topic will lead us too far. James Joyce is a great and tragic figure, and if you watch his future work you will see the unfolding of his inward tragedy. The disruptive artist displays *himself*. He dramatises his own struggle. He exhibits his own despair on his canvas.

ROSSER : Then we should pity them.

GILBERT : That would be idle. They *are*.

ROSSER : What would you do with them?

GILBERT : I've told you. As an individual I denounce them; acting with my neighbours I would treat them as we treat dangerous lunatics. Without malice but without sentimentality, I would render them harmless to the community.

ROSSER : Don't you send your homicidal maniacs to an institution?

GILBERT : Yes; and I am against that policy which ties up sane citizens to guard them. As they can never safely be allowed abroad, I would put them painlessly to death.

ROSSER : Now, Gilbert ! You wouldn't put Shaw or Joyce to death !

GILBERT : Indeed, I would; and actively assist, if called upon. The two evils of our age are sentimentality and tolerance. We ought to kill more.

ROSSER : Perhaps these gentlemen will kill you first ! You will appear extremely objectionable—and dangerous—to them.

GILBERT : Certainly ! And I tell you, Rosser, that unless we have again, in England, men who will die or be killed for their beliefs, we cannot be saved.

ROSSER : From what?

GILBERT : Decay : Disruption : Death !

ROSSER : My dear Gilbert; you're nothing but a fanatic !

GILBERT : I'm an intense reactionary. I am actuated by a faith which drives me forward. I may be destroyed by those whom I feel are enemies to the community; for they are many and strong. But I shall always believe in Old England.

Rest-Harrow and Chickory

ALL along the dusty road, weary as we go,
  Rest-harrow and chickory on the borders grow.
  All the other pleasant things shrink and hide away;
Rest-harrow and chickory still to greet us stay.
Some there are who love to think on high heroic deeds;
Rest-harrow and chickory to them are only weeds.
To humble men who walk upon the common daily road,
Rest-harrow and chickory are happy thoughts of God.

FANNY JOHNSON.

THE TEREWTH

THERE was a meeting the other day of an extraordinary body called the Naked Truth Advertisement Society, or some such name. It was connected with that curious cant recently started about the " ideal " of advertisement; and how it is highly truthful. Beyond that I do not profess to know, or care, very much about the Naked Truth Advertisement movement. Most of us entertain a philosophic doubt about whether modern advertisement displays very much truth, whatever it may display in the way of nakedness.

Like most men born in my time, I have always been in the habit of accepting advertisement as a joke. I am even still prepared to accept it as a joke. But it is too much of a joke to be asked to accept it as a religion. There is nothing intrinsically immoral about advertisement. A man has a right to paint his name over his shop; a man has a right to pay for permission to paint on his neighbour's paling a broad arrow pointing to his shop. As in everything else, what is wrong in the present condition is the proportion. We live in a society in which the figures that used to be secondary have become primary—the trader, the traveller, the tout, the pedlar. It is like a garden in which the toadstools have grown taller than the trees. There may be a miser in every village; but there is not a millionaire on top of every village. There may be a town-crier calling out private as well as public announcements; but the town-crier is the servant of the town and not of the tradesmen. With us the secondary thing has nearly swallowed the primary; the town-crier can be mainly a trade-crier or the advertisements be more important than the news. Even so, any number of entirely honourable men advertise, because they use the machinery of their civilisation; just as they pay wages even though they may dislike the wage system. They accept it, as I say, as a joke; but we must always be joking about it, or it gets beyond a joke. A continuous stream of satire must be directed against this social extravagance, which already occupies more than its normal place in society. We must make a guy of the advertiser, as men have made a guy of the dandy or the flunky or the pretentious upstart. We must be always laughing at Autolycus the pedlar and watching him to see whether he becomes Autolycus the thief.

Instead of that, we find the whole business surrounded by a sort of solemn optimism. If we really wish to know what is the superstition of our time, it would be enough to have noticed the oriental prostrations and flatteries with which a great part of the journalistic world received the Advertising Convention some time ago, and will now probably receive the adherents of the Naked Truth. People may speak evil of almost any other dignities in any other form; from the old tradition that cried " To Hell with the Pope," to the new one that is more likely to cry " To Hell with the Parliament." Anybody may say with the old Colonel that the army is going to the dogs, or with the young Conchie that it ought to go to the dogs. The weary journalist thinks equally little of repealing the Habeas Corpus Act or of scrapping the British Navy. He is allowed to announce the abandonment of patriotism and rather encouraged to announce the abandonment of religion. But he is always expected to be " optimistic " about the world of advertisement; to lay flattering unction to the soul of the Oil King and look always on the sunny side of Port Sunlight. He is not content to say that an advertisement is tolerable, he must say that it is true. Now are we really to accept all this nonsense, as the newspapers do, and carefully refrain from laughing at something that is only tolerable when it is laughable? Let us control our mirth and refer gravely to the documents.

The advertisers tell us that the essence of all their advertising is Truth. It is always the highest satisfaction of our immortal souls to seek and to find the truth, and I will therefore proceed to seek it in this fashion and to note briefly the truths that I find. Starting with the solemn proclamation of " Truth in Advertising " inside the first advertisement page of *Punch* (it is by Sir Charles Higham, and is a prose lyric in praise of a particular motor-tyre, which is presented as permanently encircling the flag of England), I pass on to the following pages exactly as they come. The next page is headed in large letters " The Cabinet You Will Eventually Buy." This is a truth of the prophetic or inspired order, implying the sort of divine fore-knowledge which some have even felt to be a little inconsistent with free-will. However, it is of some personal interest to me to know the cabinet that I shall eventually buy, even if I have no immediate intention of buying a cabinet at all. I feel it almost a duty as well as a doom to buy it " eventually "; lest I cause the prophet to stumble upon his favourite point of truth. The next page is entirely occupied by " The sweetest, most sanitary and scientific tooth-brush you ever put into your mouth." I have not put any very wide and varied multiplicity of tooth-brushes in my mouth, having the old provincial and Early Victorian preference for my own. And I am afraid I have never noticed the exact degree of sweetness even in that; not being in the habit of eating my tooth-brush. So I am willing to accept this truth on the authority of others of a more varied and voracious experience. The next is the comparatively mild revelation that the wearing of woollen underclothing of a certain sort is essentially characteristic of Men of Action. I note down this truth also and proceed to the next, which says that while there are doubtless other cigarettes in the world, yet all cigarette-smokers have been unconsciously waiting for something different, something better, which is now offered to them. This is an example of the discovery of truth, not in the future, but in the subconsciousness. It is not everybody, even among psychoanalysts, who knows what everybody else is unconsciously waiting for. The next says that everybody (presumably including myself) is saying that the best whisky is one of which I am quite unconscious of having even heard the name. The next only says that another cigarette is unique and resembles the voice of the singer after which it is named. On the page opposite Robert Louis Stevenson is represented as paying a compliment to another whisky. This truth is of a third order; the psychic rather than the psychological. Stevenson is represented as saying it in the capacity of a ghost risen from the dead, to repair the omission by which he neglected to say anything of the sort when he was alive. On the next page I learn that faith, imagination and courage are the qualities that have placed a particular pattern of Safe in the foremost position. This is accompanied by a picture of Napoleon surrounded by the smoke of an artillery battle; to indicate the sort of scenes that the business gentlemen in question have passed through, before the safe became really safe. Then we come to a remarkable motor-car which is superior in every way to much more expensive cars, but which is charitably sold for a very much lower price. Finally there are the advertisements of various medicinal salts. Each of them is admittedly better than the others. All of them produce results which are considered wild and impossible when they are promised by social revolutions or great religions; by Utopia or the New Jerusalem. The great Utopian word "perfect" is deliberately used and emphasised. One salt "keeps mind and body attuned and in perfect condition." Another provides "the joy of life arising from the possession of perfect health and high spirits." And with that we actually come to the end of the first part of the paper, which consists of advertisements, and come upon the curious survival of certain other sheets of merely literary interest, which are still wedged into the middle of it. There is another thick magazine of advertisements at the end, doubtless full of other truths for which we have all been unconsciously waiting. But it seems unnecessary to wade through them in order to prove once more what we all know already. I have taken a perfectly fair sample of the actual successive items of perfectly respectable advertisements in a perfectly respectable paper. I have not quoted any of the exceptionally bad advertisements which appear in other papers; the swindling advertisements that offer to teach what obviously cannot be taught; the quack advertisements that offer to cure what cannot in any such fashion be cured; the medical discoveries that heal contrary diseases with the same drug; the certain road to success opened by pioneers who have failed in everything else; the sex advertisements that are full of obscenity and perversion; the journalistic scares that are alive with panic and treason. I have taken ordinary advertisement at its best; and I leave it to anybody's common sense. As a lie it is a lark. Nay, as a lie it is a legitimate lark. Some sort of humour and humanity might be got out of these things considered as tall stories like Baron Munchausen's. But if those who tell them tell us that they are true, what are we to say of their "ideal" of truth?

The only defence of these statements, of course, is that nobody believes them. In other words, the only real defence, of those thus professing to tell the truth, is that we have all got used to their telling lies. But if it is a bad intellectual vice to get used to telling lies, it is a worse intellectual vice to get used to telling lies and to bragging about telling the truth. That sort of thing weakens the mind in a worse fashion. These lies may become harmless by becoming meaningless; but only when all human language and human judgment have become meaningless with them. When men really think it natural and normal to say that men of action are to be judged by their underclothing, they have lost the use of human speech. When people have reached the point of gushing over a sweet tooth-brush or describing a mild aperient as perfect happiness, they are paralysing in themselves the noble power of praise.

There are many other things to be said about advertisement and that plutocracy of which it is the gaudy banner. We may have occasion to say them in other connections; for the moment we are content to say this.

It would be far better for the souls of such people to be cynical about advertisement than to be idealistic about advertisement. There is no necessity to be either; for advertisement in itself, as I have said, is not a sin or even a scandal. Nor is it the fault of individual advertisers if it is a nuisance. It is our fault, for tolerating the rule of mere money, so that it can paint the world with its own vulgar pattern. We have none of us any right to play the Pharisee to these people; but we are entitled to draw the line when they play the Pharisee to us.

T. P. X.

ANNOUNCEMENT FOR APRIL THE FIRST

The League of Nations will settle the outstanding differences between the Polish nationality and the political ideas of East Prussia in a manner satisfactory to both sides.

The Government cure for unemployment will receive the unanimous support of all parties and be carried out with triumphant success.

The British Colonies and Dependencies will finally pledge themselves to a universal system of military service in support of the Mother Country.

The American Poet will make his appearance.

The inhabitants of California will show an enthusiastic hospitality to the Japanese and facilitate in every way their influence on the American continent.

A complete report of the Parliamentary proceedings for one night will be published in several volumes.

A very wealthy man will be punished for something.

Scientific men will discover in Spitsbergen the long series of Missing Links that would be necessary to establish the Darwinian theory of evolution.

Somebody will write a Socialist pamphlet that could be read by the poor people in whose interest it is composed.

The proposal to audit the Party Funds will be considered and carried out.

The Conservative Party will be gratified by the final establishment of Protection and the Radical Party by the disestablishment of the House of Lords—or possibly the Church of England.

A policeman giving evidence will be harshly and severely forced to reconcile his statements with each other.

Some one or other of the Prophecies of our social future, written by sociologists during the last fifty years, will come true.

The social and political world will be soothed by the disappearance of this paper.

The Patriot

[*It was suggested that in the final International settlement Jerusalem should be restored to the Jews and Brighton to the Christians.*]

IT was noses, noses, all the way,
    With eyelids mixed in my dreams like mad:
      Their bright ties seemed to blaze like day
    Their brisk legs flamed such bags they had
From the Parade they fade away.

Here they sojourned and there they go,
    I did not hate them, when all is said;
    And how they will fare when they find for foe
      Not ours but the Arab hate instead
God only knows! We are safer so.

THE THIF

(Continued from last week.)

By WALTER DE LA MARE.

FROM that day on, of course, the Thief's one thought, desire and aim was to find the Magic Egg. From loft to cellar, from roof to drains, he searched his mansion through. There never was such a scene of riot and rummaging and disorder. The contents of a thousand drawers were strewn upon the floor. His sacks of money and jewels were slit from top to bottom and lay, their contents glittering in heaps in the sunlight that could now bespread itself through his upper windows. He ripped up his ottomans and sawed through his chair-legs; and disembowelled his divans.

And there was no one to watch, help, or feed him but one puny scullery-maid with eyes black as sloes and a shock of jet-black hair. And why? Simply because she had refused to go. Six times the Thief had barred her out, having given her, for fear of being talked about, a fresh week's wages every time. Yet still for the seventh time, she had managed to creep back again into the mansion, though how, her master never knew.

Being accustomed by this time to hearing only the gnawing of the moths and the mice and the rats and the hushing drift of dust in the vacant air, the Thief could distinguish the least little sound in his mansion at night And so for the seventh time he had found himself creeping downstairs with his candle, only to discover this Susan sitting on the scullery steps with the same old band-box as before.

"Why do you keep coming back, when I have told you to go?" he cried angrily in the doorway. "It's against the law. I shall send for the P—P—P—."

But somehow or other the word stuck to the root of his tongue.

Susan's black eyes, shining like pools of ink or ebony beneath her mop of jet-black hair, looked up at him from the scullery step. "Oh, Master!" she said. "If I go, then you will starve to death, you will. In all me life I never see anyone before so drop away."

And the Thief, shivering with cold as he stood in the doorway, could feel how loose his bones were in his body. "What's that to you?" he said. "And why should you care?"

"Oh, Master," said she, "You was less unkind to me than to all the other servants, and stay here I must and will, if only to see you into your coffin."

"My coffin," cried the Thief, staring at her out of an empty face, "My coffin!"

"Oh, Master!" said she, "They comes to all, they do."

And the Thief after grumbling and grumbling (for he had never meant to be less unkind) simply because he was too weary and unhappy and restless and befogged in his wits to do anything else, let her stay on. And once more he returned to his search for the Magic Egg.

Now early one Spring morning, the Thief happened to climb up on top of two chairs in his forgotten lumber room to look over the edge of an old Carnarvonshire wardrobe. It was not a very elegant or beautiful or valuable wardrobe, and it looked queer and ugly standing up there among all the other splendours which that wicked Thief had acquired in his long life. But unlike the rest, it was an honest wardrobe, for it had been left to him in her last will and testament in his young and careless days by a widow-woman. For one bright morning the Thief had been on his way through East Honglingham to see a famous Abbey in those parts in which in old days the Monks had dined off silver dishes that had once belonged to the Grand Kham of Tartary.

And as in the bright March weather he turned the corner into the village street, he saw over an orchard wall, hanging pegged upon a clothes-line, and spread over the currant and gooseberry-bushes within, a marvellous array of laundered linen. The sun flashed down on the cherry-trees and plums in full blossom. But whiter yet was this array. Pausing—even on that rapid and dangerous journey—to admire this scene, he had with all his heart exclaimed out loud, "My, now! that's what I call WASHING."

And by chance the widow-woman herself—her sleeves tucked up to her elbow and a pink print cap on her head—was standing at that moment on the other side of the wall, and she heard these words. She drank them in. But it kindled such burning pleasure in her heart to hear her work thus praised by a stranger, that she never forgot him. And when she lay dying, she remembered him yet again. Thus it was that the Thief had acquired this old, common Carnarvonshire wardrobe.

All thought of the widow's washing, however, had vanished completely out of his mind as he clambered heavily up on to the two chairs that morning in the search that had now grown desperate for the Magic Egg. And as his eyes came over the dog-tooth cornice, his sight fastened greedily upon a small square wooden box, its top at least an eighth of an inch thick with dust. For on the side of it his squinting eyes had detected in the dim light six scrawled letters: "THE EGG."

With a groan of joy he thrust out his hand, clutched the box, the upper chair slipped from under him; and down he came toppling headlong, helter-skelter to the floor. There was no doubt about it, his leg was broken in three places, and a rare trouble it was for Susan to get him into bed. But she bound the impious leg up at last with three old silk handkerchiefs and a broom-stick.

And after a while, with the wooden box under his pillow, the Thief fell asleep in his great four-post bed. For a full forty-eight hours—two whole days and two whole nights—he lay there fast asleep. At the beginning of the forty-ninth he woke up, and having lit his candle at the bed-side, pushed his hand in under his pillow as he lay on his back and, with trembling fingers, drew out the box. And there within, sure enough, just twisted up in a twist of old newspaper and cotton-wool, was the Egg.

It was a teeny-tiny egg, of the colour somewhat of a robin's. And as the broken-legged Thief held it between finger and thumb he heard a faint, faint, faint tapping. Tap, tap, tap. And in another instant—hatched, may be, by the warmth of the Thief's swansdown pillow—the thin shell crumbled between his fingers and there flew out, full-fledged, a teeny, tiny, leetle Bird with feathers of gold and eyes like emeralds and claws like coral. And it perched on his bedrail; it tweeted a few frail notes sharper than a needle and tinier than a clover-seed; and it looked at the Thief.

Even at that moment there was a whisper of a noise at the immense mahogany door. For the ninety-seventh time during that last forty-eight hours Susan was standing there in the doorway looking in on her master; but now her eyes under that black mop of hair were fixed on this Tiny One.

And she said " Oh, Master! "

And it seemed to the Thief as he lay there shrunken almost to a shadow, and looking at Susan, that he had never seen a lovelier sight. And yet, strangely enough, the delight in her dark eyes, and on her smooth young sooty cheek as she smiled at the bird, was something no Thief—not even Ali Baba's brother himself—could steal. And his heart seemed to break into three times as many pieces as his leg, as he said, having forgotten how many times this question had been answered by the high-born with emphatic Noes, " Susan, will you marry me? "

And she said: " Oh, Master! But I don't like anything in the house at all, at all, at all. I hates it. And particularly them bags of beads and brass upstairs in the attics. And all them rats a-capering on their hind-legs in the cellar. And such a mort of carpets to sweep and marble to keep clean and windows to keep curtained. But if you truly love me I will marry you. And please may I have the little bird on the bedrail for a wedding-present."

Now there was an old happy curate that lived in the great Square nearby—the only human creature there, because all that property was of no value now and the rent a mere song. For what even comparatively honest man, after all, wants to live next door to a Thief? But the curate had other views, and he had called regularly at the Thief's mansion month after month on the first Mondays for years and years, though in the butler's day he had never once been let in. But Susan knew about him all right, oh yes; and he came round with his stole and his surplice over his arm that May Day morning, and he married them then and there.

And the Thief, having now given away everything in his house, including the glass beads and the brass, died presently after, of his broken leg. And though he was not exactly happy or good—since no man can be that for more than a moment or two together—I must say that on the day of his death there was much less of a squint than usual in his little green eyes, and he looked far less like King Henry VIII. (who could have married as many duchesses as he pleased by cutting off their heads in turn) than he had ever looked before. That may have been because in his last moments there was a little gold bird singing a song like a grasshopper on the towel rail near the window to the left of his bed, while on the right sat Susan, holding his crime-stained hand and saying how sorry she was to bid him good-bye.

And soon after the Thief had breathed his last, the tiny inmate of the Magic Egg fluttered across the bed and quite unbeknown to Susan, who had fallen asleep with grief and fatigue, at once set to building a little sort of a nest in her hair. But in spite of the fact that she, being kind-hearted, was thus prevented from combing out her hair *completely* every night and morning, the kind curate managed to get her a " place " with an elderly maiden lady living in a charming villa near a village called Silleyton in Suffolk. And this lady (seeing how good and happy and willing a creature Susan was

otherwise) did not mind her maid looking like a Zulu with that extraordinarily bunchy mop of hair. And when this old lady died, having no nephews to whom to leave her money, she left it all to Susan.

So Susan was a lady, too. And after residing quietly in the villa for some little time, the High Chamberlain of the Duchess of Anjou and Angelette, who lived nearby, presented her with a gilt-edged ticket admitting her every Tuesday, Thursday and Saturday, to walk in her Great Park. And though the children of the third under-gardener, when they saw her in her neat black weeds, taking the air under the pale-green beech-trees, would whisper audibly to one another, " Lawks, what a mop! " —for some reason Susan was as happy as a kingfisher.

And every foggy 5th of November she would take a first-class ticket and be off by the Great Eastern Railway, to a certain large cemetery near London, and make her way to the south-east corner of it. And there, under a weeping willow, stood a small rounded stone. Susan would lay her bunch of artificial forget-me-nots (the real not being yet abloom) beside the stone, and, with her black-edged handkerchief in her hand, she would once more spell out the epitaph on it:—

" Here lies my poor deer husband."

Regina Angelorum

OUR Lady went into a strange country,
       Our Lady, for she was ours
And had run on the little hills behind the houses
       And pulled small flowers;
But she rose up and went into a strange country
       With strange thrones and powers.

And there were giants in the land she walked in,
       Tall as their toppling towns,
With heads so high in heaven the constellations
       Served them for crowns;
And their feet might have forded like a brook the abysses
       Where Babel drowns.

They were girt about with the wings of the morning and
       Furled and unfurled,   [evening
Round the speckled sky where our small spinning planet
       Like a top is twirled;
And the swords they waved were the unending comets
       That shall end the world.

And moving in innocence and in accident,
       She turned the face,
That none has ever looked on without loving
       On the Lords of Space;
And one hailed her with her name in our own country
       That is full of grace.

Our Lady went into a strange country
       And they crowned her for a queen,
For she needed never to be stayed or questioned
       But only seen;
And they were broken down under unbearable beauty
       As we have been.

But ever she walked till away in the last high places,
       One great light shone
From the pillared throne of the king of all that country
       Who sat thereon;
And she cried aloud as she cried under the gibbet
       For she saw her son.

Our Lady wears a crown in a strange country,
       The crown he gave,
But she has not forgotten to call to her old companions
       To call and crave;
And to hear her calling a man might arise and thunder
       On the doors of the grave.

                              G. K. C.

THE DRAMA

The Victorian Age and Dancing Mothers

THE appeal of a Victorian piece of dramatic masonry is not immediately apparent. There are moments when we grow impatient with what seems to call for no elucidation. The reiteration of the platitudes of yesterday frets upon the stage to-day. Gradually, however, the proportions of the edifice win on us. We may resent the unnecessary basement, but the hall is spacious, the living rooms are on a generous scale, and we finally come to the conclusion that though the elevation be dated, it is not jerrybuilt, and has a quality of honest persuasion.

Mr. N. F. Grant has planned "Possessions" at the Garrick Theatre to scale. The story has grip, and though his men and women are viewed from the exterior alone, there are situations of dramatic sincerity which are convincing. The play is pre-Ibsen in its treatment. That is to say the author does not probe beneath the immediate emotion, there are none of those swift revealing touches, which in a phrase will show a corner of the mind that mere spectacular observation can never fathom. The characterisation is coherent, the types pleasantly observed and the writing has an easy quietness that is most agreeable.

The plot has two strands. We are shown the mechanical working out of melodramatic spleen and the struggle between vanity and affection. Sir William Jesmond is a self-made Scotsman—of momentary lapses into English vulgarity—with a daughter, Monica. He wishes to marry her to the Earl of Northallerton, who is quite brainless. Now the brainless we have always with us, but the manner of exhibition varies from age to age; this particular specimen is démodé. In apposition to Sir William is Colonel Wedderburn, a much-decorated hero of the type beloved of dramatists, who dashes to Cairo on Monday and turns up at the North Pole for the week end. Lady Jesmond is negligible save for her bad manners transported from a past decade.

Then we have David Arnott, a civil engineer, who has returned to marry Monica after three years of silent absence. Monica herself is shadowy; thirty years ago she might have passed for flesh and blood. During the war she nursed young Arnott who kissed her and went forth to make his fortune. Monica nourishing his memory, romantically waited his return. Now young women of to-day are, doubtless, still capable of this sort of thing. They do not, however, refuse to marry without the blessing of papa. Nothing but the housing problem ever stops them, and Arnott had already arranged the home.

The young man also accepts the situation with an Edwardian meekness and it looks as if Northallerton would win hands down when Mrs. Arnott takes the field. In the old days she was the lady of the Manor, who endowed the charity boy Jesmond with stray sixpences and Sunday clothes. But with the growth of the Jesmond fortunes the star of Arnott declined. The inevitably dissolute husband dragged the family through the mud and his widow's sole comfort is the orphan boy who wants to marry Monica.

The scene in which the mother pleads her son's cause should have been set in Manchester; there it might have seemed credible. But London has a certain levelling quality that prunes away the more distressing crudities of social intercourse. In another generation Mrs. Arnott might, perhaps, have stalked like an avenging ghost into the Jesmond drawing-room, but to-day the discussion, like the lady's garments, would be less sombre. The character is manufactured melodrama, and but for the suavity of Miss Irene Rooke would have been far too sinister.

As it is I wish Miss Rooke would modify her general make-up. There is a hint of Boadicea in the black and white of her costume, and the heavy pallor of her complexion which makes one sympathise with Lady Jesmond, whose quite un-usual rudeness precipitates a scene. On a swift crescendo of indignation Mrs. Arnott tells Sir William of his wife's intrigue with Colonel Wedderburn—who is the father of Jesmond's child!

Here is a situation of real stage value. What will the author do with it? At this point the age of this carefully plotted drama grows visible. A further complication is inserted; Mrs. Arnott recants and carefully exits. This gives Colonel Wedderburn his opportunity. He confesses to Sir William and on the ground of his paternity claims that Monica must not marry Arnott. Sir William yields. The young pair embrace with blessing and the gallant soldier leaves, never, we feel, to return.

I want to give value to the workmanlike qualities of "Possessions." It is, however, conceived for an era when the stage demanded plays of sentimentalism. The interview between the Colonel and Sir William has neither thrill nor surprise, and yet I am certain that Mr. Grant could have achieved both had he reset his point of view. Nevertheless, by the canons of the theatre it is eminently actable and very well worth seeing. Mr. Norman McKinnel plays the Scotsman with canny humour and Mr. Aubrey Smith gives an agreeable performance of himself as Colonel Wedderburn

There is nothing of yesterday in "Dancing Mothers" at the Queen's Theatre. The authors, Edgar Selwyn and Edmund Goulding, have written an American play which deserves a better title. Jazz is only an incidental. The crux of the matter is the conflict between wife and mother and father and child. Mrs. Westcourt is devoted in both capacities, though somewhat inclined to immolation on the domestic pyre. Her husband, Hugh, provides a good house and a big bank balance, but gads after flappers, while Kittens, the daughter, drinks cocktails in the rooms of Gerald Naughton, a notorious bachelor. Night after night Ethel is left alone until in a fervour of indignation she decides she will go up to town with her friend Zola Masserene.

Kittens is so extraordinarily uncivilised in speech and manner that one is inclined to wonder why the gentle Ethel suffered her to grow like that. Certainly, however, she is a provocation, and the dancing mother has our sympathy when she encounters husband and child on a roof garden with their attendant attachments. To save Kittens from further entanglement Mrs. Westcourt starts a flirtation with Gerald which has a swift culmination.

Ethel, Kittens, and Irma—an old flame of Gerald's—meet at his rooms. He never had intentions in regard to Kittens —she was just a crudish flapper who ran after him—and it is her mother's first visit to his flat. When, however, Naughton makes love to Ethel one feels that an error in taste is sometimes more questionable than an offence against morals.

In the ultimate Mrs. Westcourt decides that she can no longer endure perpetual neglect and goes to Europe with Zola Masserene—Gerald as a tame cat in attendance. We are left in doubt as to whether mother will return, a wise move of the author's.

The piece is full of witty lines and the stage craft is admirable. The acting is good and Miss Gertrude Elliott plays Ethel with a dignified tenderness that keeps the most dubious scenes on a high level. Mr. Godfrey Tearle tries hard to be disagreeable as Hugh and Mr. Leslie Faber is an engaging bachelor. Miss Elsie Lawson's brilliant sketch of Irma Raymonde is one of the best things in the production. I am unacquainted with the type of American flapper played by Miss Jean Forbes Robertson. I can only say, however, that as portrayed, Kittens is blatantly unattractive. I suggest that this young actress has a touch of trop de zèle.

"Dancing Mothers" has the swiftness and entertainment of a Riviera express. It is a cocktail with a dash of decadence.

J. K. PROTHERO.

REVIEWS

Weekend Book

THIS entertaining little book has already won much flattering attention from earlier reviewers, but nevertheless may be entitled to yet a few more words of praise as a new book for a new paper. For it *is* new in conception and accomplishment. Of making anthologies there is no end, and the puzzle to many a good compiler of such works is to think of any subject which has not already been listed, sorted, indexed, arranged chronologically or biographically, under subject heads, object heads, or no heads at all. But here is an idea. Intelligent people or rather we should say wise people get out of London for the week-end. Congenial souls meet in country cottages, country houses or even country mansions, and the brightest mind either of guest or host is often unable to supply that necessary stimulus which makes a week-end party a pleasant memory to last until the next week-end arrives and the round begins again. Now here are the hints that should make a dull week-end impossible.

The talk is of poetry the old discussion turns up again and again. What is great poetry, who wrote great poetry—the old poets, why yes, here are Shakespeare and Donne; new poets—why yes, here are Masefield and Rupert Brooke, and a further list of reminders at the end of the book. How the ardent talkers must thank the compilers of the week-end book as they wander to their host's shelves and refresh themselves and their friends with Wordsworth, Shelley or Keats. And especially will they enjoy themselves over the " Hate Poems " recited with such gusto by the young and ardent.

Of songs, too, the musical members of a week-end party want to sing when the strenuous day is done. We cannot imagine a better selection, just the air, and the words given for a mixed chorus, or for a solo be it soprano or contralto, bass or tenor. English, French, Irish, Russian, American, what you will—one song leads to another as every wise man's son doth know. Or who is for games when songs are done? Here is a list of many old ones and many new, paper games, rhyming games, problems, indoor and outdoor games, and perhaps best of all, blank pages at the end of the book where the possessor can add to the list proved games or tentative suggestions that may be developed later on.

And for the hostess on whom so much depends. She will indeed be grateful for hints on food and drink, new sandwiches for picnics, what is good and what isn't good if you have to depend on tinned goods, some hot drinks, some iced ones, and much useful instruction such as " mice in honey should be imported from China and not prepared at home." We feel sure the hint will be accepted gratefully. A puzzling part of this unique volume is the section devoted to first aid in divers crisis. That such crisis do happen at week-end parties is only too true, though sea-sickness is not often to be reckoned among them, and we hope the disease called " the morning after " is not too prevalent. But who would not be glad to know what is the remedy for sunstroke (very rare we suppose if the week-end party takes place in England, but just possible), or for stings and bites, or peripalpebral ecchymosis (black eye, a very frequent crisis, no doubt), and the receipt given to stay the Hicquet and Nose Bleed, and above all what to do " before hobnailing the liver."

Such then roughly is the outline of this entertaining volume which every host and hostess will probably hide from their guests in order that a tribute for originality at week-ends may be unjustly attributed to them, but which every guest, thinking to gain some kudos for himself or herself, will conceal he in the pockets of his plus fours, she in the outside flap of her vanity bag. Anyhow it is a book which no entertainer can afford to do without. Even the book marker is a reminder, " Have you forgotten the corkscrew? Have you forgotten the salt?" What more is there to say?

F. C.

Novels of the Day

M. JEAN COCTEAU is the most talked of man in Paris. He is like a combination of the Sitwells, Mr. Ronald Firbank, Mr. Wyndham Lewis (the artist), and Mr. Michael Arlen, plus intellect and charm. M. Lewis Galantière, his very able and fluid translator, in a preface to " * Thomas the Impostor," says of Cocteau:

" He has often been confused with *les jeunes*, and erroneously so. Cocteau stands apart from his contemporaries. They are jealous and afraid of him; he is decently courteous to them. He is a magnet, but he is also a leader, though no despot. Many young men have revolted against his leadership, prompted by personal exacerbation."

Cocteau, of course, is not so great as his admirer would have him. He is still very young and devotes so much time to being eccentric that he has little real space for work. When he is tired of being talked of by people who do not matter, he will write magnificently; at present he is satisfied to be superficial and smiling.

Cocteau, however, has already done enough to supply a score of young Londoners or Parisians with reputations. He has fourteen publications to his credit, not including an adaptation of " Romeo and Juliet " and several ballets. In America he has been identified with " Les Six," a group of young composers, blessed by Satie, which has since evaporated. Cocteau is also known—and he perhaps esteems this his supreme honour—as the official opener of a Paris bar to which he gave the name of one of his pieces.

The boy, Guillaume Thomas, of humble parentage, who masquerades as the nephew of General de Fontenoy, who assumes uniform as a fancy dress, and is welcomed into the French army without any qualifications except impudence and ignorant bravery, is a novel little creation. Guillaume is one of those admirable liars who, saying what he would like to be true, in effect makes it so. He is lucky in his fairy godmother, the Princess de Bormes, a lady so great that life is all simplicities to her.

The Princess does what she wishes, and, doing so, makes it convenable. The Princess is above suspicion; she leaves loose morals to that astounding person, Madame Valice, who is exceedingly coarse, but the only practical lay-member of the Princess's travelling hospital car, binding wounds which the Princess shudders in looking at.

Interesting as these ladies are, M. Cocteau will not permit much time with them. He is feverishly concerned with his juvenile liar and hero. It was to the boy's credit that, at the height of his luxury, he did not neglect his old aunt at Montmartre. He turned up to see her ten minutes each week, saying that he was on liaison service.

Guillaume does some surprising things in, and for the army. Nobody ever doubts that he is the nephew of a distinguished general. Everyone regards him as a man while he is still a child. Madame de Bormes' daughter, Henriette, loves him to distraction, and her mother does not forbid her doing so; but Guillaume is not excited. He cheerfully consents to being shifted from the neighbourhood of the Bormes to a supposed place of safety up the line; war continues to be a delightful game to him. When an enemy patrol advances he wisely runs like a hare, and then turns round, out of breath:

" At that moment he felt a terrible blow in the chest. He fell. He became deaf, blind.

WEEKEND BOOK. A Sociable Anthology. Nonsuch Press. 6s.

" * THOMAS THE IMPOSTOR." By Jean Cocteau. Appleton. 5s.

" ' A bullet,' he said to himself, ' *I am lost if I don't pretend to be dead.*' "

There was no need for pretence. Young Guillaume Thomas was dead, without knowing that he was.

The book is full of delicate phrases. One of them I admire especially. It is written of Rheims after bombardment: " The cathedral was a mountain of old lace."

If Mr. Geoffrey Dennis had called his terrible and telling book " † Nightmare in Poland," he would have prepared readers to summon up all their sanity and courage to meet the forces of evil.

It is some time since Mr. Dennis wrote " Mary Lee," which concerned itself with the views and actions of the narrowest of nonconformist sects. In it he dealt with the curse of Puritanism, but one felt that the curse was the book. In " Harvest in Poland," there is the horrible reaction attendant on fanatical Puritanism, with its individual judgment and its over-heated hell.

The opening chapters in the Midlands reveal young Emmanuel Lee as destined from birth to be the sport of psychic influences. Emmanuel is his own historian, and he talks (or writes) like a lunatic of genius. The description of the seance of Mr. Quince, the Medium, would have made Robert Browning laugh; but Emmanuel gets from it an increased belief in the power of evil, and the warning that he must resist certain things and a certain journey.

At Oxford he meets Prince Julian Lelewel, who invites him to spend a holiday in Poland. The Prince, like some other characters in the book, is an unconscious emissary for Evil. Young Lee in Paris experiences for the first time in his life the incursions of the World, the Flesh and the Devil. This portion of the Lee narrative makes the daring of Mr. Alesteir Crowley appear like a Sunday school tract.

There is a wild journey through Germany and into Poland, in the course of which Emmanuel's prince patron is at times devil and at times good friend. The household of the Prince, with his diabolic grandmother, his mad mother, his pervert cousin, and Zwan, the dwarf, appears much more like a corner of hell than of Poland.

Zwan is a miniature Rasputin, and the centenarian grandmother, who has two hatreds—one of Russia and the other of her family—believes in him as devoutly as the Czarina is said to have believed in his prototype.

Again and again, through the pages of " Harvest in Poland," its narrator tells of warnings and visions; and the visions are such that they have often the appearance of actualities. In the last chapters, " The Terror by Night " and " The Valley of the Shadow," Lee contends for days—or seconds—with a supreme tempter, who is, properly enough, a member of the Prince's family. The chapters are well named. Faust's interviews with Mephistopheles are farcical incidents compared with Emmanuel Lee's struggles with Count Bethlehem Zwelewely. Conveyed with entire conviction, " Harvest in Poland " is one of those dreams one awakens from with profound relief.

At a period when Mr. Phillip Guedalla despairs of the novel, the younger writers are giving abundant promise. Mr. Jeffery E. Jeffery, who has done ambitious, serious work in " Escape " and " The Burden," had written for relief, a light comedy of modern life in " ‡ An Octave," in which an extraordinary series of changes in the career of an easy-going man happens from Sunday to Sunday. The opening note is struck in the sentence: " Perseverance had brought Leila Rexon to the end of Mr. Garvin's article on the middle page of the *Observer.*"

Leila's husband, who is a publisher, is neglecting her. He is, furthermore, exceeding his interest in Rosamond Culver,

who in the early thirties, was already being taken seriously as a novelist. " She lived emotionally with the deliberate object of being able to write emotionally of her experiences; and it was common knowledge that her experiences included three lovers, by one of whom she had had a child."

Leila has a counterbalancing little affair with Hugh Sircombe, a dilettante who writes agreeably about travel; but Leila is not prepared to drift as far as her amiable husband, Tony. Both of them are devoted to their girl, Honor, who is excessively modern but a nice clean sort. Honor's feared indiscretion is marriage with a very Fabian young man, Bernard Blagden, who has six pounds a week and a rich endowment of dogmatism. The Rexon boys, Guy and Colin, present minor little problems to their parents.

Like most middle-aged men, Tony is more seriously concerned with his business than with his family or his " flirts." Rosamond Culver's MS, " The Maiden Ladies," contained much promise, as it dealt, very delicately, with three unmarried sisters who dwelt together in an upper-class suburb on a restrictive income. Two-thirds of the book outlined and filled in their respectability and their mutual relationship. The third was a slow and subtle revelation of the fact that no one of the three was a maiden and that each had succeeded in hiding the fact from the other. Tony quite finished with Rosamond when she disposed of " Maiden Ladies " to the up-to-date firm of Fiske, Kybert & Co.

The real backbone of the novel is lazy Tony Rexon's heroic efforts to save the firm of Rexon and Rust from absorption and destruction. This is one of the very few romances in which a publisher appears as a novelist's hero.

Louis J. McQuilland

WITH O. HENRY.

WILLIAM SYDNEY PORTER, who wrote under the pseudonym of O. Henry, was not only a genius but above all American; and his stories, overlaid though they are by artistry, are faithful chronicles of the raw and teeming life of those United States that he knew so well and studied so carefully. Moreover, his personality was elusive, even to his few intimates, and any first-hand knowledge of the man himself is of more than usual interest.

It is strange that his biographer should be a former bandit; but not so strange as if Bill Sykes had written of his progenitor. For, as is set forth in this book,* O. Henry had not only actually met the types of whom he wrote, but he had suffered degradation as pitiful as theirs. He wrote of what he knew, and the tragedy of his own life, far from embittering him, did but enhance his sense of pity for the unfortunate. Indeed, it might not be an unprofitable speculation to seek the causes of that ingenious device in his tales which is known as the " O. Henry twist " rather in the psychology of the man than in mere craftsmanship.

Politicians and propagandists speak all too glibly of our kinship with the Americans; they seek to revive a relationship the death of which was toasted in an unique brew of tea six generations ago. But our common language, most brittle of ties, may yet keep us together if only its strands be plentifully watered with understanding. And this book by Al. Jennings, the ex-bandit, which despite its crudity and its stories of almost unbelievable cruelty introduces a great man, may fulfil a certain destiny if it induces its English readers to study the pages of O. Henry. For it will have set before them a writer from whom more can be learnt of the Great Republic than from a library of text books and of histories.

" † HARVEST IN POLAND." By Geoffrey Dennis. Heinemann. 7s. 6d.
" ‡ AN OCTAVE." By Jeffery E. Jeffery. Leonard Parsons. 7s. 6d.

" * THROUGH THE SHADOWS WITH O. HENRY." By Al. Jennings. Duckworth. 6s.

LIBRARY LIST

MYRTLE. By Stephen Hudson. Constable. 6s.

Dedicated to Frederick Delius, " Myrtle" is a book about musical people. Mr. Hudson has a technique all his own. His present experiment in prose is the attempted revelation of the character and charm of a young girl as seen through various eyes—those of her nurse, her sister, and her various admirers. At the end of the book one knows rather less about Myrtle Vendramin than at the beginning. It may be that she is too subtle to be obvious; but one imagines that such a briliant writer as Mr. Hudson is indulging in irony at the expense of a young woman who has nothing of character to reveal. Hudson is obsessed by the previous fictional family he invented, the Kurts, and in " Myrtle" he gives that young lady to the gloomy Richard Kurt, after Richard has succeeded, to his own intense stupefaction, in divorcing his wife, Elinor—who was, of course, intensely relieved to get rid of him.

AN OLD MAN'S JOTTINGS. By Joseph Rickaby. S. J. Longmans. 7s. 6d.

Father Rickaby, in his preface, makes a wholly unnecessary apology for his age and for work " senile and fitful." There is a logic, a wit, a keenness about these notes which younger men of ability and piety might envy. He is not afraid to be political, but holds the balance evenly between class and class. It seems a judgment, he says, that after the Rationalist press comes the Soviet propaganda; but in England he holds that the Radicalism of Labour, verging dangerously upon revolution, would receive wholesome correction if working men were confined less to the unlovely surroundings of their daily toil and saw more of " this earth, this England," as God and nature made it. In social life, Father Rickaby believes, adulation may be more dangerous than drink: " Better be surrounded by a circle of champagne bottles than by a circle of admirers. Flattery flies to the head more disastrously even than champagne." The jottings are mainly religious, but they are never mawkish.

LETTERS FROM W. H. HUDSON TO EDWARD GARNETT. Dent. 6s.

The recipient of the late Mr. Hudson's letters should have been content with them as memorials of a personal friendship. The author of " Green Mansions" and " The Purple Land" is not a Southey or a Stevenson in correspondence. The present Garnett collection contains a good deal of complaint about Hudson's reviewers and too much adverse criticism of the author's contemporaries. Hudson, declaring that he was free from the adjectival " vice of cleverness," was " amused and irritated" by the cleverness of Mr. Belloc, and brought an old complaint against the Editor of this periodical, about balancing an eel on his nose. Poor Hudson had evidently lost his sense of balance. The dead naturalist was a violently Orange Ulsterian, though he appeared to have no knowledge of Ireland. He had an obsession also that Doughty's " Dawn in Britain" was the greatest—as it is almost the longest—of poems. The letters are full of *trivia*, as in the piece of news: " Last evening I fell in with a boy—a small farmer's son—carrying a duck in a basket, and we walked and talked for a couple of miles together. He was like David's brother. This would interest Mr. Garnett, but has no concern for the outside world. There is nothing of literary value either in the statement: " That paper, ' Do Cats Think? ' has brought me a lot of letters, and the editor of the *Strand* has bought the second serial rights to put it into his magazine." Decidedly, Mr. Garnett has done Hudson's reputation no good in the printing of these *ephemera*.

CHILD-LORE: A Study in Folk-Lore and Psychology. By Mrs. S. Herbert. Methuen. 6s.

This book is an attempt—and a most commendable one—to give a simple account of what Mrs. Herbert calls the " Science of Childhood." Mrs. Herbert is not over-anxious as to psychoanalysis, and escapes fairly well from the nets of those tiresome sex-maniacs, Freud and Jung. Parents and bachelors will be at one with her in the idea that the best way of keeping a child out of mischief is to give it something to do, though that line of procedure entails a lively and extended imagination. One is in entire sympathy with the little boy who said to his mother, " There is no fun in playing if you cannot get dirty." In the Folk-Lore part of the book it is interesting to learn that the negroes in Guinea place the new-born boy on a shield, as the Spartans did, and that the Montenegrins put pistol and rifle near his cradle. The latter fact may account for a lot of the trouble in the Balkans, since these weapons have more potency than the bayonets of toy soldiers.

THE ROMANCE OF EXCAVATION. By David Masters. The Bodley Head. 6s. 6d.

It is interesting, and chastening, to know that while our early British ancestors were painting themselves crudely with woad, the Egyptian ladies were sitting at their dressing tables " making-up " in the fashion of to-day. Professor Flinders Petrie discovered that in the course of Egyptian excavation. These explorers in buried cities are always sure of themselves. When the Frenchman, Mariette, going up to Thebes, saw a few columns sticking out of the sand at Carnak, he began his great task straight away. Most enthusiastic of all these Old Moles was Heinrich Schliemann, who loved as a child the stories of the old Greek heroes, especially the deeds of Homer, and said to his small play-fellows, " I am going to find Troy." That was a good joke, but a better joke came when he did actually find it after many years of working for money and studying for learning. In 1870, filled with the knowledge of years, he came to the desolate Hill of Hissarlik, standing on the Plain of Troy, a short distance from the Dardanelles, and set his labourers to work cutting the secret out of the heart of the hill.

A BOOK OF VAGROM MEN AND VAGRANT THOUGHTS. By Alfred T. Story. Duckworth. 3s. 6d.

It is a pity that the influence of Lamb plays such a considerable part in the writing of English essays, for what one likes in Lamb, one can barely tolerate in his imitators, conscious and unconscious. In spite, however, of the Elian inspiration, and a selection of very pedestrian subjects, Mr. Story's little book has no boredom in it—or, at least, very little. One reason of this is that his set-pieces are relieved by suitable stories, like that of the amiable lady of Berlin, who sang like a perfect syren, but always stood with her back to the audience because she had the face of a horse. The poor thing's cheeks were bathed in tears every night she sang because of the contrast between her music and her physique. I like, too, Mr. Story's vagrom artist who, painting a sunset, and seeing how dull his copy on canvas appeared beside the original in the heavens, would mutter, " Too lavish! Too lavish! He would ruin a colour manufactory."

BINDON PARVA. By George A. Birmingham. Mills & Boon. 7s. 6d.

The Rev. Canon Hannay, the best stage Irishman of our time, has forsaken, for the moment, his Handy-Andyisms, and has given his wondering public a volume of what are generally called ghost-stories. The tales savour of the late Robert Hugh Benson, minus his spiritual inspiration, but are remarkably good of their kind. The narrator gets them from the fictional Reverend Silvester Maturin, Vicar of Bindon Parva, who extends his religious services to former vicars and members of the parish who have been dead for hundreds of years. The opening narrative tells of a Hugh Freyne, who was parish priest in the days of the Wars of the Roses, and who committed a great sin, returning to Bindon Parva many years after as a layman, behaved as a devout worshipper, but died unconfessed and unabsolved, leaving as his epitaph *Peccator Miserrimus*. Another pastor was Felix Brandon, who preached a windy and turbulent sermon extolling Titus Oates, but who felt compunction in betraying a Catholic gentleman into the hands of that very twisted pillar of Protestantism. The chronicles are brought down to the days of the Oxford Movement. Maturin, the simple, good man, who speaks of the dead as if they continued to assist at his services, has not much common-sense, but Canon Hannay has helped him to tell quite a number of entertaining yarns.

THE HOUSE OF FINNY. By Henry J. Thompson. Herbert Jenkins. 7s. 6d.

A fair number of novels have been written about the drapery business, and this is by no means the worst of them. Mr. Robert Finny, who thinks Finny & Finny the most important words in life, is to some extent taken from the life. He is unconsciously blasphemous, in the Blanco-Posnett manner, when he speaks of the Almighty: " How about 'is thunder? How about 'is storms and earthquakes . . . why, come to think of it, there never was such an advertising agent for a business as God is for Heaven." Mr. Finny is pompous, irascible, and unable to carry a jorum of port with any dignity. He creates chaos by his frequent pouncings on unfortunate assistants, and " The House " is sustained only by its manager, Hendry. Finny decides that he will marry his capable manager to his rather unmanageable daughter, but Hendry is married already . A new broom comes into the firm in the shape of Mr. Finny's nephew, George, a Futurist artist with grandiose ideas. During Mr. Finny's frequent lapses he almost carries those ideas out, but decides instead to run off with Hendry's wife. Hendry joins an opposition firm, and is coerced back to the falling House of Finny by the bright Miranda. The book has plenty of humour of the jocose variety, but the author must simplify his style if he is to do really good work. He must, above all, beware of such sentences as " The enthusiasm of the zealot rubesced his cheek and lamped his eye." That sort of thing gives the reader a nasty jar. On the whole, however, Mr. Thompson has added to the gaiety of the circulating libraries.

"G.K.'s WEEKLY"

Every Thursday.   Price Sixpence.

NOTICES.

Tel. No.: City 1978.   Annual Subscription Rate (52 Issues) £1 10 4.

Cheques and Postal Orders should be made payable to G.K.'s Weekly Ltd., and crossed a/c payee Westminster Bank, Ltd. MSS. submitted to the Editor must be accompanied by a stamped addressed envelope

Copies of "G.K.'s Weekly" can be obtained from, or subscriptions placed with, any News dealer or News Company in the United States or Canada, or direct from *The* International News Co., 83-85, Duane Street, New York; *The* American News Co., Ltd., at Toronto, Winnipeg, Vancouver, Montreal, Ottawa, St. John, Halifax and Hamilton. Sole agents for Australasia: Gordon & Gotch (Australasia), Ltd. Sole Agents for South Africa: Central News Agency, Ltd.

Offices: 20 & 21, Essex Street, Strand, London, W.C.2.

Prepaid Classified Advertisements

RATES.

Minimum 20 Words (Two Lines)   ...   .   Four Shillings.
Every Additional 10 Words (One Line)   ...   ...   Two Shillings.
Less than 10 Words charged as a line.
Heading and each additional line set in capital letters charged as
two lines.
Instructions should be addressed to—
PREPAID CLASSIFIED ADVERTISEMENTS DEPARTMENT,
G.K.'s WEEKLY, 20-21 Essex Street, Strand,
London, W.C.2, by first post on Saturday of each week.

Appointments, &c., Vacant and Wanted.

UNIVERSITY OF BRISTOL.

The University invites applications for the following non-professional appointments :—
HEAD OF THE DEPARTMENT OF GERMAN.
HEAD OF THE DEPARTMENT OF ECONOMICS.
Stipend in each case £500 per annum.
The status and title of the persons appointed will depend on qualifications. Duties to commence on October 1, 1925.
Applications should be lodged on or before April 20, 1925, with the REGISTRAR of the University, from whom further particulars may be obtained.

UNIVERSITY OF BIRMINGHAM.

EDUCATION DEPARTMENT.
A LECTURER (Man or Woman) will be required on the Method of Modern Language Teaching and for the supervision of Language Teaching in the Schools, together with some work in the French Department of the University. A high honours degree and school teaching experience essential. Duties to begin September 1, 1925.
Stipend beginning at £300 per annum.
Applications, with copies of four testimonials, should be sent in not later than May 14, 1925, to the undersigned, from whom further particulars may be obtained.

C. G. BURTON, Secretary.

Lectures, Scholarships, &c.

STRATHEARN COLLEGE, EDINBURGH.—Post scholastic trainings in Cookery. All Domestic Arts. Gardening and Poultry (residential). Diplomas awarded. Extensive grounds. Motoring, Dancing. Summer Travel Tours arranged. Illustrated Prospectus from PRINCIPAL.

ANSTEY PHYSICAL TRAINING COLLEGE, - Erdington, Birmingham (Ling's Swedish System) offers complete Teacher's Training (Women) in Swedish Educational Gymnastics, Medical Gymnastics and Massage, Dancing, Hockey, Lacroses, Cricket, Tennis, Netball, Swimming, Anatomy, Hygiene, Physiology, etc. Three Years' Course. Prospectus on application.

Girls' Schools and Colleges.

MISS IRONSIDE'S BUREAU.
JOURNALISTIC AND SECRETARIAL TRAINING.
Prospectus on application. 73 Gower Street, W.C.1.

OVERDALE SCHOOL, FARLEY HALL, near Oakamoor, N. Staffs. Good all-round education for limited number of Girls in charming country residence, 650 ft. above sea level. Principals : Miss PICKARD, M.A. (Newnham College), and Miss KITTS.

HARROGATE COLLEGE FOR GIRLS, YORKSHIRE. Chairman :—The Right Hon. LORD GISBOROUGH.
Entrance Scholarship Examination will be held on May 20, 21 and 22, for the award of Five Scholarships varying in value, according to merit, from £30 to £100 a year, and open to girls under 14 years of age on May 1. Entry Forms must be returned before May 6, 1925, to the HEAD-MISTRESS.

Boys' Schools and Colleges.

ALDENHAM SCHOOL.—Six or seven Entrance Scholarships of the value of £50 each will be offered early in June.—Particulars from the HEAD-MASTER, Aldenham School, Elstree, Herts.

KING EDWARD VI. SCHOOL, BURY ST. EDMUND'S. Two House-Scholarships of £9 per ann., open to boys under 13. One Exhibition of £20 per ann., restricted to sons of officers deceased on active service. Examination June 9, 1925.
Further particulars from HEAD-MASTER.

Hotels, Hydros, &c.

REFORMED INNS.—Ask for Descriptive List (gratis) of 170 Inns and Hotels managed by the People's Refreshment House Association, Ltd.
P.R.H.A., Ltd., St. George's House, 193 Regent Street, W.1.

MOOR COURT, SIDMOUTH (Private Hotel).—ONLY hotel adjoining 18-hole Golf Course; stands high; magnificent sea views every room; excellent cuisine; electric light; gas-fires in bedrooms. Easy reach sea, shops, churches. Charabancs to all parts. Good Fishing. Terms, 4½ to 8½ guineas, inclusive, according to room and season. Special week-end terms to golfers. Telephone : 189 Sidmouth.

CUMBERLAND HOUSE HOTEL, 51, 53, 55 Earl's Court Square, S.W.5.—Central, pleasantly situated, good locality, large public rooms; comfort the keynote. From 2½ guineas.—Tariff S. HORSPOOL.

AT BOURNEMOUTH HYDRO visitors find Hotel Comforts with baths and other advantages of a hydro at moderate cost. Tele. : 341. Lift.

EDINBURGH.—Guests received in large Mansion House. Central, extensive grounds, tennis, golf, racquets, motor, own farm and garden produce. Separate tables. From 3 guineas. Early booking necessary. Illus. prospectus. Apply HOUSEKEEPER, St. Leonard's House, Dalkeith Road.

Tours, &c.

SIR HENRY LUNN, LTD.
£63 PALESTINE, EGYPT, PATMOS, SMYRNA, CONSTANTINOPLE, ATHENS.
£9 19 6 GOLF, BELGIAN COAST, 14 days' Hotels and Rail.
£15 4 6 MONTREUX, SWISS RIVIERA, 14 days' Hotels and Rail.
£15 1 0 BRUNNEN, LAKE OF LUCERNE, 14 days' Hotels and Rail.
Illustrated Booklet post free.
5 H.K. ENDSLEIGH GARDENS, LONDON, N.W.1.

Foreign.

VILLA BIENVENUE — LAUSANNE CHAMBLANDES, SWITZERLAND. — FINISHING SCHOOL FOR GIRLS. Special study of French. Modern languages, Art, Litertaure, Domestic Science classes, Sports. Highest references.—Principal, Miss RUFER. Escort from London.

ADVICE ABOUT SCHOOLS, AT HOME or on the CONTINENT, and TUTORS' ESTABLISHMENTS, DOMESTIC ECONOMY SCHOOLS, ets.,
is given free of charge by
MESSRS. BABBITAS, THRING & CO.,
36 Sackville Street, London, W.1. Telephone : Regent 4926.
Educational Agents. Established 1873.
Messrs. Gabbitas, Thring & Co. are personally acquainted with nearly all School Principals in the country. They will also be glad to supply full information about establishments giving a course of training in Domestic Economy, Secretarial Work, Agriculture and Horticulture.
NO CHARGE WHATEVER IS MADE TO PARENTS.

Miscellaneous.

CARSON'S PURE PAINT.—NON-POISONOUS, MIXED READY FOR USE. In over 50 colours. Specially manufactured for the finest exterior and interior decoration.
For patterns and particulars write—
WALTER CARSON & SONS, Battersea, London, S.W.11.

SOMETHING NEW FOR BAZAARS, SALES OF WORK, FETES, EXHIBITIONS, ETC. Handsome, novel, hand-coloured Pottery, Glassware, Trays, Tea-pot Stands. Certain success assured to purchasers of our Vases, Bowls, Fernpots, Trays, Tea-pot Stands. Every piece HAND-COLOURED. Beautiful colourings. Big profits. Customer writes : " Pottery supplied was much admired and sold out before anything else. It we had understood demand beforehand we should have been safe in having quite three times the amount." Write for full details.—" RAINBOW " POTTERY CO., Dept. " S," Lindfield, Sussex.

HAVE YOUR OWN BOOKPLATE.—Your own Arms, Crest, Motto, or other ideas incorporated. Artistic and original work from £2 2s. Specimens sent free.—HENRY B. WARD, 57 Mortimer Street, London, W.1.

Published by the Proprietors, G.K.'s WEEKLY, LTD., at their offices, 20 & 21 Essex Street, Strand, London, W.C.2 (incorporating THE NEW WITNESS). Telephone No. City 1978. Printed by THE ALLIED PRESS, LTD., 19 Clerkenwell Close, London, E.C.1. Sole agents for Australasia : Gordon & Gotch (Australasia), Ltd. Sole Agents for South Africa : Central News Agency, Ltd.

G.K.'s Weekly

EDITED BY G. K. CHESTERTON.

No. 4.—Vol. I.   Week ending Saturday, April 11, 1925.   PRICE SIXPENCE. YEARLY (52 ISSUES) £1 10 4.

Telephone No. City 1978.   [Registered at the G.P.O. as a Newspaper.]   *Offices, 20 & 21, Essex Street, Strand, W.C.*

CONTENTS:

ARE WE REACTIONARY?

IN our last issue Sir Henry Slesser quoted at length from the debates of the House of Commons a perfectly lucid and logical and solid criticism of the social policy which we pursue. It was by Mr. Montague, a Labour member; and apparently the only Labour member to maintain what many suppose to be the whole Labour policy. He criticised our conception from the point of view of the old Fabian intellectual; who did at least differ from many other intellectuals by the possession of an intellect. This criticism, being concerned with fundamental and essential questions of public policy, was very little reported in the press. Newspapers are necessarily limited in their space; and we who are beginners would be the last to deny the difficulties of making up a page. And if the newspapers were to admit into their columns any considerable discussion of what is to happen to the English land or the English labouring class, they would find it impossible to print at length the fourth housemaid's fifth reiteration, in the witness box, that she never saw anything particular about the demeanour of Captain Bingle towards Lady Brown. We should be driven to content ourselves with only five photographs of people paddling in the summer or ski-ing in the winter. We shall endeavour to provide Mr. Montague with an adequate reply, but we feel some pride in the fact that we are probably among the few who will give him even an adequate report.

It is necessary to deal here with the charge of being reactionary and what is really implied in it. It is popularly expressed, as our contributor has noted, in the common phrase about putting back the clock. It makes the brain reel to think how many million times we have been told that we cannot put back the clock. It is strange that people should use the same mechanical metaphor in the same mechanical spirit so many times without once seeing what is wrong with it. It looks rather as if their clocks, anyhow, had stopped. If there is one thing in the world that no sane man ought to connect with the idea of unlimited progress, it is a clock. A clock does not strike twelve and then go on to strike thirteen or fourteen. If a clock really proceeded on the progressive or evolutionary principle, we should find it was half-past a hundred in about a week. So far as the significance of the signs go, which is the only value of a clock, the case is altogether the other way. You do not need to put the clock back; because in that sense the clock always puts itself back. It always returns to its first principle and its primary purpose; and in that respect at any rate it is really a good metaphor for a social scheme. The clock that had completely forgotten the meaning of one and two would be valueless; the commonwealth that has completely forgotten the meaning of individual dignity and direct ownership will never recover them by going blindly forward to an infinity of number; it must return to reality. It must be reactionary, if that is reaction.

But if that is reaction, a great many other things are reactionary. For instance, a Trade Union was and is utterly reactionary. Indeed, when it first appeared it was regarded as reactionary; especially by the people who then considered themselves most progressive. It was regarded by the Radical of the industrial revolution as a piece of unscientific sentimentalism and ignorant discontent. And so it was, upon the principles then counted scientific. The Trade Union was reactionary if the Manchester School was progressive. And the Manchester School certainly thought itself progressive; and indeed everybody else thought so, too; it was not only praised as progressive but dreaded and denounced as progressive. What is the use, therefore, of Mr. Montague throwing the word " reactionary " at us, when his own grandfather might have thrown the word " reactionary " at him? The Trade Union reacted almost automatically towards the tradition of the Guild because individualism was driving on indefinitely to insanity; because that mechanical clock had gone mad, and was striking a million. We react towards the tradition of the peasant because the divorce between property and personality has become equally impossible; so that a man is not even a clock but one of the works of a clock.

If we can dispute with Mr. Montague over the term " reactionary," we might dispute with him still more over the term " medieval." About that we have a very simple thing to say. If Mr. Montague will get into a little boat and sail away from his native land in any direction whatever (short of the North Pole) he will probably land in a country where small ownership is a living, thriving, staring modern reality, in a greater or less degree according to the inroads of the last " progressive " fad of industrialism. If he goes west and lands in Ireland he will find it. If he goes east and lands in Denmark he will find it. If he goes almost anywhere he will find it much more fully developed than he will find it here. Everywhere doubtless it is modified or thwarted; everywhere doubtless it might be improved; but everywhere it is a thing of the present. If anything in the world is modern, small property is modern. He might as well say the decimal coinage is medieval; for almost every place which has decimal coinage has some measure of small property. He might as well say Napoleon was a medieval figure; for this tendency has largely followed the code Napoleon. In a legal or strictly historical sense, indeed, Mr. Montague's implication is wildly incorrect. Medieval civilisation was indeed *progressing* towards private property for all, when it was split asunder by that strange earthquake whether economic or theological. But medieval civilisation started with the legal fiction of feudalism, by which the land belonged to the King; that is, to the State. In other words medieval civilisation started with the fiction of Socialism. It

is Mr. Montague who is medieval. It is Mr. Montague who is reacting towards the first heraldic fictions of the feudal age. We hand him back the emblazoned escutcheon with a bow. Modern Europe, swarming with prosaic and practical peasants, is good enough for us.

Of course, we know very well what he really means, whether he knows it or not, by our being medieval. He means something that has many other euphemisms. He means something that has survived medievalism though it made medievalism, just as it survived feudalism though it mitigated feudalism, just as it survived slavery though it dissolved slavery. We know its name if he does not; and we beg to inform him that this also is an exceedingly modern institution. If he will sail round the world in his little boat, he will find out how modern. But nobody expects him to argue on the assumption of Catholic Christianity, and therefore it is irrelevant to deal with that matter here. We will only say that, if he cares for a hint about the nature of the thing in its varied effects, he will find it in the notion of the Will which is at the root of all liberty. Because that philosophy favours voluntary association, it supports Guilds and Trades Unions; because it believes in a province for volition it favours property. And he will find this study more philosophical than playing with a clock and talking of politics in terms of time. It is bad enough when he merely calls that reactionary to-day which was progressive yesterday. But as a fact he is calling that progressive to-day which was reactionary yesterday.

We shall find an opportunity elsewhere of discussing in greater detail the practical criticisms involved in Mr. Montague's most interesting speech; here we are only concerned with the particular reproach of reaction. But in a general fashion we may say this. Mr. Montague's ideal society is one in which no man will ever have any real control; even over himself. The advantage of the plan he deprecated, the plan by which each worker in a factory might also be an independent worker on the land, is that each man would have something to fall back upon, and that a fundamental. Suppose, for instance, there is a strike; presumably in that case there will be a strike fund. We certainly have never indulged in the vulgar grumbling against strike funds or strikes. But after all a strike fund must be in the hands of officials; just as all the money of the Treasury is in the hands of officials. In theory we have control over the money in the Treasury. In practise, men may come to have as little control over the Trade Union fund as over the Treasury. Of course, this will not affect one who does not want the people to rule; who would uphold the Trade Union against the Trade Unionists. But the people we want to rule are people and not offices. Against the despotic thing called Supply we set the democratic thing called Demand.

NOTES OF THE WEEK

THE issue of the paper for Easter Week cannot be what it ought to be if our civilisation were restored to its real origins and true to its holiest traditions. Perhaps, if that were so, the right way of celebrating Holy Week would be to publish no paper at all, but to attend to more important things. As it is, much of our work on this or any other occasion will seem unworthy and may even ring false. We are accused of being gloomy and of being frivolous; and we should be the last to deny that in current culture the two can be combined. We are charged with being pessimistic because we wish to restore a Merrie England in which it might have been possible merely to write a song about the sun that danced on Easter Day. We are charged with being flippant; and it is only too probable that our current comments on the neglect of Easter may sound like a very sour and even unseemly sort of flippancy. But we cannot provide, in the form of modern journalism, the antidote for these evils. We can only work for a better time and a better system that may possibly provide them. One thing is certain; if ever humanity does return to healthier and more humane conditions, it will not abolish but ratify the human custom of recurring ritual dates and feasts. They existed wherever humanity is human, even when it was heathen. They still exist, and have still in some sense a fuller meaning, in so far as we can say that we are still Christian.

* * * *

THE debate about the Naval Base at Singapore, whatever else it is, is a complete answer to the queer provincial romance set out for us in Lord Beaverbrook's papers; the illusion that we can shut ourselves up in the British Empire as if we had gone away in a flying ship and colonised the moon. A nation can be a small nation; and when it is it is often a very great nation. A nation can be a great power; and can deal in a more or less moderate and cautious fashion in relation, and probably in rivalry, with other great powers. But there is nothing but nonsense in the notion of a man wanting to own half the earth and take no notice of the other half. There is nothing but a crazy contradiction in the idea of being imperial without being international. It is a thoroughly typical case of the modern millionaire's philosophy; the philosophy of having it both ways. So he wishes to have the most respectable marriage with the most reckless divorce; he wants to eat his wedding-cake and have it. So he wants to have uncontrolled sexuality and uncontrolled birth-control; to eat his birthday cake and have it. And so he wants to cut up the whole earth like a colossal cake and continue to serve out a vast number of slices to himself; and yet to take no notice of what happens to the other slices or what is said by the other people. There is no connecting principle in his action whatever; except that he is comfortable in his indifference and comfortable in his greed.

* * * *

THIS is well illustrated in the whole discussion about Singapore. According to the New Imperialism, we are to take a great deal of notice of Australia but no notice at all of Japan. It seems to make no difference that Australia takes a very great deal of notice of Japan. We might please Australia by defying Japan or ignore Japan and snub Australia; but we cannot consult the one without considering the other. It is equally hopeless to suppose that we could know everything about Canada and nothing about America; or everything about America and nothing about the American attitude to Europe. National moods change, especially American moods; combinations and understandings shift and alter; and because we choose to forget other nations they will not be so obliging as to forget us. We may see again the rushing and the swooping of the eagles, whether they are what the Eagle of Rostand called the Black Eagles of Austria and Prussia or the Golden Eagles of Gaul and Rome. We shall not prevent such birds from swooping by becoming that highly South African bird that is said to hide its head in the sand and comfort itself, no doubt, by calling it the Illimitable Veldt. That illimitability is itself an illusion. For these thinkers only barbarian powers seem to count: and the example can be found even there. Do they suppose the Germans have forgotten their colonies, because some of us have forgotten the Germans?

* * * *

WE say therefore that we must have a foreign policy; it is absurd to suppose it can find a substitute in an imperial policy which is simply a colonial policy. The policy in which we have always believed was that which underlay the whole theory of the Great War; an enduring understanding with France, with Poland and the new nations and if possible with Italy; an alliance frankly prepared for possible barbarian eruptions in the future; but strong enough, and above all loyal enough, to put fear enough into barbarism to hold it at bay and render those eruptions less and less probable. If there were such a formal and fixed alliance, we could do what can always be done when it is really formal and fixed. We could control the action of our partners at all points where it really happened to collide with British interests. This is a policy; it is not the only one; and there are other policies for which we can see other arguments. But we can see no argument for having no policy and then calling that vast negation and emptiness an empire. Moreover, as we have urged before, it is not even as if the British people could now turn to the British Empire as a real relaxation, in the sense of a real romance, let alone as a real support. It is not only bad politics, it is even bad journalism, to beat the big drum of Empire just now. The subject is, in the dialect of the Yankee pressmen on whom these people model themselves, "cold." We have to praise England, not as a colonial power, but as a central and civilised nation—in peril.

* * * *

WE are daily warned of the dreadful danger of the Red propaganda, especially in the Red Sunday Schools, those curious institutions in which certain pious characters would seem to be honouring Sabbatarianism without Christianity. We are incessantly told of the seditious leaflets which are apparently scattered in every home except ours. In short, we are assured continually that we must destroy Socialism or it will almost immediately destroy us. Now we, as it happens, really do wish to destroy Socialism; though we doubt the wisdom of using the power of the police to do it. But if we could use the power of the police against Socialism, we have no doubt whatever about what would be the first strong and vigorous act of our dictatorship. It would be to burn all the Anti-Socialist literature and journalism and put almost every prominent Anti-Socialist in prison with a gag in his mouth, before he could say another word. If he says many more words, he will turn the Labour Movement into a landslide. We would suppress the whole issue of the *Daily Mail* and the *Daily Express* whenever they contained anything dealing with Socialism; then perhaps there would be some chance of people finding out what the case against Socialism is. At present a large number of people seem to be under the impression that Socialism consists of criticising God and the Prince of Wales, who seem to be part of the same theological system. Nobody knows the case against Socialism till he knows the case for Socialism; and if only the Socialists know that, they will quite certainly win.

* * * *

WHEN we hear that Sir Alfred Mond is indignantly attacking the Government Department called the Post Office for its indifference to the prospects of Wireless, our deepest instincts rush forth in a flood of sympathy with the Government Department. For one thing, it restores one's faith in the dignity of the human intellect to find anybody who shows an indifference to Wireless. Everybody who values the free spirit above fashion and time should rally to the support of the philosopher refusing to be dazzled by these barbaric displays of materialistic magic. Perhaps this first intellectual impulse is a little too pure and clear; it is in truth too wise for this world. But even on a worldly plane, certain doubts will suggest themselves to a worldly experience. The government official is sometimes bullied by business forces, if not merely because he is a philosopher, at least merely because he is a gentleman. He may in the present case be quite wrong and the business forces quite right; for our system of government does suffer from a bad apathy as well from a bad activity. But in the past we have suffered much more from the activity than the apathy. If we heard news in the contrary sense, if we heard that Ministers were showing splendid zeal and public spirit in speeding up the new science, if we heard the Bill was to be piloted through in a night or the triumph accomplished by patriotic unanimity at a stroke, we should know wha sort of thing to suspect and the word and the memory to mark it; Marconi.

* * * *

AN actress recently returned from America has been remarking on the Americanisation of London; which must very much spoil the natural pleasure of such a return. All true travel is a roundabout way of going home. It is the deliberate search for strange things that familiar things may lose, if not the atmosphere of familiarity at least the atmosphere of contempt. But the great travellers would have been very reasonably annoyed if when they were full of the radiant finality of home-coming they found themselves only welcomed with the wild spectacle of foreign parts. Captain Cook would have been decidedly distressed if on sailing into the port of Plymouth and looking with affection on the spires and roofs of home he had found all the English practising cannibalism or tattooing themselves in the manner of the Fiji Islanders. We do not see why it should be impossible for the English traveller to rediscover his own island without finding it fantasti-

cally disfigured in the manner of a Fiji island. There is much that is striking and interesting about the flaming advertisements of Broadway, as about the flambeaux flourished in the torch dances of many tribes. But we think it an inferior substitute for the fine curve of the great crescent of Regent Street; which really recalls a passage in our history and the classic spirit of an age. Americanism in America is an interesting and even admirable thing; and if we have to travel to see it it is in the same position as the Parisian atmosphere of Paris or the Roman air of Rome. But America in England is vulgar in quite a different sense from the suggestion that Americanism in itself is necessarily vulgar. A great many of the more glaring American features which look ghastly in London do not look so unnatural in New York. Everything is glaring there; the sky, the sun, the hard light that picks out everything with a point like steel; the architecture that has sprung up to the sky to suit the narrow island on which it stands. But there is another reason why this sort of Americanisation must be resolutely resisted in England. It is never by any chance the good things of a nation that are borrowed in this way. Especially never the popular things. Plutocracy borrows from plutocracy; but the poor seldom borrow from the poor; because communications are less easy. The poor remain therefore the most national in all nations one of the many respects in which they remain the most normal.

* * * *

WE are often reminded that the march of liberal and humanitarian ideas can now never be arrested, and it is interesting to observe in confirmation of this the statement that America proposes to substitute "a soldier for a lawyer as head of the Prohibition forces," and that the methods of this military gentleman (in dealing with any ship that he happens not to like the look of) are expressed in the formula "Shoot first and ask questions afterwards." But ships are by no means the only vessels in which prohibited liquor is conveyed to American citizens. Perambulators have been used before now; so perhaps the soldier had better shoot whenever he sees a suspicious perambulator. Even babies have turned out to be bottles of whisky, carried in a convincing embrace by a lady in widow's weeds. Several incidents of the sort were seriously reported from the Canadian frontier. So perhaps the warrior had better bring up his guns whenever he sees a sinister looking baby; or a widowed lady he does not happen to know. There are a great many precedents for this method of legal inquiry; by first committing a murder and then interrogating a corpse. Wild feudal Scotland satirised it as Jedwood Justice. But this Prohibitionist proposal, about the soldier shooting at sight, seems to be serious, for it is reported in the paper most sympathetic with Prohibition. It is also a paper opposed to Militarism.

* * * *

WE hope that equally drastic methods will not be adopted by the Hairpin King, who is announced as having arrived in London to make war on bobbed and shingled heads. He is called Sol. H. Goldberg, an arrangement of words and letters that may reveal to the prejudiced both his immediate citizenship and his remoter racial origins. We do not know how he is going to make war on the new coiffure; but we hope he will not be quite so decisive in his action as the parallel gentleman who makes war on the old drink of humanity. We hope he will not stick hairpins into ladies first and ask questions afterwards. Indeed, it seems possible that the ladies will ask questions. We hope he will not suddenly skewer a young woman in the street merely to attract her attention to the arguments (many of them very sound) which he advances against the recent fashion. Yet he would have more justification than the other man, for a man can only suspect that the ship may carry whisky; whereas he may have much more than a moral certainty that a lady with a shaven head does not carry hairpins. There have been a great many murders, at any rate in the murder stories, successfully committed, if not with hair-pins at least with hat-pins. Which raises another interesting question: when we have universal disarmament, shall we have a definition of arms? Or will they forbid all the instruments with which people have been killed, from tintacks to tea-kettles?

*   *   *   *

THE dinner in commemoration of Charles Lamb, which happened to come too late for comment last week, was a very triumphant success, for Mr. Augustine Birrell was in the chair, and he is the very best imaginable individual to speak on the subject since Mr. E. V. Lucas obstinately refuses to speak at all. The arrangements and accessories of the joke were not unworthy of it; especially the quotations from Lamb set out on the menu to mark each course of the meal. Nevertheless, there was one small matter which marks perhaps a change of manner. If Charles Lamb's friends had given him a festive dinner with a farcical bill of fare, the very first thing they would have thought of providing for Lamb would be Lamb. The modern fancy shrinks from this sort of obvious and outrageously simple joke. But the great age of Elia and the Essayists did not. As they liked the clown to knock down the policeman with a leg of mutton, they would have applauded the buffoon who knocked down Elia with a leg of lamb. At the worst they would have said that the worst pun is the best. They had no refined prejudice that the best pun is the worst point. They must go to the limbo of the punsters with Homer and Shakespeare and the other barbarians. Mr. Birrell said truly that we hear far too much of the delicate element in Elia; and too little of the robust element. That incessant pummelling of each other with puns is a good example. For the rest, there was one other curious gap in the excellent banquet. There was no trace of Roast Pig.

*   *   *   *

IT seems that a Mr. Wiggan has started talking about Eugenics again in America, that home of lost causes. A home of lost causes has its virtues as well as its faults; and there is really a sort of chivalry and fighting spirit about the way in which these hopeless things are tackled again and again by that really spirited race. The Americans really have all the advantages of high spirits, which are quite a different thing from fresh ideas. They have also the disadvantages of high spirits; one of which is the wasting of a vast amount of time on trifles and things that come to nothing. But the eugenic spirit of Mr. Wiggan is a very different thing from the eugenic spirit of Dean Inge, who seems to combine a conscious feeling that nothing is any good but eugenics with a subconscious doubt about whether eugenics are any good.

No such civilised subtleties seem to disturb Mr. Wiggan. His programme, as described in the American press, is a political programme. Apparently he would have grades of men established by law; with a beautiful innocence about the grade in which most other men would probably put him, if they were asked. He does not seem to answer the question of why he should judge them instead of their judging him. He does not, so far as we know, explain how heredity can be traced through five generations, each one of which will profess a different scientific theory on the subject. For instance, if extremes neutralise each other, they may produce a moderate result; if they break up again into extremes, they may produce madness. But there seems to be plenty of that being produced anyhow.

*   *   *   *

WE have received a number of communications in the form of answers to Mr. Belloc's two examination papers; one of which we print elsewhere as an example of the interest they aroused, and possibly as the beginning of what might be a rather new and entertaining journalistic game. Nevertheless it was very humane of Mr. Belloc to say that candidates need only answer a small number of questions; as there were a number of exceedingly important questions which we believe that nobody in England, outside a very small and often secretive minority, would be able to answer. We noticed with interest that the questions to which replies were offered were generally those dealing rather with theory than with facts. At least people seemed to take a particular interest in every kind of theory except that which is called theology. One gentleman said that theological questions did not interest him; quite arrogantly for all the world as if it were something to be proud of. As a matter of fact, the refusal to go to the roots of thought is responsible for a great deal of failure in the fruits of it.

*   *   *   *

IN this paper, we may as well say frankly thus early in its career, we must refuse to observe the modern delicacy which leaves out all allusions to the origin of the world or the only reason for doing anything. We fully recognise that we live in a world of religious divisions, and still more of religous doubts; and that, as seen by the commonsense of that community as it stands, our own religion or any other religion is not so much a religion as an opinion. But we cannot for the life of us understand why it should be the only opinion about which there is no liberty of opinion. We cannot understand why it is improper of us to defend what it is proper of everybody else to assail. This paper is in no sense directly connected with any such matter; it exists to maintain an ethical and economic, but most certainly not an ecclesiastical interest. But the human beings who write in it are human beings and have a right to express the various sides of their human nature. There is no reason why they should not defend their creeds when they are insulted. We shall always endeavour to give a fair scope for the other creeds or traditions when they conceive themselves insulted. But we have had far too much of this agnostic decorum; this new sort of Bowdlerisation and Censorship, which expurgates from human books and speeches not what is worst in the works of man, but what is best.

BANK HOLIDAYS

THE season called Easter is chiefly famous for containing two Bank Holidays. Bank Holidays, as their name implies, are institutions established by the moral authority of the Banks, like everything else in our ordered and dignified civilisation. Whether the season of Easter ever had any other significance, of some sentimental or superstitious kind, it is now idle to inquire. Allusions have been found in the newspapers to St. Lubbock; who was perhaps (as has been said) a hermit famous for his austerity and holy poverty, and especially for being infested with insects, which he had the saintly humility to describe as one of the Pleasures of Life. But these legends and links with another age need not concern us now. The nature of the Bank Holiday is expressed in its title; as the Bishop of Bumblebury said in his sermon at the dedication of the new wing of the Bank of England: " We may well lift up our hearts in solemn thanksgiving to that great Unknowable Power whose movements we may vaguely feel as finding expression in the Bank Rate; but which, we may well hope, possesses merciful as well as terrible attributes, since it gives us these beautiful holidays."

But although the foundations of the system are well assured, it has hardly yet taken on the character of an historic institution, adorned as such an institution should be with ritual and symbol. It has been suggested that we should preserve the few faint suggestions that remain from the lost legends about Easter, and incorporate them in a ceremonial system more fitted to our own use. A New Calendar for Easter is being drawn up, upon a principle which will make the whole season pivot more positively upon the two Bank Holidays, and express the fundamental principles of banking; only a few points in the scheme, however, are sufficiently settled to be noted here.

The Sunday at the beginning of Easter week is called for some unknown reason Palm Sunday; and in many descriptions of politics and high finance there is a frequent reference to some ceremony connected with palm-oil, which antiquaries have often tried to reconstruct. In any case it has been decided to dedicate this day to one of the most distinguished cadets of one of the greatest of the banking houses. It is to commemorate the occasion of Sir Herbert Samuel entering Jerusalem.

Until the establishment of the Bank Holiday, the name of Good Friday seems to have suggested nothing except the sale of some particular kind of bun, marked with a cross. For those who have a faint sentiment about the symbol, it may well be noted that the new civilisation has already retained it in a nobler form. The day will no longer be sacred to the crossing of buns, but to the crossing of cheques. In this connection we may also note some lingering allusions to some mysterious object called a Passover which was probably a primitive form of Passbook.

The full programme for the ceremonial of Easter Sunday, especially the reading of the First and Second Lessons from the First and Second Ledgers; the temple with its columns of gold inscribed with columns of figures; the new arithmetical hymns consisting entirely of numbers and free from any trace of dogma; all this may be described on a future occasion. To-day is a Bank Holiday.

EFFICIENCY—AND EFFECT

THE very interesting remarks of Sir Michael Sadler have raised the less interesting discussion, so familiar in the press, about academic culture, with its classical foundations, and its contrast with utilitarian instruction in science or commerce. The man of independent intelligence will probably have long reached the state of reaction once admirably described by Mr. J. C. Squire, in connection with old and new schools of art. We think of the don sitting in his select circle of academic " authorities," with that air of acid amiability that pervades universities all over the world. We recognise his proof that Stonehenge does not stand on Salisbury Plain; and how nobody must contradict him, because " Stonehenge is his Subject." And after settling down into that still atmosphere of cloisters and quadrangles, that world of ripe scholarship and refined debate, a man might very well stagger to his feet, saying " Take me to Leeds! Waft me to Liverpool! Take me to the foggiest, filthiest, most smoking and stinking place in the Black Country; for I can bear no more." But when he was taken to Leeds or Liverpool, when he was set down among the bustling and businesslike instructors, when he saw all the beautiful diagrams of physiology or engineering, when active and resolute men swarmed about him seeking to bear him away to a lecture on Steel Houses or a Commercial Correspondence Class, then if he were really independent and intelligent, he would fling himself to the ground groaning: " Take me to Balliol; hide me in a quad; bury me under a book-case; and let wild dons dance upon my grave." Such are the disadvantages of independent intelligence.

Now of course there is a great deal to be said against the old academic tradition in England. And nobody is better qualified than Sir Michael Sadler to attack the old social culture; because he himself attacks what he himself possesses. He is certainly not the ordinary commercial utilitarian; full of that spirit which the charity of Mr. Arnold Bennett has taught us to call the Card, but which we are sometimes tempted to call the Cad. He is certainly not the common scientific materialist, who sees every object as if it were a slightly deformed organ preserved in spirits; of the sort that may certainly be called low spirits. He is a man understanding something of tradition; and like most men with a sympathy for tradition, one having a sympathy also with liberty. If he appears on the side of the Moderns against the Ancients, it means that there really is something to be said against the Ancients. And there really is a great deal to be said against them, as they appear in their academic guise in this country. It is a mistake, for instance, to class Greek and Latin together at all; a mortal mistake to class them together as dead languages. It is true in one sense that Greek is dead although it is immortal. Latin is not dead at all. Anybody can hear it talked as a living language every morning, if he gets up early enough and knows where to go. If people were taught Latin and French together they would learn the real Outline of History. Nevertheless there is a sense in which even the don with his dead languages is right, where the whole living world is wrong.

He is right because he is concerned not with Efficiency but with Effect. It is the mental weakness of all the upholders of Efficiency that they simply stare at us in mystification if we ask them about Effect. To have a fastidious taste in sausages, even to like them burned very dry and black, is more intelligent than to worship a sausage-machine. And the pleasures of pedantry are pleasures and not merely processes. The snuffy old don who still likes to murmur as he reads for the thousandth time *formosam resonare doces Amaryllida silvas* has got something out of education. It is he and not the business man who fulfils the business phrase. It is he emphatically who gets results. It is he emphatically who is a result. He is perhaps a rather disappointing result. He is perhaps a rather deplorable specimen, to be the product of the high passion of great poets and the heroic citizenship of lost civilisations. But his enjoyment is a product of these things and it is enjoyable. He does get something out of his education. It is not much, if it does not make him wish rather to go out and shout in the woods than to shuffle about in the quad. It is not much, if it does not make him forget his petty and pedantic superiorities of social status and education, if it does not withdraw him towards the people as the poets were drawn towards the shepherds; if it does not fill him in some measure with the largeness, the liberty and the humanity of Virgil.

But it is an Effect and not a mere miserable Efficiency. His pleasure, so far as it goes, is the pleasure at which culture is directed; it is the thing to be cultivated and not an iron and rigid array of pitchforks and harrows and agricultural instruments. He is so far greater, in the sense that William Blake meant when he said that the rat and the beetle watch the roots, but the lion and the eagle the fruits. Efficiency is useless until it has effected something as subtle and insoluble as the loveliness of the Virgilian line. Business is barren until it has built up some place or situation in whch a man can have that idle joy. Science is meaningless till a man can find in the whole material universe something that pleases him as a man is pleased with a Latin tag. What is the matter with the pedant is generally that he is not pleased enough with the Latin tag, or not pleased in the right way, or not pleased so as to enlarge his conception of pleasure. What is the matter with his culture is not that it is classical but that it is not classical enough; not that it is traditional but that it is not traditional enough; not that it is literary but that it is not literary enough; not that it is unworldly but that it is not unworldly enough. But it is something; and he does get something out of being educated. The practical man gets nothing out of being educated. He gets nothing even out of being uneducated.

Before it was called Efficiency it used to be called Effort. The Victorians moralised about it before the Anti-Victorians discovered it. Carlyle, with his Gospel of Work, had called it creative before the new realists had the bright idea of calling it constructive. It means constructing ships without knowing where you want to sail and flying-machines without knowing whether you really want to fly; it means everlastingly elongating the speaking-trumpets when there is nothing to say and equipping everybody with ear-trumpets when there is nothing to hear; it means building cities for other men to think ugly and making roads along which other men

will grow tired; and drugging yourself against this dreary prospect by the mere excitement or illusion of doing something, when in truth you are doing nothing; and not doing it gracefully. Against that monstrous modern delusion even the poor old don stands up in a sort of feeble protest; for he is not merely an advertisement of what he himself is doing, but a monument of what the mighty world has done for him. He is an Effect; he is a human being who has derived a certain amount of human happiness from something that he could not have gained for himself. And he does in some dim way testify that the end of our being is not a servile and materialistic "endeavour," but a freedom and a fruition and a joy.

A Child's Zoological Garden of Verses

IF I had an elephant and he was white,
    I'd go for a ride on him every night;
    For Jumbo would shine so bright you see,
That motors would never run into me.

The lion has a hairy mane,
So has the lion's brother,
The lion's wife hasn't any—so
That's how the little lion cubs know
Which lion is their mother.

The tiger is striped and he lives in a cage,
And he always seems in a most terrible rage;
If I had a suit like the tiger's, I know
I'd be proud that the people should stare at me so.

The bear goes climbing up the pole
As if it were a stair,
But I can't see—it makes me frown—
Why—just because the bear is brown,
He's not a *polar* bear.

The crocodile is dead you think,
He simply lies and lies,
But just each now and then he'll wink
His wicked little eyes.
And he would gulp you in a trice
From toes right up to forehead;
Most animals are *somehow* nice
Excepting him—he's horrid.

You mustn't laugh at the Giraffe
Whose neck's so long and slim;
If both your hands were feet, you see,
And food grew only on a tree,
I know you'd jolly soon agree
You'd want an extra limb—
Besides he needs your sympathy
When you've a stiff neck how you cry!
Well—think of *him*.

                                        M. B. R.

An Outline of Creative Evolution

THE higher that you get
        In Creative Evolution
    The drier you will get,
        This is why
Gentle Reader you and I
        Are dry.
    It is also why the oyster
        Is comparatively wet
And the jelly-fish is moister.
                        GEOFFREY DEARMER.

MRS. MARKHAM'S HISTORY OF ENGLAND
About Lawyers

MRS. MARKHAM: And now to-day, my dears, I will tell you about lawyers.

MARY: Oh! Mamma! What fun! What fun! (*She dances about*).

TOMMY (*eagerly*): Indeed, dear Mamma, I am all on fire to hear about them also!

MRS. MARKHAM: Very well, my dears, then the first thing you must know is what lawyers are good for.

MARY: I was just going to ask that, Mamma, when . . .

MRS. MARKHAM: Mary, dear! You must not interrupt! I was saying " What are lawyers good for? What is their use? " Well, they have three uses—and you must carefully attend to this. *First* they condemn people to prison and even to death.

TOMMY: I am glad to hear that, Mamma!

MAMMA: Wait a moment! Their *second* use is to explain the law: to show us all what it really means.

MARY: I confess, dear Mamma, that I have been not a little puzzled. Are not our laws written in English?

MAMMA: Yes, my dear, and they are as plain as it is possible for honest men and women to make them: nevertheless, they must be *interpreted* when there is any difficulty.

TOMMY: What kind of difficulty, Mamma?

MAMMA: Why, for instance, the law says no one may bet on a horse in any *place*. That sounds plain enough, does it not?

TOMMY: Yes, indeed!

MAMMA: Well, think a little, what is a place?

TOMMY: Oh! Mamma, we all know what a place is. Really, I don't see what else it can be but a place.

MAMMA: Exactly, my dear, *you cannot describe it:* but until someone *does* describe it for us and tell us exactly what " a place " means, it is impossible to apply the law. Now the lawyers looked thoroughly into the matter and proved that a *place* meant any place where vulgar loose people bet, such as streets, public houses, etc. But a place where proper people and indeed lawyers themselves bet—such as a racecourse or a good bookmaker's office— is not a place. You see how important that is! No one would have known it exactly if the lawyers had not been there to explain it all.

MARY (*absorbed*): Oh! Mamma! this is *most* interesting! Can you give us another example?

MAMMA: Yes, my dear; for instance, in East Africa a Hippopotamus comes under Wild Birds and is protected as such: " *all* " licensed premises during the war were shut at certain hours, but " *all*," it was found, meant all *except* a tavern near the Temple and the drinking bars of the House of Commons: justice " *free* " to all is proved to mean " *free after due payment* ": there are hundreds of others. Indeed we should never be certain about the exact meaning of anything but for the lawyers. They also decide how much truth or untruth a witness may tell in a case and when and where and how and if, or if not. They are here invaluable.

TOMMY: And what is their third function, Mamma?

MAMMA: I am glad to hear you use that word " function," my dear. Pray use it as often as ever you can. Well, then, the third use to which we put lawyers is that of *arguing*.

MARY: But, Mamma, we can all do that!

MAMMA: Yes, my dear, so can we all speak: but we cannot all speak as well or as long or as loudly as Mr. Lloyd George or Mr. Handel Booth, or Mr. Bottomley: and they are called Public Speakers, therefore, as being specially gifted. And so it is with lawyers. They are trained to argue better and at much greater length than any ordinary person: and that is their third function.

MARY: Pray, Mamma, what is the longest any of them has argued at one time?

MAMMA: I have heard your father say that one of them, called Sir William Wugg, once argued for five whole days, with intervals for food and sleep.

MARY: Good gracious!

MAMMA: Yes, indeed! He was evidently a most talented man.

TOMMY: But, Mamma, what do they argue about?

MAMMA: I will give you an example. A man takes away your money. To try and get it back you must go before a lawyer called a " Judge " in what is called a " Court of Justice."

TOMMY (*surprised*): May I not take my own money back myself?

MAMMA: No! Certainly not! That would be most un-English! And if you even *tried* to do such a thing another lawyer would certainly send you to prison.

MARY: Oh! how *interesting* it all is, Mamma!

MAMMA: Well, you go before the lawyer and say " I want my money back." Then the person who took it hires another lawyer (or several, if he has taken a large sum), and pays them to *argue* that he did not take it; or that if he did he cannot be blamed; or that even if he can be blamed he must not be asked to give it back, and so on.

TOMMY: Then where should I come in, Mamma?

MAMMA: Why, my dear, you must then hire yet another lawyer in your turn—or several, if you have enough money left—and then your lawyer or lawyers and his lawyer or lawyers argue for several days, and the lawyer who listens to them, and is called a Judge as I have said, marks the points, or score, and decides at the end which side has won.

MARY: Does the best arguer win, Mamma?

MAMMA: Not always, my dear. Sometimes the Judge has very good private or public reasons for deciding one way though all the best argument has been on the other.

TOMMY: Then, I see, Mamma! The man may keep my money after all?

MAMMA: My dear, he always keeps the money. That is common sense: for he took it and so now he has it. But the important thing is that the lawyer called "the Judge" decides whether he *ought* to keep it or not. Sometimes he decides one way, sometimes the other.

MARY: How wonderful it all is!

MAMMA: Yes, indeed, my dear, it is most wonderful. People come from all over the world to learn to be like our lawyers, but they never succeed.

TOMMY: Do not all the lawyers become very rich, since they are paid to argue like this?

MAMMA: Not all, my dear: but all good ones do. Of course, as in all professions, idle ones become quite poor, and some have even to write for the papers.

TOMMY: Oh! Mamma, that sounds very sad! A lawyer who has to be a mere writer!

MAMMA: Yes, my dear, it is. But I am glad to say it is very rare. And most of them do quite well out of arguing and condemning to death and explaining what ordinary words really mean. The very richest become lords: and even the poorest are hardly ever sent to gaol.

TOMMY: And are the lawyers who are called Judges paid also, Mamma?

MAMMA: Yes, my dear, and so are other lawyers who get up the arguments and are called solicitors. They are paid over and over again.

TOMMY: I think, dear Mamma, when I grow up I shall become a lawyer.

MAMMA: By all means, my dear, if you have the suitable talents, I am sure your father and I would approve: but I have told you enough for to-day. Next time . . .

MARY: Next time, Mamma, will you not talk about Kangaroos?

MAMMA: Not till I have told you about the Police, my dear. It is most important you should learn about them because people who make mistakes about Policemen suffer terribly in later life. So next time we will talk about Policemen, Magistrates, Prisoners, Gallows, and all that sort of thing.

MARY: Thank you, dear Mamma, I shall greatly look forward to it.   H. BELLOC.

UTOPIAS UNLIMITED

II—Concerning Grocers as Gods

MR. WILLIAM WILLIAMS was a grocer's assistant. For many years the grocer had groced and the assistant had assisted; but of late his employer had begun to have doubts of whether he was of much assistance; and one bright and brisk spring morning he rather suddenly and dramatically ceased to assist.

As Mr. Stiggles was one of the three competing shopkeepers of a small village by the seaside, his shop had something of the general character of a village shop; and he sold several things that may or may not be defined as groceries; such as certain large vials of Home-Made Lemonade which it was William's duty at that moment to set prominently in the window. Some had been known to question some of the titles attached to the goods of Mr. Stiggles. Some had murmured that his superfine sugar had suffered contact with his sandy floor; and that his celebrated Fresh Eggs were ornaments rather of an ornathological museum than a shop. But nobody had ever disputed the title of Home-Made Lemonade; or doubted that Mr. Stiggles made it himself, by some recipe as secret as that of the Benedictine monks. Many believed sea-water to be the staple, but there was a suggestion of soap; and other ingredients such as verdigris and chopped-up grass were suspected. Mr. Stiggles came into his shop with sudden violence, to find William hurriedly concealing a cigarette; for Mr. Stiggles disapproved of smoking. It was perhaps the only suggestion of a moral sense that he ever exhibited.

"Why aren't those things in the window?" he demanded. "Pinker and Bootle have both got theirs out. Why don't you put 'em in the front where they can be seen?"

"Oh, all right," said William with a sinister air of languor. He lifted one of the large lemonade bottles and hurled it with a crash through the front window, so that it made a star of green liquid and broken glass on the cobbled street. "I should think it could be seen there," he added.

He then left the shop in a leisurely manner, and when Mr. Stiggles demanded what he was going to do, he explained.

"I'm going to pick pockets," he said. "I'm going to live with thieves and thugs and burglars. I want a little honest company."

Mr. William Williams left his village grocer, full of a fine fury against the mean tricks of grocers in competition, but he did not have any chance of comparing their morals with those of thieves; for before he could attempt it, he met somebody who profoundly influenced his life, and gave him a larger view of thieving and other things. This was a tall man he met in a lane; a man with long wisps of hair and a wide hat; he had a very kindly and encouraging smile and bulging eyes like a mesmerist's. Perhaps he mesmerised William; anyhow he made him feel very happy and good; telling him how there was a land beyond the sea where everybody was happy and good without the least apparent trouble; for instead of two grocers fighting like cat and dog, there was one common fellowship and unity of interests between the grocer and the groced.

So William went away across the sea with the old gentleman, who was called the Prophet Hinks, and somewhere on the shining plains of America he found the shining city. It was certainly very calm and beautiful to look at, with terraces of white not divided into separate houses, but marked by doors at intervals all painted an exquisite peacock green and flanked by little shrubs in little tubs, to show that the new civilisation was not indifferent to art and beauty. But the chief thing that struck William about the new civilisation, when he came to study it, was that he could not get a cigarette there. He thought at first he might get it in the Vegetarian Hostel, as tobacco is a vegetable; but his argument was sadly waved away. He thought he might look for it in the House of Joy, otherwise called (out of William Morris) "The House of Fulfilment of Craving"; but though he had a very definite craving, he could not get it fulfilled. Then he lost his temper and said:

"If you're so fond of giving people plants in little tubs, I shall grow a tobacco-plant in my little tub."

"*Your* little tub?" said the Prophet Hints in low and heart-broken tones. "*Your* little tub! How little you have understood the spirit that is here!"

And indeed he found that Professor Hinks and his Committee were the owners of the ground as well as the buildings; and that nothing could be done that they did not want to do themselves. So he thoughtfully picked up the red Russian bowl, in which his luke-warm water had been served to him that morning, and threw that also through the window with a loud crash.

"Stiggles was a stinking rat," he observed, "but at least he was only my employer and not also my landlord and my lord and my god. I'd rather go back to where they fight each other like rats, and at least show they are alive."

So he strode away and betook himself homewards; and the nearer he came to home the more his reaction rose within him and his heart went out to the rough-and-tumble tradition of his fathers. He wanted to go back to a human place, where there was a little human and kindly hatred; where everything was not chilled and frozen with universal Love. It would be fine to see the two grocers fighting in the streets, and to take sides in the funny old family quarrels; and perhaps to find friendship and marriage as well as quarrels, and try his luck at bringing up a family and die and be buried in his own land.

When he entered his own village he stood still and stared down the principal street. There were two long perspectives of stately classical buildings, along the whole frontage of which on both sides ran an inscription in gigantic golden letters. "Stiggles's Universal Stores." There was no other shop or house visible in the circle of the horizon. The solid block was divided into a series of departments, flanked by little shrubs in little tubs, to show that the new system was not indifferent to art and beauty.

What struck Mr. William Williams most about the new system established by Stiggles's Stores was that he could not get a cigarette there. For Mr. Stiggles (now indeed a nobleman) retained the one moral principle in his life. He would really have felt it an unclean and unholy thing to have gained a little more money by selling the nicotian poison along with the various quack medicines, widely advertised and dangerous drugs, alcoholic cures for achoholism and other home comforts that were provided at his Stores. But outside this honourable scruple, it really seemed that the Universal Stores was really universal, in the sense that it did really possess an inferior form of almost everything in the world. Artists might buy their colours there if they did not want the right colours; musicians might purchase violins and church organs cheaply and rapidly manufactured; indeed, people had been known to order a cathedral from Stiggles, who had put it up with the utmost rapidity, neatness and dispatch. Mr. William Williams wondered whether there was something inherently wrong in his own character, whereby a strange discontent seemed still to possess him even in the most smooth and satisfactory social conditions. His mind began to revert with another unreasoning and sentimental reaction to all the real simplicity of the lunatic under the luminous American sky. They had at least in some sort of half-witted way been looking for things that are too good for this world. William was beginning in a puzzled way to tell the people in the shop about his American adventure; but when he came to mention the name of the Prophet Hinks, they were filled with horror; and the sort of pity that is akin to loathing. "He is a Socialist!" they cried, "and Socialism is fatal to individuality."

At which Mr. Williams gave a great cry, and seizing a yellow Oriental vase from the counter, he hurled it through the window with a loud crash and leapt after it, running wildly down the street and waving his arms. For he remembered that, in the days of his childhood, there had been a dark and depressing pool just beyond the bridge, which many suicides had found suitable and convenient. But in this he was intercepted; for although this enlightened community had, of course, long outgrown any prejudice against suicide, they preferred things done in a decent and orderly fashion. So he was conducted to Stiggles's Lethal Chamber in Stiggles's Death Department; and was afterwards enclosed in one of the fashionable and universally coveted Stiggles Coffins and buried in the popular and universally frequented Stiggles Cemetery. So he had his prayer, as is given to few mortals, and died and was buried in the village that was his home.

The King's Highway

OH, the ringing hoofs of horses on the King's Highway,
How they tinkle, first crescendo, then afar, diminuendo,
Making music, making gladness on the King's Highway.

Oh, the gliding of the cycles on the King's Highway,
How they gently swerve and bend, how their lamps like jewels lend
A glory and a glamour to the King's Highway.

Oh, the grinding traction engine on the King's Highway,
Rude of form and hard of feature, like some megalithic creature,
And yet kindly of intention on the King's Highway.

Oh, the buzzing of the motors on the King's Highway;
How they rush unto their end, bringing swiftly friend to friend,
Bringing dole or healing swiftly on the King's Highway.
                                        FANNY JOHNSON.

FOUND WANDERING
By G. K. CHESTERTON.
A POLITICIAN ON PURGATORY

WHEN politicians stoop to the Church question, even journalists may aspire to it. Sir William Joynson-Hicks, the Home Secretary of the present Government, has been addressing some remarks to a crowd in the Albert Hall; remarks on which I should prefer to comment in this purely personal column. For in this column I am rather a contributor than an editor. I do not commit any of my colleagues or allies in this enterprise to what is, after all, a matter for the individual (loud Protestant cheers, from the Albert Hall).

The Home Secretary is reported as saying "We want no priestly interference, we ask for no purgatory, and we will submit to no compulsory confessional." The last clause of this declaration is especially a great relief to our minds. No longer shall we see a policeman seizing a man in the street by the scruff of his neck and dragging him to the nearest confessional-box. No longer will our love of liberty be outraged by the sinister bulk of Black Maria taking its daily gang of compulsory penitents to Westminster Cathedral. The chief social sinners of our day will no longer be forcibly attired in white sheets and driven to the door of the priest at the point of the spear. All that is to be altered now; auricular confession is no longer a part of the British Constitution, to be enforced with fixed bayonets. It is to be left freely to the choice and even the caprice of individuals, like all other matters of opinion in a truly modern state. It is to be as voluntary as attendance at a particular type of State school is for the children of the poor. It is to be left as freely to individual choice as is a particular scheme of health insurance for the working classes. It is to be as much outside the law as a particular medical theory of the curative power of cowpox. It is to be as completely voluntary as education in a modern state. It is to be as completely free as military service in a modern war. A government will no more dream of forcing a free man to confess his sins than of forcing him to insure his servants or vaccinate his children. Whatever else we may think of that Protestant progress that has led up to the modern state, everybody knows at least that in every department the modern state has abandoned the idea of compulsion. Some have even doubted whether we shall establish Prohibition.

But the passage that interests me, even more than the repeal of all the Coercion Acts that have hitherto imposed the Confessional on the English people, is the singular phrase that comes before it. I pass over the phrase "We want no priestly interference" as having worn a little too thin to hold many threads of thought; but I pause upon the very remarkable phrase "We ask for no purgatory." I do not pause merely for the obvious flippancy about the man who went further and fared worse. I do not even ask Sir William of what it is that he feels so secure that he needs no transition stage. The strictly logical inference, from a man needing no purgatory, is either that he has nothing to be purged away or that he does not want anything purged away. But these spiritual speculations are no business of ours. What interests me is not the strictly religious or theological, but the generally philosophical and logical attitude implied in saying those strange words, "We ask for no purgatory." I mean the attitude, not so much towards theological truth as towards any truth; towards the very idea of truth. It seems to imply that when Sir William reaches the gates of another world, S. Peter or some well-trained angel will say to him in a slightly lowered voice, in the manner of a well-trained butler, "Would you be requiring a purgatory?"

Perhaps a parallel may be to the point. When we of a certain philosophy open the papers and find them full of articles about Science and Religion or the Future of the Churches, we know pretty well the scope of the discussion. Our eye travels rapidly down the column until it picks out the capital G at the beginning of Galileo; and having seen that this item has been duly inserted, we are satisfied and turn to our ordinary avocations. The people who write these articles can be relied on not to disappoint us. And as Galileo is evidently the only astronomer they have ever heard of, and the stricture upon him by the Inquisitors the only decision of the Church they have ever heard of, it is natural that they should judge a great many matters in the light of this incident, so far as they are acquainted with it. I will not attempt here to extend that acquaintance at any length. I might state a number of things about Galileo that are not without interest. I might point out that whatever else he was, he was not the man they are admiring; the man who suffered for making the first suggestion that the earth goes round the sun. I might advance the paradox that the Copernican theory was propounded by Copernicus. I might point out that Copernicus taught astronomy at Rome under orthodox official authority. I might point out that long before even Copernicus stated it, it had been suggested in the very middle of the Middle Ages by Cusa; and that the persecuting Church proceeded to persecute him by making him a Cardinal. The truth is, I fancy, the very opposite of the suggestion commonly made. Galileo was not blamed for opening the question but for closing it. What annoyed people was that he said: "*Galileus locutus est; causa finita est*," or, in modern scientific language, that he said the thing had passed from a hypothesis to a law. What especially annoyed people, I believe, was that he declared the theory could be found in the Bible; a very annoying habit in anybody. But all this, though amusing in many ways, is familiar to everybody except those who are always mentioning it. And it is not in this controversial connection that I originally mentioned the name of the great Italian. Those who glorify that name so regularly and so inaccurately are in the habit of adding an anecdote which is also, I believe, inaccurate. They say that as he turned away from the tribunal which had denied the motion of the earth, he murmured, "And yet it moves." And whether he said it or not, he and the Inquisitors would at least have agreed that it either moved or didn't, and that neither they nor he could make any difference to the fact, whatever it might be.

But it never occurs to Sir William Joynson-Hicks that when he says, "We ask for no purgatory," it is exactly as if all the Catholics answered all the champions of Galileo by rising and saying in a chorus, "We ask for no Solar System." If they did, it might begin to dawn on Sir William Joynson-Hicks that the Solar System can exist whether we like it or not, and that Purgatory may exist whether he likes it or not. If it be true, however incredible it may seem, that the powers ruling the universe think that a politician or a lawyer can reach the point of death, without being in that perfect ecstacy of purity that can see God and live—why then there may be cosmic conditions corresponding to that paradox, and there is an end of it. It may be obvious to us that the politician is already utterly sinless, at one with the saints. It may be self-evident to us that the lawyer is already utterly selfless, filled only with God and forgetful of the very meaning of gain. But if the cosmic power holds that there are still some strange finishing touches, beyond our fancy, to be put to his perfection, then certainly there will be some cosmic provision for that mysterious completion of the seemingly complete. The stars are not clean in His sight and His angels He chargeth with folly; and if He should decide that even in a Home Secretary there is room for improvement, we can but admit that omniscience can heal the defect that we cannot even see.

We heard a great deal in our youth about the reconciliation of Religion and Science, and on one point real religion and real science have always been reconciled. Neither of them will listen to this curious current nonsense about being reconciled to anything that happens to be hanging about. At least they both talk as if there were such a thing as truth, whether or no they think each other's versions of it true. Biologists do not stand up on a platform in the Albert Hall and cry defiantly to a cheering crowd, "We ask for no Great Sea-Serpent." Mass meetings at the Royal Society on the subject of the Higher Mathematics, in their relation to the fixed stars, are not assisted by a politician shouting to a mob, like the old Greek, "What are the Pleiades to me?" Nobody discusses those questions as if they were solely and entirely questions of fashion and fancy; of making things more attractive or merely making them more easy. Doctors do not say that it will attract more medical students to say that spotted fever is the same as chicken-pox, and so solve the problem of "Why the Operating Theatres are Empty." Astronomers do not say that it will be more convenient for young people if the eclipse of the sun is fixed for half-past five instead of half-past six; and so solve the problem of a rising generation indifferent to signs in heaven. Nobody proposes to Brighten geology by finding live fossils in molten larva for the amusement of the young. Nobody proposes to Broaden Botany by saying that fruit-trees can grow like sea-weed without roots. In these departments nobody thinks they can gather figs from thistles or faith from the animals that feed on them. Science reports upon the facts as she finds them; we may sometimes differ about the facts, but not here at least about the nature of fact. In that sense it may truly be said, in the too common contemporary phrase, that science has a message as supernatural religion has a message. The vague visionaries of our time are fond of talking about messages; but apparently not of thinking about them. We do not want a messenger who alters a message.

Once grant that there is such a thing as a supernatural messenger, and almost all the current talk about broadening and brightening the creeds becomes very nearly nonsense. It is quite reasonable under certain circumstances to disbelieve a message. It is not reasonable under any circumstances to distort it. If a man comes to me bringing a message from my mother, asking me to come and see her in a house with a green door opposite the third lamp-post in the Old Kent Road, I either believe the message is real or I do not. I may suspect it to be a plot to entrap or murder me in an opium den, because I know my mother has a horror of the Old Kent Road or a superstitious dislike of green; in that case I shall not go at all. But it is absurd of me to accept it as my mother's message and then say. "Must we believe it is the Old Kent Road? Would it not be more hopeful, more progressive, to think she is in the New Kent Road?" as if she did not know where she was herself; or to say, "Need we agree that the door is green; I always prefer to think of it as blue," as if we were proposing to paint the door instead of proposing to find it. Nobody would allow his mind to get into such a muddle about a real mother and a real door in a real street. And if we refuse in the religious case to imitate that muddle, it is because we do regard our mother as real.

From Pinnacles of Lofty Thought

FROM pinnacles of lofty thought
   A measure of the world is made,
   The mind's keen arrows flying forth
Are shafted truths that unafraid
Send lightnings through Time's shadowed glade.

Yet all the comprehending laws
Are compassed in a tiny brain,
The beauty and the unity
Return to man himself again,
As unto earth returns the rain.   PERCY RIPLEY.

COLE ON COBBETT

By Maurice B. Reckitt.

IF modern journals were to choose for themselves patron heroes, as medieval guilds adopted patron saints, it would be difficult, in the case of G.K.s WEEKLY, to find a stronger candidate for the niche of honour than William Cobbett. It is not merely that a journal seeking to set the problem of democracy in a new light might naturally welcome association with the greatest of English democratic journalists. The tie is something closer than that : closer than the coincidence of the common weapon of journalism, or the spiritual comradeship arising from a common profession of the democratic faith—a profession which Cobbett was not greatly inclined to make as a matter of theory, though he bore ceaseless witness to it for at least thirty years in the sphere of practice. Cobbett belongs to us because his battles belong to us—battles in which, upon the front, at any rate, on which he fought them, few since his day have been willing to engage. He believed in property as a necessary accompaniment of freedom in an age which was forcing the ordinary man to see property only as the necessary accompanient of tyranny. The Industrial Revolution—the most devastating of all revolutions—which made property inhuman, made the lot of property-less man (which very soon meant nearly every man) sub-human; and riches and poverty became alike so unnatural that for those who accepted the revolution which " progress " had wrought, the champion of the ordinary liberties of the ordinary person appeared to be demanding something strange and extravagant—as indeed he still appears.

Cobbett never regarded himself as a revolutionary, and why indeed should he have done so, who stood for values, parties and associations which Cotton Kings and Enclosers were sweeping away with almost catastrophic violence? " We want great alterations but we want nothing new," cried Cobbett on behalf of the Radical movement of his age; and if the modern rebel were only radical enough he could say the same. That the common man should count as a citizen and as a worker; that his livelihood should be at the mercy of none; that he should be free to live in his own land and able to rear his own family; that financier and politician should be the servants of the public interest : these were the causes for which Cobbett contended, yet they appear in the guise of lost causes in 1925 at least as much as they did in 1825. And they are lost to-day not merely, nor chiefly, because they are still defeated, by those who might be expected to attack them, not because they have been so largely abandoned by those who might have been expected to defend them. They are lost, as little Bo-peep's sheep were lost, because when we seek to go to their aid, we do not know where to find them. *The Times* said of Cobbett at his death that " he was incorporated with no portion of our political or social frame." The writer of those words thought that this was a condemnation of Cobbett, whereas it was really a condemnation of the times—and of *The Times* which exemplified so characteristically their smug complacency. Cobbett's demands in their essentials are still incorporated with no portion of our political or social frame : nor is the outlook of G.K.'s WEEKLY. But the causes which at Cobbett's death were lost for so many decades—these it may at least find once again, though it fail, as he did, to establish them.

The relevance of Cobbett's life and writings for this generation is indeed striking. It is not merely that the large issues for which he contended are still those for which we have to fight, for these are of eternal significance and will be alive in some form or another in every age. But the very circumstances in which he worked, the particular quarrels into which he found himself drawn, remind one again and again of the problems of to-day. The burning issues of 1825 are still burning in 1925 and destroying all that comes within their reach; for no one has discovered how to put them out, or if they have so discovered, they have not been allowed to try. The burden of Debt; the results of deflation; the effect of ' benevolent reforms," and of compulsory " education "; the demand for the transportation of the poor under the guise of " emigrating " them; the alleged necessity of restricting the population— these are but a few of the controversies in which Cobbett bore a vigorous part that are still with us in substantially the same form to-day. I open *The Times* on the very morning I am writing this review and find a eulogy of Canning—an opponent of whom Cobbett entertained a particularly poor opinion—which begins with these significant sentences. " It becomes every day more apparent that the rather painful road trodden by our forefathers at the close of the last great war is the same we shall ourselves traverse for the next generation. The circumstances are different, we shall arrive at different solutions, but we shall be dealing with a parallel set of problems." It is more

---

* THE LIFE OF WILLIAM COBBETT, by G. D. H. Cole : with a chapter on *Rural Rides* by the late F. E. Green. Collins, 18s, net,

probable indeed that we shall arrive at no solution; it is certain that the nineteenth century arrived at none, or we should not be presented with " a parallel set of problems " to-day. But if we are to traverse afresh that " rather painful road " to which, after a century of circular progress, we have once again returned, it is well that we should have before us the example of one who challenged so sanely and so brilliantly those very tendencies which Canning and his tribe expressed as the guarantees of an ever enlarging happiness and prosperity.

So let us be grateful to Mr. Cole. He has given us just what we lacked—a life of Cobbett which reveals him not only as a great individual but as a great tribune, " the last great tribune of the Agrarians," who " was, by force of circumstances, also the first great tribune of the industrial proletariat." This book is, if one may be permitted to say so, not only a revelation of Cobbett, it is a revelation of Mr. Cole. It reveals the powers of a real historian, and history is a field in which its author has not until now attempted any serious piece of work. But it reveals something more— the power of sympathetic treatment of ideas and tendencies which the author can only incompletely share. To Mr. Cole as a Socialist—albeit one whose Socialism is heavily " guilded " over with libertarian values and ideas—Cobbett necessarily appears as a reformer, who, if he did not exactly take the wrong turning, at least failed to discover the right one. " The protest as he made it was hopeless . . . he could not give to the new working class a constructive gospel; that could only be adumbrated as yet by the forerunners of Socialism." It is true that Cobbett's talents did not lie in the construction of " new moral worlds "; he did not see the need for new morals, when the troubles that were afflicting his country were chiefly arising from repudiation of the old and permanent ones. He was prepared for change; he was not prepared to welcome any enormity simply because it was a change. It is certainly open to question whether industrialism need have been a change for the worse: for Cobbett there was no question that, in the forms it was taking, it was a change for the worse. If he had been told that the rule of factory kings and the corrupt politicians who served them had to be accepted as a necessary stage to factory committees and incorruptible bureaucrats, he would have replied that it seemed to him more practical to build the new England on the broad and natural foundations of distributed property and universal freedom than on the narrow and crazy framework of plutocracy. Socialists have spent a century in thinking out ways of making a plutocratic industrial system work in the public interest. Cobbett thought it wiser that it should not begin to work at all. And had the will and the resolution of the majority of his countrymen been as firmly fixed on this object as were his own, it is safe to say that it never would have done. The alliance of aristocracy and capitalism, formed to defeat Napoleon, and continued, as Mr. Cole in his admirable opening chapter shows, to defeat the English people, would have been broken. But the fact which more than any other made Cobbett's task a hopeless one was that the real revolution had taken place two centuries before the spectacular one began. Cobbett's *History of the Protestant Reformation* is not the work of an exact and scientific historian; but it goes to the root of the matter to an extent that even its author did not really suspect. The sixteenth century established the rule of the rich as such: the new technique of the eighteenth century turned that rule into a despotism. If a " constructive gospel " could not be founded on the facts of 1833, the year in which Cobbett entered Parliament, neither could it be based on the philosophy of 1763, the year in which he was born. This was the error of Cobbett—not that he looked backward, but that he did not look backward far enough. He sought too much to conserve: he should have attempted rather to restore.

Mr. Cole says, " I have found the writing of his life a fascinating task." His book shows it. The vigour of Cobbett's style has infected his own, which is more direct and vivid than has always been the case with him. The book is long, as was, indeed, inevitable: its hero lived to be seventy-three, and if ever a man " lived a full life " it was William Cobbett. He left behind him a volume of prose which in sheer quantity, to say nothing of its extraordinarily wide range, must be almost unmatched; yet Mr. Cole shows himself familiar with it all. Again and again he lets Cobbett tell the story in his own words, so that the book is not only a biography, but in large measure that autobiography which the great egotist in his later life often planned but never began. Despite a few repetitions, the interest of the book never flags; though the change of style which the interpolation of Mr Green's chapter involves is not perhaps the advantage which Mr. Cole generously affects to suppose. In this book Mr. Cole fulfils—as he has not always fulfilled—the promise of his first book, *The World of Labour*. Not since *Social Theory* has he given us anything of the same class.

Assuredly he has in this book a splendid subject. Cobbett is that rare combination—a great personality who is also a representative figure of his time. It is thus that Mr. Cole sets out to portray him: " a peasant unclassed," striving for a new foothold of freedom in a world of wheels. " It was fitting symbolism that Cobbett's birthplace was *The Jolly Farmer*. The jolly farmer, through all his vicissitudes he remained," crying out against the new regimentation which, as he complained (though writing on this occasion, for once, in a bad cause) " includes the suppression of mirth." It would be going too far to call him a lovable character. As Mr. Cole justly observes, " Cobbett had none of the Liberal virtues. He was not broad-minded or tolerant, or considerate or forgiving, or humble or charitable, or slow to anger or plenteous in mercy. His morality was of a fighting, self-assertive sort." He could never forget himself. In defending his policy on the Reform Bill, he declared that the workers would soon be convinced " that I am best consulting their good *as well as the preservation of my own character*. Relentless to his enemies, he was hardly more merciful to his friends. " I never was of an accommodating disposition in my life," he proudly declared, and the self accusation was merited. Besides a number of private feuds, he quarrelled continuously with his political associates—with Burdett and Place on the Right, with Hunt, Carlile and Benbow on the Left, thus doing much to establish that fissiparous tendency which has been so persistent a tradition of English reform movements.

But if he had, as men say, the defects of his qualities, those qualities—courage, tenacity, and a burning passion for justice—he had pre-eminently. He had the courage to change his mind and to confess himself wrong; but his root principles he did not need to change. As a young man he took the ideals of Toryism seriously; but when the logic of facts compelled him to conclude that the Tories did not take them seriously, he deserted the Tories rather than desert his ideals. Cobbett became a Radical because he was in the fullest sense radical, for he went to the root of things. At the root of

politics he found corruption and cynicism; at the root of the new land-holding system he found, as he said, masquerading under the guise of efficiency, " an outrageous invasion of private property "; at the root of the " industrial progress " his contemporaries were belauding he found the glorification of greed and the pitiless oppression of the common man. He followed always where the argument led, not were the leaders of any school were pointing. " The revolutionary *idea* was always alien to him," as Mr. Cole observes: matters would be much better, he wrote, if men were left without a press, " because they would then judge and act from what they *saw* and *felt*, and not from what they read." It was thus always that he himself was moved. He saw " the democracy of the equal chance " rendered futile by the new power of the machine lords; he felt freedom in the countryside withering and stifling, pressed to death by the enclosures. And " Cobbett and the people *felt alike* : that was the secret of his ascendancy." They were inarticulate, but he could speak for them, and in doing so give them the confidence they lacked. His crusade has seemed to some later observers Quixotic. The Englishman appears to them as futile in tilting against the great cotton mills as was the Spaniard in charging the little windmills. The simile, indeed, is not without its value, for Cobbett was never so happy as when on horseback : and amidst the rise of the towering chimneys and the gathering whirr of the machines, the " jolly farmer's " charge for freedom seems in retrospect the greatest of rural rides.

The Judgment of England

" ILL fares the land, to hastening woes a prey
     Where Wealth accumulates and Men decay."
      So rang of old the noble voice in vain
O'er the Last Peasants wandering on the plain,
Doom has reversed the riddle and the rhyme
While sinks the commerce reared upon that crime
The thriftless towns litter with lives undone
To whom our madness left no joy but one;
And irony that glares like Judgment Day
Sees Men accumulate and Wealth decay.

                  G. K. C.

I Thank the Goodness and the Grace

Red guards for Soviet, White guards for Czar,
Thank God we live where only Blackguards are.

THE COCKPIT

AFTER some consideration, we have decided to open this controversial section of the paper for the present as follows; we propose to print two or three among the many interesting letters we receive, with our own comment on their questions; and then take note of which of these skirmishes develops into the most promising general engagement. It will be understood that the letters are selected, not as being the most important, far less the most elaborate, but in proportion as they raise the sort of questions that seem to us likely to lead to some sort of illuminating debate on the chief problems of the day.

To the Editor of G.K.'s WEEKLY.

DEAR SIR,—I wish you would ask the writer of " Notes of the Week " where he learnt that this world was made only for non-Jewish races. He implies that the Jew, wherever found, is " an interloper and a nuisance," but even the poorest Jew has as much right to live as, say, the distinguished Editor of " G.K.'s." As a matter of fact, the average Jew is an honest, loyal citizen of the country in which he lives, and in spite of the many difficulties which have been and, in many countries, still are put in his way.

It is unjust to say that " the best of the Zionist Jews regard it (Palestine) as a nation given to them to rule." A Jew is a Zionist because it has been the dream of Jewry since the Diaspora to return to the land of Israel, as even a casual knowledge of the Liturgy would show.

" Sound the great horn for our freedom; lift up the ensign to gather our exiles from the four corners of the earth."

It is not freedom to rule others that the Jew desires, but freedom to live his own life in the land of his fathers, his spiritual home. A hackneyed phrase, " spiritual home," but what else can one say of the Orthodox Jew whose daily prayer is :—

" May it be Thy will O Lord our God and God of our fathers that the temple be speedily rebuilt in our days, and grant our portion in Thy Law. And there we will serve Thee with awe as in the days of old and as in ancient years."

Periodically there is much talk of a " Jewish Problem," but the biggest of all is the Jew's Problem—to cope with the hatred and prejudice of those neighbours whose eagerness for general denunciation of his race is in inverse proportion to the meagreness of their knowledge and understanding of him.—Yours faithfully,

MARGARET WEBB.

Wimbledon Common, April 3, 1925.

[Our correspondent, as we understand it, complains that we think the world was made for non-Jewish races, because we said that the Jewish state ought to be established on a larger scale. She thinks we are denying life to the Jews, because we say that such a state ought to be more solidly and consistently Jewish. She thinks we are merely prejudiced against that race or religion, because we say that it ought if possible to have a real nation, and not be put off with some half-way house called a national home. Suppose, in an almost exact parallel, we had said that the Irish could not be put off with the compromise called Home Rule, but must have a complete nation and even an independent republic. Would our critics have condemned us chiefly for our cruel prejudice against the Irish? In short, our present critic condemns us because we wish there could be a real Zionist policy instead of a sham Zionist policy. She is entirely mistaken in supposing we are without sympathy with the Zionist vision. We have often expressed our sympathy with Jewish nationalism; quite apart from friendship with many Jews. We wish that the Jews had half as much sympathy with the Christian feeling about the Holy Sepulchre or the Moslem feeling about the Holy Places as we have with the Zionist feeling about the Holy Hill of Zion. If they had, they would see what we see, the extraordinary difficulty of doing what ought to be done in the place where in many ways we should most like to do it. What is the matter with the attitude with many Jews is sufficiently revealed in the last words of the letter. It is the extraordinary delusion that there is no problem except the problem of the meaningless malice of Gentiles. Even if this were true, the lady would still have her problem. It would be the problem of why people all over the world should go mad on the subject of the Jews any more than of the Javanese. As long as a certain sort of quite intelligent Jew goes on maintaining that he and his people have never contributed at all to the misunderstanding, he will be more misunderstood than ever. That denial of all provocation is itself a provocation : that denial of the problem is itself a problem.]

To the Editor of G.K.'s WEEKLY.

SIR,—The writer of the leading article in your last number allowed that it was difficult for a man to be certain that his own age was unusually degenerate, a disheartening sentiment to appear in G.K.'s WEEKLY, had it not been immediately qualified; for the writer went on to prove by examples drawn from history that some epochs in a nation's life are more degenerate than other epochs. His readers were, therefore, permitted to infer that their faith in the uncommon decadence of the present times was probably quite justified, and might continue to despair in comfort.

I am not myself a believer in the special decadence of this age, but I admit that another article in your last number, by Mr. Bernard Gilbert, the author of Bly Market, shook my scepticism a little.

In this article, Mr. Gilbert advocates the killing of Shaw, Joyce, and other as yet unspecified writers, in the interests of Old England. Blood has been shed ere now in the olden time, on behalf of this or that religious system. The names of Henry VIII. and Bloody Elizabeth will at once occur to readers of G.K.'s WEEKLY. But persecution on behalf of the kind of tradition symbolised by Chaucer, Shakespeare, Fielding and Dickens is a new idea in the spiritual history of mankind; and an age capable of producing the author of such an idea must not be upset if excitable persons denounce it as mad, morbid, poisonous and the like.

The Renaissance Malvolio is a sane and consistent comic figure, walking in the light of day. Mr. Bernard Gilbert, as the modern Malvolio, using rack and gibbet against Illyrian dissidents from the doctrine of cakes and ale, is a Bl—y nightmare.

HUGH KINGSMILL.

5 Endsleigh Gardens, N.W.1.
   April 4, 1925.

[Mr. Bernard Gilbert is highly capable of looking after himself; and in such signed articles and individual opinions, of course, we do not necessarily claim to speak for him or him for us. We decline to think that we do believe in toleration more than Mr. Gilbert does; it is the effect of our ecclesiastical superstitions. We incline to agree that persecutions of the Tudor sort are off. But we do not think our correspondent realises the strength of Mr. Gilbert's case. It is all very well to say that Chaucer and Dickens ought to be too amiable to persecute; but what happens when they are persecuted? What happens when the amiable thing has to defend itself against the unamiable? Now the cranks do persecute. Mr. Bernard Shaw, for whom we have a great respect and affection, is in favour of prohibition; that is he would impose teetotalism by brute force. Some day he may impose vegetarianism by brute force. There is a much stronger argument than our critic allows for the view that much less force exerted earlier would have saved more genial traditions. Many a subject of the Puritan would have eaten his Christmas dinner in peace if Calvinism had been nipped in the bud— if one may associate Calvinism with a bud. Many an employee of Scrooge and Gradgrind would have enjoyed his Christmas dinner if certain utilitarian theories had been nipped in their lovely springtime. Our own deduction from this would take longer to explain, and perhaps we may some day explain it. But anyhow even kindly things must defend themselves; and as it is they often only begin to defend themselves when they are already defeated. Even Mr. Pickwick fought for his nightcap; and Sam Weller noted an affront to the name by saying " Ain't nobody going to be whopped for this? "]

To the Editor of G.K.'s WEEKLY.

DEAR SIR,—I think the first number of your weekly promises well, and I hope the paper will become a power.

As a follower of Henry George, I am not in agreement with your views, for you do not appear to make clear the distinction between property in land and property in things that are the result of labour, nor do you point out that the chiefest monopoly (that upon which all other forms of monopoly rest) is the monopoly of the land.

At the same time I say, " More power to your elbow."

Yours truly,
CHARLES AYLIFFE GARDNER.

Cardiff, March 23, 1925.

[In thanking our correspondent for his generous good wishes, which come from a reader not altogether at one with us, we should like to say first that it is very difficult indeed to make clear the whole of a political philosophy in the first numbers of a paper, especially a political philosophy different from those into which the old political world is still divided. Distinctions of all kinds have to be made clear one after another; and we ask him to be patient with us. We do not agree with the nationalisation of the land, because we do not think that the true distinction is between things that are produced by labour and things that are not, but between things which arouse the sentiment of property and things that do not. But when he says that the land is at present a monopoly, he raises our whole point. We exist to maintain that a State monopoly and a trust monopoly have the same impersonal and inhuman character. While the land belongs largely to a class, it might loosely be called a class monopoly. When it belongs to the State, it will rightly be called a State monopoly. But if we can succeed in breaking it up among thousands of small landowners free to buy and sell, it cannot by any possible stretch of language be called a monopoly. We have great sympathy with our correspondent's dislike of landlordism; but we respectfully suggest that he is more of a champion of monopoly than we are.]

To the Editor of G.K.'s WEEKLY.

" *They love darkness rather than light because* . . . ."

DEAR SIR,—If the age of chivalry is not altogether dead, and if the spirit of the *New Witness* still breathes in your columns, I shall not appeal in vain for your help in pressing for an inquiry into the causes of the dismissal of Miss Douglas Pennant from the Commandantship of the Women's Royal Air Force in 1918.

The case—I refrain from expressing an opinion whether it has been made out or not—is briefly as follows:—

(1) Miss Douglas Pennant, an experienced and devoted public servant, found the W.R.A.F. at the darkest hour of the war, in a state of scandalous inefficiency, muddle and indiscipline.

(2) No sooner had she set herself to end this state of things than she was warned that her activities were becoming a nuisance in certain influential quarters.

(3) Having been thus warned, she was subjected to every sort of petty annoyance and obstruction, but as she persisted in defying the " influences," she was dismissed, with every aggravation of brutal rudeness.

(4) The scandal having leaked out sufficiently to attract public attention, a committee of the House of Lords was appointed with the professed object of clearing the matter up.

(5) This committee not only allowed the inquiry to be side-tracked on to certain sexual scandals alleged to have taken place months after the dismissal, but it was actually ordered to be broken off before Miss Douglas Pennant had had time to conclude her case unless, forsooth, the unfortunate lady was prepared to pay the whole cost of the inquiry, estimated at £3,000 a day !

(6) Since this outrageous travesty of justice, the cue has been to represent Miss Douglas Pennant as that undesirable type of person, a bore with a grievance, one whose case has been fairly tried and quashed.

I hope, if only in the name of public decency, that this matter will not be allowed to drop. That a lady, whose life has been one long course of devotion to the public service, should be broken and ruined, without cause shown is the least important feature of the case. But that it should be whispered that honesty is not the best policy where it conflicts with " influence," and that it should be believed that this matter is being hushed up for the excellent reason that the scandal of the public services during the war is one that beggars description, is a matter of more than personal interest.

If these charges are false, let them be nailed to the counter by a fair and impartial inquiry, such as we have never been allowed to have yet. If they are true, if there is anything in the rumour that some people at home were jobbing and intriguing at the expense of those who were dying in France, then . . . ; but Greece has set us an example !

I am, Sir,
Your obedient servant,
ESME WINGFIELD-STRATFORD.

[We are very glad to print Mr. Wingfield-Stratford's letter, or any other appeal by a responsible person based on such allegations of suppression and miscarriage of justice. We have never had the facts before us for the formation of a judgment ourselves; but there seems very good reason to suppose that some sort of reconsideration is needed.]

THE NU SPELING

THE Prophet of Progress was wandering over a vast plain which he had expected to find prosperous and fruitful, but which lay ruined and bare. Being enlightened, he guessed at first that a war had raged recently; had it been a war between barbarous peoples or in superstitious ages, of course, the land would have been covered with corn and cottages again in a year or two; but by the completeness of the desolation he knew that science had here shed her light upon the human mind. On closer examination, he saw in the remaining ruins something more detailed and domestic about the destruction than even scientific education could explain. And on enquiring of the Oldest Inhabitant, who was also the Only Inhabitant, he learnt that the war had been a civil war, which is the most uncivil sort of war there is.

"All this Revolution," said the Inhabitant, "came through the New Spelling."

"Surely," said the enquirer, "that reform, though excellent for the elucidation and simplification of life, is a relatively small matter to have produced such a convulsion."

"You have not considered," replied the other, "any more than the revolutionists did, the deplorable mis-understandings due to the different meanings attached to the same sound. It is all very well to say that we should write words as they are pronounced; but there are words which are pronounced the same and only distinguished by being spelt different. It all began with the Government issuing its great proclamation which was headed "Steel Houses." When this was translated into simplified spelling, you can imagine the deplorable misunderstanding. You can imagine the effect of this permission apparently granted by the King's authority to a vast and vagrant population, none of whom had been able to get any houses for half a lifetime."

"It is a difficulty that had not occurred to me," said the prophet, "but surely it must have occurred to the constructors of the New Spelling."

"The Revolution was conducted rather in a hurry, as revolutions often are," admitted his informant, "and this possibility was overlooked. It produced many other sad misunderstandings. I could tell you stories about the interchange of Wales and Whales which would sound like a monstrous mythological epic of mountains and leviathans. Perhaps the most melancholy incident was the misunderstanding of the headline in the religious column of the *Daily Express*, which really ran "Bishop to Remain in See." But the conduct of the inhabitants of Brighton in keeping the Bishop of Chichester partially and permanently under water, and calling upon him to conduct the services with his head sticking out of the sea, was none the less natural under the circumstances."

"Very natural mistake, of course," replied the prophet and resumed his progress through the world.

He reflected profoundly and with some perplexity on what he had often heard about simplification which so often reaches the point of sensationalism. He remembered the very large letters in which the headlines were printed for him, as if he were a child learning the alphabet. He remembered the slashing and slangy language in which they were written, as if meant to be popular with the most ignorant, but really they were very obscure; and that often he had to read them three times before he knew what they meant.

THE POET AT THE BREAKFAST TABLE

IT would be needless to recapitulate the details of the discovery by Dr. Porthwaite of the tomb of Apoldezzar, King of Babylon. Everyone must remember how the news first came and set England in an uproar. Biblical students died in myriads, like wasps around a treacle pot, in their attempts to force a way into the already crowded British Museum Library. Artists went mad overnight as they sat at their easels, reconstructing the funeral of a King of Babylon. An obscure writer of popular songs leapt into immediate fame by inserting an errata slip into a composition of his which had just passed through the press: "*For coal-black mammy read light-brown mammy, passim.*" The chorus girls in a well-known revue all developed rickets in their attempts to dance like the slave maidens on a frieze in a temple at Naa-bek. A P. & O. liner sank in the Mediterranean through sheer weight of scholars, journalists, tourists, and crowned heads. Half the world went to Babylon, and the other half stayed behind to write newspaper articles about the place.

    *   *   *   *

Dr. Porthwaite sat at breakfast with a Poet. The meal was laid in a simple canvas tent, all around which spread the vast wastes of the local desert. To the left of the marmalade jar here was no town nearer than one hundred miles; to the right of the toast-rack the nearest outpost of civilisation was sixty miles away. The tea cosy was the only tea cosy in a thousand square miles of glaring sand dunes.

These were the solemn thoughts that coursed through the Poet's mind. He was not talkative. While they had been waiting for their eggs to boil, Dr. Porthwaite had chatted incessantly of his discovery: British pluck—playing a straight bat—the Empire—Babylonian *ditto*—gold and silver—sarcophagus—secret wrested from the desert of ages (this a poetic simile out of a sense of hospitality to his guest).

The Poet seemed to be sunk in a lethargy of despair; but as Dr. Porthwaite seized his egg-cup firmly in his left hand and prepared to tap the egg with his spoon, Destiny paused and Poetry soared to its apogee.

"Forbear!" cried the Poet in a voice of iron. "Is there no secret that you dare not rape?"

Dr. Porthwaite looked at his vis-a-vis, apologetically at first, then in anger, then in consternation. His guest stood menacingly over him, white and trembling, his eyes starting, his skin moist with perspiration. The Doctor's last moment had come. The native servants had retired out of earshot. If there was to be a struggle it would be a death-grapple between two savage and primeval men, blinding each other with marmalade, stabbing wildly with the triangular pieces of toast. The most effective weapon to hand for the Archæologist was the tea-pot, but this the Poet had already seized. He seemed to fill the tent as he swung that china institution over the bald head of his host.

"Forbear!" he cried again. "Have you a soul? Is it as safely hidden as the tomb of Apoldezzar? Must I snatch your secret from you by striking deep into your brain?"

"What is your discovery? A broken empire and a broken tomb! The dead has surrendered its dead! A King discrowned by Death and now by you! What have you found and what does it mean? Gold, chariots, coffers—empire, lust, greed, assassination, cruelty, perhaps a little mercy here and there. A slave girl shows kindness to a caged bear! An old hag shelters a fugitive from royal wrath! That is your secret! Take it, write books about it, mouth it through the world! Receive, for all I care, the freedom of the city of Birmingham, but do not touch my egg!"

"But my dear man," said Dr. Porthwaite, "I assure you that your egg is ready for you across the table. Sit down and eat it like a sensible fellow, and I shall go on to eat my own."

"Your egg!" screamed the Poet in a new paroxysm of anger. "No egg is your egg! Only one who has reverence for an egg may eat it! You have had the crass temerity to break into a royal tomb, and now you have the almost blasphemous folly to break into an egg! A thousand armies have marched over Apoldezzar's grave, and have not known of its existence; now it is open and its secret is known. But if one man marched over an egg it would open, and its secret would be lost! That is my discovery! An egg—a tomb that gives forth life! An egg—a secret that Babylon could not solve, nor Egypt, nor Carthage, nor Rome, nor England! What does it conjure up? The beauty of a bird in feather, a thousand peaceful farmsteads, blue sky, all ages and all countries, the whole of life, every splendid thing! Boil it and what does it conjure up—a family peace, father in a bad temper, Johnny getting ready to go to school, the whole of living, every splendid thing! And you in your basic idiocy prattle about Babylon while you boil an egg. In your narrow civilisation you have lived, and by the symbol of that civilisation shall you die!"

The china tea-pot came swiftly down upon the bowed head of the unhappy Dr. Porthwaite. And slowly, reverently, carefully, the Poet ate two eggs.

GREGORY MACDONALD.

HERCULES IN TROUBLE

THE other day a man was fined seven-and-sixpence for trying to push a bus over, and the magistrate referred to the attempt as "one of the labours of Hercules."

Now this incident provides a clear illustration of the present-day attitude towards individual endeavour. A man has not an earthly chance of pushing a bus over; he cannot even do the bus much harm; yet not only does he have to suffer the humiliation of defeat, but he is punished for making the attempt.

All the same, it must have been well worth seven-and-sixpence. There are so many things I should like to push over—or even to try to push over. If only I knew how the fining system worked, I would save up a few pounds and enjoy myself. Is the fine proportional, I wonder, to the size of the object attacked, to the muscular strength of the attacker, or to the desirability of the attack being made? Would one have to pay as much for trying to knock down the Albert Memorial as one would for "leaning up against" Queen Anne's Mansions? And would it be unreasonably expensive to have a push—just a very little one—at the lamp-post which stands so inconveniently outside my door?

All through the ages there has raged this ceaseless contest between the small and the great, between the idealist minority and the materialist majority, between David and Goliath, between Don Quixote and the windmills. And nowadays, at any rate, the odds are always on Goliath and the

windmills; and David and Don Quixote spend the night in Bow Street.

Even Hercules himself, if he were alive to-day, would be considered no Hero at all, but a public nuisance. His treatment of the Nemean lion and the Lernean hydra would be condemned (and rightly) by the R.S.P.C.A. In pursuing the Arcadian stag and the Erymanthian boar he would find himself up against the Game Laws; while even the Stymphalian birds would probably be strictly preserved. Imagine, too, the newspaper headlines on the morning following his excursion into Amazonia: "Sensational Jewel Haul. Queen's Girdle Stolen by Daring Crook." The episode of the golden apples of the Hesperides would come under the heading of petty larceny; his method of cleansing the Royal Stables would get him into trouble with the Metropolitan Water Board for tampering with the course of the Thames; while even his capture of Cerberus (though performed with the full consent of Pluto, the dog's owner) would not escape the interference of the law. For no sooner would he be seen walking down the street with the creature trotting beside him on a lead than an officious policeman would come up.

"I suppose you know," he would say, "that them two-'eaded dorgs require a *double* licence. . . . ?"

No, this is not an age for Heroes.

JAN STRUTHER.

Some Answers to Mister Belloc's Exam

1. One point.—It is "manifest" that "no Christian Religion" means "no Bishops," and there are many Bishops; which is absurd.

The Times replied that Lord Northcliffe always said there could be no "Upper House"; and has recently sent down word that "he can find 'no room' for *two* Managing Directors of the Universe."

Analysis: Euclid is the only man who never read the *Daily Mail*. He is reason enough.

4. The hon. gentlemen *meant* that "all will be well with the world if you leave us to see that nothing is ever changed for the better, and we are always in power to keep you in the place provided for you by Providence. The true philosophy of life is 'stick where you are.'" Which is a thought full of "cheer."

5. (a) Modern thought is Negation; the highest of all authorities, because none can deny it.

   (b) Admitting nothing, it cannot admit "Johannine authorship."

   (c) "Fourth" is a purely abstract conception, like all figures; the symbols of intellect without emotion. "Saint" is a material, vegetarian, idea.

   (d) A self-educated man in a "pub" once said to me: "Gloom! Garn!"—because it was "my drink."

6. (a) The text-book must have been written by a sound sleeper, who had never spent happy hours puzzling over the characteristically modern, highly developed, symphony of discords at the "open-air concerts," given nightly without charge in our city roof-gardens, by feline "stars."

   (b) Has the writer an ear for a Bach?

"I have answered four questions and that is enough." You cannot prove that four is "more than three."

THE DRAMA
Over the Top

THE Pioneer Society, under Miss Edith Craig, having achieved explorative work of real value was untimely buried. It rose from premature oblivion last Sunday when Susan Glaspell's "The Verge" was staged at the Regent Theatre.

The work of this dramatist, too casually labelled, "uncommercial," must inevitably find its public and it only needs intelligent anticipation to turn the opportunity to good account. The success of Shaw at the Chelsea Palace has demonstrated the possibilities of the drama of ideas and there is little doubt in my mind that as keen and as paying an audience would be found for Susan Glaspell as for G. B. S.

"The Verge" is very nearly a great play. The conception has a logical and an emotional appeal and its treatment, always unexpected, is humorous and tragic. Only at the end does the impetus weaken; the culmination evades the main issue; one feels the hand of the author working the wires.

The play dramatises that revolt against the perpetuation of pattern which at moments must seize upon us all. The knowledge that no act can remain unique, no form preserve a splendid isolation, that in no sense can we "break through" has its abiding depression. Routine cannot be escaped, custom must stereotype even the erratic. Miss Glaspell shows us a woman struggling against the shackles of repetition. Claire will not allow the desire of to-day to involve the morrow. She fights against the imprisonment of what she wanted—a year, a month, a day, a minute ago. She must grow out of all she has known or desired, sloughing each inhibition, breaking every obstacle to free expression.

The daughter of New England puritanism, there is something as fanatical in her endeavours to disavow her spiritual inheritance. She has divorced one husband—"a stick-in-the-mud aunt"—by whom she had a daughter, married another who "sticks" in the air and has one lover for amusement and a second, Tom Edgeworthy, who hangs back for fear he should lose her by fulfilment. Claire's mentality is hard and brilliant, she thinks with magnificent clarity and, rare combination, is possessed of feminine allure. Moreover, possessing the gift of God—those "growing hands" that can rear the frailest seedling—she has turned her genius to the evolution of a new form of plant life.

To this end, mere human needs are brushed aside. It is very cold, a blizzard nips the skin from your back, the heating apparatus does not respond to the strain. No matter—turn the heat off from the house into the laboratory, "Breath of Life" in the incubation stage may be starved. Let husband, friend and lover keep warm if they can so that the child of Claire's desire comes to fruition.

A similar course is not infrequently adopted by masculine explorers—witness the exploits of one Palissy who fed his furnace with the family bedstead to fire his pots. It is only when a woman carries research to the freezing point that one is conscious of a challenge.

The first act Miss Sybil Thorndike played with a curious, almost elfin charm. Here she cast aside all mannerisms and stage tricks and succeeded in creating an atmosphere of otherworldliness which stimulated the imagination and kept curiosity guessing. The second act rises through a series of emotional stresses to a moment of poignancy rarely equalled in modern drama. Claire has sought her tower to escape the pressure of other people's thoughts. But even here she is pursued. Adelaide, her sister, is burdened with an entire gospel—Claire must become more like other people and allow Elisabeth, the daughter, to help in the laboratory. The girl, a frankly unsympathetic young person, also desires to re-pot her mother's life.

Now the tower, like Claire herself, unexpectedly escapes from its description. This perturbs the sister who insists that a round tower should go on being round—not square.

Genuinely and aggressively alarmed, she is the expression of the true suburban mind which clings unalterably to the ideal of the same thing in the same place at the same time, world without end. Claire holds herself in check till Adelaide is reinforced by her own husband. Well-meaning and humorless, the man advances those world-weary arguments against the unusual. His wife has been thinking too much. She should have a change and consult a nerve specialist whom he has in waiting down below. This snaps the tension. Claire scents danger and cries out for Tom Edgeworthy. It is an effective moment in stagecraft. Through the trap door comes the sound of a gramophone which her voice cuts across. Silence follows and you hear footsteps slowly coming up.

Having raised the storm Harry and Adelaide flee before the whirlwind. But Claire is already soothed. She is at peace with Tom though still pressed with the urge for full discovery of her own nature and his. She pleads that they shall be lovers. With Tom she may lose that sense of self which for ever pursues her. But Tom has not the courage; in possessing her he will lose her. If he leaves her she will remain with him for ever. And then comes the cyclone. Claire calls for her husband, for Adelaide, for Dick and for the specialist.

"How do people go insane?" she screams, "It's not so easy to get out." The family cluck forth platitudes and, pushed beyond endurance, Claire throws herself into Dick's arms. She will sink as low, as low as the gutter, and he will go with her!

There is much that is fine in Miss Thorndike's rendering. She holds one in suspense and conveys the sense of spiritual outrage in every movement and inflection. But when she pleads with Tom one is conscious of a failure which somehow distorts and maims the situation. We do not see a woman passionate and ardent exulting in the sacrifice of her security; rather we behold a cold and level-headed creature presenting arguments difficult to rebut.

The working out of the problem is disappointing. It is the day on which "Breath of Life" is due to flower. Into the laboratory comes Dick chased by Harry with revolver. Anthony, the gardener—the Greek chorus of the play—prevents bloodshed, with a plea for the plants, and "Miss Claire," as the old man always calls her, composedly comes in. As always happened she imposes her own atmosphere. Husband and lover stand aside for her to speak. "Breath of Life" is brought in; Claire is justified of her faith. She has brought forth a flower new and strange as was the first rose in Eden.

But once more the sense of finality closes in on her. She has but made another prison, a form to be perpetuated over and over again. In vain she has sought to create the free and flowing pattern—what is shall always be. But even so her soul shall not be manacled and when Tom pleads for what he has refused and asks her for herself she turns on him. He is trying to imprison her in what she *wanted*. And yet she does want him and desire weights her will. This she will not endure. An explorer to the end she kills him.

It is here that the author falters. Claire, the "Breath of Life" by her side, goes mad and the curtain falls on the repetition of sister Adelaide's favourite hymn, "Nearer my God to Thee." As a study of a modern type of ecstatic, careless of suffering so the pure ideal be held, "The Verge" would stand alone. But the end begs the whole question. If Claire were mentally unsound the argument falls to pieces. Where lunacy is inevitable analysis is futile. The play should end on the note of defiance. Claire, the martyr, waiting for the faggot! Claire, the explorer, who to know life must end it, whose tilt against conventionality ends in the greatest of all conventions, death!

J. K. PROTHERO.

REVIEWS

Novels of the Day

WIT and pity seldom go together, especially in the writings of women. Miss Clemence Dane and Miss E. M. Delafield have considerable wit, but their books are hard as flints and keen as razors. They regard mankind, and womankind in particular, with contempt.

The author of " Elizabeth and her German Garden " tempers her wit and humour to shorn lambs. She cares as little for stupid, narrow people as you and I do, but some inordinate sense of fairness in her compels her to recognise that they are, after all, God's creatures.

The title of her latest book, " Love,"* is not an ironic one. The reader will take some time to find this out.

The little shy woman who had been nine times to see and hear " The Immortal Hour " at King's Cross, and the freckle-faced, red-wristed, flaming haired young man, who had been thirty-six times, were ideal figures for a certain kind of satire. When the ruddy one, who was twenty-five, got fiercely sentimental over the pale one, who was forty-seven, the situation seemed to demand severe treatment. When it transpired that tiny Catherine Cumfrit had a stiff young daughter of eighteen married to a sanctimonious and uxorious rector of forty-seven, that development seemed sheer farce, especially in the enraging effect it had on Christopher Monckton, who regarded Catherine as a helpless and adorable small girl.

The Countess Russell does not believe in farce; she knows it is a very low medium in literature. She is laughingly tender to Catherine and Chris; she makes a wry mouth over the Reverend Stephen Colquhoun and his adoring bride, Virginia; but she gives the devout devils their due. She is even fair to Stephen's formidable, beak-nosed mother.

It is held that all love is an illusion. Christopher's love for Catherine did argue a certain opacity of sight; for Catherine was by no means a merry widow, and she dressed dowdily. One precaution only she took, and that was a hat that shadowed her face. Yet even when Christopher saw that face without any garnish, it launched more than a thousand ships for him. He was an impetuous lover, and it required all his ardour to storm the heights of little Mrs. Cumfrit. It was only by an accident, the breaking down of a motor bicycle in a bleak space where pursuer and pursued spent the night, that marriage came about. Catherine's shocked and scandalised son-in-law insisted on it. Catherine pleaded limitations of age and the decency of continued widowhood. " Love isn't decent," protested the fiery Christopher, " love is glorious and shameless."

The honeymoon made a lover of placid Catherine. In course of time her love became so insistent in its care and tenderness that Christopher felt that he was sinking in a sea of treacle; but Christopher was too fond and too chivalrous to betray his youthful impatience. He brought Catherine out to suppers which disagreed with her and dances that exhausted her. She was not a modern woman, Catherine, or she would have danced Christopher down. Fatigue, sallowness, wrinkles came, and Catherine sought a beauty specialist. The specifics did not work. Then the poor thing was summoned down to Virginia's death-bed. She thought the Reverend Stephen was dying, for he was doing most of the screaming before the birth of a son. After that death Catherine resolved to give up the game of youth.

It was then that Christopher saw her—what she called the real Catherine—for the first time. She had let her hair go grey; she had abjured cosmetics; she had become sensible.

" Oh, damn being sensible," said poor Christopher. " Be what you were before. Good God, Catherine," he went on, hiding his face, clutching her knees, " do you think a man wants his wife to scrub herself with yellow soap, as if she were the kitchen table—and then come all shiny to him and say, ' See, I'm the Truth '? And she isn't the truth. She's no more the truth shiny than powdered."

There was reason in what Christopher said, but Catherine was tired of tiring herself. Don't think that is the end of the marriage, for it isn't.

There is nothing for ridicule in the quite beautiful love and marriage story that forms the contents of Mr. Compton MacKenzie's " Coral."† In his former books, especially those dealing with the fortunes of that very dull drab, Sylvia Scarlett, there was much that was tawdry and a good deal that was sinister and unpleasant. " Coral " is better than even " Guy and Pauline "; it is much better than " Carnival," to which it is a sequel. In " Carnival " a good theme was ruined by a melodramatic ending. " Coral " is sustained in its excellence from beginning to end.

As it is a good many years now since " Carnival " appeared, it may be well to recall that its heroine was Jenny Pearl, an entirely delicious ballet-girl, whom a very foolish young man, Maurice Avery, decided not to marry; Jenny was the stuff of which good wives are made. That young woman went down to Cornwall, and mistakenly wedded a lowering native named Trewhella, who shot Jenny when he found her in conversation with her former sweetheart.

In the present book Maurice, who has married suitably but dully, has a very lovely and warmhearted daughter, Coral. Jenny's little boy, Frank, has developed into an attractive man, and is at once the idol and exasperation of his aunt, May. Frank had done war service and is a competent chauffeur, but he is devoured with a desire to fly and devotes all the leisure and odd cash in his life to perfecting flying-wings, in the manner of Icarus. He falls on slack times and is at his wit's end for a job, and then he gets the post of motor-man in the household of Maurice Avery. Maurice liked him at first glance, and had the puzzled sense of a strange familarity. He saw him just in the same light as his daughter, Coral, did immediately afterwards:

He was certainly prepossessing, as slim and straight as an axle, as dark as an ancient bronze, damson-eyed, with lips red like a rowan, and ears sharp as arrow-heads. Avery noticed his hands stained with oil and coined a phrase for him in his mind. " A faun captured by Hephaestus."

That passage looks a little dangerous. It suggests that Frank is a Berta Ruck chauffeur, romantic and beautifully spoken.

It is the triumph of Mr. Mackenzie's matured mind that the young man is, and remains, a very ordinary driver-mechanic, uplifted a little by his love for Coral.

His was not the finest kind of love. When his aunt heard that he had engaged himself to the Averys she was much upset. May Raeburn detested Maurice for his treachery in love towards her sister, the adored and adorable Jenny. She has to tell Frank that his name is not Abel, but Trewhella, that Maurice Avery had made love to his mother, and that his father had been hanged for murder. Frank, though in love with Coral, determines he will revenge his mother's death on her. He thinks better of that harsh oath, but the implication of it remains.

Coral will have her Frank, and she leaves her father's house and all that it means to be the mate of a very difficult young man, a kind of Henry Straker. The peremptory husband forbids his bride all communication with her family. He bears her off to Bournemouth—he had suggested Margate—and there the wonderful honeymoon occurs. After that he

* " LOVE." By the Author of " Elizabeth and her German Garden." Macmillan, 7s. 6d.

† " CORAL." By Compton Mackenzie. (Cassell, 7s. 6d.).

bears Coral back again to his aunt's abode in Dairymaid Row, Islington.

The rest of the novel is the story of a young wife who endures ugly surroundings, coarse food, hard work, and ingratitude, simply because she is utterly devoted to her man. In the hands of most writers, Frank would have developed into a sentimental poet or a callous scoundrel. Mr. Mackenzie lets him remain a competent chauffeur with an old-fashional idea as to the duties of wives; and yet the sulky inventor cannot help but worship Coral at times.

Coral will remain one of the most real and likable girls in English fiction. She redeems everything insincere that Compton Mackenzie has ever written.

Second only to her is May Raeburn, with her never-failing grief for beautiful dead Jenny. When poor old May is going to bed rather terrified—most illogically so—at the thought of her sister's ghost appearing, she comforts herself with the thought that pretty, laughing Jenny had never believed in the like:

She hears Jenny babbling again:

"Ghosts? Don't be silly, young May. Blackbeetles. yes. Well, anyone has seen blackbeetles. But whosoever's seen a ghost? Oh, no, not in these, duck! Ghosts? Yes? then you looked again and saw it was mother's lace curtings come back from the wash."

Jenny was a very real dancing girl. Even her shadow has charm and fun.

The stupidities of luxury seem to be the same everywhere. Miss Mildred Cram in ‡" The Tide " is apparently under the impression that the dancing, cock-tailing and jazz madness are the especial possessions of New York. Regrettably it is not so. Negroes, Jews, and that ambiguous race and sex, complimentarily called " men-milliners," provide most of the so-called amusement in monied circles in London. They provide it mainly for women determined to have the best time by wearing the best clothes, but having no other ideal in life.

Miss Cram's heroine, Lilah, is not so bad as many of her sisters-in-joy. Having made a marriage which gives her her fling in all kinds of extravagance, she sacrifices the position of wife to Roger Peabody by eloping with an ex-warrior, who has the mouth of a satyr, but a badly crocked heart. It is true that Lilah brings seven trunks full of clothes with her and all the jewellery her husband gave her, including a string of pearls worth a fortune, but still she is content to be fairly poor in Florence.

The ordinary mercenary female who believes in living her own life would have given up the debilitated satyr after a month of narrow means. Lilah held out very much longer. She would have returned to her patient husband when she went to see him in Paris, but for the news of the sick satyr's approaching death. When she went back to Gabriele D'Annunzio's villa where she had had her depressing adventure, she curiously made up her mind that a reunion with Robert Peabody was impossible.

In spite of her appalling vanity, her utter selfishness and her avid desire to have everything, I almost liked Lilah, when she was compelled to do some work in New York in drapery and hat stores. It was inevitable that the poor boob, Robert, should want her again; but Lilah, at least, knew how the proletarians lived when she got back to luxury. That would afford her, at any rate, the pleasure of comparison. No wonder Lilah often thought the weary old globe, " a duck of a world! "

LOUIS J. McQUILLAND.

---

‡ " The Tide." By Mildred Cram. Jonathan Cape. 7s. 6d.

LIBRARY LIST

LENIN. By Leon Trotsky. Harrap. 7s. 6d.

The publication of this book has caused the exile of Trotsky; but there are books equally bad written every week without any specific punishment being inflicted. One suspects that both Trotsky and Lenin had a great deal of American dope pumped into them, as in the letter from an alleged peasant to the latter : "We must grasp the bourgeoisie more firmly so that they will burst in all their seams." There is not much about Russia in the book; but there is a great deal about Trotsky and quite a considerable amount about H. G. Wells. Mr. Bronstein (to give the Jew in dictator's uniform his proper name) disliked Mr. Wells at first glance; so apparently did Vladmir Ilyich (the infrequent names of Lenin). " What a bourgeois he is! He is a Philistine ", V. I. is supposed to have said after a first interview. Bronstein is very angry with Wells for his promise to clip Marx's beard. The book has no value as history or biography. It may, of course, have been entirely conceived and written by a Semitic journalist, as in the passage where Lenin is described with his left eye closed, receiving by radio "a web of bloodthirsty reserve and political cant" and resembling "a damnably proud moujik who won't be imposed upon."

LONDON LIFE IN THE 14th CENTURY. By Charles Pendrill. George Allen and Unwin. 10s. 6d.

A most fascinating result of deep search into the daily life of a London which was at once small and considerable. We are accustomed to believe that there was no beer but good strong beer in London before Dora came, but it is instructive to learn from Mr. Pendrill that in 1337 the London brewers were found to be drawing so much water from the Conduit that everyone else had to go short and, accordingly, their use of this supply was henceforth much curtailed. Again, we are always blaming the bakers; but it is illuminating to consider that when bread was standardised at one halfpenny a loaf, the weight always varied. Law and order were not carried to excess in the 14th century as evidenced by the fact that a lady of the period, sister to the Dean of St. Martin-le-Grand, supplied knives to some prisoners in Newgate with which they murdered the gatekeeper in order to effect their escape. At that time they did themselves very well in St. Paul's. Every year the clergy there were presented with a fine fat buck. The body was sent to the kitchen to be roasted, but the head was chopped off and fixed on a pole, and the Dean and Chapter with garlands of roses on their heads, carried it round in solemn procession. I fancy that Dean Inge would pass the buck if that hearty custom were revived.

THE HISTORIC BASIS OF ANGLICANISM. By Joseph Clayton, F.R.Hist.S. Sands & Co. 6s.

Mr. Clayton is the master of an English style simple, forcible, persuasive, effective, and he thoroughly knows his subject. As Dom Bede Jarrett, O.P., says in his introduction, the accuracy of the statements in Mr. Clayton's book cannot be questioned, nor the interpretation denied. The only way in which the book can be attacked is by ignoring the Reformation. This has been so persistently done for a couple of generations past that one cannot hope for an acknowledgment of the Reformation from Anglican quarters. The facts remain, however, as detailed by the author and tabled by Dom Bede Jarrett, that the founders of the Church of England in the sixteenth century were Lutheran in feeling and belief; that the three chief objects of their hatred were the Pope, the doctrine of transubstantiation and vows of chastity and celibacy, and that they deliberately wished to cut themselves off from the Mediæval Church as well as from the Church of their own time. In his final sentence Mr. Clayton puts the case of the Church in its simplest form : "The Catholic Church is a visible society whose Head is Christ and whose head on earth is Christ's Vicar, the Pope. The denial of that headship has often been made by Christians, and it has always involved for its makers separation from Catholic unity."

GROBO. By E. H. W. Meyerstein. Cecil Palmer. 7s. 6d.

Mr. Meyerstein has an air of smartness, but it is impossible to know what he is driving at; his novel is absolutely meaningless; has no resemblance to life, nor any vestige of romance. Grobo is a Spaniard from Alicante, who might be a Jew from the Commercial Road. As a child he is bought (for no possible reason) by a whiskered Englishman, jocosely called Sir William Lockjaw. When he attains years of discretion he is sent to Harrow, and is very quickly sent out of Harrow. He returns to Spain from a bandit, Saragala, is introduced to a General Gammerlommer, and is sent back to England and installed in Oxford. The Oxford chapters are, if possible, more futile than the chapters that have preceded them. It is difficult to know why this book was written, and even more difficult to understand why it ever came to be published.

BLIND RAFTERY. By Donn Byrne. Sampson Low. 5s.

Some say that Byrne's music is too sweet and his colours too bright, but he does convey glamour. Raftery was the last of the great Irish ballad-makers, who wandered through the country getting hospitality on every hand. He praised his friends over the harp-strings and damned his enemies with a stinging verse. Byrne tells how he came into Claregalway where Dafydd Evans, the base Welshman, prospered on the poverty around him, and where Raftery encountered a woman of Spain who was as dainty as a fairy and as beautiful as an Orpen portrait. The Welshman gave him Hilaria in marriage with a grin, and they travelled through Ireland together, though the old, full welcome was not there for the bard. Hilaria was filled with unhappiness because she did not come to him as a pure woman and because her presence shadowed his triumphs; but when she finally made confession the blind singer knew the reason of her unhappiness and pardoned her sweetly and royally. The book is what is called picaresque. There is much romance in it and some fine songs.

YOUTH AND MAIDENHOOD. A Book of English Verse. Chosen by L. S. Wood. Dent. 7s. 6d.

The idea of the anthology is that while childhood has been well provided for, the poetry of later childhood and early youth appears to have remained uncollected. Mr. Wood has made a very representative selection of English poets along the lines indicated. He gives his adolescents selections from Chaucer, Lidgate, Skelton, Spenser, Sir Philip Sidney, Shakespeare, John Donne, Ben Johnson, George Wither, Milton, and on through the immortals by way of Herrick, Pope, Gray, Goldsmith, Blake, Wordsworth and Scott to the definitely nineteenth century poets. He has shown a fine care in picking out " My Sister's Sleep " from the Rosetti poems. Mrs. Meynell has abundant material for him, but he contents himself with " Your Own Fair Youth," and the exquisite " Letter from a Girl to her own Old Age." Lionel Johnson's " Winchester " is here, Rupert Brooke's " Funeral of Youth," Edward Thomas's " Celandine," and Siegfried Sassoon's " In Fifty Years." The anthologist has displayed a common-sense courage in retaining Felicia Hemans' " Casabianca."

THE BEARDSLEY PERIOD. By Osbert Burdett. The Bodley Head. 7s. 6d.

A critical study of the writers and artists of the 'nineties who had the "Yellow Book" for their rallying ground. Mr Burdett has wisely refrained from dealing with the lives of his subjects, and has easily refrained from dropping into the Wilde-trap. He does justice to the "Yellow Book's" editor, Henry Harland, as a writer of charm and delicacy, and has paid a necessary tribute to the admirable work of Hubert Crackanthorpe, which was esteemed by so fine and conscientious a craftsman as Henry James. It is ironic to recall that Beardsley's designs for the fifth volume of the "Yellow Book" did not appear because one, William Watson, at the instigation of a person called Mrs. Humphry Ward, threatened to make a "last sacrifice" if Beardsley were retained. I fancy Mr. Burdett is not entirely correct in stating that the *New Statesman* was founded " to counteract from the Fabian side the vigorous criticisms of socialism and Shavian ideas that Mr. Belloc and the two Chestertons were leading." I remember Mr. Cecil Chesterton as one of the most distinguished of Fabians, and agree with Mr. Burdett that he was "the most brilliant and courageous journalist of his generation in London."

ACROSS EUROPE WITH SATANELLA. By Clare Sheridan. Duckworth. 15s.

The activity and vivacity of Mrs. Clare Sheridan are abnormal. Just as one would take a trip to Eastbourne, she suddenly makes up her mind to go to Russia on a motor-bicycle, and with that object gets her devoted brother "Peter" to provide the machine and drive it and look after it. The excursion begins in Holland and ends in the Crimea. The book has nothing special in its composition and says no new thing. That would be difficult since Europe is now so over-run by motor-bikes that it begins to resemble the front at Southend. Mrs. Sheridan, however, writes so amusingly about little things that one passes from page to page with the idea that something important is going to happen. Many visitors to Poland will quarrel with the radiant author as to her statement that the city of Warsaw has no character nor individuality. It is surprising to learn from Mrs. Sheridan that the belief still prevails abroad in the insanity of Britons. "I could not love the English if they were not just a little mad," confided a little lady to her who had taught chemistry in the University of Petrograd.

WINE OF DEATH. By Anthony Armstrong. Stanley Paul. 7s. 6d.

" I who was Amenes, Captain and Chief of the Bodyguard to Mardaka, Prince of Neptus, look back into the misty past." A number of books begin this way, and they continue—as they always continue. Mr. Armstrong has considerable imagination, but his misty characters talk in the rather concrete manner of to-day, which does not help illusion. The story, however, has plenty of action. Amenes is a hater of women, but early in his Saga he is troubled by the sweet advances of a primitive flapper, Isme. His second temptation, which he meets in the City of the Golden Gates, is a vixenish young princess, Melapa. This city is governed by an evil influence called The Voice, which resembles wireless inasmuch that it is heard but not seen. The Children of the Wave, of whom Amenes is one of the leaders, have a very bad time, and are threatened by what Mr. Armstrong calls the Sacrifice of the Wine of Death. In an extended Albert Hall there is a very large and very ugly image furnished with large knives and also with a capacious bowl. When a Child of the Waves is put on the knees of this god the knives descend and the bowl is filled with blood. The Princess Melapa just escapes the knives, and Amenes is left in the position of deciding whether he will marry the temperamental princess or the even-tempered Isme. Wisely he does neither, but makes tracks from the Golden Gates. I suspect we shall hear a lot more of Amenes.

THE ENGLISH VERSIONS OF THE SHIP OF FOOLS: A Contribution to the History of the Early French Renaissance in England. By Fr. Aurelius Pompen, O.F.M. Longmans. 21s.

This is a most elaborate and super-noted volume, full of commentaries and comparisons. When Seabastian Brant, once City Clerk of Strasburg, wrote the "Narrenschiff," as Professor of Law in the University of Basel, he had probably little idea that the first edition, printed in Basle in 1494, was to have many successors and numerous translations. The work is a satire directed against contemporary laity and clergy. Mr. Henry Charles Lea in his "Eve of the Reformation" in the Cambridge Modern History strongly indicates that the volume played a great part in European history. Everyone who had a grievance against the Catholic Church welcomed its protestant plea that man deals directly with God and is responsible to Him alone. The object of Fr. Aurelius Pompen is an attempt to bring the Barclay and Watson translations somewhat nearer to the student of English literature. He says that he is painfully conscious of one great defect in his book : that there is no unity in it. This is a very mild offence in the connection. There is no greater unity in " The Ship of Fools," with its worldly satire and schismatic sermans, than in the individualistic arrogances and acts of Luther, Calvin and Knox and other " Stars of the Reformation."

ANOTHER MAN'S WIFE. By Lady (A.) Scott. Nash & Grayson. 7s. 6d.

There is a genuine gift of characterisation here. Hetty Amery, the pretty typist, her colleagues, the decent young clerks, and Josh Wedge, her employer, are very much flesh and blood. In another station of life, Honoria Wickham, slender, gracious, quick-witted, and practically living on her wits, has all the attraction of that other creation " The Expensive Miss Ducane." With the exception of Josh, Lady Scott's men are not very vivid, the fact being that they are not intended to be. Mark Leamington, who resolved to stick to Hetty in spite of the contempt of his family for a typist who lived in the least distinguished part of Bayswater, is an average decent Englishman. Hetty is rather silly in believing Honoria's story that Mark is marrying her only from a sense of honour, and it is difficult to pardon her for wedding Josh in order to set Mark's conscience at rest. It would be most unpleasant for a girl of any sensitivity to have to share even the board of a husband who shouted out : " Have some more champagne. Thirty-two shillings a bottle, my dear, that's the stuff, my girl. Lap it up, lap it up." Of course that is only the beginning of Lady Scott's novel.

"G.K.'s WEEKLY"

Every Thursday.   **Price Sixpence.**

NOTICES.

Tel. No.: City 1978.   Annual Subscription Rate (52 Issues) £1 10 4

Cheques and Postal Orders should be made payable to G.K.'s Weekly Ltd., and crossed a/c payee Westminster Bank, Ltd. MSS. submitted to the Editor must be accompanied by a stamped addressed envelope

Copies of "G.K.'s Weekly" can be obtained from, or subscriptions placed with, any News dealer or News Company in the United States or Canada, or direct from *The International News Co.*, 83-85, Duane Street, New York; *The American News Co., Ltd.,* at Toronto, Winnipeg, Vancouver, Montreal, Ottawa, St. John, Halifax and Hamilton. Sole agents for Australasia : Gordon & Gotch (Australasia), Ltd. Sole Agents for South Africa : Central News Agency, Ltd.

Offices : 20 & 21, Essex Street, Strand, London, W.C.2.

SOME PRESS NOTICES OF No. 1.

"The new organ has the familiar political individualistic touch of 'G.K.' which is needed and welcome."—*Aberdeen Press and Journal.*

"I have received a copy of the first number of G.K.'s WEEKLY and a very good first number it is—Chesterton's personality is reflected from every page."—*Glasgow Record.*

"This sixpenny journal is bright, varied, provocative and individual. There is nothing else like it. Undoubtedly here is a journal that is alive and deserves to live."—*Liverpool Courier.*

"That Mr. Chesterton should find a platform all his own from which to address the world at short and regular intervals, is a public gain. He is one of the personalities of his time."—*North Eastern Gazette.*

"From the first number of G.K.'s WEEKLY I judge well for its prospects. . . . I have an idea that this paper. . . . will be read most widely by those who disagree most violently with its policy."—*Bath Chronicle.*

"G.K.'s WEEKLY deserves to be a success as it certainly will be, if it keeps up to the standard of the first number. The weekly should be welcomed as a bright and fresh star in the firmament of art and letter."—*Hull Daily Mail.*

"The number of weekly reviews is already large but G.K.'s WEEKLY must be welcomed because of its standpoint. The review contains notes of the week refreshingly critical from that point of view."—*Nottingham Guardian.*

"G.K.'s WEEKLY makes its bow this week to a public that has long awaited it. It is a bow with no timidity. It seems to know that its welcome is assured. It certainly knows that it can fill a niche."—*Edinburgh Evening News.*

"Although we may not always agree with Mr. Chesterton's views we are invariably entertained by them, and his suggestions for our political and economic salvation contain much with which the average person can sympathise."—*Northern E. Despatch.*

"For several years past, the world has waited, with an eagerness, deepening into anxiety, for the appearance of Mr. G. K. Chesterton's promised new journal. Its chosen title has seemed, from the first, to announce a host of good things; what could be more enticing than G.K.'s WEEKLY? Now at last the initial number appears."—*North Eastern Daily Gazette.*

"I like this new paper edited by Mr. G. K. Chesterton, the first number of which is now published. It strikes a fresh note. The leading article by Chesterton himself which opens it is as unlike the kind of thing we find in the other weeklies, as G. K. C. is as unlike H. G. Wells. I do not say it is better than any of them but it is different, unexpected, provocative. And the whimsical touch is sensible too."—*Glasgow Bulletin.*

"Mr. Chesterton enjoys a unique position among the great and famous. . . . so it is safe to assume that a large public will welcome Mr. Chesterton's new venture into journalism. He is amusing when he describes his reasons for calling his paper 'G.K.'s Weekly.' It was not his wish, he says, but that of his business advisers. Mr. Chesterton can rest assured that his paper is well named."—*Huddersfield Examiner.*

"We welcome G.K.'s WEEKLY. It is a sixpenny paper; it comes from London; it is one of the few journals produced in the English Metropolis—or elsewhere across the Irish sea—which can be recommended without a pang of conscience to the general reader. Mr. G. K. Chesterton's publication is more than interesting; if it is not a 'new departure' exactly, it is a decided improvement on the older sixpenny weeklies."—*Irish News.*

"If every issue of G.K.'s WEEKLY is as wise and diverting as the first number there need be no fear for the success of a very striking venture in journalism. The comments on current topics are ,as might be expected, pungent and to the point and the 'Notes of the Week' promise to make some of the best and most suggestive reading in the paper. The feature 'From G.K.'s WEEKLY a Hundred Years Ago' is a glorious half page of satire."—*Western Press.*

"G.K.'s WEEKLY's out at last,
And I don't think any lover
Of G.K. who sees the vast
Familiar figure on the cover
Looming large, prodigious, fat
Will (I say this humbly, meekly),
Even dare to whisper that
G.K.'s WEAKLY!
(W.H.B. in the *Morning Post*).

In reply to many enquiries from readers who did not get a copy of the Prospectus of G.K.'s Weekly, Ltd., issued in December last, and who desire to take up shares, we are reproducing particulars of the Capital of the Company together with a copy of the Form of Application for shares which was enclosed therein.

Applications can be made on the "Form of Application for Shares" given below.

Published by the Proprietors, G.K.'s WEEKLY, LTD., at their offices, 20 & 21 Essex Street, Strand, London, W.C.2 (incorporating THE NEW WITNESS). Telephone No. City 1978. Printed by THE ALLIED PRESS, LTD., 19 Clerkenwell Close, London, E.C.1. Sole agents for Australasia : Gordon & Gotch (Australasia) Ltd. Sole Agents for South Africa : Central News Agency Ltd.

G. K.'s WEEKLY.—December 26, 1925.

THE NEW WAR ON CHRISTMAS.

G.K.'s Weekly

EDITED BY G. K. CHESTERTON,

No. 41.—Vol. II.   Week ending Saturday, December 26, 1925.   PRICE SIXPENCE
YEARLY (52 ISSUES)
£1 10 4.

Telephone No. City 1978.   Offices, 20 & 21, Essex Street, Strand, W.

CONTENTS :

WHAT HAS HAPPENED

IN the issues following on the New Year it is our intention, as already explained, to devote this front page to a preliminary note on the most important thing that has happened in the week. But it is impossible to publish anything in Christmas week without recognising that the most important thing that happened is Christmas. And in this there is a certain further significance; in the fact that Christmas was something that did happen and that does happen. This quality of dramatic crisis has never been dropped out of it, in all its endless repetitions and not infrequent degradations. It is in this that it differs most notably from all the new fashions in faith or substitute for faith. Just as in their notion of peace they want men to agree about nothing, so in their notion of festivity they want people to rejoice about nothing. They have no notion of news in the old sense of good news. They cannot celebrate an event but only an evolution. Mr. Bernard Shaw said, in his fine and spirited preface to St. Joan, that the religion of the modern world was clearly going to be the religion of Creative Evolution. But even Mr. Bernard Shaw does not leap over the garden-wall and rush down the street calling out excitedly, " Creative Evolution has just happened ! " Our Aristophanes cannot act in the case of Evolution as Archimedes in the tale of Eureka. There were followers of Comte who said that we must worship Humanity as the modern god. But they never went about waving their arms and shouting, " Humanity has just happened." They could not do so, not only because shouting was hardly their strong point, but also because of the nature of the thing they had to shout. It was the whole point of those Victorians, with their evolutionary ethics, that nothing ever happened in that dramatic and decisive way; and in one sense that nothing ever happened at all. Humanity itself had only grown with infinite gradations out of the grotesque shapes of the slime. There was no moment when anyone could say " A man is made," as we say, " A child is born." Whether their evolutionary theory of origins is true or not does not very much matter. Whether their ethical inference from it is accepted or not matters very much indeed. For the modern world has really read into that story of the primeval world an entirely evil notion of setting relativity against reality. Because the beast only slowly becomes man, they argue that beastliness only slowly becomes unmanly. Harmless actions become wicked, and then become harmless again; so that a man may excuse any cruelty or treachery by merely saying that he is a little behind the time or very far in front of it. There is the same absence of the exceptional and exciting event in the more mystic moderns. Incarnation cannot be the exception in a world of Reincarnation. If God does not even recognise the material, the moment of his materialisation is immaterial. None of these creeds can tell a story; their stories are too long. But our story starts as with a ringing cry in the night; and that shock of bells in the darkness like great guns announcing battle and victory. Something has happened. Perhaps, on a true reading of history, nothing has happened since.

NOTES OF THE WEEK

Mosul and the League

AS we anticipated, the League of Nations award gives Mosul to Irak. And so long as we adhere to the Conference-of-the-Big-Nations-with-the-Little-Nations-looking-on, we must regard their decision as binding. Of course, we could walk out of Irak, but that would be good neither for our prestige nor for the cause of Christendom against Islam. We think it silly that the gentlemen at Geneva should have the power to influence our foreign policy to so vital an extent, but the harm was done when the late President Wilson stampeded us (without a peradventure) into forming a League, out of which the United States have contracted. We may be assured that membership of the League will impose upon us many onerous obligations, though not as many as if we were a small power. But there may well come a time when the League will demand from us the surrender of something as much desired by us as Mosul is by the Turks, and we shall not like it. We had not to wait for General Laidoner to inform us what like is the Turkish soldier sauntering through an enemy village, and we should be well content if the Turks were recognised by the League as a military organisation with no *locus standi* in a society of nations. But that will not happen. Either the Turks will give in, or there will be an international demonstration, and then they will give in, or there will be a war. In which case it must be a war between the League, and not England, and the Turks.

Getting Rid of our Farmers

ENGLAND continues her mad attempt to rid herself of any persons of farming experience. After January 1, married men (and even, we gather, single men) with farming experience who are going to farm in Canada will be able to get from England to Halifax, St. John and Quebec for £3, to Winnipeg for £5 10s., and to Vancouver for £9. Even a limited number of single men without farming experience may take advantage of these rates if they declare themselves going to Canada to farm. Apparently Canada's need for more agricultural workers is great, but ours is greater, if only our Government knew its business. And we should like to know what plans are being made for settling the intending farmers on the land. Formerly there were no plans at all, and we were asked by Canadian friends to warn English people against the booby trap. Are there any plans now? There is a nasty ring about the preference given to men with experience in farming when you test it against the announcement of the Canadian Government that the design of the new rates is to obtain farm-workers for farm work. Does that mean that the married men with experience of farming are needed as agricultural labourers? We do not want to be unjust to the Canadian Government, and we shall be glad to learn that the immigrants with farming experience will be given every facility to acquire land. Nor do we blame them for wanting to get our best men over there. But we blame our Government for inciting them to go.

The Case for Protection

WE fail to see how a Socialist can logically object to the Safeguarding (or Protection) of Home Industries. His theory, as opposed to the *laissez-faire* of the Manchester school, implies the right of the State to interfere with and regulate the course of trade both domestic and foreign. If he happens to be also a Trade Unionist he should see the reasonableness of robbing the product of foreign cheap labour of its resultant advantage when competing in the home market with home-made goods. We know that Protection is often to the advantage of the manufacturer and the trader rather than of the workman and consumer, but it need not be, and the business of the Labour members is to watch the operation of the Safeguarding of Industries Bill when it becomes law with a view to amendment if its incidence is unjust. This is the more necessary as at least one member of the Cabinet is interested in the trades to be safeguarded. No doubt Protection-all-round is a folly, and the trades to be protected must be carefully selected from time to time. Moreover, the protection must necessarily be temporary. If in the long run we cannot produce an article as cheaply as the foreigner, we had better produce something else. Unless it is a thing we *like* producing; but that is another matter. A protected industry is in an artificial condition, and the permanent erection of a tariff wall is as foolish as the lowering of wages. We can in England produce things of a quality which will command their own price in the world's market. Let us concentrate on those! Obviously an exception must be made in the case of stable and key industries.

Economising our Defences

THE speech made at Chelsea by Sir Samuel Hoare, the Secretary for Air, was most unsatisfactory. He stated that:—

Although our inferiority in air force as compared with that of other Powers is still notorious, and although air attack is the most dangerous form of attack to which these shores are liable, as a result of the Treaty of Locarno we are prepared to spread to some extent our programme of air defence.

Let other countries follow our example, and make it possible for us to carry out this postponement and for all Governments to avoid in the years to come a race of armaments that will be far more disastrous than any that we have endured in the past.

You will observe that we are to set the example, although "Our inferiority in air force as compared with that of Foreign Powers is still notorious." The thing is absurd. We congratulate Sir Samuel on the fact that whereas when he first took office our air force was in an inferiority of one to ten, it is now only in an inferiority of one to three as compared with that of France. But that good work must be continued. And Sir Samuel does not say how we compare with Germany, though perhaps the new Russian book of revelations might tell us.

For the Sake of a Few Shillings

THE Government will complete, stage by stage, its Home Defence Force of 52 Squadrons. But there will be a slowing down. Why? Partly because Europe is so peaceful, and partly because *the British taxpayer is clamouring for a reduction of Government expenditure*. In other words, we are to witness a cowardly surrender to the clamour of big business men voiced by the Yellow Press. Sir Samuel knows the extra expenditure is necessary, and says so.

" The rise from £16,000,000 to well over £20,000,000 would have in no way been due to Air Ministry extravagance. Inquiry after inquiry has come to the same conclusion that the Air Ministry has carried out its difficult task economically and efficiently.

" It would have been due to the sole fact that you cannot treble the strength of one of the fighting services without incurring cost, and that next year would have been a peak year in our expenditure owing to the capital expenditure for new stations being incomplete and the maintenance expenditure for half the new squadrons being already started."

The introduction of air power made this country vulnerable to a very terrible sort of attack, against which a Force comparable with that of any other nation must be our protection. The saving of £4,000,000 a year would mean a few shillings less in taxes per head of population. Is it possible to weigh the risk against the saving? What will happen is what happened before: when war is declared there will be a frantic rush to build aeroplanes at scare-prices, for which we shall pay, as we are paying, when the war is over. We note, however, Sir Samuel's hint that our action depends on that of foreign powers. We trust that means that if there are no signs of slowing down by our competitors before the end of next year our programme will be speeded-up once more.

Another Ulster Revolt

WE have greatly enjoyed the report of the Ulster police strike. Into the cause of the dispute we do not wish to go, more than to say that it was a matter of length of notice and amount of compensation. But the proceedings of the rebels must be chronicled. The "A" Specials have formed a Strike Committee with its headquarters at Prince's Dock. There a rigorous discipline is maintained, and, says the *Morning Post*, "dispatch riders dash to and fro bearing messages. Lamps have been taken into the barracks occupied in Belfast by the revolting force, who have also laid in provisions which they declare will last for several weeks. Strict prohibition has been decided on, and every man in Prince's Dock has declared off liquor until the dispute is ended." We understand the men make a point of assuring newspaper representatives that they remain loyal to the Crown, but will stand by their rights. The declaration of loyalty has the usual Ulster ring. Ulster never was " loyal " to England, she used us for her own purposes, and many a Protestant and Ulsterman refused to respond to the toast of the King at the time when the last Home Rule Bill was passed. But the revolt pleases us immensely. Does it mean that the Irish Boundary settlement promises peace with the Free State, and so the "A" Ulster specials are resolved on a war of their own? Or does the thing go deeper, and are they resolved not to have peace with Dublin? Anyhow, this is a useful case to cite when people talk about the wicked lawlessness of the Southern Irishman.

The Cave Collapses

WE regret that the Labour Cave, headed by Mr. Wheatley, has been persuaded to return to its Party allegiance. We had hoped much from the independent action of such men as Mr. Wheatley, Mr. Maxton, and Col. Wedgwood. The point of view adopted by Mr. Ramsay MacDonald and Mr. Arthur Henderson is quite logical. They want to get back into power, and they cannot hope to do so soon unless their party is cohesive and easily manipulated. But we thought the insurgent members realised that a return to power, in or out of inverted commas, was not of prime importance, and that the results achieved by the old Irish Nationalist Party suggested the best method of attack. Mr. MacDonald has become a " statesman," interested in the Party game, and resolved to play it with a proper observance of the rules. That is why he is respected in political circles and why he must not be followed by any Labour member who wants things done. We have in mind, not the ultimate establishment of Socialism, for which all parties are working, but immediate problems such as unemployment, Trade Union activities and the attempt to paralyse them, the price of commodities, especially of food, and housing, especially of the working classes. A resolute Labour Cave might have gone a long way towards their solution. A Cave in each of the three official parties, working together without prejudice, might have solved them.

On the Eve of the Holiday

WE shall not attempt to hide from you the fact that this issue of the paper was put to bed shortly after last week's issue was published. Everybody's doing it; everybody must, if they are to reach their public before the holiday. And in writing our " Notes of the Week," which are in fact the notes of a day, we feel inclined to plagiarise from the *Times*, and say that " nothing has happened except forty-eight hours." But indeed there is something profoundly real about this pause in events, which we should have felt even if we had been given a week instead of a day to write about. For the whole of the seven days before Christmas Day are the Eve of Christmas, when the world seems to stand breathless waiting for the Event. Anyhow, we shall write no more this week about Kings and Kaisers, Kabinets and Kapitalists. We are just starting our holiday, when we shall endeavour to forget there are such dreadful things as " proofs " or print of any sort. We are going to a pantomime, we are going to a party. You, sir, there, would look well in a false nose, and you, Sir, would look triumphant in purple whiskers. Madame, will you be my Colombine? In a Pickwickian sense, I mean! Pray do not take this as a declaration! Or, if you will, you shall be Prince Charming or the Bad Baron's unfortunate missus. Or a Queen, now, would you like to be a Queen? We are giving away crowns and things. But only for to-day, sir. With each half a pound of tea one crown. Please to fill in the coupon! All of which means that we wish you a Merry Christmas. God bless us, every one!

IN ANSWER TO THE COCKPIT

ON October 10, Mr. R. E. Woodfrey wrote reproving us for opposing the British Fascisti. He asked: "Whether it is as wise to risk allowing a revolutionary upheaval in the hope of snatching from the inevitable wreckage the materials for a saner National life, as first to ensure that the revolution is obviated, before legislating to erect the new edifice." Well, if the British Fascisti are not revolutionary, their plagiarism of the title of Mussolini's party seems unwarranted. If by "revolutionary" Mr. Woodfrey means "violent," then the British Fascisti have been revolutionary in their actions (they have brandished swords, they have broken up meetings, they have "borrowed" a newspaper lorry), but they seem to assume that violence is justified only in support of things as they are. They do not propose, for example, to march on Westminster, as Mussolini marched on Rome, and get rid of the political gang, as he got rid of it. Let them be assured that they will not "obviate revolution" by kicking up a dust with a few obscure Communists, or helping plutocrats to suppress a perfectly legitimate working-class movement. Mr. Woodfrey suggests that they may yet be marching side by side with us, but that will not happen until they realise where they want to go and what they must leave behind.

The need for the Editorial US to take a hand (or a a claw) in the Cockpit fight is emphasised by a letter received a few days ago assaulting us mildly for publishing Mr. Ussher's letter which was entitled: "Our Anti-German Bias." We replied to Mr. Ussher last week, but we want our other correspondent to understand that the Cockpit is an arena for those who disagree with us, with each other, and even with themselves, as well as for our partisans. And we take this opportunity of saying that even in other parts of the paper we have published and shall publish opinions widely separated from ours. In general we think that most of our readers recognise that they are not our opinions.

But in the case of the article "Henry Ford—Humanitarian" (October 31), one or two readers seem to have been puzzled, although in an editorial note we said of the writer: "His opportunity for acquiring first-hand authentic information (of Mr. Ford) has been exceptional, *whatever we may think of the conclusion he draws.*" Now in the issue of October 10 there was a sketch by R. A. Hodgson which did give our opinion of the standardised mass production which Mr. Ford and millionaires like him stand for. All the more pleased were we to receive later a portrait of the master-mind, by an admirer, which seemed to us absolutely to confirm our case. Mr. Hodgson might have written "Mr. Ford—Humanitarian" as an ironical pendant to "The Change."

On October 17 we published an interesting letter from Mr. K. C. FitzGerald, an Irish farmer. He put the point which has always been put where it has been proposed to re-distribute property. Even if families working on the land have, at a given moment, small farms, in a few years some will have prospered exceedingly, and some will have failed so completely that the choice for the men concerned will be to sink into the workhouse or to become labourers for the successful farmers. We think this is highly probable. Nevertheless, we know that in the past peasant proprietorship has endured in many parts of the world for centuries, and that France to-day, while so much else is in confusion, finds her main strength in the peasant ownership of the land. If Mr. FitzGerald, by acquiring land from bankrupt small-holders, "emerges into the large farmer class again," is his land, he asks, to be taken away from him and re-divided? Perhaps it might be. Perhaps the children of the men who had become his labourers might wish to take the risk of responsibility, and the Farmers' Guild might advance the money to buy back their fathers' land. A Distributist State could anyhow ensure that Mr. FitzGerald, who says he is a lazy man, did not become merely a capitalist who had sunk his money in land. Everything is done at present to make it difficult for the small farmer to own, and to keep possession; that process the Distributist State would reverse. But our strongest ground is that in the past peasant ownership has been found more enduring than any other system, except slavery, and that to-day in other countries, without special safeguards, it is enduring.

We note that in Russia, according to Mr. Norman Denny, who wrote in the issue of November 14, this tendency of "more enterprising, or more fortunate peasants to buy out their weaker brethren" is manifesting itself. We do not know to what extent this is the case, but we do know that the Russian peasant owner has so far been able to resist the tremendous pressure of the Bolshevik bureaucracy and its attempts to nationalise the land, and we await the issue with confidence. However, Mr. Denny scores a point against us. We had said that in negotiating with Moscow for wheat we were really negotiating with the peasant. We were wrong, and this has been made clear by the recent operations of Moscow in the wheat market. But our main position is re-inforced by Mr. Denny. He says: "The present (Russian) Government . . . is neither representative of, nor popular with, the peasantry. It is trying assiduously to ingratiate itself. Its measure of success may very possibly, in the long run, decide its tenure of power."

Mrs. Dora Russell's letter in the issue of October 3 does not really deal with the Tailpiece of September 12.

But on the new issue she raises she is wrong. It is not "a fact of woman's experience that limiting the family, whether in palace or hovel, means better health for mother and children." It is not a fact that it means better health for the mother, it is a wild assumption, and as for the children, in the majority of such cases there aren't any.

"Why," asks Mrs. Russell, "should we women not have four children instead of ten?" The answer to that is that in most cases Birth Control does not mean four children, but one or none. It means race suicide, and it means unhappiness for the childless wife and the breaking-up of homes. It means many uglier things.

We grant that while Birth Control is urged on the poor as an alternative to higher wages and better homes, it is practised by the well-to-do as what Mrs. Russell calls a way of avoiding "burdens," and what may be more legitimately called a way of escaping life. We call Birth Control a crime, but an Atheist Frenchman will tell you that it is a fatal folly.

TOP—

CREEDS IN THE CRYPT

A gentleman recently expressed the extraordinary wish to have his child baptised in the Crypt of the House of Commons. As he was a Presbyterian, it was necessary to establish the principle " that the Crypt of this ancient House is now available to all Christians of all denominations." The first Christian whose image springs to the mind is naturally Guy Fawkes; who perhaps interpreted a little too individually and intensely the right of a Christian of any denomination to pursue his activities under the Houses of Parliament. But the ceremony he attempted to perform is not (as some suppose) actually incorporated in the liturgies of his denomination; but was a spirited example of something that used to be praised as " private judgment " and is now praised rather as " private enterprise." There are many more logical deductions from the principle. For instance, Mormons are Christians of one particular denomination. Mormon marriages would seem to go along with Presbyterian christenings. It would be very interesting if a Mormon elder chose the Crypt as the scene of his wedding, or rather weddings. It is true that a Crypt is not very well adapted to Mormon marriage on a vast or multitudinous scale; to some superb and continuous pageant of polygamy, upon the Asiatic model of Solomon and all his glory. There is a good deal of polygamy in the poetry and romance of our time; and some of our novelists would require the use of Salisbury Plain rather than St. Paul's Cathedral, let alone the Crypt at Westminster, where their pent-up feelings might threaten to expand like the gunpowder of Guy Fawkes. But how, amid so many modern movements, can the Crypt reasonably be confined to Christians? We do very seriously owe an obligation of brotherhood to all men; but that is not necessarily confined to Christians. Why should it not be available to all Moslems of all denominations or all Hindus of all denominations; or even all agnostics of all denominations, of which there are a good many? Surely Mr. Saklatvala must not be shut out of the Crypt of the House of Commons; on the contrary, there are many in the House of Commons who would like to see him shut in. He is, we suppose, a Parsee and represents the old Persian cult and culture of sun-worship and fire-worship. It might be a little difficult to worship the sun in the Westminster Crypt; though (the distinguished Oriental might well retort) sometimes not more difficult than in the Westminster streets. But fire-worship would be quite feasible, if perhaps a little risky and liable to some of the objections urged against the private enterprise of Guy Fawkes. And how about facilities for the other new religions? If the trumpet give an uncertain sound, how shall Mr. Dennis Bradley prepare himself for the battle; and could it not sound regularly from such a cave? Could not all the Christian Science healers be locked up there, to give us all absent treatment?

The real history of the Crypt may seem to some an allegory. It was called in the fifteenth century " St. Mary in the Vaults "; and it has since been in turn a stable under Cromwell, a private room for Walpole, a coal-cellar, a lumber-room, and so at last a place available to Christians of all denominations.

—AND TAIL

THE SIN OF MODESTY

We noted recently that there is a new muddle in morality upon the point of the ancient virtue of modesty; a muddle chiefly encouraged by the cheap psychology of publicity. But we should never have imagined that even a politician could be so utterly and unfathomably muddled as Sir Philip Cunliffe-Lister. His speech at a recent Mansion House meeting was something like a serious repetition of a very comic song in one of the Gilbertian comic operas. He is reported as saying solemnly: " We have many virtues as a people, but we have one great defect. We are too modest about our achievements." And so, "we" being first conscious of our virtues, and then conscious of being unconscious of our virtues, proceed to inform the world, first how good we are, then how modest we are, and then how wicked it is to be so modest when we are so good. The Briton has every moral merit in every other way; the Briton is as military as Julius Caesar (who probably learnt the military art in Britain), as democratic as Danton (who lived for a short time in London, and probably picked up democracy there), as logical as Pascal (whose works are probably proved by a cryptogram to be posthumous papers of Francis Bacon), as mystical as Isaiah (which proves once and for all that we are the Lost Ten Tribes), and now all these virtues are balanced in the Briton in a beautiful harmony. But alas, there is a darker side! Alas that all these shining qualities should be blackened and blasted by a terrible sin! This paragon's possession of every moral merit is poisoned by the fact that he also possesses the humility of St. Francis of Assisi and the modesty of Colonel Newcome. But for these damning defects, how near to heaven might he not have soared! But for these vices, he might have been able to make some sort of public mention of his virtues; politicians might have talked about them; and Sir Philip Cunliffe-Lister might even have referred to them in a speech at the Mansion House.

There is something confounding in the simplicity of the man who says: " We are very admirable, but we are so humble that we never think of saying so." Of course he does not exactly mean what he says; and of course he is practically unconscious of saying it. What he really means, or at least the truth behind what he says, is something like this. " Hitherto the natural vanity of vaunting oneself (which exists in every man and therefore in every Englishman) has been modified in its manner of expression, in the case of the Englishman, by the idea of the gentleman. England being ruled and represented by a gentry, a certain kind of restraint on swagger has been fashionable and popular. Therefore our national ideal has been Colonel Newcome; but Colonel Newcome was no good in business. The great business of mankind now is to make a great deal of money, as the Americans do and as Colonel Newcome would never have done. For this reason we must drop all the decent restraints and reticences of the English gentleman and make ourselves as like as possible to an American bagman. A gentleman will hate having to push himself *in that way;* but there is money in it." That is what Sir Philip really meant; though he probably does not know it.

AN INTERVIEW WITH THE BEAN

THE first question to answer is: Should the "g" be sounded hard or soft? If hard, then the name is merely a termination, which the Very Reverend Bean never comes to—though we live in hopes. If soft, then a hasperate would seem to be omitted, though no doubt the name has then a certain definite atmosphere, resembling that of Ickenham and 'umble. Or we may suppose the word curtailed for an anagram, and the tail part to be either "—urious" or "—unction" "—enuous." But I'm inclined to think that the "g" should be hard, and that the name stands for the mark of the present participle—a perfect definition of the Very Reverend Bean. Here is no rash plumping for any state of present activity or passivity; here is no suggestion either of Christian or heathen dogma. All that is carefully deleted, and the termination boldly announced—the present participle.

Taking his initials as initials, they are good ones—none better. It is obvious that he was not born with them, and there is a rumour that he got them at his baptism, but this he will tend to deny. Baptism is, for him, fatally involved in the geocentric conception of the universe, and he has been ego-centric from his youth up.

He once promised us that he would write a book, or a series of articles in the *Morning Pennant* on "How I Became a Bean." But the scheme fell through for the lack of material.

Some have doubted that he is a Bean at all. It is true he lives in a Beanery, but a man who lives in a stable is not a horse. True again, he dresses like a Bean, but I have appeared at a Christmas party dressed as Father Christmas. Finally he is known and addressed as Bean So-and-So, and in that style are made out his cheques from the *Morning Pennant*, yet even this is not conclusive, for was not the late George Sanger known and addressed as "Lord"?

It seems safest to conclude that it is a courtesy title—courtesy, we mean, on the part of those who use it. For it can have no significance as a badge of rank or the ensignia of belief.

The Very Reverend Bean has been accused of treading the broad way which leadeth to destruction. This is unjust: he foots the tight-rope, and that nimbly—especially when you consider that the crook at one end of his balancing rod tends to unstabilise his equilibrium.

We must admire how he maintains it—how, having lost his beliefs he keeps his decorum. *Dulce est decorum,* as the Old Bean himself would say. And then they talk of the dome of St. —— toppling!

When I sought an interview with him, he said that he had signed an exclusive contract with a certain few newspapers, but he was able to make an exception in the case of G.K's WEEKLY, provided he wasn't paid for it. I assured him that he wouldn't be paid.

I began to ask him his opinion on the present controversy in the Anglican ——, but he interrupted me.

"My dear fellow, I never talk shop," he said, "for less than fifty guineas a thousand."

"Besides," he went on, "I know nothing whatever about religion. And, except that now and then I like to gird at the gross superstitions of Constantinians, the subject does not interest me. But tell me, are you Nordic?"

I said I had been, but Sir Herbert Barker put that right.

The Old Bean smiled sourly, and said he was in favour of Birth Control.

"But not," I said, "of celibacy?"

"Emphatically no," said the Old Bean. "That would spoil everything. I believe in making the best of both worlds."

"Heaven and hell?" I asked.

"There never was a heaven," said the Old Bean darkly, "and this is all the hell I want."

I had not the heart to pursue the subject.

"What," I asked him, "is your opinion of the Waterloo Bridge dispute?"

"Let us have a new bridge, by all means! The new thing is always and altogether better than the old. I may regret that this reminder of our old enmity for the decadent French should disappear, but, after all, we have the station."

"Don't you admire Rennie's bridge?"

"No, sir," said the Old Bean, "certainly not. It is geocentric. A good bridge, like a good religion, should have its foundations in the air, where they can be seen."

"But," I objected, "such a bridge would be useless as a means of crossing from this bank to the next."

"Who wants to cross?" asked the Old Bean. "A good bridge, like a good religion, should be a hiatus."

"Is it true that Mr. Epstein has been asked to design the new structure?"

"I hope so," said the very reverend. "Of course, I shall object, but it will provide a fine subject for a newspaper article—perhaps for several. . . ."

There was a wistful look in his eyes.

"Moreover," he went on, "Epstein's art is so delightfully Pagan, and it is our Christian duty to have charity for those who seem not to believe what we are supposed to."

"That reminds me, do you believe in God?"

"My dear fellow," said the Old Bean, pressing the bell, "what a very indelicate question!"

W. R. TITTERTON.

Whines from the Wood

A LITTLE sip, a little sip
    And then too much.
This is the sort of thing to grip
A duke or a duch.
But we who live the life conviv.,
We are not such.

We drink and drink, and drink and drink,
And then stop short.
"Rum!" says Achates with a wink,
But mine's a port.
The tap's run dry?
Be pleased to try
The other sort.

You don't know how, you don't know how
To broach the bung?
The milkmaid never asked the cow
When I was young.
But simply drank
As from a tank,
The grass among.

Nevertheless, nevertheless,
I am discreet.
Despite the chill of bitterness,
True love is sweet.
Though hearts may ache,
A prime rump steak
Is good to eat.

Despite the smart, despite the smart,
The Lord has had
A corner for me in his heart—
The dear old lad!
And God's my friend.
And that's the end.
And aren't you glad?

Shepherd Watching Flock

THE BRAIN STORM

By Gregory MacDonald

IN an Age of Science anything may happen.

A rumour spread through the House. It was whispered, it was spoken, it was cried aloud. Members pshawed it, derided it, canvassed it; and it grew. Its author was little Clefton (C., Grinstead East).

So long as the rumour was personal to Clefton, so long as one said to another, " D'ye hear what little Clefton says? He says—— " the story carried no conviction; for Clefton was the most abandoned and deliberate bore that Democracy had ever chosen for a representative. But in the space of a short day the rumour became a ship under full sail, free in its own element, no longer held at anchor by Clefton's name. And it was no idle rumour. It was the truth.

Stripped of all dramatic conversational additions the truth was simply this: Bilke, the Prime Minister, had no brains!

There was really no reason to doubt the fact. Clefton had it on the best authority, the authority of his own eyes, and his discovery certainly did explain why Bilke wore such an obvious wig. It appeared that the brilliant statesman, dining at Clefton's home one night, was seized with an illness which was unexpected at least by the other guests, who recalled with delight that they had never heard him score off Clefton with such dexterity and point before. But Bilke felt his illness coming over him. He caught his host by the arm and dragged him into another room.

" Not a word of this, as you value your career," he muttered hoarsely. " Not a word! Take off my wig, unscrew my head, and put the regulator to zero!"

Then he fainted into a corner-stand filled with *bric-à-brac*.

The bewildered Clefton disposed his Chief upon the hearth-rug and removed his wig. He found, to his amazement, that the Prime Minister's scalp was literally as smooth as a billiard ball: it was made of ivory. This he touched, grasped, unscrewed. It came out under his hand, like the plug from a hot-water bottle; and within the cavity usually occupied by grey-matter was revealed a complicated little machine of gleaming metals. Clefton found the regulator and moved it to zero. He tapped the Prime Minister's head apprehensively. He shook it in agony. He banged it with some violence against the fender. Noiselessly the wheels began to revolve and the scalped politician came round with a start.

" Thank you very much," he remarked placidly. " Now when you have replaced my skull we shall rejoin the company."

For the remainder of the evening the Prime Minister guyed the right honourable Member for Grinstead East with particularly happy effect. He felt that his secret was safe and he made no further allusion to it. Should Clefton threaten to expose him he would cease to use him as his butt and Clefton would drop out of politics.

But Clefton, being what he was, buttonholed every available politician throughout the next day to communicate his untoward story. Sometimes, by sheer inadvertence, he accosted the same individual twice or even thrice over. No matter. In a very few hours the House of Commons was resounding like the Zoo with the varied noises by which the representatives of the People express their disapprobation or their pleasure. Clefton was forgotten. His story was believed.

Here was stuff for a political crisis! Looked at all ways round the situation fairly bristled with perplexities. First, as to Bilke. During the lifetime of three Parliaments he had been Prime Minister. He was the most astoundingly brilliant figure in the whole history of political institutions. True, he knew nothing of foreign policies; true also, his ingenious

expedients to stave off crises in home affairs were always failures; but the failures gave him the opportunity to invent new expedients. Not by these standards are statesmen to be judged. Bilke triumphed always because he treated Parliament with the gentle hands of a master-jockey, and because he was careful to keep a trump card up his sleeve for the very last moment at each general election. No Opposition could make headway against him.

But Clefton's bombshell was, so to speak, a two-edged sword. While the more conservative landed gentry among the supporters of the Government could no longer see in Bilke one of that splendid type that made England what it used to be, they were nevertheless quick to realise that Bilke might be the first of a splendid type that was to make England what it was going to be. The man was no less efficient merely because he was mechanical. The overthrow of Bilke meant the extinction of his party; and, true to their traditions, his followers began frantically to defend what they did not dare to alter.

For a moment the Opposition was in a state of wild hilarity, but sober reflection almost induced despair. In the first place, the general public could never be brought to believe that the Prime Minister had a mechanical brain. They did not know him personally. The only hope was a revolt among the six hundred odd legislators gathered at Westminster. But, hang it all, they were gentlemen! If the Prime Minister suffered the inconvenience of a glass eye or of a cork leg it would hardly be considered gentlemanly conduct to make political capital out of the fact, and although there were no recognised rules of etiquette to dictate one's attitude towards an artificial brain—still, there it was.

At one point it almost seemed that the small Back-to-the-Land group would take over the Government. Gumble was effective when he declared that a man with an Ingersoll brain might very well have a Ford stomach. This gave rise to all sorts of horrid doubts. Bilke, for all they knew, might be a walking Industrial Revolution and he was closely scrutinised for a time. But Tinkell was generally conceded to have gone too far when, following up this train of thought, he asserted that Bilke was in the power of a small industrial syndicate which overhauled him once a year. The suggestion that the Prime Minister was in the hands of magnates was not sporting, and the Back-to-the-Land group lost its popularity.

All this time Bilke walked with his head in the clouds, affecting not to notice the political turmoil around him. His colleagues were not so tactless as to discuss their difficulty with him. The Opposition also was too well-bred to cause him any embarrassment. When Parliament broke up for the summer it appeared that Bilke had weathered the most violent storm of his career.

Not so, however. The worst of his troubles was still before him. As he entered the debating chamber on the first day of the next session, Bilke glanced casually at the Opposition benches and stood rooted to the ground in astonishment. His face was livid, a death mask; for his practised eye had noted an extraordinary change in his opponents. Horritch, Goxton, all the front bench; yes, and the Back-to-the-Landers, even Tinkell; and the Socialists, too—every man-jack of the Opposition was wearing a wig!

No wonder poor Bilke was dismayed when he realised that some diabolical agency had betrayed the whereabouts of the little German mechanic who invented all his mental processes. Over two hundred be-wigged politicians now possessed brains as brilliant as his own and they were intriguing against him. A Napoleon had arisen from the Corsica of the back benches.

The Napoleon was no other than Gumble, who had formerly distinguished himself by his passionate denunciations of machinery. But he was no obscurantist. He could on occasion bow gracefully to the inevitable. It was Gumble who persuaded the Back-to-the-Landers that the only way to save their party was to sacrifice all its principles; and in response to his appeals they took the detested machines, if not into their bosoms at least into their heads. It was Gumble who brought the Socialists to the very sound conclusion that the equality of man would be possible only if brains were standardised, or even (as he conceded) nationalised.

Only two members of the Opposition held out against the conspirators. One was Dodderington, a man whose pride was his impartiality, whose *idée fixe* was that there were two sides to every question. He, therefore, insisted upon having the material basis for his impartial spirit scooped out, but he refused to allow the insertion of a mechanical brain. And Mrs. Gumble, M.P., resisted her husband's desire for an operation because she was extremely proud of her Eton crop.

The mine was laid. But was Bilke hoisted to the moon? Not at all. At the very first division the fallacy of Gumble's arguments was abundantly demonstrated. Because all the brains of the Opposition resembled exactly the brains of Bilke there was, practically speaking, no Opposition at all. The whole body cast their votes in his favour repeatedly, and within a week Bilke was proclaimed Dictator.

In the wilderness of the Opposition benches the Parliamentary correspondents of the session saw one small oasis. Mrs. Gumble sat pale and determined, still proud of her Eton crop; and Dodderington, the impartial, beside her, twiddled his thumbs in a state of complete vacuity. Whether His Majesty's Opposition so constituted ever succeeded in overthrowing Bilke the Dictator we must leave to the historians of the future to decide.

But in an Age of Science anything may happen.

THE VILLAGE OF THE STRAGGLING STREET

ON a mountain side some miles from Innsbruck lies the Village of the Straggling Street. You could not forget that picturesque straggling street winding its way up the mountain side as if it were the main thoroughfare of a great city. A tiny street, but proud of itself and its crowning glory—the old church on its summit. Last Christmas Eve the snow lay thick on the old church steps. The Alps had disappeared into the night, waiting to rise again, white, glowering giants on Christmas morning. But on Christmas Eve the snow lay like a carpet stretching into a dim eternity.

The bells of the old church rang, calling and calling to the Village of the Straggling Street. The coloured windows of the old church glowed joyfully; never was there such a happy little church in any village on a mountain side. It pulsated with joyful importance—was it not Christmas Eve?

On the snowclad steps of the old church sat an old woman, a very old woman. She was wrapped in a shawl which had once been of bright and gay colours, but was now as faded as she was herself. She sat very still, looking before her—just listening to the bells. Through the half open door of the old church you could see that it was decorated for Christmas, and in a tiny chapel was a Crib.

But the old woman sat on the snow-clad steps staring before her—just listening to the bells that echoed down the mountain side into the valley below.

Up the straggling street came a young girl. She was very young. She went up the steps of the old church, and as she passed the old woman she stopped.

"A Happy Christmas," she said, and she gave the old woman a coin.

"A Happy Christmas," said the old woman, as she took it.

"Do you really think that I shall have a happy Christmas, old mother?" she asked.

The old woman did not answer.

The young girl bent over her.

"You see, old mother," she said, "I've lost him. He went away many months ago and said he would come back to me, but I think he never will now. Never. I couldn't have a happy Christmas without him. Tell me, old mother, do you think that he will ever come back?"

"Go and pray before the Crib," said the old woman.

"But I have prayed, old mother."

"Go and pray again," repeated the old woman, looking before her and listening to the bells echoing into the snow-covered valley below.

As the young girl went into the church a tall man and a woman came up the steps. The lady was wrapped in rich furs and she was very beautiful. Although the snow enhanced her beauty nothing could soften her expression.

"I suppose one ought to come," she said.

"One ought," answered the man.

He was very tall and looked very rich.

"Beastly nuisance the car won't climb the slope," he went on.

"I do hope it's warm in the church," said the beautiful lady.

"It's rotten about the car," the man said, "and something ought to be done about that street. It's awful. Not fit for decent people to use. It's all right for peasants and people like that, but not for us."

Then they saw the old woman.

"A beggar," said the beautiful lady.

"Better give her something," said the tall man.

"Yes, it's Christmas. It's the thing to do," replied the lady, as she opened her bag.

It was of gold mesh and it suited her expression.

But the old woman sat on the snow-clad steps looking before her and listening to the bells that echoed into the valley below. The lady held out a note to her.

"Here you are, my good woman," she said.

"I would rather you wished me a happy Christmas," smiled the old woman.

The beautiful lady pushed the note back into her bag of gold mesh. "Well," she said to the tall man, "I never did. Since the war these people are becoming so independent."

"Beggars ought not to be encouraged," he answered, and taking the beautiful lady's arm he led her into the church.

After a moment the bells stopped ringing and from within came the sound of music and the chant of voices.

. . . Singing the joyful news that Christmas was bringing peace and goodwill to all men.

The old woman drew her faded shawl of bright and gay colours around her. She was so alone.

In the old church all was warm and happy. Out in the cold the earth seemed waiting, waiting for the coming of Christmas Day. Down from the mountain side towards the Village of the Straggling Street came a young man. He looked very weary, but on his face there was an eagerness.

He looked as if he were seeking.

He passed the old church, looking straight before him, into the Village of the Straggling Street. The old woman, without moving, cried after him, "A happy Christmas, my son."

The boy turned.

"A happy Christmas, old mother," he answered. Then he came back to her, and stood close by her. "It's a cold night, old mother," he said.

"It's cold, my son, but warm within," she answered, motioning to the church.

"What's the use" he answered. "She will have forgotten me if I do not hurry to her. She lived below in the little house with the painted walls. I left her and now I cannot find her. Do you think I shall ever find her again, old mother? Will she forgive me when I do? I left the village to seek my fortune, and I have come back with nothing. Nothing."

"There is always love," said the old woman.

"Yes, there is always love," said the young man.

"I had a son once," whispered the old woman. "Some people said that he was a fool because he was not clever like the other lads in his village, but I loved him. Then he went to the war. There was no talk of his being a fool when it came to fighting, except that he did not know what he was fighting for—like many others—he was killed . . . killed. Now I'm alone—alone."

"I had a mother," said the boy. "She died of starvation in the war, and if I do not find the girl who lived in the little house with the painted walls I shall be alone, too."

"Go into the church," said the old woman, "and pray."

"But I have prayed, old mother."

"Pray again," she commanded. "Pray before the Crib. Pray to the Child Jesus, and put this in the box for the poor."

She gave the boy the coin the girl had given her.

"But, old mother . . ." began the boy.

"Do as I say," said the old woman.

The boy went into the church.

The snow on the mountain side glistened. The sound of Christmas joys came from within the church.

The Village of the Straggling Street lay still and snug in its white covering. The old woman sat still, looking before her, listening to the chant of Christmas hymns that floated from the old church into the valley below. Presently she looked up. A stranger had come up the street and stood before her; a tall stranger wrapped in a heavy cloak. He had kind eyes, and when he smiled it seemed to the old woman there was a shining in them.

"Why aren't you in the church?" he asked the old woman.

"I'm too poor," she said, "I cannot even offer the Child a penny to show that I am glad it is Christmas. I'd like to see the Crib, though," she went on, "but I'm all alone and I'm afraid to go into the church by myself. I'm old and forgotten and unwanted, but I'd like to see the Crib and pray to the Child Jesus."

"But why don't you go in?" asked the stranger. "Come now, let me persuade you. It's my duty to see that people go to the Crib on Christmas Eve."

But the old woman shook her head.

"I'm too poor, too old. I shall never go in. And yet I want to see the Child, St. Joseph, the Manger, and the star guiding the Wise Men. But more than that, I want to see Our Blessed Lady bending over the Crib, smiling. . . . But I'm too old, too poor, too faded."

"No one is too poor to see the Crib on Christmas Eve," said the Stranger. "You shall see it, old mother."

"But how?" asked the old woman. As she watched him it seemed to her that the stranger's face grew very bright, and through the darkness of his cloak there came a flash of gold and blue and scarlet. And it seemed to her that he drew a sword from his side and slashed it through the air.

The Village of the Straggling Street lay very still in its coverlet of snow.

"Look," said the stranger.

The old woman crouched on the steps and gazed before her. A star shone in the firmament high, high above her.

"It's the Star," she cried, and then beside the Star she saw the Manger in which the Child lay, and over the Child bent His Mother—His young and wondrous Mother. Around the rude cot knelt the Wise Men and in their hands they carried gifts of unsurpassing worth. With them knelt the

Shepherds, gazing. By the Virgin's side stood St. Joseph, loving, strong and tender, and through the thatched roof shone the Star of Bethlehem.

Into the Manger where he lay.

As His little hands moved, even the cattle watched adoring.

The old woman gave a little cry and hid her face. But the stranger bade her look once more.

On a throne high, high above the heavens, sat the Blessed Virgin and in her arms was the Child. Around her stood ministering angels.

"No one is alone," said the Blessed Virgin, and the Child held out His tiny arms to the Village of the Straggling Street.

"Look, look," cried the old woman, "there's my son, my son," and she pointed to one of the ministering angels, all glorious and bright.

The stranger put his hand on the old woman's arm.

"Come," he said. "Come."

The old woman looked up. St. Michael stood beside her. She arose and followed him out of the Village of the Straggling Street.

.   .   .   .   .   .

"Well, I must say," said the beautiful woman, as she walked with the rich man down the steps of the old church, "It's very cold. I shall be glad to get home and see what presents I've had sent me." And they went on, drawing their warm coats close around them.

The congregation left the church. Some still hummed the Christmas hymns and others were silent, thinking of far-off Christmas Eves. Last of all, hand in hand, came the girl and the boy.

"She told me to pray before the Crib, and now I've found you again," said the boy.

"She told me to also," said the girl.

"There she is. Let's go and thank her," he smiled.

They went towards the figure of the old woman, crouching upon the snow-clad steps.

"How still she is," said the girl.

"How still," said the boy.

"Old mother," whispered the girl.

"Old mother," whispered the boy.

"She's dead," the girl said, taking his hand.

"How happy she looks," he answered.

RALPH NEALE.

The Pantomime

So what was in the story books was true:
    There is a demon-haunted wood that hems
    The singing fountain and the land of gems;
And hark! that is the horn of the Boy Blue!
And look! in that portentous towering shoe
Hundreds of children dwell! and from the stems
Of flowers the fairies swing with diadems
Of gossamer, and fluttering wings of dew!

And now the Prince has kissed the slumbering lips;
And winter roses and midsummer snow
And sheaves of spring together fall and grow
And perish in a wild apocalypse;—
Till from a cataract of golden rain.
The mottled clown cries, "Here we are again!"

MAURICE BARING.

THE CORNER-STONES OF DISTRIBUTISM

IN the ensuing series of articles it is not the intention to draft a final policy of Distributism, but to stimulate thoughtful and constructive criticism by reducing existing theories into the form of practical suggestions. The following steps appear to be necessary in order to erect a policy :—

(1) The enumeration and acceptance of inescapable economic facts.

(2) The division of Distributism into its component parts.

(3) The survey of those vital considerations, non-fulfilment of which spells certain failure.

(4) The selection of those practical and attainable objects which shall ultimately form the approved policy of Distributism.

These articles will have fulfilled their purpose if they do but set the wheels in motion.

Mr. Chesterton's series of articles, "The Outline of Sanity," has made clear the inescapable fact that the doctrine of Distributism is one which affects every phase of economic life, both agricultural and industrial. For the principle of the widest possible distribution of wealth obviously embraces all wealth, and its ultimate form as a practical policy will depend solely upon the possibility or otherwise of various methods of distribution. So that in the necessarily slow and gradual process of evolving a policy from an ideal it will be as important to keep the limits of practical possibility in the foreground as to keep the ideal to the front. Neither the one nor the other is less important. The age-long issue of ideal and fact is joined once more.

The first point which arises from the consideration of Distributism is that it is not a doctrine of destruction. Its inmost motive is not to destroy but to create, not to tear down the economic edifice built up by the necessities and the wisdom of our forefathers, but to repair that edifice where possible and to rebuild it only where the ravages of time, and, indeed, of progress make necessary. It is a doctrine of progress, but it is also a doctrine of conservation. If it opposes the monopolies of industrialism, it opposes no less the even worse monopoly of the Collective State. And since it is founded on the principle of the distribution of wealth, then the protection of that wealth is inherent and vitally necessary to it.

If these preliminary and rather general arguments be accepted it is possible to proceed with the formulation not of a policy but of the foundations upon which a policy may ultimately be erected. And it is the purpose of this article not even to lay the necessary foundations, but merely to discuss four possible corner-stones thereof in the hope that the further discussion of them in G.K.'s WEEKLY may lead to a final adoption of the corner-stones of Distributism.

We all know that the first necessity of life is food. Agriculture, in its various forms, gives us our food. Although agriculture is the vital factor of our lives, we British are only too painfully aware that it languishes in Great Britain. We are a large population in a very small country, import two-thirds of our food, and to pay for that food have to export commodities. So we know that although industry depends upon agriculture for food, yet our industry pays for the food which we cannot produce and must import. What we do not yet realise, though its truth is being slowly and inexorably forced upon us, is that *a sound and successful system of agriculture is an economic necessity to industry*. And that, I venture to suggest, should be the first corner-stone of Distributism.

The second corner-stone of Distributism has been re-iterated constantly in G.K.'s WEEKLY. It is the principle of *the private ownership of property*. In support of this principle it were waste of time to adduce any further argument here; although it is certainly permissible to call attention to the fact, so often omitted by experts, theorists and professional reformers, that the private ownership of property is as fundamental a need of the human heart as is love itself. It is one of the main-springs of human nature, and any economic system which ignores it is fore-doomed to failure.

Capital is savings : the capital of a nation the savings of its citizens. Capitalism is thrift and the utilisation of savings to acquire potential wealth. Savings began, no doubt, with the storing of food, and progressed, by the use of gold, silver and paper tokens, which made savings "fluid," through various stages of usury to the modern system. But the main point for the Distributist to remember is that he is a Capitalist—that Distributism is a form of Capitalism. For are not peasants above all Capitalists? And is not every small shopkeeper a Capitalist? Mr. Henry Arthur Jones has pointed out that the only adults in the nation who are not Capitalists are those who are confined in madhouses and workhouses. A plain fact succinctly stated.

When the agitator yells from his tub, "Down with the Capitalists!" he is in reality shouting, "Down with myself!"—a very sensible slogan did he but translate it. When heralds of the dawn, such as the Collectivist, Mr. Sydney Webb, advocate their State Socialism they are advocating that we all should hand over our savings to the State and so create by our pauperism the worst form of monopoly yet invented. It is perhaps curious that they have not yet set the example by giving up their own private property : no doubt that will come, when a Socialist Government is in power. It would be a noble gesture and a good advertisement.

But the Distributist does not want to hand over his savings to the Government or anyone else. His creed is to distribute wealth and not to concentrate it, and—here I do invite criticism and discussion—*his main object is to create more Capitalists*.

So I suggest for the third corner-stone of Distributism the axiom that *Distributism is a form of Capitalism*.

The present writer, having been in business, knows that every business which does not improve is bound to deteriorate ultimately. Human activities cannot remain *in statu quo*. That is a remarkable and a vital truth. In England, even if the economic depression be taken into consideration, we are surrounded by examples of this truth—especially in our "heavy industries." Both agriculture and industry, in all their forms, must either progress or decline. In other words, progress is essential.

Now it is incontestable that progress must be paid for—either in agriculture or industry. And it always has, and always will be paid for out of profits. It is not merely a question of avoiding that form of national and universal bankruptcy which has distinguished the futile Communist experiment in Russia; but it is also a question of preventing that slow and progressive disintegration which must result from stagnation.

For the fourth corner-stone of Distributism, then, I suggest : *No economic system can endure unless run for profit and profitably*.

To recapitulate briefly :—

(1) Successful agriculture is necessary to industry.
(2) Property must be privately owned.
(3) Distributism is a form of Capitalism.
(4) Profits must be permitted.

Are these the corner-stones of the foundations of Distributism?

B. D. ACLAND.

THE NEW WAR ON CHRISTMAS
By G. K. Chesterton

CHRISTMAS, which in the seventeenth century had to be saved from gloom, in the twentieth century has to be saved from frivolity. The alternative need will seem natural enough if we picture any really poetical combination, as in any of the great Christmas pictures. If a man paints a rich blue sky with a single star blazing white above Bethlehem, the picture is just as much spoilt if you whitewash it and leave it all blank as if you paint out the star and leave it all blue. If there is some glowing Gothic window showing the Three Kings in the flamboyant hues of their holy heraldry, it is just as much lost whether you darken the window and turn it into a wall or smash the window and let in a white glare and a wind of winter. The dancing angels in the medieval picture will be equally limited whether you clip their wings or lame their feet; and the boy bishop ceases even to be amusing if there are no bishops except boys. Christmas, like so many other Christian and Catholic creations, is a wedding. It is the wedding of the wilder spirit of human enjoyment with the higher spirit of humility and the mystical sense. And the parallel of a wedding holds good in more ways than one; because this new danger which threatens Christmas is the same that has long vulgarised and vitiated weddings. It is quite right that there should be pomp and popular rejoicing at a wedding; I do not in the least agree with those who would have it a purely private and personal thing like a proposal or engagement. If a man is not proud of getting married, what is he proud of, and why in the name of nonsense is he getting married at all? But in the normal way all this merry-making is subordinate to the marriage; because it is *in honour* of the marriage. People came there to be married and not to be merry; and they are merry because they did. But in the snobbish society wedding the serious purpose is entirely lost sight of, and nothing remains but frivolity. For frivolity is trying to rejoice with nothing to rejoice over. The result is that at last even the frivolity as frivolity begins to fail. People who began by coming together only for fun end by doing it only for fashion; and there is no more even of faint suggestion of fun but only of fuss.

Similarly people are losing the power to enjoy Christmas through identifying it with enjoyment. When once they lose sight of the old suggestion that it is all about something, they naturally fall into blank pauses of wondering what it is all about. To be told to rejoice on Christmas Day is reasonable and intelligible, if you understand the name, or even look at the word. To be told to rejoice on the twenty-fifth of December is like being told to rejoice at a quarter-past eleven on Thursday week. You cannot suddenly be frivolous unless you believe there is a serious reason for being frivolous. A man might make a feast if he had come into a fortune; and he might make a great many jokes about the fortune. But he would not do it if the fortune were a joke. He would not be so hilarious if his benefactor, with similar hilarity, had left him bundles of bad bank-notes or a cheque book of which all the cheques would be dishonoured. The testator's action, however playful, would not be long an occasion of social festivities and celebrations; nor would the April foolery be so permanent as Christmas fun. You cannot even start a lark about a legacy you believe to be a sham legacy. You cannot start a lark to celebrate a miracle you believe to be a sham miracle. The result of dismissing the divine side of Christmas and demanding only the human, is that you are demanding too much of human nature. You are asking men to illuminate the town for a victory that has not taken place; or which they believe to be the lie of some Jingo journal. You are asking them to go mad with romantic joy because two people they like are being married, at the moment when they are being divorced.

Our modern task therefore is to save festivity from frivolity. That is the only way in which it will ever again become festive. Children still understand the feast of Christmas, they still sometimes feast to excess in the matter of plum pudding or a turkey. But there is never anything in the least frivolous about their attitude to a plum pudding or a turkey. Still less is there anything frivolous in their attitude to a stocking or a Christmas tree. They have the serious and even solemn sense of the great truth; that Christmas is a time when things happen; things that do not always happen. But even in children that sanity is in some sense at war with society. The vivid magic of that night and day is being killed by the vulgar levity of all the other three hundred and sixty four days. For this is the age in which everybody incessantly talks about psychology and nobody apparently thinks about it. Surely it is the very alphabet of psychology that a child will look more closely at one Christmas tree than if it stood in a forest of Christmas trees. Surely even a modern psychologist might know enough of his subject to know that one Father Christmas (whether detected to be Uncle William or not) is more exciting than a regiment of Father Christmases all standing in a row and all looking exactly alike. Yet the moderns are making the whole regiment of the three hundred and sixty five days look exactly alike, even if they are disguising them all in the same frivolous masquerade. They might at least establish one holiday in the year; one wild and hilarious holiday on which nobody could dance.

The battle against this barbaric blunder in psychology is especially joined in Ireland; and the chances are that the newspapers will talk great nonsense about it in England. There have been several signs lately that Ireland intends to be really independent; that is, that Ireland intends to be really Irish; and in nothing so much as in a greater restraint in the interpretation of revelry. It is something of a satire that Ireland was always taunted with being dependent on America. And now Ireland alone is making some attempt to be independent of America, while England is allowing herself to be more and more Americanised. The hard and brassy hedonism and heathenry of New York will have far less chance in Dublin than in London or Liverpool. The Irish are already appealing against jazz and jingle to the tradition of their old national dances, which are comparatively formal and even full of solemnity. The root of the difference is doubtless religious, like everything else; but our Americanised journalists will make another of their native howlers if they imagine that the protest is merely what they would call "clerical." Dignity is deep in the Irish blood and bone; as a priest once said to me, " The Irish have the passion of distinction." It is because the Irishman is an Irishman, and not only beause he is a Catholic, that he would always have objected to a young woman in tights and a top-hat becoming the only form of national entertainment. I remember hearing Mr. W. B. Yeats, who is certainly neither a clerical nor a Puritan, saying in a voice of deep indignation : " I hope to see the day when there shall be fights in the street over the attempt to force on our people the vulgarity of the cosmopolitan theatre." It is not impossible that his hope may be realised.

The English Christmas was quite as noble and national a thing as the Irish dance. It was not quite so dignified a thing because it was English and not Irish; but it was, in its very intense and intimate essence, innocent. The whole glory and gaiety of the thing collapses at a touch of anything that is not innocent. Anybody ought to be able to see that, as a mere fact of artistic unity and atmosphere, however much he may himself have lost his innocence; he ought to be able to see what sort of words or suggestions would in fact spoil an old English Carol or spoil a Dickens' story. And those are exactly the elements of that atmosphere that is coming upon us like a roaring and reeking gas out of the yawning and glaring furnace of the new frivolity. It poisons the popular instinct for pleasure, which triumphed in the old popular feasts. It is, very truly, the pace that kills.

A Carol of Unchanging Things

THE passing years bring changes
   To country and to town;
   And many a new place is built up
And many an old pulled down.

Old customs, like old houses,
   Fast fall into decay;
But Christian men shall ever praise
   Christ's name on His birthday.

When Jesus was a baby,
   And in the manger lay,
The snow that fell was not more white
   Than this which fell to-day.

Still brightly shine the berries,
   And they shone red as blood
When Mary in the stable
   Beside the manger stood.

To-night above the market-place
   Each star glows like a gem :
And so they shone that first Christmas
   Above sweet Bethlehem.

Changeless as these His mercies are
   Who came down from above
To lay within that manger
   And reign as King of Love.

" Peace upon earth ! " the angels sang
   At His nativity;
" Good will to men ! " the burden rang
   Of their high minstrelsy.

" Peace upon earth ! " our fathers sang,
   Mindful of that decree;
" Goodwill to men at Christmastide ! "
   And even so sing we.

We have no precious gifts to bring :
   We are but simple men :
But right goodwill have we to all
   Within this house. Amen.
          KENNETH H. ASHLEY.

THE COCKPIT

To the Editor of G.K.'s WEEKLY.

HOW HATH THE MIGHTY FALLEN

DEAR SIR,—May we ask why, in view of the following points you admitted into your issue of November 7 the article entitled "Henry Ford—Humanitarian. A Psychological Study of the World's Richest Man." (*a*) It does not fulfil the promise of its high-sounding title; (*b*) The article itself is (1) astonishingly bad journalism, (2) lamentably lacking in coherence and cohesion, and (3) fatuous in its triviality.

This is not the patronising criticism of those who think that their admiration for you entitles them to find fault; it is simply the desire of two bewildered readers for enlightenment on a phase of your paper which they have failed to understand.

In this spirit may we ask how you, with your decided views on philanthropy, humanitarianism and capitalism, reconcile the admission of this article with them? Was the last phrase in your introduction to the article an emergency exit? How hath the mighty fallen!

We beg the favour of a reply; please do not leave our questions exposed to the unanswered desolation of the Cockpit. —Yours faithfully,

PEC.

MENDEL AND DARWIN

DEAR SIR,—It is surprising to find in reading G. C. Heseltine's article, "Dewdrop and Diamond," that there are people, who, while presuming to write on the subject, possess so little knowledge of Darwinism as to confuse the several Darwinian theories.

The theory of the "Descent of Man" from the lower animals still stands unassailable. Apart from the evidences of "a few bits of broken skulls," we have now many proofs from the studies of comparative anatomy, embryology and pathology.

As "ismists" we prefer a theory which is rational to one which is mythical, a theory which is inspiring to one which is discouraging—in short, a theory which is possible to one which is impossible. Darwin explained the evolution of man by a process of the survival of the fittest; the fittest be it noted in adaptability and intellect, not in mere brute strength; his separate theory, "The Origin of Species," was an attempt to explain the *arrival* of the fittest. It is to this theory that Mendel has given, in the words of Morgan, the *coup de grace*.

Mendel has done more than this, he has replaced it by a sounder theory and augmented by Morgan's work on Drosophila, a more practical and tangible one.

Thus the theory of man's evolution has been strengthened by Mendel's work and nothing could be farther from the truth than to say it has been "shook to air." Why the writer should, in what appears to be a defensive tone, assume the task of eulogising Mendel, I fail to see.

In all our universities Mendel is held up by the greatest teachers of the day as an example worthy of imitation by the younger generation of experimental biologists.

Mr. Arnold Bennett is an able writer of bourgeois biographies, but as a figure worthy of consideration in modern biological philosophy he is presented, to me at least, in a new rôle.—Yours truly,

G. H. BATES.

DEWDROP AND DIAMOND

DEAR SIR,—May I ask my critic, Mr. G. H. Bates, why he found it necessary to dilate on so obvious a thing as my ignorance? He does not, however (and I venture to suggest cannot) quote a a single mis-statement of scientific fact in my article "Dewdrop and Diamond."

Had he given his more worthy critical faculty place before his indignation he would have observed that:—

(1) I did *not* "confuse" any theories of Darwin.

(2) I did *not* use the words "shook to air" with regard to "The Descent of Man."

(3) I did *not* use the expression "a few bits of broken skulls," which he apparently imputes to me since he quotes it.

(4) I am in entire agreement with Morgan's (and Mr. Bates's) opinion as to the effect of Mendel's work on the theory of Darwin referred to, and I expressed my opinion clearly.

(5) I never connected Mr. Arnold Bennett's name with "Biological" philosophy, and I hope I am incapable of doing so.

(6) The fact that Darwin and Mendel were biologists is accidental as far as I am concerned, and in no way affects my arguments. In a sense the whole point of the article may be summed up in the fact that they might have been butchers without affecting the argument. Perhaps that is why Mr. Bates as a scientist misses the point and strengthens it in so doing.

I feel sure that Mr. Bates ought to know that no *theory* is *unassailable*. Again, he must be even more ignorant than myself if he suggests that any *theory* is *impossible* to a scientist.

Since my critic joins me so heartily in my admiration for Gregor Mendel perhaps he can suggest some explanation of the fact that a thinker of such brilliant intellect and keen nose for error clung very tenaciously to a "theory" (the wrong word, but Mr. Bates's, not mine), which was "uninspiring, discouraging, and impossible."

We shall then get to the heart of the argument.—Yours faithfully,

G. C. HESELTINE.

WHY DON'T WE?

DEAR SIR,—Mr. Thomas Crompton may well observe that England has done more than any other country to deserve the divine appellation of Mother of the Arts, we may also wait long before that, or any mede of justice, is granted to her in G.K.'s WEEKLY.

I owe (as do many young men) a lot to Mr. Chesterton; I acknowledge my debt with gratitude; but it is a debt solely for past favours—the past favours of "The Napoleon of Notting Hill" and "The Flying Inn," not for present ones of G.K.'s WEEKLY.

Nothing in English political life is wholesome, no politician is to be trusted, for even if he's honest he's a fool, no men of money or in high places are decent or care a rap for England —that's the burden of G.K.'s WEEKLY. Instead of saying: "We're all English, let's pull together and get the old country out of a hole," it's: "Everything's wrong, everything always will be wrong, what's the use of trying," the keep-your-coat-on policy.

Let Mr. Chesterton realise a few facts: (1) Plenty of men in politics and in "big business" are as fond of England and as disinterestedly wholehearted in her service as he is.

(2) Perpetual juggling with words sometimes results in jugging them, and their meaning.

(3) The vast majority of Englishmen who were killed in the war were not "sick at heart and nothing afraid"; they were ordinary, jolly mortals often enough petrified with fear; and of all people they would be the last to be amused by a bickering, never satisfied, indefinite, unhelpful weekly verbosity.

Yours sincerely,

LAURENCE W. MEYNELL.

THE DRAMA

MR. ST. JOHN ERVINE has been making one of his most valuable contributions to dramatic criticism. He has launched a crusade against the murdering of the English language which goes on in theatres and places where they speak. It is a rare and an excellent thing to chance on clear enunciation and to listen in complete security to a delivery which gives full value to vowels, elides no consonants and remembers that the letter " r " has a unique value. I thought of these things when I was present recently at the Christmas play given by the pupils of Oakdene School, Beaconsfield. The cast was composed of quite young girls, few of them having reached the age of sixteen. They all spoke well, from the eldest to the youngest showed a sense of words and a comprehension of characterisation which was most refreshing.

Generally speaking, the dramatic performances given by schoolgirls at Christmas or midsummer suffer very badly from the choice of play. How often have we been called upon to listen to a childish rendering of " The Merchant " while Hubert and Arthur at all times and seasons are difficult to escape. There must be a steady demand for simple pieces suitable for young girls, and yet judging by results there must be a woefully inadequate supply. For this reason, for the benefit of those who want to know where they can find a play suitable in characterisation, subject and general scope, in which young people can take genuine interest and discover means of individual expression, I feel I am performing a really noble act in telling them that they will find all that they require in " Faith and Fable " a Masque in Two Scenes and Five Episodes by Frances Chesterton.

A CHRISTMAS PLAY

The motive of the play is simple and effective. The curtain rises on a group of children, whose floating draperies suggest old Greece. The little ones tell each other tales of the great gods, and lament their passing. The general concensus of opinion is that the gods are dead; a small party are agnostic on the point and a boy—known as the Child throughout the play—maintains his faith in their existence and sets out to seek them. The child's faith is rewarded; he discovers Vulcan sleeping by a cold forge. The lame god tells him that he can light no fires. He has passed from the memory of man; no one cares for the beautiful metal things he used to make—there is nothing for him to do. In the midst of his complaints, St. Dunstan, the patron saint of metal workers, appears. He blows alight Vulcan's dead fire, welcomes the god as brother and insists that they two shall work together, the pagan god and the Christian saint.

The child's next discovery is Orpheus, with a broken lyre. He laments the dead music; his songs no longer make glad the heart of men. There comes to him Saint Cecilia who stirs men's souls, calling them from sin as Orpheus called Eurydice from Pluto. The allegory is continued in the meeting of Diana and St. Joan, flaming symbols of womanhood, they bridge the gulf and merge their mutual glories. Then we have Pan—accompanied by four of the most adorable rabbits—who is welcomed by St. Francis. And last we see the meeting between Mars and St. George. The action of the drama never halts, and the young performers showed a very real capacity for characterisation. In no sense do these girls " act." They give a simple interpretation of the part they are called upon to play. They are, thank heaven, miles away from those pitiful little creatures, who, fresh from a training academy, mince upon the stage. Mars, for example, without any coaching, came upon the stage swelling with pride. His martial swagger was as irresistible as the pathetic droop of Vulcan by the cold forge.

THE CHILD AND THE GODS

The Masque ends with the return of the Child accompanied by the gods. who, with their attendant saints, form a procession. The final tableau was effective, and the costumes, both in colour and design, extraordinarily good. They were all home-grown, so to speak. Mrs. Chesterton, the moving genius of the whole thing, understands very thoroughly the value of suggestion. The setting for Vulcan and his forge was simply an old tree trunk with a pile of twigs, some red paper and an electric torch, which, at the pressure of St. Dunstan's fingers, blazed into light. I mention this because it goes to show what I and others of my colleagues so often labour to insist: that the whole art of stage presentment lies in the unloosing of the imagination of the audience. That tree stump, and the flicker of light, grew in our minds to a lonely forest. A stage forest would merely have closed our mental shutters—we should not have seen the wood for the trees.

I am not suggesting that the air of Beaconsfield is responsible for the amazingly good diction of the girls at Oakdene. Primarily they have the advantage of Mrs. Chesterton as a dramatic coach. But apart from this, one of the chief reasons lies, I think, in the simplicity and strength of the lines they have to deliver. Other plays by this author include " Piers Plowman's Pilgrimage, a Morality Play." This, published at 1s. 6d. net by Messrs. Samuel French, is as effective as " Faith and Fable," and its performance has been enjoyed not only by young people at Beaconsfield but has proved equally popular in other schools. The literary quality of these plays is unmistakable and there is a lilt about the songs that moves the feet to dance, and I feel that I deserve the thanks of all those who have been seeking for so long and so vainly one of the rarest things in this modern writing world—a simple, strong, well-written drama, in which such old-fashioned qualities as a love of country and a passion to defend that which we love, the blessings of liberty and the peace of home, are stressed. Such a play as this Mrs. Chesterton has written, and I commend either " Piers " or " Faith and Fable " for immediate and widespread production.

THE MIND OF THE CENSOR

I never pretend to understand the hidden springs which move the Censor to give or to withhold consent for the public performance of a play. It might reasonably be thought that a play which preaches the desirability of virtue in contrast to the soft and insidious habits of vice, would be considered fit and proper for the public. That this is not so has been shown repeatedly of late, though by the same token, plays of sheer nastiness in which emasculated men run in and out a lady's wardrobe hunting her underwear have been freely licensed. At this imagination boggles and I am constrained to remember those placid cinema films which expose " by permission of the Censor," cows at milking time, sheep grazing and ducks swimming, while scenes of an exotic character never seem to call for any such label. " L'Ecole des Cocottes," by Armont and Gerbidon, adapted by H. M. Harwood for the English stage, is one of the wittiest plays that I have seen for many a long day. Its moral lesson would appear to be that the way of ladies of this profession, though it may lead from flat to flat in an ever-ascending scale of lavishness, is not ultimately one of satisfaction. Ginette begins in a modest apartment in Montmartre with Robert, a musician after Mauger. It is explained to her by Stanislaus, Professor of Etiquette, that she is not doing her duty to society in remaining in obscurity. She has the power by the wearing of many and most expensive things to stimulate industry. She may be regarded as a revival of trade—a simple matter if she will only learn to use her knife and fork. She listens and goes from Montmartre to the Rue d'Anjou, and from there to the Avenue de Bois de Boulogne. We leave her on the eve of dining with a Cabinet Minister, who will doubtless translate her to an even more expensive domicile. The satire directed against publicists, profiteers and Prime Ministers runs like the finest play of swordsmanship—and scores at every point. The play, produced by Mr. Graham Browne and presented by the Play Actors, was brilliantly acted, and for the first time I am able to give Miss Gladys Cooper my wholehearted admiration for her rendering of Ginette. Miss Dorothy Hamilton as Amelie, an entirely dowdy and most respectable cocotte, was extremely clever, and the performances of Mr. Athole Stewart and Leslie Faber were quite perfect. The stage direction by Mr. Vere Bennett was admirable. It seems a pity that so much talent and such delicious wit should be hidden from the eager playgoer. I wish someone would explain the Censor.

MORE CHRISTMAS SHOWS I understand that Mr. Miles Malleson's play, "Conflict," produced at the Q Theatre, is coming to the West End soon after Christmas. The theme, it may be remembered, is a debating one, and the case for and against Socialism is contested. I did not see it at Q, but I look forward to its next appearance with curiosity. The author has a certain pretty fancy, and it will

be interesting to see if he can get over a serious theme expressed in witty and incisive dialogue. The cast will include Cecily Byrne, Collette O'Neill, Tom Nesbitt and Ian Fleming.

One of the most interesting of the Christmas productions will be the presentment of Cecily Hamilton's "A Child in Flanders," at the Old Vic. This Nativity play, given with old carols, will be followed by "Jack Horner"—culminating in a real old-fashioned gorgeous Harlequinade. The music of the pantomime will be founded on old English songs, adapted by that most popular of conductors, Mr. Corri. The gap between the Nativity Play and the Pantomime will be bridged by a poem by G. K. Chesterton, which will be Epilogue and Prologue in one. It is well in keeping with the Old Vic tradition that the Pantomime should have been written by the producer, Andrew Leigh, with other members of the company.

I hear that a very amusing revival has been perpetrated in New York, when that fine old melodrama "Sweeny Todd" was given in the costumes of 1830. The actors adopted the mannerisms of the period, and the whole production was extraordinarily amusing. It would seem that the States have rediscovered certain of our theatrical gems, and I hope that this good old blood and thunder epic of Fleet Street may be returned to us with the American company.

J. K. PROTHERO.

THE RETURN OF DON QUIXOTE
By G. K. Chesterton

CHAPTER IV.—(*Continued.*)

THE FIRST TRIAL OF JOHN BRAINTREE.

MR. ALMERIC WISTER was, and is, the one fixed point round which countless slightly differentiated forms of social futility have clustered. He managed to be so omnipresent about teatime in Mayfair that some have held that he was not a man but a syndicate; and a number of Wisters scattered to the different drawing-rooms, all tall and lank and hollow-eyed and carefully dressed, and all with deep voices and hair and beard thin but rather long, with a suggestion of the æsthete. But even in the similar parties in country houses there were always a certain number of him; so it would seem that the syndicate sent out provincial touring companies. He had a hazy reputation as an art expert and was great on the duration of pigments. He was the sort of man who remembers Rossetti and has unpublished anecdotes about Whistler. When he was first introduced to Braintree, his eye encountered that demagogue's red tie, from which he correctly deduced that Braintree was not an art expert. The expert therefore felt free to be even more expert than usual. His hollow eyes rolled reproachfully from the tie to a picture on the wall, by Lippi or some Italian primitive; for Seawood Abbey possessed fine pictures as well as fine books. Some association of ideas led Wister to echo unconsciously the complaint of Oliver Ashley and remark that the red used for the wings of one of the angels was something of a lost technical secret. When one considered how the Last Supper had faded——.

Braintree assented civilly, having no very special knowledge of pictures and no knowledge at all of pigments. This ignorance, or indifference completed the case founded on the crude necktie. The expert, now fully realising that he was talking to an utter outsider, expanded with radiant condescension. He delivered a sort of lecture.

"Ruskin is very sound upon that point," said Mr. Almeric Wister. "You would be quite safe in reading Ruskin, if only as a sort of introduction to the subject. With the exception of Pater, of course, there has been no critic since

having that atmosphere of authority. Democracy, of course, is not favourable to authority. And I very much fear, Mr. Braintree, that democracy is not favourable to art."

"Well, if ever we have any democracy, I suppose we shall find out," said Braintree.

"I fear," said Wister, shaking his head, "that we have quite enough to lead us to neglect all artistic authorities."

At this moment, Rosamund of the red hair and the square, sensible face, came up, steering through the crowd a sturdy young man, who also had a sensible face; but the resemblance ended there, for he was stodgy and even plain, with short bristly hair and a tooth-brush moustache. But he had the clear eyes of a man of courage and his manners were very pleasant and unpretending. He was a squire of the neighbourhood, named Hanbury, with some reputation as a traveller in the tropics. After introducing him and exchanging a few words with the group, she said to Wister, "I'm afraid we interrupted you"; which was indeed the case.

"I was saying," said Wister, airily, but also a little loftily, "that I fear we have descended to democracy and an age of little men. The great Victorians are gone."

"Yes, of course," answered the girl, a little mechanically.

"We have no giants left," he resumed.

"That must have been quite a common complaint in Cornwall," reflected Braintree, "when Jack the Giant-killer had gone his professional rounds."

"When you have read the works of the Victorian giants," said Wister, rather contemptuously, "you will perhaps understand what I mean by a giant."

"You can't really mean, Mr. Braintree," remonstrated the lady, "that you want great men to be killed."

"Well, I think there's something in the idea," said Braintree. "Tennyson deserved to be killed for writing the May-Queen, and Browning deserved to be killed for rhyming 'promise' and 'from mice,' and Carlyle deserved to be killed for being Carlyle; and Herbert Spencer deserved to be killed for writing "The Man versus the State"; and Dickens deserved to be killed for not killing Little Nell quick enough;

and Ruskin deserved to be killed for saying that Man ought to have no more freedom than the sun; and Gladstone deserved to be killed for deserting Parnell; and Disraeli deserved to be killed for talking about a ' shrinking sire,' and Thackeray——''

'' Mercy on us!'' interrupted the lady, laughing, '' you really must stop somewhere. What a lot you seem to have read!''

Wister appeared, for some reason or other, to be very much annoyed; almost waspish. '' If you ask me,'' he said, '' it's all part of the mob and its hatred of superiority. Always wants to drag merit down. That's why your infernal trade unions won't have a good workman paid better than a bad one.''

'' That has been defended economically,'' said Braintree, with restraint. '' One authority has pointed out that the best trades are paid equally already.''

'' Karl Marx, I suppose,'' said the expert, testily.

'' No, John Ruskin,'' replied the other. '' One of your Victorian giants.'' Then he added, '' But the text and title of the book were not by John Ruskin, but by Jesus Christ; who had not, alas, the privilege of being a Victorian.''

The stodgy little man named Hanbury possibly felt that the conversation was becoming too religious to be respectable; anyhow, he interposed pacifically, saying, '' You come from the mining area, Mr. Braintree?''

The other assented, rather gloomily.

'' I suppose,'' said Braintree's new interlocutor, '' I suppose there will be a good deal of unrest among the miners?''

'' On the contrary,'' replied Braintree, '' there will be a good deal of rest among the miners.''

The other frowned in momentary doubt, and said very quickly, '' You don't mean the strike is off?''

'' The strike is very much on,'' said Braintree, grimly, '' so there will be no more unrest.''

'' Now, what do you mean?'' cried the very practical young lady, shortly destined to be the Princess of the Troubadours.

'' I mean what I say,'' he replied, shortly. '' I say there will be a great deal of rest among the miners. You always talk as if striking meant throwing a bomb or blowing up a house. Striking simply means resting.''

'' Why, it's quite a paradox,'' cried his hostess, with a sort of joy, as if it were a new parlour game and her party was now really going to be a success.

'' I should have thought it was a platitude, otherwise a plain truth,'' replied Braintree. '' During a strike the workers are resting; and a jolly new experience for some of them, I can tell you.''

'' May we not say,'' said Wister, in a deep voice, '' that the truest rest is in labour?''

'' You may,'' said Braintree, dryly. '' It's a free country— for you anyhow. And while you're about it, you may also say that the truest labour is in rest. And then you will be quite delighted with the notion of a strike.''

His hostess was looking at him with a new expression, steady and yet gradually changing; the expression with which people of slow but sincere mental processes recognise something that has to be reckoned with, and possibly even respected. For although, or perhaps because, she had grown up smothered with wealth and luxury, she was quite innocent, and had never felt any shame in looking on the faces of her fellows.

'' Don't you think,'' she said at last, '' we are just quarrelling about a word?''

'' No, I don't, since you ask me,'' he said, gruffly, '' I think we are arguing on two sides of an abyss, and that one little word is a chasm between two halves of humanity. If you really care to know, may I give you a little piece of advice? When you want to make us think you understand the situation, and still disapprove of the strike, say anything in the world except that. Say there is the devil among the miners; say there is treason and anarchy among the miners; say there is blasphemy and madness among the miners. But don't say there is unrest among the miners. For that one little word betrays the whole thing that is at the back of your mind; it is very old and its name is Slavery.''

'' This is very extraordinary,'' said Mr. Wister.

'' Isn't it?'' said the lady. '' Thrilling!''

'' No, quite simple,'' said the Syndicalist, '' you will see it easily enough if you think a minute. Suppose there is a man in your coal-cellar instead of your coal-mine. Suppose it is his business to break up coal all day, and you can hear him hammering. We will suppose he is paid for it; we will suppose you honestly think he is paid enough. Still, you can hear him chopping away all day while you are smoking or playing the piano—until a moment when the noise in the coal-cellar stops suddenly. It may be wrong for it to stop— it may be right—it may be all sorts of things. But don't you see—can nothing make you see—what you really mean if you only say, like Hamlet to his old mole, ' Rest, perturbed spirit.' ''

'' Ha,'' said Mr. Wister, graciously, '' glad to see you have read Shakespeare.''

But Braintree went on without noticing the remark.

'' The hammering in your coal-hole that always goes on stops for an instant. And what do you say to the man down there in the darkness? You do not say, ' Thank you for doing it well '; you do not even say, ' Damn you for doing it badly.' What do you say is, ' Rest; sleep on. Resume your normal state of repose. Continue in that state of complete quiescence which is normal to you and which nothing should ever have disturbed. Continue that rhythmic and lulling motion that must be to you the same as slumber; which is for you second nature and part of the nature of things. Continuez, as God said in Belloc's story. Let there be no unrest.' ''

As he talked vehemently, but not violently, he became faintly conscious that many more faces were turned towards him and his group, not staring rudely, but giving a general sense of a crowd heading in that direction. He saw Murrel looking at him with melancholy amusement over a limp cigarette, and Archer glancing at him every now and then over his shoulder, as if fearing he would set fire to the house. He saw the eager and half-serious faces of several ladies of a sort always hungry for anything to happen. All those close to him were cloudy and bewildering; but amid them all he could see away in the corner of the room, distant but distinct and even unreasonably distinct, the pale but vivid face of little Miss Ashley of the paintbox, watching—

'' But the man in the coal-cellar is only a stranger out of the street,'' he went on, '' who has gone into your black hole to attack a rock as he might attack a wild beast or any other brute force of nature. To break coal in a coal-cellar is an action. To break it in a coal-mine is an adventure. The wild beast can kill in its own cavern. And fighting with that wild beast is eternal unrest; a war with chaos, as much as that of a man hacking his way through an African forest.''

'' Mr. Harbury,'' said Rosamond, smiling, '' has just come back from an expedition of that sort.''

'' Yes,'' said Braintree, '' but when he doesn't happen to go on an expedition, you don't say there is unrest at the Travellers' Club.''

'' Perhaps there is though,'' said Harbury, in his easygoing way.

'' Don't you see,'' went on Braintree, '' that when you say that of us, you imply that we are all so much clockwork, and you never even notice the ticking till the clock stops.''

'' Yes,'' said Rosamund, '' I think I see what you mean and I shan't forget it.'' And, indeed, though she was not particularly clever, she was one of those rare and rather valuable people who never forget anything they have once learnt.

(To be continued.)

THE SCRAPBOOK

THE TURKEY'S CHRISTMAS CAROL.

In this season of rejoicing,
Christmas wishes you are voicing,
But my prospects are, like Hades, very murky;
For I beg you to remember
That your feasting in December
Means a time of fearful terror for a turkey.

II.

Though the prodigal's returning
To a father who is yearning
Makes the fatted calf feel anything but perky;
Prodigals are rare, and rather
Rarer still the yearning father;
But there's no escape from Christmas for a turkey.

III.

In the farmyard I look showy,
And at Stratford-atte-Bowe
My appearance on a dish they call *rekerky*;
Hence I envy scraggy chickens,
While I hate the name of Dickens,
And lament the fate of Mr. Scrooge's turkey.

IV.

So I'm full of agitation
In this time of jubilation,
And you must admit I've grounds for feeling shirky;
You may call your Christmas merry
But I tell you that it's very,
Very far from being merry for a turkey.

T. B.

*   *   *   *

For our politicians no black shirt is meet;
We advise a white shirt, or still more, a white sheet.

*   *   *   *

LOCARNO.

Some say we know the day of Bethlehem
When rulers to high treaty set their hands;
Some say we know the hour of Calvary
By Pilate and King Herod shaking hands.

*   *   *   *

Though Christmas comes but once a year
With Christmas presents for a beano,
Valentine's Day through all the months
Brings Valentines to Valentino.

*   *   *   *

Not out of Bethlehem or the blessed star
Comes that base hour of Bloch when battles cease;
When Greek meets Greek, then comes the tug of war;
When Jew meets Jew comes worse—the tug of peace.

*   *   *   *

Fashion, we hope, will draw a line and stop,
To mark the Eton from the Dartmoor crop;
Manners, at least, some difference must strike
When morals grow so very much alike.

*   *   *   *

ON MEDIEVAL ITALY.

Men of importance; men in high esteem;
Busy with facts, some dukedom's loss or gain,
Grave politics, and many a deep-laid scheme;
Drew the world's gaze; while loitered in their train
Some unconsidered dreamer with his dream
—The Facts are fallen to dust. The Dreams remain.

EVA DOBELL.

NATIONALISM.

There was a young lady of Buda,
Whose father was born in Bermuda:
    Her mother, though black,
    Was a Czecho-Slovak
And by marriage a daughter of Judah.

R. V.

*   *   *   *

THE DISCOVERY.

[" The real issue at the elections in Belfast was the boundary which divides those who have no bread from those who have a surplus."—Mr. S. Kyle, M.P., in the Northern House of Commons.]

    While Mr. Feetham and his friends debate,
      The border has receded to Belfast,
    And thus the irony of Ulster's fate
      Reveals itself to Orangemen at last.

G. G. K.

*   *   *   *

ANOTHER SONG OF JOURNALISM.

Now harken to me if you're wanting to be
A journalist proper and " swish ":
Young Man, you must grovel, first write a Dud Novel—
And then you may write what you wish
           Young Man,
O then you may write what you wish!

In the *Daily Excess*, in that noble Stunt Press,
Do you think there to blazon your name?
Well, another good way, young fellow, to-day
Is to marry a lady of fame.
           Young Man,
Is to marry a lady of fame.

Oh, 'tis simple, you see: just the other great P,
Yet without it our little Brook frets—
They will treat you with scorn,
You will languish forlorn—
For they'll send your work back with regrets
           Young Man,
They will send your work back with regrets!

D. H. M.

*   *   *   *

" For purity," she died, and then 'twas seen.
Her memory, friends and hat alike were green.

R. N.

*   *   *   *

THE CLERK.

On Sunday through the fields I walk
And with the Higher Spirits talk:

On Monday to the office stool
I go, and scribble for a Fool.

For six week-days, I earn my wage
He only asks my soul in pledge:

On Saturday, I take it out
Shop-soiled and sadly knock'd about—

What though it be a little shrunk?
I gladly take it from its bunk:

On Sunday through the fields I walk
And with the Higher Spirits talk.

ALFRED J. BROWN

*   *   *   *

HIGHER CRITICISM.

Old Esau was a happy hunting, hearty, hale, and hairy man;
But Jacob an adulterating, devil-dodging dairyman.

R. V.

REVIEWS

A NEW VOLUME OF POEMS BY MR. CHARLES WILLIAMS *

IF to be wrath with one we love does indeed, as Coleridge averred, work like madness in the brain, then perhaps to be irritated with certain nonconformities in a good poet should disqualify one from reviewing him. Years ago, in the *Witness* (*Eye* or *New*—who can remember?) it fell to me to open the door for Williams. This present coincidence is none of my seeking, nor the author's, I solemnly assure the readers of this paper who hate all log-rolling. It is my destiny to open the door for Mr. Williams again, with a deeper bow than before, but with a whisper of protest, too.

For those who know not his previous volumes it may be necessary in a few words to situate this poet. Mr. Williams' instrument is not the penny whistle, the jew's harp or that saxophone about which *Punch* pours such a patient stream of well-bred fun. He does not expect to gather a crowd on the pavement. It is most unlikely that he will enjoy in his lifetime anything beyond a *succès d'estime*. His eventual success is sure. Rubbish, however highly praised and highly paid it may be when new, will not last—which, by the way, is a pity, because it is only an old vintage bosh that is worth anything; and then it disappears, just as it begins to acquire historical value. As we read the lineaments of the Victorian face mirrored in Martin Tupper or Lewis Morris, so our countenances will be read by posterity, reflected in—in whom? Who are the great writers of rubbish in verse? Since Miss Wilcox's death, do we hear as much as we did about the poetesses whose works sell entirely in morocco pocket editions at dressmakers' shops? Are not all best sellers in prose now? The many-headed British spinster now eats prose. Still, the market is forestalled against work of Mr. Williams' quality; the reviewers are busy talking about stuff which is freakishly, funnily bad, bad with schoolgirl naughtiness (like Miss Sitwell's productions) rather than schoolgirl goodness—like those of the late Miss Wilcox. The fact remains that modern good work, unless it has a long preparation like Housman's *Last Poems*, for which critics had been thirty years preparing a welcome, does not at once distinguish itself from the ruck, and the good poet must have patience, perhaps till his dying day. Not that I am without hope that Mr. Williams is educating readers for himself and building a public with new friends gained by each volume—this is now his fourth. But here is the rub. Neither am I without fears that he will lose good friends and make bad ones by his nonconformities. The word shall be repeated just for the sad irony of it that the poet of *Conformity* should weary of well-doing. There is one influence that has done him no good. He bids his poet, going to Rome, answer the question, "*Who now among the English wear the bay?*" by naming Yeats, Hardy and Bridges; these of the older. Among these, I fear, it is Hardy that has corrupted his admirer; though his verse is not as rusty and unmelodious as Hardy, there seems to be a new *parti pris* of avoiding tunefulness as a cheap meretricious attraction. And of a piece with this is the deliberate non-conformity of metre in, e.g., *Domesticity* and *The Two Domes*. Why should the author be pleased to turn his singing-coat and rhyme a and c, leaving b and d blank? It is as if he said to his reader: "You don't come here to enjoy yourself, my boy: in case

you might feel too easy, a pin will be stuck into you at intervals."

> Is it knowledge, is it knowledge only, and fear
>   Lest one chance of many should bring this body at last
> To burning or drowning? or exile from its dear
>   Companions and instruments, locked in a prison cell?

This is an unprovoked attack on the reader's ear. There is logic in rhyme when it closes the stanza with a clinch; but this queerness of rhyming the odds and leaving the evens blank gives me the impression of a man fixing his housedoor halfway up the stairs, and leaving his threshold open. One would like to think that it was of calculated purpose the poet devised this added irritant to enhance the awesome disquieting effect of the poem; but, alas, there are evidences elsewhere in the book that it is just a touch of nonconformity; there are here and there some dumps of raw words printed (in a sort of scheme) in the midst of finished products. One of Mr. Williams' masters, Coventry Patmore, might have taught him that words do not became poetry merely by being bad prose—any more than one becomes a Catholic merely by being a bad Protestant. Here endeth the fit of wrath. *Explicit ira incipit laudatio.*

These things would not matter if Mr. Williams were one of the abjects. But his best is of the best, not merely good but rare and, above all, highly distinctive. If it were shown you, unsigned by the author's name, without hesitation you would know for his and nobody else's work all that is best in the book; your warrant being a certain quivering supersensitiveness of the imagination, inclining to the macabre, a native elastic ease of movement, a most delicate but most unsqueamish diction, curiously streaked with seventeenth-century and with twentieth-century language. Almost unerringly his rhythm carries the words that are given it to carry, odd as some of them look; and the poet's thought—rich or quaint or grisly—is never allowed to be blunted or vulgarised just in order to avoid a word that is "unpoetical."

A quotation tells more than many lines of characterisation; here is a small specimen taken from the title-poem of the collection, *Windows of Night.*

> Around and over them the great night flows;
>   The night of genesis, the fount of all
>   Our life and height. What god, what animal,
>   Therein was our first father, when the pit
> Of space first held, running with melted snows,
>   Perception? What divine or bestial head
>   Remembers us? What hands or paws are spread
>   Upon the mighty stair to clamber it?
> Feel we not how on our interior throes,
>   Shaking the ladder of spaces and of times,
>   This living and forgotten monster climbs,
> Dragging the night behind him as he goes?

This kind of stanza fits Mr. Williams' ideas like a skin; it makes sufficient demand on his powers of workmanship never to allow him to go too easy (as in his sonnets he is tempted to do): in it he achieves effects of periodic magnificence, controlling the large movement by a most masterly management of speeding-up and slowing-down his lines. The specimen shows his preference for a full-weighted line, and his acceptance of the strict modern canon anathematising verbal inversion. His poetry does not make easy patter.

---

* WINDOWS OF LIGHT. By Charles Williams. Oxford University Press, 1925. Price 5s.

Difficult he often is; but a reader who is worth his salt, when he meets such stuff as this, ought to say: " Here is such an interesting and impressive noise that I must certainly stop and inquire what it is all about." In that case he will not be cheated or disappointed, but will find the matter almost always equally interesting by reason of the vastness of imagination, the finesse of fancy, the poignancy of sensibility, or some other quality highly personal to the writer.

I have quoted and commented on this poem because it is perhaps on the biggest scale of achievement that Mr. Williams has yet reached; though this is not the first volume in which he has shown that he understands the architecture of the great ode. There is much more here that is excellent—sonnets, each of which is the clean effortless incarnation of a simple thought; but in *Windows of Night* itself, more than in the rest, I find the satisfying assurance that the poet is going higher. *Ascensiones in corde suo disposui.*

One must not conclude without asking a question that suggests itself: What other poet has ever dedicated a book to his publisher? The fact that Mr. Williams does so is surely a very precious compliment to Mr. Milford, which the execution enhances. It is a charming example of the author's gift of style, mannered without affectation, minute without insignificance. Perhaps it is now time to remark that the most important thing to say of this poet is that he has an exceptional amount of style about him, and nearly all of it very good.

J. S. P.

A THOUSAND AND ONE!

LONDON has many moods and tenses, and it is given to few to know them all. She is most variable in her less fashionable moments—Piccadilly is eternally the same, and the people of Mayfair are almost fatiguingly well-dressed. It is when you go to the meaner of her streets that you find glimpses of a beauty so strangely concealed that at the moment of discovery you seem to see this city of a thousand facets with new eyes.

Mr. Stephen Graham knows all the fascinating byways—often cluttered up with vegetable refuse—all the secret alleys and those pleasant open spaces which in the city break the grey streets with oases of green. He opens many doors, reveals unlooked for poignancies, re-discovers laughter, that laughter which is the comment of the Cockney upon life. He has done most of his exploration at night when, as he says :—

> " London is more beautiful. There is a poetry in it which is missed by day. The night skies and the fogs hold it and brood over it, the many voices are hushed, and out of all the discordances of the day comes an issue of peace. The strivers rest from their striving, the workers from their work. . . . A feeling of exaltation creeps into the minds of those who watch while London sleeps, a sense of the majesty of seven million sleepers altogether under the one tent roof of the London night. . . ."

But it is not with those who sleep in peace and comfort that the author is concerned. He tells us of those outcasts " in twos and threes and fours on the cold seats of the Embankment . . . *disjecta membra* of our inhospitality, each with his story, his tragi-comedy, spending thus the midnight hours." The Embankment has a curious attraction for the homeless. It may be that the river has a certain narcotic influence, the impassivity of that sluggish stream seems to untie the knots in one's brain, to soothe the gnawing hunger for a bed and a hot meal. It may be that they feel there is a chance of getting the necessary coppers for a doss house in this spot; anyway, you will find there all sorts and conditions, and only on the very coldest night is it swept clean of humanity.

From the Embankment let us go to the Bohemian resorts of London, the night clubs, the cosy little supper restaurants

and the café bars. Mr. Stephen Graham knows them all, and his description of The Wooden Soldier, Au Chat Noir, and others of the same kidney, takes you right into those brightly lighted places where behind " a mahogany coloured horseshoe or lemon-shaped bar Frenchwomen and Italians dispense refreshments."

The author is on his native heath in Soho, and anyone in distress, pecuniary or otherwise, calls, as a matter of course, on him for help. He knows every corner of the quarter, and can call upon the night clubs each by its name. One of the most fascinating chapters in this voyage of discovery deals with prison life. Mr. Graham was a prison visitor at one time and he came to know the gaol types with a thoroughness that, while it brought much disappointment, never killed his sense of kindliness. He tells us that he spoke to " six hundred diminutive, untidy men in khaki with blue numbers on their chests, who sat huddled and looked curiously at me. . . . Despite khaki every man was self-developed and individualistic; the one thing they all had, however, and that was the blight of crime and punishment on their souls." And yet they still loved to laugh, and when they heard of Mr. Graham's adventures in Mexico they simply chortled with glee. They were, indeed, so pleased with their entertainment that at the conclusion it was suggested to them that when they emerged from prison, some of them might like to go there and make a fresh start. But there was nothing doing! They looked at him with sly eyes, and he realised that they would not budge from England. " Our criminals would rather enjoy the Police they have than fly to others that they know not of." Some of them are in and out all their lives, and as a whole the author regards prisons as resthouses for people who lead a life of crime. The danger is, he insists, to the beginners, for prisons are schools for the inexperienced. " No first offender should be sent to a prison where he comes into the company of the cynical and the hardened."

Then we are given a delightful pilgrimage through the London churchyards; the most wonderful of which is that of St. Botolph Without, Aldersgate. " A secluded green vale in the midst of our asphalted city, sometimes called ' Postman's Park.' Here amid old trees, tombs, a sundial and a fountain . . . tired people sit with their backs against the wall which tells otherwise only of stirring action—of Mary Rogers, stewardess of the *Stella*, who sacrificed her lifebelt and went down with the sinking ship, of William Drake, who in 1869 stopped a pair of runaway horses in Hyde Park and saved two ladies' lives, but lost his own."

A pleasant resting place this, from which we turn with a touch of regret into the West India Dock Road, where stands that institution popularly known as Charlie Brown's, a public-house with a reputation for " lurid gaiety and strange affairs." The decorations alone in this centre of good cheer are worth a visit. " There was a dried up woolly cobwebby lamb with two heads; a camel's hump; a dusty human skull without lower jaw . . . a jar of serpent's eggs, and a horrible monstrosity of a fish, but having a nose and fins."

This is but one of the many treasure stores of information included in this chapter. The scenes rise before you. You see the people's faces, hear the clink of the glasses, share in the gargantuan merriment that comes from huge dock labourers joking with barmaids behind the shining bar. And then we drive through London after midnight, starting from Throgmorton Street, down St. Paul's, past Temple Bar to empty, wide, Whitehall, and on to Queen Anne's Gates where " there are shadows of sedan chairs in the darkness." A fresh itinerary for every night, and even then you could not know London with the intimate love and understanding of the author unless you shared with him his never-ending hunger of humanity.

A human book, remarkable not only for its literary quality but for the understanding and the pity which illumines every page.

J. K. P.

---

* LONDON NIGHTS. By Stephen Graham. Hurst & Blackett. 12s. 6d. net.

NOVELS OF THE DAY

IT is delicate flattery on the part of an author to leave to the reader the full explication of his or her story. That was a method which appealed irresistibly to Henry James. He did his devotees the compliment of suggesting that they were as subtly-minded as he himself was and would resent any underlinings.

It is no bad plan in literature this of conveying life by means of veiled hints, as it makes reader and writer, as it were, partners in creation. There are thousands of potential novelists who cannot interpret themselves. To such the novel of veiled suggestion with its appeal for psychical collaboration is the highest thing of its kind.

Miss L. P. Hartley in "Simonetta Perkins"* leaves two-thirds of her task to the intelligent reader. Ostensibly, the correct and leisured wealthy young American spinster, Lavinia Johnstone, communicates her life in her secret diary. In reality she tells very little. One feels that, under a pretence of shallow emotionalism, this woman may have deep passions. Of course, her New England upbringing, the selfish conventionalism of her mother, and the fact that both ladies are glorified tourists seem to sterilise any hope of vivid reality in Lavinia's inner life. One cannot spring from Puritan stock, be submissive to maternal nagging and " do " Italy by guide-book without serious sacrifice of spirit.

It is quite possible, however, to take another view of Lavinia and to see her as a being utterly shallow and intensely self-poised, living in terms of mock drama, not touching life on any side. Even in that event, the reader has to do most of Miss Hartley's work for her in thinking out just how Lavinia succeeds in staging herself. In the diary she admits cowardice, deceit, carnality; but her admissions are somehow too generous to be true. "Simonetta Perkins" is a puzzle in psychology infinitely more well-worth than certain popular competitions which are still proceeding in the British Press. It is true no material gain will accrue from the solver of Miss Hartley's problem, but it will bring with it great intellectual satisfaction—even if the solution is wrong.

And now, as our American friends say: "Meet Miss Johnstone." She is in Venice reading a book on the psychology of love and glancing at intervals at the local architecture.

"How I hate Baroque," thought Miss Johnstone. "And this, I am told is the best example of it. It comes of being born in Boston, I suppose. And yet a Johnstone of Boston should be able to appreciate anything. Anything good, that is."

Miss Johnstone has always been impervious to eroticism of any kind. It irks her intensely to come across a passage in the irritating volume intimating that in the case of solipsistical and egocentric natures, the tide of love, long awaited in secret, may find a tortuous and uneasy passage.

"Should I call myself an egoist?" Miss Johnstone mused. "Others have called me so. They merely meant that I did not care for them. Now, if they had said fastidious or discriminating! On the whole it is a pity that Stephen Seleucis is coming next week; but he did once say, ' Lavinia, is isn't only your charm that attracts me, it's your refusal to see charm in anyone else.' "

Stephen was the last of a cohort of ardour which loved Lavinia for her looks and her prospects. She had wanted to care for all of them, but none of them could give her the tiniest thrill. It stimulated and humiliated Lavinia when she discovered that she was getting quite a number of thrills

* Simonetta Perkins. By L. P. Hartley. Putnams. 7s. 6d.

from the smiling mouth and fine eyes of Emilio the gondolier, who was not in the least romantic and more than a little mercenary. With the continuance of this disturbance Lavinia has an eager desire to bestow temporal benefits on the boatman, and writes to her friend, Miss Templeman in Rome in the following delusive strain:

" Strange things happen even in Venice, though not (as you will readily believe) to me. My friend, Simonetta Perkins (I don't think you know her—she was recommended to Mamma, who didn't like her, so she devolved upon me) has formed a kind of romantic attachment with a gondolier. She is not in love with him, of course, but she very strongly feels she doesn't want to lose sight of him. Not to see him from time to time would be the death of her, she says. She passionately desires to do him a good turn, but as she has never done one before, she doesn't know how to set about it."

These women understand one another. Miss Templeman sent a wire earnestly advising that Miss Perkins should leave Venice immediately. Lavinia was feeling the strain of her unworthy passion. She was, to herself, secretive, she wore a hang-dog air, she moved stealthily in her orbit; no wonder people avoided her. She was a liar and a cheat; scratch her and you would find not blood, but a mixture of private toxins.

To her new English friends, Lord Henry de Winton and his wife, who had been greatly taken by her, she deteriorates in spirit. Lavinia heard them discussing her:

" She's like an unlighted candle," Lady Henry de Winton was saying.
" I can't understand it."
" An altar-candle?" suggested her husband. "Well, we did our best to light her."
"No, not an altar-candle," Lady Henry said, "A candle by a corpse."

The only one who could light her was Emilio, whom Lady Henry had called an Adonis and Lord Henry had alluded to as a genial-looking brigand. Lavinia's light had failed because the Wintons had bribed Emilio to their service.

Lavinia thought deeply upon this matter of winning over the gondolier, and, at some cost to her pride, succeeded in engaging him for the evening. She had a declaration to make to him:

The canal opened out, very black and very still. They passed under the shadow of a trawler.
" Ferma qui," said Lavinia suddenly.
The gondola stopped.
" Emilio," Lavinia said, " Ti amo."
" Commandi, Signorina?" murmured the gondolier absently.
"I shall have to say it again," thought Lavinia.

Lavinia does say it again, but there is no banal or Clare-Sheridan-cum-Elinor-Glyn-esque ending. Miss Johnstone remains shallowly undecipherable.

One is a little puzzled to learn from the publisher of Mrs. Harrod's " The Triumphant Rider "† that her literary qualities used to call forth the emphatic admiration of Henry James. Of course, Henry James was a polite man, and, to some extent, a squire of dames, but he was also a conserver of literature. This is not to say that Mrs. Harrod has written a very bad book, but simply that her qualities are not Jacobean.

The worst thing about " The Triumphant Rider " is its theme or plot. Marcia Wells, the virginal and angelic daughter of a foul-mouthed prostitute, is a frankly impossible figure. The guileless girl sells herself for a consideration to one of her mother's friends. She cannot fulfil the bargain. but makes off with the Treasury notes. In her flight she accosts a young man, Anthony Fielding, who lets her rest in his flat. In a train Marcia encounters a stranger, Lady Maud Westbourne, who, confidingly, introduces her to London society. Marcia has been taught by her mother that all men are swine, but she gets on with them surprisingly well, giving nothing and taking much. Sir Willans Westbourne, the husband of her benefactress, becomes quite mad about her in a senile way; but Marcia has a sympathetic feeling for Stedman, her would-be seducer, and the feeling

† The Triumphant Rider. By Mrs. Harrod (Frances Forbes-Robertson). Jarrolds. 7s. 6d.

increases when she discovers that he is the famous Severn, who will appear to the reader a most ordinary kind of man. not the full priggishness of her type, but is quite boresome at times. One wonders that the other women tolerated her.

Marcia, alas! is a Marie Corelli kind of heroine. She has She is always harking back to her naughty old mother whose precepts and practice she cannot follow. Mrs. Wells is an affectionate mother, but she is incensed by a letter from Marcia urging her to be happy and give up paint. The irritated woman replies:

> "Why should I give up making myself look nice? The very best paint their faces nowadays. Don't come this nonsense over me. You might just as well ask one to take out one's false teeth. There's many a clean face that's rottener than a painted one."

There is a certain amount of common-sense there, and one can hardly blame the aggrieved Mrs. Wells for calling rare Marcia a stuck-up bit of goods.

Marcia makes enormous progress in Society, especially when she meets the Duchess of Kilchester, who, according to description, would heartily have agreed with her mother's views about cosmetics, having a heavily painted face. The Duchess remarks with great vivacity:

> "Come and sit by me, my wonderful child. Where have you come from?"
> "Out of the everywhere—into where?" as George Macdonald wrote.
> "How did you know?" asked Marcia, a happy devil penetrating her shyness.

Marcia makes conquests wherever she goes. Like her wicked young friend, Lady Susan Brode, who had a glittering white bosom and over-coloured lips and affected onlookers as a houri in their midst. At the Grafton Club her dreamy eyes met a perfectly strange boy's passionate, solicitous stare. The Shelley-like boy loathed Susan because she was a light woman, but he did not know that it was Susan he was treating to a solicitous stare. With a blush he invited her to dance with him. Here we get a passage of Mrs. Harrod's typical wit:

> Two women with heavy puffs under their eyes, protruding bosoms, and a discreet display of diamonds murmured lascivious jokes to one another as Susan passed. "She is out-doing herself in attitudes," one said, "she might be part of her partner's braces."
> "Unbraced to embrace," I should say. "It isn't decent."
> "It is not part of modern decency to be decent." And they moved towards the bar.

How that recalls the epigrammatic naughtiness of twenty years ago. I don't suppose anyone wants to know what happened to Marcia. One suspects that she got very badly on her mother's nerves when she returned to that indomitable raddled woman after her experiences with the aristocracy. Before that departure she had endeavoured to give Lady Susan her heart's desire in Howard Severn, but Howard was not having any, and, furthermore, he cherished a romantic passion for the fair vestal whom he had tried to seduce under his *nom-de-guerre* of Stedman.

LOUIS J. McQUILLAND.

PERSONAL IMMORALITY

THERE is an old story about a Scotswoman who told the meenister that she was aye cheered by one glorious hope, the glorious hope of immorality to come. The same delightful idea occurred to a bookseller who advertised in his catalogue: "*The Belief in Personal Immorality*," by E. S. P. Haynes. This arrested the attention of M. Yvon Nicholas, who has made a lifelong study of the subject. He purchased the book, and was disgusted to find it dealt with a theme of interest to old-fashioned Rationalists like Mr. Haynes, but of none to the modern world.

M. Nicholas, therefore, determined himself to write on " the really engrossing theme suggested by the ingenious printer of the catalogue," or by the bookseller.

He has made a good job of it.*   I am afraid that M. Nicholas, like Mr. Haynes, is a Rationalist, but he pretends to be modern enough not to be interested even in unbelief—except that he states definitely that he does not believe in God. I gather that he does not believe in reason. For in one place he says that if he were God, He would not mind how people behaved so long as they worshipped Him, and in another, that if he believed in God he would have no objection to the Pope having the final word in the matter of private morals. Again, he tells us that " Persecution in France and Germany might have died a natural death with the eclipse of the Church; but it was revived by military conscription under Frederick the Great in the 18th century and Napoleon Buonaparte in the 19th century, to say nothing of the Great War in the 20th century. In pre-war Russia and Germany moral privacy was respected even more than in Great Britain so long as the citizen was not unorthodox in politics. There was also certainly more liberty in this respect in Austria, France, Italy and Spain."

This passage contains one mis-statement and a self-contradiction. It is not true that in pre-war Germany moral privacy was more respected than in Great Britain. Unmarried couples living together were liable to imprisonment. And you will note the glowing inconsistency of stating that " Persecution . . . might have died with the death of the Church," and then going on to say that " there was certainly more liberty in this respect in Austria, France, Italy and Spain."

The author admits that if we are bound to exchange the priest for the policemen, then he is all for the priest, but he wants a new moral code devised. He sees, I think, that a code is necessary if we are not to waste half of every day deciding how we shall act during the other half, and perhaps he will see the need of having one code common to all the members of the community. In which case where does the private judgment of the individual come in?

However, you may put aside all that with the footnote that he does not believe in God, and go on to thank God that he does not believe in the policeman. His attack on the inquisition of the Industrial State is splendid indeed.

A delightful letter from the late Lord Pevensey, written shortly before his lamented death, follows the essay.   M. Nicholas maliciously suggests that the dead peer thought he was writing about immortality. How does he know? In the neat picture of Pevensey's home-life, full of delicate touches of characterisation, in the notes on his intercourse with the Woods at Caius, Cambridge, my lord never gives himself away. When he begins to quote the famous limerick:

> Exhausted and painful researches
> Conducted by Huxley and Ball.

it seems that we shall discover he is talking about immorality but he diverts us straightway to a discussion on the morality of apes. He says: " The baboon is moral, the gorilla is moral. The long-ringtailed lemur of Madagascar (perhaps our nearest relative) is essentially moral. Then why not Mr. Gladstone or the Bishop of Sodor and Man? Things are what they are, and their consequences will be what they will be. Why should we deceive ourselves?"

These are beautiful and consoling words, but they do not decisively inform us whether morality or mortality is in question.

W. R. T.

LIBRARY LIST

ADVENTURES IN UNDERSTANDING. By David Grayson. Hodder & Stoughton. 7s. 6d.

There is a considerable and continuous market for bromidal writing of a cheerful kind, dealing with the delights of the country, the glamour of well-known books and the goodness of humanity. Mr. Grayson has got the prescription, and the mixture as before will please his simple readers.

THE SINGING SEASON. By Isabel Paterson. Leonard Parsons. 7s. 6d.

A story of old Spain beginning at the time when Pedro the Cruel was killed by his natural brother Henry. The heroine of this romance is Isabella, daughter of Sigismund, a merchant of Cordova who has in his veins the blood of Moorish kings; and the hero, Isabella's lover, Roderigo, " the Virgin's Knight."

THE KEEPER OF THE RIVER. By Hamish McLeod. Hutchinson. 7s. 6d.

Very Scotch in sentiment and atmosphere, this readable novel tells of how the mysterious John McCrae came back to the island of Lubb in the menial post of Keeper of the River, and behaved with the hauteur of a king, much to the disgust of the new English owner of the castle, Sir Harold Fairchild. Sir Harold's niece, Laura, however, took a different view of the proud McCrae.

GRETA'S DOMAIN. By Bessie Marchant. Blackie. 2s. net.

It must be a little disconcerting, to say the least of it, suddenly to be smitten with small pox on board ship and left to recover on what is practically a desert island. Yet this is what happened to the Sternes, who, on the death of the father of the family, determined to return to England from Chile, where they had lived in his lifetime. It is the old story of a man and woman who live from day to day, taking no thought for the morrow, an unpardonable crime in parents. However, the careless parents produce the resourceful member of the family—a daughter. Happy-go-lucky parents, indeed, seem to have been invented to give the children a chance to prove their mettle. Greta Sterne certainly rises nobly to the occasion, pulling the family through unbearable troubles with a fortitude that is highly commendable. Would that all parents might produce such daughters. Except, perhaps, that the world would then be too full of feminists and so come to an end!

COMES THE BLIND FURY. By Raymond Escholier. The Bodley Head. 7s. 6d.

The work of translation of this remarkable French book has been most skilfully done by that practised hand, Mr. J. Lewis May. From the moment one is introduced to those very old and formal people, Monsieur Langlade and his wife, Adelaide, greeting their grandchild, Henriette, the note of tragedy is struck. Poor little Henriette is the illegitimate daughter of the old people's dead son by a worthless mother. Although Catholics, the Langlades have a Calvinist view of life, and they regard the little girl as a sinner because of the sin of her parents. Gradually she endears herself to them, but they keep her imprisoned in their narrow home. Henriette makes friends with undesirable people, and her fault is discovered. She becomes blind, but that terrible infirmity does not destroy her zest for the world. Then poor Henriette falls into deep disgrace. Her old grandmother says with conviction. " She is quite lost." The old grandfather had, long before that, cursed the unfortunate young creature.
disregarded.

* THE BELIEF IN PERSONAL IMMORALITY. By Yvon Nicholas. The Cayme Press. 3s. net.

Prepaid Classified Advertisements

Published by the Proprietors, G.K.'s WEEKLY, LTD., at their offices, 20 & 21 Essex Street, Strand, London, W.C.2 (incorporating THE
NEW WITNESS). Telephone No. City 1978. Printed by THE ALLIED PRESS, LTD., 19 Clerkenwell Close, London, E.C.1. Sole agents for
Australasia: Gordon & Gotch (Australasia), Ltd. Sole Agents for South Africa: Central News Agency, Ltd.

G.K.'s Weekly, April 10, 1926

PSYCHO-ANALYSIS

G.K.'s Weekly

EDITED BY G. K. CHESTERTON,

No. 56.—Vol. III.   Week ending Saturday, April 10, 1926.   PRICE SIXPENCE
YEARLY (52 ISSUES)
£1 10 4.

Telephone No. City 1978.   Offices, 20 & 21, Essex Street, Strand, W

CONTENTS:

AMERICA

AMERICA looms so large in all discussions, especially among people for whom anything large appears to be great, that it may be well to insert a word of warning; and to point out that the real truth about America is that America is very small. It covers a great space on the map; though even now there are spaces where its civilisation is spread very thin. It builds its houses very high, when it builds houses at all; but over a great part of its territory it cannot build anything, except more or less modernised huts. It contains great natural features, like Niagara, and is apparently entirely unable to see them; for Niagara is blocked from view on one side by something between a factory and a slum. It would be easy to go on stating plain facts of this rather flattering description; but it would be unfair, for the truth does not involve only faults but also merits. The very virtues of America are rather the virtues of smallness than of largeness. It has exactly and emphatically *not* got that indefinable quality which makes the Renaissance or the pagan epics great; what made Matthew Arnold say that the French Academy was worthily founded by Richelieu, " himself a man in the grand style." On the contrary, the virtues of America are little and local, and we should pray to be delivered from pride when we add, provincial.

The ground-work of America is still democratic, despite the detestable plutocracy which dominates great industrial cities everywhere. Great parts of it are still Christian, if only in the sense of Puritan; but they have remained Puritan and Christian by being out of the main stream of life, and not by being in it. It is much more like a civilisation left behind by the progress of the world than one which is in any sense leading the world. Exactly in so far as it seems to be leading the world, or supposes that it is leading the world, or is in any sense pressing upon or changing the world, it is the pressure of an inferior upon a superior; and it is simply, solely and utterly to be resisted. Its virtues are its own and are valid, as virtues always are, for the individual soul. But its vulgarities are the effect of it seeking to spread itself over something that is not merely older or grander, but larger, more liberal, more living. The ideas now being debated in Paris, in Oxford, or in Rome, are much fresher and freer and more promising ideas than those current in the great American cities; they are not merely more cultured than those of Boston; they are newer than those of New York. We are far from saying that America would have nothing to teach England or Europe. She has equality to teach; but she is not teaching it. She has that power of popular combination called " revolution "; but she is rather ashamed of it. The only power she is wielding, the only influence she represents, is money. She is still in part a democracy in herself. But she is a plutocracy among the nations.

NOTES OF THE WEEK

Unbeaten Yet!

THAT the private 'bus-owners have not acknowledged themselves as beaten was proved last week by their running on the accustomed routes in defiance of the edict of the Ministry of Transport. This was an event of prime importance, worthy to rank with the protests of the people of Limehouse against being turned out of their homes. The news was published by most of the newspapers, but almost entirely without comment. It was difficult to talk about Bolshevism when the men concerned in this revolutionary action were plainly upholding the rights of private property. We ask the Premier to consider the matter seriously. Here is a cloud no bigger than a man's 'bus, and yet we tell him that it is more dangerous for him to ignore the protests of these few 'bus-owners than to antagonise the Miners' Union. The 'bus-owners may be crushed, for the Combine, arm-in-arm with the Minister of Transport, is almost invincible, but this instinct for ownership, which is showing itself now, more strongly than ever since the coming of machine-production, that instinct will not be crushed. It will grow, and Mr. Baldwin must make up his mind whether he is on the side of the Private Owner or of Monopoly. Incidentally, though it appears we must not impute improper motives to a Member of Parliament (and perhaps not to any Government official), we ask Mr. Baldwin to see that nobody who has had anything to do with this backing of the Combine against the public has any interest, direct or indirect, in the price of Combine shares. With what is apparently cynical frankness it has been acknowledged that the cuts in the 'bus-services have been made to help the tramways—the dud tramways of the Combine. But Mr. Baldwin should inquire deeper than that.

And Shall the 'Buses Die?

A FEATURE of all these problems is that they become too problematical. They get entangled with long words and newspaper reports and people forget the simple issue. And so it is desirable to put the issue simply. We had a friend once who came into money and a title. We who had known him when he was poor and honest, rallied him about this. He replied with a great deal of gloom: " I don't think these privileges make any difference. If I could have a man with two long poles to walk before me in the streets and clear everybody else off the pavement to make way for me, that would be a privilege worth having! " In effect, that exactly is what the traffic combine has been given power to do: to clear everybody off the streets except themselves. If we allow the proposed restrictions to be enforced, future generations will say of us: " The people who endured that kind of thing must have been slaves." Another meeting was held last week at the Memorial Hall to protest against the restrictions. But the best protest has been made by the men themselves. Let the public help them by riding only on privately-owned 'buses, and by co-operating in any scheme the owners may evolve for stepping outside the net of the Ministry of Transport. A million Londoners have signed a petition against the Combine, but the mere act of signing a Declaration of Independence will not give us, any more than it has given America, freedom. Those million Londoners, presumably most of them passengers on the free 'buses, must act.

The Cost of Bureaucracy

WRITING on the Budget and Mr. Churchill's Balance Sheet, the *Daily Mail* says: " The serious fact which has to be faced is that for the year which begins to-day no real reduction in expenditure or taxation is to be hoped for." That is perfectly true. As our readers will remember, we never nourished that hope; and we wager that the *Daily Mail* never nourished it. In another column it gives extracts from an article by the Hon. Esmond Harmsworth, in which he shows how the staffs of the various Government departments have increased since the war, and he says some very true things about the Government and the dangers of bureaucracy. But, taking his own examples, does the increase in cost at present amount to much? Since 1914 the Foreign Office has increased its expenditure by £199,000, the Treasury by £228,000, the Ministry of Agriculture by £365,000. Altogether, that is an increase of £792,000. Now in 1914 the expenditure of these three departments was only £278,000 (or in present values about £500,000), and the increase is in itself tremendous, but it is less than half a million, and in a Budget of £800,000,000 it does not count. In fact, the Press campaign against the Civil Service is merely a stunt. And Mr. Harmsworth's call to Parliament to guard its privileges against the encroachment of the bureaucracy is a trifle funny.

Less in Income Tax

AGAIN, faced with the fact that the revenue has more than come up to expectations, the *Daily Mail* says that this, in " a time of trade depression, must be ascribed largely to the extreme severity with which taxation has been exacted." Now this is untrue. We are not in love with the methods of tax-collectors, but, though they may have been more exacting, they got less income tax out of us last year than before. It was anticipated that this tax would amount to £262,000,000; actually it brought in £259,411,000—a difference of £2,589,000. Indeed, the total yield of taxes (£684,544,000) is £2,016,000 less than the estimate of it. Only one item has increased to any extent: super tax, which shows that even in these times of depression the big incomes are growing bigger. We know as a fact that this is so, and it is so widely acknowledged that the *Daily Express* Lobby Correspondent, in making his forecast of the Budget, says: " It is anticipated that there will be an increased revenue on larger assessable net incomes, as within the last two years the profits of commercial undertakings have substantially increased." The *Daily Mail's* case won't hold water, it has got to admit that the monopolists are getting richer, and that they can stand all the taxation which is being put on them. The shrinking in income tax proper is, of course, to be far more than accounted for by the 6d. off the income tax, which cost the nation £24,000,000.

Mortgage the Mines!

MR. CHURCHILL has to meet a deficit, but his Budget shows a balance on the right side. The fact that two millions of the net surplus represent the amount of Italy's repayment of war debt may make the English feel more kindly disposed to Mussolini. As you know, it is the Coal Subsidy that has pushed the balance down on the wrong side. Now this seems to us very silly book-keeping. We agree with all that has been said about subsidising one industry at the expense of the others, and we ask once again why the subsidy is treated as money chucked into the gutter instead of an investment? It is not, in any case, money thrown away, if the coal industry can only be kept going with the help of it, but it is largely money put into the pockets of mineowners unless it is treated as a loan advanced on the mortgage of the mines. If the Government invests in English coal-mines, yet asks no interest until they are going concerns, it may ask for a partner's interest, yet need not treat the investment as a loss.

The Shrine of Shakespeare

WE are glad to see that Mr. Shaw is advising the public to subscribe to the fund for the re-building of the Stratford Memorial Theatre, and we note that he regards Stratford as the most notable birthplace in the West. - If we cannot share in this Shakespeare-olatry (John Bunyan weeps among the shades) we do at least think that English drama gains strength by constant quaffing at its fountain-head, and that the work begun at Stratford by Sir Frank Benson and continued by Mr. Bridges Adams has been invaluable. Therefore it behoves the public to re-establish Mr. Bridges Adams in a theatre as quickly as possible, and to see that the new theatre is finer than the old. Many have held, with some show of reason, that there is something artificial in having the Shakespeare Memorial Theatre at Stratford, where he was born, instead of in London, where he wrote and " produced " his plays. But a National Theatre in the West End would become a very deadly thing, and otherwise the work which Bridges Adams might do in London is being done very splendidly by Miss Lilian Baylis at the Old Vic. When she has Sadler's Wells going, London will have no need to ask for a Shakespeare Theatre.

Working C.O.D.

WE believe that Mr. Baldwin has instituted the C.O.D. service from the best of motives, and we are sure that it could be made use of to help the smallholder. But the big advertisers are already making their plans. "Like most other promising novelties," says *Truth*, "the cash-on-delivery postal service has its drawbacks. One of them lies in the opening it affords to those shady traders who make a handsome income by selling shoddy trash at high prices. For instance, it is more than likely that the mock auctioneers, who have been hounded out of their swindling occupation by the publicity given to their little tricks, will hasten to use C.O.D. as a means of breaking new and profitable ground and of unloading their accumulated stocks. People living in the country who propose to avail themselves of the C.O.D. facilities should rigorously confine themselves to reputable firms advertising in reliable newspapers." We trust that neither people in the country nor people in the towns will take this advice. An advertisement in what *Truth* calls a reputable paper means nothing except that the firm concerned has paid for the space. Naturally we do not expect consumers to deal with firms or smallholders of whom they know nothing; but we hope to see groups of smallholders securing a bank guarantee of the standing of their members, and the members getting into touch right away with the consumers. No time must be lost. It is the pleasant diversion of the modern monopolist to turn every reform to his advantage.

Inheritance

A MOST curious Press comment on the proposal that the amount which a man may bequeath should be limited was that there is no difference in principle between that and the proposal to confiscate the entire fortune at the death of the owner. It is, we are told, merely a difference in degree. That is to say, our contemporary sees no essential difference between a man leaving his son two thousand pounds and a shop and leaving him ten million pounds, a number of factories, one or two departmental stores, some mines, and effective control over a share capital of some hundreds of millions and over the lives and liberties of some hundreds of thousands of workmen. Our friend would regard the limitation of fortunes during the lifetime of the owners, say, to £50,000, as identical in principle with the wholesale confiscation of capital by the State. It is such confusion of thought which makes hard the task of explaining what private property really means. We are not ourselves disposed to support the tampering with inheritance while the larger question of monopoly remains untouched. For if Mr. Griffiths's wish were realised, the landed proprietor would suffer most and the financier scarcely at all: it is so easy for the man with wealth in the form of shares to transfer them to his " heir " before he dies. Nor do we think that the limiting of fortunes would effect much. The only way to limit the power of wealth is to bring private property, including the means of livelihood and the free use of it, within the reach of the common man.

FAKING THE PHOTOGRAPH

WE dare say you noticed and will remember that in the old *Police News* and *The News of the World* of twenty years ago the photographs and drawings of criminals showed, as a rule, a face of undoubtedly criminal type. This, which was invariably true then, when it was the plain and laudable business of the press to make the public's flesh creep at the horror of the crime, is by no means invariably true now when it may be good for circulation to paint the criminal as a romantic figure, for whom silly women, if it is a man, and silly men, if it is a woman, may feel a dreadful fascination. *The News of the World*, perhaps the most honest commercial newspaper now on the market, alone remains quite true to the original purpose of the recorders of crime, and what convincing pointers for Lavater their portraits of criminals would make!

Yet many of these fellows are quite good looking. Why do the seven deadly sins stare at you from the printed photograph? You will understand why if you turn up the file of a newspaper and look out the portraits of some well known character (1) printed while he was a reputable person; (2) when he had been charged with a penal offence. You will notice how those amiable curves and dimples have changed to the very signature of the devil. The same face, but, Lord! the difference!

We do not profess to explain exactly *how* the change has taken place, for very often the same photograph has been used for the two blocks from which these very different prints were taken. We shall not suppose that the blockmaker said in his heart (1) "This is a good fellow, we will soften down the bad lines and bring out the good ones," and (2) "This is a bad man, we will soften down the good lines and bring out the bad ones." All we know is that from similar photographs these very different results are obtained, and that no art editor would have passed that portrait of Binks charged with embezzlement as the portrait of Mr. A. Binks, M.P., the well known patriot and journalist. But somehow, somewhere, consciously or unconsciously, the press has faked the photograph.

To come a little closer to our subject, you may have been struck by the fact that Mussolini, when he first showed himself as the enemy of Bolshevism, was a fine figure of a man, and that month by month since then he has been growing more ugly and vicious-looking. Yet we are credibly informed that in fact his face is much what it was when he marched on Rome. The climax happened last week when a London daily published a print showing him beyond all question as a debauched bravo, a Hindoo Bill Sykes. The caption informed us that he was about to set out for Northern Africa escorted by fifteen battleships. You felt he was up to no good. A vague remembrance of the Barbary pirates floated through your brain, and you pitied the poor Moslem merchants who met that fleet of battleships with its ruffian chief.

Some may hold that the press gives a sort of mystical portrait like Dorian Gray's which shows the spiritual decadence of the man while his face in the flesh remains cherubic. But there are difficulties about this theory. For Binks's portrait remained beautiful while he was *committing* his crime, and, though the portrait of Mussolini and the portraits of all Frenchmen have changed for the worse, the portraits of all Germans have changed for the better. If we accept the Dorian Gray theory we must suppose that Binks only became a villain when he was found out, and that all Frenchmen have become villains and all Germans angels since the Armistice.

Binks is the real difficulty, for if there has been a fake in the photographs of Mussolini, Briand and the Herr Doctor Luther, there has also been a fake in the letterpress. During the war all the facts seemed to be in favour of our Allies, and all the facts against our enemies, but now it is quite the other way. The very papers which printed columns about the Corpse-Factory now print columns about the peace-loving Republic under the Arch-Pacifist Hindenburg, zealously fulfilling all its obligations under the pernicious Treaty of Versailles, and trying to imbue the perfidious Latins with its own angelical ideals; the very papers which wrote, and with every reason, of the matchless heroism of the French, our comrades-in-arms, and the lamentable sacking of their villages by the barbarous Hun, now point to the Frenchman as the only thing which has fallen lower than the franc, putting innocent Englishmen into prison without cause, refusing to pay her debts, and keeping alive in Europe the spirit of militarist Imperialism which Germany has done so much to kill. Has the news been faked completely to match the photographs, and the photographs to match the news? Or have our old friends become demonic, our old enemies almost divine? Have all the old spots of the leopard come out large as life and twice as natural on the lamb?

We should have thought that the public generally would have troubled to ask themselves that question, whatever conclusion they might come to. And perhaps they have asked it, for we don't know, there is no means of knowing what the public asks. There is no public opinion to-day because there is no means of people meeting together and talking over things as there used to be, and the great organs of public opinion carefully select the letters from their readers. All we know is what the press tells and what our reason tells us. Our reason tells us that the English people are not all fools, and that the press lies.

Yet no doubt some of the public are deceived as they were at the time of the Boer War, some, perhaps many Englishmen, have an idea that France is busy locking up fellow-country men of ours, while England never on any account locks up a Frenchman. Some, perhaps many, do believe that Mussolini is the brutal ruffian he looks in his latest photograph, and that all he has done in Italy is to keep the press from telling the truth. And we are afraid that some believe that, if Germany has not greatly changed, it is because she was always better than we thought her, and that the Great War was a great mistake. If that be so, we shall need all our dislike for a dictatorship to prevent ourselves crying to heaven for a dictator to stop this treasonable licence of the press.

TOP—

PETROL AND THE PICTURESQUE

We see across a popular paper a large headline which runs " Motoring an Aid to Beauty." This might of course be taken in various ways. Now that we have received a universal guarantee of the existence of Truth in Advertising, we are in a gentler mood and ready to be receptive to any extent. If we are assured that there are some persons whose features would be improved if they were hurled out of cars upon sharp and irregular rocks, we admit that features, like rocks, are of an infinitely varied outline and we are prepared to believe it. If it be suggested that some never find themselves in really graceful, arresting and artistic attitudes until they are flying over the bonnet or kicking half way through the windscreen, we concede that there may be sedentary persons who could not be induced by any other process thus to pose for the artist. It may be argued that some people look best upside down; and that some others look best of all when you can see nothing but the soles of their boots. However this may be, these speculations seem to us much more reasonable and realistic than the suggestion that people look better when they are motoring; especially if they are wearing goggles.

But if it be a difficult thing to make motorists beautiful, something has certainly been said and done about making motors beautiful. In this respect there has really been some improvement: in the appeal of motor-cars to the eye, though hardly in the appeal of motor-horns to the ear. If we wanted a small illustration of the whole big business of the mechanical and materialistic civilisation, we could hardly do it better than by comparing the bells on sledges with the horns on motor-cars. The people who go about on sledges are just as practical and even prosaic as the people who go about on petrol-engines. They want to have some sound to announce their coming and they produce an exquisitely beautiful thing for a purely practical object. The motor-horns are not only unbeautiful but ugly; and not only ugly but intentionally ugly; as ugly as they can be, as ugly as possible. It was not, however, of the hideousness of the horns of motors that we intended to speak. We have one very simple suggestion to make to the motor-lover who claims to be a beauty-lover; and only a word is needed to suggest it. If motorists do care about beauty, may we suggest that they use their influence to remove from the roads of this most beautiful land some of those loathsome and emetic posts and pumps of a jaundiced yellow or a dull and opaque scarlet, that deface the villages and kill all the colours of earth and sky? If a motorist would only run into them, and smash and be smashed, he would die the death of a hero and a patriot, and we would subscribe to his monument.

—AND TAIL

THE CHAMBERLAIN OF BIRMINGHAM

In an exceedingly intelligent and well-written French newspaper, the other day, was printed an extract from the eloquent speech of the Lord Chamberlain of Birmingham to the House of Lords. By careful exigesis and application of the higher criticism, it could be identified with a speech of Sir Austen Chamberlain to the House of Commons. We have all smiled at these French errors about England, whether or no our education enables us to note the similar English errors about France.

But there is a very much more interesting and important sort of error, which might well be illustrated from this case of that high official, the Lord Chamberlain of Birmingham. The French critic could not be expected to realise where he was wrong; but the English critics might possibly be expected to realise where he was right. And in a very real sense he *was* right; and the English critics do not realise it in the least. On the same day on which this statement appeared in the French paper, a very patronising account of Sir Austen at the Guildhall appeared in an English paper. The journalist had of course received orders to belittle, but not revile, the tentative sympathiser with our Allies in the Great War. And he did it by saying that most of Sir Austen's points fell rather flat and were received in silence; which happens much more often to the speeches of the politicians than is commonly admitted in the papers. Then seizing on a safe point, he said the only truly eloquent and moving words of Austen Chamberlain were those celebrating virtues of Joseph Chamberlain. The journalist then added that one of the most interesting figures present in that vast crowd was Sir Austen Chamberlain's son; who (it was significantly remarked) passed a great part of the time in stroking his chin. It appears that he remained quite calm; to the eye of the journalist strangely and mysteriously calm; and continued to stroke his chin instead of foaming at the mouth, rolling on the floor, kicking over the table and dancing a war dance in the ruins, as would be the more natural course of any man listening to his own father making a speech. Now we suppose that numberless people read that passage in the English paper without noticing that we have here a hereditary aristocracy, or hereditary gentility, in full swing. No nobleman handing on a coronet or a coat of arms could be more purely hereditary. Austen Chamberlain is accepted for the sake of Joseph Chamberlain, and the son of Austen Chamberlain is accepted for the sake of Austen Chamberlain. The journalist, in his simplicity, actually concluded by wondering whether the youthful oligarch intended to suggest (by his remarkable manipulations of his chin) that he was " thinking of that far-off day when " he also would be a great politician supposed to be elected by the people. Whether it was meant to make sure that he really possessed the family chin, or to strengthen his chin, or to hold his jaw, or to adjust some facial muscle for the purpose of holding a single eyeglass, we have no idea; but the journalist seemed to be enormously interested in it. Now the only reason why anybody, even the journalist, could possibly be enormously interested in this, is that he also is " thinking of that far-off day when " etc. In other words, he assumes that the young man will succeed to a seat in Parliament, a seat in the Cabinet, a seat at the Guildhall Banquet. In other words, Sir Austen really *is* the Lord Chamberlain of Birmingham; and that is a far truer description of him than any democratic description referring to representative government.

THE SCRAPBOOK

TRA-LA-LA.

S PRING-TIME is here.   Buds are bursting, and so on.
      Tra-la-la-la ! Hark to the song of the bird !
      Lassies and lads—Hey lass ! you know how
            they go on.
Scientists think them more than a trifle absurd.

Spring-time is here; am I the one to deny it?
Doesn't my heart leap like a bird on the wing?
Snow may occur, but I am the one to defy it;
That for your make-believe Winter ! Here is the Spring.

Cold in the head? Wish you were dead?
Feet in a fever? Caput of lead?
Dust in the eyes, and the throat, and the nose?
Fie on the man with objections like those !

I am afoot o'er the grass or the ling
(I don't know whether ling isn't heather)
Watching the thingabob blossoms unclose.
Here, as it seems that already I've said,
Here, anyhow, I continue to sing,
Here is the Spring !

*   *   *   *

THE SWISS VILLAGE.

It seems these wooden chalets in neat lines
Were set here by some Titan-child at play
With his toy village. Brightly painted pines
On little stands. A church. A garden gay;
(A mimic rose about the paling twines.)
When night comes will they all be packed away?
                                    EVA DOBELL.

*   *   *   *

A FLASH OF SUMMER.

The mongrel puppy wags his tail (as who
Should say, " She patted me ! "); fat babies coo,
Then laugh and fall asleep again; the sun
Peeps out a moment; solemn children run
Across the road to gaze at her and smile
As she goes by. And Life seems more worth while
To us as well, whose hair is tinged with grey.
. . . She turns the corner. . . . Brenda passed this
      way.
                                    JOE WALKER.

*   *   *   *

ADVICE TO A YOUNG POET.

My friend though it pays to be slattern
   So long as you're thoroughly neat,
Avoid (as I haven't) the pattern
   Of icily regular feet.
The many like poets who borrow
   And pay for the poets who pay,
And all the worst bards of to-morrow
   Are derived from the best of to-day.

And keep your original wit well
   Untainted and free from alloys,
And don't be as new as a Sitwell
   And don't be as old as a Noyes.
Whatever you are we all wish you
   The best of good fortune and bliss,
But do not *derive*—it will dish you—
And never write poems like this.
                                    GEOFFREY DEARMER.

RAILWAY RHYMES.
IV.—THE TICKET-INSPECTOR.
(Commonly called The Jumper.)

E VERY now and again
      The ticket-inspector boards the train
      And those who haven't paid their fare
Are not best pleased to see him there;
But those who *have*, produce with glee
Their tickets for the Jumper, he
Suspicious of their readiness
Endeavours to collect excess
From people honest as the day;
If he attempts to make *you* pay
Twice-over for a single run
Or treble for a double one—
Kick him abruptly on the shin;
If you can get a good one in,
He'll bellow " Ow " and leave the train,
In haste and, let us hope, in pain.   R. W.

*   *   *   *

ON DR. MOFFAT'S NEW TRANSLATION OF THE OLD TESTAMENT.
(*Voltaire adapted.*)

Know you why Jeremiah passed
   His life in constant lamentation?
He as a prophet could forecast
   Our Dr. Moffat's *New Translation* !
                                    PIERRE.

*   *   *   *

ETERNAL WOMAN.

Out of the sapphire depth
Of the moon-lit sea
Where the stars dance,
Her eyes I see.

And when the nightingale
Joins song with the clear
Far temple bells,
Her voice I hear.

And as the spray flings up
In the sun-kiss'd air
Glittering, cool,
I see her hair.

Than the scent of the rose
Of incense or myrrh,
Sweeter by far
The breath of her.

And because God is kind
In Heaven above,
Poor fools like I
Can win her love.   A. R. U.

*   *   *   *

THE PAST.

I said : " Your dancing eyes
Have made the past so dim,
That in this joyous life
No aching memories swim."

You smiled at me; and then,
Still smiling, shook your head.
" After the bitter past,
Life turns to dust," you said;

" And I, who cannot love,
Must live to know its pain."
And then you laughed; but those
Dark eyes danced not again.
                                    KENNETH HOPE.

BEAUTY AND THE BEAST

By HUBERT E. O'TOOLE

TRAVELLING towards Connemara in the train from Galway, with not very far to go to the western verge of Europe and longing to see that region which looks so attractive on a large scale map, strangely enough I was not accompanied in my third-class compartment by any sons or daughters of the soil, but by English visitors and one American lady. As far as Oughterard the prospect was merely well-wooded and pleasant but some distance beyond that town the train rattled into a country such as I had never seen before. The landscape suddenly became denuded of trees: small lakes appeared here and there sparkling in the sunshine, and great bare mountains rose up, of a dark green colour with a suggestion of purple in it which, when the sun caught the stony patches upon them, reflected its light in such a remarkable way that they looked like nothing more than gigantic moss-grown sapphires. There was really a suggestion if not of fairyland about them, then of a fairy land. It is in the nature of mountains to be gloomy, generally speaking, and nothing gloomy sparkles, but these mountains sparkled as if they were laughing and it was not possible to take them very seriously. I felt greatly exhilarated.

The train pulled up at a station set in a plain almost enclosed by mountains and the whole extent of country was so bare that it seemed that unless a man were indoors everything he did would be sure to be observed by somebody, or as if that were the world with the lid off. I commented on the fact that there were " very few "—there were not any—trees to be seen, to the man who was to drive me to my destination, and he burst out laughing. I was not quite sure why, unless it were that the mere mention of trees there seemed the height of absurdity—as if, for example, an explorer were to remark to an Eskimo in the Arctic Circle that there was a great deal of ice about.

Five miles we drove over a perfect switchback of a narrow winding road along the bottom of a desolate valley, to where hedges and loose stone walls began, four miles more along the side of a mountain below which swept an arm of Lough Corrib, in which was set most delightfully a tiny islet, just large enough to bear at one end a lonely castle, balanced at the other by a clump of trees rising in a manner exactly suggestive of feathery palms upon an island in the South Seas. Anything more picturesque it would be hard to imagine. Then at last, down, down, down through the most luxuriant of mossy and ferny pine woods (actually), past a lovely island-studded inlet of the lake, by a sandy way, then over the shoulder of a hill and down again to the house, which looked over the lake and was backed by a hill covered with foliage—a pleasant retreat.

I climbed up out of the wood to the open road that evening. There was no sunshine now to make the mountains sparkle. Across the lake lay a huge monster with black scars upon him descending with fearful abruptness into the water, and the wind from the west blew an awful mass of lurid mist out of a funnel of mountains until they with the billows of cloud seemed to form one stupendous whole, the dizzy heights of which were lost in the heavens. Torrents of rain threatened to descend at every moment, and the scattered people that I met seemed overawed and frightened. I came to where a sheep had slipped from the raised road into a sloping field, and its owner in a rough homespun jacket of undyed wool was endeavouring to drive it back, assisted by a dog. Just as I was passing the dog had urged it up the slope and the shepherd was below me endeavouring to hoist it bodily on the road. I bent down and caught it by the horn. "Take the lug with the horn, sir," says he; "take the lug with the horn," in a voice of the most intense apprehension for the safety of the panting sheep. I remembered that a " lug " was an ear, and duly catching the " lugs " with the horns I " lugged " it up. He thanked me and I went off. I thought I had obtained a flashing glimpse of the extreme pre-occupation of these people wresting a bare subsistence from that barren land to the exclusion of everything else.

There is surely something besides cloying sentimentality in apostrophising " Erin " as to " the tear and the smile " alleged to be present in her eye simultaneously—in Connemara, at any rate. The rain as a matter of fact did not come down at all, and when I went to my room and looked out of the window the moon at the full had risen above the mountain at the other side of the lake, and shone in peaceful steadfast splendour over the scene as if the threatening clouds had been a mere joke. But in truth the hill behind the house may have been hiding them all the time for all I know. In the following days I learned something of the fickleness of that climate which in a few minutes can change from warm sunshine that makes the mountains glisten companionably to cold mist that covers the tops of them as completely as if they had never been looked upon by mortal eyes, and change back again as rapidly, so that it was often quite impossible to imagine what the weather was going to be like.

One fine day which remained fine I climbed to the top of Mount Leckavrea with a companion. As we mounted upwards a vast extent of country began to unfold itself to our eyes, in the bosom of which lay Lough Corrib like an inland sea. A steady coldish wind blew there out of the West. How different such a wind in such a place to the wind in a city which seems to blow merely from around the corner and from every direction at once, as it were. Here it was a steady strong current like a marching army. From the summit the view, or rather series of views, was magnificent.

Turning our backs and walking towards the slope of the other side we could see the arms of the sea in the south, faintly and inextricably mingled with a vast network of lakes such as I doubt is to be seen anywhere else on earth. I bemoaned our having no camera, and solemnly declared that I would surely climb up on another day provided with one.

It was necessary to cross the lake and row some two miles to get to the foot of Mount Leckavrea from the house in which I was stopping, and true to my resolve I set off alone some days afterwards with a camera. I decided to cross first so as to be close in to the land when I moved into the unsheltered part. The lake water is black and gloomy when you look into it, and I was unable to refrain from trying to imagine what these depths beneath me might be like. Getting close to the opposite shore I followed it and arrived in due time at a favourable spot for landing to make my assault upon the mountain. At the foot of it were some fields about a cottage in which people were working at the hay. I took my leisurely way up from the water and decided to have a word with them, which I did, sitting down to rest upon the ground. They were a man and his wife (and daughter in the background) and the man gave me some hints as to the best way to take to get to the top of the mountain and in the end escorted me for a considerable distance. Following his instructions as well as I could I came to the summit without mishap to myself, and the weather remaining fine took my photographs with great care. (I was desolated to find afterwards that the films had all been over-exposed.) My boat I could see as a tiny speck below. Well satisfied with myself I commenced the descent, which I accomplished in due course. The husbandman and wife were still at work at the hay at the foot of the mountain, and asked me would I have a " cup of tea." I said I would, upon which the housewife was thrown into some confusion, and dashed before us towards the cottage muttering something about wishing she had known sooner that I was coming. I was informed on entering the cabin that if I had only come earlier in the year I could have seen the creeper roses over the door, but that they were all gone now as I could see. I was ushered into the living room the floor of which I noticed was of extraordinary unevenness and slippery dampness and seemed to be formed of great round cobble stones. There was an open hearth by way of fireplace above which was suspended a common tin can for boiling water, while beside lay a pot oven in which bread had just been baked—indeed I had it piping hot with my tea. The housewife proceeded to set a table under the window while the man of the house held conversation with me. I was conscious of the presence of one or two little boys hovering about, and the daughter sat in a corner next the fire endeavouring to pacify an infant which lay in a sort of wooden box. I thought I could observe signs of great poverty. There were one or two chairs about, obviously hewn out of solid logs as if that were the woodman's cottage of the fairy tales, and on one of these before the fire sat a little boy with tousled head, clad in fantastically ragged and indeterminate garments and the very picture of rustic bashfulness, who hid his face in his arm when he thought I was looking at him and only ventured to peep out when he thought I was not. I would dearly have liked to photograph him exactly as he was. It struck me that it would have been worth while to come all the way from Dublin merely to look upon that child. He had a great pale oval face and large dark wondering eyes, strangely beautiful, with a peculiar suggestion about them of the bloom of fruit, which somehow reminded me of some painting I knew not what. But alas, I had used all my films, and was obliged to forego my desire and could only feast my eyes. I vaguely wondered why he and his sister should not be more rosy-cheeked than they were. Surely, living in the depths of the country, they should be more robust.

I finished my tea and took my way to the lakeside through the hayfield where the man of the house was again at work, and asked him to show me some boats he had spoken to me about. He was delighted to do so, and we walked to my boat into which I stepped while he cast off the mooring chain, and, pushing her off, neatly stepped in at the last moment in a manner which I had not sufficient confidence in myself to attempt. He manned the oars thereafter while I stretched luxuriously in the stern enjoying the novelty of being rowed instead of rowing. We came to a place on the shore where he had made two little coves for his boats, of which there was only one at the time there. It was a very much better boat than the one I was using, and as he wished to cross the lake I took his boat while he took mine. Judging him to be a good oarsman, and out of pure exhilaration at having such a good boat I rowed hard to be the first over, rising off my seat at every stroke. I was an easy first sure enough, with a set of blisters on each hand, and mentioned the fact that I had raised them with pride.

I spoke to my hostess that evening about my adventures during the day and particularly how interested I had been in the lonely little homestead at the foot of the mountain and the people who lived in it, and how I had been struck with and admired the little boy who sat before the fire. The conversation ran on the people of those parts. I said that I had expected to meet people of magnificent physique, but that on the contrary, especially the girls, they appeared to be puny and lackadaisical. What could be the reason of it, I asked? The answer was startling and unexpected. "Oh," she said, "consumption is the cause of it. They don't get enough to eat. Potatoes and salt is all they ever have. They're glad to get a bit of butter. And they have to work so hard, even the little children. There's that little boy now that came round from Mr. Connolly's with the fish, he was telling me he has to go all the way to Cornamona this evening, with the donkey, to bring back a bag of flour across its back."

The plain words smote me to the heart.

STRAWS IN THE WIND
OUR CRITICS: TRUSTS AND TRADES UNIONS
By G. K. CHESTERTON

WHATEVER be the fate of a difficult venture like this little paper, supported only by small capital and that coming from very small capitalists, it will certainly last until it has seen fulfilled to the letter the prophecy with which it began. Yet even so short a time ago the prophecy appeared a paradox. Every day it becomes more and more of a fact. Before we die, even before our paper dies, we shall see a universally acknowledegd fact.

We said that Big Business and State Socialism were very much alike, especially Big Business. We said they were growing liker and liker every hour and would soon be identical. We said that the Capitalists and the Communists, so far from being mortal enemies, were already practical partners. It seemed to some people exactly like saying that black was white; indeed it was saying that black is red. So far the colours are doubtless distinguishable, where they are undiluted; and even make a sort of pattern of contrasts like a red and black chess-board. But already the contrast is a pattern and an exclusive one. And at the end of the process it would be as impossible to introduce a free yeoman or a small guild into that system as it would be to introduce a Green Knight of chivalry or a Purple Castle of romance into a game of chess played with two colours. The system has already become a Party System; that is to say, there is more and more of the system and less and less of the party. It is already at best a game like chess; and all our gallant politicians can be trusted to play the game.

I remember my brother, who was on the Fabian Executive, saying that Bland and others wanted Anti-Socialists to form one party and Socialists the other, taking the place of Whigs and Tories; that the space between the Front Benches might " be once more a true frontier." I think Mr. MacDonald said something of the same kind recently. Anyhow, the prophecy was much truer than the prophets either knew or desired. It was one of those prayers which fate accepts with a dreadful smile; those promises that prosper with a sort of ominous optimism. The bar of the House will indeed become once more a true frontier; as true as the old frontier. The question will indeed be " Are you a Socialist or not ? " and very like the question " Are you a Unionist or not ? " The Socialists will most truly take the places of the Liberals; and the Socialists can be trusted in time to become quite as anti-social as the Liberals have been illiberal. Mr. MacDonald and Mr. Baldwin will understand each other exactly as Mr. Asquith and Mr. Balfour understood each other. It did not mean that they had no differences of opinion; but it does mean that they tend more and more to a certain condition, in which they understand each other better than they understand anything else.

Now I wish to make this general position plain (and indeed it will soon be plain enough) before I go on to answer some very reasonable questions asked by Mr. Maurice Reckitt and others. In so far as Labour and Capital are still two Parties they will become one Party System. The genuine force behind the best Socialists will be the bargaining power of the big Trades Unions. But their political opponents will only be the men with whom they are bargaining. The very idea of a bargain is different from the idea of a battle. The two can bargain because they are both familiar with the article they are buying and selling; with the idea of a man's labour being sold to another man. There is a sort of silly and sentimental journalist who always tells us that Labour and Capital should have the same hope, the same high ideal, the same No-mistake Worth-while Uplift. He is a fool and he is perfectly right. Labour and Capital have got the same ideal; and a jolly rotten ideal, too. They do both at present think in terms of the proletarian principle; of great masses of wages being paid out to great masses of men by a group of comparatively few men. They have really, at the back of their minds, got the same conception of a modern state; just as the Whig and Tory aristocrats had the same conception of a state or the Victorian Liberals and Conservatives had the same conception of a state. Out of that sort of agreement you can make a state; even if it be not what we call a free state; if it be only what we call a servile state. Above all, you can make a Party System. But you cannot make a revolution or a religion or a change of heart or an act of faith, or indeed any decisive act or any fundamental change. The two parties, whether old or new, are only too lobes of one brain or two valves of one heart or two wings of one creature; a monster of huge size whose heart and brain are both rather small for its size. Anything that really divides them will split that head and pierce that heart; and that must come from outside the monster altogether; it must come from far away . . . the Green Knight riding from the Purple Castle.

Now I have supported the Trades Unions all my life and all the time during which practically the whole press condemned them. I have supported Strikes which (outside the little group of this paper) the whole press condemned. I know well that the Trade Union was the only possible organisation to meet the evil of capitalism. I still think the Strike was the only possible weapon to meet the tyranny of those particular capitalists. If that situation happened to them to-morrow, I should support them to-morrow. Where it is happening to-day I am supporting them to-day. But I do not think that the big Trade Union meets *my* particular problem. I cannot see that in itself big Trade Unions can cure the evil of big organisations. On the contrary, I observe (with great grief) the same evil appearing in the big unions as appears in every other sort of big business. I observe with regret the noble army of porters or plumbers or scavengers sinking slowly towards the condition of parliamentarians. I see them also called upon to exhibit loyalty to leaders; that is loyalty to utterly disloyal men. I see them also sitting in rows on benches while a president or a representative whom they all dislike sits above them on a platform, universally distrusted and mysteriously immune. In short, I have seen the Labour Movement become the Labour Party; and a part of the Party System.

They talk of the danger of Communism; and there really is a danger of Communism. It is the danger that it will finally confirm and perpetuate Capitalism. They rave about the Red Peril and they are right; it is the peril that this red and black mixture will make one dull universal brown like bricks made of mud. But what I am pointing out at the moment is that this notion which seemed so lately to be a nonsensical notion is now very likely to be accepted as a normal settlement. The big businesses are working with the State and are quite willing to work with the State Socialists. The State is taking the part of the Trusts; as in the case of the Trams. It will soon be hard to tell the difference between a State monopoly and a monopoly still theoretically outside the State. This is the combination of the two most powerful things of our time; and any attempt to resist it looks like a forlorn hope and may even be a risk. In considering whether we want the risk, we shall naturally consider first whether we want the resistance. Do we want to prevent this combination? There is no doubt whatever that all the most powerful people of our time want to effect it. There is no doubt whatever that unless a very exceptional effort is made in the other direction, they will effect it. I have spoken of bricks; and we are undoubtedly, in an exact metaphor, being bricked in. The semi-socialist officials started building their wall on one side of us and the managers of big commercial systems building their wall on the other; they have now built so high that the roof has very nearly met over our heads. There is still a

crack of daylight; but there is still a very deep and complex dispute about whether men really desire daylight.

Now I think it so vitally important and so vividly true that men do desire daylight, more than the most elaborate system of subterranean electricity (whether supplied by a vast private company or a somewhat smaller public authority), that I should like to say first, before I come to grips with certain questions about omnibuses and other things, that it is by this necessity that I should stand in the last resort. I do not think the great Trades Unions now need help so much as the small owner. I do not think the great Trades Unions can be a complete substitute for the small owner. I do not think the great Trades Unions will of themselves offer us any solution of our problem of the necessity of the small owner. Most of them regard a small man who has become a small owner as a man breaking away from Labour instead of a man breaking up Capital. Most of them still regard sharing the risks of an enterprise as a trap or a trick. They would, therefore, probably consider the small owner a mere " moderate " or conservative, they would probably consider the small property a compromise. But my feeling is exactly the other way. I think it is the Trades Unions which, left to themselves, will become merely moderate and conservative. I think it is the bargain about wages that is a compromise; and will probably be a more and more compromising compromise. I think that the only chance of a revolution, in the good sense of the word, the only chance of a real and drastic change, is at present in the small owner and not in the big union. The big union is perfectly right as far as it goes; but I doubt if it will go much farther. I think it is very likely indeed to slow down; just as Radicalism slowed down when it became a part of the Liberal and Unionist machine, with two parties and one " true frontier." In short, I think Trade Unionism and even Socialism, left to themselves, very likely go to sleep or to sing the world to sleep. I think nothing but Distributism is in the least likely to wake it up.

I am, therefore, in a peculiar position with regard to this problem. I propose in an article next week to do my best to explain to Mr. Reckitt why I think that the small owner is just as likely to be a good employer as the big owner, in cases where he is really established as an owner and really has to be an employer. But I might have an appearance of special pleading, or of merely minimising a genuine difficulty, if I did not thus preface my answer by saying frankly that I do not think good wages will save the world, or that the organisations demanding good wages are altogether to be trusted to save themselves. They are themselves in immediate danger of being linked up with the machinery of plutocracy.

The Song of a Town

HE knows a town whose spires
   Assault the heights of noon;
And stem the sunset fires,
   And capture the quick moon.

Here music is a quiet
   In alabaster halls.
Here silence is a riot
   When lilac-blossom falls.

Earth-deep their trees are rooted,
   Their summits hold the skies.
The branches dreamy-fruited
   Swoon perfume in men's eyes.

Here whoso will, may travel,
   To that dear town belong;
If only he unravel
   The secret of his song.

LOUIS GOLDING.

PSYCHO-ANALYSIS

IT is now an established fact that all human motive and action is due to beer; not merely among adults but also among children. The age of innocence is a pretty myth, but it is time that people threw off their sentimentalities and superstition, and looked facts in the face. This is the age of Science. . . .

The whole life of a child (of either sex) is actuated by Beer. The first action of which a child is capable is a lusty yell; we have established that this is no less than a cry for Beer, or at any rate for some kind of drink. The next action of the child is to drink. If it does not drink beer it is because its system is not yet capable of drinking beer. But behind the relish of milk is the desire for beer. These we call the primary instincts. The secondary instincts are to be found in the love of popping corks, of yellow-brown colours, of frothy substances (like soap), and so on. The child instinctively calls his father Papa (which represents the popping of the cork), and his mother Mamma (which gives the noise of the liquid being poured into a glass). All the gurgling noises of childhood go to prove the strength of the instinct. . . .

Most of our knowledge is based upon dreams, which we have taken as the most reliable evidence scientifically possible. We know (by means too long and elaborate to tell here) that even very young children dream about beer; nay more, that they dream about nothing else. When a child dreams of a boat upon a lake, what is it but a symbol of beer? Of a shower of rain, a river, a sea? Everything yellow or brown is beer. Everything frothy or sparkling is beer. Everything in something else is beer (a nut in its shell, for example, is obviously representative of beer in the bottle). Everything issuing from an aperture is beer. Everything that moves is beer, particularly quick-moving, jerky things, which are reminiscent of "hops." In fact, we may say that the child cannot dream of anything but beer. There is no dream possible but beer. . . .

Psycho-analysis has been received with cries of horror. Old ladies, disgusted to find that their whole existence has been a stifled craving for beer, have written indignantly. Lovers of children have said that our conclusions are vile and nauseating. We examined a well-known teetotaler, and discovered that he was possessed of a Bass-complex of amazing intricacy. We offered to give him a free course of treatment, but he went away in a fury. The truth is always unkindly received. . .

Here is an example. The patient was Miss X. She came to us in great trouble. "My nerves are all gone to pieces," she said. "I want you to help me." Professor Bösh questioned her, and kept her under observation. He discovered that before going to bed she was in the habit of brushing her hair. "The brush was of an amber colour, and was transparent. The patient would raise it slowly to her lips, pause and then proceed to brush her hair. This was quite unconscious. In reply to my questions it transpired that several years before she had been forbidden by the family doctor to drink anything alcoholic. She had been in the habit of taking a glass of ale every night at supper." Professor Bösh explained this to her, and at once convinced her of its truth. She submitted herself to treatment, and was soon perfectly well and strong.

Our most interesting case of the last year is undoubtedly that of Mr. Z (who lives at ——, near ——). He came to us on February 15, and informed us as follows: "A few weeks ago I had a curious dream. I found myself in a railway train which was travelling at a great pace. I was seated in the first compartment of the front carriage, but in spite of my most frenzied efforts, I began very rapidly to pass from carriage to carriage, the wooden partitions offering no resistance. In a couple of minutes I was sitting on the line. Another train appeared, and I clambered into the first compartment, but with no greater success. I was hanging on the edge of a precipice with a drop of 50 ft. into a small lake. As I fell, I noticed that I had been clinging to a very high bridge, and that I was falling straight on to a barge. There was an explosion, and I found myself eating the pieces as they came down. So extraordinary was this dream, and so unlike anything that I had ever dreamt before, that I thought it worth while to tell you."

The dream was explained thus: Mr. Z, though he would not admit it, was a very heavy drinker. The incident of the railway train was obviously a symbolisation of a visit to a public house. He stood in the front row of people next to the bar, but after he had drunk a number of pints of beer, he was violently ejected from the room. He then went to another public house, with the same result. By this time he was fairly drunk. He noticed a fly on the edge of his glass, which fell into the beer. In his dazed state of mind he connected it with his own recent ejections and falls. He connected it vaguely with "bar" (this explains the curious detail of the "barge"; the high bridge was probably a game of cards for high stakes). The explosion may have been anything, a clap on the back, the dropping of a stick. Eating the pieces is clearly his muddled impression of picking up his change on the counter. Mr. Z savagely denied all this. He said that it was sordid and altogether abominable. The next day, he went to an ordinary G.P., who prescribed a liver pill. When Mr. Z realises that this treatment is useless, he will perhaps return to us and subject himself to our more expert and scientific treatment. . .

G. WALTER STONIER.

TWO POEMS

Day's End

I CANNOT bring Thee broken offerings;
   Bearing such gifts what could I say to Thee?
     "Accept my treachery"?

Wilt Thou receive these broken offerings,
Fallen from faltering hands,
Because the road was rough and wearying?
   In trembling hands
Eager but frail, I could not hold them fast,
   They fell at last—
The road was long, and rough, and wearying.

Shall ways be gentle if the feet be wild?
   Give Me the fragments, Child.

EDNA A. KAHLA.

Sonnet

WHEN in my bitterness of soul I cried
   That love had no more power to give me
     pain,
Since he within my heart lay crucified,
   With its dear empire yielded to the brain:
Then with incredulous and wary mind,
   By reason's own dispassionate vision led,
I went my way, nor knew that I was blind
   As one who sleeping moves among the dead.

Until you came, suddenly, out of the crowd,
   You, with your strong hands and urgent words.
And I was lifted on a golden cloud,
   Surrounded by warm winds and singing birds:
And now, a prisoner, my only plea
   Is that your love may never set me free.

WINIFRED GOODALL.

The Ruins of Carthage

THE COCKPIT

To the Editor of G.K.'s WEEKLY.

BRITISH NICKEL

DEAR SIR,—Your mention of the British America Nickel Corporation in your issue of March 6 suggests that the following extracts from " The Triumph of Unarmed Forces," by Rear-Admiral Consett, might be of interest.

Page 198 *et esq.* :—" There was only one factory in Norway that produced nickel in any important quantity, the Kristiansand Nikkel Raffineringswerk, known as the K.N.R. This company was under contract to supply Germany with a certain monthly quantity, which would appear to have been about 60 tons. Norway's total nickel exports practically all of which went to Germany, were as follows :—

1913	1914	1915	1916	1917
594	696	760	722	442 tons.

" An agreement was drawn up by H.M. Government with the K.N.R. with the object of limiting the export of nickel to Germany. For this agreement, H.M. Government paid the sum of £1,000,000. The particulars of the agreement are not accurately known; but the limit agreed upon as the maximum quantity to be exported was, there is good reason to suppose, about 80 tons a month. This limit appears to have been arrived at on information supplied to H.M. Government that the K.N.R. could produce 1,500 tons of nickel a year. My own information on this point, taking the efficiency of production at the company's own estimate, was that 1,300 tons was a liberal allowance to make; but without supplies of nickel ore from New Caledonia, which ceased soon after the outbreak of war, the maximum production would be somewhere about 720 tons a year—possibly a little more.

" This agreement led to H.M. Government's being involved in transactions with the British America Nickel Corporation; and the question that comes uppermost in the mind is: Who were the advisers of H.M .Government in these transactions, and why were the latter carried through without reference to the Legation in Christiania, which had been so successful in other directors in making Germany feel the pressure of our blockade?

" The indefensible sinkings of Norwegian ships by German submarines, the loss of life they caused, and the sufferings endured by survivors in open boats created in Norway a deep and bitter feeling of enmity towards Germany. This feeling found expression in a petition by the Mates' Union to the Storthing for the cessation of all nickel exports to Germany, on the ground that nickel was the metal used in the construction of torpedoes; and soon afterwards, towards the end of April, 1917. a very envenomed attack upon the K.N.R. was made by the Norwegian Press, including newspapers of all shades of political opinion."

In the fourth paragraph of the extract quoted on page 197 from the report on National Expenditure, allusion is made to the British America Nickel Corporation. *This Corporation's interests were closely identified with those of the K.N.R.* (my italics). The managing director of the British America Nickel Corporation, Mr. James Hamet Dunn (now Sir James Dunn, Bart.), was then in Copenhagen. Conceiving it possible that Mr. Dunn might be interested in the attitude of the Norwegian Press towards the K.N.R., I forwarded to him without delay a cutting from one of the Norwegian papers, almost immediately on receipt of which Mr. Dunn proceeded to Christiania; but to no purpose; for soon after his arrival, in May, 1917, the K.N.R. works were practically destroyed by fire.

This untoward event settled the question of nickel for the time. But when the incident had been forgotten the work of rebuilding the K.N.R. commenced at once; and the company stated that full production would again be possible in January, 1918. A second agreement was drawn up by H.M. Government on much the same lines as the original agreement; but again the Norwegians came to our rescue; for just before the new works were completed a second press campaign was launched, no less violent than its predecessor of the spring. Bowing to pressure of public opinion the Norwegian Government intervened, and the K.N.R., instead of nickel, was compelled to produce electrolytic copper, of which Norway stood in need.

"On whose advice was it that . . . in the light of the knowledge in possession of H.M. Government, arrangements should have been made whereby Germany was assured of the greater part of Norway's output of nickel? And that the nickel company should have been paid by H.M. Government for sending the nickel to Germany?"

In addition to Admiral Consett's very pertinent questions. one would like to know how it happened that the managing director of a company which was closely identified with a firm supplying Germany with nickel was considered a suitable person to be made a baronet? I don't know whether " foolish " is exactly the right word to describe the proceedings outlined above, but they undoubtedly want " rubbing in."

Yours truly,
H. S. D. WENT.

THE CHARM OF NOT OWNING

DEAR SIR,—Having returned from abroad only last evening I have just seen your, very nearly, crushing rejoinder to my letter.

At the risk of becoming that plague of editors, a constant writer to the press, I hasten to reply.

I wrote as an Irish farmer, and, as such, I must completely disagree with your statement as to the difficulty of becoming a peasant proprietor. In Ireland it could not well be easier.

The would-be owner, entirely without payment of any law. or other costs, can become the owner of land by means of a system of annuity payments. These are spread over a period of 69½ years and cover the capital charge and interest at the rate of 4¾ per cent.

I am indeed a lazy man, but, alas! sir, those of us in this world who are least inclined, have often to work the hardest. I do not say that I retire to bed each evening on the verge of collapse, but at least I endeavour to pull my fair weight between the shafts of the agricultural cart.

I venture to assert that the average French peasant owner is no whit better off, except for his title, than my own labourers.

Possibly in Utopia the owner has a better time than the paid servant. but unfortunately this delightful country would appear to be very far removed from our present habitation. In any case, I greatly fear that when discovered it will be found to be a country entirely without farms—great or small.

Personally I have no hesitation in saying that I would rather work as a farm labourer, on a well run farm, than attempt to bring up my family, as yet unborn, on ten acres of land. A fair sized farm would be another matter because, as I have said, I would speedily acquire more.

I trust, sir, that my children would inherit sufficient ability to retrieve back my hard won land from the descendants of my farmer labourers!

I am, sir,
Your obedient servant,
K. C. FITZGERALD.

To the Editor of G.K.'s WEEKLY.

G.K.C.'s BLAST

DEAR SIR,—I am afraid I cannot claim to be the author of a phrase attributed to me in the letter of mine you printed in a recent number.

I like the sound of "G. K. C.'s generous blast," but what I wrote was " G. K. C.'s generous *heart*."—Yours faithfully,

EX-SERVICE MAN.

SECRET PARTY FUNDS

SIR,—The amazing collapse of the Liberal Party is surely largely due to the Secret Party Funds Scandal.

What, for instance, has happened to the money provided by Sir Alfred Mond to the funds of the Party?

It is surely worth inquiring into this whole question of Secret Party Funds.

If Sir Alfred left the Liberal Party, what has happened to his money provided by him?

Surely to leave a Party which has his money to play with is not exactly a very real separation. Possibly, however, as a good business man, Sir Alfred quits the Party outwardly while still retaining a financial interest in the concern?

Such a peculiar state of affairs calls for comment. Those who support the Liberal Party might well insist on a little enlightment. It is surely not unreasonable to ask that legislation be introduced to prohibit secret Party Funds and to make it compulsory for all Party Funds to be made public and an audited balance sheet published every year with the names of all subscribers.

Yours faithfully,

CARDROSS.

STERILISING THE UNFIT

SIR,—I quite agree with Bishop Barnes that something should be done with regard to the unfit, which does not necessarily mean the poor. I have been a member of a committee for seven years, who interview each month cases of unmarried mothers, many of whom have poor records and are physically and mentally unfit for such responsibility. I know of nothing more sad than to see these poor creatures suffering the pains of motherhood.

It would be a Christian act sterilising the unfit, many of whom become institutional drudges deprived of freedom.—Yours truly,

ADA MASON,
Chairman to the Children Act and
Boarding Out Committee, Edmonton Union, N.

FARMING IN CANADA

DEAR SIR,—I read with great interest your remarks in " Getting Rid of Our Farmers," and I felt very much that I would like to let them have a few truths on what they might expect on coming out to this country. I have been in Canada sixteen years now, intending to take up farming, and thoroughly went into the subject of ranching. It is a terrible life of hardship, conditions are entirely different out here, and if farmers have any sense they would be wise to stay at home in England; there is nothing for them out here but very hard and uncongenial work. People with money and experience come out and take up land, and in some cases become owners of large tracts of land, and that seems the finish. They work from morning till late at night, and the result is failure, they may make a bare sufficiency for themselves and family, but that is all, and they may be very thankful if they succeed in doing this. Labour is impossible to get, and no efficient man will engage to go on a ranch, where they would have everything to do, ploughing, milking, tending the cattle and some house duties besides; not as it is in England, where each man does his own work. Land is very highly priced, and if they wish to pre-empt or homestead it would be at the back of beyond, away from church, schools, and neighbours. I could tell you of numbers who have come out here full of hope, who are broken-down wrecks, and would give a great deal to be able to return to the old country, but cannot possibly scrape up the price. A man here came out with money, bought land, and settled on it with his family; he and his wife worked hard and slaved to support and bring up the young family. He collapsed, was taken to a hospital, never seemed to wake up again, and died in a few days—verdict, worn out, overworked. He leaves a wife and seven children, half-starved things, to struggle on as well as they can, and one wonders how. The greatly reduced fares will tempt many, and it would be only fair if the same offer could be made to them in six months to return, if they wished, and you would be surprised how many would be thankful to do so, and would realise how much better off they were in England. I see different societies are urging girls to come out for domestic service; I would beg girls if they have any respect for themselves and any religious feelings to stay at home. There is no proper service for domestics here; they would just develop into general servants, and very hard worked ones, too; no freedom, but a life of drudgery, children to look after, housework, cooking and washing—no convenience at all. The truth is never told them, only a wonderful glorified home life, " one of the family," dancing and pleasure, and they find out their mistake too late, poor girls. The moral atmosphere is terrible; away from all, religious influence gone, and no wish for it either, Sundays and week-days alike; men have to work the same. In fact, one may say by far the greater majority are without any thought of God. I do so hope, if anyone sees this letter, that it may discourage both men and girls from coming out to this country, unless they are going to friends.

Perhaps some may think that I have written too strongly, but if they only saw the utter misery I have witnessed they would, I feel sure, think nothing too strong.—Yours, etc.,

C. J. PITCAIRN.

WAGE-EARNERS AS SHAREHOLDERS

DEAR SIR,—In G.K.'s WEEKLY of February 27, it is suggested that the workers and staff of a limited liability company should be shareholders in that company.

I have a few shares in one or two industrial concerns. Do I feel that I am a part-owner? Emphatically no.

I most certainly should not advise any working man who was receiving wages from a company to put his savings into buying shares in that company. Supposing the company goes bankrupt, he loses his savings as well as his job.

" Don't put all your eggs in the same basket " is the stockbroker's well known advice.

What the workers want is a bonus in the shape of a percentage of the profits. If they know that 10 per cent. of the profits will be distributed among the staff, they will work all the harder, take an interest in their work, and feel that they are being fairly treated.

They want, however, that money *in cash*, and the liberty to use it as they like.

Many of them will invest it.

The other thing they want is permission for one of their members to attend all board meetings, and to look at any of their firm's books.

Give the workers a 10 per cent. bonus and a representative at all the board meetings, and they won't worry much about joint direction.

These ideas, however, are not new to industry, and many firms work on these lines.—Yours faithfully,

A. PELHAM BURN

THE DRAMA

IT is an old complaint that the cinema empties the theatre —which merely means that if the public can't get what they want on the stage they try the pictures. I have failed to notice any very serious attempt to outcompete the movies; what I do find is that some of our playwrights are seriously affected, or rather I should say disaffected by the film. There are certain stories which, though weak in plot and characterisation, " get over " by reason of exotic settings and popular emotionalism, and on the pictures this style of thing is bearable. You may feel that the drama is less than the dust, but the dust may be sufficiently attractive to hold the attention. Translated from the film to the stage, such stories fall hopelessly to pieces.

The Movie Drama on the Stage

I have seen two examples of movie dramas on the stage this week. Either of them would have been tolerable on the screen. In the theatre they are wearisome and futile.

" Summer Lightning," by Frank Denny, at the Comedy Theatre, could be dished up quite passably for the screen. The trouble is that the dramatist has approached his play from a film angle. A continual dodging in and out of cupboards, a perpetual cropping up of hidden treasure—pearls, plans or model engines—will always raise a laugh on the pictures; the swiftness of action staves off the boredom of repetition. In the same way the mysterious stranger can be surrounded by romance supplied by close-ups and flash-backs. Who can resist the allure of a man who emerges from a Moorish palace replete with harem and performing elephants; or the fascination of a sheik shown in the authentic setting of blood and sand?

A Lost Plot

The plot is of the slightest, and what there is is lost by the way. We have a prince from Eastern Europe, which at the moment has a positive outcrop of kings and rulers, who under the name of Maxwell makes love to the wife of an aviator and at the lady's request takes charge of her husband's model engine. To save the reputation of this little fool another lady takes the prince to her house, dopes him with her aunt's sleeping draught and puts him to bed. In the morning he poses as her husband, to the surprise of the authentic article, who threatens to report him to the Air Board! This sort of thing accompanied by the perpetual loss and reappearance of the engine model goes on for two acts.

In the third act we are in the saloon of the prince's yacht. An extensive game of hide and seek takes place. Husbands emerge from cabins, dash into wireless rooms and endeavour to escape through port-holes. The curtain comes down with the arrest of the unfortunate prince to whom the dramatist has done less than justice, and the triumph of the lady kidnapper who persuades an Admiral that he is not a Prince at all!

A dreary, dreary play which would have scraped through as a film.

Mr. Ion Swinley as the prince with a foreign accent deserves decoration. He contrives to imbue a painfully lay figure with vitality, and proves yet again how much an accomplished actor can do with a poverty stricken part. Iris Hoey works very hard, but she has literally no straw wherewith to make bricks, and Margaret Scudamore gives a crisp performance of an aunt.

A Tame Sheik

" Prince Fazil " at the New Theatre, from the play of *L'Insoumise* depletes the popular sheik of his glory. On the film, Henry Ainley's fine figure and rolling eyes would have thrilled the heart of every flapper. On the stage he doesn't thrill at all. The part he has to play won't let him. Prince Fazil is a tame sheik and an ill-treated one. His French wife kisses a good honest forlorn lover, who has worshipped her since childhood, on the mouth. The poor sheik sees this and like most husbands, East or West, doesn't understand. He suggests Fabienne should 'phone to the young man and tell him not to come to dinner. She regards this as a challenge and rings up Hamilton to tell him to hurry. Whereat Prince Fazil disappears into the desert.

We see him in his palace and it is a bitter disappointment. Gone are the gazelle-like creatures that on the movies sway before our enchanted eyes. We behold some dozen modern young women, who cannot wear their clothes, and who suggest an Oriental stall at Wembley, rather than the seduction of a Turkish seraglio. The sheik has come back to the land of his fathers and tries to settle down to Eastern domesticity. He is foiled by the appearance of Fabienne, who insists on returning to him. The tame harem is sent away and for six months the lady is satisfied with love.

The Return of Nature

But Mussulman law forbidding her to adventure, she gets bored and appeals to the Sultan for a divorce. Her suit not unnaturally is refused—Prince Fazil is an admirable husband—and unable to stand the monotony, Fabienne runs away with her friends. The friends include John Hamilton, who reiterates his passion on every possible occasion. The fourth act shows us the lady in a villa at Biarritz with Hamilton in decorous attendance. She has, however, once again relapsed into love for the sheik, and sits languishing and longing on a pile of cushions. Enter Prince Fazil, miraculously recovered from a blow on his head. They mutually embrace and Fabienne requests to be taken back to the harem. But Fazil isn't having any. He poisons her with a ring and she dies content in his arms. The sheik leaves his visiting card with the butler and for the last time fades into the night.

The theme is hackneyed, but even such threadbare interests properly handled could achieve emotional effects. But it is badly constructed and extremely ill-written. Never once does the play come within a hundred miles of illusion. It is pedestrian from first to last. It cannot be called a melodrama because it lacks the strength and humour necessary to that form of art. It is a film gone wrong, and I can only regret that Henry Ainley and Madge Titheradge have identified their talents with this poor substitute for the pictures.

J. K. PROTHERO.

THE RETURN OF DON QUIXOTE
By G. K. Chesterton

CHAPTER VIII.

THE MYSTERY OF A HANSOM CAB.

LOOKING down the descending curve of the dreary street, where the ranked houses seem to be reeling towards the great grey whirlpool of the sea, Murrell could only see three distinct or detachable objects that could be said to suggest life. One was quite close to him; it was a milk can left outside the low door in an area. But it looked as if it had been left there for a hundred years. The second was a stray cat; the cat did not look sad so much as simply indifferent; it might have been a wild dog or any such wanderer prowling about a city of the dead. The third was more curious; it was a hansom cab standing outside one of the houses; but a hansom cab that partook of the same almost sinister antiquity. All this happened before the hansom cab had become an extinct creature to be reserved only in museums; but this hansom cab might well have been in a museum side by side with a Sedan chair. In fact it was rather like a Sedan chair. Being of a pattern still to be found here and there in provincial towns; made of brown polished wood and inlaid with other ornamental woods or woods once meant to be ornamental; tilted backwards at an unfamiliar angle and having two folding doors that gave the occupant the sensation of being locked up in an ancient eighteenth century cabinet. Still, with all its oddity, it was unmistakably a hansom cab; that unique vehicle which the alien eyes of a clever Jew saw as the gondola of London. Most of us know by this time that when we are told that the pattern of something has been much improved, it means that all its distinctive characters have disappeared. Everybody has motor cabs; but nobody ever thought of having such a thing as a motor hansom cab. With the old pattern vanished the particular romance of the gondola (to which Disraeli was perhaps referring) the fact that there is only room for two. Worse still there vanished something supremely special and striking and peculiar to England; the dizzy and almost divine elevation of the driver above his fare. Whatever we may say of Capitalism in England, there was at least one wild chariot or equestrian group in which the poor man sat above the rich as upon a throne. No more, and in no other vehicle, will the employer desperately lift a little door in the roof, as if he were imprisoned in a cell, and talk to the invisible proletarian as to an unknown god. In no other combination shall we ever feel again so symbolically and so truly our own dependence upon what we call the lower classes. Nobody could think of the men on those Olympian seats as a lower class. They were the manifest masters of our destiny, driving us from above, like the deities of the sky. There was always something distinctive about any man sitting on such a perch; and there was something quite distinctive even about the very back of the man sitting on the quaint old cab as Murrell approached it. He was a broad-shouldered person with side-whiskers of a sort that seemed to match the provincial remoteness of the whole scene.

Even as Murrell approached, the man, as if weary with waiting for his fare, laboriously descended from his lofty place and stood for a moment staring down the street at the scene. Murrell had by this time pretty well perfected his detective art of pumping the great democracy and he soon fell into a conversation with the cabman. It was the sort of conversation which he considered most suited to his purposes; that is it was a conversation of which the first three quarters had nothing whatever to do with anything that he wanted to know. That, he had long discovered, was so much the quickest way to his end as almost to deserve to be called a short cut.

At last, however, he began to discover things that were not without interest. He had found out that the cab was quite a historical antiquity in another way, and eminently worthy of a museum; for the cab belonged to the cabman. His thoughts went back vaguely to that first conversation with Braintree and Olive Ashley, about the paintbox belonging to the painter and, by inference, the mine to the miner. He wondered whether the vague pleasure he felt in the present preposterous vehicle was not a tribute to some truth. But he also discovered other things. He found that the cabman was very much bored with his fare; but was also in a hazy way afraid of him. He was bored with that unknown gentleman because he kept him waiting outside one house after another in a tedious and interminable pilgrimage round the whole town. But he was also slightly in awe of him because he seemed to have some sort of official right to visit all these places and talked like somebody connected with the police. Though his progression was so slow, it seemed that his manner was very hasty; or what is now called hustling. One felt that he had commandeered rather than called the cab. He was somebody who was in a frightful hurry and yet had a great deal of time to spare for each of his visits. It was therefore evident that he was either an American or a person connected with the Government.

Bit by bit, it came out that he was a doctor, a medical man having some sort of official claim to visit a variety of persons. The cabman, of course, did not know his name; but his name was the least important part of him. What was much more important was another name; a name that the cabman did happen to know. It seemed that the next stoppage of the crawling cab would be a little further down the street, outside the lodgings where lived a man whom the cabman had sometimes met in the neighbouring public house; a curious card by the name of Hendry.

Murrell having, by this circuitous route, at last reached his desire, almost leapt like an unleashed hound. He inquired the number in the street which was honoured by Mr. Hendry's residence; and almost immediately after went striding down the steep street towards it.

It would be untrue to say that he had no premonition that he was approaching the chief adventure of his life. In point of fact, he invariably had that premonition whenever he turned the corner of the street. But there was something subconscious in him, as there is in the child (or, for that matter, very probably in the lunatic) which told him that his illusion was not quite real; or in other words that his play-acting was play-acting. He never doubted that his wandering life of adventure would continue. What he did not know was that he was near the place where it would stop.

(To be continued.)

Vision

EYES, I could pluck you out,
    So gadabout,
        Emptily roving here and there
To see bleak shadows in bleak air;
    And all so dull
As though the Word that made it were a fool.

Men there were known to be
    Whose eyes could see—
Could bear a light beyond the sun,
And every leaf they looked upon,
    Smiling for bliss,
    Cried, " Lo, my treasure! Lord, take this!"

ALAN PORTER.

REVIEWS

MR. T. S. ELIOT'S POEMS

MOST contemporary poetry is written in towns and under the stimulus of town life. More and more the sacred fire becomes an urban and sophisticated flame, burning without heat—but not without smoke—in a pretentious lantern. " The simple, sensuous, poignant things seem to have all been said," once wrote Sir Edmund Gosse in charitable explanation of the matter and manner of certain new poets. We shall grow more complex, and our poems with us. The multitude will understand us less than ever, but an aristocratic few handfuls of individuals trained to our symbols and ecstatic to our hidden beat, will be aware of our intentions and find joy in our performance. It is a mood that attacks most poets in their moments of inadequacy: the sense of inevitable repetition of beautiful words and images made colourless by the mighty past. The impetuous thought is to do without the past, to scrap its forms, annihilate its spirit, replace Pegasus by a Hispano-Suiza vehicle, and so get on into the light of the New Poetry. And it is a mood of false impatience, proceeding from inadequacy to a fumbling fulfilment of ill-considered intentions. Poetry is not a matter of " first-class brains " in the modern exclusive sense; and a poetry that can only be approved by rapturously puzzled coteries bears with it the odour of its own decay. It is a plant of superficial rooting, forced to a peculiar blossoming for the jealous admiration of " synthetic " horticulturists who are secretly unhappy when they consider the lilies of the field.

Here is Mr. T. S. Eliot, an acknowledged leader of the new poets, as learned and concise as any critic of our time. What is it he is trying to do, to *say*, in his collection " Poems 1909-1925 " ?* He is gay, with the terrible gaiety of an undergraduate who has drowned Divinity in drink:

" I grow old. . . . I grow old. . . .
I shall wear the bottoms of my trousers rolled.

Shall I part my hair behind? Do I dare to eat a peach?
I shall wear white flannel trousers and walk upon the beach.
I have heard the mermaids singing, each to each."

He is cleverly impressionistic:

" Midnight shakes the memory
As a madman shakes a dead geranium."

" I am aware of the damp souls of housemaids
Sprouting despondently at area gates."

He is portentously zoological:

" The broad-backed hippopotamus
Rests on his belly in the mud;
Although he seems so firm to us
He is merely flesh and blood."

He is aware of Oliver Goldsmith:

" When lovely woman stoops to folly and
Paces about her room again, alone,
She smoothes her hair with automatic hand.
And puts a record on the gramophone."

He has a fine image for personal futility:

" I should have been a pair of ragged claws
Scuttling across the floors of silent seas."

_____

* POEMS, 1909-25. By T. S. Eliot. Faber & Gwyer. 7s. 6d.

He has a vivid hospital image for an evening of quiet suspense:

" When the evening is spread out against the sky
Like a patient etherised upon a table."
which, if we are minded, we may set beside Wordsworth's:

" The holy time is quiet as a nun
Breathless with adoration."

But at the end, after we have read the seven pages of explanatory notes, in five languages—ancient and modern— we are left bewildered. It is clever jingling in the first, fourth and fifth quotations; brilliant phrase-making in the second and third; and poetry, exiguous and welcome, in the sixth and seventh. Yet over it all is a devastating air of conscious cleverness: " the simple, sensuous, poignant things have all been said ": the mind kicks out the heart, and the mind worries the mind the mind worries the mind kicks the heart mind worries mind mind mind. . . . I find the lucidity of Miss Gertrude Stein's poetic method the simplest medium to express the impression left on me. I am bewildered, for it is clear as daylight to me that, half-strangled by theories, there is a poet in this young American, a poet who gasps out beauty between whiles, as if to show the barren futility of hard brightness:

" We have lingered in the chambers of the sea
By sea-girls wreathed with seaweed red and brown
Till human voices wake us and we drown."

" I am moved by fancies that are curled
Around these images, and cling;
The notion of some infinitely gentle
Infinitely suffering thing."

There is the universal music of poetry; the gritty brightness fades and is not; we forget the posturings, the academic struttings, the uncharitable quips; we are content in a moment of reconcilement until the twisted cleverness will out again with:

" Over buttered scones and crumpets
Weeping, weeping multitudes
Droop in a hundred A.B.C.s."

a verse which even Cadby Hall would not applaud.

The trouble is, of course, not the fact that Mr. Eliot's work is written in a town atmosphere—as our opening would seem to imply—but that he has a basic disgust of life. He flies to studied coruscations from the damp souls of housemaids as he would fly from the viscid souls of milkmaids, because he has no use for their simplicities and no understanding that the marvellous world of sense and circumstance eddies about and surges within them as surely as about and within himself. He is bereft of wonder and sees weary, flat footed clerks where others have seen inspired office boys treading sunward. He sees a town of muddy streets and trampled sawdust and broken blinds and dingy furnished rooms where Francis Thompson saw a confluence of life about

" the traffic of Jacob's ladder
Pitched between Heaven and Charing Cross."

There is beauty and pity and terror waiting for Mr. Eliot in the town, and in the eyes of its denizens heavens and hells of experience:

" The notion of some infinitely gentle
Infinitely suffering thing."

WILLIAM KEAN SEYMOUR.

THE SCHOOLMASTER ABROAD

A PARODIST makes merry with the follies and mannerisms of books already published; it is a rare stroke of genius (and luck) when he so divines the enemy mind that when a subsequent offence is committed, the enemy falls plumb, automatically, into prepared pits of ridicule. Readers of *Caliban's Guide to Letters* and, yet more, of *Lambkin's Remains* will rejoice with incredulous rejoicing to find here a volume* full of sincere unconscious testimonies to the truth of those great pieces of modern irony. Here we have the Rev. Professor Knight (page 92) illustrating the Sacred Truce, which in ancient Greece obtained during the season of the Olympian Games, by this sentence: " I quote these words because they are an anticipation of our Parliamentary golf matches, when the leaders of the Government and the Opposition meet together for friendly encounters on the green." The satirist would hardly have dared to write that; it would have seemed excessive and improbable. Yet there it is, written in all seriousness; and as though it were not rich enough, the writer hastens to add: " How much I wish, ladies and gentlemen, that all the jarring sects of Christendom had their Olympic Games every few years, to enable them not only better to appreciate each other's works, but to enter into those friendly contests for superiority, which are so much better than the acrimonious strife of partisans." It only remains to add " Catering and all other arrangements by Sir Henry Lunn & Co. Book early."

In order that we may better appreciate each other's works, I cite again from the Rev. Professor Knight. Our readers will be reassured to learn that the Professor is of opinion that the Sphinx is " one of the wonders of the world " (page 96), and this bold judgment is confirmed by the information that the Rev. Professor Knight never returns to Egypt without going to see the face of the Sphinx, *and usually alone.* A moving picture—no, I beg pardon, we must not use that phrase any more; it has gone wrong—let us say an uplifting picture this, for the mind's eye; the wonder of the world *tête à tête* with the deprecator of Sectarian Jars. But how much to be regretted is the absence of a blabbing witness to certify the world what effect, if any, was produced on those inscrutable lips of stone by a confrontation with the writer of Professor Knight's prose. " A voice speaks out of that mysterious face from a region in which (as a poet says) ' time and space are not.' ". The audacity of these poets! Has one of them really said that? But ought we to mention their indiscretions? However, to return to the Sphinx, the wonder of the world; if, like her Theban sister, she dealt in riddles; one could imagine her propounding this problem. *Draw a plan showing the relative positions of the Voice, the Face and the Region in this sentence.* Or indeed she might raise an even more devastating question: *On what principles of sense or grammar does the Rev. Professor Knight connect words and phrases?* A mere reviewer, unpossessed of that stony ancient calm of mind, is disconcerted by the insensitiveness of a man who can allow a silly, slovenly lecture, delivered to a party of tourists, to appear, unrevised, as printed prose fourteen years later. Some people think that even butterflies, transfixed by pins and preserved under glass, make a depressing collection; but here we have houseflies and blowflies in a showcase.

It is only fair to admit that not all the writers—for as writers they have committed themselves to be judged in this republication—write such amorphous sludge. Yet, though they attempt the common decencies of English writing, a curse envelops them all, they are of the shop, shoppy; their sentiments and their funniments alike smell of the pulpit and desk. In all their tones we hear the hearty facetiousness of the parson at the choir-outing, as it were a little sublimated. There are some amongst the lecturers from whom we should expect an exhibition of egoism and headmasterly self-complaisance, and Imperialistic cant. Before Wembley there was Wembley-matical talk, fit to be the talk of the day among the electors and electresses of the New Canoodledum. And we are not disappointed. Here again the originals outsatirise the satirist in perfect self-unconsciousness. Mr. Waugh, Mr. McKenna and the rest of that band may hug themselves in company and sing " We told you so ! " For the debate on Athenian Imperialism is a sort of gran tutti of fatuity. That was in 1910-11, and here now in 1925 we have it solemnly reprinted, in cold blood. It comes with a queer stale smell as though the lid had been taken off some frowsy receptacle. One cannot help wondering what must be the feelings of the survivors when they read this cruel perpetuation of their remarks in print.

Of course, the lecturers are not as slipshod as the debaters; but evil communications corrupt good literary manners, and here we find even Dr. Walter Leaf guilty of such a sentence as this: " Some of you will remember the words of Horace about the herds feeding over the tombs of Paris and of Priam. That was *literally carried out* from about the year A.D. 500 to 1876." I wish one had seen the herds and been able to congratulate them on literally carrying out their feeding, instead of executing it metaphorically. Dr. Leaf in his better mind would have written " That was so." However, a mere journalist grotesqueness of reach-me-down phrasing is a trifle compared with the illiterate manner of writing exhibited by the Rev. Professor Knight.

Some of these papers contain information, and a few do at least open interesting inquiries. As an honourable exception, the late Dr. Gow's address on *Thessaly and Tempe* deserves mention. The lecture on Rhodes by Dr. Jamieson might be useful to a tourist. Dr. Caton enlightens the Pilgrims of Collective Culture on the subject of the Medical School at Cos—though he has nothing to say about the poetical school in that island. As for most of the remainder, it cannot be said that either the information is adequate for the simple reader, or that the level of ideas and intelligence is adequate to anything but the herd-mind of the secondary teacher. The inadequacy of the lecture on Crete, excusable in 1910, makes the ambitious title " Aegean Civilisations " an impertinence to the reader in 1925. It is difficult to conceive what motive can have prompted the republication of such matter in book form now.

J. S. P.

HEARSAY*

A TITLE going back to the Conquest, an army career of the usual kind and Household appointments under a Liberal Government have not provided Lord Saye and Sele with very exhilarating recollections. His best chapters deal with early days in South Africa when he did some soldiering under the old conditions. A more modern note is struck when, after his retirement from the army, Lord Saye and Sele became a brewer's agent. Shortly before the war he was involved in what became known as the " Canteen case." Feeling that the rights of the case are still in dispute, he devotes a chapter to it, and prints a number of condolatory letters from eminent friends in support of his case, including one from Lord Reading.

H. G.

---

* AEGEAN CIVILISATIONS : Essays and Lectures delivered to the Hellenic Travellers' Club in 1910-12, London. E. Benn, Ltd. 5s.

* HEARSAY. By Lord Saye and Sele. Nisbet. 15s. net.

NOVELS OF THE DAY

THE average schoolmaster is but a schoolboy of advanced years. The priggish youth is but the pompous pedagogue in first edition. Happily for the boy, he inevitably breaks out of the prison-house. The man, poor devil, remains on in its shadows, becoming more puerile as he totters piteously to old age.

The elementary school teacher has a faint chance of forgetting his dogmatic impertinences in an outside world that looks upon him with contempt, and may kick him for his soul's good. To the unfortunate creature enclosed in a public-school life offers no such betterment. Year by year, in spite of recurrent holidays, he becomes more juvenile in habit of mind, and is no longer fitted for intercourse with any but his colleagues. Judges and clergymen would be just as bad as teachers if they were herded away together for long periods each year. As it is, they suffer from the vanity of school teachers in having their most foolish utterances left unquestioned and their silliest jokes attended with some cachinnation.

Mr. Kenneth Potter strikes one as having escaped out of the darkness of a lesser public school. His novel, "The Shadow of the Chapel,"* is deeply branded with the note of experience. I would urge readers not to be put off the book by the discovery that it deals with chapel attendances, for round the chapel revolves the whole life of the school, and in that school are many studies in oil and vinegar (to quote my friend, James Laver).

Oliver Makepeace is not the worst of the masters. He might have become as tolerable as any member of an intolerable class could be if base ambition had not urged him to become a frequent figure in chapel. The head-master, though a poor Christian, was keen on those attendances, because they represented discipline. Early in Dr. Cooper's reign of religious terror Makepeace created a bad impression. He kicked at the chapel parade, with its attenders, sulky and unctuous, and that special platoon who realised that the fear of the Lord was the beginning of promotion. "Servile hypocrites," exclaimed Oliver, "I won't go." But a few moments later he ran for his gown and was just in time.

That was the beginning of the end. Passing the college windows with Lanyon, Makepeace saw on the blind of one a dim silhouette rubbing its hands over its face. "That's old Milligan," said Lanyon, "he always does that all the evening, once he's inside his room. And yet in the daytime he seems quite normal. Of course, he's been here thirty years."

Compulsory chapel would be no penance to old Milligan. It was to the less senile masters. None of them had even the right official view of religion. An indiscreet young cleric often troubled the head master by taking Christianity too literally. At school Makepeace had believed what he was told, and had taken very little notice of it. At the university he had become for a short period a fervent High Churchman, but his dislike for early rising gradually undermined his faith, and he took to the society of persons who seemed to disbelieve in almost everything. The most constant attendant, Rennie, was a Presbyterian. Lanyon was a Gallio. Blake was a sound North of Ireland Black Protestant. Then there was Summers. Summers was Makepeace's most dangerous rival for the house-mastership of Lime Grove, about to be vacated by old Marney, who was quite in his dotage. Summers looked smooth and servile. He was married, and lived on a blasted heath outside the school, in one of three small villas, with bright green gates, forlorn in the waste. Summers abode in the middle one, "Strathpeffer," between "Kia Ora" and "Chatsworth."

Summers was almost open Agnostic until the possibility of the house-mastership through chapel attendance came into view. Makepeace was pointing out that the school was intended for members of the Church of England:

"People who don't belong to the Church of England—Oh, I'm sorry, I forgot you were an Atheist."
"Agnostic," corrected Summers. "But I wish you wouldn't dwell on the subject."

Makepeace withdraws the word, saying that it means the same thing, and casually repeats that Summers does not belong to the Church of England:

"Pardon me," said Summers, "I do; I was brought up in it. It is very difficult to stop being a member of the Church of England. A wide communion, a wide communion. Its peculiar merit is that it includes all shades of belief. Haven't you ever been told that? That's why it includes me."

Makepeace had seriously outraged the head-master by reading "Bull Dog Drummond" to his Divinity Class. His improper behaviour and a number of extraneous circumstances had assured him of the house-mastership at Lime Grove. Unfortunately, dining too well with the retiring master, he missed another chapel, and Summers got Lime Grove. Immediately after this Oliver began a great agitation for the abolition of compulsory chapel, complaining also of Ritualistic practices in it. About this time Makepeace's luck turned. On a holiday abroad he had been able to help Lord Stallham, a school governor, out of some little difficulty by intervening with some intelligible French sentences. His lordship was of great use in assisting Makepeace to the headship of a small public school at Quenby. Lord Stallham was Evangelical. It was his confident hope that the new head master of Quenby would be zealous in Low Churchism. So he would have been, but for Gooch, the draper, a leader in local affairs and a member of the school governing body. Gooch had a passion for interference, especially with regard to the chapel services. After beginning life as a Baptist, he had, like so many Nonconformists grown prosperous, gone over to the Church of England, and in his case the conversion was uncommonly thorough, his zeal carrying him far into Anglo-Catholicism. Makepeace had to compromise on a High Church service.

Poor Oliver had done a number of disagreeable things to attain his object, foremost of these being marriage with prim Miss Abbot whom he had almost a physical distaste for.

Circumstances, too, compelled him to take steps as a head which he had condemned as a junior. He had to impeach a young master for smoking in the quadrangle. The last one hears of Makepeace is in the issue of a manifesto to his staff: "It must be clearly understood that masters are expected to attend chapel whenever the boys do. The religious life of the school—— "

On a day of sincerity before that dementi, he had said to himself, "What a damned nuisance religion is."

* * * *

From scholastic and sordid concerns to high romance and picturesque hazards. It is with regret that I am compelled to say that Mr. Donn Byrne has for once failed to make good use of the rich material to his hand in "Hangman's House."† He has failed lamentably with the Hangman himself, killing this most powerful figure off in an early chapter. The Hangman, Lord Glenmalure, had begun life as a Fenian, but had soon cast the folly of patriotism aside, and opened a most unscrupulous career at the Bar. By prosecuting his countrymen as political felons he had become Attorney-General, then Lord Justice O'Brien, then Lord Chief Justice of Ireland and Baron O'Brien of Glenmalure, the most implacable anti-patriot since Norbury. Mr. Byrne introduces him in his old age, and represents him

* THE SHADOW OF THE CHAPEL. By Kenneth Potter. Chapman & Hall. 7s. 6d.

† HANGMAN'S HOUSE. By Donn Byrne. Sampson Low. 7s. 6d.

as a strong man, and as such to be respected; he treats him almost as badly. in fact, as Mr. Galsworthy treats Soames Forsyte.

The book is largely concerned with Glenmalure's daughter, Connaught, who has a passion for hunting and racing. Mr. Byrne gives us plenty of fine horses. Before Glenmalure died, he had, rather stupidly for a formidable judge, married his lovely daughter Connaught to a red-bearded, undependable person, John Darcy, son of an old school-fellow and colleague of his, the Right Honourable Michael Darcy, Judge of Her Majesty's Most Honourable and Privy Council in Ireland, but better known by the Irish voter and taxpayer as " Tricky Mick." Connaught would have infinitely preferred her young neighbour, Dermot MacDermot, who loved her passionately, but let her be disposed of without any ado.

There is nothing much to these young people, whose exaltations and sorrows leave one cold. The villain husband of Connaught is a miserable creature, almost too insignificant for contempt.

The most pronounced failure of the book, however, is the Commandant Hogan, the bitter enemy of Connaught's husband. The Commandant, an Irish Fenian in the service of France, whose constant dream is of an Ireland won from England by the sword, is deputed by the Fenian chiefs in New York to go back to his native land and warn the people that a rising will be impossible.

We meet the Commandant Hogan in various disguises, in various chapters of Hangman's House, and deplore the injury done to him by his creator, Donn O'Byrne, in making him a merely pictorial figure, with little to do but look mysterious. It is shoddy of Mr. Byrne also to borrow the idea of the finale from " Kathleen-na-Houliham," when O'Hogan leaves the country to go back to his foreign service. There is weakness all through the book, and there are repetitions from earlier books as to the historical glories of Dublin and Galway. What he has concerned himself mostly with is the sporting side of Irish life, and it does not harmonise with the two or three themes which he has left at a loose end.

There is one short story in the book which does his genius credit. and that is the tale told in the smoky room in Tory Island by the Connemara bard of " Dan Hoyser, the great Irish poet, and how he met Venus in the mountains of High Germany."

The old romanticists in Ireland have the habit of borrowing from the mythologies and sagas of the world and putting them in native garb. Lovers of Wagner will shudder over their lost Tannhauser, but Donn Byrne has made of him a greater success than any of the characters in " Hangman's House." It will be observed that the tolerance of His Holiness in his talk with Tannhauser, fresh from the Venusberg, is almost excessive :

" Holiness," Dan Hoyser groaned. " For twenty years I have been sinning, and I want forgiveness and absolution."
" Well, you have it," says the Pope. " Wine and women and a throat cut here and there, don't bother yourself about that. Sure what fire of poetry would be in you if you were a mouselike habitual man."

I hope Donn Byrne's bishop will take no notice of this.
                                        LOUIS J. McQUILLAND.

LIBRARY LIST

THE LOSING GAME. By E. S. Stevens. Hurst & Blackett. 7s. 6d.
Miss Stevens can always tell a good story. She is unconventional in making her heroine, Vera Lowndes, middle-aged and passée. Vera, with very little encouragement from her husband and several warnings from her friends, goes out to join him in the oil-bearing part of Mesopotamia, leaving her devoted little daughter, Ginty, behind her. When she reaches Bagdad she feels she has made a mistake. Her husband, Gilbert, is immensely taken with Linda Vyte, who is a real charmer. Her small, almost deformed husband, Michael Vyte, is presented with great skill. While Vera is playing the losing game she hears news of her small daughter's death. It speaks much for the novelist's skill that one regrets Ginty as one would a real child.

A COMEDY OF WOMEN. By John North. Jarrolds. 7s. 6d.
The strain of " Girl or Boy " has been resumed in Mr. North's second novel, which concerns Mr. Godfrey Jobb, whose capital and income were in pills; his wife, Marjorie, who made the literary success of the year; Randal Farrer, advertising agent, who made her make it, and Randal's eccentric but charming wife, Christina, who upsets everyone's applecart. The novel is a diverting one.

BUBBSON. By Stanley J. Rubenstein. Jarrolds. 7s. 6d.
Too obviously a humorous book in which the pace is forced, as can be seen in advance from the too-facetious dedication. The idea, however, is quite a good one. Bubbston, an author, who has found it impossible to persuade any publisher to handle any of his work, plans out a will and a series of curses, with the most surprising effect.

PROCTOR'S HALF-HOURS WITH THE TELESCOPE. Longmans. 5s.
This is a new edition, revised and brought right up to date by Dr. W. H. Steavenson, F.R.A.S., of the deservedly famous little standard manual for amateur stargazers. It abounds in heavenly maps and diagrams which are invaluable to the beginner, and must be a source of sore temptation to those who have not yet begun.

LOUDOUN FROM LARAMIE. By Joseph B. Ames. Hutchinson. 7s. 6d.
There is a spate now of cowboy novels at the standard price which are not comparably near in story and style to the penny dreadfuls of our boyhood. These books, written for American joyahoos, are an insult to the lowest English intelligence. " Loudoun of Laramie " would be disdained in a home for imbeciles, though its appeal is evidently directed to morons.

WHIPPED CREAM. By Geoffrey Moss. Hutchinson. 7s. 6d.
Readers who seek for the naughtiness of " Sweet Pepper " will be disappointed here. Lindy Hawkins is, it is true, a most amoral young woman, but her divagations make for a lot of dullness. Her husband, General Hawkins, of the Brigade of Guards, is, no doubt, pictured from the life as the author was a member of that distinguished force himself ; but Sir Henry Hawkins is a frightful duffer in all non-military affairs. Lindy, who slipped into young Lord Dashwood's bedroom, while poor old Hawkins was suffering from insomnia, has a father who is as amoral as herself, and who cannot assure Hawkins that Lindy will not commit herself again. The young woman has a bad time. The book is curiously dull.

THE PIPES OF PAN. By Julia Tregenna. Hutchinson. 7s. 6d. net.

These pipes to-day are hardly used. Pan cannot be held responsible for the conduct of a silly woman who meets a strange man on the high road, talks to him all night and then complains because her husband doesn't like it. Our sympathies are with Pan.

THE DESERT LOVERS. By Gordon Casserley. Hodder & Stoughton. 7s. 6d. net.

Mr. Geoffrey Blake for some strange reason thought the desert would be nice and quiet and free from skirts—feminine anyway. He finds his mistake and gets badly mauled. He is left with a lovely slave who kisses his beautiful big boots. There are more capital letters in this book than we have ever seen before.

LAUGHTER AND TEARS. By the Hon. Mrs. Lionel Guest. The Bodley Head. 6s.

Some of the tears are very trying, streaming down the cheeks of mawkish sentimentality, but "The Practical Joke," a snake story, and "Noon To-morrow," the episode of a beautiful woman attacked by leprosy, strike the authentic note of horror. Mrs. Guest has a decided sense of humour as displayed in "The Advertisement" and "The Weighing-in Machine."

THE DIAMOND HEELS. By Winifred Graham. Hutchinson. 7s. 6d.

In hectic mood Mrs. Graham, desisting for a spell from the evils of Mormonism, tells how Natalie Nanson, of the diamond heels of destiny, glided into the ballroom at Claridge's, got into confidential talk with Colonel Caponnet, learnt about his awful mother-in-law and his motherless twins, but did not marry him. There is plenty of incident for the money in this trivial record of alleged strong passions. The book is an improvement on many of Mrs. Graham's previous novels.

THE TRIUMPH OF A FOOL. By John Ressich. Cassell. 7s. 6d.

Gideon Gilray, in spite of much care lavished on him by the author, is a quite uninteresting man. Though not born with a silver spoon in his mouth, he acquires riches by adoption and proves disappointing to the lady whom he thinks his mother. Mrs. Gilray, the vulgar snob, is the best-drawn character in the book. Gideon marries a woman who resembles a firefly and one who resembles a fish, and is unhappy with both. Paying cold-blooded Carrie to divorce him, he takes on with warm-hearted Madge, whom he wisely removes to New Zealand.

THE CELESTIAL CITY. By Baroness Orczy. Hodder & Stoughton. 7s. net.

When we were very young our ambition was to take all the "excellents" of the term. The Baroness Orczy, however, has now bagged the lot for her latest Bolshie novel. The dull, stupid, virtuous husband of the reformed thief smokes "excellent" cigars and drinks "excellent" wine and in the scrap with the bold bad Russians gives an "excellent" example of punching. Princesses (Russian and excellent) hunt missing husbands and the bad ones all reform under their royal influence. A dull book.

IN A STRANGE LAND. By H. J. Proumen. Faber & Gwyer. 6s.

Translated by E. G. Allingham, with a preface by Henri Barbusse, this is a vivid story of Belgian life in England during the war. It is not a pleasant book, but there was not much happiness in the lives of these refugees, whose faults and vices as well as their virtues are recorded with a stark fidelity. There is humour in the record, too, and a good deal of anti-war propaganda, skilfully conveyed through the mouths of disputants.

LOVE'S BLINDNESS. By Elinor Glyn. Duckworth. 3s. 6d.

The one good thing about Mrs. Glyn's novels is that they are little ones. This is the "thrilling and passionate romance" of how Hubert Lord St. Austel married the beautiful daughter of a Jewish moneylender and a Roman princess (an unusual blend). Hubert Culverdale, D.S.O., M.C., eighth Earl of St. Austel, who had "faced death a hundred times in France and Flanders with the calmest emotions," thought that Vanessa Levy was marrying him for his position, but that lovely semi-Jewess really loved him, and finally converted Hubert to her in spite of the lecherous machinations of Allice (spelt with two l's), Duchess of Lincolnwood.

THE BLACK GLOVE. By J. G. Sarasin. Hutchinson. 7s. 6d.

The mass of historical novels are written according to a formula. Mr. Sarasin conveys little of the Restoration atmosphere, but his yarn is ingenious. His portrait of the Duchess of Albemarle is the best thing in a story telling of how a chaste Court lady was forced to marry the jailbird, Captain Tyburn, because they spent some hours in an alleged plague-stricken house together. She was rather punctilious for those times. One sees, too, a great deal of a mysterious Dr. Bendo.

THE ISLE OF PHEASANTS. By E. M. O'R. Dickey. Duckworth. 7s. 6d.

Mr. Dickey is continually facetious and many of his passages suggest an echo of that conventional stage-Irishman in fiction, the Rev. Canon Hanney. Young people who want to be amused will, no doubt, get some fun from the story of Simon Ecks, one of those journalists who only occur in fiction, who to avoid the sirens of the suburbs seeks retirement in a country vicarage and comes up against a young married woman appropriately named Delilah.

JOHN ANTHONY'S SWEET TEMPTATION. By Sybil Tasker Hart. Heath Cranton. 7s. 6d.

This is the kind of novel which when badly done is silly in the extreme, but Miss Hart does it remarkably well. Her heroine, who is called Boy, is a fluffy little thing, but she has courage and works hard for a living. The modest hero, who is a journalist and novelist, is puzzled by Boy's ladylike mother, who takes strong liquors because of some heart infirmity. His sister-in-law, Annabel, is a most cleverly drawn representative of the mercenary young married women who live in tiny flats and have a vulgarly good time.

ROUND ABOUT NORFOLK AND SUFFOLK. By Rev. Canon F. J. Meyrick. Jarrold's. 2s. 6d. net.

Canon Meyrick, the well-known Vicar of St. Peter Mancroft Church, Norwich, publishes a collection of articles written at various times on various topics. To East Anglians the little book provides a fund of interest and reminiscence. The articles called "A Splendid Penance" (the story of Herbert de Losinga, founder of Norwich Cathedral) and "The Stones of Dunwich" are especially well written and reveal a happy fusion of sound knowledge and free imagination. The style is fluent, yet disciplined—coloured, yet not luridly so. To me, whose early days were spent in close association with St. Peter Mancroft Church, these fanciful flights have conjured up a world of happy days, and brought to mind many a forgotten episode. One chapter is called "The Musings of a Verger." It tells of the death of Douro Potter while helping to ring a touch on the twelve bells. He tolled his own death bell and died in the belfry. I remember Potter very well. Of all that specialised group of men who carry the wand of office in churches and cathedrals, he was the most unique within my experiences; more unique even than the verger at Durham, or the verger at Southwark or the head porter (lives he still?) at Peterhouse. There was personality in Potter's every utterance. He would not give vent to vain repetitions in conducting a party round the church, but would answer their questions with counter-questions and so "grow to a point." He loved to defend the "via media" of the English Church. On one occasion I was practising a Bach Fugus on the organ and ended by adding the "Tuba Mirabilis" for a climax. Unknown to me, Potter was discoursing to a group of sight-seers. He came over to the console and waited till the release of my final chord, then said: "I wish to take advantage of this silence to protest against an unequal competition." Canon Meyrick's delightful little book is rounded off with some unusual fishing yarns, told with unobtrusive good humour.

B.M.

Published by the Proprietors, G.K.'s WEEKLY, LTD., at their offices, 20 & 21 Essex Street, Strand, London, W.C.2 (incorporating THE NEW WITNESS). Telephone No. City 1978. Printed by THE ALLIED PRESS, LTD., 19 Clerkenwell Close, London, E.C.1. Sole agents for Australasia : Gordon & Gotch (Australasia), Ltd. Sole Agents for South Africa : Central News Agency, Ltd.

G.K.'s Weekly, May 1, 1926

THE MYSTERY OF MUSSOLINI.

G.K.'s Weekly

EDITED BY G. K. CHESTERTON.

No. 59.—Vol. III.   Week ending Saturday, May 1, 1926   PRICE SIXPENCE
YEARLY (52 ISSUES)
£1 10 4.

Telephone No. City 1978.   Offices, 20 & 21, Essex Street, Strand, W.

CONTENTS:

THE REVOLT OF THE BUSMEN

WE have been told again and again that the desire for ownership does not exist in England to-day. At least, there might be a trace of it among millionaires who own forests of factories and fleets of motor cars, and who straddle like a squatting Colossus with country seats in two shires and *pieds-a-terre* in two capitals. But certainly, we were told, it is extinct among Englishmen who own nothing except the clothes they stand up in and the furniture (probably had on the hire purchase) they camp among. There are no poor men in England who will fight for the liberty to own the things by which they live :—their shops and the tools of their trade. Can this be said any longer ? Have not the busmen disabused even the most old-fashioned Socialist of that fancy ? We confess that we, too, were blind. We knew that the instinct for ownership, if it were not active, was at least dormant in all of us. But we had thought that much would have to be done to re-awaken it. We had not hoped that so easily and so swiftly it might become a flame, a beacon.

Since last we wrote in this place the busmen have been hailed before a magistrate to show cause why they should not be punished for resisting the Combine. Their evidence told us no more than we knew, that most of them were poor men who had put all they had and all they could borrow into the purchase of their buses ; that the issue was one of life and death for them and that they were determined to fight for their lives.

But the evidence of a representative from the Yard, if it did not tell us more than we guessed, at least confirmed our guesses. We know now that the police do work hand in hand with the Combine—which was to be expected when the Transport Ministry had been working hand in hand with the Combine from the very start.

Since the local authorities, through whose areas the threatened bus services run, have declared on the side of the men, and have stated that they do not want the trams, and they want not merely as many buses as they had but more, there is no shadow of excuse for the understanding between the Combine and the Ministry.

Once again we implore Mr. Baldwin not to under-estimate the importance of the affair. He is very busy at the moment with the dispute between the miners and the mine-owners, and that is important enough, and will need all his skill to settle. But this fight of Englishmen for the right to own is of vastly greater importance. Their example will be followed. The revolt of the London bus owners is only the first of many such revolts. And Mr. Baldwin is an honourable, well-meaning man. But in deciding how these bus-owners shall be treated he is deciding how all independent owners shall be treated when they are threatened by an influential combine. He may be deciding how he and his Ministry and h's class shall be treated by the men who revolt.

NOTES OF THE WEEK

Gallipoli Day

ONCE again some of the veterans of the Great War have fallen on their old markers and felt that they were one. They were the survivors of the Twenty-ninth Division which on April 25, 1915, made its way through two lines of barbed wire to the heights of Gallipoli, first crossing in open boats from the transports a strip of still water under intense fire from the enemy on the heights, a fire so intense that, as one of those who was with them said, "the sea was red with blood." They are the survivors of that Division which was, in the course of that glorious, disastrous campaign, "wiped clean off the slate," was as constantly recruited, and remained what it had been in *esprit-de-corps* and in fighting power. Gallipoli Day was well remembered, perhaps because Gallipoli was one of our failures, and about a failure such as this there is nothing to remember but valour. There was no foolish talk about the dawn of a new era, the great mistake we made in fighting at all, the peculiar spiritual elevation of the Turk, but only a soldier's salute to the living and the dead. So we, civilians that we were perforce, salute them: the gentlemen and the workmen who died side by side, and the gentlemen and workmen who stood on Sunday side by side again, if only for an hour. There is a comradeship of the trenches we have not recaptured in our civilian life, and some of the veterans were very shabby, for all their shining medals.

The Royal Baby

WE shared the joy of the public at the news that his Duchess had presented the Duke of York with a daughter. In the first place, such an event as this assures us that the stately figures we see driving through the streets (and even that but seldom) or hear about when they open something or lay a foundation stone are really human. Life nowadays is passed in sound and sight-proof compartments; above all our Royal family live cut off from the people, instead of walking or riding among them as was the custom some centuries back. We know that occasionally an institution is visited and an old man is shaken by the hand or a child is patted on the head; we see that in all the papers, but the events are too obviously staged and too remote from the masses of us to seem real. But the birth of a Royal baby is quite another matter, and so the hearts of those like us, whose loyalty has remained intense in spite of everything, our hearts are thrilled. Moreover, this new young lady is the presumptive heir to the Throne, and we like to fancy that our children will pay her homage. Probably she will be an autocrat, our Queens are usually despotic, but she will be liked none the less for that, and a spice of autocracy in our monarch will be useful in the days to come.

Mr. Wheatley and the Subsidy

WE are glad to note that Mr. Wheatley is much in favour of subsidising the mining industry, but we cannot accept his definition of a subsidy. "It is," he says, "the intelligent way out of our difficulty." We agree. But we do not agree that "it means taking from the surplus wealth of the country an amount sufficient to maintain in a decent standard of living the workers engaged in one of the essential industries of the country." Who, to begin with, is to fix the decent standard of living? We are of opinion that at present costs of living a miner's seventy-odd shillings a week is a miserable wage. We think that the farm-labourer's longed-for minimum of thirty shillings a week is a miserable wage. But you will not put things right merely by contributing money from the Treasury. As a stop-gap, yes, Mr. Baldwin was right in making a free gift of some of the public money; but now we must put the affair on a business basis. We give our idea of how it can be done elsewhere in this issue. Nor is it very reasonable of Mr. Wheatley to talk of competitive capitalism being doomed when he knows that competition between big capitalists is almost obsolete. Perhaps he was ill-reported; perhaps he means in this connection what we mean, that there is a good chance for capitalist monopoly to survive if it can reduce the common people to the condition of slaves. But why, then, does he talk the old-fashioned Socialist stuff about us being "saturated with the competitive system"? Workmen are saturated with the idea that they must in any conceivable state of society be employed for a wage. But that is a very different thing.

American Sauce

INCREDIBLE as it may seem, America intends to prosecute the claims lodged by American shippers who suffered damage through England's blockade of Germany during the war. At least, so we learn from Sir A. Maurice Low's dispatch to the *Morning Post*, and he is a reliable witness. He tells us that what Washington proposes is that the representatives of America and England shall meet in London or Washington and engage in a sort of sifting-out process to determine which claims have merit, and which are not entitled to any consideration. But, apparently, blockade claims are not to be ruled out of consideration. Senator Borah maintains his original position, and it is stated that both President Coolidge and Mr. Kellogg stand with him. Now, as Sir A. Maurice Low points out, Senator Borah's arguments won't hold salt water. The case of the British ships seized by the United States during the Civil War is exactly analogous with that of the American ships seized by us during the war with Germany. We have no doubt that American shippers knew that the cotton they sent to Sweden was meant for Germany, and in any case it went to Germany when it got through our blockade. That, as Sir A. Maurice Low points out, is precisely the case of British cargoes sent from London to Bahamas, and rightly seized by the States. We shall think very poorly of our Government if they do not tell Washington that they will not assist at a conference on war claims until all blockade claims have been ruled out.

The Budget

WE begin this note before the delivery of Mr. Churchill's Budget speech, but there is every indication that it will be a dull Budget. With a considerable amount of skill the Chancellor of the

Exchequer has convinced his adversaries in advance, though against their will, that there is no great opportunity for a drastic cut in expenses. He frightened his own Party with the prospect of having to economise at the expense of our Defences, and the Opposition with the certainty that one of the first economies would be at the expense of education. The Economy Bill, with its trifling tilt at National Insurance, was a sprat which has caught a whale. We sincerely trust that Mr. Churchill has fulfilled expectations and brought in his Betting Tax. This is a very legitimate form of taxation, and no Puritan who buys the *Daily News* or the *Star* has the right to say that it is wicked to countenance betting. We might hope that as an immediate consequence street-betting would be legalised, but a tax on street-betting would be difficult to collect, so that probably for a time the street-bookie will remain an Ishmael.

Games on Sunday

WE are glad to note that the Ecclesiastical Commissioners will in future allow games to be played on lands leased by them. So that it seems they are not afraid of putting the clock back. A few centuries ago it was as usual to play games on Sunday as to go to church. Now, when it is no longer usual to go to church, the Commissioners make the proviso that games shall not be played while church services are in progress. The idea is, no doubt, that nobody would go to church if they had the chance of playing a game instead. But why do the Commissioners still bar games, such as football, by which the competitive spirit is invoked? Is there any game worth calling a game which is not competitive? Or do the Commissioners fear to cause occasion for betting among the spectators? We fear that the relaxation of their restrictions will be of little use to those who most need a game on Sunday if competitive games, such as football, are not to be played. And, while we are about it, is it not time that theatres were allowed to be open on Sundays? In a very fine speech delivered at the Shakespearian Birthday Dinner of the Fellowship of Players, Mr. Arthur Bourchier pleaded for the right of performing societies to produce plays on Sunday. He might have gone further and fared no worse. For all his arguments have an equal force if urged for the freedom of the theatre from Sabbatarian restrictions. "A man," he said, "may play golf or ride a horse, or drive a car, and yet be accounted worthy to be in the Apostolic succession. The heart of a minister of the Church does not beat less true because his extremities are guilty of a pair of plus fours." We do not yearn to see priests in that garb, or engaged in that quaint Scottish game, but the Lord Chamberlain (or the Ecclesiastical Commissioners) will not share our objection. And Mr. Bourchier is right in his main contention that if it is seemly for a man to play golf on Sunday it is seemly for him to act in or watch a stage-play.

The Olympian Mac

MR. RAMSAY MACDONALD, speaking at the dinner at Olympia to members and friends of the Association of Architects, Surveyors, and Technical Assistants, was eloquent. It would seem that he was moved almost to tears. We feel that we must quote his beautiful words at some length, and we thank the *Daily Telegraph* for the opportunity of doing so. Proposing the toast of the Building Exhibition (held at Olympia) he said he felt most profoundly that such exhibitions were contributing more than the tongue could tell to the peace, the happiness, and the holiness of our lives. Men and women wanted houses, not merely as shelters, but as homes which, by their walls, their aspects, and their designs, spoke to the human mind in words that were soothing and uplifting, and supplied that subtle, psychological influence which made all the difference between a happy and an unhappy home. (Hear, hear.) The fireside did not consist only of a hearth and a couple of chairs; there must be a presence—an indefinable presence—that appealed to the hearts of men and women, and which came within the category of that which was holy. Those who were engaged in the building of £350 houses, far more than the £5,000 houses, for there were many more of them—if they were going to do their work well, must be able to get hold of something of the spirit of our great cathedral builders, who were not merely masons in the sense of laying one stone on top of another, but were architects, artists, and religious worshippers in the sense that as the walls rose over their heads they felt that they were contributing something of permanent beauty and moral value. (Cheers.)

Down with Utilitarianism

"I DETEST utilitarianism in house building," proceeded Mr. MacDonald. "Utilitarianism is the death of the soul of man. When we do things in a minimum way; when there is no imperative demand in our hearts for something more than the merely useful, then we are no longer men, but mere machines. In these days of impecuniousness and penury we should be running a great risk if we built houses on the mass-production principle—just as a great deal of our furniture is made—by machinery a million at a time. If such a time should come it will mean that there is not much of the love of God left in us." We trust that the builder who is putting up a semi-detached house or a bungalow for £350 will remember these holy words, and will leave sufficient space for the gas stove. We trust, too, that Mr. MacDonald himself will remember them when next the question of Steel Houses comes up. "Utilitarianism is the death of the soul of man." That is a noble sentiment. "When we do things in a minimum sort of way . . . then we are no longer men, we are machines." And what happens to us when we are housed in a steel machine? Again Mr. MacDonald must remember that the masons built the cathedrals with strict reference to the wishes of Him Who was to dwell therein, and presumably the builder of the £350 house must be as zealous to please his incoming tenant. And if the tenant is not fixed in his tenancy, are we not likely to get later on a tenant in the house to whose human mind the subtle psychological influence of the walls, the aspects, and the designs may not speak in words that are either soothing or uplifting? Does not Mr. MacDonald see that a house is not really a man's home unless it belongs to him, so that he can inbue the walls with his own designs, so that he can, for example, knock holes through them? All the same, if only the foremen and bricklayers erecting houses in our neighbourhood could have Mr. MacDonald beside them as they work and uttering his words of holy wisdom, we are sure that their response would have great moral value.

MORTGAGE THE MINES!

THE coal deadlock continues: it was to be expected. The owners have shown no disposition to consider the point of view of the miners, and on the whole we are not sorry they have proved so intractable. For, if they behave so with the eyes of the country upon them and the possibility of Government control before them, we can foresee to what lengths they would go if and when they were uncontrolled and unobserved.

Their stupidity must have exasperated the more intelligent monopolists, it has given away the case for monopoly so completely. The nation has now taken an interest in mining which we cannot lightly surrender, and certainly we cannot afford to leave the mineowners a free hand.

We endeavoured last week to show that above all else the miners should fight for control, and the owners have proved our point for us. Whatever happy arrangements were made now, they would not long be operative unless the miners were in a position to enforce them, or unless we must contemplate recurring strikes and recurring Government intervention.

A system of mixed control with the owners and Government officials as major factors would be no more satisfactory, since, as the 'bus affair has taught us (if we needed teaching), Government officials always tend to throw their weight on the side of a Combine. No! the miners most fight for control.

Yet we agree that equally they must resist any attempt to lower their wages, which they may consider involves in itself a battle hard enough. We are of opinion, however, that if Mr. Baldwin knows his business that battle will be lightly won.

Though nobody has adopted our watchword, "Mortgage the mines," a number of publicists (Mr. Garvin chief among them) have accepted our main proposition that public money handed over to the mining industry should be regarded as a loan. But mortgage is the better word, for it implies the right of continued supervision.

Now, if we are to raise a mining loan to provide the purchase price of mining royalties and money to be lent on mortgage to the mines, that will relieve the taxpayer of a burden. As Mr. Garvin points out, the interest on part of the loan would be met by the return from the mining royalties, and, as he admits, the interest on the major part of the remainder might be a charge on the industry.

But why, ultimately, only of the major part? We realise that at present the industry might not be able to pay all the interest due on the full amount of the mortgage. But there is no reason why it should not be entered in the ledger against them, to be paid when, with the help of the money advanced and the reconstruction promised, the industry is on its feet. Nay, more, why should not the transaction follow more nearly the usual lines of a mortgage, so that after a period to be fixed a proportion of the sum advanced would be repaid with each instalment of interest?

There is no doubt that this could be done; there is no doubt that such a transaction, instead of being a burden on the ratepayer, might be a profitable investment. And, also, there is no doubt that it would be ridiculous to raise a loan large enough for all other purposes, but not large enough to put a reduction of wages out of question.

The two things necessary in regard to mining are that the miners who produce the coal should be satisfied, and the public which consumes the coal should be satisfied. The owners plead that they must live, but we do not see the necessity; they are not owners at all in the true sense of the word, they are concessionaires, and the industry could get on very well without them. The owners are to be helped to stand on their own feet, but surely not on the feet of the miners or the public.

Wages are a first charge on the industry, and they are not too high. We are told that the industry is not prosperous enough to pay them, but we are also told that it cannot afford to pay anything, and that unless it is reconstructed and otherwise helped it must stop. Very well then, it must be helped; but then so generously that the present wages may be maintained, and only on condition that they are maintained. There must be other conditions. The owners must agree to the scheme of reconstruction suggested in the Report and approved by the Government and the miners, and they must agree that the miners shall be given a large degree of control over the working of the pits and the conditions of labour in and round about it.

By the action he has taken Mr. Baldwin has virtually superseded control by the concessionaires. Control by the miners is the only decent and logical alternative. The concessionaires are bankrupt and should have nothing to say. What is the alternative? A strike! A strike that will cost much in money, more in temper, and still more in lost opportunities for trade. Even if this strike be avoided, by some sort of illogical compromise, the risk of strikes must remain, unless strikes are declared illegal and the workmen are once and for all acknowledged as chattel-slaves. This is, if we do not give the miners control!

Monopoly is not a state of Society, it is a state of war, and can only be carried on by battle between the two armies of men and masters with intervals of armistice and arbitration. The class-war which the Bolshevists preach exists, and should be ended. It can only be ended by healing the cleavage between "master" and "man."

TWO SONNETS

PHANTOM the world is; we, too, tirelessly
　　Vaunting our restless egos with loud cries,
　　And shrill announcing trumpets, even we,
Brief particles of dream, move phantom-wise.
Shadows surround us, we ourselves are shades
　　Wrought unsubstantially, and all our might
Of towers and arms and thought and songcraft fades
　　To a far flicker of a little light.
Rameses died, and Alexander, she
　　Whose beauty sang to rapine and to flame,
And Antony and Cæsar, Deirdre,
　　They died and are but phantom and a name;
And we, as they, frail tossing ghosts of time,
Are nought save in the sanction of a rhyme.

WILLIAM KEAN SEYMOUR

AND so shall I till life holds naught but song,
　　And blood is beating to the beat of verse
　　And life is lovely as a dream, perverse
As air, and yet as calm as rain, among
The crocus lawns before the sun is down.
Thus, then, I would that you and I might live,
Thoughtless of common cares, and loving, give
Our dual minds an individual crown.

When, in the night, as fear, with wakeful wing,
Shall steal my wealth of sleep and leave me pain,
Shamefully bowed and dumb and sick, I'll bring
My sleeplessness to you: I'll feel your eyes
Spreading peace upon the dark; again
You'll take me home, most strong, gentle and wise.

PHILIP HENDERSON.

TOP—

A SOCIETY PARAGRAPH

The following paragraph in a daily paper has given us a subtle and even a solemn joy. " You cannot help noticing in these political gatherings nowadays what a number of women are looked upon with interest and respect by the men of their party. Dame Helen Gwynne Vaughan was always a centre of earnest talkers, and Lady Lawrence, Chairman of the Ladies' Imperial Club, was sitting and talking with Lord Younger for a long time. Lady Kinloch-Cooke, just down from Cardiff, told me that she had been making a good many speeches in her husband's constituency during the Easter recess." This followed upon another political paragraph devoted to Lord William Cecil, Lord and Lady Askwith, Sir William and Lady Joynson-Hicks and Sir Alfred and Lady Mond ; so that the surging and dangerous democracy of modern politics is aptly illustrated by two solid paragraphs in which there is not a single person without a title. We have no animus about the individuals involved, beyond a profound and heartfelt compassion for the unfortunate lady who is always the centre of earnest talkers. Indeed we conceive ourselves capable of regarding the ladies in question with " respect," even without having the privilege of being " men of their party." The habit of men, of various parties, looking at women with " interest " does not seem to us to be entirely new. In our researches into the barbarous past, we have come upon many cases in which women were apparently looked at with marked interest by men. In this case, however, the point appears to be that the ladies were looked upon with respect as well as interest ; and that the men of their party, instead of elbowing them out of the road, hurling them out of the room, roaring them down, rolling them over, or otherwise reverting to the more ordinary way of treating a female companion, exhibited an unconquerable patience and a strained and almost unnatural politeness. Such are the trophies which triumphant woman has gained for the first time by the possession of the vote.

We can never quite make out whether the people who talk like this about the position of the " modern " woman mean anything particular or not. Nothing that they say bears the remotest resemblance to any reality that we ever knew or heard of, in connection with our own mothers or grandmothers or great aunts. That the world is better for women having certain particular political functions is a perfectly reasonable opinion. That the world was ever so wicked or stupid as to present the contrast implied here we have great difficulty in believing. Did these people actually have experiences which make that remarkable society scene appear truly remarkable ? Did they live in some country of the blind where women were never looked at with interest ? Did they dwell in some den of savages where women were never looked at with respect ? Was there ever any society of intelligent people, in which it was impossible to see a lady acting as the centre of earnest talkers ? Certainly not in the society of Cleopatra, or of St. Catherine of Siena, or of Diane of Poitiers, or of Mary Queen of Scots, or of Mrs. Thrale, or of Madame Roland, or of George Eliot, or of George Sand. The truth is that the old-fashioned woman is becoming a wilder and wilder fable every day. It is bad enough to have a mythical monster for a remote ancestor in the Stone Age or the Neolithic epoch. It is too much to have our own mothers turning into mythical monsters. In due course, doubtless, our own contemporaries of the other sex will take on these rude and repulsive features of antiquity ; but for the present we feel ourselves quite capable of talking to a woman with interest and occasionally with earnestness, even if she is not in Parliament—and even if she has not got a handle to her name.

—AND TAIL

PROFANITY AND PROPORTION

The recent row in America about the entertaining Mr. Mencken, who defiantly sold a magazine said to be improper and was apparently pursued by the police for doing so, continues to leave a trail of comment in the American papers and magazines. And doubtless it was a significant incident, though it is not easy for English people to understand all that it signifies. Mr. Mencken is a clever and bitter Jew, in whom a very real love of letters is everlastingly exasperated by the American love of cheap pathos and platitude. There is a great deal to be said for him ; and it is all quite negative. His own philosophy is the sort of nihilistic pride, which belongs to a man with a sensitive race and a dead religion. He has nothing to defend and he defends it splendidly. To be just to him, we must always remember the vast prairies of flat and vulgar sentiment with which he is surrounded. We might fairly say that it is only just to Mencken to remember that he has to put up with America and only just to America to remember that it has to put up with Mencken.

An article in the American *Bookman* reveals a further and quainter quality in the situation. What makes it most difficult for people of our own tradition to judge the truth in such a quarrel is the national values involved. We should normally be in sympathy with the Americans who are defending morality ; only that the Americans seem to have such an extraordinary morality to defend. We believe that Mr. Mencken, who makes himself a champion of Nietzsche and delights in shocking the Christian as well as the Puritan sensibility, is quite capable of praising works which we would not touch with a pitchfork. But when we come to the actual attacks made in America upon these things, we are much more bewildered by the attack than the defence. The *Bookman* mentions a controversy in which also Mr. Mencken was involved, concerning the works of Theodore Dreiser, the famous American writer of realistic fiction. It seems that an institution called the Anti-Vice Society appointed a committee to draw up a list of all the examples of " immorality and profanity " to be found in one of this gentleman's studies of daily life in America. As the novel consists of seven hundred pages, which had to be carefully considered word for word in this fashion, it is clear that the examiners were called upon for not a little industry and close attention. However, by uniting all their forces together in one great corporate effort, the members of the committee managed to read the book. They then apparently made out long lists of disconnected words and phrases, including not only anything which savoured of sexual impropriety but the most casual conversational exclamations which the philologist could remotely connect with religion. It seems that expressions like " Oh, Lord ! " or its more American variant of " My Lord ! " were gravely written down in the dreadful indictment. As no social type in these social studies was permitted to say " Oh, Lord," it is needless to say that not even the most squalid and degraded miscreant in the criminal classes could even be conceived as saying, " Oh, hell ! "

What strikes us as extraordinary is not so much that anybody should object to this or that rather meaningless exclamation, as that anybody can possibly class it with questions affecting the dignity and decency of the relation of the sexes. But that is the world in which Mr. Mencken has to live ; and it must be remembered as an excuse for him.

THE SCRAPBOOK

RAILWAY RHYMES.
VII.—THE GUARD.

DO not be hard on the Guard,
    His is a difficult case.
    When he wants to jump in,
At the risk of his skin,
Don't slam the door bang in his face,
Nor form yourself into a "barrage"
And let him go leaping in vain;
Remember—when Guard's in his carriage
All's right with the train.   R. W.

* * * *

SCHOOL GHOSTS.

On winter nights long years ago,
When all the land was white with snow,
And fellows blew upon their hands
And wished themselves in warmer lands,
And everybody's nose was red,
And still it wasn't time for bed—
We'd creep in through a classroom door,
And group ourselves upon the floor
Or, better, on the radiator,
And start with tales—how some one's mat.
Once knew a nun who'd seen a spectre.
How could one doubt and still respect her?
And then we'd tell, a little daunted,
How well we knew the School was haunted.
We'd ghosts to reach from there to Beenham,
Although 'twas other chaps who'd seen 'em.
Huddled and breathless, bound by spell,
We'd whisper on until "the bell"—
Unless, before those jangling sounds,
(The classrooms being out of bounds)
We happened to be caught, and then
Were soundly whacked by holy men.

Still I remember very well
The horrid tale of Mangey Nell,
A servant who bagged watches, lockets,
And petty cash from fellow's pockets.
One day they caught her doing this
And gave her up to P.C. Bliss,
Who took her off to Reading Gaol,
Where Nell, who had been looking pale,
Pegged out before the judge could sentence,
And died without a true repentance.
Though the poor thing went off to—well,
A certain place which rhymes with Nell,
Her ghost returned to haunt the School,
Knowing the corridors were cool,
And made herself a perfect pest.
Her groans robbed every one of rest;
And fellows swore they wouldn't stay,
And several of them ran away—
Until at last, as you've surmised,
They had to have her exorcised—
And we agreed it served her right
For giving people such a fright.

There was a ghostly matron, too,
A thin and wisp-like lady, who,
Not being strong, had died of shocks
While helping Martha with the socks.

She did her haunting everywhere:
You sometimes passed her on the stair
Or saw her in the infirmary
Preparing quarts of senna tea:
It scared all those who'd sooner trust
A living matron more robust.
And then there was a dog which haunted
All places where he wasn't wanted—
A spotted hound whose eyes flashed fire.
(Young Jobson, who's an awful liar,
Says he saw him gnawing bones,
Lying outside on the stones.)
This spotted dog was paler, thinner
Than Spotted Dog we met at dinner.
The tale was steep, but did not follow
'Twas not the easier to swallow.

And then there was a boy named Jim
Whose shadowy spectre, pale and slim,
In Haydock Hall wrote hard all night
Till crow of cocks released the wight.
He wrote with labour undiminished
"Lines" which in life he hadn't finished.
His master made an awful fuss
Because he wrote "Non volumus,"
And banged him hard upon the head
Until he found the boy was dead.
Although such things were rarely done
Except in playfulness and fun,
The master, sad to say, was hanged
Because he'd killed the boy he banged.
(I never quite believed in Jim:
It happened I invented him.)

But I must not forget—Good Gracious!—
A certain Father Indignatius
Who used o' nights to haunt the chapel.
You couldn't move your Adam's apple,
You felt that you must choke and die
When *that* blood-freezing shade came nigh!
One night the undisputed fact is
He came and spoiled a choir practice.
And nobody, they say, ran faster
Than Mr. Blank the music master;
While one poor boy jumped like a flea
And cleared the choir gallery,
And fell below upon a seat
And broke a leg and hurt his feet.
The choir was afterwards immune
Because it learned to sing in tune.
(And I should like to add, this mystery
Is well-authenticated history.)

* * * *

Now all the ghosts are laid, they say:
They're sheet-and-turnip spooks to-day.
But when I climb Woolhampton Hill
I know that ghosts await me still—
The poor sad ghosts of youth gone by,
The little chump who once was I,
With every fear, ambition, hope,
And—all that minor poets' dope.
Don't start that "blurb." Come on, you fool,
They're on the touch-line, yelling "School"!
                              A. M. BURRAGE.

THE JEWS
An Imaginary Conversation by Bernard Gilbert

BERNARD GILBERT : Hullo, Lavrin, how goes your work ?

JANKO LAVRIN : Slowly.

GILBERT : Writing serious criticism in England must be a slow business.

LAVRIN : It takes me all my time to get my books published.

GILBERT : Which brings me to what I wanted to ask you. You know what is being produced all over Europe without having to wait—as I do—for the successful to be translated. Tell me, is there in any corner, vital literature coming forth?

LAVRIN : No !

GILBERT : Not anywhere?

LAVRIN : Europe—with the possible exception of Russia, about which it is impossible to learn much—is one dead level of sentimental uprooted mediocrity.

GILBERT : A sad statement.

LAVRIN : What of it? You don't ask me if there is anything vital in England or America, because you know.

GILBERT : I have come to certain conclusions about England and wish to see how far they are applicable to other countries.

LAVRIN : I saw what you said to Eustace Kyme. You take it, briefly, that between Alfred and Henry VIII, your nation was more or less homogenous, with one church, one law, one king, and that, with the irruption of the New Learning, the unity began to disappear?

GILBERT : Religion feeling the attack first, as it must.

LAVRIN : You mustn't mix up the Renaissance with the Reformation. The former started with the fall of Constantinople, according to historians, and the consequent spread, throughout Europe, of those who bore with them the seed that——

GILBERT : Infected all nations. Ours amongst them—mine, I should say.

LAVRIN : You're very English.

GILBERT : I hope so. Why not?

LAVRIN : You were born and bred in a rural community which you did not leave until you were thirty, and to which you are now returning. You are essentially English, including all the shortcomings, all the prejudices——

GILBERT : As we say of Samuel Johnson——

LAVRIN : You want to turn out all aliens, all Communists—

GILBERT : Anyone who tends, by his presence, to disrupt the community.

LAVRIN : Including me?

GILBERT : You shall have a visitor's ticket with the utmost extension.

LAVRIN : Being so thoroughly imbued with the lore and language of the Saxon Bible, and using it so often as you do, has not the symbolic story of the Garden of Eden struck you? Though there was no return, there was an alternative.

GILBERT : You refer to the central motive of Christianity : that man having fallen, cannot save himself ; so that there is no return to Eden ; but he can be saved by a vicarious sacrifice ?

LAVRIN : The motive appears in many early religions ; as you see in Frazer.

GILBERT : I was talking about that, the other day, to Robson, the Engineer to the Gulland Commission, down in Bly——

LAVRIN : Is that your idea of a joke ?

GILBERT : Racial humour ! Robson pointed out that the Jews, as a race, have acclimatised themselves to city-life ; to an existence without root ; a more startling example, even, than the Chinese. Is it possible that salvation for our civilisation will come from the Jews ?

LAVRIN : I've considered that.

GILBERT : If this present civilisation is to be saved——

LAVRIN : It *must* be saved.

GILBERT : There are seventeen hundred million of us, Lavrin, and that's a round number to forecast about. The Jews have apparently solved this problem, having learnt to exist and cohere, though totally uprooted and dispersed from their native soil. They have persisted so long that one cannot overlook the example.

LAVRIN : Being thus in advance, as it were, of the other white races ?

GILBERT : Who knows but that from amongst them some new Gospel will arise ? Is it that that you would say ?

LAVRIN : It has arisen.

GILBERT : Indeed ! Where ?

LAVRIN : Socialism is essentially a Jewish doctrine.

GILBERT : From which of their ancient Books of the Law do they derive it ?

LAVRIN : Not from the orthodox religion. It is, however, a gospel coming *from* Jews.

GILBERT : Were you ever under the Bolshevists ?

LAVRIN : Not in Russia. I was in the Hungarian affair ; and that made me thoughtful.

GILBERT : So that the white races—if their civilisation continues—will be massed in great cities, becoming gradually acclimatised under the example and leadership of Jews ?

LAVRIN : Go on.

GILBERT : The governments will be purely bureaucratic.

LAVRIN : You have it !

GILBERT : Already over Europe, democracy has broken down.

LAVRIN : The inevitable outcome of the accretion of Man into communities so large that its members cannot know each other.

GILBERT : Democracy being a plant of slow growth that will not bear transplantation into unfavourable soil.

LAVRIN : Impossible soil.

GILBERT : " Unless the inhabitants meet together with a sufficient knowledge of each other."

LAVRIN : The Greek knew it, three thousand years ago. Democracy had broken down, or shall we say quietly decayed by the end of the Nineteenth Century, in nearly every European country. The war made it apparent.

GILBERT : One of the signs being the lessened interest in politics ? You would add that, in the future that we are envisaging, our Parliament will be of as little importance as a Board of Guardians.

LAVRIN : Less !

GILBERT : What do you know about Guardians ?

LAVRIN : Nothing. It must be less. The new city-caste is the civil service, an all-powerful class with ironclad walls. We are already more in their grasp than you may imagine.

GILBERT : I notice that in revolutions, the bureaucracies are little disturbed.

LAVRIN : Machinery must go on in a modern state. The bureaucracies are themselves largely revolutionary, if you examine them.

GILBERT : Shall we have a new race of Janissaries ?

LAVRIN : With hereditary chieftans ?

GILBERT : The future lies delightfully in the mists.

LAVRIN : What we are examining, is here, now. It becomes clearer every week.

GILBERT : That is not so delightful ! But what were you advancing about the salvation of mankind ?

LAVRIN : Do you wish to live under this new regime of a socialistic bureaucracy, bolstered by scientific materialism ?

GILBERT : No. Nor can it continue. It's an adjustment of despair, and cannot last.

LAVRIN : Those uprooted Jews have lasted nearly two thousand years.

GILBERT : As parasites upon more settled races only. They're like our Quakers and Conchies, who are able to refrain from fighting because the majority will fight to defend them.

LAVRIN : That is possible.

GILBERT : It IS. Your adjustment, I say, is one of despair, and cannot endure. Down, presently, comes our Civilisation : Gentile and Jew together.

LAVRIN : The roots being gone.

GILBERT : Down come ivy and oak. It has taken Man millions of years to learn how to live together in small communities, such as the one I was bred in ; which I am picturing in my Old England ; and not yet has Man shown any sign of being able to adjust himself to the conditions which are thrust irresistibly upon him as soon as he settles, multiplies, becomes wealthy and industrial, and loses touch with the soil and the tribe.

LAVRIN : You said, yourself, that we cannot forecast for a whole world.

GILBERT : I speak now of the immediate future. I cannot interest myself in the next civilisation. A few centuries is as far as one may reach. It's all very well for Bernard Shaw or H. G. Wells to run ahead for thirty or fifty thousand years for salvation——

LAVRIN : Despairing, as, one by one, their illusions drop from them ?

GILBERT : Their only hope that Man shall grow into Gods or Supermen, either by the aid of physical science or by living to a thousand.

LAVRIN : For all that, I believe a new Community will arise which will save humanity.

GILBERT : Where are the tokens of your Third Community ? Who are its forerunners ? Is it Marx or Lenin ?

LAVRIN : Socrates was one ; Jesus another.

GILBERT : Both were members of the most settled communities of the old type that we know. The Jews and the Greeks were compressed by a ring of enemies, and fiercely cohesive. I often use them as examples of my thesis. Jesus and Socrates were the flowering of the deepest-rooted tribes.

LAVRIN : They foreshadowed something new.

GILBERT : They could never have been produced by an uprooted race. It is fitting for the modern Jews to have given us Socialism and Communism. Since their Dispersion, they have offered the world nothing with root ; nothing alive.

LAVRIN : There *must* be some hope for humanity ; otherwise all is despair.

GILBERT : Not at all ! I'm not a pessimist : I do accept the world. If it moves in a given direction then it must

An Imaginary Conversation by Bernard Gilbert.

move so ; and we can only note that. It doesn't fill me with despair to consider the fall of the Roman civilisation, the total disappearance of old Egypt, or Nineveh, or Babylon.

LAVRIN : You are a member of this civilisation and cannot detach yourself. There must be some way of salvation.

GILBERT : Having left the Garden, Man enters on a dark path.

LAVRIN : What of the vicarious sacrifice so deeply planted in the human breast as a sign of hope ?

GILBERT : It is hard to draw a parallel between the individual and the race. Sometimes I am tempted to compare the return of the uprooted native (when he does return ; not being completely severed) with the salvation of the Christian. Love for his fellows ; love for his native soil ; the spirit of the tribal community ; the Spirit of Affection ; drawing him back.

LAVRIN : Not very convincing.

GILBERT : No !

LAVRIN : We are compelled to take careful note of ancient myths and legends that underlie old religions.

GILBERT : None more than I.

LAVRIN : Let me then press this problem to your notice. In its interpretation lies the hope of humanity.

GILBERT : It is a dark mystery.

LAVRIN : All spiritual truths are dark mysteries until some one reveals them to his fellows.

GILBERT : When they stone him.

STRAWS IN THE WIND
THE MYSTERY OF MUSSOLINI (II.)
By G. K. CHESTERTON

AN intelligent Englishman said to me the other day : " I could forgive Mussolini anything if he were not so fond of rhetoric." And it is this rhetorical quality in Latin politics that is perhaps the commonest form of a curious misunderstanding in this country. Let us begin by considering for a moment what this rhetoric actually is, which the Englishman compared with the sound, solid, business-like tone of his own business Government.

Mussolini, when a bullet had just been fired bang into his face, had his face plastered up a little, mounted upon a platform and made the following highly rhetorical remark : " If I advance, follow me ; if I retreat, kill me ; if I die, avenge me." Now we can all imagine what would be the nearest rendering of such a florid and flamboyant phrase into the language of our own sphere of practical politics. We know what a British statesman would say, or at least would be expected to say, if he said anything at all, after having his nose nearly blown off by a pistol. It is possible, of course, that he would immediately become a strong, silent man and retire to bed. But if the practical politician had to say anything of the same sort, it would be something like this : " It is a matter of great gratification to me, Mr. Chairman, to be permitted on so important an occasion as that of the seventy-third biennial meeting of the Anglo-Semitic Bankers' Protection League, and in the presence of this large and enthusiastic meeting gathered in support of the cause that we all have at heart, to assure you of my continued confidence in the principles and prospects of our great Party, the Party of Hink and Potter, the Party of Atkinson and Bins, and I will venture to say, ladies and gentlemen, that it is with equal confidence that I can advance to grapple with the great problems of Empire which the well-meaning ineptitude of our irresponsible opponents has left in a confusion which I conceive to be unprecedented in our national history ; with confidence I repeat, that in judging those questions frankly and firmly I can count on the support of a loyal and united Party. I hope that I am well aware, Mr. Chairman, that this magnificent loyalty and this patriotic devotion are not directed personally to me, but to those great principles of Progress combined with Conservation which I have the privilege to represent ; and I do not doubt, Mr. Chairman, it would be grossly improper for me for one moment to doubt, that did I in some period of political aberration prove false to those great principles, did I fail firmly and resolutely to apply them, did I shrink from the fulfilment of my pledges with regard to them, you would be the first to condemn my weakness and you would be fully entitled to remove me from my position. But so long as I am privileged to enunciate those principles and to hold that position, I need fear none of the motley and partisan factions that are gathered to resist the will of the people ; and I for one will make bold to say, Mr. Chairman, that the public opinion to which this great meeting so eloquently testifies would alone be a warning to those opponents that the removal of my own modest personality would not suffice to stifle the indignant voice of the Empire ; and that without any assistance that I can give, and even in the event of any such assistance being for some reason withdrawn, this great movement would still go on its way ; and that any political or other misfortunes falling upon me would be fully balanced and blotted out by the victory that must at last attend upon the forces of authority and order ; the resources of civilisation are not exhausted and, as the great Lord Balfour said upon the glorious field of Mitchelstown, you will not hesitate to shoot." I have shortened my quotation from this great speech very considerably ; but I hope it has not lost a certain air of largeness and even of leisure.

"If I advance, follow me; if I retreat, kill me; if I die, avenge me." It will still appear a paradox to many, in our own political tradition, if I confess that some of us do not quite see that Mussolini's words *are* so very much more rhetorical, in the sense of florid and artificial, than the other remarks which the big business politician addresses to the big meeting of bankers. It may seem strange; but some of us are not quite sure that the passage I have quoted, from our own practical political speaking, is so very much more practical than the frenzied rhetoric of the Italian. In the British oration there are more figures of speech; there are certainly more fictions about fact. To say the least of it, the British oratorical observation takes a little longer to say. We are told that time is money; and there are times when time is life. And when bullets are flying about men's heads, and they are within an inch of instant death, there is no time to be businesslike. There is no time for business government or really practical discussion. Too many things are being done. There is time for nothing but rhetoric.

Now I have taken this as a text because our own sort of rhetoric is specially stamped, not merely with pomposity, but with hypocrisy. It seems to me that the chief problem which the whole modern parliamentary epoch has presented to us is the problem of hypocrisy. There is a motive in that long-winded way of talking; and the motive is the desire to disguise a thing even when expressing it. It is the desire to say a thing and not say it. For after all, in his own way the plutocratic dictator does say it. The politician does mean that his party is to follow him as blindly as any battalion could follow a military leader; only he has not the honesty to give the word of command shortly and sharply as if it really were a word of command. I do not say the politician does really mean that in certain circumstances he himself ought to be killed. At that point, I am inclined to think, he would pause; at that point his humanitarian sensibility would recoil from the horror of taking human life. But he does not necessarily recoil from taking anybody else's human life. Human lives were taken at Mitchelstown; they were taken at Featherstone; they were taken at Denshawi, at Amritsar, at any number of other places over which our placid parliamentary apologists presided. They were not afraid of hanging men and women for wearing of the green; of avenging with awful cruelty the cruelties of the Indian Mutiny; of sending secret orders for spreading the anarchy of the Black and Tans. They were not afraid of violence and vengeance; of doing deeds of blood and deeds of darkness. What they were afraid of was using the language of violence and vengeance; talking in the terms that come natural to men breathing the very air of death. What they were and are afraid of is the presence of plain words and short sentences; as in those three sentences of Mussolini. They are afraid of rhetoric; it is too real.

The friendly critic who has challenged me on this question seems to be somewhat in doubt about whether I can be serious in merely throwing doubt on the rumours about the dictatorship of Rome. Yet my attitude is very simple; and is the same which I adopt towards many foreign questions that I do not profess fully to understand. I do not see how it can be "uncritical" to confess ignorance about the things of which I am ignorant. I said again and again that if I were an Italian, if I were in Italy, if I were near enough to feel the facts as facts and not as "news," I very probably should find the Dictator doing things I strongly condemn. Meanwhile I am an Englishman, I live in England, and I find that the English newspapers are certainly telling lies, whether or no the Fascists are telling the truth. Now it may appear odd; but it seems to me a more important question for an Englishman whether the English newspapers tell lies than whether one particular Italian gentleman with a bullet in his nose is telling the truth. Any number of despots and demagogues have held dictatorships in the varied and vivacious history of Italy; most of them have been accused of crime, sometimes falsely, sometimes truly. It seems to me possible for a man who suspends his judgment about one particular case (of which he knows very little) to continue to say that Italian history must be understood in the spirit appropriate to it; and that it annoys him when his countryman, the British journalist, in discussing so great a matter, acts like a knave and looks like a fool.

For instance, any number of historical notes are needed to settle the disputed question of whether Danton did or did not share any of the responsibility for the Massacres of September. After most English people had assumed for nearly a century that he did, I believe the more authoritative conclusion now is that he did not. But it is quite certain that he and his friends, confronted at that moment with his enemies, did think much less of human life than the Victorian English did, and took part in many actions at which such people were very much shocked. But I do not think it was a good thing that people should be merely shocked. I do not think it helped the world that our statesmen and scholars should look at the French Revolution with about as much understanding as if they had all been timid maiden aunts in Cheltenham. I do not think the world was wise because Danton was exhibited as nothing but a great grinning and gory ogre to two or three generations of his neighbours. For Danton was not merely a gory ogre; and would not have been, even if he had really stretched the desperate cynicism of those dreadful days to the extent of winking at the wild and wicked raid upon the prisons. He was a number of things less fabulous than an ogre and well worth the world's understanding; a Frenchman; a son of the soil and of the farmer class; a manager of mobs and armies; a natural diplomatist with a policy that affected the world; above all a patriot and a man of popular sympathies. Yet the Massacre of September was very much worse even than the murder of the Italian politician, about which I do not profess to know the disputed details. In either case my position is very simple. I do not want England to make a fool of herself again over the Fascist revolt as she did over the French Revolution. I do not want the Englishman exhibited to the world as a pompous and preposterous Pharisee who has covered all his own killing with his own hypocrisy; and then lectures men writhing in mortal combat because they talk of their own killings with candour. That is the exact extent of my uncritical acceptance of Fascism; and it is not strictly speaking an acceptance of Fascism at all. It is not so much that I want the Fascist to be admired as that I want the English journalist to be respected; and not despised and derided throughout the new Europe for talking nonsense about Fascism. Whether or no one man was or was not culpable in one act, the whole national movement has to be considered as we consider great historical events. Happy is he who can be really historical about contemporary things. Without that sense, all his comments will in a little while look as ludicrous and clumsy as old *Punch* cartoons about Abraham Lincoln or Parnell. And the only thing of which I profess to be certain in the matter is that, when Christendom has reacted, however violently, into some sort of really representative government, the enlightened and liberal comments on Mussolini will look very like the writings of those laborious gentlemen who were busy proving, a hundred years ago, that the French Revolution was a gross violation of the British Constitution.

Epitaph

For those, inspired with certainty, who going
   Exultant ways to death, obeyed high laws;
And for those others who, bitterly knowing
   Their cause was futile, stayed to serve their cause.

RUPERT CROFT-COOKE.

POLAND AND THE LEAGUE COUNCIL—I.

By B. Szczepkowski

DISCUSSIONS on the subject of the extension of the Council of the League of Nations have naturally given rise to the greatest excitement in Poland. It is comprehensible that Polish opinion, appreciating the significance of Germany's entrance into the League, and in particular the obtaining by Germany of a permanent place in the League Council, is disquieted in the highest degree by the uncertainty of the situation which has been created by the discussions that have been taking place on this, the most important political subject of to-day. And it cannot be wondered at that Poland looks with peculiar anxiety upon the course taken by the discussion of this matter in Great Britain. The Poles understand perfectly well the important part Great Britain is playing in the pacification of Europe, and all the dangers which may threaten the work of peacemaking in case the Germans succeed in carrying through their most secret plans of revenge. Only a mind that can see but a short way before it cannot perceive in the wronging of Poland the full success of the German plans for revenge.

It is to be regretted that whilst people in Poland know very well, or at least most of them know, what is happening and what is being said in Europe, on the other hand Europe knows very little or is falsely informed as to what happens in Poland. If it were otherwise, that is, if people in the rest of Europe understood the part which Poland is playing in the east of Europe, which, strictly speaking, she is called upon to play, there would undoubtedly be a different attitude taken up by the diplomats of European states towards questions in which Poland is directly interested. To-day the state of things is such that everything which German propaganda states is, in many cases, accepted as true. This explains the extraordinary fact that in certain democratic circles in Europe, Poland is looked upon as a hindrance to general peace, whilst in reality Poland always was and will be the chief key to peace in Europe. During the time when Poland was not on the map of Europe, peace was always menaced. If to-day Poland were not there, there would rise before the face of Europe the phantom of a new war far more terrible than the war of which we were recently the witnesses. European civilisation could not stand up against this new war. And who could guarantee that the outbreak of hostilities on the Polish-German frontier would not transform itself into a general world-conflict? Yet the Germans, made ever bolder by the continual concessions made to them by the Great Powers, are tending just to that.

Why is Poland obliged to demand for herself a permanent place in the League Council? Just because she cannot allow the violation of the fundamental principles of peace by the Germans, since she is very much concerned in the maintenance of that peace. Whilst the Germans want to incite quarrels between all the nations, want to keep up a state of continual disturbance, of intrigue and conspiracy in Europe, Poland must necessarily tend towards the maintenance of such relations between the nations as would secure them from the horrors of a new and dreadful war. And not only for the sake of her own safety, not only in her own interests, which, in this case, completely correspond with the safety and the interests of the other nations of Europe, but in homage to the highest ideals of humanity is she obliged to require that she be given a permanent seat in the League Council, the Council in which the Germans will also sit.

Persons who think very simply, who do not wish to look a little into the distance, imagine that it will be possible to placate the Germans at the expense of Poland. That is a most regrettable mistake, which already to-day is revenging itself cruelly wherever this kind of false opinion is maintained. It is just the other way round, for every concession made to Germany at the expense of Poland is a serious menace to European peace and tends directly towards the realisation of the world-destroying plans of Germany. Every weakening of Poland is a victory for Germany and an increase of the danger of war threatening tormented Europe. Only the strengthening of Poland, the making of her into a strong bastion on the east of Germany, can be a sure hindrance to those world-destroying plans of Germany, can be a source of security to peace.

In Poland we are accustomed to look upon Great Britain as the chief defender of law and order in civilised, cultural Europe. Every Pole understands that the maintenance of the power of the British Empire is the surest means of maintaining equilibrium and peace. That being so, no Pole can understand why in Great Britain German propaganda against Poland is so frequently listened to and is so successful. For if Great Britain strains every nerve to maintain peace on the continent of Europe, why should she do it in such a —let us speak openly—dangerous manner? For it is quite clear that the method of weakening Poland cannot be the method favourable to the interests of Great Britain. Who is to hinder the Germans from making what changes they wish in the east of Europe if Poland forms no obstacle in their way? Who will have the strength to hinder all the changes which may take place in Russia to the advantage and in the interests of Germany? The casting down of Poland for the sake of Germany means an open road to the East, an open road to the causing of a new world war, the results of which are difficult indeed to foresee.

If some people in Europe are troubled by the present uncertainty of the situation in the east of Europe, they should remember that it is not by way of supporting Germany at the expense of Poland that the east can be pacified. That way leads inevitably to the transference of the conflagration in the east to the west of Europe. But Poland cannot care even less for her own position than others care for it. Poland knows very well what way she must go in the immediate future as regards her foreign policy. Poland is not an island, and her frontiers on the east and on the west are not of a kind to make her feel in a perfectly safe position. Hence Poland must seek security for herself by means of such a solution of that most important problem as will guard her interests and will not harm in any way the interests of the world or of Europe. Thus whilst the Poles understand perfectly well that there can be no question of their working together with Germany, as the relations between Poland and Germany remain in a condition of continual uncertainty, everyone knows quite well that there is no hindrance to the closest relations between Poland and Russia. Still to-day the position in the east is such, at least to a great extent, that prevents such a proper understanding between Poland and Russia, indeed it prevents it between Russia and every other country in Europe. Relations with Russia of to-day may be correct, though even as to that there must be certain reservations, but there can be no question of any closer bonds, of any permanent agreements. Anyone who thinks differently is making a mistake and has no real idea of what Bolshevism is.

(To be continued.)

JIX IMPERATOR

THE COCKPIT

To the Editor of G.K.'s WEEKLY.

RELIGION AND PEASANT OWNERSHIP

DEAR SIR,—It is not quite clear to me why Mr. Fordham should be so angry over the comments of Mr. Blundell on his recent article.

I support Mr. Fordham in the main, most enthusiastically; I sympathise most heartily with the social ideas promoted by your journal; except, as in the case of Mr. Fordham also, in your conclusions on the inevitability of a religious basis for a peasantry.

Mr. Blundell has drawn correct conclusions from incorrect premises, and Mr. Fordham—*vice versa*.

Most of those, who like myself and Tolstoy's Ivan, smell of the soil and the barn, need little urging of a religious nature, to impel us to the settled life of the independent peasant, when we get the chance of attaining it.

Having lived from childhood among the most rooted traditional type of rural Britons, and conveniently close to a cluster of villages, which have been predominantly peasant and in an almost Utopian state of Distributism for centuries, you may be interested to learn that I have found the most stable elements to be the most irreligious.

The same may also be said of the ex-Service men small owners (a few of whom in this locality, acting upon the excellent advice of Sir Richard Wenfrey, "Our Dick," as the old men call him, reserved their funds until the council land boom had died down, and then bought or leased their farms privately). These men, and I know them intimately, are hardly ever known to visit any places of worship, and their views on such matters are well exemplified by the old Army saying: "We're here—because—we're here."

Frankly, my view is that your ill-advised, though undoubtedly sincere attempts, to propagate religion with a peasantry, will have the effect of leaving the majority of the British *would-be peasantry* to be plucked by Mr. David Lloyd George.

At the same time, however exasperated we may be with your views on this point, we do not under-estimate the value of your thought-provoking journal.

For this reason, I remain, sir,

Your Obedient Servant,

WILL SMITH.

FARMING IN CANADA

SIR,—The letter from Mr. C. J. Pitcairn published in your issue of April 10 is so unrelieved in its pessimism that one is tempted to think you can only have printed it with your tongue in your cheek. For undiluted gloom Mr. Pitcairn is, in fact, a whole-hogger. Every man on the land and every girl in domestic service is, according to him, either on the verge of starvation, worn and enslaved by hard work, morally destitute, or all three at the same time. I wonder whether Mr. Pitcairn knows anything at all first hand about farming—obviously he knows nothing from experience about domestic service. I am inclined to think he does not. He has lived in Canada for sixteen years; "intended to take up farming and thoroughly went into the subject of ranching." Well, if a man intends to take up baking and thoroughly goes into the subject of plumbing, he does not get very far. Farming is not ranching and ranching is not farming. He elaborates his confusion by stating that a man on a "ranch" will have to "do ploughing" and "some house duties besides!"

But, Sir, since you quote this unqualified pessimist at such length, will you permit me to quote briefly three cases of a very different character that have come under my observation during the last seven days?

First, Mr. Fred Tarlton, who went to the Dominion thirteen years ago from Derbyshire, writes to a friend in this country:—

"Canada is without doubt the finest land under the British flag. Our neighbours to the south are looking on with longing eyes. Indeed, they are doing their utmost to Americanise Canada.

"As President of Gadsby Board of Trade, I ask any intending immigrant to write our secretary for particulars of our district before deciding to locate elsewhere. We have among us five families which came out last year under the 3,000 Families Scheme, and are all getting along finely. . . . We do not want trade specialists. My remarks refer chiefly to the agricultural requirements of the country. A man has to work. He needs lots of 'pep,' ambition and initiative. If he possesses these qualifications he will make good.

Second, Mr. R. U. Hurford, who is home on a visit to his mother at Highbury, went to Canada twenty-four years ago when he was nineteen years of age. He had been working in a boot warehouse. On his arrival in Winnipeg he refused an offer of £25 a month for a job in the same trade to take up work on a Saskatchewan farm. Four years later he rented land for himself in British Columbia, worked, prospered and bought adjoining property. He then went in for pure bred Jersey stock, and to-day computes his fortune at £13,000. "What I have done can be duplicated by any man," he told me. "I believe opportunities in Canada to be just as good now as they were when I went out."

Third, Miss A. Thomas, formerly of Aberystwyth, who went to Canada seven months ago as a domestic help, writes me as follows:—

"My experience in a Canadian home varies from that in an English home, and it is very interesting to know the different ways and things to cook for the Canadians. They are very thoughtful towards the domestic maids, and they see that they get fair play. Domestics in Canada get two afternoons off every week, Sunday and either Wednesday or Thursday. That is more than I had in England, and I worked very hard, and only had 10s. weekly, but in Canada you can earn £6, £8 and £9 monthly, and not work so hard as you do in England.

"We can also save money in Canada. I am delighted at the treatment given to me, and every other girl says the same. All the girls I know who come to the Hostel come in with smiling faces. We have plenty of music and dancing, and also fancy dress dances.

"I am only twenty-two, but I have been in service ten years, and I can say that since I have been in Canada I have had more chance and more fair play than ever before in my life."—Yours, etc.,

W. T. CRANFIELD, *Director*.

THE LEAGUE OF NATIONS

DEAR SIR,—I was distressed to read in a recent issue, articles entitled "Wilson's Folly" and "The Geneva Farce." Surely it is the duty of all Catholics to work for peace, and that which Mr. Belloc refers to as "the rather comic artifice called The League of Nations" has done more in that direction than any other human effort since the war.

May I refer you to the "Topics of the Month" in *The Month* for March and April. These notes are surely more in keeping with the Catholic aims than the two articles in your WEEKLY.—Yours faithfully,

C. EVELYN KRALL.

'WAGE-EARNERS AS SHAREHOLDERS"

Dear Sir,—In a letter on April 10 Mr. A. Pelham Burn expresses himself as in favour of a plan of giving all employees of a business a share in the ultimate profit, but is against the compulsory accumulation of the whole or part of this in the capital of the concern. He states that he holds a few shares in one or two industrial concerns, but that does not make him feel a part-owner. I suggest that if these shares were held in the business in which he was working he would feel a sense of proprietorship.

I found my belief upon the expressed opinion of many workers in gas companies—particularly representatives of the 9,000 workers in the South Metropolitan Gas Company, who between them own shares to the value of some £700,000.

While we welcome schemes of profit-sharing. and, I believe with Mr. Burn, that they give the worker an interest in his work, and the feeling that he has been fairly treated—my own opinion from a long study of the matter leads me to believe that this is very much stronger where part at any rate of the profit received by the worker is accumulated in the business in which he is working. Schemes of profit-sharing which have led to capital holding seem to me to be more permanent and more successful.

When the workers own capital in the business and are feeling a responsibility for its success a Works Council is of great value; its influence will carry great weight with the directors and ultimately it may be found possible to arrange for representation of the workers on the Board. This has been done in the case of the South Metropolitan Gas Co., the South Suburban Gas Company, Messrs. Ford, Ayrton & Co., Ltd., as well as in several cases in America and other countries.—Yours faithfully,   E. W. Mundy, *Secretary.*

April 13, 1926.

CONTRA MUSSOLINI

Sir,—I should like to give emphatic support to the protest by " Anxious and Perplexed " in your issue of this week against your attitude towards Fascism and foreign problems in general. I fear that after all the letters of Mr. Scott-Moncrieff I remain an entirely unrepentant enemy of Signor Mussolini. To justify this position, I do not need to refer to the " garbled " reports of the Press (incidentally, the biggest syndicate of all—the Harmsworth—favours Fascism), but only to the things for which he is praised in your columns. and to his own declarations.

You seem to welcome Mussolini as the prospective leader of a Latin " bloc " against the " barbarians," and as one who will finally exorcise the miserable spirit of the League of Nations from the peoples of Europe. It is for precisely the same reasons that I regard him as the enemy. For if the Latins exhaust themselves, their opponents, and all Europe by perpetual open or latent hostility, the result must be that European culture, Latin included, will sink into a sea of barbarism, and the world will be left to the Americans, which Heaven forbid.

You also admire Fascism for its contempt of Parliamentary institutions. But its leader's statements show that it does more than despise Parliamentary Government; it is opposed on principle to the whole idea of government by persuasion and counting heads rather than by force and breaking heads. Here we come down to the fundamental creeds of men, and as a believer in the former ideal, I am bound to oppose Fascism, no matter how the democratic ideal has been perverted in practice, and no matter what degree of material prosperity has been brought to Italy by Fascism—though it is arguable that this prosperity might have come in any case with the gradual settlement after the war, and is likely to be rudely shattered by the foreign adventures in which Mussolini will probably indulge.   English Radical.

April 19. 1926.

THE TIME FOR ACTION

Dear Sir,—After regularly reading G.K.'s Weekly for a considerable length of time, and also reading various books on social and economic questions—and here I should like to mention particularly that magnificent outburst of Fr. Vincent McNabb's " The Church and the Land " one feels constrained to ask: " When is the time coming for action, for attempting to do something in the way of putting principles into practice? "

So far it is all propaganda work, and this will continue to be necessary long after a start has been made in the way of trying to realise the ideals of Distributism. But obviously, either Distributism will never get beyond being a matter of purely academic discussion amongst well-intentioned people, or it will result in an attempt to translate theory into practice; and how is this going to be done?

In the present state of things it would seem, if anything, more likely that we should get help from the moon or from Mars than that the country should obtain salvation from Government. We enjoy a highly democratic constitution, which has attained a truly admirable degree of inefficiency and—but I will leave it at that. Apparently then we must either look for a sudden revolution, which would end by defeating its own object, or a start must be made by a number of people numerous to constitute an economically self-sufficing community. It would apparently be hopelessly impracticable under present conditions for isolated individuals to return to the land and attempt to win from the soil a sufficiency of necessaries and decent comforts for themselves and their families. But it would seem possible to establish a small homogeneous community on the land under such conditions that it would be capable of supporting itself, and of finding a satisfying degree of physical, mental and spiritual well-being and social intercourse.   Yours truly.   Alpha.

THE DRAMA

"THE Marvellous History of St. Bernard," at the Kingsway, as adapted by Henri Ghéon, makes one hunger for an unembroidered rendering of the play. In part, the native simplicity and real beauty of the legend are unimpaired, but there are moments when the line of the structure sags. The plan of the design melts into meaningless ornament, modernity jostles medievalism with a patchwork effect that is unpleasing.

Renunciation that does not Renounce

The setting of the first act is admirable. We have a glimpse of heaven, with Our Lady flanked by the Archangel Gabriel and St. Nicholas. Valerie Taylor gives a simple and beautiful rendering, but Dennis Blakelock as St. Gabriel, with his egg-like dome and complacent expression, is the most unheavenly thing one can imagine. Grosvenor North as St. Nicholas is not inspiring, and his beard waggles incessantly. We see the trio only at intervals, each appearance marking a stage in the history of St. Bernard. It is in this, the characterisation of the chief figure, that the play seems to go wrong. The story is of a young, virile man, with all the pleasures of life before him. He is brimful of vitality and his lovely fiancée appeals to his mind as well as his taste. He receives a call. He is marked out by heaven to fight Satan, who yearly takes his toll of the pilgrims passing over the mountain side. He obeys the call and leaves home, sweetheart, and a brilliant future for the poor monastery, where he defeats the devil. Now the essence of the business is to mark the sacrifice. We must feel that young Bernard is giving up those things that he desires. Never for one moment does Robert Harris faintly suggest this. He plays in a detached monotone. He is indeed a sort of a male Gummidge who sees neither satisfaction in this life nor glory in the life to come. For this reason his renunciation appears null and void. One cannot really believe in his spiritual ecstasy.

Gwen ffrangcon-Davies as Marguerite is very lovely. She lends pathos and dignity to the part of Bernard's fiancée. I have not liked her more in any play. Scott Sunderland as Bernard's bustling father is admirable, and Charles Maunsell as Satan is creepily effective. For the rest the company is negligible. The pilgrims are careless as to their make-up, their beards are ill-adjusted and they show no evidence of fear when they approach the devil's lair.

A Sad Ravel

If there are loose ends in "St. Bernard," the play at the Duke of York's bearing that name is a positive ravel. Dion Titheradge—under the pseudonym of Geoffrey Warren—has written a drama about a man who had been in prison for fifteen years for murder. He meets the heroine out motoring, very shabby and sullen, and explains himself by saying he runs an Australian ranch. The heroine who, we are told, is an actress, falls in love and marries him. Why she does this it is difficult to understand, for six weeks after the wedding she is barely conscious of his presence and spends all her spare time out of the theatre in cavorting with her cocktail friends.

These same friends are a little the worse for wear. We have met them many times of late in Noel Coward drawing rooms and at Lonsdale parties. Unlike their originals, however, these persons are quite devoid of wit, and their society makes one yearn for a respectable ratepayer of Streatham Hill.

One of the pillars of the cocktail party is Winton Penner, as futile a travesty of a pressman as even a playwright ever put on to the stage. He discovers that Malcolm Forres, the husband of the actress, has a past, and immediately the whole story of the "murder" appears in a leading Sunday paper. There would appear to be a distortion of facts in the account, as we learn that the dead man deserved what he got. He seduced Malcolm's sister, abandoned her and drove the girl to suicide; whereat her brother shot him through the head.

Meanwhile it is indicated that the actress has loved Malcolm all along. Nevertheless, she accepts the story of his crime without a protest, though the leader of the cocktail ones, Brenda Farren, loudly protests. The characterisation of Brenda is good and she is brilliantly played by Mollie Kerr. She admits she loves Malcolm, who is quite obviously interested in her. The true end of the play would be the disappearance of these two to discover a common future. But the dramatist thinks otherwise. He rings down the curtain on the departure of Malcolm "for a year," when he will return and claim his wife's love. The wife meanwhile insists that she will keep her soul in prison for that period.

Dion Titheradge was quite clever as Malcolm. He is handicapped by his lack of inches, but suggests—so far as his part will let him—strength of character. Mary Merrall has a bad part with which she does little.

The Astaires' Burden

The manifestation of genius at its highest point affords a rare joy to the beholder. For that reason I looked forward with intense anticipation to the return of the Astaires. The producers of "Lady Be Good" at the Empire Theatre consider perhaps that amusement unalloyed is not good for any man. For that reason, emulating a slightly Calvinistic providence, they sandwich the Astaires between long and unadulterated tracts of utter boredom. I doubt if it be possible to discover any book quite so dull as this. It has no vestige of plot and its ramifications are grey and dispiriting. You sit and ache for the Astaires, and when they come you forget everything but the inspiration of their dancing. But they appear too seldom, and the glimpses that we have of them are all too short. Further, there occurs a separation between these twin feet which should be forbidden by all the laws of fitness. Deprived of her brother, Adele's genius is shorn of its full expression. Without his sister Fred grows dim. He is paired too often with a character called Shirley, largely I suppose because the inane workings of the feeble plot demand a so-called love affair. But even so it is worth while to bear the heavy burden of a general boredom by reason of the sudden flashes of relief the Astaires give. But why must they be made to carry the onus of this dire machinery? Surely it should be possible for this heavenly pair to Oompah Trot in brighter surroundings.   J. K. PROTHERO.

THE RETURN OF DON QUIXOTE
By G. K. Chesterton

CHAPTER IX.—(Continued.)
THE HANSOM CAB.

"DO you know what that means?" she asked. "That brute there has come for father."

Dismissing the notion that the brute could be the cab-horse and stoutly refusing to admit that it could be his friend the cabman, Murrell rapidly concluded that it was the mysterious official in the cab. And a dim premonition of the probable state of affairs began to pass across his mind. He knew that a number of new and rather sweeping laws, which in practice only swept over the poor streets, had given medical and other officials very abrupt and arbitrary powers over people supposed to fall short of the full efficiency of Mr. Harker, the manager of the stores. He thought it only too likely that the discoverer of the remarkable scientific theory of colour-blindness as a cause of social decay might appear to fall short of that efficiency. Indeed, it would even seem that his own daughter thought so, from her desperate efforts to steer the poor old gentleman away from the topic. In plain words, somebody was going to treat the eccentric as a lunatic. And as he was not an eccentric millionaire or an eccentric squire, or even in these days regarded as an eccentric gentleman, it was probable enough that the new classification could be effected rapidly and without a hitch. Murrell felt what he had never felt fully since he was a boy, a sudden and boiling rage. He opened his mouth to speak, but the girl had already struck in with her voice of steel.

"It's been like that all along," she said. "First they kick him into the gutter and then they blame him for being there. It's as if you hammered a child on the head till he was stunned and stupid and then abused him for being a dunce."

"Your father," observed the visitor doubtfully, "does not strike me as at all stupid."

"Oh, no," she answered, "he's too clever, and that proves he's cracked. If he wasn't cracked, it would prove that he was half-witted. If it isn't one way it's the other. They always know how to have you."

"Who are *they*?" asked Murrell, in a low and (for anyone who knew him) rather menacing voice.

The question was in some sense answered, not by the person to whom it was addressed, but by a deep and rather guttural voice coming up the black well of the staircase, from somebody who was mounting the stairs. The crazy stairs creaked and even shook under him as he mounted, for he was a heavy man, and as he emerged into the half-light from the little window on the landing he seemed to fill up the whole entrance with a bulk of big overcoat and broad shoulders. The face that was thus turned up to the light reminded Murrell for the first moment of something between a walrus and a whale; it was as if some deep-sea monster was rising out of the deeps and turning up its round and pale and fishy face like a moon. When he looked at the man more carefully and less fancifully he saw that the effect came from very fair hair being very closely cropped in contrast with a moustache like a pair of pale tusks, and from the light of the window on the round spectacles.

This was Dr. Gambrel, who spoke perfectly good English, but never lost a faint air of being foreign; which, among his poorer patients, was perhaps merely due to his being fussy, not to say impatient and irritable. It was quite obvious that he was impatient and irritable now.

"Why didn't you say you'd left the door open?" he said, sharply. "I had to waste two minutes waiting before I found it wasn't really shut."

"Oh, I meant it to be really shut," said Miss Hendry, rather grimly.

"Now don't let us have any more of that nonsense," said Dr. Gambrel, gruffly. "It's much the best thing for him. I believe he knows it himself. I'm not going to make any fuss about it if he will come along quietly in the cab."

"I dare say he'll come along quietly," said the girl, bitterly. "I dare say you've persuaded him it's hopeless. It doesn't need much persuasion to show anybody that, nowadays."

"Well, I can't wait here for ever," said the doctor.

"What about waiting somewhere else?" asked Murrell. "I admire that hansom cab of yours enormously and the landscapes round here are very beautiful."

"Who the devil are you?" demanded the scientific gentleman with the glasses; and something in the sudden change in the key of his voice made Murrell look at him with a new notion in his mind.

"I am not quite sure who I am," he said, after a moment of ripe reflection, "but I rather think I am a celebrated collector of old and curious cabs. You should see my collection. The truth is, it may appear on the face of it improbable, but you have just given me an idea."

While he spoke with exaggerated slowness and an air of leisure, he watched the medical gentleman very carefully, and noticed that that scientific character was playing a very rapid tune on the balustrade with his fingers, and that waves of formless and apparently unfamiliar emotion were passing over his face. Suddenly he spoke, and his tone was entirely new.

"What are you talking about, damn you?" he said.

"I was thinking more intelligently than I was talking, I fear," said Murrell candidly. "I was thinking whether I would throw you down the stairs. But it seems to me that the resources of civilisation are not exhausted."

With these words he slipped rapidly into the room and closed the door, leaving the other two on the landing.

(To be continued.)

A Poem

ONCE, standing in the fields, the Mother heard
    The happy children shouting at their play,
    While near at hand a tawny, tuneful bird
Sang sweetly, then flew merrily away.

But Mary, sad at heart, forsook the hills,
    Thinking of Jesus, and began to creep
To the deep ghost-woods, where dead daffodils
    Shone like pale spectres from the land of sleep.

Here, with bowed head and tender, lovely face
    She waited God, because she knew Him dead,
Watching the flowers nodding in that place,
    And light to dew, and shade to shadow wed.

Watching the large gloom folding to her breast
    Flower and fern, and leafy bough and trees,
She mused how her dear Son had erstwhile blest
    The little children for their happiness.

It was the loved John brought the news to her:—
    "Jesus hath conquered," then away he crept.
She smiled, then kissed the children, half in fear,
    And, for the first time since His death, she wept.

G. F.

THE GOLDEN AGE OF THE UNIVERSITY OF EDINBURGH

By Professor Charles Sarolea

V.

THE influence of the Town Council may no doubt explain some of the abuses which continued till the nineteenth century. It was quite natural that the business mind should look upon learning mainly from the practical point of view, and that it should consider the possession of a Chair as a vested interest. The practice became more and more general of selling and transmitting a Chair, just as one would transmit any other form of property. The practice was all the more natural because the salaries were very small, because pensions were unknown, and because intellectual capacity was really transmitted by heredity, as in the famous dynasties of the Monros and the Gregorys.

The political and moral changes of the new regime were reflected in one drastic innovation in the methods of teaching. The time-honoured system of Regents was abolished and was replaced by the professorial system. Henceforth each essential subject had a professor attached to it.

Historians of the University seem to me to attach far too much importance to this change, which they represent as the main cause of University expansion. Pedagogues, even to-day, are apt to overrate enormously the importance of educational methods and regulations. In fact, both the professorial and the tutorial systems have their advantages and disadvantages. The prosperity of a University depends on causes more far-reaching. I feel profoundly convinced the deeper cause of the marvellous prosperity and expansion of Edinburgh University in the eighteenth century was the introduction of a freedom which is unknown to any University even in our own days.

One must be familiar with the inner history of the institution to realise how absolute that freedom was in the Golden Age of Edinburgh University. The professor might teach whatever he liked and the student might learn whatever he chose. The University was not bound by one thousand and one regulations as she is to-day. There was no unwieldy Calendar of 1,000 pages. There was no curriculum. There were no examinations. There was practically no graduation. In vain did the University authorities try to bring graduation again into favour. The students and the public resisted their efforts. Until the beginning of the nineteenth century the University enjoyed long before the German Universities a "Lehrfreiheit" and a "Lernfreiheit" which even a modern German University might have envied.

There was one other form of liberty which may seem to have been less desirable. Professors considered themselves not only free to teach what they liked, but they did consider themselves free not to teach at all. They were much more inclined to take the law into their own hands. Those were the days when promising young noblemen were expected to prepare themselves for political life by a grand tour on the Continent. When Professor Adam Ferguson was asked to accompany a young aristocrat as travelling tutor for two years he applied for leave of absence for two years. The town authorities refused. The refusal did not prevent the Professor from starting on the grand tour and from being reinstated in his Chair on his return. Nor did it prevent him from taking the same liberty when ten years after he was given a chance of going to America on a political mission, entrusted with the duty of reporting on the condition of the colonies.

VI.

It may be interesting in this connection to recall that it is this very absence of examinations and graduation which was the paradoxical origin of the Honorary Degrees which play such a spectacular part in our modern Universities.

Owing to the disfavour of the ordinary graduations and owing to the absence of ordinary degrees, even professors found themselves without those qualifications which would recommend their merits to the outside world. They were only able to get a degree by the very expensive process of spending several years at a foreign University, such as Leyden or Utrecht, which were in the eighteenth century the favourite resorts of Scottish students. The lamentable result was that most of the professors had no magic letters after their names. In the eyes of the man in the street this might prove a serious disqualification.

At the beginning of the eighteenth century, in order to make the situation less uncomfortable for its own teachers, the Senatus thought it expedient to confer the Honorary Degree of Master of Arts on three of its professors. That trivial expedient is the humble origin of the solemn ritual which was destined to become such a prominent feature of our University life.

VII.

There remains another cause which seems to me to explain very largely the prosperity of the University in the eighteenth century, namely, that spirit of universality which is so characteristic of the eighteenth century generally. Here again, the conventional historian is wrong in his interpretation of the facts. Historians of the University tell us that the advantage of the new professorial system over the regent system was mainly that it made for specialisation. That view seems to me entirely mistaken. The introduction of the professorial system for several generations did not make for specialisation, rather did it tend to produce a far greater versatility, for the simple reason that professors were not tied to special subjects. Nothing is more remarkable than the facility with which professors in those spacious days moved from one subject to another subject which had absolutely no relation to it. Thus, Adam Smith in succession taught English Literature, Political Economy, Moral Philosophy, *et quaedamalia*!

VIII.

Whatever may have been the causes of the expansion of Edinburgh University, certain it is that for several generations it was a hotbed of genius. Not even the sensational beginning of the University of Berlin after the disaster of Jena can show such a galaxy of men of genius and men of talent. Principal Robertson is the renovator of historical literature. David Hume is the father of modern philosophy. Adam Smith is the founder of political economy. McLaurin is the most illustrious mathematician of his age. Joseph Black is proclaimed by Lavoisier as his inspirer and his master.

IX.

There was one very paradoxical though very natural result of the fame of Edinburgh professors and of the easy and liberal system of teaching. The University of Edinburgh, which to-day is one of the most democratic of Europe, was for several generations one of the most aristocratic. To-day the Scottish middle-class parents are increasingly disposed to send their sons to Oxford, partly because Oxford is supposed to have a better social standing and also because it provides better opportunities for social intercourse. In the eighteenth century English noblemen sent their sons to Edinburgh, because intellectually it stood much higher than the southern universities. In the eighteenth century Oxford, as we know from the concurrent and independent testimony of Adam Smith and of Gibbon, was sunk in sloth and ignorance. On the contrary, Edinburgh was world famous. Such was the prestige of Edinburgh professors that the English aristocracy were not content to send their sons to the University, they also engaged the services of its teachers as travelling tutors on their Grand European Tour.

(To be continued.)

MR. BELLOC

By E. S. P. Haynes

THE name of Mr. Hilaire Belloc is not nearly so well known in this country as it should be. He is, in my opinion, and in that of many more competent judges than myself, the best living poet (with the possible exception of Dr. Bridges and Mr. Hardy) and a most scholarly writer of prose. His historical work and verse for children and travel books are well-known to those who care for good literature; but his versatility has perhaps obscured his reputation, for in this country editors have a rather German habit of putting everyone into little compartments and not allowing them to wander outside.

Belloc's reputation has also suffered from the fact that he has taken from time to time an unpopular line in politics and because his point of view is very different from the contemporary point of view. In politics he made a considerable sensation by adhering to his election pledge in regard to Chinese labour when he first entered the House of Commons in 1906, and again by his articles on the Marconi crisis in 1911. He also strongly advocated the auditing of the party funds in regard to such matters as the sale of honours. Much of what he said and wrote in the past is now admitted to be true; but that is because his criticisms were after a suitable interval repeated by more cautious and conventional publicists who waited until the first impact of Mr. Belloc's remarks had ceased to shock or surprise. Even to-day when the sale of honours has been generally deprecated there is still a marked disinclination to discuss any question of auditing party funds.

Then in regard to his point of view one must remember that his enthusiasm is reserved for the Catholic Church and Europe to the exclusion of the Non-Catholic civilisation of Great Britain and North America. I ought perhaps to distinguish between Great Britain and North America because Great Britain, as Mr. Belloc would be first to admit, has many deep roots in the faith and culture of medieval Europe. I need only mention that incense was used as late as 1750 in Ely Cathedral. Mr. Belloc's idea of civilisation is highly individualist, for he wants every citizen to have some little property of his own whether it be in the form of money or of land, and he cordially hates the industrial system (the beginnings of which he traces back to the Reformation) under which the great majority of citizens are wage-earners of a servile type with no property at all. This system he thinks was due to the decay of the Catholic belief that men are equal in the sight of God, and have immortal souls. On the other hand his Catholic bias is combined with an enthusiasm for Rousseau and republican ideals more recently tempered by a taste for absolute monarchy. I am, however, not concerned at this moment to expound Mr. Belloc's opinions on Church and State, and merely refer to them because I think they have accidentally obscured his gifts as a literary artist.

They have seldom been better displayed than in his last volume of essays entitled " Short Talks with the Dead and Others,"* though that is only the title of the first essay, and the other essays are infinitely various. One of the best is a satire on the intolerable persons who are always making modern cities hideous and dragooning their inhabitants into standardised servitude. Mr. Belloc does not understand why Venice is allowed to remain as it is. He writes in his best ironical vein :—

" While the Venetians are about this vigorous cleansing up of their world and ridding it of the old nonsense, it occurs to me that they might do worse than fill up their canals."

After advocating the abolition of religious services in St. Mark's he discovers another scandal :—

" The bad water supply of the town (which has not really

* SHORT TALKS WITH THE DEAD AND OTHERS, By Hilaire Belloc. Cayme Press, 7s. 6d.

been rectified even yet) has led to another appalling evil, worse, if that be possible, than the dreadful statistics of infant mortality.

" The people of Venice, as is apparent to the most casual observer, have been driven by the absence of a proper hydraulic, or perhaps I should say hydrological system, to drinking quite common red wine habitually as a beverage, with all the evils attendant upon so fearful a practice.

" I am glad to say that this habit is now somewhat declining among the wealthier classes through the introduction of champagne, Asti, soda water, and other common sorts of aerated waters, but it is still appallingly common. Things have gone so far that I have myself observed with my own eyes a priest enter a common bar near the Capo Nero, talk familiarly with the owner thereof, who was his brother, and in broad daylight drink a large glass of red wine as though it were so much milk.

" The subject is too unpleasant to be dwelt upon at any length. Nothing but a strong sense of duty has made me touch upon it even in the briefest way."

He ends up on a more hopeful note :—

" However there is some hope for the future. An active group of American and English ladies and gentlemen (with whom are acting, I am glad to say, a certain number from the Dominions) have recently formed a society with offices in Kingsway entitled, ' The V.R.C.' or ' Venice Reconstruction Company,' and there is every hope that when the present irresponsible régime in Italy comes to its natural end, and free institutions are restored, this admirable and disinterested body will be given the concession which it has in vain sought from the existing Government at Rome. If difficulties are still put in their way, they will appeal to the League of Nations."

Irony, Mr. Belloc thinks, is best secured by poverty, because poverty makes men appreciate reality. As he says :—

" Poverty has a yet nobler effect by its introduction into our lives of irony; and irony I take to be the salt in the feast of intelligence. I have, indeed, known rich men to possess irony, but only by importation, just as a man may possess a picture which he has bought. Poor men possess irony as native to themselves, so that it is like a picture which a man paints for his own pleasure and puts up on his own walls. All the poor of London have irony, and, indeed, poor men all over the world have irony; even poor gentlemen, after the age of fifty, discover veins of irony and are the better for them, as a man is better for salt in his cooking. Remark that irony kills stupid satire, and that to have an agent within one that kills stupid satire is to possess an antiseptic against the suppurative reactions of the soul.

" Poverty, again, makes men appreciate reality. You may tell me that this is of no advantage. It is of no direct advantage; but I am sure it is of advantage in the long run. For if you ignore reality you will come sooner or later against it like a ship against a rock in a fog, and you will suffer as the ship will suffer "

With his usual exactitude he defines poverty as follows:

" Poverty is that state in which a man is perpetually anxious for the future of himself and his dependents, unable to pursue life upon a standard to which he was brought up, tempted both to subservience and to a sour revolt, and tending inexorably towards despair."

Whether one agrees or disagrees with the definition or the opinions based upon it, the passage shows a strong Johnsonian vein in Mr. Belloc, who through his mother, long known in old days as Bessie Parkes, comes of an old Unitarian family in the Midlands. There is a certain virile hatred of cant and hypocrisy running through this sturdy English stock which expresses itself more pointedly in combination with French wit, but is none the less essentially English. Mr. Belloc often talks like Dr. Johnson in the same vein of melancholy tempered by common sense and dislike of unreal sentiments. I mention this side of him because his French name and origin sometimes obscure it from his readers.

NOVELS OF THE DAY

"TRADITION wears a snowy beard, romance is always young," said, or sung, Whittier. Mr. John Masefield is evidently of the same opinion in "Odtaa,"* which has been profanely explicated as "one damned thing after another." The juvenile hero of this book, Highworth Foliat Ridden, mercifully called Hi, is the genuine article in adventure. He does not care what happens to him so long as the happening is coloured and dangerous. He falls in deepest love with a lady a little older than himself. He knows he can never possess her, but he pours out his heart in full stream to the beautiful one, and even idealises her fiancé.

His father had the lowest view of Hi's attainments. Ridden senior was entirely devoted to horses, and he thought his youngest son was a fellow common and debased because he desired to be an engineer; so he ships him out to Santa Barbara to make good, if he can, in any of the native industries of a turbulent land. Unfortunately sugar and copper are a bit shaky when Hi arrives, as the Reds and the Whites have finished a struggle in which the Whites, or clerical party have been worsted, but are preparing to fight again.

Mr. Masefield, who has been knowing enough to order a wonderful coloured map of the Santa Barbara territory for the jacket of his tale, is equally clever in making the politics of Santa Barbara as simple as possible. There are no blacks, greys, greens, browns, or drabs in the unsettled constitution of this fiery land, but simply white for conservative purity and red for bad blood.

The Riddens had some connection with the country, and they had friends there in the Piranhas, who were Whites, and dangerous to know. Hi had no misgivings, and was delighted to meet his girl playfellow, Rosa, again. No; Rosa was not the angel of his life; she was quite plain, badly made-up and affected a masculine style. Rosa's cousin, Carlotta de Leyva, was the goddess of Hi's finest dreams. Masefield had made Carlotta live in that bright, divine beauty of hers by painting her portrait in prose through the medium of Hi's admiration:

> There suddenly stood before him a woman who realised all his dreams of what a woman should be. Yet she was not like any other woman. She was as little like a woman as a humming bird is like a bird. She was a small, perfect, spiritual shape, glowing like a humming bird. He had once heard somebody say that you only get perfection in small things. He had thought the man an ass at the time, but remembered it now. This woman was perfect. Her hair was of a most deep, dark brown, very abundant, but caught close to her head by a narrow fillet of gold. This gave her something the look of a boy, enough, perhaps, to establish a sympathy with a boy like Hi. The eyes were darker than the hair. They shone as though the brain behind them was one glow of light. . . The nose was straight. The ears which are seldom beautiful, even in the beautiful, were perfect in her. The cheeks were of a rich colour as though the life within were very intense. The mouth was the great distinction; it was of a faultless beauty. All fun, all thoughtfulness, all generosity, were in those gentle, sensitive, proud curves.

Most boys want to make some impossible sacrifice at the throne of their first goddess. It was the privilege of young Hi to go on an errand of desperate danger for Carlotta. The goddess's fiancé, Don Manuel, was to be recalled from the bedside of his dying mother at Encarnacion to rescue Carlotta from the hands of the Reds. The task was the easier for Hi as he revered Don Manuel, whom he had summed up at his first introduction to him: "This is an extraordinary man, either splendid or very queer, perhaps both." The stately Spaniard had also treated the boy with the courtesy which the young so seldom get.

"Odtaa," it must be borne in mind, is not really a love-story at all. People who are sick of love might read it with the greatest interest. It is well, however, to get the guiding motive of Hi in his desperate journey to Medinas. Hi did not care very much about the blasphemy of Don Lopez de Meruel, Dictator of Santa Barbara, proclaiming himself God. He was not overly concerned to hear of the assassination of the military leader of the Whites, General Chavez. He was intent, however, in getting Carlotta's message through to Don Manuel at any cost. When he had first seen her he had stared and stared at her and thought: "She is lovely, lovely. O God, I wish I could fight for her or do something for her." Of course, that idolatry spurred him on in his nightmare journey by sea and land; but he would have enjoyed the special mission anyhow. Hi preferred any risk or discomfort under heaven to dull security. He should have been a son of that other intrepid performer of incredible tasks, Sard Harker.

When Hi learned that Carlotta has been captured by the Reds and that Don Manuel, with all the White troops he could muster, was the only possible deliverer, he sped out hell-for-leather, but at every stage of the journey he was held up, baffled, battered. He suffers tortures from man, beast and insect. He parches with thirst and swoons with starvation. Everywhere he meets new obstacles and agonies. Only once in a dream does he feel utter peace in the vision of his girl friend, Ruth, whom he had not seen for years, but who came to him in the domains of sleep with a strange tenderness, an exquisite compassion. Nowhere on the journey was Hi making good. He was being turned back again and again, while his humble friend, Ezekiel Rust, was speeding on on horseback to the summoning of Don Manuel.

It is a curious feature of "Odtaa," that in spite of its boyish bravery, it is a book of heart-breaking frustrations. The message which Hi cannot deliver and which Ezekiel Rust does, summons Don Manuel to Santa Barbara, but Manuel is not popular with the leaders of the Whites and they do not rally to his standard. One of the most doleful chapters in a tragic book is that in which Hi and his friends hear in their prison the guns of the conquerors—and discover to their chagrin that the said conquerors are the Reds, the Whites have been swept away like chaff in the wind. By unexpected magnanimity Hi is permitted to join an English ship leaving the country of mistakes and futilities. With tears running down his cheeks, he says: "Oh, God, I have made a mess of it." Carlotta had been killed a week before this. Roberto Mandariaga said of her: "None can describe her, nor would one understand, if she were described. She was sent like a light from God."

Romance is coming back to English fiction. Masefield has picked up the torch that fell from Joseph Conrad's hand.

     *   *   *   *

Novels about writers and journalists are perpetually unconvincing. Not since George Gissing wrote "The New Grub Street" have we had a book which truthfully portrays the writing type. It would be difficult to do, since half of the craft perpetually make moan about its miseries—they don't really mean this—and the other is engaged in froward boasting. I have found Vernon Knowles's story, "Beads of Coloured Days,"† disappointing in its attempt to present a group of artistic people. I refuse to believe in the success of any of these callow youngsters. Alec Holt himself, who fails as a poet and succeeds as a translator, has more to him than any of the young genii who surround him. How hollow is the fame of these intelligensia:

> All his friends: talk, laughter, plans. Success coming. Paulton: now reader for a firm of publishers; his own book of short stories shortly to appear. Mitton: with a landscape accepted by the Academy, and two hung in the Salon. Greenway: delighted and something of a hero; his exhibition at the To-Morrow Club of Interpretations, as he called them; portraits executed in convex mirrors, copper tubing and a dozen other extraordinary oddments; the talk of artistic London, and the subject of a cheerful sneer in *Punch*. Rawlson: hard at work with rehearsals of his play, and writing a new one.

---

*ODTAA. By John Masefield. Heinemann. 7s. 6d.

†BEADS OF COLOURED DAYS. By Vernon Knowles. Gardner Darton. 7s. 6d.

They are all impossible to believe in these successful young men, especially Rawlson, who has big manly, brutal ideas about drama, which would arouse the tamest Censor to action. It is possible that Mr. Knowles may write and say that all these characters are taken from life; that would not make them any more credible or tolerable, though Greenway *may* exhibit his monstrosities at the To-Morrow.

I don't think any reader of this periodical would have cared much for the literary frenzies of Alec. His infancy had been nurtured by Tennyson and Swinburne. The introduction to a publisher's nephew led him in his teens to all those people who figure in the critiques of literary weeklies:

Among the novels that he read, Rolland's *Jean Christophe* stood out foremost and made profound impression on him. *Sinister Street* and *Sylvia Scarlett*: George Moore and some of D. H. Lawrence and May Sinclair showed him life a thing of vividness and glowing interest. James Joyce arose on his horizon like a vast sun, sending crude, terrible light into the most secret corners. *Ulysses* left a wound behind.

There is some frantic nonsense in this. Without any desire to be coarse, one would have believed more in the literary taste of Alec Holt if he had said that Joyce arose on his horizon like an average latrine. I don't believe that Alec ever read any of the daring dulness of the author of that extraordinarily stupid play, *Exiles*. It was doubtless the custom of the young people who persuaded him of their genius to utter " Ah, Ulysses! " as the young Swinburnians used to intone, " Dolores."

One satisfactory feature of the book is that Alec still retains his job in the office of Waring & Co., machinery manufacturers, and is on the point of marrying a very beautiful violinist of the first grade shortly after the death of his lovely wife, Ruth, who was dreadfully hurt that Alec did not become a great poet.

Mr. (or is it Miss?) Vernon Knowles's " Street of Queer Houses " showed a most brilliant and humorous imagination. " Beads of Coloured Days " is sentimental and shallow. It will probably have a measure of success at the circulating libraries, and be ardently discussed in South Kensington.

LOUIS J. McQUILLAND.

LIBRARY LIST

MARTIN HANNER. By Kathleen Freeman. Jonathan Cape. 7s. 6d.
A most dryasdust book which in its gritty hardness might have come from the pen of Mr. John Middleton Murry. Miss Freeman describes her novel as a comedy. It is intensely depressing, dealing as it does with two miserable provincial universities and the ambitions of a bloodless professor, and what are termed his love affairs—two very rigid courtships with young women destined by Providence for welfare work. The critics have been praising this book. Dullness is still regarded as a virtue by some superior people.

THE SPECTACLES OF MR. CAGLIOSTRO. By Harry Stephen Keeler. Hutchinson. 7s. 6d.
An entirely impossible story of a wealthy American who leaves to his son a few dollars a month provided he wears for one year a hideous and cumbersome pair of spectacles supposed to have been originally the property of the famous Cagliostro. Those spectacles eventually enabled Jerome Herbert Middleton to pick out from his foolish father's electric signs directions for finding hidden bullion. The only sensible interest the book has is a description, extending over many pages, of life in a lunatic asylum, where modern methods of psycho-analysis are employed on the patients of whom the millionaire's son is one.

THE LAUGHING MASK. By Cosmo Hamilton. Hurst and Blackett. 7s. 6d.
Conventional magazine stories served up by Mr. Cosmo Hamilton with a cynicism insulting to any intelligent reader. Mr. Hamilton is loudly by way of being an English gentleman in these rather terrible performances in sentiment of which the most atrocious is the tale of a little aristocrat who has got a burglar's equipment among his nursery toys. A real burglar arrives on the scene, and the hardened professional criminal is so melted by the comradeship of the impossible child that he abandons his swag. The only thing that remotely resembles literature in the book is a clever study of a feminine cuckoo in the nest in " The Safe Miss Seaton."

KALI'S JEWELS. By Helen M. Fairley. Hutchinson. 7s. 6d.

Rich and rare were the jewels that adorned the brow of a new brand of goddess one Kali. To capture these a family party set out from their nice clear home and meet with a lot of stale adventures on the way. Indeed even the new brand of goddess savours of Woolworth's bargain basement, and the nice clean family are so dull that our sympathies are with the blacks who leave them to be eaten by crocodiles. We hope the crocodiles had a good digestion.

POSSESSIONS. By Bernard McCarthy. Hutchinson. 7s. 6d.

A familiar plot, an old fashioned style with certain elements of human strength and human weakness. The story centres round the rivalry between two sons for the inheritance of their father's business, complicated by the discovery that the eldest son is not a blood relation, but just "adopted." His supposed mother did this to placate her husband who, like the ancient Jews, reproached her as a barren woman. Our sympathies are with the unfortunate person who against his will was co-opted. He deserved the business as a compensation.

THE STORY OF SELMA. By Isobel Clarke. Hutchinson. 7s. 6d.

A simple maiden on the Cornish coast meets a singularly unpleasant Vicar. The bleakness of Cornwall rather than the warmth of his affections tempts her to take him as a husband. But the gods of that strange country are revenged. The Vicar is a miser who hoards crusts and begrudges butter. From this land of margarine Selma flies and finds peace in the arms of a convenient cousin. Lest, however, anything should be wanted to her complete satisfaction the author kills the Vicar and the cousin becomes the husband. We award the palm to Death.

POOR DEAR ESME. By A. M. Burrage. George Newnes. 2s. 6d.

As in "The Smokes of Spring," the plot is far-fetched, yet this story of a boy masquerading as a girl in an academy for young ladies will be appreciated by children and grown-ups alike because of the racy and vigorous manner in which it is told. Esmé, initiated into the mysteries of feminine attire and deportment at very short notice, makes a most creditable girl. The tale of the bricks which he drops during his chequered career at St. Mildred's is inimitably told. He induces four chosen comrades to smoke cigarettes in his bedroom with disastrous results, secrets beer bottles under his bed, and tumbles in and out of every scrape which Mr. Burrage can devise.

NOT UNDER THE LAW. By Grace Livingstone Hill. Lippincott. Two Dollars.

Miss Hills' heroine, Joyce Radway, is a pretty girl and a mighty good cook. She is kind hearted, obliging and generous. As against these qualities she is a bone-headed Fundamentalist. She is filled with indignation when a clergyman deprecates the idea of an angry God who wants sacrifices of blood; she is annoyed that Christians should attend Christy Minstrel shows, and she is constantly quoting scripture and singing crude Salvation Army hymns. There is a handsome young man in the book called Darcy Sherwood who is accused of abducting Joyce and burying her. Joyce has not been abducted. She has left cruel relatives in order to pursue her own salvation, Darcy has not buried anybody, but has been hoarding illicit rum. Being acquitted of the murder by the presence of the body in Court, he confesses to the rum-running and is let off with a fine. He has become truly repentant, and one gathers that he and Joyce will spend the remainder of their lives together swopping edifying Scripture texts. It says much for Miss Grace Livingstone Hill's attractiveness as a story-teller that one follows Joyce's more worldly little adventures with very considerable interest. Joyce certainly can cook. Her speciality dishes are described at length in the novel.

THE UNPUBLISHED DIARY AND POLITICAL SKETCHES OF PRINCESS LIEVEN TOGETHER WITH SOME OF HER LETTERS. Edited with elucidations by Harold Temperley. Cape. 12s. 6d.

The career of a Russian ambassador's wife who was the mistress of Metternich and later of Guizot, and a close friend of George IV, Castlereagh, Canning, Wellington, Earl Grey and others, ought to be full of interest. Mr. Temperley's book will appeal to political students rather than to the general reader. Some new facts emerge but they will chiefly concern those who wish to have a detailed grasp of politics in the early years of the last century. Without under-estimating Princess Lieven's undoubted power politically and socially it must be confessed that she was a typical *intriguante* who is not really interested in causes but only in the men who attract her attention at the moment. No doubt the Princess was extremely useful to those who were responsible for policies, as, for example, when a considerable amount of smoothing had to be done to keep England and France quiet about the Polish revolution. One piece, printed at the end of the book, since it has already appeared in German, is very interesting. This is an account of the murder of Czar Paul I, and is a recollection of the Princess when she was "fifteen years old, of a gay humour, loving eipsodes, and regarding any catastrophe very lightly."

LEGACY OF THE ANCIENT WORLD. By W. G. de Burgh, M.A. MacDonald and Evans. 15s.

This is an admirable résumé of the trend of those ancient civilisations which formed the basis of our own. The author has a wide grasp of the essentials on which these ancient worlds were built. When, however, he comes to the discussion of their philosophic significance he is less clear. He inclines towards the theory of progress and somewhat stresses his argument in favour of "relatively coherent evolution." But if we cannot accept his conclusions we are at one with Mr. de Burgh in rendering tribute not only to the grandeur of Rome and the glory of Greece, but to that amazing civilisation of Egypt with its scientific triumphs and engineering feats. This is a book students of history and sociology should read. It is a valuable acquisition to the library.

The directors of **Robert Holden & Co. Ltd.,** offer a prize of £100 for the best novel submitted with a view to publication, by an author who has not yet published a novel in book form. In addition to the award of £100, payable on day of publication, the usual royalties will be paid. The publishers will require an option on the next two novels written by the author, who will receive, in respect of each of those as an advance on account of royalties a sum equal to one half of the amount earned by the preceding novel.

This seems a very practical proposition.

Published by the Proprietors, G.K.'s WEEKLY, LTD., at their offices, 20 & 21 Essex Street, Strand, London, W.C.2 (incorporating THE NEW WITNESS). Telephone No. City 1978. Printed by THE ALLIED PRESS, LTD., 19 Clerkenwell Close, London, E.C.1. Sole agents for Australasia: Gordon & Gotch (Australasia), Ltd. Sole Agents for South Africa: Central News Agency, Ltd.

G.K.'s WEEKLY May 22nd, 1926.

THE PRIDE OF ENGLAND.

G.K.'s Weekly

EDITED BY G. K. CHESTERTON,

No. 62.—Vol. III.   Week ending Saturday, May 22, 1926.   PRICE SIXPENCE
YEARLY (52 ISSUES)
£1 10 4.

Telephone No. City 1978.   *Offices, 20 & 21, Essex Street, Strand, W*

CONTENTS:

WHO WON?

WE said last week in our typewritten strike-issue that the men have won, and we see no reason to modify our judgment. It is true that the T.U.C. called off the strike unconditionally, but they believed that they had arrived at a satisfactory understanding with the Government; and though at the moment there is some ground for thinking either that they took too much for granted, or that the Government has let them down, we have no doubt that *the miners are in a stronger position than they were on May 3*. Let us not forget that the fight was to get a fair deal for the miners. If there had been no strike they certainly would not have got a fair deal. If now they get one, it is certainly because of the strike. Therefore, the men have won.

We acknowledge that they have had to pay a high price for the victory, but so have the Combine, whom it cost in cash about five times what it cost the unions. But the concessions made by the men when returning to work are of more consequence. In several ways the power of trade unionism has, nominally, at least, been restricted. We think the restriction is only nominal, for the unions have *shown* their power, and the combines have felt it.

Why were the masters so anxious that the men should acknowledge in writing that they had been naughty boys and that they would never do it again? Because, in spite of the backing of the Government, the armed forces of the realm, and the well-dressed classes, the strike dealt them a heavy blow. If it had been as ineffective as they boast it was they would not be so anxious that it should never happen again; they could rely on trade unionists not wanting it to happen again.

You may argue, indeed, that since the general strike has been declared illegal it cannot happen; but this argument won't hold water. It would be quite easy to arrange for a number of separate strikes on separate issues to happen at the same time. We have no doubt that another general strike will happen, though it may be given another name.

The best reason for calling the settlement a victory for the men is that what the combines meant to do they failed to do, and failed utterly. They meant to destroy trade unionism. And they did not cripple it. Their intentions were made plain to the most incredulous by the joyful haste with which, immediately after the publication of that lying phrase " Unconditional Surrender," the masters prepared to gather the spoils of the victory which, in fact, they had not won. For a few sweet hours they thought that the unions *were* broken. The Premier undeceived them.

We are asked by one of our most valued readers, Mr. E. S. P. Haynes, how we justify the general strike. Our answer is that trade interests are now so interlocked that a general strike has become identical in character with one in a particular industry. But, of course, the recent strike needs no such justification, for it was the only possible reply to a deliberate conspiracy to smash the unions.

NOTES OF THE WEEK

Back to the Miners

THE negotiations between the miners, the owners, and the Government may well have been renewed before these lines are published. The representatives of the coalowners' associations are to meet in London on Thursday (20th), while, on the same day, following on a number of meetings of the Miners' Federation Executive, apart and with the Premier, a full delegate conference will be held. We anticipate that Friday or Saturday will see the re-opening of negotiations. It is, of course, impossible to forecast what will be the result of them, but we trust that a compromise will be reached which will provide for a continuance of wages at their present level until the scheme for re-organising the industry has been prepared, and approved both by owners and men. As we have said repeatedly, we think the Government would find it a cheap investment to subsidize the mines until they begin to make a profit, and so render unnecessary even a temporary cut in wages. But the subsidy must take the form of a mortgage on the mines.

The Owners' Book

BEFORE the compromise is reached we trust that the Government will ask, and a little louder than Sir Josiah Stamp was in a position to ask, for all the books of the owners necessary to establish their claim to have lost heavily on the running of the mines during the past year or two. It will be impossible even then to trace some of their manœuvres—such as the selling of coal below cost price to themselves, as steel manufacturers, or to themselves, as coal-merchants, or to themselves, as shippers. But Mr. Baldwin ought to be able either to allay or to confirm the strong suspicion of City men that the mine-owners' figures, given in evidence before the Coal Commission, were all bunkum. We know how cleverly they watered their capital during the war to avoid paying the tax on excess profits, and their refusal to produce all the books asked for by Sir Josiah Stamp leads us to suppose that they have been as clever and patriotic now.

Civil War in Poland

THE state of civil war at present existing in Warsaw will inevitably stir the antagonists of Polish independence to renewed advocacy of a German suzerainty. For this reason it is important clearly to understand why and how this dispute has come to pass. To the mind of the majority of Poles of varying political opinion, Pilsudski stands for patriotism. He is the one man of eminence who has consistently refused to admit the advantage of an alliance either with Russia or with Germany. Whatever may be said of this attitude in regard to foreign politics, it has undoubtedly consolidated the Polish people in his favour. He is the symbol of that persecution under which Poland suffered for two hundred years. He was imprisoned by the Germans; and he was imprisoned by the Russians; the two national hatreds are united by his blood. His picture hangs on the walls of the peasants' and the workmen's homes side by side with Sobieski and Kosciusko. He has been accused of many things. It has been alleged against him that he has made

a fortune by trafficking with the Jews. But in no case have these allegations been upheld. Nothing has been discovered to his discredit. He remains a soldier, who has proved his military genius by successes against the Ukrainians and the Bolshevists, and at the moment when Haller was completely routed his arrival by forced marches saved the situation.

Pilsudski's Aim

THE system of proportional representation which holds in Poland has produced a Seym in which no party has been sufficiently predominant to form a Cabinet. For this reason governments have existed only by the tolerance of the various "Blocks," and a general weakness of administration has ensued. Pilsudski has seized the moment for the assertion of his personality. Whether he succeeds or not he should in no sense be credited with a desire to gratify ambition at the expense of his country. The Left is solid for him, the peasants, politically allied to Witos, cherish him as a national hero; elements of the landowning class on the Right have thrown in their fortunes with him. At the moment of going to press the battle outside Warsaw between the Poznan troops under Haller and Pilsudski's regiment is in progress. By the issue of the encounter the immediate position will be affected, but whatever the consequence, Pilsudski cannot ultimately be dethroned as the idol of a passionate and a romantic people. Pilsudski lives moderately, with no show of state. An undistinguished looking man with a resemblance to General Grant, you are suddenly aware of that curious light in the eyes which bespeaks the fanatic. He centres his whole being in one aim—Poland one and indivisible.

Where the Crooks go in the Strike-time

ONE of the most interesting news "stories" since the strike was published in the *Daily Graphic* of Tuesday, May 18. Scotland Yard chiefs, it says, have been discussing a mystery which has baffled not only "The Big Four," but every detective in the Force. It lies in the question: "Where do crooks go during strike time?" The *Daily Graphic* tells us that from May 3 to May 17 there was no crime worth mentioning in London. "Cat burglars deserted Mayfair, and family jewels remained undisturbed. Warehouse thieves and motor bandits downed tools. Confidence tricksters . . . also suspended operations." And what do you think is the answer to the conundrum? You would never guess it. "It now appears," says the *Daily Graphic*, "that when the strike was declared, the crooks of London, at a secret meeting at Hackney Marshes, decided to offer themselves as volunteers for emergency work. Thus, while some of the crook community were trundling milk-churns at King's Cross, others were unloading ships at the docks." This is a really wonderful discovery, and we are glad it has been made, not by the *Daily Herald*, but by Scotland Yard and the *Daily Graphic*. But will the companies who want to retain their strike-breakers be able to keep them, now that work is no longer an adventure? Scotland Yard, we hear, thinks that they won't.

THE LESSON OF THE STRIKE

EVERYBODY, except the Trade Unionist, is talking just now about what the strike has taught them. It has not taught us much. English workmen have kept their temper. But we knew they could do that. The upper and middle classes with the armed forces of the Crown behind them, are said to have beaten the working classes. If they did, it is not much to boast about. People who commonly dress like gentlemen have shown that instinctively they take sides against people who commonly work with their coats off, but we knew they would do that. The " black-coated workman " has always been the tool of the Combine ; most of the volunteers were such because it was the swagger thing to be.

But we must admit that many had a nobler impulse : they went into the thing because it was a good rag. It was an adventure. And much heroism is needed to realise that standing still and doing nothing may be the biggest adventure of all.

We suggest, therefore, that in the next General Strike, the G.H.Q. Workers should find work for the men to do. They cannot promise the easy contract of the volunteers : " justifiable homicide if you kill, murder if you get killed," with nobody there to kill them ! Indeed, violence must be out of the question. But they must find the men something to do.

The T.U.C. offer to run minimum services was refused ; need that have bothered them ? It was not illegal to supply food and fuel to the working classes and to take working people not on strike to and from their factories and offices. This should be done. The T.U.C. ran a newspaper ; it could run other services.

It could, for example, run bus services. But to do that efficiently it must have buses at its command. And there we come to the root of the matter. Though the T.U.C. had no quarrel with the private bus owners, and let their buses pass without the most pacific picketting, its interests were not theirs. In the next strike they must be. The private bus owner must be a member of the Union. If the Trade Union is to keep itself alive in times of strike against the Combines it must have small holders to depend upon.

We suggest that the Unions should encourage their members to set up trading ventures, and should advance the money needed, on the understanding that the small owners thus created should remain members of the Unions and should help to support men out of work when on strike against the Combines.

If we are to resist and in the end to defeat the Combines, we must have a City of Refuge. Small-ownership will give us that. Small-ownership will give us a minimum national service which can carry on when the monopoly services have stopped working. And do not believe, because a few monopolist papers have said that the working classes are beaten, that we throw up the sponge ! The war is only just beginning. We, the workers, have started later than our enemies. But our resolve is as stern as theirs, and our strength has yet to be tested.

AN OPEN LETTER TO THE HOUSE OF LORDS *

MY LORDS.—For a thousand years we have been partners in the first work of mankind, you and I. Between us we have kept this land green and pleasant, fair and fertile. We have fed its heroes and philosophers, its poets and its kings. Upon our labour and upon the wealth we have brought her by the fruits of the earth and the wool from the sheep we have tended, has been built England's greatness and prosperity.

You have held and ruled the lands—we labourers have had them in our keeping content to serve you and to labour for the joy of tilling English earth, taking as the material reward of our toil plain food, rough clothes and small homes. We have denied ourselves your comfort and your culture content that you should enjoy it through the surplus wealth which our labour has produced in abundance.

When you would stand as leaders of men we have given you our loyalty in peace and you have reigned as kings in the shires. We have answered your call to arms and died under your banners in battle without knowing or asking why.

In whatever age you have come to us to complete your ennoblement—the king may give right and title, but it is the possession of land which ennobles a man—we have held your estates ready for you. We have not cared whether your rank was the reward of bravery in battle or service of the State, of political knavery, the concealment of a king's follies or the care of his concubines. We have regarded neither bar dexter nor sinister. It has been sufficient for us that you have come back to the land and turned from foolish things to the splendid sanity of the soil.

In these later days when our food has become dearer and poorer in quality and we may not eat our own, when you have taken from us—you will say by economic necessity—the perquisites which have been ours by right for generations, the vegetables, skimmed milk, pig offals, ale and cheap cottages, have we not endured these things dumbly for the sake of you and your estates, and our blessed land in its travail? Do you not rely on us and our stability (which some call stupidity) as your bulwark against the forces of revolt and anarchy?

And now, my Lords, when the spirit of business and usury, of cheating and money-changing reigns in high places, when the loudest voice in the land is that of fools who say that man can live by trade, by insuring and banking, by coal and railways and statistics, you who know with us that men live by bread, though not even by bread alone, have listened to the lies and left us! You who have shared with us the first of man's vocations have denied us even the worth of thirty pieces of silver !

You have said that every labourer is more worthy of his hire than the agricultural labourer, and to the least of them you have granted more than we have presumed to ask. We have not asked our worth for we nor no man knows it.

Do you forget that your action ranks with wilful murder, the sin of Sodom, and the oppression of the poor in the quartet of sins crying to Heaven for vengeance?

And if any man should ask us, my Lords, why you have thus forsaken us and the land we serve, leaving us contemptuously in the lowest place, how shall we make answer?

For shame, my Lords !

I am, my Lords,

Your humble and faithful servant.

WHO FEEDS YOU.

* The House of Lords has recently rejected a Bill to secure a minimum wage of thirty shillings a week for the agricultural labourer. In many districts wages are below this amount and they very rarely exceed it.

AM I A DISTRIBUTIST?

1.—Wanted: A Practical Policy

By Arthur J. Penty

FROM time to time, in recent years, I have called myself a Distributist and I have often wondered whether I am entitled to so describe myself. Perhaps the best way for me to start will be to begin by explaining to what extent I am and I am not a Socialist, for Socialist I am by tradition. I was attracted to the Socialist movement in my youth because it proposed to abolish economic individualism, to replace the present competitive society by one based upon the principles of brotherhood and co-operation. To that extent I am a Socialist still. I accept the informal Socialist philosophy with its belief in brotherhood, mutual aid and co-operation. My differences with the Socialist movement are due to the fact that I arrived at the conclusion that the official economic theories to which the movement subscribes have nothing whatsoever to do with the principles of brotherhood and co-operation, or in other words, that there is no correspondence between the moral impulse of the movement and its economic faith. The aim of all my writings has been to promote such a correspondence by getting rid of the official economic theories which hang like a millstone round the neck of the Socialist and Labour movements, and to put in their place an economic theory that is in harmony with their aspirations.

I began by attacking the bureaucratic ideal of Collectivism as a method of industrial organisation, and by promoting the idea that industry should be organised under Guilds as it was in the Middle Ages. The idea found much support among Socialists, but in their hands Guilds became a form of Collectivism. That the Guild idea misfired was to me proof positive that I had not got to the bottom of the problem, or that I had not explained clearly what I understood by a Guild. There was evidently something more fundamental that I had not attached. What was it?

When I had travelled thus far I became interested in Distributism. According to Distributists the root trouble of the Socialist movement was to be found in the fact that they connected all the evils of society with the institution of private property and demanded its abolition. This is certainly true, if it is not the whole truth, for it was the desire to abolish the private ownership of property and what goes with it—the private management of industry—that drove Socialists into the hands of bureaucracy, while it was undoubtedly responsible for transforming the Guild idea into a form of Collectivism; for Guild Socialists did not abandon the idea of abolishing private property.

My reason for saying that Guild Socialism was a form of Collectivism is that experience of its workings showed that it developed similar symptoms. The defect of the Building Guilds was that they developed an extraordinary multiplicity of committees which, owing to the fact that the average committee man got lost among the complexity of details, tended to transfer power into the hands of the officials. Thus the Guild movement, which began as a reaction against bureaucracy, ended by creating an inverted kind of bureaucracy.

So far as I can see there is no remedy for this tendency of activities to-day to lose their way in committees and bureaucracies except by acknowledging the legitimacy of private management which in turn involves a recognition of the principle of private ownership. Up to this point I am a Distributist.

But I am not sure whether Distributists will travel with me any further, for it appears to me that in controverting the Socialist idea of abolishing private property they often fall into the opposite error of exalting private property into an end in itself; just as if there was something peculiarly blessed about the possession of private property. The Puritans had some such idea, but I cannot find any authority for it in the teachings of Christianity or in history. The teaching of the Gospel as to the perils of wealth is unmistakable, while, if tradition counts for anything, the example of the Early Church at Jerusalem suggests that the Christian idea of society is communistic.

But Communism is difficult. It is an ideal, but it can only be lived by ideal men. It is impossible, apart from discipline, and as the majority of men are unwilling to accept a discipline—Communism has in the tradition of the Church been confined to religious orders—a modified Communism that we know by the names of the corporate or common life having been deemed a more practicable ideal for the life of the workaday world. The Fathers of the Church did not idealise property. They held it to be contrary to nature, but necessary because of the presence of sin in the world. It was a consequence of the Fall.

That appears to me to be the right attitude. It is, I am persuaded, wrong to exalt private property as an ideal, but right to accept it as an expedient in view of the corruption of human nature. Distributists, it seems to me, are right in seeking a redistribution of property, but wrong in so far as they idealise property, for ownership should not be absolute. The mediæval idea was that property should only be held conditionally upon the fulfilment of duties. It is to this attitude towards property that I desire to return.

This brings me to a consideration of the principle of Function, which was the principle underlying the organisation of mediæval society, and it is the principle to which we must return. It is the principle which insists that activities are only justifiable when subordinated to a social purpose, in the light of which private property can only be justified in so far as it is necessary for the performance of function. By which is meant, for instance, that land can be held for cultivation but not for speculative purposes. From this point of view, from the point of view of Function, a redistribution of property is necessary because apart from it functions necessary to the well-being of society cannot be properly performed.

But how can property be redistributed? That question is not easy to answer, and because of this many take refuge in the idea of revolution, seeing no remedy by constitutional means. But can revolution be seriously regarded as a remedy? In an agricultural community where there is a peasantry on the soil, where the problem of property is the problem of breaking up great estates, a revolution may be effective. But I cannot see that a revolution could do anything to solve the problem of property in this country, where there is no peasantry on the soil, and where the concentration of property is dependent upon the manipulation of finance and the ownership of machinery. For industrial workers cannot seize their share in machinery as peasants can seize a share of the land.

It is clear, therefore, that if Distributism is to emerge as a practical, political policy Distributists will have to come to definite conclusions about machinery and money which are the two key problems of modern civilisation. One of the hopeful signs of the times is that people at last are beginning to think about them.

(To be continued.)

TOP—

BY DEED POLL

A gentleman of the name of Whisker has changed it for another. We do not mean that he has reversed the usual process, and taken the name of his wife. It is true that the Central Feminist Committee is now drafting a Bill to legalise the assumption of the wife's surname by the husband. But the gentleman who was Whisker had no such freakish design. He changed his surname because it was the cause of unseemly jesting.

Now we admit that Whisker is not as fine a word as Beard, though it has an austere nobility which Moustache or Moustachio can never rise to. And there are a hundred other surnames which a man may be less proud to wear. We know that a cat wears whiskers, including that great cat whose sign is in the heavens, but whiskers have been worn by many a stout sea-captain, by many a hardy peasant, and, in Victorian times, by many a statesman, poet, and innkeeper. We should be sorry to think that the silly freak of side-whiskers or the equally silly modern scorn of all facial hairiness has brought the word into worse repute as a surname than such common appellatives as Catchpole, Mutton, Coward, Swindley, Squirl, or Onions.

A man named Cohen, Levi, Samuels, or Bierbaum, has a sound commercial reason for calling himself Gordon, Montague, or Howard, and an actor may be pardoned for choosing a *nom-de-guerre* which will look well on a play bill. But we think Mr. Whisker was ill-advised to cast off a fine old English name merely because people laughed at it.

He might have made it famous. When Mr. Oliver Onions was making a start in novel-writing a publisher offered to buy his next three novels if he would take another name. Mr. Onions proudly refused. Who thinks now of vegetables when he sees that name on the jacket of a novel ?

A man and his name are one. Shakespeare, as an artist in words, was not at all of the opinion he put in the mouth of one of his characters that " a rose by any other name would smell as sweet." He knew that it wouldn't. And how uneasy seems an English wild flower when decked with a learned termination ! Even the signature of a writing man influences his work (if " Fiona Macleod " and " William Sharp " is an extreme example) not only because of what the signature means to the world, but because of what it has come to mean to the man who has lived with it. *Noms-de-guerre* are sometimes necessary, but they are always a mask. That name we grew up with is our stark face. We fear that even for a fortune of £50,000 we should not adopt the name of Wurzel-Flummery, or of Plantagenet either.

—AND TAIL

SPEEDING UP THE WORMS

A fine example of what may be effected by Mass Production is to be afforded us shortly by the silk-worm. Though not as notorious as the ant or the busy bee, we believe that the old-fashioned silk-worm, working as it were from hand to mouth, is an industrious creature. But the new rivalry of artificial silk, evolved not by worms from a perusal of mulberry leaves, but by other operatives from wood pulp, has persuaded the Silk Kings that the old process is too slow. Therefore a radical transformation of the present domestic requirements of silk-worms (we quote from the *Silk Journal*) is to take place. The new method has this special advantage that " most of the requirements of labour are eliminated." We gather that this means that hardly any human labour will be needed in the process. For " all the work referring to the collection, transportation and distribution of the mulberry leaf and silk-worms, the change of the rearing beds, the cocoon forming of the worms and the collection of the cocoons is conducted through the assistance of special machines working in an absolutely automatic manner ; so that labour has only really the task of surveying the machines in question."

We should imagine that it surveys them with awe.

" During their birth the silk-worms are placed on a continuous band which moves forward at a constant speed. . . . They are shifted automatically from band to band, each fresh band moving faster than the last in relation with the increase in size of the worms."—Until the worms are ripe ! Then comes the beautiful climax of the scheme.

" When the silk worms are ripe they meet the twigs necessary for the cocoon forming, that move forward also at the same speed as the silk-worms, and when the cocoons have been formed they are separated automatically and transported to the drying plant. The leaf on its part is also supplied automatically through an opposite distribution carriage."

This is mass-production more efficient than anything Mr. Ford of America ever devised ; and we draw the attention of his son to it, in the hope that he will be able to adapt the system to the requirements of motor-car-assembling in his new English factory.

Trade unionists need not fear that the conditions of life will be bad, for we read : " The silk-worms are reared in special dispositions divided into various compartments that are perfectly isolated from one another, and are supplied with a warming plant and a cooling plant, and with ventilation for maintaining the silk-worms all through under the most ideal conditions."

But you will observe that you must catch your worm young, and though we may obtain good results by placing the ripe workman on an endless band and arranging that he meets the parts of the car which he must assemble, as well as his meals and his recreation automatically, only the very best results will be reached when the infants whom Mr. Ford should acquire have moved along a sufficient number of endless chains to make them ripe for their life's work. We do not know, of course, if the worms have been consulted. We don't suppose they have. They have merely been informed that on and after a certain date the new system will be in operation. And there lies the danger. It may be thought that if English miners are willing to work under conditions very like those (shall we say ? yes we think we must) adumbrated in the *Silk Journal*, it is by no means certain that the silk-worms will be as docile. For a worm will turn.

THE SCRAPBOOK

"ADVENTURE."

YOU "Man who runs on wheels,"
  Bound tightly by
  Conventions—Beastly, Bold, Beautiful—
I heard you sigh the other day, and say
  That you were bald.

It seems the tragedy was caused by Hats,
High, Hard, and Hideous,
And trains for which you always had to run.
  And Perspiration.

Man! hast never wished yourself
Armed to the eyes with every sort of gun,
With fierce red hair upon your upper lip,
Mounted on mustangs—yes, you've learnt to ride,
Hast never wished yourself
Callous and Cynical?

Or is the greatest venture in your life
The pulsing moment when you give
Your 'Bus seat to some Lady with Hard Eyes?
                                        W. A. K.

LLYN IDWAL.

THEY were bathing in a mountain tarn beside a
    lichened boulder,
  And their bodies shone like flowers in that wild,
    grim place:
One was like a man with muscled thigh and shoulder,
  The other was a woman with a fairy face.

It was in my mind to run down to the water-side and play
    with them,
For their beauty seemed to call me, and I knew they
    were my kin;
But then I thought, maybe they'll have the power to make
    me stay with them,
  And no more shall I come back to the friendly inn.

And so I went no nearer across the ling and heather,
  But lay there in the sunshine, half hidden by a stone;
I looked up to the sky and saw a curlew drop a feather,
  And when I scanned the pool again the fairy folk had
    flown.
                                        C. J. N.

On the Rails Again

TO CASSANDRA.

When I behold thee splendidly alone,
—With thy fair thought, sufficient company—
Thy head a little bent, apart from me
Withdrawn and from the world that I have known.
I often long to greet thee on thy throne,
To come into thy dream; but timidly,
Not daring to be messenger to thee,
Speech crouches twixt my lips, and makes no moan.

Bedazzled by the radiance of thy grace,
My body shakes to tremors of my soul,
And tongue and voice come not to my relief:
Only my sighs, only my mournful face
Speak for me now; but they reveal the whole
Passionate secret of my love and grief.

(From Ronsard) by ARMEL O'CONNOR.

A NORTHERN TOWN GARDEN.

The trees were sombre and the sky was grey,
The garden sulked; but the nasturtium bed,
Flaming with yellow, orange, scarlet, red.
Caught every gleam of light——
She was so gay
That first the sky relented,
Then the sun
Peeped down and smiled upon her just for fun.
                                        H. L.

*   *   *   *

THE BLACK COUNTRY.

He makes his furnace of the fields of God,
  Mammon the wastrel, from whose presence fly
Nature and grace to leave, where he has trod,
  Wan corpse of earth beneath wan shroud of sky.

                                        H. E. G. ROPE.

AN ARRANGEMENT IN BLUE AND GREY

By MARGERY SHARP

ONCE they stole a Mayor.
They lived in a forest of dim wisteria, whose giant vines twined their writhen arms down long fantastic avenues where the pale blossoms drooped like lanterns, or towered up in great swaying pillars, all twisted and enwreathed and hung with purple pennons. There were winds in the forest, small cold winds that never dropped, so that the air was filled with a twilight mist of blown petals, and they could not see clearly down the slanting terraces. Sometimes the winds would seize on a drift of powdered hyacinth that lay heaped about the archways and sweep it up in a lovely tumult of blue and grey; and then they would be caught in a sudden passion of beauty and dream away a century under the lanterns.

But once they stole a Mayor.

He was round and pink and shiny, and smelling very strongly of Pears soap, with three nice little chins and hands that were dimpled and soft like a baby's. And his name was Alfred Rotherhythe Higgs. (And he lived in a house called " The Cedars " with a wife called Mabel and a dog called George.) He was quite a new Mayor, and so proud of his fine new robes that he used to try them on in secret (under the cover of an address on Economics and the Plain Man, or Hygiene, or Civics in the Schools, as the case might be) when his wife had gone to Evening Service; which was how he came to be stolen.

Alfred Rotherhythe Higgs had just climbed on to the ottoman (having first removed his shoes, for he was a tidy little Mayor) in order to observe the fall of his scarlet robe (for the mirror didn't come quite to the floor) when he saw three of them sitting on the back of the easy chair.

Despite his surprise, which was considerable, and his alarm, which shouldn't have been there at all, Mr. Higgs' first thought was of his wife.

" Excuse me," he said politely, " but you're crumpling the antimaccassar."

They took not the least notice, but simply went on regarding him in a rapt manner that was undeniably flattering. Indeed, they would have been quite prepared to go on gazing at him for the next century or two, had not a sudden remembrance of their shadowy home swept them all up in a whirl of scented mist, out through the window and into the sky, where the Mayor's fluttering robe clashed tempestuously with the last tatters of an exceptionally fine sunset.

He woke up with a strange faint fragrance in his nostrils and tried to pull the sheets up higher; but they melted through his fingers in a fine cool powder, and he couldn't find the eiderdown. Alfred Rotherhythe Higgs opened his eyes and looked about him. He could see nothing whatever but a dim expanse of bluish grey that stretched away on all sides without any apparent end. He shut his eyes quickly and tried again. This time he perceived, sticking up just in front of him, two small dark objects that seemed vaguely familiar. He sat up cautiously to see what these might be, and they immediately moved nearer, so that he recognised his second-best pair of heather-mixture socks. . . . The Mayor stood up.

They were all about him, so many and so swift that he could scarcely distinguish them from the bunched purple blossoms. Indeed, it seemed to him that the whole forest was alive, that every flowered stem and pennoned column was leaning closer, edging a little nearer, sometimes silently drawing back to make way for a dim perspective of tangled arches that pressed forward behind them; the blown petals fluttered about him like moths. Alfred Rotherhythe Higgs stood perfectly still, his robes of office bunched up in his little pink hands, his little toes in their heather mixture socks dug deep into the scented dust. He was trying hard to feel indignant.

" What is the explanation of this? " he demanded at last, letting down his robes an inch or two, for the sake of majesty. But instead of his best official voice, the one he used when addressing girls' schools, he heard a scared little pipe that sounded like the wind in the wisterias. So he let down his robes another inch or two and added severely (but his voice was fainter than ever):

" Very well, I shall go and find a constable." (He called them constables because he was a Mayor.)

And with that the Mayor pulled off his heather mixture socks (as though it were the most natural thing in the world) and paddled away down the nearest avenue, kicking up the petals behind him and looking for a policeman. Before he reached the end he had quite forgotten what he set out to find.

They loved their Mayor. They loved every bit of him from his clean little heart (where the smell of Pears soap was strongest) to the entrancing pinkness of his bare toes. They followed him in great wisteria-coloured troops as he trotted happily about the endless twilight mazes, crooning to himself odd snatches, of whose meaning he was rapturously ignorant, out of the Economics of the Plain Man.

He spent much of his time looking for his socks, for the twisting galleries were all so much alike that he could never remember exactly where he had left them neatly folded over a convenient bough. He was suspicious, moreover, that the forest was not always quite the same; once he had trotted down an avenue of arches, and, turning, found an avenue of towers. But nothing bothered the Mayor now, not even the great stains of green and lavender that had begun to appear on his gay red robe, nor the fact that his socks, in which the purple now predominated, were getting more and more difficult to tell from the wisteria flowers. The Mayor was entirely happy.

He might never have remembered, might have gone gaily kicking up the blue petals for ever and a day with never a thought of his house " The Cedars," or his wife Mabel, or his dog George, had it not been for a sudden glimpse of a lamp-lit avenue that looked so remarkably like the High Street on a Saturday night, that he took up his socks and trotted down it to find a constable. With every step it grew more familiar; the wisterias were fewer and less luxuriant, till at last you might quite easily have taken them for lamp-posts; the flower-dust thinned and scattered under his scurrying feet, and once he stubbed his toe against a manhole; in fact the pavement was now so hard and scrubby that the Mayor was just going to sit down on the kerb and put on his socks when he saw to his horror that the people were coming out of Evening Service. Alfred Rotherhythe Higgs forgot all about the constable (for the second time) and fled like a blown leaf for his own front garden. His glorious speed seemed the last fading traces of his gay enchantment, that and the practiced facility with which he swarmed up the wisteria outside his window (and this surprised him most of all, for it was a thing he would never have dreamed of doing in the forest).

But then he did not see his wife Mabel extract from the bureau drawer about two days later a pair of dead wisteria flowers, rather smaller than usual, and almost the colour of heather.

THE PRIDE OF ENGLAND
By G. K. Chesterton

THE first article which I wrote in the first number of this paper, with its excellent principles and its execrable title, I inscribed with the name of " Found Wandering." And I was really and truly found wandering by the most sensational news of modern English politics; for I had been obliged to go abroad for what ought to have been for a few days, when those sudden barricades were thrown up that might have meant, for all I knew, exile for a few months. At such a moment I would rather express something of the first sentiment that surges up in the soul than any very full or final criticism of the situation. And the first sentiment that surges up in me is the pride of England. It is necessary to see something of the common conditions of the Continent to realise that, from a distance, England really looks like an island. I had not realised that, from a distance, it also looks like a mountain. And perhaps all the more like a mountain at the moment when it happens to look like a volcano.

And yet, by a paradox, it looks all the more of a mountain because it is so little of a volcano. I have been bored, like all national people, by the merely mechanical praises of English moderation and order. I know well that they have often been merely praises of snobbery and apathy. I know well that they have missed many opportunities by which nations at once more logical and more impetuous have done great things. But as a man grows older he begins to understand how hard it is for people to practise even their own virtues; how impossible to practise other people's. And in this business the English are practising their own virtues so as to be a wonder of the world. The first news I found was in a French newspaper, sold on a little stall in Tarragona; and the very intelligent French journalist who wrote on the English strike remarked, with a sort of bottomless wonder, " Nobody seems really irritated with the strikers; it is more common to sympathise with their misfortune and the reduction of their wages." That was written from the capitalist standpoint; but even that gave me a sudden movement of pride. If I speak with the tongues of men and angels and have not charity—the English gentry speak with the tongues of geese and donkeys : but they have charity.

Moreover, from the other standpoint, there is a very just and logical reason for being proud of the comparative calm of the English revolution. It really is essential in this case, apart from all newspaper nonsense, that the proletarian party should remain strictly peaceful and law-abiding. It is not merely a part of the policy, it is something much nobler; it is a part of the argument. English strikers would really throw away their whole case if they struck—in the sense of hitting somebody on the nose, however tempting some noses may appear. It is the whole case of those who sympathise with Labour principles that a strike is simply a stage in a bargain or the refusal of a bargain. A man has a right to sell his labour as he has to sell his land; for what it will fetch. It is a perfectly free commercial contract, like buying a hat or selling a house. Of course, in the ultimate moral and spiritual sense he is bound to consider the glory of God and the good of mankind in making or refusing his bargain. So he is bound to consider the glory of God in buying a hat or the good of mankind in selling a house. But in the ordinary legal sense it is nobody's business but his own what he chooses to give for his hat, or to take for his land, or to take for his labour. Now it would obviously destroy all this doctrine of free bargaining if the free bargain always ended in a free fight. It ought not to be necessary to say of a man, " He thought the price of the hat too high and yet he did not murder the hatter." It ought not to be possible to say, " She refused to let lodgings at Margate for less than so

much; but as yet there has been no bloodshed on Margate sands." Fighting and killing have their value in their own place; as *we* at least are ready to admit in the case of wars as well as revolutions. But they are quite out of place when men are claiming their lawful rights to a peaceful bargain. Any striker who breaks or burns is giving away the whole case for the strike. He is accepting the servile doctrine that a refusal of wages is itself a sort of riot.

It is therefore with an undivided mind that I am proud in this case of the English good humour which mystifies the French journalist. This does not mean that I cannot see the advantages in the French spirit also, of which I have written often enough. But if anyone wants an amusing comedy of contrasts in the matter, let him consider that the English strike happened at the same time as the French celebrations of the festival of St. Joan of Arc. The general strike had always been regarded as the end of the world; the absolutely final and all-destroying crash between the incompatible universes of Capital and Labour. On that everyone would have to take sides, as on the Judgment Day, dividing hell and heaven. And when it came in London it seems to have been treated rather like a London fog. On the other hand, the one thing in the whole world on which all Frenchmen agree absolutely is the admiration for St. Joan. Atheists adore St. Joan; blasphemers adore her; devil-worshippers, I imagine, have a weakness in her favour. And this being the one and only point on which Frenchmen do not differ, the result was that they fought each other all along the street; the police charged the mob, and all sorts of people were injured and arrested, including at least one priest. It takes all sorts to make a world.

Above all, the pride in England is the pride in the Trade Union. It was England that invented the Trade Union; and foreigners in any number of places still talk of " le trade union " as they talk of " le train." The English invented the locomotive engine and the modern substitute for the guild; and heaven knows they have more reason to be proud of trade unions than of trains. The foreigners among whom I have myself been moving have all identified this form of liberty with something local and national in our own island. The trade union was not indeed as rational and satisfactory as the guild; perhaps this was partly due to the place, but even more to the period in which it appeared. It was an instinctive popular protest rather than a part of an ordered democratic system. But it was the inevitable reaction of Christian democracy against the abnormal concentration of capitalism in a morbid period of economics. It seems fairly obvious that it is the very existence of this great English institution that has been attacked in the present crisis. And while we ourselves have always preferred the policy of small property, we have never hesitated to defend the proletarian organisation as the only actual defence of the classes without property. If that institution falls in England, the newspapers will give all sorts of names to the incident; it will be attributed to this or that trivial politician or paper, hardly known in any other country and not known at all at any later time. But those who watch England from afar, like a mountain in a sea, will say that the flag of freedom has fallen from a height. It seems to me quite plain that the employers have planned and timed this lock-out to occur exactly when it did occur. They hoped that if it came then, and failed then, the whole power of the poor to defend their wages would disappear. They hoped, of course, to restore the old leonine contract between the isolated poor man and the sole owners of food : though nobody acquainted with the hypocrisy so essential to our public life will expect them to say so.

"My Dominions, Right or Wrong."

THE COCKPIT

To the Editor of G.K.'s WEEKLY.

**THE
GENERAL
STRIKE**

SIR,—Late last night I received the current issue of your paper, exhorting your readers to " Stand by the Strikers," and setting out the claim of the miners to higher wages. The case of the miners is no longer in issue, and they may well wish to be saved from their friends. The right to strike does not include the right to make war on the community.

For about two years after the war solicitors were quite inadequately remunerated as compared with other professionals, considering the rise in the cost of living. There were cases of very serious hardship in which business could not be carried on, and clerks were thrown out of work. Do you suggest that in order to accelerate the increase subsequently granted by statute the Bench and Bar ought to have denied justice to the public, that the transport of food should have been endangered, that newspapers should have been abolished, and that mob law should have been established?

This strike combines gross breach of contract and a conspiracy to bully the community by brute force. It would not have been possible but for the cowardice of the Liberal Party in passing the Trades Disputes Act, 1906. If that Act is not repealed the country will have, for all intents and purposes, a Soviet Government.—Yours, etc.,

E. S. P. HAYNES,

May 9, 1926.

**THE
ANGLICAN
POSITION**

DEAR SIR,—Many of Canon Dorrity's historical statements are so astonishing that I beg leave to offer the following remarks which I don't think any honest and competent historian will deny. The editor of G.K.'s WEEKLY does not require any assistance in controversy; but the subject is so interesting, and the Canon's misconceptions so common, that I claim a few moments in the Cockpit.

We don't know *very much* about the Church in Britain during the Roman occupation. We do know that St. Gildas (6th century) in his " Epistles," uses this phrase: " To St. Peter and his successors Christ said, ' To thee do I give the keys of the kingdom of Heaven.' "

We do know that in 402 Pope Innocent the First excommunicated the eminent British heresiarch Pelagius.

We do know that in 314 three Bishops (of London, York, and possibly Caerleon) attended the Council of Arles convened by Pope Sylvester. We also know that Bishops from Britain were present at Nicaea, Rimini and Sardica in 325. 359, and 347, respectively. We do know that after Sardica, the assembled Bishops addressed Pope Julius the First in these words: " It will be seen to be best . . . that the priests of the Lord from each of the provinces report to the head, that is the See of the apostolic Peter."

We do know, to turn to the Saxon period, that the See of Canterbury was founded by a Benedictine monk sent to Britain by Pope Gregory, who committed to his care " all the bishops of Britain ": and that whatever be the whole truth about the famous interview between St. Augustine and the British (or Welsh) Bishops, the Christian Welsh at this time hated the pagan Saxons worse than the Devil, and absolutely refused to attempt their conversion.

We know that the See of York was refounded by the Roman missionary, Paulinus, in 626, and that at the Council of Whitby in 664 the Celtic Church, issuing from Iona, came into line with the rest of Europe about keeping Easter.

We know that the Pallium came from Rome to all the Archbishops of Canterbury till Elizabeth's Matthew Parker, and that this signified Papal recognition and Papal authority. The Pallium is *still* in the arms of the Anglican See.

We know that in spite of Papal misgovernment in the later Middle Ages, no Englishman (except the Radical don Wyclif) ever denied the Pope's spiritual headship of the Church Universal, and his claim to be the successor of St. Peter.

Finally, three queries. (1) Cardinals. Why did the English medieval Church contain Cardinals, and why were those Englishmen after the Reformation, who were made Cardinals, Roman Catholics and not Anglicans, if there was no break in religious continuity? (2) Why did Queen Elizabeth turn the Benedictines out of Westminster Abbey, the Order that gave Canterbury its first Archbishop and England many of her cathedrals, if there was no break in religious continuity? (3) Why did Henry VIII. execute Blessed Thomas More for *adhering* to the ancient belief in the Pope's spiritual supremacy, if there was no such break?

The Church of England really cannot have it both ways. If she is to side with those British bishops against the founder of her chief See, she can claim neither part nor lot in the glories of the English church from Augustine to Cardinal Pole. But *if* she claims continuity with the Church of Anselm, Beckett, Grosseteste and Wolsey, she is logically bound to acknowledge the claims of the Pope.

Yours, etc.,

N. R. CHILDE.

**THE
AMERICAN
CHARACTER**

DEAR SIR.—The American colony here read your reflections on America with mingled feelings. They felt not so much angry as hurt at the strange conglomeration of half-truths from the pen of one they had always admired and respected for his clean-cut logic and fairmindedness; for Americans believe, above all, in fair play. However, they did admire your frankness.

Alfred Noyes recently gave to an English paper the best analysis we have seen of the mingled idealism and realism of the American character. Whoever says our people will not fight for an ideal was not in America during the war. Why, even Senator Borah was an idealist then, but he, like the rest of us, was disillusioned by the Peace Conference. American cartoons explain better than a thousand words the exact reaction of the average American to-day to European criticism.

Not until after the Eucharistic Congress will even Catholic Englishmen suspect the truth about the religious revival amongst us.

Yours, etc.,

JAMES F. KEARNEY, S.J.

To the Editor of G.K.'s WEEKLY.

A SCOURGE TO EUROPE

SIR,—One would be a fool to deny that, incidentally, Mussolini has conferred important benefits on Italy, though the abnormal condition in which he found that country must always be remembered.

But can a man who proclaims as his creed that " Only the strong have the right to resist," ever be acceptable to those who delight in G.K.'s WEEKLY—much less to its editor?

When I saw this dictum of Mussolini's in *The Times* many months ago, I hoped to see it dealt with as only G. K. could deal with it. I can only suppose that it escaped the editor's notice, for I cannot but believe that it would have roused his wrath, and made him understand why many who admit Mussolini's greatness are convinced that he will yet prove a scourge to Europe.

I am, etc.,

F. W. LEWIS.

Cardiff.
April 23, 1926.

MUSSOLINI (continued)

SIR,—Although I have examined Mr. Moncrieff's quotation several times I have not yet found the "one important word " which he accuses me of having " altered." He evidently read this biography carefully, and has treasured it; I did neither, and quoted from memory. It is true that—if I were Irish—and had nothing but a rifle against a lorry of machine gunners, I should probably retire behind a hedge or anything convenient, but if I had to throw stones, it would seem unnecessary to " sharpen " them. " Utterly reckless," I ignore all the rigmarole Mr. Moncrieff cites as affecting my extract; indeed, I should not be surprised if most of the detail and even the incident itself were imaginary. The essential feature is the gloating of its author: " Once, twice, thrice! " Young Benito was probably a nice lad; his progressive deterioration is depicted by photographs which culminate in an offensive marble effigy by Wildt.

Sir, I only wish I were paid—by the Pope presumably, to denounce this Dictator. Alas, I am a Nordic, and unsuitable for such enterprise: Protestant, Individualistic and English —though not one hundred per cent., I have never associated with Jews or Freemasons, and so am no doubt an easy victim of their dishonest propaganda, the vision of which, perhaps by depriving Mr. Moncrieff of his sleep, has evidently blinded him to reality.

It is part of your doctrine, Sir, that France, Poland and Italy are privileged by culture, religion, honesty, or what-not, to do as they please in the garden, and even to break up the furniture of Europe if they cannot amuse themselves otherwise. Francesco Coppola, delegate to the League Assembly, wrote in *La Politica* last December that " it is a vital necessity for Italy to acquire lands *of her own.* If we are not to perish we shall be forced to *seize* land and raw material by a modification of the map of the Mediterranean *through an act of force,* for though unemployment does not exist in Italy at the moment, we are Running the Risk of it! " His italics, but my capitals and note of admiration.

I admit I have been prejudiced against a Greater Italy ever since the Tripoli atrocities, and the calculated desertion of the Central Powers at the right moment did not improve the national reputation, but I am no more fond of the Beautiful French Army or the Br. Empire Ltd. This vapacious trio have again come to a businesslike agreement: we have got Mosul, nothing is to be said about a little roughness in Morocco and Damascus, and Italy will presently grab Smyrna or again endeavour to protect Abyssinia against its own ruler. And to what end? The effect of Imperialism on Commerce is like that of Gold on Industry: one provides jobs for chartered companies and undertakers, the other gives profits to Financier and Underwriters; the people pay for both.

" Patriotism," said Janal-ed-Din to Wilfrid Scawen Blunt, " is a virtue in weak nations, a vice in the strong." Like property, it is improper in bulk.

According to an Associated Press dispatch from Rome—not Berlin—the principles of the Brenner Guard " include "— (what more do they want?):—

1. The divinity of Italy.
2. Italian products are the best in the world.
3. The Italian landscape is the most beautiful in the world.
4. The most unworthy Italian is worth a thousand foreigners.

Up the Nordics! Every day in every way we grow bigger and better, more beautiful and blessed. Foreigners need not ridicule Fascismo, its own propaganda is enough.

Mr. Moncrieff's heavy sarcasm at " Ws " rather obvious irony shows a lack of humour not surprising in one who can so admire this operatic Napoleon, but what does he mean by " Obedience "? His time and your space, Sir, are no doubt of some value, but self-assertion of one's own wisdom, and the folly of those who do not agree with it is unimpressive. Of the same curious interest as the patriotic appropriation of right and honesty, it fortunately differs from that *credo* in that it is diverting without being dangerous. It is funny but rather vulgar.

GEOFFREY BIDDULPH.

March 21, 1926.

MUSSOLINI (concluded)

Mr. Scott Moncrieff writes from London :—" So far as I can remember at this interval of time and space Mr. Biddulph in his earlier onslaught omitted to mention that Mussolini at the time of the alleged incident of the sharpened stone was seven years of age, and in every way outmatched by his opponent. He has now invented the delicious touch that Mussolini *threw* the stone three times in succession, but does not say whether the clever little boy caught it on the rebound or stooped to collect it from the ground. It may, of course, have been sharpened into a boomerang. It seems a pity that Mr. Biddulph should launch so violent an attack upon a book which he admits that he did not read carefully and has not preserved. I did not read the book carefully and certainly did not praise it; all that I said was that any life of Mussolini was better than none, and that a life by an intimate contemporary was of more value than the posthumous work of some professor. To revert to the question of stones, I can well remember being stoned in my early boyhood in Clydesdale; but always by boys bigger than myself and by two or more at a time, which elements are essential, I suppose, to Mr. Biddulph's idea of fair play."

[NOTE.—This correspondence must now cease.—EDITOR.]

CONSCIOUSNESS

SIR,—It would be interesting to know concerning Doctor Jane Ellen Harrison (whose book was favourably reviewed in your columns of February 6):

1. Whence she derives her confident knowledge that her consciousness began with her body;
2. When she supposes that her body began to be.

Sincerely yours,

T. BATY.

Japan.
March 7, 1926.

THE RETURN OF DON QUIXOTE
By G. K. Chesterton

CHAPTER IX.—(*Continued.*)

THE HANSOM CAB.

"HOW many lunatics do you keep here?" demanded Dr. Gambrel, who seemed to be needlessly moved by the incident, to the point indeed of trembling with temper.

"I suppose I'm a lunatic, too?" Miss Hendry replied, shortly. "I'm quite ready to be anything my father is supposed to be."

"Well, well, it's all very painful," said the doctor recovering his composure and with it something more like a callous benevolence. "But there's nothing to be gained by shilly-shallying over it. You'd much better let me see your father at once."

"Oh, very well," she replied. "I suppose I shall have to."

She turned abruptly and opened the door which let them both into the little dingy room where Dr. Hendry was sitting. There was nothing very notable about it except its dinginess; the doctor had been in it before, and the young woman had hardly been out of it for the last five years. It is therefore perhaps a rather remarkable fact that even the doctor looked at it with a vague surprise, the cause of which he was at the moment too fiercely flustered to define especially. As for the young woman, she looked at the room with a stare of stony astonishment.

There was no other door to the room; Dr. Hendry was sitting alone at his table, and Mr. Douglas Murrell had totally disappeared.

Before Dr. Gambrel could remark on the fact or even become fully conscious of it, the unfortunate Hendry had hopped up from his seat and seemed thrown into a flutter of mingled surrender and expostulation which stopped any other line of conversation.

"You will understand," he said, "that I protest formally against your interpretation of my case. If I could put the facts fully before the scientific world, I should not have the smallest difficulty in showing that the argument is entirely the other way. My intellectual position has been misunderstood precisely because it does, in fact, represent the intellectual norm; the mere fact that the abnormal has become numerically superior to the normal at a certain place and period of history does not, according to the definitions of any serious philosopher, disturb the essential distinction between the normal and the average. I admit that, at this moment, the average of our society has, owing to certain optical diseases which——"

Dr. Gambrel had the power of the modern state, which is perhaps greater than that of any state, at least, so far as the departments over which it ranges are concerned; he had the power to invade this house and break up this family and do what he liked with this member of it; but even he had not the power to stop him talking. In spite of all official efforts, Dr. Hendry's lecture on Colour-Blindness went on for a considerable time. It continued while the more responsible doctor edged him gradually towards the door, while he led him down the stairs, and at least until he managed to drag him out on to the doorstep. But meanwhile other things had been happening, which were not noticed by those who were listening (however unwillingly) to the lecture which had begun in the room upstairs.

*　　*　　*　　*　　*　　*

The cabman perched upon the ancient cab was a patient character, as he had need to be. We have already noted how he whiled away the hours of waiting outside various houses, by getting down from his seat and getting up again, and

other artless arts. He had been waiting outside the house of the Hendrys for some time, when something happened which was certainly more calculated to arouse his attention and entertain his leisure than anything that had happened yet.

It consisted of a gentleman apparently falling out of the sky on to the top of the cab, and righting himself with some difficulty in the act of nearly rolling off it. This unexpected visitor, when eventually he came the right way up, revealed to the astonished cabman the face and form of the gentleman with whom he had had a chat recently a little further down the road. A prolonged stare at the newcomer, followed by a prolonged stare at the window just above, revealed to the driver that the former had not actually dropped from heaven, but only from the window-sill. But though the incident was not by definition a miracle, it was certainly something of a marvel. Those privileged to see Murrell fall off the window-sill on to the top of the hansom cab might have formed a theory about why he had originally been called Monkey.

The cabman was still more surprised when his new companion smiled across at him in an agreeable manner and said, like one resuming a conversation:

"As I was saying——"

It is unnecessary to go back after all these years, and the adventurous consequences they brought forth, to record what he was saying. But it is of some direct importance to the story to record what he said. After a few friendly flourishes he sat himself down firmly with his legs astraddle on the top of the cab, and took out his pocket book from which he produced some of the considerable sum of money he had thoughtfully put there for his adventure. The cabman eyed him with a fascinated silence, and eventually he leaned across at the considerable peril of pitching over, and said, confidentially: "Look here, old fellow, I want to buy your cab."

(To be continued.)

A Craftsman's Prayer

When eager to my work I rise,
And climb, hotfoot, my workshop stair.
Thus runs my strange unwilling prayer
To the Great Craftsman in the skies :—

I.

Oh, Thou, Who o'er Thy Work canst bend
Unwearied, through Thy timeless year,
Grant me to know my time to end,
To down the tools and pack the gear !
By these my days of sight and power,
When I grudge not my best to Thee
I pray Thee, curb me in the hour
When power and vision wane from me !

II.

Some turn the outrun glass again
Nor from the applauded task will cease,
So they the full day's wage obtain
And die in harness and in peace.
But *I'll* accept the idler's ban,
I'll bear the blank years' dull unrest,
If just, as artist and as man,
I may add nothing to my best !

G. M. HORT.

THE DRAMA

"CONFLICT," by Miles Malleson, at the Queen's Theatre, is a clever example of what can be done with an old plot in a new setting. It is always the angle of approach which counts, and the author has given an original twist to a situation familiar and beloved of every playgoer. A rising financier wants to marry the daughter of his titled partner. The lady refuses to be his wife, but agreeably becomes his mistress. He is renewing his plea for a more permanent alliance at three o'clock in the morning—father is of a trusting disposition, before and after, when a face appears suddenly at the window. The face does this several times, the tension being skilfully worked up, and at last a young man in a state of destitution enters through the French windows, to be received by Lord Bellingdon accompanied with a pistol, the lady having gone to bed. His name is Smith. He was at Cambridge with the rising young financier and having lost all his money in the war suggests a loan.

He partakes of sandwiches and whisky, becomes a little drunk, and confesses that, desperately hungry, he once took a pound note off a coffee stall. Sir Ronald Clive is not too shocked, but Lord Bellingdon is outraged. He declines to consider anything but the principle of honesty, which he declares has been violated.

Eighteen months later, Smith, neatly dressed and looking very well, calls once again. He is not prepared to return the £120 previously borrowed, but wishes to state that he intends to stand as Labour candidate in opposition to Clive, nominated in the Conservative interest. He wants a straight fight. Will his hosts agree not to mention the matter of the pound note? They do agree, and Smith departs, having made the acquaintance of Lady Dare Bellingdon, who immediately interested, develops a keen curiosity in Socialism. She invites him to tea, calls at his bed-sitting room after a meeting, and returns his inevitable kiss.

The last act is cleverly written. Lady Dare tells her father she has been to Smith's room, Smith is sent for, and a general auditing takes place. The old peer says he will disclose the theft of the pound. Whereat his daughter threatens that if he does this to Smith she will publish the fact that Ronald Clive has made her his mistress. This spikes the old man's guns, and the curtain falls on the discomfiture of the Conservative candidate and the embrace of the young couple.

This is not a conflict of ideas, but of temperaments. The theme is skilfully handled and the slight soupçon of politics gives it a modern flavour. The play is in no sense a clash of economic philosophy. There is none of the thrust and counter thrust of Shavian drama. But it is a workmanlike piece, with witty lines, coherent characterisation, and a sense of dramatic values.

Mr. Granville Barker's translation of "Dr. Knock" at the Royalty Theatre is admirably done. This brilliant skit on the methods of a section of the medical profession suffers, however, from being set in France. Dr. Knock who, buying a practice minus patients, contrives by suggestion to build up a profitable clientele, is as familiar in this country as in any other. Why, therefore, should the types presented of credulous women and impressionable men be entirely French? We have all of us met the hypochondriac who yearns to be told of an obscure disease, the *malade imaginaire* is always with us. It was Somerset Maugham in "Penelope" who gave us some unforgettable specimens of the habitues of a fashionable physician's consulting room. I wish Mr. Denis Eadie could have set the scene of Dr. Knock's practice in London or the provinces. For the rest this witty play, with its absence of sex, is taken too slowly. The tempo should be hurried, the intervals between the acts halved, and for those who do not consider brilliant dialogue sufficient entertainment for an evening a one act play could be introduced. Mr. Eadie is clever as the young doctor, but just a touch too commercial, Miss Barbara Gotte is extremely funny, and the smaller characters are most adequately played.

I am a devout admirer of Komisarjewsky, but it is the privilege of an admirer keenly to resent any falling off in his pet genius. In his production of Gogol's "The Government Inspector," Komisarjewsky has made a bad mistake. He has underestimated the intelligence of his audience. The play is a roaring farce. We have a small provincial town enchained by the political corruption which we choose to think flourishes only in Russia. The postmaster, like his English country colleagues, opens the letters before they are distributed. He learns, therefore, that a Government inspector will shortly appear. Imagination works quickly and fastens on an agreeable scallywag, staying at the hotel, as the great man *incognito*. Accordingly all the officials visit him, tender the usual bribes and place their houses and their female relatives at his disposal. The young man fleeces everybody gaily and departs in a blaze of glory, having promised to marry the Governor's daughter.

The Governor, in a transport of satisfaction, sketches his future as a Field Marshal in Petrograd, when the postmaster enters to say that he has opened another letter—this time from the scallywag who confides the truth to his friend. There falls on the stupefaction of the fleeced ones the knell of the arrival of the real inspector. And the curtain drops.

Komisarjewsky produces the play on the lines of "Chout," one of the least successful of the modern Russian ballets. The actors play on a raised platform, perpetually revolving like a merry-go-round. Its gyrations make you dizzy, and it is not until the middle of the second act that you are able to separate the platform from the players. Further, certain of the characters are purely pantomimic. Like Tweedledum and Tweedledee, they are obscurely symbolical. This curious method of production on two planes—straight farce and pantomime—handicaps the play heavily. It is absurd to suppose that an audience keenly appreciative of Tchehov is unable to gauge the childlike humour of Gogol. What should have been an amusing romp has been turned into a highbrow marionette performance. It may be that this method of production would appeal to a Russian audience. It does not and cannot help an English one.

I must, however, say a few words for the most delightful stage horse I have even seen.

J. K. PROTHERO.

THREE CENTURIES OF CHEMISTRY *

DR. IRVINE MASSON has given us a fascinating story in this account of " Phases in the Growth of a Science." It is a courageous attempt to show the development of the Scientific Method in our inquiries into the nature of matter, and on the whole a successful one. Yet, without in any sense belittling the work of experimental science, we can still question its arrogant assumption of superiority to " the dry lamp of reason or argument unfed by facts." For, as this book shows, the " facts " of yesterday are often the myths of to-day—the strongest facts of the " phlogistonists " have given place to the newer knowledge. But there is no fundamental reason why the facts of our generation should be on that account more factual than those of three hundred years ago—the generation of Bacon and Shakespeare.

It is becoming increasingly difficult for any but the specialist to know how much of a modern scientific statement is based on pure theory and how much on experimental evidence. The specialists' interpretation of evidence varies widely, despite their honesty of purpose and love of truth. And where are we when we come to the more advanced chemistry which is so inseparably involved with physics and pure mathematics?

Dr. Masson tells us that he addresses " those who do not understand the technicalities of chemistry and physics, but are interested either in the evolution of modern thought or in applied logic." We venture to think that he would address them in vain, for but few except those conversant with the technicalities of both chemistry and physics could follow his chapters on the physico-chemical implications of the Ionic Theory, for example. And this despite the fact that the matter is throughout eminently lucid and readable.

In this connection it is surely evident to the author that modern chemistry cannot wholly escape the scorn which Boyle directed against those alchemists who described their works by such titles as " The Philosophers' Dragon which Eateth up her own Tayle," and " Knock the Child on the Head." (To digress here, one can hardly miss the aptness of these titles to the modern Science of Eugenics.) We may have thrown over the allegorical touch, but with the best of intentions the chemist remains darkly obscure to all but the chemist. The habit of pleading the normally reasonable excuse of " literary algebra " was hardly ever more abused than it is to-day, when every discovery seems to breed a new language.

The author's reference in the beginning of the work to the " theory-mongers' aloofness from experimental evidence as opposed to deference to authority," forces into sharp relief the fact that he gives as much as a third of the book to the foundation of the Royal Society ! The deference to that body as the custodian of right-thinking, and therefore, in reason, to its authority, could hardly be more marked. It is indeed a truism that without a slavish deference to authority in the foundations of his knowledge the modern young scientist would never get anywhere.

We might wish that Dr. Masson could have gone to greater length, and thus been able to make his intriguing story more easily readable by the general reader. As it is, we must be grateful for a very lucid and straightforward account. And if we cannot accept its implications in their entirety it is because Priestley himself has warned us—and his warning extends to all chemists :—

" We may take a maxim so strongly for granted that the plainest evidence of the sense will not entirely change, and often hardly modify our persuasions ; and the more ingenious a man is, the more effectually he is entangled in his own errors, his ingenuity only helping him to deceive himself by evading the force of truth."   H.

* THREE CENTURIES OF CHEMISTRY. By Irvine Masson, D.Sc. Ernest Benn, Ltd. 15s.

NOVELS OF THE DAY

THE war that was to end war almost killed civilisation. The next struggle of the nations will do it effectually. Mr. Shaw Desmond in " Ragnarok "* depicts a conflict beside which the Great War 1914-18 was an affair of outposts.

I gather that before writing his book Mr. Desmond interviewed politicians, soldiers, sailors, airmen and scientists in Europe and America, and asked them for their views as to how another world-struggle would be likely to develop when the combatants had taken the air, the sea and the land. Behind this " shocker " there is a considerable, and a disconcerting amount, of scientific plausibility. Mr. Desmond does handle an epic subject with great power ; but it is much to be regretted that such power is confined to the descriptive and philosophic sides of the book, and that he has not troubled, apparently, to make the leading characters correspond to life. If the *dramatis personæ* had been in keeping with the drama, " Ragnarok " would have been a book to command universal respect. As it is, the leading figures are thoroughly unlikely people. Miss Joan Trefusis, a kind of super girl-guide, in charge of an unofficial aerial force, is just as improbable as " Chinese Lillith," who is also a power in the air. Even more surprising, Desmond Darcy, the little monkey of an Irishman, who is an " Ace " of the first magnitude, is as impossible as the Cockney, Tom Battershell, or Miss Vixen Riggs, " The Illinois Terror." I have to chide Mr. Desmond also for placing a foundling fat baby in a battle-plane.

If, however, the characters are dismissed as lay figures, there is enough left of " Ragnarok " to justify its title as a super-shocker. Its terrors and agonies seem beyond human endurance, but that is the way scientific fighting proceeds ; the human element is not considered. If mankind breaks under the strain of intolerable odds, so much the worse for a world that has ceased to have any cautionary power of self-preservation. Shaw Desmond, in his Armageddon of the little gods, pictures a globe in which all the old landmarks are swept away, using for his text a paraphrase of Scandinavian mythology :—

And the gods looking down upon the earth and seeing how the men crawling thereon tormented one another, saw that it was time to make an end. So it was that they gathered themselves together from the uttermost parts of the heavens and the hells to Ragnarok.

At the period in futurity Mr. Shaw Desmond begins his thriller, Japan has been aiming at a weird co-operation, the domination of China's four hundred and fifty millions and the unification of those millions with India's three hundred millions of Brown Men and with the Russians, themselves really Asiatics ; and with this unification of Asia to challenge the White Race with the cry of " Asia for the Asiaties." France, with her millions of coloured troops, has entered this dangerous coalition in ignorance of Japanese future policy. England has lined up with Germany and America has kept preserving the Monro Doctrine.

The World goes to war with Japan's aerial onslaught on New York. Death descends on the city in sprinkling glass like fine rain, alighting in streamers of silver, like an April shower in a light wind.

America for generations had been anticipating a Japanese raid via San Francisco, but in this final war, the expected things were never done. The element of surprise was the

* RAGNAROK. By Shaw Desmond. Duckworth. 7s. 6d.

strongest weapon any nation had—surprise and attack. The defenders were like unarmed men against a gas warfare which exploited different forms of torture and death according to the chemical genius of each country engaged.

From a position of vantage Joan Trefusis and Desmond Darcy see the " Dripping Death " fall on New York, and its attendant horrors :—

When they came out by the Hudson terminus, they found the street a seething torrent. Resistlessly, they were carried by the screaming throngs into the lower end of Broadway with the human tides sluicing through it as a freshet sluices through a canyon. From high above, floating down to them in the stone canyon in which they were confined, there came a muffled roar. Joan saw the Woolworth sway a little in the night under the electric suns, and then there was a crimson splash from the heart of it, and the whole of the enormous facade, thousands of thousands of tons, had crashed downward into the narrow gully, damming it completely.

The purely material destruction was terrific, but the new liquified gas with its property of spreading its deadly fumes indefinitely after dropping, was horrible in its effects on humanity. There were bitter enemies to the United States in its very heart, notably Rastus Silver, the " Black Emperor." America went mad hunting Asiatics first of all: then the Ku-Klux-Klan assumed a prominence it never had before in endeavouring to exterminate Jews, Catholics and Irishmen. The negroes were lying low and so did not provoke assault. A time came, when, faced with the Coloured Danger in its fiercest form, even the Klan admitted that a man might be a Catholic and yet go to heaven. It took, however, a Day of Judgment, to cause that tolerance.

In the London *Times* there were guarded hints as to the danger to the Empire, and especially to Australia, if the Yellow Man were allowed to defeat America. At the same time there was a recrudescence of Red propaganda among the British troops and, indeed, of Red activity everywhere, but this propaganda had become so common a feature of European life that people were not much concerned about it.

What did disturb England as by a menacing gesture was that Plekanov, the Red Dictator, in whose hands rested the destinies of one hundred and fifty millions of people, had been received in audience by the French President, and had even been present at a great review of French troops in the Champs Elysées, where the fierce discipline of the Senegalese had aroused the admiration of the onlookers. France had stated quite openly that she had seventeen millions of these black warriors from whom to draw her armies of the future " when the day came."

France, however foolishly and without reason, had accused England of betraying her at the time of the Ruhr occupation because of England's refusal to press the Germans for reparation—and France never forgets. Germany's alliance with England had roused French anger to fever-height.

When Death on the Pale Horse came to London, it came in the quietest guise from overhead, with a noise like the bursting of a paper bag. A little man underneath the first faint explosion beat the air about him with his hands as though he were struggling with something invisible. Then he lay down in the roadway in the path of the streaming motor cars coming into Hyde Park, where he began to vomit very freely and comfortably over the white macadam. There was nothing in sight to account for his sudden indisposition. Presently people around him began to fight with their hands above their heads as though they had been bitten. Then they threw themselves down and followed the example of the sick little man. They, in the phrase of the day " sucked the gas," and died in intolerable agony. Gradually a great number of what looked like silver fishes dropped lightly on London and the gas was freely released. The initial rush was for the Underground :

The first comers had surged into the lifts and started them down, and those above, thrust helplessly forward, had fallen down those

shafts until they were filled to the brim with suffocated and dying people. . . . The tunnels were by this time stuffed with people who had fallen electrocuted on the live rails, the fresh waves of humanity getting the current through them, and the bodies lifting under the rhythmic surge of the pulsating current.

When the poison wave passed the Submerged People came out from the East End and wrecked the West:

As the current rushed forward the length of the Strand, the old church of St. Clement Danes, set in the middle of the roadway, acted as a breakwater to part it. It was here as though by instinct and the memory of long marches of the unemployed from the Thames Embankment, the torrent threw off two waves—one down Norfolk Street and the other down Arundel Street, down to the Embankment under the leadership of a man who called on them to wreck " the bloody hotels and clubs " in Northumberland Avenue. These two spates, perhaps forty thousand strong, literally went through the facades of the Constitutional Club and hurled themselves against the Metropole and Victoria Hotels. They went through these places barehanded, the blood streaming from face and hand as they climbed through the windows.

A second gas wave was to come to London, and then the Senegalese. The black troops found a first landing from the air in Richmond Park. From this Royal Park, the Senegalese were distributed about the seven terminal electric stations which at this time fed this part of London, and as the armies of escaping people poured along the electric tracks they were met by these blacks under their white officers :

It was about five o'clock in the grey dawn that the blacks in their tasselled fezes and voluminous blue jeans made their appearance outside the old Richmond Bridge, over which already many thousands of those who had escaped the gas had passed towards Epsom and Ham until they had reached Leatherhead. About five thousand of them just thrown out of the carrier planes, came marching down the hill from Richmond Park, the white eye-balls rolling in the black faces. In all cases the refugees were given the choice of going back into the gas or dying under the knives of the soldiers.

Much more thoroughly Germany dealt with Paris :

There were no tearing night-bombers flinging down unquenchable phosphorous bombs, exploding with deafening detonation. There was from first to last very little gun-firing, because the target was practically invisible to the ground gunners. There was just the passing of a cloud of tiny planes like the flight of a cloud of locusts . . . and then there was nothing . . . nothing but the results. There was a fire-torn city in which the inhabitants were burned as in huge ghats. There was a city of millions in which large areas were poisoned and full of corpses which polluted the air. And then, after a while, there was typhoid and plague.

On land the Germans had made complete preparations for thoroughly occupying French territory. Large masses of them had collected in the Sedan basin, and it was here that the French planes came upon them to spray the grey mass beneath with death. It took the Teutons a long time to realise, in spite of the deadly efficacy of their own flying service that a single airman in a single poison plane was worth a hundred army corps. Five millions of young dead Germans were left behind on the broad fields of France.

The British Empire and all the civilised comity of nations went by the board. In London, as elsewhere, people were living very miserably in the underworld :

Thus passed the great White Civilisation which had endured for three thousand years; and thus came the beginnings of the Yellow, Brown and Black Civilisations which were to follow in the eternal cycle of evolution.

Not a cheerful book this, but even in its exaggeration a justified indictment of that coming war in which poison gas is so cheerfully prophesied by men of war as the main weapon of the future from that sky which children of this world so childishly regard as one of the envelopes of heaven.

LOUIS J. McQUILLAND.

LIBRARY LIST

THE RED PLANET. By W. J. Locke. The Bodley Head.

This is another of the reprints in the 2s. edition. "The Red Planet" is not one of the best of Locke's books and nothing like as good as "The Beloved Vagabond," but there is good stuff in it, though it does not seem so fine as when we read it while the war, of which it treats, was still on.

CLAD IN PURPLE MIST. By Catherine Dodd. Jarrolds. 7s. 6d.

Readers of "The Farthing Spinster" will encounter severe disappointment in this record of bucolic folk in the Isle of Man. The novel is severely local and gives us all the detestable colloquialisms of Manx life. Even Hall Caine can do this better than Miss Dodd. If this clever lady is to do anything with her future work she will have to restore the Farthing family in London.

KATHLEEN AND I AND OF COURSE VERONICA. By Richmal Crompton. Hodder & Stoughton. 7s. 6d.

Papa, Mamma and Baby have been the subjects of countless episodes in the fiction of England and France. Mr. Crompton is to be commended that in their presentation again he has found a method of his own. Each brief occurrence to the family of three is done with admirable humour and some originality.

TURBOT WOLFE. By William Plomer. The Hogarth Press. 7s. 6d.

Uncommonly well done this seemingly simple tale of a strange white trader in Africa. Turbot Wolfe astonishes people by his morality and his outspokenness. He has few other qualities. The book is a record of the people he encounters at his trading station, who are distinctly unconventional and who pay little attention to the colour line in sex. The record has a kind of madness in it as of one raving in the heights of what novelists call brain-fever, but has the merit of being thoroughly interesting. The characterisation of Turbot as indicated by himself is rather remarkable.

YELLOW CORN. By Upton Gray. Hodder & Stoughton. 7s. 6d.

All the strength of the English countryside is in this admirable first novel. As regards the human element the strength inclines to a bitter obstinacy as in the case of John Simpson's bitter determination that his daughter, Clary, shall not wed the upright son of a crooked enemy. Simpson's favoured suitor is Ned Amyon, a well-to-do farmer with miserly instincts. The course of true love does not run particularly smoothly, and this is part of the truth of "Yellow Corn."

THE LONGS OF JAMAICA AND HAMPTON COURT. By Robert Mowbray Howard. Simpkin Marshall. 36s.

These Colonial families are the most intensely English of any. You have to go to the Longs of Jamaica to realise what English nationalism really means. But there is more in the book than that. There is a lot of half-intimate history in the middle eighteenth and early nineteenth centuries, and it is a book to be studied along with the Virginians. Some of the correspondence of the Longs has an excellent dignified simplicity.

THE GRIP-FAST ENGLISH BOOKS. Longman Green. 1s. 6d. each.

It is always bad to acquire knowledge but these little books extract most of the poison from the process. The titles are somewhat high-falutin' :—(1) "The Spirit of Childhood"; (2) "The Opening Gate"; (3) "When the World was Young"; (4) "The Spirit of Adventure." But there are some jolly good selections in the various books which lead one from "Bethlehem," by Laurence Housman, to "The Race for the South Pole" (Capt. Scott).

BOOTH AND THE SPIRIT OF LINCOLN. By Bernie Babcock. Lippincott. 7s. 6d.

Mrs. Babcock has already written two unnecessary books about Abraham Lincoln. The third one is even less effectual than its predecessors. The idea of the story is fairly good. It represents the assassin of Lincoln, John Wilkes Booth, as actually escaping from the hands of the law, and, in his long flight, being pursued by the spirit of the martyred president. Such an idea requires a distinction of treatment that Mrs. Babcock is utterly incapable of.

THE AUTOBIOGRAPHY OF A SUPER TRAMP. By W. H. Davies. SELECTED PREJUDICES. By H. L. Mencken. WIDE SEAS AND MANY LANDS. By Arthur Mason. Jonathan Cape. 3s. 6d. each.

This is an excellent series of reprints. A stiff cloth cover and good print. Davies's autobiography needs no bush. Mencken is by no means a fool although an American. Of course he underlines his sentiments but you can get a very good idea of what America is and might be from his somewhat pompous and slightly acid criticisms. Arthur Mason's sea book is a classic. It has the real touch of the salt,

but we are sure that all our readers have read it, or read about it, and we need only recommend them to buy this very excellent edition.

THE SECRET THAT WAS KEPT. By Elizabeth Robins. Hutchinson. 7s. 6d.

Elizabeth Robins has done so much good work that we have a tenderness in approaching this, her latest volume. It is written with something of the author's old flair for description and emotional tenseness—but there are large long tracts of tedium which, faint yet pursuing, we impatiently traverse. While we retain our old admiration for the author we do not think much either of the secret or the way it was kept.

SEA-GIRT JUNGLES. By J. C. L. Collonette. Hutchinson. 18s.

This is a fascinating book, written with swift imagination and that eye for detail which will discover more in a walk through Balham than many a one can unearth in an expedition throughout Africa. The sport of photography makes excellent reading and the various dangers and difficulties of the camera man set the reader palpitating with envy and admiration. A rattling good yarn. We commend this book to everybody.

BEYOND THE BOSPHOROUS. By Lady Dorothy Mills. Duckworth. 15s.

Adventures, as we know, are to the adventurous, but there is little of the romance of the open road in this account of a visit to the land of romance and harems. Jerusalem in particular does not seem to have inspired the author with anything but a desire for fine writing. There are many purple passages in this book which are passable. It is when Lady Dorothy Mills merges into philosophy that we are fatigued. There are many finely finished and interesting photographs.

WOODROW WILSON. By William Allen White. Ernest Benn. 21s.

The American people have always dramatised their Presidents. National heroes have been poured into a popular mould with such persistence that it is difficult to perceive their natural features. The same process has been adopted in the life of President Wilson, wherein William Allen White has followed in the footsteps of custom. The author tells us of the great man's home life; his early love passages; and his academic honours. We get no fresh light on his psychology, however, there is nothing of the Strachey scalpel in this memoir, which is amiably written and very well disposed.

Published by the Proprietors, G.K.'s WEEKLY, LTD., at their offices, 20 & 21 Essex Street, Strand, London, W.C.2 (incorporating THE NEW WITNESS). Telephone No. City 1978. Printed by THE ALLIED PRESS, LTD., 19 Clerkenwell Close, London, E.C.1. Sole agents for Australasia: Gordon & Gotch (Australasia), Ltd. Sole Agents for South Africa: Central News Agency, Ltd.

G.K.'s WEEKLY, November 6th, 1926

DOWN TO TWOPENCE

G.K.'s Weekly

EDITED BY G. K. CHESTERTON.

No. 86.—Vol. IV.   Week ending Saturday, November 6, 1926   PRICE TWOPENCE
YEARLY (52 ISSUES)
10s. 10d.

Telephone No. City 1978.   *Offices, 20 & 21, Essex Street, Strand, W.C.2.*

CONTENTS:

TWOPENNY TRASH

WITH the present issue this paper appears for the first time as a twopenny paper, of reduced size and with a special and relatively limited purpose. It has been found possible to continue in this form, and the course has been adopted for reasons that refer to the new principle of propaganda; the formation of the League. The League was at one time tentatively described as The League of the Little People. It was afterwards felt that the title was rather too much of a good joke to be a good definition. In this connection it has something of a serious significance. We fear that the little people will now have to accept a little paper; but it is rather more relevant that they will have to pay a little price. Whatever may be said for the sixpenny standard in a magazine that is sold like a book, it was felt to be quite impossible in a paper that is to be sold like a pamphlet, or almost like a leaflet. In other words, the mass of people attending meetings or joining leagues are, if not to be dismissed as small people, at least to be congratulated on being types of small property. By changing from a literary to a social basis, the movement becomes much more definitely democratic; and is conceived as covering many more people than can commonly afford to take in a literary weekly. Henceforth this paper, if it continues, will continue as the organ of a general organisation; and will therefore be justified in being (what such official organs usually are) rather more business-like and more brief. The paper has sufficed to found the League. The League may suffice to circulate the paper. But the kind of paper which a League circulates is at once more popular and more practical than the kind of paper which can outline the philosophy for the founding of a League. The League is what the paper has done; the paper henceforth will be what the League can do.

Cobbett's Register, in which appeared the last notes of that normal ideal we represent, before it disappeared in the darkness of nineteenth century plutocracy, was called Twopenny Trash; first by its enemies in contempt and then by its editor in pride. And it is something of a consolation to reflect that the remarks of that rowdy demagogue have passed into classical literature, when so many things then counted classical are forgotten; when so many Elegant Extracts from the Classics, so many Lines by a Noble Lord and Essays by a Person of Quality, remain as lumber in neglected libraries. It would be audacity to suggest that the elegances of our time also may pass; and that posterity may not read all our literary weeklies, with their exquisite translations from the Russian and their gems of Imagist poetry. There was a time when ours also might have been a literary weekly, if it could have worked with the commercial system of the age; that is, if it could have printed on one page a graceful essay by a don and on another page an advertisemen of a toothpaste calculated to make him sick. But we are working against the commercial system of the age, as was Cobbett in his own time; and the only consolations of such a condition are laughter and the love of friends—and of foes.

NOTES OF THE WEEK

Down to Twopence

SINCE last we appeared before you we have been banting. And though it has been decided not to associate our League by name with The Little People, it will, as long as we live, or until our circulation becomes much more active, be associated with a very little paper. We are half the size we were, but we are only one-third as expensive, and if, as we hope, we have kept the features you want most, then you will find us far better value for money. The prime arguments used to persuade us to this reduction in price (and consequently in size) were that if G.K.'S WEEKLY is to survive it must be as the organ of the League, that the League needs an organ, and that for League purposes a twopenny paper is far more valuable than a sixpenny. For example, it is obvious that strangers at public meetings of the League will not pay sixpence, but might pay twopence, to discover what these queer people are driving at. Again, we could not ask members of the League to buy a number of copies of a sixpenny paper, but we can and do ask all of them to *buy three copies of the new Tuppenny, and give two copies away.* But please buy them through your usual newsagent!

Wanted, a Song!

WE have lost a number of valuable features—notably the weekly articles on Novels of the Day, by Louis J. McQuilland, and on the Drama, by J. K. Prothero. The Scrapbook page was the peculiar pet of the Assistant Editor. He has seen it scrapped with some emotion. McQuilland, Prothero, and the contributors to the Scrapbook are not lost to us, they are working in the League, and if and when the paper waxes fat once more they will be at our call. Meanwhile, it is possible that the League may have from time to time debates or discussions on literature and the theatre, for we suppose that it will gain in strength by attracting to it members of the public who are not at present interested in social and political theories. As for the Scrapbook, we trust that at some of our meetings there will be songs, and that some of them will be intentionally funny. Here, indeed, is a question of vital importance: we must have a marching song; who will give it to us? In the early days of the Socialist movement it had a number of fine songs, and it went wrong completely only when it became obsessed with that mournful ditty: " The Red Flag."

The Maintenance Fund

THE following contributions have been received:— K. L. S. and K. M. H., 10s.; K. H. Josling, 6s. 3d.; B. Orford, 12s.; J. B. Trinick, 2s. 6d.; R. J. Collins, £1; 10 Bedians, 15s. Now we have to point out that during the past few weeks some of the half-crowners have not sent in their contributions; that the reduction of price to twopence is in the nature of an experiment, and that at the end of four or five weeks we shall inform the League how much it will have to find each week if it wants the paper to continue as its organ. We know that most of the delinquents are busy supporting the League; but the burden will be all the heavier if we are deprived of the support on which we depended.

The League

THE next public meeting of the League will be at the Chatham Town Hall at 7.30 on Monday, November 15. The Editor of the paper will speak. The Chatham Branch, which has organised the meeting, is proving itself very energetic. An informal canvass of likely supporters has been taken, and the sale of the paper is being pushed briskly. The secretary is Mr. J. Murphy, 55 Paget Street, Gillingham, Kent, with whom intending members should communicate. Equal activity is taking place in Croydon. An interesting letter has been sent by Mr. H. Cullen, 39 Bishop Street, Cheetham, the secretary of the Manchester Branch, to his members. We quote part of it:—" May we offer the following suggestions to our members and sympathisers:—(1) To spend the same amount of money, viz., 6d., for their usual copy, in purchasing three copies at the new price. (2) To circulate the new price amongst their friends and acquaintances. (3) To make enquiries for the Paper at newsagents and free libraries. (4) To obtain permission to show the Paper's placard outside any shop or house on a main road or thoroughfare. (5) It is essential that any increase in the circulation of the Paper should flow through the customary trade channels, viz., newsagents and retailers, so as not to antagonise them, and not ordered from head office." We shall publish a report of their meeting held Wednesday, November 3, in our next issue. We hear from Oxford that the demand for G.K.'S WEEKLY exceeds the supply. This must be seen to. A small meeting will be held this week, when the branch will be formed. The next meeting of the Liverpool Branch will be on Thursday, November 11, in the Grenville Café (opposite Exchange Station), in Titheburn Street, Liverpool, at 8 p.m. A secretary is needed for the very lively branch at Bath. Mr. Green-Armytage, c/o G.K.'S WEEKLY, will be very glad to hear of one.

THE CENTRAL BRANCH

The Central Branch will meet on Friday, November 12, at 5.30 p.m. in the Essex Hall, Essex Street, W.C.2. This is to be a business meeting to enrol members, elect a working committee, and decide on a practical policy for the Branch. Anyone interested in the League may attend.

A set debate has been purposely omitted in order to give free and ample discussion of what has been done, what has not been done, and what you want to be done.

It has been suggested that in addition to the Branch meetings at the Essex Hall, there should be informal meetings every Friday at which members may discuss problems at issue between themselves. It has therefore been arranged for a supply of Distributists to be on tap every Friday evening at 5.30 at " The Devereux," Devereux Court, off Essex Street.

The next monthly meeting, with debate (after November 12), will be on Friday, December 17, at 5.30 p.m., in the Essex Hall.   G. C. HESELTINE.

Hon. Secretary, Central Branch.

TOP—

THE EXAMPLE OF MOND

There are some who take an academic and abstract interest in the probable price of coal, and the methods of obtaining it; and to these theorists it may be of interest to know that a scheme like that urged in the *Daily Express* and elsewhere will probably take shape at no distant date. A great Trust will be formed by all the commercial interests involved, who will possess themselves of all the coal obtainable, so that it will cease to be obtainable by anybody else. It will be managed on the sane lines of private enterprise, free from the strangling restrictions of State responsibility. There will be no pedantic fancies of fixing a price or a wage; but business men of ripe judgment, having obtained all the coal in the country, will adjudge the price with reference to the reasonable and legitimate interests of their great business. There is no intention of forming a Monopoly; and Sir Otto Goldstein, in making this disclaimer, declared that he had no other motive but a desire to protect England from the influence of foreign capitalists.

It is a happy coincidence, tending to cover conveniently a number of parallel cases, that a commercial combination for the purpose of purchasing Wood in all its forms has also entered the field with every promise of success. Nobody can question the energy and thoroughness of this great public work; including as it does all trees, twigs, sticks, matches and shavings on the floors of carpenters' shops; from each of which the fortunate speculators will be able to extract a considerable profit. Needless to say, they have no thought of creating anything resembling a Monopoly, and Mr. Karl Guggenheimer, the controller of the combination, explained that he was moved only by indignation at the thought of foreigners obtaining a commercial footing in our markets.

Somewhat similar in character, though even wider in scope, is the bold proposal that Fire as such, wherever and however it may come into existence, should *ipso facto* become the property of the Imperial Light & Heat Co., Ltd., so that the amount of warmth in each room may be regulated by a central and responsible authority, which will be free from all the soulless tyranny of Socialism, but empowered to make sure that the habits of striking matches, lighting candles, smoking pipes and similar actions are kept under a closer control. The very thought of a Monopoly has never crossed the minds of these eager public servants; and the most important of them, Sir Joachim Jugend-Jacob, declared with tears that he would forswear all monopolist pleasures, if once he could see his England freed from the wicked foreigner.

Fortunately ours is a country in which progress, though steady, is prudent and slow; and as Professor Emanuel Gottlieb-Strauss wittily said, the proposal to apply the principle of private enterprise and private property to Air is as yet only in the Air. For all his good-humoured jesting, however, the Professor is a man of deep and earnest purpose, nor has he been idle touching the scheme which he thus lightly sketched. We are informed that before long a prospectus for a company owning all the Air of these islands will be offered to the wealthy investor; and that the present chaotic and careless use of air will be reduced to reasonable order. There is nothing in all this that even savours of the idea of Monopoly; and the very name of Gottlieb-Strauss is warrant for the patriotic purpose, which is that of a national defence against the conspiracy of Aliens.

—AND TAIL

THE DEVIL IN SOLUTION

If anyone wants to know what certain wild and violent persons mean by the stink of Parliament, the stale and corrupt savour of cant which really seems to stop the nostrils like a poisonous atmosphere, which has discredited our decayed parliamentarism everywhere and raised both the Fascists and the Bolshevists against it, he will find everything he wants in one small newspaper paragraph; in the episode of people severely rebuking a Labour member for saying that M.P.'s were occasionally drunk. There is every sort of offence in the thing, each worse than the last. There is (1) the claim of Members of Parliament to be a privileged class of priests or nobles, not to be criticised by the populace, in spite of the contrary pretence that they are representatives and messengers of the people. There is (2) the idiotic idea that it would be possible to collect six hundred human beings in a community which (thank God) still drinks wine and ale, and in their cases can afford to buy it, and then imagine that by the mere act of being elected to Parliament, the whole lot of them become physically and psychologically incapable of ever taking a glass or two more than is quite good for them. There is (3) the low and smelly sentimentalism (borrowed from the richest and therefore worst elements in America) which supposes that excess in a particular liquid, or even moderation in that liquid, is somehow a sin set apart; something with a savour of superstitious horror. There is (4) the sort of fixed and frozen falsehood that is quite independent of reality; that can pull a long face that is as unreal as a mask about something that everybody jokes about; something that is talked about casually in every club; not as a scandal, but as a pretty probable ordinary occurrence or accident of daily life in a large society. There is (5) the sort of snobbishness which is also sneakishness; which implies indirectly rather than directly that while anyone may make jokes about drunken cabmen or drunken navvies, nobody above a certain income must be supposed to get drunk at all. There is (6) the strange instantaneous instinct by which the spirit of Fuss, which is also the spirit of Futility, rushes in to make the very most of something which it professes to deplore as distressing and indecent; the spirit that cannot leave anything alone, even when any sane person who really regretted it would have ignored it; the spirit of advertisement that must advertise everything. There is (7) the insolent inequality on which Dr. Salter remarked with very just indignation; by which we shut up the drinking places of the poor and keep open this drinking place of the rich; on the pretence that they never drink. Lastly, there is (8) the amazing ignorance of the world outside the House, as it is to-day. The rising generation is, if anything, rather too lax and cynical about such things. We have seen a play, supposed to be funny, in which two refined young ladies gradually get drunk. Is it supposed that the whole public will be prostrated by the rumour that two middle-aged politicians once drank a superfluous glass of port? Those who know anything of politicians will not think it the most superfluous or the most sinful of their acts. It would be much better even if politicians were tipsy in the House than that they should be venal and treacherous in the House; and men are better engaged in taking beer than in taking bribes.

PARLIAMENT FROM WITHIN
By Sir Henry Slesser, K.C., M.P.

THE necessity to continue that species of martial law which the Government have now employed for six months during the coal dispute, made it necessary for Parliament to re-assemble last week. It is my opinion that the framers of the Emergency Powers Act never intended that Regulations made under it should extend to the abrogation of the common law and the creation of new, hitherto unknown, offences. Were the Regulations to be considered in a Court of Law, it is quite possible that it would be decided that some of them were beyond the powers of the Act itself which speaks only of the making of Regulations to secure the necessary supplies of the commodity which is the subject of the dispute and the preservation of peace; but in the absence of any such legal determination, the only thing possible to do is to point out in Parliament the extent and danger of these extra-legal edicts. This demonstration, which is of the utmost importance to all lovers of liberty, is consistently ignored in the Press; indeed, every time an attack has been made on these governmental decrees, the Press has confined itself to a chronicle of some wholly ephemeral or histrionic topic, and the great majority of the people to-day fail to realise the extent and ambiguity of the powers which the Government, under the Act, have vested in the magistracy. The Regulations, for the most part, are taken, without modification, from the Defence of the Realm Act and assume the existence of an enemy—a view quite consistent with that of a noble lord who, speaking recently in the City of London, compared the deprivation of the means of livelihood from the miners to the blockade of the Germans and did not seem displeased with the analogy.

Under the Regulations a new offence, unknown to the law—the offence of disaffection—is created. It is undefined except in so far as it has been considered to be one of the elements of sedition and gives power, apparently, to the magistrates to make criminal the expression of any opinion with which they may happen to disagree. The Home Secretary, in justifying the continuance of this martial law, was at pains to explain that the merit of the Regulations was their leniency; but apart from those cases where new offences are created—cases in which no conviction could have been made in the ordinary law and where consequently no question of leniency could arise—as a matter of fact the Statutory penalties against intimidation of workers are less severe than the penalties laid down in the Emergency Powers Act. For in the case of the Act of 1875, where the term of imprisonment, three months, is the same as in the Regulations, there is an alternative fine of £20 in the place of the £100 penalty which the Regulations prescribe.

It has been my lot to have to point this out to a cynical and attenuated House on many occasions; but there is no doubt that so long as this dispute continues this power will be jealously preserved.

That the Regulations are indefensible is made very clear by the exercise of the police of their power under them to prohibit meetings held by miners' leaders. I have recently come from a mining area, and it is the unanimous opinion of the people on the spot that feelings of disaffection are far more readily kindled by the prohibition of what they assure me has always been an orderly meeting than by its permission, and, so far as the miners are concerned, they ask nothing better than that the Government should continue to interfere to prevent their case being stated to the men; but, if a wider view be taken, it is surely directly against the public interest that, on the plea of a fear of a breach of the peace, the argument should be weighted so much in favour of the coal owners that they may be allowed to publish, as they are allowed to publish, the most vehement attacks on the miners' leaders in the form of leaflets and other propaganda while the miners are prevented from replying.

The Government appear now to be in the last stages of demoralisation. In the Prime Minister's speech all suggestion that there is any solution to the coal difficulty, except that of driving the men back by means of privation, was abandoned. We heard little or nothing of the lamentable departure from the terms of the Commission's Report; re-organisation was never mentioned, nor was there any real defence attempted by Mr. Baldwin of the owners' refusal to negotiate a National Agreement. It is even uncertain whether, if the men agreed to district agreements, the owners would consent, and so this dispute drags on day after day, week after week, while industry is destroyed and credit vanishes and a vast mass of ill-feeling and suspicion is being created which Bolshevist agitators may envy, but which must cause grave anxiety to every patriotic citizen.

House of Commons.

Rhymes for the Young Londoner

THE ROUND POND.

The man who gave this pond its name
Was really very sound.
I doubt if many ponds there are
Quite so rotund or circular—
To put it bluntly—round.

Here is a splendid place to sail
A schooner or a yacht,
A steamer or a brigantine—
If you posses such things I mean—
I, being poor, do not.

Let me forewarn you of one risk
You must prepare to take—
The wind at any time may drop,
Whereon—your ship will simply stop
Half-way across the lake.

I knew a boy whose bran-new boat
Became becalmed this way.
He's hung about—excuse these tears—
Awaiting its return for years,
And now he's old and grey.

Adopting my superb device
The risk is very slight.
Obtain a hundred yards of string:
Hitch one end to the ship, old thing,
But hold the other tight.

Be sure the knot is firmly tied.
And *do* for goodness' sake
Hang on to *your* end. This prevents
All risk of loss or accidents—
Unless the string should break.

L. N. J. & R. W.

STRAWS IN THE WIND
THE YANKEE AND THE CHINAMAN
By G. K. CHESTERTON

PERHAPS it would seem a little abrupt to leave Mr. H. G. Wells with the single word of farewell I appended to his last letter; and yet there is really nothing else to say. I cannot now comprehend what his difficulty is or why he cannot accept a perfectly plain statement. Catholics believe that the Fall of Man did definitely happen. The words Fall of Man do not in the English language mean a snake twisted round an apple-tree; any more than the words Fall of Troy mean a snake twisted three times round the neck of a priest, as in Virgil's description of the Trojan disaster. The words mean, in their natural sense, a descent from a higher state to a lower. That man did so descend, and not merely ascend, is an important dogma; and we all hold it. Its precise relation to time we do not profess to know; for the very obvious reason that a spiritual change might take any time or no time; it might be instantaneous or millennial; it might mean the loss of a whole civilisation, or the silent surrender to evil of a solitary contemplative, leaving no terrestrial traces at all. It is palpably futile to look for the place or period; because an internal beatitude might exist in any place or period. What I cannot understand is why anybody should deny us the right to say that Troy came to an end, because he has seen certain pictures of the Wooden Horse and we will not answer for all the details.

The Fall reminds me, however, of another scientific character even more bothered by abstract conceptions. As Mr. Green-Armytage truly said, the real point about the Fall is pride; and I know no point more difficult to make clear to most modern people as an abstract conception; even when they themselves accept it as a concrete conception. Nothing indeed is quainter than the way in which modern people often profess to see nothing wrong about pride; but do in practice find something very wrong indeed about any man who is proud. Any chance collection of clubmen, with the conventional morals and manners of the modern world, would probably dismiss as a mere mystical paradox a dogma which said: "Pride is worse for the soul than profligacy or intemperance." But they do in practice dislike the conceited man in the club much more than the man who reads French novels or drinks unnecessary brandies and sodas. The truth is too near to them in practice to be visible to them in theory. Their instincts have already acted on it, before their intellects come to consider it and reject it. An undergraduate may be ready to go all the way with the philosopher Nietzsche; but not to go on a walking tour with the Superman. In short, those who think it theological nonsense to say that self-sufficiency is a sin have not the smallest difficulty in recognising self-sufficiency as a nuisance. And they are not half such good critics of the doctrine they do not know as they are of the man they do know.

But there is another and smaller but still very practical product of this problematic self-esteem. One perfectly practical objection to self-praise is that it produces rudeness. It produces it not only in the arrogant person, who is the aggressor, but in the other or ordinary man who is acting in self-defence. It is very difficult to see how there can be any other defence. When a man bases his whole argument on the implied first principle, "I am an example of the sort of social type which the world should encourage," there is not only a natural temptation but almost a logical necessity to answer, "You are not." It is the amusing weakness of the self-satisfied that they always, with quite a flourish, lay open their guard to this riposte. We all know the sort of prosperous person who thinks it quite enough to say, "Well, I went to that sort of school" or "When I began, I was in the same position" or "If I hadn't, I shouldn't be what I am now." The mildest disputant will be disposed to ask the question, "What are you now?" The less mild disputant will be disposed to answer it.

Starting with the most amiable intentions, and without the least personal hostility, I am disposed to talk like this when a great American like Mr. Edison, for instance, disposes in a radiant and rapid manner of the whole problem of the moral quality of a mechanical civilisation. It is due to him to say that in this case it is not of himself personally, but of his countrymen collectively, that his remarks are so radaint. But they raise exactly the same question; for the reasons already suggested; that they *assume* that the social type he represents stands for universal satisfaction; whereas it seems to some of us that it only stands for a self-satisfaction. And the awkwardness of that argument, as I have said, is that it is very hard to answer it simply without being rude.

Mr. Edison says, in an interesting article in the *Forum* that the proof of the superiority of mechanical civilisation, as compared with an old civilisation like that of China, is to be found in the sort of American who is alert and eager and inventive; that is, in the sort of American that he is himself. How on earth is one to answer that; except by saying point blank that we do not think quite so much of him as he thinks of himself? He speaks very scornfully of the Chinese; but there are any number of Chinamen who understand everything that matters much more " alertly " than he does. He would probably not understand what we meant if we mentioned some Chinese superiorities; but that only shows how very little he understands. If we compare the life described in " Babbitt " with the life described in a remarkable recent book about the Chinese family, we shall be struck chiefly by one thing. It is that both lives are bound on every side by convention and tribal taboos; but that those of the American are dowdy, threadbare and third-rate; while those of the Chinaman are dignified, poetical and bright with colour. Poor Babbitt confessed that he had never once really done as he liked; and perhaps he would be puzzled if I told him that what he missed most was that generous outward gesture of sacrifice and dedication, by which the Chinaman burns joss-sticks to his ancestors and the Christian candles to his patron saint. But the point is—how can one say how much there is of Mr. Babbitt in Mr. Edison with proper politeness to the latter?

The strange thing about scientific genius is not only its narrowness, but the stupendous sort of stupidity that it can show outside its narrow limits. That is what makes America startling; and a country of comparatively diffused light, even if it be twilight, like China, so much more soothing. We all know what marvels Mr. Edison has made; but none of them are so marvellous as something I once saw that he said. He was reported in a serious American magazine as saying that he would now subject all this spiritual notion to a new scientific test; and if there really was a soul, he would find it. Now no educated Chinaman could be so stupid as that. He might doubt whether there was a soul, or say with Confucian agnosticism that he knew nothing about the soul, or with Buddhistic pessimism that renunciation was the release of the soul; but he would know that a soul is by definition something like a thought or a memory or a relation. And any philosophic Chinaman would know what to think of a man who said: " I have got a new gun that will shoot a hole through your memory of last Monday " or " I have got a saw sharp enough to cut up the cube root of 666 " or " I will boil your affection for Aunt Susan till it is quite liquid.

THE RETURN OF DON QUIXOTE

By G. K. CHESTERTON

CHAPTER XIV. (Continued).

THE PARTING OF THE WAYS.

OUTSIDE in the dark streets the crowds had grown thicker and thicker; and there were murmurs about mystifications and delays. Like all men in the unnatural posture of revolt, they needed to be perpetually stimulated by something happening; whether it were favourable or hostile. A defiance on the other side would do; but a defiance on their own side was the best; and there had been promises of a great demagogic display that evening. There had been as yet no positive unpunctuality; but something told them that there was somewhere a little hitch. And it was five minutes later that Braintree amid a roar of cheers, appeared on the balcony.

He had hardly said a dozen words before it became apparent that he was talking in a tone that had been unusual in English politics, even in what had been called by its critics revolutionary politics. His voice sounded as iron sounds amid a clatter of tin; nor could those who applauded him understand, any better than those who opposed him, the finality and sense of having come to the end of a road or the edge of a precipice, that was really the burden of that iron voice. But he had also something to say that was of the final sort. He refused a tribunal; and in that there is something of the sort that always moves the deep element of epic poetry in a mob. For nothing can really be approved or applauded except finality. That is why all the ethics of evolution and expansive ideas of indefinite progress have never taken hold upon any human crowd; and why the speeches of modern politicians are less and less reported; and why they hide themselves in ignominious safety behind the veils of wireless broadcasting and every indirect and impersonal method.

The new scheme of government had set up a seat of judgment, or chamber of inquiry, for the settlement of the strike which Braintree led. It was a strike now largely confined to the Trade Unions of his own district; which were engaged in the manufacturing of dyes and paints, originally derived from coal-tar. The very genuine energy that supported the new government had grappled immediately with the industrial problem in question; and promised to treat it in a larger and more imaginative spirit than had been possible to many of the conventional committees of the past. It was probable that it would be settled on somewhat saner and simpler lines than those of the complicated compromises of the old professional politician. But it would be settled. That was what the new rulers very legitimately claimed. And that was what Braintree and the strikers very legitimately objected to.

" For nearly a hundred years," he said, " they have thundered at us about our duty to respect the Constitution: the King and the House of Lords—and even the House of Commons. We had to respect that too. (Laughter.) We were to be perfect Constitutionalists. Yes, my friends, we were to be the only Constitutionalists. We were the quiet people, the loyal subjects, the people who took the King and the lords seriously. But they were to be free enough. Whenever the fancy took them to upset the Constitution, they were

to be indulged in all the pleasures of revolution.. They could in twenty-four hours turn the Government of England upside down; and tell us that we were all to be ruled not by a Constitutional monarchy but by a fancy dress ball. Where is the King? Who is the King? I have heard he is a librarian interested in the Hittites. (Laughter.) And we are summoned before this revolutionary tribunal—(cheers)—to explain why we have for forty years, under intolerable provocation, failed to resort to revolution. (Loud cheers.) We do not mind talking to their lunatic librarian if they like. We will confront this ancient traditional order of chivalry that is ten weeks old; we will face the profound Conservative principles of continuity that never existed until the other day. But we will not submit to its judgment. We would not submit to lawful Toryism. We will not now submit to lawless Toryism. And if this Wardour Street curiosity shop sends us a message that we must yield; our answer is not in doubt; you will give it as readily as I."

He turned with an abrupt gesture on the balcony and another roar shook the building.

(*To be continued.*)

NOW WHAT ABOUT IT?

PEOPLE who have been clamouring loudly for something practical to be done are now given the chance of helping to do it. Therefore, the directors of G.K.'s WEEKLY have consented to the experiment of continuing to run at a loss, in order to give the League an opportunity of extending the paper's radius of action as an organ of the League's principles.

This experiment must be justified, and in a very few issues too, by something like a fivefold increase in the circulation. There is no tolerable alternative. Here then are some practical suggestions for the practical people.

It must be a point of honour with every reader not to take advantage of the reduction in price—yet. In other words *every reader who has been buying one copy at sixpence must take three copies at twopence* until his two surplus copies have secured two new readers. They must be bought and distributed with that end only in view.

That is the general reader's job if he wants the paper to thrive and return to its former size and glory.

League members and branch secretaries have a further and more important reason for securing and restoring the paper.

The League without this organ of expression will thrive about as well as a dumb tipster. It is not exaggerating the position to say that most probably the League will have to make itself responsible for the success of this experiment and save the paper which gave it birth or die of inanition, for it is certainly not yet strong enough to leave its mother.

These facts are of *immediate* importance. Therefore every League member must take extra copies for distribution. They may be given away intelligently or left lying about in propitious places which the wit of members may select. Any member with a glimmer of enthusiasm will make a dozen copies a week his minimum. He will also pester newsagents and bookstall-keepers who do not show the paper.

Branch secretaries must make it their first business to have an ample supply on sale at every meeting, and see that it is sold. Those who have not yet organised meetings must do so within the next two or three weeks if they want to save the organ and give the League an effective start. They should notify the Editor in good time for notices to appear.

It cannot be too strongly emphasised that unless effective steps are taken *at once* the development of the League and the propagation of its principles will be seriously restricted

The Executive of the League has taken the initiative—it is now up to the critics and Dutch uncles to follow it up and see that it is not lost. The first and most practical support they can give is to increase the effective range of the organ of the League's principles.

THE COCKPIT

To the Editor of G.K.'s WEEKLY.

THE FALL OF MAN

DEAR SIR,—I fancy that Mr. Wells will be content with his heresy for some while yet. Father McNabb has been summoned; and, really, I am not yet positively certain that he didn't give that quotation from Aquinas as a joke, as a little test to see whether we were awake or not.

The Catholic, apparently must say to himself "I will hold the first chapter of Genesis without wavering. When, however, I discover—as I discovered at school—that there are several conflicting and even contradictory versions, I will make a choice between them. Further difficulties can always be met by symbolical interpretation."

It may seem to many that that is not holding the first chapter of Genesis without wavering. The flippant suggestion might be made that under these terms we would undertake to hold anything, however slippery.

But Mr. Chesterton's reply is not very much better. He ingeniously and somewhat irrelevantly gives us a number of variations on an old Provincial air. It is not until the last paragraph but one that he tackles his opponent. He says—

"What I complain of in the evolutionary ethics of Mr. Wells and Mr. Shaw is that if good is only before us, a thing to be grateful for, and in no sense behind us, a thing to be regained, I cannot see what eternal test we have of whether any entirely new development is good or not.

That is a very reasonable objection, and the whole point of such philosophy has been to answer it. I will not insist that Mr. Chesterton is provincial, because he has read the theory and is still asking the question. As Mr. Wells has probably remarked more than once in the course of this controversy, life is always striving, going in a direction. How do we know that it is the right direction?

Individually, we do not know. Any more than Columbus knew where the Atlantic was leading to. Or Mr. Chesterton knows what Adam looked like before the Fall.

Yours,

G. WALTER STONIER.

DR. OSCAR LEVY AND CHRISTIANITY

SIR,—After reading Dr. Clarke's letter, I think I can sum up the affinity between Judaism and Nietzschean philosophy. Both stress the importance of the organism over the individual, as, for instance, the purpose of marriage in Judaism and the conception of the State in Prussianism. The individual purpose is subordinated to that of the group activity, whether that be State, Race, Nation, Religion or anything else. Christian philosophy stresses the importance of the individual. The opposite one which is shared in particular by the Jews and the Prussians, is the most dangerous to individual liberty yet conceived, and often obtains unthinking acceptance by those who ought to know better. It is well backed by International Finance, and can be observed at work in all forms of internationalism. Further, it is the basis of all forms of what is called "Socialism," and it must not be overlooked that Karl Marx was a Jew. It can even be discerned in the Trade Union movement, where the interests of the individuals comprising that movement are being subordinated to the interests of the group or "organisation." Here is a philosophy for The League to fight.

Yours, etc.,

JOSEPH O'NEILL.

JEWS AND CHRISTIANITY

SIR,—I appreciate the difficulties of Mr. Maurice B. Reckitt, but I think they arise from a disbelief in his own Scriptures. Like every other book, sacred or profane, everyone gets out of the Bible that which he brings to it. If he brings an "historic" belief, he gets out of it what it takes for history. I am on the side of St. Paul, whose faith was of a different kind. He said that the story of Abraham and his two wives and two sons was "an allegory," and, therefore, *not* history. Christ also said practically the same thing. When the Jews were boasting about being sons of Abraham Christ pointed out to them that the stones of Jerusalem had just as much right to the claim as they had—that is to say, none at all. There is another Scripture which I most fully believe in, but about which most Christians are complete atheists. It is again St. Paul who says it: "The latter killeth, but the spirit giveth life."

Mr. Reckitt refers to Christ being "in the succession of the Hebrew prophets." The prophets were great, but the people were not. I cannot find one of the prophets who has a good word to say for Mr. Reckitt's "great race." The great race stoned them, and afterwards built their sepulchres and boasted—as Jews boast to-day—of what fine fellows their prophets were. They treated Christ, who was in the succession in this respect, in the same way, except that they have not yet built His sepulchre. They have never understood Him, any more than Nicodemus did, and though they may become bishops or archbishops, Roman or Anglican, they never will understand Him until they deny themselves, that is, their Judaism, and are born again as Christ said.—Yours faithfully,

JOHN H. CLARKE, M.D.

THE RETORT COURTEOUS

DEAR SIR,—Will you kindly break the following story to Mr. Burrage?

Once upon a time a manager produced a play; what it was about I do not remember, but the critic of the *Daily Express* was surprised at the good reception given to its ill-chosen situations.

He wrote a criticism for his papers which was something like this:

" I do not understand why, but the audience laughed at a joke in doubtful taste, laughed at a timeworn situation, and they laughed at another aged platitude. I do not understand it, but they laughed."

Now the point of the story is that the enterprising manager of that theatre plastered the Underground lifts with a notice which read:

" The audience laughed—and laughed . . . and they laughed "

and signed it *Daily Express.*

Thus—not only misrepresenting the unfortunate critic, but also making it appear that he advocated that which he hated.

I would have been interested to give Mr. Burrage some results from real experience in mumming, and projecting an idea—as against his theories—but I will refrain even from telling him where he could see some of these plays produced.

Please reassure him. I have no desire to become his keeper.   Yours sincerely,

MOYA JOWETT.

LIBRARY LIST

THE LIFE OF SIR THOMAS MORE. By William Roper, his Son-in-Law. Blackie's Library of Golden Prose. 1s. 3d.
This is a handy series; the books slip easily into a pocket, and are well got up and printed.

THE RIVER FLOWS. By F. L. Lucas. The Hogarth Press. 7s. 6d.
As may be guessed this river flows in a triangle—the eternal triangle, to boot. The author takes his characters dreadfully seriously, not in a way that swamps his sense of humour, which is excellent, but in a way that intensifies their not very extraordinary emotions beyond recognition. The war passages are vivid.

THE OXFORD BOOK OF FRENCH VERSE. Chosen by St. John Lucas. Oxford: At the Clarendon Press. 8s. 6d.
This is a new edition of a work too well known and too widely appreciated to need further recommendation. The editors of the Oxford Books of Verse have an almost uncanny knack of finding the best things in the language. This has over 500 pages of them.

THE TRAIL OF THE BIG BEAR. By William Bleasdell Cameron. Duckworth. 7s. 6d.
We are, as a nation, keenly interested in Red Indians. But we are apt to be sentimental about them. Mr. Cameron's narrative, which deals with the Frog Lake massacres of 1885, will give a true idea of their characteristics, at any rate at that date. It is yet another proof of the truism that truth is stranger than fiction.

THE MIDNIGHT COURT AND THE ADVENTURES OF A LUCKLESS FELLOW. Translated from the Gaelic by Percy Arland Ussher. With a Preface by W. B. Yeats and woodcuts by Frank W. Peers. Cape. 6s.
Mr. Ussher, whose name is already familiar to readers of this journal, here shows himself in a new and more refulgent light. " The Midnight Court " was written by Brian Merriman early in the Eighteenth Century; it is a long satirical poem with a certain breezy vividness and no sense of proportion. But it has what Mr. Yeats calls in his preface " vitality," and Mr. Ussher's version is all poetry, which is more than can be said for most translations. The "get-up" of the book is superlatively good, so are the woodcuts.

THE LIFE OF ALFONSO DE CONTRERAS. Written by Himself. Jonathan Cape. 12s. 6d.
This is a great book of adventure. Alfonso who tells us here his own story was a Spanish soldier of fortune who ran away to the wars at the age of fourteen and rose by his valour and resources from the office of turnspit to the dignity of a Knight of Malta. He was of the same kidney as Sir Dugald Dalgetty and the acid touch of his scepticism is a nice contrast to the hazardous adventures he endures. We do not understand Spanish, but Mr. David Hannay's translation reads very well.

Published by the Proprietors, G.K.'s WEEKLY, LTD., at their offices, 20 & 21 Essex Street, Strand, London, W.C.2 (incorporating THE NEW WITNESS). Telephone No. City 1978. Printed by THE ALLIED PRESS, LTD., 19 Clerkenwell Close, London, E.C.1. Sole agents for Australasia: Gordon & Gotch (Australasia), Ltd. Sole Agents for South Africa: Central News Agency, Ltd.

G.K.'s WEEKLY, January 22nd, 1927.

G.K.'s Weekly

EDITED BY G. K. CHESTERTON,

No. 97.—Vol. IV.   Week ending Saturday, January 22, 1927.   PRICE TWOPENCE
YEARLY (52 ISSUES)
10s. 10d.

Telephone No. City 1978.   Offices, 20 & 21, Essex Street, Strand, W.C.2

CONTENTS:

VIVISECTION

THE campaign against the vivisection of dogs has just now increased in vigour, and to a considerable extent we are on the side of the campaigners. But not altogether ! If it could be proved that the sacrifice of our old friend, Quoodle, would save the life of the Secretary of the League we should not hesitate, but hand over the poor old fellow to the vivisectors, though with tears.

But we take it that this condition, or a parallel condition, is not always fulfilled, and that sometimes dogs are vivisected in the general interests of scientific discovery. In that case we should want to be very certain that the discoveries anticipated were likely to benefit humanity. And we gather that the dog and the man are not so alike in organic construction that the results of his vivisection would afford a trustworthy analogy.

Our two points, you will observe, are : (1) that we dislike cutting up a pal ; and (2) that we place the interests of a man higher than those of a dog.

The strange thing is that many of those who clamour most loudly against the vivisection of a dog, do not in the least mind cutting up a pal when the pal happens to be a man. For they are of the cult so quaintly styled " humanitarian," and they are responsible for all that shoddy gospel of social science which is based on the vivisection of man.

To parallel the statement of a great Parliamentarian, who once remembered that he was not an agricultural labourer, we observe that we are not all psycho-analysts, and there are many of us who would not sit, as a foreign princess has just sat, for hours with a condemned murderess, studying her psychology. We feel that France should beg the condemned murderess's pardon for this outrage. But we know that our English humanitarians are busy studying the psychology of their countrymen, who are not murderers,

even if they have been condemned to poverty, and perhaps to death.

And we know that all the welfare work of humanitarians is vivisection of the poor, all the " vital " statistics of the reformers have been obtained by the vivisection of the poor, all the philosophy of the humanitarians is based on the assumption that the poor are there to be analysed and vivisected.

Some few of the humanitarians are of a nobler sort. They are cold scientific fellows who would vivisect you a rabbit, a frog, a dog, or a man with equal readiness ; their bloodless yet insatiable scientific curiosity has no limits. Their curiosity is rather an awful thing, yet we respect them far more than those smug sentimentalists who smile to see a conscious man on the rack and shriek when a chloroformed dog is strapped down on the operating table.

We want to assure all such people that until they repent there is no place for them in our League. We shall not put the poor under the microscope, whether the poor is a poor smallholder, or a poor craftsman, or a poor shopkeeper, or a poor devil of a journalist. We shall not publish statistics to prove that it is difficult for him to live on £2 5s. 3d. a week, and morally impossible for him to live on £2 4s. 1½d. Many well meaning but misguided persons have published working-class budgets, showing how much the very poor spend on coal, how much on bread, how much on beer, and how much (1¼d.) on other amusements. And many ill-meaning persons have gloated over them. Damn their impudence !

The thing is, we suppose, that humanitarians do regard the dog as a pal, and do not regard the poor as a pal, but as a queer and rather frightening creature, who must be dissected for their own sakes, if not for his.

NOTES OF THE WEEK

The Cruisers Start for China

THE Government is quite justified in sending the First Cruiser Squadron to China. The situation at Hankow is extremely difficult, and we can best preserve peace between ourselves and the Nationalists if we show, as we have shown, the Nationalist Government that we are well disposed towards them, and the Nationalist rank and file that we are a strong Power. But Mr. Baldwin must not be persuaded by the Bondholders to choose the easy path and slip into war. A war between England and China at the present moment would be a catastrophe—even if we posed as the supporters of one of the several factions. As the *Observer* acutely remarks, that would be playing the Russian Bolsheviks' game. If war does not happen it seems highly probable that a stable government will shortly be established in China, and in that case it is certain that the Government will be Nationalist.

Mr. Baldwin's Task

THE Nationalists are not Bolshevik, it is not Bolshevik to want China to be free of foreign control. To state, as the *Daily Telegraph* does, that the Cantonese Government is using the crowd in its anti-foreign propaganda is not merely mischievous, it shows a lack of understanding of the force of Chinese national feeling. It would be truer to say that the Russian Bolsheviks are trying to use the anti-foreign feeling of the crowd for their own ends. We concede that the English Government will find it hard to convince the Chinese people, as distinct from its Government, that it is all in favour of its Nationalist aspirations. Here, in fact, is a chance for honest and courageous statesmanship, by which not only the merits of Mr. Baldwin as a leader, but of England as a great power, will be judged.

Land or Water

MR. ROBBINS reproves us for recommending that unemployed miners should be invited by the Government to help in bringing the canals up-to-date, and suggests that they would make ideal agriculturists. He may be right in thinking that the normal miner is a ready-made farmer. And we are sure that he would make a good digger. We should like to see him working on the land for good pay, we should like still better to see him farming his own land. But it is all a question of the best point of attack. Now we think that the ruin of the canals is one of the most striking examples of the way Monopoly works. We think that a majority of the English people could at the present moment be convinced that in ruining the canals the Railway Companies committed a crime. And we think they could be made to realise that if the canals were acquired by the State and made usable by motor barges the cost of living would go down. Therefore we are unrepentant. We still urge that one of our first endeavours should be to gain the freedom of the canals.

Books for Distributists

WE are now able to add considerably to our list of books which might be useful to Leaguers. *Rural Rides;* W. Cobbett; Nelson; 1s. *Guild Socialism;* F. Coldwell; C.S.G.; 3d. *Fields, Factories and Workshops;* Peter Kropotkin. *Deer Forests, and how they are bleeding Scotland White;* J. B. McDiarmid; 3d. *The Church and the Land;* Fr. Vincent McNabb; Burns and Oates; 2s. 6d. *The Real Democracy;* Mann and others; Longmans; 4s. 6d. *Guilds, Trade and Agriculture;* A. J. Penty; Allen and Unwin; 3s. 6d. *Old Worlds for New;* A. J. Penty; Allen and Unwin; 3s. 6d. *Agriculture and Unemployment;* Penty and Wright; Labour Publishing Co.; 2s. 6d. *Conditions of the Working Classes;* translated by Parkinson; C.S.G.; 3d. *Distributive Justice;* J. Ryan, D.D.; Macmillan and Co., N.Y.; 6s. 6d. *A Primer of Social Science;* Parkinson; King & Son, Ltd.; 3s. 6d.; *The Acquisitive Society;* R. H. Tawney; G. Bell & Son; 4s. 6d. *The Town Labourer;* J. L. and Barbara Hammond; Longmans & Co.; 6s. *The Village Labourer;* J. L. and Barbara Hammond; Longmans & Co.; 6s. *Political Economy;* Devas; Longmans & Co.; 8s. 6d. *The Return of Christendom;* M. B. Reckitt (Epilogue by G.K.C.); Commonwealth Press, Letchworth; 2s. 6d. *The Servile State;* Hilaire Belloc. *Economics for Helen;* Hilaire Belloc; Arrowsmith; 5s. League members will like to know that the articles which appeared here under the title of " The Outline of Sanity " (with additions) have been republished in book form by Messrs. Methuen, price 6s.

The Maintenance Fund

THE following contributions have been received :— F. J. Toole, 11s. 6d.; G. Beaumont and Friend, 5s.; H. Fletcher, £1; East London South Africa, 2s.; Harrow, Middlesex, 2s.; B. Coldwell, 2s. 6d.; J. B. Trinick, 2s. 6d.; E. M. T., 5s.; H S. Paynter, 5s.

SAUL AMONG THE PROPHETS

"IF we live in smaller communities where the tension of living is not so high, and where the products of the fields and gardens can be had without the interference of so many profiteers, there will be little poverty or unrest."—HENRY FORD. " My Life and Work," page 88.

" If a man is in constant fear of the industrial situation he ought to change his life so as not to be dependent upon it. There is always the land, and fewer people are on the land now than ever before. If a man lives in fear of an employer's favour changing toward him, he ought to extricate himself from dependence on any employer. He can become his own boss."—HENRY FORD. " My Life and Work," page 220.

" But wherever it is possible a policy of decentralisation ought to be adopted. We need, instead of mammoth flour mills, a multitude of smaller mills distributed through all the sections where grain is grown. Wherever it is possible, the section that produces the raw material ought to produce also the finished product. Grain should be ground to flour where it is grown. . . . This is not a revolutionary idea . . . This is the way we did things before we fell into the habit of carting everything around a few thousand miles and adding the cartage to the consumer's bill. Our communities ought to be more complete in themselves."—HENRY FORD. " My Life and Work," page 232.

" Foreign trade is full of delusions. We ought to wish for every nation as large a measure of self-support as possible. Instead of wishing to keep them dependent on us for what we manufacture, we should wish them to learn to manufacture themselves and build up a solidly found civilisation."—HENRY FORD. " My Life and Work," page 242.

TOP—

AN ERROR OF JUDGMENT

Some very degraded and dirty-minded people leave poison lying about for dogs. The American Republic, raising it to a higher civic plane, leaves it lying about for citizens. The establishment of the principle that it is one of the privileges of a ruler to poison his subjects is an interesting one in itself; and especially inspiring as coming from the great democracy that threw off the yoke of kings. If Mr. Calvin Coolidge had read (among other equally reliable historical facts in his youth) that the Pope and the Italian Cardinals habitually left goblets of poisoned wine standing about that people might drink them, it is possible that he would have called it an example of ancient cruelty and corruption. If he had also read that they excused it, by saying that it would encourage people in saintly abstinence and fasting, he might conceivably call it a very horrible hypocrisy. It is all the more interesting to watch Abraham Lincoln expanding into Alexander Borgia.

But there is one part of this amazing piece of news which puzzles us a great deal. It appears that these remarkable rulers and reformers are careful to collect what they call alcoholic liquors and to put poison in them. But we always understood that this was quite unnecessary. It seems less redundant to paint the lily than to poison the deadly nightshade. It is indeed like gilding refined gold to add venom to the refinement of pure arsenic. And an earnest study of Prohibitionist literature has always left us under the impression that alcohol is itself a poison. Can it be that there is any mistake in the chemical analysis? Is it not a notorious fact that a glass of beer strikes down the strong man in the street and leaves him a helpless wreck for ever after? Can it be doubted that the pure young American, who has put his lips to a single glass of wine, is from that moment a mass of disease and vice? Why poison a poison? Why slay the slain?

Properly considered the Prohibitionist is paying rather a handsome tribute to liquor. He is giving an official contradiction to the current reports about the danger of drinking it. So robust are the victims of this much-abused habit that a special service of State poisoners has to be organised in order to lay them out. The political authority in question was faced with the serious problem that a man might go on day after day, perhaps, to the age of eighty, drinking wine or whisky, without ever realising that he had been consuming something as fatal as prussic acid. Obviously, the only course for responsible rulers and reformers is to give him the prussic acid as well. But it is only too probable, we fear, that sophistical and ingenious men may twist this necessity into an argument for the horrible conception of the harmlessness of wine; and may argue that the drinkers can hardly be engaged in killing themselves, when it becomes the duty of a humane and enlightened administrator to kill them.

—AND TAIL

WHERE TENDENCIES GO TO

As there has recently been some discussion about our relation to the Liberal tradition, accompanied with some discussion about the history of the Liberal party, we should like to write here one reminder about that one point.

We ourselves were in earlier days at least counted not only Liberal but Radical. We were especially associated with that wing of Radicalism which was considered especially Radical because of its opposition to Imperialism. We made ourselves very unpopular by regretting the independence that was taken away from the Boers and scarcely less offensive by asking for about a fifth part of the independence that has since been given to the Irish. We do not propose to debate that question here; but merely to record that fact, with reference to certain other prospects at the present time. The prospects of the present time are, as we so often repeat, those of great capitalist combination ending in Monopoly. We are now told at every turn that there is no escape from the big mantrap of the big monopolist shop. Our critics continually tell us, and none more (we are sorry to say) than many Liberal critics, that the whole tendency of the time is towards big combinations, and that the time of isolated and individual enterprises has gone by. Soon, presumably, law and medicine will cease to be guilds and become commercial departments. Poetry, philosophy and religion will be under sound commercial management. Harrod's will provide a priest or prophet along with a manicurist or a barber.

In any case, these Liberals have surrendered to what they call the tendency of the time. And our memories go back to another time, when Liberals surrendered to another similar tendency for a very similar reason. They called themselves Liberal Imperialist and supported Rhodes and Kipling in painting the African map red—very red. Asquith and Haldane and Grey and Rosebery, all the most respectable leaders, thought it the most reasonable lead. For that school said that the tendency of the time was towards the consolidation of great empires; and that the time of the isolated and individual nation had gone by. They pointed to the perfect pattern of the German Empire; the necessary character of the Austrian Empire; the permanent invincibility of the Russian Empire. Men pointed to those immense inevitable combinations exactly as their representatives to-day point to the immense inevitable commercial combinations. They dreamed that the Hapsburg system was as immortal as the Harrod system. They supposed in their simplicity that William of Prussia was as much an instrument of Providence as Woolworth or Whiteley; and that the empire of Russia had been dowered by God with a divine immortality, just as if it was Selfridge's.

Since then we have seen some odd things. President Wilson; the Fourteen Points; Self-Determination and the springing up of a score of small separate nations. It may be good or bad; but it is a significant comment on the value of " tendencies " and " times."

TRANSPORT

DURING the recent Mining Lock-Out almost all the facts were mentioned in the papers. But some were shouted, and some were whispered. And, since truth depends on justice of emphasis, the result of the several noises was alway a lie. Now the main truth about coal-getting is that the cost at the pit-head is an inconsiderable fraction of the price to the consumer. That was whispered. It was probably true that the mining industry could not make a profit unless wages were reduced or hours lengthened (that was shouted) or unless the mines were re-organised (that was whispered), or unless the sellers of coal stopped profiteering. And this last proviso, which was at the heart of the controversy, was ignored.

Quite recently, however, Lord Beaverbrook was honest enough, or brazen enough, to give the game away, and to show that Rockefeller, Carnegie, and other masters of combines triumped by controlling the selling end of the business. In commenting on his lordship's utterance we endeavoured to show that the typical monopolist was a middleman.

The middleman in any particular case is seldom an individual or an individual concern. This party and that party gets a rake-off, and then there is the carrier. It is of the carrier we propose to speak to-day.

Our great general carrier is still the railway company, for so far the road motor-lorry has done no more than challenge its supremacy. And the railway company is all in favour of the big middleman, he gives less trouble, and so it gives him easier rates. The small dealer of any sort is reckoned of small account. This, of course, helps the Monopolist tremendously. If you or I bought coal at the pit-head and traded it in London we should find it an expensive hobby—if ever the coal got to London. And yet we ought to be able to halve the current London prices, for the middleman's profits are monstrous. But railway freights which are far too high in any case are ludicrously high in the case of small parcels. It is possible, nay probable, that even were freights reasonable the smallholder would find co-operative marketing essential. But he will naturally be looking for an alternative method of transit.

And here every consumer in England and a very large number of producers will be with him. The recent announcement by the railway companies that they were about to advance their freight charges is causing a good many people to ask if we can do without the railway companies. The answer is that we can. The *Daily Mail* says: " On the practical side it is doubtful whether the increase will in the end prove to be of advantage to the companies themselves. The railways are already suffering severely from the ever-growing competition of motor transport. It is true that the taxes on heavy motor vehicles have just been very heavily increased. But it is at least probable that the forthcoming addition of 6½ per cent. to the railway charges will prove to be more than the traffic will bear, and will drive a great deal of traffic that at present uses the railways to the roads. If, at the same time the recovery of trade is checked the railway companies may lose more than they gain; and their position may become much more difficult than it is now."

Well, we think a great deal of the traffic *will* be diverted from the rail to the road, and we think that the frequently contemplated increase of rates is merely speeding up an existing tendency. The railways (anyhow, as goods carriers) are out of date, and if we had good special motor roads criss-crossing England everywhere nearly all the goods traffic would soon be on the road.

Yet the road is not the cheapest, though it is the speediest form of goods-transport.

Last week we commented on Professor Gilbert Murray's proposal that the unemployed—miners and others—should be set to work on the draining of the Severn, on the construction of the canals, and on the re-claiming of the Wash. We approved all those suggestions, but we urged that there was another great work on which the unemployed might be engaged: the restoration and development of the canals.

Some years ago a motor-engine was patented which, with the normal-sized motor-barge developed 40 h.p. for ten hours at the cost of 9d. In view of our alleged hostility to the House of Mond, we may mention that the motive power was gained by driving " Mond gas " through anthracite. The inventor thought it the very thing for our canals. But he had no chance of trying it out on them, they were all covered with weeds. It is now being largely used for shallow craft in the tropics.

But our canals *are* all covered with weeds. On some of the canals the weeds are cleared from the fairway one day per year to allow the directors to pass in a stately barge, on some of them things are never disturbed.

The canals would provide a cheap and efficient method of inland transport. But the railway companies control them, and they have been allowed to weed up and silt up, their banks have been left unrepaired, and never reinforced to stand the passage of motor barges because the railways did not want a competitor.

Even if the railways were likely to become an efficient and a reasonably cheap means of transport, it is essential that the canals should be developed as an alternative means. Indeed no other means can justify itself as efficient and cheap unless it has to face the competition of this more normal method of transit. The canals will never be developed while they are controlled by the railway companies, nor, indeed, is it reasonable that these public highways should be in private hands.

Therefore we urge that (1) in order to provide useful work for the unemployed, and (2) in order to afford an alternative method of transport, the canals should be at once acquired as a matter of urgency by the Government, and adapted for the use of motor-barges.

Wedding Rhymes
THE BRIDESMAIDS.

The Bridesmaids should by rights attend
The Bride and not the Bridegroom's friend,
But, it is only fair to say,
The Best Man is their lawful prey.
And so they lure him to a game,
I don't precisely know the name,
But male participants admit
The ingénueity of it
The victim from the moment " Go "
Is volleyed to and jockeyed fro
Until he's in the net, poor fool.
He *may* escape, but as a rule
A *faute accomplie* means a catch,
And constitutes both game and match.
Lucky is he who wriggles out
Of all this bandying about
And cheats the Hymeneal Corps
Of shuttlecock—and bachelor   R. W.

STRAWS IN THE WIND
ON MR. WELLS AND MR. BELLOC
By G. K. CHESTERTON

BEING forced to cut down this paper, we are forced unfortunately to cut out reviews and things not relevant to our special cause. This must be my apology to many, including those who have suggested that we ought at least to review Mr. Belloc's critique of Mr. Wells, touching both the two large books and the two smaller pamphlets. Another difficulty is, of course, that I cannot review it impartially—whatever that may mean. And by this I do not imply that I always agree with all Mr. Belloc says, or that when I do I should always say it as he says it. Friends, thank God, are not so much alike as that; and fellow-Catholics can include the widest contrasts in the world. On a point of detail, for instance; Mr. Belloc is learned in the matter and I am not; but I should doubt whether he is right in speaking quite so contemptuously of the idea that Arianism was a simplification. That Arian theologians stated it in a hair-splitting style I can well believe, for all the early Trinitarian controversy was like that; but it might still be a subconscious relapse towards a facile simplification; as was Islam afterwards. And, more generally, I should not so fiercely accuse Mr. Wells of ignorance, for the simple reason that he is really ignorant. It is clear from the "Eden" correspondence in this paper that he really does not know any Catholic philosophy; and, therefore, ought to be given the chance of liking a thing so entirely new to him.

But, allowing for differences in detail and method, what is the sense of a reviewer pretending not to see the truth when he sees it? The main truth about *The Outline of History* seems to be this. Every man has an interesting part of his mind, which comes from God and himself, and an uninteresting part, which comes from accident and convention. If I talk about machinery, say about motoring, I can only utter platitudes; as that inventions are wonderful or that motoring too fast is missing the scenery. But Mr. Wells can take that matter of machinery and project out of it, by combining technicalities and imagination, a vision like The War of the Worlds. Mr. Wells writing fictions about the future is Mr. Wells; a person and a poet. Mr. Wells writing facts about the past is not Mr. Wells, but the leavings of all Mr. Wells's most worthless teachers and taskmasters, far away back in the worst period of English elementary teaching. This is what Mr. Belloc substantially says; and this is what he quite clearly proves. The particular case of Darwinian Natural Selection only stands out as a very startling example of stubbornness in such a dowdy and dusty Victorian loyalty. As Mr. Belloc points out, if Mr. Wells simply said, "The Darwinian hypothesis still convinces me, in spite of all that has been said against it," he would be talking sense on one particular side, on which doubtless there are still sensible scientific people. But that he should pretend that nothing particular has been said against it, that no sensible scientific people are now writing against it, is simply astounding and stupefying; and I cannot understand it. I am no biologist; but biologists to whom I have talked have made no disguise about the revolt against Darwin. It is just as if I (in defending private property against Mr. Wells's Collectivism) were to shout louder and louder, in furious obstinacy, that there had never been any Socialist movement or Fabian Society, or any sort of reaction against the pure individualism of Herbert Spencer. Darwin and Spencer are of the same date—and equally dated.

But, as I say, that is only a stubborn outstanding example; it is the same stale stuff all through. The man who wrote that the medieval Church founded schools not to educate the people, but only to impose her dogmas, is not the Herbert George Wells who used to *think*. Not even he who used to think against thinking; as in a delicate piece of destruction like "Doubts of the Instruments." It is simply cant and claptrap sixty years old; and it means nothing. I might equally well say that he writes history, not to educate people, but to impose his theories about peace and progress. What the devil should a man impose, except what he thinks is the truth; and how can he be expected to regard anything else as education? I disagreed with his old "relative" scepticism, but I did not despise it. Despising this later sort of thing is not despising Mr. Wells, but only some cheap atheist in a billycock hat whom he had the bad luck to meet when he was a boy.

If I were reviewing the books in detail, I should remark that Mr. Wells says little in defence of what seem to some of us the most indefensible assertions; e.g., those about the psychology of early man. The two most astonishing statements in his book, I think, were, first, that there seemed "no room" in the lives of the Cro-Magnan artists and hunters for speculation and philosophy; and, second and still more staggering, the suggestion that men buried a rotting corpse with careful rites regarding weapons and other provision, because they did not know that the corpse was dead! Touching the first, we can only recall the man who said he had no time, and was told he had all there is. A man intelligent enough to draw and paint, wandering alone between earth and sky, may or may not have enough room for philosophical speculation; but he has all there is. Touching the second, it is almost impossible to know what to say. In a world without undertakers, without clothes, without coffins, how long did it take humanity to discover that a dead body decays? Of course, as Mr. Belloc remarks, those who say such crazy things can always cover them by saying that men were not men, that there are no such things as men, but only mutable transition types. But those who say this seldom seem to see what it involves. Among other things it involves throwing The Outline of History into the fire even faster than in the course of nature. For it renders all history intrinsically and totally impossible. Moses may be a man and Mr. Wells may be a man; and it may, therefore, be interesting to hear Mr. Wells on Moses; perhaps more interesting to hear Moses on Mr. Wells. But if Mr. Wells can impute anything whatever to Moses, because he was not a man and nobody knows what he was, it is obvious that nobody can make any remark of the smallest interest about him. Anybody is free to suggest anything; and we have no test of the truth of anything. If I choose to say that men walked about on their hands because they liked to think they were walking on the sky, I have as much authority for saying it as anybody has for saying anything else. Under these conditions the School of History does not flourish.

The Birth

Only the cricket chirps; no nightingale
Floods the deep hour of darkness with her song.
Earth with her lovely burden in her womb
Labours in whispered pain, and staggers pale
In star-watched agony. Not long! Not long
Oh Mother; even now the moments loom,
And the moon-midwife with her lethal lamp
Searches thy deathlike bosom for a sign.
With birth-dew now thy shrouded hair is damp.
Hasten, Oh God! complete this work of Thine!

                             RICHARD CHURCH.

THE DRAMA

Wind-Mills

THE second edition of the "Blackbirds" serves to re-emphasise the supremacy of Miss Florence Mills and her company over any similar entertainment in London. It is one's fortune at the generality of revues to brighten at one item and sadden at three. Time goes on and you hope against hope that a stimulating moment is at hand, and then depression sets in until at last as by the grace of God a glimmer of genius lightens the gloom.

The Black Pavilion

At the London Pavilion there is none of this periodic melancholy. The sheer vitality, the amazing pressure of talent to the square inch progresses the whole evening. For my own taste I hunger for more part singing. The beautiful velvety negro bass, comparable only to the Russian, too seldom sounds in the present programme. We have, however, a negro cabaret in which we get a taste of the company's musical qualities. Miss Edith Wilson contributes not a little to the gaiety of the evening by a Black Bottom dance and a new song "It doesn't Pay to Advertise your Man." An item I could have wished left out is "Hades," set with appropriate flames and grinning devils, in which the company appear as scarlet imps. It is not that they are lacking in zest, gaiety or aplomb but that the number could have been included in the most ordinary programme. It is unworthy of the genius and the dash of the Blackbirds—that is my complaint.

Oh Blackbirds, Blackbirds, Flying South !

The dancing is superhuman in its fantasy and lightness. I could never tire of watching Miss Florence Mills or the inimitable three who run the whole gamut of boneless posturing. London will be infinitely sadder with the departure of the Blackbirds and it is my hope that they will be with us for a very long time.

* * *

A Happy Marriage

"Lido Lady" at the Gaiety is quite another story. The plot is familiar in that it includes the rag, tag and bobtail of the most popular of its genre. Its sole use indeed is as a vehicle for the genius of Mr. Jack Hulbert and Miss Cicely Courtneidge. The whole burden of the show is on these two and as they are seldom absent from the stage the mediocrity of the dialogue, the mechanical action of the chorus, does not really matter. Mr. Hulbert has the quality of the unexpected. You never quite know what he is going to do with his incomparable legs, and he is almost as agile with his voice. Miss Courtneidge has developed her sense of the eccentric and can do wonders with the most obvious situation. I like also the little fat man with the big voice who bursts into a violin solo in mid-ocean. "Lido Lady" is a good title but a more appropriate and descriptive one would be "Cicely and Jack." This expresses and fulfils the show.

* * *

Beccles Cake

"Ask Beccles," by C. Campion and Edward Dignon, now running at the Comedy Theatre, is quite a good melodrama of the crook variety. Beccles is a human person with an irresistible desire to acquire famous gems. Occasionally he has qualms of conscience and returns the historic trophies he has lifted. The play opens with an indignant and somewhat blatant *nouveau riche* who complains that she has lost her diamonds. She calls in the police and the chase begins. Never for a moment are you in doubt as to Beccles's guilt. This is quite apparent. The excitement consists in seeing how he will extricate himself. He baffles the police, gets the best of a notable receiver—admirably played by Mr. Lewin Mannering—and finally returns the diamond to its setting by plunging the room in darkness. This last feat is a little clumsy—Beccles is discovered leaning against the switch, the suggestion being that he got there accidentally and by a sudden movement switched it on again. The end is peace for everyone. Beccles captures his sweetheart and secures the release of the time-honoured mortgage on her father's estate. He promises the lady a ring; she begs him "to buy it" A light, bright, frothy trifle.

J. K. P.

THE COCKPIT

To the Editor of G.K.'s WEEKLY.

A RENT IN THE WASH

DEAR SIR,—Surely the farmers of the land, which Professor Slater suggests should be reclaimed from the Wash, would have to pay rent. Apart from the actual reclamation there would be houses and buildings to be built, roads to be made and a system of drainage to be elaborated, etc.

It would hardly be fair for the taxpayer to provide all this without any return.

As a matter of fact I believe that the average rent for agricultural land at the present time represents a poor return for the capital expended to make it productive.—Yours faithfully,

ARTHUR EMPSON.

WORK FOR THE UNEMPLOYED

DEAR SIR,—I am surprised at you. Professor Slater says that the unemployed miner is a competent navvy ready made, and suggests that he be employed on Severn electrification, ship canals and the reclamation of the Wash. You agree, and add only the improvement of inland waterways.

But the miner, in surprisingly large numbers, is something even more obvious and satisfactory than a navvy. He is a competent and ready-made land worker. He works down a pit until he sickens for a sight of the sun. Then he gets himself a job as a farm labourer. After a time the starvation wage of a land worker drives him back to the pit. And so on.

Could there be a clearer case for the re-creation of a peasantry from the debris of industrialism? The largest industrial group, with a very large minority not only willing but able to work a holding! And you have missed it!

England needs reclamation a great deal more than the Wash, which it will be time to tackle when the blessed "Law of Diminishing Returns" is really in operation elsewhere. At present not a million acres in England are in sight of it.

Of course, the Government won't agree to Professor Slater's suggestions, nor to yours, nor to mine, but that is no reason why we should not point the moral. Our opponents tell us that the re-creation of a peasantry is an idle dream, industrial workers being neither able nor willing to go back. We can produce up to a quarter of a million unanswerable answers. Here are men in plenty, meeting both conditions, and only waiting for the chance.

And, as Professor Slater says, "Any financial calculations to the contrary are delusive."—Yours,

H. ROBBINS.

THE NEW READER

DEAR SIR,—The members of our local branch of the League have asked me to make this suggestion; that in *every* issue of your weekly the objects of the League should be set out simply and briefly in prominent type. All leaguers are striving to increase the circulation of G.K.'s by giving copies to people outside the League. Now it is not easy for an absolute stranger to deduce the simple creed of Distributism from the brilliant articles which delight the initiated. Give him a simple clue, and he will then see what you are driving at. At present he is mystified.

A statement such as that which is printed on the first page of the League leaflets would suffice. Why not give the new reader this help? It will also help us to get new readers to take G.K.'s regularly.—Yours faithfully,

J. P. ALCOCK (*Liverpool Branch*).

FREE SPEECH

DEAR SIR,—Your correspondent "H.H.," in a recent letter, described Mr. Baldwin as *lackey to the gang of thieves and murderers who have enslaved men and starved women and children to death. . . ., and as a coward and a hypocrite.* I do not write to champion the cause of Mr. Baldwin; my opinion of him would matter almost as little as "H.H.'s" does, but whatever may be your opinion of him (which does matter), it is difficult to imagine that the publication of such letters as "H.H.'s" will assist the circulation of this journal. For my own part, I shall wish to be a subscriber for as long as you continue to direct it and contribute to it; that must be the view of many of the supporters of it and of the League; but it is disappointing to see valuable space allotted to an individual whose method of stating a grievance consists in melodramatic vituperation screened by anonymity. It is a method quite irreconcilable with any aspect of G.K.'s WEEKLY.—Yours faithfully, RALPH COOKE.

[NOTE.—Our own opinion of Mr. Baldwin has been plainly expressed on many occasions. We think it right that the opinion of our readers should be expressed in the Cockpit. And so we print Mr. Cooke's letter. —The Editor.]

CANTOS

THE editor of this paper, in a memorable editorial, once warned us about confusing " bigness " with " greatness." Here is a poem* which by its very size is remarkable, appearing, as it does in an age of sudden lyrics. It is written in the stanza of Chaucer's ' *Troilus and Criseyde*, and runs to nine cantos of about thirty stanzas apiece. And I am confident that it is no confusion of terms which makes me call it a great poem.

The very fact of its appearance is an answer to the disgruntled folk who claim that this is no time for poetry, that poets cannot get a hearing, and that if Milton were " living at this hour " his *Paradise Lost* would get as little notice as it did when it was first published. *Dymer* makes a sizeable book and there is nothing sensational to recommend it; its appearance can only be due to complete confidence of the publishers in its actual literary merit. And it justifies that.

Mr. Clive Hamilton has great powers of sustaining his eloquence. There is no single stanza of all his long tale which could be picked out as bad art. Sometimes he rises passionately to the occasion with a rush of words :—

> She said, for this land only did men love
> The shadow-lands of earth. All our disease
> Of longing, all the hopes we fabled of,
> Fortunate islands, or Hesperian seas
> Or woods beyond the West, were but the breeze
> That blew from off these shores; one far spent breath
> That reached even to the world of change and death.

> She told me I had journeyed home at last
> Into the golden age and the good countrie
> That had been always there. She bade me cast
> My cares behind for ever—on her knee
> Worshipped me lord and love—oh, I can see
> Her red lips even now! Is it not wrong
> That men's delusions should be made so strong?

He has facility, but it is not a dangerous facility, and he has a certain bright manner of realism which almost staggers one :—

> That moment in a cloud among the trees
> Wild music, and the glare of torches came.
> On sweated faces, on the prancing knees
> Of shaggy satyrs fell the smoky flame,
> On ape, and goat, and crawlers without name.
> On rolling breast, black eyes, and tossing hair,
> On old bald-headed witches, lean and bare.

And he has a certain mastery of phrase that is wholly satisfying :—

> " You will grow full of pity and love of men
> And toil until the morning moisture dries
> Out of your heart."

Perhaps his failing is a vagueness of intention, a certain lack of absolute consistency, which is born, I think, of his crowding his canvas too much with splendid imagery. In that he reminds one of Mr. James Branch Cabell, and in moments there is a touch of Byron, and in others a hint of James Elroy Flecker. But on the whole this is an intensely original poem, and represents, in a way, a test set up. It will be most disheartening if it is passed by.

RUPERT CROFT-COOKE.

---

* DYMER. By Clive Hamilton. Dent's. 6s.

LIBRARY LIST

THE BREAKDOWN OF SOCIALISM. By Arthur Shadwell. Benn. 10s. 6d.

Read as an appendix to Mr. Joseph Clayton's " Rise and Decline of Socialism " this book has a certain definite value. It is an enlargement of a number of articles written for *The Times*, after a tour of investigation through Europe. But Mr. Shadwell is a little too anxious to explain, even to excuse, his use of the word " breakdown." It needs no defence.

THE STORY OF THE STREAM. By A. M. Young. Heinemann. 6s.

A book of essays, many of which are reprinted from *The Observer*, Mr. Young deals confidently and soundly with his subject " jolly angling," but in his descriptions of Nature he is far too ornate, as : " Who that has been out on the river when the first faint flush of awakening dawn kisses the dark and slumbering eyes of night, in which the stars are veiled, and calls her once more to life and loveliness? Who that has seen the pearl white river mist rolling before the flame-maned horses of the morning, seen the crimson banners of Apollo sweeping across the sky. . . ." and so on, *ad lib.*

BLINDED KINGS. By J. Kessel and H. Iswolsky. Translated from the French by G. and K. de Teissier. Heinemann. 7s. 6d.

This novel deals with the mysterious figure of Rasputin. The history of the earliest chapters of the Russian revolution is far too obscure as yet for it to be possible to say whether its facts are correct. But certainly the characterisation is powerful and the " atmosphere " is there.

PIERRE LOTI. By Edmund B. D'Auvergne. T. Werner Laurie. 16s.

One is always a little suspicious of books that open in the manner of this one, especially if the books are biographies, " One April evening, some sixty years ago, a boy sat at the window of a top room in the French seaport town of Rochefort." But Mr. D'Auvergne is not quite the kind of biographer that we should gather from it. True he is rather too sentimental, rather inclined to idealise in a way that becomes wearisome towards the end of the book, but he makes up for it by his painstaking presentation of details that matter. One gets a very clear picture of Loti, and learns much about his eccentricities.

SIXTY-FOUR YEARS IN CEYLON. By F. Lewis. Simpkin & Co. 15s.

This is an unassuming book about life in Ceylon and its very modesty gives it a tone of its own which is attractive. Every now and then Mr. Lewis rises to a point where the reader suspects more than modesty and recognises genius. But the quality of the prose is regulated by the matter. Thank heaven! there are no purple patches. The book is much too long but it can be read easily and those who know Ceylon will find much to interest them, whilst those who have never been there will get a clear vision of a wonderful island.

TRANSITION. By Edwin Muir. The Hogarth Press. 7s. 6d.

This book has the sub-title " Critical Essays on Contemporary Writers," and it is evident to anyone who reads the last two essays in the book, on " Contemporary Poetry " and " Contemporary Fiction," that the author misuses the word " contemporary." For him it means only the writers who have not yet come into their own. He treats exhaustively of James Joyce, D. H. Lawrence, T. S. Eliot, etc., but the book has nothing to say of the writers who have any real sway over modern thought, outside the cliques. Yet it seems to me that Mr. Muir promises as much as most of them. He is an indulgent, but a clear-sighted critic.

SKIN FOR SKIN. By Llewelyn Powys. Jonathan Cape. 9s.

Mr. Llewelyn Powys is a stylist, in the narrowest sense of the word. He has a truly Flaubertian love for the " elusive adjective." He likes similes for similes' sake. (Some of them in this book are really beautiful, as, " I caught her bare hand and held it fast. It was tremulous and warm, like a live thrush.") And by the unfortunate circumstances of his life—he was a victim for many years to incipient consumption—he has been given something intensely moving to put into his exquisite prose. Perhaps his outlook is rather a bitter one, but it is surprisingly free from morbidity.

THE ORIENT I FOUND. By Thomas J. McMahon. Duckworth & Co. 15s.

The Australian who writes this volume of travel has already made a name for himself and if he does not proceed with a searchlight of dazzling power we are at any rate spared the strong shadows that a strong light creates. He tells us of British Borneo, China, Japan, Manila and Honk Kong. He likes Japan and does not believe that she is a menace to peace. He does not attempt to solve the Chinese problem, but contents himself with remarking that once China gets European customs she will go ahead. It might, however, be argued that the attempt to graft European customs on an Eastern race has been the main cause of trouble both in India and China.

AMONG THE BRANCHES

CENTRAL BRANCH.—*Secretary*: G. C. Heseltine, 20/21 Essex Street, Strand, W.C.2.

The discussion at the Devereux on January 14 followed an interesting and able paper on " Distributism as I see it," by Mr. Gregory Macdonald, who dealt with the philosophic basis of distributist theory. The subsequent contributions by those present were as keen and stimulating as usual, but there was a very persistent tendency to argue the position with regard to machinery and mass production. In view of the importance of this subject it is hoped to arrange an early debate to be opened by Mr. Cargill. A paper on " Local Government " was suggested and will be arranged.

At Marble Arch, Hyde Park, Mr. Geo. Coldwell took the field for the League at three o'clock and he was followed by Messrs. McNamara and G. C. Heseltine until five-thirty. The large crowd showed a very lively interest and there is no doubt that these meetings are going to be an important part of our propaganda. More Leaguers should turn up to work amongst the crowd, particularly at the end of the meeting.

There will be no meeting at the Devereux on Friday, the 21st. For particulars of meeting to be held at the " Six Bells," Chelsea, on Monday next, please communicate with secretary.

BARNET.—*Secretary*: T. McNamara, 70 Berkeley Crescent, Barnet.

BIRMINGHAM.—*Secretary*: K. L. Kenrick, 7 Soho Road, Handsworth.

BRIGHTON.—*Secretary*: C. B. Harrison, 21 Alexander Villas, Brighton.

CAMBRIDGE.—*Secretary*: H. E. Wood, King's College, Cambridge.

CHORLEY.—*Secretary*: James Power, Woodlands, Rotherwick Avenue, Chorley.

COVENTRY.—*Secretary*: R. E. S. Willison, 102 Westwood Road, Coventry.

CROYDON.—*Secretary*: Stormont Murray, Turret House, 4 Campden Road, Croydon.

A debate on Distributism between G. K. Chesterton and Lieut. Com. A. S. Elwell-Sutton (prospective Liberal candidate for South Croydon) will take place on Friday, January 21 (8 p.m. sharp) at The New Gallery, Katherine Street, Croydon (opposite Public Library). Mr. Gilbert Foan (prospective Labour candidate for North Croydon) will take the chair. Seats in front rows 1s. (reserved); admission to hall free. Tickets can be obtained from 20-21 Essex Street, Strand, W.C.2, from 4 Campden Road, Croydon, or from door of hall on the night of the debate. Will all members of The League in the London area please endeavour to attend? Nearest station " East Croydon "; frequent train service available from Victoria or London Bridge.

EDINBURGH BRANCH.—*Secretary*: Jas. Turner, 69 St. Leonard's Street, Edinburgh.

The first meeting of the Edinburgh Branch will be held in Room 5, Oddfellows Hall, Forrest Road, on Friday, January 21, at 7.30 p.m. All interested will be welcome. It is hoped Mr. Boyle, of the Glasgow Branch, will be present to give us the benefit of their experience.

GLASGOW.—*Secretary*: A. McGregor, 128 Hope Street, Glasgow. Meetings Monday, 7.15 p.m. at offices of secretary.

Thirteenth meeting, " Practical Distributism in Scotland: Fourteenth Report of Board of Agriculture of Scotland further considered." Report was presented to Parliament, July, 1926. Total acreage taken over by Board for land settlement schemes—346,087 acres; total acreage already allotted to small holdings—241,747 acres; capital payments made for land acquired—£485,973; annual payments for lease and fens—£27,446; applicants settled since 1912—4,498; applicants still to be settled—10,055; fresh applications last year—705; number of settlers who have given up holdings since 1912—257; applicants were settled chiefly in Argyllshire, Sutherlandshire and Skye. Re progress of settlers, the Report (p. 16) states :—" Reports received by the Board show that holders generally are making a success of their holdings. This is noticeable more particularly in the case of holders who have been in occupation for a period of five years or more and who are now beginning to overcome their difficulties. . . . keeping in view the qualities required for the successful working of a small holding, credit is due to the settlers for the manner in which they have faced the initial difficulties of their new life. The success attained by the majority of the holders is increasing the demand for settlement."

LIVERPOOL.—*Secretary*: J. P. Alcock, Melwood, Deysbrook Lane, West Derby, Liverpool.

MANCHESTER.—*Secretary*: James Hammond, 20 Verdun Road, Monton, Eccles.

A meeting was held on Wednesday, January 12, at 8 p.m. at the Cosy Café. A paper on " Distributism and the Rights of the Individual " was given by Mr. Wilson. Considerable discussion took place, it being finally agreed that the Distributive State was the only one which safeguarded the rights of the individual. Various sub-committees were formed and the usual business,

correspondence, etc., dealt with. The next meeting will be held on Wednesday, January 19, when a paper on "Arts and Crafts" will be given by Miss M. Lee. One new member.

MEDWAY.—*Secretary*: J. Murphy, 55 Paget Street, Gillingham, Kent. Next meeting, 55 Paget Street, Gillingham, on January 13, at 7.30 p.m.

NEWCASTLE-ON-TYNE.—*Secretary*: J. Finlayson, 20 Goldspink Lane.

It has been decided to hold a public meeting within a fortnight. Further particulars next week.

NORTH SHIELDS.—*Secretary*: J. J. Rogan, 28 Windermere Terrace, North Shields, Northumberland.

OXFORD CITY AND DISTRICT.—*Secretary*: R. R. D. Paton, The Old Farmhouse, Black Bourton, Clanfield, Oxford. Will Leaguers in and around Oxford please communicate with Mr. Paton?

OXFORD UNIVERSITY.—*Secretary*: R. C. S. Ellison, Merton College, Oxford.

SOUTHAMPTON.—*Secretary*: W. S. Ellsby, Banister Court, Southampton.

THANET.—*Secretary*: G. Victor Taylor, The Bungalow, Lymington Road, Westgate-on-Sea.

WEST MIDDLESEX.—*Secretary*: J. V. Jenks, 108, Milton Road, Hanwell, W.7.

The area of this branch extends from Acton and Chiswick on the east side to Southall and Hounslow on the west, and from Harrow and Willesden on the north to Brentford and Isleworth on the South. Will sympathisers in this inclusive area (which also includes Ealing and Hanwell) please send a postcard to the secretary, in order that he may acquaint them with the date, time and place of the next branch meeting. Leaguers transferred from Central Branch will hear from him shortly. One new member, making our number ten in all.

Branches are in process of formation at the following places and until secretaries have been appointed intending members should communicate with the Leaguers whose names are given :—BANFFSHIRE.—G. Beaumont, The Elms Hotel, Dufftown, Banffshire. BELFAST.—J. R. Ross, 14 Woodland Avenue, Cliftonville. BRADFORD.—Mrs. G. Healey, 4 Rossifield Road, Heaton, Bradford. BLACKPOOL.—Miss E. M. Taylor, 37 Norbreck Road, Norbreck, Blackpool. CARDIFF.—Wm. P. Hogan, 17 Amesbury Road, Penylan, Cardiff. HUDDERSFIELD.—Norman R. Turner, 12 Belmont Street, Huddersfield. LEEDS.—T. Byrne, 141 Leeds Terrace, North Street, Leeds. ROCHDALE.—M. P. Keating, 15 Chatsworth Street, Whitworth Road, Rochdale. SALFORD.—James Burns, 8 Trafalgar Square, Regent Road. SHEFFIELD.—Canon Wm. Collingwood, Bamford, Sheffield. WEYBRIDGE.—Mrs. Helen A. Reckitt, Marrowells, Weybridge, Surrey. WINDSOR-ETON-SLOUGH.—Hubert S. Paynter, Rainbow Cottage, Christmas Common, Nr. Watlington, Oxfordshire.

APPLICATION FORM FOR MEMBERSHIP

I wish to become a member of THE LEAGUE, *with whose objects I am in sympathy, and I enclose herewith* ...., *being the annual subscription of one shilling, and* .... *as a donation.*

Name ....

Address ....

To The Treasurer, The League,
   20-21 Essex Street, Strand, London, W.C.2.

Published by the Proprietors, G.K.'s WEEKLY, LTD., at their offices, 20 & 21 Essex Street, Strand, London, W.C.2 (incorporating THE NEW WITNESS). Telephone No. City 1978. Printed by THE PRESS AT COOMBELANDS, LTD., London and Addlestone. Sole agents for Australasia : Gordon & Gotch (Australasia), Ltd. Sole Agents for South Africa : Central News Agency, Ltd.

G.K.'s WEEKLY, January 29th, 1927.

THE END OF "THE EMPIRE"

G.K.'s Weekly

EDITED BY G. K. CHESTERTON,

No. 98.—Vol. IV.   Week ending Saturday, January 29, 1927.   PRICE TWOPENCE
YEARLY (52 ISSUES)
10s. 10d.

Telephone No. City 1978.   Offices, 20 & 21, Essex Street, Strand, W.C.2

CONTENTS:

ARE YOU A PRO-CHINAMAN?

WE were Pro-Boer in the nineteenth century, and some of our then sympathisers wondered that in the twentieth century we were so resolutely Anti-German. There was no change of front on our part, but only on the part of the enemy. We were always Pro-English, and if to-morrow we may have to call ourselves Pro-Chinese it will not be through any faltering in our patriotism.

Last week we stated that we considered the Government had done well in sending cruisers to China, while continuing to manifest their desire to come to just terms with the Canton administration. We are still of that opinion. And it is plain that if we are to make a naval demonstration it must be in force. So that we cannot logically object to the dispatch of further troops to the East.

But there is in the air a certain feeling, difficult to analyse, but unmistakable, which is always there before a war-cloud breaks That note is in the Press, and there it is easier to analyse. For example, in Monday's *Express* their Special Correspondent has a long story about a rival Chinese war lord. Somebody is gunning for a war.

We think we know who that somebody is : the Bondholder. If the Chinese Nationalist Government becomes stable no doubt the " English " holder of Chinese securities will lose money. China has been victimised shamefully in the past; for instance, it has been made impossible for her to use her waterways freely, so that she was compelled to have resort to the rail. And it is plain that the Nationalists mean to secure for the Chinese

full control over the whole of the country and its resources.

With that intention we, and every decent Englishman, will have every sympathy, and the Bondholder will have none. Mr. Baldwin has shown that he sympathises, and we are sure that if left uncontrolled he will do the right thing. But we know from the experience of the Lock-Out that if Finance gets to work on him he cannot be trusted. It is possible that the Bondholder may drag him (and us) into a war.

Of course, it will not be a war with China, it will be a war in the first place to protect the poor English residents, and in the second place on behalf of China (represented by Chang, or somebody) against the Bolsheviks who have captured the Government of Canton. You will remember that the Boer War began to protect the down-trodden Uitlanders who were dying for a vote.

Now we are not going to appeal to Mr. Baldwin's good sense, for that is needless. He sees the situation plainly enough. Nor do we need to appeal to his good feeling. His heart is in the right place. If he does wrong he will know he does wrong, and the greater will be his sin.

Therefore we shall just threaten him. If he goes to war with China he will put Labour in power for a generation—*in power!* Does he want to do that? It does not matter to us. Whichever party is in power Trust-Socialism will be its philosophy. But the utter defeat of the Tory Party means almost as much to Mr. Baldwin as the dishonour of England means to us.

NOTES OF THE WEEK

China

WE plead elsewhere in this issue for a sober mind in regard to the Chinese question. And, as an example of the state of mind which should not be cultivated, we quote a passage from Monday's *Morning Post*: "In the meantime the banks are said to be reopening in Hankow, an experiment which may or may not be justified by the event. The Cantonese, who are vindicating the principles of Nationalism by invading another province, are said to be badly off for money, and it remains to be seen whether an open bank will not prove an irresistible temptation to those humble followers of Lenin." This is disgraceful. And we invite the authorities to consider whether or no such perilous stuff should be printed. The re-opening of the banks at Hankow is a sign that the bankers there have confidence in the Nationalist Government. Hence the anger of the *Morning Post* and its ill-bred jeers. As for the invasion of another province, we take it that an English Nationalist Government would not think itself false to its principles if it invaded Cornwall, and we seem to remember that the *Post* had no qualms when England invaded Ireland. Finally, the Cantonese Government are not followers of Lenin. The Duke of Northumberland's fellow-feeling for the Bondholders should not make him so completely blind to the facts.

Semi-Detached

WE do not understand on what terms Viscount Grey will stand with Mr. Lloyd George. There are not to be two Liberal Parties. The Party will be one and indivisible, but it will have two heads, and, apparently, two organisations, though only one exchequer, for the " million fund " is fairly mythical. And the fun of it is that the two groups have not a *Liberal* principle between them. The Grey group will accept no endowment from the Lloyd George fund, since it entails a "moral obligation" towards the donor. " In these circumstances it is proposed to form within the Liberal Party a new body: the Liberal Council, which, though in no wise antagonistic to the existing organisations, will, nevertheless, remain entirely independent both of the fund and of the obligation attaching to its acceptance. The Liberal Council, which will include in its membership men and women on equal terms, will work for all Liberal causes, supply speakers, and give advice and assistance to candidates when desired to do so." But will the Grey group in the Commons receive the Lloyd George whip? And if they do, hadn't they better accept the endowment? Of course, if they boldly declared that a secret part fund is immoral, and that they would have nothing to do with a party which is caucus-controlled, not only would the split with George be a real one, but a great step towards the cleansing of politics would have been taken. But they won't do that.

The Whitley Council

IN writing of Trade Unions, the " heavies " emphasize the fact that better trade depends on the goodwill of the men. *The Daily Telegraph* urges that the Whitley Council is the best means of arousing and harnessing that goodwill. It says:—" No industry belongs to capital, or to labour, or to management, of itself, for every industry is dependent for its prosperity upon the co-operation of all sections. The Whitley Council was a means of expressing and guiding that co-operation, touching not wages alone, but hours, conditions, health, apprenticeship, and education." This, we submit, is an unfair way to put it, for " management " may refer to men who are mainly capitalists, or men who are solely wage-earners. Yet there is a real distinction between capitalists who are engaged in an industry and shareholders who know nothing of the industry except that they draw dividends from it. Again, the capitalist-manager is often, if not usually, entirely uninterested in the trade he profits by, except as a milch-cow. Both he and the absentee-shareholder are parasites, and no Whitley or other Council could secure reasonable co-operation with them.

Garlanded Chains

IT is time we stopped talking about " capital " as something that walks about on two legs. An industry is run by men who pursue it. They are workers. They need capital; that is to say, they need cash or credit to buy plant and raw material, and cash or credit for running expenses. In a civilised society it would be possible for a master-craftsman or a number of master-craftsmen of known stability of character to obtain the cash or credit required. But there would be no question of the person who advanced the money obtaining any sort of control over the industry. And the true cause of labour discontent is that workmen vaguely feel that the mere financier in business is an intruder and an exploiter. No re-adjustment of wages and hours or improvement of conditions will get rid of that feeling. Nor, finally, do we think that men will be satisfied until they own the trade they live by. Whitley Councils are no better than wreaths of roses round the chains.

The Maintenance Fund

THE following contributions have been received:—J. B. Trinick, 2s. 6d.; B. Coldwell, 2s. 6d.

The Menace of the Leisured Woman

TIME and Tide wait for no man. Owing to the broadcasting arrangements for the debate between Lady Rhondda and Mr. G. K. Chesterton on the above subject, to be held at the Kingsway Hall, on Thursday, January 27, it is especially important that Mr. Shaw should be able to begin his opening speech punctually at eight o'clock. Ticket-holders are, therefore, requested to be in their places not later than 7.50 p.m. We are asked to state, in order to avoid disappointment, that all tickets for the debate, including the unreserved seats at one shilling, are now sold.

On Jollity

FROM a letter by Sir W. V. Harcourt (see his *Life*, by Gardiner, Vol. 1., page 608), on Itinerant Showmen and Travelling Shows:—

" The best social reformer is the man who realises most the best thing you can do for the people is to make them *jolly*."

" All attempts at regulating jollity are a mistake and a failure."

" There is nothing so doleful as the class of people who seem to consider that the whole duty of man is summed up in going about in a tall hat and a black coat."

TOP—

NOW WE ARE THROUGH

FIRST VOICE: Hello!

SECOND VOICE (*severely correcting the other*): Hullo!

FIRST VOICE: Say, is that England?

SECOND VOICE: It was once. Is that America?

FIRST VOICE: No; it's New York.

SECOND VOICE: Oh . . . I was always taught that New York is in America.

FIRST VOICE: I guess not. America is in New York . . . sometimes; comes up for the bright lights and the hard drinks.

SECOND VOICE: Oh . . . I understand . . . are there hard drinks?

FIRST VOICE: Yep. And hard drinkers. Say, if you've ever seen Broadway——

SECOND VOICE: Yes, I've seen "Broadway."

FIRST VOICE: And I reckon you've seen American life on the movies.

SECOND VOICE: I've never seen any other life on the movies.

FIRST VOICE: And I hear you've got the bright lights in your little burg now; and the old man Woolworth is making things hum over there.

SECOND VOICE: Yes . . . how wonderful it is to be able to talk like this to strange lands and learn all their curious manners and customs!

FIRST VOICE: Isn't it just wonderful? (A pause.) Wonderful to think we should be talking like this!

SECOND VOICE: Very wonderful.

FIRST VOICE: Wonderful to think we're really telephoning from London to New York!

SECOND VOICE (*more briefly*): Wonderful.

FIRST VOICE: Telephoning right across the Atlantic.

SECOND VOICE: Bright thoughts flashing to and fro every instant.

FIRST VOICE: Yep.

SECOND VOICE: A torrent of fresh and creative ideas pouring over our two respective countries.

FIRST VOICE: Yep.

SECOND VOICE: The things we have so long wished to say to each other leaping to our passionate lips.

FIRST VOICE: Yep.

SECOND VOICE (*severely*): Yes.

FIRST VOICE (*enthusiastically, but with a slight effort*): Isn't it just wonderful to think we're telephoning right across the great Atlantic?

SECOND VOICE: Very wonderful. Quite mysterious, in fact.

FIRST VOICE: I guess I don't quite get you.

SECOND VOICE (*dreamily*): I said it was mysterious. Why . . . *why* are we telephoning right across the great Atlantic?

FIRST VOICE (*with abrupt cheerfulness*): Wal, we thought maybe you'd like to know something about Little Old New York——

SECOND VOICE: Well, if we've got bright lights just as you have, and you've got hard drinks just as we have——

FIRST VOICE: You'll never get a big boom in hooch till you have Prohibition.

SECOND VOICE: There may be a few further modifications needed to make us exactly alike. But when once we are, well——

FIRST VOICE: Well.

SECOND VOICE: Well, there you bally well are.

FIRST VOICE (*suddenly returning to the charge*): Wonderful to think——

OPERATOR: Time's up.

—AND TAIL

VIRTUE AND VULGAR ABUSE

A week or so ago a correspondent remonstrated very sternly with us, not for anything that we had said, but for something we had allowed somebody else to say. It was something against ourselves, but more especially against Mr. Baldwin, to whom we had paid a personal tribute. Altogether, we seem to suffer a good deal for Mr. Baldwin; if we are to be abused for praising him; and then abused for being abused for praising him. It almost looks as if we might be remembered in the next Honours List. But there is one Socialist habit we think worse than abuse; and that is the pedantry of always using long words like "proletarian" instead of plain words like "wage-earner." And this scientific trick raises a question even more essential to our own case for property.

Abuse is easily abused; in both senses of the word. It is easy to revile such revilings; and it is undoubtedly only too easy to revile anything. It is only too likely that human sinners in a rage will revile the wrong thing. But there is this much to be said for vulgar abuse and vituperation; that it must be moral. It must appeal to morality; and it must in practice appeal to the old morality; because there is no other to appeal to. And when the great Socialist said that property is theft, he really said at the same time that property is not theft. For if there is such a thing as unlawful theft, then there must be somewhere such a thing as lawful property. The very language that he was forced to use in denunciation of ownership was drawn from the old traditions of ownership. You may be able to murder a man with machinery; you may be able to poison a man with chemistry; you certainly are able to bamboozle a man with economics and science. But you cannot slander a man except with morality.

It is the same with the sort of violence of which the correspondent complained. It may be very much out of balance for a Communist to call Mr. Baldwin a thief. But even in calling him a thief, he is talking more against Communism than against Mr. Baldwin. He is falling back, as all human beings do ultimately fall back, on the fundamental sense that something belongs to somebody; or ought to belong to somebody; and that it is possible for somebody else to take it away. When the Communist says that many modern rich men are robbers, he is perfectly right; but he is not particularly Communist. He is pointing out that in the past poor people have been robbed by rich people; as they have. But he is conceding the moral evil of robbery. If ever Communists do shed the old morality altogether, their conversation will become one vast arid void of depressing politeness.

THE END OF "THE EMPIRE"

LAST Saturday night was a melancholy occasion for many. Those of us who in our youth delighted in the music-hall have felt a fresh pang every time one of the old halls went over to the enemy. Perhaps my worst moment was on the last night of the Tivoli, when Joe Wilson, the manager, burst into tears, and for the first time blotted his shirt front. The Pavilion and the Oxford passed with a flourish of trumpets proclaiming the new King. We were not allowed to weep in peace into our tankards.

The Empire has been luckier. Either the new people were wiser, or the old people had the pull. Or they were overcome by the goodness of the " story." It is a good story, for the Empire has cut a figure in its time.

There was jollity in all the old halls, and in the Empire there was style. Perhaps in the nineteenth century we had not quite forgotten the age when men carried themselves with an air. Certainly you remembered it when you entered the Empire; in that spacious hall, too proud to call itself a palace, there was room to ruffle it, with the hat at a slant, a hand on the hip, and a cane like a sword by your side. So I have seen Randal Charlton walking—the last of the Regency bucks.

Everybody had been to the Empire. The Assistant-Commissioner of Boola-boola, playing " Take me Back to London " on a cracked banjo, dreamt that he smelt Crosse and Blackwells' pickles, and saw the pretty ladies and swimming lights of the Empire promenade. It was here that Winston Churchill made his first public appearance—on the highest peak of a barricade of chairs. And it was here that Mrs. Ormiston Chant and Mr. McDougall scored their most spectacular victory.

That victory killed the Empire. Though it has been a long time a-dying, it has been dying from that day. And I want you to consider to what extent the triumph of the Puritan has benefited public morals. That it has tended to stifle public jollity there can be no doubt.

I was myself less perturbed by the closing of the Empire promenade than by the forbidding of the sale of drink in the auditorium. The never-ending audacity of elected persons never went farther than that. If man may drink with his meals, which some have held (though they were heretics) to be bad for him, why should he not drink with his songs, which nobody can deny is wholesome for him? And why the hell should anybody be allowed to say that here and now he may drink, and there and then he may not? Of course, I know the assumption; and may the blight of perpetual dryness be on the man who first assumed that old ale, the nut brown, that would put the soul of ten men into a weaver, is an evil thing.

When you could no longer drink with your liquor there was an end of it; not so much because you would certainly want to drink, though beer and wine are fine symbols of good fellowship, but because you could not when you would, and you felt the ghostly policewoman watching you. Of course, we ought to have rebelled, but " the Flying Inn " had not yet been written, and rebellions for things that really matter are hard to come by.

I was, in those days, one who drank to a song, and when, between drinks, I promenaded at the Empire, I saw too many pretty ladies (thousands of them) to be beguiled by any. As Mr. Pickwick (or was it Solomon?) says, there is safety in numbers.

But I realised as clearly that it was absurd to forbid ladies to circulate on the promenade as my soberer friends did that it was absurd to forbid drink to circulate elsewhere in the hall. " You cannot," the war cry ran, " make people moral by Act of Parliament or L.C.C. regulations." And I think most of us meant that men would not be more moral even if

they refrained, on compulsion, from liquor and the ladies, and listened munchance to the song.

And, as a matter of fact, they did not refrain. The Puritans have killed the music-halls, and clapped hands on it. There is now no Empire promenade, there is now no Empire, no Tivoli, no Pavilion, no Oxford Music Hall. But Sir Wm. Joynson-Hicks and the Bishop of London are seriously perturbed by the growth of night clubs and the light behaviour of young persons of the opposite sex.

I do not think there is much harm in night clubs. I have been to most of them, and my main complaint is that they are so beastly dull. But there is no doubt that they are less wholesome as well as less jolly than the old music-halls, and that I would rather have taken my wife, my sister, or my daughter to the Empire, or the Tivoli, than to any of these caravanserais of shingled pleasure.

Of course, the poor do not go to night clubs, and I suppose the suppression of the music-hall was an attempt to reform the poor. At the Halls the classes met in a way they never meet now. Where do the poor spend their leisure to-day? Horrible thought! I suppose they go to the pictures, and rush out torrentially to pump in as much drink as possible before closing time.

Then, for those not quite poor, there are, as well as the pictures, the public dance-halls. Not much harm in the dances, perhaps, yet one stern reformer has called them (unpleasant fellow!) a bath of sex. You could not so have styled the entertainment which let us chorus one of Marie Lloyd's jolly songs five times over.

Have we lost liberty? Well, all that is gone. Even without song, and pinned to a bar, the clock controls us. Soon they will try to turn the tap off altogether; and what will happen then? There will be more night clubs and worse ones. And drink will be sold at the chemist's, as in that memorable shop whose windows shattered, when the people rose, like the breaking of the windows of the world.

W. R. TITTERTON.

Rhymes for the Young Londoner
BUCKINGHAM PALACE.

Pay no attention to popular fallacies
Whether they're modern or whether they're old,
Do not imagine that Buckingham Palace is
Builded of silver and panelled with gold.
Philip and Eleanor, Arthur and Charity,
How could you ever believe such a thing?
Don't you perceive that such blatant vulgarity
Never would do for the House of the King.

See the brave soldiers on permanent sentry-go
(Surely those hats must be fearfully hot!)
Dubious persons attempting an entry go
Out at the double—or else they are shot.
And rightly say I, for displaying such vanity
How could we ever permit such a thing?
How could we have all the dregs of humanity
Bolshing about in the House of the King?

Hector and Herbert, Godiva and Gloria,
Come you from Sussex, or come you from Kent,
Hie you to London, hop out at Victoria,
Turn to the left to a certain extent.
Outside the Palace behave yourselves graciously,
Don't do a common, a terrible thing—
DON'T touch the bell and then scamper audaciously!
Stand, and touch hats to the House of the King.

L. J. R. W.

STRAWS IN THE WIND
THE HOUSE OF FULFILMENT
By G. K. CHESTERTON

FAMILIAR as I naturally am with controversy by fire and faggot, I do not wish to persecute Mr. H. G. Wells in the literal sense of pursuing him as an escaped enemy; or even of pursuing him as an endless topic of conversation. But his recent article in the *Sunday Express*, devoted to denying that Man exists as a fixed type (or indeed that he exists at all) has one particular aspect which is specially antagonistic to the views that we advance here. It is obvious, of course, that the whole notion of Man as a mere transitional type, melting from shape to shape like a cloud, is antagonistic to our scheme of social justice. It is also antagonistic to any other scheme of social justice. All men desire a human society that can be a home; a home that will fit a man as a hat fits a head. But it is no good interviewing a hundred hatters, and trying on a thousand hats, if the head is always swelling and twisting and turning into different shapes like the smoke out of a chimney-pot. We cannot build a house for a man who is not always a man, but sometimes a mammoth and sometimes a whale and sometimes a minnow or a tittlebat. And it is obvious that those who wish to disregard men's necessities will be only too delighted to hear of the mutability of their needs. The man who wants to feed his servant on chopped hay will be charmed to hear that the servant may be evolving into a creature as vegetarian as a cow. The man who wants to feed his servant on carrion will be glad to hear that he may be growing as omnivorous as a carrion-crow.

But it is not that general evil in the evolutionary monomania to which I refer at this moment. The point at which Mr. Wells's last utterance specially cuts across the lines of our own movement is the point about the family. Mr. Wells, in urging his theory that man has changed, makes the strange remark that he has become less sexual. That is hardly the impression of most people who can look calmly round at the life and literature of our time. But it soon becomes apparent that Mr. Wells does not mean what he says; but something quite different. He means, apparently, that man has become less domestic. He means that he is less settled in his sex relations; and he seems in some mysterious way to regard the mere relaxation of sex relations as a retrenchment of them. Darby and Joan are sexual; but Don Juan and Lothario are not sexual. Baucis and Philemon are a shocking case of sexuality; but Jupiter turning into a bull, a swan, and a shower of gold, to pursue his profligacies, is an illustration of how completely a divine being disdains the sentiment of sex. It seems to me quite obvious that Mr. Wells is simply using sex as a term of abuse; with a curious trick of employing Puritan denunciation in defence of Pagan philosophy. Hissing the word " sexual " in that fierce fashion betrays the eternal Manichee inside the Materialist.

Now the principle which primarily concerns us is this. Sex is an instinct that produces an institution; and it is positive and not negative, noble and not base, creative and not destructive, because it produces that institution. That institution is the family; a small state or commonwealth which has hundreds of aspects, when it is once started, that are not sexual at all. It includes worship, justice, festivity, decoration, instruction, comradeship, repose. Sex is the gate of that house; and romantic and imaginative people naturally like looking through a gateway. But the house is very much larger than the gate. There are indeed a certain number of people who like to hang about in the gate and never get any further; who do in the exact words of Swinburne's poem " play with light loves in the portal." They generally prefer to do it in somebody else's portal. So far as I can make out, Mr. Wells does not think that *they* deserve to be branded with that dreadful adjective. But even they are not so silly as to

say that the house is only a gate; that the world contains no houses and nothing but gates; or that domestic people have no sense and nothing but sexuality. But Mr. Wells, whether he means this or not, does certainly lay himself open to a considerable doubt about what else he can mean. When sexual relations are used to create non-sexual relations, he is shocked by the expanding power of sex. When sexual relations are merely repeated at random, and reproduce nothing whatever except themselves, he does not seem to mind them half so much. There again we see for an instant, as if brown and withered and looking out from its gilded Byzantine tomb, the mad face of the Manichaean. But anyhow, the long and the short of it is that sex can be used seriously to make something or loosely to mar anything; and Mr. Wells seems rather to prefer it when it mars and not when it makes.

It is perfectly obvious, for instance, that the free lover is simply a person attempting the impossible idea of having a series of honeymoons and no marriage. He is building a long arcade consisting entirely of gates; with no house at the end of them. As he is always trying to repeat the sexual part of the programme, and not go on to the non-sexual part of it, it would seem mere lunacy to say that he is freed from the obsession of sex. And yet it is of a society at least conceived in that spirit, and full of that general philosophy, that Mr. Wells has the calm audacity to say it. Now we are very much concerned, not only for ethical but for economic reasons, to say the opposite. Property in its proper sense is simply the economic aspect of that positive and creative Thing which is started by the instinct and ends in the institution. It is simply the housekeeping of that solid house, of which love is the romantic gateway. Property must be private because that family wishes to be private; because it wishes to be in some degree separate and self-governing; because the home insists on home rule. And even the enemy bears witness to this link of property and domesticity; because he reviles them both.

This domestic institution doubtless is now seen under great disadvantages; battling for its life and almost battered to pieces by the forces of capitalism and materialism. I will not say it is not at its best; for I suppose this human institution, like humanity, is never really at its best. It always falls short of a divine plan; and there was no complete human family except the Holy Family. I would rather say it is now at its worst; but mainly because its enemies have done their worst against it. It has lost the sane sense of the protection of property; because most have no property and a few have too much protection. Its own internal creative power, in arts and crafts and games and graces and dignities, has been crushed inwards with the weight of the outer world and all its blatant banalities and booming platitudes. It will be a problem to trace its real outlines in the tangle; and a great struggle to build it anew. But if it is lost, liberty is lost and lost for ever. Nothing is left but the remote mechanical search-lights of the Servile State, shot like death-rays into every corner of existence and killing everything that grows by its own life.

Wedding Rhymes
AUNTS.

An Aunt in bombazine will glare
And be extremely peeved
If, by the young and happy pair,
She is not well received.
The thoughtless couple may not care—
The Aunt is grim and grieved.

Sagacious Brides, at Aunt-alarms,
Should hurry up on deck,
Attract the Aunt with simple charms
And fall upon her neck.
An Aunt received with open arms
May write an open cheque.   R. W.

THE DRAMA

"THE RINGER," Mr. Edgar Wallace's inspiriting melodrama, will undoubtedly prove the forerunner of innumerable descendants. Already we find Dr. Noel Scott's " The Joker " on the Royalty stage. A mystery man is always a sure card in a crook play, though it is essential that until the psychological moment he should remain a mystery; but whereas the hero of the Wallace drama remains concealed until the curtain is about to fall, the identity of the joker is made plain to an inquiring audience within the first five minutes of the action.

He is rather a tiresome person, this same joker. He owes his success not to his own brains, but to their absence in other people. Indeed it is a little difficult to decide whether he, or the rogues and vagabonds he tracks, are the more destitute.

We have an innocent, trusting, but mentally deficient heroine, Jill Vane, charmingly played by Miss Phyllis Y. Titmuss. She resides with her step-uncle, Major Borwick, who is described as the genius of the gang. The gang exist by theft and blackmail. Arthur Mainwaring at one time had an intrigue with Jill's sister. She got over it, however, and married a wealthy man. Mainwaring meanwhile has kept her letters and proceeds to extort large sums as a bribe to keep silent. Before the matter went too far, however, Jill insists that it was she and not her sister who was the heroine of the liaison, whereat her brother-in-law throws her out of the house and she takes refuge with the wicked Major.

Jill is not all she seems. That is to say, she is not a poor orphan but a rich heiress. Her father had a farm—those wonderful Australian farms—which the Government buys for £100,000. Mainwaring decides he wants the money and will marry the girl, who will shortly come of age. In the meantime he returns to his blackmailing device over the letters. Their plans, however, are spoilt by the joker, who has a pleasant habit of leaving that particular playing-card about the scene of his exploits. He waylays one of the gang, steals the letters; he visits the flat of another, and thoroughly searches it; last, but not least, he gets hold of a stolen diamond en route to a receiver in Holland. He is in love with Jill, is attached to the Intelligence Department, is called Peter, and is played by Mr. Dennis Eadie.

As a member of the Intelligence, one is not surprised that he hands the letters back to Jill, who puts them into her vanity bag. The said bag is stolen and Jill chloroformed, and the gang departs for Wapping, leaving the joker to face a murderous ex-convict.

The scene in Wapping has a few genuine thrills. There is a trapeze act over the roofs of the adjoining houses, some admirable sleight of hand with a pistol and the final triumph of the Joker. The fourth act following his marriage with Jill, is as weak as the first, and not even the admirable acting of Miss Minnie Rayner, all too late, can redeem it. Mr. Lewin Mannering gives a brilliant portrait of Hemming, the one member of the gang who shows intelligence, and Mr. Cronin Wilson is very good as the blustering Mainwaring. Mr. Dennis Eadie remains polished and unchanged.

*   *   *

The Gate Theatre is running a series of foreign plays, beginning with " Melodrama " by Georg Kaiser. This is a most delightful satire. We have the beautiful young wife betrayed by a callous husband, who married her only for money. We have the infant heir spirited away by his fond mother to America; the wicked Count being supplied with a common child whom he regards as his own son. There is an emotional uncle, an aristocratic great aunt, a faithful steward, and a woman from the gutter—mother of the substituted son.

All the high-faluting speeches that melodrama has included, all the snobbish sentiments voiced by the Squire throughout the ages, are dished up with the most wonderful sauce piquant; this brilliant skit played with perfect elan, is one of the most pleasing entertainments in London. Norman Shelley as the Count, is inimitable; Caroline Keith as the great aunt has almost Shavian riposte. Molly Veness, as the Countess, does not please me quite so much; she should deliver her preposterous rodomontades with complete seriousness. As it is, she allows a sense of humour to punctuate them, so that the full richness of their absurdity is obscure.

The productions at this little theatre are remarkable. Their settings have the requisite touch of suggestion which appeals to the imagination. Here is an opportunity for enjoying good acting and an extremely witty play. " Melodrama " runs only for a fortnight; I don't think anybody ought to miss it.

J. K. P.

THE COCKPIT

ANTI-VIVISECTION

DEAR MR. CHESTERTON,—I must protest most emphatically against the manner in which, in this week's leader, you lump together the opponents of vivisection and the " humanitarians whose welfare work is a vivisection of the poor." Surely there is this enormous difference between them—the anti-vivisectors are passionate, while the C.O.S.-ites are passionless; in short, just like the vivisectors.

Your readiness to sacrifice Quoodle does credit to your heart. The secretary might accept the sacrifice; and, if it be not too sentimental to make the suggestion, Quoodle—if he knows the secretary—might be ready for the sacrifice. But who is to judge of the necessity for the sacrifice—the experts? It is asking us to put more faith in them than many of us can.

Quite recently in an American laboratory a cat (I think) was burned alive in order to discover how far burning affected the amount of carbonic acid in the lungs. The evidence was required to " prove " whether a woman had been killed before being burned or whether burning was the cause of death. Scores of doctors must have held scores of p.m.'s on human victims who had met their death by burning. If doctors are the scientists we are led to believe, they should have been in possession of such evidence, which, since it came from the human body, might have had some value.

As to the " smug sentimentalists who smile to see a conscious man on the rack," why warn them that the League is no place for them? Have any applied for membership? Are any likely to do so? I should be greatly surprised to hear that the charity-mongers had been crowding into the ranks of the Distributists!

A man may have a very decided objection to vivisection without being a " sentimentalist." You appear to have *some* objection yourself. My own view of the matter, for what it is worth, is that the practice is so horrible that it cannot be right, and although in certain circumstances a man might well succumb to the temptation to sacrifice an animal in this way—to save a fellow man's life—yet, since the whole business *is* so horrible and so doubtful, to *anticipate* the circumstances is quite another matter.

LOUIS A. DESSURNE.

VIVISECTION AND UNEMPLOYMENT

SIR,—Your article on vivisection does not hold water. You say you would not experiment on dogs unless you were sure some useful knowledge about disease would be the consequence. Unfortunately, you never can be sure about this. Often a physiological experiment which appears at the time to be entirely academic, is subsequently found to be of great importance to the exponents of medicine and surgery. Also experiments for the purpose of tracking down disease are not the only experiments which are useful. Experiments to find out how the body works normally are just as important. To draw an analogy, you cannot mend a puncture in a bicycle tyre unless you first observe how the tyre should be in its normal state.

May I now change the subject entirely, and bring your attention to certain points which you may have overlooked:—

(1) That the medieval guilds have been revived in Spain.

(2) That H.M. Stationery Office is supplying manufacturers and distributors with statistics of unemployment in their areas.

The *Times* says this is " to adjust sales activities to the changing prosperity of local areas or to make due allowance for such changes in judging the effectiveness of advertising or salesmanship."

Now I may be balmy, but it sounds incredible that unemployment figures should make a difference to the advertising of a factory. If there is an increase in unemployment, shall we live to see the happy day when the big firms will tear down their beastly advertisements in despair? If half the population of England became unemployed, I admit it would make it necessary for the factories to make changes in salesmanship, etc., but surely a relatively small local increase of unemployment would not incur all this bother.

I have a suggestion to make. A surplus of goods brings the price of those goods down, a surplus of labour brings the price of that labour down. Therefore a little unemployment might be good news to the manufacturers. However, this is only a suggestion, but it is a suggestion suggested by certain rumours I have heard connected with Sheffield. Sheffield often receives paragraphs to itself in certain newspapers. Trade is said to be booming there, there is a great demand for labour, and everybody is immensely happy—except the unemployed who troop there encouraged by the good news. Why shouldn't they be happy, too? Why, for this reason, when they get to Sheffield there is no demand for their labour, they have been deceived. But the manufacturers, bless them, are happy. And why? Because there is now a surplus amount of labour, thanks to the newly arrived unemployed.

However, the manufacturers may have a good excuse to offer for these " statistics of unemployment," or perhaps you can correct me and find an excuse for them.—Yours faithfully,

G. P. B. WHITWELL,
Guy's Hospital.

P.S.—The statistics of unemployed may be obtained for £5 annually to subscribers only.

MISS TENNYSON JESSE AND TOUSSAINT L'OUVERTURE

WHILE the youth of England is busy with the Charleston, the Black Bottom and other survivals of nigger obeah and voodoo, it may not be interested in the slightest degree in a negro who was a great soldier and statesman, lawgiver and Christian. We owe a good deal of our knowledge of the spirit of Toussaint L'Ouverture to William Wordsworth before he became an old sheep. The sonnet remains while the inspiration of it is well-nigh forgotten.

Miss Tennyson Jesse will revive, among the intelligent, an old enthusiasm for freedom in her presentation of the man who was called the Black Napoleon and who would fiercely have resented the appellation. Toussaint is the most remarkable negro of the centuries. He was literally a king among men, though he bore all the physical stigmata of an enslaved race.

In "Moonraker"* or "The Female Pirate and her Friends," Miss Jesse tells the story of young Jacky Jacka, who, in the year of our Lord, 1801-2, ran away from home to take ship on the *Piskie*, which was boarded by the pirate, Captain Lovel, with his fierce and beautiful craft, *Moonraker*. In the later capture of a French vessel, Lovel rescued from summary death a young Frenchman, Raoul de Kerangal. There is a most ingenious story as to the entirely unsuspected feminine element abroad *Moonraker*, and the amazement the final disclosure caused to everyone, even clever young Jacky Jacka; but the real pith of the book is in the purpose of Lovel, entirely persuaded by his young French friend, to rescue Toussaint from the French legions and French treachery.

The tale is told by Miss Jesse but it reads as if the boy himself had transcribed it. It is an astounding record this of the negro general and his colleagues fighting against the mighty forces of the greatest military power in the world, and fighting successfully until his own generals betray him. As Governor-General of San Domingo, Toussaint had incurred the displeasure of Napoleon, and that great-little man, in one of his fits of baseness, resolved to exterminate L'Ouverture and his Republic of Haiti.

It is a pathetic and fantastic picture that Miss Jesse (or her Jacky) paints of the slave who became a ruler:

Jacky saw that the Governor-General had several front teeth missing; he was ugly and sad-looking, like a sick monkey, and yet you felt he was a great man, though he was as black as the Earl of Hell's riding-boots.

Toussaint believed absolutely in the honour of the French Consul and the French people. Well, the people are scarcely ever to blame in cases of unjust and unnecessary war, but the generous soul of France should have risen in protest at the scurvy treatment its military heads accorded to a chivalrous foe.

The young ship's boy and the young Frenchmen meet as staid middle-aged buffers after a very long lapse of time. Raoul tells the friend of his youth of the lonely fortress near Besancon, of the unanswered letters to the First Consul and of that last winter morning, when dead from starvation, the black General was found lying with his grey head leaning forward on a cold and empty stove, his teeth all fallen out and his limbs distorted with rheumatism. Death in those distant years saved Toussaint the ignominy, anyhow, of teaching the Black Bottom to degenerate whites.

LOUIS J. McQUILLAND.

---

* MOONRAKER. By F. Tennyson Jesse. Heinemann. 6s.

LIBRARY LIST

GOOD—BETTER—BEST. By J. A. T. Lloyd. Holden. 7s. 6d.
This is the sort of book that makes one simply cry out for a good old shocker. It deals with the psychology of a criminal, and its atmosphere is unreal and nauseating, its style laboured.

PAGES IN WAITING. By James Milne. John Lane. 6s.
Mr. Milne talks entertainingly of the book world; he has what must be an almost unique knowledge of such matters as the history of publishing houses, and pioneers of the cheap reprint. When he is in satirical vein he is not quite so interesting, and the best thing in the book is his " Word of Preface " to the " Dear British Public."

THE FRINGES OF EDINBURGH. By John Geddie. Chambers. 7s. 6d.
This is an elaborately illustrated book on the great city written by one who evidently knows it supremely well, and loves it. Edinburgh's bibliography is already enormous, but this is a worth-while addition to it.

THE BOOK OF ROBERT SOUTHWELL. By Christobel Hood. Blackwell. 7s. 6d.
All lovers of great religious poetry will rejoice at this very well produced memento of a noble and scholarly mind, too long neglected. Southwell's poetry has a fire which will warm us when the legion of more voluble and famous poets leaves us cold.

THE HINDU VIEW OF LIFE. By S. Radhakrishnan. G. Allen and Unwin. 5s.
Not being Hindu we are hardly qualified to comment on the subject matter, but it would seem to be undoubtedly authoritative and it is certainly presented in a very clear and readable prose. It comprises the Upton lectures delivered at Manchester College, Oxford, in 1926.

THE REIGN OF BRASS. By Charles C. Jenkins. Duckworth. 7s. 6d.
In spite of its grandiose language, which is rather feebly forcible, the writer tells a good yarn of a poetic Canadian youth who became a barrister, a junior reporter, an English naval officer, and finally a whisky-smuggler of the Great American Lakes. It is significant of the America of to-day that it finds its highest exponent of manhood in a boot-legger.

AMONG THE BRANCHES
GENERAL NOTICES

Will members interested in the formation of new Branches of the League kindly send their names and addresses, for publication in G.K.'s WEEKLY, to the secretary of the League, 20-21 Essex Street, Strand, W.C.2

Branch secretaries are reminded that reports should reach head office by first post on Monday of each week for insertion in G.K.'s WEEKLY.

E. GORDON DUNHAM, Sec.

———

CENTRAL BRANCH.—*Secretary*: G. C. Heseltine, 20/21 Essex Street, Strand, W.C.2.

The usual weekly discussion will take place at the Devereux on Friday at 6.30.

BARNET.—*Secretary*: T. McNamara, 70 Berkeley Crescent, Barnet.

BIRMINGHAM.—*Secretary*: K. L. Kenrick, 7 Soho Road, Handsworth.

BRIGHTON.—*Secretary*: C. B. Harrison, 21 Alexander Villas, Brighton.

CAMBRIDGE.—*Secretary*: H. E. Wood, King's College, Cambridge.

A public meeting will take place at the Guildhall on Sunday, January 30, at 8.30 p.m., when Sir Henry Slesser and Mr. G. K. Chesterton will speak on "Is Liberty Dead?" For further particulars apply to the secretary.

CHORLEY.—*Secretary*: James Power, Woodlands, Rotherwick Avenue, Chorley.

COVENTRY.—*Secretary*: R. E. S. Willison, 102 Westwood Road, Coventry.

CROYDON.—*Secretary*: Stormont Murray, Turret House, 4 Campden Road, Croydon.

EDINBURGH BRANCH.—*Secretary*: Jas. Turner, 69 St. Leonard's Street, Edinburgh.

GLASGOW.—*Secretary*: A. McGregor, 128 Hope Street, Glasgow. Meetings Monday, 7.15 p.m. at offices of secretary.

LIVERPOOL.—*Secretary*: J. P. Alcock, Melwood, Deysbrook Lane, West Derby, Liverpool.

A business meeting was held at the Grenville Café on Thursday, January 20. Committee and officials were elected for 1927, and a tentative programme was discussed. Mr. E. R. Gill kindly took the chair. The next meeting will be on Thursday, February 3, at No. 6 Lord Street, at 8 p.m. prompt. A discussion "Is Big Business Efficient?" will take place. The members of the study circle hope to make it lively, and the opposition will be there. Visitors will be welcome. Attendance at meetings might still be improved.

MANCHESTER.—*Secretary*: James Hammond, 20 Verdun Road, Monton, Eccles.

A meeting was held at the "Cosy Café," on Wednesday, January 19, at 8 p.m. Mr. J. P. Alcock, the Liverpool branch secretary, was present, and he advanced much helpful criticism as well as various ideas which his branch were carrying out. One or two of our own members may possibly repay the visit in the near future. Miss Lee gave a paper on "Arts and Crafts," considerable discussion ensuing. The next meeting is to be held on Wednesday, the 26th inst., at the "Cosy Café," when Mr. Murphy, the chairman, is to give a paper on "Education and Distributism." The paper down for discussion on February 2 is that of Mr. Irving, on "Co-partnership."

MEDWAY.—*Secretary*: J. Murphy, 55 Paget Street, Gillingham, Kent.

A report of the debate between Mr. G. K. Chesterton and Mr. S. F. Markham will appear next week.

NEWCASTLE-ON-TYNE.—*Secretary*: J. Finlayson, 20 Goldspink Lane.

The first meeting will be held on Thursday, February 3, at 7.30 p.m., in Crown Hotel, Clayton Street. All interested are invited to attend. Anyone wishing to send a paper, or having any item for inclusion in the agenda, is asked to write to the secretary as soon as possible.

NORTH SHIELDS.—*Secretary*: J. J. Rogan, 28 Windermere Terrace, North Shields, Northumberland.

OXFORD CITY AND DISTRICT.—*Secretary*: R. R. D. Paton, The Old Farmhouse, Black Bourton, Clanfield, Oxford. Will Leaguers in and around Oxford please communicate with Mr. Paton?

OXFORD UNIVERSITY.—*Secretary*: R. C. S. Ellison, Merton College, Oxford.

SOUTHAMPTON.—*Secretary*: W. S. Ellaby, Banister Court, Southampton.

THANET.—*Secretary*: G. Victor Taylor, The Bungalow, Lymington Road, Westgate-on-Sea.

WEST MIDDLESEX.—*Secretary*: J. V. Jenks, 108, Milton Road, Hanwell, W.7.

The area of this branch extends from Acton and Chiswick on the east side to Southall and Hounslow on the west, and from Harrow and Willesden on the north to Brentford and Isleworth on the South. Will sympathisers in this inclusive area (which also includes Ealing and Hanwell) please send a postcard to the secretary, in order that he may acquaint them with the date, time and place of the next branch meeting. Leaguers transferred from Central Branch will hear from him shortly. One new member, making our number ten in all.

Branches are in process of formation at the following places and until secretaries have been appointed intending members should communicate with the Leaguers whose names are given:—BANFFSHIRE.—G. Beaumont, The Elms Hotel, Dufftown, Banffshire. BELFAST.—J. R. Ross, 14 Woodland Avenue, Cliftonville. BRADFORD.—Mrs. G. Healey, 4 Rossifield Road, Heaton, Bradford. BLACKPOOL.—Miss E. M. Taylor, 37 Norbreck Road, Norbreck, Blackpool. CARDIFF.—Wm. P. Hogan, 17 Amesbury Road, Penylan, Cardiff. HUDDERSFIELD.—Norman R. Turner, 12 Belmont Street, Huddersfield. LEEDS.—T. Byrne, 141 Leeds Terrace, North Street, Leeds. ROCHDALE.—M. P. Keating, 15 Chatsworth Street, Whitworth Road, Rochdale. SALFORD.—James Burns, 8 Trafalgar Square, Regent Road. SHEFFIELD.—Canon Wm. Collingwood, Bamford, Sheffield. WEYBRIDGE.—Mrs. Helen A. Reckitt, Marrowells, Weybridge, Surrey. WINDSOR-ETON-SLOUGH.—Hubert S. Paynter, Rainbow Cottage, Christmas Common, Nr. Watlington, Oxfordshire.

APPLICATION FORM FOR MEMBERSHIP

I wish to become a member of THE LEAGUE, with whose objects I am in sympathy, and I enclose herewith ...., *being the annual subscription of one shilling, and* .... *as a donation.*

Name ....

Address ....

To The Treasurer, The League,
20-21 Essex Street, Strand, London, W.C.2.

Prepaid Classified Advertisements
RATES.

Minimum 20 Words (Two Lines)... ... ... **Four Shillings.**
Every Additional 10 Words (One Line) ... ... **Two Shillings.**
Less than 10 Words charged as a line.
Heading and each additional line set in capital letters charged as two lines.

Instructions should be addressed to:—
PREPAID CLASSIFIED ADVERTISEMENTS DEPARTMENT, G.K.'S WEEKLY, 20-21 Essex Street, Strand, London, W.C.2, by first post on Monday of each week.

Appointments Vacant.

CANVASSERS WANTED TO OBTAIN Subscribers to Important Weekly Newspaper. Good commission terms.—Box 32, G.K.'s WEEKLY, 20 Essex Street, Strand, London, W.C.1.

Educational.

ST. THERESE'S CONVENT, Sunbury Manor, Sunbury-on-Thames, Middlesex.—High-class residential and day school; girls; kindergarten. (35 mins. Waterloo.).—Apply, Mother Superior.

Miscellaneous.

WHAT BETTER GIFT than a bound volume of G.K.'s WEEKLY? Volume I, 6d. copies (Nos. 1-26), pages 1-624, with index. Few volumes available at 10s. 6d. a volume. Later volumes in preparation. Binding cases 2s. 6d. a volume. Address, Business Manager.

All "G.K.'s Weekly" Advertisements are Guaranteed.

Published by the Proprietors, G.K.'s WEEKLY, LTD., at their offices, 20 & 21 Essex Street, Strand, London, W.C.2 (incorporating THE NEW WITNESS). Telephone No. City 1978. Printed by THE PRESS AT COOMBELANDS, LTD., London and Addlestone. Sole agents for Australasia : Gordon & Gotch (Australasia), Ltd. Sole Agents for South Africa : Central News Agency, Ltd.

G.K.'s Weekly January 28, 1928.

THE EQUALITY OF SLAVES.

G.K.'s Weekly

EDITED BY G. K. CHESTERTON.

No. 149.—Vol. VI.   Week ending Saturday, January 28, 1928.   PRICE TWOPENCE. YEARLY (52 ISSUES) 10s. 10d.

Telephone No. City 1978.   [Registered at G.P.O. as a Newspaper.]   Offices, 20 & 21, Essex Street, Strand, W.C 2

CONTENTS :

WHAT DOES STALIN MEAN?

THIS is a question which the Monopolist Press never asks, since it knows the answer. It talks a lot about him, generally praising him and calling him a realist, by which it means a man who is too sensible to have moral principles. But it never asks what he means. For it does not want its readers to know.

We think that Mr. Garvin wants them to know, but that he himself is not sure of the answer. For he says that Stalin wishes to form a Socialist or semi-Socialist state in a capitalist world, and that Lenin, had he been alive, would probably have supported him. But we think that the most important implication escapes him.

There is no doubt that (1) Stalin's Socialism is not the Communism of which the British Communist dreams, (2) it is not the Communism of which Lenin dreamt, (3) it is not what Lenin established.

The British Communist dreams of a state of society in which the ownership of property by the nation means complete freedom for the individual. Lenin desired much the same, but with greater emphasis on national ownership; and if the peasants had been amenable he might have attained the latter—for a time. The peasants resisted, and Lenin's scheme was wrecked. Its operation was mainly confined to the industrial problems of the town. Yet until Lenin died, the theory that the workman was the master, and that though he worked under compulsion, it was he who compelled, was maintained.

The other half of the Bolshevik theory was that the social revolution must be international. A logical sequence of this was intensive propaganda in all foreign countries—propaganda working for a general overthrow of existing social institutions the world over. But the difficulties of establishing Russian industries without the aid of foreign capital and the free entry to foreign markets was enormous. And this, while it supported the case of the Internationalists, rendered the internal equilibrium of Russia unstable. For some time the attempt was to undermine capitalism from below, while seeking its support from above.

This was the position when Stalin came into power, and he realized its absurdity. Gradually he has made it plain that he is far more eager to establish Russian industry on a paying basis than to further the world revolution. Increasingly he has permitted the capitalist exploitation of raw materials and manufactured goods in Russia. And the manœuvres of his secret agents have been devoted less to subversive propaganda than to the nominal espionage of an Imperialist government. More than ever the Russians are bent on conquest, but now it is undisguisedly by force of arms.

Russia, in fact, tends to become the ordinary capitalist state—with this difference : that since it started with a dictatorship and with many industries organized on a monopolist basis, it will be easier for it to take the final shape of capitalist monopoly.

Men like Sir Alfred Mond feel that Stalin is on their side, and they are waiting for a good excuse to enter into free negotiations with him.

And that is the meaning of Stalin. Trotsky has gone into exile because he still nourishes the ideal of international dictatorship of the proletariat, and supports the means of subversive propaganda. He is more honest and he was less dangerous than Stalin. For Stalin and Mond will come to terms.

NOTES OF THE WEEK.

The Ramsgate Poll.

THE poll of the local government electors of Ramsgate on the Ramsgate Corporation Bill, 1928, was taken on Tuesday of this week, and the result is not known at the moment of going to press. The main fight is over the proposed transfer of the Ramsgate Harbour from the Ministry of Transport to the Corporation. It is maintained by the opposers that the reason why the Ministry is so anxious to make the gift is that the Harbour has been for years a dead loss, and there is no prospect of an appreciable greater revenue, and that the Harbour works are in a state of decay. It is further held by some that, since the Harbour is Crown property, it cannot be alienated in favour of the Corporation. That point we do not propose to argue, nor do we see that a big general question is involved—unless, as some fear, the Corporation is likely to sell the Harbour to a private company, should the burden on the rates become heavy.

The Insignificant Hawker.

FOUR questions are put to the electors, and only one seems to us of grave importance. Just as in the Bill itself hawking is referred to in one small clause in a subsidiary part of the Bill, so in the circularized questions we find hawking mentioned only at the tail of a footnote : " Resolution No. 3 relates principally to provisions for preserving the amenities of streets and the convenience and safety of persons using them; safeguarding the public health; provision of clauses for dealing with slaughter houses; the control traffic and hackney carriages and the prohibition or regulation of the distribution of handbills, the soliciting of alms and touting and hawking." Thus once more an attempt is made to kill the hawker without fuss. The coupling of the hawker with those who distribute handbills, solicit alms, and tout, is peculiarly illuminating. Now, as we say, we do not know what is the result of the poll. But whatever it is, and whether or no the electors of Ramsgate have decided to take over the Harbour and the Burial Boards and the Slaughter Houses, to control traffic and hackney carriages, and to prohibit or regulate the distribution of handbills, the solicitation of alms, and touting, we trust that all the friends of the hawker in Ramsgate and elsewhere will bother their respective members of Parliament to secure an amendment of the Bill in his favour if and when it is presented.

Poland and Its Enemies.

AN article in the current number of the *Nation* reminds us that the left wing of English political opinion looks forward to another partition of Poland. The writer describes the regime of Pilsudski as an opportunist and makeshift government, inspired by opportunism yet better than either parliamentarism, or anything the right wing of Polish politics could produce. The torrents of abuse poured upon the latter—the nationalist and clerical, monarchist and fascist parties—are the outcome of rage rather than mere prejudice, and suggest crimes too fearful to be specified. They appear to be a desire to relieve Poles in the Eastern provinces from learning Lithuanian or Ruthene (described as a passion for " persecuting racial minorities "), a desire to keep the Polish state from Prussian and Bolshevik encroachments, and a resistance to an influx of foreign capital, bringing in its train the international tyranny of monopolists and financiers—beloved of the *Nation*.

The Railways and the Roads.

WHEN Combines fall out, the citizen comes to his own. When the Combines are united, they won't fall out. We note that the Transport Committee of the Federation of British Industries has recommended strenuous opposition to the Bills that the railways companies have presented to Parliament for power to compete with road transport. The committee holds that, armed with the powers sought for, the railway companies would crush competing carriers, and would then put up their rates. And so railway rates would be maintained and road charges increased. With this point of view we are in absolute agreement. This is universally the effect of a monopoly, and this would have been the effect of the Traffic Monopoly in London had not Lord Ashfield met with the heroic resistance of the independent 'bus-owners. For long the railway companies considered themselves a monopoly, and behaved as such. All suggestions for improvement in their methods of traffic have been scouted. And now the one idea in their silly heads is to become what they thought themselves to be. But Combines are *so* effective. What would happen to the railways if the canals were acquired by the nation, and brought up to date?

Another Tittlark.

THE fatuity of news as the modern news editor sees it, is well illustrated in the bold announcement that the sparrow is not the most common bird. In spite of the expert ornithologists who spring this epoch-making discovery on a startled world, it is probably quite untrue; nobody really cares, nor does it matter, whether the number of sparrows per square mile is more or less than those who have nothing better to think about think it is. When the statement that the titlark is more common than the sparrow has been repeated solemnly several times by a few nonagenarian ornithological " experts," it will no doubt pass into the Category of Scientific Fact. Like most alleged " Scientific " facts it will have no relation to the reality of human experience. The sparrow will remain the commonest bird to all but a few pedants, because it is the bird they most often meet. Not one Englishman in ten thousand knows a titlark if he sees or hears one; and to the rest all birds less than pigeons are sparrows, thanks to modern education, and the industrial soot. It has been suggested that this paper is a Titt-lark, but we think this needs confirmation by competent ornithologists.

Beauty and the Beasts.

THE Ministry of Health's fear for the beauty of the villages, attacked by the jerry-builder, is a little belated, and the appeal to be made to architects and builders is a nice example of the simple faith of the politician in the profiteer. Anybody but a Minister of Health or a Housing Authority would know that already the post-war rabble-coops are falling down all over the country, whilst the inhabitants are building themselves rustic sheds in the garden. In a few years the subsidized houses will have all subsided and been bought up by scrap-iron-and-rubble merchants. Ugly as most of the sheds, bungalows, and standardized houses of the common people are, they are neither so ugly nor so difficult to efface as the hideous villas and mansions of the new rich.

The Second Cecil House.

THE Lord Mayor performed the opening ceremony at the second Cecil House (Women's Public Lodging House Fund) for homeless women on Wednesday, January 18th, at 3 p.m. The new House at 47/51, Wharfdale Road, King's Cross, N.1, will accommodate 61 women and six babies with a good bed, hot bath, hot tea, and all washing facilities, for one shilling a night. Some 11,054 beds have been provided at the first Cecil House at No. 35, Devonshire Street, Theobald's Road, W.C., since it was opened in March last.

Stop Press News.

BY two and threes the Ministers are coming back to town. Though Jix is on *Le Côte d'azure,* and Hoare is in the Alps, And Amery's in Canada, and gaining great renown By climbing up a mountain, and then by climbing down, While the Labour Opposition is a-waiting for their scalps. There is diligent activity among the Party hacks. And Baldwin's sent a letter to a present candidate . . . An interesting Budget is expected, with the axe For the Army and the Navy, and a lessened income-tax. But the Labour Opposition resume their hymn of hate. Yet the Labour Opposition have made friends with Alfred Mond, And his masterly proposals will receive their kind regard. And Mr. Cosgrave (President) has crossed the herring pond, And found Chicago's Thompson if anything too fond. And Simon's gone to India, and called, and left his card. We hear they treat his mission with considerable phlegm. We hear they've called a boycott, but John will see it through. For India is the brightest—stone in Britain's diadem. We hear that good Queen Vic. at times disliked the G.O.M. We hear that greyhounds love to fight; then why not me and you? We hear a foreign gentleman is buying music-halls. We hear the railways want to run the motor-transport too. We hear that British Broadcasting is buying up St. Paul's. We hear that Mr. Coolidge is angry with the Gauls. We hear the worst of Mr. Cook; but doubt if it be true. We hear that Mussolini's mad. Then why not me and you?

W. R. T.

FUN WITH THE CALF.

"The allegation was that the man supposed to have been in a trance had three meals a day supplied by Morritt, and the police declared that when they tickled the man's feet he rose and left the casket."--*A Sunday Paper.*

With silent dignity!

"This would be treating M.P.s as if they were children."—Sir Thomas Inskip on the bishops' latest proposal.

We are not aware that the bishops have a particularly low opinion of children.

"Additional work would be impossible for ordinary men, but Sir Herbert Samuel, *as we all know,* is not an ordinary man."—*The Nation* on Sir Herbert standing as a Liberal candidate. (Italics ours.)

We know. *We know.* WE KNOW.

"We are all holy—bishops, dustmen, criminals, and prostitutes."—*The New Leader.*

And capitalists, of course. It's convenient for "Labour" papers to have nice religions like this; it is bad for the circulation to excuse monopolists openly.

"If there were no small shops, and everybody had to go to big ones, everybody would be better served in price and quality."—*The Observer.*

Who will want to buy tripe half cooked after 8 on Saturday night, when they can get it in a state of decomposition in the *Observer* the next morning?

A PIONEER.

From *The Oscillator*, A.D. 1947.

WE have only time, just before going to press, to make a few—and how inadequate—comments upon the news of the sudden and tragic death of Mr. Saul McJurgen Sleim.

Is it too platitudinous to say that almost universal regret, not only in the City, but in the nation at large—certainly, at large—will be experienced? Indeed, it is safe to assert that no home in Britain will mark without a sigh, the passing of one whose name was in every sense a household word.

The great work that made the name of McJurgen Sleim respected and loved throughout Britain, and almost adored in the garden city of Dermiston, which he designed, surely cannot need mention here. Yet it is fitting that some bare outline of his life should be attempted, if only to remind us of what man this was, who has gone and left us poorer for his going.

Saul McJurgen Sleim, son of a grocer of Shoreditch, was born in 1880. He inherited his father's tiny shop, and was moderately successful, but soon perceived that his real artistry (may we say?) favoured a larger canvas. He sold out, and, acquiring a controlling interest in a small laboratory and plant, became known to the industrial world as the first man to produce a really saleable form of powdered milk. The immediate success of his preparation was partly due perhaps to the attractive packet in shape of a churn, with the astute announcement in large red type on the label : " This milk powder should on no account be exposed in the presence of cats."

Shortly after his initial success, Mr. Sleim made a journey to India, and returned to startle the Press and send dismay into every suburban home by his declaration that natural rice, as he had seen it grown, was a harbour of bacteria and a menace to our physical well-being. Simultaneously, Professor Lucent Babilon, already well-known through his monumental work on Navels, proved that the eating of natural rice was the sole cause of arrested mental development among the children of sedentary workers. (Type X7.)

Within a month every City stores and every village " general " was supplied with a sufficient stock of " Rico," made by the McJurgen Sleim Corporation, to answer the immense demand aroused by up-to-date publicity. " Rico," a germ-free, semi-digested compound of glucose and desiccated coconut, was soon a staple food wherever English customs have taken root. An intriguing romance of industry and science was disclosed when later Professor Lucent Babilon gave his name to the charming Miss Sleim, at the tranquil old-world Lombard Street Registry Office.

Yet now appeared one of those reverses which must at times be encountered even by a field-marshal of Industry. Sleim's Milk Powder was as perfect as chemistry could make it; " Rico " was admitted by Harley Street specialists to be a scientific triumph. And yet, through some inexplicable reason, housewives found the new rice-pudding not quite an ideal product. Every known method of cookery was used : every conceivable temperature tried ; without the desired result. The pudding was perfect. But it had no skin.

McJurgen Sleim was the only man unmoved by the noise of debate. His way, he said, was—right or wrong—action. At the end his hair was white, his physique all but shattered. But his superb energy had won through.

What new thing can be said of that victory? To-day, Sleim's Synthetic Skin for Rice Puddings is demanded by stern women at every counter from Camden Town to Killiecrankie : its syllables are lisped from cradle to cradle by the tiniest tots. There is no need for rhetoric. Let bare facts speak. Last year the national consumption (that is, leaving out the huge exports) of Synthetic Skin averaged 1,000 sq. ins. per head, representing the immense total of 150 million square feet—enough Skin to cover a rice-pudding the size of Epping Forest !

One thing is certain—not the wildest revolutionary would have ventured to grudge Mr. Sleim his admittedly colossal wealth. For years his works at Dermiston Garden City, ever increasing in extent, have been humming unceasingly to keep pace with the shoal of contracts from prisons, orphanages, sanatoria, the Army and Navy, with the incessant public appetite, and with the stream of orders from every clime from Peru to Baluchistan. Standarization has not destroyed variety : to-day the Synthetic Rice-Pudding Skin is available in sheets of three different thicknesses, measured to suit seven sizes of pudding dish. The Research Department at Dermiston is now engaged on the perfecting of a Skin that shall be washable, and that may therefore be used for several Puddings.

And the man himself? It is typical of him that, when pressed to accept a title, he replied : " The plain McJurgen Sleim is a name with a niche in the stomach of every Britisher. Why should I change it? "

Modest, ever calm, yet like an intellectual tornado when at work, Mr. Sleim of late years had been almost wholly devoted to his pastime of moth-collecting. He had thirty assistants engaged under the direction of a first-class entomologist. " I love my moths," he would say, simply. He was, too, a man with a warm pulsating love of humanity and a belief in its destiny. Ten expert philanthropists, with an office staff of many hundreds, carried on the work of establishing Sleim parks and libraries, and those splendid free hospitals for the treatment of the fearful gastric disorders which of late years have so alarmingly increased. One—and one only—little foible he indulged : his love of tall buildings. His main factory chimney was, he playfully boasted, twice as high as York Minster. His study at his residence near Dermiston is half a mile above the lawn level, reached by a magnificent flight of marble steps.

And it was to this innocent fancy that Mr. Sleim owed his fatal mishap. It was his custom to walk from bottom to top of the marble stairway to his study, daily after breakfast. Yesterday morning he climbed as usual. Unhappily, one of his secretaries, anxious to observe for himself the effect of sunlight on a new colour-scheme for the Skin, had placed a square of it on the top stair of the flight. Mr. Sleim, whose eyes had long been failing, stepped upon the moist sample of Synthetic Skin, slithered, and descended, with a horrible rhythmic sound, head first, the entire five thousand marble steps. He never regained consciousness.

Rightly, the Nation honours its poets and its soldiers with public funerals. Shall we do less for Saul McJurgen Sleim, the man who, by his discovery of the Synthetic Skin, saved Rice Pudding for posterity?

KESTON HAYES.

TOP—

THE JOKE OF JOURNALISM.

HAVE we ever succeeded in conveying to our readers a something, a soupçon, an indefinable element about the daily Press of our day, that does not wholly satisfy our highest dreams of the dignity of man? Has any such faint indication of faultiness been wafted from our pen? We do not know. At the best, we can but give rather random examples; in the hope that some suggestion of our meaning may be reached, if only by repetition. For example: a distinguished journalist's description of Thomas Hardy's funeral, in the *Daily Express,* is head-lined in large letters, "Funeral Without a Tear." The writer attacks this grave matter immediately, beginning with the words: "The interment of Thomas Hardy's ashes in Westminster Abbey yesterday was a funeral without a tear. The widow was very bowed, but in the congregation—scores of people had been sitting, waiting for the funeral, for four hours—no eye was damp." We really prefer to risk being flippantly profane rather than sentimentally profane. And we can only be mildly surprised at the assiduous journalist, who examined scores of people so closely as to make sure they were not concealing a tear anywhere about their persons. We really do not know how he could be absolutely certain that no eye was damp; except by the careful application of blotting paper all round. But towards the end of the same description there is another paragraph that intrigues us even more than that about the chemical tests for the lachrymal glands. The writer makes some extraordinary remarks about Mr. Bernard Shaw; apparently founded on the idea that Mr. Shaw can never have been inside a church before. Then follows the mysterious paragraph.

"Shaw must have been wondering why the Abbey Canons wore such strange-looking vestments, not remembering, perhaps, that they had been handed down from another age."

So far as we can make out, Mr. Shaw thought that a Canon had cut out a cope or a cassock merely for fun that morning, and shaped it entirely according to his own taste and fancy. Mr. Shaw is under the impression that stoles and chasubles were spontaneous jokes specially invented for the funeral of Thomas Hardy. Not having at hand the rich traditional scholarship of the *Daily Express,* he could not be expected to know that any clergyman had ever worn a surplice before. We have ourselves occasionally criticized Mr. Shaw for an undue indifference to some ancient traditions and historic ideals. But we really think it is a little hard on him to assume that he *must* be ignorant of the fact that priests in the past have not unfrequently worn vestments. The man who stage-manages his own plays so vigilantly though so kindly, and who stage-managed with special vigilance the stately ecclesiastical scenes of *St. Joan,* was surely not quite so much surprised as all that, to find that a church dignitary does not perform the church service in his shirt-sleeves. But we merely give these two examples as faintly indicating a certain *tone* in current journalism, which we should modestly desire to modify; and which we rather regret to see becoming the universal culture of the age.

—AND TAIL

THE EQUALITY OF SLAVES.

The millionaire who recently presided with so much propriety over the council summoned to give a higher status to the manual labourers of England, was very particular in pointing out that there ought in future to be no distinction between those simple labouring folk and the clerks working in offices. The sentiment was probably meant genially, and may be accepted genially. Our own tastes are egalitarian, and we are very willing to dispense with social distinctions. We should be very glad indeed if bank-managers and cashiers could be raised to the status of bricklayers and joiners. We should be sorry to see any demonstrations of social superiority against them. It may be that, in the intangible instinct and subtle atmosphere of human history, it will always be difficult for the man who merely handles money, or manages exchange, to have quite the same honour and dignity as the man who actually makes or grows things by his own strength and skill. It may take some time to rid mankind of the natural haunting feeling that a miner is more of a man than a money-changer. It may long continue to be a sort of temptation to the shipwright to assert his obvious superiority to the shipbroker; let alone the shipbroker's underwriter's clerk. It is in a sense a subtle and delicate matter; a matter of emphasis; like the exact amount of romance we can tolerate in the position of the soldier. No sane person wants soldiers to swagger and browbeat normal society. No sane person wants the picturesque appeal of the soldier entirely to disappear. The best is that delicate social balance which can exalt one thing without lowering the other; and in the same way, we can agree with the wise of all ages in saluting a special grandeur in the labourer, without suggesting any abasement in the clerk.

Whether this was exactly what the millionaire intended, by his generous gesture of equality, we cannot be quite certain. Nevertheless, we believe that the remark of the great capitalist was in another way really true and really important. As we have spoken of the fundamental reasons for the dignity of the manual worker, it is only fair to note that there is, or was, another sort of excuse for the more snobbish sort of superiority sometimes attributed to the scrivener or clerical assistant. It was not only because he wore a black coat, or, in darker instances, a billycock hat. It was also, partly, because there did still linger over his lot a fiction that he was in some more settled sense a householder; that the man who was something in the City had the more definite status of a citizen. With that there went always some shadow of the idea of property; distinguishing a citizen from a serf. What the millionaire really meant was that, now that nobody has any property, least of all in connection with his work, it is really needless to preserve this shadowy distinction. When the factory hand is always turning somebody else's handles and not his own, and the typist is always copying somebody else's letters and not his own, it is idle for one to turn up his nose at the other. All men are equal in their loss of manhood.

THE SOCIAL SWIRL.

By A LADY OF FASHION.

August Memories.

My dear, I am in a thrill of excitement. I have just spent the week-end at Brighton (in the company of a maiden aunt), and we occupied the suite at the Prince's which in turn has been graced by the tenancy of the Duke of C—— and Lord Arthur B——. The latter was engaged at the time in drawing up the Peace Treaty, which some dreadful Frenchmen described as *Pretty Fanny's Last Play*. Most ill-natured, 'I think. The town was full (when I was there, I mean) of distinguished people. As witty Sir Horace Chauffé said to me over a *sole Colbert* at the Metropole, you couldn't see the piers for the Peers. Lord Ewe Settle came down with a car full of books. Church history, no doubt. That Prayer Book does so weigh on the poor dear's mind. Couldn't they refer the dispute to the League of Nations?

The Admirable Sartor.

I wonder why so many ex-officers have become dress-designers! Is it a revulsion from Khaki? or the effect of a visit to G.H.Q.? Anyhow, my dear, they are fine fellows, and the other day at Cheero's one of them (Captain Turmut) uttered an immortal aphorism. Speaking of one of our Royal Princes, he said: " He introduced the loose sweater, the loose-fitting dinner-jacket, and the flexible dinner tie." That might almost be used as an epitaph. The Captain is all for the evening tail-coat. He said to me " If you set a man in a dinner-jacket alongside a man in an evening tail-coat you will notice a distinct superiority in the latter." Personally, I think it depends on what you do with the tails. Should you sit on them, fold them around you, or let them flap? I suppose that must be governed by your contour; but the question puzzles me.

Steps and Legs.

I have heard all sorts of opinions on the success of the attempt to revive old dances. At one or two of my favourite night-clubs the waltz has certainly caught on, and at a Hunt Ball last week I saw a hundred people perform the Lancers with the utmost dignity and decorum. But the Marchioness of Tum-tum said to me at the Legation Club last night: " Nonsense! You can't dance *The Blue Danube* in a Kilt." To which my reply was that the late Isadora Duncan danced it (and to perfection) in her shift. *But she made it a step-dance,* as I hold it should be, don't you? All the same, the modern girl's legs are so ugly—but there! You know my bee. What they will look like if the skirt comes to an inch or two below the knee, I don't know. It should be all or nothing with legs. Which reminds me that nowadays young girls are not taught deportment, and I think it's a pity.

Sea Murmurs.

I darted across to Monte the other day (with the aeroplane so cheap and handy, it's almost like a suburb of London) and cannoned into leonine Sir Henry Brass. I asked him what luck. And he said he was there conducting concerts. When I ventured to express surprise, he asked me (with a smile which robbed the remark of its malice) if I thought that the Riviera was exclusively devoted to misconducting. It was at Monte that I heard the news of poor dear Sir Ralphy Tubb's *contretemps* with an octopus. It is sad that after having escaped so many dangers he should almost fall a victim to a fish. Some people call him an Octopus of the Theatre, but that of course, my dear, is only a figure of speech or *nom de guerre*.

Love and Diet.

Do you think that there can be platonic friendship between a young man and a young woman? I put that question to Professor Mumb O'Jumbough the other day (we were skating together at St. Moritz), and our greatest psychologist said : " Yes, and even between two young men." I found the remark cryptic. Yet really you know, my dear, the sort of young men and women you see about couldn't be anything but platonic. Is it underfeeding? I know that some statistics just issued are said to prove that most of us die from over-feeding—or so dear Pirrip Nodin told me at the British Museum the other day. But I doubt it. For it mentions clergymen and farm bailiffs as the two professional classes who eat least and live longest. Well, it is quite possible that the cloth may bant; but farm bailiffs, my dear! And I *know* that some society women have brought their ration down to one or two raw carrots a day in order to keep their figures. Which reminds me that the latest fashion is for a hostess to receive male and female guests while in her bath, with a lid on. But I shall never bring myself to it.

Political Notes.

People seem less and less inclined to adorn themselves in fancy dress. At the Charity Ball I noticed, to my horror, a number of people who were not specially dressed for the occasion. I fear that another wave of pessimism is overtaking us. One of the most striking costumes was that of Lord Yeasmith who came as a smith's hammer-man with a broken hammer. But the foolish rumour that his lordship intends to join the Labour Party is founded on a witty remark by a member of the Diplomatic Corps, which was well represented. " You will observe," said his Excellency, " that the hammer is broken." Of course it was rather late in the evening. I saw a marvellous Russian Cossack, but he turned out to be a Wing-Commander. By the bye, why do they call it the *Tnree Arts Ball*? I suppose it had something to do with Chelsea originally. At least, so one of my partners told me. He said that in Paris they have a Charity Ball, but that there nobody dresses. I should think it was rather dull, my dear.

Educational Announcements.

CONVENT OF THE ASSUMPTION
RAMSGATE.

London Matriculation, Oxford Locals, Associated Board of Music, and Royal Drawing Society Examinations. Games; good playing fields.
Apply to the REVEREND MOTHER.

ST. JOSEPH'S COLLEGE
(MARIST BROTHERS),
DUMFRIES.

Senior and Junior Courses University Entrance Exams, Oxford Locals, Matriculation, Higher Leaving certificate etc,

Friar Row, Caldbeck,
CUMBERLAND.

Co-educational modern school. Very healthy and beautiful situation, affording great scope for the use of regional study and occupational experiences. Fees moderate and inclusive; entire charge if desired.
Principals:
Dr. Mabel Barker, B.Sc., & Miss Gertrude Walmesley

Hillside Convent College,
The House of Residence is at
FARNBOROUGH HILL,
HAMPSHIRE.

Formerly the Home of the Empress Eugenie. High Class Boarding School for Girls. Conducted by the Religious of Christian Education, under the Patronage of His Lordship the Bishop of Portsmouth.
Ideal situation. Grounds about 80 Acres. Home Farm. Riding. Tennis, Golf. Cricket, Hockey, Netball, Etc. Preparation for University Degrees, Inter. Arts, Matric., Oxford School Certificate. Modern Languages by Native Teachers. Secretarial Training. Handicrafts, Music, Art, Elocution.—For Particulars apply,—**Rev. Mother.**

The "MADONNA"
NURSERY & PREPARATORY SCHOOL
Under the Patronage of
His Eminence the Cardinal Archbishop of Westminster.

Children admitted from two years of age.
Fees from £75 per annum.
Also TRAINING COLLEGE FOR NURSE-GOVERNESSES. Apply to The Lady Principal, "The Madonna," Letchworth, Herts.

SOUTHSEA.
St. JOHN'S COLLEGE.
Conducted by the Brothers of the Christian Schools.

One of the healthiest situations on South Coast Extensive Playing Fields. Football Cricket. Tennis. Swimming. Preparatory Classes. Oxford School Certificate. London Matriculation, London Chamber of Commerce Exams. Entrance Examinations to Army, Navy, and Air Force.
Inclusive terms if desired. Apply to: Rev. Bro. Director

HALIDON HOUSE SCHOOL
ESTABLISHED 1871.
SLOUGH, BUCKS. (Near Eton, Windsor and Iver).

Girls of all ages receive a thorough education; also Boys under 12, in a separate house. Splendid health record. Good examination results. Vacancy for Student to train as School matron. No Premium.

Distributist books

Most of the books recommended in "G.K's Weekly" for study by Distributists may be obtained from the C.T.S. Lending Library, which also has a very interesting collection of books on Catholic doctrine, history, apologetics, etc. Over 6,000 titles—2 books at a time to Town—3 to Postal —and still more to Overseas Members—for 10/- a year.

Write for particulars now to the Hon. Librarian,
C.T.S. LENDING LIBRARY,
(Formerly Bexhill Library)
74, Victoria Street, London, S.W.1.
——ROE——

In Case of any Difficulty in Getting G.K's. Weekly

will readers please write to the Publishers, G.K's. Weekly, The Marshall Press, Milford Lane, Strand, W.C.2, giving name of retailer. The change of publishers may cause some delay in certain quarters, although your local newsagent can get it for you regularly.

THE SCRAPBOOK.

WINTER MONODY.

The Northwind flourishes a wand
  As he troops through Hackettstown,
He stirs a little heap of dust
  And weaves a sudden gown,

Then dances down the vacant street
  As if he owned the place,
But when he halts to take a rest
  You cannot see his face.

The dervish whirls before my house
  With elbows on his hips,
Whistling a vague, nostalgic tune
  Through his high-piping lips.

Somedays he thumps the window pane
  Or shakes the picket fence,
Or rides upon the stable door
  With a gamin's impudence.

He calls the dead leaves back to life,
  And they scamper from the trees,
To follow him across the lake,
  Ten thousand Argosies.

He wrestles with complaining pines,
  But poplars in his clutch
Writhe with a strange, hysteric sway
  Transcendent at his touch.

The autumn goes, the winter comes;
  He steals the mountain gold,
And when you meet him in the dawn
  His finger tips are cold.

The Northwind flourishes a wand
  As he rides through Hackettstown,
But now he takes a gust of snow
  And spins a suit of down.

                    A. M. SULLIVAN.

TO A CERTAIN LABOUR POLITICIAN.

You worship power, and love the smooth career
  From handicraft to statecraft, well begun
  In honest toil, until at last is won
The guerdon of much glibness and no fear
Of breaking faith. Naught but a facile sneer
  You give those trusting souls for whom you spun
  Your web of lies, whose faces now you shun—
Pledge-trafficker and promise-profiteer !

Yet have a care, right honourable lout,
  That those who raised you up cast you not down,
    Deceived, enraged, with execrating howls.
So shall you fall, brief triumph turned to rout,
  And men shall hail you legislator—clown,
    The joy that strutted with the guinea-fowls.

                    CLAUDE L. TASKER.

MARY'S GARDEN.

Mary Mary, quite contrary,
  How does your garden grow?
With chimney stacks and cinder tracks,
  And factories all in a row.

Walls of bricks upon every side
For mass production of London Pride,
With sound of wheels in hut and in shed
From dewy dawn until time for bed;
With hooters hooting the flying hours,
The voice that speaks for the unseen powers,
That hurry men forward, line on line,
Hurry to breakfast and hurry to dine,
And hurry them back from meal to toil
With wood to shape and metal to boil;
And how in the world should this be done
If they stood outside to see the sun?
Wheels to rumble and pulleys to pull,
How if the packages be not full?
Levers to lever and breaks to act,
How if the packages be not packed?
How if the jolly old town stand still
Waiting and waiting and waiting until
Red revolution sweeps on the tide,
When London can't wait for London Pride.
For flowers in factories must be made
Artificial with engines to aid,
Since in the garden when Mary goes
No longer the smallest flower grows.

Mary, Mary, quite contrary,
  Why did your garden go?
The Millionaires thought it was their's
  And I fear they're right, you know.

                    J. D. GLEESON.

THE SHROPSHIRE LADS.

(Ardent admirers of Mr. A. E. Housman's verse must often have speculated as to what befell the youthful characters of whom he sings. These lines supply the much-desired information).

When sun had set on Severn
  I'd munch a currant bun,
And eye the Ludlow hussies
  Who after Jack would run.

And Dick would play his bagpipes,
  And Tom stand on his head,
Till neighbours vowed they ought to
  Be spanked and put to bed.

Now Dick in Madagascar
  Trades cocoanuts and oil;
While Tom at stone of Portland
  For many a year must toil.

And Jack, obese and gouty,
  May nevermore take beer :
His hair 'tis sparse and scanty,
  And cut but thrice a year.

                    D. R. LOCK.

STRAWS IN THE WIND.
THE UNSEEN CATASTROPHE.
By G. K. CHESTERTON.

THE case of Mr. Guedalla and the Wireless Debate proves, as he truly says, that the old thing called a Censorship by the Government has been set up in broad daylight. It is a queer story. It has been common in modern novels to describe heroes, and especially heroines, afflicted with what some call the artistic temperament and some bad temper and some divine discontent. Anyhow, it was always suggested that their captive spirits struggled in the cage when they might have soared to the clouds; or, generally speaking, that their minds were too large and liberal for the petty routine of our prosaic daily life. It seems to me that this sort of fiction is not only fiction but actually the reverse of fact. What amazes me about the modern world is that the most colossal and catastrophic things are happening, and that it is the modern mind that is too petty and prosaic to realize them. So far from it being an eagle in a darkened cage, it seems to me more like an owl in broad daylight or in the blazing sun of some more than tropical summer almost burning up the earth. Perhaps the nearest image we could get for the newspaper state of mind would be a snail only faintly conscious of the necessity of keeping pace with an earthquake; or a diary of the day of judgment written by the slow finger of a sea-anemone. The modern minds seem too small for the modern changes; and instead of brooding imaginatively in Balham, they seem to be chatting prosaically in Sodom and Gomorrha. Those of us who realize what is really going on can hardly find words sufficiently large and simple to describe it to the dull and bemused spectators. It is awkward to describe something as plain as the sun turning green or the moon falling into the Thames; and to find that people only understand it sufficiently to answer that the weather is certainly very changeable.

The truth is that tremendous changes are passing over the world; the sort of changes that appear in history because men struggled with them; but which do not appear in journalism, because men do not struggle. Our fathers sometimes exaggerated their own wars and revolutions; we are perhaps the first generation of men who under-rate them, or are even unconscious of them. Some may doubt this generalization, and may murmur that our great scientific discoveries are fully demonstrated and displayed. This is true; but these are not the really remarkable changes; and it is not the remarkable part of them that is displayed. In so far as they are a continuation of the comparatively commonplace notion of increasing speed and decreasing space, we do indeed boast of them; but it is already a very old boast. For centuries it has been a recognized matter of gossip that the new coach is quicker than the old coach, that the new steam-engine is quicker than the new coach, and so on and so on. It is only because we have got thoroughly used to this sort of self-flattery that we can accept it from the newspapers in any quantities. But any real news about events that are really new is still for all practical purposes forbidden.

If it is a novelty to say about the aeroplane exactly what the Early Victorian said about the steam-engine, we are indeed a race of daring innovators. If it is fresh and original to join with Lord Ashfield in talking about the tubes exactly as we should have joined with Lord Wolverhampton in talking about the telephones, then we are indeed original and fresh. But we shall probably not be told the real story of the tubes, any more than the contemporary public was told the real story of the telephone. But when we turn to the other side of the matter, even from the standpoint of these our immediate ancestors, the case is very much the other way. Those ancestors would have been astounded at the open story of monopoly and tyranny that we all take for granted. Suppose you had told some of the old Whigs, let alone Liberals, that there was an entirely new type of Printing Press, eclipsing all others; and that as this was to be given to the King, all printing would henceforth be Government printing. They would be roaring like rebels, or even regicides. Yet that is exactly what we have done with the whole new invention of wireless. Suppose it were proposed that the King's officers should search all private houses to make sure there were no printing-presses; they would be ready for a new Revolution. Yet that is exactly what was proposed for the protection of the Government monopoly of Broadcasting. Suppose even Lord Wolverhampton, when he was in the Liberal Government, had suggested that he should telephone to everybody else, but nobody else should telephone to him. Even the Liberals would have been moved to make some protest for liberty. Yet such a one-sided telephone would be essentially the same thing as the new monopoly of telegraphy. There is really no protection against propaganda of the most unfair and aggressive sort being entirely in the hands of the Government; except indeed the incredible empty-headedness of those who govern; who, as was apparent in the case of Captain Berkeley, would still be unable to argue even if nobody is allowed to answer.

Nobody knows that for one enormous instant the doors stood open for freedom; nobody knows how promptly and with what a clang they were shut again on our captivity. There was a moment when the new power of the Word, given by the Wireless, might have broken the whole servile silence which the printed word preserves. For one wild instant a man might have told the truth to ten thousand people; and a roar from the whole Press and Parliament could never have covered or recalled the secret that had broken loose. The next moment the Government, grumbling at and haggling and delaying all sorts of other nationalizations, lost not an hour or a minute in nationalizing the new telegraphy. On that sort of thing, at least, we are all Socialists now. It is wicked to nationalize mines or railroads; but we lose no time in nationalizing tongues and talk. The public of to-day had that huge opportunity without knowing it. They had that huge disappointment without knowing it. We might once have used, and we shall now never use, the twentieth century science against the nineteenth century hypocrisy. It was prevented by a swift, sweeping, and intolerant state monopoly; a monster suddenly swallowing all rivals, alternatives, discussions, or delays, with one snap of its gigantic jaws. That is what I mean by saying we cannot see the monsters that overcome us. But I suppose that even Jonah, when once he was swallowed, could not see the Whale.

BOOK OF THE WEEK.
THE MIXTURE AS BEFORE.

THIS is a book about Spain by a hearty stamping Anglo-Saxon freethinker with a zest for artistic language.

> The priest got out at the next village, lowered himself with some difficulty. He said good-bye in a bland cloudy voice, somewhat sculptured, " Vayan ustedes con Dios, Senores." The marble baroque tone of the complete ecclesiastic. His short blunt fingers flickered cherubs . . . .

If you like that sort of writing and think it good, this is a book you will like. Mr. Pritchett uses it to convey dislike and disapproval not only of Spanish priests, but also of Spanish churches : as of Badajoz Cathedral :

> It ate too much, that church—too many tithes, too many souls, too many priests, too much sun. It slept too much. Its bell snored harshly the hours.

Why the Devil do people write like this, even to please the readers of the *Christian Science Monitor,* in which part of this book appeared? One might equally say of the main door of the Stock Exchange that it is replete and glutted with the white arched stomachs of stockbrokers, cunning, drab with secret thoughts of Surrey, vulturine . . . Not that this furious toil for the picturesque grouping of epithet does not occasionally land Mr. Pritchett in felicity. For example, the cry of the night-watchman of Plasencia :

> The words fall like a crash of rods in the street, a sneeze of iron.

Except for its second half this sentence is just and graphic.

There is exhaled from this book a perfect rude animal and material health, a keen savouring of the external and occasional flashes of decorative charm in translating it— " The sky was green as ice, and the stars white as little houses "—and a complacent, uninformed, and bustling Nordic contempt for the Catholic Church and all its manifestations. Arthur Symons (a better observer than most) has said that the Spaniard likes to see the blood on his crucifix. Mr. Pritchett's variations on this simple theme are like Saturday morning in Smithfield. His summing-up of the Spanish character ("mystical and superstitious. They do not admire the French rationalism ") is that of the ordinary Cook's tourist, like Mr. Arnold Bennett, who was so justly rapped over the knuckles by the Spanish Ambassador some little time ago. This is the common attitude of the Nordic. Such a traveller can perceive (by peeping distastefully through the door) the crowds at Mass in France, and then go away and write quite gravely in his diary that the French never go to church. Doctors call it conscientious myopia. Most of our Anglo-Saxon tourists in Spain have it. Spain, with its strong national pecularities, is their meat : and all tourists do not travel in trains. Compare Mr. Pritchett's book with (say) Palacio Valdés's autobiography, *Le Roman d'un Romancier,* just published in Paris, and the grave extent of this myopia is at once apparent.

There is a profoundly pathetic chapter in Mr. Pritchett's book, about a Scottish missionary and his wife who are living in Badajoz for the purpose of converting Spain—

MARCHING SPAIN. By V. S. Pritchett. Ernest Benn, 10/6.

to the tenets of which sect is not apparent. The people in and around Badajoz do not much care about being converted, and although indolent they sometimes rise up and hit Don Francisco (who assists the Scottish missionary to distribute Protestant Bibles and tracts) very hard with big thick sticks. Of these reactionaries, as Mr. Pritchett records from Don Francisco himself, one was afterwards stricken from Above with syphilis, another was shot dead in a quarrel, and a third forced to leave the neighbourhood, " and led, as I afterwards heard, a ruined life." That shows what happens to people who won't be Spanish United Frees.

Mr. Pritchett, who reveres Unamono, is apparently an Englishman, though from the ripe general nature of his reflections (" I was happy, and a happy man needs no glory, no religion, no extraneous God, for happiness is God." " It seems that the old dogmas are no longer worth fighting for"—This! And when you consider the fierce, unending, huge, bitter warfare in France to-day !)—from the nature of these one might almost take him for that type of American Mr. Kipling has lately drawn; a gold-filled mouth champing and relishing great mouthfuls of ethics and wind and betterment and uplift and words and whoobub and locutions and Almighty God knows what. If he had only walked Spain as a walker, this book, for all its orgies of picturesqueness and artistic self-consciousness, would have been worth reading, for Mr. Pritchett has a talent for graphic, if baroque (a good word) description, and an eye for colour. But—alas !

This Spain is a bad business. Why don't Cook's do something about it, in conjunction with the Fabian Society, the Food Reform League, the Unitarian Council, the Birth-Control Committee, and the Advertising Convention?

LIBRARY LIST.

SOLDIER BORN. By Conal O'Riordan. Collins. 7s. 6d.

Mr. O'Riordan has established an Irish dynasty. In the present novel he harks back to Sir Desmond Tyrconnell Quinn and his agreeable son, David. In David I seem to see glimpses of the youth of the author. The period of the novel is the time of the Union in Ireland and of "Prinny" in England. Mr. O'Riordan knows his history and his topography, and gives us an amazing and amusing portraiture of the Tomboy Princess Charlotte, and of David at Westminster School with Tony Dazincourt. There are glimpses of old Dublin that would delight that fine Irish fictionist, Donn Byrne.

PASSIONATE PARTICLES. By Margaret Peterson. Ernest Benn. 7s. 6d.

A strong study in egoism and hate. Little Ann Fabian was not wanted by her beautiful mother, Felicity, and the child was conscious of this from her earliest time of understanding. Felicity had another child by a lover. She adored Dolores. Ann was admired by nobody, but she had a morbid liking for her half-sister, who was later to wreck her life by taking from her the love of the only man who ever cared for her and who became her husband. There was a tragedy attached to Ann's youth. A child friend of hers had died in mysterious circumstances. When her half-sister was apparently on the point of death from poisoning, Ann partially relented. A second murder was obviated. A more ambitious book this than Miss Peterson generally writes.

THE MAN WITH SIX SENSES. By M. Jaeger. The Hogarth Press. 7s. 6d.

Michael Bristowe was rather a miserable little creature whose one gift was that he had a marvellous sensitivity as a "diviner." He could not only locate water and metals by his sixth sense, but see and feel with an intensity not given to ordinary men. The narrator of the story tells how Bristowe made havoc in his little world and how he made havoc with it.

OUTSIDE THE LAW. By Sir Frederick Pollock, D.C.L., LL.D., K.C. The Cayme Press. 7s. 6d.

At the age of 82 Sir Frederick Pollock has published some of the recreative products of his agile mind. There are essays on mysticism, and Shakespeare's attitude towards the technique of war and diplomacy as dramatic material, serio-comic parables in an eastern setting, verse, and an imitation of Rabelais on the subject of cats. None of these pieces are of great value, and it is in no spirit of irony that we hope Sir Frederick found more pleasure in writing these trivialities than we did in reading them.

THE STAR OF SATAN. By Georges Bernanos. The Bodley Head. 7s. 6d.

This book is the authorized English translation of the French volume, *Sous le Soleil de Satan.* It has a remarkable theme for a novel—that of a blameless priest who is constantly mortifying his flesh and spirit lest the Devil should claim him. The conscience-stricken penitent becomes a saint in spite of himself.

OUTSIDE THE BULL-RING.

I WILL confess that the most vivid mental pictures that I brought back from Madrid were of the *corrida de toros* on Easter Sunday. It is said that most English travellers find their way to a bull-fight once, and that few go a second time. Those who have not been often accuse those of us who have of having gone to satisfy a morbid curiosity, and they tell us that we have gained an ineradicable blot for our escutcheons; but if we travel with minds open to receive new and genuine impressions of other peoples, and not with minds sealed with conceit that often passes as patriotism, I fail to see how we can ignore the bull-fight. You may talk enthusiastically of Spanish *futbol,* but that does not alter the fact that all Spain goes to the bull-fight. At the bull-ring you will sit with—and feel for a time a part of—all Spain. Ladies in *mantillas* whom, you confess with disappointment, you have not yet seen off the English stage, will be there. Officials, soldiers, men, women, and children, of every conceivable social rank will be represented in tier upon tier of seething faces, half in brilliant sunlight, half in deep shadow. You will never forget the concentrated atmosphere of colour and hubbub that almost overpowers you, as you wait with something approaching fear, fascinated by that glaring yellow sand, whose dark rings spell blood, and suggest that, for a moment, you are back in Ancient Rome.

And then, afterwards, the interminable arguments about bull-fighting and fox-hunting, sport and cruelty, not to mention the false herrings of Sabbath-breaking across the trail!

I had taken the trouble to go to that bull-fight armed. I had listened intelligently to a very kindly Spaniard's point of view, and I had accustomed myself to the ritual and the sacrifice by studying picture-postcards. I would be fair, I had told myself; I would give to the bull-fight the chance that I would give to anything else in sport, or art, or science, that I hoped to understand. My genial friend explained to me that these bulls live on the fat of the land for years, with every comfort and no work, and die fighting gloriously before thousands of admirers; whereas other bulls slave under the yoke for a whole lifetime, and die ingloriously in their senile decay. I could not say the same about English hunting, where the notion that the fox or the stag or the hare enjoys being chased to earth and torn to death by wild dogs is palpably absurd. I will not say that I believe that the bull enjoys a bull-fight, but I do submit that the balance of cruelty lies with the stag-huntsman.

In truth, argument about cruelty is of little value: cruelty is so entirely a matter of custom. We believe now that the flogging a nineteenth-century boy got for false quantities in Latin was cruel, and probably our grandchildren will think that the mild caning a twentieth-century boy gets for breaking bounds is cruel. The Englishman condemns bull-fighting as cruel, because it is strange to him; he does not condemn fox-hunting as cruel, because he has been brought up to take it for granted. He only thinks, with John Masefield, of the appeal to the eye and to the imaginaiton of a meet, of the appeal to the ear of the horn and the baying of hounds, of the exhilaration of the ride across country. Fox-hunting to him means beautiful red coats, and horses, and dogs, in an old-world setting of manor houses, open country, and grey skies. The Spaniard thinks, in a similar way, of the appeal to the senses; and bull-fighting to him means brave men and wild beasts, skill and strength, in a setting of sunshine, colour, and passion.

If he agrees with us so far, the Englishman will argue that the bull-fight is not sporting: the bull has very little chance of escape; as if the *matador's* final thrust were the main point of the fight. As well might he say that the sport in the hunting of a fox or a stag lies in the ghastly last act. No, it is the skill displayed and the risks taken in the chase that differentiate the sportsman from the butcher. It is exactly here that the bull-fight struck me as being superior to the fox-hunt: it is the elemental struggle of man and beast, skill and cool daring against brute strength and hot rage. The *torero* may lose his life, but the huntsman's risks are merely those of any horseman. The fox has cunning on his side and the stag speed, but neither is matched with man: he is matched with a pack of hounds, directed by man. The bull dies splendidly, the fox shamefully.

You may tell me not to forget the wretched horses of the arena. There is little fear of that; their death was the most ghastly sight I have witnessed. The *picador,* with calves well protected, riding a broken-down cab-horse, which has been deprived of its vocal chords and is bandaged round one eye, is a mere butcher. As a young American, with his native land's love of horses, said to me, " It's the horses that get you." The rôles are reversed: the heroic figure in the English hunt becomes the ignominious sacrifice in the Spanish bull-fight. I failed to get an adequate reason for this from my Spanish friend. He shrugged his shoulders and said, " Yes, it is cruel, but . . ." So I came to the conclusion that it was not an essential part of the bull-fight, as it is in countries where they employ skilled horses and *picadores,* but just custom again. Blood inflames a man's lowest nature, and gives him a certain morbid, sensual pleasure. In England, if executions were still public, as they were in the " age of reason " and in aristocratic Georgian days, I wonder if the market-square would be empty, or Tower Hill deserted! I think there would be crowds, and I believe it would be quite untrue to say that every member of those crowds was abnormally morbid or cruel. No, most of us would be there, all who do not turn their eyes away from scenes of torture the film-producers give us sometimes, or from tales of the Inquisition in history-books. As it is, crowds collect outside the gaol on the morning of an execution, hoping to hear a bell, or to see a flag, and thus to take part in a small way at the kill.

Personally, I found that the short interlude of the *picadores* had the effect of taking the edge off the cruelty to the bull, and of enhancing the glory of the last acts, when I was thrilled by the grace and agility, the skill and the coolness of the *banderilleros* and of the *matador* himself. But this did not last to the end. As the great beast lost strength, all my sympathies went out to him, and I became one of his supporters. I found myself, kind Englishman that I am, earnestly hoping that he would reach that maddening gladiator with his horns, and toss him across the sand; and I pictured to myself the bull being finally led off in triumph to retire on a pension to some grassy plain in Andalusia.

JACK HOOD PHILLIPS.

THE DRAMA.

ELMER RICE'S *The Adding Machine*, at the Court Theatre, has a special interest for readers of this paper. The author shows us the soul of the clerk; the deadening influence of a routine that has in it no element of production. Zero has lost his soul, the machine has destroyed God.

Zero married as a young man in the fond hope that he would be promoted from ledger to ledger, until he became the head of the store. But at the end of five and twenty years he is doing the same thing as on his first day of employment. His wife tells him what she thinks of him, in a monologue punctuated by hair curling and references to a little prostitute who lives next door; whom Zero, in a panic, reports to the police, and she is sent to prison. In his daily task, the girl who calls out the figures he takes down used to be young, but now—he speaks his thoughts aloud—her neck is getting scraggy, and she doesn't dress smartly. The girl herself is conscious that he no longer takes an interest in her; there was a time when he might have kissed her. Zero endures his life only through the illusion that one day the boss will promote him. He will be sent for and rewarded for his service. He is sent for. The boss tells him that the work he does can be more cheaply performed by an adding machine; he will draw a month's salary—and go. Zero cannot stand the shock. He takes a bill file and stabs the boss to the heart. He goes to the chair with nothing but a rambling statement.

We next meet Zero in the graveyard. He meets one Shrdlu, a youth whose " sinful nature " had led him to read a profane book, *Treasure Island*, after which he tried to go to sea. His saintly mother brought him back, however, and apprenticed him to a settled job. One Sabbath at the mid-day meal, when he was called upon to carve the leg of lamb, his mother with kindly forethought held the dish for him, and instead of slicing the meat he cut her throat! The youth finds comfort only in the fact that he will be called on to endure eternal torment. Even this comfort is denied him, for when he and Zero find themselves in the Elysian Fields he finds everything very different from what it ought to be. There are no flames, no racks, no thumbscrews, there are even no conventions; married people walk about with illegal partners quite unconcerned. This disturbs Mr. Zero, who by this time has been joined by Miss Devore, the girl who used to work with him. She has committed suicide because without Zero the world is blank. But Zero is too conventional to be happy. He is a married man and can't forget it, and leaves her and the Elysian Fields behind.

The final scene. Zero has been reborn throughout the ages, and the time has now arrived when he must return to earth. He has become steadily worse throughout his incarnations: having started as a monkey he is now a mere clerk. He has gone through æons of suffering and experience that " the big toe of his right foot may press a super-adding machine which shows the output of every collier in a coal mine."

Mr. Frank Randell is a touch too robust as Zero, whom one visualizes as a spineless little man. Miss Carrie Baillie is terribly efficient as Mrs. Zero, and Miss Dorothy Turner plays well as Miss Devore. Mr. Charles Maunsell as Shrdlu is extraordinarily good.

J. K. PROTHERO.

THE COCKPIT.

To the Editor, G.K.'s WEEKLY.

THE LAND MONOPOLY.

SIR,—Mr. T. G. Rogers wrote an article in a recent issue, in which he pointed to the enigma (in words that reminded one of the introduction to Henry George's *Progress and Poverty*) of the persistence of poverty amidst plenty.

I believe that land monopoly stands in the way of a better distribution of wealth, and that the only effective way of breaking down land monopoly is by taxing land values, as was taught by Henry George. I don't know what Mr. Rogers believes, but he says (on 31st Dec.) that Henry George failed to prove his case (or words to that effect).

Now, Henry George's *Progress and Poverty* is acknowledged to be a masterpiec of logic, and I would refer your readers to it. If Mr. Rogers can't see the point that is not the fault of George.

Yours faithfully,
C. A. GARDNER.

A PROTESTANT PROTEST.

SIR,—I am one of those who, though not members of the League, derive from the reading of your WEEKLY great instruction, very great exhilaration, and not a little exasperation. If the admirable article of Mr. Ellison in a recent issue, with its wise tolerance of outlook, really represented your point of view, I think your members would very rapidly multiply. But does it? In particular I shall be glad to know whether you welcome Protestants among your ranks. Can a Protestant be a Distributist? I assume, as a Protestant, that he can; and if so, I could wish that your paper would indulge rather less in the constant, if covert, derision and caricature of Protestantism—especially of Nonconformity—of which a flagrant example is the "Top and Tail" of December 31.

I have no wish to raise irrelevant theological issues, but surely no one should venture to write about Protestantism who does not realize (a) that many Protestants are not Calvinists (e.g., Wesleyans and Quakers), and that (b) even the theology of Calvinism cannot be without travesty summed up by a few references to Total Depravity or Predestination, and (c) in the sense in which Calvinism is held to-day it derives quite as much from St. Paul and St. Augustine as from John Calvin.

As regards the paragraph in "Tail," one can only envy the writer the sublime assurance with which he diagnoses the motives and inward spiritual state of the Members of Parliament who composed the majority in the recent Prayer Book debate. Another weekly review assured us, with as much—or as little—authority, that practialy all the well-known agnostics and atheists in the House voted with the minority. Who is to tell? One can only say that it seems *prima facie* more probable that those of the Tories who had *no* religious conviction of any sort would vote as the Prime Minister, the House of Lords, the Bishops, and the almost unanimous voice of the newspaper monopolists urged them to.

But to repeat my former question: is a continual baiting of Protestants necessarily a part of your Distributist propaganda? Do you only want political adherents who agree with you in their religious allegiance?—Yours, etc.,

J. W. HARVEY.

A DISTRIBUTIST PRACTICAL POLICY.

DEAR SIR,—Birmingham Branch is on right lines in discussing a "Constructive Housing Policy in View of Possible Ownership."

The first essential is to secure a site, but Mr. Lester has indicated the Taxation Way of making available cheap sites. Just now building materials, through rings and restricted production, are dear. Only from *some* land are building materials being extracted. When *all* land with these materials is being developed through the new revenue-raising system, the intensified production will lower prices, plenty of construction will naturally follow, personal liberty will be restored, and men will easily be able to employ themselves through millions of acres of land being in the market for use.

J. O'D. D.

NOTE.—A long letter has been received from Mr. Dudley Heathcote in reply to Mr. Karel Capek's and Mrs. Wilton's criticisms of his article on the Slovak Problem. Pressure of space compels us to hold it over until next week.—EDITOR.

A CONFERENCE ON

Agriculture and the Small Farmer

has been arranged between the Rural Reconstruction Association and The League, for

Saturday, February 4th, from 3 p.m. to 10 p.m.

at The London School of Economics, Houghton St., Aldwych, W.C.2.

Speakers for The League: Mr. G. K. Chesterton, Fr. Vincent McNabb, Mr. G. C. Heseltine.

Speakers for The Association: Dr. Gilbert Slater, Mr. Montague Fordham, Mr. R. Borlase Matthews.

Addresses will be followed by open discussion.   For details apply to the Secretary, The League.

AMONG THE BRANCHES

CENTRAL BRANCH.—*Hon. Sec.*, A. M. Currie, 20/21, Essex Street, Strand, W.C.2.

Meetings held every Friday at 6.30 for 7 p.m., at the Devereux, Devereux Court, Essex Street.

At the Devereux last Friday the debate with the Young Fabian Group drew a full house. The proposal before the meeting, "That the only alternative to Distributism is slavery," was carefully avoided by most of the speakers, but this did not detract in any way from the interest or enjoyment of the debate. Mr. Gregory Macdonald, supported by Mr. Currie, led off for the League, while Mr. Thompson, supported by Mr. Andrade, replied for the Fabians, an open discussion following. The visitors put their case well, and the Socialist idealism formed a sharp contrast to our own hard-headed grasp of affairs—which had hitherto been unsuspected by most of us. No vote was taken, so that it is impossible to estimate what casualties may have been inflicted upon Distributist or Fabian convictions. The broad conclusion which emerged was that the Socialists, appalled at the industrial disorganization of Canaan, are legging it for Egypt, where, as their prophets assure them, the standard of living is high and where labour conditions are settled. On Friday we passed in the desert. We reached agreement only in condemning the sand and in grumbling at the maggots in the manna.

On Friday next, at the Devereux, at 6.30 for 7 p.m., Mr. H. E. Humphries will open a discussion on Trade Unions.

WEST LONDON GROUP.—*Hon. Sec.*: A. Ardern, 25, Felden Street, S.W.6.

The next meeting will take place on Monday week, February 6th, at 8.30 p.m., at the Six Bells Hotel, 197, King's Road, Chelsea.

Mr. Kavanagh will open a discussion on the Mental Deficiency Bill, and it is expected that Mrs. Cecil Chesterton will be present to give us the benefit of her experience.

A further announcement will be made next week.

BIRMINGHAM BRANCH.—*Sec.*: K. L. Kenrick, 7, Soho Road, Handsworth.

The first of a series of meetings which will be devoted to a discussion of the chapter-headings of Mr. Humphries's book, *Liberty and Property*, was held at the Guildhouse, off Broad Street, on January the 20th. The Secretary introduced the discussion on "The Principles of Distributism." He took the four principles of Equality, Freedom, Justice, and Private Property. He defined Equality as the statement that we have no means whatever of even beginning to decide which of any two men is the better man or which is of greater value, because in order even to begin to do so we should have not only to know the whole man, body, mind and soul, but we should also have to know the whole universe and all eternity. Speaking of Freedom, he said that if you don't believe in Freedom you were bound to believe in slavery. Justice he defined as meaning merely that the judge should not be bribed. Private Property he defined in the words of an essay written many years ago by Bernard Bosanquet as "that material nucleus in the outside world of things which enables a man to distinguish himself from an animal, a child, or a slave." A very interesting discussion followed as to whether Mr. Humphries's statement that "a landlord has no right to say that no public-house shall be opened on his estate" could legitimately claim a place in the same chapter on "The Principles of Distributism," as the sentence "Liberty is the right of a sane adult to do anything he pleases that is not forbidden by law as injurious to the equal rights of other men."

The next meeting will be held on Friday, February 3rd, at the Guildhouse, at 7 o'clock, when Mr. Bradford will open a discussion on "Capitalism."

LIVERPOOL.—*Sec.*: J. P. Alcock, Melwood, Deysbrook Lane, West Derby, Liverpool.

Please note our new meeting place, 13, Salisbury Street (opposite St. Francis Xavier's College).

January 26 (Thursday), at 13, Salisbury Street, commencing at 8 p.m. Discussion: "Distributists and Politics."

January 27 (Friday), a debate with the Liverpool Fabian Society. The League speakers will oppose the motion "That Socialism, and not Distributism, is the Path to Greater Liberty." At the Grenville Cafe, Tithebarn Street.

The Hon. Treasurer is now Mr. D. Dixon, 9, Warburton Road, Seaforth.

Fortnightly discussions will be held at 13, Salisbury Street, as follows:—

All correspondence should be addressed to the Secretary of the League (G. C. Heseltine), 20/21, Essex Street, W.C.2.

Thursday, February 9.—"Co-operation in Industry." Opened by Mr. F. C. South.

Thursday, February 23.—"Shall the League Live?" Opened by Mr. R. Velarde.

Thursday, March 8.—Six Solutions. Six members will put forward their own opinions on the line of action which should be taken by the League if it is to accomplish any work of value.

All the above meetings commence at 8 p.m. prompt.

MANCHESTER.—*Sec.*: John A. Toohey, York Mount, Bury New Road, Prestwich.

A meeting of the members of the Branch was held on Wednesday evening, the 18th inst., at the Metro Café, St. Peter's Square, Manchester, Mr. Hammond in the chair.

Mr. R. J. Finnimore, a journalist member, gave us a capital paper on the "Modern Press." He summarized the

---

RICHMOND AND KINGSTON.

Will members of the League, and others interested, in the Richmond, Twickenham, East Sheen and Kingston districts please communicate with Mr. W. J. C. Evers, 29, Marlborough Road, Richmond.

---

gradual development of the newspaper from the broad sheets, down to the modern daily. He pointed out that the small sheets which were issued during the General Strike were like the old broad sheets.

The present Press monopoly was referred to, and Mr. Finnimore pointed out two of its dangers, i.e., that the journalists themselves were half-enslaved, and the readers of the daily papers are gulled and misled respecting the realities of our present economic position. The only two newspapers which can be really said to stand for social justice, and which endeavour to give a correct version of our present economic realities and the perils inherent in this growth of monopoly in every sphere, are the *Daily Herald* and our ouw little weekly newspaper, *G.K.'s Weekly*. Mr. Finnimore drew our attention to the difficulties of keeping two newspapers of this kind in existence, the great capital required in order to launch a modern paper, and the fact that advertisements provided most of its income.

Mr. Finnimore was heartily thanked for his excellent paper, and an interesting discussion followed.

Prepaid Classified Advertisements.

The charge for these powerful Small Advertisements is 1/3 for the first 7 words and 2d. a word afterwards. Seven insertions are given for the price of six.

Advertisements (with remittance) should reach us by Monday morning to ensure insertion in the current week's issue.

Small Advertisement Manager, G.K.'s WEEKLY, 20/21, Essex Street, London, W.C.2.

Personal.

EXPRESSION, DEBATE, DELIVERY
A Psychological Aid to Memory and Fluency of Speech. The Rhetorlogue Mnemonic Wheel, 21/-; Book and Speakers' Charts, 21/-. From OWEN BENNISON, 46, Bessborough Place, Westminster, S.W.1 Money Orders crossed " & Co." Kindly mention this paper. Details sent post free.

Appointments Wanted.

PUBLIC-SCHOOLMAN, studying for Teaching Diploma, seeks post as junior master or tutor to young boy. French, Latin and usual English subjects. —Box P. S., G.K.'s WEEKLY, 20/21, Essex Street, W.C.2.

GIRL (20), living near London, anxious to work as artist's or photographer's model; good blonde colouring, slim build, medium height, hair unshingled.—"JUNE," Box 61, G.K.'s WEEKLY, 20/21, Essex Street, Strand, W.C.2.

Astrology.

HOROSCOPE. Personally calculated. Two years' influences. Excellent unsolicited testimonials. Send birth date, 1/6. —" BELPER," Irving Road, Bournemouth.

HOROSCOPE. Guide to success, with 5 years' future prospects. Knowledge is power; forewarned is forearmed. Send 2/6 with birth-date, time and place.—M. VEGA, 165 (G), Maughan Street, Newcastle-on-Tyne

Books, Etc.

BOOKS.—New and Second-hand. Enquiries made for any book free of charge.—L. H. DAVIS, 7, Downton Avenue, London, S.W.2.

BOOKS for Better Business and other interesting subjects. Send stamp for illustrated Catalogue.—W. T. BROWN, 45, Nicholas Street, London, E.1.

Clubs, Etc.

THE LIGHTHOUSE, 117, Union Street, Borough, S.E.1. Good accommodation at less than popular prices. Nice little hall to rent; nominal fee. Apply: MANAGER.

Gramophone Exchange.

GRAMOPHONE Records exchanged. London. Write or call: Book Store, 110, London Road, S.E.1

Dress Agency.

MRS. BARLOW pays utmost value for Discarded Clothing. Everything confidential. Promptness.—" Castleway," Hanworth, Middlesex.

Literary, etc.

GREAT Vocal Discovery.—Develop a beautiful, powerful, resonant voice. Wonderful silent method. 3d. stamp, particulars and wonderful testimony.— PROF. REID, 541g, Wigan Road, Bolton, Lancs.

Medical.

BLOOD pressure, indigestion, constipation, sleeplessness, giddiness, loss of memory, headaches, depression, rheumatism, nerve and heart troubles, varicose veins, etc., are mostly due to hardened arteries. DR MLADEJOVSKY'S (Professor of Medicine, Prague University) simple treatment. Wonderful results. Booklet free.—DROSIL (Dept. A6), 26, Sun Street, London, E.C.2.

TUMOURS, Gallstones, Piles, Lupus.— Booklet describing successful home herbal treatment sent free to sufferers.— STROOPAL (Dept. K), Hartfield Road, London, S.W.19.

Restaurants.

DISTRIBUTIST Restaurant. — " The Owl," 3, Kingly Street, W.1. (behind Robinson and Clevers, Regent Street). Luncheons and Teas. Members of the League can meet each other here.

Typewriting, Duplicating, Etc.

LITERARY Typewriting carefully and promptly executed. MSS. 1s. per 1,000 words; carbon copy, 3d. per 1,000.— MISS NANCY McFARLANE (J.), 44, Elderton Road, Westcliff-on-Sea.

TYPEWRITING and Duplicating. Authors' MSS. typed 10d. per 1,000 words; carbon copy 3d. per 1,000 words. Testimonials, circulars, etc., duplicated. Envelopes addressed. Prompt and efficient work.—MARION YOUNG (C), 7a, Station Road, Balham, S.W.12.

TYPEWRITING and Duplicating.— Moderate terms.—MISS HILL, 36, Church Street, Kensington, W.8.

TYPEWRITING, literary work intelligently done. Envelopes addressed, etc. Moderate terms.—JEAN McCANCE, Porlock Weir, W. Somerset.

NEAT ACCURATE TYPING
Intelligently executed. MSS. 1/- 1,000 words.
Quotations given.
Miss N. Netherwood, 128, Park Road, Loughborough.

The Proprietors exercise all possible care in the acceptance of advertisements for "G.K.'s Weekly."

Property.

HAMPSTEAD GARDEN SUBURB
HOUSES TO LET OR FOR SALE.
Contract built under Surveyor's continual supervision, 3 or 4 Bedrooms; with or without Garages. Good Gardens. Completed to tenant's requirements. The finest value obtainable. Write for illustrated brochure :
COPARTS, LTD.,
Agents for Houses in
LONDON'S MOST BEAUTIFUL SUBURB, 12, North End Road, Golders Green, N.W.11.

Tuition.

DAVIS Correspondence College.—Bookkeeping, Shorthand, Languages.— Terms: Overcreek, Park Road, Leigh-on-Sea.

ITALIAN.—Short, rapid courses.—T. BALESTRERI, 16, Coram Street, Russell Square, W.C.1.

MENTALISM.—The study that imparts confidence, effects good memory, develops the brain and increases earning ability; 1/2.—H. REASON, Publisher, Gt. Crosby.

Accommodation To Let and Wanted.

BED-SITTING Room to Let in Bloomsbury Flat; gas stove and ring, electric light, use of bath-room, geyser, and telephone. Professional woman, student or social worker preferred.—Write: Box 44, G.K.'s WEEKLY, 20/21, Essex Street, W.C.2.

CONVENIENT, sunny, 4-roomed furnished Bungalow; garden; healthy, quiet village; sea 1½ miles; main water; drainage. Daily help possible. Long or short let.—MILLER, St. Nicholas at Wade, Thanet.

FURNISHED, with attendance, good sitting-room and bedroom, with use of bath, full attendance and cooking. Well recommended. At South Benfleet. To let for 3 months, 35/- weekly; for shorter periods, £2 weekly.—Write: PORTLOCK, 15, Pindar Street, London, E.C.2.

LADY would let 1 or 2 Rooms, either furnished or unfurnished; near South Norwood Park, Golf and Tennis Club.— Write: LEASGILL, G.K.'s WEEKLY, LTD., 20/21, Essex Street, W.C.2.

WANTED, in March, Part of House or Flat, for two ladies with maid; unfurnished; quiet position, use of garden; ground, first or second floor, not basement. Two sitting, three bedrooms, kitchen, bath-room, etc. Locality: Stanley Crescent, Ladbroke Square, Chepstow Villas.—Please write " MARY," 14, Mayfield Road, Sanderstead, South Croydon.

Published by the Proprietors, G.K.'s WEEKLY, LTD., at their offices, 20 & 21, Essex Street, Strand, London, W.C.2 (incorporating THE NEW WITNESS). Telephone No. City 1978. Printed by THE MARSHALL PRESS, LTD., 7, Milford Lane, Strand, London, W.C.2. Sole agents for Australasia: Gordon & Gotch (Australasia, Ltd. Sole Agents for South Africa: Central News Agency, Ltd.

G.K.'s Weekly

EDITED BY G. K. CHESTERTON.

No. 171.—Vol. VII., p. 225.   Week ending Saturday, June 23, 1928.   PRICE TWOPENCE
YEARLY (52 ISSUES)
10s.   10d.

Telephone No. City 1978.   [Registered at G.P.O. as a Newspaper.]   Offices, 22, Essex Street, Strand, W.C.2

CONTENTS :

VOTES FOR WOMEN.

WE too would pay our homage to Mrs. Pankhurst, as an inconsiderable voice in the universal Hail and Farewell. We who always recognized her virtues, salute her, as a splendid enemy. They that splashed her with filth weep over her as a lost friend.

Well, this sort of inverted disloyalty is a part of the English character, a trait that the Latins and the Gaels find it very difficult to understand. And to repent their hatred of the Germans is one thing, to repent their hatred of Mrs. Pankhurst is quite another. Indeed, we too tend to forget that we had ever quarrelled with her when we recall her greatness.

For she was a great, a fine woman. We have seen her ruling a crowd, a crowd quite hostile, save for a little band of devotees clustered round her. We have seen her proud eyes light up, her nostrils dilate and her lips smile with the gay joy of battle, which is the greatest joy in life to the fighting man. We have seen her dragged along by two . . . no, three or four policemen, dishevelled yet not undignified—unlike the other poor creatures who served her cause.

And that is the gravest point in our indictment of the great lady :—*Her followers*! They marched so proudly in procession, they looked so fine; but in a tussle with the police, or worse still with the mob, they looked so pitiful—so shameful—so bedraggled, with soiled garments disarranged, and robbed of their crown. We have known many admirable girls who were broken and some few who were killed under the wheels of this splendid, devoted, high-souled Juggernaut. And you must pardon us, ladies, who will consider this as an additional insult;

but, though it is good to fight and if need be to die for your country or for any other great cause, these were things we did not like to see.

We grant them St. Joan, though we cannot consider the gaining of the votes for women as important as the saving of France. We grant them other great women-leaders in war—such as Queen Eleanor. But, in every case that we can remember, they were leaders of *men*, and in the case of St. Joan it was only she who suffered martyrdom.

There is no doubt that Mrs. Pankhurst suffered martyrdom. Even had we not heard the details of her abominable torture, a glance at her photograph taken when she was newly come from her imprisonment would tell us that. And she suffered unflinchingly. And miraculously soon the gay dancing valour came back to her eyes.

Oh, had you been in Trafalgar Square that day when the platform began swaying, and brutal hooligans from West End suburbs, with lustful gloating faces, swirled close to catch her, and had you seen that proud measuring glance and the gay scornful toss of the head, you would have loved the woman and longed to serve her ! There were some anti-Suffragists got broken heads for her sake that day.

And, had she been leading an army of men, her tactics were, up to a point, so right. The Suffragists indulged in mad extravagances. But so did the Irish when fighting for their freedom. We do not justify arson, still less the burning of churches; the squirting of vitriol into pillar-boxes was the trick of wanton children ; and there were some more deplorable things, such as the suicide of a Suffragist on the race-course at Epsom on Derby Day.

But Mrs. Pankhurst and her party made themselves so unpleasant that in 1914 the Government was waiting for a dignified excuse to give them the vote. And that is how we shall get Distributism : by making ourselves damned unpleasant.

We cannot justify the way the Government behaved. It was nonsense to tell us that they could not yield to force. Apart from bribery, corruption, and cheating, force is the only thing any government yields to, even if sometimes (as in this case) the force merely causes intense discomfort. And it was dangerous to say that only a minority of women wanted the vote. Only a minority of people wanted the pubs closed in the afternoon, but the Government was cheated into closing them

Therefore it was foolish to say that the Government was compelled to resort to utmost severity in order to stop the Suffragist campaign. That the vote has now been granted by a Conservative Government to all women above the age of 21, is proof that the pre-war Liberal Government (not opposed in principle to woman's suffrage) was wrong to feed women forcibly and to subject them to so many other unnameable humiliations.

And indeed we cannot admit that the torture of the women is ever to be tolerated. But that is part of our case against votes for women.

To think that such a brave battle was fought and such sufferings were endured to give women the vote ! And at a time when, almost by general consent, the vote is regarded as entirely valueless !—when the weakness of Parliamentary institutions has become patent, and many Continental nations have turned for truer representation towards dictators ! That is the monstrous irony of the thing ! To think of it, Mary Gawthorpe, Annie Kenney, and you others, splendid girls, who proved so much more clearly your devotion to your cause than as yet we have proved our devotion to Distributism—all dared and suffered for a vote !

Well, as a matter of fact they didn't. The Suffragists had some motives far more admirable and some far less. There was in certain Suffragists more than a touch of that silly antagonism to Man which is called Feminism, and manifests itself in a desire to abandon most of the habits of women. But there was in many a genuine desire to help poor women who lived in slums, poor women who slaved in factories, poor married women who were pestered by officials, poor women who were down-trodden anywhere and in any way. Of course many of them, perhaps most of them (but not Mrs. Billington Grieg), emphasized unduly the undoubted fact that some women are badly treated by their husbands. And, since they tended to ignore the fact that some men are badly treated by their wives, their passion for justice went askew.

That is a matter for argument. But Mrs. Pankhurst stands above all argument as one of the noblest women of our time.

NOTES OF THE WEEK.

Alarums and Excursions.

WE have heard it stated that Mr. Fitzalan Hope, the Deputy Speaker and Chairman of Ways and Means, asked that his name should not be considered when a successor to Mr. Whitley as Speaker was in question, because of the multitude of his business. We have also heard it said that he thought that his being a Catholic would make his selection, at this present moment of excitement, a cause of greater excitement. Anyhow, he was not thought of, or, if thought of, was not spoken of ; and that harmless person Captain Fitzroy, the member for Daventry, will be Speaker. We hear, too, that Dr. Hensley Henson, Bishop of Durham, may succeed the present Archbishop of Canterbury, his qualifications being that he was once a Modernist, and is now almost a High-Anglican. This appointment and this prediction are fairly reasonable. But what are we to think of the suggestion that the preposterous Jix may be the next Conservative Premier ? This weak, pompous spitfire is the very man to make a revolution. Do the bosses want it ?

Nero Fiddling—But no Rome.

THE Sunday Express, inspired no doubt by the visit of Prince Potenziani, by the arrival of Sir Ofori Atta, and by the renewed American invasion, has been assuring its readers that London rivals ancient Rome in the time of Nero. That cosmospolitan crowd in the streets (Rome had no Americans !) Those quaint black faces ! The Coliseum—stern reminder of our glory ! It may be all true and we hope it is. But if London were as accustomed as ancient Rome to the visits of dusky potentates it would assuredly not greet them with such headlines as the following : SIR OFORI ATTA—JOVIAL AFRICAN CHIEF.—GOLD CROWN AND DANCING PUMPS.—EGGS AND BACON. There is growing up in London a kind of provincialism which is not born of a pride in local things. It is the result of small barbarians from small places capturing the organs of public opinion.

A Rare Honour.

THE invitation of the University of Oxford to the Abbé Brémond to accept an honorary degree of LL.D., confers upon him as a Catholic priest a rare honour which he shares with H.E. the Cardinal-Archbishop of Westminster. M. Henri Brémond, who was born in 1865, is a member of the Académie Française, a distinguished littérateur and equally eminent in the affairs of the Church and the State. His *Historie du Sentiment Religieux en France* won the Grand Prix de Gobert in 1923, and his *Prière et Poésie* caused a considerable stir when it appeared. He is a specialist in *pure poetry,* the new school in France which seeks to restore music to verse.

A MOTTO FOR THE LEAGUE.

Mr. Ellis Roberts suggests that the League take the following lines as its motto :—

Let the superfluous and lust-dieted man,
That slaves your ordinance, that will not see
Because he doth not feel, feel your power quickly ;
So distribution should undo excess,
And each man have enough.

King Lear. Act IV. Sc. 1.

Feeding Ourselves.

IN a leaflet on the *Possibilities of Food Production,* published by the Rural Reconstruction Association, Sir John Russell, D.Sc., F.R.S., Director of the Rothamsted Experimental Station, is reported as making some very remarkable statements in support of a contention often urged by Mr. Heseltine in these columns, namely, " that we *can* feed ourselves if we wish." On the subject of wheat he says, " England, thanks to its climate, is one of the best known countries for growing wheat, for it has the needed temperate moist climate. We have also Square Head Master and Revil Wheat, the heaviest croppers in the world, whilst the new wheat known as Yeoman II. has all the qualities of the best mixtures that English bakers use." He goes on to say that we might reasonably expect to raise our average of 30 bushels to the acre to 40 bushels, and then we could grow all our wheat on seven million acres, which is less than half of our present arable and a quarter of our cultivated land. He adds cautiously that this might not be sound policy, *but it is not impossible.* He says also that " we might hope to produce all our own poultry and eggs, pork and bacon, commodities of which we produce about half in all at the present time."

Is Agriculture a Business?

IN addition to this the same expert gives it as his opinion that "Agriculture has not the characteristics of a business : it is a ' method of life.' A cow is not a machine to produce day by day an equal supply of milk . . . . There is a daily fluctuation . . . . It is the same in every branch of agriculture." He is impressed by the keenness and alertness of farmers, and contradicts the common cry of the town critics that English farmers are slack and unenterprising.

Robbing England of Men.

WE ourselves have not a strong faith in " experts," but we suggest that if the Government is to heed any, it can chose none more competent in his sphere than Sir John Russell. Instead of bolstering up industries with little or no hope of doing more than holding their own, it might give some attention to agriculture, which has still such great possibilities. On another page the Birmingham Branch of the League suggests diverting some of the unemployed on to the land instead of paying them to be permanently idle. We note that the Government is training some miners for agriculture—*and then making a present of them to Canada!* Meanwhile England starves for farmers.

Shaw's New Book.

MR. BERNARD SHAW, who once gave all the reasons for living three hundred years, has lately been giving his reasons for refusing to live for ever. They seem to be chiefly based on the assumption that he has not lived at all. For no man has lived who has not seen something worthy to be perpetually possessed. But we happily have no fears of his not living till next week, when a review of his latest book, by the Editor of this paper, which comes too late for this number, will appear. It is inspiring to see him fighting on so many fronts.

FUN WITH THE CALF.

MISS MARY PICKFORD.

Trunks held up by U.S. Customs.—*Daily Mail* headline.

Rather elephantine.

LOURDES CURE CLAIM.

Woman who suffered from infancy.—*Daily Mail* headline.

Second childhood?

THIS WEEK'S FAIRY TALE.

ON the Day following the Loss of his Mother, the Great Industrialist Lay Weeping, Moaning, and Writhing. So that his Friends, Thinking to Comfort him, Came to him and said : " There, there, we understand. But did you not Agree only Yesterday that, Owing to her Old Age and Failing Eyesight, it was Necessary, in the Interests of Economy, that she should be Put Away? " And the Great Industrialist Answered : " Of course, I did, You Mutts, but if I had only kept her until To-day, Instead of Pushing her Under the Train Yesterday, I should have Received £12,500 from the *Daily Purge,* instead of a Paltry £10,000. The cost of maintaining her for this Period could not have Exceeded 2s. 8d., Including all Overhead Charges, so that as a Result of my Thoughtlessness and Precipitancy, I have Lost No Less than £2,499 17s. 4d." And his Friends went Sadly Away, Knowing that for the Greater Sorrows of Life, Time is the Only Healer.

UNEMPLOYMENT.

A DISTRIBUTIST SOLUTION.

[The following scheme has been drawn up by a Sub-Committee of the Birmingham Branch of the League, and has been endorsed by that Branch. It is being submitted to the Executive Committee wth a request that it be considered for adoption by the League. In the meantime criticisms and suggestions will be welcomed.—H. R.]

I.

THE outstanding social feature in this country for the past eight years has been the existence of a body of men and women, varying from one to one and a half millions strong (but never falling below the smaller figure), for whom the industrial organization of society can find no means of livelihood.

The cause of this is the decline of our foreign markets. The practical monopoly of industrialism with which this country began its career as the Workshop of the World was the result, not of any essential or permanent title to such a monopoly, but of a series of political and economic accidents purely temporary in their effects. We were the first to discover coal and iron in juxtaposition, and we were the first to exploit that discovery. Other nations did not make, or did not choose to make, the same discovery. Moreover, during the Napoleonic Wars the rest of Europe had other preoccupations, and by the end of them England easily led in industrialized production.

But our lead was gradually disappearing throughout the nineteenth century. By the end of it, we were reduced to a position of bare equality with many younger industrial nations. By 1914 we were definitely in a position of inferiority to several of them whose natural resources were fresher and more extensive.

This relative decline was masked throughout the period by the constant opening-up of new foreign markets. It required the war of 1914-18 to make clear to us two things of the first importance—that our lead was lost, and that there were no more new markets. Industrial exploitation had covered the globe. Even in " undeveloped " countries such as China and India, industrialism reared its head and supplanted British products.

It is quite certain that our industrial decline is permanent. It is still the fashion in a section of the daily Press to speak of it as temporary, but the Federation of British Industries knows better. The brightest forecast to which any honest economist would now commit himself would be the bare maintenance of our present position.

But that present position—the *best* to which we can reasonably look forward—involves the permanent existence of a million unemployed. That is, there are and will remain in this country a million or more unfortunate souls who are condemned by no fault of their own to an undignified, unsought, and demoralizing idleness and poverty.

Possibly out of compassion, but more probably as an insurance against civil commotion and even revolution, the governing powers of the State have introduced a system of subsistence payments for the unemployed : largely paid for, it is true, by the working classes themselves, but degraded in our speech and usage as the Dole.

The payment of actual subsistence to these innocent victims of the failure of a system which never gave them more than a bare living, is an obligation of the strictest justice. But unemployment benefit can be justified on no intrinsic ground. It is a permanent unproductive charge on the community, and it is a material agent in the progressive demoralization of those constrained to accept it. But the various sugestions made by financiers, industrialists, and others, to devote these payments to the relief of industry by employing men at a low wage, to be made up by the Dole to Trade Union rates, must be utterly discountenanced. The whole amount of these payments would not suffice to regain our distant markets, captured by better-equipped or nearer competitors; and the practice itself would lead to abuses only too familiar to the working classes. It is the very definition of the Unemployment Problem that there are already more men in industrialism than industrialism can support. To add still more men, under any conditions short of the Coolie Standard, will merely intensify that problem.

To suggest reluctant emigration—exile from friends and country—unless it be demonstrated that there is no more milk in the breasts of England, is a remedy more appalling still. They who advance it should receive the punishment of men who despair of the State.

It is the purpose of this statement to advance a scheme which, while costing the community little or no more than the present unproductive relief, will restore to the unemployed their dignity and independence, give stability and wealth to the State, and if pursued to its logical end ultimately extinguish the present cost of relief.

As it is notorious that our export trade is in permanent decline, so it is notorious that the land of this country is more neglected and more wastefully farmed than that of any country in Europe. We import five-sixths of our food and on account of the decline in our trade we may soon be unable to pay for the whole of that. On every ground therefore, we must produce more food for ourselves. We need a peasantry. It is also true that in industrialism may be found a large number of men alike able and willing to work the land if given a reasonable chance. This is especially the case in the most depressed of all our industries. In most mining districts, many men alternate between farm work and mining ; and many more cultivate large allotments, keep pigs, and goats, and so on.

An unemployed man (not necessarily the same individual) with an average family of a wife and three children receives in a year in unemployment benefit the sum of £78. For the reasons already given, this sum may be regarded as a permanent annual charge on the community. Capitalized at 4½ per cent., this amount will yield a capital sum of £1,733. For a very little more than this capital sum a family can quite certainly be settled in a holding of a reasonable size (say of 25 acres) equipped for straight farming, supplied with enough stock and seed for a start, and given subsistence on the unemployment scale for fifteen months pending the maturing of his first crops. The total average cost of this settlement would be £2,060. Of this sum, £1,733 would be raised as already suggested, by utilizing the unemployment benefit of £78 per annum to pay interest on a Government Loan. The balance of £327 would be similarly raised, and would after two years be covered by the repayments of the man concerned. During the first two years the interest (a total of £30 in round figures) would have to be paid by the State. This sum of £30 represents the only direct additional expense to the State. Full details are given below. Administration expenses would cancel out as between the Ministries of Labour and Agriculture.

(To be continued.)

TOP—

BACK TO THE BEARD.

WE all remember the once fashionable sport of spotting men with beards and calling them beavers. They were so called because beavers have no beards; on the same principle on which monopolies are called private enterprise, and politicians are called right honourable gentlemen, and the fancy of a millionaire for printing his private opinions on a million sheets of paper and scattering them about the country is always called "an organ of public opinion." But over and above the maxim of *lucus a non lucendo* having become the general modern motto, there was much that was quaint in the selection of that particular image. The joke against the bearded man was partly against the old-fashioned man; and partly against the Bohemian. In other words, having a beard is not playing the beaver, though it may be playing the goat. It may be merely copying the bearded composure and conservatism of the oyster. But such quaint Early Victorian individualism seems the last thing to be logically associated with beavers. Beavers are Communists; and like many other Communists, highly respectable and rather dull. Beavers are class-conscious proletarians of the Tenth International; and are not interested in anything except Labour questions, chiefly connected with the building of dams. Nothing would seem to be less like the bearded eccentric surviving in a beardless age who might in this be compared rather to the last specimen of the Dodo or the Great Auk. Perhaps the notion of the beaver beard carried some shadow of reminiscence of the beaver hat.

By this time the beaver joke is almost as antiquated as the beaver hat; and the counting of beards seems as remote as the collecting of scalps. And yet the memory rises again in the mind when we gaze, as we have just been gazing, upon a row of shiny newspaper portraits, inscribed, "Young Men of To-day," and accompanied by a rapturous article describing the present-day as a golden age of the young. One of the portraits apparently represented young Mr. Selfridge; and there was a very poetical passage about the first linking up of a long chain of shops. We approve of the word "chain." There were other young men also, of course; but we merely mention the matter to record the first momentary impression, which is not without significance. After looking at it once (and there is no particular reason for anybody looking at it twice) the general effect was that the young men all looked very much alike. Now we hear a great deal about Victorian stodginess; and we ourselves are no mere eulogists of Victorian custom. But we think it certain that the heads all in a row would have looked less alike, if they had been those of the young Carlyle, the young Huxley, the young Tennyson, the young Trollope, and the young Dickens. All would have worn their hair longer, but the length would have differed more; some might have worn beards, and none of the new young men dare be seen in a beard. Now we do think it is worth a note, and is a text for some little meditation, that at this time when everybody is talking our heads off about Being Natural, about letting things sprout spontaneously and come of themselves in freshness and freedom, we are even more ruled by the razor than Lord Chesterfield or Beau Nash.

—AND TAIL

EFFACING THE IMAGE

IN the Ideal Homes Exhibition there was an extraordinary contraption that was called the House of the Future. Weird as it was, perhaps the weirdest thing about it was classing the House of the Future as an Ideal Home. There may be somebody somewhere for whom this sort of thing would really be an ideal. We need not dwell upon what it would be for us; beyond saying that we suppose so modern a mansion will at least contain a lethal chamber. It would be the pure-minded modern substitute for a wine-cellar. And certainly we should be tempted at an early date to look for that room, if we were obliged to live in that house.

But there is one particular point about the House of the Future which concerned us more seriously, if anything about it could be serious. At least it concerned the oblivion of a very vital truth; a truth forgotten by a great many modern people much more sensible than the lunatics who manufactured this enormous mantrap of steel. It was gravely explained, in the leaflets and other explanations given to the public, that this particular sort of mansion is not intended to last, any more than a motor-car. At first our spirits will be naturally cheered and uplifted by the thought of it perishing so rapidly; only to be dashed down again by the information that the householder will then go into another house exactly like it. Or else he will gradually put together a new house

out of standardized parts, in the manner of a Ford car; anyhow, he will as quickly as possible throw the old house away. Castles and cottages will follow the swiftest cars to the scrap-heap; such is the superior strength of the new materials.

Now even a nonsensical antic like this illustrates what is wrong with the world. What is wrong is decivilization or the return of barbarism; because it is the loss of man's *real* lordship of matter. Man's true power upon this earth was that he could stamp it with his image; make it respond to his spiritual appetites; almost make it speak, as with a voice like his own. It was the whole point that he could humanize mud and stone and clay and timber. He poured so much of his inspiration into the garden that the garden could pour back the inspiration into him. He could make the trees talk to him and the flowers salute him; like a magician in a fairy-tale. Materials were no longer materialistic; they had undergone a silent fermentation of affection and memory; and a spirit had passed into them: the impress that is unique in the physical universe; the image of the image of God.

This is the element called Property, misued and profaned like every good element to evil ends; but now, in the new barbarism, for the first time merely ignored and forgotten. When man wishes merely to break up or forget his house, he has relapsed into the straw hovel or ragged tent of the desert, and is near to all the numberless and mindless creatures that pass and perish and leave no mark upon the land.

THE SCRAPBOOK.

MEMORY.

Touch not the shades of blurred regret,
Leave the soft colours there.
The deeper hues we loved we would forget—
They are too near despair.

Leave but the faded wistful greys
Time softens with his brush,
Where Beauty, with old dreams half-captured, strays,
And whispers in the hush.

Call not the reds to life again,
Nor wake the dazzling white.
Kind Pity, who has soothed the stabbing pain,
Dulls our once eager sight.

We are not strong enough to gaze,
Now the last words are said,
On rainbow tints of long-forgotten days,
And dreams we know are dead.

M. K. M. B.

THE EMPTY HOUSE.

Ah, dark the rooms and thicker than the dust
    Crowd fast the lonely ghosts on silent feet;
    And all the shadow'd nooks lost dreams secrete—
Last words of lovers' pain and broken trust.

And ghostly in the trees the mournful wind
    Eternal tryst keeps with the twisting leaves:
    Upon decaying walls the ivy weaves
A last wreath for the wraith Death left behind.

MARY ANTONY GEORGE.

THE WIDEST SENSE.

When Joynson-Hicks says " Transubstantiation,"
Apostrophizing Savidge and the Nation,
    He uses it in the very widest sense!
Stretch, ye vocabularies! O words, begin
To wobble slightly! so Hicks enters in,
    Speaking in accents Protestant and tense.

For why should words have meaning? Romish art
From which, Hicks knows, all our dire troubles start,
    Alone makes narrow thus our words and thought.
Away with meaning! Birmingham can show
How black is white, faith unfaith, and yes " no "
    And any numeral reduced to nought !

Yet, Hicks, if in the very widest sense
We looked at you, firmly, without pretence :
    I do believe there'd be no Hicks to see—
Or at the best a small cherubic boy
Whom only dear Mamma's prophetic joy
    Could ever fancy as Home Secretary !

R. E. R.

THE MINSTREL IN BELEM.

I made a golden mantle
    For a Nativity Play;
The most terrible of the Magi
Wore it on Christmas Day;
    I gave words to say.

I made three golden finches
    For the shepherd Hobinol
To give to his Dear Darling,
    Who is the King of us all
        To play withal.

I made of my sorrowful heart
    A gorgeous crystal cup,
And I pressed the grapes of the world
    For a wine to fill it up—
        Mary, give Him to sup.

WILFRED CHILDE.

RIDE A COCK HORSE.

Fine lady, fine lady, upon a white horse,
Where are you going? " To Banbury Cross."
Fine lady, fine lady, why will you go?
" To buy a fine bell for my little big toe."
Fine lady, what will you do then all the day?
" I'll ride a-cock horse while the fiddlers play."
Fine lady, fine lady, when homeward you make,
Fine lady, please bring me a Banbury cake.

UNA PHYLLIS DOD

ORION.

Up above the station roof
Is Orion far aloof,
Gleaming four-square in the sky
Like a bed where I could lie,
With a star at every post,
Blessing me as I need most.
Mark and Matthew at the head
Of my starry posted bed;
Luke and John as it is meet
Burn their tapers at my feet;
And, as every dog should do,
Sirius winks and watches too.

S. R. HURST.

THE MOLE ON HER BELLY.

Back to ceiling and belly to floor
Burrows the mole on the peaty moor.
The whortle is rooty; but on she squirms
After her booty : worms, worms, worms !

P. G. S.

STRAWS IN THE WIND.

IN PRAISE OF COUNTER-JUMPERS.

By G. K. CHESTERTON.

LET him that does not understand the story of the shops, or the nature of the small shopkeeper, consider philosophically the case of the Counter-Jumper. The term was used some time ago in contempt of the common trader. It has already become a compliment: a compliment to something more and more uncommon.

Despite our excitement about exceptional acts of adventure or enterprise, as touching those who fly the Atlantic or swim the Channel, it will sometimes be wise to correct it by comparing our heroes, not so much with the heroes of the past, as with the ordinary people of the past. For we live in a time when even heroism has become a form of specialism. We do not underrate the heroism when we say that it has become almost professional, like any other form of sport. We may note here the curious paradox of the old comic novels; in which even the cowards were in a sense more courageous than many moderately courageous moderns. Many people in the pit of a theatre have roared with laughter at Bob Acres standing trembling on the duelling-ground, who would never themselves have gone to the duelling-ground at all. And while men still laugh at Mr. Winkle nearly falling off a horse, many of them would never have had the courage of Mr. Winkle in getting on to a horse; especially when he could not ride. And it will generally be noticed in the novels of the early nineteenth century that the riding of a horse, which is now becoming so specialist a sport, was regarded as normal to any number of commonplace and even prudential persons. In the tales of Jane Austen, the dull and timid and stay-at-home types trot about on horses exactly like the dashing or romantic ones. It is not necessary to dogmatize here on the loss and gain in such changes of fashion. But it is important to remember that even the mockeries and terms of derision, that were then fashionable, often give us a glimpse into a world in which certain feelings were common to many which are now confined to few. Something in the very tone and turn of phrase often indicates that real though rather indefinable spirit. And nothing of that spirit could be more spirited than the phrase that called a common shop-boy a counter-jumper.

The patient customer to-day might walk down the long avenues of some ten or twelve departments of Selfridge's without observing any attendant suddenly jump over a counter. Nor is the whole air and deportment of the attendants such as to suggest that they have but a moment before, or will but a moment after, whirl their legs aloft with such a flying leap. The whole attitude and atmosphere implied, even in this damning description by an enemy, must have been much more really bold and boyish to have been described in such terms at all. And indeed we do feel the presence of this bravado when we encounter such figures in fiction. Mr. Richard Swiveller would certainly have jumped over the counter. Even Mr. Jobling or Mr. Chuckster would have done it, with a touch of more languid grace. The two apprentices in the *Christmas Carol,* in the early life of Scrooge, had actually slept under the counter. It is a very real satisfaction to hope that employees now sleep in somewhat more comfortable places; though the improvement is not due, as some seem to suggest, to the original class and creed of Mr. Scrooge. It is due to the employees themselves having banded themselves together in Unions of which Mr. Scrooge and his modern representatives strongly disapprove. It is a good thing that the protest of the working-classes has begun to have its effect, even on the workers in the middle-classes. But we are talking here of a tone and the atmosphere of a generation; which was, by the way, the generation in which the first and most heroic and most hated of the trades unionists began their battle. And it is impossible not to feel, in reading the fiction and phraseology of that generation, that there was more of the spirit of battle in all their gestures and their jokes. The first barbarous movements of the industrial revolution had not broken their spirit half so much as the last polished and orderly discipline of the industrial rule seems to have broken the spirit of their grandsons. The prentices in the *Christmas Carol* slept under the counter, but they jumped over the counter. And it is no exaggeration to say that they jumped for joy. There was much more even in Sim Tappertit than Dickens ever detected. For that absurd swagger, about saving his bleeding country, was indeed the vague memory and inheritance of a history in which the prentices had really been historical characters. It went back to the days when the narrow and crooked streets of London had echoed with the cry of " Clubs, clubs ! " in many a quarrel of King or Guild or Parliament, in many a brawl about Frenchmen or Scots or Jews. And it made a difference to the island story when the London counter-jumper leapt over his counter and seized his club.

Compare with all this vulgarity the soothing presence of the shop-walker. The shop-walker is the typical figure of our time, because he becomes more important as there are more avenues and departments in the emporium. Miss Rose Macaulay, in her recent and fascinating satire, has pointed out that the shop-walker invariably observes " straight through "; and she asks (in her sceptical and destructive manner) " Through what? " For when the shop has become a labyrinth, the mere guide becomes a sort of leader; but the shop-walker is not only not a shop-leader, he is hardly even a shop-man. He has not even a counter to himself, let alone a store; he is as nomadic as the nocturnal policeman. He does not even stand behind a counter; and certainly nobody can imagine him wildly leaping over one. He is simply there to oil the wheels of somebody else's enormous and complicated machine; and therefore, perhaps, it is not his fault if his manner is a little oily. I spoke in my haste, perhaps, when I said some time ago that England is no longer a nation of shopkeepers, but a nation of shop-walkers. But the same truth can be put more temperately by saying that the shop-walker gives what his admirers would undoubtedly call " a tone " to the new shops and therefore to the new society. But whatever eles it is, it is not a very tonic sort of tone. It is not a tone of spirit and vivacity, even of a vulgar sort. And if the new shop-walker ran a race with the old counter-jumper, it would hardly be the walker who would win.

BOOK OF THE WEEK.
THE RUSSIAN DICTATOR.

THIS* is by far the clearest and fullest account we have had in England of Vladimir Ilyitch Ulianov, the Russian Dictator, known to the world as " Lenin." (It was the name his brother Alexander had taken; Alexander, who had planned the assassination of the Tsar in 1887, and was himself hanged instead; the police having, as usual, full knowledge of the conspiracy. Seventeen-year-old Vladimir Ilyitch decided, on his brother's execution, that the old methods of the revolutionaries in Russia would not do : " No, we shall get nowhere along this road ; it is not the right one.")

The man of a book—Marx's *Kapital*—was Vladimir Ulianov : a man of Theory ; the author of this biographical study makes that plain. Lenin " from his twenty-second year had a passion for thick statistical volumes." At twenty-four he was a convinced Marxist. In London he spent long hours in Highgate Cemetery, " and sat by the tombstone of Karl Marx." The historical theory of Marx possessed Lenin. History became his " deity," and his " providence." His atheism was utter and complete. Other followers of Marx might deny an objective truth and teach that truth could only be "an ideological form." Lenin would have none of this subjective truth. It made Christian belief possible : " Even Catholicism is an organized form of human experience."

Yet he was no mere doctrinaire, Lenin. Over and over again the theory had to be bent or broken as events might demand. At the last, when he held power, the communism to have been established was frustrated. The peasants simply wouldn't have communism. Lenin changed his policy : " his strength lay in his capacity to divine the changing moods of the nameless multitude." He was Russian, this son of a small government official of Astrakan, and understood the peasants. " He remained rooted in the countryside ; in spite of all the influence of the humanitarian philosophy of the industrial West, he was only concerned to secure what the countryman wanted." Communism was, of course, inevitable. The " class conscious proletariat " would in due time be all in all. Meanwhile the peasants needed ploughs and machinery. " At the summit of power, more and more securely established, he lost nothing of the inexorable rigidity of the Theory." But the peasant or workman, ignorant of theory, knew, as Lenin pointed out, " that capitalism at least was able to provide for his needs. . . The peasants reply to us is : ' You Communists are splendid folk, but you are not equal to the task you have taken on. . . . The work of the capitalists is more than you can do.' " Lenin insisted that the peasant was right.

" What is wanted now," said Lenin in the fifth year of the Republic, " is no longer politics, but the most prosaic of detail work. For this the people will be grateful, and only if we realize what the people want shall we be able to rule." Communism, the Theory, remained impregnable ; how to reach it was still the problem. The Dictator frankly admitted mistakes. " As no one else was allowed to criticize, he felt bound to do it as publicly as possible himself." The first thing to be done, the country being cleared of invaders, was " to build a solid bridge which shall lead us to Socialism."

Before his death the Dictator was working for the stabilization of the rouble and the restoration of the heavy industries : " Our salvation lies not only in a good harvest nor only in good conditions in the light industries, we still need the heavy industries. If we are without these we are still doomed as a civilized country."

The ultimate aims of Dictatorship vary. The methods of the Dictator are the same in every land. His first business is to put down anarchy and consolidate power. Terror and the suppression of opponents were as necessary in Russia as elsewhere if the country were to be saved. The man who had long ago declared himself a Jacobin and for thirty years had never faltered in his loyalty to Theory, " was not to be bound, in face of reality, either by his own or anyone else's books." Tolerance was never included in the Theory. " Nothing in thought or aspiration seemed to Lenin more incomprehensible than tolerance." Despotism was in the blood of this Asiatic. " In him the element of domination and Cæsarism found expression in the handling of theory." " He learnt from Karl Marx that freedom of thought which he prohibited in others."

The endless talk, the continuous flow of words in the written articles of his earlier Russian comrades in the Marxist movement, led to nothing, it seemed to Lenin. Divisions and sub-divisions in the Socialist ranks made the hope of effective unity vain. Lenin sat at the feet of his elders in exile and grew impatient of it all. Exile tends to distort the view of most. Lenin never ceased to keep in touch with realities. He, and he alone, it seemed to him, could save the situation in the general break-up of Russia in 1917. With other refugees he hastened home through Germany on the downfall of Tsarism, to organize and wait for the hour when he could grasp the power he needed for the saving of Russia and the social revolution. The incapacity of Kerensky, the treachery of others to the Theory, drove him to act. He saw himself as the Jacobin, " closely in touch with the organized proletariat, the real revolutionary social democrat." The Girondist " who thinks in terms of professors and students, and babbles about the absolute of the Democratic claims, is an opportunist."

This book helps us to understand Lenin and his place in European history. It describes the environment in which he worked, his activities, his ruthlessness, his indifference to personal comfort, the refusal of riches. Hatred, the author tells us, " was the flame that warmed him in days of cold despair "; and " this hatred supported and strengthened him." It was no private wrong, no sense of personal injury that kept the hatred alive. It was the consciousness of the sufferings of his neighbours, " all the tragedy of Russia," that made Lenin merciless to enemies of the Theory. When we ask, How did it come about that Lenin, before he died, had won so wide an affection? this book gives the answer : " In the cottages of town and village in which exhausted men sat at unspread tables, on whose hard beds and broad stoves children played and wrinkled old women fell asleep, there still throbbed the unending tired murmur of the suffering. To bring contentment into these homes was the one great task. He had never forgotten it ; and instinctively the great mass of people began to feel this love."

JOSEPH CLAYTON.

* LENIN. By Valeriu Marcu. Translated by E. W. Dickes. Victor Gollancz. 21s. net.

Small Workshops.

BASKET WARE
Rustic wicker furniture for outdoors. Log Baskets, Dog Baskets, Laundry and Travelling Hampers. Cane and coloured Shopping Baskets. Carriage paid. Illustrated catalogue and price list free.
BLACKWELL & SON, 20, Cross Street, BARNSTAPLE.

LEATHERWORK
Stools, motor cushions, log tubs, blotters, hand-made gloves.
KATHARINE COCKCROFT,
37, Belsize Park, N.W.3.

EMBROIDERY
Embroideries in wool on jumper suits and waistcoats.　KATHARINE COCKCROFT,
37, Belsize Park, N.W.3.

VISITING CARDS
Persons desiring Visiting Cards. Write for exquisite examples of refined society's latest fashion.
NICHOLLS, 294, Church Road, BRISTOL.

PRINTING
Good printing at moderate charges. Specimens and price free.
HATHERLEY, 43A, Trentham Street,
Southfields, LONDON.

THE FOREST TOYS
Wooden animals of all kinds, hand carved and painted. Price list post free.
F. H. WHITTINGTON, Brockenhurst,
HANTS.

VEGETABLE-DYED, HANDSPUN AND HANDWOVEN MATERIALS
Curtains, cushions, rugs, scarves and dress materials. Goods sent on approval. Vacancy for pupil.
DORIS JEWSON, 18, Colegate, NORWICH.

DECORATOR & PLUMBER
All house decorations done. Moderate charges; good work.
F. STONE, 5, Heath Villas, VALE OF HEALTH, N.W.3.

PHOTOGRAPHIC ENLARGEMENTS
Artistic Postcard Enlargements from your small films. 3/- dozen. Hand-woven cushion squares, 5/6. Table runners, 7/6. Fadeless Blue and Golden Brown.
ARTS AND CRAFTS, St. Osyth,
CLACTON-ON-SEA.

IRISH HOUSEHOLD LINENS
Direct from the Manufacturer. Coloured dress linen, very fine quality, 36 ins. wide, only 1/9 per yard, post free. Catalogue, samples and remnant bargain. List free.
J. HENDERSON, Milner Street, BELFAST, N. IRELAND.

GLOVES
Irreproachable gloves hand-made by expert. Original button holes. Every kind of handwork. Disabled Soldiers and Invalids employed. Bazaar and Trade should apply. Very moderate prices. Write for list.
HANDICRAFT HUT, PATTERDALE.

UPHOLSTERER & HOUSE FURNISHER
Restful Easy Chairs made in small workshop by practical working upholsterer. Covered in Damask, £5. Velvet or Moquette, £5 17s. 6d. Carriage paid anywhere in United Kingdom. Samples of coverings and designs on request.
R. STREET, 27, Albert Road,
COLNE, LANCASHIRE.

HOME DECORATIONS.
Hand-worked Pictorial Friezes. Beautiful exclusive designs for Home and Nursery. 108-in. repeat from 6d. per yard. Patterns on request.
(Specimens can be seen at the office.)
A. & F. MAYGER, designers,
14, Argyle Avenue, HOUNSLOW.

KNITTED WEAR.
Reader would like orders for Hand-made Silk Socks, Matinee Coats, Pull-overs, etc., also strong Boy's Stockings and Gents' Socks.
BOX 12, G.K.'s Weekly
20/21, Essex Street, STRAND, W.C.2.

TOYS
Christmas Dolls. English made. All kinds and prices. Speciality attractive cuddley dolls. Soft animals in great variety. Dolls mended. WINTER, Catbrook, TINTERN.

TAILORING. LADIES & GENTLEMEN
Bespoke and ready-to-wear. Good materials. Alterations and renovations carried out. Moderate charges. Patterns on request.
F. WALKER 18, Gt. Portland Street,
LONDON, W.1.

HAND MADE FURNITURE.
Hand-Made Furniture, mainly of English-grown woods, and to original designs from the simplest to the finest styles.
A. ROMNEY GREEN, Woodworker,
25, BRIDGE STREET, CHRISTCHURCH,

HANDWOVEN MATERIALS
Handspun and vegetable dyed, in silk, wool, and cotton. Dresses, jumpers, shirt lengths, scarves, curtains, cushion covers, and materials for all decorative purposes.
THE KINGSLEY WEAVERS (Leo & Eileen Baker), Chipping Campden, Glos.

GENTS SOX
Guaranteed All Wool and every pair made at home. Mixed colours, 2/3; plain colours 2/6. Postage paid.
G. MERRIKIN, 28, Shene Bldgs.,
Bourne Est., HOLBORN, E.C.

LEATHER GOODS.
Leather Comb Case, 1/6.　Raffia Sprays. Woven Scarf, 7/6.
MASON, Cowesby, Northallerton, YORKS.

PRINTER & PUBLISHER
Posters. Catalogues sent on application.
H. D. C. PEPLER.

SCULPTOR, CARVER & LETTER CUTTER
in wood and stone. Tombstones, Wall Tablets, Stations of the Cross, Altars, Holy Water Stoups, Sanctuary Lamps.
H. J. CRIBB.

WEAVER-DYER
Suitings, Homespun Tweeds, Serge for Habits, Vestments.　J. V. D. KILBRIDE.

WOODWORKER
Household and Ecclesiastical Furniture, Weaving Appliances. BUILDER.
Address above :—　G. MAXWELL.
DITCHLING COMMON, HASSOCKS,
SUSSEX.

DRESS ORNAMENTS
Hat and Frock Ornaments; Pin Trays; of single or cut sea-shells. Colours, bronzes. From 1/- each.
BIELBY, Alfriston, SUSSEX.

HANDWROUGHT FURNITURE
Davies' Handwrought Furniture. "Distinctive" for the past 25 years. Davies' Handicraft Furniture has been known for its fulfilment of all the ideals that actuated the old craftsmen. It is entirely handwrought in solid oak and other fine furniture woods, beautifully polished to show to best advantage the natural grainings. The designs are original, simple in taste, artistic in effect, but comfortable and adaptable in every respect for everyday use.
W. H. DAVIES & SONS, Mount Street,
BOLTON, LANCASHIRE.

HATS
Raffia trimmed hats and baskets.
ROSE AGENCY, Hanover Buildings,
SOUTHPORT.

NEEDLEWORK
Pictures, landscapes, all silk, from 10/6.
KATHARINE CHEVALLIER,
247, Dover Road, FOLKESTONE.

VIOLINS.
Hand-made Violins of exceptional tone. £5-£15. Also ship models.
BOX V.2, G.K.'s Weekly,
22, Essex Street, STRAND, W.C.2.

WOODCUTS OF OLD ENGLAND
Engraved, printed and published by Molly Power. List on application.
MEDIÆVAL CRAFT, Wells, SOMERSET.

HANDWOVEN PILE RUGS
Something new! Made in any size, colourings and depth of pile required. Prices from 25s. Send for samples.
THE HAND LOOM CENTRE, NORWICH.

LINGERIE
Orders taken for hand-made lingerie, and embroidery.
SANDERS, 122, Ramsey Road,
SOUTHAMPTON.

For the Table and Farm Produce.

FLOWERS.
Cut fresh daily from our own Nurseries. We have flowers for all occasions. Through the Florists' Telegraph Delivery Association we can " Say it with Flowers " to your Friends, Anywhere, Any time.
ORD BROTHERS,
Horticultural Distributors,
32 & 33, Grainger Arcade, Newcastle-on-Tyne.

FISH
Fish from sea, 4 lbs. 3/- upwards; cleaned; carriage paid. Schools, etc., supplied.
IMPERIAL FISHING CO.,
GRIMSBY. Est. 1897.

HAMPER
Lovely Hamper of Fresh Dorset Farm Produce. Deliciously tender Spring Chicken or Duck ready trussed, Fresh Farm Butter, New Laid Eggs, double thick Cream, pure Farm Honey, Cheddar Loaf Cheese, Double Cream Cheese, Farm-cured Bacon, etc., sent carriage paid for 20/-. You will be glad you sent. Guaranteed fresh arrivals. Hundreds of Testimonials.
M. JENNINGS, White Farm, Ashington,
WIMBORNE, DORSET.

REAL DEVONSHIRE CLOTTED CREAM
½ lb. 10d.; ¾ lb. 1/5; 1 lb. 2/6; post free.
BOLES, Heathfield, Holsworthy, Devon.

POULTRY
Tender boiling fowls, 7/- and 7/6 pair. Fatted ducks and roasting fowls, 8/- and 9/- pair, trussed, ready for cooking. 36 well-rooted fern plants, varieties, in lovely soft moss, 4/-. Primrose roots 1/- per dozen. Post paid.
A. BELL, The Glebe,
ROSSCARBERY, CORK.

FARM PRODUCE.
Flowers and Vegetables. Let us post you some lettuce, or flowers fresh from the garden to the table, the Postman the only Middleman. Send 2/6 and you shall receive a parcel of fresh flowers and lettuce twice a week.
J. REILLY, Market Gardener, Westbridge,
KIRKCALDY.

POULTRY
Large roasting fowls and ducks, 7/6 pair. Boiling fowls, 6/- pair, trussed.
MOLLIE O'DONOGHUE, The Convent Road Shop, ROSSCARBERY, CORK.

POULTRY
Delicious large spring chickens, 8/- pair. Large tender boiling fowls, 6/-, 7/-, trussed. Postage paid.
MISS DEMPSEY, Poulterer,
ROSSCARBERY, CORK.

FISH
Fish straight from the sea. Basses of best selected fish, cleaned, ready for cooking, from 3/-.
J. WILLINGHAM, Fish Docks, GRIMSBY.

IRISH HONEY SECTIONS
Delicious clover honeycombs from Co. Cavan, 16/- half-dozen, 30/- dozen, carriage paid; also English honey, jars.
THAMES VALLEY BEES,
TEDDINGTON, MIDDLESEX.

POULTRY
Plump Roasting Fowls, 7/6 pair; nice tender Boiling Fowls, 6/6 pair, trussed.
MRS. ANNIE RYAN, Fairfield House,
ROSSCARBERY, CORK, Ireland.

ASPARAGUS
A healthful table delicacy. 120 good quality, nicely packed. Buds sent every week for 7 weeks, £1 16s. 120 only, 5s. 6d., post paid.
P. G. H. FIELD, Grower, Church Road,
HAMPTON, WORCS.

BEST FRESH FRUIT DIRECT FROM THE FARM
Strawberries, 5/- for 4 lbs. Currants and raspberries in season. Carriage paid. Cash with order.
A. P. GRENFELL, Old Manor, Stawell,
BRIDGWATER.

MRS. MARKHAM ON AMERICANS.

By HILAIRE BELLOC.

MARY: Now that you have talked to us on elephants, dear Mamma, will you not talk to us on Americans ?

TOMMY: Yes, Mamma, you promised me to talk about these fascinating beings.

MRS. MARKHAM: The phrase " Fascinating beings " seems to me, my dear Tommy, inappropriate, and (*looking at him severely*) I am not quite sure that your intention . . . .

TOMMY (*eagerly*): I assure you, dear Mamma, the words were used in a flattering sense, and my eagerness for information perhaps oustripped my discretion.

MRS. MARKHAM: Doubtless . . . .Well, then, I must first inform you that the Americans are our cousins.

MARY (*interrupting*): You told us that long ago, Mamma, when you were talking about Evolution.

MRS. MARKHAM (*sharply*): Never mind whether I have already told it you or not, it is important for you to remember it always. The Americans, I say, are our cousins; for we descended from a common stock which is called the Anglo-Saxon, that is, the people who come from Anglia and Saxonia.

TOMMY: Where is Anglia, Mamma?

MRS. MARKHAM: Anglia proper, my dear, is somewhere in North Germany, and so is Saxonia; but East Anglia is to the west of Anglia, across the North Sea.

TOMMY: Incredible! Then East is West?

MARY (*pleading*): Please, Mamma, do not listen to him, but go on.

MRS. MARKHAM (*to Tommy, severely*): Your ignorance, my child, as is too often the case with ignorance, is attached to your vanity. The East Anglians who inhabit Norfolk and Suffolk are only eastern relative to the middle Angles who inhabit the middle part of this country, though they are indeed Western relative to the other Angles who live in Anglia proper.

MARY: Let us look up Anglia Proper on the map, Mamma.

TOMMY (*sighing*): Oh, please, no! I want to hear about Americans.

MRS. MARKHAM: You are right for once, Tommy; and now that you know that Americans, like ourselves, are descended from Anglo-Saxons, it is sufficient.

TOMMY: When did they branch off from us ?

MRS. MARKHAM: In the 17th century, my dear; that is three hundred years ago, for you must know that at this time the Government was so wicked that they would not allow people to worship God according as they felt inclined, on which account a number of noble men and women got into a boat called " The Mayflower " and sailed away for a distant land where they might pray in the fullness of their hearts.

TOMMY: Who paid for the boat, Mamma?

MRS. MARKHAM: These good men and women paid for the boat themselves.

MARY: Then surely, Mamma, they must have been very rich. Could you and Papa pay for a boat to take you over to America?

MRS. MARKHAM (*hurriedly*): I know nothing of all that, my dear. Let it be enough for you that these people were called Pilgrim Fathers.

TOMMY: What about the Mothers?

MARY: Yes, Mamma, and the little boys and girls?

MRS. MARKHAM (*continuing*): And they landed at a place called Plymouth Rock, where they founded the City of Boston which became the chief city of the United States—for so they called themselves.

TOMMY (*curiously*): Why did they call themselves " United States," Mamma?

MRS. MARKHAM (*solemnly*): To show that they believed in freedom and in the worship of God without restraint.

MARY (*still more solemnly*): Oh, Mamma, it does me good to hear those words !

MRS. MARKHAM: Next I am sorry to say there was trouble between them and ourselves, which was like a quarrel between brothers.

TOMMY: Or at any rate cousins.

MRS. MARKHAM (*to Tommy*): I don't want any of your interruptions !—(*to Mary*)—You understand, my dear, that at that time we were virtually brothers.

MARY (*humbly*): I do indeed, Mamma.

MRS. MARKHAM: But there happened something which I am sure will make you very sad to hear; which is, that some of these good people going down into the hotter part of America were wicked enough to use negro slaves.

TOMMY and MARY (*in chorus*): Oh, Mamma, how horrible; did they actually enslave the poor negroes?

MRS. MARKHAM (*sadly*): Yes, my children, truth compels me to admit it though they were of our own blood, they did enslave these poor negro men who knew no better than to say " Yes, Massah," and yet were often flogged to death. They toiled in what is called " Plantations " and lived a most miserable existence. Then the real Americans who lived in the healthy climate of the North, and of whom many also had English blood in them, said " This shall not be ! " So they made war against the wicked men in the South and freed all the slaves.

MARY (*clapping her hands*): Oh, that is good news, Mamma; and what happened to the slaves?

MRS. MARKHAM: They became American citizens, my dear, and have ever since then poured out praise and glory to their benefactors.

TOMMY: Did they turn white?

MRS. MARKHAM: No, not exactly, for it must take some time before the last benefits of civilization shall reach them; but they can now vote whenever they are allowed to do so, and many of them are barbers, or conductors on tramways, or prize fighters, or engaged in some other useful trade—while others compose music which is very popular everywhere, for they are great musicians.

TOMMY: What happened after that, Mamma?

MRS. MARKHAM: After that, my dear, the Americans, being blessed by God on account of their having freed the slaves, expanded vastly in wealth and numbers, and are now the richest people in the world—and the most numerous after the Chinese, Indians and Russians. They are also the most progressive, and even the poorest of them possess what even rich people in this country would think luxuries: such as Ice cupboards, Ford cars, Telephones, Megaphones, microphones, gramophones, and things of that sort.

MARY: I hear, dear Mamma, that the United States are a democracy.

MRS. MARKHAM: They are, indeed.

TOMMY: And what does that mean, Mamma?

MRS. MARKHAM: It means, my dear Tommy, that like ourselves they are governed by themselves; and not by any foolish King, or rich people or anything of that sort, still less by foreigners. They vote from time to time as to who shall govern them in each City and each State, and also for who shall govern the whole country. In this way they do not fall into the wickedness of fighting to determine who shall govern them, but everything is orderly and right.

MARY: I am very pleased to hear this, Mamma. And pray what is the name of the gentleman who is elected to be the Governor of the whole of the United States?

MRS. MARKHAM: He is called President, my dear. Sometimes he is called one thing and sometimes another. The one who is President to-day is called Calvin.

MARY: Then I am sure, Mamma, he must be a good man.

MRS. MARKHAM: You are right, my dear.

TOMMY: Who will be the next President of the United States, Mamma?

MRS. MARKHAM (reverently): That is what we none of us know, my dear; but we can be quite certain of this, that God will guide them in the right way, and whoever it is will be a very great and good man.

MARY: The Americans are indeed fortunate, Mamma, to be thus directed by the Most High. Can you not tell us anything more of their good deeds?

MRS. MARKHAM: Yes, my dear, but it would be superfluous to insist, for their virtues are much the same as our own. Moreover, I must tell you that they sternly repress folly and disorder on the part of such few people as have come to them from other places than England.

TOMMY: What, Mamma, are there then in America men of lesser breed who are not of our blood?

MRS. MARKHAM: I am sorry to say that there are! In the past Americans were too generous and admitted into their State Irishmen, Poles, and even Italians. But now they have seen the error of this, and they are preventing the increase of such undesirable elements.

MARY: Really, Mamma, these people seem to have all the good qualities than anyone can possess.

MRS. MARKHAM: But I have not yet exhausted the list; for you must know that they have forbidden drinking wine or beer or any kind of thing on which anybody could get drunk, so that now no one in America knows even what Drunkenness is. And not only that, but they are now going to outlaw war, so that there will never more be war anywhere in the world, and no more shooting at people or dropping bombs on them from the air, or making them unhappy in any way.

MARY (dissolving into tears): Oh, Mamma, surely this is too good to be true! (Sobs.)

MRS. MARKHAM (patting her on the shoulder): There! There! my dear, your generous emotions do you credit, and I can but sympathize with them.

TOMMY; Why do we and other nations wait so long in copying the noble example of the United States, dear Mamma?

MRS. MARKHAM: It is in the mysterious designs of Providence; but you know, Tommy, that the world gets better and better, and therefore we may expect it to be at last perfect as America is to-day. (A pause.)

MARY: Please, dear Mamma, who are the principal American Poets, Sculptors, Architects, and Theologians?

TOMMY: What!

MARY: I was only asking Mamma out of a book I have been reading where that question was put about Czecho-Slovakia.

MRS. MARKHAM: I will not go into Czecho-Slovakia, but I can easily tell you who are the principal Poets, Sculptors, Architects, Theologians, and Jurists. The principal sculptor was Mr. Hiram Power, the principal poet was Longfellow, and the principal theologian was, I am glad to say, a lady called Mrs. Eddy; but there have been many others, for theology prospers in the New World.

TOMMY: Does everyone love the Americans?

MRS. MARKHAM: No, my dear Tommy; I am sorry to say the only people who really love them are the English, though of course on account of their being so powerful other people pretend to love them, notably the degraded French. Yet everybody ought to love them, because they lent money to all who were in necessity during the Great War, and yet (is this not sad?) we are the only people who are paying them back!

MARY: Then I hope, dear Mamma, the Americans will make war on all these wicked people and make them pay heavy interest as well!

TOMMY: Yep! Blow 'em out of the World!

MRS. MARKHAM (reprovingly): Nay! My dear children, these are not sentiments the Americans themselves would approve. They will, I am sure, apply only peaceful forms of pressure such as those suggested by Mr. Otto Kahm. Meanwhile, we can all have recourse to prayer (rising). And now, my dear children, that is enough for to-day. Next time we will learn something about newspapers.

TRAVEL NOTES.

THE KENTISH COAST.

IF you have thoughts of circumambulating the Kentish coast, it is advisable not to begin too casually; 'twere better you picked your point of departure, or you may mix yourself up hopelessly in the maze of derelict islets and forgotten waterways that lie between Gravesend and the mouth of Swale. 'Twere better you took a wide jump to Whitstable, whose oyster fame spreads a bright reflective glow upon bivalves of such diverse races. Whitstable is quaint and odd and ancient, and full of queer corners and unexpectedness, and honourably dirty and untidy from its trade.

From Whitstable make your way quickly along the low cliffs to Herne Bay. The sudden taste of the sea so short an hour from London may tempt you to linger, but there is better to come. At Herne Bay (but where is the bay?) the sands stretch far, and the pier is long. The hotels and private mansions blink on the parade through discreet though corpulent early Victorian bay windows. The houses here are mostly of stone. The crowd of tents on the beach, with the bathers running between them and the water, has the look of a barbaric encampment. Away from the waters the houses are villas of brick, very suburban of air, rather pleasant, and a little boring. The small village of Herne, a half-hour's walk away, is gabled and old, and had Passion Plays in mediæval times and summer visitors in the days when metropolitan man still found the courage for a walk of half an hour to his sea. In the embattled parish church of Herne (St. Martin's by name) is a figure of Ridley the martyr, once its vicar, pressing a Bible to his breast.

From Herne Bay the cliff mounts continuously up to Reculvers and its twin ancient square spires, crowned grotesquely with up-to-date skeleton signalling gear. Through the triangle-topped central windows the sky looks bluely at you. And here the coast sinks and grows more jagged and winding, and encloses innumerable tiny sanded bays; and at one of the turnings suddenly high whiteness strikes you, and these are Birchington cliffs and the beginning of the chalk. This is undoubted Thanet; behind you as far as Reculvers one may suppose that once the Wantsum ran.

Where to Stay.

BENFLEET, near Canvey Island.—Furnished rooms, with or without attendance. Bath, gas, and every comfort. Board-residence can be arranged.—Write PORTLOCK, 15, Pindar Street, London, E.C.2.   A.

CHILDREN.—Country and seaside, Essex. Lady will take sole charge of children for holiday or longer periods. Good home comforts and food; very moderate terms.—Write Box G.T., G.K.'s WEEKLY, 22, Essex Street, W.C.2.   A.

DOUGLAS, I.o.M.—Bed and Breakfast, 5/-; other meals optional, Comfortable, clean.—Mrs. FLETCHER, Sydney House, Bucks Road.

EASTBOURNE.—Ready July. Board-Residence from three guineas, week-ends one guinea. Near Beachy Head, sea, golf links.—Address: CLAPHAM, Fernleigh, Beachy Head Road, Meads, Eastbourne.

FOLKSTONE.—Gentlewoman received as paying guest, Pleasant house; good views; from 35/-.—CHEVALLIER, Bank Top, Dover Road.

IRELAND.—Visitors excellently catered for; MISSES CARMODY, Cliff Cottage, Howth, Co. Dublin. Medically recommended. Mountain and sea air. English references given.   630

JERSEY, Rosebank.—Superior board-residence; central, near Church. Excellent cuisine; every comfort; highly recommended; moderate.—H. MILLEST.

JERSEY, "Bethanie," St. Aubin.—Catholic Guest House; French cuisine; all comforts; ideal view over the whole bay; near church. Highly recommended.   630

LOWESTOFT.—Lady guests received. Delightful situation on sea front; bracing, sunny, home freedom; excellent catering.—ST. MARY'S CONVENT, Kirkley Cliff.   91a.

MATLOCK.—Presentation Convent. High-class boarding and day school for girls. Home life. University, music and elocution examinations, if desired. Ideal situation. Qualified mistress for games, swimming, advanced music, painting, modern languages. Paying guests received.

RHYL, N. Wales.—Lady Guests. Minute sea; shady garden; tennis; bracing air; home freedom; excellent catering.—Apply SUPERIOR, St. Mary's Convent.

ST. LEONARDS.—Melville House, Magdalen Road. Board-residence; overlooks Convent. 2 mins. sea and White Rock. Splendid views; moderate.   526

VENTNOR.—Noel Boarding House. Overlooks Church; reliable; 4 good meals. Catholics welcome Catholics. 50/55. Stamp. PROPRIETRESS.

YORKSHIRE HILLS.—Board residence; home comforts; moderate. Weaving lessons.—MASON, Cowesby, Northallerton, Yorks.

Hotel Directory.

ALDERNEY.—Scotts. Purest bracing air, long sunshine. Brainfagged's retreat, Rundown's reconstruction, Insomnia's cure, Consumptive's hope; perfect rest. Special terms long stays. Terms moderate.

DEAN FOREST, Severn-Wye Valleys.—Beautiful Holiday Home (600 ft. up); 70 rooms; 5 acres; billards; motors, garage; 60s. week. Prospectus.—Littledean House, Littledean, Glos.   314.

HAWKHURST.—Queen's Hotel. Residential or Luncheons or Teas daily. Garden and Garage.—'Phone: 7, CLEMENTS, Proprietor.

LAKE District.—Victoria Family Hotel. Beautiful Buttermere via Cockermouth. £4 4s.; electric light; mountain air; A.A. and R.A.C.; grand centre.

LANGOLLEN, Hand Hotel. Extensive garage attached to hotel.—J. S. SHAW, Proprietor.

LANGOLLEN.—Royal Hotel. Most comfortable in N. Wales. Good food; good service; moderate charges. Sunday Mass. Proprietress: Mrs. HARVEY, late of the Albion Hotel, Lincoln.

MANCHESTER, All Saints.—Sydney Family and Commercial Hotel. 25 bedrooms.—MRS. A. I. COLLARD. 'Phone: Ardwick 3731.

MANCHESTER.—Kilronan Private Hotel, 40, Manchester Road, Chorlton-cum-Hardy. Tel.: 1771 Chorlton. Cars 12, 13. Opposite Savoy Picture House. High Tea, Bed and Breakfast, 10/-.—MISSES FREEMAN KELLY.

MATLOCK (Derby) Chatsworth Hydro. Tel.: 9.—Write free souvenir.

MOVILLE, Co. Donegal.—McConnell's Hotel. Comfortable. Apply Manager.

NEW FOREST, Brockenhurst Hotel.—Ideal country house; comfortable winter quarters at moderate inclusive rates. Excellent chef. Gas fires, bedrooms; contsant hot water; garages; near links. Telephone: 74.

SLOUGH, Bucks.—Old Crown Hotel. Affiliated A.A. and R.A.C. Full Table d'Hote Service; garage free during meals.

TEIGNMOUTH.—Minute sea; small, snug. Strand private Hotel. (Northumberland Place).

VENTNOR (I.o.W.).—Metropole and Beach Hotels. Sea front. Moderate terms. Open all the year.

MUSICAL JOTTINGS.

Triple Bill at the Court.

A CURIOUS admixture of Vaughan Williams, De Falla, and Schubert, form a tasty repast for opera lovers at the Court Theatre season of light opera. The Schubert opera, *The Faithful Sentinel*, is presumably included in honour of the composer's centenary, as the work itself hardly merits resurrection on its own merit. With the exception of the duet for soprano and contralto at the end of the first scene, and the orchestral interlude, the music is only interesting as foreshadowing the composer's later genius. I found the quaint pantomime suggestion of the rhymed dialogue very delightful; and the production was incidentally responsible for some of the most beautiful singing that could be desired, on the part of Miss Dorothy Silk (Kätchen), Miss Astra Desmond (Lady Agatha), and Steuart Wilson (Heinrich Duval).

The Shepherds of the Delectable Mountains, by Vaughan Williams, founded upon Bunyan's *Pilgrim's Progress,* is an attempt to express musically the Pilgrim's first vision of the city of Mount Zion and his triumphant passing through the river of death to his final home. There is an atmosphere of hushed solemnity about the music that is admirably suited to the spirit of Bunyan's mysticism. The shepherds take their contented state very seriously; they do not even smile. The Pilgrim expresses ecstatic joy once; when his heart is pierced by the symbolic arrow of the celestial messenger; but otherwise he, too, seems to be influenced by the atmosphere of twilight melancholy; while the bearing of the Messenger suggests that even the Celestial City must be a rather dreary place. The orchestral scoring is admirable, and in Vaughan Williams's usual scholarly manner. Of the singing, the most distinguished is the delicate interpretation by William Biggs of the part of the Second Shepherd.

It was with mental and spiritual relief that we turned to the virile humanity of the music of Manuel de Falla. *The Puppet Show of Master Pedro,* an adventure of Don Quixote, is a completely delightful work depicting the gallant rescue by the obsessed Don of the cardboard Don Gayferos and his lady, Melisendra, from the pursuing Moors. The puppets were admirably worked, and the humour was never overdone. Miss Kathleen Beer—as Master Pedro's assistant, explaining the various scenes—was excellent; so, too, was Arthur Cranmer, as Don Quixote. His final peroration—after breaking up the puppet show—contained all the pathos as well as the humour of the madman's sincerity in his knight-errantry.

Some Recitals.

A N interesting recital of songs and duets was given at the Wigmore Hall by Misses Janet Christopher and Beatrice Beaufort, including a cantata for soprano and contralto, and the soprano aria—with violin, from the opera *Enrico Leone,* by Agostino Steffani. Both vocalists possess a keen musical sense, while the violin playing of Miss Dorothy Hayward and the pianoforte accompaniments by George Reeves were beyond reproach.

The second of the three Schubert recitals at the Wigmore Hall was distinguished by the brilliant performance of the Grand Duo for two pianofortes by Frederick Wührer and Angus Morrison. In other items Miss Adila Fachiri displayed her usual mastery of the violin, and Harold Dahlquist sang with much charm and ability.

V. N. L.

THEATRES, CINEMAS, Etc.

THE COCKPIT.

To the Editor, G.K.'s WEEKLY.

SUNDAY AMUSEMENTS.

DEAR SIR,—I am a Protestant minister, desirous of soliciting your support, and that of all Leaguers, on behalf of Sunday observance. Most decent Britishers would object to Sunday opening of theatres, but they are not quite so opposed to the opening of other places of amusement. I notice the Tivoli, which advertises in your columns, a place which was once the glory of British variety, but has become a picture house, opens on Sunday. We are soon to have another American invasion; and the Tivoli, like other big picture houses, will sooner or later have to fall into line with the new policy of picture-variety programmes. With Sunday opening, it is difficult to see how variety artists can escape a seven days' week. Daily matinees are a certainty, and, as is the present method in many picture-variety houses in London, many split weeks, when artists will have to move their props., often long distances, and probably their lodgings as well. I believe the Church to which you belong prides itself in the fact that it has made Sunday a holiday or holy day, when the labourer is free to be a man, and even a clown, if he so desires. This, no doubt, leads many Catholics to advocate Sunday amusements; not realizing that under present conditions it involves the loss of that holy day to those who are to be numbered among the wage slaves of to-day, the artists, who depend for their living upon theatrical trusts, which are as soulless as other trusts your paper denounces.

Take first of all the religious standpoint. I believe your paper, like myself and the Wee Frees, is old-fashioned enough to believe that religion does count for something. That is to say, that it does not matter so much that a few million people are deprived of amusement for one night in seven, compared to the calamity of one man being deprived of religion for seven days of the week. Now even the Catholic, while it is true he can go to church on other days, has his right to keep the Sabbath Day holy by going to Mass. Sunday is the day when artists have to travel, and with baggage and settling with landladies and catching trains, Sunday morning is a busy time. With Protestant artists, the only chance of worship is on Sunday evenings, provided they can get lodgings in the new town and settled down by that time. There are Protestants, no doubt, who claim to be Christians without requiring a church; but they don't interest me, nor, I am sure, do they interest you. I believe you admire principles and beliefs and dogmas sincerely held, even although they don't happen to be your own. Surely, then, to deny Protestant artists, who are an overwhelming majority, the opportunity of worshipping according to their custom and belief, is not to help Roman Catholicism, but merely to play into the hands of the pagans, who care nothing for principles or religion of any kind, and merely regard the Protestant Sunday as an irksome restraint on the box-office receipts.

I start on religious grounds because I believe that, in your paper, unlike the trust papers, these grounds will be first. The secular grounds are secondary but obvious. Even supposing variety artists are not church-goers, but out-and-out Bohemians, why should they be denied their Sunday clubs, of which there are many of old standing, when other people can have social intercourse on other evenings denied to stage artists? The very nature of their work makes it impossible for them to take turn about having nights off during the week, like 'bus drivers; and unless their Sunday holiday is preserved, then they are going to become the worst victims of the new combines which are destroying the liberty of our land. Even exercise and free air become difficult with often long journeys in the London area to daily matinees; and home life and the intercourse of their children rendered impossible even on Sunday. You have recently fought for 'bus owners and costermongers. Do you not think that the time has come to take notice of the gigantic combines which are seeking to control our amusements; and defend the ancient liberty of our comedians and other stage artists in this matter of a holy day, which the Church in times past won for our people?

11, Lansdowne Crescent,   JOHN KENNEDY.
Glasgow.

THE VIRTUOUS INGES.

SIR,—Dean Inge has been at it again. He has been hymning to the Oxford Eugenics Society the merits of his own upper middle class. This, of course, is no new thing. He has told us before of the virtues of his own relatives, how one was a scholar of this College, another a Fellow of that, very meritorious people, no doubt. But we do not remember hearing that one of this illustrious family was ever ploughing champion of Little Bumbleton, or that one bore the prize for his vegetable marrows at Much Grundlingham. Also we have seen no distinguished pugilist, market gardener, or poacher, among the Dean's noted kinsmen; nor yet one in great local demand for his powess at thatching, or who drove a 'bus with more eminent skill than his fellows. Honourable men as the Dean and such Eugenists may well be, they forget that in this world, too, are many mansions. Although we may not all attain academic excellence, in a final reckoning it may be found that those men of little showing who have dug and hedged hard and truly, may also have deserved well.

PENNAI.

AMONG THE BRANCHES

CENTRAL BRANCH.—*Hon. Sec*, A. M. Currie, 2, Little Essex Street, Strand, W.C.2.

Informal meetings held every Friday during the summer months at the Devereux, between 6 p.m. and 7 o'clock.

WEYMOUTH.

The Secretary of the League will be in Weymouth on Friday and Saturday, June 22nd and 23rd. Will any member in Weymouth who will act as convener of a meeting of other members please communicate with him?

WEST LONDON GROUP.—*Hon. Sec.*: A. Ardern, 25, Felden Street, S.W.6.

NORTH LONDON BRANCH.—*Sec* (pro. tem.): J. Macnamara, 72, Berkeley Crescent, New Barnet.

BOURNEMOUTH. — *Sec.*: Miss Mott, 4, Dingle Road, Boscombe.

BRIGHTON. — *Sec.*: C. B. Harrison, 21, Alexander Villas, Brighton.

FYLDE BRANCH.—*Sec.*: Miss E. M. Taylor, 37, Northbreck Road, Blackpool.

SALFORD.—*Hon. Sec.*: J. Burns, 8, Trafalgar Square, Regent Road, Salford.

BRADFORD BRANCH.—*Hon. Sec.*: J. Gosney, 35, Buxton Street, Heaton, Bradford.

COVENTRY.—*Sec.*: R. E. S. Willison, 102, Westwood Road, Coventry.

EDINBURGH.—*Hon. Sec.*: Jas. Turner, c/o Dunne, 5, Keir Street, Edinburgh.

NEW MILLS.—*Sec.*: J. Boak, 46, Hyde Park Road, New Mills, nr. Stockport.

LIVERPOOL.—*Sec.*: J. P. Alcock, Melwood, Deysbrook Lane, West Derby, Liverpool.

An informal meeting will take place at the White Café, Cook Street, on Tuesday, June 26. Commences about 7.30. Anyone welcome.

Watch for announcements of informal meetings during summer months. A group have arranged to meet on the FIRST MONDAY of each month in the restaurant at Creedon's, Elliot Street. Anyone welcome. Other informal gatherings will be arranged.

NORTH SHIELDS.—*Sec.*: J. J. Rogan, 28, Windermere Terrace, North Shields, Northumberland.

Proposed New Branches—

NORTHAMPTON.

Will members and others interested in the Northampton District please communicate with Mr. T. S. Mann, 106, Beech Avenue, Northampton?

JERSEY.

Will any members or readers in Jersey please communicate with Mr. W. Rice, 41, Belmont Road, Jersey, with a view to forming a local group?

TEIGNMOUTH.

Will any members or readers in Teignmouth please communicate with Mr. A. W. Couch, Strand Private Hotel, Teignmouth, with a view to forming a local group?

The DISTRIBUTIST LEAGUE

(founded in conjunction with "G.K.'s Weekly" for the restoration of liberty by the distribution of property).

President: MR. G. K. CHESTERTON.
Secretary: G. C. HESELTINE.
Office: 2, Little Essex Street, London, W.C.2.
Telephone: City 1978.

There are many readers of this Paper who are not members of the League. All who believe that ownership in the means of livelihood is normal to man, and necessary to liberty, and all who dislike and distrust the concentration of control advocated by Socialists and practised by Monopolists, should join the League. There is no other tenet for membership, and no other obligation than 1/- subscription, although active work is welcomed from all who can give it.

THE LEAGUE offers the only practical alternative to the twin evils of Capitalism and Socialism. It is equally opposed to both; they both result in the concentration of property and power in a few hands to the enslavement of the majority.

THE LEAGUE stands

For the Liberty of the Individual and the Family Against interference by busybodies, monopolies, or the State.

Personal Liberty will be restored mainly by the better Distribution of Property (*i.e.*, ownership of land, houses, workshops, gardens, means of production, etc.).

The Better Distribution of Property will be achieved by protecting and facilitating the ownership of individual enterprises in land, shops, and factories.

Thus THE LEAGUE fights for:

Small Shops and Shopkeepers against multiple shops and trusts. Individual Craftsmanship and Co-operation in industrial enterprises. (Every worker should own a share in the Assets and Control of the business in which he works). The Small Holder and the Yeoman Farmer against monopolists of large inadequately farmed estates.

And the Maximum, instead of the minimum initiative on the part of the citizen.

GLASGOW.—*Hon. Sec.*: A. Mason, 55, Exeter Drive, Partick, W.1.

During the summer months a group will meet at 6, Blytheswood Drive, W. (McConaghy), every Monday evening. It is hoped that as many as possible will roll up, as there is business to consider of importance to our autumn campaign.

OXFORD (Cobbett Club).—*Sec.*: E. St. J. Hoogewerf, St. John's College. Treasurer (to whom apply to join): A. P. Tory, St. John's.

MANCHESTER. — *Sec.*: John A. Toohey, York Mount, Bury New Road, Prestwich.

PORTSMOUTH. — *Hon. Sec.*: Miss Ellen Flanagan, 30, Nelson Road, Southsea.

BIRMINGHAM BRANCH.—*Sec.*: K. L. Kenrick, 7, Soho Road, Handsworth.

The 39th meeting of the Branch was held at the Guildhouse on June 15th. A vigorous discussion arose on the point of " Good Husbandry " under the Scheme for the Settlement of the Unemployed on the Land. There was a very strong feeling against the appointment of any kind of inspectors to decide what constituted " Good Husbandry." The main topics of discussion for the evening were the profit-sharing scheme of Imperial Chemical Industries Limited, and the new Government scheme for the relief of rates. It was decided that Distributists could not possibly approve of Mond's Profit-Sharing Scheme, good and generous as it was from a purely business point of view. The question of Rating-Relief is to be brought up at a future meeting when further information has been obtained.

Next Meeting—Friday, June 29th. Mr. Dealey on " The Attitude of Distributists to the Man in the Street."

BOOKS TO READ.

The Servile State, by Hilaire Belloc. (4/-).

The Outline of Sanity, by G. K. Chesterton (6/-).

Economics for Helen, by H. Belloc. (5/-).

Liberty and Property, by H. E. Humphries (1/3).

Guilds, Trade, and Agriculture, by A. J. Penty (5/-).

Fields, Factories, and Workshops, by P. Kropotkin (2/6).

The Acquisitive Society, by R. H. Tawney (4/6).

Primer of Social Science, by H. Parkinson (3/6).

The Church and the Land, by Vincent McNabb, O.P. (2/6).

The Change, by G. C. Heseltine (2/6).

The above may be obtained through booksellers or direct from the Secretary of the Distributist League, 22, Essex Street, W.C.2.

LEAGUE LIBRARY.

A number of books of interest to Leaguers, including those on the the recommended list, are available at the office. Rate: threepence a week, and one penny a day afterwards.

All correspondence should be addressed to the Secretary of the League (G. C. Heseltine) 2, Little Essex Street, W.C.2.

Prepaid Classified Advertisements

The charge for these powerful Small Advertisements is 1/3 for the first 7 words and 2d. a word afterwards. **Seven insertions are given for the price of six.**

Advertisements (with remittance) should reach us by Monday morning to ensure insertion in the current week's issue.

Small Advertisement Manager, G.K.'s WEEKLY, 20/21, Essex Street, London, W.C.2.

PERSONAL.

EXPRESSION, DEBATE, DELIVERY
A Pyschological Aid to Memory and Fluency of Speech. The Rhetorlogue and Glossary of Logic, 21/-. The Rhetorlogue Mnemonic Wheel, 21/-. The Rhetorlogue Practice Charts, 1/-, post free. From OWEN BENNISON, 46, Bessborough Place, Westminster, S.W.1. Money Orders crossed " & Co." Kindly mention this paper. Details sent post free.

OFFERED busy woman, quiet artistic retreat, week-ends.—MISS GRAHAM, The Oast House, Burwash Weald, Sussex.

PROFESSIONAL Man who regained fitness without drugs will send details to health-seekers. —G., 47, Huddlestone Rd., Cricklewood, N.W.2.

APARTMENTS.

COUNTRY Farmhouse, quiet, sea and mountain air.—WILLIAMS, Tymaur, Bryncrag, Tonynonsea, N. Wales.

BOOKS, ETC.

BOOKS. — New and Second-hand. Enquiries made for any book free of charge.—L. H. DAVIS, 7, Downton Avenue, London, S.W.2.

CLUBS, ETC.

THE LIGHTHOUSE, 117, Union Street, Borough, S.E.1. Good accommodation at less than popular prices. Nice little hall to rent; nominal fee.—Apply : MANAGER.

CONNOISSEURS, COLLECTORS, ETC.

£100 BARGAIN.—Four beautiful Oil Paintings by noted Landscape Artists (British and Dutch), massive gilt frames. Private collection.—Apply KENNEY. South Elmsall, near Pontefract.

DRESS AGENCY.

ECONOMY Dress Agency, 11, Riseholme Road, Lincoln, sells on commission Gentlepeople's Clothing to workers of all classes.

MRS. BARLOW pays utmost value for Discarded Clothing. Everything confidential. Promptness.—"Castleway," Hanworth, Middlesex.

GARDENING.

BEDDING Plants, Asters, Antirrhinum, Alyssum, Stocks, Marigolds, Nemesia, Lobelias, Sweet Peas, 6d. per dozen, post free.

VEGETABLE Plants, Cabbage, Savoys, Kale, Sprouts, Reds, Cauliflower, 1/6 per 100, post free.—J. REILLY, Nurseryman, Westbridge, Kirkcaldy.

LITERARY.

GREAT Vocal Discovery. — Develop a beautiful, powerful, resonant voice. Wonderful silent method. 3d. stamp, particulars and wonderful testimony.—PROF. REID, 541g, Wigan Road, Bolton, Lancs.

NOVELS, Children's Stories, Poems, Plays, etc., wanted for Book Publication.—CLAUDE STACEY, LTD., 27, Chancery Lane, W.C.2.   A

STORIES, Articles, Serial and Verse wanted. Payment on acceptance. Post MSS. to Secretary, P.L.A., Pinders Road, Hastings. (Est. 1911.)

TUITION.

ITALIAN.—Short, rapid courses.—T. BALESTRERI, 16, Coram Street, Russell Square, W.C.1.

MISCELLANEOUS.

BILLIARD Cloth, Rubbers, any length cut; send table size.—ALFRED GRICE, Wharf Street, Dewsbury.

EASILY MADE MONEY. Sell Linen Bargains in your spare time. Particulars from J. HENDERSON, Milner Street, Belfast, N. Ireland.

FORTUNE Telling Doll. " Fairy Fortune Telling Doll." A great novelty and delight ; 2/6 post free. Sample at the office.—Box 36, G.K.'s WEEKLY, 20/21, Essex Street, Strand, W.C.2.

GOOD Printing at low trade rates. Specimens and prices free.—HATHERLEY, 43A, Trentham Street, Southfields, London.

HANDSOME profits assured by our excellent money-making opportunities. Highly recommended. Send stamped addressed envelope for particulars free.—GREEN & Co., 17, Church Lane, Hull.

IDEAL Window Decorations.—Write for Peach's new catalogue. Curtains, New Nets, Casements, Muslins, Cretonnes, Linens.—S. PEACH & SONS, LTD., 180, The Looms, Nottingham.

IRISH Hand-woven Tweed, 28 ins. wide, pure wool, 8/- per yard. Irish Tweeds, 56 ins. wide, 11/6 yard. Patterns free.—LARGEY, 40, Lr. Ormond Quay, Dublin.

LOOK ! Chance of a lifetime. Our 112 page book (Key to Success) will show you how to improve your financial position. Price only 2/6, post paid. Worth pounds.—EYRE, 120, Preston Road, Winson Green, Birmingham.

NEEDLE Cases for Bazaars, Masonic Ladies' nights, etc. Buy direct from Factory. Send for 5/6, 10/6 or 21/- parcel of assorted kinds. Post free.—Dept. G.K., B. HAMPTON SON & Co., LTD., Victoria Street, Redditch.

ON WITH THE MOTLEY. Splendid choice of Costumes at lowest possible prices. Dix's 57 varieties of Face Paint.—The Butterfly Shop, 277, Brixton Road, S.W.9. Brixton 5032.

PRINTING, 1,000 Handbills or Billheads at 3/3 per 1,000 . Memorandums, Postcards, Duplicate Books, Envelopes, Posters, etc. Large range of samples, 3d. postage.—MEAD & SON, Dept. P., Sandy Bedfordshire.

REAL Shetland Hand-Woven Tweed, 28 ins. wide, 8/6 per yard. Scotch Tweed, 56 ins. wide 12/6 per yard. Patterns free.—FAIRCLOTH (Dept. 55), Stromness, Orkney.

SUPER Quality OLIVE OIL. Buy your Olive Oil from the actual importers; it is fresh and quite different from the stale stuff usually sold in shops. Do you like the real taste of Olives? Send 2/9 for sample pint, post paid. 7/6 ½-gallon, post free.—QUICK & Co., LTD., Peckford Place, Brixton, S.W.9.

WHY NOT have a Pencil Day? Pencils with Special lettering for Bazaars, Sports, Building Funds, etc. Lists free. — GRETA PENCIL MILLS, Keswick.   630

XMAS Chocolate and Cigarette Clubs. Spare time Agents wanted. Fry's, Rowntrees, Cadburys, etc. Excellent commission. No outlay. Particulars free.—SAMUEL DRIVER, South Market, Leeds.

MUSIC, INSTRUMENTS, ETC.

BANJOS, Mandolins, Drums, Violins, Guitars, Ukuleles, Accordeons, Saxophones, Xylophones. Lists free.—PALMERS, Dept. J., 135, Linthorpe Rd., Middlesbrough.

GRAMOPHONE Records exchanged. London. Write or call : Book Store, 110, London Road, S.E.1.

RESTAURANTS.

DISTRIBUTIST Restaurant. - " The Owl," 3, Kingly Street, W.1 (behind Robinson and Cleaver's, Regent Street). Luncheons and Teas. Members of the League can meet each other here.

TO LET.

ATTRACTIVE, beautifully situated house, 5 bedrooms, bath, h. and c. throughout; garden. August. Near R.C. Church. Possible arrange domestic help.—MILLER, Chipping Campden, Glos.

THORPE BAY.—Lovely modern house; sea, links; 40 minutes London. £110 p.a.—Write Box T. B., G.K.'s WEEKLY, 22, Essex Street, W.C.2.

TYPEWRITING, REPAIRS, ETC.

TYPEWRITERS from £2; easy payments arranged. Repairs. Duplicators. 'Phone : Central 8210. Typewriter Experts, 55, Little Britain, E.C.1.   77

TYPEWRITER Mechanic would do repairs cheap. Any make. Good references.—GILL, 100, St. George's Rd., Peckham, London, S.E.15.

TYPEWRITING, DUPLICATING, ETC.

AUTHORS' MSS. Revised and made saleable. Intelligent typing.—VOISIN, Corbiere, Jersey, C.I.   512

AUTHORS' MSS. and Technical Typewriting correctly executed; 10d. per 1,000.—MRS. CLIFSTONE, 11, Cromwell Avenue, Bromley, Kent.   103

LITERARY Typewriting carefully and promptly executed. MSS. 1s. per 1,000 words; carbon copy, 3d. per 1,000.—MISS NANCY McFARLANE (J.), 44, Elderton Road, Westcliff-on-Sea.

TYPEWRITING, 8d. thousand. Enormous experience. Authors highly recommend.—TYPIST, "Belmont," Hanham, Bristol.   62

TYPEWRITING and Duplicating. — Moderate terms. — Hiss Hill, 36, Church Street, Kensington, W.8.

TYPEWRITING and Duplicating. Authors' MSS. typed 10d. per 1,000 words; carbon copy 3d. per 1,000 words. Testimonials, circulars, etc., duplicated. Envelopes addressed. Prompt and efficient work. — MARION YOUNG (C), 7a, Station Road, Balham, S.W.12.

TYPEWRITING.—8d. thousand. French and Spanish translations (into English), 9d. a folio. — NEWCOMBE, 36, Wilson Street, Middlesbrough.

NEAT ACCURATE TYPING

Intelligently executed. MSS. 1/- 1,000 words. Quotations given.
Miss N. Netherwood, 128, Park Road, Loughborough.

SPECIFICATIONS — CONTRACTS,

TECHNICAL Mattor of all kinds accurately typed from rough drafts. Duplicating, MSS., Translations. Envelopes addressed. — LEOLINE HARTLEY. Est. 1894. 422, Mansion House Chambers, E.C.4. Tel. : City 2787.   72

NURSING HOME, ETC.

SMALL, comfortable Home for invalid folk. Good cooking and fires. Trained nurse. Moderate terms, really cheap.—RAVENHURST, Old Hastings.

MEDICAL.

GREAT Herbal Asthma Remedy; most successful. Stamped envelope particulars.—MASON, Cowesby, Northallerton, Yorks.

BLOOD Pressure, Heart Attacks, Giddiness, Strokes, Headaches, Indigestion, Constipation, Insomnia, Loss of Memory, Asthma, Depression, etc., are mostly due to arterio-selerosis (hardening of the arteries).—Dr. Mladejovsky's simple remedy DROSIL. " Numerous experiments have proved the value of this discovery."—*Daily News.* Booklet free.—DROSIL AGENCY (Box B6), 26, Sun Street, London, E.C.2.

DIABETES

FOR TRUTHFUL EVIDENCE
of the wonderful results of " VINCULIN " Tablets, Africa's famous remedy. A Godsend to sufferers. No Drugs. No Injections. Write ·—

INGHAMS COLONIAL PRODUCTS Co.
(Box 30), Carnarvon, N. Wales.

The Proprietors exercise all possible care in the acceptance of advertisements for "G.K.'s Weekly."

Published by the Proprietors, G.K.'s WEEKLY, LTD., 22, Essex Street, Strand, London, W.C.2 (incorporating THE NEW WITNESS). Telephone No. City 1978. Printed by THE MARSHALL PRESS, LTD., 7, Milford Lane, Strand, London, W.C.2. Sole Agents for Australasia : Gordon & Gotch (Australasia, Ltd.). Sole Agents for South Africa : Central News Agency, Ltd.

PRICE : SIXPENCE.

G.K.'s Weekly

EDITED BY G. K. CHESTERTON.

No. 208.—Vol. VIII.,   Week ending Saturday, March 9, 1929.   PRICE SIXPENCE.
YEARLY (52 ISSUES)
28s. 0d.

Telephone No. City 1978.   [Registered at G.P.O. as a Newspaper.]   Offices, 2, Little Essex Street, Strand, W.C.2.

CONTENTS :

ON LLOYD GEORGE.

BEFORE Mr. Lloyd George made his promised speech at the Connaught Rooms we had reserved this space for a careful examination of the policy which he was to have outlined for the benefit of Liberal candidates at the forthcoming election, and though his speech was such a disappointment, we must not let the occasion pass unrecorded.

We had heard beforehand that the Liberal commander-in-chief, for such, after a strange series of promotions, dismissals, and re-instatements he appears to be, was to assemble the band of five hundred hardened and intensively-trained shock-troops which he is to fling into the field for the Big Push next May, and to harangue them in a martial speech which would not only explain to them the plan of campaign, but fill them with that fighting spirit which wells so profusely from his own indomitable bosom. What Cæsar and Napoleon did for their great armies in the way of oratorial encouragement, he was to do.

Sickness and the toll of previous engagements reduced his effectives to some four hundred on the day of the big parade, but they must all have been keyed up to a high pitch of efficiency and enthusiasm when their leader, surrounded by a staff of officers who had sunk all their recent animosities to assist him, mounted the rostrum.

The result was disappointing to the ordinary non-combatant; it must have been doubly so to the crack Liberal Army unless they are less intelligent than the civil population.

We had, of course, all the rhetorical ease which Mr. Lloyd George has never been denied, even by his bitterest opponents, to possess. During the Boer War he did not make the mistake animadverted upon by Kipling of " killing Kruger with his mouth," but it has never been doubted that—(as in the more recent war)—had he desired to do so, he could have done it as well as any man to any kind of opponent.

So on this occasion we were not disappointed in Mr. Lloyd George in that respect. He had all the old tricks of badinage, the flashes of ridicule, the play of bludgeon and rapier in which he is a past master. But such weapons strike one as far more suitable to a mass meeting of ordinary electors, out for one of those evening's entertainments which the Englishman seems to derive from a political gathering, than an official speech by the leader of an important political party to his candidates.

They surely can think up their " ad captandum " arguments for themselves ; the little jokes could safely be left for the circle of armchairs round the fire after a good dinner at the National Liberal Club. What they needed, what the country eagerly awaited, was a clear pronouncement of Liberal principles, a definite statement of Liberal policy. Certain very grave issues confront the country. Millions are unemployed, many of them starving and unclad. Discontent is rife. A ranging view through the Empire and through the world in general shows more for concern than for rejoicing. Certain questions are printed across the heavens in letters of fire. To these we awaited an answer.

We have not got it. The last hope has died of expecting any answer from any of the three chief political parties.

We knew that Conservative and Socialist were so much preoccupied in the first place with the party game, in the second place with the policy they share of dragooning the citizen into mute obedience to a rule-of-thumb bureaucracy without hope and without mercy, that little was now to be expected of them; there was just a hope that Lloyd George, who has imagination, would rise above himself and declare boldly for a deliberate cutting away of the mess and muddle of opportunist legislation that is hampering our feet, a reverting to those principles of personal independence, of private ownership, of the concentration on essentials like the national food-supply rather than on putting money into the pockets of foreign financiers, which seem to us and our readers so self-evidently important and desirable, so urgent for salvation.

There was nothing to " get hold of." True, Mr. George threw out his famous declaration that he could reduce unemployment to normal proportions within a year. He did not say what he regards as " normal " in this connection. Presumably that permanent number of unemployed persons which existed before the war, and was regarded by Liberal statesmen not only as a necessary evil, but as a desirable feature of the labour market, since it kept down wages and ensured obedient conduct among those in work under the fear that others were standing by to take their jobs if they misbehaved.

His plan is to revise the English road system. We should not deny that, as modern traffic has developed —though what proportion of modern traffic is necessary, either for business or pleasure, is a question to be argued—our roads must be increased in number, strengthened, straightened, widened and so on. But apart from the needs of the pleasure-motorist, it seems possible that one might have a marvellous system of roads with no merchandise to carry along them, great arteries dry of the life-blood which alone makes them necessary. What trade is to follow these new and improved routes we do not know. It is sufficient that large numbers of people can be herded into the great task of making them.

Normally one would imagine that these workmen would have to be paid, but Mr. George assures us that we need not worry. Not only have he and his subordinates had time during the enforced leisure of exile to reconstitute the roads of England on paper, but they have worked out a scheme to get them made without a penny of extra cost either to the taxpayer or the ratepayer. This is true wizardry. Enormous as the Liberal Party Fund is rumoured to be it surely is not great enough to stand the cost of putting, say, a million and a half of unemployed into permanent work. Or is Mr. Lloyd George going to hand over our roads to a company of big capitalists, not necessarily of British birth or residence, in exchange for some fresh stranglehold on the throats of the nation and its finances?

NOTES OF THE WEEK.

It would be dangerous to build a case against the Home Secretary or the Postmaster-General on the facts surrounding the confiscation of Mr. D. H. Lawrence's poems. The official explanation, that Mr. Lawrence sent them through the post in an open packet, which was examined in accordance with recognized and reasonable regulations, is probably the true one; and once the minor official, who looked for a technical infringement of rules, had found what he regarded as obscenity his superiors were bound in duty to order their retention. What should concern us, then, is not the fact of examination, but the nature of the poems examined. And we have only a Puritanical Minister's word for it, that the poems really are obscene. A competent tribunal will decide in due time, no doubt, if the seizure of the packet was justified. Meanwhile, we hope that good may come from the uninformed and hasty clamour of the Press; as it will do if the authorities decide to put a limit to officiousness and to establish a legal definition of indecency, less vague and more comprehensive than the one obtaining. In present circumstances a magistrate is safe in condemning almost any combination of words that does not accord with his personal taste.

*   *   *   *

By a curious coincidence, a film scenario by Mr. H. G. Wells and a play by Mr. C. K. Munro, expressing opposite conclusions, have appeared in the course of a few days. Mr. Wells suggests in *The King who was a King* that amalgamation among industrial undertakings can guarantee world-peace. Mr. Munro presents a combine in *The Rumour,* the directors of which deliberately foment war. And the difference between the two conclusions may be defined in the words that Mr. Munro dislikes combines as much as Mr. Wells dislikes war. What interests us most in this connection is that both authors have mirrored a state of civilization in which armies and national ideals and human lives are pawns in a financial game. That is where we draw the line and find the moral. Mr. Wells may regret that Mr. Munro and himself have started from the one premise to arrive at contradictory conclusions. The critics may decide obtusely that both these authors are arguing for pacifism. The real point is that both are exposing the evil springing from financial domination which allows a few industrialists to betray the aspirations and destroy the freedom of their fellow-men. Whether a combine helps to preserve peace or provoke war, its objects are selfish, and its methods tyrannical. The public is as much indebted to Mr. Wells as to Mr. Munro for making that quite clear.

*   *   *   *

The *Daily Mail,* famous for its patriotic campaign against Soviet Petrol, " stolen petrol," announced the increase in the price of petrol without a word about Russia or robbery. Nowhere in that issue did it advertise its posters for display by every patriotic petrol-monger. Gone was the cry, " No Soviet petrol sold here," " Don't buy stolen petrol." From which we concluded that the campaign had been completely successful. Whether it had succeeded in banishing the last drop of Russian Oil Products from the land and inspired every motorist with such fervent self-sacrifice and patriotism that he cheerfully and proudly paid the Anglo-American Combine the higher price and was even distressed when the Combine was forced to reduce it, or whether it had scared the Russians into a proper mood for discussions with our Ambassador of Empire, Sir Henri Deterding, we do not know. We do know that the country has been covered with R.O.P. pumps, empty and idle, of course, along the roads, and that now Sir Henri says they may be used and we may buy R.O.P. We hope that the *Daily Mail* has not had too many posters left on its hands and that its staff will not be unemployed in consequence. We feel sure anyway that such an enterprising journal will be able to utilize the waste paper and the staff on some other equally noble and patriotic campaign.

*   *   *   *

The feverish campaign in favour of " British Eggs " is giving the home poultry farmer and egg-producer the assistance he has needed very badly for the last ten years. For most of the smallholders who started after the War, this assistace has come too late. It would be interesting to know what or/and who has prompted the Press at this particular time, and why? Whilst we are all in favour of urging the necessity for supporting our own food producers, we strongly suspect that the present campaign in favour of the British Egg is too generous and too long maintained to be inspired from purely disinterested motives. We now await the cry for efficient co-operation, the formation of top-heavy Co-operative egg marketing concerns and the prospectus of the new parent organization which will develop our egg-industry on modern and progressive large-scale lines, particularly in the marketing direction. English smallholders will then find themselves secure and secured, as are so many Danish egg producers.

*   *   *   *

The pages of cinema history frequently provide a commentary, by analogy, on matters of wider interest. That is why we paused this week to read reports of the acquisition of an interest in the Metro-Goldwyn-Mayer Corporation by Mr. William Fox, the President of the Fox Film Corporation. The price paid by Mr. Fox is said to be in the neighbourhood of £45,000,000, and the consequence of the deal is that his company, which owns enormous studios in Hollywood, a film distributing company in this country, and a large number of cinemas in America will associate with one of the most powerful producing and distributing companies in the world. Of course negotiations to such an end as this could hardly have been conducted secretly; but the news must come as a surprise to those who paid attention to previous rumours. In 1928 the President of Goldwyn-Mayer denied reports of negotiations with another concern in the strongest terms, and practically suggested that they would be amusing if they were not so silly. In 1929 Mr. William Fox reveals their prophetic accuracy. We now await confirmation of equally discredited rumours of yet another big merger in the film trade.

*   *   *   *

Some months ago, when the *Daily Express* was inveighing against the iniquity of the Oil Combine, with particular reference to the boycott of the Russian oil interests, which was then being attempted, we expressed the hope that when eventually a truce was arranged between the two, the *Express* would continue its campaign. Perhaps somewhat to our surprise, but certainly to our intense gratification, this pious wish has been fulfilled. For the past week, indeed, at least two columns of that lively journal have been devoted to the most energetic expression of views which we have been endeavouring to propagate for many years; and we feel that we may for the present refer to Shoe Lane any enquiries for our opinion of this particular topic. We may now await with interest the application of the same arguments to the Traffic Combine, the (prospective) Coal Trust, the Steel Cartel, the Chemical Trust, the Milk Trust, the Drapery Trust, and even, with that cold relentless, Spartan logic, which invariably directs the policy of our Press, to the Newspaper Trust.

*   *   *   *

The day of Salesmanship as a catchword may be shorter even than was predicted in these pages last week. Already, from the mouth of Mr. Lloyd George we have had the suggestion of a successor—Public Works. We are inclined to regard the building of roads, bridges, or, for that matter, pyramids, as a form of employment preferable to the somewhat artificial task of persuading one another to buy the things which as is primarily implied, nobody wants. That Mr. Lloyd George himself will not be permitted to put the scheme into operation seems certain, but it is quite probable that his proposals will force some similar policy upon the other parties. Perhaps, on consideration, some such paroxysm of public energy might provide a fitting climax to the industrial era. At least it would provide food for the curiosity of future historians—such roads, such drains, such monuments, such parks, such palaces; what a nation ! And there will be no one to mention that minor disadvantage of the civilization : that it failed to produce any free men.

*   *   *   *

The scene is the House of Commons. A member of the Capitalist Government is speaking on unemployment, which he attributes to the effects of the War and the General Strike. From the Stranger's gallery comes in quiet but penetrating tones the one word, Capitalism. We now envisage a day when a member of the Socialist Government is speaking on unemployment, which he attributes to the War and the General Strike. From the Stranger's gallery comes in quiet but penetrating tones the one word, Socialism. And, in truth, one is as good as the other, for they are both alike in this : that neither seeks the only real remedy, the liberty of man to work and make that which he desires and can do. Both seek the liberty of the citizen through his enslavement; the one to a vague amorphous thing called Big Business; the other to a vague amorphous thing called The State. In reality, in both cases it means enslavement to a bureaucracy controlled by a few. Doubtless both will endeavour, like Mr. Lloyd George, to reduce unemployment figures to something nearer the normal. The point is that in either Capitalism or Socialism unemployment should be regarded as normal.

A CRISIS IN ROLIA.

By Our Carrabad Correspondent.

KING LEO'S unprecedented action in giving his assent to the Electoral Bill, before its passage through the Rolian Parliament, is the one subject of discussion here in Carrabad. The effect on government cannot be estimated yet, nor is it possible to say what policy will be adopted by the political parties in relation to the crisis.

Many people with whom I discussed the Act think that the Party leaders and the Cabinet will agree to oppose the Bill and defy the Crown. If they do so, the King is certain to order a dissolution and a temporary dictatorship. But my view is that political opinion will be submissive; for, while the Press is silent, the people are clearly on the side of the King.

I can think of no parallel in English history to the present course of events. The situation is unique in form, if not in essence. But imagine the Barons being forced to sign *Magna Charta* by King John, or Cromwell having a detailed reason for removing the bauble. Those are rough and dangerous comparisons; yet I think they help to clarify a *précis* of the Act.

The purpose of the Electoral Act is really to destroy the machinery of party politics, by placing Government on a more democratic basis. To that end, a domiciliary qualification is demanded of candidates for Parliament, and the Premier's portfolio returns directly to the Parliament and the King.

With regard to elections, it is laid down that every Parliamentary candidate shall be nominated by twenty-five householders in the constituency for which he wishes to stand; that he himself shall be a registered voter in that constituency and have a vote in no other; that he shall not be required to pay a deposit on nomination; that the legitimate cost of his election campaign shall be fixed by the local authority; and that election shall be for a normal period of four years.

To lessen the danger of abuse, it is further enacted that no national political organization shall intervene locally, by providing speakers, or distributing election placards or literature. Power is given to local councils to prosecute and unseat a successful candidate, whose campaign is judged on sufficient ground to have been in contempt of Parliament. Also the meaning of bribery and corruption is extended to cover election pledges of a false or extravagant nature, gross flattery and offers of transport facilities. Incidentally, provision is made for the free use of public transport service by *bona fide* electors on polling days.

The purpose of this section of the Act is to ensure, if possible, the election of members who are genuine representatives of their constituencies. Whether or not it will be workable, remains to be seen. I doubt myself if the introduction of the Alternative Vote, which is required also by the Act, will ease the difficulties thus created; but the experiment is at least a bold one, deserving of respect.

Following a General Election, which may not be held again without an interval of four years, the *de facto* Government remains in office for one calendar month, during which both Houses of Parliament (Citizens and Nobles) must meet to elect new Ministers. The Act requires candidates for the Premiership to be nominated by Members of Parliament, who will proceed to discussion and a vote, a majority of two-thirds being required for election. Subsequently, the Premier-elect will form a Cabinet, subject to blackballing by a Select Joint-Committee of both Houses, and will then submit his own certificate of election and the names of his approved colleagues to the King, whose assent is not likely to be given automatically.

The new Cabinet will be formally inaugurated on taking office, when each member will be sworn in as a Privy Counsellor. In effect, it will become the executive committe of the Privy Council, which will meet regularly to approve or amend Cabinet decisions and the complementary members of which will be selected by the King himself.

The Government will be answerable during its tenure of office to Parliament and the King; and, while normally existing for four years, may be censured by a three-quarter vote in both Houses, or by Royal Proclamation. In that event, a new Premier will be elected at once as before.

I should emphasize here that the new procedure is aimed directly at the Party system, sicne there is little likelihood of any Premier-elect imperilling his Cabinet at the outset by confining his selection to members of his own Party. One vital clause in the Act prohibits the soliciting or regulation of votes in Parliament by political organizations, which means that balloteers (as whips are called in Rolia) will vanish from the poliitical scene; with them, of course, must go the power of the parties.

I understand that the first election under the Act will be held in the third week of April, and so propose to defer a more detailed description of its clauses until effects can be judged in the light of experience. At the moment the circumstances of its promulgation threaten to confuse the issue, which will be affected further during the actual campaign by the news of other changes which the King is believed to favour. As these include the introduction of a Bill to fix the maximum growth of commercial and industrial undertakings, no effort is likely to be spared by financiers and others to make the Act unpopular.

ADAM QUINN.

HAUNTED.

Down lonely ways, through every crowded street
I hear near mine, your little hurrying feet.
Keen winds that wail heart-breaking outside
Sounds as if somewhere, oh! my sweet, you cried.

In each flower-face, some grace of you I see,
A passing smile, a glance you gave to me,
Soft winds that blow where scented gardens lie
Bring me your fragrance that can never die.

There is no place in all this whole world wide
That I can reach, but you are by my side,
No word I say, but you are there to hear;
When mean thoughts come, it is your look I fear.

Closer you come when day slips into night,
Holding my soul within your white soul's light,
So will it be till life and death are one,
When re-united we shall journey on.

JOAN DESTIN.

TOP—

THE NEW MOORE.

OLD MOORE is still popular as a Prophet; and, indeed, the art of prophecy seems to be more fashionable than ever. Even the critics of Old Moore have nothing to say against him except that he is old. As soon as he chooses to call himself Young Moore, he can prophesy with all the old confidence and all the old scientific spirit and authority. The name of the New Moore seems to become Professor A. M. Low, who recently writhed and foamed upon the tripod of inspiration at the Caxton Hall.

Like all preternatural prophets, he simply predicted, saying "man will " or " the world will," without darkening counsel by doubts or arguments. And some of the things he predicted were very interesting. He said that the world was growing better and better, and mankind rising higher and higher. He gave illustrations. " We are already losing hair, teeth, eyesight and sense of hearing. Our descendants will have mechanical aids. There may be some radio beam method of sight." We sincerely hope so. We do not like that first faint quaver of doubt in the word "may." Still less do we like it linked with the still unshaken certitude that we certainly *shall* go blind. There may be an interval of an evolutionary æon or two, while a totally blind race does its best to look for a radio beam that may or may not exist.

But Young Moore gets better as he goes on—just like evolution. " Parts of their bodies will be transplanted wholesale, and I can quite imagine the necessity of a future law to stop a man selling his ears and nose." We can quite imagine a future law to stop a man using his ears and nose, in the present higher evolution of social liberty. As to his using his brains, there is no danger of that, so long as a higher evolution is going on. But it is certainly an alluring thought that we might have a composite politician, made of different parts of the existing politicians. It is an idea that may well be commended to another and more lucid gentleman of the name of Low. We can imagine that brilliant artist sketching a pleasing monster, with the cheek of Mr. Winston Churchill, the nose of Lord Melchett, and the all-seeing Eye of Jix. It would lend a new meaning to a Coalition Cabinet.

So far as divine inspiration need ever descend to reasons, the professor's reasons for thinking thus are (first) that three hundred years ago witches were sometimes treated in New England very much as niggers are still sometimes treated in Texas, and (second) that an elderly stockbroker has not always heard about a new vacuum-cleaner. This is a sort of progress, or prophecy out of the void, in which there seems to be more vacuum than cleaning. It is a pleasing coincidence that the paper which trumpets the prophecy has the next column devoted to the entirely new and hitherto unheard of notion that Dreams may Come True. We rather doubt if the nightmares of the New Moore are prophetic. It is hard enough to believe that he is real, let alone his bad dreams. For (if we may speak in the rude style of one who, having no vacuum-cleaners, could not use his mind or make anything worth considering) Professor Low is such stuff as dreams are made of, and his little life is rounded with a sleep.

—AND TAIL

THE EVIL LAUGH.

As ugly a thing as we have seen for some time is the newspaper note that " Ironical cheers " were the only greetings to the Labour member who introduced a mild measure dealing with the Audit of the Party Funds; or, in other words, suggesting that the Mother of Parliaments might some day be made almost as clean as any common little club or shop that publishes its balance sheet. The project was not even hopeful enough to produce protest and anger. All those things have died away in a ghastly silence in which nothing is left but a giggle. It is called in Parliamentary reports an ironical cheer. There is certainly a double irony in calling it ironical: but anyhow it is the sort of cheer that is not very cheering. For it means we have passed the point of uncovering shame: and can only uncover shamelessness.

Nobody can offer any argument for not auditing Party Funds. Nobody ever has done so; nobody ever has attempted to do so. Bonar Law said feebly that such a rule would be evaded. In other words, he said that his own profession was so dishonest that it would cheat any attempt to detect its dishonesty. That is the nearest to a spirited enthusiastic defence of the Secret Fund that anybody has offered. There is no defence; there is even no defiance; there is only that curious noise; dreary, desolate; horrible as the howl of a dog in the ruins of a dead city.

We hear a great deal nowadays about the value of a sense of humour. The sentimentalists have managed to make even humour sentimental; they have managed to make even humour serious. We ourselves have occasionally in the past been detected in the act of making jokes, and been severely rebuked for it; we have been called flippant and facetious and paradoxical, and the Lord knows what; we have been criticised in other days for pantomimic tricks and lack of dignity. But it is one thing for a man as part of an occasional pantomime to stand on his head, it is another for him to think it a part of his normal social life to crawl on his stomach. Humour, even especially in the sense of good humour, has been put to a very bad use. The moderns, having vulgarized dignity, have now vulgarized even the inversion of dignity. Even the holidays of the mind, in elf-land and wonderland, are to be over-run with trippers and touts. As it has spoilt everything else, it has spoilt the original truth (bracing and even bitter in great works like *Don Quixote*) that it is well for a wise man sometimes to laugh at his own enthusiasms. But there is a way of doing it that is like the grin of the detected culprit or the smile of the street-walker, or the ironical cheer of the Member of Parliament. Laughter is a good thing and we have enjoyed a good deal of it; but God in His mercy forbid that any of us of any moderately decent trades, from scavengers down to scribblers, should ever laugh at ourselves like that.

ACROSS THE BAR.

The Hicks Rumour.

IT is distressing to hear the proposals which are being made for the removal of Sir William Joynson-Hicks to the House of Lords. Even supposing that it is possible to obtain the necessary certification (which entails, I believe, the signature of two doctors and a magistrate), what sort of treatment is this to mete out in maturity to one who has sacrificed in his country's service all the flickering intelligence of youth? Indeed, should we not rather reward him? Surely somewhere in the City there is an empty desk, or one that could be emptied; some vacancy in the world of coal or steel or silk or soap or cheese, to which he might be promoted? This vindictive tendency to stigmatise the unpopular politician can be productive of nothing but evil; for, if there is to be no certainty of real achievement at the end how can we hope to attract to public life that type of mind and ambition which has in the past provided the whole impetus to our Imperial achievement? Let us hope that if the shameful thing is done the victim will have the courage to appeal to the justice of his fellow-countrymen against the spiteful punishment of his leaders.

No Flies on Him.

Mr. Heinrich Q. Klintenbacher, the well-known American Steel King tells me of a new and ingenious ruse which is being employed by a certain gang of confidence tricksters, one so artfully conceived that Mr. Klintenbacher did not mind admitting that he had himself fallen a victim to it. Before coming to England he had been warned about gold-brick men by his mother, and when he was approached in the vestibule of his hotel by a man who, after curt preliminaries, offered to sell him a large block of yellowish-looking metal for $250, he was inclined, without enquiry, to send the fellow about his business. Happening to glance at the brick, however, he perceived, stamped across the face of it, the words "Real Gold." Although his own commercial interests are almost exclusively confined to the baser metals, it was evident to him at a glance that a block of real gold of such a size must certainly be worth more than the price asked for it. The opportunity seemed, indeed, too good to be missed, and after some negotiation the brick changed hands for $200. It was his intention to have the metal worked up into a little statuette of himself for his famous Long Island home, and we may judge of his chagrin to learn, on submitting the metal for this purpose, that it was not gold at all, but some composition of lead and copper, the deceptive words having been added, intentionally no doubt, to lend verisimilitude to a story which his natural business acumen would have led him to suspect.

Trying it Out.

The following letter has reached me, possibly owing to some confusion of envelopes :—Sir,—In reply to your request for an unsolicited testimonial to the value of your Correspondence Course in French, I have not the least hesitation in recommending it. *Au contraire,* indeed, I am inclined rather to praise it *à outrance.* For anyone who would, *sans souci,* acquire such a command of the language as to enable him on every occasion to find the *mot juste,* and only that *mot,* may confidently be indicated as the system *par excellence.* Before taking the course my accent was *écru,* my grammar *distrait*: now there are few feats of *traduction* or enunciation which I do not regard as *à portée.* For a *homme d'affaires* like myself this knowledge and the power which it gives me are of incalculable value. To wish you and your future students *bonne fortune,* now that my own instruction is a *fait accompli,* is the least *gage de grace* which I can offer.

Art in the Home.

Yet another gallant adventurer has descended into the stern melée of commercial life in the person of Lady Jessica Flinders. At her tastefully-designed consulting-room in Bond Street she has established herself as an adviser on matters relating to decoration. Her fees are modest: twenty-five guineas for a consultation, but she hopes to add some reasonable amount to her income. When I consulted her the other day I was surprised at the instinctive grasp of her subject which she displayed. " At the top of your room, you say, is your ceiling. I think you should paint it yellow with red spots. And your walls; yes, of course you must let them stretch right down to the floor and cover them up with some sort of paper, a soft green would be suitable. And for furniture I should suggest chairs and tables, and perhaps one or two sideboards or cabinets. If you have a bookcase, you should keep the backs of the books outwards. And you must have pictures—blue pictures to harmonize with the underlying scheme." That was all : but what a genius ! One felt that she visualized the scene, that, as she drew her hands before her eyes she imagined herself actually in a room, looking at it. And all this for twenty-five guineas from one of the most gifted of our nation's women !

AGAG.

BABEL.
A Rhyme for Children.

The sea washes England
Where all men speak
A language rich
As ancient Greek.

The world wide over
Man with man
Has talked his own tongue
Since speech began.

Yet still must sorrow
Move the mind;
He understands
But his own kind.

The voices lovely
Hollow, and near,
Of beast and bird
Beat on his ear;

Eye into eye
Gaze deep he may,
Yet still through Babel
Gropes his way.

WALTER DE LA MARE.

STRAWS IN THE WIND.

THE ISSUE OF THE INDISCRIMINATE.

By G. K. CHESTERTON.

As the prospects of this paper have grown more doubtful or even desperate, my own spirits have risen with a sense of the scale of the modern danger. When I began it, I merely thought it reasonable that there should be one weekly paper to represent a reasonable alternative to conventional Capitalism and academic Socialism. But I now realize, with ever increasing joy, that what we have taken on is something much bigger than modern Capitalism or Communism combined. I realize that we are trying to fight the whole world; to turn the tide of the whole time we live in; to resist everything that seems irresistible; I may therefore be pardoned a bright, though probably brief, period of almost exaggerated cheerfulness.

For the Thing we oppose is something of which capitalism and collectivism are only economic by-products; something which is quite as likely to betray its soul, or its soullessness, in some chance change of etiquette or some trivial trick of costume. It is so vast and vague that its offensiveness is largely atmospheric; and it is perhaps easier to defy than to define. But it might be approximately adumbrated thus; it is that spirit which refuses Recognition or Respect. It will not pause upon anything or allow the limits of anything; it will not halt anywhere as upon a frontier; it will not recollect itself as before a shrine; it will not stop to give thanks before the feast or to ask for admission before the door. This is the thing with which we are at issue in the most lofty and in the most trifling affairs. We are averse, for instance, from Gate-Crashing; not because we cannot appreciate crashing, or a reasonable amount of juvenile enjoyment in the crash; but because we can appreciate Gates; and think that, properly understood, they are themselves dramatic and exciting like the Gates of Heaven and Hell. When we support religion we in no sense support superstition; when we say a man should take off his hat in church, we do not mean that he should take off his head in church. But we do mean that he should use his head, so as to perceive that there is a difference between the outside of the church and the inside. We do mean that he should understand, like George Herbert, the lesson of the Porch and the difference between one thing and another. And we hate the sort of Universal Religion that denies the dignity of the shrine as much as the sort of Universal Stores that denies the dignity of the shop. When we have to do with Gates, we do not ask for rioters to bring clubs, for craftsmen to make keys. But this is not because craftsmanship is more quiet, still less because it is more slow. It is because it is more interesting; since it is possible to be interested in the key as well as in the door, and in the door as well as in what is behind the door. And we ask the man to take off his hat in the church, or for that matter in the house, not because we want him to be passive, but because we want him to be active. And the act of removing a hat is an act; and involves taking an active part in the service. It is the act of Recognition; or the appreciation of the dignity of difference. And the whole modern world is a monster marching to destroy it.

This is what explains the paradox that must still puzzle many of those who have the sense to see it. I mean that the same age which tends to economic slavery tends to social anarchy; and especially to sexual anarchy. So long as men can be driven in droves like sheep, they can be as promiscuous as sheep; so long they are yoked together like cattle, they can, in one sense, breed as casually as cattle. What is lost in both cases is the sense of distinction; first the master's sense of the difference between man and man and then the man's sense of the difference between woman and woman. Plutocracy does not specially fear the natural appetites, because they also, like industrial organization, bring all men to one level; not unlike the level of the beast of the field. Plutocracy only objects to the artificial appetites, such as those for liberty, honour, decency, and private property. So long as it can make sure that a man's work is adequately monotonous and material, it will allow him the sort of pleasure that is really equally material and even monotonous. It offers the bribe of free love to ensure the loss of free labour.

This is also the explanation of all that element of Gush which flows through all the Publicity that is the expression of Plutocracy. Gush is exactly the right word; because the whole thing has become liquid and has no more lines or frontiers than the sea. It cannot cut itself off from anything; even from anything good. It cannot renounce anything; not even the truth. It cannot attack the best things in life; it can only defile them. It can only sprawl all over them and spoil them, like some loathsome oily substance spilt over beautiful things. It can only degrade Democracy into True Democracy. It can only befoul Christianity with True Christianity. It can only bury the Gentleman (poor old boy) under a mountain of mud and stick up a monstrous mud effigy of the True Gentleman. It has almost fatally poisoned the noble function of Praise, and generally prefers to describe it as Optimism.

Long ago when I was a little boy, and later when I was a not much older minor poet, I felt that there was not enough in the world of a sort of wondering recognition, or pause of mystical respect, before any ordinary object, whether a lamp-post or a flower. For that reason I resented the despair of the Decadents of the nineties, and for that reason I resist the opposite evil now. For though the ogre has two horrible heads, one devouring everything and the other vomiting everything, his name is the Indiscriminate and I hate him.

DIRECT RULE.

DEMOCRACY has reached such a pitch nowadays that even the man in the street is affected by it. Granted the means, indeed, he cannot escape from it. For one penny he becomes a democrat of Fleet Street. For ten shillings (or for nothing, if he has the pluck and an inside aerial) he becomes a democrat with the compliments of the B.B.C. For one-and-threepence he becomes a cushioned, darkling democrat of Metro-Goldwyn-Mayer and the Provincial Cinematograph Theatres, Ltd. He need say nothing. He need think nothing. He need desire nothing. So long as he is willing to read, listen or look, with a sufficient number of fellow-men in the street, all these things are added unto him on the principle of mass-production. Everything is arranged by a few oligarchs at the top, and that is why democracy has recently been so popular.

Profound observers have even noticed in the past year a sudden intensification of democracy in a series of popular movements that have come, as such popular movements always do come, from above. To cite one example, woman has at last asserted her supreme political intelligence by being given the vote as a gift from Conservative Party Headquarters. Not only that, but she is now receiving from the same source (and even from rival concerns) powder-puffs, vanity cases, small combs, free bridge teas and double tickets for dances, to which she may admit the young man whose politics happen to satisfy her critical taste. This is democracy beyond the wildest dreams of theory, a kind of democracy that gives new life not only to politics but to trade.* Nobody but an embittered aristocrat would regard this sweeping wave of democratic acceptance as a simultaneous insult to the intelligence of a woman and to the value of the franchise : the intelligence of a woman is equated to a powder-puff and the value of a powder-puff is equated to a vote. But the democratic feeling is that woman will use her critical faculties in assessing the rival merits of the Conservative, the Liberal, and the Labour powder-puff. With her usual instinct, she will follow her nose.

Another popular innovation that has made the past year an epoch to the political historian is the coming of theTalkies. It was a principle laid down years ago in the rather snobbish and exclusive period of the City States that the size of a State should be determined by the capacity of the ruler to know all the ruled by sight. This principle in itself limited the ideal State to a few thousands of population; it became increasingly impossible to carry out as democracy advanced, and as the doctrine gained ground that democrats should ignore each other unless they were provided with an introduction.

It has been succeeded, in the days of the photograph and film, by the more workable principle that all the ruled should know the ruler by sight. Who does not appreciate that the flat and smudgy shadow of Mr. Baldwin presented daily at breakfast on a large sheet of semi-

*Economists declare that, although in the past General Elections have resulted in trade depression, the Flapper Vote opens a new era of industrial hope. Trades engaged in the manufacturing of feminine *bric-à-brac*, and the catering trade, will be working at a trebled pressure that should absorb all those thrown out of employment in the textile, engineering, and mining industries. See the *Report of the Three-Party Economic Conference on the Relations between General Elections and National Prosperity* (p. 6).

blotting paper, or the flickering and unsubstantial wraith of Mr. Baldwin flitting every night across a thirty-foot sheet, has led to the recent, wildly democratic acquiescence in the principle of De-Rating, and to the popular absent-mindedness which had the result of placing the currency system of this country in the hands of the Bank of England?

And now, as if to strengthen the mute agreement of the many with the benign policies of the few, come the Talkies, and with the Talkies new political vistas. It appears at once that when the people know what Mr. Baldwin looks like, and also how he talks, they must know the whole vibrant personal thing that is Mr. Baldwin. Art demands form. The Talkies demand action and plot. Rightly, therefore, are the Headquarters of the political parties preparing dramas in the new Talky technique that will give in the round a human picture of the political leaders. It would be monstrous if a generation that knows to the last gesture the reaction of Charlie Chaplin to a well-aimed custard pie were to be ignorant of Mr. Baldwin's actions under such an assault.

It is pleasant to look forward to the deafening outburst of silence with which these Talkies will be received by the democracy in the Cinema. The Conservative plot may concern a stately Baldwin of the County Families living in his cultured home with his charming wife, say, the Duchess of Atholl. They engage, after a suitable interview, in which Mr. Baldwin discourses on Safeguarding and Lord Beaconsfield, one Mr. Ramsay Macdonald as butler and his wife, say Miss Ellen Wilkinson, as housekeeper. But by subtle machinations, in which they are aided by coachmen and scullions like Messrs. Maxton and Cook, who accompany their actions with a flood of rather alarming Communist chatter, the butler and housekeeper contrive to instal themselves as lord and lady of the manor, relegating the cultured and aristocratic Baldwin couple (who are born to rule) to their own menial positions. The public will then be expected to notice the bumptious, arrogant, and parvenu behaviour of the usurpers in contrast with the restrained and intensely conservative attitude of Mr. Baldwin, who waits at table with dignity though in Opposition, and of the Duchess of Atholl, who discourses on Loyalists while she darns the table linen.

The Liberal plot is likely to be of a more recondite and historical character, showing John Stuart Mill and Cobden restoring England by a solemn and philosophical pledge to do for England free of charge everything that Mr. Lloyd George should have done by the outlay of pounds, shillings, and pence, ten years ago. This will give real scope for the eloquence of the Talky technique : the high-light of the film will be a tableau based upon Millet's *Angelus,* showing Mr. Lloyd George himself and Mrs. Runciman pausing in prayer over the turnip fields of England.

The Labour plot—but why go on? The silent horde of the electorate will receive the spectacle of Mr. Ramsay Macdonald in a toga pronouncing a funeral oration over the body of Capitalist Cæsar with the same vague indifference. For the seats are comfortable, the theatre is dark, the atmosphere is conducive to rest. It is sufficient that the ruled know the rulers by sight, how they talk, how they act. That is what the publicists praise as the modern democracy preparing for what the publicists have already described as the Mechanical Election.

Arthur Midgham.

POLITICS.

THE result of the Covent Garden Election was declared on Tuesday, as follows :—

Sir M. de Courcy (Lab.)	6,801
John Smith (Cons.)	5,432
Miss Dora Option (Lib.)	3,367
Isaac McIsaacs (Dist.)	0.3

No change.   Lab. majority 1,369

The by-election was caused by the application of Mr. Eric Little, M.P., for the Chiltern Hundreds. In the General Election, he defeated the Conservative candidate in a straight fight by 100 votes and polled 10,342.

Exactly sixty per cent. of the electorate went to the polls. It is presumed that the Distributist candidate has forfeited his deposit.

Comment on the result in the daily Press is illuminating. It seems to be generally agreed, except among Conservatives, that a blow has been aimed at the Government and that Covent Garden is yet another fulcrum on which the Cabinet will be levered out of office.

" Covent Garden has thrown a winged thunderbolt into the Tory camp," writes " Centre Forward " in the *Daily Socialist,* " and the result may safely be taken as a test of public opinion. Labour has increased its majority in the division by over 1,200 votes, despite the presence of two more candidates, so that the new member has clearly received a mandate from the people.

" Obviously the Government's misconception of the meaning of ' gradualness ' has contributed to this sweeping victory. But increasing recognition of the fact that Toryism, as a political creed, has been discredited by the progressive ideals of Socialism, remains the principal factor determining the result. We march on, heartened, to the battle."

" Westminster," of the *Evening Banner,* begins his comment with a playful sally, suggesting that the holding of the election at a moment when " income tax collectors were applying for summonses " had something to do with the defeat of the Conservative candidate.

" Anyway," he continues, " that is as good an explanation as any other. It is worth noting that the new member failed to secure a clear majority over the other candidates and that he has actually polled 3,541 fewer votes than were cast for Labour in the General Election. He cannot claim, therefore, to have captured either the interest or the support of the majority of his constituents."

The Liberal Press emphasises the fact that only sixty per cent. of the electorate voted. " As a result," says the *Daily Sun,* " a Socialist is in on a minority vote, while both the leading candidates have been given far fewer votes than at the General Election."

" Profundus," writing in the *Newsman,* takes a similar line. " The Socialists imagine," he says, " that they have received a bouquet from Covent Garden, while the Tories are pleased at having dodged a tomato. To my mind, the latest product of the ' Market ' division is Dead Sea fruit.

" The truth of the matter is that Liberalism has proved once again that it holds the balance of power. Miss Option's votes, added to those secured by either of the leading candidates, would have ensured her election. And had either stood down, she would probably have won. In the circumstances, Liberals have no cause for discouragement."

As for the Distributist view, the following remarks are made editorially :—

" The result of the election leaves us pretty much where we were before. However, two points emerge : one that Mr. McIsaacs would probably have secured more votes if more people had voted ; the other that the payment of a deposit by nominated candidates is manifestly wrong."

E. J. M.

THEATRES, CINEMAS, Etc.

BOOK OF THE WEEK.

ZOLA AND HIS TIME.

By MATTHEW JOSEPHSON. Victor Gollancz, Ltd. 25s. net.

"I DO not expect justice," wrote Zola. "I know that I must disappear." And at another time: "But how can we writers of the nineteenth century survive with the colossal mass of our work? The ancients bequeathed us one or two masterpieces which posterity could cherish: An *Iliad*, a *Divine Comedy*, a *Don Quixote*. But we, with our twenty to fifty volumes, how can posterity select, how can it know which to keep? They will not even approach our works."

So far as England is concerned, Zola has already disappeared, except that his short and brutal name still hangs about the fading legend of Dreyfus. But what the Affaire Dreyfus was all about, whether Zola was a Jew and Dreyfus an enthusiastic *Camelote du Roi*, what Zola attacked in *J'accuse*, who was Esterhazy: all these vague questions about the great European scandal of the last century are losing their importance year by year. "I do not expect justice; I know that I must disappear."

That passion for fame and that obession of oblivion were, as a matter of fact, characteristic of Zola. On the one side he had great powers for literature, a burning apostolic desire for truth and honesty, extraordinary powers of mind and body: qualities that were wedded by an intense egoism to a dangerous introspection, a preoccupation with the indecent, a lack of proportion in his outlook on life.

Englishmen will never quite understand, and Mr. Josephson in this volume does not explain, how and where the eccentricity of Zola emerged into the normal and French attitude towards literature. Zola was the acknowledged head of the Naturalist School of Literature in the century of Positivism and Mechanism, of Revolution and chaos. He formed a regular habit, which no outward circumstances were allowed to alter, of writing each morning four sheets, one thousand words, depicting every sort of aberration and irregularity in human life. Attempting the detached and scientific spirit of his time (and failing in it with his time, as Lombroso did, as Bertillon did), he went about with his notebook to all the savoury and unsavoury haunts of Paris taking notes unabashed of his observation. It was a grand opportunity for the practical joker; it was an impartial investigation with the verdict already settled; and the great cycle of Zola's *Rougon-Macquart* novels, which included every type of human character and destiny in the many branches of one family tree, showed that Zola understood as much and as little of life as do most human beings.

The Naturalistic School was preoccupied with the unnatural, with aberration, with corruption. Consequently, it was self-conscious and artificial. But (and here is the character of the individual Zola merges with the spirit of French literature), it had power, clarity, a ruthless desire to be honest in the light of a fixed body of beliefs. At the beginning of the century French writers called themselves Romantics, gloried in Romanticism. They worked out Romance by syllogisms, carried their battles into the streets and into the theatres, issued manifestos and counter-manifestos. When Romanticism was finally overthrown they went the full swing of the pendulum to Naturalism. They worked out Reality by syllogisms, carried their battles into the streets and into the theatres, issued manifestos and counter-manifestos. The English are more inclined to take their literature as a hobby and to preserve an even course between the rival schools. But behind the extremes of the French schools is one spirit of which they are expressions. The works are less likely to live than the enthusiasm that produced them. Zola will live as the spirit of the place, as the man who was romantic over reality, and as an outstanding example in the two parts of his career of the French mind which refuses to divorce literature from life.

This life of Zola is an untidy and a diligent book, a vast mass of material put together with extreme care, but with no great skill in writing. It presents, however, very clearly the personal problem of Zola, a man who gloried in his infirmities, which were many. Reared in Provence, he was poor, langorous and idealistic. In Paris, where he sought fortune, he continued lazy, he lived in squalor, he lost his ideals. Suddenly he threw over the artistic life, took a small job as a clerk in Hachette's, became obsessed with writing, and decided to show the world the power of one whom the world had always regarded as a pariah. As a matter of fact, however, the world had never bothered its head about him, and the feeling of being a pariah was entirely a thing of Zola's imagination. Marriage turned him more and more to realism, but a childless marriage increased his disappointment in life. It was a liaison that gave him children, that gave him the combativeness and the power to stand by Dreyfus in the face of the French nation. Then came a voluntary exile, and, after the virtual vindication of Dreyfus, an honoured and mellowed old age wherein the Realist became gradually the ameliorist and the Utopian. Zola had far more success than falls to most men, but he was a complete egoist, nerve-ridden, changing his beliefs and his expression with changing circumstances of his private life. Unfortunately for him he lived in the period when psychologists were first running amok in Europe: a fact which explains both his preoccupation with his own eccentricities and with the eccentricities of humanity—a study which he called Naturalism.

G. M.

BOOKS FOR EVERY MAN.

SEEING THE FUTURE. By Christabel Pankhurst. Harper and Brothers. 7s. 6d. net.

Miss Pankhurst believes on the evidence of sight, and the thesis of this book is that we must see more clearly.

It is, of course, an admirable suggestion, but there are any amount of difficulties which the author overlooks rather than looks over. The chief difficulty is that even sight is a matter of faith; it cannot be proved that what the mind receives the impression of beholding is actually what is there. Quite apart from the question of angles and perspectives, there are all sorts of other varieties of view, due to delusion, illusion, myopia, reflects and heaven only knows what else.

Miss Pankhurst's point of view may or may not be admirable but what is to happen when another equally sincere point of view denies what she declares in the true vision? The author's pious hope is a most beautiful spectacle, but it does not really solve or even clarify the difficulty of seeing a way out of this dark wood into which civilization has strayed.

CRAZY DAYS. By Martin Bruce. Hurst and Blackett, Ltd. 7s. 6d. net.

The title is not inapt to describe the matrimonial and other adventures of a pecuniary English nobleman and a rich American heiress. It is written in very light vein, and, though occasionally there are unnecessary references to things of which it was once considered not good manners to speak, there is a certain point in the satire that underlies the frivolity.

BLIND CIRCLE. By Maurice Renard and Albert Jean. Victor Gollancz, Ltd. 7s. 6d. net.

The two authors of this thriller have between them produced a most fascinating horrible plot. It is not only a detective story. To tell the story here would be to weaken very much the thrill of future readers, but the idea of four identical corpses of one man is an ingenious one; and if the solution of the mystery seems at times improbable, it loses nothing in effect.

INSPECTOR FROST'S JIGSAW. By H. Maynard Smith. Ernest Benn, Ltd. 7s. 6d. net.

This tells how a woman is murdered, without any apparent motive or reason and with nothing but the most battlingly simple facts upon which to base a solution. Inspector Frost fits his Jigsaw together in the same calm and unemotional manner in which the author has written the book. It is a fascinating achievement.

WOMAN AND SOCIETY. By Meyrick Booth. George Allen and Unwin. 8s. 6d. net.

On May 1st the new woman electorate comes into being. On March 5th is published Mr. Meyrick Booth's book, one of the most valuable discussions of the problems of feminine emancipation that has been written for some time.

It is obvious, as the author points out, that no one book could possibly give all the *pros* and *cons* of the discussion, but as a sketch of the problems it is amazingly comprehensive. The whole question is reviewed afresh from the standpoint of modern science, and the review is one that should be read by all who realize how vital to our civilization is clear thinking on this matter, and how intolerable is the present chaos.

The treatment is as impartial as any treatment of the subject by one of the sexes can be, though it is probable that neither those who believe in "the old-fashioned ideas about marriage and the woman's place in the home," nor those of the more intense feminist persuasions, will think Mr. Booth's treatment of them fair. Nevertheless, the author gives nearly all sides of the argument an airing, and the many authorities from which he quotes show how wide has been his research.

TRADE UNION DOCUMENTS. Compiled and edited by W. Milne-Bailey. G. Bell and Sons, Ltd. 8s. 6d. net.

The Trade Unions, a necessary part of Industrialism, have from a comparatively humble beginning now grown to be one of the greatest forces in the modern State, and the backbone of organized Labour movements and political parties. The story of their growth and development, and of how legal and political recognition and representation was won step by step, is of extraordinary interest.

Mr. W. Milne-Bailey tells the story by documents—a very valuable way of telling a story, even if the romance of the tale is left to the imagination. Many documents have, of course, been omitted; it would be impossible in one volume to include them all; but what are here cover most of the field of research; and for those who wish to study the matter more closely and thoroughly, there are many works of reference given to which they can turn.

The edition is divided into four parts, each with an introduction and inclusion of the appropriate documents. Part I. deals with the value, aspirations and objects of Trade Unionism; Part II. with the Structure and Organization. Part III. with Functions and Methods. Part IV. with the Place of Trade Unionism in the Community.

THESE PEOPLE.

These people of the deep blue eyes,
And brown, unruly, hair,
What innate secret of the skies
Mayhap, is hidden there;
What dreams of infinite delight,
Are hidden by that brow—
Soft, fair, and wonderfully white:
I sometimes wonder how
They bear the dreams
That hide behind their eyes,
What scorn they all must hold for us,
Who only deal in lies;
What swords now rusting, what romance
Now dead, would live again,
If only they could voice the thoughts,
That live behind their brain.

These people . . . are the sufferers:
The rest of all mankind
Pass on, not caring what their fate,
Happy, heedless, blind.
Yet they live on, and their great thoughts
Are left to us alone,
To us, who partly understand,
But never can atone.
Your dreams will die, sweet people,
You work, and suffer—yet,
The world is unromantic,
The world—will soon forget.

　　　　　　　　　　　　　　　A. L. WOOLF.

MUSICAL JOTTINGS.

THE British National Opera Company opened a week's season at the Lewisham Hippodrome on Monday, February 25th, with a performance of *Aida*. Considering the severe handicap of the small stage, a quite lavish spectacle was provided. Radonnes, in fact, upon returning from his triumph among the vast and unknown Ethiopian lands, must have experienced very vividly that sentiment of affection for small and local things, which is so much valued by Distributists. Mr. Walter Widdop, who impersonated the great warrior, was in good voice. The male cast was generally good; Mr. Norman Allin (though obviously suffering from a severe cold) being impressive as the High Priest; Mr. Anderson duly magnificent as the King; and Mr. Arthur Fear an intense Amanasro. The name was taken by Miss May Blyth, whose make-up hardly carried the conviction of her dramatic expression, nor the charm of her voice. Miss Constance Willis was somewhat terrifying as the Princess, but she found the music well suited to her voice. Mr. John Barbirolli conducted with much spirit, and the orchestra was well above the average.

The Berlioz *Damnation of Faust* was a happy choice for the Hallé Orchestra, conducted by Sir Hamilton Harty, at the Queen's Hall, on Friday last. The B.B.C. series of concerts have given much this season, for which our gratitude is due, and it is doubtful if we shall again get a performance so nearly approaching the adequate as was this last. It raised again the old question of a resident conductor. I doubt whether individually the Hallé Orchestra is better or as good as the Philharmonic or the London Symphony, but there can be little question that as an ensemble it far transcends either of them. Sir Hamilton Harty is, of course, a magnificent conductor, but the question is more whether even with a conductor of less talent the discipline of a resident director is what is chiefly needed to bring our London orchestras up to the standard which, as individuals, the players can certainly reach.

The soloists on Friday last were disappointing. The best was Miss Stiles-Allen as Margaret, and Mr. Herbert Simmons in the by no means magnificent part of Brander. The Mephistopheles (Mr. Harold Williams) was obviously handicapped by a severe chill, caught, presumably, by being so long away from the warmer atmosphere of his domain, while the Faust of Mr. Tudor Davies was far too vocal. All singers should aim at command and beauty of tone, but the aim should be achieved before they reach the concert platform or operatic stage. By that time the technique should be so mastered as to be almost unconscious, and the aim be that of dramatic expression. Conscious tone-production mars our artistic performance.

The Budapest String Quartet on Wednesday last were responsible for some magnificent performances of Beethoven, particularly that of the tremendous A minor quartet. The players are admirable individually and together.

The return of Louis Godowsky was an occasion of much pleasure at the Wigmore Hall on March 1st. This young violinist has made great progress since his last performance in London some years ago. Particularly pleasing was the performance of the Glazounow Concerto.

V. N. L.

THE DRAMA.

THAT *The Rumour,* at the Court Theatre, should be as complete a commercial success as *Journey's End* at the Savoy is significant; given a strong play, with a direct appeal, a public is inevitably forthcoming. Mr. C. K. Munro has pruned and cut his work since the initial performance by the Stage Society, and has done it admirably. The play, however, could still do with further tightening up. The politicians' speeches are overlong, and their continued repetition needless. The majority of people spend their lives in avoiding the fulminations of Cabinet Ministers, and it is a little hard when on an evening's entertainment to be compelled to listen to inevitable platitudes.

These, however, are but minor criticisms. *The Rumour* has a vitality and a movement that carries the audience from start to finish. The author tracks cosmopolitan intrigue with the dexterity of genius. He postulates a not impossible war precipitated entirely by the machinations of finance. He shows us innumerable wires set in motion—the Press, the public, panic, revolution—each and every section doped, exacerbated with mass suggestion.

There are moments of poignant humour; the contingents raised by the City to avenge the death of Lena Jackson—Lena's Own Scouts who march away bedewed with sentiment. The shifting panorama gives no time for boredom, the whole gamut of emotion is run through.

Mr. Stanley Lathbury as Ned, the Spider who weaves the whole web is persuasively evil. He gives extraordinary significance to a small part, purposely small as showing the seed from which a Stock Exchange ramp is raised. This rendering is an admirable foil to the actor's delineation of Sir Robert Mortimer, one of our less virile Die-hards. Mr. Michael Sherbrooke as La Rubia is explosively effective, and Mr. Robert Breed as the newsboy amazingly good.

Fashion, removed from the Gate Studio Theatre to the Kingsway, is also a commercial success. The original company has not been retained in its entirety, which is a pity. Miss Betty Potter has been succeeded by Miss Marie Dainton, who plays Mrs. Tiffany on the lines of musical comedy which throws the study of the nouveau riche somewhat out of gear; but we still have Miss Helena Pickard as the adorable Seraphina, and Miss Viola Lyell as Gertrude. This picture of society in 1850 still remains one of the most delightful shows in town. Additional songs, Victorian gems of bathos have been included, and the settings are well in the period.

J. K. PROTHERO.

Small Workshops.

NAME PLATES.
Guaranteed Firth's stainless steel 10" x 3" up to 10 letters 8/6 each.
J. B. DAINTY Pensnett, near DUDLEY.

LEATHERWORK.
Stools, motor cushions, log tubs, blotters, hand-made gloves.
KATHARINE COCKCROFT,
37, Belsize Park, N.W.3.

METALWORK.
Antique and Modern of all descriptions, in brass, copper, and iron, to own or customers' designs. Speciality, Electric Light Fittings, Electrical accessories and general hardware of exceptional value.
J. F. GARROD, LTD., 72, Charlotte Street, LONDON, W.1.

WHO'S NICHOLLS?
Why, the hand-done Visiting Card King. Specimen packet designed free.
256, Church Road, BRISTOL.

PRINTING.
Good printing at moderate charges. Specimens and price free.
HATHERLEY, 43A, Trentham Street,
Southfields, LONDON.

HATS.
Raffia trimmed hats and baskets.
ROSE AGENCY, Hanover Building,
SOUTHAMPTON.

VEGETABLE-DYED, HANDSPUN AND HANDWOVEN MATERIALS.
Curtains, cushions, rugs, scarves and dress materials. Goods sent on approval. Vacancy for pupil.
DORIS JEWSON, 18, Colegate, NORWICH.

DECORATOR AND PLUMBER.
All house decorations done. Moderate charges; good work.
F. STONE, 5, Health Villas, VALE OF HEALTH, N.W.3

PHOTOGRAPHIC ENLARGEMENTS.
Artistic Postcard Enlargements from your small films. 3/- dozen. Hand-woven cushion squares, 5/6. Table runners, 7/6. Fadeless Blue and Golden Brown.
ARTS AND CRAFTS, St. Osyth,
CLACTON-ON-SEA.

HAND BEATEN METAL WORK.
Restored to original design and finish. Any metal. 45 years' experience. References.
CLARK, Radioville, Ashstead, SURREY.

ARTIST CRAFTSMEN.
Hand work in Iron, Bronze, or Stainless Steel, Electric Fitings, Lamps, Fire Iron, Stools, Trivets, Gates, Ornamental Ironwork, Bronze Grilles, or any artistic metal work in Silver, Brass, Bronze, Iron, for Ecclesiastical or domestic use. Clients' own designs sympathetically carried out, otherwise all work designed and carried out by
R. P. ROBERTS and PHILIP HODSON,
Artistic Craftsmen, the Forge, Limited, Beechlawn, Beechwood Road,
AIGBURTH, LIVERPOOL.

UPHOLSTERER AND HOUSE FURNISHER.
Restful Easy Chairs made in small workshop by practical working upholsterer. Covered in Damask, £5. Velvet or Moquette, £5 17s. 6d. Carriage paid anywhee in United Kingdom. Samples of coverings and designs on request.
R. STREET, 27, Albert Road,
COLNE, LANCASHIRE.

THE FOREST TOYS.
Wooden animals of all kinds, hand-carved and painted. Price list post free.
F. H. WHITTINGTON, Brockenhurst,
HANTS.

GLOVES.
Irreproachable gloves hand-made by expert. Original button holes. Every kind of handwork. Disabled Soldiers and Invalids employed. Bazaar and Trade should apply. Very moderate prices. Write for list.
HANDICRAFT HUT, PATTERDALE.

EMBROIDERY.
Embroideries in wool on jumper suits and waistcoats. KATHARINE COCKCROFT,
37, Belsize Park, N.W.3.

TAILORING, LADIES and GENTLEMEN.
Bespoke and ready-to-wear. Good materials. Alterations and renovations carried out. Moderate charges. Patterns on request.
F. WALKER, Mortimer Hall,
93, Mortimer Street, Regent Street, W.1.

BASKET WARE.
Rustic wicker furniture for outdoors. Log Baskets, Dog Baskets, Laundry and Travelling Hampers. Cane and coloured Shopping Baskets. Carriage paid. Illustrated catalogue and price list free.
BLACKWELL & SON,
28, Cross Street, BARNSTAPLE.

NEEDLEWORK.
Pictures, landscapes, all silk, from 10/6.
KATHARINE CHEVALLIER,
247, Dover Road, FOLKESTONE.

HAND-MADE FURNITURE.
Home-made Furniture, mainly of English-grown woods, and to original designs from the simplest to the finest styles.
A. ROMNEY GREEN, Woodworker,
25, Bridge Street, CHRISTCHURCH.

HANDWOVEN PILE RUGS.
Something new! Made in any size, colourings and depth of pile required. Prices from 25/-. Send for samples.
THE HAND LOOM CENTRE, NORWICH.

HANDWOVEN MATERIALS.
Handspun and vegetable dyed, in silk, wool, and cotton. Dresses, jumpers, skirt lengths, scarves, curtains, cushion covers, and materials for all decorative purposes.
THE KINGSLEY WEAVERS (Lee & Eileen Baker), Chipping Campden, GLOS.

GENTS. SOX.
Guaranteed All-Wool and every pair made at home. Mixed colours, 2/3; plain colours 2/6. Postage paid.
G. MERRIKIN, 28, Shene Bldgs.,
Bourne Est., HOLBORN, E.C.

THE
London School of Weaving
13, Bryanston Street, Portman Square, W.1.
NOTED FOR ITS WONDERFUL FABRICS
DAILY CLASSES.
Patented Table Looms Weaving any Patterns, Contractors to Government for Looms, etc.
Established 1898   Telephone Mayfair 6595
PRICE LISTS ON APPLICATION.

MIRRORS AND FRAMES.
Mirrors and frames bordered with fruit and flowers, lovely colours. From 12/6. Also embroidered waistcoats and overalls.
THEA HOLME, Sussex Lodge, Champion, Hill, S.E.

PRINTER AND PUBLISHER.
Posters. Catalogues sent on application.
H. D. C. PEPLER.

SCULPTOR, CARVER & LETTER CUTTER
in wood and stone. Tombstones, Wall Tablets, Stations of the Cross, Altars, Holy Water Stoups, Sanctuary Lamps.
H. J. CRIBB.

WEAVER-DYER.
Suitings, Homespun Tweeds, Serge for Habits, Vestments. J. V. D. KILBRIDE.

WOODWORKER.
Household and Ecclesiastical Furniture, Weaving Appliances. BUILDER.
Address above :— G. MAXWELL, DITCHLING COMMON, HASSOCKS,
SUSSEX.

DRESS ORNAMENTS.
Hat and Frock Ornaments; Pin Trays; of single or cut sea-shells. Colours, bronzes. From 1/- each.
BIELBY, Alfriston, SUSSEX.

HANDWROUGHT FURNITURE.
Davies' Handwrought Furniture. "Distinctive" for the past 25 years. Davies Handicraft Furniture has been known for its fulfilment of all the ideals that actuated the old craftsmen. It is entirely handwrought in solid oak and other fine furniture woods, beautifully polished to show to best advantage the natural grainings. The designs are original, simple in taste, artistic in effect, but comfortable and adaptable in every respect for everyday use.
W. H. DAVIES & SONS, Mount Street, BOLTON, LANCASHIRE.

KNITTED WEAR.
Reader would like orders for Hand-made Silk Socks, Matinee Coats, Pullove.s, etc., also strong Boys' Stockings and Gents' Socks. BOX 12, "G.K.'s Weekly,"
2, Little Essex Street, STRAND, W.C.2.

VIOLINS.
Hand-made Violins of exceptional tone. £5—£15. Also ship models.
BOX V2, "G.K.'s Weekly,"
2, Little Essex Street, STRAND, W.C.2.

LEATHER GOODS.
Leather Comb Case, 1/6. Raffia Sprays Woven Scarf, 7/6.
MASON, Cowesby, Northallerton, YORKS.

LINGERIE.
Orders taken for hand-made lingerie, and embroidery.
SANDERS, 122, Romsey Road,
SOUTHAMPTON.

IRISH HOUSEHOLD LINENS.
Direct from the Manufacturer. Coloured dress linen, very fine quality, 30 ins. wide, only 1/9 per yard post free. Catalogue, samples and remnant bargains. List free.
J. HENDERSON, Milner Street, BELFAST, N. IRELAND.

BRASS RUBBINGS
and other Medieval subjects. Engraved printed and published by Molly Power. Lists on application.
MEDIÆVAL CRAFT, Wells, SOMERSET.

For the Table: Farm Produce.

SHAMROCK.
Shamrock Trailing Sprays, generous boxes, 1/-, 2/-, 3/-, 5/-, 10/-, to £1 each. Harps and emblems 4d. Also best fatted Fowls, 7/6 pair, trussed; all post paid.
MOLLY O'DONOGHUE,
The Convent Road Store, Rosscarbery, Cork.

POULTRY.
Splendid young roasting cockerels, 7/6 pair. Boilers, 6/-. Fatted geese, 7/6 each, trussed; postage paid.
MISS GREENWOOD, Rosscarbery, Cork.

Best roasting fowls and ducklings, 7/-, 8/-, 9/- pair. Splendid boiling fowls, 6/6 pair; larger 9/- pair. Plump turkeys, 14/-, 16/-, 20/-, 25/- each; all trussed; postage paid.
A. BELL, The Glebe, Rosscarbery, Cork.

Specially fatted roasting fowls and ducks, 7/6, 8/6 to 10/- pair. Tender boiling fowls 7/- pair. Fatted geese, 10/-, 12/6 each; all trussed; post paid. Mrs. A. REGAN,
Fairfield House, Rosscarbery, Cork.

Large Roasting Fowl and Ducks, 7/- pair. Large fat boilers, 6/- pr., 2 prs. 11/-, trussed. Shamrock sent to your friends in foreign lands on receipt of address and 1/6. All post free.
MISS JORDAN, Rosscarbery, Cork.

CHOCOLATES.
Home-made of Fresh Cream Milk, pure Butter and new-laid Eggs. Boxes and baskets from 2/-; lacquer boxes from 5/-. Postage extra. DELANEY, 40, Brooke Street, E.C.I.

REAL DEVONSHIRE CLOTTED CREAM.
¼ lb., 10d.; ½ lb., 1/5; 1 lb., 2/6; post free.
BOLES, Heathfield, Holsworthy, Devon.

THE COCKPIT.

To the Editor, G.K.'s WEEKLY.

DANGEROUS LAWS.

SIR,—Your article on "Dangerous Laws" prompts me to tell you of a law under which I recently suffered; not so much a dangerous law as a silly one.

I entered the "Old Crown," R———, on a recent occasion for my lunch of bread, cheese, and beer, which was ordered well before two o'clock; at two o'clock the landlady told me I must go. In spite of my protest that the food and drink were ordered before two o'clock she persisted; so I had to bolt my beer and take my bread and cheese out and eat it in the street, where it was raining. I have thought since, that I was a fool for my pains, for I was three miles from home, and could, I suppose, have qualified as a bona fide traveller. Some good may perhaps accrue to the British Empire by restricting the sale of beer to a certain hour, but what harm can come from eating bread and cheese after two o'clock is beyond any effort of mine to imagine.

MURRAY RUMSEY.

BLOOD OR BLISS.

SIR,—May I avail myself of this opportunity to thank Mr. Geoffrey K. Coen for his stinging criticism of my letter. Let me inform your correspondent, with all due respect for his literary abilities as a letter writer, that sarcasm is only used by those who do not possess enough initiative to reason sensibly.

I am sorry that Mr. Coen objects to there being such a thing as idealism, but why should he have to split straws over a word? Then he writes "a vague idealism means nothing unless there be a very definite ideal." He might just as well argue that King Charles was beheaded only when his head was cut off. Later he proceeds "If once such an ideal is found there will be no *unconscious* urge towards the destruction of that which opposes the ideal." I do not disagree with this brilliant circumlocution, but I did not say in my first letter that there would be an "unconscious urge" when the ideal state was existent. I said that the "urge" is present now, and the idealism is looked forward to in this age.

Mr. Coen supposes I have some sort of vague idea of my ideal in my mind. Why should he suppose? I suggest that he has gone too far with his psycho-analysis, and that he should not attempt to take the mote out of my eye before he removes the beam from his own. One other point I would mention is that your correspondent seems to have overlooked the fact that my letter was an argument against crime fiction—not a debate on exaggeration.

E. A. JONES.

THE SECRET OF THE SECRETARY.

SIR,—May I draw your attention, if it has not already been drawn, to a rather interesting reply made by the Home Secretary to a question by Mr. T. J. O'Connor, M.P., in the House of Commons. The reply was to the effect that it would not be in the public interest to make any statement on the steps which had been or are being taken to prevent a recurrence of the offence committed by Ex-Sergeant Goddard; but the importance of the matter is fully appreciated, and there is good reason to hope that the various steps being taken will produce the desired results.

Now I can understand that it would be inconvenient, at least, to publish abroad all the rules and regulations and ways and means by which law and order is maintained, but in the present case it is of some importance that public confidence in the police should be restored, and this sort of secretiveness is more likely to shake it still further. Either it means that the police have to be kept in ignorance of the methods adopted to detect their fall from duty —which is not very encouraging to our high opinion of them—or else the public are to be kept in ignorance as to how the police force is organized and managed. This might be in the interest of the bureaucrats, but how can it be in the public interest, as stated?

JOHN MASTERS.

The Distributist League.

(founded in conjunction with " G.K.'s Weekly " for the restoration of liberty by the distribution of property).

President: MR. G. K. CHESTERTON.
Secretary G. C. HESELTINE.
Office, 2, Little Essex Street, London, W.C.2.
Telephone : City 1978.

There are many readers of this Paper who are not members of the League. All who believe that ownership in the means of livelihood is normal to man, and necessary to liberty, and all who dislike and distrust the concentration of control advocated by Socialists and practised by Monopolists, should join the League. There is no other tenet for membership, and no other obligation that 1/- subscription, although active work is welcomed from all who can give it.

CENTRAL BRANCH.

CENTRAL BRANCH.—*Hon. Sec.* : J. Desmond Gleeson, 2, Little Essex Street, Strand, W.C.2.

On Friday night last at the Devereux Mr. W. K. Scudamore gave a most interesting and intellectual lecture on " Eugenics." Good citizens beget good children, and bad citizens beget bad children. That may, or may not, be a sound proposition, but when by good citizens is meant citizens with money, and by bad citizens, people without money, then the proposition becomes very unsound indeed. Mr. Scudamore showed clearly that the idea behind Eugenics is to get rid of the poorer people and thus cut off a serious burden of the rich. The repressive side of the eugenic scheme includes the principle that persons should in progressive classes beginning with the lowest scale of poverty, be prevented by a simple surgical operation, from having children. It seems unnecessary to add to that.

Next week Mr. W. R. Titterton will speak on " Should the Theatre be Abolished."

LIVERPOOL BRANCH.

LIVERPOOL BRANCH.—*Hon. Sec.* : F. C. South, 132, St. Anne Street, Chester.

A debate with the Liverpool League for the Taxation of Land Values has been arranged for Monday, March 11th, at the Wedgwood Café, Hackins Hay, Dale Street, at 8 p.m.

At 6, Lord Street, on March 21st, the discussion on the Guild State will be continued. As this is the last meeting of our programme for the winter session we should like to see a good attendance. It is proposed to hold a Hot-Pot supper after Easter. Details will be announced later.

AT THE DEVEREUX.
7 p.m. Friday, 8th Mar., 1929.
W. R. TITTERTON
on
SHOULD THE THEATRE BE ABOLISHED ?

BIRMINGHAM BRANCH.

BIRMINGHAM BRANCH.—*Acting Hon. Sec.*: H. Robbins, Weeford Cottage, Hill, Sutton Coldfield.

A meeting was held at the Guildhouse, Oozells Street, on March 1st. The inclement weather affected the attendance. The position created by the recently launched campaign for sterilisation of the unfit was discussed at length. It was agreed unanimously that Distributist action was called for, and a special sub-committee was appointed to report to the next meeting.

Mr. E. A. Bradford gave an admirably lucid account of Leninism. Lenin himself was revered and almost worshipped as a prophet. His doctrine, a development of Marxism, laid down the division of all men into exploiters and exploited. This " economic interpretation of history " involved the axiom that force should be used against the exploiters, and the Bourgeoisie could be, and were, killed without any reference to moral standards. Against this immoral standards must, in fairness, be set the very real improvement in the condition of the bottom dog in Russia.

In a passage of real eloquence, Mr. Bradford compared and contrasted this dictatorship from below with the dictatorship from above expressed by Fascism. Both were hateful to Christian men who valued spiritual liberty above all things. Would they be able to keep apart from the great clash between these two theories, and, if not, on which side would they be found?

The subsequent discussion was unfortunately hampered by lack of time. If members would remember that 7-30 means 7-30, more business could be transacted. Next meeting, Friday, March 15th, at the Guildhouse, 7-30 p.m. prompt. Report of the special sub-committee, and decision on action to be taken.

NORTH LONDON BRANCH.—*Hon. Sec.*: J. O. Strong, 29, Southwood Lawn Road, N.6.

OXFORD (Cobbett Club).—*Hon. Sec.*: B. J. Wall, Brazenose College.

PORTSMOUTH.—*Hon. Sec.*: Miss Ellen Flanagan, 33, Kent Road, Southsea.

MANCHESTER.—*Hon. Sec.*: John A. Toohey, York Mount, Bury New Road, Prestwich.

SALFORD.—*Hon. Sec.*: J. Burns, 8, Trafalgar Square, Regent Road, Salford.

WEST LONDON GROUP.—*Hon. Sec.*: A. Ardern, 25, Felden Street, S.W.6.

GLASGOW BRANCH. — *Hon. Sec.*: A. Mason, 55, Exeter Drive, Partick, W.1.

BOURNEMOUTH.—*Hon. Sec.*: Miss Mott, 4, Dingle Road, Boscombe.

BRADFORD BRANCH.—*Hon. Sec.*: J. Gosney, 35, Buxton Street, Heaton, Bradford.

COVENTRY.—*Hon. Sec.*: R. E. S. Willison, 102, Westwood Road, Coventry.

EDINBURGH.—*Hon. Sec.*: Jas. Turner, c/o Dunne, 5, Keir Street, Edinburgh.

NEW MILLS.—*Hon. Sec.*: J. Boak, 46, Hyde Park Road, New Mills, nr. Stockport.

NORTH SHIELDS.—*Hon. Sec.*: J. J. Rogan, 28, Windermere Terrace, North Shields, Northumberland.

NORTH LONDON BRANCH.—*Hon. Sec.*: J. O. Strong, 29, Southwood Lawn Road, N.6.

BOOKS TO READ.

The Servile State, by Hilaire Belloc (4/-)

The Outline of Sanity, by G. K. Chesterton (6/-).

Economics For Helen, by H. Belloc (5/-).

Liberty and Property, by H. E. Humphries (1/3).

Guilds, Trade, and Agriculture, by A. J. Penty (5/-).

Fields, Factories and Workshops, by P. Kropotkin (2/6).

The Acquisitive Society, by R. H. Tawney (4/6).

Primer of Social Science, by H. Parkinson (3/6).

The Church and the Land, by Vincent McNabb, O.P. (2/6).

The Change, by G. C. Heseltine (2/6).
Do We Agree?
by G. B. Shaw and G. K. Chesterton (1/6).

The above may be obtained through booksellers or direct from the Secretary of the Distributist League, 22, Essex Street, W.C.2.

THE LEAGUE offers the only practical alternative to the twin evils of Capitalism and Socialism. It is equally opposed to both; they both result in the concentration of property and power in a few hands to the enslavement of the majority.

THE LEAGUE stands
For the Liberty of the Individual and the Family Against interference by busybodies, monopolies, or the State.

Personal Liberty will be restored mainly by the better Distribution of Property (*i.e.*, ownership of land, houses, workshops, gardens, means of production, etc.).

The Better Distribution of Property will be achieved by protecting and facilitating the ownership of individual enterprises in land, shops, and factories.

Thus THE LEAGUE fights for:
Small Shops and Shopkeepers against multiple shops and trusts. Individual Craftsmanship and Co-operation in industrial enterprises. (Every worker should own a share in the Assets and Control of the business in which he works). The Small Holder and the Yeoman Farmer against monopolists of large inadequately farmed estates.

And the Maximum, instead of the minimum initiative on the part of the citizen.

Small Advertisements.

The charge for prepaid advertisements is 2/- per insertion up to 24 words, and one penny per word afterwards. Advertisements not paid for in advance cost 3/- per insertion for 24 words and twopence per word afterwards. Space costs 5/- per inch. Thick type in all cases 20 per cent. extra. Seven insertions for the price of six.

EXPRESSION, DEBATE, DELIVERY

A Psychological Aid to Memory and Fluency of Speech. Rhetorlogue and Glossary of Logic, 11/-. The Rhetorlogue Mnemonic Wheel, 21/-. The Rhetorlogue Practice Charts, 1/-, post free. From OWEN BENNISON, 46, Bessborough Place, Westminster, S.W.1. Money Orders crossed " & Co." Kindly mention this paper. Details sent post free.

INTERNATIONAL PLAY CLUB. — Members wanted for Education Dramatic Work (Shaw, Galsworthy, Barrie, etc.), at home and abroad. Successful tour in Germany last Whitsun. Subscription moderate. Auditions for beginners. Free membership experienced amateurs.—Apply SECRETARY, 1, Aberdeen Court, Aberdeen Rd., N.5.

NATURE Can Cure You. Helpful Guide free.— NATUROPATH, 47x, Huddlestone Road, London, N.W.2.

HOTELS.

EDINBURGH. St. Mary's (Private), 32, Palmerston Place. Fine situation. Convenient train and tram. Liberal table. 'Phone 23872.

DEAN FOREST, Severn-Wye Valleys.—Beautiful Holiday Home (600 ft. up); 80 rooms; 5 acres; billiards; dancing; motors; garage. 52/6 to 70/- week. Prospectus.—Littledean House, Littledean, Glos.   314

CLUBS, ETC.

THE LIGHTHOUSE, 117, Union Street, Borough, S.E.1. Good accommodation at less than popular prices. Nice little hall to rent; nominal fee.—Apply MANAGER.

DRESS AGENCY.

ECONOMY Dress Agency, 11, Riseholme Road, Lincoln, sells on commission Gentlepeople's Clothing to workers of all classes.

LITERARY.

AUTHORS invited contribute "Writer's Own Magazine," 6d. monthly. Specimen free. MSS., all kinds also required for Book issue.— STOCKWELL, LTD., 29, Ludgate Hill, London.

PRETTY laughable Plays. Moderate Royalties. List 2d.—Miss BOILEAU, Knockeven, Southbourne, Bournemouth.

STORIES, Articles, Serials and Verse wanted. Payment on acceptance. Post MSS. to Secretary, P.L.A., Pinders Road, Hastings (Est. 1911).

RESTAURANTS.

DISTRIBUTIST Restaurant.—"The Owl," 3, Kingly Street, W.1. (behind Robinson and Cleaver's Regent Street). Lucheons and Teas. Members of the League can meet each other here.

APARTMENTS.

COUNTRY Farmhouse, quiet, sea and mountain air.—WILLIAMS, Tymaur, Bryncrag, Tonynonsea, N. Wales.

CHEERFUL Bed and Dressing-Room, use sitting, good cooking; suit elderly gentleman. — White Rose Cottage, All Cannings, near Devizes.

The Proprietors exercise all possible care in the acceptance of advertisements for "G.K.'s Weekly."

MISCELLANEOUS.

"COTTAGE Antiques." Old Lancashire spindle-black, ladder-back and Windsor chairs, oak corner cupboard, carved oak chest, Staffordshire figures, brass candlesticks; beautiful Paisley shawls and other genuine antiques at moderate prices.—Mrs. HARRISON, Highcroft, Park Lane, Burnley, Lancs.

EASILY MADE MONEY. Sell Linen Bargains in your spare time. Particulars from J. HENDERSON, Milner Street, Belfast, N. Ireland.

GOOD Printing at low trade rates. Specimens and prices free. — HATHERLEY, 43A, Trentham Street, Southfields, London.

HANDKERCHIEFS, fancy, printed, scalloped Irish manufacture, suitable Bazaars, etc. Sample dozen, 3/3 post paid.—MANUEL, Standford. Bordon, Hants.

HARRIS TWEED. Any length cut. Patterns free. — JAMES ST. TWEED DEPOT, 392, Stornoway, Scotland.

HOMEWORKERS wanted, whole or spare time. Rug-making. Earn 30/- to 70s/- weekly. — YORKS RUG COMPANY, Redcar, Yorks.

HOUSEKEEPER, thoroughly experienced, stores, linen, staff, etc., desires position, hotel or private; could relieve cook.—Samble Cottage, Llanreath, Pembroke, Dock.

THE SUNBEAM, a little paper for the deafened, 1/3 annually, post free. Also join the Friendly Corner, a cheery postal club for the deafened. 2/6 annually. 2/6 entrance fee.—X22, G.K.'s WEEKLY.

LADY Specialist in excellent substitutes for impaired hearing can supply hearing aids and lip-reading lessons, both of great assistance in business and social life.—X32, G.K.'s WEEKLY.

LOVELY, warm Men's Home-Knitted Socks, 2/6 pair.—SCORE, Station Road, Liss.

MONEY easily earned in spare time by selling Rubber Stamps; particulars free.—RICHFORD, Ltd., Snow Hill, London.

NEEDLE, Cases for Bazaars, Masonic Ladies' nights, etc. Buy direct from Factory. Send for 5/6, 10/6 or 21/- parcel of assorted kinds Post free.—Dept. G.K., B. HAMPTON SON & Co., Ltd., Victoria Street, Redditch.

PRINTING 10,000 Handbills or Billheads at 3/3 per 1,000. Memorandums, Postcards, Duplicate Books, Envelopes, Posters, etc. Large range of samples, 3d. postage.—MEAD & SON, Dept. P., Sandy, Bedfordshire.

REAL Shetland Harris Wool Hand-Woven Tweed, 28 ins. wide, 8/6 per yard. Scotch Tweed, 56 ins wide, 12/6 per yard. Patterns free. —FAIRCLOTH (Dept. 55), Stromness, Orkney.

SHOWCARDS, Pictures, Letters, in Colours Simultaneously. Owen recent invention. Directions 7½d.—WRIGHT, Willis's Place, Wisbech.

SWEETMAKING, complete course, 2/9 post free; CAKE DECORATION, complete course, 2/9, post free. Both courses 5/-, post free. Or send for Free Particulars and Price Lists to see complete contents before purchasing. — G. R. LAMB, M.A. (Cantab.), C.D.A., Dept. HL., Newent, Glos

"ELBIE" DUSTLESS DUSTERS. Antiseptic, Sanitary. Absorbent Healthy. For Household Use. Office, Store and Garage. Tested and Approved by "Good Housekeeping Institute." Awarded Certificate of Merit by "Institute of Hygiene." Awarded Gold Medal at Paris, Brussels, Bristol. 1/- each p.f. The dust is collected in the fabric. The article dusted is polished as well. No shaking required; it leaves no lints. After washing is as good as new. Sold by all ironmongers, stores, etc., or BATLEY & CO. (K. Dept.), STOCKPORT.

WEARING APPAREL.

LADIES' Coloured Cambric Underwear, lovely embroidered, full fashioned; sky, white, lemon, helio or pink; 4 garments; 2 chemises, 2 knickers, 6/6; O.S., 7/6, post free.—GOLD, 48, King Street, Ramsgate.

EDUCATIONAL.

ST. JOSEPH'S PREPARATORY SCHOOL
Burwash, Sussex.

CONDUCTED BY THE SALESIAN FATHERS. Most healthily situated midway between Tunbridge Wells and Hastings. 1½ hours from Charing Cross. Ages from 6 to 14. School matron. Central Heating. Modern Sanitation. Wireless. Electric Lighting. For Prospectus apply to the PRINCIPAL.   29

OFFICES.

CITY Office (share of) with 'phone, 10/- week, address only 3/6 week.—REILLY, 8, South St., E.C.2. (Clerkenwell 1581).

TYPEWRITERS, REPAIRS, ETC.

TYPEWRITERS from £2; easy payment arranged. Repairs. Duplicators. 'Phone Central 8210. Typewriter experts, 55, Little Britain, E.C.1.

TYPEWRITING, DUPLICATING, ETC.

AUTHORS' MSS. and Technical Typewriting correctly executed; 10d. per 1,000. — Mrs. CLIFSTONE, 11, Cromwell Avenue, Bromley, Kent.

DUPLICATING EXPERT offers 50 extra copies free—SCHOOLMASTER, 71, Brackenbury Road, Preston.

INCREDIBLE! Unbeatable! Duplicated typewritten matter, 3/- per 100. — E. S. COY, 1, Homer Terrace, Bootle.

LITERARY Typewriting carefully and promptly executed. MS. 1/- per 1,000 words; carbon copy 3d. per 1,000.—Miss NANCY McFARLANE (J.), 44, Elderton Road, Westcliff-on-Sea.

LONDON'S Premier Typewriting Service. 1,000 words 10d., carbon copy 2d. Perfect work guaranteed. Authors' MSS. a speciality.—"FLEET" Typewriting Agency, 153, Fleet Street, E.C.4.

TYPEWRITING and Duplicating Expert. MSS. typed, 1,000 words 1/-; carbon 3d.—Miss HILL, 48, Kensington Park Road, W.11.

TYPEWRITING accurately executed; 1,000 words 1s.; carbon 3d. Free specimen. Shorthand.—Miss THAYRE, 22, Gray's Inn Residences, E.C.1.

TYPEWRITING and Duplicating Authors' MSS typed 10d. per 1,000 words; carbon copy 3d. per 1,000 words. Testimonials, circulars, etc., duplicated. Envelopes addressed. Prompt and efficient work.—MARION YOUNG (C.), 7a, Station Road, Balham, S.W.12.

TYPEWRITING. — 8d. thousand. French and Spanish translations (into English), 9d. folio.—NEWCOMBE, 36, Wilson Street, Middlebrough.

NEAT, ACCURATE TYPING
Intelligently executed. MSS. 1s. 1,000 words. Quotations given. Miss N. Netherwood, 128, Park Rd., Loughborough.

MUSIC, INSTRUMENTS, ETC.

BANJOS, Mandolins, Drums, Violins, Guitars, Ukuleles, Accordions, Saxophones, Xylophones. List free. — PALMERS, Dept. J., 135, Lathorpe Road, Middlesbrough.

MEDICAL.

THINNING Bath Salts. Excessive fat just vanishes. Excellent for rheumatism, tired feet. 1/9 post free.—HELEN TEMPLE, 171a, Sloane Street, S.W.1.

RHEUMATISM.—For particulars of an invigorating cure that does not cause depression send addressed envelope to CHILD, 234, Eastern Road, Brighton.

GREAT Herbal Asthma Remedy, most successful. Stamped envelope particulars.—MASON, Cowesby, Northhallerton, Yorks.

BLOOD Pressure, Heart Attacks, Giddiness, Strokes, Headaches, Indigestion, Constipsion, etc., are most due to arterio-sclerosion, ets., are mostly due to arterio-sclerosis (hardening of the arteries).—Dr. Mladejovski's simple remedy DROSIL. "Numerous experimenters have proved the value of this discovery."—Daily News. Booklet free.—DROSIL AGENCY (Box B 26, Sun Street, London, E.C.2.

Published by the Proprietors, G.K.'s WEEKLY, LTD., 2, Little Essex Street, Strand, London, W.C.2 (incorporating THE NEW WITNESS). Telephone No. City 1978. Printed by THE MARSHALL PRESS, LTD., 7, Milford Lane, Strand, London, W.C.2. Sole Agents for Australasia: Gordon & Gotch (Australasia, Ltd.). Sole Agents for South Africa: Central News Agency, Ltd.

GK.'s WEEKLY, DECEMBER 28, 1929. THE EXODUS FROM EUROPE: By G.K.C.

G.K.'s Weekly

EDITED BY G. K. CHESTERTON.

No. 250.—Vol. X.   Week ending Saturday, December 28, 1929.   PRICE SIXPENCE. YEARLY (52 ISSUES) 28s. 0d.

Telephone No. Temple Bar 1978.   [Registered at G.P.O. as a Newspaper.]   *Offices 2, Little Essex Street, Strand, W.C.2*

CONTENTS :

THE END OF A DECADE.

ARBITRARY and artificial as a division of time, the decade is generally ignored by its own generation. The 'Nineties never spoke of themselves as Naughty, the 'Eighties never thought of themselves as Elegant, or as 'Eighties, or as anything as the Present. It is not until another ten or twenty years have passed and the period has acquired an interest in the eyes of history, that the more casual student, in order to fasten his impressions to some sort of rough-and-ready chronological mooring, adopts the decade and credits with a distinctive character.

The Nineteen-Twenties complete their course this week; and it happens that the end of the decade coincides quite nearly with the end of a distinct phase in our history and the world's, just as the beginning of it coincided quite nearly with the beginning of that phase. So that whether in half-a-century's time they speak of us as the Terrible 'Twenties, or the Triumphant 'Twenties, or the Tiresome 'Twenties, or the Tawdry 'Twenties, they will be at least to that extent right if they speak of the 'Twenties as of a period distinct.

It was in 1919, by the prestige of Wilson, that that doctrine first assumed importance, the wide acceptance of which has shaped the story of the subsequent eleven years. It is a doctrine not easy to define in a few words, unless we take the easy course of accepting its own terms and call it post-war idealism. It would be more accurate to describe it as a cold, material cynicism, deriving ultimate authority from the fear of death. It is that theory which teaches men to value

peace above honour, comfort above freedom, security above courage, life at any price above death in any cause.

In its first expressions it was applied to international relations, and there it met, and bent before, the resistence of the older traditions of civilisation. The memory of Belgium and the little nations was still vivid enough in 1919 to force the establishment, under precarious guarantees, of Poland and Jugo-Slavia. Anger against Germany still ran too high to be ignored; if it failed to put the Kaiser's neck in a noose, it did at least succeed in extracting fine promises of reparation. But although the new, cold humanism bent before the pressure of Justice and Anger, it did not break. An enormous propaganda machine was created which ceaselessly dinned its precepts into the mind of men. Peace before honour. Comfort before freedom. Safety before courage. And the constant dull repetition had its effects.

From imposing this theory on the former conception of international relations, its exponents passed on to apply it to domestic affairs, to industrial problems. In industry the doctrine adopted such slogans as Organisation, Centralisation, Rationalisation, the Elimination of Wasteful Competition. First it was argued that it was better for two tradesmen to agree upon a high price and to divide the business peacefully than to compete: better still for them to unite and to become one tradesmen. Then, that it was better for a master to pay his men subsistence wages than to risk a strike; that it was better for the men to accept his terms than to incur hardship. It was better to merge than to compete. It was better to compromise than to strike. It was better to buy your enemy, or to be bought, than to fight.

That teaching has now secured general acceptance; if it is not yet universally acknowledged by the Latin and the Slav, it has at least established itself in North Eastern Europe and America. There the old traditions are forced on to the defensive and are losing ground; and for the first time man's weakest failure to maintain his own standards is preached with the authority of gods and governments as his highest duty.

That triumph is the achievement of the decade. In the next ten years it must be disputed if those standards are ever to be re-established from which all civilisation have derived their authority. For this is the sign of the new humanism, which is not to be found in doctrines more violent and more evil : that it rots the minds and hearts of men and takes from them courage to revolt. It is well that the 'Twenties are over.

NOTES OF THE WEEK

Our estimate last week of the voting on the Coal Bill was quite frantically wrong. Towards the middle of the week, the *Morning Post,* which besides being frequently honest was in this case particularly interested in the rejection of the Bill, lashed the Conservative Party into action, with a vigour which commands our admiration. At the same time, the Cabinet, without committing itself, hinted broadly that whatever the result of the division, it had no intention of resigning. The danger of a new election somewhat diminished, the Conservative Whips responded heartily to the castigation of the *Post.* Leave was cancelled for those M.P.'s who had intended to start their Christmas holidays on the Thursday, and a hundred telegrams were sent recalling those who had already gone out of town. There is no doubt a way of making it clear to the recipient that a whip is really meant to be obeyed, and not merely intended to impress the public. As a result the Conservatives turned up in such strength that the Liberals, who had committed themselves to the bluff, had to stand down six of their members and lend two to the government in order to avoid bringing the Socialists down. As it was, the issue was close enough to cause them some anxiety.

*   *   *   *

The Bill will no doubt undergo modification in committee; but it is to be doubted whether, even when it emerges for the third reading, it will call for unqualified praise. In several respects it makes changes in the right direction. The provision for the reduction of half-an-hour in the working-day of the miner will meet with general approval. The argument that it must increase the price of coal to the consumer, even were it proved, is invalid. The first charge upon any undertaking, large or small, must be the decent maintenance of its workers. The faults of the Bill lie mainly in the elaboration of the scheme, which it projects, radiating from Whitehall. While, if we accept the reasonable view that minerals are the property of the State, there must be machinery centralised to the extent that may be necessary to protect the State's interest. No one, with the interests of the miners, or of the community at large, can view with anything but concern the prospect of the concentration of all effective authority in the Board of Trade. The Bill has evidently been drawn up by the present Government with the prospect in view of trouble in the future between the State authorities and the miners. There is a place in the scheme for well-behaved Trade Unionists who pass the scrutiny of the Board of Trade; but there is a careful grip retained by the central executive. We believe that the miners as a whole are satisfied with the Bill. We offer it to their consideration that, under it and the million amending Bills, orders and regulations to which it will give birth, a strike will be crime, to be put down by all the forces at the disposal of the State. We are not altogether as pleased as they appear to be to see a million families placed under this servitude.

*   *   *   *

Captain Eckersley, a recent acquisition to the Socialist platform, has been expressing his views on the B.B.C., of which he was at one time chief engineer. He objects to the inclusion in the programmes of such items as cricket, football and racing results. The B.B.C. is a national institution, and, as such, should broadcast only national or world news. The minority (he actually refers to them as a minority) who want information on these and other frivolous subjects should wait till next day's newspaper supplies their need. But we presume that in the Socialist Utopia all our newspapers would be national institutions, and that the same objection would arise to their supplying news, other than that of national importance. However, the problem may not arise, as by that time racing, cricket and football will probably have been prohibited. Capt. Eckersley would also rather see bulletins issued upon the style and meaning of Mr. Vernon Bartlett's talks than upon the society gossip columns of the *Tatler.* The snobbery of the snobbish is objectionable, but on the whole we prefer it to the snobbery of the intellectual.

*   *   *   *

Some of the romance of Polar exploration has gone now that the explorers can keep in touch with civilisation by means of wireless. There are three expeditions in the neighbourhood of Antarctica at present and we hear morsels of news from one or another of them almost daily. The news is generally not of a sensational character but often amounts to little more than a jotting in a diary recording events with a brevity which does not call up a mental picture for the reader. Reviewed in perspective in a book those same events take on a significance they cannot be expected to have when set down in isolated paragraphs. The real value of wireless will be seen if it ever becomes necessary to send out a call for help. Wireless would not have saved Scott and his companions, nor is it certain that it would have helped Shackleton in the rescue of his men from Elephant Island, for even when he reached Valparaiso he had the utmost difficulty in getting a relief ship for them. Certainly that was during the War, but would he have got that ship any sooner by a wireless appeal? Perhaps he would, but for the sake of the present explorers we hope that the need for a test of this sort will never arise. There may be occasions when the explorer asks himself whether the apparatus is worth its weight in food. That is a searching question and the answer ought to be in the affirmative.

The true nature of the new Education (School Attendance) Bill and its implications are unlikely to be known to the general public until its provisions are in operation. Its ostensible purpose is to continue compulsory elementary education from 14 to 15 years by amending the Education Act of 1921. The Government is concerned not so much with Education as with the state of the labour market, and the extension of official control of the working classes. By this ruse of using the Compulsory Education System it will be possible to keep children off the labour market for another year and at the same time extend the dependence of the working classes on the State by extending the dole system to children of 14 to 15. This Bill provides for a dole of 5s. per week per child, subject to the usual examination of the family affairs by the official Inquisition. No one in his senses can pretend that the little extra smattering of algebra and spelling which the children may learn will make them any better as machine-minders, or dole-drawers, or whatever similar calling the Socialist State prepares for them. The cost to the parents who do not want their children so mis-educatd and pauperised, and the citizens who save the State the burden of children, will be five and a half million pounds in the first year, rising rapidly. Does any normal citizen want it?

* * * *

In its career of crime the germ of Influenza has found many a curious habitat, but none so strange as Chicago, that famous American health-resort on the shores of the Great Lakes. It is readily understandable, however, that, in a city so noted for the purity and peacefulness of its inhabitants, the presence of anything so criminal as this notorious wrong-doer could not remain long unnoticed, and it must have been a comparatively easy task for Professor Falk to effect its isolation. Influenza, as its Spanish name implies, is of alien origin, and despite its menace to the well-being of our Empire, we have allowed it far greater freedom than our American cousins, whose detestation of aliens is only equalled by their toleration of them. We would, nevertheless, feel more assured that Influenza had at last been cornered and conquered if we were convinced that it differed in any appreciable degree from the ague of our grandfathers, or from the colds and catarrhs of to-day. If the mere finding of a certain speck under a microscope, and the subsequent preparation of a serum which caused a number of monkeys to cease using their aseptic handerchiefs presaged the certainty of a cure, we would be the first to congratulate the discoverer, but, alas, we have been stung too often. We seem to remember that during this century the germ of every disease to which flesh is heir, has been isolated and has received due adulation in the Press, complete with photographs and family history. Yet, in not more than six cases of well-known diseases has the provision of even a palliative followed; various sera and anti-toxins have been prepared and lauded to the skies; they have cured and killed in almost equal proportions, and have been successful in direct ratio to the amount of publicity they enjoyed. The wholesale chemists and patent-medicine mongers have reaped the harvest, and the public has continued to sniff and suffer. Our grandfathers, using a corkscrew instead of a microscope, and a tumbler in place of a serum syringe, found, in a glass of hot toddy, as good a specific against " Influenza " as any bio-chemist or bacteriologist has ever discovered.

IN PARLIAMENT

We have always suspected that the Prohibitionist movement in this country, as in America, is largely a matter of vested interests. On Monday, Lady Astor confirmed our suspicions. In an unguarded moment she begged that the Minister of Agriculture would " . . . always bear in mind the brewers' profits." The occasion of this revelation was a series of questions by Mr. Wise on the possibility of Government control of barley imports. Lady Astor does not allow her sense of perspective to be upset by whatever the interests are that move her, for on the same occasion she also asked, "Will the right hon. gentleman remember that bread is more important than beer ! "

The Minister of Agriculture is to issue a circular to County Councils on the desirability of their exercising their powers for acquiring land for smallholdings, but, all the same, we feel that the Smallholdings Acts will remain a dead letter. While replying to Viscount Elmley and Captain Bennett, Mr. Buxton revealed incidentally that one of the effects of the late Government's much vaunted Smallholdings Act has been to remove the Ministry's power of forcing the hands of defaulting County Councils by acting for those who refuse to provide smallholdings.

We never for a moment believed that Mr. Thomas's monstrous programme of relief works would have the slightest effect either way, and it has therefore come as a considerable surprise to us that the regulations under which the works are carried out have already led to an increase in unemployment. Grants are calculated on the basis of wages paid to labour recruited from the ranks of the unemployed. We have just been informed of cases in which permanent employers have been dismissed, left on the dole for a fortnight, and then taken on again, in order that the maximum grants might be obtained.

This state of affairs is similar to that which has arisen under the Local Government Act. The administration of various services was to be improved by their transfer from the District Councils to the County Councils, the transfer to be as from 1st April, 1930. The immediate result of the Act has been to throw those services into such a chaotic condition that, when the County Councils take them over, straightening them out again, let alone improving them, will absorb all their energies for many years to come. Many Rural Councils, believing that the County Councils would be left to " hold the baby," have dismissed their highway staffs and spent nothing on road maintenance during the past year. The deterioration which has resulted will take many years to remedy and will greatly add to the burden of county rates. The same applies to other local services, but though duly authenticated cases have been laid before the Ministers concerned the Government remains officially ignorant and incredulous.

Captain Crookshank was vastly indignant with Miss Bondfield who was " exactly one minute and a half in proposing to the Committee, at a quarter to twelve, a Vote of £3,500,000." He did not expect even a Socialist Government to deal with national finances in that spirit. A somewhat grim contrast to that airy lavishness was revealed when Mr. Adamson blusteringly endeavoured to dodge the issue, raised by Major Wood, of whether the recent East Anglian fishing fleet disaster was not attributable to the Government's refusal of credits to enable fishermen to replace their worn-out boats and gear.

Dictator or Parliament?

By Gregory Macdonald

ON the Feast of Guy Fawkes the sittings of the Polish Sejm were postponed for one month by the Speaker, after a dramatic conversation with Marshal Pilsudski, because a large group of Army officers, supporters of the Marshal, refused to leave the building. From that time until December 5th, when the Sejm met once more, political activities were openly expressed only by the propaganda of the Party organs, the frequent confiscation of anti-Government newspapers, and the carefully-prepared speeches of various Cabinet Ministers in the principal towns. There were no major sensations. There was only a flicker of national indignation when some British Socialists reverted to the Victorian habit of preaching the theories of Walter Bagshot and John Richard Green to a nation that had seen Napoleon. But almost immediately the interference of the British Socialists was seen in its right perspective, and forgotten.

Under the Constitution of 1921, the meeting of the Sejm for the Budget Session could not be postponed for a longer period than one month. During that period not even the most experienced politician could forecast what would happen in December. The mastery of the situation lay in the hands of Marshal Pilsudski, a soldier-politician whose chief weapon has always been the weapon of surprise. Purely as a Minister responsible to Parliament he was awkwardly placed. His own supporters, the Non-Party Block of the Centre, were outnumbered by the Opposition of the Right, led by the National Democrats, and of the Left, led by the extreme Socialists. The National Democrats, whose programme is one of a Catholic Renaissance, were the old enemies of the Marshal during the Partition period, when he sided with the Central Powers, while they placed their hopes for the future in the Triple Alliance. They have always been his opponents. The Socialists, on the other hand, were his supporters during the events of 1926, and only in the last three years have they swung over to the Opposition. His old enemies and his late friends combined could easily pass a vote of No Confidence against the Government of which he is actually the leader, though nominally only the Minister for War. The Budget prepared by the Minister for Finance (whose predecessor had already been impeached) could be rejected. And the Marshal's determination to reform the Constitution in the direction of the American model, so as to increase the power of the President at the expense of Parliament, could not be achieved in that chamber.

But it was also clear that Marshal Pilsudski would never admit the politicians of the Sejm to be his final judges. He has always regarded the Sejm as an institution worth preserving in hopes of better things; though its past record has been one of sub-division into a number of weak Parties, and of a succession of Cabinets formed out of their ephemeral coalitions, during the critical years when the foundations of a new Poland were to be laid. Marshal Pilsudski took office after a *coup d'état* supported by the Army in 1926. The work of his Government has been decisive and varied. In the last resort he relies upon the Army still; although there is in the country a great body which regards him with more than the reverence paid by the Italians to Mussolini.

Pilsudski, after all, was imprisoned by the Czar and by the Kaiser, was exiled, recruited the armies of Poland, defeated the Bolsheviks at the gates of Warsaw, and then took his part in the reconstruction of the State. But the opposition to him in the country at large is not to be despised. It is made up of his old opponents in the complicated politics of the Partition period, together with a large number of the intellectuals, of the Socialists (who control the Unions), of the *petite bourgeoisie,* and of the students, who are important as the politicians of the future. Of these last, eighty per cent. belong to the National Democrats. For the Socialists the present régime is too reactionary. The intellectuals and the students object to it as a confederacy of Free Masons and Jews. Yet nobody can deny that the Government is led by the greatest personality in Poland, or that its practical policies have been carried out with remarkable success. It is also clear that the Opposition in the Sejm, united only against Pilsudski, could not combine for long to form an alterative Government.

The careful speeches of the Cabinet Ministers were built around one recurring passage: that the Government would carry out its policies, and especially the policy of reforming the Constitution, by force if force were necessary. It was expected, then, that Marshal Pilsudski would intervene at the Sejm, that possibly he would have it dissolved and appeal to the country by a General Election, or that possibly he would suppress the Sejm altogether and establish a personal Government in its stead. However, the Sejm met in comparative calm, without the intervention of the Minister for War. A vote of No Confidence was proposed and passed by some 240 votes to 120. The Prime Minister, Switalski, delivered the resignation of his Cabinet to President Moscicki, who accepted it. The next move lay with the President; but it must be remembered that the President was nominated by Marshal Pilsudski, with whom he works in the closest collaboration.

This review of the situation is written in the middle of a crisis which will produce the unexpected at every turn. At the present moment it is to be expected that the President will invite another one of Pilsudski's followers, possibly M. Matuszewski, to form a Government, which will continue the same policies as the old, and with nearly the same Ministers, but which will lean rather more towards the Socialists of the Left. The crisis has turned, then, into an invitation to the Socialists to co-operate more closely with the Pilsudski régime against the parties of the Right. If the new Government also suffers an adverse vote (for the Sejm will never see eye to eye with Pilsudski on the constitutional question or on the question of liberty of the Press) the alternative remains of a personal rule based upon force under the ægis of the Marshal. Pilsudski's ultimate sanction is the Army. But first he may assume the Premiership himself. Or he may withdraw from active politics for a time so as to demonstrate the futility of the politicians who oppose him, so that he may return with increased power to carry out his policies without the impediment of the Sejm.

So far as an outsider can form an opinion upon the extremely complicated politics of modern Poland, it seems that the rulership of Pilsudski is the practical necessity of the moment. There is no respectable alternative. But Pilsudski is unlike Mussolini in leaving behind him no scheme for perpetuating his own power—the constitutional reform calls either for one strong man succeeding the other, or else for a President invested nominally with wide executive powers but in fact the tool of vested interests, like the Republican President of the United States—and it is certain enough that the rulers of Poland in the future will belong increasingly to the National Democratic Party or to its allies.

On the one hand, then, this crisis means that the *coup d'état* of 1926 must be either justified or disowned. Or it may be regarded as the temporary unsettlement of a new State, to be expected after the first efforts of construction. The salvation of it all is that primarily the present quarrel is a politicians' quarrel. The people are not seriously divided on any question; but the politicians cannot forget the real differences caused by the Partitions, when a century of division among three Empires engendered many philosophies radically different. If Marshal Pilsudski can maintain his power without perpetuating in the new generation the bitter animosities of the old, he will be succeeded, in fact, by his political opponents, but by younger men who have not had to endure his history. Their rule may express itself in Parliament, in oligarchy or in autocracy, but it will stand first of all for the unity of the Polish people.

[The above article was mailed to us from Poland by our contributor. Obviously, in a political situation such as he describes, events follow very rapidly, and there have been further developments since he dispatched the article to us. The situation, however, does not seem to have altered fundamentally, though, in any case, we welcome the article as being one of the very rare reviews of Polish affairs that the British public gets first hand.—ED.]

A Wordy Warfare

By Van Norman Lucas

THERE is a fight coming which is going to be great fun to watch, or rather listen to—for it will be literally a verbal fight. Not the least of the fun arises from the fact that the perspective combatants do not seem to have realised yet the fact that they are to fight. Perhaps they have; perhaps already secret diplomacy is at work finding a way out; but it is difficult to see how a fight can be avoided, as *one* of the two must win, there can be no compromise. Neither, of course, of the two will lose in any way except pride; the sufferers, if either win, will be as usual the general masses.

The fight that is coming is between the B.B.C. and the American "Talkie" kings.

Let us look at the facts. When broadcasting became the latest fad it succeeded for a time on the appeal of novelty. The deficiencies and insufficiencies were not noticed at all seriously until the novelty began to wear off. But they were many and inevitable. Entertainers can be roughly divided, dialectically, into five classes. There are those of the "posh," the well-off dialect; the "Irish" dialect; the Lancashire or Yorkshire pronunciation; the "farmers" and country yokel type; and the foreign pidgin English (which covers French, Italian, Spanish, German, Swiss or Dutch—except that the last two require a certain additional technique in yodelling).

These stage dialects were all right so long as they were used only to audiences in the large towns, especially in London. The truest to type was the Lancashire entertainer, chiefly because he really did come from Lancashire. He came, in fact, in such quantity that it simply was not worth while imitating him. The "posh" and well-off

accent always went down very well, chiefly because the "posh" and well-off type is too ridiculous to allow of exaggeration. The others were only successful in places foreign to and ignorant of the real type and speech.

But broadcasting upset all this nice arrangement. Real Irishmen not only listened-in but broadcast (a nasty shock to those many who only regarded the receiving set as a sort of home extension of the music-hall or theatre). So did farmers and country yokels. So did all sorts of real people. With the result that we had simply a glut of music (an universal language). But the B.B.C. obviously did not think it good enough; so they issued proclamations, issued papers and journals, and began to instruct the people as to the *correct* pronunciation of the English language.

Then, following quickly upon broadcasting came the "Talkie" fad; and now we are in a mess. For not only are there now various English dialects, but those of America to contend with. Mr. Atkinson, the well-known film critic, in a recent article summed up the situation very well. I quote the following passage :—

" A problem that seems to defy solution is that presented by the prevailing or characteristic American voice, as distinct from dialect.

" Dialect, in any form, is not necessarily unpleasant, and some American dialects are pleasing to the ear, but there can be no doubt about the strong reaction in this country against the " tinny " note in the characteristic American voice, irrespective of the slang or colloquialisms in vogue.

" The ruling factor is that American audiences, for whom films are primarily made, have not taken kindly to the purely English voice, and profess to find a difficulty in understanding it.

" What pleases them we call ' nasal,' and what pleases us they call ' adenoidal.' "

And this is where the fight is going to start. It is unnecessary and quite useless to imagine that a remedy will be found in making British " Talkies " for England, and American " Talkies " for America. At least it is useless for the moment or for some considerable time yet. Eventually, in all probability, unless it becomes feasible and possible for all the world to talk one language and all to talk the same way, some departmentalisation will be evolved; the limitations of " Talkies " as a medium recognised; but there is too much vested capital at stake just now to hope for any such sane solution for a long time.

So who or what is going to win? Will the nasal predominate or the adenoidal? Shall we say " guy " or " fellōh "? It is going to be very interesting. I quote again from Mr. Atkinson :—

" Britain's strength would appear to be in the cultured, English voice, but as there seems to be no demand in America for the cultured English voice it is difficult to say what kind of talkie made in Britain would appeal to the American masses. . .

" Our industry will recover, but as it is dependent mainly on America for the installation and efficiency of the apparatus which will enable it to compete with America, the initiative is likely to remain with our Transatlantic rivals for a long time . . ."

Oscar Wide once remarked that there was little difference between English and American except, of course, in the language.

The Newfoundland Fisherman

By W. R. A.

THE main premise of Distributism, that it is better for a man to be his own master, and have a means of livelihood securely dependent on his own exertions and not on the whim of employers, has always seemed to me indisputable. But in deference to the waywardness of things in general, G.K.'s WEEKLY, for example, rightly recognises that the principle cannot everywhere be applied, and contents itself with the proposition that a wider ownership of property is desirable. Railways and coal mines require co-operative effort, directors and directed, or certain types may find the moral strain of independence too burdensome and actually prefer set hours at set tasks. I have recently had the opportunity of observing the economic situation in a country of small property owners—Newfoundland, the oldest and perhaps the least known British Colony—and possibly a brief account of conditions there may be of interest to Distributists. It will illustrate the complexity of the modern commercial world and the intellectual difficulties besetting the convinced believer in small ownership.

In Newfoundland the majority of men are to-day independent. Practically all fishermen by trade, they own their own boats, tackle, houses and land. As a rule their whole livelihood is from the fisheries and the amount of money a man makes during the fishing season, at any rate in good years when cod is plentiful, depends on his own skill and industry. Agriculture, which is confined to vegetables, and the keeping of a little livestock, both difficult in some parts owing to climatic and other conditions, are secondary considerations to the Newfoundlander. His wife is left in charge of the cabbages and goats. He is primarily a man of the sea.

He does not often work completely on his own. Small crews are needed to man boats and haul in heavy cod traps, and to help with the splitting and salting of the fish. The schooners which run up to the Labrador fisheries in the summer require crews of 10 to 20, and generally the whole business of cod fishing (as now organised) is better handled by small groups of men than by single men in very small boats. To-day these groups are often family groups—a father and his sons, with cousins, uncles and nephews thrown in, while wives and daughters often accompany the men to Labrador on their schooners. When the members of a group are not related they are usually near neighbours and work on a strict profit-sharing basis. Every schooner, and every shore fishing crew, must have a skipper, but he is only *primus inter pares,* with full command over his crew only in the emergencies of the sea.

Now this virtual independence in men following a skilled and dangerous calling produces a crop of virtues. The Newfoundlander is up to a point a very fine fellow. He greets a stranger without embarrassment as a man and a brother; with great respect for learning and piety (*e.g.,* doctors and clergymen) he has no sense of personal inequality. He will welcome you to his house with dignity and good manners, and often scarcely understand the offer of payment for a meal. Hospitality, as in all scattered and simple peoples, is usually free to the traveller. But it is on the sea that the Newfoundland fisherman is at his best. To take a trip in a Newfoundland fishing boat in a lumpy sea with the crew shouting crude jests at one another and visibly enjoying the exhilaration of wind and waves, is to realise that one is among free men.

The remote parts of Newfoundland are about 100 years behind the times. Old English words and sea chanties still linger; there are interminable sad ballads of schooners that struck shoals and were seen no more. An old fashioned puritan simplicity prevails.

There is, of course, another side to this pleasant picture. The Newfoundlander is often extremely obstinate and stupid in opposing changes obviously to his own advantage. Like all men of the peasant type he is intensely suspicious of the wisest reforms. He is often totally uneducated, and not very interested in anything except fish. Though he rarely swindles his immediate fellows he is completely dishonest in his dealing with large organisations and the government.

His precise economic situation is peculiar. He cannot produce all his own food, and flour, beef and many other things must be imported. Such necessities are usually bartered to the fishermen by fish merchants in a small way, or by agents of big firms, who take in return part of all of the annual catch. In the old days when few could read or write fishermen often found themselves unable to shake themselves clear of debt to the local trader; a little clever manipulation of accounts by the merchant kept him in thrall all his life. To-day a multiplicity of fish buyers and increasing education have made such slavery uncommon. It is also worth noticing that the hardship was not always on the side of the fisherman; in bad seasons the merchant often had to give families their winter supplies without return, for otherwise they would starve during the severe weather from January to May.

The present difficulty is that the whole system of fishing needs re-organisation if it is to compete with the highly organised fisheries of Scandinavia and Iceland. Newfoundland has lost several markets because the fish is prepared for export in 1929 in precisely the same way as it was in 1729. The by-products of the cod are not sufficiently utilised. Larger and faster boats and more up-to-date tackle would greatly increase the annual catch. The multiplicity of competing fish merchants prevents effective grading and supervision of the fish and no firm has by itself the power or capital to carry out reforms. In consequence of lost markets the price of salt cod remains low, and since the price of necessities such as flour, fishing tackle and clothes is rising, the Newfoundlander finds it harder to live every year. At present he is emigrating enthusiastically to the United States.

I have often thought that in his peculiar circumstances the Newfoundlander would be better off if the whole industry were in the hands of a trust. A trust could insist rigidly on a certain standard of fish and supply up-to-date fishing gear. Nominally, of course, the fisherman would be as independent as ever, but with only one firm to buy his fish and to supply him with stores he would have to toe the line, and there is no guarantee that a trust, once it achieved its monopoly, would give him a square deal. In this case the best solution of the difficulty would be energetic action on the part of the Government, but this happens to be outside the sphere of practical politics, while a move in the other direction is possible at any moment.

The truth is that it is difficult for independent men to exist in the world to-day at all, resisting the general pressure in the direction of standardisation and monopoly. We deplore the modern drift, but in certain special circumstances it may bring immediate obvious advantages. In the particular case in question it is difficult to balance exactly the gains and losses.

Straws in the Wind

EXODUS FROM EUROPE

By G. K. CHESTERTON

EVERYONE knows that, in the present collision of continents, we might say of hemispheres, England has taken the side of America. I regret it, for I wish she had taken the side of civilisation. There are a great number of things that I very warmly admire in America; but the moral superiority felt by a few Baptist millionaires, supported by their Baptist ministers, to the whole historic, heroic, poetic, patriotic and religious culture of Christendom is not one of them. Of all the qualities of any man of any nation, his superiority is the least likely to be superior. I know that the Englishman in his time was purse-proud; but I am not proud of such pride. Nor am I called upon to admire the particular sort of Yankee globe-trotter, who combines an irrational passion for looking at things with an impatient passion for looking down on them. Nevertheless, I have far more respect and sympathy for the honest, simple-hearted, thoroughly regular guy from Kansas or Omaha, who can hardly conceal his contempt for relics or ruined temples, to the pure-minded politician from Washington or Boston, who has exactly the same contempt for flags that have been like the last visions of martyrs or frontiers that have been traced in the blood of heroes. I think the man from Omaha is a thoroughly nice, jolly, genuine fellow; and I have drunk many a lager with him to the confusion of Prohibition. If he doesn't understand classical temples, he doesn't pretend to; and if he despises European social ranks, he is probably right in the sight of God. But the international idealist of America pretends that he does understand the nations of Europe; and then calmly proposes to abolish them; or at least to act as though they were already abolished. He chooses to suppose that there is no more difference between France and Germany than between Florida and Georgia; and then, when we tell him that the danger has really gone deeper than he knows, he treats his own ignorance as an intellectual superiority. And the joke of it is that, if even that deep division now closes up in a yet deeper European unity, he will understand that least of all. He has been plaintively wondering for a century why the French and German do not agree; and when they do agree, it will be in order to disagree with him.

It is unjust to judge any country by its politicians; but I must confess to a mild but rising resentment against a certain tone that threatens to drown all our own traditions; a certain drawling nasal duet of the Scottish and American accents, which is supposed to be very soothing, but which I for one find very exasperating. I do not think that very sentimental Scotch-American song will even do very much to put men in the mood for Peace; and I am quite sure it will not put them in the mood for Justice. I am not impressed when politicians point to themselves and say "Blessed are the Peacemakers," even when they have made some faint and hesitating efforts to disarm everybody except themselves. Nor, indeed, do I think it a very safe proceeding even in the practical world of problems like Disarmament. We have clung to the American skirts, not because of what is best in America; but rather because of what is worst and even least American. It is the mere fact that America happens to be the *pied a terre* of the wandering international financier. We have dipped the Union Jack in surrender to the Stars and Stripes, out of respect for the sort of Jew who cannot get into any club in New York. This is idiotic as well as ignominious; but anyhow it is simply a surrender to power; not even an effort to make a balance of power. We are not even siding against a powerful rival because he is powerful; as we did in the case of Louis XIV., of the great Napoleon or of the poor old Kaiser. We are merely siding with him because he is powerful; though we cannot share his power and may share some very upleasant results of his power. There has never been a power that was thus powerful without producing a great combination against it. Suppose such a combination comes swiftly, suddenly or perhaps with violence, what about us? In plain words, it looks to me very much as if we are to be smashed from the air by France and Germany, some little time before our whole population can take refuge in Chicago or some similar haven of peace and love.

But I do not mention this last point immediately for condemnation; but only to hold up my hands once more in dull amazement at the absence of controversy. It is certainly not impossible that some such catastrophe should be the result of the alliance; there is at least a case for the criticism of so vast a shifting of our centre of gravity; and yet it has hardly been criticised at all. In its ultimate upshot, it has hardly been discussed at all. A number of other things, or other words, have been discussed; such as Disarmament and Blockade and the obvious advantages of peace among nations. But the point which really was a matter for judgment has not been judged. After all, the cant against Secret Treaties and the diplomacy that produced the Great War, we are far less warned than we were before the Great War. There is far less frank and fundamental debate about an alliance with America than there was about an Entente with France. There was a far more organised *claque* for Mr. Snowden than there ever was for Sir Edward Grey. There are now far fewer voices pleading for the whole great civilisation of Europe than there were pleading, just before the War, for the pompous and unpopular militarism of Potsdam. Among the few who thus plead for the traditions of the central civilisation I am very proud to count myself; even if I were the only surviving Englishman to value the title of a good European.

Science and Morals

By G. C. Heseltine

MR. Bertrand Russell, besides holding a number of academic degrees, is a Fellow of the Royal Society, the most exclusive and distinguished scientific body in this country. He is the author of works on International Affairs, Social Science, Education, and Philosophy, including an "Introduction to Mathematical Philosophy." Therefore he may fairly be called a scientist. He is recognised as such by his contemporaries and by the literary and scientific Press as well as the general Press. Reviewers of his works and commentators on his opinions invariably refer to him as a scientist, a thinker, and a philosopher.

Whether he intends it or not, whether it is justifiable or not, his published works are in consequence put before the public as serious contributions to intelligent discussion on the subjects with which he deals. They are given the prestige of his reputation as a thinker and a scientist; therefore, unless he makes it clear that he is joking, his works will be taken seriously. It will be assumed that he has employed the careful thought and exact scientific method in handling his subject that his reputation as a scientist suggests and that any scientific enquiry, especially mathematical, demands. If he does not do so, he imposes upon younger and less well-trained minds than his own, and takes advantage of their ignorance and their respect for his scientific integrity to propagate unscientific, and therefore in the scientific sense, immoral principles.

His recent book *Marriage and Morals** will be widely read, especially by the adolescent, because the subject matter interests everybody most intimately, because he has been "outspoken" on matters of sex, and because many modern hedonists seek to salve their consciences by finding scientific and authoritative support for their sexual hedonism. Mr. Russell's book may not even attempt to justify such hedonists, but it will be expected to do so.

In estimating the value of this book it is necessary to consider the author's methods of argument, the soundness of his premises, the value of his evidence, the quality of his logic, the extent of his adherence to scientific method in the examination of his evidence, and in his inferences, and his regard for truth. This last will necessitate examining misstatements of fact, if any, and considering whether they are deliberate or due to ignorance, culpable or otherwise. It will be further necessary to consider to what extent he has allowed personal prejudices and bias to influence the discussion.

It is impossible to do this thoroughly in the course of a short article. The nature of this particular case demands, in fact, a book of rather greater length than Mr. Russell's. Let us therefore consider a few points at random. Unfortunately, since Mr. Russell has chosen, reasonably enough, to take the Catholic Church as the chief and most extreme advocate of the views to which he is opposed, I must make it clear that I am not here concerned with the Catholic Church as such or to defend its teachings. Catholic doctrine and practice is only considered here to test Mr. Russell's work on points of fact. In his own words, "We wish to appeal to reason" (p. 51); "We

* MARRIAGE AND MORALS. By Bertrand Russell (Geo. Allen and Unwin. 7s. 6d.)

must content ourselves with neutral and scientifically accurate phraseology " (p. 52).

On page 48 we find " Catholicism has always had a certain degree of toleration for what it held to be sin . . . and has been prepared to give absolution for fornication provided the sinner acknowledged his fault and did penance." The three conditions for effective absolution in the Catholic Church are stated in numerous standard works of reference. Mr. Russell here misstates them, omitting, either deliberately or through culpable ignorance, the one condition which is fatal to his accusation of toleration of sin.

On page 47 "Catholics . . . must hold that the great majority of Protestant children whom their political action causes to exist will endure eternal torment." Mr. Russell either knows this to be untrue or he is ignorant of what he can know for the asking.

As as example of Mr. Russell's method we may notice his assertion that " *the political action of Catholics* (in opposing state advocacy of contraception) *causes Protestant children to exist.*" In these ten words used to convey Mr. Russell's idea of linkage between cause and effect, there are at least ten disputable points which if disputed would reveal several implied misstatements of fact.

He consistently suppresses evidence which he knows to be fatal to his argument. For example he quotes St. Paul's words for a particular occasion and assumes that to be the whole teaching of the Church, except where he can quote the Fathers in support of extension of such teaching, insisting repeatedly that he states the whole case fairly. He makes great play with instances of verminous religious. He adduces no evidence in support of his statement that "to be covered with lice was an *indispensable* mark of a holy man " (my italics). In all his evidence against the Christian ethic this scientist is concerned not so much to examine that ethic critically as to discredit some individuals who are presumed to have accepted it. Even then his quotations are taken in every case from anti-Christian writers. The absence of quotations from Christian authorities on Christian teaching and practice is most marked throughout. Has Mr. Russell read them? If so, why does he suppress them, or write as if he had not read them?

Mr. Russell also appears to be driven to other strangely unscientific shifts to make his case. " The view of the orthodox moralist may be fairly stated as follows " (p. 81), is followed by : " It is possible to keep a girl in ignorance until the night of her marriage," " A boy should also be taught that in no circumstances is conversation on sexual subjects permissible, not even in marriage," and many such statements. In fairness, I must add that Mr. Russell precedes this sort of thing with " I fancy," but we might expect facts rather than fancies from a scientist of his eminence.

Then, in addition to putting his own view of his opponents as theirs, a common enough trick in politics or the more disreputable sort of controversy, Mr. Russell in discussing what he calls the "Taboo on Sex Knowledge" ignores the possibility of knowledge in any case being injurious. He mentions " Governmental activity is concealing facts—for example, the desire which every Government feels to prevent all mention of a defeat in war, for the knowledge of a defeat may lead to the downfall of the Government, which, though usually in the national interest, is, of course, not in the interest of the Government.'' He here ignores the possibility of such knowledge not being in the interest of the nation. Reticence about sexual facts, has its origin, he tells us, in a similar motive.

The passage about the Government contains an instance of the cheap sneer, which he also uses against the Christian moralist. It is a poor case, and a poor scientist, which needs to fall back on such sneers. Then he has also a general contempt, which he expresses arrogantly, for the opposite point of view, '' the silliness of the majority of mankind '' (p. 50); '' the well-known fact that the professional moralist in our day is a man of less than average intelligence '' (p.72) (this presumably refers, *inter alii,* to the Bishop of Birmingham); '' Whoever oppose these deduction must face the fact that he or she is not in favour of justice to the female sex '' (p. 72-3).

This sort of '' argument '' will not, of course, impress intelligent readers. Nor will it increase their respect for scientific bodies in which Mr. Russell is accepted as a scientist, a thinker, and a philosopher. Poor Science has been so much maligned by her devotees that the public treats her with more curiosity than respect. I do not know whether Mr. Russell regards culpable ignorance or suppression of the truth as the more scientific. It is for him to decide. For on that decision we may measure his services to contemporary thought and science.

On Blowing Out One's Brains

By J. D. Gleeson

LIKE many apparently simple tasks, that of blowing out one's brains is far more difficult than it sounds. It is not merely a case of getting one's affairs into a hopeless tangle and then taking up one's automatic and settling the whole business with a flash and a bang. The affair, like all serious matters, must be approached in a methodical manner. In the first place, as the professor would say, it is necessary to make certain that there are any brains to blow out.

Consider the case of the unfortunate Mr. X, which, indeed, is a case in point. Mr. X conceived the satisfactory idea of ending his days by blowing out his brains. It was on account of the last of a long series of complicated '' deals ''—for the path of true business seldom runs straight. He took up his great big *44,* after having left a note for the undertaker (he was always particular in small details) and another note for his wife—though why at such a time he should want to worry *her* was more than his friends could make out. He took up his shooter, I repeat, he took a fair aim and he fired . . . And nothing happened. Not a trace of a brain was blown out, and he stood there bewildered and angry, feeling not a little ridiculous, with a neat little hole drilled in his head. He tried again, and yet there was nix of the brain stuff flying around. In a fury of desperation he then went on firing at random all round his head. He made a fair pepper-box of it, he turned it upside down and shook it, and yet his efforts were rewarded with no sign of the grey matter. It is little wonder that he became a confirmed pessimist, refusing ever after to see any gladness in life.

The second essential is to know how to shoot straight. Nothing is more deplorable than to watch a man aiming at his own head and missing the mark. It is as bad as being bowled out with the first ball—a thing monks often do by way of penance, but still not calculated to raise a man in the eyes of his fellows. But the worst of missing your own head is that you may hit someone else's head. Many a friendship of a life-time has been brought to a sudden and unexpected close because a man has not taken pains to perfect himself in the use of the revolver. If a fellow elects to blow out his brains, moreover, he should be careful to choose a lonely spot for the deed. Journalists, to whom the pastime may appeal, should never on any account select Fleet Street as the scene of their sport. If in aiming at yourself you merely succeed in shooting another journalist, be assured he will never forgive or forget. Nor for that matter will his friends, and as a result of your rashness, you will speedily find yourself cold-shouldered out of the Street of Adventurers.

It is useful, too, in this connection to know the size of your own head. If it is merely a fat-head you are tolerably safe, but if it should be one of those slender, refined, little heads that some few of us contrive to wear with distinction, you are advised to exercise the greatest caution.

The next important point to drive home in this matter is that everyone who feels that he may at some moment give way to the lonely joy of parting with his own brains, should invariably carry his revolver about with him. Do not leave your canister at home; it is dangerous. Only the other day a man of the highest character came to the conclusion that the time was ripe for blowing out his brains. He had, however, left his revolver at home. He went to fetch it. In crossing the Haymarket he was run over. He had only himself to blame, it was not their fault. Nevertheless, it was a tragedy, and one that a more efficient man would not have been involved in.

It is, of course, highly useful also to make sure that your's are the brains that should be blown out, before you blow them. It may conceivably happen that the greater service would be done by blowing the other fellow's brains out. In matters such as this, one must not be selfish. The narrow view may, in the long run, be the lesser one. After all, the really generous man should be very hard up for material before he draws upon himself. One's creed should be more open, more all-embracing. If your first impulse is to shoot yourself because, let us say, you cannot face the landlord, think again and perhaps you will then conclude that it is better to shoot the landlord. Do not delude yourself with the strange idea that, of all men roaming around to-day, you are the one to be most easily spared. Look about a bit more and you will widen your views.

This business of blowing one's brains out, then, is not nearly so simple as you thought. There are difficulties in the way that the novice would never foresee. A strong, silent man might get over them, it is true, but then, who wants to be a strong, silent man? Let the strong, silent men shoot themselves strongly and silently, if they like, and if only they will. For us there are easier paths and brighter. It is merely a question of borrowing a shilling, and very few friends would mind lending that when they were informed to what practical purpose it was to be put. Most friends would consider it a good speculation. There is, however, just one little hint I would give you (rather than myself) and then I have done. Do not delay. Already the Electric rival is invading the Englishman's castle. A day will come when your shilling will drop into the meter just too late.

Book of the Week

THE EYE OF THE ORIENT

A HISTORY OF NATIONALISM IN THE EAST. By Hans Kohn.
George Routledge & Sons Ltd. 25s. net.

WHEN in due course the attempt is made by people of the future to assess or value the Industrial Age (through which we are now passing), I suppose the point that will strike them most forcibly will be the astonishing manner in which each nation concentrated upon the task of wasting its natural resources. To-day we are wasting generously and freely. Coal is thrown at the head of every potential purchaser in the world, until in sheer desperation he throws it back. Petrol is poured by the thousand gallons upon the roadways and newer and wider roadways constructed that more may thus be poured away. The conservation of energy is not an Industrialist's crime. Natural resources, moreover, are, of course, of two kinds, the replacable and the irreplacable, but the waste of our time makes no distinction between them. One other resource that should not be considered under either heading is likewise wasted, the resource known as Man, and sometimes, unfortunately, as Manpower.

It is obvious that when you are desperately engaged in wasting your materials for the maintenance of an Empire, you will also be doing quite a number of other things that you do not desire and, in fact, that you did not know you were doing. Thinking in terms of trade, you may be starting movements, changing systems, raising oppositions, and so on in dim remote places. These things have no part in your plans, they are accidental to them and still they may become a distinct embarrassment to your future. But if you do not know precisely what you are doing in the distance, it is highly probable that some watchful foreigner will have noticed the signs, and will let the world have the benefit of his vision, or, at least, views. In this roundabout way you will eventually learn what are the results of your late actions, only you may possibly hear the news too late.

The " watchful foreigner " in the present case is Herr Hans Kohn and his "views" are rather amply expressed in his vast volume, *The History of Nationalism in the East*. In this work he searches the world, not indeed from China to Peru, but from Egypt to India; that is, the eastern world that has been touched (in more senses than one) by British Imperialism. Briefly, we have stirred up the East with a long stick. We have broken the slumber of centuries and aroused a spirit that is not new to the world, but new to the present ways of the world. Herr Kohn calls the spirit " Nationalism," but Pride might be a more suitable word. The point of real importance however is this : that to the western world generally, and to the Empire particularly, this spirit is hostile.

The awakening of the East may be only the winking of the East, but it is well to know that the eye of the Orient is open. White men are being seen in the eastern daylight, and the legend they once created about themselves is no longer believed. When the westerner first went out East, equipped with the lastest weapons known to science, he was invulnerable. Nothing could avail against him. If he was an enemy, it was one who could not be killed, one who must be tolerated and one with

whom it was better to make terms. Moreover, it was always known what terms he wanted—and he got away with it. The westerner, in fact, created a great illusion around himself, and the East was duly impressed. He was invincible, he was a ruler, and he had not come out for his health. Herr Kohn is, however, wrong when he says that the white man conveyed the idea to the East that all white men were brothers, who did not fight against each other. In the East they had seen too much of the White Man's Burden being pinched by one white man from another; they had heard too many very varied types of missionaries preaching, too many varied types of creed ever to believe in the peacefulness and solidarity of the West. This dream was not, therefore, shattered by the Great War, when the East was brought in by one set of westerners to oppose the other.

Still, a very creditable legend of western supremacy had been created in the East, and how was it shattered? I think that the Boer War started the business. The whole idea of that particular War, together with the unpreparedness of the Army for that type of war, started the swing of the pendulum the other way. The lords of the East were held, as it were, by a handful of farmers, and that news was not hidden, but rather advertised, by others of our western brotherhood. But undoubtedly the real turning point was 1904, the Russo-Japanese War. There is much that is eastern about Russia, but it was as a western power that it opposed the Japs, the babes of the East. There was much that was western about Japan, but it was as an eastern power that it opposed Russia. In that struggle the hitherto invincible West went down. The giant was knocked sideways. It was seen that the East *was* able to meet this terrible White Man, that he *was* after all vulnerable, and that the future of the East was not to be dictated by the West. In the East those who had never heard of Japan rejoiced at the Japs' victory. All non-Europeans indeed rejoiced, and even in darkest Africa was the defeat of the White Man celebrated.

The Great War did nothing to re-establish Europe's claim to supremacy, but rather stressed the opposite. Yet the greater event in the East was undoubtedly the Russian Revolution, for in 1917 Russia ceased to be a menace in the East, and became an ally. The old Russian imperialistic dreams perished at a blow. Constantinople became safe from Russia, for the first time for a great many years. Russia renounced her old claims in the East, and now allied herself—at least in propaganda—against the capitalistic designs of the West. A new peril was discovered on far-flung frontiers. The West had grown to rely much on the East, to depend upon it for necessities, and it was in the weak points, in the remote places that Russia now appealed, supporting them against the West. The enterprises of capital from Europe had created vast stretches of proletarian patches, and with these Russia sought to link itself. Workers of the World Unite ! India, for instance, began to teem with new problems.

It was not always necessary for the Bolsheviks to create unrest or to invent crimes of capitalists against India. The cotton industry was more or less deliberately ruined in India, in order that the work might be done in Lancashire and the mass-produced goods be sold in India. Indians were not likely to forget, but Russia helped them to express their remembrance. Macaulay's educational schemes in India, moreover, helped to work against this country. They were planned on English models, and the teaching was in the English language. But the English model makes patriotism to one's country almost the centre of the affair. The Indians, too, came to know that they had a country. They were ruled by a very distant race, the administrators of which took no root in India. Officials came for their brief years and departed. Others followed, and, in turn, went. And as the shadow of the White Man grew and grows less in the East, it is not surprising that Indians dream of the day when the last Englishman shall depart, when his last wasted effort shall be spent, and India be free. For that is the impression, that the Westerner in the East is a passing fancy, and his doings, judged by Eastern standards, a wasted gesture. Everyone interested in either Empire or the East should read this book, which is excellently translated.

J. D. G.

Short Reviews

WRITING FOR CHILDREN: A MANUAL FOR WRITERS OF JUVENILE FICTION. By Arthur Groom. A. and C. Black, Ltd. 2s. 6d. net.

This is an addition to the useful series which contains *The Writers' and Artists' Year Book,* and gives an interesting account of the pitfalls awaiting the young writer of Juvenile Fiction and the possible reward awaiting those who follow the rules of the game. The author is himself experienced in that delightful and difficult field, and his advice is valuable. But many people will refuse to agree with him that a child's story should begin thus and thus, and that certain subjects are out of date. Children are always much the same, and their literature need never be machine-made. The lists of children's publications are useful.

CAPTAIN SCOTT, by Stephen Gwynn (The Golden Hind Series). The Bodley Head, 12s. 6d.

The latest addition to this useful series of biographies of great explorers, is also the latest of British Explorers and one of the greatest. When all the tumult and the shouting of the Press and the public platform, with the straining after the dramatic and sensational, has been discounted, Scott remains great both in his achievements and in his person. His story is recent enough to be forgotten, but it may be re-read from his own accounts and those of some of his companions, which are, or should be, in every intelligent library. In addition to the fascination of his story and the Antarctic continent as he describes it, Scott has an epic of heroism to relate and he does it in good English and without jingoism.

The object of this latest volume is to present a more intimate and personal picture of the manner of man that was Scott. Mr. Stephen Gwynn undoubtedly succeeds, and he does so not only by his own words but largely by judicious and generous quotations from Scott's reports, diaries and personal letters. One might well regret that the intimate letters of so fine a nature, especially those to his wife, should be butchered to make a Roman holiday, but it was no doubt inevitable if the author was to achieve his end. That he has done, and the result is an intimate and very readable biography which will take some superseding. One rather irritating typographical defect must be mentioned—it may have been due to a shortage of colons or quotation marks, but whereas some of the actual quotations from Scott's writings are indicated, in most cases there is no indication of quotation at all. Often it is not necessary, sometimes it is. In any case the author (or printer) should be consistent.

THE HUNDRED BEST ENGLISH ESSAYS. Edited with an Introduction by the Right Honourable the Earl of Birkenhead, P.C., D.L. Cassell. 8s. 6d. net.

On the first page of his introduction, Lord Birkenhead states that he does not put forward his selection as being the best essays in the English language. Further on he points out that the word essay is indifferently and wrongly applied to-day to any prose piece, but adds that this broadening of scope has definitely occurred and must be accepted, " as we accept the mechanisation of physical life." Indeed, he accepts as essays all that are so named " by authors of merit." But he goes even beyond that. His first " essay," here reprinted, is an extract from one of Latimer's sermons. Another is a passage from Pepys' Diary. And there is a quotation from Bunyan's "Grace Abounding." Another is a discourse by Sir Joshua Reynolds to students of the Royal Academy. Another is quoted from " The World of William Clissold." There are, of course, some essays in the book and there is a certain justification for so labelling the texts of speeches. We should be interested to hear, however, how the book acquired its title, why Lord Birkenhead bothered to explain that essays have form, and what policies he pursued in writing the biographical notes that precede his selections. We must add, in fairness, that a number of great essayists of the seventeenth and succeeding centuries is suitably represented and that the best of their work will repay the purchaser who wants a compact, reasonably priced volume—so long as he realises exactly what he is buying.

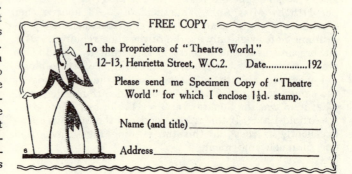

Musical Jottings

Before The Holidays

IT is good that the committee of the Wednesday Evening Concerts at the Wigmore Hall are to continue the series in the New Year. Five concerts are arranged : on January 22nd, February 5th and 19th, and March 5th and 19th. The last of this year's series, given on December 4th, at which the finest items in a fine programme were the Mozart *Sonata in E minor for pianoforte and orchestra,* played by Harold Samuel and Isolde Menges, and two Bach cantatas, sung by Dorothy Silk, delicately accompanied by wood-wind and strings, inspired eager anticipation for the new series.

The last of the B.B.C. symphony concerts of the year was given under Sir Thomas Beecham on December 11th, the evening being given up to Granville Bantock's *Omar Khayyam.* That the work achieved the effect it did is largely due to the magnificent performance which the conductor inspired. In itself the work is unequal and can be more fully appreciated as music when divorced from the significance of its title and its text. It is difficult to imagine quite such vivid emotionalism displayed by the cynical poet.

Constant Lambert's *The Rio Grande,* played under the composer's baton by the Hallé Orchestra on December 13th, confirmed the impression that we have in the young composer a musician of far more than average ability. The work itself has been described as " making music out of jazz "—whatever that may mean exactly : it implies an exact definition of what music is and what is jazz, and where they conflict, a definition which does not exist. Actually what Mr. Lambert has done is to use several of the musical rhythms, evolved rather than created by jazz, in a symphonic form, and he has done so very brilliantly. Criticism of the work is handicapped by the appeal and interest of novelty, but it seems probable that when the novelty has worn off the work will still be appreciated as a fine piece of orchestral composition.

A performance in its entirety of the Bach *St. Matthew Passion* is a rarity, and to-day, when the fashion is against long performances, its attempt is courageous. It speaks well, therefore, of the performance given by the Bach Cantata Club at St. Margaret's Church, Westminster, that for the whole time (from 5 p.m. to 10.15 p.m., with a break of an hour for refreshment) a crowded audience (or should it be congregation?) was held in rapt attention. Special congratulations are due to the organisers of the performance, and to Mr. Kennedy Scott under whose direction the excellent performance was achieved.

One of the most pleasant of the late memories that we shall cherish of the old year is the recital given on December 11th by Miss Anne Thursfield of " An hour of her Favourite Songs "; an hour, as she explained in a programme note, was only a tithe of the time required. Her sincere and profound artistry is such that we should like many more hours. Perhaps these will be forthcoming?

I was only able to hear one item of the recital given, the same evening by Cecil Bouvalot and Suzanne de Livet. That item was the *Sonata No. 2 for Violin and Pianoforte,* by Arnold Bax. If the artists rendered the other items as excellently as they did this the evening must have been one of much enjoyment.

V. N. L.

The Drama

Napoleon

NAPOLEON wanders stiffly and dejectedly through *Madame Plays Nap,* striking the traditional attitudes and wearing the famous uniform, but looking for the most part as if he doubted the reality of himself and his environment.

I know exactly how he feels. I felt that way myself while watching a performance at the New Theatre. The play seemed to be an exercise in play writing, with cardboard characters and emotionless scenes, which could be regarded in a spirit of complete detachment.

That may have been the fault of the authors. Or it may have been the fault of the actors. I am inclined to blame them all for settling down with too much conscientiousness to the creation of farce. Had they tried to give us comedy, the characters might live.

The first scene is in a pawnbroker's shop. The pawnbroker and his wife are royalists, disguising their feelings in the midst of Revolution. It is not surprising then that we should see them next at St. Cloud, where Madame is regarded by Napoleon as a model wife. He is, in fact, so fond of exhorting the other ladies to follow her example that two of them conspire with a corrupt Chamberlain to damage her reputation.

Accordingly her husband receives a forged letter summoning him to a friend's house. Madame is then urged to travel home in the carriage of one Venatier, whom she encountered first in the pawnshop, after which Napoleon is given to understand that she has accepted Venatier's advances. But Madame escapes, returns, braves the anger of Napoleon, and defeats her enemies.

Not only has she evidence against them. She traps them into resurrecting a story about her supposed association during the Revolution with an officer whom she hid above the shop. They describe him to Napoleon as a most unfavoured wretch, whereupon Napoleon is reminded of a day when he pawned his watch, which the husband still carries in his pocket.

The situations here are presented at the right moments, and the authors have written appropriate dialogue. But not much more than that can be said in favour of the play. It does not really seem to matter at the beginning of the third act whether Madame or the conspirators win. Watching her game with them is very much like watching a game of cards when one is not an enthusiast.

As Madame, Sybil Thorndike gives one of the worst performances of her career. She is so anxious to express vivacity that she afflicts the nerves. There are excellent reasons for her decision to give tragedy a rest, but few would base agreement on the evidence of her acting here. And Lewis Casson, an actor of really high standing, is very unimpressive as Napoleon. Others in the cast vary from being reasonably good to being unreasonably bad.

M. C. C.

Small Workshops

GLOVES.
Irreproachable gloves hand-made by expert. Original button holes. Every kind of hand-work. Disabled Soldiers and Invalids employed. Bazaar and Trade should apply. Very moderate prices. Write for List.
HANDICRAFT HUT, PATTERDALE.

LEATHERWORK.
Stools, motor cushions, log tubs, blotters, hand-made gloves.
KATHARINE COCKCROFT,
37, Belsize Park, N.W.3.

METALWORK.
Antique and Modern of all descriptions, in brass, copper, and iron, to own or customers' designs. Speciality, Electric Light Fittings, Electrical accessories and general hardware of exceptional value.
J. F. GARROD, LTD., 72, Charlotte Street,
LONDON, W.1.

WHO'S NICHOLLS?
Why, the hand-done Visiting Card King. Specimen packet designed free.
256, Church Road, BRISTOL.

PRINTING.
Good printing at moderate charges. Specimens and price free.
HATHERLEY, 43a, Trentham Street,
Southfields, LONDON.

UPHOLSTERER AND HOUSE FURNISHER.
Restful Easy Chairs made in small workshop by practical working upholsterer. Covered in Damask, £5. Velvet or Moquette, £5 17s. 6d. Carriage paid anywhere in United Kingdom. Samples of coverings and designs on request.
R. STREET, 27, Albert Road,
COLNE, LANCASHIRE.

DECORATOR AND PLUMBER.
All house decorations done. Moderate charges; good work.
F. STONE, 5, Health Villas, VALE OF HEALTH, N.W.3.

PHOTOGRAPHIC ENLARGEMENTS.
Artistic Postcard Enlargements from your small films, 3/- dozen. Hand-woven cushion squares, 5/6. Table runners, 7/6. Fadeless Blue and Golden Brown.
ARTS AND CRAFTS, St. Osyth,
CLACTON-ON-SEA.

TAILORING, LADIES and GENTLEMEN
Bespoke and ready-to-wear. Good materials. Alterations and renovations carried out. Moderate charges. Patterns on request.
F. WALKER, Mortimer Hall,
93, Mortimer Street, Regent Street, W.1.

NAME PLATES.
Guaranteed Firth's stainless steel 10 in. x 8 in. up to 10 letters 8/6 each.
J. B. DAINTY, Pensnett, near DUDLEY.

THE FOREST TOYS.
Wooden animals of all kinds, hand-carved and painted. Price list post free.
F. H. WHITTINGTON, Brockenhurst,
HANTS.

GLASS.
Three-fold Dressing Table Mirrors in decorative gold mouldings from 50s. Hand-carved three-fold Mirrors gilded in English gold leaf from 77/6. Also Shields and Armorial Bearings in stained and painted glass for window decoration.
JOHN S. DUNN,
8, East Chapel Street, Curzon Street, W.1.

HATS.
Raffia trimmed hats and baskets.
ROSE AGENCY, Hanover Building,
SOUTHAMPTON.

EMBROIDERY.
Embroideries in wool on jumper suits and waistcoats. KATHARINE COCKCROFT,
37, Belsize Park, N.W.3.

CLOTHES OF CHARACTER.
Lounge Suits from 5 gns. Dress Wear from 6½ gns. Overcoats from 4 gns. All hand finished.
S. G. HUNT, 47, Eastcheap, E.C.3. Tel.: Royal 0807. 1 min. Monument and Mark Lane Stations.   P.

BASKET WARE.
Rustic wicker furniture for outdoors. Log Baskets, Dog Baskets, Laundry and Travelling Hampers. Cane and coloured Shopping Baskets. Carriage paid. Illustrated catalogue and price list free.
BLACKWELL & SON,
28, Cross Street, BARNSTAPLE.

NEEDLEWORK.
Pictures, landscapes, all silk, from 10/6.
KATHARINE CHEVALLIER,
247, Dover Road, FOLKESTONE.

HANDWOVEN PILE RUGS.
Something new! Made in any size, colourings and depth of pile required. Prices from 25/-. Send for samples.
THE HAND LOOM CENTRE, NORWICH.

HANDWOVEN MATERIALS.
Handspun and vegetable dyed, in silk, wool, and cotton. Dresses, jumpers, skirt lengths, scarves, curtains, cushion covers, and materials for all decorative purposes.
THE KINGSLEY WEAVERS (Lee & Eileen Baker), Chipping Campden, GLOS.

GENTS. SOX.
Guaranteed All-Wool and every pair made at home. Mixed colours, 2/3; plain colours 2/6. Postage paid.
G. MERIKIN, 28, Shene Bldgs.,
Bourne Est., HOLBORN, E.C.

BRASS RUBBINGS
and other Medieval subjects. Engraved printed and published by Molly Power. Lists on application.
MEDIEVAL CRAFT, Wells, SOMERSET.

PRINTER AND PUBLISHER.
Posters. Catalogues sent on application.
H. D. C. PEPLER.

SCULPTOR, CARVER & LETTER CUTTER
in wood and stone. Tombstones, Wall Tablets, Stations of the Cross, Altars, Holy Water Stoups, Sanctuary Lamps.
H. J. CRIBB.

WEAVER-DYER.
Suitings, Homespun, Tweeds, Serge for Habits, Vestments. J. V. D. KILBRIDE.

WOODWORKER.
Household and Ecclesiastical Furniture. Weaving Appliances. BUILDER.
Address above.—G. MAXWELL,
DITCHLING COMMON, HASSOCKS,
SUSSEX.

DRESS ORNAMENTS.
Hat and Frock Ornaments; Pin Trays; of single or cut sea-shells. Colours, bronzes. From 1/ each.
BIELBY, Alfriston, SUSSEX.

HANDWROUGHT FURNITURE.
Davies' Handwrought Furniture. "Distinctive" for the past 25 years. Davies' Handicraft Furniture has been known for its fulfilment of all the ideals that actuated the old craftsmen. It is entirely handwrought in solid oak and other fine furniture woods, beautifully polished to show to best advantage the natural grainings. The designs are original, simple in taste, artistic in effect, but comfortable and adaptable in every respect for everyday use.
W. H. DAVIES & SONS, Mount Street,
BOLTON, LANCASHIRE.

HAND BEATEN METAL WORK
Restored to original design and finish. Any metal. 45 years' experience. References.
CLARK, Radioville, Ashstead, SURREY.

HAND-MADE FURNITURE.
Home-made Furniture, mainly of English-grown woods, and to original designs from the simplest to the finest styles.
A. ROMNEY GREEN, Woodworker,
25, Bridge Street, CHRISTCHURCH.

LEATHER GOODS.
Leather Comb Case, 1/6. Raffia Sprays Woven Scarf, 7/6.
MASON, Cowesby, Northallerton, YORKS.

LINGERIE.
Orders taken for hand-made lingerie and embroidery.
SANDERS, 122, Romsey Road,
SOUTHAMPTON.

IRISH HOUSEHOLD LINENS.
Direct from the Manufacturer. Coloured dress linen, very fine quality, 30 ins. wide, only 1/9 per yard, post free. Catalogue, samples and remnant bargains. List free.
J. HENDERSON, Milner Street, BELFAST,
N. IRELAND.

MIRRORS AND FRAMES.
Mirrors and frames bordered with fruit and flowers, lovely colours. From 12/6. Also embroidered waistcoats and overalls.
THEA HOLME, Sussex Lodge, Champion Hill, S.E.

For the Table: Farm Produce

XMAS POULTRY.
Plump Turkeys, 15/-, 20/-, 25/- each. Fatted Geese 8/6, 10/-, 12/6 each. Splendid Roasting Fowls and Ducks 7/6, 8/6, 10/- pair. Boiling Fowls 6/- pair; all trussed; post free. Order early.
A. BELL, The Glebe, Rosscarbery, Cork.

Best Christmas Turkeys, 15/-, 20/-, 25/- each. Splendid fatted Geese 8/-, 10/-, 12/- each. Plump Roasting Fowls and Ducks 8/-, 10/- pair. Boilers, 6/6 pair; trussed; post paid.
ANNIE REGAN, Fairfield House,
Rosscarbery, Cork.

Excellent Large Roasting Fowl and Ducks, 6/6 pair, 2 pairs 11/6. Fat Boiling Fowl, 5/- pair, trussed ready for cooking. Post paid.
MISS GORDON, Rosscarbery, Cork.

TURKEYS.
Prime Xmas Turkeys, 12/-, 13/-, 14/- each. Large cocks, 18/-, 19/-, 20/- to 25/- each. Large roasting fowl, 8/- pair. Fat geese, 10/- each, trussed, ready for cooking; post free.
MISS CAINE, Produce Stores, Rosscarbery.

SWEETS.
Home-made. 3/- brings ½ lb. mixed sweets or 1 lb. toffees.
L. SHORTT, Fivecross, Moreton, Dorchester.

CHOCOLATES.
Home-made Chocolates and Sweets. The use of fresh cream, milk, pure butter and eggs guaranteed. Price 3/-, 4/- and 5/- per lb. Luncheon and tea rooms.
DELANEY, 40, Brooke Street, Holborn;
27, Kirby Street, E.C.1.

REAL DEVONSHIRE CLOTTED CREAM.
¼ lb., 10d.; ½ lb., 1/5; 1 lb., 2/6; post free.
BOLES, Heathfield, Holsworthy, Devon.

HOME-MADE TREACLE TOFFEE.
For postal order 2/6, I will send 1 lb. tin, post free.
Mrs. POWNALL, High Bank, Glossop Road, Gamesley, Derbyshire.

THE COCKPIT

To the Editor, G.K.'s WEEKLY.

SITUATION IN IRELAND

SIR,—I had not the advantage of hearing Mr. O'Duffy's address to the Central Branch on " Ireland and Economic Ideas," and must judge of his thesis from the brief account in your columns. No economic system has either failed or succeeded in Ireland. There was a *political* system, which failed—rather badly—and it monopolised the attention of Irishmen to the exclusion of social and economic considerations. Its successor is barely in the saddle, and to generalise on its achievement would be premature.

But this is as good an occasion as any of pointing out what Distributism is not. It is not a system where nobody does anything but keep stock or cultivate land. The essence of the Distributist State is balance, and with the important exceptions that they are in contact with reality and cannot be starved to death, a nation of land-workers is as unbalanced as a nation of factory-hands. Both have to sell their surplus to purchase other necessaries from a distance, both therefore lack an important element of social and economic stability, and both are victimised by finance and transport.

In such countries as Denmark, this lack of balance is masked by vigorous Government action in marketing, but this has not yet been possible in Ireland.

The weakness of the present position in Ireland, which will have to be remedied if Distributism is to become a reality there, is the absence of local crafts and industries to provide material for community life and local reciprocal markets. I agree that there is little sign of the necessity being realised there at present. That is deplorable, but it is not an argument against Distributism.

And was Slavery bad only for the Slaves? When Mr. O'Duffy has established his Robots, he will still have to find a new way of avoiding the fate of Athens. Even that magnificent youth of the world could not survive the fatigue of being waited on, and now we are rather tired to start with!—Yours faithfully,

H. ROBBINS.

DISTRIBUTISM OF OLD

SIR,—I thought I knew Thomas Love Peacock pretty well as a clear thinker and a hater of all faddists and cranks and humbugs, but it was only on re-reading him the other day that the following passage from *Crotchet Castle* struck me as being about the clearest and simplest—as it must be, I imagine, the earliest—statement of Distributism I have come across anywhere.

Mr. MacQuedy, the Scots Political Economist, has been talking his usual blether of confused economics and Peacock, in the person of the Rev. Dr. Folliott, answers him thus :—

Rev. Dr. Folliott : " You have given the name of a science (*i.e.,* Political Economy) to what is yet an imperfect enquiry, and the upshot of your so-called science is this; that you increase the wealth of a nation by increasing in it the quantity of the things which are produced by labour; no matter what they are, no matter how produced, no matter how distributed. The greater the quantity of labour that has gone to the production of the quantity of Kings in a community, the richer is the community. That is your doctrine. Now, *I* say, if this be so,

riches are not the object for a community to aim at. *I* say, the nation is best off, in relation to other nations, which has the greatest quantity of the common necessaries of life distributed among the greatest number of persons; which has the greatest number of stout hearts and strong arms united in a common interest, willing to offend no one but ready to fight in defence of their own community against all the rest of the world, because they have something in it worth fighting for. The moment you admit that one class of things, without any reference to what they respectively cost, is better worth having than another; that a smaller commercial value with no mode of distribution, is better worth having than a greater commercial value with another mode of Distributism; the whole of that curious fabric of postulater and dogmas which *you* call the science of Political Economy, and which *I* call *Political Economiæ inscientia,* tumbles to pieces."

Crotchet Castle was written in 1831; one hundred years ago. Of course, if all Distributists know the passage well and it is only I who have hitherto missed it—or missed its full significance—please do not print this letter. Peacock is full of passages of a Distributist " spirit," but none quite so clear and terse as this.—Yours faithfully,

WILLIAM BLISS.

WILL IT REFORM?

SIR,—In your issue of the 30th Nov. you state that the failure of the B.B.C. to please everybody means that broadcasting is not likely to change human thought and activity.

In your next issue we shall be reading that because Caxton got his printing types mixed, books cannot influence the mind of man.

CECIL B. LEADER.

P.S.—A reader since number one.

EMPIRE FREE TRADE

SIR,—According to Mr. Belloc the politicians are subservient to the bankers and other monopolists. At the same time, he says, the politicians (and therefore the financiers and bankers), are subservient to America who has obtained a mastery over us.

How does this square with Beaverbrook's " Empire Crusade" which is backed by Melchett and a number of other monopolists? The Empire Free Trade campaign is obviously the antithesis of subservience to America. The object of it, according to Beaverbrook himself, is to set up an amalgamated Empire to counteract the growing power of America.

If that is so it can only lead to strife between the two countries. There is no need to mention the folly and absurdity of this so-called " Crusade " and the strife it cannot but engender between England and her colonies, whose normal development it proposes to check.

I merely ask for an explanation of this seeming paradox and contradiction; the people who are supposed to be subservient to America concocting a scheme which can hardly fail to act (should it ever be tried, which God forbid) directly against American interests.

P. HEARNSHAW.

The Distributist League.

(founded in conjunction with "G.K.'s Weekly" for the restoration of liberty by the distribution of property).

President: MR. G. K. CHESTERTON.

Hon. Sec.: F. KESTON CLARKE.

Office, 2, Little Essex Street, London, W.C.2.

Telephone: Temple Bar 1978.

There are many readers of this Paper who are not members of the League. All who believe that ownership in the means of livelihood is normal to man, and necessary to liberty, and all who dislike and distrust the concentration of control advocated by Socialists and practised by Monopolists, should join the League. There is no other tenet for membership, and no other obligation than 1/- subscription, although active work is welcomed from all who can give it.

CENTRAL BRANCH.

CENTRAL BRANCH: *Hon. Sec.*. C. T. B. Donkin, 2, Little Essex Street, Strand, W.C.2.

A Christmas meeting was held at the Devereux on Friday, December 20th, and the gravity which often marks the weekly discussions there was entirely suspended, like the free list. The Central Branch lost its centre of gravity, in fact, and became magnificently eccentric. Mr. W. R. Titterton was in the chair, and, in consequence, the fun began at the beginning, and was not nearly finished at the end. It was hoped that everyone would contribute either a song or a ghost story, so that any excessive levity occasioned by the singing of "King Solomon had Ten Thousand Wives," or "The Stormy Nore," might be quelled by blood-curdling tales of headless spectres, clanking chains, faces at windows, and noises in the night, and conversely that the dentures set chattering by such stories might become manageable again to the tune of "Stop Your Tickling, Jock!" To some extent these hopes were realised, though it is practically certain that what some of us thought was the chattering of teeth was really only the clinking of glasses.

A prize of a bottle of port was given to the teller of the best ghost story, and it must be admitted that the good ship "Ananias" never deserved (and got) a better reception on coming into port. The judges who awarded the prize were the assembled ladies, each of whom was offered, and most graciously accepted, a memento whose value it would be difficult to under-estimate. Incidentally, we are informed that the lady who received one sapphire earring would be glad to get into touch with the lady who got the other, with a view to arranging terms of partnership.

Other meetings are as follows:—

December 27.—No formal meeting.

January 3.—W. R. Titterton on the Dictator.

January 10.—T. Davies on Distributism.

BIRMINGHAM BRANCH.

BIRMINGHAM BRANCH.—*Hon. Sec.*, K. L. Kenrick, 7, Soho Road, Birmingham.

The 64th meeting of the branch was held at the Guildhouse on December 13th. Mr. Bradley read a paper on "Distributism and Money." He traced the history of currency and finance from the early days of barter to

---

the present day of banking monopoly and defaulting company directors. He showed how paper-money had increased out of all proportion to real value, and how in consequence the control of credit put the whole wealth of the country in the power of a few individuals. Messrs. Harris, Emblem, Thistlethwaite, and the chairman and secretary took part in the discussion which followed. The secretary gave notice that at the next meeting (January 10th) he would bring forward a motion to ask the Executive of the League to urge the Government to appoint a Royal Commission to enquire into the possibility of putting the land of the country to its obvious and just use of supporting a free, contented and self-supporting peasant population on a basis of occupying ownership. Next meeting January 10th. Mr. Bradford on "The Idea of Government."

GLASGOW BRANCH.

GLASGOW BRANCH.—*Hon. Sec.*, A. Mason, 59, Truce Road, Glasgow, W.3.

On Monday, December 16th, members and friends met in the Knights of St. Columbas Halls at a Smoker. There was a very gratifying attendance, and the evening passed from success to success to a fitting climax when the fun ran highest. The worth of meetings of this nature was emphasised by the enrolment of four new members. Thanks are due to Mr. McConaghy for the refreshment arrangements. The whole evening was a model of true Distributist informality.

The next meeting will be on Monday, January 6th, when a programme for the second half of the session will be arranged, and at which Mr. McKay will advance the proposal "That the Branch start a fund for promoting a definite Distributist enterprise."

LIVERPOOL BRANCH.

LIVERPOOL BRANCH.—*Hon. Sec.*, S. Anderson. 3, Leopold Road, Kensington, Liverpool.

At the Grenville Café, Tithebarn Street, on Wednesday, December 18, Mr. J. P. Alcock spoke on "Distributism and a Mechanical Civilisation, are they compatible?" He pointed out that, provided society kept machinery in its place, and regarded it in its true perspective, machinery and Distributism could be close allies. To-day machinery enjoys a prestige it does not deserve, and has a dominating effect on society. In a Distributist State this could not be, for the machines would be man's servants, only needed when called upon.

Thursday, January 2. Song rehearsal for Annual Dinner, 7.30, at the Alligator. On this date, at the Alligator, a committee meeting will be called, which will not interfere with the song rehearsal.

January 9, 1930. Annual Dinner held at the "Angel," Dale Street. Tickets 4/6, can be had from the Secretary, F. S. Anderson, 8, Leopold Road, Kensington, Liverpool.

MANCHESTER BRANCH.

MANCHESTER.—*Hon. Sec.*, John A. Toohey, York Mount, Bury New Road, Prestwich.

The last meeting of the members of the Manchester Branch for the year 1929 took place on Wednesday evening, the 18th inst., at the K.S.C. premises (in the small lounge), Chapel Street, Salford. Mr. Cummings presided.

Mr. J. Cosgrove, who has visited Denmark several times, gave the members present an interesting account of his impressions of the social life of Denmark, and during the course of his paper he brought out in a very clear and effective manner the contrast between several aspects of social life in a country like Denmark as compared with an industrialised country like Great Britain. His deepest impression was the very genuine democratic feeling of the Danish people, which democratic spirit Mr. Cosgrove remarked began to manifest itself on the steamer from Harwich to Esbjerg, as he travelled on a steamer belonging to a Danish shipping company with an entirely Danish crew.

Mr. Cosgrove also mentioned that the one-time leaseholds had gradually been transformed into freeholds, and he stated that practically two-thirds of the Danish agricultural land was farmed by freeholders.

A point to which the speaker drew attention was the rather ominous fact of many of the farmers and agriculturists being indebted to the Co-op. Banks and Agricultural Credit Societies for loans, which might later give the lenders too great a grip on the farmers and their holdings.

Mr. Cosgrove referred to the fact of Prohibition having been defeated in Denmark, also touched upon the Danish educational system, and in concluding stated that he had carried back with him as the result of his various visits to Denmark the most agreeable and lasting impressions and happy souvenirs.

BRADFORD BRANCH.—*Hon. Sec.*, J. Gosney, 35, Buxton Street, Heaton, Bradford.

COVENTRY. — *Hon. Sec.*, R. E. S. Willison, 102, Westwood Road, Coventry.

EDINBURGH. — *Hon. Sec.*, Jas. Turner, c/o Dunne, 5, Keir Street, Edinburgh.

NORTH LONDON BRANCH: *Hon. Sec.*, J. O. Strong, 29, Southwood Lawn Road, N.6.

BOOKS TO READ.

The Servile State,
          by Hilaire Belloc (4/-).

The Outline of Sanity,
          by G. K. Chesterton (6/-).

Economics for Helen, by H. Belloc (5/-).

Liberty and Property,
          by H. E. Humphries (1/3).

Guilds, Trade, and Agriculture,
          by A. J. Penty (5/-).

The Mystery of Trade Depression,
          by F. E. Holsinger (7/6).

The Acquisitive Society,
          by R. H. Tawney (4/6).

Primer of Social Science,
          by H. Parkinson (3/6).

The Church and the Land,
          by Vincent McNabb, O.P. (2/6).

The Change, by G. C. Heseltine (2/6).

Do We Agree?
          by G. B. Shaw and G. K. Chesterton (1/6).

Rural Rides, by William Cobbett (1/6).

The above may be obtained through booksellers or direct from the Secretary of the Distributist League, 2, Little Essex Street, W.C.2.

Small Advertisements.

The charge for prepaid advertisements is 2s. per insertion up to 24 words, and one penny per word afterwards. Advertisements not paid for in advance cost 3s. per insertion for 24 words and twopence per word afterwards. Space costs 5s. per inch. Thick type in all cases 20 per cent. extra. Seven insertions for the price of six.

EDUCATIONAL.

UNIVERSITY EXTENSION LECTURES
(University of London).

THE DEVELOPMENT OF THE ART OF THE THEATRE. A course of ten lectures by Miss Elsie Fogerty, on Mondays at 6.30 p.m., at Kingsway Hall, Kingsway, W.C. Admission free to first lecture on October 7th.

ENGLISH LITERATURE.—DRYDEN to COLERIDGE. Twenty-four lectures by Dr. Arthur Compton-Rickett, on Mondays, at 6.30 p.m., at Bishopsgate Institute, Bishopsgate, E.C. Admission FREE to first lecture on September 30th.

Particulars of these, and of eighty-five other courses on HISTORY, LITERATURE, MUSIC, ECONOMICS, ART, and other subjects may be obtained from the University Extension Registrar (Dept. L.), University of London, S.W.7.

LITERARY.

SONG POEMS wanted. Successful composer invites known or unknown Authors to submit Lyrics for prompt consideration. Send MSS. and stamp, " Composer," (288) c/o Ray's Advert. Agency, Cecil Court, London, W.C.2.

G.K.'S WEEKLY.—Wanted, copies of Nos. 1, 4, 7, 60, 61 and 150.—Reply to " R. & M.," Postal Dept., Wm. Dawson & Sons, Ltd., Canhon House, Pilgrim St., E.C.4.

CATCHY MUSIC set to Lyrics by Maurice Scott, the famous composer of scores of popular songs (reference any London Music Publisher). MSS. edited and revised. (Terms mod.) Booklet on Popular Song-writing free (stamp for postage).—15, Tufnell Park Road, London, N.7.

BOOKS. — New and Secondhand. Enquiries made for any book free of charge. — L. H. Davis, 19, Trinity Road, Upper Tooting, London, S.W.17.

PRETTY, Laughable Plays. Always liked. List 2d.— Miss Boileau, Knockeven, Southbourne, Bournemouth.

CATHOLIC and General Literary Bureau.—Principal, Wilkinson Sherren. Special attention paid to Literary Aspirants and Young Authors. MSS. read, advised upon, and, when approved, offered to Editors and Publishers.—Particulars from Wilkinson Sherren, (temporary address), 119, Nether Street, North Finchley, London, N.12.

NEW Anecdotes and Jokes by Mark Twain. Published for the first time, with portrait. Price two shillings, post pair.—Mark Twain Society, Mayfield, California.

RESTAURANTS.

DISTRIBUTIST Restaurant. — " The Owl," 3, Kingly Street, W.1. (behind Robinson and Cleaver's, Regent Street). Luncheon and Teas. Members of the League can meet each other here.

MUSIC, INSTRUMENTS, ETC.

BANJOS, Mandolines, Drums, Violins, Guitars, Ukuleles, Accordeons, Saxophones, Xylophones. List free.— Palmers, Dept. J., 135, Listhorpe Road, Middlesbrough.

TO LET.

CHEERFUL Bed and Dressing - Room, use sitting; good cooking. Suit elderly gentleman. — White Rose Cottage, All Cannings, near Devizes.

MISCELLANEOUS.

GOOD Printing at low trade rates. Specimens and prices free. — Hatherley, 43a, Trentham Street, Southfields, London.

HANDKERCHIEFS, fancy, printed, scalloped Irish manufacture, suitable Bazaars, etc. Sample dozen, 3/3 post paid.—Manuel, Standford, Bordon, Hants.

HARRIS TWEED. Any length cut. Patterns free. — James St. Tweed Depot, 392, Stornoway, Scotland.

IRISH HANDWOVEN TWEEDS for Suits and Costumes. Patterns free from Joseph Largey, 40, Lr. Ormond Quay, Dublin.

LOVELY, warm Men's Home-Knitted Socks, 2/6 pair.—Score, Station Road, Liss.

MONEY easily earned in spare time by selling Rubber Stamps; particulars free.—Richford, Ltd., Snow Hill, London.

NEEDLE Cases for Bazaars, Masonic Ladies' nights, etc. Buy direct from Factory. Send for 5/6, 10/6, or 21/- parcel of assorted kinds. Post free. — Dept. G.K., B. Hampton, Son & Co., Ltd., Victoria Street, Redditch.

PRINTING : 10,000 Handbills or Billheads at 3/3 per 1,000. Memorandums, Postcards, Duplicate Books, Envelopes, Posters, etc. Large range of samples, 3d. postage. — Mead & Son, Dept. P., Sandy, Bedfordshire.

SHOWCARDS, Pictures, Letters, in Colours Simultaneously. Own recent invention. Directions 7½d.—Wright, Willis's Place, Wisbech.

THE SILENT METHOD OF VOICE CULTURE.

THE SILENT METHOD Produces amazing results. Builds up the voice that excels in volume, range and purity of tone; eradicates all vocal difficulties, weak voice, harshness, huskiness, limited range; infallible cure for STAMMERING. Send 3d. stamp for particulars and astounding testimony from delighted students the world over.

Prof. W. R. REID, 541g, Wigan Road, Bolton, Lancs.

THE " SEMPER " Screwdriver with four blades, each instantly available, for screws of all sizes. Well made, simple, powerful; guaranteed hand-tempered steel. Handy and reliable. Price : 4/- post free, from C. A. Blamchet, 168, Regent Street, London, W.1.

Advertise in G.K.'s Weekly

Among the many testimonials that we have received, the following is typical :

"You will be interested to hear that G.K.'s Weekly pulled more business than £30 spent by a well-known firm of advertising agents in magazines they recommended."

TYPEWRITING, DUPLICATING, ETC.

MEMBER OF AUTHORS' SOCIETY, expert typist, will type authors' MSS. at usual rates. — S. W. Powell, 38a, Curzon Rd., Boscombe, Bournemouth.

TYPEWRITERS from £2; easy payments arranged. Repairs. Duplicators. 'Phone Central 8210. Typewriter experts, 55, Little Britain E.C.1. 77

AUTHORS' MSS. and Technical Typewriting correctly executed; 10d. per 1,000. — Mrs. Clifstone, 11, Cromwell Avenue, Bromley, Kent. 103

DUPLICATING EXPERT offers 50 extra copies free. — Schoolmaster, 71, Brackenbury Road, Preston.

INCREDIBLE! Unbeatable! Duplicated typewritten matter, 3s. per 100. — E. S. Coy, 14, Homer Terrace, Bootle.

LITERARY Typewriting carefully and promptly executed. MSS. 1s. per 1,000 words; carbon copy 3d. per 1,000. — Miss Nancy McFarlane (J.), 4, Elderton Road, Westcliff-on-Sea.

LONDON'S Premier Typewriting Service. 1,000 words 10d., carbon copy 2d. Perfect work guaranteed. Authors' MSS. a speciality.—"Fleet" Typewriting Agency, 153, Fleet Street, E.C.4.

TYPEWRITING and Duplicating Expert. MSS. typed, 1,000 words 1s.; carbon 2d.—Miss Hill, 48, Kensington Park Road, W.11.

TYPEWRITING accurately executed; 1,000 words 1/-; carbon 3d. Free specimen. Shorthand. —Miss Thayer, 22, Gray's Inn Residences, E.C.1.

TYPEWRITING and Duplicating. Authors' MSS. typed, 10d. per 1,000 words; carbon copy 3d. per 1,000 words. Testimonials, circulars, etc., duplicated. Envelopes addressed. Prompt and efficient work.—Marion Young (C.), 7a, Station Road, Balham, S.W.12.

TYPEWRITING. — 8d. thousand. French and spanish translations (into English), 9d. a folio. — Newcombe, 36, Wilson Street, Middlesbrough.

TYPEWRITING. MSS. 8d. per 1,000 words. Carbon 2d. Pitman's transcribed. Outside work undertaken. Best work, lowest charges. Accuracy guaranteed.—I. Watkins, 40, Verulam Street, E.C.1.

MSS. TYPED, 1/- per 1,000 words, 3d. carbon copy. Translations (French and German into English).—Miss Pollard, 36, Ampthill Square, N.W.1. Museum 3965.

STYLISH and accurate Literary Typewriting, 10d. per 1,000 words. Revision undertaken. French copying or translation. — P. Gregory, 34, Pleasants Street, Dublin.

NEAT ACCURATE TYPING,

Intelligently executed. MSS. 1s. 1,000 words. Quotations given.
Miss N. Netherwood, 128, Park Road, Loughborough.

HOTELS.

EDINBURGH.—St. Mary's (Private), 32, Palmerston Place. Fine situation. Convenient train and tram. Liberal table. 'Phone 23872.

DEAN FOREST, Severn-Wye Valleys.—Beautiful Holiday Home (600 feet up); 80 rooms; five acres; billiards; dancing; motors; garage. 52/6 to 70/- weekly. Prospectus. — Littledean House, Littledean, Glos. 314

CHIPPING CAMPDEN, Gloucestershire (Cotswolds). A few guests taken in comfortable old house for three guineas weekly. Catholic church.—Mrs. L. K. Baker, Westcote House.

KIRKLEY, Lowestoft.—Ladies received at Convent. Magnificent situation on sea front. Excellent catering — Separate tables optional — Home freedom. 10/- day. Apply :— St. Mary's Convent.

Published by the Proprietors, G.K.'s Weekly, Ltd., 2, Little Essex Street, Strand, London, W.C.2 (incorporating The New Witness). Telephone : Temple Bar 1978. Printed by The Marshall Press, Ltd., 7, Milford Lane, Strand, London, W.C.2. Sole Agents for Australasia : Gordon & Gotch (Australasia, Ltd.). Sole Agents for South Africa : Central News Agency, Ltd

G.K.'s WEEKLY, FEBRUARY 22, 1930.

THE DRINK PROBLEM

G.K.'s Weekly

EDITED BY G. K. CHESTERTON.

No. 258.—Vol. X.   Week ending Saturday, February 22, 1930.   PRICE SIXPENCE.
YEARLY (52 ISSUES)
28s. 0d.

Telephone No. Temple Bar 1978.   [Registered at G.P.O. as a Newspaper.]   Offices 2, Little Essex Street, Strand, W.C.2

CONTENTS:

THE RESPECTABLE REBELS

IT is not really long ago since people who held " Labour " opinions were looked upon as rather revolutionary characters. The shadow of the French Revolution was still thrown across their track and they were pictured (and loved to picture themselves) as Dantons and Robespierres, directing the crowds and putting to its proper use the Guillotine. It is not really long since Labour leaders were thus disreputable, not fit to be mentioned in the daily press, save only in terms of contempt and abuse. It is not long, indeed, since they were alive and free, but so rapidly and thoroughly have they changed that the English revolutionaries seem now as ancient as the French revolutionaries; only it was the English revolutionaries who were revolutionised, and the English nation that was left alone.

The most noticeable fact of our political life during the present generation is the conversion of Labour politicians to respectability. There may have been a time when Ramsay MacDonald did not always wear a clean collar, or when Henderson's trousers went uncreased. There may have been such a period, but it sounds incredible. When the Labour group became a real Party, it entered into the full political system on the emphatic understanding that it would observe all the rules laid down by Parliamentary precedent. The revolutionaries agreed to follow in the steps of the " tyrants " and on no account to find a path of their own. They were elected to the best club in London on condition that they would be good clubmen, would carry out the regulations as laid down by the authorities and would never indulge in more than a mild

rag, as was the custom of members of that club when they wished to let off high spirits.

The Labour Party accepted the conditions when they entered Parliament and, by God ! they have kept them. In return they were allowed to have their photos in the papers, were given invitations to Burlington Gallery and generally became men about town. They were praised by those who had recently been their opponents. They were called " good Parliamentarians." No greater insult could have been offered to the old group of revolt that had marched with banners to Trafalgar Square, but the converted crowd accepted the title with gratitude. In the days of William Morris they had talked of destroying the Houses of Parliament, of blowing them up or, more picturesquely, of shelling them from the river : a delightful idea. But now their one aim is to preserve Parliament, to make it permanent, to make it safe.

The consequence is that we are now (in one sense) back in Victorian days. Parliament is a machine that moves with its old-time smoothness. Parties have confidence in each other that they will never let one another down. Revolt must come from without. Any change in the system, that is becoming increasingly repugnant to public taste, must be imposed upon parliamentarians. The old group from which the Labour Party sprung must be re-created. The old Socialists of the Morris type—and some of them were almost as much distributist as socialist—are wanted to-day more than ever, now that their descendants have been converted to security. The worst kind of Parliament is that kind that is safe for Parliamentarians. This type should be forced to live dangerously. The governors should walk in terror of the governed. The representatives of the people should go uneasily, lest at some point they fail to represent the people. No men should be watched so carefully as politicians. Nothing moves them so strongly as fear. But to-day there is no popular movement in this country against the Parliamentary system. Now that the rebels have been brought in, or bought in, there is no determined body to supply their place. The politicians, therefore, have no fear of the people. Unless such a movement of revolt again appears in popular life, the so-called leaders will continue at their parliamentary game until events, which they are unable to control, bring everything crashing down to ruin. For though the machine works to-day much the same as it did in Victorian days, the situation in which it works has changed completely. The Victorian solidity has disappeared. To mention one thing only, imports to-day exceed exports by a figure that will shortly become unbearable.

But as things stand the Labour crowd will continue to be good Parliamentarians. They will read carefully the book of rules of the club to which they belong and avoid breaking them. Their old beliefs are left far behind. At one time, they believed in something they called equality, but to-day they believe in sending their sons to the Public Schools. On the Continent you will find schools, not private or public or elementary, but just schools. All children attend at them unless they have something wrong with them. But here we have schools to suit each type of pocket, and the Labour men, who once believed in democracy, have not a word to say on the subject. Of course, they have no cure for Unemployment, for to find a cure you might have to break the rules of the Club, and that would never do.

Everything that they once knew how to do, they must not now attempt. Therefore it is that they talk much of Peace. War to them is unthinkable, especially—though they do not say it—Class War. They repeat dully the worst phrases of the worst War Books. And in such fashion do they keep their pledges to the electors.

NOTES OF THE WEEK

Last week Mr. Ramsay Muir, as a spokesman of the Liberals, extolled the positive virtues of a Three Party System. He may have been right, or at least, wise, when he declared definitely that a minority Government was the only possible one. Immediately afterwards, Lord Beaverbrook announced that his intensive campaign had produced 200,000 Empire Crusaders (who, formerly, had been pogostick fiends, cross-word puzzlers, Mustard Clubmen, and Froth-Blowers) although it is to be assumed that one half of them are discredited politicians, and that one half of the remainder are seriously distracted by the rival claims of the Kerb Step. However that may be, the new party is formed: the United Empire Party. May it do good things. Various European countries, which have copied the Parliamentary system invented by Walter Bagehot,

have spoilt it by a multiplicity of Parties, and gone back to Dictatorship. England is still in the position of copying the countries which have copied her. Before we have a government we shall have a multiplicity of Parties. But we doubt if Lord Beaverbrook will lead even one of them for long.

*   *   *   *

The news that the Premier has refused to renew his membership of the Independent Labour Party confirms this view. Now, among the shades of opinion professed in the Labour Party, are Labour, Independent Labour, and Communism. If the industrial position grows worse, the position of Communism will grow better. But, as long as the Parliamentary system continues, it will degenerate year by year in a series of ineffectual coalitions. The Wops and the Dagoes seem to have reached our conclusions before we have reached them ourselves.

*   *   *   *

Lord Monkswell was taken to task last week by the *Daily Express* for having alleged in the House of Lords that many important newspapers refused to publish anything adversely criticising the railways because their advertising managers would not permit it. Lord Monkswell has also declared that he was not referring to the *Daily Express* when he made his speech. In an editorial comment on the subject, it was stated that " the advertisers would be the first to resent any suggestion that they influence, directly or indirectly, the editorial policy." Yet any journalist who knows anything about conditions in Fleet Street, is quite aware of the influence of advertisers over editors. The *Daily Express* may be immune from this influence, but we doubt very much if other newspapers have the same honest, independent outlook. In fact, we could cite a number of instances, if to do so were not to betray confidences, in which the knowledge that advertising contracts were in jeopardy persuaded editors not to print or at least to stress certain " stories " that they had to hand. When advertising revenue helps to support a newspaper, the editorial policy is naturally framed in accordance with commercial policies and the editor becomes a departmental head. The *Daily Express* may deny that advertisers would think of implementing their power, but few will agree that the power does not exist. After all, it is possible still to exercise common-sense.

*   *   *   *

Three of our most distinguished economists—Mr. J. M. Keynes, Mr. G. D. H. Cole, and Mr. R. H. Tawney—have been appointed members of the Government's new Economic Advisory Council. This is a clear indication that, as we have long suspected, the economic condition of the nation is so complicated and confusing, so perilously unsound, that the politicians are baffled and dare not attempt of themselves to effect any radical reform lest they should do more harm than good. Hence the Economic Council, a particularly interesting body when it is set up by the Socialists, who have been offering economic cure-alls in the market place for years and years. As for the composition of the Council, Mr. Keynes is perhaps too academic to be very helpful, but Mr. Cole we know to be honest and well-intentioned, and with much for which Mr. Tawney stands we sympathise. There are other members, however, and a clotted secretariat below. While we admire the impartiality of the Premier in his choice of men for his little Economic Privy Council, we can only speculate as to the nature or the unanimity of its advice.

* * * *

The campaign against Russia, which broke out in the course of a short month, seemed to us to be suspiciously unanimous. A Russian General is kidnapped; Mexico breaks off relations; Germany proves Soviet forgeries of banknotes. The Pope declares against persecution; the Archbishop of Canterbury follows suit. France meditates a rupture; Henderson bows to the storm; but the reply of the orthodox bishops, in a series of questions and answers with Soviet journalists is such a piece of puerile propaganda that we must imagine either an interview entirely faked, or else a hierarchy completely bought. Acceptance of either view goes far to prove the case against the Soviets. The fact seems to be that Stalin is proving himself a good Communist by a vigorous home and foreign policy on Communist-Atheist lines. He will not succeed in the end; neither need the Bolsheviks cry havoc over war, for there is no country in Europe ready to fight them, and none even rich enough to declare an economic boycott.

* * * *

" Applied scientifically, advertisement is a very definite economy," says Mr. W. Buchanan-Taylor, publicity manager for J. Lyons and Co., Ltd., " not only to the manufacturer, but also to the actual consumer. Advertised goods are generally the best, since the advertiser must live up to his claims or go by the board." If we are to believe that Mr. Buchanan-Taylor is sincere where he makes these remarkable statements, he is quite obviously entirely out of touch with reality. Applied scientifically, or any other way, advertising is not an economy but an extra, the price of which (and the price is increasingly heavy) must be paid by the consumer. It is an additional tax put on food, or any other commodity, and the only reasonable thing to do is to have as little of it as is possible. No man with his feet on the ground would dream of calling it an economy; as well refer to the Income Tax as an increase on income. As for the advertiser living up to his claims, he spends his life living them down. The thing that Mr. Buchanan-Taylor would like to believe is that the people who have the most money to splash about on advertising are the people who make the best goods, but the fact is that they have the most money precisely because they get rid of the worst goods. Modern advertisement is a kind of smoke screen put up between the consumer and the goods, so that he cannot see what he is getting. The advertiser, moreover, does not go by the board, but to the board; the board meeting that declares the latest and least justifiable dividends.

* * * *

London is threatened by an invasion of the latest architectural—or rather scenic—device of " Plastic Lighting " which has already transformed New York and Berlin into Cities of Dreadful Light. We are told to admire—at the St. James's Park Underground Offices for instance—the contrast between the remorseless austerity of the building and the prodigal cost of its nightly illumination. And,

indeed, the sheer perversity of the conception is impressive, after a Satanic fashion. To run up a palace on the cheap, and then to spend thousands on keeping it fit to be seen, is an admirable example of Efficiency. Gaunt, bare, repellent, and only capable of a certain nightmare effectiveness by artificial light and at an extravagant cost, these fashionable edifices are very like fashionable women. Caligula would have liked both.

* * * *

We published an article a few weeks ago about the remains of a Dinosaur recently discovered at Tetuan in Morocco, and we are now able to append a footnote which proves our contributor to have been almost as right as he was wrong. He poured sly scorn on the tentative scientific theory that the prehistoric beast was an American species and had migrated across the lost continent of Atlantis (raised for the occasion) to a well-earned grave in Africa. But, according to latest advices, it is now proved quite definitely to have come from America, though from Canada, not the United States. In fact they have discovered its name-plate which, in the case of this particular species, always bears the country of origin. The skeleton, which was covered with earth—the result of a landslip—has now been completely exposed, and tests have proved it to be metallic, the most notable feature being its great curved ribs of steel. Their rakish appearance impressed the members of the scientific mission from Madrid, and investigation showed that the Dinosaur was, in actual fact, a derelict hay-making machine. So down goes poor Atlantis to the bottom of the sea again.

PARLIAMENT

THE Charing Cross Bridge controversy may well prove a turning point in English constitutional history, for in the course of it the supposed rulers of this country have one by one proved impotent in the face, not of public opinion perhaps, but of a small and determined opposition. First of all the all-powerful financial interests, represented in this case by the Southern Railway, hearing talk about the scheme, announced that it was their railway bridge. They did not propose to allow any such scheme, and such talk had better cease. The Southern Railway was told that it did not govern this country, but it looked over its list of shareholders and directors, and gave a satisfied wink. In spite of that wink it was propitiated, and the L.C.C. next appeared on the scene.

After years of talk the present scheme was produced in a couple of months. It proposes to obstruct a site possessed of endless artistic and architectural possibilities with a structure only less unsightly than the present railway bridge. The requirements of road and river traffic are equally disregarded.

Though £14½ millions may be involved in compensation to various interests and in the construction work, a steel bridge (and at one time a suspension bridge seriously was considered) is to be built in order to save a couple of hundred thousands. Mr. Thomas, who has the financial interests of the steel industry very much at heart, made special arrangements for the easy passage of the Bill through Parliament without discussion. Modifications were made in the standing orders for that very purpose. Then, to the dismay of the conspirators, opposition appeared on the scene.

The fight put up by Sir Banister Fletcher, Sir Reginald Blomfield, Sir Martin Conway, and their associates, must ever be an inspiration to those who attempt to assert the rights of the individual or of the public against a seemingly omnipotent autocracy. They have carried on their indefatigable struggles in the face of overwhelming odds—the L.C.C., the Ministry of Transport, and endless vested interests. Sir Percy Simmons, the chief villain of the piece, took their opposition as a personal affront. In a fit of pique he has announced that if, as the result of the machinations of the Royal Institute of British Architects, his Charing Cross Bridge Bill is defeated in the Commons on Wednesday night, he will have Waterloo Bridge pulled down " just to larn 'em to be pigs."

The defeat of the Bill on Wednesday night would certainly be disastrous, for it would probably mean the dropping of the whole matter and the perpetuation of the present abomination which only Mr. G. Bernard Shaw loves. An amendment has been put down, however, requiring that, before work be proceeded with, further designs be obtained by means of an open competition or otherwise. An open competition can obviously be of no use in this particular case, but such an amendment would certainly provide the engineers with an opportunity of producing a more satisfactory scheme than their last hasty effort.

The champions of the Local Authorities (Enabling) Bill,

which passed its Second Reading on Friday, revealed that its chief purpose was the removal of the small dairy, butcher and baker. The supply of bread, according to Dr. Salter, needs rationalising, because the large bakeries cannot meet the competition of the smaller ones. If the smallers ones are eliminated and the larger municipalised, it will be possible to carry on the production of bread as wastefully and uneconomically as the largest plant can do it. There will be no competition, and if any misguided people really object to dearer bread the extra cost can be put on the rates. Captain Gunston looked forward with great pleasure to the day when Dr. Salter, having eliminated the redundant bakers, tries to reduce an equal number of redundant doctors. The Bill was the culmination of a campaign initiated many years ago in the drawing room of the Fabian Society, and the Government not having the courage to introduce it, was sneaking it through the House on a Friday morning, as a private member's Bill. In supporting municipalisation, Major Milner pointed out that the multiple store also uses public money, but provided by shareholders, and that in neither case is the management financially interested. That, of course, is the Distributist objection to both.

Sir K. Vaughan Morgan emphasized that the Bill proposed to remove the present safeguards of the individual against abuses by local authorities : the present direct appeal to Parliament, giving interested parties opportunities to be heard, and the discretion of Parliament itself were to be swept away. The Bill was a constitutional challenge to the powers of Parliament and the liberties of the citizens and ratepayers.

THREE BUSINESS VIRTUES.

I.—PUNCTUALITY.

Why write this letter?
Aeroplanes fall,
Mail-bags disappear,
And your spelling's queer
—Don't write at all—
Better, far better.

II.—TRUTH.

Never tell lies :
They return, like flies,
And buzz round the cerebellum.
—Get other people to tell 'em.

III.—EFFICIENCY.

Into grandma's snuff
James put *just* enough
Cyanide.
Grandma' died.

H. V. T. BURTON.

The Drink Problem
A Distributist Solution
By H. S. D. Went

NEARLY twenty years ago it was pointed out in *The Eye Witness*—in an unanswerable " Open Letter to a Temperance Reformer "—that the real Drink Problem is the problem of how to supply drink to the people, so that the supply may be as good, cheap, and wholesome as possible. With the exception of the Distributist League no organised body has attempted to solve that problem.

Probably the simplest, and most sensible solution would be to return to the medieval practice of Free Trade in drink, combined with a strict local inspection to insure good quality. A century of Pussyfoot propaganda has, however, so emasculated the minds of the bulk of our contemporaries as to render such a common-sense measure impracticable. Recognising this, we have worked out, and now offer for your consideration, an alternative solution which is perfectly practicable, and—to any reasonable person who has not got an axe to grind—unexceptionable.

First and foremost, we demand—we do not suggest or ask—that all restrictions on the manufacture, sale, and consumption of excisable liquors imposed since August 4th, 1914, shall be removed forthwith. We base our demand on the pledge given by Mr. Lloyd George on April 20th, 1915. He was then asking the House of Commons to empower the Central Control Board (Liquor Traffic) to impose restrictions, and said : " These powers are for the purpose of the War only—limited to the period of the War. We do not want to raise any issue beyond that." That pledge has been shamelessly and repeatedly broken by every Government which has held office since the War ended. First by Mr. Lloyd George himself, then by the late Mr. Bonar Law, by Mr. Baldwin (twice), and by Mr. Ramsay MacDonald (twice). After the War was over the Coalition Government made the bulk of the " war-time " restrictions permanent, by the Licensing Act of 1921. This was an " Agreed Act"; that is to say it was the result of an agreement between the Pussyfoots and the Trade, the former getting as many vexatious restrictions as the nation would stand, and the latter getting their profits and—as they thought—freedom from further Pussyfoot pestering. The people were not consulted as to this agreement, and it is with considerable amusement that we recall that the King's signature was hardly dry upon the Act before the Pussyfoots began to " double-cross " their accomplices and work for additional restrictions. We demand that the crime against the nation committed in 1921 be undone, and the pledge of 1915 honoured.

The next essential to a good supply of drink is that there should be plenty of places where drink can be obtained. Since 1904 all our Governments have pursued a policy of reducing licences on a plea of " redundancy." To the ordinary mortal it is obvious that a public-house which was really redundant would very soon be closed by its owner ; just as is a redundant butcher's, or baker's, or candle-stick-maker's—for people do not keep public-houses for fun, but to make a living by keeping them. The Temperance Reformer, however, thinks otherwise, and—as he has a pull with the politicians—committees of local big-wigs (many of whom are Pussyfoots) called Licensing Justices are empowered to close such public-houses as they—in their wisdom—consider that the public does not want. A man who has only to go round the corner to get a drink is not likely to drink so much as he would if he had to go two or three miles to get one. In a crowded bar there is no opportunity for rational talk, games, or music ; or in fact for doing anything but drink. If a public-house is crowded, the landlord has great difficulty in seeing that none of his customers has had more than is good for him. A policy of reductions for " redundancy," which leads to a scarcity of public-houses, conduces, therefore, to a low standard of sobriety. Anyone who doubts the truth of this can verify it by referring to the Home Office *Licensing Statistics* which are published annually. Figures will be found there which prove that—in town and country alike—where there is a large proportion of public-houses to population there is, almost invariably, a high standard of sobriety ; and where there is a small proportion of licences to population there is, almost invariably, a relatively low standard of sobriety. We therefore propose that " redundancy " should no longer be considered a ground for refusing a licence.

Having by these two simple measures provided that the supply of drink shall be good, we have now to deal with the question of cheapness. The obvious way to reduce the price of drink is to reduce the grossly unjust load of taxation which drink now bears. When you pay 7d. a pint for beer to-day, you are paying nearly $3\frac{1}{4}$d. in tax. Before the War, beer of the same strength was sold at $2\frac{1}{2}$d. a pint, of which $\frac{1}{4}$d. was tax. Before the War a bottle of whisky could be bought for 3/6. To-day a bottle of the same brand, but lower strength, costs 12/6, of which 8/5 is tax. At the present time about forty-three per cent. of what the Pussyfoots call " the Nation's Drink Bill " goes to the Government in the form of taxes which cost very little to collect. If the substantial reductions which justice demands were made in these taxes, the Government would find it difficut to find the money to pay for their grossly inflated staff of officials. We realise, therefore, that such a reduction must be accompanied by a large reduction in public expenditure. For this reason we have no great hopes of achieving this item of our programme in the near future.

(To be continued.)

The Chair-Leg Maker
By Hugh Camborne

IN this mechanical age it is somewhat surprising to find that chair-legs, even the cheap ones, are made by hand. Other chair parts are made by machinery, but the making of legs and " stretchers " is a rural industry, the son taking up his father's work.

The legs are made in the villages of the Chiltern Hills. When cut, they are laid out on the garden hedges to dry, which here and there are broad and flat from the weight of them. But the leg-making industry is older than the hedges. It grew up with the beech-woods.

Beech is used for this craft because for generations the hills have been covered with beech trees. It is cheap to buy, which is essential, and it is on the spot.

There is no fortune in the industry. The manufacturer receives for each article from three farthings to a penny half-penny. The orders come from the chair factories.

At the price, the hand-turned legs are actually as profitable to the factory owner as they are when made by machinery. For the maker a week of full work produces only the equivilent of a labourer's wage.

The industry is depressed for lack of new recruits. It is kept alive by family tradition. To a stranger it may seem to lack variety—and it is curious that there is no evidence that it formerly embraced the manufacture of the whole chair. According to local opinion it has always been confined to the lathe-worked parts, the legs and "stretchers." No doubt the seat, arms, and back each have their own history, but it seems to have been written elsewhere.

Yet to the owner of a " shop," as he calls it, the work is of absorbing interest. As he wanders through the beech-woods, a grotesque figure, one could imagine that he had sprung up out of their rugged roots. He is examining the trees which are marked for cutting, and will bid for those he fancies at the autumn and winter sales. He calls such a day in the words his " holiday." He is equally happy at the bench in the work and its problems—planning how to discharge an order within the time limit, disposing of the by-products of chips and logs for firing. Always he has the dignity of a man who is working for himself.

" We Scientists"
By Q. U. O.

SCIENCE—KNOWLEDGE. Such is the first and most simple definition of the word in question given by Doctor Johnson in his Dictionary. There are two other definitions which are subsidiary and more limited. These need not occupy our attention. The main definition is obvious. The Doctor, for all his knowledge of the English language, never condescended to unnecessary elaboration in expressing himself.

Science in its true sense is Knowledge. But we live in a more enlightened age than Doctor Johnson lived in, or we think we do; and there is more knowledge in the world now than existed in his day, or we like to think there is. And there are more scientists, or persons who call themselves such.

Was Doctor Johnson a scientist? He possessed great stores of knowledge of varied character. He was probably the best informed man of his day. No other person then living could have performed what he performed in the compilation of his Dictionary practically unaided. No one of the present-day could equal his feat. We may, therefore, assume that he was a scientist of pre-eminence. But would scientists of to-day admit this?

What is a modern scientist? A modern scientist is, broadly speaking, a specialist of narrow outlook and, I fear, of narrow habit of mind. Broadly speaking, I say, for there are exceptions of importance but of limited number : persons of deep penetration and acquistive powers; of open minds endowed with critical faculties. But clustering around these like the exterior of a nebula; or pendant from them like the tail of a comet, what do we find? Why, this. An indescribable mass of formless, shapeless satellites, almost invisible in their tenuosity, almost indistinguishable in their nebulosity; possessing minds of jelly-fish, revolving in orbits so circumscribed as to appear stationary.

Who or what are these small souls, if souls they can be called? I cannot tell you who or what they are. But I can tell you what they call themselves. They style themselves " We Scientists."

And what do they do? They usurp the functions of the Creator. They create to-day the universe after their own ideas; and next year they re-create it on a different principle; just as a child builds an edifice of bricks, knocks it down and rebuilds on a different plan. And how they love the crash.

Like busy ants with a piece of straw, so they with their theories. They pull, push, tug, turn over, revolve, and in the end they regain their original formation having accomplished nothing. The chemist, the physiologist, the geologist, the theologist, the biologist and all the rest of the crowd—they batter each other, they shriek, yell, howl at one another; they curse each other, they embrace one another, they rush together, they fly apart, and they achieve—nothing.

Are they truly scientists? God forbid. They do well enough for our cheap journals. That is their metier. And their limit.

But if Science does not dwell with these, where is it to be found?

My answer is that it dwells in the hearts and minds of those who do not separate geology from chemistry, chemistry from theology, and so on; who recognise all knowledge centred in one authority; who do not seek for facts in one branch to disprove or to stultify facts in another branch; who seek to co-ordinate rather than to separate; who take no unholy joy in endeavouring to create disbelief in what others endeavour to prove; who get something worth out of everything; who do not lose themselves in a maze of half-baked theories; who through the dim perceptions of our limited intelligences see shining in the distance a Great Light.

BALBUS BUILDS A WALL.

Winston's task is nearly done.
(*Blow the bugle, slap the brick* !),
Does the labour count as fun?
Not in his arithmetic.
He's an amateur of all
Arts of life and politics;
It's a sort of tariff wall.
(*Blow the bugle, slap the bricks* !).

Not a wall that circles round—
Heavens high and inches thick—
All his dear ancestral ground
(*Blow the bugle, slap the brick* !);
But a safeguard here and there—
Not one tax upon the tum—
Quite a workmanlike affair.
(*Blow the bugle, beat the drum* !).

Winston's wall is rather chic.
(*Blow the taxes* ! *Slap the stick* !)

W. R. TITTERTON.

Straws in the Wind

THE PRIEST OF THE RED CZAR
By G. K. CHESTERTON

MANY of those most deeply familiar with Russia believe that the Bolshevists only conquered the many other revolutionary parties in the Revolution, because they alone secured the services of the Secret Police of the old regime. It was the natural beginning and full assurance of the dawn of light, liberty and peace of mind to know that the police were even more completely concealed than the criminal classes. Naturally, they often dressed up as each other; and this general tone of imitative colouring led to many confusions, even to confusion of mind. Sometimes the policeman himself was not quite certain whether he was a policeman or a dynamiter disguised as a policeman, or yet again, perhaps, a policeman disguised as a dynamiter. He never could be quite sure (it would seem from some wistful Slavonic fragments) whether he was conspiring against himself, or spying upon himself, or betraying himself to himself for the destruction of all existing things and the good of Holy Russia. All this increased the simple bewilderment in his blank blue innocent Russian eyes. According to the stories of the old regime, it really troubled him that he could not be sure whether he was a policeman or a criminal. With the new regime, having presumably discovered that he can be both, he seems to be more lively; and anyhow, as I say, there are some of experience of authority who think that his liveliness has been responsible for the success, in the brutal sense, of the Bolshevist revolt. In that case, it is only fair to withdraw some of the exaggerated charges against the mere nihilism of the new Russia. It is not fair to say that the Bolshevists are mere destroyers. They have destroyed the great golden shrines and the holy eagle of Constantine and the last traditions of Byzantine culture. But they have preserved the spies and the executioners and the torturers with all reasonable care.

But there is one other queer little relic that the Bolshevists have taken over from the Czars, besides the notion of a Secret Police. They have set up as a sort of side-show in their great exhibition a curious sort of semi-official Church. Though the avowed and active creed of the whole system is a wild materialism, they keep a poor old priest on a string, as something between a curio and a captive of war, on condition that he is not " agin' the government "; or, in other words, on condition that he does not protest against anything they choose to do and say. It is, of course, a repetition of the one really bad mistake made by the great men of the French Revolution. Instead of leaving the Roman Church alone, as something on another plane (as the American Republic very wisely did), they tried to construct a new artificial Roman Church to fit into their own civil service; and found they had nothing but a few discredited and cynical abbés, whom all the real Catholics despised as traitors and all the other people despised as priests. It is the representative of this curious new official Orthodoxy in Russia, who is represented as having piped up his melancholy notes to answer the Pope about religious persecution. I say it is supposed to be; for doubts are thrown on the authenticity of such news from Russia; and it would be unjust to the Metropolitan Sergius to assume that the notes are necessarily his own.

Anyhow, they are very unmistakably the notes of a captive bird. Even in an utterance like this, of course, there are some things that are true enough. The speaker says that the old Orthodox Church was too much disposed to identify itself with the old Government. We can only add that the new Orthodox Church is following in father's footsteps; and seems quite as conscious of the worldly wisdom of identifying itself with whatever is the existing Government.

Of course, it is only to be expected that a person in such a position says that nobody in Russia is persecuted for religion, but only for really diabolical things like objecting to the Government. I never heard of any persecutor, or apologist for persecutors, who did not rightly or wrongly say that. The Early Christians were martyred, not for any matter of religion, but merely for implying that some adventurer or debauchee, chosen by the Legions, was not a god when he said he was a god. The English Martyrs were not hanged, drawn and quartered for heresy, but only for treason in going to Mass when Queen Elizabeth said it was treason to go to Mass. It is always easy to base persecution on politics; and the very cases where this is most tenable are those to which the critic refers as the persecutions attributed to Rome. The Spanish Inquisition really was Spanish much more than Roman; an effort to dig out the Moors and their allies. The Bartholomew was a popular Paris revolution against nobles who wanted to loot in France as they did in England. I am not going into that long story now; but it is broadly true that Roman persecution was the protection of a popular religion against alien aggression. The Russian case is just the opposite; an alien few destroying what everybody knew to be the solid soul of Russia.

There is one other touch, which always alienates me from Bolshevism; it is bookish. The apologist says utterly unreal things, like calling the Pope a financier, or allying him with English land-holders; most of whom hold land stolen from his Church. The Sacred Book of Marx, having been written sixty years ago, doubtless conceived British milords as millionaires owning the earth; to-day the landowners are pretty dicky even about owning land. That is more than the blunder of the foreigner; it is that of a man blind to the living world around him. A few English landlords have been Catholic or Anglo-Catholic; of many it would be not unfair to say that they had no religion except a dislike of the Pope. To talk of the two conspiring is to rave at random; and above all to miss the main modern fact; that the really powerful Capitalist forces of to-day are not Christian, but every bit as Pagan as the Bolshevists—and rather like them.

Slipping The Sign

By Agag

IT is said that while Seddon, the poisoner, was standing in the dock to receive sentence he waggled a masonic sign—or, it may have been, winked a masonic wink—at the judge, who was also a mason. In spite of this, the judge sentenced him to death, although they say that his voice was broken with tears as he pronounced the dreadful words.

This kind of anecdote is as good as an annuity to an enterprising journalist like myself, a Press College graduate, a Free Lance With a System Who in His Leisure Hours Can Make Anything from £50 to £500 per Week by Note of Hand Alone—I mean, by His Pen. There may be a few subjects which it would be difficult to introduce by the narration of this simple story, but for the moment I cannot think of them. My only concern is to decide which treatment is likely to be of most benefit to you, dear reader, to your mind, to your morals and, above all, to your Efficiency as a Unit-Force in the Great World-Struggle for Prosperity, Production and Brotherhood.

The article on " Blind Justice," dragging in Brutus and Abraham; emphasising the high standards of incorruptibility maintained throughout the ages by our British sense of straight-dealing; striking off at Herod and Russia, by way of contrast; and winding up on a high note of Service—" But the British judge, when he takes office, must learn to steel himself, not only against financial temptation and the calls of blood, but also against appeals more powerful and more spiritual. With broken and bleeding heart, he must maintain, whatever the cost to himself, those standards of English justice and fair-play, which have, etc.—that article would, as you have remarked, be a wow, a certain three guineas from *Tim o' Tooting's* or any of the pop-eyed weeklies; but to a craftsman like myself, it seems a trifle obvious. There are more subtle lessons to be drawn from the story.

More workmanlike would be the article on " Forethought in Business." " Too many of us, like Seddon, are apt to go through life without any serious thought for the morrow. We flounder along from day to day until we find ourselves faced with a crisis. Not until then do we consider the dangers which encompass us. Not until then do we think of slipping a sign to the authorities. Are you like Seddon? Will *you* wait until you are in the dock—until the chance has passed and the Great Recorder is closing your account with those sad words : ' Too Late '? Or will you be one of those who look forward? Will you plan ahead—not days, but weeks and years ahead? Get into the habit of seeing the authorities before you do the job. Work it all out at the Lodge and take the advice of more experienced men. You may say that this requires thought, trouble and organisation; but remember that no great prize is ever won without exertion." And so on.

Or, again, treating the incident as an allegory, we could strike rather a neat line on Empire Free Trade. " A scene not unlike that which was witnessed many years ago in that tragic court-room, is being enacted again to-day, but with this difference : the court-room is the world; the prisoner is represented by our Dominions and Colonies, shackled as they are by our obsolete tariff policy; we, the people of these islands, are the judge. The Empire is making a masonic sign to us—the sign of that great brotherhood which was established by Drake and Rhodes and Cromwell. The decision is with us. Will we ignore the sign? Are we too hidebound by our shibboleths to heed their call? Will we sentence them to death? Or will we rise and take them by the hand—the people of our own blood, the members of a fellowship as great in its own way as the Masonic Craft? Speaking at the opening of the annual Flower Show at Norbury, yesterday, Councillor T. C. Mutton said, etc."

The sales-provoking article on " Specialisation : To-day's World-Need " would, it is true, find a wider market among both the dailies and the weeklies. " The square peg in the round hole is a pitiable object and we can well sympathise with the emotion expressed by the judge. Perhaps until that moment he had been unaware that Seddon was on the square. In a flash, the tragedy of the man's life is revealed to him. He is a mason, but a mason with overweening vanity and confidence in himself. He is not content to hold to the traditions of his craft. Blackmail, perjury, coining, pocket-picking, forgery, bucket-shopkeeping, and the long firm fraud are not good enough for him. He thinks that, without training, without experience, he can take on the ' other fellow's ' job. He doesn't care whether murder is a masonic sort of crime or not. He can do it. Too often is this attitude adopted in modern business to-day. Too many men who have been successful in putting out forged scrip, who have devoted themselves to it the whole of their lives, think, as Seddon thought, that it will be as easy for them to make money at some other industrial enterprise. And too often they learn to their cost, as Seddon learnt, that specialisation is the keynote of success in the field of modern commerce."

For the Vegetarian, the Buddhist, and the Labour Press, something might be worked out on the " No More Punishment " line. " Picture the agony of the judge. The man whom he is to sentence to destruction is—as he suddenly finds—a man like himself. They have perchance sat at the same table, drunk together the health of the Great Architect of the Universe. As brother masons they may even have exchanged greetings : ' Worshipful Junior Grand Warden, is the Lodge properly tyled? ' ' Worshipful Senior Grand Deacon, the Lodge is about as properly tyled as it is darn well going to be to-night. And now, what about a quick one? ' This is the duty which we impose upon our judges—we who hold ourselves to be a civilised people. At any moment of the day they must be ready to sentence fellow-men, fellow-members of lodges and tennis-clubs, to death, or worse, to the brutal and degrading ' cat,' which, necessitating, as it does, removal of the prisoner's shirt, deprives him of all moral sense and lowers him to the level of the beasts. This is the sort of punishment which we cause to be inflicted, instead of providing teachers to show misguided convicts how wicked it is to kill people and bang children about. Cinema pictures showing the pain which such acts cause would do more towards making the world a garden of peace than all the hangings and lashings which now take place. And, once the initial cost was defrayed, it would probably be cheaper."

But on the whole, I am inclined to think that the best articles would be those on Prayer, on Saluting, on Sportsmanship, on Putting it Across, on the World-Faith of the Future, and on the Ad. That Pulls.

Poor devil, if he hadn't broken down at the last moment no one would have known that he was a mason.

Edwin Pugh

By J. D. Gleeson

EDWIN Pugh died a week or so ago, and the event was practically unnoticed. Pugh has suffered an eclipse during the last years. The glory of his first achievements belongs to an older generation, and he never took the trouble to reproduce them for the present age. He belonged to the 'nineties in one sense, that he made this period the period of his literary career. He began his work at a time when such work was accounted really worthy work; before the novel had become cheap. It was realistic novel work, studies, character sketches, and so on, in the same tradition as Dickens, but a Dickens seen through the by-no-means-clear glasses of Gissing. It was Dickens without Dickens, so to speak, which sounds the very dickens. Anyway, Pugh was welcomed by Henley and his shouting young men, many of whom had something really worth shouting about. They were an earnest band of workers and a jovial band of players, and Pugh worked and played with the best; rather better indeed than the best.

It was the study of the Cockney type that he made his special task and he really did succeed in uncovering, that is, discovering, the actual human being that lurked beneath the London exterior. It was the Cockney soul that he was looking for, and he found it; but the soul itself was sad and the author saddened with it. It was, in fact, the character of the kind of work that Pugh did that the centre itself (when found) was invariably an object of pity. The band with which he worked, and in some sense to which he belonged, was eternally gay in its talk and eternally sorrowful in its work. When they were together in their leisure, their spirits rose higher and higher; then they were alone with their thoughts, their spirits sank and fell. The truth, perhaps, is that they were all pagans at heart. They feasted for to-day, but put to-morrow in their books.

It was probably Pugh's misfortune that his first real book was his masterpiece. A masterpiece may rarely be repeated, for if one manages to put all, or most, of one's inspiration into one work, the rest must seem comparatively uninspired. But it is a double misfortune if this should happen at the commencement of one's career, for in that degree the career is over; the rest is anti-climax. At any rate *Tony Drum* was written at the beginning of Pugh's literary life, and the critics hailed it for what it was, an outstanding work of genius. The author took his place in the front rank of the novelists, meeting them all on equal terms. He enjoyed himself for a while, and then he wrote another book. It was not a masterpiece, and the critics did not fail to say so. With the cheerful inconsistency of Fleet Street, the reviewers turned round and began to take back the good things they had said about Pugh. He was a sensitive man, and the hostile attitude of his late friends seems to have been taken to heart.

The first pleasure of literary success was over, and Pugh probably felt a keen anger towards the critics who now spoke in hard terms of his new works. Pugh knew how to hate, and how to keep on hating. It was a quality he did *not* share with his Cockney characters, who do not know the meaning of sustained hate. But Pugh, though he had found the Cockney and drawn his picture for the world to see, and though he had been brought up in London, was not himself a Londoner. He was a Welshman. Though he had discovered the mystery of London, he was himself trapped in the mystery of Wales. It was from this older and alien race that he got his enmity, and sometimes when you looked into his deep brown eyes, you would find fires that you did not understand.

But though he might be dissatisfied with his critics, there were other reasons why Pugh did not retain his enthusiasm in his trade. It is possible that if his critics had at this time been kinder, if they had encouraged instead of discouraging him and making him resolve never to please them again, he would have repeated his first success. On the other hand, it is possible that he questioned very sharply whether the work he was doing was worth doing. I mean, he had become a first-class novelist rather too easily, and he asked himself what was the value of the position he held. I think that he came to the conclusion that the importance of the novelist is overrated, that novel writing is a pleasant hobby, but a poor profession. At any rate, he let his position go without any particular effort to retain it. He suffered his light to be hidden under a bushel, and it did not depress him. He saw his sales diminish and his name eclipsed by lesser names, and he still lived on cheerily, talking of this, that and the other, refusing to worry about Pugh the novelist. Occasionally he would speak of " Regaining his London position," but he seemed to say it because he expected that you would expect him to say it; and he never did regain his position, for the excellent reason that he never tried.

The best books of the later years were not novels at all, and the last great book that Pugh wrote was never even published. The books on Dickens were a worthy contribution to the literature of that great subject, and the book on London, *The City of the World*, is, in its way, a classic. But the really great book was the volume on H. G. Wells that Pugh did not publish. *Big-Little H. G. Wells* appeared somewhat over ten years ago serially in *The New Witness,* and just as in earlier days Pugh had searched for the soul of the Cockney, so now he searched for the soul of Mr. Wells. The development, greatness and limitations of H. G. W. are only to be found in that unprinted book. It was a study of a living character, frank yet friendly, and one which lived with a life of its own. Wells objected to it at the time, but the book should have been published. It does him no injustice, but it does a very big justice to Pugh.

Pugh will not be forgotten by those who knew him. The tiny white-haired man, with the trim pointed beard and the large kindly eyes, stands out like one of his own drawings; and that is a big compliment to his work. He would take his place in the arm-chair and talk and talk about literature, sport (especially boxing), Dickens, beer, all things. He would tell of a review he had just written on Barry Pain, for instance, beginning: " We once thought that Barry Pain could write anything—and now he does," or he might be threatening to fight you. His friends were always persuading him not to fight one of themselves. And then for long periods he would disappear, returning eventually after weeks or months, to drop again into the chair and resume the conversation at the point where it had dropped. His friends were accustomed to these sudden but prolonged absences, but now Pugh has really disappeared.

Books of the Week

PERSONAL RESPONSIBILITY

CONTINENTAL STATESMEN. By George Glasgow. Geoffrey Bles. 10s. 6d. net.

THE TIGER, GEORGES CLEMENCEAU, 1841-1929. By George Adam. Jonathan Cape. 10s. 6d. net.

AS a preface to his sketches of continental statesmen, Mr. Glasgow has prefixed a remark made by Mr. Baldwin to the House of Commons, on July 26th, 1929. " If disaster comes, if bloodshed comes, as it often has in our history, the politicians always escape. The worst that can happen to the politician is loss of office ; and the men who give their blood are generally those whose hands have had nothing to do with the laying of the train that led to the explosion."

That observation is correct when it applies to the politicians of this country, but it is difficult to see why it should be made a text for a book on the statesmen of Europe. Mr. Glasgow deals as fully as he can with a random selection of politicians from France, Spain, Italy, the Balkans, the Slav countries, Russia, Germany, even from Scandinavia. He is distinctly honest, both in his selection of characters and in what he writes about them. As a correspondent abroad and as Foreign Editor of the *Contemporary Review* he has acquired material and formed judgments. After that experience he might easily have turned to books by other people and mugged up complete little essays so as to cover the gaps in his knowledge. But, in fact, he sets down what he knows about a man, leaves unsaid what he does not know about him, peppers his prejudices over the pages, and delivers the salad for the opinion of his public. When he is wildly wrong, or one-sided, it is probably because he has no material to work upon. Consequently, the book is readable and journalistic without being sensational copy ; and an example of his good judgment is shown in his remarks on Primo di Rivera, which have been partially verified in the past fortnight. But still he leaves the mystery unsolved why he used as a text the remark by Stanley Baldwin that the politician always escapes. True, he writes nothing about the dead politicians who have not escaped. But, even of those with whom he deals, Mussolini escaped by a hair's breadth with a bullet through the nose, and Dr. Seipel suffered a bullet wound through the lungs. Venizelos fled Greece for his life ; and Greece has been notorious since the war for a massacre of politicians. Raditch was shot in the Diet of a country which had already seen the slaughtering of its royal family. The fact is that politics take on quite a different character in countries where the politicians are personally aware that they may not escape, though they may be in the right, if the people, or even their political opponents alone, are really exasperated.

One of the results of this situation is that braver men go in for politics. Mussolini may now have shaken nerves, but he has fought in the trenches and made light of assassins. Smetona and Pilsudski have shown personal courage all their lives. Masaryk and Hindenburg are unlike in every other characteristic but that. And, among the dead statesmen of whom Clemenceau does not speak, Clemenceau stands out as a man afraid of nothing.

Mr. George Adam has written a very interesting book on Clemenceau, although it must be kept in mind that the Tiger is but recently dead. Settled opinions take some time to form ; and many of the twists and turns in Clemenceau's chequered career Mr. Adam does not attempt to explain. He may, however, be taken on the whole as a real admirer of the old cynic. And, in fact, it is easy to admire a man who faced hostile crowds imputably whenever he had to, who fought duels whenever they were necessary, and who constantly dared his parliamentary opponents to tear him out of the tribune if they must. The odds were that they might ; but it is difficult to imagine the most violent English politician being even torn away from the despatch-box by his friends on the other side of the House.

In other respects, too, Clemenceau's life was something quite remarkable. He was born in the year that saw the body of Napoleon placed in the Invalides. He was in America during the Civil Wars and entered Richmond with General Grant. He was a mayor in Paris during the Franco-Prussian War. He was a middle-aged man when he took on the championship of Dreyfus. And he should have been an old dotard when the war began which made him supreme ruler of France and the man who dictated the terms which were meant to reverse the result of Sedan ; after that he settled down to philosophic works which gained him the admiration of all sorts of people in the new Europe.

He was one of the great figures, and now there is an end to him. He was made for a period of five years, when he mobilised France by denying all his previous principles ; and in those five years he atoned for the obscurities of his previous political life. But neither then nor at any other time did he ever think or state that the politician always escaped. He knew his own responsibilities. But in England they order things very differently.

ARTHUR MIDGHAM.

LONDON'S PUBLIC SCHOOL

MERCHANT TAYLORS' SCHOOL　　Basil Blackwell. 10s. 6d.

THE history of the English Public Schools has been a very chequered one, but its general aspect has been more black than white. The older foundations have suffered from the fact that they were richly-endowed and always worth plundering. Materially they have not suffered very much in the long run because they have been re-endowed by the rich whose special preserve they have become. But their material status has been maintained at the expense of their educational value and their foundation statutes. These last, based as was Winchester the first and the model of the rest, on sound moral as well as educational principles, were finally thrown away by the Act of 1868 and other enactments of the past century. The *pauperes et indigentes* of Wykeham's Statutes stand a poor chance of receiving the free education provided for them at Eton and elsewhere, though theoretically it is still accessible to them.

On the other hand certain of the old foundations retain more of the virtues and less of the vices of the Public School system as we know it. Chief amongst these are

St. Paul's and the Merchant Taylors', whose history is now before us. These, being day schools, do not deprive the boys of the home influence which we still believe, despite the chaotic state of the modern home, to be essential to a proper education. They spare the boys the barbaric bullying and the immediate moral dangers which were prominent features of the public schools of a few generations ago and have not wholly disappeared. Whatever Spartan qualities may have been implanted on those hard and insensitive enough to survive, and however famous the survivors may have become in politics, the City, or the Army, there is no doubt that they ruined more good men than they made.

Schools like the Merchant Taylors', or perhaps we should say schools following that model, have suffered less change than the boarding-schools. On the whole they have retained more of their old traditions and pursued the " even tenor of their way " more peacefully. Perhaps that is why the present volume on the Merchant Taylors' School is on the slight side and falls back on its historically interesting neighbours, the Charterhouse and St. Etheldreda's, Ely Place, to provide bulk to the book. In fact, of course, these do more than that. No history of the School, any more than any other history, is complete without its local historical setting and background. It is educationally essential to realise that one is a part of a living stream of history. In this case the end chapters complete the book.

Wisely the school society has allotted the several chapters to various members. The result is cohesive and very readable for the general public as well as the particular. The history of a public school, particularly one so situated in the heart of London and so specially the school of its citizens, great and small, is surely a matter of public interest. O.M.T.'s will rejoice that this timely volume has been so well produced.

Short Reviews

ON GOING TO PRESS. *By F. L. Stevens. Methuen, 3s. 6d. net.*

Descriptions of experiences likely to befall the young journalist form the greater part of this book, which Mr. Stevens has tried to keep free from the " pedagogic note." We would recommend it for what it is worth, were the author less tendencious. But when he remarks that the journalist of yesterday " worked at odd hours . . . was an example of splendid loyalty to his newspaper and foolish indifference to his own and his family's wants," and thus differed from the journalists of to-day, who " are anxious to take their place in the world as men of culture and dignity," we are reminded of the statement of the jacket, that his " professional growing-pains are not yet ended." If some of the activities referred to in this book are illustrative of the work of cultured, dignified men, it becomes necessary to ask Mr. Stevens for definitions of his definitions.

Allowances must be made, of course, for satire. But the preface suggests a curious blindness to essentials. We are told that " if journalists organised not only to increase wages but to improve the standard of writing, to insist on some academic qualification, they might benefit both prestige and pocket." There are such things as purpose and understanding and loyalty to belief, as well as prestige and security. There is still such a thing as independence, even in journalism.

In the last chapter it is said that the journalist must ally himself with his fellow-craftsmen, for purposes of protection, training and culture, as he has done already by means of a union which " has won for him very real victories in the matter of wages and hours." While hating to intrude in the domestic politics of our own craft, we should be glad to know what is meant by " culture " and why the Institute of Journalists, which wisely stresses the professional status of the true journalist, has been so clearly ignored.

One of the gravest dangers facing journalism at the present time is that journalists themselves are becoming fatalistic. Their object now seems to be, not to stand out against the commercialisation and degradation of the Press, but to accept servitude with the manner, if not with the mind, of Uriah Heep. Mr. Stevens has neglected to comment clearly on this important tendency.

WHO'S WHO IN THE THEATRE. *Edited by John Parker. Isaac Pitman. 30s. net.*

The sixth edition of this important work contains a synopsis of playbills issued during the past five years, biographies of leading artists, authors, producers and critics, geneæological tables, seating plans, tables of stage dimensions, and other information of value to people associated with the theatre. The editor, who is the secretary of the Critics' Circle, can be charged with very few omissions, and must be congratulated on the accuracy of his detailed notes.

Gramophone Notes

February Records

THEODORE CHALIAPINE, the great Russian bass, has returned to the fold of the Gramophone Company, the early February list including his rendering of Dargomwijsky's *The Old Corporal* and Flegier's *The Horn,* fine records both (H.M.V. D.B. 1342).

Mischa Nevitzki, accompanied by Sir Landon Ronald and the London Symphony Orchestra, plays effectively Liszt's somewhat flamboyant Pianoforte Concerto in E flat major (D.1775-1776). Liszt has been popular of late with the gramophone companies. So, too, have the Viennese waltz type of composers. This month there is a record of Dr. Leo Bleech and the Berlin State Opera Orchestra in Henberger's *The Opera Ball* overture (C.1799), and of the International Novelty Orchestra performing the *Carmen Sylva,* waltz and the waltzes from the operetta *Eva,* by Lehar (C.1808).

The mid-month issue includes a fine record of Debussy's *L'Après Midi d'un faune,* played by Leopold Stokowski and the Philadelphia Symphony Orchestra (D.1768); another Bach organ record, the *Fantasia and Fugue in G minor,* played by G. D. Cunningham on the organ of St. Margaret's Church, Westminster (C.1812); Mendelssohn's *Ruy Blas Overture* by the Symphony Orchestra, conducted by Malcolm Sargent (C.1813); and some excellent dance records by Jack Hylton and others.

Two special issues of the month are of interest. One is of selected Irish music, the other of H.M. the King's Speech at the opening of the Naval Conference in London. This last, which is issued in specially decorated discs, is an excellent piece of recording.

The Columbia Gramophone Company have as large a list as usual, mostly of the light variety. Two excellent music-hall records are of Will Fyffe, the Scottish comedian (9928), and one of Will Hay's amusing sketches (5695-5696). Miss Irene Scharrer is at her pianistic best in Liszt's *Hungarian Rhapsody* (9920), and Miss Yelli D'Aranyi's beautiful violin tone well reproduced in Brahm's *Hungarian Dance No. 8,* and *Souvenir* by Drdla (5681). An interesting contrast in lyric tenors is obtained by a record each of Hubert Eisdell, singing *Mary, My Mary,* and *Best of All* (5686); of William Heseltine in *Ailsa Mine* and *Mountain Lovers* (9923); and of Francis Russell singing Wagner's *Prize Song* and Handel's *Sound an Alarm* (9924). Paul Whiteman and his orchestra return to the fray with special arrangements of Rimsky-Korsakov's *Song of India* and Liszt's *Liebestraum* (9798), and Sir Dan Godfrey and the Bournemouth Municipal Orchestra are heard in *Whispering Pines* and *Zip Zip* (5683).

The mid-month issue is also chiefly of a light nature. The best record is one of Kit Keen singing *Lily of Laguna* and *Little Dolly Day Dream* (5720), both of which he renders in a manner worthy of Eugene Stratton. Another amusing record is that obtained of Mr. Flotsam and Mr. Jetsam (5709).

The Decca Records include in an excellent February issue, thirteen of A. A. Milne's "Pooh" songs, set to music by H. Fraser-Simson, and sung by Dale Smith. The records are two double-sided discs (M.105-106). There is also a record of Olga Olgina, soprano, singing Rossini's ever popular *Una Voce,* accompanied by orchestra, conducted by Basil Cameron (M.92).   V. N. L.

The Drama

Michael and Mary

MR. A. A. Milne has tried his hand again at the Three-Act play. This time he is more successful, though in *Michael and Mary,* at the St. James's Theatre, the flats are still badly joined, and the main love theme suffers from a criminal sub-plot.

The story opens charmingly on a seat in the British Museum, where a young lady, in the terrifying costume of 1904, encounters a young gentleman. She is pretty and forsaken. He is literary and romantic. He learns that her husband has left her without a penny, and that she has no prospect of work. He insists on dividing with her his capital of £100, and they make an agreement to meet at the Museum every month to discuss progress.

In the second scene we find them established on separate floors in respectable lodgings in Islington. He has achieved some journalistic success, and she has got a job. They are ecstatically in love, but Victorian scruples—or should one say Edwardian—prevent him from speaking. She has a husband! At this point the play creaks badly with the introduction of Michael's father, a fictional clergyman, who all but leads his son in prayer. He extorts a promise that Michael will marry Mary for fear lest a lapse from grace might ensue. Michael keeps his promise, and the two young people deliberately commit bigamy.

We next see them after the War, in 1919. Michael is making money, and Mary has borne a son, now at school. Moreover, she has been interviewed in the evening Press with accompanying photograph. This mild publicity is their undoing. There enters Mr. Weston, Mary's legal husband, who has just returned from the States, noticed the paragraph and come to levy blackmail.

But Michael is not having any, and promptly knocks the fellow down. He incontinently dies of heart disease, leaving his corpse upon their hands. There follows a rehearsal of the story to be told to the police. Weston asked for money as an ex-Service man in Michael's old regiment; was discovered in a lie; grew truculent, and under a slight push collapsed. The whole scene is painfully unreal and quite out of the picture. Never for a moment does Michael convince us of being capable of engineering the business. The tale is accepted by the police, and there follows an interval of ten years.

Here we meet David, the son, a modern-mannered young man with his father's Victorian principles. He has just married Romo, also a modern. The ceremony was casual and none of the relations knew about it. David breaks it to his father, who then decides that the boy and his young wife must hear the story of Michael and Mary. David condones the offence, and the curtain falls on tears and kisses.

The author has achieved some very exquisite moments —pathos, humour and wit. But these are jostled by cumbrous interludes of stark, and, what is worse, unbelievable melodrama. But the mixture will please most people, and the play will run a long time. Mr. Herbert Marshall, Miss Edna Best and Frank Lawton give accomplished performances.

J. K. PROTHERO.

Small Workshops

GLOVES.
Irreproachable gloves hand-made by expert. Original button holes. Every kind of hand-work. Disabled Soldiers and Invalids employed. Bazaar and Trade should apply. Very moderate prices. Write for List.
HANDICRAFT HUT, PATTERDALE.

LEATHERWORK.
Stools, motor cushions, log tubs, blotters, hand-made gloves.
KATHARINE COCKCROFT,
                37, Belsize Park, N.W.3.

METALWORK.
Antique and Modern of all descriptions, in brass, copper, and iron, to own or customers' designs. Speciality, Electric Light Fittings, Electrical accessories and general hardware of exceptional value.
J. F. GARROD, LTD., 72, Charlotte Street, LONDON, W.1.

WHO'S NICOLLS?
Why, the hand-done Visiting Card King. Specimen packet designed free.
256, Church Road, BRISTOL.

PRINTING.
Good printing at moderate charges. Specimens and price free.
HATHERLEY, 43a, Trentham Street,
                Southfield, LONDON.

UPHOLSTERER AND HOUSE FURNISHER.
Restful Easy Chairs made in small workshop by practical working upholsterer. Covered in Damask, £5. Velvet or Moquette, £5 17s. 6d. Carriage paid anywhere in United Kingdom. Samples of coverings and designs on request.
R. STREET, 27, Albert Road,
                COLNE, LANCASHIRE.

DECORATOR AND PLUMBER.
All house decorations done. Moderate charges; good work.
F. STONE, 5, Health Villas, VALE OF HEALTH, N.W.3.

PHOTOGRAPHIC ENLARGEMENTS.
Artistic Postcard Enlargements from your small films, 3/- dozen. Hand-woven cushion squares, 5/6. Table runners, 7/6. Fadeless Blue and Golden Brown.
ARTS AND CRAFTS, St. Osyth,
                CLACTON-ON-SEA.

TAILORING, LADIES and GENTLEMEN.
Bespoke and ready-to-wear. Good materials. Alterations and renovations carried out. Moderate charges. Patterns on request.
F. WALKER, Mortimer Hall,
        93, Mortimer Street, Regent Street, W.1.

NAME PLATES.
Guaranteed Firth's stainless steel, 10 in. x 8 in., up to 10 letters, 8/6 each.
J. B. DAINTY, Pensnett, near DUDLEY.

THE FOREST TOYS.
Wooden animals of all kinds, hand-carved and painted. Price list post free.
F. H. WHITTINGTON, Brockenhurst,
                HANTS.

PEASANT ARTS SOCIETY.
17, Duke Street, Manchester Square, W.1. Selling off entire Stock at very great reductions. Lease expires 25th March. Hand-made articles by country craftsmen. Hand-weavings, Earthenware, etc.

GLASS.
Three-fold Dressing Table Mirrors in decorative gold mouldings from 50/-. Hand-carved three-fold Mirrors gilded in English gold leaf from 77/6. Also Shields and Armorial Bearings in stained and painted glass for window decoration.
JOHN S. DUNN,
        8, East Chapel Street, Curzon Street, W.1.

HATS.
Raffia trimmed hats and baskets.
ROSE AGENCY, Hanover Building,
                SOUTHAMPTON.

CLOTHES OF CHARACTER.
Lounge Suits from 5 gns. Dress Wear from 6½ gns. Overcoats from 4 gns. All hand finished.
S. G. HUNT, 47, Eastcheap, E.C.3.   Tel.: Royal 0807. One min. Monument and Mark Lane Stations.   P.

BASKET WARE.
Rustic wicker furniture for outdoors. Log Baskets, Dog Baskets, Laundry and Travelling Hampers. Cane and coloured Shopping Baskets. Carriage paid. Illustrated catalogue and price list free.
BLACKWELL & SON,
                28, Cross Street, BARNSTAPLE.

NEEDLEWORK.
Pictures, landscapes, all silk, from 10/6.
KATHARINE CHEVALLIER,
                247, Dover Road, FOLKESTONE.

HANDWOVEN PILE RUGS.
Something new! Made in any size, colourings and depth of pile required. Prices from 25/-. Send for samples.
THE HAND LOOM CENTRE, NORWICH.

HANDWOVEN MATERIALS.
Handspun and vegetable dyed, in silk, wool, and cotton. Dresses, jumpers, skirt lengths, scarves, curtains, cushion covers, and materials for all decorative purposes.
THE KINGSLEY WEAVERS (Lee & Eileen Baker), Chipping Campden, GLOS.

BRASS RUBBINGS.
and other Medieval subjects. Engraved printed and published by Molly Power. Lists on application.
MEDIEVAL CRAFT, Wells, SOMERSET.

LEATHER GOODS.
Leather Comb Case, 1/6.   Raffia Sprays Woven Scarf, 7/6.
MASON, Cowesby, Northallerton, YORKS.

PRINTER AND PUBLISHER.
Posters. Catalogues sent on application.
H. D. C. PEPLER

SCULPTOR, CARVER, & LETTER CUTTER.
in wood and stone. Tombstones, Wall Tablets, Stations of the Cross, Altars, Holy Water stoups, Sanctuary Lamps.
H. J. CRIBB.

WEAVER-DYER.
Suitings, Homespun, Tweeds, Serge for Habits, Vestments. J. V. D. KILBRIDE.

WOODWORKER.
Household and Ecclesiastical Furniture, Weaving Appliances. BUILDER.

Address above.—G. MAXWELL,
DITCHLING COMMON, HASSOCKS,
                SUSSEX.

DRESS ORNAMENTS.
Hat and Frock Ornaments; Pin Trays; of single or cut sea-shells. Colours, bronzes. From 1/- each.
BIELBY, Alfriston, SUSSEX.

HANDWROUGHT FURNITURE.
Davies' Handwrought Furniture. "Distinctive" for the past 25 years. Davies' Handicraft Furniture has been known for its fulfilment of all the ideals that actuated the old craftsmen. It is entirely handwrought in solid oak and other fine furniture woods beautifully polished to show to best advantage the natural grainings. The designs are original, simple in taste, artistic in effect, but comfortable and adaptable in every respect for everyday use.
W. H. DAVIES & SONS, Mount Street,
                BOLTON, LANCASHIRE.

HAND-BEATEN METAL WORK.
Restored to original design and finish. Any metal. 45 years' experience. References.
CLARK, Radioville, Ashstead, SURREY.

HAND-MADE FURNITURE.
Home-made Furniture, mainly of English-grown woods, and to original designs, from the simplest to the fines styles.
A. ROMNEY GREEN, Woodworker,
                25, Bridge Street, CHRISTCHURCH.

LINGERIE.
Orders taken for hand-made lingerie and embroidery.
SANDERS, 122, Romsey Road,
                SOUTHAMPTON.

IRISH HOUSEHOLD LINENS.
Direct from the Manufacturer. Coloured dress linen, very fine quality, 30 ins. wide, only 1/9 per yard, post free. Catalogue, samples and remnant bargains. List free.
J. HENDERSON, Milner Street,
                BELFAST, N. IRELAND.

MIRRORS AND FRAMES.
Mirrors and frames bordered with fruit and flowers, lovely colours. From 12/6. Also embroidered waistcoats and overalls.
THEA HOLME, Sussex Lodge,
                Champion Hill, S.E.

For the Table: Farm Produce

POULTRY.
Excellent Roasting Fowls, Ducks, 7/- pair. Tender boiling fowl, 5/6 pair, ready for cooking. Post free.
Miss CAINE, Poultry Stores, Rosscarbery, Cork.

Real Shamrock; generous boxes, 1/-, 2/-, 10/-; £1 each. Harps 1/- each.
Also large boiling fowls, 6/- pair; turkeys, 15/- each, trussed. All postage paid.
MOLLIE O'DONOGHUE, Convent Road
                Store, Rosscarbery, CORK.

SWEETS.
Home-made. 3/- brings ¾ lb. mixed sweets or 1 lb. toffees.
L. SHORTT, Fivecross, Moreton, Dorchester.

HOME-MADE TREACLE TOFFEE.
For postal order 2/6 I will send 1 lb. tin, post free.
Mrs. POWNALL, High Bank, Glossop Road, Gamesley, Derbyshire.

CHOCOLATES.
Home-made Chocolates and Sweets. The use of fresh cream, milk, pure butter and eggs guaranteed. Price 3/-, 4/- and 5/- per lb. Luncheon and tea rooms.
DELANEY, 40, Brooke Street, Holborn;
                27, Kirby Street, E.C.1.

REAL DEVONSHIRE CLOTTED CREAM.
¼ lb., 10d.; ½ lb. 1/5; 1 lb., 2/6; post free.
BOLES, Heathfield, Holsworthy, Devon.

THE COCKPIT

To the Editor, G.K.'s WEEKLY.

WE OUGHT TO GO

SIR,—I am surprised that you should think it worth while printing such an article as J. D. Gleeson's attack on the Italian Exhibition. That sort of " making a case " is the worst form of sheer sophistry.

It is all very well for moneyed folk who can afford to go and see the world's great masterpieces in their national homes, but the great majority of English men and women, of which I am one, cannot afford these luxuries, and in our gratitude for the opportunity which the exhibition at Burlington House offers us, we resent such a snobbish attack as your contributor makes.

Of course, such pictures are not hung in "pubs." The kind of man who goes to a " pub " to drink beer does not want to waste his precious time looking at masterpieces of art. There may be a few good pictures in some of the richer clubs, and it is significant that Mr. Gleeson speaks of the man suddenly discovering a masterpiece pausing with his *glass of wine* in mid-air. Most of us have to do without wine. It is a pity if we have to do, as well, without the pictures just to suit the taste of philistines.   WILLIAM ORANGE.

COLUMBA, STERN AND WILD

SIR,—Though Mr. Kavanagh's concession of Columba to Scottish Presbyterianism had ironical intention, it is in happy accord with the broad and tolerant attitude of his Mother Church, in waiving all question of doctrinal divergence and canonising the great Irishman.

The dogmatical basis on which Scottish Presbyterianism was established at Iona definitely denied the essential Roman tenets of auricular confession, priestly absolution, prayers to the dead, interposition of the saints, and transubstantiation. After thirteen centuries of almost unceasing struggle against the imposition of Roman and Anglican prelatry, the National Church of Scotland was recently consolidated on the same dogmatical basis in relation to these tenets, and is as strongly as ever imbued with the anti-sacerdotal tradition. I much admire the logical sense (lacking in some of his co-religionists) of Mr. Kavanagh in choosing the English and not the Scottish doorstep on which to plank down the unwanted Roman brat, John Calvin.   JOHN CARGILL.

[This correspondence must now cease.—ED.]

MORE PARTIES REQUIRED

SIR,—" Lawyer's Clerk," in his letter on " Are we a Party? " raises an interesting question. Distributists have been much too shy of entering politics. The comparatively little progress that Distributism has made in the country since the inception of the League, seems to indicate that we should adopt new tactics. Possibly the best (and certainly the most heroic) are those advocated by Fr. McNabb, and practised by the Scottish Catholic Land Association. But few of us are in a position to adopt them. We are continually denouncing Sodom and Gomorrah, but few of us are really anxious to leave the Cities of the Plain.

But the advantages of political action by the League would be two-fold. Almost all that we want could be accomplished by Act of Parliament; but before we see a Distributist Party at Westminster, I fear it will be necessary for us to start a campaign for the abolition of deposits and so on at elections, and make Parliament open to poor men.

I see in my paper this morning that Lord Beaverbrook has started a new party. This seems to suggest a line of action which might well be taken up by those who dislike Parliament and desire the restoration of the monarchy or the establishment of a dictatorship. Evidently we have only to start enough new parties, until we have about twenty, including Vegetarians, Pentyites, Tawneyites, and all the rest, in order to render Parliamentary procedure impossible, whereupon some Distributist, unless the Vegetarian is too quick for him, may step into the breach as Monarch or Dictator.   P. I. JONSON.

ARE WE A PARTY?

SIR,—As is not altogether unusual with lawyer's clerks, your correspondent is begging the question. Because the Distributisti can be defined as a party it does not prove that political parties are not iniquitous. I cannot at the moment recall an absolute instance of an assertion in this paper that political parties are iniquitous, but I admit that such a condition seems generally assumed.

But surely it was never suggested that the banding together of those with similar political views is inevitably iniquitous. What has been attacked is the Party System, a system, that is, which makes party more important than politics. In other words, though it is true that what we call the " political parties " of to-day are almost completely corrupt, it is not because they are political parties, but because they are not political enough. They have used the fine science of politics upon which to hang their petty and selfish professional careers.

If Distributists do the same they, too, will in their turn, become an iniquitous party. Perhaps, however, they will be the exception which proves the rule.   JOHN MASTERS.

RATIONALISATION

SIR,—Mr. Thomas has openly stated in the House of Commons that he is favouring a policy of Rationalisation in industry although he knows that the inevitable effect will be to add hugely to the number of the unemployed. It is easy to see from this that Rationalisation has nothing to do with Ratiocination. It is truly amazing that this statement has not evoked any noticeable protest from the electorate, and that the Press should actually praise Mr. Thomas for being brave and outspoken.

Thus, from the economic standpoint, it is evident that Rationalisation is merely harmful; but there is another side to the question which is not often mentioned. In practice Rationalisation seems to mean the subjection of the workers to a tyranny. The effect of Rationalisation in the gramophone, clothing, and other industries has been the lowering of wages, increase of hours, harder work, with detrimental effects on the health.

The earliest instance of Rationalisation seems to have been the Egyptian edict that the Israelites were to produce the full tale of bricks without the usual supply of straw. Rationalisation is clearly a further step towards the Servile State, and it is therefore somewhat shocking to find *The Church Times* expressing in a recent issue a tentative approval of this infamous system.   PHILIP KILWARDBY.

The Distributist League.

(founded in conjunction with "G.K.'s Weekly" for the restoration of liberty by the distribution of property.

President: MR. G. K. CHESTERTON.
Hon. Sec.: F. KESTON CLARKE.
Office, 2, Little Essex Street, London, W.C.2.

Telephone: Temple Bar 1978.

There are many readers of this Paper who are not members of the League. All who believe that ownership in the means of livelihood is normal to man, and necessary to liberty, and all who dislike and distrust the concentration of control advocated by Socialists and practised by Monopolists, should join the League. There is no other tenet for membership, and no other obligation than 1/- subscription, although active work is welcomed from all who can give it.

CENTRAL BRANCH.

CENTRAL BRANCH: *Hon. Sec.*, C. T. B. Donkin, 2, Little Essex Street, Strand, W.C.2

Mr. E. J. Macdonald spoke at the Devereux on Friday last on "The Press." He pointed out that the present state of journals, journalism and journalists is due partly to the progress of mechanical invention, and partly to popular education. Now that we have the modern paper-making and printing machinery, and an enormous reading public to consume the output therefrom, it has become almost inevitable that the control of newspapers should fall into the hands of monopolists, for the machinery must be kept busy in order to be profitable, and it cannot be kept nearly busy enough if there is widespread competition. Nevertheless, he said, the Press is not so bad as we of the League paint it. We have a Beaverbrook, a Rothermere and a couple of Berrys, certainly; but we might have had a Hearst. The ingenious English journalist still has some chance of expressing an opinion, and even of telling the truth inconspicuously now and again.

In the discussion Mr. Titterton said that journalists were all right, but oh! their masters! He advocated the issuing of broadsheets by the League—broadsheets written in words of two syllables; but Mr. Reece wanted to know how they could be adequately circulated outside Fleet Street, and Mr. Currie suggested that even broadsheets, distributed by the editorial staff itself, would cost money. Mr. Macdonald, in replying to a discussion that barely touched his main points, emphasised the desirability of being fair to the modern Press. It might be a great deal worse, in view of modern conditions, for there are several journalists who have never heard the word, writing perfectly good Distributism.

On February 21 Mr. G. C. Brend will give extracts from an Anti-Distributist Anthology.

BIRMINGHAM BRANCH.

BIRMINGHAM BRANCH. — *Hon. Sec.*, K. L. Kenrick, 7, Soho Road, Birmingham.

At the next meeting, to be held on Friday, February 21st, the Chairman, Mr. H. Robbins, will open a discussion on Medieval Government, in continuation of the series, "Distributism and Government."

NOTICE.

We regret that owing to indisposition Mr. Chesterton will be unable to debate with Mr. Scrymgeour on February 28th. The debate has, therefore, been postponed to a later date. Money already sent for tickets will be returned.

IMPORTANT NOTICE

TO ALL MEMBERS

The Secretary desires to thank all who have responded, with sums ranging from 1/- to £1, to the Appeal for funds, with which to carry on the work of the League.

Many more donations are still required before the position can be regarded as satisfactory. We ask that every member will make it his duty to contribute. Remember that upon the success of this appeal depends the success of the League's effort during the coming year.

A member of the Central Branch, who has already given £1 has offered a further £5 if another Leaguer will give a like amount. Can any member take up this generous challenge?

Donations may be sent through Branch Secretaries or direct to the League Office.

LIVERPOOL BRANCH.

LIVERPOOL BRANCH: *Hon. Sec.*, S. Anderson, 3, Leopold Road, Kensington, Liverpool.

The Liverpool Branch held its first debate of the year on Tuesday last, February 11th. The Larkhill Debating Society provided the opposition and the subject was "That the present system of Parliamentary government is Democratic." The Liverpool Branch took the negative.

Our opponents had no easy task and had to content themselves in setting out the democratic nature of Parliament in theory, and in betraying a simple trust in politicians. Mr. A. C. Tait, leading for the Liverpool Branch, soon pointed out their errors, and showed that if Parliament was democratic in theory we, at least, were not getting the benefit of it. The result was an overwhelming victory for the Liverpool Branch.

Wednesday, February 19, 1930, Grenville Café, Tithebarn Street, 8 p.m., "The Guilds an Essential of the Distributist State?" Mr. A. C. Tait.

All members are urged to attend and bring their friends.

MANCHESTER BRANCH.

MANCHESTER. — *Hon. Sec.*, John A. Toohey, York Mount, Bury New Road, Prestwich.

An interesting debate and discussion between the members of the Manchester Branch and the Salford Council of the K.S.C. took place on Friday evening, February 7th last. The topic chosen was "Unemployment and the Revival of Agriculture," and the Birmingham Branch scheme of settling the unemployed men in small holdings was vigorously advocated by the members of the Branch. The debate was adjourned on Friday evening, the 7th inst. and continued on the following Friday evening, the 14th inst., and the chief objection the Distributists present had to deal with was the statement that Great Britain, owing to climatic disadvantages and lack of agricultural knowledge, could not compete with the foreign countries such as Denmark, the Argentine and Canada with respect to producing the necessary foodstuffs for the support of the population of Great Britain.

The members of the Manchester Branch found it difficult to persuade those non-distributists present of the urgency of the problem of a better distribution of property and a more rational distribution of the population, although we gave some figures of rural and urban population which came as a surprise to the members of the K.S.C., Salford.

Messrs. Cosgrove, Cullen, Lynch, Cummings, Brennan and Williams, also the Secretary of the Branch put the case for the Distributist proposals and outlined the Birmingham scheme of small holdings, and the Secretary begs to thank those members of the Manchester Branch who were present to lend a hand in the discussion.

PROPOSED NEW BRANCH.

H. G. Weston, Member of the Central Branch Committee, has recently settled in Leicester and is anxious to form a new branch of the League in that centre. Will anyone who is interested write to him at:—

Fotheringhay,
158, New Walk,
Leicester.

Small Advertisements.

The charge for prepaid advertisements is 2s. per insertion up to 24 words, and one penny per word afterwards. Advertisements not paid for in advance cost 3s. per insertion for 24 words and twopence per word afterwards. Space costs 5s. per inch. Thick type in all cases 20 per cent. extra. Seven insertions for the price of six.

EDUCATIONAL.

UNIVERSITY EXTENSION LECTURES
(University of London).
THE DEVELOPMENT OF THE ART OF THE THEATRE. A course of ten lectures by Miss Elsie Fogerty, on Mondays at 6.30 p.m., at Kingsway Hall, Kingsway, W.C.
ENGLISH LITERATURE.—DRYDEN to COLERIDGE. Twenty-four lectures by Dr. Arthur Compton-Rickett, on Mondays, at 6.30 p.m., at Bishopsgate Institute, Bishopsgate, E.C. Admission FREE to first lecture on September 30th.
Particulars of these, and of eighty-five other courses on HISTORY, LITERATURE, MUSIC, ECONOMICS, ART, and other subjects may be obtained from the University Extension Registrar (Dept. L.), University of London, S.W.7.

LITERARY.

AUTHORS desiring advice about revision or publication of MSS. (Novels, Poetry) should consult Oscar Cook (Author, Editor), c/o Scammel, 10, Duke Street, Adelphi, London.

SONG POEMS wanted. Successful composer invites known or unknown Authors to submit Lyrics for prompt consideration. Send MSS. and stamp, "Composer" (288), c/o Ray's Advert. Agency, Cecil Court, London, W.C.2.

G.K.'S WEEKLY.—Wanted, copies of Nos. 1, 4, 7, 60, 61 and 150.—Reply to "R. & M.," Postal Dept., Wm. Dawson & Sons, Ltd., Cannon House, Pilgrim Street, E.C.4.

CATCHY MUSIC set to Lyrics by Maurice Scott, the famous composer of scores of popular songs (reference any London Music Publisher). MSS. edited and revised. (Terms mod.). Booklet on Popular Song-writing free (stamp for postage). —15, Tufnell Park Road, London, N.7.

PRETTY, Laughable Plays Always liked. List 2d.—Miss Boileau, Knockeven, Southbourne, Bournemouth.

CATHOLIC and General Literary Bureau.— Principal, Wilkinson Sherrin. Special attention paid to Literary Aspirants and Young Authors. MSS. read, advised upon, and when approved, offered to Editors and Publishers.—Particulars from Wilkinson Sherrin (temporary address), 119, Nether Street, North Finchley, London, N.12.

NEW Anecdotes and Jokes by Mark Twain. Published for the first time, with portrait. Price, two shillings, post paid.—Mark Twain Society, Mayfield, California.

RESTAURANTS.

DISTRIBUTIST Restaurant. — "The Owl," 3, Kingly Street, W.1. (behind Robinson and Cleaver's, Regent Street). Luncheons and Teas. Members of the League can meet each other here.

MUSIC, INSTRUMENTS, ETC.

BANJOS, Mandolines, Drums, Violins, Guitars, Ukuleles, Accordeons, Saxophones, Xylophones. List free. — Palmers, Dept. J., 135, Listhorpe Road, Middlesbrough.

SITUATIONS REQUIRED.

LADY, with or without own car, wants work, chauffeuse or Secretary, or would help cakeround, market garden, animals; keen worker.— BM/ZVLO, London.

MAN, age 60, strong, willing, any capacity, Grocer or Labourer or Storeman, Caretaker. Chatham district preferred.—Murrell, 19, Gad's Hill, Gillingham.

MISCELLANEOUS.

"FREE HOROSCOPE." Year's principal future events, advice on life. Send birth-date, 1s. —9, Kingsgrove, North Morecambe.

GOOD Printing at low trade rates. Specimens and prices free.—Hatherley, 43a, Trentham Street, Southfields, London.

HANDKERCHIEFS, fancy, printed, scalloped Irish manufacture, suitable Bazaars, etc. Sample dozen, 3/3 post paid.—Manuel, Standford, Bordon, Hants.

HARRIS TWEED. Any length cut. Patterns free. — James St. Tweed Depot, 392, Stornoway, Scotland.

IRISH HANDWOVEN TWEEDS for Suits and Costumes. Patterns free from Joseph Largey, 40, Lr. Ormond Quay, Dublin.

LOVELY, warm Men's Home-knitted Socks, 2/6 pair.—Score, Station Road, Liss.

MONEY easily earned in spare time by selling Rubber Stamps; particulars free.—Richford, Ltd., Snow Hill, London.

NEEDLE Cases for Bazaars, Masonic Ladies' Nights, etc. Buy direct from Factory. Send for 5/6, 10/6, or 21/- parcel of assorted kinds. Post free.—Dept. G.K., B. Hampton, Son & Co., Ltd., Victoria Street, Redditch.

PRINTING : 10,000 Handbills or Billheads at 3/3 per 1,000. Memorandums, Postcards, Duplicate Books, Envelopes, Posters, etc. Large range of samples, 3d. postage.—Mead & Son, Dept. P., Sandy, Bedfordshire.

SHOWCARDS, Pictures, Letters, in Colours Simultaneously. Own recent invention. Directions 7½d.—Wright, Willis's Place, Wisbech.

HOROSCOPE.—Generous readings at low fees; careful, accurate work. Genuine. Testimonials from all over the world. P.O. 1/-, birth-date.— "Belper," Irving Road, Bournemouth.

THE SILENT METHOD OF VOICE CULTURE.

THE SILENT METHOD Produces amazing results. Builds up the voice that excels in volume, range and purity of tone; eradicates all vocal difficulties, weak voice, harshness, huskiness, limited range; infallible cure for STAMMERING. Send 3d. stamp for particulars and astounding testimony from delighted students the world over.

Prof. W. R. REID, 541g, Wigan Road, Bolton, Lancs.

THE "SEMPER" Screwdriver with four blades, each instantly available, for screws of all sizes. Well made, simple, powerful; guaranteed hand-tempered steel. Handy and reliable.

Price: 4/- post free, from C. A. Blamchet, 168, Regent Street, London, W.1.

TYPEWRITING, DUPLICATING, ETC.

MEMBER OF AUTHORS' SOCIETY, expert typist, will type authors' MSS. at usual rates. —S. W. Powell, 38a, Curzon Road, Boscombe, Bournemouth.

TYPEWRITERS from £2; easy payments arranged. Repairs. Duplicators. 'Phone Central 8210. Typewriter experts, 55, Little Britain, E.C.1.   77

AUTHORS' MSS. and Technical Typewriting correctly executed; 10d. per 1,000. — Mrs. Clifstone, 11, Cromwell Avenue, Bromley, Kent. . 103

DUPLICATING EXPERT offers 50 extra copies free. — Schoolmaster, 71, Brackenbury Road, Preston.

INCREDIBLE ! Unbeatable ! Duplicated typewritten matter, 3s. per 100. — E. S. Coy, 14, Homer Terrace, Bootle.

LITERARY Typewriting carefully and promptly executed. MSS. 1s. per 1,000 words; carbon copy 3d. per 1,000.—Miss Nancy McFarlane (J.), 4, Elderton Road, Westcliff-on-Sea.

LONDON'S Premier Typewriting Service. 1,000 words 10d., carbon copy 2d. Perfect work guaranteed. Authors' MSS. a speciality.—"Fleet" Typewriting Agency, 153, Fleet Street, E.C.4.

TYPEWRITING accurately executed; 1,000 words 1s.; carbon 3d. Free specimen. Shorthand. —Miss Thayer, 22, Gray's Inn Residences, E.C.1.

TYPEWRITING and Duplicating. Authors' MSS. typed 10d. per 1,000 words; carbon copy 3d. per 1,000 words. Testimonials, circulars, etc., duplicated. Envelopes addressed. Prompt and efficient work—Marion Young (C.), 7a, Station Road, Balham, S.W.12.

TYPEWRITING. — 8d. thousand. French and Spanish translations (into English), 9d. a folio. — Newcombe, 36, Wilson Street, Middlesbrough.

TYPEWRITING MSS. 8d. per 1,000 words. Carbon 2d. Pitman's transcribed. Outside work undertaken. Best work, lowest charges. Accuracy guaranteed.—I. Watkins, 40, Verulam St., E.C.1.

MSS. TYPED, 1s. per 1,000 words, 3d. carbon copy. Translatins (French and German into English).—Miss Pollard, 36, Ampthill Sq., N.W.1. Museum 3956.

STYLISH and accurate Literary Typewriting, 10d. per 1,000 words. Revision undertaken. French copying or translation. — P. Gregory, 34, Pleasants Street, Dublin.

NEAT ACCURATE TYPING,

Intelligently executed MSS.
Miss N. Netherwood,
41, Arthur Street, Loughborough.

HOTELS.

EDINBURGH.—St. Mary's (Private), 32, Palmerston Place. Fine situation. Convenient train and tram. Liberal table. 'Phone 23872.

DEAN FOREST, Severn-Wye Valleys.—Beautiful Holiday Home (600 feet up); 80 rooms; five acres; billiards; dancing; motors; garage. 52/6 to 70s. weekly. Prospectus. — Littledean House, Littledean, Glos.   314

CHIPPING CAMPDEN, Gloucestershire (Cotswolds). A few guests taken in comfortable old house for three guineas weekly. Catholic church.—Mrs. L. K. Baker, Westcote House.

KIRKLEY, Lowestoft.—Ladies received at Convent. Magnificent situation on sea front. Excellent catering. Separate tables optional. Home freedom. 10s. day. Apply.—St. Mary's Convent.

Published by the Proprietors, G.K.'s Weekly, Ltd., 2, Little Essex Street, Strand, London, W.C.2 (incorporating The New Witness). Telephone: Temple Bar 1978. Printed by The Marshall Press, Ltd., 7, Milford Lane, Strand, London, W.C.2. Sole Agents for Australasia: Gordon & Gotch (Australasia, Ltd.). Sole Agents for South Africa: Central News Agency, Ltd.

G.K.'s Weekly, May 23, 1931

THE PRESS AND SPAIN. By Hilaire Belloc. P. 164

G.K.'s Weekly

EDITED BY G. K. CHESTERTON.

No. 323.—Vol. XIII.   May 23, 1931.   [Registered at G.P.O. as a Newspaper.]   Sixpence.

Temple Bar 1978.   2, Little Essex Street, London, W.C.2.

CONTENTS :

FORTY YEARS ON

THE most important event of the past week was the fortieth anniversary of Pope Leo XIII.'s Encyclical *Rerum Novarum*, known in its English translation as *The Condition of the Working Classes.*

This Encyclical, in its few but brilliant pages of wisdom and exhortation, presents so clear an outline of that social philosophy we call Distributism, and for the furtherance of which this paper exists, that no excuse is necessary to Distributists of any creed for reminding them of a book so bound up with their aims and so characterised by humanity and vision.

The present Pope, Pius XI., deserves the gratitude of Distributists, as indeed of the whole world, for deliberately advancing the jubilee of *Rerum Novarum* by ten years in order to draw attention to its supreme applicability in present social and industrial conditions. His broadcast speech of May 15th and the Encyclical which he proposes to issue in corroboration of Leo XIII.'s pronouncement of forty years ago, confirm, if they can attempt to add little to the work of his predecessor.

It may be worth recalling that Leo XIII., born in 1810—between Trafalgar and Waterloo—and early distinguished as scholar and poet, did not reach the Papacy until 1878, having spent a great part of his life, both as a layman and after ordination, in the conduct of civil affairs. He was an experienced and far-seeing administrator when, at the age of 68, he was elected Pope.

His first Encyclical on the Equality of Men issued in the year of his election, showed at once that no better choice could have been made. Further pronouncements in which the authority and dignity of his high office enhanced the shrewd (and probably unpopular) analysis of current events by a man who had given his life to their study and who, both as Christian and statesman, was appalled by their trend, culminated in the Encyclical of 1891 in which the evils of both Capitalism and Socialism as they then existed, were unhesitatingly condemned and man's right to liberty and property reaffirmed.

It is of these things that the present anniversary is meant to remind us, and it is amusing to note the reactions of different types of men to so important and abrupt a restatement of the things they prefer for their own advantage to forget, or which have been kept from them by the sedulous or credulous apes to whom they surrender their souls with their suffrages.

Mr. Lansbury, a Socialist, says that if the Pope came to England—a startling occurrence which no doubt Mr. Lansbury would leap from his bathing-dress to armour to prevent—he would " see the folly of trying to stop Socialism." Even well informed people feel that the Pope must have been misunderstood or mistranslated, and that he cannot mean Socialism, but some foreign exaggerated un-English thing called Communism.

It is more than probable that he means, as Leo did, exactly what he says : the attempt to set up a State monopoly and control in matters where it has no competence or right.

Similarly, of course, our preposterous Capitalist press, the laughing-stock of Europe, while not neglecting the possibilities of Vatican ceremonial as a news-story for its Catholic readers, prefers to over-emphasise the attack on Socialism while disregarding the equally trenchant criticism of capitalism, monopoly and the establishment of the servile state.

We can only be thankful that by the anniversary of *Rerum Novarum* and the publication of the forthcoming *Quadragesimo Anno*, a great section of the public will be reminded by a leader of influence and authority that man has an inalienable right to the mastery of himself and his labour, his person and his family, and to the acquisition and protection of that material and spiritual independence which individual property, however small, alone can give.

NOTES OF THE WEEK

The High Commissioner for Canada has assured the Press that the Conference of representatives of the wheat-producing countries " does not seek to exploit the consuming countries of the world in any way whatever." Then what gave him the idea of making this contradiction? The object is, if possible, to devise some scheme for the more equitable distribution of the wheat of the world. We can offer the High Commissioner and the Conference a most valuable, effective, and in every way desirable suggestion. It is that they should take steps to prevent the operations at Winnipeg and Chicago whereby the supposed " glut " has occurred and the farmer of North America has been cheated of " the reasonable return for his labour " which this Conference proposes to secure for him.

*   *   *   *

The present difficulties of the wheat growers, wheat gamblers and millers are due, as everyone knows, to the fact that the North American gamblers held up enormous stocks of wheat to secure an unjust margin of profit from the consumers. The plan failed because the Argentine would not join in but continued to sell its wheat, and as there was a good supply, the price remained at a fairly just level. You cannot hold wheat for ever, in the first place because it will not keep for ever, and in the second because it needs special accommodation and the next harvest will not wait for you to clear the stocks. The result of these circumstances was that the gamblers were forced to sell and the buyers were on top. The loss was passed on as it always is, to the farmers and the investors in small American and Canadian Banks. Farmers are discouraged, put out of business, and will not grow so much wheat. This will partly correct the difficulty for the Gamblers of the Wheat Pit, but not entirely. The obvious thing to do is to get together, have a heart to heart talk with the blacklegs, and see that it does not happen again. We can see the hard-headed business men, the hundred and one percenters, knocking their heads together with a devilish clatter. " What we want is more equitable distribution and a fair deal for the farmer. Damn the money. Don't let us think of sordid gain. The prices, as the President says, will adjust themselves. We must all get together. What we want is Co-operation, harmony and brotherly love in this business." There will be no need for anyone to use such

bad words as ring, corner, world-combine, conspiracy in restraint of trade. Nothing stronger than rationalisation of selling organisations will be needed.

*   *   *   *

The days, and even the nights, as the Prime Minister has observed, are short, but that does not excuse any Government for failing to exert itself in the right way. Mr. MacDonald feels rather sorry that Labour has not been enabled already to score the goals planned by his predecessors in the Labour Movement. He seems even to blame the defence of the opposing team ; as if full backs were expected to make no show at all of opposition. We must confess that the Liberal and Conservative backs have been sufficiently complacent to please any forwards. But Mr. MacDonald was talking not of football, but of politics, which is a very different game.

*   *   *   *

Perhaps the most enlightening clause in the suggested new unemployment benefit law is that which states (according to the official Labour journal) that " benefit will not be paid in such cases (transitional benefit) if the applicant's family is adjudged to be in a position to keep him or her." It is a complete admission that unemployment insurance *qua* insurance has collapsed and that " dole " is a correct name for the present system. The justification for the general reduction of benefit, plus increase in contributions, that " cost-of-living has fallen since the present scales were fixed " is, of course, ludicrous and should deceive no one, not even the most innocent of registered persons. It is so obvious that the fund is bankrupt, and so increasingly obvious that Britain has not the means to support a bankrupt fund, that we wonder a Royal Commission could be so naive.

*   *   *   *

We have said many things against compulsory State Education on many grounds, but it has been left for the *Evening Standard* to hold its unfortunate victims up to ridicule and to complain that, what with illiterate servant girls and errand boys, the middle-class taxpayer is not getting his money's worth. As if citizens of the State are educated as a commercial investment for middle-class taxpayers ! A very graphic, though ill-phrased letter from a servant girl was printed as an example of illiteracy, quite without her consent ; though many a middle-class taxpayer might have been shamed by it ; and in the correspondence which this called forth, one indignant matron said triumphantly that when she asked her servant to spell racquet the compulsorily State educated failure spelt it racket. As who wouldn't ? Another letter was in better perspective, " I know nothing of the writer of the letter ; and neither, apparently, do you. But it does strike me that she may well be a good citizen (even if she cannot spell), and that she may have profited quite considerably from such education as she has had (if she has had any)."

*   *   *   *

The following account from an evening paper is of a contemporary happening which seems to call for close local investigation :

Bromley (Kent) magistrates to-day refused a mother's application to make an order against Bromley Guardians Committee compelling them to restore to her the custody of a child born in 1919 before her marriage.

Resisting the application, Mr. P. J. D. Wily, Public Assistance Officer, said that the child was now in an institution for the blind. He asked for the name of the institution to be kept secret, so that there should be no interference.

The mother said that she was hard-working and had brought up a large family respectably. She added :

" I have been allowed to see the child once only in ten years. Whatever I may have done, I am entitled to see my child. Can I see it occasionally ? "

The Chairman, Alderman R. W. James, after a private discussion with Mr. Wily, said that the magistrates had no jurisdiction.

Mr. Wily : If the woman calls at my office, she can have information from time to time about the progress of her child.

The Mother : You can keep your information. I am the child's mother, and I have a right to see my child.

It would be interesting to know who has got jurisdiction in the matter. Is it the Public Assistance Officer who is alleged to have asked the name of the institution to be kept secret and to have offered the mother official interviews or is it the mother herself ?

Parliament.

" Uncle Arthur " really excelled himself last week before he left for Geneva. It may be, as he clearly holds, the duty of a Foreign Minister to say the thing that is not, but the office requires that it should be done with a certain skill. It would be interesting to know what first put it into the head of this hard-working trades union organiser that he ought to be at the Foreign Office. Certainly the riotous imagination of the political satirist never imagined a more incongruous appointment. Even the present House of Commons gasped when Mr. Henderson solemnly denied the breakdown of the Anglo-Russian sub-committee. He subsequently explained that he denied it " according to the information at my disposal."

*　　　　*　　　　*　　　　*

Poor M. Briand ! He survived that round of golf with Lloyd George a few years ago, but I suspect that Uncle Arthur's telegram of good wishes really did him in. Or was it a propaganda *canard* put about by his opponents ? The impropriety of a British Cabinet minister indirectly telling the French how they shall vote is plain enough. M. Briand has obvious faults and limitations, but mental agility has often served him none too badly in the absence of culture, and from the point of view of Anglo-French relations his disappearance from the scene may well prove regrettable. But the spectacle of our Mr. Henderson wandering about in a Europe described pretty accurately by Mr. Simonds in *The Times* last week is positively frightening.

*　　　　*　　　　*　　　　*

The India debate was more interesting than most because there were economic realities behind it. To disentangle all the principles involved in any discussion on India would be a long and difficult task. From a purely political angle the position of the Conservative Party shows how powerful is the Rothermere-Beaverbrook combination, though not at all in the way it would wish. I should say that eighty per cent. at least of Conservatives are with Churchill on India. The dominance of Baldwinism is due entirely to the fact that if outsiders begin throwing half-bricks at a gentleman, a party which remains on the whole gentlemanly, will sympathise with the target rather than the marksmen.

*　　　　*　　　　*　　　　*

I hear, but do not believe, that the proletariat was organising " Hands off Odhams " committees when it became known that harsh things were being said about the workers' own daily. In other quarters there is a good deal of indignation and it is justified. The forecast of the R.M.S.P. summonses

was one of many indications that this particular paper has sources of information which are not open to others. When it is " political information " it doesn't matter a row of beans. Who cares whether we learn of the latest Government folly a day or two earlier or later ? Paragraphs announcing the intention of the public prosecutor to take criminal proceedings are quite a different matter, and on any reasonable theory of public conduct they ought not to appear. Some members of the Government combine an unprecedented degree of secrecy in things the public has a right to know with an irresistible tendency to blow the gaff on matters that are legitimately private.

*　　　　*　　　　*　　　　*

A shrewd parliamentarian declared at the beginning of the present parliament that this Labour Government, like the last, would fall on the question of Russia. We have not heard so much about it lately, but the prediction is worth keeping in mind. Mr. MacDonald appears to have no conception of the real nature of the risks he is taking, and is content if he can score off some extravagance by " anti-reds." It all reminds one of the attitude of those pre-war Liberals who thought they had disposed of all discussion of Prussia's ambitions, by proving the improbability of an unexpected landing of German troops at Dover.

*　　　　*　　　　*　　　　*

It is surprising to find an indictment of the Servile State in the *Daily Express*, which has, however, published an account of the conduct of factories in Czecho-Slovakia. If ever the term " slavery " were applicable to factory workers, the epithet must be applied to the conditions described. We are therefore grateful to the *Daily Express* for having carried an argument to its logical conclusion.

Current Affairs

THE PRESS AND SPAIN

By HILAIRE BELLOC

THAT unending theme, the condition of our Press, has received another fine piece of nutriment in the reports of the Spanish troubles and the comments upon them.

The English papers of the more reputable sort (we may neglect the Harmsworth and Max Aitken press for the moment as not even pretending to write for an educated public) has treated the Spanish troubles in two fashions. The great majority of the papers and reviews have merely stated the facts, so far as the little tyrannical clique which has seized power in Spain has allowed those facts to come out. A small minority of the press has commented slightly on those facts : the comment has always been the same, sometimes the " populace," sometimes the " mob " has been described as furiously " anti-clerical."

Further, our press has treated the whole affair as something of a secondary order, sensational but of no great international importance.

Now let us set down in their order certain facts which are known and which are almost certainly true because they have been recorded throughout Europe and in some cases testified to by eye-witnesses. I will put these facts in a table and enumerate them.

1. Many days after the revolt of the army and particularly of the artillery had compelled the King to fly, although the majority of votes had been given in favour of his regime, there was tranquility. The nation awaited the promised general elections which were to take place in a few weeks.

2. The scratch lot of politicians who, without a pretence of popular mandate, had installed themselves in power—the army not interfering with them as not being worth while—published general statements in their own favour but gave no detailed figures of voting.

3. The same politicians, of whom the active organising members are strongly anti-Catholic Freemasons, published their decision that little children in school should no longer be taught their religion (this was called in our press " the first step towards freedom of religion ").

4. The primate of Spain issued a declaration advising everyone who cared for the future of religion in Spain to vote at the coming elections in favour of candidates who would support religion. This perfectly normal proceeding was called by the clique in power a challenge to political freedom.

5. Some days later simultaneous attacks were made in many of the great cities upon the Churches, the ornaments and the Reserved Sacrament therein ; and the habitations and schools of clerics and nuns. Three features marked these attacks ; (*a*) they everywhere were exactly the same, taking the form of arson, organised and carried out in the same fashion at much the same moment, with a central movement against Jesuit buildings.

(*b*) There was no injury to persons. No violence of any sort against them, apparently not a single case of rough treatment such as angry people will always give to those whom they are attacking.

(*c*) The army looked on and so did the excellently organised long service national police and no effort was made by public authorities to constrain, still less to punish the perpetrators of the crimes.

6. No attack was made upon the house of a capitalist or upon any great capitalist work or upon a bank. There was no attack upon anything that stood for organised wealth : only upon selected houses of religion.

Now look at those plain facts and ask yourself what anyone possessed of the most elementary powers of reasoning must conclude upon them ? It is perfectly clear that there was an arrangement made supported by the authorities, prepared and well organised to do what was done. That its object was to produce an effect of popular hatred against religion and of divorce between the Spanish people in the mass and their Faith. There was nothing spontaneous about the affair from beginning to end, there was none of that haphazard violence which accompanies spontaneous popular movements : most extraordinary of all, there was no attack upon that wealthy irreligious middle class to which the Masonic body belongs and from which it is recruited. You may say that their aims in attacking the Church are admirable or the reverse—that has nothing to do with the plain facts of the case. The thing was quite clearly organised, prepared and supported by the public authority. Has our press said a word on that ? Not a word. Has it even made a pretence to understanding what has happened ? It has not even done that. Whenever it has commented on the affair it has treated it as a sort of confused movement on the part of the Spanish people as a whole in their detestation of a religion which they detest about as much as Englishmen detest public-houses and race-courses.

Ponder upon these things. Europe is big with very great events indeed. They may burst forth in civil fighting or in international fighting, they may come less violently though rapidly in some other way—and how are we prepared to meet them, so far as the instructions given us by our press can prepare us ? Whether it be these official outrages in Spain, or the threat against Poland, or any one of the twenty issues which are bringing us to the edge of catastrophe, we are left ignorant and misled while all the rest of Europe is understanding, discussing and preparing.

Those who think that when the European changes come this country will stand apart as a happy neutral, may regard the condition of the press with indifference ; but then the opinion of the people who think that—they are themselves largely the uneducated controllers and owners of the popular press—is worthless. Yet there is no one to take their place.

THE DISTRIBUTIST LEAGUE

For the Restoration of Liberty by the Distribution of Property.

President : G. K. CHESTERTON.

Hon. Secretary : F. W. OSBORNE.

2, Little Essex Street, Strand, W.C.2.

Telephone No.—Temple Bar 1978.

Good Faith in Politics

By A. U. Dax

ONCE upon a time, in the days when the railways did not exist even in the imagination of people, a king set out from his castle to visit his domain. On the abominable road—all roads then were like that—the horses, which dragged the massive coach, made slow progress. What with the early start, the dust, the heat and the jolting, His Majesty was tired. He also had a mighty thirst. So, when, about the dinner hour, the spires and then the walls of a good town of his came up on the sky-line, the king was pleased. The coach rolled across the drawbridge, it was about to enter the coolness of the gate-tower, when it stopped. In the roadway, on their knees, were the city magistrates. The fat mayor began to stutter: "Most High Majesty . . ." "Yes, I know," said the king, "you love me." "All highest Sovereign, the humblest of your servants crave to be pardoned . . ." "What is that?" the king exclaimed. "Speak up, man! I want my dinner." "Your Majesty, the royal salute! We have not fired the salute. But, Most High Majesty, there were many reasons. First, we have no gunpowder, then . . ." "I do not need your many reasons," shouted the king. "The first is the best. Coachman, whip up! I want my dinner."

The mayor with his "many reasons" for the silence of the city artillery, was ridiculous. Still he had had the sense of giving his best reason—the lack of powder—first, and this is more than are able to do some of our distinguished contemporaries. They volubly explain the why and the wherefore of an event, but never seem to get near to its true reason. Either they are afraid to speak out, or they are themselves ignorant of the matter. In the domain of politics we constantly meet with such impotence in so-called statesmen. They may speak about an internal problem, like unemployment or about a point in foreign policy, like the peace of Europe, always they fail to express in plain words the real cause of the trouble. The vagueness of modern mental processes is exasperating. Its victims are mirrored in a sentence: "they know not, whether they believe in God, or not, and they know less, whether they want their soup salted, or not." Like the king, who ached for his dinner, the world cries out for prosperity and peace. It is impatient to have them. Instead, it is fed with excuses, and, try as it may, it cannot get at the real source of the delay.

An accusation, supported only by an anecdote, with a few fine words thrown in, is like the thrust of a tin knife in a play. But to back our view on modern statesmanship we have proof of a more substantial nature. Like the absence of gunpowder in the old story, a good reason exists, which makes other excuses superfluous for the failure to achieve peace and prosperity. This is the lack of good faith in political life. In every case, I am convinced, this lack of good faith, that is honesty in the relations between politicians and between governments, can be shown to be responsible for the failure. As Europe is to be thrown into a new crisis by the raising of the problem of the German-Austrian *Anschluss* immediately, and by that of disarmament early next year, I will use these issues to illustrate my meaning.

The League of Nations, contrary to the views held by its fanatics, is not a panacea against war. Neither is it entitled to play the part of a Super-State in the world. Still, within the strict limits of the Covenant, the League possesses considerable powers, which can be used to strengthen the cause of peace among the nations. These powers flow from the obligations accepted for themselves by the signatories of the Covenant, because they are contained in the clauses of the latter. Great Britain, having signed the treaty, is as much bound by it as any other state in Europe. May we ask, if the people of this country are acquainted with the nature of these international obligations? Are they aware that they exist at all? The answer is in the negative. This, because politicians of all parties, in their fear of injuring their electoral position, have refrained from telling the British people that, since the signing of the Covenant, embodied in the Treaty of Versailles, they are free no longer to do as they like, to isolate themselves from Europe, or to pick and choose political combinations. The people of Great Britain are not being reminded of the fact that Mr. Lloyd George and his colleagues of the British delegation have tied them to Europe by the signature given in Paris in 1919.

To keep the people of Great Britain in ignorance of the real state of affairs is an act of bad faith. An act, grosser still, is to try to quieten the doubts, which from time to time arise in the public mind in respect of the British position, by the argument that, anyhow, as the decisions of the Council of the League have to be unanimous, nothing contrary to British interests can ever become binding. To tender such advice is not only dishonest, it is immoral, because it is a well-known principle in the unwritten law of international relations that the breaking of a treaty cannot be excused by the consideration that otherwise national interests will suffer. British politicians have forgotten how to express in simple words what is their unquestionable duty. An example of this we had only the other day, when the Secretary of State for Foreign Affairs answered a question in the House about a declaration made by his Belgian colleague about the reliance which Belgium can place on Great Britain in the case of an attack by a third Power. This, naturally, was a reference to the Treaty of Locarno, concluded in 1925 to guarantee territorial integrity between France and Belgium on one side, and Germany on the other. In his reply, Mr. Henderson referred to the Belgian's declaration as to "his" interpretation of the Locarno obligations. Mr. Henderson evidently has a different interpretation? Then why does he not state it outright?

In the question of the *Anschluss* British politicians are torn between the fear of committing themselves to common action in Europe, and a desire to play the part of arbiters in the dispute. As the method of having your cake, and eating it, has not been discovered yet, the result is a sequence of diplomatic pirouettes to avoid the need of definite decisions being taken. I hope that I shall be permitted to continue this exposition later on.

Within the Law

By James Mark

I.

WE have hitherto viewed Administrative Law mainly in those aspects wherein it departs from the accepted principles of our constitution. It is fundamental in our politics (I use the term in its strict sense) that there should be a nice balance of power between the three branches of government: the legislative, the executive and the judiciary. Ultimately all actions should be appealable before the Courts which should judge them according to laws applicable to all and everyone. Now the system known as Administrative Law is called into being when this balance is upset, when a greater proportion of the power is attributed to the executive side of government, which is at the same time extracted to that degree from the curbing influence of the other two. In so far as extensions of this sort have been made in this country, their effect has been almost invariably bad : firstly, because they have been made insensibly and in a hidden fashion ; secondly, because no safeguards were devised at the same time, against the wrong exercise of the new powers attributed to the officials. For this reason, most of what I have had to say on the subject has been in the nature of destructive criticism.

But though the present furtive manner in which this system is being introduced into this country leads us very rightly to subject it to our closest scrutiny, the subject is well worth further consideration and constructive thought. This becomes obvious, when we consider for a moment, the general trend of politics to-day. Old frames are apt to break when we enclose within them new and growing plants, and Administrative Law is certainly a plant which is destined to grow ; it is asking for trouble to try and keep it within a cadre designed for another system. One may safely make the generalisation that States are taking a greater and greater part in regimenting the individuals that compose them. This is sometimes spoken of as paternal government, meaning that the individual is left less to his own devices and is controlled and looked after more, in his life, by the State. It is a little difficult to say, without precise knowledge of the facts in each case, in what countries and to what extent this paternal tendency is most manifesting itself, but there can be little doubt that it is well marked in England. I do not wish to suggest that we should accept this state of affairs and encourage it ; as a rule, we have little for which to thank the State for its interference with the family, but we may admit readily enough that, in certain matters, its influence has been for the good ; and I do not think it can be denied that, in certain spheres, those in which it is particularly beneficent, this influence might, with advantage, be extended still further, *provided effective means are devised of keeping the actions of officials strictly within the bounds within which they are intended to act.*

There is another reason why we should not confine ourselves to destructive criticism, but should bring some constructive thought to bear. Whether we desire it or no, the tendency towards paternal government is going to continue, even though its only object be to bolster up the present state of affairs, which we believe, in the end, spells perdition. And paternal government means more power given to officials. We are almost too tired of hearing complaints of the incompetence and inefficiency of Parliament. The reason behind it all is, that Parliament is trying to retain the government of the country and failing to do so, because, owing to the multiplication of matters with which governing is concerned, it has neither the necessary knowledge nor the time to handle them effectively. In the end, the probable upshot will be either a dictator (in one form or another) or a central committee for discussing matters of general policy, aided by a system of local governments which will do the work. Whichever way things go, we are bound to have an increasing army of civil servants to handle the work which the individual will no longer be allowed to do for himself. Now, if we are to be made to swallow the pill, we may as well have something to take the taste away ; if we are going to be regimented by Sergeant-Majors, we may as well keep them within the bounds of King's Regulations ; that is : if we are going to have full-fledged bureaucracy, we want a skilfully devised set of laws, in the manner of a framework, within which the system shall be worked. Only in this way may be obtained the maximum of benefit coupled with the minimum of

injustice, from a system we may well deplore, but which, i seems, we are more than liable to have thrust upon us.

It must be realised that Administrative Law is new to thi country—its growth is confined practically to the last half century—and what there is of it will bear no comparison, as a developed system of rules, with what may be seen, for instance in France. These rules deal with such subjects as the liability of officials when acting in their official capacity, the formation of special judicial bodies which have jurisdiction to determine such matters, and with the procedure for bringing culprits before them. Now in England we have no such thing. In fact it is diametrically opposed to our traditions we have always thought it natural that all persons should have their cases tried before the ordinary Courts and judged by the same laws. However, it is with such topics as I have mentioned, that we shall be dealing, and though we may be unwilling to accept, on principle, the setting up of administrative agencies of a judicial character, yet the point must be clearly grasped and the fact faced, that if we are not going to have administrative lawlessness then we must have some form or other of administrative law. It may be objected that the administrative functions of government might be increased and still exercised in accordance with ordinary law. In theory this might be so ; but I hope that the moral I have tried to point, notably in connection with the " in this Act " clause, has not been entirely vain. In practice it has been found that the Minister could not exercise effectively the powers conferred upon him, unless he were given a certain amount of autocracy.

Readers who desire a full exposition of the case for the introduction of Administrative Law into this country are referred to the very able work of Dr. Robson, *Justice and Administrative Law.*

Straws in the Wind

THEY ARE ALL PURITANS

By G. K. CHESTERTON

THERE is supposed to be a sort of Civil War raging in America, in the literary sense, between the Puritans and the Anti-Puritans. In this case, obviously, we cannot say between the Puritans and the Cavaliers. For the active Anti-Puritans are men like Mr. Sinclair Lewis and Mr. Mencken, whose one remaining link with the Republic is probably their disinclination to draw swords and die for the King. But they can be called the Puritans and the Anti-Puritans; and a stranger from England or Europe, after studying the two factions, will be tempted to make a certain assertion about them both. At least I am tempted to make it; though I recognise that it is a simplification and perhaps an over-simplification. I am tempted to say that they are all Puritans; especially the Anti-Puritans.

Of course there are the usual exceptions and marginal differences and debates about definition. The religion that remains in the ruck of American villages doubtless differs, as is pointed out in an interesting article in *Scribners*, from the origins from which its sects arose. It is not pure Puritanism; it is something rather impure that is the only practical product of Puritanism. It might be called, in the more general sense, Prohibitionism. But then pure Puritanism did not exist for more than a generation or two of unnatural exaltation and exclusion; in the course of which it did some extraordinary things, outside the normal, and certainly outside the nineteenth century Nonconformity. The Puritan substituted a God who wished to damn people for a God who wished to save them. He pushed the Parliament to oppose the king and then wrecked the Parliament in order to kill the king. He revived the barbaric butchery of all prisoners of war, in the case of the Calvinist ministers after the defeat of Montrose. He created the Scottish Sabbath, compared with which the Jewish Sabbath is jolly. But every man has a sane spot somewhere; and he was not a teetotaller. The particular scruples of the modern Puritan differ from the particular scruples of the original Puritan; save in the essential point that both have always been at once violent and trivial. The essential of the Puritan mood is the misdirection of moral anger. It is having righteous indignation about the wrong thing. That the new Puritans have added some new wrong things, to the old heretical heritage of wrong things, does not alter the essential qualification; that they take care to be wrong about what they think wrong.

To the old vices of gambling and gambolling, they have added the vice of beer-drinking; but whether we call the new amalgam Puritanism or something else, it exists and we must call it something. The English name given in my youth was the Nonconformist Conscience; but in England it is dead, while in America it is still considerably alive. It is in this sense that I say that the Anti-Puritans are Puritans; are almost more Puritan than the Puritans. Mr. Sinclair Lewis is a Puritan. The ordinary detached freethinker or freelance, like Mr. Walter Lippmann is a Puritan. The late Mr. James Huneker was a Puritan. Mr. Mencken is a Puritan. They are all Puritans.

What I mean is this. Between the two extremes of Mrs. Carrie Nation smashing saloons with axes and the Bohemian in Greenwich Village sipping strange culture with absinthe, there are of course a thousand shades of common sense or common senselessness. There is every sort of sane American citizen between the mad Puritan and the mad Pagan. But from my own standpoint, which is neither Puritan nor Pagan, there is one rather curious thing that is common to them all. For instance, one kind of man will say in effect, " I don't believe a man can be a good citizen unless he's a good Christian; and the Bible that was good enough for my mother is good enough for me. I don't say I've never taken a drink, but I don't allow it in my house; and I'd give anything to save my sons from gambling." Then there is a second sort of man who will say, " I'm afraid I can't believe in any creed myself, though of course I've a great respect for Christ and good Christians. It's all very well for them; but naturally I don't go in for being a saint; I take a drink from time to time, though not as a habit; and I'm not above a game of poker." Then we have a third type of man who says more impatiently, " Oh, these Christians are too good for this world, or they pretend to be; though lots of them are dirty hypocrites and drink on the sly; they aren't so darned Christian when you come to know them. I make no pretences; craps and whisky and this world's good enough for me." Next to him we have a wilder specimen who says, " Christianity's been nothing but a blasted blight on all the fun and freedom of humanity. I'm not ashamed of saying, ' Eat and drink for tomorrow you die.' All the Christian ever says is, ' Don't drink and hardly eat for tomorrow you're damned.' You read what Mencken says about the ministers who want to cut out gambling, etc." Then of course there is the more logical and philosophical culmination of the same philosophy, as in Mr. Mencken himself. Now there are any number of intelligent and kindly and jolly people of all those shades of thought. But what I remark about them is that they are all Puritans; at least they are all what we call in England Nonconformists. They all have the exact but extraordinary Nonconformist scale of moral values. They all have the same fixed but astounding notion of the nature of Christianity. Some of them accept Christianity and therefore refuse wine or whisky or games of chance. Some of them hesitate about Christianity; and therefore hesitate about wine or whisky or games of chance. Some of them reluctantly reject Christianity; and therefore (almost reluctantly) accept wine and whisky and games of chance. Some of them deliriously reject Christianity; and therefore deliriously accept wine or whisky or games of chance. But they all seem incurably convinced that things like that are the main concern of religion. It is a pretty safe bet that if any popular American author has mentioned religion and morality at the beginning of a paragraph, he will at least mention liquor before the end of it. To a man of a different creed and culture the whole thing is staggering.

There is another side to this truth, which I hope to suggest in another article. For the moment it is enough to note that to such a stranger the Puritanism of Mencken is more of a puzzle than the Puritanism of Moody and Sankey.

The Bashful Bad Men

By J. Desmond Gleeson

A NEW and delightful series of articles is running in the world's best morning paper under the general heading, " The Worst Thing I Ever Did." Perhaps one should rather say that the series was running, for these things change with such bewildering rapidity that the whole business may be entirely forgotten before these lines appear in print. One hopes, nevertheless, that the series will not be forced to die abruptly, but allowed to continue indefinitely. There are rather a number of people from whom one would like to hear the worst thing they ever did. There must be a large gang of crooks in high places whose worst deeds would be well worth hearing. After having passed long, busy and mis-spent lives, it would be a matter of some delicacy to pick out the most shocking of their many misdeeds. But I think the thing should be made into a competition. Cabinet Ministers, newspaper proprietors, financial sharks— I mean magnates, of course—literary cranks, Irish gunmen, screen stars and society entertainers should be encouraged to come forward and discuss their vilest actions with that fearless frankness (or is it frank fearlessness ?) that we admire above most of the virtues of our enlightened age. Each should display his own particular gem of crime in its proper setting, and add a tender note, showing why it stinks beyond the crimes of the other competitors. Each should endeavour to point out how much filthier he is than are the rest. They should cap one another's stories with one baser than the last, and each time one feels that one has descended to the lowest depths a fresh voice will ask, " Ah, but what did Mr. So-and-So do in '96 ? " and there will follow a new tale disclosing dirtier depths still further below.

Such a feature would add greatly to the interest in newspapers, which I understand is the object of Editors. Not only would the public be the judges in this competition, giving or withholding their votes at the end, but they would be treated to a thrilling instalment every day. New and startling revelations would follow one another with breathless rapidity across the news-sheets, and people would discuss them with animated pleasure for hours. Many a dull office would awaken to new life when the inside news about past deals became the stable topic of conversation, and poor little clerks would feel their admiration rising and their pulse beating the faster as they came to see their bosses in a new and better light. Admiration and awe, long lost to view, would struggle to the surface and ambition, revived and invigorated, would inspire the more adaptable of the clerky hearts. Even the despised suburbs would feel a lovely pride in the shocking condition suggested by these narratives of national depravity. Men would return by the city trains provocatively haughty, envied by the whole neighbourhood, because they had some slight subordinate dealings with a shady character who had just been making public the blackest secrets of his villainous career. And far away in country towns and villages, aged ladies would eagerly absorb the details of the deeds that made old England's name, and those of the better sort would vow to live worse ever afterwards.

It cannot be said, however, that we are yet within distance of the beautiful picture I have just drawn. Those who have started this brilliant series of articles are not getting the best out of their contributors. There seems a strange reluctance on the part of the crooks to come forward. There seems an even stranger modesty about the gentlemen who have so far come forward to recount their sins. Perhaps they are begin-

ning gently, so that they may work themselves (and ourselves) up gradually to the dark climax they have in view. After all, truth is not so easy to arrive at. You may have to chase it over a long stretch before finally you corner it. But anyway the series has not yet risen to its natural height, and the title is infinitely superior to the articles that follow it. One would think that the mere request to tell the worst thing you ever did would be inspiration in itself. It should put the writer on his mettle. It should be accepted as a challenge and a challenge met. But the writers do not quite enter into the spirit of the contest. There is Mr. Gilbert Frankau, for instance. Searching his mind for villainous actions well performed, Mr. Frankau discovers that he neglected to kiss his mother on the day of his wedding. Come, come, Mr. F., say we, that's not good enough. Those who have studied their Frankau, both in the libraries and on the bookstalls, expect better crimes than that. From inferior folk this would merely evoke looks of indifference, but from a best-seller it gives a feeling of being let down. There is James Douglas again who, dauntless as ever, enters the lists. But even the Douglas does not pick up the gauntlet. What particular crime it was he confessed to I do not now remember and probably neither does he at this time of day. And if the worst thing he ever did cannot even be recollected a week later it is at least probable that it was not the worst thing he did.

What can it be that comes between the writers and their readers when they attempt to set down their distinguishing crimes ? What wayward spirit takes hold of their pens and hurries them away in the wrong direction ? Would it be the same if they were writing, not of their own rottenness but of the rottenness of each other ? Here I think we touch on an important point which should immediately be brought to the notice of those whose privilege it is to run these articles. It is possible, nay, it is highly probable, that if these gentlemen were writing *on one another* and not on themselves they would feel less self-conscious, more natural and altogether more able to do justice to their subject. There would be a freedom about their work, a wholesome lack of restraint that could not fail to find reflection in the articles that they wrote. Admitted that Mr. Frankau does not shine when he is asked to confess his sins, could he not, however, find among his friends one with a better memory than he himself possesses who would thoroughly enjoy telling us what was the worst thing that Frankau ever did ? And the Douglas, too, surely in his large circle there is to be found the candid friend one who knows him better than he knows himself, and who would give us the benefit of his knowledge.

Before coming to my conclusions I have discussed this serious matter with many thousands of readers, as is my habit. Together we have thrashed the matter out in many bars and even while we went home singing through the rain. Among all these readers of the world's best morning paper I have been especially struck by that section which took the business literally. When they saw that the heading ran " The Worst Thing I Ever Did " they naturally jumped to the conclusion that what followed was the worst article that the writer had ever written. They thought it strange that the artists should publish their worst articles, or rather strange that they should boast of them as such. For such modesty they were not prepared, nor, as they hastened to point out, was it a quality that they expected to find on the central page of their favourite paper. For my part, I present the view of these literal people as one might present a minority report. And though their estimate is rather sweeping, it is possible that it is quite right.

Bits and Pieces

By Agag

YOU CANNOT HELP BEING THRILLED—

There is a certain school of literary thought which despises, or affects to despise, Mr. Edgar Wallace's facility for manly and straightforward narrative. It deplores his lack of subtlety, the simple honesty of the man which makes his villains show villainous through the most immaculate attire, his persistence in clinging to a conception of a world in which vice is organised and efficient, and through which virtue muddles its way somehow—generally with the aid of a couple of pretty startling coincidences. It is not my purpose here to defend Mr. Edgar Wallace's view of life, or to draw the close analogy which could be drawn between Mr. Wallace's work and some earlier and even better-known moral writings: I am concerned to boost him in another capacity—in the capacity of literary controversialist, which he filled with sudden and startling success last week. There appears to have been a feud standing for some time between Mr. Wallace and Mr. Hannen Swaffer. Mr. Wallace had already launched one direct attack in print, and it had rolled off Mr. Swaffer's back without effect, as these things do. Mr. Swaffer is proof against such methods. Whether he is slapped on the face by an angry actress, or slapped (figuratively) on another part by an exceedingly contemptuous Bernard Shaw, Mr. Swaffer remains equally at ease. These are mere occupational inconveniences, like the snubs which a Strand tailor's tout must endure in the course of his daily work. Mr. Wallace, his fire drawn and rendered ineffectual, revised his methods and succeeded in one short Press interview in scoring more points on his somewhat unimpressionable target than most men can claim who have been shying bricks at it, on and off, for years.

—BY THE VANISHING AUNT.

Mr. Wallace told the *Daily Express* that he had been nursing a certain rancour against Mr. Swaffer and that he had sat down to write another article criticising him, when a ghostly voice came to him telling him to desist. He went upstairs and when he returned his manuscript had vanished. He went to bed and was awakened in the early hours of the morning by an elderly female figure who told him that she was the materialised spirit of a deceased relative of Mr. Swaffer, enjoined him once more to be good and kind to Hannen, chatted indifferently for a while on horse-racing and such matters; and then vanished. All this the *Daily Express*, needless to say, printed quite solemnly. The following morning a well-known clergyman warned Mr. Hannen Swaffer's deceased aunt that if she should venture to visit him, he would stand no nonsense, but would report her immediately to his bishop. So far as I am aware, Mr. Hannen Swaffer, for all his interest in spiritualism and for all his late relative's interest in him, has not yet made any comment upon Mr. Edgar Wallace's remarkable psychic experience; but I trust that Mr. Wallace will not let the matter rest here. It seems to me that Mr. Wallace, having fallen so readily into line with the suggestion of Mr. Hannen Swaffer's deceased aunt (I will call her Mrs. Prendergast, although it is extremely improbable that that was her name), must have established a certain influence over her, and that, with a little tact, he might be able to persuade her to take part as a character in one of his future novels. The place of the Fourth Just Man still remains empty, and I cannot imagine a more useful ally for the other Three than Mrs. Prendergast. Or, if Mr. Wallace prefers it, he might prevail upon her to act as guide and counsellor to Lieutenant Bones in his continual struggles against the wiles and cunning of Bosambo (was it Bosambo?) and the other African chiefs. I leave the details to Mr. Wallace, so long as he will promise that we shall hear more of this engaging, whimsical character.

BARGAINS IN BALDERDASH.

And, talking of African chiefs (how slender are the threads which connect one line of thought with another!) I have noticed recently another form of the once-thriving trade in the export of worn-out hats to negro countries. Top-hats are not concerned, and it is not we who are doing the exporting. The Americans are exporting, we are importing, and the commodity is the comic strip, that form of humour which, at its worst, consists of six bad drawings to express or, rather, to expose, one pitifully feeble joke. You may have noticed recently that a number of papers have announced the publication of new and frantically funny weekly or daily comic strips. It is a fact as well worthy of notice as anything else connected with these papers, that the majority of the strips are American in origin, were drawn, published, perused and pulped in America anything from five to fifteen years ago and are being sold over here in job-lots. Just as we used to send our top-hats out to the Guinea Coast when we had done with them and had stored them in an attic for half a generation, so are the Americans sending their humour to us. Just as the savage chiefs used to swagger before their less fortunate subjects and brag about the value and virtue of their battered foreign headgear, so are our savage chiefs of Fleet Street boasting and blowing about their acquisition of these stale fragments of slender alien humour, And these same papers are the ones, by the way, which most persistently urge upon the public to "Ask Whether It Is British Before You Buy."

THE LUCK OF THE LORDS.

It is good news for those who have at heart the honour and dignity of the Peerage of the United Kingdom that Mr. Snowden may shortly be sent to the Upper House (or, more appropriately, that the Upper House may be sent down to Mr. Snowden). Nothing is yet settled, but should Mr. Snowden decide to accept the ermine it seems overwhelmingly probable that, following and even overtaking the example of some of his more recently-created colleagues, he will decline to be addressed as Lord Snowden of the Elephant and Castle (or whatever his formal title may be) but will insist on being called "Phil," or "Cocky," or "Matey," or "Hi," as in the past.

A LAMENTABLE ADMISSION.

I am an Englishman, I am a provincial, I have not that quick, logical, Latin appreciation of reality which is so much to be desired in one who speaks publicly of public things. That is why, when I read that D'Annunzio, whom I have seen described by some intelligent people as the greatest genius alive, and by others, equally intelligent, likened to an evil plague—when I read that that man has spent an afternoon steaming about on a toy warship, in a cocked hat, firing salutes to Mr. Kaye Don, writing poems to Mr. Kaye Don, placing spells on Mr. Kaye Don, kissing Mr. Kaye Don, and all the time talking the most unutterable nonsense that I have ever had the pleasure of reading—then, in my provincial English mind I decide that that man, whatever he may have been or done in the past, is to be regarded at the present moment as a rather glorious joke, to be preserved at all costs for the delight of our dreary generation.

Should Prohibition Come

By G. C. Brend

DEAR GREAT-GRANDCHILD,

I AM writing to you from that far-off period which we called Modern Times but which you will probably call the Later Middle Ages. Year after year, one, Edwin Scrymgeour, M.P., has introduced a bill into the House of Commons for the total abolition of alcohol except—let us be fair—under certain restrictions for medicinal purposes. Year after year the Bill is thrown out. It seems to me impossible that my fellow countrymen will ever be mad enough to pass this Bill, but it must be remembered that to my great-grandfather the idea of it ever being introduced into the House of Commons would have appeared equally fantastic.

Let us therefore assume the worst. Prohibition has arrived. Drink has been abolished (officially). The inn, that foul gin-palace of the past, has been swept away. For who can doubt that the thorough-going Prohibitionist would pull down the very building itself, that stood for such decadent barbarity. In its place we should have the boarding-house and the large well-lighted restaurant. And you, great-grandchild, are returning in your new car to your model home to welcome your smiling wife and happy children. And I, thank God, have died many years ago.

Just a word then, great grandchild, about that sink of iniquity, the pub, which you are destined never to see. You will never see the *Cat and Fiddle* silhouetted on the sky-line, high up on the moors above Buxton. You will never sit in the ivy-covered gallery of the 600-year-old coaching inn, the *New Inn* at Gloucester, and in the same delightful town you will never dive into the underground vaults of the *Monk's Retreat*. (O wise monks!) You will never sip rum punch in the *White Horse* at Shere. You will never exchange a bitter with a gentleman's gentleman in that discreet little Mayfair backwater, the *Running Footman* and just as the *Running Footman* runs away from you, so also will the *Running Horse* of Leatherhead. You will never see the Americans pouring into the *Lygon Arms* at Broadway, in such numbers that Broadway, Worcestershire, almost appears to be Broadway, New York. You will never step out of *Jack Straw's Castle* on a summer's evening to gaze at the lights of London twinkling far below in the gloom. You will never step out of the *First and Last* to hear the Atlantic breakers roaring their way up the Cornish coast. You will never drift along in a punt up to the *Bells of Ouseley* where Surrey touches Berkshire. You will never drink a pint at a single gulp, for a bet, in the *Star*, at Alfriston. You will never play skittles at the *King's Head*, at Roehampton. You will never sleep in the room in which Charles the First once slept in the *King's Head*, of Monmouth. You will never make that miraculous journey in Chelsea from the *World's End* to the *Man in the Moon*. You will never wear your landlord's boots in the *Bear*, at Devizes, your own having been soaked by the rain. You will never study interesting autographs in the visitor's book of the *Lamb*, at Burford. You will never sit in the *Cottage of Content*, at Mersham and watch the endless stream of traffic along the Brighton road. You will never stand outside the *Falcon* on the desolate Yorkshire moors with despair in your heart whilst sixteen of your imbecile companions attempt to give an exhibition of folk dancing. You will never wander along the banks of the Wye by moonlight after a meal at the *Green Dragon* in gloriou old Hereford. You will never dine with the *Marquis o Granby*, at Epsom, with *Dick Whittington and his Cat*, a Highgate, with *Bedlam Tom*, at Redbourn.

But like yourself, I become tired of this " You will never refrain. Let us therefore vary it. Pluck the *Feathers* fror Ludlow. Butcher the *Bull*, at Peterborough. Expel *Adar and Eve* from their Cotswold Eden near " Cranham's sobe trees." The *Bear and Castle*, at Marlborough, will g So too will that extraordinary gentleman, the *Trusty Servan* of Minstead, in the heart of the New Forest, he who has th legs of a stag, the head of a pig and the ears of an ass. Tw or three miles away *Sir John Barleycorn*, of Cadnam, wi also be a casualty. We shall have to say good-bye to th *Fighting Cocks*, at Horton Kirby, to *Bel and the Dragon*, a Cookham, to *Dick Turpin's Cave* in Epping Forest and t that funny little pocket pub, the *Sportsman*, on Walton Heath Salisbury of the soaring spire will undoubtedly starve, fo at one stroke she will lose her *Shoulder of Mutton*, her *Haunc of Venison* and her *Round of Beef*. More than one ghos will turn uneasily in its grave when the *Cricketers*, of Dunctor are no more and the same may be said about the *Swan*, a Fittleworth. No longer will man wonder what the *Durhar Ox* is doing in Leicestershire, how the *Hampshire Hog* ha found his way into Chiswick and why the *Essex Serpent* is i Covent Garden and the *Rose of Normandy* in Marylebone Then there is that strange creature the *Swan with Two Necks* Why with two necks ? Apparently because it dates back t the days when there was only a picture and no writing o the signboard and it was meant to typify the *Two Swans* Now the way to draw two swans, is to draw one complet swan, with the neck and head of the second just visible o the far side. Hence the swan with two necks.

In one final holocaust the Prohibitionist will sweep awa the *Case is Altered*, the *Who'd Have Thought It?* the *Hit o Miss*, the *Goat in Boots*, the *Goat and Compasses*, the *Bull i the Thorn*, the *Devil and the Bag o' Nails*, the *Saracen's Head the Hole in the Wall*, the *Four Alls*, *His Lordship's Larder the Mechanic's Larder*, the *Crooked Billet*, the *Magpie an Stump*, the *Fortunes of War*, the *Valiant Trooper*, the *Kentish Drover*, the *London Apprentice*, the *Dancing Maids*, the tru *Lover's Knot*, *Ye Olde Beare's Paw*, the *Pillars of Hercules* and the *Hero of Waterloo*. Perhaps however he may hav enough perverted sense of humour to keep the *World Turne Upside Down* and perhaps for a moment—but only for moment—he may halt in his destructive work when his ey alights on the *Live and Let Live*.

And that, great grandchild, will be your world. Th pub will have gone but not the drink. That will continue though even by 1931 standards, it will be pretty foul stuff In place of the pub will be the speakeasy. Perhaps you wil even get an extra kick out of the fact that your drinking i illegal, but personally I would not exchange your lot for mine However, the outstanding fact is that you in your speakeasy will be drinking, just as we in our lifetime used to drink ir the pubs. That at least is a bond—perhaps the only one— between us. It may not be much but it is something. And so, dear great-grandchild, from the depths below I drink to you.

Your affectionate Great Grandfather,

Nineteen Thirty-one.

Books.

Christian Democracy

A BULWARK OF DEMOCRACY. *By Augur. Appleton. 5s.*

IT is appropriate to review such a book as this on the anniversary of Leo XIII.'s *Rerum Novarum*. For that charter of the working masses was not written by an economist or a philosopher, some sanctified Marx, with a theory to apply to industrial conditions. It was not written by an Italian Conservative, disturbed by an alteration in the economic balance of his own country. *Rerum Novarum* was written by an international statesman of the first rank, with a central position, with a living tradition of history and statecraft, and with the most intelligent of agents in every country of the world.

Leo XIII. was the first modern Pope who wore the three-crowned tiara without the exercise of temporal power. That very isolation among monarchs gave him a clearer view of the over-mighty state which was already making monarchy a sham. And long before the Allied Powers gained their doubtful victory, Leo XIII. had carried the struggle with the over-mighty state of Bismarck and the *Kulturkampf* to an unambiguous conclusion. When Bismarck made his peace with the Holy See, he claimed that the *Kulturkampf* had been launched only to check the Polish menace in the Eastern Provinces—in Pomerania and West Prussia, now more properly known as Poznania and Pomorze. The claim was false. But it was true that Leo XIII. found the people of those Provinces among his allies ; and when, in 1891, he wrote *Rerum Novarum* to express the ideals of Christian Democracy, he had seen them already put in practice by the Poles of Poznania against the doctrine of blood and iron which was avowed in nineteenth century politics, as it was tacitly followed in nineteenth century industry.

A century ago the position of the Poles was hopeless, and for long it seemed to remain so. If there was a rebellion in Russian Poland, Germany came to the assistance of Russia. If there was a rebellion in German Poland, Russia saw that her interests, too, were threatened. If, after the Crimean War, Napoleon III. thought to exact freedom for Poland from Russia, a plan in which he had the support of Great Britain, both Prussia and Austria exerted diplomatic pressure against it. After the failure of three rebellions which shook Europe, it seemed that the Polish question was closed forever. In German Poland there was no hope of national revival. The nobles, who had represented the nation, were in exile, or powerless on their estates. The peasants were passive : and it was one of the reasons for the fall of Poland that the peasantry had not been allowed to share the national sense. The towns were filled with solid German burghers who prospered at the expense of Poles. Von Flottwell and Von Grolman—both picked out for special praise by Prince Bülow in his *Memoirs*—were initiating a drastic policy of prussification, which was, in Flottwell's words " to link up the province with Prussia by the gradual abolition among the Polish population of those views, habits and inclinations which are contrary to the connexion."

Flottwell, however, made a curious mistake, quite apart from his attempt to make the German language obligatory, quite apart from his establishment of a German bureaucracy to replace the Polish land system (and it was this bureaucracy that defeated the Rising of 1848), quite apart from his foundation of Catholic seminaries under German auspices. The mistake he made was to look upon the nobles as the chief enemies of Prussia. He thought that by improving the economic condition of the peasants and the small townspeople he could use them as allies against the nobles and the clergy. He did improve their economic condition, and thereby gave them the opportunity for national pride.

The reason for the title of this book, and its connection with the *Rerum Novarum* of Leo XIII., lie in the developments which followed. Before and after 1848 the Poles of Poznania were gradually developing a new policy. Instead of trying to regain independence by forlorn military hopes, they began to build up a democracy within an empire, using every national, economic and religious means at their disposal. A Dr. Marcinkowski came back from exile with a scheme for a society to help poor youths obtain a higher education. The Church encouraged him. Soon the society was built up from branches to executive through the whole of Poznania, with all classes supporting it, and in all its branches a focus for Polish nationalism. The police could not touch it, even when it took disputes between Poles out of the Prussian Courts and settled them by arbitration, imposing a fine which went to the society. And other societies grew up alongside it, with Marcinkowski as their guiding spirit : notably a revived Association for giving credits to Polish landowners ; Flottwell had already begun a policy of buying them out, and the whole strength of this democracy was to come from ownership.

Maximilian Jackowski became convinced in his turn that rebellion was fruitless, and so he began wandering around the country like Cobbett, awakening the peasants to their national tradition. Here again a network of societies was formed, but they might not have prospered much if Bismarck himself had not started making mistakes. He attacked the Catholic clergy, secularised the schools, substituted German for Polish in education. The school-war broke out. The peasant knew now that he was being attacked ; and Jackowski's societies jumped from 11 to 105 in four years. They began to cover Poznania, a network of local committees grouped around their Vice-Patrons, discussing all local affairs, and meeting 1,000 strong, at a General Assembly in Poznan. Soon the new ideas became so widespread that a boycott began of German traders, of Jewish shopkeepers, of doctors and lawyers who were not Poles.

All this was a prelude to the most remarkable events of all, which followed Bismarck's new policy for destroying Polish feeling in the Eastern Provinces. Taking advantage of the poverty of the large landowners he set up a Commission, with a first credit of one hundred million marks, to buy them out. Before that Commission was disbanded, it had received credits of 700,000,000 marks, and 150,000 German colonists had been settled on Polish lands. But at once Jackowski's organisation had taken the field. A week after Bismarck's campaign was launched, a Bank of the Union of Co-operative Societies was founded to fight the Commission with its own weapons : its directors were an ex-school-teacher, a parish priest, a country doctor and a lawyer ; and from 1896 to 1914, according to German figures, the Poles took back from the Germans more than ten times what the Germans acquired from the Poles.

In those years after Bismarck's policy began, the whole face and spirit of German Poland changed. The peasants became active participators in the national struggle, the nobles were proud to join the peasants, the townsmen built up their own trades. The large estates changed into a vast mass of small properties. The bishops and priests took a leading part in the co-operative movement, so much so that an Archbishop wondered whether a bank manager was necessarily a good shepherd of souls ; and three priests made themselves famous, Szamarzewski, Wawrzyniak and Adamski as apostles of co-operation.   By the time that Bülow had come to the cowardly policy of expropriation, by the time when the Ostmarken-Verein had begun its Germanising activities, which the author here compares with the work of the Cheka, the Polish democracy of Poznania was formed.   It remained only for it to complete its work in the restoration of Poland.

Augur is already known for his brilliant ordering of a mass of facts and documents.   This book is a fine example of his powers, and no brief account of it can do more than confuse his issues by compression.   He takes into his survey and illustrates with some excellent maps, the part played by Poznan in 1918, the whole history of the struggle between German and Slav, and the history of Poland to the Partitions. It is a book with a particular value, all the more because it is the only account in English of a historical battle between a defenceless people and the strongest of empires.   To say no more than this is praise enough : it describes fully and graphically the victory of Distributism.

GREGORY MACDONALD.

I SAILED WITH CHINESE PIRATES. *By Aleko E. Lilius. Arrowsmith.* 15s.

Mr. Lilius has written an interesting account of his experiences among the pirates of the China Seas.   He spared no pains in his search for material, even going to the length of getting himself locked up in a Hong Kong prison in the hope of finding someone among his fellow-prisoners who would bring him in touch with the pirate leaders.   In the end his efforts were successful and the story of his adventures, quite well and plainly told, involves a pirate queen, a secret brotherhood, an execution or two, a number of kidnappings and escapes and a Chinese servant who is faithful to death.   The ordinary, casual reader may find some of the incidental descriptive passages quite as interesting as the more exciting parts of the narrative. The description of Macao (one of the most amazing towns in the world) in itself makes the book worth reading.   Personally I found his most exciting adventures not so incredible as the pidgin-English which he puts into the mouths of his Chinese characters.   Pidgin-English, like any other dialect or language, has quite distinct forms of its own : the mere substitution of the letter " l " for the letter " r " and the liberal sprinkling about of the " ee " suffix do not constitute a really adequate translation from the English.

A.M.C.

THE WORLD OF THE NEW TESTAMENT. *By T. R. Glover. Cambridge University Press. 6s. net.*

Dr. Glover, who combines academic scholarship with a knack for clear writing, has long been known to the general public as a writer on religious subjects in a daily paper.   In this more scholarly description of the Ancient World in the first days of Christianity he achieves something like a triumph.   His lucid style is admirably fitted for an exposition of complex historical situations, his arrangement of matter into full chapters on *The Greek, Alexander, The Roman, The Jew, The Roman Empire, The Hellenistic Town,* and *The Man of the Empire* give him the necessary space for expansion, and the detail of his knowledge is apparent everywhere.

It is the tradition for academic scholarship not to admit enthusiasm, so the reader would only guess in a few places that Dr. Glover has many prejudices in common with Dean Inge.   That may be what is wrong with academic scholarship.   His task is to study " a civilised world with a great education and a splendid past, a world with a literature, a philosophy, an art, a spiritual ancestry, familiar

and beloved for centuries, a world with postulates, the axioms and inhibitions that make man, a world made one by the Mediterranean . . . . . ."   An example of Dr. Glover bursting through his scholarship is his shrewd attack upon linen surplices, which hardly seem to merit such a marshalling of history and literature.   " If, in Milton's caustic phrase, ' the ghost of a linen decency haunts us yet,' the sacred use of linen, the surplice, is a last heirloom from the priests of Isis.   But, as we shall see, Christendom had nobler gifts from Alexandria."   Probably Cotton Week.   But this sort of farce is extremely rare in a good book.   It is a pity that it has no index.

THE ARCHÆOLOGY OF BERKSHIRE. *By Harold Peake, M.A., F.S.A. Methuen. 10s. 6d.*

A volume on the archæology of Berkshire may not be to everybody's taste who does not know that county.   It should be explained that this is one of a series, *The County Archæologies,* under the general editorship of Mr. T. D. Kendrick, M.A. ; three volumes have now appeared and four more are in preparation.   So each to his own choice.

Mr. Peake's work on Berkshire compresses, supplements and brings up-to-date the information contained in the *Victoria County History* and he seems to have made a vow not to omit mention of a single arrow-head, scraper, beaver's skull, Roman coin or Anglo-Saxon brooch that has been reported in the county since research began. The bones of beavers, by the way, are unexpectedly important because of a theory that peat beds are the last results of beavers building their dams in river valleys : the archæologist is jubilant if he discovers the skull of a beaver at the bottom of a bed of peat. And this book teems with odd information of the kind.

Its subject is the whole county from the beginning of time to the Norman Conquest.   Berkshire is probably a good county by which to illustrate geological changes, the spread of population from uplands to lowlands, along river valleys and through diminishing forests, the rise and fall of the Roman power, the coming of the Anglo-Saxons and of the Danes.

There are numerous illustrations of objects that have been discovered from time to time, and a full gazetteer at the end lists all possible finds, with references, under the names of villages.   The author's information about Wayland's Smithy and the White Horse will be of general interest.   One of my own surprises was to learn that the Roman road from Silchester to Speen passed right through the marshy valleys of the Kennet and Enborne to the Bath Road at Thatcham Newtown.   The *County Archæologies* promise something more than an archæological interest.   Anyone who lives in the country may now be fired by enthusiasm and dig for one of those pots of Roman coins which seem to have been left lying about here and there.   It is as easy a way of making money as any other.

G.M.

Gramophone Notes.

May Records

THE Opera Seasons at Covent Garden and at the Lyceum create an obvious occasion for the issue of appropriate gramophone records.   But so similar are the operas and the artists at Covent Garden to those of previous seasons that the gramophone companies are hard put to it to find new subjects for recording ; while at the Lyceum so unexpectedly dissimilar is the occasion to anything we have had that, except for the excerpts from the operas popularised by the Diaghileff Russian Ballet and several Chaliapine records, the gramophone companies have little on stock to meet the situation and little time to replenish their stocks.

So that new operatic records this month are scarce. Next month it is possible that the efficient organisation of the big companies will have caught up with the operatic interests of the moment. At present, however, interesting records are confined to a new issue of Gounod's *Faust* sung in French and as performed at the Paris *Opera*, including the Walpurgis Scene and the Ballet (H.M.V. C 2122-41) ; to some fine singing by Mme. Toti dal Monte, accompanied by members of La Scala Orchestra of Milan, of excerpts from Verdi's *Falstaff* and Bellini's *La Somnambula* (H.M.V. D.B. 1317); and to an effective but rather brittle colorature performance by Mme. Lily Pons, of the " Mad Scene," from Donezetti's *Lucia de Lammermoor* (H.M.V. D.B. 1504).

The Columbia Company are content with an issue of *Merrie England*, performed by the Columbia Light Opera Company, under the personal supervision of Sir Edward German (D.B. 478-483). Columbia are, however, responsible for the best orchestral record of the month : that of William Mengelberg and the Concertgebouwe Orchestra of Amsterdam, in Beethoven's glorious *Leonore Overture No. 3* and the same composer's unfortunate *Turkish March* (L.X. 129-130). H.M.V. give us Schumann's *Symphony No. 1*, very well played by the Chicago Symphony Orchestra, conducted by Frederick Stock (D 1889-1892).

Instrumental records include a fine pianistic performance by Friedman of Mendelssohn's *Songs Without Words* (Columbia, D.B. 454-457) and by Benno Moiseivitch of Beethoven's *Andante Favori* (H.M.V., D. 1874). There are several delightful humorous and light records, including two by Miss Gracie Fields (H.M.V.) and an unusually large selection for this time of the year of dance band records. Possibly dance tunes are more popular to-day for river and sea-side trips than they are in the dance rooms.

V. N. L.

The Drama.

" Lean Harvest "

"LEAN HARVEST," by Ronald Jeans, is a most vitalising departure from stereotyped production. The theme is ordinary, its development at moments almost sterile, but it is presented with such force, adroitness and vivacity that it hold the interest all the way through.

" What you put into life, broadly and generally you get out of it " is the underlying motif. Mr. Leslie Banks plays the part of the young man who sets his will for power through money. Mr. J. H. Roberts is the brother without ambition and, generally speaking, content with the second best in literature as well as life. The first is engaged to a very mild young woman who becomes impatient at the perpetual postponement of their wedding. The young man simply will not accept the pedestrian situation and turns down one job after the other because they do not offer him sufficient scope. And then he has the chance of a position at £700 a year, which means marriage and a small villa with some of mother's furniture. Into this milieu there arrives Celia, a beautiful creature whose sheer appearance demands luxury. The sight of her, the take-it-for-granted attitude of the family as to his future suddenly irritates him. He switches right round, refuses the job—Celia takes the telegram—and the villa, marriage and Anne fade into the background.

This first act is emotionally rather barren. It is difficult to reconcile the driving force of the character with his long acquiesence in the tepid domestic surroundings in which we find him. Village life of this particular suburban type may do much to impose stagnation, but neither Anne, the mother, nor the brother show the smallest mental or affectional reactions. You feel that this prodigal son would have marched out of the villa years before.

The next meeting with Celia is shown in the film manner. She comes out of one telephone box, he comes out of another, and in two minutes contact is made and the playwright saves twenty minutes of explanation. These short, crisp scenes would stimulate the palate of the most jaded playgoer and urge the action on each time.

The couple marry, and Anne pairs off with the literary brother, but our Napoleon only comes to love his wife after marriage and then she is a bad second to finance and power. He makes money, she spends it. He creates gigantic trusts, she makes social successes, and every time one or the other tries to break through the walls of self that keep them from each other, they realise more and more completely how far apart they are.

The climax comes when Celia's faithful admirer finally decides he has looked at the unobtainable so long and so hopelessly that he can bear it no more. For Celia has remained faithful to her husband though the fidelity is mechanical. Finally she leaves her husband ; it is a difficult parting. You feel the pain on either side, the hopelessness, the irreconcilibility of the two temperaments. For fundamentally it is not money that has come between them. The trouble is that they are both takers rather than givers. Each is so self-centred that they cannot reach out to the other.

The last act is a triumph of expressionism. The brilliant financier, left in his study utterly alone, calls on his gods of power, money and authority, but the strain has been too much. He is a sick man and his will breaks. You see the creatures of his thoughts mocking him, voices shouting the odds of life, echo and re-echo, jeering faces peer at him, clutching hands, evil shadows come and go. The lighting is magnificent, the setting a triumph.

Mr. Leslie Banks has never achieved a better piece of acting. He succeeds in presenting the growth of years, the hardening of the arteries, the blurring of the features with little in the aid of make-up. It is a marvellous and rather terrifying study. Mr. J. H. Roberts as the mild author of Jacobite love tales is very pleasing, and Miss Diana Wynyard is superbly right in everything she says and does.

The end of the play is Mr. Ronald Jeans at his most cynical. The financier leaves his money to his brother and Anne, and immediately the two start quarrelling. The man wishes to settle in the country, the woman longs to travel—Venice, Sorento, where Celia and her lover have already gone.

J. K. PROTHERO.

AMUSEMENTS.

THE COCKPIT

[Letters on this page express the views of readers, not of the Editor. Correspondents are asked to limit themselves to 200 words. Short letters are always more likely to be printed than long letters.]

"A CABINET DECISION"

SIR,—In asking for a reasoned explanation of the statement that birth-control is opposed to the integrity of the family, Mr. Baines is setting us what is admittedly a difficult problem. The short answer to his request, against which he enters his caveat at the outset, is that in the last resort the integrity of the family depends upon a certain view of chastity to which modern birth-prevention is as utterly abhorrent and loathsome as cannibalism. I believe that that view may with as perfect justice be called the Puritan view as the Catholic view. Personally, I believe in distributism for no other reason than that I believe in chastity. Distributism means chastity for all; the Servile State means chastity for the privileged few. On any other view the Servile State is streets ahead of any other form of economic organisation.

Since, however, Mr. Baines refuses to allow us this primary argument, we must do our best with the secondary arguments :

(1) Historically, the industrial revolution was followed by a great increase of population, and the first experiments in birth-prevention were upon the squalid and swarming populations of the industrial North. Its later development and real success have been among people who do not know what poverty and squalor are. These people want industrialism to continue because it is the source of their prosperity. But they want industrialism without its squalor, and it looks as if birth-prevention could give them this. But a successful industrialism, that is, an industrialism deprived of its revolting features, would mean the end of the family because it would make the family an economically unnecessary institution.

(2) A case is known by the company it keeps. The case for birth-prevention is inextricably interwoven with the case for the sterilisation of the unfit, the case for easier divorce, and the case for the moral non-necessity of marriage. They are absolutely essential to each other and logically and psychologically they form a perfect organic unity.

(3) The establishment of a wide-spread system of State Clinics for the teaching of birth-prevention would give the State another excuse for interfering with family life and another method of doing so. And it cannot be too strongly emphasised that the modern State is the enemy of the family. The modern State cannot tolerate an *imperium in imperio*.

(4) One of the functions of marriage is to try to make the man bear a part of the burden and take a share of the responsibility which Nature would appear to have placed almost unfairly on the shoulders of the woman. Under a widely-practised system of birth-prevention, the man gets almost completely rid of his share of responsibility. *But the woman doesn't.*

(5) Birth-prevention means that marriage can be entered upon more light-heartedly and even recklessly. This possibility is in itself an enemy of the family.

(6) Our case is that when two people marry they should be endowed with private property to enable them to provide for their children. To the argument " But they needn't have children if they cannot afford it," there is no reply.

(7) The optimist who thinks that birth-prevention will not be abused is a similar sort of person to the optimists who once maintained that the dole would not be abused, and has just as much knowledge of human nature.

(8) We are asked what we propose to do when our distributis agricultural state becomes over-populated. We will face tha problem when it arrives.

K. L. KENRICK.

[This correspondence may now cease.—ED.]

INDIA

SIR,—May one at least of your readers register his astonishment an disgust at the appearance of the unsigned—and so presumabl editorial—article on " India " in a periodical taking its title from M G. K. Chesterton. An article which finds " the crucial point of th problem " in India to " concern the safety of the immense Britis interests " there, finds Mr. Winston Churchill " in principle qui right," and contends that " British rule in India must remain fo the protection of our interests " is the merest conventional apolg of predatory Imperialism. I grew up to be thrilled by the courag eous and incisive attacks launched by Mr. Chesterton upon the im perialism that involved us in the shameful war in South Africa, an it comes as a shock to find a writer employing his paper thirty year later to urge a " fight to a finish " against Indian nationalism o behalf of British investors who have been draining the wealth of tha country for generations.

No doubt the efficiency and relative impartiality of British admini stration have brought benefits to India, but at a terrible cost i taxation and exactions of every sort from the impoverished masse of that land. A Distributist paper might have been imagined t show less concern for " our [whose ?] immense interests " there, an rather more for that process of " agrarian deterioration " which th Indian Agricultural Commission reported in 1927. Their investiga tions showed that there had been a growth of " landless labourers from 7½ millions half-a-century ago to over 25 millions to-day and Dr. C. A. Bentley, the Director of Health for Bengal, declare some three years ago that " the present peasantry of Bengal are in a very large proportion taking to a dietary on which even rats could no live for more than five weeks." The root of the Nationalist move ment is economic, and whatever its faults, it represents a justifiable conviction that the joint burden of taxation involved in imperial rule and the toll taken by " our immense interests " is becomin intolerable.

The publication of such an article as this is a disgrace to the liberty loving traditions of G.K.'s WEEKLY, and one can only imagine casual ignorance to be the explanation of it.

MAURICE B. RECKITT.

NIETZSCHE AND DARWIN

SIR,—My youth and lack of experience in polemical warfare make me reluctant to enter the lists with Mr. Chesterton as my opponent, and yet I feel that a recent statement of his in his article, " The Absence of Argument," cannot be allowed to pass uncorrected.

He says that " Nietzsche accepted the Darwinian theory," yet we find that in " Beyond Good and Evil " Nietzsche speaks of Darwin as a " respectable but mediocre Englishman "; in " The Will to Power " there is a lengthy aphorism entitled " Anti-Darwin " with the sentence : " I incline to the belief that Darwin's school is every where at fault "; his " Skirmishes in a War with the Age " also contains a chapter headed " Anti-Darwin." Of course, the error into which Mr. Chesterton has fallen was foreseen by Nietzsche, for in " Ecce Homo " he explains the true meaning of the word " Superman," and in the next paragraph goes on to say : " Other learned cattle have suspected me of Darwinism on account of this word."

JOHN L. BEEVERS.

THE DISTRIBUTIST LEAGUE

CENTRAL BRANCH.

A CONFERENCE on Social Credit was held at The Devereux, on Friday, May 15th. The Marquis of Tavistock, who graciously took the Chair, opened the meeting by saying that the tragedy of the modern world was that, in spite of ample plant, more than ample labour, and ample means of distribution, people were dying of famine and wheat was being burnt by farmers. Economy was a pernicious red herring, as were tariffs and communism. We must nationalise the control of purchasing power.

Opening the case for Social Credit, Mr. Arthur Williamson read a well-written paper in which he said that Social Credit was based on a new philosophy of life incompatible with the industrialist system. The question was Can you replace poverty with plenty? Earth is the final raw material, but nothing can be accomplished without money. Money, in Mr. McKenna's words is "all currency in circulation among the public and all bank deposits which can be drawn by cheque." The limiting factor to the creation of money is psychological. It is only necessary to devise a mechanism in order to break the present irresponsible power of Finance and introduce an era of democracy and ordered plenty. The necessary mechanism was the system of Social Credit and National Dividends.

Mr. W. T. Symons, following up Mr. Williamson, said that Distributists and Social Credit supporters had common ground—the desire for Liberty, decentralisation, and variety in life. But he thought that Distributists took a "scarcity attitude" and lacked any practical constructive proposals. Also the Distributist view of society was incomplete, or at least there was too much emphasis on agriculture and not enough on industry. And Distributists always gave an impression, though they probably did not intend to, of wishing to go back rather than to go forward to a new social structure. The moral objection to the present system was not on grounds of avarice. The controllers of the present system were not out for wealth but for power. The remedy was the issue of money upon the authority of the community in order to enable goods to be *consumed* and a system of National Dividends by which every citizen would be assured of an income and would therefore have leisure to develop himself in whatever way he chose.

Commander Herbert Shove was the first to speak from the Distributist point of view. He said that he had come prepared to bless the Social Credit scheme as after reading some of its literature he had come to the conclusion that it was an extremely ingenious and admirable plan for breaking the power of the Banks and demolishing the present credit system which was responsible for so much evil. But having this evening heard an exposition of the philosophy which underlay the scheme, he could not support it. From Mr. Williamson we had heard that he did not believe in original sin and that St. Paul was out of date; from Mr. Symons we had an expression of admiration for the Bolshevist State in Russia. The philosophy which we had been told informed Social Credit he could describe only as damnable.

Mr. Frederic Holsinger attacked the Social Credit people on the ground that they had no conception of realities and especially that they did not use economic terms (such, for example, as money) in the ordinary sense accepted by economists.

Mr. J. R. Colclough, B.Sc., (Econ.) said that he too had been much puzzled by the special and unorthodox meaning which exponents of Social Credit attached to ordinary economic terms. Furthermore, he had spent many years in trying to discover what Major Douglas and his followers meant, but had not yet been successful. He found the Social Credit scheme quite unintelligible.

An interesting discussion followed, and Mr. Williamson and Mr. Symons answered many questions. This was the most interesting discussion on economics of the present session and several Distributists, notably Mr. G. Davies, said that they thought that there was much which Distributists might learn from the Social Credit people, and that some members of the Central Branch ought to make a closer study of the subject.

Before closing the meeting Lord Tavistock made a brilliant speech in which he answered certain questions which Mr. Symons and Mr. Williamson had been unable to deal with owing to lack of time. In conclusion His Lordship said that an evening of this sort was of great value as nothing was more desirable than that all idealists who were working to remove the terrible oppression and injustice under which the labouring masses at present suffered should meet and exchange views. Distributism, however fine an ideal, was, he thought, defective on the practical side, and Social Credit (which was not an end in itself) offered a means towards the end for which we were striving.

It is proposed that, if sufficient support is forthcoming, a Distributist Summer School shall be held during this year. It is suggested that it shall take place during the week-end which includes the August Bank Holiday and shall last about four days. Ditchling Common has been suggested as a suitable place as being the centre of the Mid-Sussex Branch of The League and within easy reach of London. These ideas are quite tentative; whether the scheme will come to anything depends entirely on the amount of support forthcoming. It has been suggested more than once in the past that it was desirable that The League should hold a Summer School; all other sociological movements of any importance do so, and it would be an excellent experiment for The League.

FORTHCOMING MEETINGS.

Central Branch.—At The Devereux, Devereux Court, Essex Street, Strand, W.C.2. Fridays at 7 p.m. Admission Free (non-members welcome).

Friday, May 22nd. A Distributist Reading. Six members will give a ten-minute criticism of the following books of Distributist interest : *Rural Rides* (William Cobbett) ; *The Servile State* (Hilaire Belloc) ; *The Devil's Devices* (Douglas Pepler) ; *Art-Nonsense* (Eric Gill) ; *The Fairy Ring of Commerce* (Commander Shove) ; and one other book. A discussion on Distributist Literature will follow.

Friday, May 29th. Mr. A. M. Coles (of the Governing Council of the National Socialist Movement) on "National Socialism."

Friday, June 5th. Mr. Frederic E. Holsinger (Author of *The Mystery of the Trade Depression*) on "The Realities of Money."

Friday, June 12th. Last Meeting of the session. Mr. T. A. Raman, B.A., LL.B., on "Gandhi and his Methods."

Birmingham Branch.—At Bullivant's Hotel (Carr's Lane entrance). Friday, May 29th, at 7.30 p.m. Mr. W. Pagett on "Impressions of Distributism in France."

Published by the Proprietors, G.K.'s WEEKLY, LTD., 2, Little Essex Street, Strand, London, W.C.2 (incorporating THE NEW WITNESS). Telephone: Temple Bar 1978. Printed by THE LEICESTER CO-OPERATIVE PRINTING SOCIETY LTD., 99, Church Gate, Leicester; Kettering and London. Sole Agents for Australasia: Gordon & Gotch (Australasia, Ltd.). Sole Agents for South Africa: Central News Agency, Ltd.

G.K.'S WEEKLY, October 17, 1931.   THE ESSENTIAL By Hilaire Belloc P. 85

G.K.'s Weekly

EDITED BY G. K. CHESTERTON.

No. 344—Vol. XIV.   October 17, 1931.   [Registered at G.P.O. as a Newspaper].   Sixpence

Temple Bar 1978.   2, *Little Essex Street, London, W.C.2.*

THE HORROR
By G. K. Chesterton P. 87.

THE ESSENTIAL
By Hilaire Belloc P. 85.

THE BREAK-DOWN

CAPITALISM never was a theory, but rather a series of opportunities for a few men who held the passes of the world. When their power appeared to be secure, and their wealth stable, the economists who were their servants elaborated a kind of theory and a set of laws which have now been smashed to pieces. For the plain fact was that Capitalism built its brief triumph by creating a proletariat of men without property who lived in slums, defenceless against exploitation. When the Capitalists had exhausted their first market by the direct exploitation of the labour of the proletariat, they created a second market and a new form of exploitation by selling cheap goods and nasty luxuries to the proletariat itself. It was the truck system magnified; it was called an improvement in the standard of living. It resulted in an even more complete divorce of the working man from the true necessities of life. It resulted in the bankruptcy of Capitalism. And when that bankruptcy came, Capitalism immediately tried to meet it by a new attack upon the poor, so manœuvred as to withhold from them the true necessities of life and yet to preserve their access to the secondary market of unnecessary luxuries.

If there is discontent now among the poor, that discontent is more than justified. If we are all in danger from the bankruptcy of Capitalism and from the destitution of workless men, it is no more than we have deserved for accepting the wrong values set before us. The poor have their wrong values too, but for that they are less to blame. The middle classes, the professional classes, the black coats, the 'intelligentsia' have for generations accepted the comforts procured by sweating the slums, and in consequence they find themselves involved in the bankruptcy, without the strength or the means to fend for themselves, and without realisation of the issues involved by the present breakdown. In justice and by necessity all the middle classes should now be on the side of the poor, applying with them the possible remedies for the restoration of England. In truth, however, the middle classes have been taught only to admire success. They admired Capitalism while it seemed to be a success. Now, the more acute among them admire Russia because there they imagine Communism will be a success. The more stupid among them cling blindly to a broken Capitalism in the frightened hope that what seemed a success in the past will once more be a success in the future.

The most striking achievements of Capitalism in this country, when all is said and done, have been to make the whole population dependent in one way or another upon industry and its markets, to make the people look upon machine industry and wage employment as ordained by nature, immutable; and to deprive the people of sources of food in their own country. England has been proudly called the workshop of the world. To-day, so many millions stand idle among the idle machines, depending upon an insolvent State for the food which they no longer grow themselves. No wonder if they turn to Socialism or Communism with its own mad plan of regimented machine industry. No wonder if they come to rioting and to panic and to starvation among the idle machines of what was the workshop of the world.

The present General Election is a turning-point in the history of this country. It may be a major crisis. And we are not going to say at once that all those who oppose concentrated Capitalism as an evil should support only those political groups and parties which seem also to oppose it. One consideration is that a great part of the nominal opposition is as much an expression in politics of Capitalist dictatorship as the Federation of British Industries itself. Another consideration is that, as the main issues become clearer, the effective opposition will prove to be dogmatic Socialism, or Communism, which is also an attack upon man, but a coherent attack, a real system, one might say a religion. A third consideration is that the immediate results of a radical upheaval now would not be an alternative system peacefully begun, but a withering of the pound, a breach in the organisation which exists for the supply of food to a foodless island, anarchy in clotted towns, and the end of what we know without prospect of what we wish.

If Capitalism has broken down, then, we are not going to swing sheep-like to an alternative which is worse. Our whole salvation lies in the fact that Capitalism never was a system, that it never did succeed. The main traditions of England survived it, continued hidden beneath it, and can grow up again to new life through its cracks and fissures. Any alternative than to feed upon a decaying Capitalism for the restoration of older things—the alternative of chaos or the alternative of Communism—would cut clean across the main traditions of liberty, property and the family which have been attacked and numbed but never destroyed in this country.

So far as the individual considers that his vote has political value for the future of England he must use it with the main idea of avoiding an easy chaos and of employing the decay of Capitalism to save the better traditions of his country, not with the idea of setting up a new system, even though it be a successful system. He must not use his political power, such as it is, to support the few rich against the many poor, but he must use the collapse of the rich to help the poor, making public at every opportunity the principles which he supports, and tying-down the candidate (so far as that has value) to professed obligations for the restoration of property, in land and in the means of production, to the great masses of the people. If we survive the present crisis at all we shall find that a belief in the virtue of concentrated wealth and monopoly in a few men has been widely destroyed. Great numbers of the people themselves will seek property for their own security and they must have it, or perish, or be slaves.

NOTES OF THE WEEK

After reading the manifestos and statements issued by the various parties in the various parties, the uninstructed voter must feel bewildered. Selecting from them a few examples, we note that the Conservatives support the Prime Minister's plea for a " doctor's mandate " while pointing out that one of the remedies they will try to impose on the doctors is that of tariffs. The Liberals on the other hand, while not insisting vehemently (in the Nationalist group at any rate) on Free Trade, desire the stabilisation of currency and the lowering of tariff barriers throughout the world. The Labour Party alone, attempts to diagnose the country's malady and to offer constructive proposals; but does not succeed. Its arguments are counterbalanced by its plans, which, where they are constructive, threaten us with as grave a danger as the danger of unlicensed capitalism.

*   *   *   *

The Labour Party points out that the capitalist system has broken down, and immediately suggests the need for a new capitalism. Where all the king's horses and all the king's men failed, the Socialists intend to succeed. They are going to put Humpty-Dumpty together again and set him up on a wall, not in Threadneedle Street, but in Whitehall. They say that we must plan our civilisation or perish, put an end to the domination of vested interests (by creating new vested interests) nationalise the banking and credit system and bring power, transport, oil, steel and coal under public control, while initiating the scientific development of agriculture. There is little difference really between a policy of that type and the policy of the monopolistic servants or partners of finance; and while the Labour Party has at least perceived, however dimly, the causes of the crisis, its purpose seems to be to lead us on towards another.

*   *   *   *

More blatantly than in past elections the Parliamentary candidates and the Press are exploiting the fact that women outnumber men in the electorate. The Prime Minister seems confident of success because he has captured the hearts of the women in his constituency; and the reports of one of his meetings have been reduced to absolute fatuity by one newspaper which printed in heavy type the remark made by one woman that she would vote for him because he was " some mother's son "—a reason that should oblige her to vote for his opponent as well. In another constituency the return of an Admiral is confidently predicted, apparently on the ground that every nice girl loves a sailor. And one of the popular cartoonists has had published a picture of a gentleman labelled " Mr. Season Ticket " galloping on an animal that looks uncommonly like a carthorse, towards national recovery. His hands are not on the reins, which are held by the buxom lady who is perched behind his saddle. It looked some weeks before the election campaign began as if there would be a ramp of this kind. Now there is no doubt at all in the matter.

*   *   *   *

It is reported that 80,000 wireless licenses have resulted from the campaign by the Post Office detective vans. Other genial results, proving the fine spur that this campaign has been to encourage the old "Britons never never shall be slaves " spirit in the nation, are also reported. Here are some: " The search by the vans has revealed that women have more sensitive consciences than men. When the vans appear, with the aerial visible on top, there is always much fluttering of consciences, and one elderly woman rushed into her nearest post-office with ten shillings and exclaimed breathlessly, " Give me a wireless licence, quick—the van is in our street!" " Many persons," states another report, " are apprehensive of taking out a licence in case they are cross-examined by the Post Office officials." But we are assured by the same report that a person calling for a licence will be asked no questions. It is intended to continue the campaign in London until the end of the month.

* * * *

The Round Table Conference has reached an inevitable deadlock on the subject of " Minorities." The Hindus seem ready to leave the matter to British arbitration—a striking commentory on the official Congress theory that England maintains her rule in India by purposely encouraging Hindu-Moslem dissensions. As a matter of fact a British dicision would be far more likely to favour the Hindus; and the Moslems know it. Sir A. Patro's suggestion that each Province should settle its own communal difficulty in its own way seems obvious common sense. It would not, of course, immediately solve the problems of Bengal and the Punjab; but it would give the other provinces a chance to get a move on. But there is no chance of this solution being accepted, for it would involve a danger of Separatism, and the Indian politicians would rather see the independence of India indefinitely postponed than sacrifice their ideal of One Big India.

* * * *

The enlightened members of our race are not in the habit of seeking guidance from a Central American republic; which explains possibly why the measures adopted by the Government of Guatemala to meet the economic crisis have not been reported or commented upon in the English Press. These measures are decidedly interesting as they show a sense of realities and fundamental needs too little found in industrial Europe. They involve the breaking-up of national lands into small holdings to be given free of charge for an indefinite period to those who are prepared to keep them in continuous cultivation. And it is laid down that any beneficiary who fails to work his land shall be obliged to give up the smallholding for transferal to another applicant.

* * * *

This national scheme offers a definite opportunity to those who wish to return to the land but lack the means to do so; and we shall watch its application so far as information can be secured, with very great interest. It deserves to succeed, particularly as its framers are evidently men of vision and understanding who have tried to make it serve the best interests of peasant proprietorship. For instance, the decree by which it has been introduced stipulates that the chief use of the holdings must be the cultivation of cereals and food for immediate home consumption, or sale in local markets and thus encourages the farmer to think in terms of real wealth rather than of currency. It is further laid down that the amount of land granted shall vary from four " manzanas " (a " manzana " corres-

ponds to 1.72 acres) in the case of a single person to five " manzanas " in the case of a family; and another clause appears to grant all rights of ordinary legal possession to holders, with the exception (additional to the provisos already mentioned) that they are not entitled to transfer their land to others than their heirs.

* * * *

We do not know how far it would be possible in the near future to apply a similar scheme in this country; though we invite our readers to study in comparison, the scheme put forward some time ago by the Birmingham Branch of the Distributist League. But if action cannot or will not be taken along these lines, there seems to be no reason why an effort should not be made to persuade large landowners voluntarily to assist. The various land associations now in being provide suitable machinery for such an effort. It should not be difficult, with the co-operation of a few owners of huge estates, to settle families on the land without heavy expense and under similar conditions to those imposed in Guatemala.

* * * *

The Moseley party, to judge by their newly-published organ, " Action," resemble Miss Arabella Allen, in that they seem a good deal surer of what they don't like than of what they do like. As regards the former, they are in complete agreement with ourselves, being equally opposed to the National Party, the Labour Opposition, and the Communists. Of their positive policy, all we can say is that they show a tendency to Fascism which, however, is counteracted by their very genuine distaste for the Fascist policy of repression. And Fascism without repression is an impossibility. It is not impossible that when they really find out what they are, they will find out that they are Distributists.

Responsibility
By A. M. Currie

IF that cloud breaks which is now hanging over Western civilisation and, most threateningly, over our small corner of it, the time for writing will be past, and it is well that certain things should be recorded now, while writing is still securely in fashion. It may be, of course, that the cloud will disperse, or, more probably, that it will be drawn to earth as a fog, noiselessly and without shock, to choke and blind and paralyse the spirit of liberty for a generation.

But it is well to recognise this: that if the storm does break, the heavy responsibility for the chaos that must ensue will lie, not with the millionaires and the politicians whose crimes and follies have precipitated it, but with us, who have forseen it. We, who have written in this paper; you who have read and have agreed with us; those few thousands of others, who have neither read nor written with us, but who have foreseen the danger looming as we have foreseen it— on the day when chaos breaks loose, it is we who will deserve to stand as the murderers of all the decent things that will die. The crooks, the cranks, the fools, who have been our constant butts, will throw their hands to heaven and cry in honesty: " We played with things we did not understand. We did not know, oh Lord, we did not know!" and will disappear to claim the mercy of God and of history for their simplicity.

But we shall have no claim upon that mercy : our part must be to stand and say : " We foresaw this thing, and we did this and this and this that it might be averted."

This and this and this ! My God, what have we done ? If this catastrophe fell to-morrow, what kind of record could we present in justification ? We have churned out epigrams in defence of liberty, and shared them amongst ourselves, and licked our chops over them. We have met triumphant tyranny with a gibe, and counted the tyranny resisted. We have talked largely to ourselves, and cleverly of abstract things ; so cleverly that common people, counting us prigs, have listened rather to the simpler stuffs of the Socialists and of the *Daily Mail*.

We have kept ourselves smug and clever and clean. We have never descended into the gutter of common human affairs. We have kept aloof from politics, for politics were too dirty to touch. We have forborne to address ourselves to the very common people in very common language, because the language was so common and, we gravely suspected, the people were too silly to teach.

We have kept ourselves select by careful heresy-hunting. We have built up a secret language for our own private use. Oh, yes, and we have met on committees and have passed resolutions in praise of freedom and of property, or, more daringly, in condemnation of tyranny. A few of us have plotted and schemed and contrived to break clear of the mess that is modern England, to plant this individual or that on a small-holding, to found one colony or another of six or a dozen families ; conceiving that the saving of this handful was more important than the saving of England.

We, who should have been leading a rebellion against the new, unnatural, insecure order of society—we have seen England come to the brink of chaos and we have done nothing about it that was not genteel. We, who have known the danger that all English things might slip down into ruin—have we acquitted ourselves of our responsibility by uttering a few scornful, but quiet and gentlemanly, protests ? Will it satisfy ourselves, or any man, to prove that, knowing the peril, we have been content to meet it with half the fire and dash and courage of an average branch of the Women's Institute ?

It is possible, indeed probable, that the cloud will not break yet, even that it will lift for a while, to descend upon us again. In that case, we shall be given a breathing-space in which to consider, in the light of the peril that has been postponed, the adequacy and the virtue of our former methods of resistance, and it may be that we shall find it necessary to amend them. Or it may be that a more frankly and firmly established slavery will come instead of chaos ; and in that case the whole character of our protest will be changed by force of circumstance. Or it may be that the crash will come immediately, that we are even now stepping down into chaos, the end of which no one can foretell. And if that is the journey upon which we are embarked, it is well that we should start upon it with no smug or priggish satisfaction at our powers of prophecy ; but responsibly bearing our own heavy share of the blame.

Bad News

A correspondent tells us that the political situation reminds him of a lump of sugar in a glass of warm water.

———

Because they thought it expedient to give a lead in the crisis, the directors of Imperial Chemical Industries have advised their employees, numbering tens of thousands, which way to vote on polling day.

———

A Director of the Bank of England states it is all nonsense for the Socialist Party to say there was a bankers' ramp. " We, as financiers, simply went to the Socialist Cabinet and advised them of the enormous withdrawal of gold that was taking place. The Cabinet said : ' What do you suggest, and what policy can you offer ?' We replied : ' That is not our business ; you are the Government and you have to decide the policy.' "

———

" In those happy days, before our nation became industrialised," said Mr. Baldwin, " we all spoke our own tongues without shame, and used old country words without being called vulgar. We have lived now to a day when most of us try to talk like the B.B.C., and in the sacred name of progress our language is gradually being formed on the model of the captions of the Hollywood films."

———

Where Governments have wasted tens of millions, the nation has been squandering hundreds of millions annually by buying from others things which it could have made or grown for itself.—*Mr. L. S. Amery.*

———

Labour denounces protected tariffs as a sinister movement of inefficient capitalism to press down still further the wage standards of the world.—*Mr. Stanley Hirst* (Transport and General Workers' Union).

———

Mr. Robert Lynd suggests that, as civilisation progresses, we may " gradually come to take as much pleasure in the noises of civilisation as in the noises of nature.

———

Mr. H. G. Wells has told a reporter that although he is " an anti-revolutionary " he feels that Russia is succeeding, and is stimulating the Western world. " We shall have to adopt a plan that is not based on private enterprise ; but it need not necessarily be on the same lines."

———

In order to make sure of a svelte figure and good carriage women are being advised by beauty experts to stand on their heads. Alternatively, they are told, the thing for them to do is to lean against walls and allow their minds to be empty ; which, if they intend to follow the advice, should not be difficult.

———

The owner of a greyhound which has won a number of races is credited with the statement that it receives " more love letters than a matinee idol."

THE ESSENTIAL
By HILAIRE BELLOC

THE essential at this moment is for all to understand the extreme gravity of the peril which menaces this country.

There are many aspects of the crisis which crowd upon the mind, each of them of high importance—notably the certain effect it will have of still further debasing and rendering contemptible the professional politicians. These may be dealt with in due order later on, but the essential, I repeat, the *one* thing to be hammered in now, is the scale as well as the character of the danger.

This is the more necessary because there was never a greater divorce between our official press, especially of the popular type, and the truth, than on the present occasion. We have had a perfect orgy of lying and of suppression, and the gulf between reality and what is presented to the befooled public is wider than ever before. There have been cataracts of sheer nonsense which have made us the derision of our rivals, and even of our friends, in Europe. One would think, to read the stuff, that this lamentable business was a sort of triumph, that the national default conferred on us a high benefit, and that the destruction of that stability which made the pound sterling the universal currency was something to chuckle over. There has been a drunkard's revel of falsehood and if we don't take care the awakening will be serious indeed. We shall not be allowed time to sleep it off.

Perhaps the worst sign of this is the insane fantasy that we can force a debased currency upon the rest of the world. The press has been full of schemes for inventing all manner of imaginary new currencies which shall in some magical way make those who cannot pay their debts in full suddenly more prosperous than those who are solvent. Each of these vagaries is sillier than the last. Whatever currency men adopt, the man who spends more than he has breaks; and what is true of men is true of nations.

The peril is of two kinds—financial and economic; and of these the second is the graver by far.

The financial peril is that of delay in the stabilisation of the pound at a lower level, of prolongation of this period of mortal anxiety and incertitude; with the possibility always present of a sudden and violent fall in the pound sterling.

So far that worst misfortune has been avoided. At the moment of writing (Thursday, October the 8th) the fluctuations of the pound have been for some days slight and the estimate that it might ultimately be stabilised at a gold value of round about 15s. to 16s. is supported by its current quotations. At the news that those in favour of an early election had won against those in favour of postponment, the pound rose somewhat.

Whereas the ounce of fine gold cost some days ago 115s., it costs to-day—the 8th of October—nearly 10s. less. This means that the foreigner and the more important dealers at home estimate that a stable government with a large majority, and unpledged, will result from the elections. A large majority unpledged to any specific action will leave the controllers of our great monopolies, including the chief of them, the bankers, free to work out a policy of which the professional politicians would be the docile spokesmen. The lowering of real wages and the cut in the money wages of public employees of all kinds, the reduction of succour for the destitute to starvation level, all that is necessary to restore, so far as it can be restored, the immediate position of industrial capitalism in this country, will, it seems obvious to these observers, be carried through without interference.

There is a great deal to be said for this point of view, which is clearly the conviction of New York at the moment of writing. There is no serious opposition party. The pretence of opposition on the part of the so-called " Labour Party " is a sham so glaring that no one could be taken in by it. Retail prices have not yet moved, those immediately affected by the cuts are but a fraction of the nation; the rest have little of what is called " class-consciousness " and have never been in the habit of using the vote as an instrument of policy. The idea of enforcing the national will by a general popular vote on a clear point is one which has never been accepted in this country. It is alien to the habits and traditions of the people.

It looks, therefore, as though for a time confidence would be restored, but there are two objections to so simple a conclusion, and only time can show whether either of them will upset the prediction. First, as we saw in the election of 1929, the new unwieldy electorate with its great masses of young boys and girls and its growing indifference to politicians is incalculable. Everything had been staged in '29 for a big Labour majority and as we know it did not quite come off.

The second objection is that there may arise during the course of the election some violent storm of protest which will make the foreigner uncomfortable and inclined to withdraw his remaining balances before the event is decided.

Even if on the financial side all goes well, and according to plan, there remains the much graver economic side. The plan for lowering real wages may work perfectly, there are plenty of stocks of food and other necessaries in the country and as general prices are still falling, the process of lowering real wages may be masked until the mass of Englishmen are used to them and the standard of living is definitely lowered. The pound may be stablished at so high a level as 16s. gold value or over. But there would still remain the economic problem, *to make the country pay its way.* If that problem is not solved the crisis will recur, and we shall be like a man going down a flight of steps from one stable platform to another: from one accepted lower standard of living to another yet lower. We shall be like a man who having paid 16s. in the pound and started again in business must again be embarrassed and default again, and, after that, default for a third time and for a fourth.

When people have outrun the constable there are only two alternatives before them—to earn more or to spend less. Spending less in some degree is achieved by the lowering of the standard of living—but only in some degree. And not in our case in a sufficient degree. For our main trouble is a bad economy in consumption, and it takes a full lifetime to change the habits of a people. The European rivals of our workmen are well fed, well housed and well clothed for sums upon which an Englishman cannot live. If you doubt it, go and look. A lower standard is but a part solution. The real problem is to increase the income of the nation.

Now the income of a nation such as Great Britain consists in three parts; what it produces for its own consumption, what surplus of its produce it can exchange with the foreigner, and what it receives as tribute from abroad—that is, payment which foreigners make for the services of those resident in this country; profits upon insurance and upon international finance, profits on foreign investments, salaries and pensions spent in this country but paid by subjects overseas, etc.

We can produce at home far more than we are now producing—but only of some things. Even at full capacity we could not produce half our vital necessaries. We import to-day between £70 and £80 per family—nearer £80 than £70—and of this more than 70 per cent. represents necessaries. We cannot produce the wheat, the leather, the wool or even the meat which we normally consume and the exotic products which have become necessary to us, such as petrol and tea, we cannot produce at all. We have nothing like a sufficient supply of raw material in the way of metal, still less have we a sufficient supply of wood. And even in articles which are classed as manufactured, a restriction of import would heavily impoverish us. For instance, doors and window frames. We could make them all at home but at a cost which would send up the cost of housing or lower the standard of housing—whichever way you like to put it. It is sound to talk of restricting imports, but we must remember how limited is the area over which restriction is possible

and how disastrously restriction—even in many things we could make ourselves—would impoverish us.

In the second category, the exchange of surplus, a depreciation of currency is obviously an immediate advantage. For we can feed and clothe the labourer out of existing stocks until these are exhausted. That is as much as to say that we can pay lower wages without the wage-earner knowing it, and while we are doing this we can undercut the foreigner. But against this there are three considerations. First that the stocks won't last for ever and that when the prices begin to rise the wage-earner will probably make trouble. Next, that all the world is ready with tariffs to meet our new advantage. Lastly, that certain of our customers have followed us in debasing their currency and against these we have no advantage whatsoever. There is also, for what it is worth, the consideration that raw material will cost us more in our currency; but that will not out-weigh lower wages.

The third category, which I have called tribute, is the most doubtful of all in the near future, yet it was precisely upon that category that we most depended in the past for our margin of prosperity. The country with a debased currency, which may be debased again, does not maintain itself as a centre of international exchange. Import for re-export, with its accompanying profits, tends to disappear; and we all know that our returns from investments overseas are declining and may continue to decline. We are still, for instance, getting, or are promised that we shall get, 25 millions annually from the Australians, part in legitimate interest and part in usury. But we know how very difficult it was to coerce them, even for this one year, and we are not at all sure that the full payment will be permanent year after year. A mass of German interest due has been postponed and some great part of it will never be received, while profits on the eastern trade have a doubtful future. We cannot rely on permanently receiving the old revenues from any of these sources.

There are the facts—and they must be faced. No amount of metaphysical arguments in favour of imaginary currencies, no amount of boasting, no amount of heartening parallels from the past will get rid of those facts.

Straws in the Wind.

THE HORROR
By G. K. CHESTERTON

NEARLY all newspapers and public speakers are now entirely occupied with finding harmless words for a horrible thing. In one sense, of course, they are always trying to do something of the sort, and they find it easy to tell people to take things easily. Simple persons call this the age of Realism; but it is, on the contrary, the age of Euphemism. We see this even in the mystifications in the mere matter of money. Refusing to pay your debts is a thing that everybody understands; and therefore it is mentioned to nobody. ' Going off the Gold Standard ' is a thing that nobody understands; and therefore it is mentioned to everybody. So far, it is all part of their training for the last forty years. Everybody was taught to use the word ' temperance ' to mean refusing to any man even the chance to be temperate. They talked about Birth Control when they meant preventing birth, just as they talked about Liquor Control when they meant forbidding liquor. But these hypocrisies were partly homages to virtue, in that they were homages to a sort of idealism. It was rather a weak and washy sort of idealism; but it was always some sort of humanitarianism. What confronts us to-day, like a chasm and a precipice, is sheer stark inhumanitarianism. Ten years ago—two years ago—even a year ago, it would have shocked us and plunged us into shame. To philanthropic Capitalists, of the school of Ford or Benn, quite as much as to philosophic Socialists, of the school of Wells or Shaw, it would have seemed a prospect so startling and so ghastly as to make them catch their breath, as men would at an abyss suddenly opening in an upward road. It is inhuman. It is horrible. I should not so much mind these scribes and pharisees saying it is inevitable, if only they would say that it is horrible. As it is, they are only trying to think of a mild geological formula to cover a cleft that goes down to hell.

For the first time within mortal memory, the Government and the nation has set out on a definite deliberate campaign to make the poor poorer. Even Industrialism and Individualism *pretended* to make the poor richer. Even Smiles and Self-Help promised to make the poor richer; or at least some of the poor richer. Every dirty little limited liability company professes to make some of the poor richer. But to-day the little professional politician, telling the truth for the first time in his life, threatens to make the poor poorer. As far as I can make out, he threatens to make some of the poor poorer than they can possibly be, without starving in the street, or falling back in another form on support by the State. People who are already clinging with their teeth and finger-nails to the edge of the chasm are to be formally and legally kicked into the chasm. It is no longer even

a matter of the old leonine contract of the wicked philanthropists, who made a man swear away his liberty before they would throw him a rope. The whole point is that we are refusing the rope; we are even cutting the rope. We are no longer pretending to be philanthropists or social reformers, whether moderate or advanced. The success of our Economy, in the name of the nation, is to be measured by the impoverishment of the people.

Now if that sort of thing were really a necessity, one would think it would be taken at least as seriously as a natural calamity. Men would write and speak of it as they would of a pestilence or an earthquake; with a certain lack of gaiety; with a certain suspension of the lighter note; with a certain gravity born of sympathy with the houses buried in the earthquake or the corpses rotting in the streets. There would be a certain deficiency of that Optimism which *The Daily Express* so uproariously sustains. If these poor men were all private soldiers captured after an overwhelming military defeat, men whom our retreating armies were forced to abandon, or our victorious enemy could refuse to liberate, we should consider that the ' necessity ' was not exactly a thing to sing about. But endless talk about the horrors of war seems to have left us dead to all sense of humiliation about the horrors of peace. If these workers had been left buried in a mine, and we had at last and reluctantly come to the conclusion that all the engines of science and all the heroism of humanity were impotent to save them, we should hardly march from the deserted mine and the deserted men singing music-hall patriotic songs. After such surrenders there would be a certain feeling that, if they were necessary, they justified the name of necessary evils. Most people would be gloomy; many people would be bitter. But as nobody must now be bitter or gloomy, the talents of our teachers and leaders are occupied with thinking of the nicest way of describing a mine disaster or a military defeat. I would suggest that deserted men dying in a dark hole might well be called ' social stratification '; and that soldiers sold into slavery by barbarians might be known as ' the ethnographical permeation policy.'

But the main point is that, while it might ultimately mean a rebirth of idealistic Socialism, it is at least the death of idealistic Capitalism. It is the end of all that pretence that the new Capitalism would go on paying higher and higher wages, till the men who worshipped gold had brought about a golden age. It is now part of the Capitalist case that Capitalism cannot afford to be generous. The business that pays properly will not pay at all. Mr. Penty wrote in this paper, a long time ago, that the modern issue was really between Gandhi and Ford. Perhaps the visit of Gandhi, to this country, at this moment, is something of an apocalyptic symbol. The spinning-wheel sounds louder and nearer, weaving perhaps new garments of destiny like a fate; and the Ford Car is wrecked upon every road. I do not claim to read the signs of the times; but at least I refuse to read the mere impoverishment of the poor as a happy sign. I have fought for fair wages all my life; and I will not now join the pomp of these New Pharisees; who sound a trumpet before them—not when they give money, but when they take it away.

Traveller's Tales

By J. Desmond Gleeson

RUSSIA has always been the land of mystery and, presumably, will always remain so. We in the West, who with our colossal impudence have tended to look upon Europe as the world, have been content to look upon Russia as something just outside the world, a patch (and rather a large patch) of no man's land, where anything may happen. The Russian novelist, on the other hand, is inclined to regard his country as a place where nothing ever does happen, a bad blank sort of stretch, upon which souls may stagger around until at length they are finally blotted out. The stage is always set, but the actors are too gloomy to play their part, though the novelist frequently admits quite frankly that things would probably be rather worse if they did play their part. But the rest of us have never believed that Russia could be anywhere near as black as the novelist painted it. We have taken our Russians with a pinch of salt— and found them pretty tough even so. To us Russia has always been the stage upon which anything might happen and, to do ourselves justice, it generally has. In the old days of travellers' tales, while it was still possible to tell tall stories for the sake of tall stories and not merely to prove some preposterous theory, Muscovy invariably offered a fair field and full favour. No one could deny you your dog-headed men, for instance, or your strange beasts if you chose to put them in Russia. You had a new country in which to work off your inventions. You could use that magic term, "The East," about which more nonsense has been talked than—oh, shut up!—and still pretend you were talking about Russia. It was the Mecca of magnificent liars, the point to which all travellers returned when they had very rapidly to make up their minds where it was that their gravely doubted experiences took place.

It is curious that Russia should always have had this character, that it should always have been the nation (if you could, or, indeed, can, call it a " nation ") that other nations choose in order to illustrate their own fantastic ideas. The ancients knew the country as Scythia, which is merely to say that they did not know it at all. But did this stop them from talking as if they knew all about it? It did not. They were as willing in those days to pitch steep yarns about Scythia as they are in these days to talk wonderful nonsense about Bolshies. Hippocrates, for instance, who could hardly have known much about what he was talking goes out of his way to suggest what manner of people these Scythians were. "Their bodies are gross and fleshy," he says, whose own body

was more like a tub than a respectable carcase, "the joints are loose and yielding; they have but little hair and they are all very much alike." It was nothing to the descriptions that were to follow, but is useful as showing how early the West began to get fresh at the expense of Russia. But if Hippocrates is comparatively sober when he looks at Russia, or rather Scythia, the same can hardly be said of Herodotus. In his usual manner Herodotus goes off the deep end without turning a hair. He describes a country the like of which never was on earth and, while we are still groggy, he suddenly weighs in with the marvellous story of Targitans and the wonderful plough that fell down from heaven.

You see, already the habit had started. From this point tall tales became the order of the day—and what a day when it happens in Russia! Nevertheless, there was a time when it looked as if things might go wrong, as if a period might be put to the gigantic possibilities of this country; as if, in a word, Russia might be made respectable. It was the Church (of course) that attempted this remarkable conversion. The Church never could leave things alone. At any rate, a very determined effort was made from Constantinople to make Christians of these Russian people. Fortunately it failed. The Russians never have been Christians and (in spite of appearances) are not even Christians to-day. But had the effort succeeded there is no doubt that Russia would have been drawn into the concert of Europe. It would have left off growing just outside the world, would no longer have existed as a land of dreams and nightmares, and we should have been forced to get our news from nowhere from somewhere else. Fortunately, however, rescue was at hand. It came from that ridiculous old East, about which more nonsense has been talked than—oh, shut up! It arrived to the tune of The Mongols are coming. The Khans came, conquered and settled, and Russia quickly drifted away from Europe and was herself again. Even taller and more incredible tales were now possible. A whole set of new scenery had been added to the stage, and travellers had the time of their lives.

And so Russia took on a new lease in life. Nothing was too romantic, nothing too fantastic to happen in this new Mongolian country, which had added to its natural impishness by embracing the Mahometan faith. But this happy state of affairs could not last. It was too good to remain true. Moreover, it is not in the nature of Mongolians to continue long at the same level. The Khans decayed with great rapidity. Russia, however, declined to depart from her fate. By now this great country had begun to appreciate her destiny, to understand that her duty lay in providing material for tall tales to the travellers of the world. Deprived of her Mongols she did not bewail her lot, but immediately set about the task of finding new stuff for still more extraordinary stories. Chief interest soon began to centre round the new figure of Ivan the Terrible, a great character in himself, but nothing like the character he might be made into, once the travellers got seriously to work. His was a well-chosen name, as perfect as anything that fine traveller, Edgar Wallace, has invented. And when Ivan was safely packed away in the last act, there was always Boris Godounov to turn to. Poor Boris suffered the fate of most sequels, but still he was always worth writing home about—which was, of course, the purpose for which he was required.

But even in Russia life cannot always be jolly, but must occasionally be real and even earnest. And so with the coming of the big bourgois, Peter—a carbon copy of an Emperor—a distressful period of respectability nearly did set in. For a while Russia actually does disappear from the tales of travellers and, as a direct result, we find the tales becoming dull and flat. Something has gone out of the lives of travellers, something that made their tales worth telling and also worth hearing. A new type of tale began to appear, a winding, endless tale of no interest, made into heavy books, mostly written by parsons, and illustrated with ridiculous woodcuts.

But it could not last. Russia, we all said, would soon be herself again. Russia was a damned sight greater than Peter and would one day put the old gentleman in his place. Reawakening was at hand—in the flabby hand of old man Marx, as it happened. Suddenly, and when it was least expected, Russia became again the centre of travellers' tales, the heart of romance. One night it looked respectable and the next it was just Russia. And to-day men come from the East and from the West and they see Russia and, not believing, rush back to tell us of the hundred and one impossible things that are happening in that country just outside the edge of the world. Well may they tell us for there is much to tell, but even the boldest travellers must pause in admiration to listen to what Russia has to tell them. For Russia intends to maintain her reputation. The latest news is almost the best news. It would seem that the Russian Carrolls and Lears have got together and decided to invent a new animal, a real Soviet animal, which shall be a mixture of the cow, the sheep and the goat. Won't the workers of the world be delighted, though not, perhaps, the cows, the sheep and the goats of the world. But, at least, all men will now acknowledge that Russia is herself again.

Public and Private Houses

By Peter Quince

I HAVE a grievance. "Nothing original in that," you say. "Yes," I reply in tones reminiscent of some beautiful hand striking a preliminary chord upon a harp. "There is this much original about it," I continue, changing my tones to those of an angered sea pounding the sides of a gallant stranded ship, "that whereas you, my fellow countrymen, every man Jack of you (I except the silly cranks) have also grievances you never air them,—either because you don't know how or you don't know where. I *do* know how and where and therefore I *will*."

I maintain and shall continue to maintain, irrespective of blows and bloodshed on the question, that the use of the adjective " public," as qualifying the noun " house," and standing in the order here written, when applied to an English inn to-day is not merely a misnomer, it is a gross and disgusting deception.

An English inn to-day is about as public a house as the House of Commons is a " private " house.

And now that I have linked the noble tradition of the English inn with the decayed and mud bespattered tradition of the House of Commons, let me tell you something about this latter which every Englishman should know but which on account of the way England is run very few do know. In the House of Commons the men we elect, like the fools we are (or rather you are, for I have voted but once and my candidate, happy man, was defeated) to govern us may drink *all day* and, unless I am mistaken, all night too when they get it badly.

That, if you like, is a " public " House, or nearer to it. Now notice two things. We, the ordinary citizens who make up the State (oh! precious word!), may not have a drink either before nor after a specified time, the time being specified by those whom we have elected to govern us and who remain free from the restrictions on individual liberty which they impose on us, and they in their turn under the thumb of the huge vested interests of a few extremely wealthy brewers who are daily becoming more wealthy. One further point in this vastly entertaining subject of the modern English inn (ye gods! a man called Burke, I believe, wrote a book about the English inn the other day and he didn't think to mention the House of Commons, because he didn't *know*, I suppose).

The English inn, this " public " house if you please, does not belong to the man who keeps it. Oh dear no! It belongs to Mr. Greedy Guts Brewer (he usually carries a handle in these exalted days!) and the man who " keeps " it is merely his tenant *paying rent* for this " public " house and retailing Greedy Guts' chemicals when everybody would far rather drink a composite mixture of water, hops, malt and sugar—sorry, I mean beer.

Now, for your crowning piece of hypocritical nonsense and this word " public " house. If you linger on the premises after the time stipulated for closing by those who can drink what they can afford whenever they like (and incidentally are placed in that position by our votes), you are had up on a charge of " trespassing."

No, I must give it up. It is too rich for my humble bread and cheese stomach! But before I finish, here's the sequel. When this news first came to my ears, myself and half a dozen friends agreed to write to our members asking for an explanation. A prize was awarded to that letter which showed most imbecility combined with cunning. The prize winning letter came from the secretary of one of our members and read to the effect that " so far as So-and-So (the member) was aware *there was no change in the drinking hours of the House.* That is the gentle art of begging the question if you like, but it's not much of an answer to the plain question: " Why has there been no change," etc., etc.!

But as to the burden of this article and the question of writing to your members, it is a matter of " Go thou and do likewise." If every reader of *G.K.'s Weekly* will write to his or her member on this rather peculiar and certainly disgusting state of affairs, it will do no harm. It might at least provide a little ginger with their beer.

Books.

Hades: Or the Future of Faustus

THE OUTLINE OF MODERN KNOWLEDGE. *Gollancz.* 8s. 6d.

TWELVE M.A.'s, four D.Litt's, two F.R.S.'s, two M.D.'s, two LL.D.'s, three B.A.'s, two PH.D.'s, half a dozen D.Sc.'s, a D.D., an F.R.A.I., an F.R.S.E., an F.R.I.B.A., to say nothing of an O.B.E. Also ran: Mr. J. W. N. Sullivan and Mr. Roger Fry.

This, as you so aptly remark, Mrs. Bouncer, is a bit tough. It certainly does take some swallowing. But what I want to know is where and how Mr. Sullivan and Mr. Fry flung away their misspent youths. When their present colleagues were drinking the tonic and dessicated air of Cambridge, Heidelberg or Yale, did they sneak away blackberrying or, worse, poaching? Or were they the Terrors of the Fifth, incorrigible and ineducable? Or—monstrous thought —can it be possible that they are the children of those who dwell in canal-boats? It can. Anything is possible.

Anything. Even an Outline of Modern Knowledge is possible. It has been done, by the extraordinary array of scholarships itemised above, assisted by the obtuse Mr. Sullivan and the inattentive Mr. Fry. It is published by Messrs. Gollancz and nobody will grudge this enterprising firm credit for a very remarkable achievement. For one thing, I have pleasure in stating that the book is all that the publishers' advertisements claim, that " it offers an invaluable survey of some of the most important fields of thought and knowledge." It has twenty-four sections, totalling half a million words, each written by an established authority. Moreover, since this enormous length allows some 20,000 words to each section, the result is rather a collection of introductory treatises than of mere outlines; and each little treatise has been specially written. If the test of a book is, Does it do what it sets out to do?, this volume certainly survives any reasonable criticism.

But there are more interesting questions than that of whether a novel object has really been achieved. Is it novel, and is it worth achieving, and what does it signify? Curiously, Messrs. Gollancz do not claim the kind of novelty they really furnish: they associate this venture with other " omnibus " publications and point out that this is new work with the advantages of compact reprint. But the object of previous omnibuses has been the cheap conveyance of all the members of particular literary families, some of them depressingly suburban families; while this is a waggonload of assorted and unrelated professors drawn in triumph through the streets to inflame the populace. It differs from other " omnibuses " in being cultural, and from other " outlines " in being comprehensive. It is a new kind of book, and the reader must ask not whether it is good of its kind but whether the kind is good. I have, in these columns, given some description of an almost century-old experiment in tabloid adult education: "Information for the People," published in the forties when modern science was a lusty child and honest doubters had a wild enthusiasm for the Solar System. But that work aimed at the distribution of facts; this at the distribution of philosophy. The contrast is interesting and even alarming; a century ago we needed information, and now we know too much; the mystery story, opening with fascinating clues in all directions, is involving into a complexity of horror. We demand unity, if only the mechanical unity of compression into a single book.

Knowledge is becoming something to be won without dust and heat; it is made attractive, and there is such a thing as a fatal attraction. As Mr. Chesterton has said, when a man tries to get the universe into his head it is his head that splits. And I am wondering what will happen to people who buy this tome and read it conscientiously through for self-improvement. No doubt there are such creatures, just as there are obscure zealots who chastise themselves with knives and fire. Both are apt to become snobbish; and the four and twenty elders who have produced this Outline will have given the worst form of high-browism a new lease of life.

I admit it might have been worse. Twenty-four sections, ranging from The Idea of God to Finance and from Psycho-analysis to Music, mean that there must be, thank heaven, notable omissions. An even more ambitious editor might have considered cinema æsthetics and motorcycle anatomy as parts of modern knowledge. Many respectable departments of learning remain, for the present, safe from the amateur; and if any of your pie-faced acquaintances show signs of having read more than a quarter of modern knowledge you will still be able to floor them with a simple problem involving taps and washers or the result of the three-thirty. And now, prehensile reader, you can no longer contain your morbid curiosity. Your shuffling feet and roving eye betray the suspicion in your bloodshot soul. You want to know whether *I* have read it, all of it.

That is my secret, and it shall perish with me.

But I will say this. I have read some of it. I can tell you why the Aurignacians were such hot stuff at cave decoration, and what an irrational number is, and the truth about Freud. Ontology is my washpot, and over finite space do I cast out my shoe. My friends say I look more distinguished (the phrase they use is "like nothing on earth") and I enjoy a growing sense of poise and power. I trust you have observed this. For, mark, the "Outline of Modern Knowledge" is no soufflé. About previous Outlines there has been a suggestion of lightness, almost of frivolity: they have had fanciful illustrations and sensational chapter-headings; they have not scorned the appeal to baser passions. But this is, seriously, a sober, grave and scholarly work. Grave do I say? It is monumental. It is more: it is positively sepulchral. Here is no syncopated science nor red-hot history for the tired business man. One evening, a little jaded, I abandoned Social Anthropology and turned with anticipatory relish—as doubtless you will—to the section on Sex. But there were no whoopee babies, not even with Mendelian determinants; and in fact I read one of the spiciest passages—all about the chromosomes of the parasitic Rafflesia—to the assembled family without evoking so much as a raised eyebrow; though of course this may be due to modern emancipation and the efforts of Mr. Aldous Huxley. My hat! That explains everything! It has just occurred to me that this compendium of modern science and philosophy is designed as an introduction to modern fiction. Well, whatever its weight it is an honest piece of work. It does explain abstrusities in general terms.

But it is a bit tough on the poor sweated reviewer. What couldn't I do to a lager!

F. KESTON CLARKE.

Russia Again

MY RUSSIAN VENTURE. *By Mrs. Cecil Chesterton.* Harrap. 8s. 6d.

"MY Russian Venture" is an account of an uncharted and unescorted journey made by two Englishwomen through White Russia and the Soviet Ukraine, during which they travelled "hard," sampled Soviet hotels of varying quality, slept in peasant's homes, did their own shopping, explored the mysteries of the rouble rate of exchange, and visited a collective farm.

Mrs. Chesterton says little which has not been said before but her story is written with an absence of prejudice which is, unhappily for relations between this country and U.S.S.R., all too rare in the copious literature dealing with the Communist experiment. Having journeyed over part of the author's route recently (I recognise some of the Soviet officials she mentions as friends), I recommend this volume as a refreshingly accurate and clear account of the conditions under which live the "ragged millions which are the sign and source of Soviet strength."

The author showed wisdom at the outset of her journey by ignoring the cities with their tourist itineraries and plunging straightway into the heart of peasant Russia, thereby revealing a sense of proportion as well as a sense of journalism, for of the 160,000,000 people living under Communism, only 30,000,000 dwell in urban areas. The rest are the raw material for the agrarian revolution now changing the face of Russia.

Entering Russia with an open mind, Mrs. Chesterton has sufficient courage to explode some of the myths which, however true they may have been of the years immediately following the revolution, are certainly not true of the Soviet Union to-day. Thus concerning the food position as she found it, not on paper but in the actual co-operative stores and markets, the author states:

"I must very definitely challenge the statement current in the English press that the Russian nation is starving because of the exportation of wheat. This is not so. The people do not eat and never have eaten white bread. The Russians, like the Poles, consume rye bread—the rye bread which is sold in Soho *cafes* as a *delicatessen.* Palatable, nourishing, it is a bone-making muscle-building food on which millions exist—"

Again, the author shows that she appreciates the psychological importance of a real equality of sacrifice —an equality which has played a larger part in rallying the Russian masses behind the Five Year Plan than the capitalists always realise:

"The material sparseness does not press too heavily upon a breed inured for centuries to the utmost rigour of existence. Their meagre diet is unsoured by the acid of envy. Desire for the rich food enjoyed by more fortunate ones no longer churns the stomach . . . This impulse of equality has invigorated their outlook. To them the Soviet is a personal and acute possession. They regard themselves as actual particles of a living organism which embraces the whole of the country."

Eminently sane and true. Sanity is, indeed, the keynote of this book. Those who prefer more highly coloured accounts, infected with the "pro" and "anti" virus to taste, should look elsewhere. But those who want a truthful, if somewhat superficial, picture of one corner of the U.S.S.R. as it really is —including the absence of plumbing(!)—will find in "My Russian Venture" a wealth of interesting information.

Many who know Communist Russia will be especially grateful to Mrs. Chesterton and to her companion for helping to explode the erroneous idea, discourteous to the kindly Russian people, that those who visit Russia unescorted are "mad." The truth is that while conditions away from the centre are primitive and the delays unbelievable to those who know not Russian railways and officialdom, in no other country in Europe is the foreigner so safe or so welcome.

If this book helps the timid to refuse that elementary fact, it will have been abundantly justified.

H. HESSELL TILTMAN.

Book Views

TRADE DEPRESSION AND THE WAY OUT. *By R. G. Hawtrey. Longmans Green and Co.* 2s. 6d.

The world's financial system is a sort of intellectual Tom Tiddler's ground strewn with gold and silver theories for anyone's picking; and the reputable economic metallurgist has to apologise for butting in on the char-a-banc parties. Mr. Hawtrey does not profess to have discovered the philosopher's stone, but he tells us where the gold has gone and what the Banks are doing with the paper. The currency engineer, he argues, may not remove all the troubles of the valley but at least he can harness the floods. That is all very well, so long as the works and dykes are permanent. In this book we are given a very lucid and informative account of international finance with particular reference to the gold standard, world markets and the positions of London and New York; the whole advocating action by the banks to expand credit. The essay, reinforced as it is by clear and up-to-date statistics, is interesting and vigorous though perhaps a little too concise for the inexpert reader: some examination of the motives for gold accumulation and of the economic position, internal and external, of countries such as Australia and the Argentine who have been "driven off the gold standard," would have been welcome. Mr. Hawtrey has a good deal to say on the "vicious circles" of expansion and contraction, and he says it well, but apparently he does not regard them as firmly geared to the larger and more vicious circle of industrialism itself.   F.K.C.

THE INTRIGUING DUCHESS. *By Dorothy de Brissac Campbell. John Hamilton.* 15s.

The intriguing Duchess is Marie de Rohan, Duchesse de Chevreuse, who was in the forefront at the court of Louis XIII, the friend of Anne of Austria, the brilliant enemy of Richelieu. Miss Campbell must have gone to very considerable pains to write this life, for it is compact with details and with observation of character, and particularly easy to read because it is written in a clear style, with few of the hackneyed tricks so popular with historical biographers. Like most other biographies, however, it is very much of a chronique scandaleuse, and certainly the court of Louis XIII gives opportunity to describe every imaginable fact, sin and abnormality, with unblushing frankness. Nevertheless, Miss Campbell says no more, and probably hints rather less, than the diarists of her period, so this may be taken as a faithful picture of her subject, to whom she gives full justice. Her portrayal of the other actors, of Louis, of Anne, of Richelieu, of Buckingham, and the rest. is always clear cut and true to life. It is a book which will interest its readers and be remembered by them.   K.C.M.

STUDIES IN SHAKESPEARE. *By Sir Arthur Quiller-Couch. Cambridge University Press. 5/-.*

To the beautifully porduced series of pocket-reprints of the essays and lectures on literature of Sir Arthur Quiller-Couch, more affectionately known as " Q," the Cambridge University Press has added an eighth volume which should be as universally popular as its predecessors and share their distinction of being as constantly referred to in college libraries, as they are sold at railway bookstalls for pleasant holiday reading. In none of his literary criticism do the humane and gracious mind, the close scholarship and the supreme common-sense of the author, shine more brightly than in his Shakespearian studies, not least of their virtues being Sir Arthur's insistence throughout in remembering that Shakespeare was first and foremost a practical craftsman in the theatre, the key to whose intentions and achievement can be found only in the theatre. Readers of daily newspapers are often asked to compile a list of books essential to life on a desert island. I should certainly save " Studies in Shakespeare " from the wreck, even at the expense of the fowling-piece or burning-glass.   A.B.

ART IN THE LIFE OF MANKIND: *A Survey of its achievements from the earliest times. By Allen W. Seaby. Vol. III. " Greek Art and its influence. Vol. IV. " Roman Art and its influence." B. T. Batsford. 5/- each.*

The first two volumes of this valuable series carried the history of art through prehistoric and Babylonian and Egyptian art as far as the culture of Nycenæ and Crete. In the two volumes just issued the art of classical times is widely surveyed. Greek art carries its influences into India and about the Mediterranean, Roman art reiterates Greece in its own fashion throughout Europe. This carries the history of our own culture into the Dark Ages, touches Persia and Egypt, and explains the development of the Byzantine, and gives some account of early Celtic and Scandinavian. The author's knowledge of his subject is wide, and he is able to compress a great deal into a small compass and yet remain interesting. It is no small feat to compress so vast a subject into 100 pages, and in the end to present so clear a picture. The illustrations, photographs and line drawings are excellent.   K.C.M.

ALL ABOUT WOMEN. *By Gerald Gould. Methuen and Co. 5s.*

There are a number of us who would always read Gerald Gould, the eminent—he objects to the term " well known "—reviewer of books, while we would for no consideration on earth read the books he reviews. We have always thought what a mighty penance it must be for the man, and wondered what the sins must have been in the first place to call for so stern and savage a sentence. But even Mr. Gould has his holiday moments when he is released from under a load of the latest novels, and this little volume shows how he spends his busman's holiday. Here we have Mr. Gould talking, telling lively lies about himself and Mrs. Gould, giving his views on this, that and the other, correcting us where we were right, misleading us to Potsdam, trailing us behind him in his little car, and, generally, losing us in the St. John's Wood. Afterwards, I suppose, he returns to his modern fiction, but I shall stay with these Women whom he has told us all about.   J.D.G.

THE GOLDEN FOUNDLING. *By Sinclair Murray. John Murray. 7/6.*

Pirrie, foundling of the Caribou gold rush trail, meets Dolph Hudson at her adopted father's mine. They love, and his friends take her to England, despite unscrupulous opposition from Hugh Purdey, a miner who loves her. How she makes good, discovers her origin, defeats Purdey and marries Dolph makes a good yarn, a pleasant companion for an hour's idleness.   K.C.M.

The Symphony Concerts

As addendum to the events notified last week I am asked by the Philharmonic Choir to announce a prospectus issued for the coming season. It is not easy to run choral societies in London these days and the considerable deficit which Mr. Kennedy-Scott's excellent choir suffered last year warranted an appeal for assistance and support, published in *The Times* last May. The result unfortunately was negligible. But despite all, the Society is launching out again this year, with a broader subscription basis and reduced prices for many seats. Two concerts are announced: The first on Wednesday, November 11th, at the Queen's Hall, includes Dame Ethel Smyth's *The Prison*, which she will herself conduct, Bach's *Cantata No. 68* and Purcell's *Praise the Lord, O Jerusalem*. The second concert announced for January 17th, at the same venue, will consist of two works by George Dyson. All who are interested in preserving the tradition of English choral music should make what effort is possible either to attend these concerts or help in some other way. Particulars can be obtained from D. Ritson Smith, 28, Flanchford Road, W.14.

The British Women's Symphony Orchestra gives their first concert of the season on Saturday of this week, with a programme including Beethoven's " Emperor " concerto (soloist Stanislaw Szpinalski) and Brahm's *Symphony No. 4*. Dr. Malcolm Sargent will conduct as usual. Meanwhile the recital world has got into full swing, with a preponderance, as last season, of pianists. Paderewski on Tuesday last, and on Saturday Myra Hess at the Queen's Hall and Harold Bauer in a welcome return to the Grotrian Hall, is generous fare for the most fastidious of tastes. Very fine performances were given on Tuesday last by Harry Isaacs and the Griller Quartet of Bax's *Quintet in G. Minor*, and of Elgar's *Quintet in A Minor*, two very different works, demanding different approach and understanding. Excellent results too, were obtained on Friday, by the Kutcher String Quartet in a proprogramme including Mozart's *Quartet in G*, and Debussy's *Quartet in G Minor*.   V.N.L.

"Elizabeth of England"

"ELIZABETH of England " at the Cambridge Theatre, has a pronounced German flavour, not only in the presentation of the Virgin Queen but in its glorification of mechanics. It is a riot of spectacular rhetoric; an ingenious arrangement shows us Elizabeth in St. Paul's Cathedral on one side of the stage, Philip II. at his devotions on the other. Mr. Charles Rickett's settings have considerable beauty and no expense has been spared on the costumes. But of characterisation, of drama, there is not a whit and stripped of its trappings the play would not hold the mind or stimulate the interest.

It is said that the German dramatist founded his play on Lytton Strachey's brilliant " Elizabeth and Essex " but there is little to suggest this fount of inspiration, and it would be of interest to know how or why Elizabeth is presented as a woman of unwieldy figure and gross flesh which never for a moment is surmounted by a flash of personality.

Elizabeth, we know, was very tall, but she was not fat, and Miss Phyllis Neilson-Terry, concealing her own graceful contours shows us the Queen fairly waddling with adipose tissue. Her Majesty's voice is also a surprise. Miss Terry adopts a curious high pitched cackle voice which at times is unintelligible, so that one long for a moment of the clear diction usually associated with this actress.

The play, episodic in treatment, shows us the Queen and Essex in sportive mood, presents Essex again in company with Bacon conspiring for the capture of the Queen, which culminates in a clumsy scene with Eiizabeth dodging in and out of secret doors and finally throwing her cloak over Essex's head. We are also given the latter's execution. Essex behind bars makes his confession while Elizabeth listens and waits outside.

Interspersed with these scenelets we see Elizabeth at Council, still undecided as to whether she will go to war with Spain. Alternatively we hear Mr. Philip moaning. It is indeed one long moan, very adequately given by Mr. Matheson Lang who, however, deserves a better opportunity.

All the way through the author is obsessed with the German view of women, which holds the innate inferiority of the female sex. Mr. Ashley Dukes has not been able to remove this impress, neither has he eliminated the suggestion that the defeat of the Armada was wholly due to climatic disturbance. We have reason to know that the winds and tempest were on our side, but some small amount of credit must be given to our surperior navigation and the fact that owing to our fore and aft rigging we were able to sail into the eye of the wind.

As it is the weather gets all the praise!

From the upholstery of Elizabeth it is a relief to turn to the melodrama " The Anatomist " at the Westminster Theatre, by James Bridie. The play, which deals with the crimes of Burke and Hare who carried on a flourishing business in the supply of corpses for dissection, has its moments of pity and of horror. The first act in Edinburgh 1828, shows us Robert Knox, M.D., the great anatomist, with his favourite demonstrator, Walter Anderson, in the drawing room of the Disharts, young Mary Belle and her elder sister, Miss Amelia. Already rumours have run about the city as to the means by which dead bodies are supplied to Surgeon's Square and Mary Belle insists that Walter shall choose between his love for her and his devotion to Knox. He refuses to give up Knox, however, and in despair goes to the Three Tuns Tavern.

The tavern is an admirable piece of stage setting, with its sinister, shadowy depths reached by a flight of steps which from the first has something of the murderous. To this cellar comes Mary Paterson, a woman of the town, with a young companion, Janet Mary has red hair and an allure that life has not yet taken from her. Warm hearted, sympathetic, Walter already in his cups, turns to her for consolation. She pillows his head in her lap and soothes him to sleep until he is taken home, still dead drunk, by a fellow student. Burke and Hare admirably interpreted by Mr. J. A. O'Rourke and Mr. Harry Hutchinson, keep an appointment with the porter of Surgeon's Hall. Another body is wanted, lots of bodies, and he has come to the Three Tuns to arrange terms. They agree for £10, but the corpse must be well-nourished. You see the thought in the murderer's minds. Mary will suit their purpose admirably. Her young companion Janet senses evil and tries to persuade her friend to come home. But Mary refuses to listen. The men buy her drink and at last induce her to go home with them.

Miss Flora Robson plays Mary with great poignancy. You feel the fundamental appeal of the poor creature, struggling to express itself through all the miasma of bad drink and human misery. She rises almost to heights of tragedy when she leaves the cellar. You feel she knows that the end of her tragic life is near.

Mr. Carleton Hobbs is equally moving when he discovers that the latest subject for dissection is the girl with the beautiful red hair.

The last act goes back to comedy. The two lovers are reconciled and Knox, who has been stoned by the crowd assembled to see Hare hanged, delivers an oration to his admiring students.

This is a play which succeeds through its drama and its acting and therefore should be seen. I liked Mr. Henry Ainley in the part of the anatomist.

J. K. PROTHERO.

THE COCKPIT

"WHAT HAS HAPPENED."

Sir,—It is a great pleasure to read your leading article "What has happened," and to discover that there *is* a man who has grasped the simple economies of inflation. After all the excruciating nonsense which has issued from alleged statesmen and economic experts in Germany, France and this country, it is an infinite relief to find that the world still contains a man who is sane. Even after four years of hectic inflation in Germany, I know from experience that it was impossible to find there one banker, stockbroker, writer or politician who could make an intelligent observation on this simple subject.

May I suggest that your paper should give prominence to four corollaries of the effects of a depreciated pound to lucidly set forth in "What has happened," because they are not immediately apparent unless put into words.

First. Every debtor of a pound of currency is one fifth *richer* than he was before the pound depreciated.

Second. If you buy £100 of boot-stock *on credit* before the price rises you do even better than in the example quoted because when you sell it for £125 you make a *real profit.*

The action taken by the Stock Exchange Committee in banning purchases on credit was not the fine moral gesture implied in your article on "This Emergency," it was dictated by the bankers to save their pockets.

Third. The credit of this country when the "National" Government took office was 130 million pounds—that was the total credit which the government could raise abroad. The amount corresponded exactly with the amount of gold in the Bank (for strangely enough the credit of a country, like that of an individual, is still limited to the amount which people believe he can pay). The 130 million credit was thrown down the drain by the "National" Government in one week and the 130 million pounds worth of gold is 'earmarked,' that is *pawned* to America and France. Thus the amount of gold behind the currency is infinitesimal and therefore if any Distributist is in a position to induce someone to accept a "Sterling Bill" at 60 days, let him hasten to the bargain.

Fourth. Not only wage-earners but also exporters will be bamboozled by the higher nominal value of 'things,' and a vast amount of goods will be given away to the foreigner before the cheering dies down. Only at a late stage will the Government step in with measures (export licences) designed to prevent British manufacturers selling at a loss. Let Distributists get a competent person to work out the proper selling price of anything they have to sell, or they will find themselves after hard work and an apparently prosperous year, hard put to it to pay the grocer.

R. G. HENNESSY.

COMMUNISM.

Sir,—I shall be grateful if you will allow me this opportunity of commenting upon the two letters you have published from Mr. Arthur Dickens, as I feel I understand the problem which worries him, and so many others (increasing in numbers and influence to-day) with leanings towards Communism as a solution of the world's difficulties.

It can, I think, best be stated like this : Capitalism, the state of society in which men are left to make for themselves the greatest fortune they are capable of making, has resulted in an appalling inequality in which, despite wonderful progress in labour saving and wealth producing inventions, the great majority toil as heavily as ever for the benefit of a small, monetarily wealthy and leisured class, controlling, by means of their money, the distribution of the real wealth produced by the working classes. This concentration of money and the control of money has resulted in the channels getting choked up, and we are now faced with what is called "The Crisis," where we are in peril of being starved of the necessities of life; without, however, there being any actual shortage in production.

Now this state of affairs, say the Communists (and so said Karl Marx many years ago) is inevitable with the competitive Capitalist theory, and there is no solution of it but the abolition of individual control and the substitution of communal control; by which each man, woman and child shall do each his or her appointed task, and receive each his or her equal share of the fruits of production—which include not only the bare necessities of existence but all which is normal or natural to the ordinary life of mankind. We must, as Mr. Bernard Shaw stated to the Distributist meeting two weeks ago, organize work and organize for leisure. And Mr. Dickens wants to know what is the Distributist answer to all that.

Well, your answer is, and if I may, very humbly, say my answer too is, "that we believe liberty to be natural to man." And when we say that Mr. Dickens must believe we mean it literally, not as a statement of our ideal of man, not what man *ought* to possess, but what actually is natural to man. For then it follows fairly obviously that Communism cannot and will not work, without (a) the popular and voluntary acceptance of a special vow of obedience such as is necessary to religious orders (which is possible but highly unlikely), or (b) the forced obedience of the proletariat to an all-powerful State (which is possible and highly likely).

There is another answer, which was very admirably put by Mr. Kenrick this week in an article entitled "Oikonomia" (which I hope Mr. Dickens has read). Mr. Kenrick shows that both Capitalism and Socialism share the delusion that property, to be productive, must be in large units—and Communism works for the largest attainable unit. It comes to this in the end : that Communism is not the alternative to the present system ; it is an extension from it ; and, I think, a logical extension and one based on far more just appreciation of economic facts and factors. But as it is of the system, the system which Mr. Belloc rightly calls the Servile System, it must stand or fall with the system. At the moment the system is tottering. It is, as Mr. Dickens quite rightly suggests and as you, Sir, rightly defined as a real red peril, very possible that the system will be saved, temporarily, at any rate, by Communism, mild in form at first but gradually growing to its fruition. And then that too must fail ; or man cease to be man as we know him to-day, man to whom liberty is natural. If I may quote you, Sir, the Communists propose to distribute income; we propose to distribute power.

JOHN MASTERS.

NEW LAMPS FOR OLD.

Sir,—You may be interested to hear that the Marquess of Londonderry, opening the new factory of Aladdin Industries Ltd., near my home, at Greenford, Middlesex, commented upon the trend of industry to move from the north to the south of England, and stated that "he was glad that these new areas were better, cleaner, more airy, spacious and pleasant to the eye, and caring more for the health and happiness of the workers."

I suggest that the areas are even better and more clean as agricultural lands, and as such are calculated to care very much more for the health and happiness of the workers of this nation. It was in the old lamp that the old Aladdin found power to work miracles; the new lamp was merely efficient. It did not make him happy or prosperous.

W. F. NAUNTON.

A MERGER.

Sir,—Harrods, the Giant Squid of the general stores, has just taken to its fond embrace the Haymarket Stores. The Chairman of Harrods assures the world that "In every case where we have taken another business over we have found that its trade has improved." I may be permitted to observe that another trend of the times which has marched in step with amalgamations and mergers is unemployment, despite Sir Woodman Burbidge's assurance that such events as the closing of the Haymarket Stores which employed a staff of some 300, means more, not less employment. Another trend of the times, also parallel with amalgamations and mergers, is reducing the value of the pound sterling. Now that the housewife will have to make 16s. go as far as 20s. went a short time ago, she may pause to consider whether the glitter and "service" of the monster store is worth the colossal advertising bill and the 20 per cent. dividend she pays to Messrs. Harrods shareholders.

ARTHUR TRIMBLE.

THE DISTRIBUTIST LEAGUE

A CALL TO ACTION.

We are nearing the end of a session which, in its earlier stages, looked as if it might witness the disolution of The League, and the substitution for it of an organisation—or organisations—with narrower grounds of appeal, and therefore, with greater promise of unity and activity within more circumscribed limits. Fortunately, there were those amongst us who had faith in The League and its mission, and The League not only survives, but has taken a new lease of life. If we recall the persistent campaign which has been conducted on their behalf, in this page and at Central Branch meetings, we do so in no mood of recrimination or of petty triumph, but rather in the hope of emphasising what is the new determination with which The League is infused, and what are its intentions and prospects for the coming session.

That campaign in favour of a greater objectivization of our ideas reached its climax in the Summer Conference. There it was agreed that The League's immediate task is to convince men that there is a *practical* alternative to Capitalism and Socialism, *by shewing them how to set about achieving it.*

This commitment has been officially endorsed by the Executive which is shortly to retire, and it has been accepted by the branches as the conscious aim of their future propaganda—the Central Branch in particular, having accepted it as a challenge to itself to take its rightful lead in the work of fashioning and propagating Distributist policies. This means that material provision has to be made for the organisation of study and research as well as for the more efficient propaganda of the constructive wisdom it will call forth. This again means the cultivation of The League's resources measured not only in terms of membership and funds, but also in terms of personal service and sacrifice of time.

Membership and funds would seem to hang together. The bulk of The League's income is derived from the subscriptions and donations of its members; and these have for some years averaged out at some 5s. per member. By comparison with the 1s. subscription imposed, this is generous; and the inference would seem to be that improvement is to be sought in the direction of increased membership. The responsibility here lies immediately with individual members: and in exhorting them to private propaganda amongst their friends, we would urge on them the duty of prompt payment of their own subscriptions. It is safe to say that until The League's present income is *doubled* it cannot hope to do its new job efficiently.

But given the funds, and given all the enthusiasm of the sort that effloresces at conferences and general meetings, there still remains the necessity for voluntary service of the more persistent and less spectacular sort, whether it be in the study, the archives, the committee room or on the platform. We earnestly exhort those who are possessed of talents for research and investigation, for administration, or for public speaking, to place their leisure time services, at least, at the disposal of their elected officers. And in justice to those who may respond to this appeal—as also to The League as a whole—we ask that where considerations of distance, private affairs, or pre-occupation with other forms of Distributist activity, militate against constant and unbiassed application to their affairs of a working committee, a member should profer his services in some less exacting capacity.

CENTRAL BRANCH.

FUTURE MEETINGS. At The Devereux, Devereux Court, Strand, W.C.2. Fridays at 7.15 p.m.

Oct. 23.—Extraordinary General Meeting. Important.

Oct. 30.—Informal Meeting. Eve of League A.G.M.

WHAT TO READ.

The Servile State by Hilaire Belloc. 4s. 6d.

Economics for Helen. Hilaire Belloc. 5s.

The Outline of Sanity. G. K. Chesterton. 3s. 6d.

The Change. G. C. Heseltine. 2s. 6d.

The Church and the Land. Vincent McNabb, O.P. 2s. 6d.

Liberty and Property. H. E. Humphries. (The League Textbook). 6d.

The Fairy Ring of Commerce. Herbert Shove. 2s. 6d.

Pamphlets.

The Drink Problem: A Distributist Solution. 1d.
Unemployment: A Distributist Solution. Gratis.
The War on the Weak. 2d.

TYPEWRITING, DUPLICATIONS, &c.

AUTHORS' MSS. typed accurately and promptly by educated gentleman (war disabled), 1s. per 1,000 words; carbon, 3d. Highly commended.—GRIFFITHS (A.), 18, Upwood Road, Norbury, London, S.W.16.

TYPEWRITERS from £2; easy payments arranged. Repairs. Duplicators.—'Phone: Central 8210. Typewriter Experts, 55, Little 77, Britain, E.C.1.

AUTHORS' MSS. and Technical Typewriting correctly executed, 10d. per 1,000.—Mrs. CLIFTSTONE, 11, Cromwell Avenue, Bromley, Kent.   103.

DUPLICATING EXPERT offers 50 extra copies free.—SCHOOLMASTER, 71, Brackenbury Road, Preston.

INCREDIBLE! Unbeatable! Duplicated typewritten matter, 3s. per 100.—E. S. COY, 14, Homer Terrace, Bootle.

LITERARY Typewriting carefully and promptly executed. MSS., 1s. per 1,000 words; carbon copy, 3d. per 1,000.—Miss NANCY McFARLANE (J.), 4, Elderton Road, Westcliff-on-Sea.

LONDON'S Premier Typewriting Service.--1,000 words, 10d.; carbon copy, 2d. Perfect work guaranteed. Authors' MSS. a speciality.—"FLEET" TYPEWRITING AGENCY, 153, Fleet Street, E.C.4.

TYPEWRITING and Duplicating.—Authors' MSS. typed, 10d. per 1,000 words; carbon copy, 3d. per 1,000 words. Testimonials, circulars, &c. duplicated. Envelopes addressed. Prompt and efficient work.—MARION YOUNG (C.), 7a, Station Road, Balham, S.W.12.

TYPEWRITING.—8d. 1,000 French and Spanish translations (into English), 9d. a folio.—NEWCOMBE, 36, Wilson Street, Middlesbrough.

TYPEWRITING MSS., 8d. per 1,000 words. Carbon, 2d. Pitman's transcribed. Outside work undertaken. Best work, lowest charges. Accuracy guaranteed.—I. WATKINS, 40, Verulam Street, E.C.1.

TYPEWRITING of all kinds, including French and German, from 1/- per 1,000 words.—Miss POLLARD, 36, Ampthill Square, N.W.1, Museum, 3965.

FREE Typewriting, prompt efficient work on new machine, 1s. 1,000 words, carbon copy 3d. 1,500 words free to new clients. Duplicating 2s. 7d. 100 copies post free. The best service available. Mrs. G. Crossley, Merlin, Anthony's Avenue, Parkstone, Dorset.

CLASSICAL SCHOLAR, able to use typewriter and correct proofs, wants secretarial work. —Miss TENNANT, Forest Hill, Eddleston, Peeblesshire.

DISTRIBUTIST ENTERPRISES.

The Distributist Workshop organised by the Glasgow Central Branch of the League, has found excellent premises for which a capital sum of £50 is required.

1,000 Shares of one shilling each are available, and Subscriptions are invited.

Full particulars to:

A. Mason, Hon. Sec.,
     59, Truce Road,
         Glasgow, W.3.

ARTS & CRAFTS.

MEMBERS of the Manchester Branch are advised that Mr. Lockhart, a craftsman, produces all kinds of knitted woollen goods on his own knitting machine. Jumpers, pullovers, men's socks, boys' stockings, cardigan jackets, etc. Support your own local craftsman. Send a postcard to Mr. W. L. Lockhart, 34, Broadlea Road, Kingsway, Burnage, when requiring any of the articles mentioned.

CRAFTSMEN'S work wanted: Handcarving brass and Metalwork: Handmade Jewellery: original lines.—José Devaney, Arts and Crafts Shop, Brunswick Street, Newcastle, Staffs.

HAND-MADE FURNITURE.

THE natural beauty of English Timbers and the splendid traditions of English craftsmanship are revealed in the original furniture and innumerable smaller articles designed and made by STANLEY W. DAVIES, M.A., Windermere.

THE FOREST TOYS.

WOODEN Animals of all kinds, hand-carved and painted. Price list post free.—F. H. WHITTINGTON, Brockenhurst, Hants

---

HAND WEAVING.

HAND WEAVING.—Lessons desired in Hand Weaving from experienced Weaver in the evenings; London, preferably Chelsea.—Melland, 2, Oakley Street, Chelsea.

LITERARY.

CATHOLIC AUTHOR-JOURNALIST offers complete literary service. Personal direction. Advice, criticism, revision, placing. Moderate fees. Inquiries invited.—JOHN QUINLAN, 275, Spring Bank West, Hull.

MISCELLANEOUS.

"SACRED HEART HOME OF REST." Beautiful rooms in a beautiful Convent; every comfort; gas fires; part central heating; cosy, cheerful, warm sitting-room with log fires. Nuns loving care for the elderly, the delicate. Good food. A really happy Home. Terms 2 guineas weekly.—Apply Superior, Convent, Aldeburgh, Suffolk.

HARRIS TWEED.—Any length cut. Patterns free.—JAMES ST. TWEED DEPOT, 392, Stornoway, Scotland.

IRISH HAND-WOVEN TWEEDS for Suits and Costumes.—Patterns free from JOSEPH LARGEY, 40, Lr. Ormond Quay, Dublin.

CLOTHES OF CHARACTER.—Lounge Suits from 5 gns. Dress Wear from 6½ guns. Overcoats from 4 gns. All hand finished.—S. G. Hunt, Monument Chambers, Eastcheap, E.C.3. Next to Monument Station.

WOODCUT Christmas Cards reprinted from Golden Bowl. Prices from 2/- to 6/- dozen. Send for sample book from Selwyn Dunn, Kelmscott, Dapdune Road, Guildford

---

Published by the Proprietors, G.K.'s WEEKLY, LTD., 2, Little Essex Street, Strand, London, W.C.2 (incorporating THE NEW WITNESS). Telephone: Temple Bar 1978. Printed by THE NUNEATON NEWSPAPERS, LTD., "Observer" Buildings, Nuneaton. Sole Agents for Australasia: Gordon & Gotch (Australasia, Ltd.). Sole Agents for South Africa: Central News Agency Ltd.

G.K.'s Weekly

EDITED BY G. K. CHESTERTON

No. 401—Vol. XVI.   November 19, 1932.   Sixpence

Temple Bar 1978.   Registered at G.P.O. as a Newspaper.   2, Little Essex Street, London, W.C.2.

THE OUTLINE OF SANITY

NO dramatist, seeking in the world around him the materials for those ironic complications necessary to his most poignant effects, need ever search beyond the newspaper files of one week. The past few days have been rich enough in examples, and if we choose one for emphasis it is because that one comes nearest to our own business, and because the irony therein is a twist of hope and encouragement, not of tragedy and defeat.

On Tuesday last we were given the Majority Report of the Royal Commission on Unemployment Insurance. Though the features of that Report are by now familiar, we are tempted to stress one or two items, after the fashion of the good caricaturist who, by artful exaggeration, makes his subject more easily recognisable if only through its weaknesses. We like, for instance, the remark that "the unemployment from which the great majority suffer is occasional in character, occurring in a life of more or less regular employment." An examination of conditions in the depressed areas shows, on the contrary, that the employment from which the majority can hope to benefit is occasional in character, occurring in a life of more or less regular unemployment; and particularly is this so in respect of those aged up to twenty or so, whose "working lives" have been "regular" only in Labour Exchange attendances. "The Commission attribute this phenomenon to something more than the transient effect of the war." This remarkable pronouncement is very like the police statements which, after prolonged consideration of the body and the bludgeon, attribute the fatality to foul play. Still, the business of the Commission was the study of insurance, not unemployment itself, and we have no wish to appear unkind. Nor do we propose in this place to attempt a detailed commentary on the recommendations, much as they invite it. That is a fight in which we are not directly concerned. We reject the philosophy behind State Unemployment Insurance, and we prefer to leave its administrative problems to the individualistic Tories who find themselves obliged to defend a super-bureaucratic Means Test, and the communistically-inclined Labour stalwarts who attack, with fire and wrath, an officialdom that is the essential basis of all they hold most dear.

That little circumstance, though perhaps extremely ironic to the historian or the disinterested planetary observer, passes without notice in an age so accustomed to Party contortions that any reasonably consistent politician would inevitably be branded as an obstinate fanatic. We give it casual mention and pass on.

What is to us even more ironically interesting, is the pleasant fact that the man who twenty years ago forced through Parliament the Unemployment Insurance Scheme, a measure to which our social philosophy is essentially opposed, the man who inaugurated the legislation resulting in the chaos, insolvency and injustice that necessitated the Royal Commission—he it is who now stands forth in Parliament and the Press as advocate of *our* solution; as belated pleader for that simple and rational policy which would have avoided the whole problem: avoided, not solved, for the problem would never have existed.

Mr. Lloyd George, in his speech during the Unemployment debate last week, gave Parliamentary utterance to arguments this paper has iterated and re-iterated week after week for years. "Are we likely," he asked, "to recover our pre-war international trade? After consulting some of the best authorities in the country without reference to party, I don't see any prospect of our doing so in the immediate future. . . you will never get rid of this permanent evil of unemployment until you place at least a million of your workers either actually on the soil or in ancillary occupations . . . can you find anything which will be more productive of the happiness and employment, the wealth, contentment and strength of this country than the settlement of half a million people on the land? You will strengthen this country in peace and in the dread prospect of our ever going to war. You are spending 110 millions a year on the defence of the realm. This is a branch of the national defence."

We would not support Mr. Lloyd George merely on the strength of that part of the argument, though it might have been taken bodily from our back numbers. It is the negative aspect of the case, and might lead to anything, including rural industrialisation or semi-military harvest-camps for proletarians without remotest hope of proprietorship. But in an interview published in Sunday's *Observer* we get something that reads very like an Outline of Sanity. A State loan for the revival of agriculture; a survey of all cultivable land in Great Britain; cottage holdings as a beginning, with the chance of economic smallholdings for all who can and will work them; decentralisation as the keynote; County Agricultural Committees that really do their jobs; a countryside revivified not by ordinances from above but by the natural energy of half a million working owners and half a million craftsmen.

We do not propose to accept the chapter and verse of Mr. Lloyd George's scheme, whatever it may be, in advance. He has not said how the land is to be redistributed, nor upon what form of ownership or tenure his new peasantry is to be based. Neither do we propose to turn a cold eye on any detail of his proposals merely because their present Parliamentary advocate has incurred our hostility in the past. At present there seems good hope that one prominent politician at least has seen what we are driving at, and though we may permit ourselves a comment on the irony of the situation, we have excellent authority for making joy over the one sinner that repenteth.

NOTES OF THE WEEK

Mr. Baldwin's recent speech in the House of Commons painted a terrible picture of attack from the air on practically defenceless cities, but few would attempt to claim that the picture was too highly coloured. There can be no doubt that a practical step towards disarmament would be the regulation or abolition of fighting air services, though such a step would be of no more value than any other agreement of the kind on paper, so long as the various Governments were in a position to convert passenger and cargo aeroplanes into troop carriers and bombers. All that would happen would be that the people in the countries at war would feel the effects of air raids less severely than if air forces were maintained at their present strength. Still his warning was not a mere waste of words, while his suggestion for some sort of international control of civilian aviation may be worthy of more detailed consideration. We cannot believe that the views of those who claim that war can be abolished by a pact forbidding armaments are any more sensible than was the idea that Prohibition in America would put an end to drinking; but any check effectively placed on the perfection and collection of lethal weapons may mitigate the horrors of another war or delay its declaration.

* * * *

We suspect, by the way, that there was more in Mr. Baldwin's speech than a warning and an appeal to European statesmen. It will have been noted that a British Note to the U.S. Government was presented at Washington almost immediately after the results of the Presidential Election were known. That Note did not announce default, but offered suggestions for an agreed revision of the present system of debt payments and it was accompanied by Notes from other Powers. Are we wrong in thinking that Mr. Baldwin had that Note in mind when he prepared his speech? If so, it must be a coincidence that while influential politicians, now fighting for power in the United States, are trying to force a decision from Washington opposed to Revision until European nations promise to disarm, a leading member of the British Government has spoken so strongly against the third fighting service. There is just the possibility that America is being asked to look upon a good example of diplomatic window-dressing.

* x * *

The London Chamber of Commerce, with the backing of the Associated Chambers of Commerce, the Federation of British Industries and the National Union of Manufacturers, has tabled an international barter scheme in an endeavour to overcome the difficulties of trading with the 35 countries which have instituted exchange restrictions. It has been described and heralded as a "return to simple, primitive barter," but its complexities and technicalities, as set forth in a memorandum by the Chamber, hardly justify the emphasis on the primitive. What is important, from the Distributist point of view, is that the launching of the scheme under such impressive commercial auspices, marks a definite and influential effort to bring the banks to heel; and what is disappointing, from the same point of view, is that after fulminating against the impotence of the banks to give a lead in the economic depression, the sponsors of the scheme have evolved a system that still relies mainly on the co-operation of the central banks of the participating countries. It seems as though those plotters in the metropolitan square-mile sacred to bankers, suddenly took fright at having lighted on an almost elemental truth, and decided to temper their boldness with compromise. The atmosphere at the conference at which the scheme was made known, might be described as heavy with masked resolves and hidden threats. Sir Stanley Machin, the senior vice president, in the absence of Lord Leverhulme, readily admitted that the monetary system had broken down; that the position of trade was becoming daily more serious and that unless something definite were done immediately there was no foreseeing how drastic the consequences might be.

* * * *

It appeared that the Chamber, with other British Chambers of Commerce, had made repeated representations to the Department of Overseas Trade, without avail; and at that Department's suggestion had met the bankers in a conference which " proved abortive owing to the inability of the banks' representatives to commit themselves to any definite expression of opinion." Here, then, was a golden opportunity for the men of commerce to make their barter purely primitive: goods for goods, on a value basis to be determined by the rate of exchange between the two trading communities. But the system they have chosen involves the creation of what is virtually a new international currency which is named " Bartex " for simplicity's sake. " Bartex " is defined as " the internal par value of an external trade barter unit " as fixed by the central bank of the country. Thus " Bartex " would vary in value according to the exchange variations between the participating countries. This, of course, would involve legislative sanction, and separate agreements between Great Britain and each of the other countries that may be concerned, tempted or coerced to join the scheme. The Department of Overseas Trade has already intimated that the barter scheme is not acceptable to the National Government; and maintains that the local arrangements which it is at present making to overcome the exchange difficulties in the various countries where trade has been most handicapped, will in time achieve as much as, or more than, a system of barter. But the London Chamber of Commerce and its supporting bodies beg to differ and counter-intimate that they will take their scheme to the Commons forthwith.

* * * *

Printed in English and containing " cordial greetings " from Sidney and Beatrice Webb, copies of the *Moscow Daily News* have been sent to the English Press as a reminder of the anniversary of the October Revolution. The contents of the issue include a letter from Lord Marley, who ends with the pious hope that increasing success may crown the efforts being made in the Soviet Union, and a message from a Mr. Joseph Reeves, whom the paper erroneously describes as the Secretary of the Royal Arsenal Co-operative Society. We understand that Mr. Reeves is secretary of the Society's Education Department. Anyway this is what he is credited with having written.

On behalf of the British co-operators who view with increasing satisfaction the unprecedented development of both consumers' and producers' co-operation in the Soviet Union, I desire to convey their fraternal greetings on the Fifteenth Anniversary of the October Revolution.

The co-operators of Great Britain, representing as they do the birthplace of the great Co-operative Movement, wish to extend to co-operators of the Soviet Union their congratulations on the contribution which the co-operative movement of the Soviet Union has made to the fulfilment of the Five-Year Plan. A study of the progress of Russian co-operation reveals a startling difference in the rate of progress of co-operation under a socialist economy as compared with capitalist countries.

The statement of Lenin that " Socialism could only be built through co-operation " is being fully justified by the course of events, and the amazing achievements of the great consumers' movement of the Soviet Union fill British co-operators with a desire to see a similar regime established in Great Britain.

It should be noted that the expressed desire in the last paragraph refers directly to the consumers' movement in Russia. That Movement, we are informed by an official of the Co-operative Party, must be presumed to be a voluntary movement, as it is associated with the International Co-operative Movement. Nevertheless, we doubt if all members of co-operative societies in England will subscribe wholeheartedly to these fraternal greetings, however innocuous they may be.

They Are Beginning To Learn
By Hilaire Belloc

IT is well worth while writing articles in *G.K.'s Weekly*. They are read in the right places and they have effect—which is more than one can say for the articles in the official press or even the articles in the gutter press nowadays, except in so far as the gutter press does have some emotional effect upon the herd; but not for the purposes of direction. The effect of *G.K.'s Weekly* is produced in another fashion. It is read by the men who write. It is read in Fleet Street, it is read by the editors of the various papers, and apparently even by one or two of the owners.

Now in the effect of *opinions* on England as she now is I have no great faith, save in so far as they may influence the herd by mere reiteration. But in the effect of *fact* I do have great belief. If some yellow-press owner hired ten thousand men in Essex and armed them to attack the people of Kent, proposing to march at some safe distance behind them, invade that county and waste it by fire and sword, I do not think he would be affected very much by reading the words, " Wicked yellow-press owner! Heaven will punish you if you attack the innocent people of Kent!" But I think he would be affected if he read, " Ignorant yellow-press owner! Learn that there is a wide and deep river between you and the people of Kent, and you can't get at them until you have made arrangements to cross it.'' He would make enquiries of those who could read a map—and would pause.

When the word went round from those who govern us—and a mixed lot they are, permanent officials, bankers, big business, and here and there the squeak of a politician—that Prussia was to be supported in her idea of a new partition of Poland and her claim for what is impudently called " The Corridor," sundry truths were printed (in this paper alone, I think) pointing out certain obstacles to the policy.

(1) The so-called " Corridor " is not inhabited by Prussians, but by Poles, and has been thoroughly Polish from the beginning of history. It appears on the old maps of Poland, and it was seized by Prussia in a violent Partition of Poland—of which Prussia was the chief author.

(2) It contains to-day the very large and important new port of Gdynia, rapidly on the way to becoming the chief port of the Baltic, a port wholly Polish in character and serving, with Dantzig, as the outlet for Polish export by sea.

(3) If all this tall talk about re-partitioning Poland and handing over Gdynia and the Poles of the Pomorze to a renewed course of Prussian bullying should come to action, there would be war in Europe.

(4) If there is war again in Europe, England will be a heavy sufferer and will probably suffer mortally; because England, highly industrialised, no longer strategically an island, unable to provide herself with food or with material for her manufactures, is on a more delicate balance than any other European nation; and because England with her vast possessions, the inheritance of a secure past, has to-day everything to lose and nothing to gain from any results of a new disturbance.

Now these things are not opinions, but facts; and facts are what the ignorant man should have, for they make him less dangerous. I have no doubt that when the owners of the gutter-press (of whom in this country we make lords) began their insensate campaign for a new partition of Poland they were ignorant of these four points. None of them had even heard of Gdynia. They had no idea that the Pomorze was Polish. They might vaguely have thought that war was possible but they could not have told us why, and they still firmly believed that if there were war, England would not suffer. Wiser and better instructed men than they were of the same opinion.

When I left for the Continent some little time ago these truths had not yet begun to appear in the popular press; on the contrary, the most astonishing articles were still coming out, the like of which for ignorance I do not remember to have seen paralleled in my time. Thus I found in one of the Aitken group of papers a whole two columns about " The Revision of the Treaty of Versailles " (which means the partition of Poland) compared with the revision of the Treaty of Vienna. In this article the liberation of Catholic Belgium from the Protestant Government of Holland was described as a triumph of English policy; and the writer imagined that the liberation of Belgium was an *English* policy due to Lord Palmerston! Another article in the same paper described the " Corridor " as being cut out of the living heart of Germany.

The point that is still hanging fire a little—but it

won't hang fire long—is the point about England's interest in peace. The reason that it hangs fire is that the ignorant owners of the yellow press can here find some support from men whose opinions are worth having and whose instruction is high. When they ask in the rich houses where they dine whether indeed these things are so, they learn from their fellow-guests (infinitely better educated than themselves—as for instance from some diplomat or historian) that the Pomorze is indeed Polish; that Poland was indeed partitioned; and that the partition of Poland is at the root of many of our modern troubles. They learn that Poland has not forgotten that tragedy and does not intend to have it repeated. They may even learn that the Poles are a warlike people, and, in spite of their Catholicism, not to be attacked with impunity—not sharing the lamb-like qualities of the Irish, the Spaniards, and other Catholics. They may even learn that war will certainly break out if this cynical policy of Prussian rapine materialises in eastern Europe; but on the 4th point (which is the essential) they may be told by very many of these men who are their superiors in education and judgment that England could keep out of war, and that if she did so she would suffer no evil consequences.

On returning from my sojourn abroad I found that the tone of the press had changed. The first three points I have here enumerated had all come to be accepted, but the 4th point had not yet been grasped. And I take it that that is because the 4th point is not a matter of fact but judgment. It has been learnt that the three other points are plain history or plain common sense, but the 4th point is indeed debateable. When we say that England would necessarily be involved in war on the continent, this does not mean that England would necessarily find herself fighting the moment that fighting in Europe began; it does not even mean that, highly possible as it is, we should be dragged into the fighting during the course of it; but it does mean that in the ultimate results of such a war England has everything to lose and nothing to gain. After backing up the Prussian aggression, she would probably find that aggression defeated quickly and this poisonous irritant got rid of. In the other alternative, a renewed Prussian power would require a good many things at the hands of England, and would be in a position to obtain them. Meanwhile England from within, living all the time on the brink of war, might develop a social condition of the greatest instability.

These things ought to be commonplaces. It ought to be a commonplace that England above all other powers is in need of peace.

Perhaps if we go on pointing it out long enough that commonplace will be accepted. The other truths have been accepted, so there is some hope. Those who still hanker after a partition of Poland have come to pin their hopes to the distracted weakness of the French government, represented as it is by professional politicians and despised by the nation which it misrules. Such calculations are very ill-founded. If the French professional politicians and their financial masters abandon Poland that will not make the Poles accept foreign domination. That will not save us from war—and war once begun, all Europe is ablaze.

When peace returned, there might indeed by a revision of the Treaty of Versailles—but not on the lines which that phrase connotes to those who to-day are so insanely playing with fire.

Is Beer a Luxury?
By G. C. Heseltine

SIR JOSIAH STAMP, in an interesting radio talk on taxation, referred several times to beer, among other things, as an example of a convenient commodity for taxation, because it was an extra, or luxury, and not a necessary. The burden of indirect taxation is not felt so severely, if inflicted through luxuries, as it would be if inflicted through necessaries. The only limit to taxation through luxuries appears to be that imposed by the law of diminishing returns. There comes a point where taxation ceases to yield full revenue because of the decrease in consumption of the commodity taxed. Revenue experts and economists favour the principle of indirect taxation because the taxpayer is less aware of the full extent to which he is being bled, and does not kick until he is bled so weak as to have no strength left for kicking.

In deciding what are luxuries and what are necessaries for this purpose, the economists make the same error as the pseudo-temperance, or prohibition, fanatics. Both converge on beer as a commodity eminently suitable for taxation, the one because it is found to yield large revenues with a long resistance to the law of diminishing returns, the other because excessive taxation effectively reduces consumption. For this second reason the no-beer maniacs press for more and more taxation, direct and indirect, on beer, and support the revenue authorities. But the revenue authorities will only respond to such pressure, up to the point at which the law of diminishing returns becomes effective.

Both assume that they are able to pursue their policies safely because beer is a luxury and not a necessary. In this they both commit the same error. In common with the economists, they fail to make a proper distinction between necessaries and luxuries.

It does not follow that because you *can* do without a thing, that it is not a necessary but a luxury. Nor does it follow that there is any virtue in abstaining merely because you *can* abstain without apparent harm. Virtue only comes into the picture when the motive is definitely and deliberately virtuous, as in religious asceticism or setting an example of self-control to the weak, and so on. Abstinence, as from beer, may be, and in the case of the prohibitionist and anti-beer fanatics it is most frequently, not a virtue but a vice—a funking of the exercise of self-control, a lying condemnation of beer as bad in itself, a contempt for the bounties of nature. Since it makes such abstinence easier if you can persuade people that beer is an unnecessary luxury or a superfluity, the anti-beer cranks, who eagerly use any statement, true or not, that serves their end (on the ground that the end justifies the means) use this one persistently. So persistently that we find most people accepting it. Is it true?

Some men can live, and apparently, in good health without meat. Excessive meat eating, in the same way though not in the same degree as excessive beer drinking, brings personal and social evils in its train. There is hardly a single article of diet that some men cannot be found able to do without, or find a substitute for. We know that most people, deprived of certain foods (such as those containing specific vitamins) will develop diseases, and that such deprivation, if universally applied, would exterminate or seriously damage the human race. Again, there are cases where adults can abstain from foods that are vital to growth in children, and children can abstain without harm from foods that are vital to the health of a normal workingman. The truth of the saying that one man's food is another man's poison, is universally admitted. The mere fact that individuals, even many individuals, can abstain from certain foods and drinks without apparent harm, does not justify us in assuming that such foods and drinks are not necessaries but luxuries and that the rest of mankind can safely do without them.

There is no doubt that very many people would continue to live quite healthily if deprived of meat, suddenly and totally. Yet no competent body of scientists would dare to recommend such a step, in view of some dangers that are known, and the possibility of many more that are unknown. Nobody knows the full value and importance of beer (and with beer I include wine and all brewed drinks) to mankind as a whole. Nobody knows what results might follow, physical as well as mental and social, if the human race were suddenly and totally deprived of beer and wine. Therefore it is impossible to say to what extent beer and wine are necessary or unnecessary to the human race. But there is no justification for concluding from this that beer and wine are unnecessary or unessential luxuries.

This is not a plea that beer is a necessity, on negative grounds, that is, because we know nothing or we have not sufficient evidence or information to justify the conclusion that it is unnecessary. On the contrary, there is a very large and formidable body of evidence which commonsense must forbid us to ignore.

When we find that mankind throughout its history, in almost every climate, civilisation, and condition, has had certain habits and articles of diet in common, it would be a good deal more than rash to assume that such things are not in some way, though we may not know *exactly* how, essential and necessary to humanity.

Though some men have lived solitary, men are naturally gregarious; though some men have been vegetarians, men are naturally carnivorous; though some men have lived on water, the history of mankind shows men are naturally drinkers of fermented drinks like beer and wine. These parallels are quite sound. In all of them excess is evil, moderation is good. The excessive herding together of men, as in modern industrial towns is evil, just as cannibalism or excessive meat eating is evil, just as drunkenness is evil. There is no substantial evidence, as large in scope as this, to show that the opposite extreme is not also evil. There is nothing, in the face of this, to justify the assumption that these common factors are not necessary, and that prohibition or excessive restriction will not be harmful.

Unemployment

—*By Powys Evans*

Straws in the Wind.

THE NEW NEW WORLD
By G. K. CHESTERTON

I HAVE made one or two notes here on the way in which men accused of worshipping new things are really only too faithful in their worship of old things. Of course, there are at least three senses in which men speak of things as old. They say that Stonehenge or the Egyptian mummies are old; meaning that they are dead. On the other hand they say that their country, or their Catholic Faith (if they possess it) is old, just as they say that an old friend is old; meaning that he is alive. Lastly, there is a third sort of thing which they say is old; as the more unchivalrous of them would say that an actress is old; meaning that she has gone on for a devilish long time being young. This third class is the one I am most concerned with here; the things that are theoretically supposed to be new; but which have been new for such a long time, that their very novelty has become an antiquity. So in the case quoted, it is one thing to admire an actress, or respect a woman, or respect an old woman; and another to think she can go on playing Juliet for ever. So there are many, even among the ideals I do admire, or the principles I do respect, which are now weakened rather than strengthened by the pretence that they are always progressing, when, as a fact, most of them in the modern world are fighting with their backs to the wall. Liberty is a lady with whom I am still very much in love; but she is admittedly celebrating her hundred and fiftieth birthday; and I doubt whether she can go on playing the Infant Phenomenon for ever. The appeal of democracy always had its doubts and difficulties, in relation to the literary and artistic classes; it was so much dependent upon a choice of words. Even the poets supposed to reverence the people were ready to revile the public. And now these rhetorical confusions are thinning a little; and something like a dead set at democracy is being made by numberless writers and in numberless ways. To take one particular point, among those myriad points, I think that the noblest and most necessary popular institution, the permanent and normal protection of freedom, is the Jury. The Jury is the only really representative Parliament; because people do not want to serve on it. But note what thousands of legal, scientific or normally vulgar pens are writing about the Jury. You will guess that the Jury will soon be in the Dock.

If there is one part of the world which is supremely and stupendously lumbered up with old things, that are still supposed officially to be new things, it is the world of America. As I have said, some of the things are good and some bad, but none of them is new: and each of them is supposed to be new. One stratum is the deposit of a seventeenth century Calvinism that I dislike; another the deposit of an eighteenth century republicanism that I like; yet another of a nineteenth century industrial individualism that I again dislike; but they are all deposits of the dead past; and there is no country so much clogged and choked by its own dead past as the United States.

The huge upheaval of Democratic voting, which has just overthrown the great static majority that stood for Hoover, may be the beginning of the end of this; an earthquake overthrowing these cold volcanoes; for nothing is colder than a cold volcano and America is covered with the cold lava of dead fanaticisms. Little importance is to be attached to a Party System; and not too much even to a vote. For the voting-machine, like every other modern machine, is one of those things that are still supposed to impress us by their freshness, and in fact only bore us by their staleness. But in this case there were more real and even religious traditions involved; there were things older than all our parties and native to mortal man; such as beer. And here again, in the whole business of Prohibition, we have the same fallacy about the new and old. It is intensely typical that Mr. Hoover himself did not talk of Prohibition as an institution; he talked of it as an experiment. I think he said it was a noble experiment. It is as if Lincoln, in his early hesitations, had said that Negro Slavery was a noble experiment. It is quite true that, far back in the seventeenth century beginnings, some sectarians had thought the negroes were benefited by being dragged in chains to the paradise of Puritan religion. And so some sectarians had originally thought that citizens were benefited by being bludgeoned by the police into drinking water, or its inferior substitutes. But Slavery was rather more than an experiment by the time Lincoln was President; and Prohibition was something more than an experiment by the time Hoover was soon to cease being President. In so far as it had ever been regarded as an experiment, it had long been regarded as a failure; and had been abandoned everywhere, except in one place where it was supposed to be a fixture. Now this election may mean that the Americans are really getting tired of having failures as fixtures. That is, that they are tired of having perfectly hopeless institutions prolonged as hopeful experiments. They are tired of accepting antiquated things on account of their novelty. Of course men like Mr. Ford clung to the noble experiment; explaining how noble it was that workmen should buy his own cars, instead of drinking with their own friends. Capitalists are naturally more alarmed, when a man talks politics over a pot of beer, than when he is shut up in a rattling machine in which he cannot talk at all. But the election looks as if this plutocratic pressure had weakened; and that some people had been talking politics after all. It may mean, as I say, the shifting of many old promises that had become mere prejudices. It may mean the shaking of that queer intolerant individualism, and dread of *all* State action, which kept New York in 1932 at the exact stage of old Manchester in 1851. There is something symbolic in those very names of the New World; New

York and New Orleans and New Jersey. They are already very old cities and provinces; and historic in a good as well as a bad sense; but they have had the name of novelty tied to them; and it has helped to make them things of the past.

A Lost Germany

By J. Desmond Gleeson

NOT long ago any one who prided himself on his knowledge of European affairs took it into his head to explain to me what was going on in Germany. It was (and for that matter, is) his hobby to interest himself in Continental politics. Reading the situation at any particular time was what he felt himself supremely capable of doing, though his reading was generally singularly inaccurate. Nevertheless he travelled far and wide and it was while I was on my own modest travels that I met him. He had but recently come out of Germany and thus he felt it was his duty to explain Germany to me. He was very satisfied with his own explanations, as such men frequently are, though the explanation sounds slightly odd to-day. It is not without interest, especially as many more than he held it.

According to his view there was not one Germany, but two and each was at war with the other. The first Germany, and I gathered that he reckoned it by far the superior, was what might vaguely be called the Germany of " All Quiet on the Western Front " and " the Road Back." It was a Germany sick at soul, pacifist at heart—indeed pacifist at heart because it was sick at soul. The astonishing sales of Remarque well-known works had clearly impressed this critic. These books, he said, were what everyone was reading in Germany and they were reading them because the mood thus conveyed was exactly the mood of the German people. The experiment of 1914-18 had resulted in finding out War, in the sense of seeing through it. It was not the experiment which failed, but the people. They had failed to carry it out and they had so failed because human nature was not equal to such awful experiments. All Quiet merely meant that all was damned on the Western Front and the Road Back merely showed that there was no such road, since no human beings remained sufficiently human to walk it. War was too barbarous a curse for the sensitive nations of to-day and never again should flags and frontiers command the attention of the German people.

This, then, I was told, was the prevailing mood in Germany. War was not merely a question of killing and being killed. It was more terrible, so to speak, for the survivors than for the dead. It set a sickness of mind upon the living, blighted all those who took part in it. A kind of moral paralysis had overtaken the people which now found only one voice, the voice of pacificism. This, I was informed, was the real voice of Germany, a Germany which had waged its last war and which on no pretext would ever be able to get its sick sons back into the trenches once they had started on that Road Back.

There was the second and less favourable Germany, the Germany of the Military Mob. (I noticed, by the way, that this second Germany was increasingly inferior as our conversation continued. Whereas it had started as something almost equal to the first Germany, it seemed now to shrink with each successive sentence. Having commenced as something of a giant, it was rapidly dwindling to pigmy proportions.) This Germany was, of course, the Germany of the pre-war survivors, the country of the Old Guard who were too old to learn anything by experience or example. It was that part of the Machine which simply went on working because it was not intelligent enough to see that the whole Machine had broken down. It seemed rather a difficult process for a mere remnant of a machine, but I fancy the point was that it functioned automatically, through discipline and not through thought. It was this Germany which continued to dream of flags and frontiers and a return of the Monarchy, which looked on the War as a temporary set-back, but which was entirely persuaded that nothing could permanently stand in the way of what was termed Germany's destiny. It is true that they looked upon the first, and superior, Germany as something standing in their way, but this also they looked on merely as a temporary set-back.

These were the two Germans, supposed to be facing one another but a short while ago, the shell-shocked battalions of Remarque on the one side, and the rather wooden militarists on the other. They had many names and I think my acquaintance actually did endeavour to distinguish them as Republicans and Monarchists. At any rate, he had no doubt whatever that it was the sick of soul who were on their way to Victory. Whatever might be the significance of that " Road Back," there was no possible suggestion that it led back to arms and armies. If it led anywhere at all, it led exactly in the opposite direction. Where then is that war-shattered multitude to-day? What has become of that superior Germany on which we were all told to fix our attentive eye?

The curious thing is that it has utterly vanished. At election times (and they occur with remarkable frequency) it invariably uses its vote in favour of armies. If it were opposed to any type of patriotic fire-brand, it would be opposed to Adolphe Hitler, yet the opponents of Hitler are not pacifists, but merely another kind of militarist. It is not to be found among the Socialists, for the Socialists, and especially the Communists, are a most orderly set of people, whereas the noisy " All Quiets " were a most disorderly gang, whose republican principles were precious near to anarchy. It is true that they were so shell-shocked that they were scarcely intelligent and may therefore easily have been misled into joining the Storm Troops, but the more reasonable explanation is that this particular Germany never really existed. That crowd of neurotics on the Road Back was something very like a phantom army, created by a great poet or, perhaps, a great propagandist. But the propaganda was exceedingly useful, delicately misleading, serving a most convenient purpose during a few critical years. And when the purpose was accomplished that shell-shocked Germany simply disappeared, so that to-day you will not hear its voice, though, in point of fact, it is challenged by every public element in Germany.

But the more curious thing is that none of our own pacifist propagandists have even condescended to notice that this Germany has disappeared. Its appearance they hailed with every symptom of approval. They called on us to admire this new national spirit and above all to notice how neatly it chimed in with our own mood. Germany would stand no more war and, as for ourselves, we were determined never again to engage in it. The two late opponents might therefore march hand in hand to Geneva, with the brilliant lights of publicity turned fully upon them, to demand general disarmament with one voice. But our peace companion has since undergone a rapid reformation and is at present polishing his steel helmet. If he was asleep before, he is now rather wildly awake and all our own pet publicists can find to say is that after all he is only demanding his rights; that his claim to equality is merely just; that you cannot indefinitely keep down a first-rate nation, and much more of the same sort. But they decline absolutely to acknowledge that a certain Germany has disappeared and that one of the very opposite character has now taken its place.

Various Opinions
By G. Gregory Macdonald

THE Russians have changed the lovely name of Nijni-Novgorod to Gawky—they hate tradition in names; I hate tradition in spelling—to honour their famous novelist. No doubt they think that the legend of the writer will endure longer than the legend of the merchant-republic. Storied Kiev should next disappear from the map, in favour of some shocker out of Tauchnitz, and the wonder is that Moscow has remained at all. Better revolutionaries would have tried first to make a better Nijni-Novgorod, instead of just giving it a title, like the peerage sought by a *parvenu* with a guilty conscience in capitalist England.

* * * *

I don't know whether all our literary circles are dabbling in Communism, but the house-organ of one great publishing firm announces this piece of news with smug assurance, as though it could be taken for granted that its readers looked hopefully to the Soviets. "Is there any other instance of such a massive tribute to a novelist?" (Yes, Mrs. Wotherspoon got buried under a ton of pig-iron when she was going through the Black Country in search of local colour.) "Whose name, one wonders, will appear on the Red Ordnance Survey in lieu of Manchester or Canterbury?" As a matter of fact, we Red Ordnance surveyors have arranged all that. Manchester will be Mitcheson (with memories of the Mitcheson School and the biological doctrine of *les affaires*). Canterbury will be Noel, to preserve some slight savour of a Christian tradition. Reading cannot do better than adopt the name of Red-Inge. The quiet cathedral town of Wells will, appropriately enough, remain the quiet cathedral town of Wells. Bury St. Edmunds will never do; it may be changed either to Murry T.

Middleton or to Bury T. Murry—but this is a point of literary criticism still under debate in the Red Ordnance Local Soviet.

* * * *

People who insist upon breaking so abruptly with tradition always believe that their own new tradition will be continuous. It would be more logical to stop at once the tradition [already begun] of calling Nijni-Novgorod by the name of Gorki. The name of Leningrad, too, has gathered legend. So has the motor car, yet these people regard the motor car as a sign of progress. Let us all start again from scratch in 1933, with no dead weight of custom upon us, pretending that we don't know a thing about what has happened from Neanderthal Man to President Hoover. The trouble is that the generations which succeed iconoclasts go to endless trouble in piecing the statues together again, and they despise the iconoclasts for their pains. For instance, Henry VIII's Commissioners (or Commissars) destroyed priceless manuscripts in Duke Humphrey's Library at Oxford, because they were Popish. Some years later the University of Oxford itself sold the very benches upon which the readers in that Library used to sit. Yet along came Camden, and Bodley, and Cotton, building it all up again.

* * * *

Whenever I think of Henry VIII I say to myself, " Diamond, Diamond; you little know what you have done." This Law, enunciated by Isaac Newton, applies with equal force to the Bolsheviks.

* * * *

Another Diamond is Mr. Garvin, whose weekly bright idea about the Polish " Corridor " (I beg everybody's pardon, but Mr. Garvin started it) now takes the form of a narrow German Corridor across the Polish Corridor. As an amendment, I move an even narrower Polish Corridor across Mr. Garvin's German Corridor, and so *ad infinitum*. But since English publicists are so anxious to be statesmanlike over the problem, I may mention two aspects of it within the scope of statesmanship which they seem to have ignored. One is that if Prussia regains Danzig and Gdynia, she will have a near-monopoly of transit, as against England, over sea-borne trade with all the Central and East Central countries of Europe. At present, for instance, Czecho-Slovakia has a choice for export between Gdynia, Danzig, and the German ports. Then, if Prussia takes the second easy step of forming the Austro-German Customs Union, she closes the exit by Trieste and the Adriatic.

* * * *

The second point of statesmanship (which takes the long view) is that while the German birth-rate is rapidly falling, the Slavonic birth-rate is rapidly rising. It is true that on account of the high birth-rate between 1890 and 1910 Germany now has more men of military age than she has ever had; but since 1898 the excess of births over deaths has fallen from 15.6

per thousand to 6.4 per thousand. Her peak population of 65 millions will decline, if the present rate is maintained, to some 50 millions. On the other hand, the Polish excess of birth over deaths rose from 15.5 in 1922 to 17 per thousand in 1930. At the present rate her population will equal Germany's population by 1975; at present it is just one half. These are factors which encourage Prussia to make an effort for Polish territory at once; but it is already a myth that Germany wants room to expand, and the future will see an increasingly active Polish population demanding the free use of its own ports. Then we shall have the trouble over again, despite the English publicists whose statesmanship is, as usual, a question of preserving all the European yesterdays.

* * * *

By the way, as Mr. Lloyd George has pronounced most excellently in favour of a restoration of agriculture, to include small-holdings, decentralisation and the exclusion of the middleman, he may have looked into the possibilities of popular banks in peasant countries; for the productive use of savings in local areas has before now given prosperity to barren countrysides. Venezia is one example. The Westerwald in Germany is another. There must be decentralisation in credit as in property.

Ballade of Shrewsbury

It was a city wrought by rhyme
Of the flood waters' overflow
From the foundation stones of Time;
With walls for bannered pomp and low
Squat towers; sullen swords a-row;
And clanging echoes of the tread
Of spearmen in the street below.
    I sing a city of the dead.

It was a city set a-chime
As noon-day pealed out—to and fro';
With drone of bees in elm and lime,
And river-murmur cool and slow,
Old red brick with an orange glow—
Laughter and running feet that sped—
A golden girl for every beau.
    I sing a city of the dead.

It is a city. Apes a-climb
Along its streets with "pep" and "go."
Extend Bank premises sublime,
Multiple shops with window-show
Of celanese and even, oh,
To boyhood's morals, final blow!—
Pyjamaed Juliet a-bed—
    I sing a city of the dead.
    ENVOI.

Sabrina fair, although I know
With decent shame you hang your head,
You've been bought up by ...... and Co.
    I sing a city of the dead.
              DAVID EDWARDS

Books

Contrast

HUNGRY ENGLAND.   By A. Fenner-Brockway. Gollancz. 2s. 6d.
    " . . . he called them untaught knaves, unmannerly
    To bring a slovenly unhandsome corpse,
    Between the wind and his nobility."

" This collapse has plunged the whole town (Great Harwood, Lancs.) into unemployment. During one month actually 74 per cent. of the workers were unemployed; the percentage is now 38.9 . . . Three thousand are undergoing the Means Test; that is, they have been unemployed continuously more than six months."

" Man, wife and son of 17. Their allowance under the Means Test is 23 shillings. Rent 7s. Coal 3s. Margin for food and clothing for three adults per week 13s." Son, whose earnings are the " Means " in question, has never earned more than 9/6 in a week and in the week of the author's investigation earned 2s. 9d.

Nine in family. Rent (one room) 14s. Poor relief allowance 35s. 3d. Margin for food and clothing for nine persons per week, 21s. 3d.

Total rent received from one house 89s. per week. Seven families, twenty-seven persons, nine rooms. (Birmingham.)

Farmworker's budget (five in family, wages 36s.). Rent 3s., bread 5s., meat 2s. 6d., milk 2s. 11d., margarine, etc., 3s. 2d., bacon 2s. 6d., cheese 2s., coal and wood 2s. 4d., sundry groceries 7s. 7s., Union, sick club, pocket money and clothing 5s. (East Anglia.)

Estimated number of workers 9,600. Unemployed nearly 7,000. On Means Test over 5,000. Receiving poor relief 1,200. (Jarrow.)

" The population of a condemned slum area has been removed to a new Council estate situated in a healthy district and composed of houses with all modern conveniences for sanitation and cleanliness. . . Yet the death-rate among these people has gone up by leaps and bounds. The children on the estate are 66 per cent. physically unfit as compared with 26 per cent. for the whole of the town . . . they are paying the rents at the cost of food. In the slums they paid 2s. or 2s. 6d. a week. Now they are paying 8s. or 10s. It is healthier to live in a slum with the minimum of nourishment than on a housing estate minus nourishment." (Stockton.)

Mortality rate for infants under one year 91 per thousand. Rate for England and Wales 60 per thousand. Medical Officer's report states that the unfavourable housing conditions and the economic conditions generally account for the large number of deaths in the later months. (Merthyr.)

" Thomas Cast, 48, a labourer of West Lane, was found dead in his home with a razor wound in his throat. His wife stated that he was suffering from bronchitis and two children were in bad health. He was very worried because he was out of work and his twenty-six weeks' benefit had come to an end. He feared that he would be knocked off benefit by the Public Assistance Committee. On the morning that he was due to go to the committee he brought her a cup of tea in bed and said he would go downstairs and light the fire. When she went downstairs she found him on the floor with his throat cut. The coroner entered a verdict of " suicide while of unsound mind." (Rotherhithe.)

Well, I think perhaps that is enough to show you what goes to fill the 224 pages of Mr. Fenner Brockway's book. The book is the report of his investigations in certain distressed areas, and it contains very little padding. The paper cover says, " The facts themselves are shameful, whatever the causes, and whatever the solutions, and they are facts which no decent person can ignore."

But I must fill out my space somehow, so what about a spot of light relief? And I feel in the quoting mood.

Placard displayed in London during the recent approach of unemployed contingents: " *Miseries of the Marching Dupes.*" Definition of a dupe: An unemployed man with a hungry family who comes to Westminster for help.

Home-page paragraph headed "Elegant Economy": " The most popular beauty specialist is the one whose preparations last the longest and serve more than one occasion . . . in one Bond Street parlour the favourite face-powder shade is a Rachel with a peach-like glow in it which is equally suitable for day or evening use."

More Mayfair cheeseparing: " Though tea and coffee, not to mention huge bowls of clotted cream, were available, there was not a single *sweet* thing to be seen. Endless savouries abounded. It was difficult indeed to choose between the attractions of thin rounds of brown bread lightly spread with *pâti-de-fois-gras* with a slice of truffle in the middle, or other thin slices covered with wafer-like portions of smoked salmon with an anchovy curled up in the centre, or a similar arrangement of brown bread and some paste, which formed a bed for a little heap of caviare." (*Daily Telegraph* account of Mrs. Emile Mond's musical at-home.) The Merthyr bread is also thinly cut and lightly spread, but not with *pâti-de-fois-gras. Chacun son gout.*

Back to stark reality—again in Mayfair: " For the first time in the history of modern Mayfair, hostesses are meeting in famous drawing-rooms for lectures on the art of washing-up, the dignity of housework, . . . Sinks were among the subjects discussed by interesting women after the first lecture . . . Sitting down to work, another idea recommended by the lecturer, has already been adopted by Lady ——. This hostess who is keenly interested in her kitchen has installed an adjustable stool for her cook to use at her work." (*Daily Telegraph.*)

Any paper, any day: " Moscow agitates and inspires English hunger-marchers!"

Queer, isn't it?

F.K.C.

A STUDY IN CREATIVE HISTORY: THE INTERACTION OF THE EASTERN AND WESTERN PEOPLES TO 500 B.C. *By O. E. Buxton. George Allen and Unwin.* 10s.6d.

The author belives that about the year 500 B.C. the stage was set for international action. "What has happened since and what is happening to-day is largely conditioned by the philosophies of life worked out to that date." Although the symbol B.C. in his title presumably means

something, there is no mention of Christ in the book, so we have chapters on Egypt, the Phoenicians, the Assyrians, Babylon, the Israelites (here the author unloads his knowledge of modern biblical criticism,) the Medes and Persians, Mazdaism, India (Buddha), China (Confucius), Greece and Rome. If we grasp what was worked out by 500 B.C. we may have hope for the future. "There is a living historical process connecting Croesus, son of Alyattes ...lord of all the nations west of the river Halys...the first of the barbarians who had dealings with the Greeks," and "such modern movements as Swaraj, Christian missions to the East, the operation of Western capital in China and Hindu labour in Fiji. If we can grasp the ascending sweep of this great process wheeling and circling upward from the dawn of history to our own time, we shall have a fuller knowledge of the immense problems men of our age are heir to, gain some ground perhaps for optimism and some guidance for our activity." I don't believe it.

G.M.

BY THE WAY. *By Beachcomber. Sheed and Ward.* 3s.6d.

This "Beachcomber Pocket Omnibus" contains as entertaining a collection of characters, admirably illustrated by Nicolas Bentley, as you will find in the whole of the L.G.O.C. Fleet. They are garnished with the spices and the sauce with which the "Daily Express" wisely tickles the palates of its readers to keep them to swallow the nauseous rubbish that makes up the rest of its daily intellectual feast. No home need now lack the jolly company of Dr. Strabismas (Whom God Preserve) of Utrecht, Lady Cabstanleigh, Prodnose, Mrs. Wretch, Mr. Roland Milk, Mr. Wal Hogwasch, and Boubon Fauncwaters. The book needs no more commendation when it is said that it is the pick of the By the Way Column for six years, produced up to the publishers' usual high standard at less than half the price of the world's worst novels.

G.C.H.

THE HEART OF ENGLAND. *By Edward Thomas. J. M. Dent and Sons. 3s.6d.*

It is most appropriate that this collection of Edward Thomas's brief rural essays should form one of the first of the reprints in "The Open-Air Library." Despite the pretentious title these sketches are instinct with the beauty of the English Countryside, as perceived by a poet. They are genuine in their inspirations and written from the heart. The prose is skilled and finely turned, and if it is not entirely free from affectation and preciosity, it shares these defects with the rest of the specific literature of the Countryside to a less extent than most. The editor of the series Mr. Eric Fitch Daglish contributes a few fine wood-engravings and a burbling preface, as conventional as it is superfluous.   G.C.H.

SONGS FROM THE BAD CHILD'S BOOK OF BEASTS. *Verses by H. Belloc. Music by Dudley Glass. Pictures by B.T.B. Duckworth, Ascherberg. 3s. 6d.*

I cannot feel that the composer has quite caught the spirit of Mr. Belloc's amusing verses, which surely have a little more in them of the sting of satire than these very conventional settings suggest. The drawings are those which accompanied the original publication of the verses. Messrs. Ascherbergs, the music publishers, have done their part well, and the whole makes an attractive volume. Ten songs are included : *The Yak; The Elephant; The Dodo; The Hippopotamus; The Crocodile; The Microbe; The Lion; The Tiger; The Python;* and *The Big Baboon.*

FORTY YEARS OF MAN HUNTING. *By Ex-Supt. A. F. Neil. Jarrolds,* 12s.6d.

This is a volume of reminiscenses by the last of the original Scotland Yard "Big Four." It is written, as the author has stated, without "records, notes or diaries," but I imagine one does not lightly forget incidences such as Mr. Neil has experienced, even if they are but incidences all in the day's work.

The experiences cover such famous crimes as the Jacoby case, the Malty murder and suicide, the Brides in the Bath affair (during which his zeal won for the author a written appreciation from the Director of Public Prosecutions), up to the more recent murders of the child, Ivy Godden, in Kent, and of Louisa Steel on Blackheath Common. It is some consolation to know from such an authority that many "unsolved" murders are in fact solved, at any rate to the satisfaction of the police; and that it is only lack of definite proof which prevents arrest and prosecution. At least it means that the police have their eye on the parties.

The book is generously illustrated, but an index should have been included.

STRANGE GUEST. *By Sylvia D. Hooke. John Murray,* 7s.6d.

Cressida, child of a very Victorian and suburban family, clings to an imaginative and uncomprehended vision. Life must mean something. Her sister Rachel's social ambitions, her brother's brilliant prospects, do not satisfy her. A school teacher fires her with ambitions for social service to which she clings, despite parental horror and sisterly scorn; in the event, her troubled life of poverty and effort is far happier and more satisfying than the glittering career of brother and sister. The book is genuine, and if not outstanding, has much to commend it,—even though parental lack of sympathy is a shade over-emphasised, and juvenile selfishness a shade too much approved.

THE ART OF SPEECH. *By Kathleen Rich. Methuen and Co.* 3s. 6d.

This book will be welcomed by all interested in elocution. The author has avoided the use of technical language and the result is a competent little book that should be of value both to the beginner and to the advanced student.

FAMILY HOLIDAY. *By W. R. Calvert. Putnam.* 5s.

An ever-so-whimsical account of a motoring holiday in Wales and the Marches. The car is "Old Mole," the writer is "The Scribe," his passengers are "The Baron" and "The Duchess." The book gave me a melancholy pleasure; it brought a lump to my throat to meet again the good old jokes of long ago—haggard and emaciated, some of them, but still the same. All this clever-clever modern stuff—"Tramp Abroad" and "Three Men in a Boat"— and so on seems somehow pale and shallow in comparison. Cunningly mingled with the Facetious Bits are Gems of Description and Informative Details. Still, all guides are fairly horrible and to anyone making the Wye-Hereford-North Wales tour this will be found as useful and readable as most.   F.K.C.

TINKLE THE CAT. *By Norah C. James. Dent,* 5s.

This rather sophisticated attempt to get inside the mind of a cat—a very domestic cat— is saved from banality by the clever animal studies by Miss Dorothy Burroughes, who here comes out in the open and admits herself to be an R.B.A., and an F.Z.S., as well as the witty creator of Selina Squirrel. Both text and pictures speak of careful observation—but the pictures contain something more—and the sketch of the policeman is as delightful as the pictures of the cat.

Music

A GLOWING performance of Balakirew's sinister and exciting *Tamara* opened the second of the series of sixteen Sunday afternoon concerts which the Philharmonic Orchestra is giving at the Queen's Hall. Miss Florence Easton followed, singing *Come Scoglio* from Mozart's *Cosi fan Tutte* with fine understanding and confidence, despite that the upper vocal register was at times a little uneasy at the demands put upon it. I very much regretted that I was unable to wait for the Verdi aria she was to sing later in the programme, as Miss Easton is too seldom heard in London, and the aria is one which, I imagine, would show her artistry at its most magnificent. I was able, however, to remain a little longer; long enough to hear a performance of Hadyn's "Paukenwirbel" Symphony which; for strength, delicacy, charm and all round brilliance I do not think even Sir Thomas Beecham has equalled before. Certainly no one else has, at least not in post-war London. Sir Thomas Beecham and the Orchestra are engaged at the Albert Hall next Sunday, with Menuhin as soloist, but four more Sunday concerts are to be given at the Queen's Hall before the Christmas and New Year break.

Undoubtedly those concerned in the production of *Cosi fan Tutte* at the Old Vic deserve all congratulations and thanks. Fears have been expressed that Mr. Clive Carey's staging lends itself too much to farce, which, once the company gets over the first restraint and can afford to let itself go, will introduce a false element into Mozart's delicate humour. But such fears are entirely anticipatory; at the moment the whole production is charming. Mr. Buesst achieves an altogether lighter and more brisk playing than has been evidenced recently from the orchestra. Joan Cross and Winifred Kennard are excellent as the flirtatious sisters (the former easily maintains the high vocal standard she set herself as the Countess in *Figaro* last week); Henry Wendon and Sumner Austin make amusing contrast as the respective husbands; and Arnold Matters, as the old cynic, has found a part which suits him admirably.

If Miss Thelma Reiss-Smith fulfils the promises of her recital last week and of the other occasions on which she has appeared before the public during the last two years, she may easily rank as one of the great 'cellists of the world. It is not so much that her technique is above the average. That can be achieved by mere practise. What she possesses far above the average is musical intelligence. In a programme including, among others, Bach, Arne and Hindemith, there was nothing she played in which one could not immediately sense her understanding of the composer's intention, combined with a strong personal sense of phrasing and emphasis. Miss Reiss-Smith should do well if she avoids the pitfalls of early and too easy success.

On Tuesday next the Philharmonic Choir gives its first concert of the season at the Queen's Hall, under Mr. Kennedy Scott; and has chosen for the occasion a new version by Steuart Wilson and A. H. Fox-Strangways of Hadyn's *The Creation*. At the second concert, on April 4th, the programme is to include a new work by Napier Myles, entitled *Ode to a Grecian Urn;* also the *Songs of Farewell* by Delius. In the interim the Choir is engaged in choral and orchestral concerts by other societies and under other conductors, notably by the Royal Philharmonic for the *Messiah*, conducted by Sir Thomas Beecham; by the B.B.C. for *Sea Drift* (Delius), conducted by Dr. Boult; and by the Courtauld Sargent Club for the *Songs of Farewell*, conducted by Dr. Sargent. A letter from the Secretary states that " in spite of the acknowledged achievements of the choir, and its evident popularity, there is still much difficulty in obtaining

singers, especially men, and Associate Subscribers are also urgently needed." He will be pleased to supply full information to anyone interested. The address is at 28, Flanchford Road, London, W.12,

V.N.L.

Drama

MR. LONSDALE is losing touch. At all events, "Never Come Back" at the Phœnix shows no advance in method, no new tricks and—worst of all—no new epigrams. One of the characters, indeed, complains that " Us titled fellahs are always being used for some trick or other " and although nobody minds that except the titled fellahs (perhaps) it is a little depressing to find that it is always the same trick. I wondered what Miss Ellis Jeffreys, whose wholly adorable performance in " On Approval " I shall always cherish among my theatre memories, thinks of her present part, in which not even she can convey an illusion that her lines contain a laugh.

Certainly not even the theatregoing public is likely to be persuaded that " Never Come Back " is any daring departure. When you write about charming crooks operating in rather less charming high society, the simple variation of first a girl and then a boy provides a not impenetrable disguise. And when you realise that you have not, after all, seen the last of Mrs. Cheyney, you also recognise the ignoble noblemen who damn and grunt their way through the piece as equally familiar denizens of the Lonsdale reservation.

The first act seemed to be disjointed and verbose—possibly because of a piece of machinery which the

Phœnix management kept in busy competition with the actors for the attention of the back rows, possibly for reasons less esoteric. One gathered that a Mr. Mortimer was entertaining a party of English and American best people at his villa in Cannes for no creditable reason; that the Duke of Bristol, young and surly, had discarded, by means of a cash payment, the wife of Sir John Moynton, to facilitate a more conventional ardour towards Miss Linkley, an ardour welcomed with unconcealed delight by her mother but not by Miss Linkley herself, who fancies a lean, dark mystery-man named Smith. Smith, in a private chat with Mortimer, exhibits his morning haul of pilferings, and the plot is thus released.

In Act II, we spend what seems to be a very long time bantering and back-chatting after a poor dinner at Mrs. Linkley's country house before we learn without surprise that her diamond necklace is missing. The detective arrives and suspicion is focussed on Smith. He realises that Miss Linkley, wishing to bolt from her odious duke, has taken the jewels, so gently steals them from her and places them in the Duke's pocket where in due course they are found. This provides a delicious curtain which unfortunately has nothing to do with the play, as we learn in Act III. Smith is under worse suspicion than ever, Mortimer having lost his nerve and left in a hurry. Moreover, he is strangely, innocently, susceptible to the policeman's bluff of confessions and exhortations to come clean, and things are looking ugly when Miss Linkley intervenes, Smith declares his love and promises to be good in future, the detective contributes a manly exordium not untinged with admiration, and we fumble for our cloak-room tickets.

This is, frankly, thin stuff, and only the quality of the acting makes it tolerable. I boldly pronounce Mr. Raymond Massey as the best all-round actor of his generation, not so much because of his performance as Smith, which is necessarily immaculate, but because he is a racehorse who can trot round a circus-ring and probably draw a milk-cart if necessary. Mesdames Adrienne Allen, Nora Swinburne and Viola Tree make good use of what good lines are afforded them and Mr. Athol Stewart presents a disgruntled peer with more humour than seems possible at this time of day. But Mr. Lonsdale should really give them all a better chance next time.

With some diffidence, I looked in during the week at the Cambridge theatre for the Guitry play " La Jalousie." It is a simple-hearted trifle on the usual theme but I feel it necessary to issue a warning that unless your French is above the average you are not likely to be greatly entertained. M. Guitry speaks nearly twice as much and at least twice as fast as the other members of the cast, and although for vanity's sake I tried to pretend that it was his expressions and gestures which helped me out rather than the printed synopsis, I have my doubts. In any case we have still with us Mr. Seymour Hicks, whose soundless vocabulary is infinitely more subtle and more complete than that which the famous French player shows. But I must admit that Mlle Jacqueline Delubac is delicious.

BENEVIDEO.

The Cockpit.

[Letters should not exceed 300 words in length and must bear the names and addresses, not necessarily for publication, of their authors.

The Editor can accept no responsibility for opinions expressed by correspondents.]

" PINS AND NEEDLES."

Sir,—I have read Mr. Baines' two recent articles with great interest, but I must confess that I am not convinced; certain of his arguments, in fact, are not at all convincing. He says that " The price of an article (so the law of rent tells us) is the cost of its production under the least favourable conditions." Well, if the law of rent tells him that, then the law of rent is an ass. Agreeably to such an axiom, the price of most articles would be their cost of production at the North Pole. I hope it is not presumption to suggest that what the law really says is something nearer this: given a number of manufacturers, the price of the manufactured article will tend to equal the cost of its production by the least efficient of those manufacturers. Even so, the statement requires heavy modification; modification so heavy in fact as to render the rule almost unrecognisable. But thus corrected the law comes in curious contrast with Mr. Baines' preceding paragraph where he says that " the price of a manufactured article has to bear the cost of the exactions of the urban landlord, etc. . . . which are *not* part of the cost of production. I would like to suggest just one question to Mr. Baines. If he is really convinced that there is an economic advantage in maintaining one industry at the general cost of the community, at the cost of reducing imports and therefore of exports also, at the cost of diverting capital, labour and purchasing power from the other industries to the favoured one, would it not be better to pay directly for its encouragement rather than develop the political corruption and parisitism that protective duties invariably engender?

JANE PARADINE.

THE ANNUITIES.

Sir,—Mr. Mark's article of October 8th would give an average reader the idea that the British case, as regards what he rightly calls a vital point—namely, the question whether the Annuities do or do not form part of the National Debt—is based on an elementary blunder.

Mr. Cosgrave's advisers, he says, were unanimously guilty of a " mis-statement of a very important fact," in that they stated that the Guaranteed Stock was not included in the Return of the National Debt for 1921. As a matter of fact, it was not included in the body of the Return, but in an Appendix showing " Contingent and Indirect liabilities "; and the whole British case, as regards this point, is that contingent liabilities do not form part of the National Debt, since the British Government are not the debtors but only the guarantors. It is possible (though not, I think probable) that Mr. Cosgrave's advisers may have been inaccurate in their reference to the Return in question; but this obviously does not affect the rights of the matter, which can best be studied in a White Paper (price 4d.) giving the statements of the British and Irish representatives at the Conference of last October. I do not propose to go into the various arguments used on that occasion: I would merely observe that the British representatives definitely claimed that the Stocks had never been shown as part of the National Debt in the United Kingdom accounts, and that the Irish representatives in their reply do not attempt to make what would have been the obvious retort had Mr. Mark's view been, in their opinion correct —namely, that the Stocks had been shown in the Return of the National Debt for 1921 (or any other year).

I repeat, I am not trying to decide the issue one way or another. It is open to anybody to read the White Paper. and decide for himself. This is not altogether satisfactory from the British point of view, since the White Paper allows the Irish representatives the last word; and much of what they say is doubtless open to further retort. But at least it is more satisfactory than trying to discuss abstruse juridical technicalities in the " Cockpit." A narrow arena is suitable only for broad issues.

WESTLANDER.

MECHANISATION.

Sir,—Many people must have been refreshed to hear that realities were discussed in Parliament last Friday. A good deal of what Mr. Lansbury said about industrialisation and agriculture was admirable. He quoted a letter of Mr. Bowden's that had previously appeared in the *Times*, which raised the real issue, viz. :—

1.—Machinery has been for many years visibly displacing men from employment in all industries.
2.—Purchasing power is in the main distributed as a reward for labour, which is being less and less required.

The problem, therefore, is, how to distribute purchasing power when industry is mechanised.

Mr. Bowden, however, added the following statement which Mr. Lansbury apparently accepts : " An agricultural revival, emigration, an universal 5-day week, would act as palliatives, but *the mechanisation process will inevitably continue and be intensified.*" (Italics ours).

But in the name of sanity, why must we accept an *inevitable* mechanisation process, however disastrous and anti-social the consequences? Is it not strange superstition for us to believe in a kind of inevitable force that drives us more and more to machinery and yet more machinery?

Surely the truth is that we change our methods of production because for one reason or another we are not satisfied with them as they are. The usual cause for dissatisfaction seems to be that production is not quick enough. With quicker production we can produce the same amount with less men, sack the rest and pocket their wages. Thus the usual motive for increasing mechanisation is that we may increase our own purchasing power and this is always at the expense of our employees, though they do not feel it as long as the markets for our products are expanding.

In other words the decreased purchasing power of the workers is not an unfortunate accident of the mechanisation process, but on the contrary it is the chief reason for its adoption. We must be careful not to assume that what is good for us individually is necessarily good for the community and what we do for our own profit is inevitable.

Of course, whenever machinery produces *better* articles without decreasing the personal interest of the workmen in their work, it is justified, but not otherwise.

E. C. BENSON.

Published by the Proprietors, G.K.'s WEEKLY, LTD., 2, Little Essex Street, Strand, London, W.C.2 (incorporating THE NEW WITNESS). Telephone: Temple Bar 1978. Printed by THE NUNEATON NEWSPAPERS LTD., "Observer" Buildings, Nuneaton. Sole Agents for Australasia: Gordon & Gotch (Australasia, Ltd.). Sole Agents for South Africa: Central News Agency Ltd.

G.K.'s Weekly

EDITED BY G. K. CHESTERTON.

No. 427—Vol. XVII.
Temple Bar 1978.

May 18, 1933.
Registered at G.P.O. as a Newspaper.

Sixpence
2, Little Essex Street, London, W.C.2

THIS WEEK

THE DOLLAR AND THE POUND

IT is very important, in analysing and trying to understand any public matter, to distinguish between motive and effect. The motive for which a thing was done may be very different from the effect which it produces, and the motive gets mixed as the effect develops. Moreover the motive may be and nearly always is of a mixed sort to begin with; and that part of it which is the principal part at the beginning of the action may be the less important part later on.

We see the importance of distinguishing thus between motive and effect in almost any historical matter. For instance, in dealing with the seizing of Charles I by the Army, the original motive was probably or certainly not to put him to death but to hold him as a sort of pawn in the Army's game with the Parliament; but later it was obvious that this capturing of the King was the first step towards his execution. Or again, in trying to understand a battle, very often a blunder at the beginning of an action may be turned into the cause of victory at the end of it. Or some motive which made a general act in such and such a fashion before an action may be changed in the course of the action itself. Napoleon did not know before Austerlitz, when he retired, what the Russians were going to do, and we do not know to this day why he retired; but we do know that after the retirement the Russians put themselves in such a position as enabled him to use his retirement in such a way as to produce the victory.

Now all that is profoundly true of the present great duel engaged between the dollar and the pound. That duel has emerged as a *secondary* consequence of the American repudiation undertaken last month, but people will soon understand that this duel now overshadows all our future policy. It is very grave indeed.

The primary motive for the American repudiation, that is, for America's suddenly refusing, with half the gold of the world in her pocket, to pay a dollar where a dollar had been promised—it is euphemistically and inaccurately called "going off the gold-standard"—was the fear in which the bankers stood, and particularly Kahn and Morgan (who are the chief figures in the American banking system) of their debt-slaves. The whole banking system of the United States was in the position of a creditor to whom the mass of the people—millions of them directly by mortgage, nearly all of them indirectly—owed a regular recurrent tribute in dollars : that is, in so much weight of gold, which gold has now a far greater purchasing power than it had had when most of the debts were made. The banks had lent to a farmer a thousand dollars when a thousand dollars was worth so much weight of wheat, and he had bargained to pay them fifty dollars a year when fifty dollars was worth so much weight of wheat— and now he still had to pay them fifty dollars a year, though that now meant the payment of double the amount of wheat—or more than double. The debtors were in revolt. There was serious danger of riot and worse, and not only the bankers but all those in authority were thoroughly frightened. Therefore was it determined to call that a dollar in future which was not in fact a dollar at all, but something a great deal less. So that the debtor from whom fifty dollars was due next June should have to pay the equivalent of, say, only thirty-five dollars.

But meanwhile other motives were coincident with this; and the most obvious of these other coincident motives was, as in the case of our own repudiation, in 1931, *the lowering of American wages to meet our own lowered wages in England*. And that is why the trick was played against England just while our absurd politicians were at sea and so taken by surprise.

Remember that in a capitalist system of production wages are the basis of all cost. When working men by their organisation have got wages up to a certain level in terms of a particular currency—say, twenty dollars or four pounds a week—you could not directly challenge the position by law, compelling the wage-earners to accept a smaller wage, without fear of revolution. But you *can* trick them into believing that they are receiving the same wage when really they are receiving much less, and you can do this by paying them in exactly the same pieces of paper printed in the same fashion—bearing on them the same numbers—but representing in reality a smaller amount of gold than the old sound currency used to do. In this way the man goes on taking his twenty dollars or four pounds a week contentedly, under the impression that his wages have not been changed, though in reality you are giving him only fifteen dollars, or three pounds a week.

We have seen how in this country a secondary motive of the same sort got to work. Our bankers and great industrialists did not repudiate voluntarily in September '31—they were forced to repudiate and to go bankrupt in the matter of the pound. But once that had happened it was obvious that they had at the same time lowered wages, so that English capitalists would in future have a great advantage in export, for they could now trick their employees into working for less wages and so lower the cost of what they had to sell abroad. An effect of this which was not very slow in appearing was the better chance for English coal in the Baltic. Our miners being paid only some two-thirds to three-quarters of what they used to have, we could sell our coal in Scandinavia at a less price than before, and could compete better in that market with Polish coal.

Now the Americans in the same way, though it was not their primary motive, had for a secondary motive this lowering of wages. But by the lowering of wages they at once began to undermine the advantage enjoyed during the last two years by the English capitalists from their newly depreciated currency. An American capitalist wishing to export a motor-car, for instance, had to pay five hundred dollars to his workmen in labour for the making of it. The English capitalist had to pay, let us say the same amount of labour on a car, one hundred pounds. After the bankruptcy of the pound, the English capitalist, though he still seemed to be paying one hundred pounds for his labour was really paying only seventy pounds or 350 dollars, while the American capitalist was still paying five hundred dollars. Thus the English capitalist could now undersell the American one in the matter of cars. But when the Americans repudiated the other day, they in their turn lowered wages; and the more they allow their currency to depreciate the more the English advantage will tend to disappear.

Therefore once this game of repudiation begins, there is a tendency for each party—or for each of many parties, now that so many nations have repudiated—to keep on ruining their currency more and more for the advantage it gives them in lower wages. That is the prime fact which arises out of the American repudiation at the present moment. A furious battle has begun between the pound and the dollar, not as to which shall be the highest but as to which shall be the lowest. *For in this kind of trickery the capitalist who can cheat most about his money, and so gets the proletariat to work cheapest, has the advantage over one who cheats less.*

Now the vital point to seize at the present moment is that in this perilous duel wherein we in England are engaged we are heavily handicapped. And the reason we are heavily handicapped is this :—

When we repudiated in September '31 the prices of the commodities which our wage-slaves ordinarily consume did not rise. Bread, bacon, margarine—all the rest of it—remained much the same in terms of the pound, or became even cheaper than they had been when the pound was worth twenty shillings. For some wealthy people the change has been a burden, but the proletariat have not felt it. This was partly because the change was very cleverly managed, vast quantities of stores being imported before the new tariffs were put on, but especially because a general fall in commodity prices accompanied the break-down of the pound. This fall in prices has now come to an end. If we try to lower the pound *now* relatively to the dollar the working-class would inevitably awake fairly soon to the trick that was being played upon them—and it is doubtful whether our capitalists would dare to risk the social friction that would ensue.

A considerable number of hot-headed people (who, to do them justice, had never learnt the ABC of economics) clamoured in the Press for keeping the pound down below the dollar in proportion as the dollar fell; but we have not been able to do so and presumably we shall never be able to do so, because were we to force the pound down any lower the working-class would discover for themselves that they were being impoverished through the rise in the prices of the things which they buy. It would not happen at once, but it would appear soon enough to cause trouble, probably within the first year of the change.

The same is not true of the United States; the American capitalist can see the dollar fall much further without fear of social friction, on the contrary, he is probably relieving social friction by such a fall. There are two reasons for this :—

The first is that so large a proportion of the American people are producers of primary products on the land, and their first interest is to raise the price in dollars of what they sell—they are little concerned with wages. The second reason is that the Americans being almost entirely self-sufficient, internal prices for their wage-slaves would not rise, for a long time at least, in proportion to the depreciation of the currency. Wheat, for instance, might be dearer, but by the time it was in the shape of bread on the artisan's table the lowered wages of those who had worked at transporting it, grinding it, baking it, etc., would make the price of the loaf less high in proportion than the price of wheat.

In general, the United States, or rather their great banking interests who are directing them for the moment, hold the trumps in this game that we are playing with our very lives. For if in the duel between the dollar and the pound they win in the near future, we shall be heavily embarrassed indeed.

But we have a chance of escape which is not to be neglected. It lies in this—that the English people are still politically the most united in the world : they will obey whatever direction they receive and even without knowing that they have received it; whereas among our rivals there is a lively public opinion, which the governing capitalist powers cannot ignore. We shall therefore in this country be able to manœuvre, at first, in security, the further lowering of wages—if lower them we must—by just so much and no more and carefully watching our game; while over there the demand for inflation may run away with them. For inflation makes everybody feel much richer for the moment and the temptation for democracies to inflate is sometimes irresistible.

If inflation does run away with them in America, their economic system will break down : but if their depreciation which has already begun is managed with anything like the skill with which we managed ours after the crisis of '31—then we cannot meet them. They hold the trumps. And therein lies the gravity of the present situation.

NOTES OF THE WEEK

Monday, May 15.

In more than one aspect the Nazi triumph in Germany did not mark a revolution at all but a faithful fulfilment of post-war developments. The past few weeks under Hitler have been a microcosm of fifteen years of diplomacy which began with the negotiation of the Armistice in the forest of Compiègne. The policy is to rely alternately upon hopes and threats, to make pledges and to break them, to create an atmosphere of tension during negotiations, to rely upon a threatening series of separate shocks, and all the while to pour out propaganda that Germany alone is the peaceful victim attacked by scheming neighbours. So in the past few weeks we have had Hitlerism plainly calling for arms and at the same time proclaiming peaceful intentions towards Poland. We have had Herr Rosenberg's idiotic mission of peace to London while Herr Nadolny was obstructing the London plan at Geneva. We are about to have—that inevitable device—a meeting of the Reichstag (which Hitler despises) as an outlet once more for propaganda that all of Germany's peaceful aspirations have been flouted. Meanwhile every doubtfully legal opportunity is exploited at Danzig; and although the explicit provisions of the treaties may be observed for some time to come (unless we overrate the Nazi sanity) there is no doubt that the series of shocks will continue so as to perpetuate an atmosphere of tension.

*   *   *   *

Present events in Danzig are also parts of a consistent series, as English people ought to have known long ago in the days when the truth about Danzig was obscured by German propaganda. At the Treaty of Versailles, Germany renounced all rights and titles over the territory of the Free City. Nevertheless, Berlin has persistently dictated the interior politics of the Free City and filled its official posts with Prussian bureaucrats. We may mention only the President of the Free State Senate, Dr. Sahm, who left that position to become Burgomaster of Berlin, *ob meritu*. Or we may mention the unjustifiable intrusion of Nazis, who take their orders from Hitler, into the political life of the Free City, which now they bid fair to control. This has created an intolerable atmosphere for the Poles who have their own limited rights over the Free City, but not until lately have the Prussian provocations been openly recognised by the rest of Europe. The attack upon the Danzig trade unions is another example of seizing upon an opportunity for creating tension, an opportunity which affords some shadow of legality; and everything depends upon the personality of the League Commissioner, who has considerable powers to call in outside assistance and considerable latitude of discretion. At present Mr. Rosting appears to be using his discretion; if he calls in outside assistance, Poland is foreseen as the probable military guarantor; and Poland would be in a difficult position if she occupied Danzig at this juncture. The probable reason for the present developments is that Berlin wishes to force Poland into this difficult position. Danzig would then be the martyred city of Germany.

*   *   *   *

In any event, the chances of war in Europe have been multiplied ten-fold. It may yet be avoided, for the Reich is not yet ready to strike though it certainly intends to do so at the earliest moment it can, but a situation has been created by which hostilities may be begun in spite of the irresponsible men now leading the Germans to disaster. In this paper, almost alone in the English Press, we have insisted upon the perils attaching to the almost uninterrupted support given by our foreign policy to the Prussians as against the Poles. The practical value of such warnings has had nothing to do with their moral value; it was obvious that morally our foreign policy was backing up the aggressor, but the practical point is that when or if hostilities shall begin England will in the long run be the principal sufferer. Now that a situation has been created which must sooner or later, and may at any moment, lead to war it is imperative that the public should grasp the danger into which the nation has drifted.

*   *   *   *

As in 1914, but with far less excuse, the authorities (the professional politicians of course, but also the more instructed permanent officials) have taken it for granted that they can keep out of hostilities and that no ill consequences will fall upon this country from an outbreak of war in Europe. Such an attitude is hardly sane. It shows a complete contempt for facts as they are. The control of Asiatic trade and of India, which is half the strength of this country, is already in jeopardy; and of all nations this nation alone has no margin left for further taxation and increased expenditure; and of all the nations this nation alone is dependent for its very food upon supplies from overseas—which supplies it can no longer secure, as it could a few years ago, by its own maritime power. There may yet be time for those who are responsible for the fate of the country to save us from the disaster that threatens, but the margin of safety will not be very much prolonged and unless there is a definite declaration of policy, and of intended action to support policy, that disaster will be upon us.

*   *   *   *

There has been no allusion that we know of in the English Press to what is perhaps the most important point of all in the German capitalist revolution. It appears, according to the account of one who is in favour of the Revolution and who has written supporting it in the *Universe*, that German capitalists can now not only dismiss a workman at will, through the crushing of the Trades Union organisations, but *can have any workman whom they choose to regard as*

subversive imprisoned indefinitely without trial. The statement (which is made by a responsible journalist attached to the *Cologne Gazette*) is quite explicit: the capitalist has only to denounce any workman as a Communist and that will be his fate. Of course any employee whom the capitalist may want to suppress or make an example of can be called a Communist and there is no publicity or evidence whatever. The man simply disappears. This is by far the worst enormity that has appeared in any western country since the war, and should be as widely known in England as possible. For it is a very great step forward towards the Servile State.

*   *   *   *

Mr. Ramsbotham, M.P., must be added to the growing list of those who have begun to lose such faith as they may have had in the Big Unit and Mass-Production. Assuming (as the Parliamentary Secretary to the Board of Education is bound to assume) that education makes for intelligence; he realises that an intelligent man is not inclined to pass his life as an unskilled factory-hand; and he foresees a coming reversion to " smaller industrial units and more individual work" in the more civilised countries, while mass-production will be relegated to countries where the workers are still at the coolie level. The idea is an interesting one: we may yet live to hear the streets of Wigan humming, like an Indian bazaar, with all the sounds of infinitely varied industry, while the only surviving power-looms are to be found in Bombay and Osaka. But possibly this picture is not altogether so fantastic as it sounds.

Fresh Fields

IT is nonsense to regard a dirty and congested social system that is little more than a century old, as permanently essential to human happiness and forever unchangeable. The system of herding people in large towns, forcing them to live on the smallest possible wage that they will accept without revolt, giving them the alternative of working for the anonymous masters of the cartels and combines, with intervals of doing nothing on the dole, or starving to death, is a rotten system.

It will be equally rotten when the same system is taken over by the state and called the Dictatorship of the Proletariat; because the proletariat is never allowed to dictate. The employed man, under any system, does as he is told, and puts up with what he gets, kicking feebly and peevishly now and then to remind himself that he is a human being. It is nonsense to say that the mass of ordinary decent men and women, the bulk of the population of this country, will put up with such a system indefinitely for the sake of the movies and canned jazz. As the present economic condition of this country shows no signs of mending, or, more likely, gets worse, we shall see an accelerating drift from the towns to the country.

As these words are being written, a press report is to hand (for what press reports are worth) to the effect that in America (the other great victim of excessive urban concentration) " it is estimated that more than 1,000,000 people have gone back to farms each year since 1930." " The farm population of Oklahoma has increased by 75,000 since the 1931 census." "Seventy per cent. of the Texas unemployed have signified their desire to go ' back to the land.' " A most significant sentence in this press item, an unconscious indication of the mind of the journalist, and typical of most peoples' minds on this matter, is as follows: " *With the general town-to-country exodus, a survey has shown that country folk are reverting to their former independence. Country ' sociables ' and schoolhouse ' box suppers ' are again the order of the farm family's life.*" Of course, they order things queerly in America, but they are still human. And the fundamentals of this matter are common to human nature everywhere.

The drift from town to country in Britain is as yet slow but it is positive and increasing. So far it has no official encouragement. The destitute unemployed of the towns have no means of moving their homes and settling in the country, though some of them have tramped out into the country seeking odd jobs on the farms. But farmworkers themselves are unemployed owing to the depression of agriculture, leaving little room for newcomers. Now that there are some signs of an agricultural revival this condition of things may be mended somewhat in the future.

Meanwhile there are very many unemployed in the towns who are not included in the official figures of unemployed because they have not come within the scope of the unemployment insurance scheme. Their position is even more desperate than that of the workers in the grades below them because they cannot draw a dole. When they are unemployed they are completely destitute once they have exhausted their savings or raised what little money they can on their small personal possessions. In this class suffering is acute. A certain sense of personal dignity and independence prevents them from applying for poor-law relief, which indeed they cannot get until they have reduced themselves to utter destitution. It is amongst this class that there is a desire and willingness to work on the land, however hard and unaccustomed the conditions, rather than seek state relief, sponge on their friends, or starve with their families. Numbers of these stalwarts venture into the countryside whilst they still retain a little capital, feeling that they can at least grow a fair proportion of their own food.

To this class must be added many of their fellows who have not yet lost their employment but are daily expecting to do so, as a consequence of some new amalgamation or ' economy ' or the bankruptcy of their employers. Then again there are many members of the professional classes whose incomes are decreasing rapidly with the decrease in their clients' incomes —some of them are beginning to eat into their capital and savings and feel that it would be a sound plan to " dig themselves in " in the country, where they may have at least a fair chance of securing a reasonable amount of wholesome food from their own small bit of land.

It is in times of economic distress like the present that men begin to put first things first and realise that food and shelter, self-respect and independence, are fundamentally more important than the fal-lals of the town:

" *Fate cannot touch me: I have dined to-day.*"

The Jews
By Hilaire Belloc

SOME years ago, shortly after the War, I wrote a book with the title of " The Jews." Many of my friends when they heard that I was going to write it begged me to pause before running so fearful a risk—the most dreadful things were going to happen to me if I were to break the taboo. I was to be boycotted, imprisoned, starved, maligned, all sorts of other things all at once. Such is the terror inspired by Israel, and very comic it is to watch its effects.

Then there was another group of advisers, and a good deal larger, who gave me to understand that anyone writing on the Jewish question wrote himself down by so doing as a fool, a crank, or even lunatic. But I knew all about that, so I paid little attention to it.

When you come to think of it, what an extraordinary thing it is that this one interesting public question should, in this one country of England be treated in so absurd a fashion! Of course there has been a close understanding between our commercial-aristocratic state and the Jews ever since the 17th. century; most of our great families have Jewish blood by this time, and it has always been taken for granted that support of the Jews was as much part of patriotism as persecution of the Irish. But even allowing for that, I cannot think that there is any sense in the old taboo of silence. It was not required by decency, nor was it to the advantage of country. Praise Jews by all means: worship them if you like. But why pretend that they aren't there at all?

Anyhow, I published my book, which bore the motto (in Hebrew), " Peace to Israel," and the thesis of which was very simple and clear. It was to this effect:—

There is a grave problem everywhere in the modern world called " The Jewish Problem," and it arises from two facts in combination: one, the fact that a particular race with strongly marked characteristics and a strong feeling of racial solidarity among themselves is spread at large throughout the world; second, the fact that as a rule there is friction between the members of this race and the members of the other races among whom they find themselves.

Here are two facts which you can no more deny than you can deny the Great War, or the sun and moon. They are perfectly plain truths, and they are important because it is self-evident that between them they create a grave problem. They create a grave problem because there necessarily arises through them the danger of cruel and senseless attacks upon the Jews which do a double harm: they obviously do harm to the Jews themselves, and they lead to widespread and long-enduring antagonism against the people who persecute them.

I said that the principal factor in the problem was the conclusion which the Jews appear to have reached, that their best policy is one of concealment. And it is here that what is special to my thesis came in; for the rest of it consisted simply of plain facts which people elaborately pretended to be non-existent but knew very well to be true. Is it better for the Jews themselves and for the world that this elaborate pretence should be gone through that the Jews are not Jews but Englishmen, or Frenchmen or Irishmen, or what not? Many people think it *is* better so. In England at that time nearly everybody thought it better; and I think most people think it better even to-day. Now I maintain that on the whole the policy is not a good one, and that it would be a much better thing to base ourselves on truth, to admit the existence of the separate race, give it a special position of its own, and frankly and openly discuss the dangers which beset it and the best way of avoiding them.

It was astonishing to note what a hubbub this simple proposition of well-known truths and of quite clear, though debatable, policy produced. I got masses of letters denouncing me for that kind of lunatic called an anti-Semite. One magistrate in America denounced me in public when I visited the United States ten years ago as a man who ought to be deported, and one of their leading publicists accused me of writing with what he called " a poison pen." I discovered this to mean in the local idiom a piece of writing which says one thing while suggesting another; something like our English proverb, " Don't nail his ears to the post."

Now my thesis may have been right or wrong; there is a great deal to be said against it. It is perfectly true, for instance, that Jews loyally serve through the greater part of their lives the country in which they live and in much the greater part of circumstances act as other citizens do. In fact one may say they always so act except when they feel their own security attacked. It is also true that long habit and association give them a great deal in common with the other races among whom they live. I for one believe that the feeling of affection which they have for their surroundings, though perhaps not as strong as ours, has a considerable strength, and that when they express it it is genuine. They possibly feel it more strongly for one kind of society than another; but still, there is a sense in which one can say that Disraeli was an Englishman or that the generous Doctor Rothschild is a Frenchman. There is nothing untrue or grotesque in calling one English and the other French. And in the same way one may say that Signor Sonnino was an Italian. Also, it may be argued with great force that conventions involving a proportion of falsehood are often useful and necessary. The convention which prevents, for instance, lese-majesté; the convention which makes us wear clothes; the convention by which we ask sympathetically after the health of people of whom we care not a rap whether they are flourishing or in agony.

But the point about my little book, which I think did a good deal of good in its way, the point which I would recall now, in 1933, was a certain prophecy which it contained. It is unwise to prophesy—and nine times out of ten it is actually silly. It is a habit I have avoided in my writing, because I have always appreciated what a fool a man looked when his prophesy did not come off. Thus though during the War I wrote millions of words on the operations I never allowed myself one prophecy of what the future would show, save, I regret to say, the risky one that Bulgaria would be the first to break away from the enemy coalition. I happened to prove right—but I

ought to have said that it was probable, not that it was certain.

Now in this matter of the Jews also I did make a prophecy, because it seemed to me so certain that it could be predicted, as one predicates the necessary consequence of observed physical facts. I said that sooner or later there was bound to be an explosion against the Jews in this or that white, western country as yet not to be decided. I said that the 19th century convention could not be indefinitely maintained, the strain was too great and the lie too enormous: where the crack would come I could not tell, but that it would come somewhere I was pretty certain. All the past was there, to prove the unhappy cycle of the Jews, persecuted in one country, received as welcome immigrants in another where the persecution was denounced, and then in time getting at loggerheads with their new hosts and suffering a new persecution. Indeed it was because this was so obviously the teaching of history that I drew my conclusion, and said that the only way of breaking that wretched cycle of cause and effect was openly admitting their difference and giving the Jews a special position of their own.

Well, the prophecy has come off. The old Hohenzollern prophecy of the Middle Ages is reported to conclude abruptly with the accusation that the Jews would be to blame for the breakdown of the Hohenzollerns and would pay for that act with their lives. " *Israël infandum . . . morte piandum.*" Whether there really be any such mediæval prophecy I know not, though I have seen the reported printed text of it.

The present trouble is an effect of the Dreyfus case at long range. The new Prussian revolutionaries have access to all the archives: they know what a Jewish agitation may work against a nation and did work against France and the French army; they already ascribed to the Jews the evils Prussia had suffered through her own fault, they feared to suffer as France had suffered, and the result is before us.

My prophecy has come off. And the culprits in this case are the Prussians.

I do not think that the way in which the Jews have been treated by Prussia, abominable as it is, will lead to any particularly bad consequences for Prussia itself. I think that if Prussia gets into trouble it will be through her own grotesquely swollen head and her consequent total misunderstanding of her true position among national forces to-day. Already I see the Jews throughout the press of the world making excuses for Prussia; and I note that no great Jewish banker has suffered at the hands of the Prussians—which is significant! I also note that the great Frankfort paper which is the chief expression of Jewish policy in Europe welcomes the new Prussian régime.

But I do think that one important consequence will follow from the abominable actions of these hysterical fools in Protestant Germany. I think that they have brought the Jewish question out into the open, and that it will remain there. In so far as they have done that, good will come out of evil: for I am still convinced, as I was all those years ago, that the conventional falsehood upon the Jewish question, especially as practised in this country, much as there was to be said for it, is bad policy as well as bad morals.

Straws in the Wind

WHO IS DICTATOR?
By G. K. CHESTERTON

I HAD already sent in my last week's article, pointing out that there is a case for Hitlerism and certainly a case against the critics of Hitlerism, before I saw Mr. Michael Derrick's very interesting and suggestive letter published in the same issue. I trust this fact will convince him that I did not even need his intelligent stimulation to make me do justice to a system which I think in other ways is unjust. But the question which Mr. Derrick raises remains in another way rather questionable. Briefly and broadly, it is his thesis that Hitler's raving appeals to racial pride and hatred and (what is worse) contempt, were assumed entirely out of policy in order to ensure popularity. All the time, he had within the tranquil glow of an ideal of international friendship, and felt nothing but the charity and humility of a true Catholic towards his fellow-Catholics and his fellow-creatures. Thus, when he told the Germans that their outlet was choked by " the lousy Poles," it was merely for convenience that he chose this form of expressing his affection for Poland; and when he indicated, in the same sentence, the well-known fact that Frenchmen are Negroes, and (worse still) are afflicted with Militarism, he did but dissemble his love in the manner of Hamlet, by wilfully pretending to be insane. Perhaps the last accusation, by the way, is the most interesting of all. Blackness is a matter of taste; the Ethopian visages of Foch and Poincaré and Maurras and Maritain rise before our memories with varied effect according to our moods. But to think that any nation should defile itself by Militarism! To suppose that any Prussian Imperialist or German patriot could be expected to pardon that!

Now I do not mean to sneer at Mr. Derrick's explanation, when I say that it is really rather a difficult business to recast one's opinions of a man, on the avowed principle that he meant the opposite of what he said. But there is another difficulty raised by this theory; and it is really my own difficulty in the whole matter. It might be expressed by saying that it is not merely the question of whether Hitler is entirely Prussianist, but of whether the new Prussianism is entirely Hitler. For on this point we must follow Mr. Derrick's argument carefully. In effect, it is this; that Prussianism in Prussia was so strong, so stiff, so rooted, so ineradicable and incurable, that any man hoping to have any hearing was forced to begin by flattering it. He was cœrced into talking nonsense about lousy foreigners, because if he had dared to say a word of Christian common sense, the Prussian pride and prejudice would have been strong enough to crush and silence him. Now this may or may not be true; but if it is true, it raises another serious question. If the old narrow Prussianism was as strong as that a few months ago, is it not possible that it is as strong as that still? If the Catholic and humane Hitler was forced to obey it then, is it not possible that he will be forced to obey it now? And though he himself may have abused the Poles without any

desire to attack the Poles, may not the most militaristic gang in Europe, the old guard of the Junkers, determine on their own account to attack Poland, and over-rule the remonstrances of Hitler by quotations from the eloquent and moving speeches in which he has himself abused Poland? In other words, the question is, even if Germany is a Dictatorship, who is really the Dictator? And surely we may be allowed to doubt whether the Dictator must of necessity be the same man, whom his own admirers and defenders excuse as having talked entirely at the dictation of somebody else. A Dictator may be all sorts of things, good or bad. But a Dictator is not dictated to; and Hitler was dictated to, even by Mr. Derrick's own version of his story.

In short, the difficulty is that the powers and influences are indeterminate; and that is in another way the difficulty of the whole German problem; and what makes the Hitlerite problem different, for instance, from the Fascist problem. Hitler has not risen to power by enunciating a certain theory of the State; certainly not by any of the very excellent later experiments, in which he has shown the increasing influence of the Distributist State. He has admittedly risen by appealing to racial pride; and the racial pride of the Germans really is a rather peculiar thing, and different from normal patriotism or even Jingoism. Its frontiers, for instance, are curiously vague and shifting. Mr. Derrick asks why a man should not desire to restore order in his own country. But Hitler did not restore order in his own country. He went to what would normally be called a foregin country, except that it was linked up by some loose theories about Aryans and Teutons and the heathen worshippers of the Swastika. In this sort of anthropological atmosphere, what is his own country? Where *is* the German's Fatherland? Or rather, where is it not?

If it happened to be convenient to Hitler to annex two English counties, as it was convenient to Moltke to annex two French provinces, he could annex Norfolk and Suffolk without calling a blush of Aryan blood to his cheek. Are they not the North Folk and the South Folk? Are not their very names in the true-hearted German folk-speech spoken? If ever that situation arose, it would be quite useless for you and me to say that Nelson was a Norfolk man; and that it is infernal nonsense to say that Nelson was a German. A hundred professors would leap up to explain that Nelson was true, valiant, a Viking, a sea-saga's-hero, and therefore obviously was a German . . . Do you think that is fantastic? It is not one shade more fantastic than, it is indeed identical with, the claim actually made by Germans to the whole province of Lorraine. I have seen long and learned German arguments, showing that Joan of Arc was a German; because she was brave and true and pious and lived in Lorraine. A young woman lives and dies to crown the French King in the French shrine, fights under the French oriflamme to clear the French soil of foreigners; and the German professors say she was a German. The German soldiers agree with the German professors; or rather the German professors agree with the German soldiers. The German soldiers ruled for fifty years in Lorraine: and they may yet land in Norfolk. That is the sort of thing I am troubled about; not the precise balance of the theories of Dictatorship and Distributism in the mind of one man, who has admittedly expressed all sorts of other ideas in an entirely unbalanced manner. I can quite believe that Hitler has his good points; I know that he has his good policies. But admittedly, he disguised his policies out of policy; and who dictated that policy? I want to know whether the old Prussia is still leading the Germanies. If she is, I know that she will lead them into war.

The Smallholder's Prospects
By G. C. Heseltine

Better boil herbs, thou toiler after gain!
                    Theocritus, Idyll X.

BETTER boil anything, even your head, than toil after gain on a smallholding. Large holdings in Throgmorton Street are a more sensible proposition for toilers after gain, but even they are no more bound to succeed than smallholdings at the other end of Watling Street are bound to fail. But when you have toiled after gain in vain, or you are no longer allowed to toil after gain, not even after somebody else's gain, you may think it better to boil herbs than to stew in your own juice; especially if they are your own herbs. You are far more likely to boil herbs successfully on a smallholding than on 'Change.

If, on the other hand, instead of toiling after gain you wish to do a little honest business, and trade hard work for a healthy independent life, a man's life, you will get your full money's worth on a smallholding. That is to say, if you work hard enough, and intelligently enough, you will get the abundant living which is your due. If your efforts are not worth much, you will not get much: you will fail.

There are those who will tell you that smallholdings are a failure. It is just as true to say that banks are failures, butchers' shops are failures, or publishing businesses are failures. Except that smallholdings are never quite the failures that the other ventures are when they fail. For the smallholding does the smallholder some good honestly, even when he fails to make a financial success of it. And it does the country some good because more food has been produced on it than if the land were left idle, or worked in a more extensive and less concentrated manner by a general farmer. Smallholders sometimes fail for the same reasons that men fail at other ways of making a living. But on the whole the proportion of smallholders that fail is small. Smallholders nearly always fail to make fortunes, but few of them fail to make a living. There are exceptions. Mr. Montague Fordham, in his very interesting book "Britain's Trade and Agriculture" (1932, Geo. Allen and Unwin, 7/6), tells of a smallholder in the Fen country who ' con-

fessed to having made £15,000 in a very few years,' whether honestly or not we are not told, but you are not remotely likely to repeat that feat. That smallholder told of how, not very long ago, he had had twenty acres of potatoes, got ten tons per acre, and sold them for ten pounds a ton—he got £2,000 for that one crop, and certainly pocketed £1,000 profit, probably a good deal more. On the other hand, a neighbouring farmer, a year or two later, told of how he sold his last crop of potatoes for £1 a ton, and thought himself lucky to get it.

Mr. F. N. Blundell, himself a landowner and farmer, in his book " A New Policy for Agriculture " (Philip Allan and Co., 1931, 7/6), says " Small holders are, in fact, making a living where large farmers are unable to do so (Report of the Work of the Land Division of the Ministry of Agriculture for 1924). The percentage of failures, where properly selected men have been placed on properly selected land, has not been high. The Report of a certain Smallholdings Committee to a County Council for February 1931 mentions that arrears of rent since ' the 1926 valuation ' amounted to £177 12s. 10d. on a total rent roll of £13,489, or 1.31%. Of how many private estates of comparable size could the same be said?

" There are districts in which the proportion of failures has been considerable and others in which it has been very small. But, taking all the schemes together, it would probably be true to say that the failures are much less numerous than in any of the postwar settlement schemes overseas. If the failures were analysed, it would be found that the cause lay, not in the size of the holdings, but in the unsuitability of the man or of the land. The pages of the *County Councils' Gazette* in 1929 and 1930, in which accounts are given of the experience of different counties, bear witness to the truth of what has been written above. They also supply much evidence that townsmen, without previous experience, are making good."

Beware, by the way, of taking too much notice of figures and statistics on the subject of smallholdings (such as those referred to by Mr. Blundell and indicated in the County Councils' Gazette). Figures are often misleading, firstly because of the recent wide fluctuations in values, secondly because they are never the whole story, thirdly because in the hands of the expert they can be used to prove anything. That is by the way.

The important point about Mr. Blundell's view is that he considers smallholdings on the whole successful, and he emphasises the very important point about the right man for the job.

In this, his opinion is confirmed by general experience. Viscount Lymington, in his highly readable and interesting book " Horn, Hoof and Corn " (1932, Faber and Faber, 6/-) says: " The preliminary requisites for success *lie in having the right men and their wives for the work and then in having first of all, the right type of agriculture for smallholding. . .*" and again: " Smallholdings must depend then, not on theory or prejudice, but on the opportunity for the right man to be a smallholder, and on the right place being chosen for him in which to own his smallholding." Observe the word " own."

One more word on this point from Mr. Blundell:

" On the credit side of the smallholdings there is much to be said. New capital values are created in the country, and new rateable values. In the case of one smallholdings scheme it was estimated that the increased rateable value was equal to the proportion of loss borne by the county concerned. The smallholder, even more than the large farmer, is a customer for the home manufacturer. He does not want the immense machines manufactured in the U.S.A. or Canada; he wants the smaller plant manufactured at home. He wants the implements he can see and buy in local shops."

Smallholdings have been variously defined. A hundred acres begins to be a small farm. Most holdings are not more than fifty acres, a very large number under ten. A man has been known to make a good living on a holding of one acre, but you are not likely to do it

The yield per acre on smallholdings is much higher than that on general farms, and the labour expended per acre must be higher also. Conditions vary so widely on smallholdings that statistics are generally misleading. The size of your holding will depend on the capital you have for buying it, the locality and quality of the land, and what you propose to do on it.

Rough pasture and waste land that is of very little value to the general farmer may be used to good advantage by the smallholder for pigs, poultry, and goats, for example. Such land can be bought or rented cheaply.

Hitherto, smallholders have been discouraged and handicapped by a depressed and declining state of agriculture in general. If they have succeeded against such odds, the prospects of smallholders under an agricultural revival are good.

In Memorandum

By F. Keston Clarke

IN response to innumerable requests that I should desist, I have much pleasure in publishing further otiose and irrelevant extracts from my notebook. First, however, let me say a few words about myself. It was on an evening of early Spring, back in far-off 1897 . . .

Oh.

All right. But let me tell you this, you scoffers. If the memoirs and diaries and autobiographies and collected correspondences and reminiscences and impressions and personal recollections and intimate revelations and inner glimpses and piquant sidelights and exclusive confessions of the footling and worthless lives of practised publicity-hogs that issue from the publishers by the daily ton, at two guineas a quarter-hundredweight, were one-tenth as vital and vivid as mine, I would break the vow I made fourteen years ago and read them. And I can't say fairer than that. *Dixi.* (Latin for saucepan.)

*   *   *   *

Observation. Contemporary craze for undressing and bathing with or without water. Makers of soap and of hot-water systems state nation cannot possibly be healthy, strong and energetic unless it spends hours a day simmering gently in slipper-baths and slubbing

its bodies with suds and scented fats. Nudists say even this insufficient; we must also lie about naked at odd times and odder places in order to become straight-souled and sinewy-limbed. Obvious that what with the ever-increasing proportion of our lives taken up by education, athletics, washing, vocational training, sun-bathing, mind-strengthening, soul-stretching, vitamin-absorbing, patent-medicine taking and Preparing For Higher Posts, soon nothing whatever will be done because we are all too busy getting fit and ready to do it. Most curious point is that if there is one thing that men and women of the most inspiring and adventurous types have had in common throughout ages it is dirt; just ordinary comfortable homely Dirt. Primitive Greeks and Romans (not late degenerates)—Normans –– Elizabethans — Victorians; warriors — priests; poets—artists; queens—dames—beauty and power; disputers of Oxford and old Sorbonne; seamen — adventurers; counsellors — kings; all greatest moulders of world's destinies have been Great Unwashed, and in many cases definitely lousy. Two propositions incontrovertible : —

(a) Nation not been so well-tubbed and hygienically-clad for a thousand years.

(b) Not for thousand years has n. been so generally neurotic, inefficient, listless and mentally and morally incapable.

Comment would be an impertinence. Henceforth I am determined to wear my clothes until they fall off. They always do anyway.

*   *   *   *

Si monumentum requiris. At Runnymede on Thames-side, there is a pleasant grassy tract which, according to local legend (doubtless inaccurate) belonged of old time to the people of Egham. Later it was taken away from the people of Egham and given to the National Trust, who put a few curious buildings where there never had been buildings before, and gave it back to the people of Egham, who were— and still are—wretchedly ungrateful. Not that it matters. But the buildings include four pylons or obelisks or cenotaphs—four big stones anyway; and each stone is carved on two sides. There are two inscriptions, each of which thus appears four times.

1. *In these meads on the 15th of June 1215 King John at the instance of deputies from the whole community of the realm granted the great charter, the earliest of constitutional documents, whereunder ancient and cherished customs were confirmed, abuses redressed, the administration of justice facilitated, new provision formulated for the preservation of peace, and every individual perpetually secured in the free enjoyment of his life and property.*

2. " In perpetual memory of Urban Hanlon Broughton 1857-1929 of Park Close Englefield Green in the County of Surrey sometime Member of Parliament, these meadows of historic interest, on 18th December 1929 were gladly offered to the nation by his widow Cara Lady Fairhaven and his sons Huttleston Lord Fairhaven and Henry Broughton."

*   *   *   *

Jolly bad luck.

*   *   *   *

Dates to Remember : 1870 Education Act . . . ditto 1876 . . . ditto 1880 . . . ditto 1891 . . . ditto 1897

. . . Board of Education Act 1899 . . . Education Act 1902 . . . Lots of Acts, 1906, 1907, 1910, 1914. Fisher's Act 1918. Consolidation 1921 . . . War, 1914-18, abolished class distinctions. 1918-1932, public school and university men flocking into Police Force. Educated democracy is the hall-mark of the age. 1933 . . . Police Chief reports constables uneducated; ranker officer system, all right before compulsory education began, now no good. Immediate action by Government.

In view of admitted efficiency of State education and failure of Public Schools, it is confidently predicted that in future 'varsity and Public-school men will have to stay in the ranks while educated democracy cools its tea with its hat at Scotland Yard.

*   *   *   *

Meanwhile, the growing habit in America of calling off the police while thugs and victims carry on direct negotiation, inspires the hope that soon it will be possible to jail the police and hand over administration to gangsters. (Loud cheers.)

*   *   *   *

Further Educational Note. Met that Mrs. Quelch this morning; she very upset, trouble with servants as usual. Poor creature been abroad many years, can't adapt herself to the modern menial. "What do you think?" says she. "Yesterday at dinner Samuel and I wanted to discuss something rather private, so of course when the servants were in the room we continued our conversation in French, just as we used to do when we lived in Cheltenham in '07. And would you believe it, every time we went off into French, the *wretched* butler and maid began talking to each other in very loud Latin; a language I *never* could make head or tail of. Such impertinence! Really, Keston, the lower classes are getting simply *frightful*. I almost hope that terrible man Mosley gets power. He'd castor-oil 'em, which isn't very nice but what *are* you to do with such *malignant* intellectualism?"

Personally, whenever the scullions are about, the missus and I continue our confidences across the table, using the tic-tac language employed at the races. Until that also becomes an optional Matric. subject we are quite safe.

*   *   *   *

From a recent official message sent by President Roosevelt to the Prime Minister of Great Britain:

"Do come and spend a week-end with me. I am sure that in a week-end we can do more for God than has been done for a long time."

*   *   *   *

God: "Really—I—this is too——"
Roosevelt: "Not at all, my dear fellow. Don't mention it."

*   *   *   *

Life goes On. Heart-cry from any popular newspaper, any Sunday morning: *Is Faith Dead?*

Moving Appeal from any preacher, any Sunday evening: *Can Faith Be Revived?*

I should worry. I have before me a carton of "Chipmunk." According to the advertisements, "Chipmunk" builds body, bone and brain; is 100% vitamin, is positively essential in infancy and is three-quarters of the battle of life. It is the greatest dis-

covery in dietetic science of this century and is destined to supersede all other food.

Now, "Chipmunk" looks like bran, smells like bran, feels like bran, tastes like bran, and in my opinion *is* bran. Its sales are colossal.

Well, I'm no authority on Faith, but, as Grinder C. J. remarked in *Chawl v. Chobble*, "A nod's as good as a wink to a packed jury."

*   *   *   *

Intelligence Test. All the following questions should be answered within three weeks:

1.—Is it true to say that the average bankruptcy is caused more by good luck than good management?

2.—If the British can't do what they dam well like in Moscow, what is the meaning of Empire day?

3.—Which cross-Channel steward first remarked: "Heave away, my hearties"?

4.—Which celebrated boating song is funny without being Volga?

5.—Assuming that a person is liable to be compulsorily (*a*) Castor-oiled in Italy; (*b*) Sterilised in Germany; (*c*) De-tonsilled in England; (*d*) Vaccinated in America; (*e*) Inoculated in Japan; and (*f*) Circumcised in Palestine, what is the average expectation of life among future professional globe-trotters?

6.—What do you suppose is the Intelligence Quotient of people who think up Intelligence Tests?

YEARS   AGO

[From time to time we propose to publish under this heading quotations from speeches and writings which seem to have a special significance after a lapse of years. Some of these quotations are from the works of men who were essentially in agreement with the views expressed in this paper. Others may cause surprise in view of the causes with which the authors were identified. Readers are invited to suggest suitable items.

The following paragraphs form the humble petition of the Rev. Sydney Smith to the House of Congress at Washington, written ninety years ago to-day. They suggest to-day that if the States concerned were to pay what they owe, with nominal compound interest (say two per cent.) it might be possible for this country to afford the balance without further argument.]

"I PETITION your honourable House to institute some measures for the restoration of American credit, and for the repayment of debts incurred and repudiated by several of the States. Your petitioner lent to the State of Pennsylvania a sum of money, for the purpose of some public improvement. The amount, though small, is to him important, and is a saving from a life income, made with difficulty and privation. If their refusal to pay (from which a very large number of English families are suffering) had been the result of war, produced by the unjust aggression of powerful enemies; if it had arisen from civil discord; if it had proceeded from an improvident application of means in the first years of self-government; if it were the act of a poor State struggling against the barrenness of nature—every friend of America would have been content to wait for better times; but the fraud is committed in the profound peace of Pennsylvania, by the richest State in the Union, after the wise investment of the borrowed money in roads and canals, of which the repudiators are every day reaping the advantage. It is an act of bad faith which (all its circumstances considered) has no parallel, and no excuse.

" Nor is it only the loss of property which your Petitioner laments; he laments still more that immense power which the bad faith of America has given to aristocratical opinions, and to enemies of free institutions, in the old world. It is in vain any longer to appeal to history, and to point out the wrongs which the many have received from the few. The Americans, who boast to have improved the institutions of the old world, have at least equalled its crimes. A great nation, after trampling under foot all earthly tyranny, has been guilty of a fraud as enormous as ever disgraced the worst king of the most degraded nation in Europe.

" It is most painful to your Petitioner to see that American citizens excite, wherever they may go, the recollection that they belong to a dishonest people, who pride themselves on having tricked and pillaged Europe; and this mark is fixed by their faithless legislators on some of the very best and most honourable men in the world, whom every Englishman has been eager to see and proud to receive.

" It is a subject of serious concern to your Petitioner that you are losing all that power which the friends of freedom rejoiced that you possessed, looking upon you as the ark of human happiness, and the most splendid picture of justice and of wisdom that the world had yet seen. Little did the friends of America expect it, and sad is the spectacle to see you rejected by every State in Europe, as a nation with whom no contract can be made, because none will be kept; unstable in the very foundations of social life, deficient in the elements of good faith, men who prefer any load of infamy however great, to any pressure of taxation however light.

" Nor is it only this gigantic bankruptcy for so many degrees of latitude and longitude which your Petitioner deplores, but he is alarmed also by that total want of shame with which these things have been done; the callous immorality with which Europe has been plundered, that deadness of the moral sense which seems to preclude all return to honesty, to perpetuate this new infamy, and to threaten its extension to every State in the Union.

" To any man of real philanthropy, who receives pleasure from the improvements of the world, the repudiation of the public debts of America, and the shameless manner in which it has been talked of and done, is the most melancholy event which has happened during the existence of the present generation. Your Petitioner sincerely prays that the great and good men still existing among you may, by teaching to the United States the deep disgrace they have incurred in the whole world, restore them to moral health, to that high position they have lost, and which, for the happiness of mankind, it is so important they should ever maintain; for the United States are now working out the greatest of all political problems, and upon that confederacy the eyes of thinking men are intensely fixed, to see how far the mass of mankind can be trusted with the management of their own affairs, and the establishment of their own happiness."

Ploughshares Into Swords

THE GERMAN PARADOX. *By A. Plutynski. Wishart. 6s.*

THE story goes that Hitler will break down the large estates of East Prussia into peasant holdings. The further statement is often made that Hitler will thereby destroy the power of the Junkers. The simplicity of these forecasts is deceptive; they do in fact involve the basic contradictions of recent German history, the paradoxes of recent German policy, which M. Plutynski here examines in the light of official statistics and reports. The agriculture of Germany, the agriculture of Eastern Germany, and the management of East Prussia in particular, are at the very heart of the complicated economic problem facing Hitler to-day. It is worth noticing that in many respects the economic tendencies of Germany run parallel with the economic tendencies of these islands, so that over and over again M. Plutynski's analyses apply directly to Great Britain. The book should certainly be read by everyone interested in the contemporary movements of Germany, but also it should be read by everyone who is fighting for the restoration of agriculture in this country.

East Prussia, to take that aspect of the problem first, is a distinct province (known to German historians as a *Kolonialland* or *Kolonialstaat* before there was question of complaint about its territorial separation from the Reich) with a poor soil and a sparse population. Since the industrialisation of Germany began there has been a constant flight from the land, away from this eastern province towards the industrial regions of the west; a movement unwittingly encouraged by German social legislation in the interests of the factory operative.

But East Prussia is also the source of Prussian patriotism, the stronghold of the Prussian ruling class and the pathetic Cinderella of the German lands since the Treaty of Versailles, to be supported at all costs against an imagined threat of invasion. Consequently, after the war, the East Prussian interests still ruling in Berlin used the province as the meeting-point of many policies. The Junkers, who conducted the war in partnership with the industrial clique, attributed defeat to a shortage of food and pointed to the German East as the destined granary of the Reich. At the same time a school of economists was preaching the doctrine of self-sufficiency, especially of autarchy in foodstuffs; and so the policy was initiated of placing very heavy duties upon all foodstuffs from outside. This went together with a policy of subsidy for East Prussia, so as to keep the standard of living of that poor agricultural province artificially level with the standard of living in the industrial west. The Junkers were to be " quids in " from the taxpayers of the rest of Germany, and the subsidies were abused, as the hastily suppressed disclosures of the Osthilfe scandals recently showed.

The Junkers and the industrial clique were now using a policy dictated by a desire for revenge, but using it for their own interests. Their demand for a restoration of agriculture was also a demand for the mechanisation of agriculture, after the deceptive example of Canada and the U.S.A., with the result that the iron industry benefited and the desertion of the land by East Prussians became more noticeable. The chemical industry was equally benefited by the increased use of artificial fertilisers. Germany secured the leadership of the world in the production of synthetic nitrogen and a virtual monopoly in the potash industry. The re-constitution of plant was achieved during the inflation period and by private capital attracted into Germany afterwards in huge sums at high rates of interest.

The policy was so far successful that two of Germany's most powerful war industries, iron and chemicals, were helped by the cry for the restoration of agriculture. The high agricultural tariffs also did their part in shutting out the foodstuffs of the Vistula and Danube valleys; but for the same reason the people of Eastern Europe were unable to buy Germany's industrial products. (Here is one of many contributory causes of the present collapse in European trade.) The mechanisation and chemical exploitation of agriculture within Germany meant in its turn that agriculture was paying a subsidy to industry; the flight from the land meant an increase in the town population; an increased town population adopted what is called a higher standard of living, using tea in greater quantity and rejecting rye bread (the rye grown in East Prussia) for wheat bread (the wheat imported under tariff from the Argentine). East Prussian rye then began to be exported overseas under bonus—another subsidy for East Prussia and another burden for the taxpayer of the Reich, already impoverished by increased social charges and higher prices due to the tariff policy.

In large measure, then, the economic distress of Germany has been due to long concentration upon the interests of East Prussia, a northerly province of slight natural resources, at the bidding of the war clique, who have penalised the agriculture of Eastern Europe, the agriculture of Germany itself, and by a logical process the very industry of Germany, for its own private advantage and to satisfy a desire for revenge. Here is a pretty commentary upon ten years of Republican "pacifism"; a commentary also upon the frequent prophecy that Hitler will be able to outwit the Junkers and the industrialists. They could not easily be shaken off by Hitler, and they will not be shaken off by Hitler so long as he also is inspired by the motive of revenge.

It is, however, conceivable that Hitler is already damned just because the dictated economic policy of the Reich runs counter to natural developments. On the gamble of war he may win anything or lose anything. But if he attempts to consolidate his position by masterly statesmanship through a short period of peace he will become increasingly the victim of economic contradictions, so long at least as he preserves the older forms of European life; with Bolshevik methods of confiscation and forced labour he may be more successful for a time. Whatever Hitler does, some of the paradoxes pointed out by M. Plutynski must persist, chief among them the political attempt to direct the German population

eastward while all the time it is naturally moving westward. The mighty efforts of Bismarck and Bülow, with the help of the *Ostmarkenverein* and a policy of subsidies, never arrested the desertion of the "German East"; it has gone on steadily since the war to the tune of 20,000 emigrants per year out of East Prussia alone. The bare eastern provinces have no attraction for the German from the south or west, while a policy of subsidies has only corrupted the patriotism of the subsidised.

It would be an ideal solution if East Prussia could become a province of peasants and find its own economic level. On this point, which concerns all the industrialised countries, M. Plutynski is particularly interesting, for a flight from the land is as noticeable as a reluctance to return to it. He quotes Dr. Hainisch, the former President of Austria, in the statement that a flight from the land becomes more marked the more rationalistic modes of thought are made accessible to the agricultural population. Rationalistic modes of thought are among the accompaniments of materialistic industrialism, so it may be concluded that in Europe a restoration of peasant agriculture will follow the acceptance of older Christian ideals. Consequently the restoration will be gradual. In an industrialised country a sudden campaign to encourage agriculture for the sake of self-sufficiency *alone* will play into the hands of the industrial clique and the chemical magnates, who will use the land to subsidise their own business interests. So, in an industrialised country, self-sufficiency cannot be regarded first as a national aim but as the moderate aim of families based upon property, accompanied by a breaking-down of concentrated industrialism, and the whole process dictated by changed modes of thought. Moderate self-sufficiency on a rational scale will follow after that. Yet at present, despite fragmentary items in Hitler's programme, there seem to be few signs of the real change in Germany; and there are equally few, for that matter, in England.

GREGORY MACDONALD.

VOODOOS AND OBEAHS. *By Joseph J. Williams, S.J. The Dial Press.* $3,00.

In the days of slave-trading, the snake-worshipping tribesmen of Dahomey were carried off to Hayti, where they were lucky enough to find their deity (or a colourable imitation of him) comfortably established. Thus the cult continued without a break. Of course ophiolatry must always seem disgusting to Europeans, but the early Voodoo-worship of the Haytians seems to have been almost as innocuous as the non-poisonous boa which they worshipped. Later, however, the sinister shadow of "Don Pedro" is thrown across the stage, and what was (to the contemporary European observer) no worse than a "disgusting ceremony" degenerates into a "nameless orgy." As the author observes, you can never tell what a negro means when he is dancing; and he can get more dangerously drunk on rhythm than on rum. The old planters who confiscated the drums of their slaves had good reason to do so. There seems to be no doubt the secret of modern Voodooism is a secret that has to be guarded not because it is believed to be holy but because it is known to be shameful. Whether the emotional indulgence that it offers goes to the length of ritual murder and cannibalism is a debated point: the author is of the opinion that, in some cases, it does. The sacrifice of the "goat without horns" is a sinister periphrasis, paralleled by that of the Indian terrorists who talk of "sacrificing a white goat to Kali." These speculations may not be without practical importance for the white races, in view of the fact that our dance-orchestras seem permanently to have adopted the negro technique for exciting emotion.

When we turn from Hayti to Jamaica, we meet a quite different set of conditions. The Jamaican "Obi" —despite the etymological temptation to connect it with the same root as " Ophiolatry "—has nothing to do with snakes. The Ashanti tribes from whom it derives seem to have been an altogether more practical and businesslike folk than the Dahomeans, and their wise-men were fully alive to the advantages of physical science. Therefore, while not despising the shows and trappings of superstition, they based their real power on a sound working-knowledge of poisoning, with the result that the Obeah-man in Jamaica has always been a person of commanding influence. It is a curious fact that, nevertheless, owing to their mistaken methods of training (especially the deleterious practice of staring at the sun), they are usually physical and mental wrecks. But the Jamaicans have " white " magicians as well as black (the adjectives are of course figurative) who devote themselves to combating the malevolent activities of the Obeah men. Sometimes (as one may well suppose) it is difficult to distinguish the one from the other. Both appear to deal in bene-ficent charms, and a catalogue of these reads curiously like an American advertisement column. The difference is that Negro methods are more direct. Thus, where-as the American wizard will teach you, by means of a pamphlet of instructions, how to increase your will power, or hold down your job; the Negro achieves the same result quite simply by means of a " Boss-fixing Powder."

We must apologise for dealing thus frivolously with a scholarly and obviously important work, written by an eminent Jesuit who is an acknowledged master of his subject. But Father Williams is also an extremely lively and interesting writer; and it is merely as such that we have presumed to appraise him.

C.E.B.

THE GREEN LANTERN. *By Augustus Muir. Methuen. 3s. 6d.*
  Mr. Muir warns us in his dedication of what kind of story this is: impeccable hero, ditto heroine, Eastern villain, and so forth. But it makes a good story; and why Mr. Muir should presume that it requires any explanation—almost an apology—I do not know. Who is Lord John? And what is the connection with the impeccable heroine? For 3s. 6d. it is very good moneysworth (comparative with the usual prices for new novels) to find out.

V.N.L.

Music

LISTENING-IN is a very, very second best to listening. But if sufficient allowance is made for what is lost, and added, by amplification, selection and the rest of the mechanical paraphernalia, it is possible, granted a knowledge of the original, plus a powerful imagination, to form some idea of what that which is being broadcast actually sounds like. On such unsatisfactory basis I would say that, with one exception, the present German season at Covent Garden is much the same as last year's season. Under Heger the " Ring " has had a steadier performance, if not so brilliant, than Sir Thomas Beecham secured last year. But there is really little more to say than has been said a score of times before of Frida Leider, Lotte Lehmann, Maria Olczewska, Lauritz Melchior, Friedrich Schorr, and the rest. The one exception has been the orchestra, a now magnificent instrument, from which Beecham, in particular, has got the most glorious effects; and one cheerfully excused the occasional lapses in the " Ring " for the pleasure of having an orchestral performance not dulled by familiarity. Even on the radio the freshness of the attack has been evident.

Meanwhile at Sadlers Wells last Saturday the Vic-Wells Company wound up what has been on the whole a successful season, with a rousing performance, under Albert Coates, of *The Snow Maiden*. Not even the vigour and the verve with which Mr. Coates imbued the whole performance could convince me that Korsa-kov's opera is not overlong, patchy and, at moments inordinately dull. But certainly we were recompen-sed by the rich glamour of the good patches, and again one was impressed by the extraordinary rightness of little Miss Olive Dyer as the snow-maiden. I wonder how much of the whole atmosphere created by the performance would be lost without her. I imagine a very great deal.

It is good to have Serge Koussevitzky back in Lon-don, and the B.B.C. Festival Concert which he con-ducted on Monday evening last is not one which will be easily forgotten by those present. By the time these lines are in print a second concert will have been given, including Walton's cheerful *Portsmouth Point* Overture, the sonorous and rather gloomy Second Symphony by Arnold Bax, and a Wagnerian selection. On Friday (to-morrow) Beethoven's Fourth Symphony and the great "Ninth" are to be given. Monday's concert, which consisted of Prokofiev's *Symphonie Classique*, the Seventh Symphony of Sibelius and Tchaikovsky's Fifth Symphony, is chiefly memorable for the Sibelius work. Frankly, I do not know enough of Sibelius to be a fair judge of how true to the com-poser's intention is an interpretation such as we had last Monday. I have neither heard enough of his works nor studied them sufficiently. Sibelius is un-doubtedly the most original and probably the greatest musical mind at work amongst us to-day; though he has had to live over seventy years before this country knew anything of him beyond *Valse Triste*. The full appreciation of his genius is still to be gathered, and his place in musical history. At least we can say of the glowing performance which Koussevitzky gave us of the Seventh Symphony that it will, apart from the immediate satisfaction and pleasure, awaken a deeper interest to know more and understand more of what the composer has to say. I fear I cannot be moved to the same interest in Prokofiev, despite the exquisite delicacy with which the charming score of the *Symphonie Classique* was treated; and there is not much more to be said of Tchaikovsky.

V.N.L.

THE COCKPIT

[*Letters should not exceed 300 words in length and must bear the names and addresses, not necessarily for publication, of their authors.*

The Editor can accept no responsibility for opinions expressed by correspondents.]

SOCIAL CREDIT.

Sir,—I congratulate you both on the fairnesss and the wisdom of your policy in allowing the case for and against the Credit Scheme of Major Douglas to be argued at such length in your columns. Alas! that so much of it is over my head; that I, swamped in this flood of economic learning, must feel, with Mr. Reckitt, that " I know my place " —and a very unsatisfactory thing it is to be swamped, to know my place is not as one who rides the flood; and as a Distributist I do not like it at all.

Yet it is true that the theory of Social Credit is a growing influence in this country. So, too, is the theory of Communism; and of Fascism; and of other policies which appear to offer the most direct—if not necessarily the most violent—change from the present; and, as I have said, I think it is wise as well as fair of you to have permittted the discussion we have just had between Commander Shove and Mr. Symons. All your readers could not have been so engulfed as Mr. Reckitt and myself; and those who could swim in that sea have by now surely struck out for one shore or the other.

I myself, *de profundis*, can only see one snag (apart from mixed metaphors) and it is that it seems so very optimistic to anticipate that all those in charge of the Credit System, if and when it is adopted, will be of the high integrity and disinterestedness of Mr. Symons. I would not mind Communism nearly so much if I thought all Communists were like Mr. Shaw. But there it is. Human nature is like that: and I cannot quite get free of the conviction of original sin, even to be a Douglasite or a Shavian.

There is an old saying in that cynical tradition to which I belong to the effect that the devil you know is better than the devil you don't know. I hope Mr. Symons will forgive the discourtesy of the implication, but that is roughly what I mean in regard to Social Credit. At least we all agree on the devilry of the controllers of the present financial system; and some of them are very clever devils. The question is, can we, when we have driven them out, and swept and garnished our house, keep it clear of other devils, worse than themselves?

JOHN MASTERS.

N.F.U. AND THE TRADE PACTS.

Sir,—My attention has been called to a report published to-day in regard to a meeting which took place yesterday at the House of Commons between representatives of the Agricultural Party and certain Members of Parliament in regard to the trade agrecments with Denmark and Argentina. The report states that

" The visitors were, without exception, greatly incensed at the action of the leaders of the N.F.U. in having accepted the assurances of the Minister of Agriculture that the trade agreements with Denmark and the Argentine would not operate against the interests of agriculture."

Two of the spokesmen of the delegation are stated to have contended that

" As the question could not have been discussed by the Council of the (National Farmers') Union or the County Branches, the leaders had no authority to commit the rank and file of farmers to the trade agreements with the Argentine and Denmark."

I shall be glad if you will allow me to make it clear, for the guidance of your agricultural readers, that the two interviews which I and my colleagues had with the Minister of Agriculture on the subject of the Danish and Argentine agreements were designed solely to elicit the full facts in regard to their bearing upon home agricultural interests. If those members of the Agricultural Party delegation who are members of the N.F.U. had cared to call here before proceeding to the House of Commons we should gladly have placed the facts at their disposal. Not one of them did so.

It so happens that yesterday we had a conference in London of County Branch Chairmen and Secretaries from all parts of England and Wales. I gave that conference a brief account of our interviews with the Minister and it will interest our critics to know that not a breath of criticism was uttered against our action. The Council of the Union will have an opportunity next week of hearing the facts and I do not anticipate that our action will be repudiated.

I need only add that the National Farmers' Union owes no allegiance to the Agricultural Party or any other political Party and it is difficult for that reason to appreciate why any action of the leaders of the Union in the direction of securing facts for the guidance of our own members should have so incensed the representatives of a political Party organisation.

B. I. GATES,
President.
National Farmers' Union.

May 11, 1933.

LORD TRENCHARD'S REPORT.

Sir,—It is disappointing to see *G.K.'s Weekly* repeating the claptrap of the gutter press in its rather thoughtless note on Lord Trenchard's Police Report. In what sense can the police force be called a " civilian body " or a " democratic body," and in what way does it differ from a military body when it is required to quell civil disturbances? Why should appointing ex-soldiers or ex-officers to the Police Force " militarise " it, beyond at worst introducing a military discipline. which has been found eminently satisfactory in its own sphere, and is in fact in force, though perhaps more loosely applied, in the Police Force. The establishment of a special officer grade should not prevent men of ability rising from the ranks, any more than it does in the army. Your note indicates a strange change of front. You have not long had such an affection for the average police-sergeant, or such respect for his impartiality and discerning wisdom, that you would like to see him running the show. Your final cut at Lord Trenchard's administration, and your general objection to graduates from the Services, and to militarisation, suggests that the writer of the note has no acquaintance with military discipline or organisation.

JOHN BETHWIN.

" THE DANCE OF DEATH."

Sir,—Thank you for your eloquent and spirited protest against the holocaust on the roads. It is not yet everywhere known that there exists an association—the Pedestrians' Association, on behalf of which I am writing—whose objects are to make the roads safe for pedestrians and to secure to the pedestrian (or to his or her relatives) just compensation in case of injury or death.

The Association has drawn up a programme which it believes if adopted would make the roads safer not only for pedestrians, but for motorists themselves; indeed, the Association has among its members many motorists anxious to secure safe roads for both those afoot and awheel.

The Association is non-commercial, non-political and non-sectarian, and has no objects other than those stated. To those all its energies and funds are devoted. Its effectiveness depends upon the size of its membership, and I should be pleased to hear from those of your readers who would like to know more about our work.

T. C. FOLEY,
Secretary.
The Pedestrians' Association.

134, Fleet Street, E.C.4.

Can We Agree?

Members of the Distributist League believe that :—

Man possesses free will, and therefore the right to exercise that free will.

Do you agree?

Man's birthright is liberty.

Are you free?　Do you wish to be free?

Man has a duty to himself, his family, his neighbour, and the State.

"Who says duties, says rights."

In this country the State has taken away the individual's liberty.

Have you not felt this?

The present governmental machine has usurped despotic powers and seeks to enslave the people.

Could you break free?

Under the present industrial system no merely nominal freedom of action can enable the individual to lead a full and free life.

What Freedom has the working, or even the professional class?

The possession of property is the guarantee of liberty. The possession of private property is not only the individual's right but his natural desire.
But that comparatively few are able to possess enough property to give them security.

What security in life have you?

Security is not only desirable; it is essential. It is almost impossible under the present system.

If a financial crash shook our economic system, what would happen to you?

You agree so far?

Then is it not worth your while to find out more about Distributism which aims at the restoration of liberty by the distribution of Property?

Write to the Hon. Secretary,
　　2, Little Essex Street, W.C.2.

League Meetings

Arrangements are almost complete for holding the Annual League Conference at St. Michael's Glossop (near Manchester) during the Bank Holiday Week-end (June 2 to 5).

Accommodation 5/- per head per day, at St. Michael's. Members bringing their own camping outfit may camp out in the grounds on the same terms. Accommodation can be arranged for ladies in the vicinity, if due notice is given.

Subject: "The Distributist Programme."

Members intending to be present must notify the Hon. Secretary, The League, not later than Monday, May 22.

CENTRAL BRANCH
May 19. Fr. Vincent McNabb, O.P.: "The Common Ethical Evils of Capitalism and Communism."
May 26. Mr. Hilaire Belloc.
June 2. Mr. G. K. Chesterton.
These last meetings of the Session will be held in Carr's Restaurant, Aldwych, at 8 p.m. prompt. Admission Free. Silver Collection.

BIRMINGHAM BRANCH.
Meetings at Bellman Buildings, 39, Carr's Lane, Birmingham, at 7.30 p.m.
May 26. Mr. John G. Milne, of the Birmingham Social Credit Group, on "Social Credit for Distributists."
June 9. Delegates will report on the Glossop Conference of The League.
June 23. Mr. J. F. Galleymore on "Hitler in the Rhineland."
July 7. Miss N. Careless on "The Reconstruction of Property."
July 21. Subject and Speaker to be announced later.

LIVERPOOL BRANCH.
May 25. Branch meeting at "The Alligator," Paradise Street, Liverpool.

MANCHESTER BRANCH.
The usual monthly meeting of members of the Manchester Branch will be held on Friday evening, May 19, at 8 p.m., at the Craigwell Cafe and Restaurant, 26a, Peter Street, Manchester. In view of the approaching League Conference, all members of the Branch are earnestly requested to attend this meeting.

BRADFORD BRANCH.
The discussion following Mr. E. Wilson's paper on "Co-partnership" was so animated that it was decided to continue it at our next meeting, to be held on Monday, June 12, at St. Cuthbert's Guild Rooms, Wilmer Road, Heaton, at 7.30 p.m. Mr. M. White will open the discussion with a short paper on "Why Distributists should not support Co-partnership." Branch members are invited to bring their friends.

SOUTHAMPTON BRANCH.
Meetings are held every fortnight at 123, Warren Avenue. Write to the Secretary for particulars.

GLASGOW BRANCH.
A considerable increase in membership has resulted from the formation of the Ladies' Group, which meets weekly and holds a monthly Joint Meeting with the Branch. Ladies desirous of joining should communicate with the Secretary—Miss D. Meiklejohn, 17, Cunningham St., Glasgow, C.2.

BOURNEMOUTH BRANCH.
Readers of G.K.'s Weekly living at or near Bournemouth who are interested in the work of the Distributist League are invited to write to Mr. R. H. McCausland, 43, St. Luke's Road, Bournemouth, with a view to increasing membership of the Branch and planning future activities.

NEW SCOTTISH BRANCH.
The new Branch holds its meetings in the Queen Anne Restaurant, Argyle Street, Glasgow, every Wednesday at 7.30, where new members are being enrolled. Secretary: Mr. J. MacNamee, 513, Alexandra Parade, Glasgow.

The Distributist League
2, Little Essex Street, London, W.C.2.

LITERARY.

WHERE TO STAY.

EDUCATIONAL.

MISCELLANEOUS.

Published by the Proprietors, G.K.'s WEEKLY, LTD., 2, Little Essex Street, Strand, London, W.C.2 (incorporating THE NEW WITNESS). Telephone: Temple Bar 1978. Printed by THE NUNEATON NEWSPAPERS LTD., "Observer" Buildings, Nuneaton. Sole Agents for Australasia: Gordon & Gotch (Australasia, Ltd.). Sole Agents for South Africa: Central News Agency Ltd.

GK's WEEKLY

EDITED BY G.K. CHESTERTON

JUNE 8, - - 1933
VOL. XVII. No. 430

Registered as a Newspaper.   SIXPENCE.

HITLER AS DISTRIBUTIST

IT is typical of a complex situation in Germany that the Hitler Government should announce, with all the trumpets of the Kremlin, a series of economic measures not at first sight unlike the measures one might call Distributist. A Press rigidly controlled by the Nazi organisation bids a people rigidly controlled by the Nazi organisation to rejoice, because the Four-Year Plan is inaugurated with the publication of the Law for the Reduction of Unemployment. And the Law will almost certainly work itself out unchecked to success or failure. Strict measures have been taken to see that no opposition can be engendered by the local patriotism of the German States. A body of bureaucrats is at command to execute its provisions. A special branch of political police has been formed to watch narrowly the doings of suspected classes, groups or individuals. Never were Distributist measures passed under happier auguries in a centralised modern State.

But not only is this State highly centralised within its present compass, so that all local particularism has been destroyed and all personal initiative subordinated to the least whim of the Central Executive. The Germany of Hitler expects to extend its present compass by invoking a new (and perhaps rather vague) doctrine of Race, so as finally to embrace all the more or less Germanic communities of Czecho-Slovakia, Austria, Switzerland, the Low Countries and Scandinavia. When the Northern Tribe has been gathered together under one War-Lord, con-siderations of strategy, if nothing else, will insistently demand the acquisition of natural frontiers, at least beyond the Vistula, the Danube and the Rhine. The centralised State is introducing what might be called Distributist measures with an eye to an Empire founded upon a theory of Race.

Here, we may say, is an example of the imitative German mind picking out of the political systems around it the various ideas which may promise success-ful exploitation, and exploiting them with a scientific solemnity unknown to any other people. As with the general, so with the particular : the idea of the family, expounded by the Distributist, is applied in Germany with the mass methods of the Communist. An official of the Ministry of National Enlighten-ment and Propaganda explains to assembled journal-ists how questions of race hygiene are to be treated by the German Press in the future. The "family idea" is to be fostered in every possible way. The old habit of poking fun at the fathers of large families is to be avoided. Every opportunity is to be taken of pointing out that this or that successful man is one of a large family. In its own way all this is ex-cellent, even as a mechanical treatment of a more spiritual idea. But we may well ask whether this Distributist idea is advanced for a Distributist motive ? Is the family valued as the primary community, as the unit of political life ? In particular, how does it square with the older argument that an over-populated Germany must have room for expansion, must at least have colonies ? No, it appears at last that the German birth-rate has fallen from 2,000,000 a year at the turn of the century to a bare 1,000,000; that it is still falling; and that the birth-rate of neighbouring countries is outstripping it. The mass propaganda of the Ministry is turned on to the task of creating the primary unit of the State. But the purpose is not to create a primary political unit; the purpose is to create the birth-rate.

The same doubts arise when we see in one of our own papers that Hitler, "with one stroke of the pen," has put women back into the home. In itself, this is an idea often debated in England, and no doubt in every other industrial country where employers have sought women as employees because they could pay them less. But that very complex of circumstances, connected with machine industry, which has turned woman into the wage-earner, has also destroyed the home to which she might have returned. None of this entire restoration can be effected with a stroke of the pen. And even allowing for journalistic exaggeration, it seems to be true that Hitler has simply forced women out of the labour market into the marriage market. The thing is done suddenly, not by the free choice of the community, and without the comparable restoration in other departments which might balance out the possible abuses of the change.

Of course it can be said that desperate diseases require desperate remedies; and the disease of the industrialised State is so desperate that no poison could bring worse than death. It is not beyond the bounds of possibility that the last results of Hitlerism will be the salvation of Germany, only because the measures now introduced will be caught up and transformed by those Germans who understand the spirit in which they should be enforced. But the very fact that Hitler introduces measures nominally Distributist (generously interlarded though they are with a hotch-potch of Communist and Junker philosophies) may bring saner measures of the same inspiration into being in other countries dying of industrialism. The real Distributism is the only practical politics.

NOTES OF THE WEEK

Monday, June 5.

If Mr. Baldwin finds it as easy to stamp out the heresy on India, when he addresses the whole Tory Party on June 28, as he presumably found it a few days ago to bring the Commons land-tax rebels to heel, he will at least have the satisfaction of leading a party more united in the national sense than the National Government can claim to be. Once again the Parliamentary rebels numbered about 200; it looks as though there is a steady group of 200 Tory members who are finding the myth of National unity rather too

irksome to support for much longer. They had their way, more or less, in the matter of the distressed areas; this time, despite their reported determination to bring about the repeal of the dormant Snowden land tax, they have bowed to the eloquence of Mr. Baldwin and the Chancellor, both of whom, be it said, desire as Tories to wipe off the Snowden measure, but as loyal Nationals, desire to keep their Socialist colleagues sweet. It is reported that the occasion brought forth an enquiry whether the Government—the National Government—would go to the country as a Tory Government at the next general election; and that Mr. Baldwin replied with disarming frankness—and irrelevancy—that he did not know when the next election would take place, nor in what circumstances.

*   *   *   *

There are those at Westminster and elsewhere who are ready to prophesy that there will be a general election long before the National Government has run its full, natural course. A year hence has been hinted at as a likely time, though with nothing more substantial to sustain the limit than a feeling that this National "Unity" will hardly be able to stand the strain for much longer. It becomes more apparent every month that the cord which binds the party factions is getting frayed. In the past month alone, rumours not to be put aside too lightly, have had it that Sir John Simon contemplated resigning the Foreign Secretaryship; that Mr. Runciman was incensed to the point of resignation over the trade pacts; and now, that Mr. Baldwin intends to stand or fall as leader of the Tory party by the result of the meeting on June 28. There seems to be general hesitation on all sides to accept the Prime Minister so staunchly as of yore, as Sir National Oracle; or to repose with such dutiful docility beneath the stern inflexibility of the Chancellor's financial rectitude. It is obvious that nothing can be allowed to upset the political apple-cart until after the Economic Conference; but if the Conference itself does not do it, directly or indirectly, the timbers will surely fall apart not very long after. We wish we could feel sure that these sporadic revolts that keep cropping up signified the awakening of individual consciences and the assertion of wills grown tired of the cracking of party whips. But for the most part they indicate Tory-industrial restiveness under a regime of lip-service loyalty. However, it will be interesting in the extreme to see the country's reaction to the old party pettiness when the election does come. All this vaunted economic recovery—how will it go down with an electorate growing rapidly poorer?

*   *   *   *

Propaganda in favour of the raising of the school-leaving age would appear to be on the increase. Last week we referred to a pamphlet which urges that children should be kept at school until they reach the age of sixteen and that adults should be retired from work and pensioned when they are sixty—in order to prevent unemployment. This week we note reports of speeches by Miss Rathbone and Mr. Morgan in the House of Commons, the former suggesting that the "glut of teachers" be met by the addition of a year to the school age, the latter saying that education authorities ought to demand evidence of prospective employment before allowing children between 14 and 15 years of age to leave school. To complete a vicious circle, it might be added that an ex-school-mistress has been forbidden recently to teach her children the simple sciences at home. She would appear to be a qualified instructor, but her children are obliged now to travel several miles every day in order to attend classes. In other words, Government, judged in action or according to the tendencies displayed in Parliament, suits the convenience of the Government rather than the best interests of the people.

*   *   *   *

We trust that the Government will succeed in carrying out its declared intention to obtain from the Mining Association a renewed guarantee, for a further twelve months, that wage rates will be maintained; for despite the assurances given by Mr. Evan Williams, chairman of the Association, members of the Miners' Federation are prepared to sanction a national strike, after July 8, should reductions be imposed in any one district. Mr. Williams has made it clear that any attempt to reduce wages is unlikely, but the Federation has yet to receive a formal notification, involving guarantees, from the owners. A strike now would increase still further the hardships of the miners; yet the owners would be very ill-advised to think that fear of distress would cause the men to come to terms. If the Government understands the situation, it should not find it difficult to persuade the Mining Association to reach agreement with the Federation. If persuasion fails the Government should feel obliged to act in the miners' interest. Too little is being done on their behalf as it is.

*   *   *   *

The motto of our bureaucratic governors seems to be " let not thy right hand know what thy left doeth." Did not the Chancellor recently strike terror in the hearts of the industrial optimists by declaring that the problem of grave unemployment is likely to be with us for at least ten years—a conservative estimate at the present rate of progress? And now from the Ministry of Labour we have a Guide to Public Assistance Committees, in which it is set forth that an applicant for transitional relief must show that he is " normally employed." The suggestion is cynical, though probably unintentionally so. To start with, the applicant for transitional benefit has gone so long without a regular job that his insurance benefit has expired; therefore his normal state is that of unemployment. Then we find (to quote a press report) that if he has had little or no employment for a long time, in order to satisfy the " normally " condition, he must prove that " he has taken such steps to obtain employment as he should know may lead to finding it."

*   *   *   *

What that might mean, it would be difficult to say; the poor applicant is likely to find it so, even though he find the Government on his side to the extent of declaring that " the cultivation of an allotment does not jeopardise a claim for benefit." This magnanimous proviso goes further: a market-gardener or small-holder is to be regarded as unemployed if he can

normally work it outside his ordinary working hours; does not make an average over a year of more than 3/4 a day net profit, and can prove that he has not turned his back on his insurable employment with the intention of getting his livelihood from the small-holding. What a niggling and muddle-headed business has Government become, when a Minister can issue a document proclaiming by its very nature that unemployment is a normal state, and demanding that the unemployed shall prove that they are normally employed, except at those moments when they are engaged in a husbandman's task.

*   *   *   *

However much we may dislike Conferences, it is undoubtedly true that, for a variety of obscure and somewhat unpleasant reasons, a total failure of the World Economic Conference will bring us all down another horrible bump to a lower landing of the depression. Therefore, politically speaking, everything depends upon the success of the gathering. The qualification unfortunately necessarily is that even success can mean little more than the success of the international interests of trade and finance, secured it may be by the efforts of our own statesmen, whose policy is directed entirely to international ends. The nations will fare best whose more acute representatives wish to use the temporary alleviation of improved trade throughout the world to build up the resources of their own peoeple against a repetition of the present calamity. We have in mind the representatives of many countries who will work like fun for a successful conference, but only so as to secure themselves a breathing-space. Our own political leaders do not yet seem to have learned the obvious lesson. Give them a year in a fool's paradise, with deceptive indications that there will be a revival of trade (a mathematical impossibility it is that a true revival can ensue) and they will forget every idea they ever had of an internal reconstruction of English economie life.

*   *   *   *

The absurdities that can be caused by unnecessary, restrictive legislation were illustrated by two cases heard last week at the Law Courts. In one, a test case brought by the police, it was ruled that magistrates in the area of Steyning, Sussex, had exceeded their authority by increasing the opening hours during the summer by half an hour. They had come to the conclusion that the summer months constituted a " special occasion " within the meaning of the Act; but the police disagreed and the police won. The pity of it was that one of the few attempts by those who decide when and where a man may buy a glass of beer to assist rather than to hinder him proved in the end to be abortive. But blame attaches most to the laws that have been passed; not to those who have to administer them. Curiously enough the newspapers that made such a fuss of the Hotel and Restaurant Bill, devoted comparatively little space to the Steyning affair. What do newspapers care about the little man championed by one of the leading cartoonist? He is not an advertiser, but merely an item on a circulation sheet.

The other case concerned the Tote clubs which had recently to be closed because of a High Court judgment that they were illegal. The management of a particular club had allowed itself in consequence to be sued and when the action came before Mr. Justice du Parcq, he ruled that Tote clubs might in certain circumstances be conducted legally. Soon, we may assume, Tote clubs will spring into being again throughout the country. Possibly they will encourage far too much gambling. Possibly therefore they will be responsible for the extension of an evil. But it must be recognised that the campaigns against gambling of which one hears are usually directed against the small clubs and the small book-makers. The large organisations, organised for bet-ting purposes—the Stock Exchange is one—remain in the odour of respectability. If people must be prevented from betting, it would not be at all a bad plan to impose the first restrictions on those who can afford to amuse themselves in other ways.

*   *   *   *

It was thought for a time that Don Alcala-Zamora, the politician-President of Spain, would decide to resign rather than give his signature to the Religious Orders Act, which confiscates the property of the Church in Spain, bans the Catholic schools and even imposes penalties for the teaching of religion. Forced to choose between conflicting loyalties, he has evi-dently decided to remain in office and risk excom-munication. When the present Government assumed power its aims and methods were described in these columns, and we propose to devote what space we can to the present situation in Spain during the next few weeks. It is important that people in England should know—unfortunately the Daily Press is un-likely to tell them—that persecution is rife elsewhere than in Germany. Given consistency and a real sense of news-values, nearly as much information would by now have appeared in the Press as was splashed on the front pages while Hitler was busy occupied with Jew-baiting.

*   *   *   *

At a recent meeting held at the Charing Cross Hotel, it was decided to form a new political party, to be called the Distributist Party, its main objects being the development of domestic agriculture, the support of the small owner and trader against the combine, the abolition of bureaucratic interference with the liberties of the subject, the reform of Parliamentary and local government machinery, the transfer to local bodies of a greater measure of authority in matters of purely local importance and the maintenance of adequate forces for national defence. A committee was appointed and arrangements were made to pre-sent a complete programme to the public within the next few weeks. There is no doubt of the need for public action along the lines indicated by the objects of this new party which is of course an independent body, not connected directly with the Distributist League. Differences of opinion may show themselves as to the usefulness or advisability of direct political action, but positive action of any sort may be wel-comed so long as its aim be true. The temporary address of the Party is 333, Grays Inn Road, London, W.C.1.

The Bath and West Show, held at Wimbledon last week, came to a bigger centre of population than for many years past, and proved a financial success, but the admittances were not as high as at numerous previous shows held elsewhere. On Saturday 22,377 people paid at the gate and during the four days the visitors totalled 50,612. We do not know how these figures compare with those for Wimbledon's more familiar attraction, but making all necessary de-ductions for people of agricultural or other kindred pursuits who attended the show as a matter of course, the returns appear to justify the satisfaction expressed by the honorary director, Lord Radnor. Before the show opened, he said he felt convinced that the Londoner would wish to see how his foods were pro-duced. On Saturday he informed a *Sunday Times* correspondent that he was proud of the results, which proved " that the Londoner has deep in his heart a love for the well-being of the countryside." If the Show has served no other purpose than to awaken in the hearts of a few thousand Londoners some sense of what the urban life lacks, it will have more than justified itself. We should like to feel as convinced about it is Lord Radnor; but our impression has been that the Londoner is palpably indifferent as to how his food is produced, or where—let alone how it ought to be produced!

*   *   *   *

The fifth report issued on behalf of the Cecil Houses begins with the very satisfactory statement that the fifth Cecil House is now " definitely on its way towards completion." Our readers need not be reminded of this splendid work, initiated by Mrs. Cecil Chesterton, to provide public lodging houses, of the best possible type, for homeless women in London. We wish now to draw their attention to the new report, copies of which can be obtained from Cecil Houses Inc., 11, Golden Square, W.1., and to urge them to assist the administrators by contributing to the fund, which makes it possible for new houses to be opened and placed on a self-supporting basis.

The Bedaux System Again

By a Special Correspondent

OVER a year ago accounts appeared in *G.K.'s Weekly*, of the Bedaux industrial methods which were causing trouble with the employees of a factory in Leicester. Since then various attempts have been made to introduce them in the Mid-lands, the latest being at a large works near Birm-ingham. The result has been a strike already lasting eight weeks and involving over 800 men. The em-ployers' side of the question has appeared in the press, and it was felt that some statement of the men's position should also appear; your correspondent has therefore paid two visits to the scene.

Passing the works' recreation ground now bearing a promising crop of hay, one arrives at the tea-rooms which form the Strike Committee's headquarters. Thence is issued their printed manifesto and there an interview with the Chairman elicited further informa-tion.

The system involves observation of the men at work, by the Bedaux experts, who by means of stopwatches time every operation on a particular job. They then determine what movements and actions are wasteful and by cutting out these decide what is the minimum possible time in which the operation can be done. This is taken as the basis of the piecework price and any improvement on that results in a bonus. Not all this bonus accrues to the workmen, but is shared by the non-productive staff—foremen, staff and progress men, who thus have a direct incentive still further to speed up the work.

Every day two boards are put up in the shop, one bearing in red the names of those who have earned a bonus and one in black of those who have fallen behind. Continued appearance on the black board results in a different job being found for that man; unfortunately it is usually the job of calling daily at the Labour Exchange.

An example was quoted of how the system works; a job was set of dressing off 8 frames in a certain time, and 200 men were tried at this before the 20 most skilled were selected. The Bedaux task was then set at 13 frames in the same time. No wonder the men were unable to stand the pace, one indeed showing such signs of exhaustion that " his mates began to draw on the floor designs . . . of a coffin." Other workers were constantly taking days off, and altogether constant trouble was experienced, the men vehemently protesting against the system. Finally the Bedaux speed merchants were chased out of the shop, and the workmen tried to interview the management. The only reply was an order to re-commence work, and at this the strike commenced.

The workmen have formed their strike committee and have called in an ex-trades union organiser to advise. Very few of them were trades unionists, but many have since joined and meetings have been held between the management and men and the trades union officials. Always, however, the same reply is received from the management: call off the strike and re-commence work and then we will discuss the position. Considering that the system was imposed with only a cursory notice and without discussion with the workers, this position is not conducive to a settlement.

There was little trades unionism in the works and although the men constantly tried to interview the directors, they were unable to break through the ring of foremen and supervisors. The published statement by the Employers' Federation points out that they have fully established with the Unions the principle of mutuality in piece-work conditions, and that the men are thus safeguarded. It is difficult to reconcile this statement with the firm's policy of employing chiefly non-union men, and with not even a works' council, any negotiation in the past would seem to have been impossible.

As to the system itself, while one welcomes any effort to improve workmanship, there is something derogatory to the dignity of man in this use of the stop-watch, and detailed supervision; and the workers' condemnation of the system as " inhuman " will find an echo in the mind of every man who reacts against the evils of the industrial system. It is a putting back of the clock on the efforts that are being made to bring together the two partners in industry, and even to give the men some partnership in the business.

Bearing on this is an article in *Blackfriars* which compares the old slavery with the possibility of a new. The former involved a state of serfdom to an individual—a master—often even possessing the rights of life and death. The latter may contain men and women under orders from the State—" a State containing a class servile by law."* It is there suggested that this latter condition will not be so undesirable as the old, but such systems as the Bedaux are a terrible foretaste of what may be expected under the new regime.

As to the future, the lines of reconciliation can only come by a frank discussion of the whole position without asking the men first to surrender. The strike was entered into because the management would not discuss matters and therefore left the men the only alternative of a strike to draw attention to their views. It is surely not too much to ask the former to recognise this, and coupled with the settlement, to inaugurate a system of works' councils. Distributists further would emphatically add that no settlement will prove lasting which does not contain the germs of co-partnership—a share in the ownership, the management and the profits. The alternatives are Communism or Fascism. Is either party willing to risk one of these two?

It's a Long Long Way to Vienna
By J. Desmond Gleeson

THE age of the great pilgrimages may now be over, or, as some might suggest, temporarily suspended, but there are still a few stray pilgrims to be found making their ways to obscure, and even unexpected, shrines. No longer may one see the jolly crowds turning their steps towards Canterbury or the more serious mobs pressing on to Glastonbury. Even those solitary figures, who favoured black patches over the eyes and who preferred out-sizes in walking sticks, are no longer common upon the highways. Nor is it quite fair to blame the motorists for chasing such pilgrims from the straight and narrow paths. The unfortunate fact is that the religious revellers lost the inclination to seek shrines before the motors appeared; or, as the Germans love to say, the will to pilgrimage was lacking long before the petrol menace turned up. But, as I say, casual pilgrims may still be discovered on their way to remarkable destinations and proceeding thither in what may moderately be called, eccentric fashion. Consider this gentleman, for instance, whose acquaintance I have made through the good services of Mr. Garvin, yes, *the* Mr. Garvin.

At the end of April, an unemployed chauffeur at Graz, who gave himself the name of " Marathon," started to walk on his hands from the Styrian capital to Vienna, a distance of some 120 miles. After completing about a third of the distance his hands became poisoned, and he had to go to hospital. He

---

* S. Humphries, O.P. " The Servile State Reconsidered," Blackfriars, May, 1933, p. 355.

intends, however, to continue his journey as soon as he is well again.

The stout old Graz breed, you see. You can't keep the boys at home once they've made up their minds to go to Vienna. And I don't blame Mr. Marathon for going from Graz to Vienna, for though I do not know Graz I *do* know Vienna. In fact, I can only blame him for not having gone earlier. While he was still a chauffeur who was employed he might have made the journey of 120 miles with greater ease. Even after he had lost his car he might have walked the distance in some ten days or so. But disdaining all normal methods of travel, he elected to go forward in a manner wholly his own, and one can only hope he will be as successful as he deserves.

All the same, he will hardly be surprised if people wonder why, if he had decided upon Vienna as the object of his ambition, he should choose to go forward hand over hand. It may be, of course, that being a chauffeur he had forgotten how to walk. Accustomed to trundle his auto up and down jolly old Graz, it is possible that his legs had lost their meaning. To use another fine phrase served up by those who know how to do this kind of thing properly, that is, profitably, he may have lost his leg-sense. When he found that they had taken away his car, therefore, he may very well have halted in a bewildered manner, "gazing" first at his feet and then at his hands while he wondered which of them a motor-less man should use. No doubt he made some efforts to put his best foot forward, only to find that there was no best (or even better) foot amongst them. He may even have made the unpleasant discovery that he had not a leg to stand on; though should he actually have two legs to stand on, the fact would not bring him a step nearer Vienna. Anyway, whatever may have happened to his legs, it would seem that he found eventually that he could rely on his hands. Not only had they not lost their cunning, but they had gained a new cunning which made even the placid people of Graz stare. We may picture the scene outside the "Monk and Mountain" (that fine old tavern to which Graz turns its evening step) when Mr. Marathon strolled up to say good-bye to his friends. As he strides lustily forward, left hand avoiding the drains with fine skill, right hand marching sturdily forward, there is a tremor of emotion among the loafers outside the "Monk." Kind-hearted men bring their friends out of the bar to see what is approaching. Then they all gather in a circle round the up-turned Marathon while he spins them his yarn.

As he looks up and they look down it may begin to dawn upon our Marathon that there are disadvantages in his position that he had little dreamt of. By the time one of his friends offers him a drink he will have no doubt of it. His two boots pointing skywards will be powerless to accept the proffered hospitality. Possibly they will end by placing his tankard on the pavement before him, but even so I conceive he will have some difficulty in slaking his thirst, unless they provide him with a straw. And when he goes off, striding grotesquely through the gloom, the interrupted workers return to the bar with a new and arresting topic of conversation.

And thus Marathon started on his lonely pilgrimage confident, at least at one time, that he would eventually reach Vienna. Whether that confidence still remains with him is another matter, though it is noteworthy that he intends to continue, even if he has only advanced one third of the distance since April. But it is not given to every pilgrim to gain his shrine and Marathon may ultimately be forced to content himself with a different sort of distinction. For he has at least done something that very few have done: he has seen the world upside down. Among the men who can claim this record stands St. Peter first of all, though "stands" is scarcely the appropriate word in this connection. St. Peter, too, holds other records. But what stands out about the present pilgrim is that the journey has taken a very long time. Not one fleeting glimpse of a world upside down did Marathon take while passing to another and more stable sphere, but a long and steady impression, lasting over several days. Looking down the long roads that led to Vienna he has seen everything upside down until he can hardly know whether he is on his head or his feet, or which side of the world is the right side up. And really it was hardly necessary for him to take all his special pains (and poison) to arrive at that conclusion. By using his feet as a normal citizen he could not have come to a different result. By using his eyes, with his head uppermost, he would have seen things quite as funny and as silly as a man walking on his hands. As it is, he may see Vienna and die—which is not quite fulfilling the proverb—but even a chauffeur should know that if you wish to use your hands as feet you should first take the trouble to provide them with boots.

Straws in the Wind

THE DON AND THE CAVALIER
By G. K. CHESTERTON

MR. CHRISTOPHER HOLLIS has written an excellent book on John Dryden. It is an instructive book; it is also an amusing book; but not so amusing as some of the reviews of it. And it concerns me here, at the moment, mainly in relation to the general position to-day of the school of academic critics, who have upheld for so long a time the historical theory which is often called Parliamentarism and is in fact Plutocracy. It is of some moment to the movement we support; because it was the official defence of this policy which made possible the dispossession of the populace. Now about the present position of that official criticism there are several rather curious things to note. The first is its *tone*; which is quite queer in its difference from the tone used in my youth, when historians were as simple as Macaulay; I might almost say when scholars were as ignorant as Macaulay. For a man can be very learned and very ignorant; and Macaulay achieved the combination to the admiration of heaven and earth. Macaulay would make short work, or imagine that he could make short work, of any young man who played at being a Jacobite; he was impatient with him as with a crank; but he was *honestly* impatient; his impatience was a sort of innocence. The critics on the same side to-day have lost their innocence. They know perfectly well that they have been defeated in battle after battle upon the big facts; and they have a curious carefulness in dealing only with very small facts. Anybody who said thirty years ago that Charles the First was not in fact a tyrant, dethroned by an indignant democracy, could really be treated as a sort of Mr. Dick, with a weakness for weeping over King Charles's Head. The modern critic does not really dare to-day to appear as the executioner (even though the critic, like the executioner, can wear a mask and remain nameless); he has not now the nerve to shake King Charles's Head at the people and shout confidently, " Behold the head of a traitor." So he becomes more fussy and particular than ever over the ancient, profound, pressing and all-important question; " Out of which window in Whitehall did Charles the First step to have his head cut off?" And that, as Disraeli very truly observed, is one of the two or three quite infallible ways of becoming a bore.

And the new professor of the old history is rather a bore; but what is much worse, he is a nervous bore. He not only drawls; but he also stammers. And his tone, as I have said, has achieved a most peculiar accent of acrid timidity. I read one criticism of Mr. Hollis's book, in a highly learned and authoritative weekly; and it largely left me wondering whether the critic who wrote it had read that particular passage in it, in which Mr. Hollis, contrasting the methods of Dryden and Pope, quotes the whole of the latter poet's famous satire upon Addison. Whether or no it was like Addison, it was exactly like the critic.

" Willing to wound and yet afraid to strike,
Just hint a doubt and hesitate dislike;
Damn with faint praise, assent with civil leer,
And without sneering teach the rest to sneer."

Again, over and above this unmistakeable tone, there is the change in the method; which I have compared to the change from laughing at Mr. Dick over King Charles's Head to quarrelling about which window-sill had the honour to be bestridden by King Charles's legs. There was an excellent example in this review, of the method of avoiding battle on the main issue and picking a quarrel about a trifle. Mr. Hollis made the general remark, which is a true and valuable remark, that it is rather a disadvantage of revolutions that they often have to be followed by new and rigid repressions, set up by the revolutionists themselves. He gives the example that William of Orange's Government censored a sort of controversy which under the last Stuarts was much more free. The critic then suggested that the whole book and its author were historically unreliable, upon some verbal interpretation of William of Orange's Government; because the censorship was removed later; I think in 1695. The point of general interest is that there was a new censorship; and the critic's way of proving that there was not a censorship is to say that there was a censorship, that lasted for about eight years. Now Mr. Hollis's general philosophy may be right or wrong; but Mr. Hollis's general remark was perfectly philosophical and a quite reasonable comment on this and many other cases of the same truth. The critic's correction, if his correction is correct, is not of the slightest philosophical or rational interest to anybody; it has no relation to the point that was really raised; it only says that somebody did something, but did not do it all the time. That is what I mean by the one side being concerned with triviality and the other side with truth. Mr. Hollis's suggestion is of some intelligent importance to us, who are living among real revolutions; Bolshevist revolutions or Hitlerite revolutions. It is not necessarily a complete condemnation of revolutions. It is simply a note on the natural history of revolutionists. But his history really is natural history, and the academic and pedantic history has become utterly unnatural.

There is a saying that a great silence broods over the great battle-fields. There is certainly a very astounding silence over the great recent defeats of the Orangemen's theory of history. Mr. Hollis begins his book by noting the picturesque coincidence that Dryden sat fishing in the river upon which Mary Stuart had looked out from the Tower of Fotheringay. The storming and taking of that Tower, with all its secrets, was a struggle that once made an amazing noise, that has now been followed by a more amazing stillness. Hardly anything is said about its sensational termination; simply because the main part of the old accepted case against the Catholic Queen has completely broken down. Considering how frightfully important it was that the Casket Letters were all certainly genuine, it is very funny to find how unimportant it is that they are most of them probably forgeries. The war was so fierce and ruthless while they thought they were winning it; it is so very quiet and casual and gentlemanly, now that they know they are losing it. That intellectual interlude at least is over; England is returning to her own past, and could hardly march under a better battle-sign than what Macaulay himself had the magnanimity to call " the towering crest of Dryden."

In the Chilean Andes
By G. A. Hinkson

IT is the Southern Summer. The February sun is just appearing over the crest of the Andes. Only thirty kilometres away is the mountain of San Ramón, more than 4,000 metres high. There are many ranges of mountains, one behind the other with the smaller ones in front; and these are visible and distinct when one is close, but from a distance it appears one great single mountain. San Ramón is the highest in this immediate neighbourhood, and the snow on its summit is still resisting the rays of the sub-tropical sun.

The light is already flooding the plain, but the mountain slopes are still darkened by shadows. The early morning train is about to leave Santiago for Puente Alto—a village 19 kilometres to the South. The air has a fresh nip in it; for here the nights are cold, even at midsummer. The railway station is almost empty. Country folk hurry along the platform carrying large bundles; and, just before the bell rings to indicate the departure, newsvendors appear with the morning papers, shouting:—' El Mercurio,'—'La Nación'—' El Diario,' dwelling mournfully upon the penultimate syllable. A Franciscan priest, who is rather large, passes along the narrow corridor with some difficulty, and, finding a half-empty compartment, sits down heavily in the corner, panting. The bell rings, and the train, which is driven by electricity from overhead cables, moves slowly out of the station. Leaving the flat roofs of the town behind, the train passes through a countryside which is parched and dusty; for the climate is rainless from October to May. It stops at every station on the short journey to Puente Alto, and swarthy peasants walk across the line and clamber on to the high foot-boards. Small boys and girls are selling oranges and red-flesh melons. The sun is higher in the sky now, and the grey rocky face of San Ramón is bathed in light. Owing to its great height and deceptive distance, the mountain still appears from the same angle. One must travel far along the plain to obtain a fresh landscape.

Puente Alto lies at the base of the Andean foothills, and is on the edge of the plain of Maipo. It was near here that the Chilean Patriot army won a great victory over the Spaniards more than a hundred years ago. It is the terminus of the electric railway. From here a miniature steam train goes to El Volcán, a village in the heart of the mountains near the frontier of Argentina. It is a narrow-gauge mountain railway built for strategic reasons some thirty years ago when war was threatening between Chile and Argentina. It is owned by the State, and operated by soldiers of the railway corps. The little engine burns wooden blocks as fuel, and rarely exceeds a speed of fifteen kilometres an hour. The line follows the Río Maipo, a mountain stream which is fed in Winter by the rains and in Summer by the melting snows. It winds in and out among the foothills, and as the train rounds the sharp curves, the sun appears first on one side and then on the other. The vegetation consists of bamboo and eucalyptus with orange trees here and there near the cottages. On the lower slopes of the mountains there is only dried grass and prickly scrub. Huasos, the Chilean equivalent of the cow-boy may be seen on horseback in the fields, or on the hot dusty road which runs near the railway and leads to the small mountain villages. The huasos wear the old traditional dress of a century ago—a broad Spanish hat, high boots, and a poncho over the shoulders. The poncho is like a small square carpet with a slit in the middle through which the head passes; it gives great warmth during the cold mountain nights, and, when not required can be thrown back over the shoulders. The huasos also wear enormous antiquated spurs with rowels of two inches in diameter.

As the little train halts at the village stations with much puffing and whistling, the inhabitants gather on the platform to meet it. They have little diversion of a sophisticated kind, and the arrival of the daily train is the most entertaining moment of their lives. At each station the height above sea-level is shown in metres painted on a black notice board in white. There are high mountains now behind as well as in front, and the other side of Ramón is visible to the rear.

El Volcán, where the mountain railway ends is like any Andean village. It has a post of Carabineros (Police), a combined post-office and general shop, and some twenty flat-roofed houses. On the other side of the river, which is crossed by a wooden bridge, there is an hotel and restaurant with tables in the garden. As is common in Chile the tables are separated from each other by partitions of pale green bamboo trees, while a vine stretches overhead and provides shade against the hot sun. El Volcán is some 1,600 metres above sea-level. At midday, when the sun is almost directly overhead, it is very hot; but, quite early in the afternoon the sun goes down behind the steep mountain, and, as the shadow spreads over the valley, the temperature falls appreciably.

At half past four in the afternoon, the little train starts off on the return jouney to Puente Alto. On leaving El Volcán, there are few passengers. Amongst these is a very large and genial looking German dressed in mountaineering outfit. He is talking to a Chilean girl who evidently lives in El Volcán and is on her way to Santiago for a holiday. He speaks loudly in Spanish—but with a pronounced German accent. She is young and pretty, and is dressed tastefully, although obviously of a country type.

The German makes jokes incessantly, and his big frame shakes with laughter. His companion smiles. a little uncomprehendingly; for, the German type of humour is rarely understood by Chileans. His laughter soon becomes contagious, and the other passengers have difficulty in retaining their composure. Some of the jokes are quite silly; but, when the German laughs he shakes the tiny train. The Western mountain slopes and the valley is now in the shadow, which is already creeping up the opposite side. As the train stops at the various stations more passengers enter, and soon it is half full.

The monologue of the hilarious German becomes drowned in the general chatter of conversation.

It is a single line railway, but here and there is a loop to enable trains to pass each other. At one of these, the driver crosses the points at an imprudent speed, and there is a violent bump followed by swaying and wobbling of the train. He pulls up promptly, but it is evident that the two front wheels of one of the coaches have already jumped the metals. Immediately, everyone tries to look out of the windows. They are asking questions, and all talking at the same time. Above the chatter, loud voices can be heard abusing the driver. He makes a desperate bid to rectify the error, and the train moves slowly backwards. He evidently hopes that the wheels will jump back on to the metals. There is another jerk and a stop.

Now all four wheels are off. This is followed by further cursing and shouting. Railwaymen appear from the station a little way back, and an officer rebukes the driver for his carelessness. It seems that we are there for the night. Some of the railway staff go in search of a jack and other necessary instruments. The passengers become bored, and walk up and down the line complaining. Suddenly, it is cold, for the sun has almost set, and its last rays give a deepening pink to the snow on the peaks. Twilight is short in these latitudes, and soon it is night. There are no lights on the train, so the passengers start striking matches. Then the railway staff appear with candles and lanterns. The villagers come out to see what has happened, and there is a general excitement. The passengers who have been strolling near the line return to their seats and try to sleep; but the cold keeps them awake. It is quite dark now, and there is no moon.

After three hours, or so, the derailed coach is lifted on to the metals, and the train descends slowly to Puente Alto. Here there is another delay of an hour, for the connection has been missed. It is nearly midnight when the lights of Santiago appear in the distance.

Books

Theonas

THEONAS. *By Jacques Maritain. Sheed and Ward.* 6s.

THESE eleven philosophical essays, cast in dialogue form, ' conversations,' though written originally a dozen years ago, are not a day out of date. The important philosophical movement on the Continent filters very slowly into this country, yet it is likely to be a most potent factor in resolving the present chaos of our civilisation. M. Jacques Maritain is one of the leading exponents of what may be clumsily called Neo-Thomism, the philosophical system of St. Thomas Aquinas adapted to deal with current conditions of life, in view of the present state of knowledge and the changes in outlook that have occurred since St. Thomas wrote. "To Thomism alone," says M. Maritain, " the privilege belongs of reconciling metaphysics and the natural sciences. Thomism alone is an essentially progressive philosophy, loves movement while holding stability in honour, gives us an exact sense of the renewals necessary in human things . . . and contains germinative energy potent enough to burst asunder the superannuated framework of ' bourgeois ' and ' anti-bourgeois ' thought."

Readers of *G.K.'s Weekly* will find in M. Maritain's Thomistic writings a remarkable support for the social philosophy of Distributism—remarkable because Distributist ideas owe little or nothing directly to the Thomist movement on the Continent. M. Maritain attacks the same fallacies, in the philosophical manner, pseudo-science, pseudo-Progress, Marxism, and the rest, that have been attacked in the more direct, popular manner in this journal and its predecessors since their inception, and on the same fundamental grounds. The writings of Mr. Chesterton, from the earliest, teem with the same fundamental truths, expressed in the terms of everyday life and applied directly to the affairs of the day. This is not to say that in reading M. Maritain you will be merely reading the same old thing. M. Maritain illuminates the subject, throws new light on it, by approaching it from the angle of pure philosophy, thus demonstrating the essential agreement between the theoretical and practical aspects of the same ideas. The language of philosophy is normally about as difficult as, say, another European language, easy enough when you know it, but never free from the variations of local dialect. It requires, in addition, a little extra exercise of the grey matter. That is why most people are frightened away from it. It is in fact a most abominably trying and confusing, not to say irritating business when the jargon of philosophy you happen to be reading is mishandled by the modern cheap-jack pseudo-philosopher. Hence readers should welcome the information that M. Maritain's writing is not only more sound but more readable than most of what looks the same, sounds the same, but is not the same. These particular conversations being largely controversial in theme—"The Theory of Success," "The Myth of Necessary Progress," "The Theory of the Superman," "The Philosophy of Revolution"—the style is lighter and more popular than it might have been otherwise.

In "The Mathematical Attenuation of Time," M. Maritain offers a stimulating criticism of the Einstein theory of Relativity. There are many who will be surprised to learn that that theory, which they took for granted as an unassailable discovery because journalists who could not understand it said it was and made a stunt of it, is by no means so readily accepted amongst scientists as might be supposed. Criticism of it is increasing in amount and authority. Dr. Arthur Lynch's recent brilliant book is an example. The assumption that because only two or three people in the world were supposed to be able to understand Einstein, therefore he was right, is an assumption of the sort that is only too common,—an emphatic proof of the need for Thomism and M. Maritain.

Mr. F. J. Sheed has rendered the English reading public a valuable service in translating the book so lucidly (? "nor" for "or" on p.98, l.20), and in producing it, through his firm, in such satisfactory form and at an accessible price.

G. C. Heseltine.

Napoleon II.

Napoleon II. *By Octave Aubry. Routledge. 12s. 6d.*

THE tragic story of the King of Rome, Napoleon's son, whom Metternich, partly out of vindictiveness and partly out of fear of the blood of the Corsican, made into an Austrian, and called the Duke of Reichstadt, is one of the most human and moving stories in the history of Europe. The Emperor made the boy the apple of his eye, set all his hopes in him to carry on the rule he had established in France, and maintain France where he had placed her by his swift and brilliant subjugation of Europe. But the Allies when they yapped like excited terriers round the fallen lion saw to it, by the ingenuity of Metternich, that Marie-Louise was seduced from her allegiance to her once mighty and always devoted husband. So that whilst Napoleon was in exile, eating his heart out for a word from her and news of his son, she was provided with a paramour, set to rule a petty state, and their son was brought up amongst his enemies, in ignorance of his great birth. As he grew to manhood he learned what a sire he had had, was fired to fit himself to live worthy of him, for his sake and France. He was allowed to overtax his constitution, fall into a consumption and die of it, diplomatically murdered, and so removed from the sphere of European politics. That, at least, is M. Octave Aubry's view of the proceedings and it cannot be denied that he has sound grounds for it. His book is the result of exhaustive research amongst the correspondence and diplomatic material of the time, some of it hitherto unrevealed, and his text is abundantly documented.

The work has the considerable merit, in an uncommon degree, of high literary as well as historical quality, being alive and intensely interesting throughout, yet without resort to the more obvious artifices of the sensational school. It maintains a reasonable temper of restraint, without at any time descending to dullness or pedantry. For the successful carry over of all this into the English version, much credit is due to the translator, who, unlike so many English translators, does translate into English.

Basel, Berne and Zurich. *By M. D. Hottinger. Dent. 5s. 6d.*

Canterbury Cathedral. *By M. A. Babington. Dent. 2s. 6d.*

The first of these books is part of the well-known Medieval Towns series. Though all Continental towns of any size are medieval towns in the sense that they have a medieval history, they are by no means all equal in medieval historical interest and it is therefore a sound plan to include these three neighbouring Swiss towns in the compass of one handy volume. The author has neatly covered the historical interest of the towns for all guide book purposes, well aided by three maps and fifty illustrations.

The volume on Canterbury, equally generously illustrated, is part of the Cathedrals, Abbeys, and Churches series, covers the ground well, with a proper impartiality in the historical portion. In addition to the Cathedral itself, there is a chapter on St. Augustine's Abbey and another on ancient neighbouring church. The handy format and production well maintains the firm's high standard in this regard, and both volumes are full value for money.

G.C.H.

R.I.P. *By Philip Macdonald. Collins. 7s. 6d.*

Mr. Macdonald's tale of vengeance, completed with the meting out of justice to the avenger, is one of the most turgid novels it has been my misfortune in recent months to read. I welcomed the sight of his name on the jacket because he is the author of some excellent fiction; but appreciation faded rapidly, indeed very rapidly, after I weathered this passage :—

" George Crecy breathed deep through nostrils squeezing themselves with effort above his fierce, flat-brushed almost white, moustache."

The other characters are described, and accounts of their actions are written in the same general style.

E.J.M.

THE FACE OF DEATH. *By Mark Gault. Methuen. 7s. 6d.*

A dilettante with more money than intelligence finds a woman dying in a room next to his in a *pension* in Florence (that most romantic city). She is poisoned; he is suspected; why, and the whole story, is told in his own words. The story is not bad, but his own words (as he has artistic leanings as a dilettante) become rather irritating.

SPIES ARE ABROAD. *By J. M. Walsh. Collins. 7s.6d.*

This is an exciting yarn of the British Secret Service. Veiled girls, mysterious knifings, bold adventurers and even bolder adventuresses, anonymous notes of warning, and so on. There is a great plot against the British Empire. The East's awake. It is all very thrilling, and, for once, Moscow is not the seat of the revolution.

V.N.L.

YEARS AGO

[*From time to time we propose to publish under this heading quotations from speeches and writings which seem to have a special significance after a lapse of years. Some of these quotations are from the works of men who were essentially in agreement with the views expressed in this paper. Others may cause surprise in view of the causes with which the authors were identified. Readers are invited to suggest suitable items.*

The following is extracted from a report of a debate in Parliament in 1601, when monopolies were, as now, of vital public interest.]

MR. FRANCIS BACON: . . . " I confess the bill, as it is, is in few words, but yet ponderous and weighty. For the prerogative royal of the prince, for my own part I ever allowed of it, and it is such as I hope shall never be discussed. The queen, as she is our Sovereign, has both an enlarging and restraining liberty of her prerogative. . . . I say that we ought not to deal or meddle with or judge of her majesty's prerogative."

Dr. Bennet: . . . " He that will go about to debate her majesty's prerogative royal must walk warily. In respect of a grievance out of that city for which I serve, I think myself bound to speak that now which I had not intended to speak before; I mean a monopoly of salt. It is an old proverb (*Sal sapit omnia*); fire and water are not more necessary. But for other monopolies, of cards (at which word Sir Walter Raleigh blushed), dice, starch, etc., they are, because monopolies, I must confess, very hateful, though not so hurtful." . . .

Mr. Francis Moore: . . . " Mr. Speaker, I know the queen's prerogative is a thing curious to be dealt withal, yet all grievances are not comparable. I cannot utter with my tongue or conceive with my heart the great grievances that the town and country, for which I serve, suffer by these monopolies. It bringeth the general profit into a private hand, and the end of all is beggary and bondage to the subjects. . . . Out of the spirit of humility, Mr. Speaker, I do speak it; there is no act of hers that hath been or is more derogatory to her own majesty, or more odious to the subject, or more dangerous to the Commonwealth than the granting of these monopolies."

Mr. Secretary Cecil: . . . " If there had not been some mistaking or confusion in the committee, I would not now have spoken. . . This dispute draws two great things in question; first, the prince's power; secondly, the freedom of Englishmen. I am an Englishman, and a fellow-member of this House; I would desire to live no day, in which I should detract from either. I am a servant to the queen; and before I would speak or give my consent to a case that should debase her prerogative or abridge it, I would wish my tongue cut out of my head. . . For my own part, I like not these courses should be taken; and you, Mr. Speaker, should perform the charge her majesty gave unto you at the beginning of this parliament not to receive bills of this nature; for her majesty's ears be open to all grievances, and her hand stretched out to every man's petition. For the matter of access I like it well, so it be first moved and the way prepared."

Cinema

" Don Quixote "

THERE are certain scenes in films that fix themselves on the memory and will not let go. I remember particularly isolated incidents in " The Nibelungs," the Keystone police, Snub Pollard, some of the Drew comedies, bits of " Sunrise," "The Student Prince " and " The Waltz Dream," and the Oceana Roll in " The Gold Rush." To these I must now add the windmill scene in " Don Quixote."

I remember a previous version, in the silent days; one in which George Robey played Sancho Panza. A deplorable exhibition (for which George Robey was not to blame) which convinced me that the camera was almost incapable of interpreting a work of any importance. But Pabst has redressed the balance of argument; aided by Chaliapine and George Robey. And the treatment of the windmill scene convinces me once more that the film can capture the imagination, and that film-makers can use their subjects with understanding as well as skill.

In this picture (which is now at the Adelphi Theatre) the character of Don Quixote has been presented reasonably and with just enough sympathy to make him real. Hollywood might have surrounded him with the creatures of sophistication, Pabst has tried to surround him with his own people. It may be said by someone coming from the theatre who had never heard previously of Don Quixote: " There was a madman." Yet most of them, if they studied the implications of the picture must have felt that they were put in the possession of bewildering sanities.

From the first scene to the last (despite a certain over-emphasis in the library scenes) one sees a genuine effort in interpretation. On that account George Robey is entitled to special praise; since his Sancho Panza is never George Robey but a man created by him with his own appreciation of Sancho's character. As for Chaliapine (whose singing it is not my job to appraise), I felt while watching the picture that I was in the presence of an actor of giant stature. The impression was by no means due to the size of the figures on the screen.

In recent months a great deal of wasted footage has been projected on the screens of cinemas. Therefore enthusiasm may easily cause a loss of balance when an ably produced, intelligent film can be seen. " Don Quixote " may be full of faults; but I wish that half the other films produced contained as many virtues.

EDWARD J. MACDONALD.

Music

ANYONE who has heard the mighty volume of Chaliapine's voice resounding throughout the vast spaces of Covent Garden and the Lyceum or echoing around the Albert Hall must have wondered, with no little trepidation, what exactly would be the result if that voice were to be amplified in proportion to the huge stature which human beings assume on the cinema screen. *Don Quixote* will set any such fears at rest. The twenty, thirty, fifty-foot, or whatever it is, man which appears on the screen does not produce much more volume of sound than the original six-foot Chaliapine. There is not, of course, anything approaching the same range of expression. That could not be expected from any mechanical reproduction, particularly from one which is so undeveloped as the present " Talkie " apparatus. Nevertheless it is true that the glorious voice has been more or less successfully " canned "—as a film critic described it— that there is, incomplete and crude as it is, a record by which posterity can realise something of what their fathers mean when they talk of the great days of Chaliapine. What he has to sing in *Don Quixote* is not of much musical value, and it is rather unfortunate that the exigencies of " the trade " necessitate him singing in English; as the words given him to interpret are not always of the best tradition of the language of Shakespeare. As for the acting, it is not for me to say. Apparently what constitutes good cinema acting is a secret known only to a few experts, and it seems obvious enough that to make an effect on the screen requires a special technique. All I can say, as a rare film-goer, and for what it is worth, is that the dramatic force of Chaliapine on the screen, while it is not what it is on the operatic stage, is something that few film stars can begin to understand. And I would also, again for what it is worth, pay a tribute to George Robey's Sancho Panza. It is rather more English than Spanish; and Mr. Robey simply can't help being funny in a particularly English way; but throughout he has kept the character of the servant, really fond of his mad master, really frightened of the scrapes he is led into and yet facing them with a humorous bravery in the manner of the traditional Cockney " Tommy "; in other words, making poor Sancho a convincing human person. I suppose, if there are sufficient films of this nature produced to entice me to the cinema, I shall in time get accustomed to the strangely distorted " synchronised " music which the art of the Talkies has introduced, and be better able to compare the excellence of one reproduction with another. I am as yet unable to pass judgment in the matter.

Nor am I in the least bit able to tell you whether Mr. Charles B. Cochran's production of *Music in the Air* is to be successful. I am sure it deserves to be. It is brilliantly put on, Jerome Kern's music is in its way delightful, and Miss Mary Ellis in addition to looking charming and acting superbly, sings the part of the operatic star extraordinarily well. Mr. Horace Hodges has got the pathos and the sentimental kind-heartedness, if not the single-mindedness, of the Bavarian musician, and he must have found his daughter a sore disappointment—vocally, anyhow. Charles V. France's music publisher is excellent. I wonder whether he would have undertaken publishing Jerome Kern. It would have paid him. Mr. Bruce Carfax does not have so easy a time as the provincial school teacher-lover, but Mr. Margetson, as the playwright, is fortunate in being so able to interpret to his players what playacting should be. A play must have a plot and the jealousies of temperamental musicians is sufficiently well known to make the plot of this play credible. The most interesting statement made is that the purpose of art is to deliver the goods; which naturally raises the old question of who is to decide what is the goods. Whether the kind of West-end audience which likes this kind of West-end entertainment will decide that once more Mr. Cochran has delivered the goods is, as I have said, a matter which is not for me to decide. I can only say that *Music in the Air* provides an amusing and an interesting evening, for more than just tired business men.

V.N.L.

The Cockpit.

[*Letters should not exceed 300 words in length and must bear the names and addresses, not necessarily for publication, of their authors.*
The Editor can accept no responsibility for opinions expressed by correspondents.]

THE LAND.

Sir,—Two articles in the issue for May 19 deal with the professional man's dilemma, referring specifically to the individual practising on his own account. But there is also the professional man employed by a large firm who finds his salary reduced and forsees the possible entire loss of his position at the end of a long-drawn out period. Further with a large family, every penny of spare income may be taken by school fees in trying to give his children an education which bears some relation to his own. Possibly he may see the youngest settled in life and have paid off arrears of school bills by the time he is sixty or so. He may even have saved a few hundreds by the time his job has to be given up, but how is he to live on that? These are the cases where a small-holding is appreciated; one that has been developed and organized while a man's energy is still fresh, not to speak of his wife's. Even if developed in spare time and farmed very lightly for a period a fair sized piece of land can soon be developed intensively. But as Mr. Heseltine points out land costs money, although the house itself can be built and paid for through a building society, over a period of years.

The renting of land as against ownership has been condemned on Distributist principles for such reasons that improvements tend to accrue to the landlord; and further any general increase in agricultural prosperity is an excuse for the raising of rents. As to purchase the writer feels that with so many people concentrating on poultry and market gardening, mixed farming is the only reasonable solution. This will necessitate 20 or 25 acres of land costing anything round £600 within reasonable access to a town.

It is therefore suggested that the form of tenure known as "Copyhold" might be revived where a landowner is willing. Under this system the land remains permanently in the possession of the family who farms it so long as a fixed annual rent is paid. Reasonable security is thus provided, not so great as freeholding, but sufficient.

Copyhold was brought into existence when the serfs were emancipated and paid a fixed sum of money in commutation for their labour services. During the fifteenth century two classes came into existence, copyholders and tenants paying a rent fixed by custom. The rents of the latter could of course be revised and were as a matter of fact raised to four or five times their original amount with the increased value of land after the Reformation. Copyholders were very much more difficult to deal with and those that lost their rights only did so by illegal means or by pressure. During the enclosures they were often persuaded to exchange their copyhold tenure for leases at the end of which they became mere tenants, or else the fines payable in certain circumstances were largely increased. But if those in power are determined to obtain the land, they can almost as easily dispossess the freeholder as the copyholder and the increased security of the former is to that extent visionary.

It would be interesting to hear the views of other readers on this suggestion, but it does appear to offer one solution of the present difficulty in obtaining the land.

ELSMERE HARRIS.

Sir,—We cannot often congratulate our daily press on its advice or sentiments; all the more reason therefore to give the *Daily Express* a pat on the back for its leading article on Monday, May 29th. Under the caption "SPEND!" it reminded its readers that during the week the Government would be distributing £35,000,000 dividend on War Loan Stock. Then followed the advice: "Spend this money *here*. Re-invest it in *productive industry* in Britain. Build......*Buy land......*!" These last words are as significant as they are timely. But it is not easy for us all to go out and buy our individual little plots. May I suggest to readers of G.K.'S WEEKLY who may be participating in this forthcoming dividend to watch for the forthcoming announcement of the proposed Marydown Farming Association, an enterprise which, while appealing particularly to Catholics, will offer to all sympathisers with a back-to-the-land movement an opportunity of following the excellent advice of the *Express* in an eminently practical way.

T. W. C. CURD.

SOCIAL CREDIT.

Sir,—While looking forward to reading replies by Mr. Reckitt and Mr. Symons to the article this week by Mr. H. Robbins, I wonder if the latter has given *full* consideration to the advantages of the proposals advanced by Major Douglas.

Were I obliged to choose under which banner I proposed to fight—*either* that raised by Major Douglas *or* that raised by the Distributists—I would naturally choose to be a Distributist, since Social Credit can hardly promise liberty, security in small ownership and the well-being of the family. But are we forced to choose? Can we not regard Social Credit as a means to an end; as something at least that can overcome the money-power and put us in a better position strategically for continued conflict with all the enemies of the small man's freedom? Mr. Robbins would seem to doubt it. So would Commander Shove. But how many really believe that the two movements can go forward together until the one can give place quietly to the other?

A. M. LINDEN.

Sir,—May I support Father Drinkwater's plea for a change of attitude on the discussion now proceeding in your pages under the above title? It must be possible to find out where the Douglasites and the Distributists are in agreement, and much good might come of willingness "to build on that." I would suggest that some gifted person, not identified with either movement be asked to read the articles and letters that have appeared in G.K.'S WEEKLY with a view to summing up the evidence for both sides and delivering his judgment. Neither side would be committed, but both might conclude that they could accept his verdict.

P. R. HARPER.

The Restoration of Property

On May 26, Mr. Hilaire Belloc addressed a meeting of the Distributist League (Central Branch) at Carr's Restaurant, Strand, W.C.2, on "The Restoration of Property." We quote the following extracts from his speech:—

"THE difficulties before us in the restoration of property are twofold. They are, first of all the philosophy under which the modern world, particularly in this country, has been created and has lived increasingly during the last 300 years; and secondly, the actual state of society produced by that philosophy. I distinguish between the two. A philosophy—or a religion, which is the only practical form of any philosophy—is a state of mind, a mood, an attitude towards the universe, and in the long run that produces its fruit in institutions, examples of action, of manner, of little daily details which flow from the philosophy. But you must distinguish between the two, because the first is not easily approachable in the same way in which the second is approachable.

"Let us take things in their logical order. There is a certain philosophy called natural religion we all have in us, and under which we should all live were we free of tradition (which of course is impossible to man) or had we nothing but an unpolluted tradition; and it must be justly taken that under those conditions property exists, in the sense, that is, of property well divided. One can imagine no more normal human society, no society more normal to man as we know him, as he is. A society in which men live in security, such that every production of wealth with that which they possess maintains them in the community, and can be handed on to their posterity. That is normal to man. All our folk lore, all our fairy tales, morals, proverbs, point to that as being our norm. If I steal my neighbour's watch I am not punished—a poor man would be punished, but I should not be—I am blamed on the theory that it is property which I am infringing. We all think normally, in our human consciences, in terms of property. That, I say, is a fundamental which we must all admit.

"Of course a man naturally owns, and naturally will have the tradition and security that goes with ownership, but to that philosophy was added another philosophy which came in slowly over the Græco-Roman world, and happily got through to our world, called the conversion of the Roman Empire. There was a slow transmogrification from the old Pagan religion into a more conscious, more active and more dangerous, but perhaps more developed state of mind, which was called Christendom, and under that again property was established, and in a very interesting way; because the Christian religion, having baptised the Græco-Roman world, had such an effect upon it that slowly and inevitably the slave became an owner. By very slow degrees it happened, and before the end of the Middle Ages, throughout the west of Christendom, on the whole and taking it by and large, there had been a commonwealth established in which most men owned and most men could transmit what they owned to their posterity. There was the guild for the craftsman and the village community for the peasant.

That was the norm of that society, and men were pretty happy under that society, and the test of normality is whether people are happy or not. If you doubt whether they were happy or not, go to the places which they carved, and see the songs which they sang, and compare them with the songs which we sing. As for carving, well go and look at the carving.

"Now that philosophy was warped by a great revolution which began after the Black Death, and was growing in the early 16th century; but after a tremendous fight, by the middle of the 17th century, Europe had decided to divide into two camps from exhaustion. The old tradition could not conquer the new revolt, and the new revolt could not conquer the old religion. One of the camps said, 'I have done with all the old things, I have got some new principles altogether,' and the other said, 'No, I am going on,' but did not only say it was going on, but organised itself for resistance lest it should be swamped; and those two camps in Europe went on. You will remember that in those days the Greek Orthodox Church hardly counted.

"Now under those two philosophies, the first philosophy, the rebellious philosophy, won. The general term for it is Protestant, but it was much more, it was also the general emancipation from the clerical system of the Middle Ages spread out in all sorts of ways. There is no generic term for it, but it won, and having won it produced very slowly, by stages of which many are familiar, after generations, what is known as the Capitalist System, in which efficiency was produced not by the supervision of work or by the guild, but by competition; in which the peasant, because he was the less instructed, was destroyed under competition; in which, not exactly because men worshipped Mammon but because they worshipped the competitive idea, the rich man ate up the small man until we arrived at the state of affairs where we are now, called Industrial Capitalism. . . .

"Now let us proceed to the second point, which is part of the first. I say this philosophy has produced Industrial Capitalism. What do we mean by that? Not the use of certain machines, because they might just as well be held by a guild as by an individual. What we mean essentially is plutocracy. We mean that the mass of men have lost their security and their choice of how they shall live within the limits wherein men should normally have such choice. So that I cannot to-day, and Mr. Chesterton cannot to-day, write what we think, as we would have done in the 17th century or even in the 18th, without the agreement of a few vulgarians who happen to have the money.

"Our second point is that this philosophy has produced a certain state of society. The change in philosophy is our root difficulty, but the second is that it has produced a certain state of society. It is a state in which by far the greater part of men are attuned to being wage slaves, that is, a state of society in which a man is more afraid of losing his job than of anything else. It is that which controls us all. Of course the mass of the people who are really poor are entirely wage slaves. They have withdrawn themselves from the worst of the conditions by a certain amount of organisation, but still, that is the norm of our society; and the great struggle among the few who are free from this condition is to avoid being a wage slave, and the greatest misfortune is to die a wage slave. But we are all attuned to that state of mind in this country. Think for instance of the extraordinary phrase 'Unemployment.' The Rothschilds, if there are any left, are unemployed. It is not having nothing to do which is the disaster, it is not getting money for doing things. The disaster is in not having security. . . .

"We have had during the last fifty or sixty years inventions and discoveries, such as the internal combustion engine and the distribution of electric power, which might have aided enormously the distribution of property if our philosophy had been right. But more important in my judgment is this. Industrial Capitalism has broken down. It has broken down for a very simple arithmetical reason—it distributes less purchasing power than it creates. I am not going to speak of Major Douglas's scheme of Social Credit, because that is merely an indirect method of distributing property, which I prefer to achieve by direct means. Industrial Capitalism has broken down, not because it is tired or old or wicked, but because it is producing an amount of wealth greater than it is distributing purchasing power for that wealth; and to put it very crudely indeed, if I want to make a hundred thousand boots, or rather employ men to make those boots, by the time the boots are made I have distributed to the men who make them the money wherewith to purchase thirty thousand boots, and what am I to do with the seventy thousand boots left? I must sell them to niggers, or to the Colonies, if you prefer that term. And supposing they also learn to turn a handle, and produce the boots themselves, where are you? That is why Industrial Capitalism has broken down.

"One of the results is that people are getting disgusted and saying something must be done. We cannot tell people what to do in a cut and dried system. No man attempting the restoration of property, or Distributism as it is sometimes called, can say, " Here is my cut and dried plan." You cannot do it, because it is normal to man, organic; it is not mechanical, it is not theoretical. What we can do is to advance something on the way, to propagate the idea, to propagate its results, to insist upon it here and there, in this reform and that, by blocking this abuse and that, until there shall be established in society a certain growth which will lead ultimately towards better distribution of property. We do not want, and it would be folly to attempt, and it is not human to regard, and it is futile to desire the equal distribution of property. If you have a society in which the norm, it may not even be the majority, but the determining number of men are possessed of security in what they do, producing with their personality and with their production fully secured for the future, you have established a healthy state, you have reconstructed property; and if you will consider that, doing it organically, without revolution, you may, in spite of the enormous obstacles in front of you, do the trick. That is the rule I put before myself, and which, if I could come back to life after my death, I should probably find completely ruined."

League Meetings

CENTRAL BRANCH
The activities of the Central Branch will continue through the Summer. Members of the Branch, and non-members are invited to a Social Evening on June 16. Details of arrangements will be published next week. The Central Branch Committee is now engaged upon the compilation of a Speakers' Handbook, notes and suggestions for which will be welcomed. Members interested may attend a meeting of the Committee at the Devereux, June 9, from 7.30 p.m. It is hoped to hold a public meeting on Credit Unions, addressed by Mr. Roy F. Bergengren, the American organiser, at the end of the month. All London Distributists are asked to co-operate actively in the work of the Branch.

BIRMINGHAM BRANCH.
Meetings at Bellman Buildings, 39, Carr's Lane, Birmingham, at 7.30 p.m.
June 9. Delegates will report on the Glossop Conference of The League.
June 23. Mr. J. F. Galleymore on " Hitler in the Rhineland."
July 7. Miss N. Careless on " The Reconstruction of Property."
July 21. Subject and Speaker to be announced later.

CLYDESDALE BRANCH.
The Branch holds its meetings in the Queen Anne Restaurant, Argyle Street, Glasgow, every Wednesday, at 7.30, where new members can be enrolled.

BRADFORD BRANCH.
The discussion following Mr. E. Wilson's paper on " Co-partnership " was so animated that it was decided to continue it at our next meeting, to be held on Monday, June 12, at St. Cuthbert's Guild Rooms, Wilmer Road, Heaton, at 7.30 p.m. Mr. M. White will open the discussion with a short paper on " Why Distributists should not support Co-partnership." Branch members are invited to bring their friends.

SOUTHAMPTON BRANCH.
Meetings are held every fortnight at 123, Warren Avenue. Write to the Secretary for particulars.

GLASGOW BRANCH.
Meetings will be held in the Highlander's Institute, Elmbank Street, at 7.45 p.m., on the following Mondays:—
June 19. Mr. McGlinchey—"Lithuania."
July 3. Discussion on " National Self-Sufficiency."
Hon. Sec., J. J. Lynch, 122, Quarrybrae Street, Parkhead, Glasgow, E.1.

BOURNEMOUTH BRANCH.
Readers of G.K.'s Weekly living at or near Bournemouth who are interested in the work of the Distributist League are invited to write to Mr. R. H. McCausland, 43, St. Luke's Road, Bournemouth, with a view to increasing membership of the Branch and planning future activities.

NEW SCOTTISH BRANCH.
The new Branch holds its meetings in the Queen Anne Restaurant, Argyle Street, Glasgow, every Wednesday at 7.30, where new members are being enrolled. Secretary: Mr. J. MacNamee, 513, Alexandra Parade, Glasgow.

The Problem of Machinery
By C. T. B. D.
A study of importance from a Distributist's point of view
PRICE 6d.

The Distributist League
2, Little Essex Street, London, W.C.2.

Published by the Proprietors, G.K.'s WEEKLY, LTD., 2, Little Essex Street, Strand, London, W.C.2 (incorporating THE NEW WITNESS). Telephone: Temple Bar 1978. Printed by THE NUNEATON NEWSPAPERS LTD., "Observer" Buildings, Nuneaton. Sole Agents for Australasia: Gordon & Gotch (Australasia, Ltd.). Sole Agents for South Africa: Central News Agency Ltd. (London Agents: Gordon & Gotch, Ltd.)

GK's WEEKLY

EDITED BY G.K. CHESTERTON

SEPTEMBER 28, 1933
VOL. XVIII.   No. 446
Registered as a Newspaper   SIXPENCE.

MANY MANŒUVRES

SO far, this present month has been a tranquil and satisfying season for the English newspaper reader. There was some talk of drought; but this did not affect the suburbs of London and therefore did not develop into a National Question. There were heath fires; but even our most vigilant watchdogs of the Press failed to scent any Communistic torch-bearers. Politicians have been speaking; but as Parliament is not sitting nobody need listen. True, there was a momentary stir over the Tschekedi show-down; but at least no self-appointed "international legal" tribunal had the fatuous indecency to stage a trial in Vienna or Madrid before we could sift the matter for ourselves.

Yes, even the mock Reichstag inquiry we had the discourtesy to shelter in London, has fortunately been forgotten in the sensation of the Leipzig fight; and in the contemplation of that great debate we again find occasion for insular complacency. Such things do not happen in England. There comes, certainly, a passing twinge of middle-aged regret as we observe the ebullience of Nazi youth. What a grand gesture that was (if indeed the Nazi agents were the incendiaries)—to burn down overnight a Senate-house for which one would have no further use ! We shall show, we fear, no such magnificence in cutting our losses : when our own Parliament-house loses its last dignity, it will be abandoned to squalor and decay, like the Alexandra Palace.

Then to add relish to our season of piping peace, there have been the Service manœuvres, to remind us

that, while we have an isle of peace to be thankful for, we are prepared to hold it. Salisbury Plain has been the cockpit of a pleasant little civil war in which nothing much has been gained except the knowledge that both sides won and ours is a jolly fine Army anyway. Of greater public interest have been the Naval and Aerial exercises in the North, from the reports of which ordinary citizens do (rightly or wrongly) hope to form some idea of our resources against dangers more real than Red armies. But the importance (to watchers) of these exercises, enthralling as they were, is diminished by the laconic reminder of the Naval Staff to the effect that this kind of thing would only work provided our air squadrons knew exactly when and where the enemy ships proposed to attack, and that in any case the function of a navy is not invasion but the rupture of the sea communication of its opponent's country, and the preservation of that of its own.

Which brings us at last to the one news-item which suggests that there are definite steps, and steps of undeniable utility, this country can take, *now*, for its defence in time of war; and moreover that even in this comfortable and soporific autumn somebody has found the energy to think of our own affairs and our own welfare. The coal merchants and the colliery owners are combining to raise an appropriation of £60,000 annually for a "sustained publicity campaign" to encourage the home consumption of coal in an effort to re-instate the industry. And the Miners' Federation proposes to "use every effort to increase the use of coal as against the importation of foreign oil and petrol, not only as a means to the greater use of raw coal, but in addition to assist the development of processes to produce oil and petrol from British coal.''

The objects of the publicity campaign are worth noting. They include ''Sales promotion in its widest sense, including publicity. In this connection it is stated that 'the claims of the Press for a substantial share of any advertising appropriation are strong and well recognised'; training of salesmen and coal executives; substitution of efficient modern appliances for the antiquated grates and stoves found in so many homes; the organisation of an adequate research service; the elimination of waste in retail distribution by systematic marketing; and the production of an efficient smoke eliminator, for which a substantial prize will be offered.'' The Coal Utilisation Council's Report, from which the foregoing clauses were taken, refers also to ''the present ruinous competition, due to the excessive number of retail distributors.''

Much of this will, we fear, sound vaguely familiar to our readers; and lest a sense of disappointment causes irritation we hasten to point out that we merely claimed somebody was finding the energy to think about this nation's welfare—not that the thinking was proving successful. Still, it is invigorating to find that the £60,000 is going to deserving persons like publicity experts, super-salesmen, and coal trade executives (whatever they may be) and that the claims of the impoverished Press will be heard. By the time these are satiated, and the inventor of the Smoke Eliminator has received his substantial prize, we hope (but scarcely expect) that a large slice of the £60,000 will be left for the ''organisation of an adequate research service''; this being, presumably, the effective part of the scheme to assist the home-production of oil and petrol.

We have not space for an immediate discussion of the proposals to eliminate small independent distributors whose only vice is that they are independent; or to eliminate antiquated grates whose only virtue is that they warm the house. What first concerns us, and everybody, is the futile and footling way in which this grave national problem—of our own mining industry in chaos while the liquid-fuel imports leap up year by year—is left to the irresponsible attention of powerful but unofficial bodies. Economic independence, and diffusion of property, is the backbone of our social philosophy; but we have always allowed that some few matters are in their nature a national concern. The coal-mining industry is one of them. It is vital to our present economy, and it cannot be distributively organised to advantage, as can agriculture and practically all other industry. Furthermore, coal-getting is coal *getting*, not coal-manufacturing. We possess a fund of coal, strictly limited in extent and availability. On this, in time of war, our munitions and transport and ships—our lives, in fact—may depend. The only golden rules in economics are justice and expediency. Hence we advocate national handling of the coal supply, and a distributist basis for agriculture, for identical reasons: because they will work best that way; and we cannot afford to have these industries working any but the best way. This coal manœuvre then is the least satisfactory manœuvre of the month. Still, we have had the Reichstag fire trial to look at: something which has nothing whatever to do with us; and which in the upshot will probably be found to have nothing whatever to do with anything.

NOTES OF THE WEEK

Monday, September 25.

The Prime Minister, anxious for the return of another '' National Labour '' candidate, made a speech last week at Kilmarnock full of windy praise for the Government he is supposed to lead and containing assurances that all will be well so long as he remains a tenant in Downing Street. Much of what he said has been heard before and calls for no special comment here. But one new statement must not be allowed to pass unchallenged. That statement was to the effect that he and his colleagues '' can look the housewife in the face and we can prove to her that our efforts in trying to get her husband into work by increasing the wholesale prices of certain commodities have not lowered for her the purchasing power of her shilling.'' Does the man live in the clouds, or were his words chosen deliberately as a defiance of fact?

* * * *

Ask any housewife who has to count the shillings carefully and she will tell you the truth of the matter. She will tell you that in the course of a few weeks eggs, butter, meat and other vital foodstuffs have had to be used more sparingly because they cost more to buy. She will admit that prices tend always to rise at this time of year, but she will add that they have risen beyond expectation. There is no doubt whatever of the increased cost of living; no doubt either of the hardship caused by the drastic application of the means test, and the continuance of reduced salaries. But perhaps the operative words in his speech were '' our efforts.'' Perhaps he meant that the price of food was one of the things the Government had not attempted to control. If so, his subtlety suggests a warning that he should talk plainly and sensibly or not talk at all.

* * * *

Incidentally Mr. MacDonald's assurances read strangely when accompanied in the newspapers by reports of a speech by Sir Herbert Austin who opposed, in a debate, proposals for a forty-hour week in industry.

" This forty-hour week is based on a fallacy. Industry is not able to support any added burden of higher wage rates, whether by higher scales of pay or shorter hours. There may be a move in the opposite direction. There may be a reduction. I say that with a full knowledge of what is going on. Hours may have to be advanced and wages placed on a more economic basis.

"Although this may be considered a move in the wrong direction, it would nevertheless have a much greater chance of solving the unemployment problem than the one we are discussing to-day."

Thus spoke the industrialist. Luckily for him he was not asked nor had to volunteer to explain what was likely to happen to the purchasing power of the housewife's shiling.

*　　*　　*　　*

Two weeks ago Mr. H. H. Hutchinson protested in these columns against the misleading statements made in connection with the Milk Marketing Scheme. He asked how many farmers were entitled to register in the first place; how many farmers did in fact register; and how many farmers voted in favour of the scheme. He added:—

" Until these figures are known, all talk of approval by an overwhelming majority of farmers is either guess work or deception."

We are still waiting, not very hopefully, for the publication of reliable, informative figures. Meanwhile most commentators in the Press have shown an unfortunate readiness to accept official statements at their face-value. Even Mr. Christopher Addison, ex-Minister of Agriculture, author of the Agricultural Marketing Act from which the scheme was derived, says, in *John Bull*, that it has been approved " by an overwhelming majority of the producers." Since officialdom is silent, will Mr. Addison enlighten us?

*　　*　　*　　*

Rumour has it that Chief Tshekedi is about to be re-instated according to the terms of an agreement by which he admits that Europeans should be tried only by Europeans and that a white man, however black, is unable to lose the whiteness of his skin. If this be true, a grand parade of marines and howitzers has been wasted, and the criticisms levelled against it by the South African Press have been justified. A satisfactory outcome of a most unfortunate dispute may be in prospect. We hope, however, that a strict enquiry will be instituted by the authorities into the conduct of all the people concerned; and that, if laxity be discovered, no fear of lowering prestige will be allowed to prevent the exercise of justice.

The Approach of War

By Hilaire Belloc

THESE lines are written on Wednesday, September 20th at a moment of crisis in Europe of which some faint echoes are heard in London.

It has been insisted in these columns, and in these columns alone out of all the English Press, that the policy of this country towards Prussia would inevitably lead ultimately to an immediate peril of War. That moment of peril has come.

It has further been insisted upon in these columns that England of all countries should have taken most trouble to avoid the situation which those who govern her destinies have created. To use once again the phrase we have used fifty times—"We have everything to lose and nothing to gain by a further outbreak of War."

It is notorious, and it is taken for granted now throughout the World, there could not be any further mobilization here for the purpose of War abroad. That is one of the permanent factors of the situation: the factor on which all Europe counts, and no one more than Prussia.

Meanwhile England has control over great masses of subject populations in Egypt and India and the Crown Colonies, and what are hypocritically called " mandates." Such control still (though precariously) produces great revenue, and that revenue is envied by others. In the old days this privileged position (as it then was) could be envisaged in contemptuous security. The Fleet was invincible; the frontiers of Britain in War were shores of her enemies. The Island itself (the wounding of which would involve a crash of the whole scheme) was absolutely invulnerable and immune. There was no danger from within, for Aristocratic Government had made it the most united of all the States in the World. There was no danger from without; the narrow seas were then broad enough; no craft could challenge the immense superiority of England on the surface of the water; attack by air was unknown; there could be no serious interference with a dominating Navy. To-day all that has gone. Yet men so live in the past that they have treated the situation after the Great War on a mere copy of what was done after the Napoleonic Wars. The idea was to raise up the defeated enemy—Prussia—so that there should be a balance in Europe, and to reduce the victorious Ally—France—proportionately.

This Policy was not wholly, or even mainly, the Policy of the Foreign Office. It was the Policy of what is to-day far more powerful than the Civil Service: the Banks, the big Newspaper Owners: Big Business generally, and for what they are worth—the Politicians. It showed what may yet be fatal to us —a deep ignorance of Europe. Prussia restored to sufficient strength will certainly attack.

You hear men maundering in speech and print about some policy of " Disarmament " or what not. Maundering is the word. No pledge; no paper arrangement can prevent Prussia both re-arming, and when re-armed—attacking. Probably she will be defeated, but when she is defeated there would be a re-arrangement of world affairs heavily disastrous to this country. There is only one thing to be done, and there is yet time to do it, but only just time. That is, for the Policy of this country to reverse engines: even now a Public declaration from even one responsible man—one of the "puppet" Politicians would do so long as he was connected with what is called "Government"; so long as he was " official." One speech would be enough, and our rapid approach to the abyss would be checked.

Hitherto there has been no sign of any such clarity or wisdom, and it is awfully probable that, as in 1914, and as in the breakdown of English credit and trade two years ago (the consequences of which fools try to hide) there will be a drift into disaster. But there is yet time. It is the Eleventh hour: when the twelfth strikes many will suffer, but the ignorant who still nourish a vague inherited sense of security, who say that they need take no part in a catastrophe involving all our civilisation, who imagine they can avoid the consequences of their vanity and self-sufficiency, will suffer more than any, except perhaps the unfortunate dull Germans themselves.

Annie Besant

By W. R. Titterton

I MET Mrs. Annie Besant but once. I forget the occasion—except that I was to interview her for the Press. But I know that I got nothing out of her. She seemed like a cloud a long way off.

So different from Ghandi, that other Mahatma, with his humanly broken teeth, and his eagerness to convert you. Mrs. Besant stayed put, like Madame Humbert's safe. Oh, those women!

When I was very young Mrs. Besant was a Fabian, and so was I. Already it was ancient history that she had been Bradlaugh's partner, stumping the country for Atheism and Birth Control. Socialism at that time was out for creative things—fellowship and so on—and the negation of God and the negation of birth seemed coeval with the Great Exhibition.

But what struck me (us, I think) about Mrs. Besant was that she was so dreadfully emotional. All emotion, and no logic. And I, as yet uninstructed, found it queer that this ex-Rationalist should so gush over.

In fact, being young, and intolerant, I disliked her and her aura very much. Bradlaugh I could stomach. Because—but you've read *The Babe and the Cross*. Them's my sentiments. Mrs. Besant's pleasant-Sunday-afternoon Fabianism worried me. You can't anchor yourself to a dissolving view.

I was very glad when she abandoned this life, and became a Theosophist.

Mind you, in the nineties or thereabouts all the Ists were friends. Provided that you rebelled against Samuel Smiles and the Prince Consort you were one of us. In the gatherings of the period I have rubbed shoulders with comrades the most abominable, and knew that I must put up with them because they were Ists.

So that it was not felt that we had lost Mrs. Besant when she embraced the immemorial East. After all, Herbert Burrows was a Theosophist, and so in a way were H. R. Crage and A. J. Penty.

But I was beginning to acquire a vague hint of reasonableness, and I told myself that Annie had always been a loose bundle of emotions, and that Theosophy with its wide toleration for all sorts and sizes of religions gave her the finest opportunity for stopping over. Well, she stopped.

And, being a woman of great urge, though not strength, of personality, she stopped wide and free. She didn't invent Theosophy—Madame Blavatsky did that—but she certainly popularised it.

And that brings us to another point. Mrs. Besant was a follower. She followed Bradlaugh, she followed Sidney Webb, she followed Madame Blavatsky. She had something given her that she could enthuse over. She was a Miss Slade who adopted herself as her own Ghandi.

Mind you, I don't think it was a big jump from Atheism to Theosophy. It's as easy to accept anything as to deny anything. To have a definite outline and stick to it—that's the devil of a job.

Of course I haven't the faintest idea what Theosophy is, and I don't know why this universal religion, with Christ, Mahommed, Buddha, Socrates, and the rest of them as commissionaires in the vestibule had to be Hindu. That gets me. Ghandi I can understand, but not this universal balanced-ration with a Madras label.

You have heard Mrs. Besant speak? She was wonderful. She thrilled you. The cloud became fire, and lightning struck out of it. If you were asking for it she carried you away. If you weren't you had to kick yourself to keep calm. But that's often the case when the orator has no more than rudimentary intelligence.

Was Mrs. Besant intelligent? I think not. I don't know, because, as I have said, when I met her I could not get near her. I think that she was chock-full of facile emotion, and had a highly magnetic personality, which she could switch on or off at will. I think that she had the best of intentions and the conviction that Annie Besant was one of the saviours of mankind.

Either she or somebody in her entourage was a good business person. Theosophy was put on the market with great skill, and she got herself and her clique accepted in India—even by the Brahmins—in a way that astonishes all students of Hindu life.

It was clever of her to reside in Madras—a boiling hot place, where they have nine hot months and three months hotter, but where all the natives speak English. So that she was able to publish a paper in English and address the natives in English. I believe that she spoke a number of the languages of India, Tamil for example, but I don't suppose she could have been eloquent in Tamil.

She was a great figure at all the many Hindu festivals, and once at least she and Ghandi addressed the same great open-air gathering in Madras. A friend of mine who was present said that what Mrs. Besant achieved by sheer oratory Ghandi got by quiet persuasion. But then she was a foreigner, and Ghandi was a native saint.

My friend is a doctor, and he went to Mrs. Besant's palace to fit her with spectacles. He saw two youngish and sleek Americans there, also in Hindu dress. And there was a troop of young girls, the daughters of well-to-do Brahmins. He notes that two miles away he had passed a Catholic monastic school where the monks educated the Eurasian children abandoned by fathers who had gone back to Europe. He said that the Americans were ablaze with jewels.

Yet I don't think that Mrs. Besant was a Mrs. Eddy. I think that she was a simple soul who believed sincerely that she was a prophetess. She believed as sincerely in her Theosophy as she had in her Atheism, her Birth Prevention, and her Fabianism. Those three things have all the terrible drab insanity of sheer logic without reason. I do not wonder that she found the sounding brass and tinkling symbols of Hinduism more attractive.

Why such a good few English Socialists of a generation ago turned to Theosophy I don't quite know. They turn now to Spiritualism, which seems to me less entertaining and more degraded. The pull with Spiritualism seems to be that it gives you the religious thrill without the bother of moral obligations. However Theosophy was more decent than that. The only things wrong with it as a religion were that it wasn't a religion and it wasn't true.

Running a new religion is always profitable. I suppose that Mrs. Besant would have found it difficult to avoid getting rich. And perhaps she used the great bulk of her wealth for the cause, and felt that her personal decorations were sacradotal.

There is no doubt she was a remarkable woman, well equipped to have been a housewife, to do parish work, to run committees. If she had happened a little later she would have been in the Suffragist movement, and the inevitable collision between her and Mrs. Pankhurst would have been worth watching. I think Mrs. Pankhurst would have won.

How stupid of me! I've just remembered what it was that I used to hate about Theosophy. Not the dissolving views and the mystic humbug, but something inhuman and dreadful at the heart of it. Something that linked it with Darwinism and Fabianism, and will awaken an answering thrill in the scientific lobe of the heart of Mr. H. G. Wells. It is Progress with a big P and with a big G. It is universal tolerance, because, sez you, evil does not exist. It is the wiping out of pity and compassion because, sez you, there is nothing to forgive. To tolerate all is to despise all—or rather to be indifferent to all. Yes, that was the phrase—blast it!—" the centre of indifference."

There was no sin, there were no sinners: men and women were at various stages on the road to perfection, that was all. Oh yes. what a legacy Annie Besant has left to reformers who would scoff at her name! Mental Deficiency Homes, indeterminate sentences, the scornful denial of the prime dogma of democracy that all men are born free and equal, the scornful denial of a prime dogma of Christianity that all men are born sinners, the scornful denial of the fine Christian virtue of humility, the glorification of the dirty sin of spiritual pride.

Why should I pity my weak and erring brother? He is merely some way (probably a damned long way) behind me on the road to Perfection. Oh blast that beastly road. To hell with that highly superior perfection!

Ship me somewhere west of Suez
Where the best kneel with the worst,
And we've got our Ten Commandments,
And the Devil is accurst,

For my old church bell is calling
And it's there that I would be,
A Sinner among Sinners
With a Faith that sets us free.

But I see now, don't you?—why Mrs. Besant looked after the selected children of high-class Brahmins, and couldn't be bothered with those Eurasian bastards. The Brahmin kids were so much farther on the road to Perfection. Oh my sainted Aunt!

[N.B.—My Sainted Aunt had a very bad temper. I wonder what would have happened if I'd told her that it was because she was not so far as I was on the road to Perfection? No, I don't wonder. I jolly well know.]

Mr. Selfridge's Solution

By Gregory Macdonald

MR. GORDON SELFRIDGE has informed the Boston Conference on Retail Distribution that both in England and in America there are too many shops. Thus, the population of the two countries, when divided by the number of stores and shops, allow only about eighty customers each; but the large and very large stores take from the whole much the greater share of the possible daily customers, so that hundreds of thousands of small shops could expect the daily custom of about seven or twelve families, no more. There are too many stores and shops; there are too many men trying to sell to those too many shops too much merchandise; there are too many people knocking at the doors of those stores begging for work. Was it not, he asked, perhaps a practical proposition to put a limit on the number of retail businesses which should be licensed and thus take one step in relieving the country of a heavy over-supply?

The proposition is definitely a practical one. It would, of course, restrict the market of consumption by taking the occupation away from many small shopkeepers, their employees and the travellers who call on them; though Mr. Selfridge was kind enough to point out that most of those inexperienced managers or owners were attempting to do work for which they were unfitted either by temperament or ability. It would also increase the numbers of people knocking at the doors of the licensed shops, begging for work—an extra commissionaire or two could deal with that. But it would be an eminently practical scheme in so far as it would allow fewer and bigger shops to have more customers without all the fuss and bother of competition.

Mr. Selfridge even added one or two details of his scheme. The licensing of business and the consequent half closing of the gate through which now anyone could pass and crowd still more an already over-crowded activity would be a help, but the licensing body could only act efficiently if made up of a board of merchants entirely free from the deadening hand of politics or of any Governmental association or control. " The surplus of shops," he said, " is an uneconomic proposition. A possible remedy is a reversion to the old guild system under which no person could enter into a business either as proprietor or employee without the official sanction of the particular guild.''

Here Mr. Selfridge makes a significant statement, and his plea for a reversal to the guild system may well become historic. Carried into practice it would, however, have the effect of increasing rather than decreasing, the number of shops. First of all, the large stores would be forced to close down, for it was always strictly seen to by the guilds that various trades should be kept distinct. Butchers could not also be cooks. A baker could not also be a clothier. The modern department store, with its cooks and butchers and bakers and haberdashers all jumbled up together is the very antithesis of guild ideas. The usual practice was for the cordwainers, the tanners, the butchers and so on, to congregate according to their trade or craft along certain streets. This meant that they could be more easily supervised—for the quality of the goods sold was considered important*—and the mediæval housewife had no farther to walk from street to street than the modern housewife from department to department.

Not only would the revival of the guilds do away with the large stores (and chain-stores subsidiary to them); it would also curtail the powers of those who live by exchange. Mr. Selfridge, say, retains his Fabric department and becomes a licenced clothier, a member of the guild, in accordance with his very practical proposition. He will be a member of an association of which the object will be to ensure a fair price to the consumer and a fair reward to the seller; consequently any attempt to forestall the market by buying cheap or in great quantities and selling dear, or more cheaply than others, will be opposed. Instead, all buying and selling will be conducted openly, and any member of a guild will be able to claim a share of a bargain made by one of his fellows; or the members will make common bargains as a guild and share the profits. This, it may be noticed, will ensure better prices for primary producers, who are often at present the leonine victims of the large establishments. They will defend their own interests by forming associations within their craft. Mr. Selfridge will thus do away with the present distinction between the few men who supply

capital plus energy, ability, foresight, vision, temperament and sanctifying grace, and the many who work for them on wages or, worse still, knock at their doors vainly begging for work to do. '' The essence of the guild system,'' notes a modern historian, '' lay in the control of industry by the industrial workers themselves, through an elected authority appointed by them. In the capitalist system, on the other hand, this control is transferred to men who stand outside the ranks of the industrial workers, and are frequently in conflict with them.'' It will be the best safeguard for Mr. Selfridge's new system to take care that craftsmen and merchants are not members of separate guilds, but allowed to share common interests.

These common interests will be many. If Mr. Selfridge is sick, he will be visited and supplied with necessities. If he falls upon evil days he will be granted a loan out of the community chest. If he dies poor he will be buried handsomely at the expense of the guild, bread and beer being distributed to other poor men on that occasion. And if Mr. Selfridge prospers he will not neglect to work magnificently for the public good by erecting market-crosses, adorning the municipal buildings, paving streets, providing gates, quays, bridges, wharves, harbours, sluices and aqueducts—just as Richard Whittington laid out his wealth upon the water supply of London.

Mr. Selfridge's proposal to revert to the old guild system might be elaborated at much greater length, and more closely than is here possible. In essentials the proposition is practical. Undoubtedly it will mean an increase in the number of shops, but Mr. Selfridge himself remarks upon the fact that at present a few large stores engross the trade of many small shops, so what he would desire is really a matter of adjustment. Indeed, something like Mr. Selfridge's idea has already been put forward by another outstanding figure of our day: '' The demand and supply of labour divides men on the labour-market into two classes, as into two camps, and the bargaining between these parties transforms this labour-market into an arena where the two armies are engaged in combat. To this grave disorder which is leading society to ruin, a remedy must evidently be supplied as speedily as possible. But there cannot be question of any perfect cure, except this opposition be done away with, and well-ordered members of the social body come into being anew, vocational groups namely, binding men together not according to the position they occupy in the labour-market, but according to the diverse functions which they exercise in society. For as nature induces those who dwell in close proximity to unite into municipalities, so those who practise the same trade or profession, economic or otherwise, combine into vocational groups. . . . True and genuine social order demands various members of society joined together by a common bond. Such a bond of union is provided on the one hand by the common effort of employers and employees of one and the same group joining forces to produce goods or give service; on the other hand by the common good which all groups should unite to promote.''

It is conceivable that Mr. Selfridge had some such idea as this at the back of his mind.

---

*Lord Snowden recently wrote: "Japan's commercial success is due to her adaptability to the needs of the markets." "For the countries with a low purchasing power she produces an attractive cheap article of such a low quality that the British manufacturer says he would be ashamed to make it." An indignant Manchester merchant replied in the same paper: "This statement shows an appalling ignorance of the actual conditions and is completely incorrect. Manchester to-day is making cotton goods from 1¼d. per yard upwards and of qualities which are actually inferior to those sold by Japan." "Callisthenes" commented in *The Times*: "It is futile for a man to manufacture above his market and for a Store to offer the public not what they want but what they ought to want. Purchasing power in the world rises and falls, and the firm which would give good service (and there is no other road to economic soundness) must not be 'ashamed' to study the income of its customers. It must not insist on supplying an article which will last two years when the customer wants one that will last two months."

FREE THINKERS AGAIN
By G. K. CHESTERTON

I BELIEVE I am in possession of a piece of news which, as we say in Fleet Street, has a certain news-value. It is hardly fitted to be flashed along the telegraph wires or blazoned in the big posters; it does not definitely involve an individual but rather generally a school; but it is a historical event; something that has happened and has hardly been noticed among the many changes of the day. The substance of the news is this. The sort of man we once knew as a Secularist has become a religious maniac.

Of course he is not actually mad, in the medical sense; nor, for that matter, is he religious in the religious sense, or perhaps in any sense. Yet the words I have used, to cover very varying stages of the malady in a fairly loose group, are the only words that convey the sharpness and importance of the incident. I mean that the *tone* of the old Fleet Street atheism, which I knew and loved of old, has entirely altered. It has come to resemble almost exactly the tone of the Seventh Day Adventists or the Millennial Dawnists, or all those queerly prosaic and even prim fanatics, who wander about handing out pamphlets, crowded with texts and vivid with italics, in which a new heaven and a new earth can be made out of a neglected cloud in the Book of Daniel, or an unusually Little Horn in the Apocalypse. Perhaps the shortest way of distinguishing between the two literary styles is to record that the first was readable and the second is unreadable. The old atheist arguments, inherited from Bradlaugh and Foote, were always crude and therefore a little heavy, even for any agnostic with some background of history and philosophy. But they were at least as clear as they were crude; and we should all of us have agreed that a paper like the *Freethinker* was easy to read; even if some of us would have added that it was easy to answer. The *Freethinker* as it is to-day is not easy to read. I know, because I have just been reading it. Its editor has kindly sent me a copy, containing what appears from the frequent mention of my name to be an attack on myself; and when I am thus personally addressed, I think it only polite to answer. If it is now not so easy to answer, it is simply because it is now not so easy to understand. It seems to be about a book I wrote on Victorian Literature several years before the War; but the Freethinkers of Fleet Street, ever on the alert for fresh developments, have pounced upon it already. I have read the critique over patiently several times, and am still somewhat puzzled by what the critic can possibly mean by some of his allusions and complaints. I remember that in that very able book *The Flight From Reason*, Mr. Arnold Lunn narrates a similar experience with the same paper. He prints the whole of the Freethinker's criticism on him, and, naturally not being able to make head or tail of it, simply leaves it to the reader in despair. It was something about how anybody, who thinks there is good historical evidence for the Resurrection, is logically bound to believe the story of Aladdin in the *Arabian Nights*. I have no idea why. But what I would first emphasise, before trying to explain my critic's remarks to myself and him, is the curious character of this change in the Secularist Press, from a tone that was crude to a tone that is really crazy.

We might take a working parallel; fortunately outside the sphere of religion. I can imagine a jolly old Radical working man talking in the old mutinous manly fashion against the King or the House of Lords; saying with surly geniality and some repetition: " What do we want with a King? Why should 'e 'ave a golden crown on 'is 'ed and me only my old boko? What's 'e blasted well doing in Buckingham Palace?" —and so on. Now I like that sort of man. I like him very much. I know what he means. I think there is, in the last resort, a lot to be said for it. It is not in the style of the *De Monarchia;* it hardly appreciates the subtleties of M. Charles Maurras. But it has truths behind it; the equality of men and something that is right in republican simplicity. But suppose that man, who begins by saying he is as good as the King, broods and eventually goes mad, saying that he *is* the King. Suppose his grievance becomes a personal grievance about his great-grandfather, and he goes about boring people with plans and pedigrees to prove his Plantagenet blood. We know the whole atmosphere will alter; but chiefly in clarity. Everybody knew what the grumbler meant; nobody will listen to what the lunatic means. That is very like the difference between the Old Secularist and the New Secularist—or the Millennial Dawnist.

Take some puzzles out of this page about me. " Chesterton uses his talents tyrannously in the service of the most reactionary of all Churches."—to which he didn't belong at the time. And how do you use talents tyrannously? I wish I knew. " He has nothing but the crudest insults for the great intellectuals." Well, there is the book; anybody can see what I really said about Mill, about Meredith, about Matthew Arnold, about Huxley, even supposing that nobody is an intellectual unless he is an agnostic. To say I had " nothing " but crude insult for them is—well, something that could be described still more crudely. Swinburne, it seems " is accused of composing a learned and sympathetic and indecent parody on the Litany of the Blessed Virgin." And the critic adds mysteriously, " an ironical suggestion in a Protestant country." I do not know what the word " accused " means here. If the critic has read Swinburne, he knows that an early verse in *Dolores* is a parody of the Litany of the Virgin. It is hardly an accusation to call it learned and sympathetic; by which I meant artistically sympathetic in an archaic Gothic mode; as were the profane Pre-Raphaelites as well as the pious ones. Whether such a thing is indecent may be discussed; but he is quite wrong in fancying that only Papists thought it indecent. The indecency of *Dolores* was denounced, more harshly than I dreamed of denouncing it, by the first Free-thinker in English public life, the late John Morley.

Finally, here is one wonderful example of how the Freethinker gets hold of the wrong end of the stick, even when I actually offer him the right end. He writes the amazing sentence, " Even the great authors of the nineteenth century do not escape his Romish censure, and are dubbed, spitefully, ' lame giants'." It is not very spiteful to call an author a giant; but anyone consulting the book will see that the men I called ' lame giants ' were not " the great authors of the nineteenth century," but specially the English authors of the Victorian time; whom I compared unfavourably with the franker and bolder Freethinkers of France and the Continent. Thus I praised Renan as a more logical sceptic than Tennyson, who was a lame sceptic, hampered by respectability and provincial religion. You would think a Freethinker would recognise that as an obvious concession to Freethinkers. But the new Freethinker does not *read* a book. He looks through it feverishly for texts to be twisted in favour of a prejudice; like the religious maniac with the Bible.

Odds and Ends
By James Donald McGleeson

AN OFFICE IN THE AIR.

"AN aeroplane, fitted with an office and designed to speed up commercial travel, will leave Portsmouth for Glasgow this morning. Its equipment includes a typewriter, card index receptacles and filing facilities." Doesn't it just show the shocking slackness and inefficiency rampant in business circles, and explain how trade is falling away and everybody is becoming depressed? No Captain of Commerce in this flying office, no salesmen, and above all no customers. Not even a sports girl tapping at the typewriter—merely a few filing facilities for stowaways. And they call this speeding up commercial travel! I wonder when business men will begin to put a little madness into their intolerable method. There should, of course, be a Monarch of Industry seated at a desk in this aeroplane office. He might not be allowed to smoke a cigar in the aeroplane, but there is nothing to stop him from chewing it, and sticking out his chin. There should also be a bright young Salesman full to the brim of persuasive eloquence. Then, just as the aeroplane was on the point of starting, a few customers should be kidnapped and hurled into the office. Before they had recovered from the shock the Salesman would start in on them. While he was stunning them with his persuasive eloquence, the Monarch of Industry would pick their pockets. In this way might the aeroplane office be made profitable instead of merely a waste, and the card indexes and filing cabinets would really be used. And by the time the 'plane landed at Glasgow the typist would present each of the customers with a neatly typed bill. Thus would speed and commerce be happily united.

THE BAD MAN IN THE BAND.

The weekly band concert at Wenatchee, Washington, had to be postponed because someone had stolen the big drum. It was, of course, the big drummer who stole it, though the conductor was too delicate to say so. As a race these big drummers are sad specimens of abandoned manhood, the reason being that the big drum gives more temptation to crime than do the lesser musical instruments. Neither violins nor trumpets offer much scope for irregular practices, but the drum can cover a multitude of sins. You might conceal a quantity of beer in a trombone and suck it up during the performance, but in a drum may be hidden bottles and bottles of the stuff. But it is quite a common thing for the drummer to carry his bar about with him and keep the band going during the performance. The trouble begins when the drummer goes outside the orchestra, so to speak, and lets out his drum for all manner of doubtful purposes. One drummer, for instance, was accustomed to hold captives to ransom in his drum and used to whack the thing harder and harder whenever his victims squealed. Another would put his drum on wheels, plaster it over with advertisements concerning a vile night club in which he was interested, and hired some ruffians to drag it through the town. But the drummer of Wenatchee had a scheme of his own. He furnished his drum with bed, chairs and table and let it out as a holiday residence. But when the band night came round his tenants refused to leave. Neither appeals nor threats availed to persuade them to leave their little house. The band assembled without the drum and when the drummer appeared with his drumsticks he had to pretend the thing had been stolen, though nobody believed him.

A VICTORIAN ECHO.

In the new life of Andrew Carnegie, recently published, it is revealed that the hero had a deep affection for his mother which found expression in a strange manner. " The millionaire took a sudden dislike to the writings of J. M. Barrie." Few will remember the consternation this caused, as it happened so long ago; way back in Victoria's reign, in fact. Fortunately I recollect the occasion with some vividness. When the news was first made public that Carnegie had ceased to care for Barrie's work, the Victorian world was struck dumb with amazement. They were fine fellows in those days, however, and quick to recover from the half-arm jabs of Fate. The eminent Victorians speedily got together to consider the situation. A movement to open Carnegie's eyes to the true beauties of Barrie was quickly got under way, in which many of the most famous people took part. It was towards this great end, for instance, that Tennyson penned his great poem, in which he affectionately addressed the millionaire in filial terms:

" He's not so bad as you fancy, dad," and so on. It was this poem, more than all else, which brought him the laurel wreath, but it also provoked a counter-blast from the opposition firm of Alfred Austin and Co., whose poem employed the word " cad " in place of " dad." But Tennyson's was only one move in the great offensive. Gladstone also played a part. One evening, putting all political business aside with commendable kindness, he called upon Carnegie, disguised as Peter Pan. The details of this singular meeting have not been preserved and will probably never now be given to the world. It is well known, however, that the whole Cabinet took a hand in the affair of bringing the millionaire to reason, the full pack of them turning up as fairies at the bottom of Carnegie's garden. About the same time, moreover, at least one lord appeared as a fish for an entire afternoon. The occasion is likewise made memorable, for when they reported these things to Queen Victoria and she said she was not amused, a young lordling brought a little welcome disgrace upon himself by observing that she might not be, but nevertheless she " was demmed amusing." But as for the project of turning Carnegie from his strange and sudden distaste, the movement was not a success and the millionaire continued to dislike the writings of Barrie.

VAIN WORDS.

The other day a lady complained very justly to the Willesden magistrate, " My husband said he intended to kill me to-day, but this morning he said he had put it off until another day," and I wish enthusiastically to support her in her complaint. This dismal, damnable procrastination is eating into the manhood of our nation. Men are growing lazy from the inside, so to speak. This eternal curse of putting off until another day what should have been done the day before yesterday is making us a laughing-stock in the eyes of the world. Moreover it used to be our proud boast that an Englishman's word was his bond, but how can any wife retain confidence in a husband who breaks his word, merely on account of procrastination. While our men are thus unreliable, speaking wild words, but recoiling cravenly when the time comes to translate them into action, what hope can there be for our race? Not until we have recovered our forefathers' motto " Do it now!" can we expect to rise above the disgrace of our present national level.

From Foyles to Fleet Street
By a Book Reviewer

I.

" IF the llama at the Zoo is like a disappointed literary man—"
　" Who said that ?" I interrupted.
" A literary man who had not been disappointed yet," she answered mildly. " But you must let me finish. If a disappointed literary man is like the llama at the Zoo, to what creature would you compare a disappointed literary woman, like me?"

She was small and quick and her clothes were anyhow. She stood looking up at me with her head on one side, and she was more like an excited terrier puppy than anything else, so I said so. Her appreciative smile seemed to play all over her face, just as a puppy's pleasure ripples forward from its tail.
" You don't look as though disappointment weighed heavy on you," I said. " Are you sure that you are one of the unsuccessful ones?"

She nodded emphatically, and adjusted the tottering pile of new novels on her arm.
" Thank heaven," she said. " Have you ever met a successful literary person, one who knows and wallows in her own success?"
I shuddered. The day had been fitful, and as we stood where we had so casually met and begun to talk, on the muddled corner of Cambridge Circus, the sunlight faded and a cold wind sprang up, snatching hats and papers and throwing them into the dusty chaos of the traffic. She caught at her own hat just in time, and her hair blew about her head and into her eyes so that she looked more terrier-like than ever.
" It's like hunting for Truth in her well," she gasped, and for a moment I did not follow the sequence of her thought. " You have to go through such a lot of cold water before you can reach her. Never mind. Let's explore London. This is just the right kind of a day."

*　　*　　*　　*

Charing Cross Road always robs me of my sense of humour. That ballast gone, it is difficult to keep your feet on the ground, and easy to float into a ghostly atmosphere. As the Irish poets used to tell us, between one step and the next you never know when you will be in fairyland.
It had begun to rain. Our brief mood of summer content was past, and already the pavements began to assume a drab and greasy look. There are parts of London that are always draggle-tailed. The air was dull, and the people passing were furtive and ill-shod.
" There were two poets of the same name," she said, " and both were derelict here. Walking in this place at times it is not difficult to understand. The City of Dreadful Night is built of grimy shadows, of life made hideous and ruined. And yet the other saw so different a vision, only a few minutes away.

　　The angels keep their ancient places
　　Stir but a stone and start a wing—
There are stones I would not dare to stir, fearing to start crawling and unpleasant things. And yet—it is not a mood to hold. Both poets slept under the same shadow:
　　But (when so sad thou canst not sadder)
　　Cry;—and upon thy so sore loss
　　Shall shine the traffic of Jacob's ladder
　　Pitched between Heaven and Charing Cross.
You never know what the sun may bring. And here it comes again, and here we are."
Indeed, the rain had stopped as suddenly as it had begun, and the sun looked out tearfully between the drifting, purposeless clouds. We left the street, and climbed a stair to the Buying Department of Foyle's Bookshop. And when we came into the little partitioned room, there sat Psyche on the counter dangling her sandalled feet, her bright hair paled and softened in the dusty filtered sunlight of the bookshop, her golden robe warm-coloured against a background of piled-up and lurid novels.
Her greeting was friendly. The books that we had brought to add to the glories of her throne she welcomed. And yet her gentle beauty put them to shame. There is a type of novel that seems to con-

centrate the whole of its plot, theme and interest in the top-line of each right-hand page. At least, after reading it in this way we feel that we have missed nothing of importance. But after six or seven of them have been digested in such a fashion, we suffer all the discomforts of repletion. Psyche did not notice our thoughts, for she smiled on us, and laid a protective hand on the topmost volume.

There were others in the crowded little room, but they paid no attention to us. "I always see them through," murmured Psyche, as she lovingly followed with her finger the contours of a cover-design. But as it was meant to startle rather than to rest the eye, she was soon brought up with a jerk. She turned to us again. "Have *you* written any of them?" she asked, and looked a little dashed at our hasty disclaimer.

We added, by way of apology: "You see, we have had to read so many"; and in unspoken thought: "And they are all the same." But she caught at that. "They are all the same." she repeated exultingly. "The old, old story of Cupid and Psyche, over again, and over and over again." Reverently she lifted from the pile a novel in a mustard and purple jacket.

"Not that one, Psyche, lest the end of your story be lost in a bog of disillusion. To that one there could never be a happy ending. Do you remember how your sisters told you that your hidden lover was a monster most hideous, and how you believed them for a while?"

Her face changed, and she put it down. But her look rested on the wild-coloured jacket as though it intrigued her. After a little hesitation she took up another, decorated diagonally in peacock and magenta. "Put it down, Psyche, put it down. It is not for you to learn that Cupid grew old and bald and fat before he died."

She stiffened. "Love is immortal," she cried angrily, and the frail sunshine seemed to fade for a moment from the little room. But she dropped the second volume as though it had stung her.

We grew suspicious. "Have you read *any* of them?" we asked. "There were so many," she murmured, shamefaced. "And I got behind. But I have read the story of Cinderella, and it is just like mine. And I have read the story of Nicolette, and the Lay of the Ash-tree and ever so many more." Doubtfully she fingered another, lido and mauve in tone, and almost pleadingly she spoke her little piece again: "The old, old story of Cupid and Psyche, how she became the bride of the unknown, and the zephyrs bore her to his palace and he came to her unseen: and how her sisters envied her good fortune, and they gave her evil counsel, and when she lit her doubtful candle she saw the sleeping Cupid. And he left her in anger, and she searched for him through earth and hell and heaven until she found him again."

But the book twitched angrily under her fingers and began to pour out scornful and jeering words:

Cupid is a monster and Psyche is a fool.
We learnt that before we went to school.

She thinks she is a Queen when she's nothing but a pawn,
And she doesn't even know how a cauliflower's born.

What more might have come I do not know; but just then half-a-dozen novels fell with a crash to the ground. The place had grown dark. Somebody apologised for keeping us waiting, and handed us a written slip. But as we left the department, and started down the stairs, we heard a little sniff, as though somewhere behind the bookshelves a child was on the verge of tears.

A Reply

By

Lt. Com. the Hon. J. M. Kenworthy, R.N.

IT is an unusual privilege for an author to be allowed to reply to criticism of his work. I particularly appreciate the opportunity of making a reply to criticisms of my recent book "Sailors, Statesmen—and Others."

The Press has been kind to my book; and this despite my deliberate frankness in writing my biography. Indeed, the principal criticisms, so far, appeared at the end of an otherwise friendly and generous review by "E.J.M." in *G.K.'s Weekly* of September 14th. E.J.M. picks out two episodes of the stormy post-war years which I described and commented upon. The first was the far-reaching plan for an alliance between the British and German iron and coal industries made possible by the proposed partition of Upper Silesia; the other the series of events ending in the repulse of the Russian Red Army before Warsaw.

Because E.J.M. disagrees with my views on these two subjects he writes that they "suffice to destroy any confidence in Commander Kenworthy either as a statesman or as a critic of statesmanship."

E.J.M. reminds me of the saying attributed—perhaps falsely—to Dr. Johnson: "Mankind is divided into two classes: those who agree with me, and scoundrels."

E.J.M. does not agree with me, so he says I am no statesman. Modesty forbids me from claiming the quality of statesmanship. But let us examine the facts.

By methods of chicanery the richest coal and iron field and the most efficient heavy industries on the mainland of Europe were handed over to the Poles when a large part of Upper Silesia was torn from the Reich. Recent events in Germany should not blind us to this monstrous injustice. The German industrialists were rendered powerless. The Poles used these magnificent mines to dump coal on the market, particularly in the Baltic and Scandinavian countries, and this seriously injured the British export trade in coal. The resulting distress in the British coal industry led, directly, to two long drawn out and disastrous mining disputes; and, indirectly, to the General Strike of 1926. The proposed marriage between the British and Silesian coal interests would have avoided these injurious disputes in a great home industry. E.J.M. says this would have "subordinated once more the interests of people to the interests of private economic groups." It is a little difficult, I submit, to separate the interests of an economic group represented by a million British miners and their families and the British people as a whole; or between a hundred thousand Silesian miners and their families and the Silesian inhabitants as a whole. But let that pass. My answer to E.J.M. is that the sooner economic interest prevails over nationalistic folly the better. Most of the present troubles of Europe to-day are directly attributable to an exaggerated nationalism with its high tariffs, quotas, exchange restrictions and the rest of the present-day nonsense which cripples trade and impoverishes whole nations.

If, on the other hand, E.J.M. objects to international economic alliances because they are only possible, under present conditions, between capitalists, he is blind to the facts of the present day. We are living under the capitalistic system, whether we like it or not. Until it is replaced by something better we have to make the best we can of it.

Now as to the episode of the "Jolly George," the munition ship which the London dockers refused to load for Poland. This was an important happening in a series of tremendous events. If I may recall the happenings, it will also explain my attitude to the "Battle of Warsaw."

Egged on by the French and a section of the British governing class and departments, the Poles had invaded Russia. Their objective was the Ukraine. The invasion was a wanton act of aggression. When it failed the Poles were flung back within their own borders. In their turn, the Russian Red Armies, following hard after the retreating Poles, advanced on Warsaw. It was then proposed that Britain and France should intervene in defence of Poland. A new war with incalculable consequences would have commenced. The action of the London dockers and the sympathetic attitude of the general public to this example of direct action was a danger signal to the Governments in London and Paris. Wiser counsels prevailed, especially in the British Cabinet, and intervention was called off. Thousands of lives and much treasure were saved as a result.

E.J.M. complains that I did not describe in my book how and why the "Jolly George" incident may be regarded as a turning point in history. If I have not now made it clear, let me add that from then onwards a saner attitude was adopted towards Russia, despite the passions aroused by the revolutionary history of that immense country. Russia is now pursuing a peaceful policy and has recently concluded pacts of non-aggression with her Western neighbours, including Poland. The result would have been achieved sooner, and with benefit to a score of nations, if my criticisms in Parliament and the Press of so-called statesmanship had been listened to earlier.

May I sum up my reply by remarking that, like my other critic, Viscount Snowden, E.J.M. should get his facts right before he attacks either my recital or my conclusions.

The Science of Peace

THE SCIENCE OF PEACE. *By Lord Raglan. Methuen. 3s. 6d.*

THIS book has a refreshing quality of which we get a foretaste in the picture on the jacket, which represents Tweedledum and Tweedledee scared from their historic contest by the sudden appearance of the Dove of Peace in the form of a big, black crow of repellant aspect. Lord Raglan evidently thinks it is time that the cause of Peace should be saved from the intolerable advocacy of the Pacifists; it is possible to disagree with him without being irritated—and we may say at once that while we agree with much of what he says, we unreservedly reject his main proposition.

He treats of War, very rightly, as "a deep-rooted disease in the body prolific of the human race" which can only be treated by a scientific study of its origins in the light of anthropology, history, and psychology. Speaking generally, we agree with his psychology and are prepared to defer to his authority as an anthropologist; but when it comes to history and the conclusions he draws from history, we fail to follow him.

Briefly his thesis is that Militarism, which was (as we agree) an essential feature of the primitive tribe, is equally an essential feature of the modern nation, and that only by abolishing nationalism can we hope to abolish war. For nations he would substitute Empires, with frontiers so arranged as to render them strategically and economically as vulnerable as possible. Thus they would be afraid to fight, just as a man with heart-disease is afraid to cough.

Now, if we except the supreme horror of the world state (which the author, to do him justice, would reject) we can imagine no more disastrous solution. And that it should commend itself to so clear a thinker as Lord Raglan is merely a proof of the sinister hypnotism which any suggestion of "The Big Thing" exercises on the modern mind.

The war-spirit of the primitive tribe was an instinct which, in its proper environment, had a certain survival value. When civilisation substituted for the purely natural organisation of the tribe, the rational organisation of the nation—the Civitas—the war-spirit, like other instincts, became gradually subjected to rational control; the nation went to war not merely because it "felt like it," but because it hoped to secure some tangible benefit. Moreover, being rational, it could now make peace as well as war: that is to say, it could frame a contract with other rational bodies; and it was found that in an increasing number of cases, this paid better than war. Unfortunately, however, the subordination of instinctive mass-emotion to reason comes more slowly in big groups than in small. Thus the small civilized nations were in constant danger from big, barbarous groups (or Empires). And these Empires, despite their barbarism, often had (like the social insects) a highly-specialised power of organisation—especially in matters of communication and transport—which made them formidable in war, and which has won them the admiration of modern thinkers who believe, with Kipling, that "Transport is civilisation.'' The Persian Empire (which Lord Raglan commends) was one example of this; Genghis Khan was another.

To-day however the war-spirit is, generally speaking, under control—partly owing to a real advance in civilisation, and partly because commercial nations are, like the man with heart-disease, '' afraid to cough.'' Nevertheless the bigger groups are still imperfectly civilised—especially the new nations which have only recently come under the civilising influence of nationhood. Thus the small nations are essentially pacific as are the old nations such as England, France, and Spain. It is from such nations as Germany and Italy that the danger comes; for in these the old tribal spirit is still insufficiently disciplined.

This is not to say that England and France would never fight; they might even fight for an unjust cause; but they would not fight for an irrational cause. The wars which led to the growth of the great commercial empires of the eighteenth century were often unjust, but they were strictly rational; for they achieved their object—namely, the enrichment of the plutocracies which waged them. But the days of such wars are over; and Norman Angell has shown to the satisfaction of all reasonable people that nowadays '' War does not pay.'' Therefore it is not acquisitive militarism but emotional militarism that is the danger to-day. And the only effective guard against this is to subordinate the tribal instinct to reason. This only nationalism can do.

Lord Raglan generally manages to avoid the ordinary pacifist clap-trap; but he accepts the curious notion that modern nations consistently preach hatred of their neighbours. And yet everybody knows that most modern education is very pacific: English children are taught that Joan of Arc was just as noble a patriot as Nelson, and that Washington was a better man than Clive; they learn that the French are very polite, the Dutch very clean, and the Germans very industrious. It is true they also learn that the natives of Asia and Africa are benighted savages; but then (in Lord Raglan's view at least), they *are* benighted savages; and ought to be incorporated as soon as possible in one or other of his half-dozen white empires, where they will soon learn to forget their barbarous traditions.

When we come to examine his case in detail, we find that he is driven to the strangest arguments to defend his anti-nationalist thesis. Thus he defines a nation as a '' community organised for war,'' and denies that Luxemburg is a nation because it hasn't an army! But in that case, what about Denmark who has publicly and expressly proclaimed her complete disarmament? He suggests that the League of Nations is fundamentally a militaristic institution because it admits Guatemala which is armed, and excludes California, which is not. The obvious answer is that the League of Nations is a league of sovereign states—although, for cogent reasons it has admitted the British Dominions which, technically, are not sovereign states. But there is no such cogent reason in the case of California. Again, in support of his plea that Empires make for peace, he says that war between England and France is unthinkable because it would mean disaster to the African Empires of the two combatants. But such a war was by no means unthinkable in 1898—and for no other reason but a clash on our African frontiers! In fact, when we recall the various war-scares of our generation, we find that practically all of them arose from points of imperial policy. The very names Fashoda, Agadir, Sarajevo prove this.

The fact is that the author refuses to follow his own admirable arguments to their right conclusion. He very nearly does so on page 148 where, in suggesting various methods of world-organisation which might ensure peace, he says: '' Another alternative method might be to divide the world up into a number of small states,'' and proceeds to give several excellent reasons in support of his solution; but suddenly he shies off and dismisses the idea because of the '' obstacles which a multiplicity of different codes would place in the way of commerce and intercourse generally.'' In other words, we must not adopt the one sure road to peace for fear of offending the Internationalist and the Marketeer.

I have dealt principally with the points on which I disagree with the book, but there is much in it that is admirable. His remarks on the attitude of women towards war are full of common sense, and a wholesome corrective to the sentimental hysteria which that subject so often arouses. His chapter on over-population also furnishes much food for thought. Also he deals faithfully with the militarist argument of war as a biological necessity, '' Nature's pruning-hook '' and all the rest of it; though one doubts whether at this date it is worth while wasting powder and shot over such pseudo-scientific rubbish.

C.E.B.

Music

IT is hard luck on the Courtauld-Sargent Concert Club that it should be deprived by the prolonged illness of Dr. Malcolm Sargent from his services as conductor for the coming season, which opens on October 16th next. But, under the circumstances, no member of the club, nor for that matter, of the general public, can complain of the fare provided.

The programme which includes the most interesting item of the season—the first performance of the Fifth Symphony by Arnold Bax—is being undertaken by Sir Thomas Beecham, on January 15th and 16th. Robert Heger conducts the first concert, and, incidentally, his first concert in England. Leslie Hewart is engaged for the second concert on November 13th; and Julius Harrison for the fifth, next February.

On December 11th, Georg Széll, whom I am informed is regarded on the Continent as being of the first rank of conductors, makes his debut in London, with Huberman as soloist, in a programme consisting of Hadyn's ''Oxford'' Symphony, Beethoven's *Violin Concerto in D* and Schumann's *Symphony No. 4.*

To Leslie Hewart falls the task of conducting the first performance since 1766 of Mozart's ''Adelaide'' Concerto for Violin (soloist, Miss Jelly D'Aranyi). This Concerto was composed at an age when our more highly civilised, compulsorily educated youths are tasting their early impressions of public schooling— '' aristocratic '' or '' democratic.'' Adelaide was

Madame de France, eldest daughter of Louis XV, and a student of the violin under Guignon. In the dedication, signed by J. G. Wolfgang Mozart, it is written that the work '' has been presided over and singularly facilitated by your august presence, and if you will graciously permit the name Adelaide to extend its protection over this modest effort, it will remain engraved on my heart for all time.'' Mozart was born in 1756. The date of the dedication is May 26th, 1766, and it was played that year. Now, after many years—and on second thoughts—the work has been deemed of sufficient interest for Marius Casadesus to harmonise and orchestrate to meet the requirements of modern presentation.

I am asked to state that 150 seats are still available for societies, groups, and others wishing to take advantage of the Club arrangements, and that the prices of seats for the general public are reduced. Full particulars can be obtained from the Secretary, Concert Club, 12, North Audley Street, London, W.1.

I have received from the Hon. Secretary of the Philharmonic Choir a letter from which I give the following extracts :—

'' Owing to the generosity of a friend of the choir, the deficit on last season was considerably reduced, and we are embarking on another season in the hope that support will be forthcoming in an increased degree. The choir provides opportunities for singers (good readers with good voices) for studying and performing the great choral works—classic and modern, while for musical people who do not sing there is Associate membership, subscribers to which are entitled to privileges including tickets for concerts. The Junior Choir caters for musical young people, and at rehearsals excellent musical training is given by Mr. Kennedy Scott, while promotions are made to the Senior section from time to time. There are vacancies in all sections and information will be given on application to me at the above address.''

The above address is 28, Flanchford Road, London, W.12. Bach's B Minor Mass will be given at the first of the Queen's Hall Concerts, on November 27th.

Despite the comparatively poor attendance at the Queen's Hall Sunday Afternoon Concerts last season Mr. Holt has decided to try again this year, and a series of twelve concerts by the London Philharmonic Orchestra commences on November 19th. As before, Sir Thomas Beecham will be the chief conductor, but the services of Albert Coates, Pierre Monteaux and Robert Heger have also been obtained. The first is to be a Wagner programme (a composer curiously unfashionable this autumn and winter). Eva Turner is the soloist. Details of the later concerts are not yet available, but if the general standard is equal to that of last year it will be Londoners' own tragedy if the attendance does not encourage these concerts to become annual events.

Meanwhile the '' Proms '' are carrying on gallantly to the end (which is on Saturday week). Honegger's *Symphonic Movement No. 3* (first English performance); Hindemith's *News of the Day* Overture; Poulenc's *Concerto for Two Pianofortes*, and a Sibelius night have constituted the most interesting of recent events. I hope that more will be said next week of the Sibelius programme.

At Sadlers' Wells opera is getting into its stride. An excellent performance of *La Bohème* promised well for the season. The outstanding performance was that by Miss Joan Cross as Mimi. Her singing was always good and at moments truly beautiful. Sumner Austin's Marcelle was also excellent. Henry Wendon, the Rudolph, has improved considerably since last season, particularly in his sense of the stage. But he is still uneasy in his movements and uncertain in his singing. Some of the tempos adopted by Albert Coates were strange to ears trained to Puccini, particularly that chosen for Musetta's song; but he inspired the orchestra to a lively performance. The general level of orchestral playing was higher than in past seasons. V.N.L.

The Cockpit.

[Letters should not exceed 300 words in length and must bear the names and addresses, not necessarily for publication, of their authors.

The Editor can accept no responsibility for opinions expressed by correspondents.]

MENTALLY DEFECTIVE?

Sir,—The case to which you refer illustrates a most serious state of affairs. Sir Ernest Wild, K.C., in suggesting an *independent* examination supports the demand, constantly made by this Society.

The present system of lunacy administration is a scandal of the first magnitude otherwise the Royal Commission would not have recommended '' an entirely new lunacy code.''

The National Society for Lunacy Law Reform is striving to prevent cruelty to children in the form of wrongful classification as mental defective. This error accounts for much misery and, once made, it is extremely difficult to rescue the victim from its effects.

Large numbers of children are classified as mentally deficient and consequently detained in these institutions who are merely backward at school and have no right to be so regarded within the meaning of the Act.

This Society comes into contact with case after case where the Mental Deficiency Acts have been wrongly applied with disastrous consequences. It is high time that the term mental deficiency was more clearly defined and that due safeguards were provided against erroneous classification.

Independent specialists are available who, realising the serious state of things, are prepared to offer their services in order to rectify matters.

FRANCIS J. WHITE, Secretary.

THE FIGHTING FIF.

Sir,—It is difficult to answer an attack made by a man, who has apparently read nothing one has written except one brief letter, the point of which he has misunderstood.

The aim of my letter was not to exult over Catholics whose faith is fortified by their emotional experiences, as in the passage quoted from Mr. Belloc, nor to ask Mr. Chesterton how he can account for his attitude to the first chapters of Genesis. My letter was intended simply to suggest that Catholics owe some of their conviction to their intuitive sense of reality, and that it is therefore misleading to state bluntly that they rely on "external facts," as opposed to internal feelings.

Mr. Chesterton asks whether I really think that Mr. Belloc saw his religion in the Alps for the first time, and did not know what religion he belonged to until he saw that there was snow on the Alps, and might have had another religion if the Alps had been at flat as Flanders.

Mr. Chesterton's habit of conducting both sides of a dispute enables him to handicap his opponent with any imbecilities that occur to Mr. Chesterton's fertile mind. But on this occasion there is no necessity to conjecture what I think about Mr. Belloc's thoughts on the heights of Weissenstein, for they are clearly summarised by Mr. Belloc himself: "Since I could now see such a wonder and it could work such things in my mind, therefore, some day I should be part of it. That is what I felt."

Even if Mr. Chesterton could not gather from my letter that I was not criticising his attitude to the first chapters of Genesis, he ought, before adding me to his Chamber of Modern Horrors, to have glanced through my books, or have deputed some long-suffering friend to undertake the task for him. In one of these books Mr. Chesterton, or his deputy, would have found the following tribute to Mr. Chesterton: "A magnificent, and though severe, not ungenerous, attack on Mr. Wells' inability to understand the philosophy of the Fall of Man. Nothing finer in defence of the idea of Original Sin against the modern idea of the steady upward progress of humanity from sub-human beginnings has been written in this generation."

HUGH KINGSMILL.

"MONEY POWER."

Sir,—I am afraid that to many of your readers, as to me, the London Chamber of Commerce Journal to which Old Traveller refers us for information on the Debt payment to America, is as remote as that of Tibet. If, however, it confirms Old Traveller's account of the transaction I suppose it does really illustrate "ignorance in high places."

I have no references, but I think the Chancellor stated at the time that the gold was being obtained from the Bank of England at par value, the "profit" from the sale of the gold at round about 28 million being paid into the Exchange Equalisation Fund. The Bank had the Government's guarantee against loss in respect of its gold holding, and as the payment was followed by a series of Bank "purchases" of gold of which the Treasury (the Equalisa-

tion Fund) was "presumed" by all the City Editors to be the seller, my impression was that the Treasury bought gold as and when it could and repaid the Bank its shareholders' gold, 19½ million. The cost to the nation was certainly more than 19½ million in interest-bearing debt; but the gold was and is quite properly the property of the Bank's shareholders and nobody else. The Exchange Equalisation Fund being, of course, just another mountain (or hillock?) of debt, the Bank may thus be presumed to be raking in the interest on whatever amount is active, *except* on the difference between 19½ and 28 million, bufit inclusive of the cost, if any, of buying 19½ million (par) at more than 28 million (sterling) and of course inclusive of the 19½ million if for convenience we regard the payment as having been made out of the Fund.

Again it does not appear to me that the war finance can be usefully erected into a special case, either of ignorance or cupidity. On the side of the Treasury it should be remembered that Treasury Notes were offered the Banks on the outbreak of war and that the Banks refused to handle them. The Banks on their side naturally preferred to finance that war as they had financed earlier wars, provided Ways and Means, and all the rest of it. I do not say it was not iniquitous, but it was not specially iniquitous because it was specially big.

The Treasury Note introduced a fresh element which handled by somebody other than the Cunliffe Committee, might have been used as a lever for dislodging the Bank from its strong position—though only by completely upsetting the basis on which the Bank and the City had rested for generations, a step for which there was not then, nor is there now, anything approaching effective popular clamour.

The upshot of it all is, then, that when the coin and the trinkets which the patriotic citizens so readily yielded up were squandered all over the earth in partial payment for the war, the Shareholders of the Bank held on to their gold; when the war inflation had reached such proportions that something had to be done about it, *our* Treasury Notes were "deflated" for us, but the Bank held on to its private fiduciary issue of Bank of England notes.

It is all very instructive, but I cannot subscribe to the suggestion of Old Traveller and others that the "social and economic disasters" of this and earlier ages are to be exclusively identified with defective monetary systems and their deflations, inflations, and vast credit expansions and contractions. All that jargon, it seems to me, can be reduced to the simple formula: fluctuating prices (or returns) from whatever cause, including monetary causes: fixed charges (and long dated contracts)—elements which arise irrespective of the monetary system wherever there is large inequality in the distribution of real wealth; for, save under slavery or feudalism, great wealth tends always to express itself in some sort of fixed charges on the less wealthy. It is the peculiarity of *our* monetary system and commercial practice that to the very wealthy is given the added power of the moderately wealthy with which to browbeat the least wealthy.

JOHN BOAK.

THE WISDOM OF THE HILL COUNTRY.

Sir,—I am sorry to disturb in any way Fr. McNabb's idyllic dream of the Cumberland grandmother. But I have a Cumberland grandmother. And she quite recently paid her first visit to London. She was enchanted.

What, I asked her, you like this foul, smoke-begrimed, lonely waste of brick, concrete, wood and tar? And there was the strange spectacle of a Londoner born and bred, trying to convince a Cumberland grandmother of the folly of liking his city; while she would retaliate with lurid descriptions of the monotony and the narrowness of the life of the fells.

My wife comes from Cumberland too,—But this is no place for domestic squabbles.

VINCENT LAWRENCE.

WILL

YOU

HELP?

The Distributist League aims at the restoration of liberty by the distribution of property.

It opposes the concentration of wealth and property in the hands of a few and holds that good government cannot be assured by large-scale capitalistic control, Socialism or Communism.

It opposes the usury of modern finance, corruption in politics, the power of the combines and the growth of bureaucracy.

It looks forward to the extension throughout the country of small ownership, which alone can guarantee the freedom of the individual, the security of the small farmer and trader and the safety of the family as the true unit of the State.

If you are not a member, you should join the League at once. If you are already a member, you should persuade your friends to join.

Write for particulars to the Hon. Secretary, The Distributist League, 2, Little Essex Street, London, W.C.2.

The annual subscription is one shilling.

League Meetings

ANNUAL GENERAL MEETING.

The Annual General Meeting of The League will be held at The George, Strand, W.C.2 (opposite the Law Courts), on Saturday, October 7, commencing at 11.30 a.m.

The Annual Dinner will be held at The Cock Restaurant, Fleet Street, W.C.2., on Saturday, October 7, at 7.30 p.m. Tickets, 4/- each, may be obtained from Hon. Sec., The League, 2, Little Essex Street, Strand, W.C.2.

BIRMINGHAM BRANCH.

The following meetings will be held at the Victoria Hotel, Corporation Street:—

Friday, Oct. 6.—" Distributism for the English." Mr. K. L. Kenrick.

Friday, Oct. 20.—Report of Delegates to Annual General Meeting.

Friday, Nov. 3.—" A Visit to Denmark." Mr. E. Knight.

Friday, Nov. 17.—" Distributism for the English." Mr. B. McDonnell.

Friday, Dec. 1.—" Distributism for the English." Mr. C. O'B. Donaghey.

Friday, Dec. 15.—Exhibition of Arts and Crafts.

GLASGOW BRANCH.

Hon. Sec., Mr. J. J. Lynch, 122, Quarrybrae Street, Parkhead, Glasgow, E.1.

CLYDESDALE BRANCH.

The Branch holds its meetings in the Queen Anne Restaurant, Argyle Street, Glasgow, every Wednesday, at 7.30, where new members can be enrolled. Secretary: Mr. J. MacNamee, 513, Alexandra Parade, Glasgow.

SOUTHAMPTON BRANCH

Meetings are held every fortnight at 123, Warren Avenue. Write to the Secretary for particulars.

BOURNEMOUTH BRANCH.

Readers of **G.K.'s Weekly** living at or near Bournemouth who are interested in the work of the Distributist League are invited to write to Mr. R. H. McCausland, 43, St. Luke's Road, Bournemouth, with a view to increasing membership of the Branch and planning future activities.

HIGH WYCOMBE & DISTRICT BRANCH.

Until further notice, meetings will be held at 28, Crendon Street, High Wycombe, on the 2nd Tuesday of each month. Hon. Sec.: Stormont Murray, 28, Crendon Street, High Wycombe, Bucks.

LEICESTER BRANCH.

Future meetings will be held at the Wyvern Hotel, Leicester.

Sept. 28.—Mr. Leslie Green on " President De Valera and Distributism."

Oct. 12.—Report of delegates to the A.G.M. Miss Mee on " The necessity of a political party."

MID-SUSSEX BRANCH.

Hon. Sec.: Mr. M. G. S. Sewell, S. Dominic's Press, Ditchling Common.

The Annual Meeting of the Branch will be held at The Sandrock, Ditchling, at 7 p.m., on Friday, September 29, 1933.

The Distributist League

2, Little Essex Street, London, W.C.2.

G. K.'s WEEKLY

The paper that stands for and appeals to the small and independent craftsman, trader and shopkeeper.

The charge for prepaid advertisements on this page is one penny per word minimum 2s. Special discount rates are allowed, as follows : Thick type in all cases is 20 per cent. extra.

4 insertions at 2s. per insertion costs	7/6
9 insertions at 2s. per insertion costs	15/-
15 insertions at 2s. per insertion costs	£1/2/6

Space is charged for at the rate of 5s. per inch.

Advertisements not paid for in advance cost 25 per cent. extra to above charges.

NEW WITNESS. Bound Volumes, Nearly Complete Set (from No. 1—Nov. 1912, to No. 21—May, 1923) For Sale, together or separately. Any reasonable offer considered.—Apply Box 453.

WHERE TO STAY.

THE FELLOWSHIP CLUB, LTD., 46, 51, 52, Lancaster Gate, London, W.2. An International residential centre, situated in a quiet square close to Kensington. Excellent vegetarian diet. Running hot and cold water and gas-fires in bedrooms. Shower-baths. Attractive drawing-room, library, smoking-room, lecture and recreation rooms. Very near tube station and 'bus routes. Single rooms from £2 5s. Double rooms from £4 4s. Partial Board. Full Board Sundays. Bed and Breakfast from 7s. 6d. Lunch: 1s. and 1s. 6d., Tea: 6d. Dinner: 3s. Telephone Pad. 7697.

HAMPSTEAD (Belsize Park Tube, 12 mins. Oxford Street). Charming rooms, furnished or unfurnished, in quiet and pleasant house. Meals and service (moderate) if required. Rents 12/-—25/-. —22, Belsize Avenue, Prim. 1043.

WEEK-ENDS AT OXFORD. Food, comfort and service outstanding for quality and economy at THE CASTLE HOTEL. Tel. 2844.

LOWESTOFT, SOUTH. Ladies may stay at St. Mary's Convent; Magnificently situated on sunny sea front; hard court; excellent catering; home freedom.—Apply Superior.

LONDON Visitors: Westminster Bridge; central; bed-breakfast, 3/6 per night, £1 1s. 0d. weekly.—Powell, 75, Lambeth Palace Road, S.E.1.

TYPEWRITING, Etc.

LITERARY TYPEWRITING promptly executed and Secretarial work undertaken.—Miss K. Flaxman, 51, Tavistock Square, W.C.1. (Tel. Mus. 5186).

TYPEWRITING, every description accurately and promptly executed, 10d. 1,000; carbons, 2d.—Miss James, 16, Feltham Road, Mitcham.

AUTHOR'S MSS. neatly and accurately typed. Expert in deciphering difficult handwriting, 1/- per 1,000 words. One-third extra for each carbon copy.— Miss E. M. Compton, 44, Buxton Road, Thornton Heath.

LITERARY.

STELLA MARIS, a Catholic Magazine, contains interesting Religious Articles for all who want Certainty—Father Lester's Answers to genuine questions— Stories—Verses. By post 2½d.; 12 months, 2/6.—MANRESA PRESS, Roehampton, London, S.W.15.

FAIR WARNING! Only 15,000 copies will be printed of The Capuchin Annual (1934). 336 pages. Order now, By post, 2/6d.—Box 105, G.P.O., Dublin.

£100 CASH OFFERED FOR NOVEL. Full particulars and Current Catalogues on application. MSS. of all types also invited for prompt publication. Advice free.—Stockwell, Ltd., 29, Ludgate Hill, London. Established 1898.

MISCELLANEOUS.

HOME MADE SWEETS. Boxes of mixed Fudge—Toffees. Peppermint Lumps, etc.—sent for 2/6 lb. box. Carriage paid from Mrs. Sparrow, Talybont-on-Usk.

INCOME TAX. Expert advice. Books written up. Appeals conducted. Overpayments recovered.—Box 9333.

IRISH COTTAGE FINE ART INDUSTRIES. Pure Irish Linens of every description, hand embroidered by Ulster needle-workers. Write for full particulars to KENNEDY'S, Bellaghy, Co. Derry, North Ireland.

DONEGAL Handwoven Tweed, Hand-knit Stockings, etc., always in stock. Tweed patterns free on request.—Manager, Lissadell, Sligo, Irish Free State.

FIRST-CLASS POSTCARDS from any photograph or sketch, 100 for 7/6d. Enlargement 10 x 6, mounted 15 x 12, included free.—NUVA, Nuva Works, Smethwick.

LONELY? Then write Secretary: U.C.C., 16G, Cambridge Street, London, S.W.1.

MEMBERS of the Manchester Branch are advised that Mr. Lockhart, a craftsman, produces all kinds of knitted woollen goods on his own knitting machine. Jumpers, pullovers, men's socks, boys' stockings, cardigan jackets, etc. Support your own local craftsman. Send a postcard to Mr. W. L. Lockhart, 34, Broadlea Road, Kingsway, Burnage, when requiring any of the articles mentioned.

BEAUTIFUL hand-woven woollen plaid Scarves; soft colourings. 12 ins. wide; 10/6 each.—Stuart, Bucklerburn, Peterculter, Aberdeenshire.

Published by the Proprietors, G.K.'s WEEKLY, LTD., 2, Little Essex Street, Strand, London, W.C.2. (incorporating THE NEW WITNESS). Telephone : Temple Bar 1978. Printed by THE NUNEATON NEWSPAPERS, LTD., " Observer " Buildings, Nuneaton. Sole Agents for Australasia : Gordon & Gotch (Australasia, Ltd.). Sole Agents for South Africa : Central News Agency, Ltd. (London Agents : Gordon & Gotch, Ltd.).

GK's WEEKLY

EDITED BY G.K. CHESTERTON

MARCH 15 - - - 1934
VOL. XIX.   No. 470

Registered as a Newspaper   SIXPENCE.

IN AND OUT

ASSUMING that the London County Council can properly be called a municipal unit, it is the largest in the country and its elections are therefore of considerable public interest. Elections were held last week. They resulted in the defeat of the Municipal Reform Party, which has held a safe majority for many years, and the success of the Labour Party which achieved a net gain of 34 seats and has now a majority of 14 over its opposition. The Liberal Party disappeared and Communist candidates polled very few votes indeed.

It cannot be said that this reversal represented a drastic change in voting. The candidates of the Municipal Reform Party received an aggregate of 592,334 votes, as against the 561,520 votes cast for them in 1931—an increase of 30,814. The Labour candidates received 681,143 votes—an increase of 258,196. The percentage of the electorate who voted was 32.8, as against 27.8 per cent. in 1931. So, many more people voted than at the previous election and the success of the Labour candidates was due to the fact that they received the support of a larger proportion of the new voters. The small percentage points to apathy, but we do not suppose that the Municipal Reformers were less active in canvassing than their opponents. Had they been so they would not have succeeded in increasing their poll.

Among the points that come up for consideration as a result of this election, may be taken first the bearing of the voting on politics as a whole. Elections in Maine generally forecast the result of Presidential elections, and a like similarity has been noticed in this country between the return of local councillors and the return of members of Parliament. That seems to suggest that a General Election this year would reduce the huge majority of the National Government possibly to vanishing point. The landslide that overwhelmed the Labour Party in 1931 is recalled by the minor landslide that overwhelmed the Municipal Reform Party last week. As in 1931 proverbially "safe" Labour seats were taken away by "National" candidates, so unexpected victories were gained by candidates for the L.C.C. In one instance so few votes separated the winners and the losers in a district where Conservative tendencies are most clearly marked, that had the Communists saved themselves the trouble of fighting the election, the Labour candidates would certainly have won. Crowd feeling shows itself in the polling booth as much as in the market-place and crowd feeling on this occasion was on the side of Labour.

This was contributed to as much by propaganda engineered on behalf of the Municipal Reformers as by the efforts of the Labour Party. It may be that many people voted, who might otherwise have abstained, and voted for the Labour candidates, simply because they were disgusted by the tactics of the Beaverbrook Press. On the eve of the poll Lord Beaverbrook attended a meeting at Camberwell in support of the leader of the Municipal Reformers, "the Prime Minister of London." Neither he nor any other speaker was able to obtain a hearing. The next day the "Prime Minister" was defeated. But while the polling booths were open readers of the Beaverbrook Press were being appealed to by poster and headlines to "keep out the hooligans." Terrifying pictures were drawn of Socialism in practice. Once give power to the hooligans and rates would go up, property rights would be endangered and the security of the independent trader would be placed in jeopardy. The attempt to stampede the electors failed—the effect was very different to that intended. The next day it was announced that a special article on his plans for London would be contributed by the new "Prime Minister," Mr. Morrison, to the *Sunday Express*.

We can assure Lord Beaverbrook's readers that his fears are groundless. Someone said a few months ago that the one event likely to check Socialism in England would be the return of a Socialist Government. The same may be said of local politics. Capitalism which is really irresponsible Socialism has governed the actions of the past administration as effectively as Socialism is likely to govern the new. Solicitude for sound government might have recalled the fact that the London County Council was not controlled by its Labour members when the owners of cinemas were told that the law would be disregarded if part of their takings on Sundays were given to charity. Labour was not in control when the bureaucracy became powerful. It is just possible that changes made will be changes for the better. But we very much doubt if any of London's citizens will notice any difference in methods of administration. The bureaucrats will remain; money will continue to be the ruling factor. The transfer of power from one party to another, nowadays, is a change of label, and has no real significance at all.

NOTES

Monday, March 12.

General Göring's speech on the glories of Potsdam was full of the old Prussian spirit even while he contemplated the submergence of Prussia in the Reich. Her soul goes marching on; and the full implications of the Prussian doctrine of duty in war give effectual contradiction to Hitler's new-found policies of peace. Observers in every country are now satisfied that Germany's military preparations are well advanced—even the theoretical ten year period of peace may be drastically curtailed—but it is possible even yet that the new rulers have bitten off more than they can chew. The enthusiasm whipped up to fever-heat by the departure from the League and the national vote has had some winter months in which to cool. The next excitement is about due. And Hitler's own latest speech reflected some more practical issues when he declared that " reducing unemployment is less important than the regeneration of the German people." The fact is that few problems have been faced by the

National-Socialists in a year of effort, while innumerable other problems have been created. Unemployment remains, and the religious quarrel is very far from at an end.

*   *   *   *

Note should be taken of the declaration by Diels, the chief of the Prussian Secret Police, that Torgler cannot be released from " protective custody" while 8,000 " enemies of the State " are under detention in concentration camps. To release him, he said, would be to accord him favoured treatment. If a Prussian official could exercise a sense of humour, Diels would have been unable to deliver this pronouncement without punctuating it with loud guffaws. If a Prussian official could exercise a little commonsense, Diels would not have spoken at all in order to make himself less ridiculous.

*   *   *   *

Torgler was arrested on a charge of complicity in the conspiracy to fire the Reichstag. He was acquitted, but was kept in custody. Later favoured treatment was accorded to his brave companion Dimitroff who is now in Russia. But Torgler must remain in prison, apparently, no matter how flimsy the pretext. Communists in the concentration camps have not been tried at all. Many of them, no doubt, are not Communists. Torgler, on the other hand, has been tried on specific charges and has been declared in court to be innocent. So long as he remains in prison Europe will have before it an example of Prussian rule, and so long as people like Diels continue to excuse his detention, Europe will be reminded of Prussian stupidity.

*   *   *   *

The report that President Roosevelt proposes a reopening of the World Economic Conference makes interesting reading. His recent activities in the United States certainly suggest him as one of the few men who could get constructive results out of the Conference to end Conferences. On the other hand, the example of President Wilson is not one to encourage imitation any more than the memory of the World Economic Conference is one to encourage resumption. With Mr. Eden's subdued tour around Europe the Conference business may be said to have ended for a time so far as this country is concerned. Yet in itself the tour was a hopeful sign, implementing what Mr. Belloc wrote in these pages last May: " Most of our modern professional politicians had not travelled nor known the delights of the Riviera and the rest till they were in middle life. It was natural that the opportunities for getting such an unexpectedly good time ' on the nod ' should carry them away. But even for such men there comes the phase of boredom, which to those born wealthy commonly appears in the thirties. Sooner or later even your Labour leader and pacifist has seen enough of Palace Hotels and *wagons-lits* and Pullmans and Alps and luxury suites on great liners, and jazz bands, and all the other accompaniments of high politics. You will begin to notice the turn of the tide when only the second rank of minor politicians are sent off upon such jaunts. When you see that symptom, rejoice. Your deliverance is nigh.

You will have just as heavy taxes to pay; but you will at least have the satisfaction of knowing that you are not providing a mass of nobodies with free advertisement and free wine and free food and free everything at your expense."

*   *   *   *

The Archbishop of York's public suggestion that a Budget surplus should be devoted first of all to the restoration of cuts in unemployment benefit has aroused quite a spirited controversy. Lord Melchett supported the idea with reasoned argument. The Bishop of Gloucester denounced it with something approaching acrimony. The Chancellor of the Exchequer himself snubbed the Archbishop in a public speech and Lord Grey drew attention to the curious constitutional theories of M.P.s who had called His Grace ' impertinent '; for the suggestion was that constituents who agreed with the proposal should write to their member and say so. " Since when," Lord Grey asked, " have M.P.s claimed immunity from having to listen to the opinions of their constituents? Or is there a special ban on any member of the House of Lords venturing to address his M.P.? How else can he hope to influence financial decisions? Had Dr. Temple been a trade union leader he would at least have been listened to with courtesy. Being merely an Archbishop he is called impertinent." The L.C.C. elections put a new face on the argument half way through, but quite apart from expediency the proposal of the Archbishop is surely an expression of common justice. Wages are the first charge on an industry; the poor are the first charge on a community.

*   *   *   *

One would not expect Mr. Ramsay MacDonald's position to be any more secure as a result of the L.C.C. elections. If the elections presage the defeat of the National Government in two years' time, the obvious policy for the Conservatives is to get out from under as quickly as possible; otherwise they will be held responsible for all the failures of the National Government when that respectable institution dies of old age. At the present moment there is still time to fasten the failures upon Mr. Ramsay MacDonald and Sir John Simon while the Conservatives may claim credit for the successes. A vigorous Tory revolt against the inanition of the Prime Minister, a swift appeal to the country on a sweeping policy of action, a change in Conservative leadership, a propitious opportunity such as may appear when the Budget surplus is tactfully allocated either to the unemployed or to the middle classes—these are the possibilities of success. As matters stand, the country will never vote for another MacDonald Administration or for another Baldwin Administration, unless something out-size in the way of a Zinovieff Letter is produced at the last moment. This does not even mean that the country is firmly determined to put in the Socialists. But there is certainly widespread discontent everywhere, and it is increased by inevitable comparisons with the activity of a Roosevelt, a Mussolini, even of a Hitler. The National Government is remarkably like one of the races described by the traveller Sir John Mandeville; it is all shoulders and no head.

Whither Austria ?
By C. F. Melville

ABOUT the time this article is published Signor Mussolini, the Italian Dictator, Dr. Dollfuss, the Austrian Chancellor, and General Gombos, the Hungarian Premier will be meeting in Rome. The object of their meeting is to discuss Signor Mussolini's scheme for a close Austro-Hungarian politic-economic association under Italian ægis.

The Italian scheme is aimed at the preservation of Austrian independence. It is the Duce's final effort to prevent Austria being submitted to a process of Nazi *gleichshaltung;* for the continuance of Austria as a buffer state between Germany and Italy is the only way for Italy of obviating the menace of a Greater Germany on her own northern frontier.

But the Italian scheme also has other aims. It is calculated, for instance, not only to keep Germany out of Austria, but also to prevent the realisation of the Little Entente plan whereby the Austrian problem could be solved within the framework of a general Danubian co-operation. For either a Germanised Austria or a Danubian Confederation would mean the end of Italian hopes of dominating the Danube.

Italy has previously tried to dominate the Balkans, and to this end she sought to encircle Jugoslavia from without and to disrupt her from within. All this failed. Her new attempt to dominate the Danube by means of an Italo-Austro-Hungarian bloc, with a possible Hapsburg restoration in the background, would seem also to be doomed to failure, because the economic part of the Italian scheme has no real value apart from its underlying political motive, and, after all, it is economic revival rather than political adventure which will really be efficacious in enabling Austria permanently to resist Germanisation.

It seems, therefore, most likely that for a time—but only for a time—Italy will be able to conduct Austrian affairs according to her own interests, but after that the Italian plan will in all probability prove inadequate to its purpose, and there will then be a weakening of the Italian influence in Austria and a corresponding strengthening of the German.

There will most likely be some kind of eventual compromise. Austria will retain her independence but will, as it were, form part of a Germanic bloc. For the new Austria is likely to become increasingly akin to the new Germany, but with certain important differences due both to the Austrian particularist tradition, which is opposed to German totalitarianism, and to the influence of the Catholic Church which is uncompromisingly hostile to the quasi-paganism and extreme racialism of Nazism.

The fact that the best solution of the Austrian problem—i.e., as part of a general Danubian arrangement—has not materialised is due at once to Italy's policy of prestige and the ineptitude of the Western Powers. France, in her anxiety to prevent any kind of Austro-German union, more or less gave Italy a blank cheque to do as she liked for the preservation of Austrian independence, and Britain, not wanting to be involved one way or the other, acquiesced. Perhaps it is too late to cry over spilt milk? At all events, the solution is not now going to be the ideal one, and so it will probably be necessary to make the best of a bad job.

In this connection it should be borne in mind that however regrettable the methods which ushered in the Fascist regime in Austria—however deplorable the shooting down by the Heimwehr of the Socialists in the Vienna tenements—nevertheless Austro-Fascism is a lesser evil than German Nazism. Both abolish the Democratic State. That was in any case inevitable. But whereas some forms of liberty are to be retained under Austro-Fascism, not any kind of liberty would exist in Austria if German Nazism were to establish itself there.

In all this the Catholic Church seems destined to play an important role. The Church, whilst not favouring an out-and-out Fascist state, is favourable to a corporative form of society in Austria. Dr. Dollfuss's project for a Christian Corporative Constitution is based mainly on the Papal Encyclical " Quadragesimo Anno." Thus, if the influence of the Church continues to prevail over the more hot-headed Fascist elements amongst the Heimwehr leaders, we shall see in Austria a Corporative state with a Fascist leaven, rather than the tyrannical totalitarian Fascist state which exists in Hitlerist Germany.

Thus it would seem that the Austrian situation is tending towards some sort of compromise which, whilst it will not be to the liking of western democracies, will nevertheless be something much more humane than Nazism. For so long as even a vestige of Austrian independence remains the worst results

of Hitlerism will be kept out of the Danubian regions.

As to the future possibilities for Europe, this is too big a subject to be dealt with at the end of a short article like this. It can only be said here that out of the Austrian developments new European groupings will probably take shape leading eventually to the creation of a new balance of Power. What final form this will take it is, of course, not yet possible to forecast.

This Liberty
By W. R. Titterton
An Open Letter to the Editor of the "News-Chronicle"

Dear Sir,—I was keenly interested in the Manifesto on Liberty signed by so many illustrious people which you published in your columns. And with equal interest I have followed the comments of your readers. Some of those comments touched upon the ground I should like to cover, but the criticism was dispersed, and taken altogether it does not cover all my ground.

With the general indictment of the totalitarian State, whether Fascist or Communist (that is: Socialist), I heartily agree. The totalitarian State is the last and worst of the tyrants. It is the absolute negation of freedom, of the prime doctrine of any civilised community, that the State exists only to safeguard the private citizen from attack—either by members of the community, or by forces outside it. You and I hold, sir, that the true function of the government is to police the country and its frontiers, and there's an end of it. I need not point out to you or any of your readers that the totalitarian State goes a lot farther than that.

But has not England for a long time now given house-room to some totalitarian ideas? Have not members and even leaders of the Liberal Party, which should be the party of freedom, at least coquetted with the idea that government has the right to make the private citizen moral by Act of Parliament? I grant you that the most prominent devotee of this undemocratic theory is a Conservative M.P., yet I think that if Liberals search their consciences they will find that the Party has been seriously infected with the virus.

Again, I suggest that the attack launched by the Manifesto is wrong in emphasis. Undoubtedly it is in the guise of Fascism that the danger presents itself to-day on the Continent. But in England Socialism is a far more formidable force, and we shall soon see registered in a general election that sharp swing to the Left which has already taken place in the country. Since Hitlerism and Leninism are essentially the same, it is valuable to have them bracketed in one condemnation. But the hope of co-operation between Liberals and those members of the Labour Party who are more liberal than totalitarian should not blind us to the realities of the situation.

Thirdly, it is needful for democrats to admit how far, even in England, parliamentary institutions have fallen short of the democratic ideal. We know how easy it has been of late to sweep the electorate off its feet with a scare-campaign, and I trace a connection, foreseen or not, between the granting of the flapper-vote by the Tories and the triumph of the "National" Government.

We know that an elector has never a free choice. Commonly he must choose between three Caucus candidates, and say whether he will be stifled in mud, seethed in the milk of human kindness, or fried in butter. The *deposit* keeps the plague of independence within manageable limits. We know that in Parliament sound business reasons are given for the members working with the machine and betraying their election-pledges, though when the Opposition is very weak Government members on the Back Benches indulge in the harmless sport of rebellion.

We know that our parliamentary procedure is complicated and slow—so much so that the Government is forced to wolf almost all the time of the House for its own measures, and the private member has about as much power of changing the law as the orator in Hyde Park.

We know that of late more and more power has been taken away even from this shackled Parliament, and instead of Acts of our Houses we have Orders in Council.

By all of these signs we know that the present Government is in fact a dictatorship, and that any alternative government likely to be elected would be only a shade less so. If a shade less! For the Labour Party Machine functions more rigorously than either of the others.

We know, moreover, that, if our Parliament has not been as corrupt as some legislative assemblies abroad, yet it has been corrupt. Honours have been bought and sold—that we know. And there is grave reason to suspect that policies have been bought and sold. We have yet to see the public auditing of the Party Funds.

Finally the Manifesto does not mention a third approximation to the totalitarian State which is at present at least as great a danger to English liberty as any. I mean the growth and interlocking of those very big businesses which we call Combines. I submit that civic liberty does not exist in a community where the private-trader—the true one, not the fake fellow who is whining just now as he grinds his multiple-axe—liberty does not exist, I say where that small man in industrial, commercial, or agricultural enterprise maintains himself only on sufferance in a world run by big business.

Do I over-emphasise the danger? I think not. It is true that in many spheres of enterprise genuine private-trading still continues. But it is no less true that it tends to disappear—and that swiftly. Equally true is it that the big businesses tend to come to agreement among themselves for the ruling out of competition. We must look forward to a Britain which, so far as agriculture, industry, and commerce is concerned, is ruled by a committee of business men. Such rule might be efficient, though that is doubtful, and no democrat will agree that efficiency is a good excuse for the abolition of freedom.

You may say that even if I am right in my forecast a good share of our personal freedom will be left un-touched. Can you believe it? Mr. Ford dictates to his employees in the matter of their personal habits. Can you doubt that the business-controllers of Britain would do at least as much?

You may suggest that Parliament will bring them to book. Rubbish! It does not bring them to book now; will it do so when they are firm in the saddle? No, sir, Parliament will be then in full what it is now in part—the servant of big-business.

From that condition of things it will not be a wide step to the totalitarian State. Should Parliament at long last venture to show independence the step would be taken to the orchestral accompaniment of guns. Therefore if we would be free we must deal now with big-business.

But since I restrict the true function of government to that of the police, how do I justify interference with trading? Why, because the police have the right to stop conspiracy in restraint of free trade. That was granted in principle long ago by the United States, though practice has lagged behind. For centuries in England the principle was accepted—and acted upon. But the danger of trade-conspiracy was never so dreadful as it is to-day.

Never before was it so necessary that a strong Liberal Party should exist in the country and find its just representation in Parliament. But it must have a clear idea of the meaning of liberty—liberty within the party itself, liberty in Parliament, liberty in private life. It must know that it alone rides free between the rocks of the Combine-State and the Fascist or Communist-State. It must awaken Britain to those twin dangers. Or rather it must appeal to the inarticulate millions who are instinctively aware of the dangers, and are awaiting the call.

Will the *News-Chronicle* give that call? Or is it content with that brave Victorian Manifesto?

Yours truly,

W. R. TITTERTON.

YEARS AGO

I SAID that his principles had been poisoned by a noted infidel writer, but that he was, nevertheless, a benevolent good man. *Johnson.* " We can have no dependence upon that instinctive, that constitutional goodness which is not founded upon principle. I grant you that such a man may be a very amiable member of society. I can conceive him placed in such a situation that he is not much tempted to deviate from what is right; and as every man prefers virtue, when there is not some strong incitement to transgress its precepts, I can conceive him doing nothing wrong. . . .

" Hume, and other sceptical innovators, are vain men, and will gratify themselves at any expense. Truth will not afford sufficient food to their vanity; so they have betaken themselves to error. Truth, Sir, is a cow which will yield such people no more milk, and so they are gone to milk the bull. If I could have allowed myself to gratify my vanity at the expense of truth, what fame might I have acquired! Everything which Hume has advanced against Christianity had passed through my mind long before he wrote.

Always remember this, that after a system is well settled upon positive evidence, a few partial objections ought not to shake it. The human mind is so limited, that it cannot take in all the parts of a subject, so that there may be objections raised against anything."

*   *   *   *

He talked in his usual style with a rough contempt of popular liberty. " They make a rout about *universal* liberty, without considering that all that is to be valued, or indeed can be enjoyed by individuals, is *private* liberty. Political liberty is good only so far as it produces private liberty. Now, Sir, there is the liberty of the press, which you know is a constant topic. Suppose you and I and two hundred more were restrained from printing our thoughts: What then? What proportion would that restraint upon us bear to the private happiness of the nation?"

This mode of representing the inconveniences of restraint as light and insignificant, was a kind of sophistry in which he delighted to indulge himself, in opposition to the extreme laxity for which it has been fashionable for too many to argue, when it is evident, upon reflection, that the very essence of government is restraint; and certain it is (says Boswell) that as government produces rational happiness, too much restraint is better than too little. But when restraint is unnecessary, and so close as to gall those who are subject to it, the people may and ought to remonstrate; and if relief is not granted, to resist. Of this manly and spirited principle, no man was more convinced than Johnson himself.

*   *   *   *

Talking of trade, he observed, " It is a mistaken notion that a vast deal of money is brought into a nation by trade. It is not so. Commodities come from commodities; but trade produces no capital accession of wealth. However, though there should be little profit in money, there is a considerable profit in pleasure, as it gives to one nation the productions of another; as we have wines and fruits, and many other foreign articles, brought to us." *Boswell.* " Yes, Sir, and there is a profit in pleasure, by its furnishing occupation to such numbers of mankind." *Johnson.* " Why, Sir, you cannot call that pleasure, to which all are averse, and which none begin but with the hope of leaving off; a thing which men dislike before they have tried it, and when they have tried it." *Boswell.* " But, Sir, the mind must be employed, and we grow weary when idle." *Johnson.* " That is, Sir, because others being busy, we want company; but if we were all idle, there would be no growing weary; we should all entertain one another. There is, indeed, this in trade;—it gives men an opportunity of improving their situation. If there were no trade, many who are poor would always remain poor."

*   *   *   *

Mr. Ferguson, the self-taught philosopher, told him of a newly-invented machine which went without horses: a man who sat in it turned a handle, which worked a spring that drove it forward. " Then, Sir," said Johnson, " What is gained is, the man has his choice whether he will move himself alone, or himself and the machine too."

—*Boswell's Life of Johnson.*

Straws in the Wind

THE BLUNDER ABOUT REACTION
By G. K. CHESTERTON

I AM accused of a diplomatic coyness almost flattering: a correspondent suggests that there is some dark secret in our policy about Austria that I refuse to reveal. I would reveal it at once: only it is so very dark and diplomatic that it is not revealed to me. What I think of Austria as a whole, and the historic foundations of her present difficulties, I explained, I fear, at rather too great a length, in a series of three or four articles some months ago. Anything that needs to be added to such a survey I am perfectly willing at any time to add. It is only necessary to say, at this stage, that there is an Austrian tradition, not merely mechanical or numerical; that, historically speaking, supporting Austrian Nazis is not supporting Austria, but supporting Prussianised Germany; and supporting Austrian Communists is not supporting Austria, but supporting Bolshevist Russia. I have repeated my reasons for deleting Prussianism and Bolshevism often enough to explain my relative preference for a third party. But Mr. Porter starts with a simpler axiom.

" There are many who hold," he observes, shaking his head with the utmost solemnity, " there are many who hold that the Catholic Church (as distinct from individual Catholics) would stop at no brutality to maintain its power." Well, there are many who hold many similar propositions, though not perhaps quite so many as there were. There were many who held that the Papists caused the Great Fire of London; and others who hold other opinions on the Popish Plot, to judge by a recent review in the *New Statesman*, which are on a similar educational level. There are many who still believe that every Catholic going to confession hands the priest a handsome tip, in return for the absolution; while the priest doubtless touches his biretta in return for the tip. There are many in the less sophisticated parts of the Middle West or the Black Belt of America, who believe that the Knights of Columbus are verbally vowed to dash out the brains of all infants of other denominations; and their simple faith stands firm under the most intolerable provocation of proof to the contrary. It was the same set of faithful witnesses who believed that the election of a Catholic as American President would be instantly followed by the appearance in the sky of the Pope in an enormous white aeroplane, come to take up his permanent lodgings at the White House. I should hesitate to say of any of these persons that their sense of scientific fact is equal to their power of religious faith. But I think all of them, without exception, are enormously more sane and sensible than anybody who can believe that the Catholic Church worked the present political reaction in Europe. After all, few Englishmen, however broad-minded, have actually hidden in a confessional box to overhear the confession; and few Americans, however enterprising, have actually performed the ceremony of the Knights of Columbus. But we have eyes, most of us, to see the facts that are now filling all Europe, and the facts flatly contradict the whole of Mr. Porter's new version of the Popish Plot.

It is enormously astonishing to notice how men can see the most staggering and stupendous facts; not only without learning anything, but without even realising that they have seen anything. If there is one thing outstanding and obvious in the whole modern movement that began with Fascism, it is that it was originally entirely a secular movement, and for some time even an anti-clerical movement. What it really has to teach anybody, who happens to be capable of learning anything, is this not unimportant fact: that the longing for order every bit as much as the longing for liberty, and the temptation to tyranny every bit as much as the temptation to anarchy, come out of the mortal mind and natural heart of man; as all four of them came forth, again and again, when men were entirely pagan and before there was any such thing as the Catholic Church. Towards the end of the eighteenth century, when Mr. Porter found many more people to agree with him than he will find now, in the nineteenth century, when his sympathisers could still be called " many," there gradually grew up a legend that the whole world was finally moving towards democracy and away from despotism. There grew up along with it another legend; that the Church had always been, and would always be, on the side of the despots. If those who loved these legends had happened to know anything at all about the history of the Church, or even anything reasonably wide and well-informed about the history of the world, they would very quickly have discovered that their identification could hardly be stretched to cover more than about fifty years of any period in the past. The Church, as a human diplomatic agent, has been on the side of despots and of all sorts of things. But it was not supporting the despot in the quarrel of Iconoclasm; it was not supporting the despot in the quarrel of Investiture; and it was not supporting the despot in the new theories of despotism that arose after the Great War. With the most famous and luminous of those theories, that advanced in the *Action Française*, it was furiously at war.

Our vague humanitarians, while still desperately trying to prove, in the teeth of all the facts, that the Papists did burn down London and the Pope did start a storm of tribal militarism plainly contrary to all his counsels, have missed the whole point of the position: for the same reason that always prevents such men from learning a lesson; because it is a lesson against themselves. The dogma that has really vanished, the illusion that is really gone, is the very notion that is at the back of all their own notions. It is the whole nineteenth century notion that humanity, unhampered by a Church, unhelped by a God, will grow of its own nature into more and more large and liberal and humanitarian ideas. The truth is that humanity, quite certainly without a Church and to some extent even with it, will go on as it has always gone on; blundering and barging about from one extreme to another; righting something of what was wrong in the old regime, but eternally tempted to forget what was right in the old regime; sometimes incidentally opposed to religion when men are in a mood of revolution; but certainly not needing any help from religion when men are in a mood for reaction. A human reaction happens when something has become an ordinary human bore; and democracy, combined with industrialism and parliamentary corruption, had become a thoroughly human bore. Having pointed out this basic error in ideas, I will deal later with the facts—which are also nearly all of them errors.

Heels of Achilles
By K. L. Kenrick

THE strenuous efforts of the dictators and their friends to cut themselves off from reason and logic and to become quite completely mad are not meeting with the success they deserve. It is easy to profess open scorn for the "immortal principles" of justice and right, but not so easy to frame a philosophy or to map out a programme which shall be wholly purged of the principles so scorned. If there are three possible courses of action of which one is good and the other two bad, the mere decision to avoid the good one at all costs affords no guidance as to which of the two bad cases is to be preferred. Up to the present the history of the dictators shows a pathetic leaning to the particular bad one which happens to show some slight superficial resemblance to the good one which has been so determinedly rejected. For how much longer this form of weakness will be tolerated remains to be seen.

Of the dictators' advocates in this country one of the most celebrated has recently suggested painless extermination as the method to be adopted by the Utopian dictator of the future for dealing with his opponents. But why painless? If justice is to be henceforth anathema, why boggle at a spot of torture? Is there not here some squalid and reprehensible relic of former democratic scruples? Would Mr. Shaw expect a crook who is prepared to forge a cheque for a thousand pounds to have qualms of conscience about stealing a five-pound note? Or does he think that if he inures himself to the Oriental potentate's "Off with his head," he will find it quite easy to refuse to the executioner his other well-known perquisites of the rack and the wheel?

There are writers in these columns who desire, and desire very ardently, "a certain type of civilisation and culture," but so far from desiring to exterminate Mr. Shaw, either painfully or painlessly, they would much prefer to keep him alive for ever, in the hope that some day they might convert him and save his soul. If Mr. Shaw were to reply that he would regard such prolongation as a most acute form of torture, and that he would prefer painless extinction to the joys of interminable argument, nobody would believe him.

However, while Mr. Shaw was penning his vigorous denunciation of such of the immortal principles as are to be found in the words sin, penance, punishment, and expiation, Moscow itself, of all places in the world, was giving further proof to an astonished humanity of the extreme difficulty of getting completely away from these words, and indeed, of living without them at all. At the recent Congress of the Communist party held in that city the chief feature was a chorus of penitent sinners, who were permitted to express their contrition and to promise better behaviour for the future.

One of the penitents made a complete list of the heresies he recanted. Another described his struggle against the dictator as his " vast sin before the party, which he must wipe out at all costs." Another chose the following formula to express his repentance, " Before me lies the sad obligation at this congress of victors to present a record of defeats, of mistakes, blunders, and crimes, to which any man is doomed who tears himself away from the great teaching of Marx, Engels, Lenin, and Stalin." Most abject and full-throated in his expressions of penitence was the speaker who said, " My sin before the party is very great. I, who was able to learn directly from Lenin, and after this from Stalin, went off the road and placed myself in the position of an apostate. . . If I had been in quite healthy, direct, simple relationship with the Central Committee, I should have been obliged . . . etc."

It was thus that the excellent Russian correspondent of *The Observer* revealed to the world that all good Communists carry Christian prayer-books in their pockets, from which they recite quite long passages when they have anything of real importance to say to the party.

We have still to learn whether these prayer-books are in Latin or in Greek. But in either case the only suggestion a pious Christian might make would be that the substitution of harsh grating sounds like Marx, Engels, Lenin, and Stalin was hardly an improvement on the softer and more gentle euphony of Mary, Michael, Peter, and Paul. Even the most truculent anti-Christian pro-dictator could hardly be expected to cease from his blasphemy and to break forth into lyric rapture at the substitution of a Central Committee for a *Sancta Ecclesia*. For what precise points of superiority can penance in a Committee have over penance in a Church?

But we need not go to Moscow to find the same baneful spirit of compromise with what is left of Christian democracy. Our dictators in this country are called experts, being of the same essence but not of the same stature as the Continental dictators. They pursue the search for the ideal of truth and justice with the same relentless zeal as their Continental brethren. When they have found it their attitude towards it shows the same hostility, and their efforts to oppose it and to evade it are equally ingenious. And in the end the same lingering and limping compunction robs them of their triumph.

A few years ago they decided that the sale of contraceptions was to be pushed for all it was worth. The campaign was in charge of an arch-priestess and met with phenomenal success. According to Lord Dawson of Penn, the sale has gone up almost by leaps and bounds. One firm at the present time turns out 8½ millions per year—another turns out 72,000 per week, and is reinforced by large importations from abroad. According to Sir John Robertson of Birmingham these things now litter the streets—like so many other factory products. But instead of being delighted with the success of their efforts to dethrone a historic virtue, the experts are shocked and alarmed. " Is there anything," asks Lord Dawson in the House of Peers, " more perturbing than precocity in youth?" Well, to a Funniman Islander or a Whattosh tribesman from Bunkumboland such a question would have no meaning. The only people to whom it can reasonably be addressed are the people who still live by the European and Christian tradition of two thousand years. Is there not here again a stickiness left over from other times and other manners? The merest half-wit could see what was going to happen if the arch-priestess had her way; and now that it has happened the experts who supported her are calling upon the somewhat decrepit loyalty of bishops and archbishops to save from the horrors of their own handiwork.

What is the moral of it all? It would be difficult to find three better representatives of the modern world than George Bernard Shaw, Lord Dawson of Penn, and the Moscow communist. Their three messages are one and the same message. After centuries of revolt against Supreme Authority, they tell us that revolt in itself is but another name for intolerable anarchy. They tell us that new authorities must be set up which must claim the right to commit every crime of which the old Authority was ever accused. They are teaching the world, in language as plain as ever language can be, that the new Popes will be no better than the old ones, and will in all probability be a good deal worse. When will they learn this lesson themselves?

Odds and Ends

By J. Desmond Gleeson

THE WINNING WORDS.

THOSE who hold that the Australians do not play cricket will unhappily find encouragement for their view in the new slogan Captain Woodfull has seen fit to give his troops. Here it is:

" Straight up the Centre; No Short Passes; Boots and All!"

No word about bats and balls; no reference to the tea interval. It may be said that there are some Slogans whose meaning is more readily apparent. Presuming that centre means centre, i.e., a point, how does one " Straight up " it? Anyway I suppose it must be a winning move, so we must make an effort to understand it. The next part " No Short Passes " is obviously a case where the " s's " have got mixed up. No one need look at it twice to realise that Woodfull is telling the boys that " No Shorts Pass." You may wear your shorts in Tennis and other inferior games,

but try any such tricks on in the sacred area and you'll be lucky if you are only unfrocked. As to " Boots and All," that last word may be understood to include knuckle-dusters and life-preservers if the game is going ill. Otherwise the " All " may be left out and by " Boots " just understand plain hob-nails.

A SHROUD AS WELL AS A SHIRT.

" And if, my dear James, it should be necessary for me to slash at you with a razor some dark night, you will not, I know, impute to me any bad motive or dream of bearing malice?"

" On the contrary, my dear Horace, I shall deem that you have but done your duty and acted in accordance with the high dictates of your own conscience—and your commanding officer. And if, in the same fracas, it should be my felicity or perhaps, opportunity to land you one on the jaw that shall lay you out for the rest of the affair, I feel that your generous soul—when it awakens—will nourish no ill-will towards me."

Conversations between brothers, such as the above, are taking place all over our country to-day. Who has spared a thought for the wretched plight of devoted brothers suddenly severed by the colour of a shirt? In homes where peace and unity so recently reigned there has abruptly appeared the difference between a black and a red. Going forth in search of adventure, many a splendid son has been conquered and converted by the principles of Marx, thrust suddenly upon his virgin mind, only to find on returning home after the good day's work, that his brother has been sucked up by the contrary faction. Here's a pretty go when over the dinner table each unlocks his secret soul and speaks of the great doings of to-morrow. Picture the consternation as each unrolls his precious bundle and displays before the dazed family the colour of his new shirt. Though under the same roof-tree the brothers' ways are now strongly divided. If one is to hold a meeting, the purpose of his brother must be to break it up. If one is to bear a banner, the duty of the other must be to tear it from his hand and trample it under foot. Held by the sacred ties of brotherhood, they yet belong to divided brotherhoods, and when with their fellows they meet in the street, it must be in battle. Consider the divisions of loyalty eating at their loyal hearts and then (if you have any feelings left) consider the thoughts of each as the dining-room door swings open and in stalks the dignified dad, nicely tied up in a bright green shirt.

THE APPEARANCE OF THE BIG STIFF.

The Loch Ness Monster may be a myth or merely a business proposition, but there was no myth and precious little business about the original monster recently washed up on the French coast. It measured nearly thirty feet from nose to tail and was some species of which we have no record. We speak of the sea giving up its dead, but when it merely gives up its living, it makes more of a sensation. Now how can beasties of this sort suddenly turn up as if it were the day after creation, instead of being near the end of the world? The universe is running down like a clock (as one section of my sage guides assures me), and yet something new in the way of monsters has only just learned how to pull for the shore. If he had left it many centuries later he might even have been too late. But what's he been doing all this time? Mankind (or, more colloquially, Me and my Mates) have been poking around in this world for quite a number of years now. We have given our care and attention to all manner of things in our time. We have climbed the mountains and plumbed the depths and all the time this chap has been eluding us. And one cannot help wondering if there are any more at home like him, or worse than him, and also where is his home that we have failed to find? I feel almost inclined to blame the scientists who have kept me in the dark all this time. It is no excuse to say they also were in the dark. Their business is to turn the light on. If monsters are abroad, we must prepare for them. It is no good looking for St. George when the Dragon has arrived. We want to make sure of him first. Perhaps a search party for St. George should be organised.

Thatch and Cob
By J. S. Fisher

THE glorious adventures in cob building which Mr. Hill has experienced were of much more than passing interest to myself, for at the time his article appeared, I was trying to negotiate the purchase of one of these old cottages for a home. Having been born in one of them it is perhaps natural, after years of town pavements and " amenities," that a desire should possess me to return to my "come from."

An agent having such a one on his books, it was with excited pleasure that I took his " order to view " and began to go into details connected with its purchase. Here let me say that those wonderful old craftsmen who built in cob—for craftsmen they were —would have done well to have concentrated on more of that art. Their works were more valuable than they knew. Could they see the prices smart agents,— who don't know what cob is,—are able to charge in our "improved" age for the work of our rude ancestors, there would be several revolutions in each grave. They would wonder anew " what things was a'comin' to."

The house I "viewed" was standing on about three-quarters of an acre of ground, part of which was a tired looking cider-apple orchard. It was half a mile up a lane off the main road, and was certainly two centuries young. It comprised, if my memory serves in the case of a house that had been " made up as you went along," of seven rooms—one divided into two; it was thatched, and this badly needing attention; and it was three miles from the town. The sanitary arrangements were of the original builder's devising. The water supply was a pump in the garden, and the price was a modest £475.

New villas, with just as many rooms, were springing up in its neighbourhood, complete with every modern gadget, awaiting occupation at £525.

It is this comparison that makes me feel those old cob builders lost a chance. They were ahead of themselves. They should have built more and poached less when the enclosures were making criminals and exiles of them. Think of the financial advantages they would have handed on to their heirs. Fifty years is a fair span of life for the modern "delectable villa" residence. Two hundred years find cob still going strong. But there are snags.

And this brings me to an item Mr. Hill passed over —the thatch. " Apart from foundations, and wages to the Ancient, the cob cost me £25," he says. "But plastering, chimneys, etc., cost hundreds; windows, doors, roof and floor, more hundreds."

It is the roof I wish he had been more detailed about. The Ancients whom I have interviewed all shake gloomy heads in long silences. When they eventually speak it is to tell me to " leave thatching alone." They admit all its virtues—heat in winter, coolness in summer seems most prominent—but " let it alone; 'tis a mortal moneyish job."

Their estimates have varied between " a lot of money," " a hat full o' money," and " Oh! pounds and pounds." One optimistically told me that a thatch would make a hundred pounds " look sickish."

Another sturdy old man of the moors, who confided to me that he had bought his cob house " one flower-show day over two cups of cider," took great pains to explain that the mere lime washing of his outer walls had just cost him six pounds, and that reed for thatching cost eighteenpence a bundle. When I say that to discover that small item it was necessary to go through the history not only of the purchase of his house but a dozen other deals—mostly horseflesh,—it may be imagined that I felt thatching was going to be a formidable job. He was quite definite about the absence of good thatchers, and very definite about the difference between thatching a rick and a house. "Ricks are one thing and houses another."

There were two thatchers, he told me, living at Norton, twenty miles away, and one who had been " cleverish " but was now " oldish " living out to Shepton, the other end of the county, but it would be a " dearish " job. Then we stuck till he thought of Benjy. This gentleman " couldn't thatch but he knew all about it." Benjy, a full-whiskered son of the soil, has a habit of keeping one eye perpetually closed while he talks with you, as if he is engaged in making measurements. I found out that he only opens both eyes when he is listening. Even then if he catches you looking at him he "measures" again. He took some time to consider and question me— several cups of cider in length, his cogitations were, his final decision being that with reed at what it was, it would run to about 3/- a square foot. That would be quite apart from the time "coming and going" which a thatcher would of course charge for. Twenty miles the nearest! Would he walk, night and morning!

My own calculation now leaves the roof, which will have to be done before next winter, as costing somewhere about £120, apart from " walking time." That assumes rafters and beams to be able to stand it. Slates seem out of place on cob. Secondhand tiles from a builder's yard will cost round about £50, but a modernist bungalow owner has suggested to me asbestos tiles. Dare one insult cob with asbestos? Which reminds me, insurance companies charge double premiums on " thatch."

Mr. Hill's estimate of £25 for cob is no doubt correct, but, oh! the " incidentals."

Age not only adds enchantment but money value to a cob house. That is why I now think that those dispossessed peasants of two centuries gone neglected their chances. They should have filled the fields with cob houses and left night poaching alone, then they or their heirs would have been " worth something " to-day. Pity is, of course, they were hungry.

See how my prospective bit of cob has increased in value from its original £25, notwithstanding that during the last two ownerships nothing has been done to roof or walls beyond colour wash.

It was sold, since the war, with the orchard, for £200. Its price when sold to the present owner was £450. He will sell it to me for £475 " or a near offer," and he has it let to a tenant,—who wants to leave it and live near his work in the town,—at 10/- weekly and an annual rate of £3. Its present owner is said to have bought it as an " investment." That is a dignity which to cob must be almost an indignity. The builders of these old houses, quiet thinking men, no doubt foresaw a lot. They never foresaw it as an " investment " or they would have stuck to it.

I think I shall buy the old house—if the smart agent will let me—and let the roof alone. After all, if it has stood all these years it will last me out. Besides, I can take my caravan—my present abode— with me into the orchard. It will come in handy for wet nights. But I wish thatch was not so expensive.

Limited Liability in Family Life
By K. Bogue

THE nineteenth century initiated the principle of limited liability in business, whereby the shareholder was freed from responsibility for the full amount of the commitments contracted by his fellow-investors. More recently and without legislation, there has come about a similar limitation of the individual stake in family life.

The symptoms are most apparent in working-class households, in which the weekly wage-earner attains financial independence at an age when boys and girls at public schools are still thinking in terms of pocket-money.

As soon as Bert or Gladys can earn more than the modest sum ear-marked for household expenses, the balance is at his or her disposal. At first it is a negligible quantity; but as the years pass, the housekeeper's share comes to bear less and less proportion to the income of the grown-up son or daughter. In normal times, however, the family muddles through in traditional British style, and no question is raised as to the ethical or economic soundness of the system. Father does not concern himself with domestic finances so long as no inroads are made on his privy purse; Mother, the chancellor of the family exchequer, is contented so long as she can precariously balance her budget. Now and again a fractious philanthropist may enquire why the fact that Bert is requiring charitable help to obtain a surgical boot has no apparent bearing on the consumption of silk stockings by his sister Gladys; but usually some deus ex machinâ supplies the boot and Gladys pursues her care-free, silk-shod way.

Thus it has become tacitly understood that the obligations of sons and daughters to the home do not extend beyond the payment of bed and board, even though in some cases they may be receiving larger wages than the head of the house; the limited liability principle is as firmly established in the house as the gas-stove.

Hence many tears over the recent Means Test, founded on the startling assumption that the members of a family are something more than shareholders in the domestic company or boarders in the home hotel, and that it is, in current phrase " up to " them in time of need to pool their resources and so preserve household solvency.

To the Berts and Gladyses of to-day the idea is as fantastic as a hansom-cab. The disintegration of the family has of late years been pursued with as much zeal as that of the atom, and with considerably more success. The present generation is being taught to look forward to a golden age in which the State shall be, in the Eastern phrase, " the father and mother " of its citizens. A glance at Russia might arouse misgivings whether the new parent will be quite as complacent as the old. Board and lodgings will, indeed, be provided; but the acquisition of private property, whether in the form of gramophones or silk stockings, seems likely to be discouraged, and cash remuneration may rather resemble pocket-money on a niggardly scale than earnings liable to income-tax. But Russia is a magic ink-pool, in which the enquirer is apt to see only the reflection of his own desires.

Perhaps one of the disguised merits of the slump may prove to have been its rehabilitation of the principle of the corporate responsibility of the family; and if this salutary doctrine could only be accepted in the time of our tribulation, it might bring the time of our wealth perceptibly nearer.

But the matter goes deeper than this, and the theory of life which it connotes has effects more far-reaching than the inclination to rely on Public Assistance or the pawn-shop rather than on family co-operation.

Limited liability may be a concept of priceless value in the realms of business, though a dispassionate review of world conditions to-day is apt to breed scepticism as to the infallibility of those who were responsible for the jerry-built commercial splendours of the last century. Still it may be both right and desirable that a pound, without undue risk to the owner, should be able to gain, not merely the ten for which there is scriptural warrant, but the hundreds promised by the company-promoter's prospectus. What is certain is that this arithmetical progression does not apply to life in general and to family life in particular.

Bert and Gladys will bring to married life no more generous ideals and no more exacting standards than those in which they have been educated, and the rule —which still prevails in nature, though not in commercial arithmetic—that none can hope to sow sparingly and reap plenteously, will once more be proved. Family life can scarcely fulfil its purpose if the much-vaunted team-spirit has always been left in the back-yard with Bert's football boots or Gladys' swimming-kit. Limited liability in the vital things of the family means that legal separation—or divorce when the cost ceases to be prohibitive—will sneak in by the back-door when love flies out at the window and that preventive methods will be adopted to ensure that parental responsibility shall not curtail the liberty or pleasures of the young couple. It means, in other words, that the eggs of human happiness will be counted too precious and too brittle to be entrusted unreservedly to the basket of family life.

Perhaps something depends on the make and condition of the basket. Perhaps young Bert and Gladys are not altogether to be blamed if gramophones and silk stockings seem to them the most satisfying prizes in life. They can hardly be expected to show much enthusiasm for a home, or a succession of homes, consisting of two or three cramped and dingy rooms in someone else's house—rooms where one must needs eat and sleep, but in which one spends as few as possible of one's leisure hours. Neither father's unskilled casual jobs nor their own monotonous factory work can supply any sound foundation of family coherence. Here, perhaps we have the clue to many rash ventures in house-buying, and still more rash attempts to start small businesses. England is strewn with the wreckage of such endeavours, because present-day conditions have no place for such individual initiative. The one-man show does not conform to the standardised pattern of commerce; it is a rough-hewn stone which spoils the symmetry of the marble halls of big business. Yet many men of the best type are eager to risk their meagre all for the sake of owning something into which they can put ideas and effort and self-denial, some foundation on which to build a family commonweal. Peasant proprietorship and the family business have their drawbacks, as any impartial survey of French conditions will show; but they provide a focus for united effort which is lacking in English family life to-day.

Bert and Gladys are no more incapable of enterprise and sustained work than are their prototypes in newer and more progressive lands; what they lack is a daily round which can offer them an interest strong enough to rival the attractions of the films or the football match. If by any economic cataclysm, if by any rainbow-blessed abatement of the flood of big business, homes could replace cubicles and family businesses multiple-stores, limited liability in family life would be born away on that ebbing tide to rot in some limbo of discredited philosophies. But as yet the master man like the dove finds no rest for the sole of his foot.

Books.

A Christian Panorama

FOUR SPIRITUAL CLASSICS: THE PASSION OF SS. PERPETUA AND FELICITY: THE GOLDEN EPISTLE OF ABBOT WILLIAM: THE DEVOTIONS OF B. ROBERT SOUTHWELL: THE LIFE OF LADY LUCY KNATCHBULL. *Sheed & Ward.* 6s.

BY putting out in a single volume four classics that were separately issued some years ago, the publishers have presented us with an Omnibus book of considerable range. From third-century Carthage to England of the Reformation is a long journey. Nevertheless there is in the completed volume an obvious unity, since from Perpetua in the Roman arena to Lady Lucy Knatchbull in her convent of exile at Brussels is really no distance at all.

The very exquisite story of the martyrdom of a young Roman matron with her maid servant, begun by herself, and completed by eyewitnesses of her death, is strange reading in these comfort-loving days. It is none the less touching and authentic. The *Golden Epistle* of Abbot William is not so tender or so harsh, for it belongs to another place and period altogether. Abbot William was the intimate friend of St. Bernard of Clairvaux, so close a friend, in fact, that this *Epistle* was long attributed to the latter. External conflict, save in controversy with the wayward Abelard, was not demanded of Abbot William, and he spent his life among the followers of St. Benedict, in his later years submitting to the greater strictness of the Cistercians. And this little treatise on the religious life was written to the Carthusian brethren of Mont Dieu.

Of Robert Southwell it is hardly necessary to give an account here. A poet established in our literary heritage, the contemporary and perhaps in some sort the friend of Shakespeare, and connected with the family tree of Shelley, his martyrdom comes home to us more painfully than that of any other Catholic priest executed under Elizabeth. Yet this only recently discovered manuscript is more revealing than his poetry.

" Sweet Lilies indeed, but a fetid root "—
That line is already familiar to us in a poetic paraphrase. But these are notes, made for his own use and meant for no other eyes.

The Life of Lady Lucy Knatchbull reintroduces us to Tobie Matthew, and to the Catholic exiles of the 17th century. The four pieces, with introductions and careful editing, provide a varied and interesting panorama of an aspect of Christian history.

K.C.M.

Music

ON Thursday last an inaugural meeting was held of what is hoped will become an important Society in the English world of music. It is known as the First Performance Society and its chief aim is the giving of music of contemporary musicians —of all countries and schools—under conditions enabling the audience (by discussion, debate, question, etc.) to understand better all that modern composers are attempting to achieve. " It is hoped," says the published statement of aims, " that concert goers of all kinds will apply to the Society for information and advice, and that the publishers of music will, on occasion, find it in their interest to consult the Society's committee. Such a medium has not hitherto existed, and it is hoped that it will prove of real service to the cause of music ". . . . . " In order that the scheme may be rendered as far-reaching as possible its promoters have decided to adopt a nominal subscription of 5/- per annum."

So, composers, send along your scores, and supporters, send along your five bobs. Or, at any rate, write for particulars. The address of the Society is The London Music Club, 22, Holland Park, London, W.11.

There seems little doubt that a Society of this nature can be extremely valuable. There is obviously need for a medium by which the creators of the modern music can get into closer touch with an audience, anxious to learn and able to appreciate and to criticise with knowledge and understanding. There is appallingly little understanding of the development in music which is going on before our eyes. Those of the older tradition will for the most part condemn it wholesale. Much worse, bright and rootless young things will shriek indiscriminate praise of anything which they are told is new and revolutionary.

I do not myself think there is a really great master blossoming forth just yet. There is too much, inevitably there must be, of experiment and ' exploring all avenues '—so many of them cul-de-sacs. Historically, it would seem that a great master selects, co-ordinates and establishes more than originates—or rather, perhaps, the way is prepared before him. But someone has got to prepare the way; and a society such as this First Performance Society offers real opportunities of discovering in what direction the way is leading and the material of which it is composed even if it cannot yet see the end of the road.

V.N.L.

The Cockpit.

[*Letters should not exceed 300 words in length and must bear the names and addresses, not necessarily for publication, of their authors.*
The Editor can accept no responsibility for opinions expressed by correspondents.]

" EYES RIGHT."

Sir,—Far be it from me to skulk behind a " compositor's error." In a moment of mental aberration I did actually write " Politiques " instead of "Patriotes." This is all the more distressing as I read in to-day's *News-Chronicle* that there are 90,000 of them all " armed with knuckle-dusters." I can only plead in extenuation that I wrote in physical pain thanks to one of M. Daladier's bullets.

The point raised by your correspondent about the participation of the " petit fonctionnaire " is of more importance. I have the issue of " L'Action Française " open before me to which he refers. In spite of the figures quoted the fact remains that a large pro-

portion of the " Manifestanty " with whom I conversed were in the service of the State. All the more honour to them. I wrote purely as an observer. One thing however is certain: France is undergoing an immense re-birth. Nor the Press nor the Wireless can suppress the fact for ever. Where once was sold pornography is now sold Maritain and Daudet and Claudel. The churches are crowded with *men* even on week-days. There is Thunder from the Right, a thunder that seems to echo from the dome of the Sacré Coeur to the Calvary on Dieppe Quay and back again to Lisieux.

EDWIN GREENWOOD.

THE AIR FORCE AND THE NEXT WAR.

Sir,—As Mr. Currie has dealt so fairly and sympathetically with the main argument in " The Navy and the Next War," may I say that I find myself in almost exact agreement with his letter on so-called " air power " in your issue of to-day. He rightly exposes the military danger of the Socialist Electrical Grid. To his example I would add the Naval oil storage Depots for which great sums are now being voted for defence from aerial bombardment. Perhaps Mr. Currie will agree with me that economy and defence would be better served by the abolition of Naval oil storage Depots rather than by increasing them, and then constructing aeroplanes to defend them.

B. ACWORTH.

Sir,—In his letter on this subject which appeared in your issue of March 8, Mr. Currie seems to me to accept Captain Acworth's conclusions as to the relative uselessness of aircraft for all purposes of war, rather too easily. He more or less assumes that aircraft will be no more effective in the next war than they were in the last—a rather hazardous assumption in view of the enormous progress made by the science of aviation during the last fifteen years. Besides the "last" war is never a safe basis upon which to calculate the character of the next war. We should do well, I think, to bear in mind some words used by the late Marshal Foch in a public address shortly before his death: " I must impress upon you gentlemen to forget the last war—not to imagine that the next one will begin where that one left off. The next war will be as completely different from the last as the last one was from the one before." It is at least possible that aircraft will play a big part in creating this difference. But let me deal with one or two points raised in Mr. Currie's letter.

1. He accepts the view that the inherent limitations of the aeroplane render it comparatively valueless as a deliberate military weapon, and adds that " in naval operations it can play no valuable part at all." Are we to conclude then that Air Power offers no serious menace to the exercise of Sea Power at all, that our Naval authorities need not worry their heads

about the bombing activities of hostile aircraft, and that surface ships have nothing whatever to fear from aircraft even in narrow waters? This is not, I think, the view held by the majority of Naval experts in this or in any other country.

2. "There is no reason to suppose," says Mr. Currie, "that the effects of aerial bombardment upon civilian life and property will be more serious in the next war than they were in the last." This strikes me as unduly optimistic. I quite agree with Mr. Currie that much of what is talked and written on this subject is hysterical nonsense, and badly needs "debunking"; I think, however, that his healthy delight in "debunking" the nonsense has led him to the other extreme, and that he greatly underrates the horrors that may await our civilian population from mass air attacks in the next war. The destructive potentialities of aircraft are infinitely greater now than ever before, and they are always increasing; and we may be quite sure that in the event of war every belligerent native will exploit them to their maximum capacity and in every way possible. Such being the case, I find it hard to believe that the slaughter and destruction that will result from the air raids of the future will not be a far more hideous affair than anything we experienced in the air raids of the past—which does not mean, of course, that I think they will come up to the horrific expectations of some of our prophetic scaremongers. Unfortunately we are far more open to this mode of attack than any other country. Besides, so long as our Navy remains on top, it is the only way a neighbourly enemy can get at us—as a German officer once genially remarked to me!

3. But, says Mr. Currie, quite a moderate force should be sufficient to overcome any possible attack, "because the advantage in air fighting must always be overwhelmingly with the defence." I rubbed my eyes when I read this statement. I always thought it was the other way about, and that the diabolical thing about aerial warfare was that the attacking force had everything its own way. Certainly our Air exercises have shown that the problem of defending London from aerial attack has so far proved too much for all the aviatic brains at the Air Ministry!

CONRAD BONACINA.

"VIENNA."

Sir,—With reference to the letter in last week's issue from Mr. J. Porter (Delphi or Adelphi oracles apart), perhaps a short statement would make the position clear. The discipline of Fascism is inimical to personal liberty. The Fascist state rests on the willingness of the people to accept its discipline. The workers of Vienna, suffering from their mild dose of Bolshevism, were not so willing, therefore they struck. The workers in Germany were not disposed to defy the discipline, therefore they accepted it. The purpose of my paragraph was to point out that the case was not one of the good management of Hitler versus the bad management of Dollfuss, as the newspaper I quoted asserted, but rather the disposition of the people. I was not suggesting cause or responsibility. If such had been my purpose I should have pro-

ceeded along these lines. There are in Europe to-day two, and only two, fixed poles, and they are fixed in opposition. These are Moscow and Rome—and by Rome I would be understood here as speaking in a political sense only; of Mussolini's experiment and not of the Vatican. The poles, moreover, are magnetic. They attract, and in the post-War uncertainty, all Europe is attracted in some degree to each, or even to both, poles; to its own effort towards unity, but also to its own confusion. The one pole represents a "workers" movement, but the other is largely a middle-class rally against it. It is the Class-War that Marx expected, but scarcely as he expected it. Now in a small state such as Austria, when large sections of the people are attracted by both poles at once, some by Moscow, some by Rome, there is likely to be an explosion. There was. Personally I dislike both ideals, but not evenly, though that is neither here nor there.

With the anti-religious experiment of the Vienna workers it was hardly to be expected that the Catholic Church would be friendly. To put it mildly, the two scarcely mix, though my heart leaps up when I behold the return of the slinking Jesuit, if not in all his glory, at least in all his furtiveness against the background of European politics. Such a rascal one would hesitate to believe; even when he said he was a Jesuit. It is a little hard, however, to saddle the Catholic Church with the responsibility of Fascism—in Italy, in Germany! in Austria or even in England. If Sir Oswald thought the Pope was behind him, even he might pause to think. The responsibility rests with those twin, stable points at opposite sides of Europe, Rome and Moscow—or rather with the forces that made it possible for them to rise and tower above the rest of the shaky nations.

J. D. GLEESON.

Sir,—Can you not give us more articles like Mr. Hill's pleasant account of his house-building? Individual enterprise has so gone out of fashion that when it is suddenly required of us we are helpless and unprepared. Yet other generations have considered it perfectly normal and natural to build or make the commodities that are too expensive to buy. We have unfortunately come to such a pass that any effort of the kind is considered a little mad, a little illegal, a little unpatriotic. The producer (as admonished in "Self Help" by Smiles) has given place to the consumer, in whom any kind of self-help at all is discouraged as detrimental to the well-being of the state.

At the back of it, of course, is a dread lest the machinery of trade break down. Thrift and private enterprise are luxuries that we must forego, lest the wheels we have set in motion should come to a standstill. But there is something wrong. For while these virtues are discouraged in the poor, they are not forbidden to the rich.

As for thrift, a Rockefeller may live to an honourable old age on dry biscuits. A manufacturer may economise on his employees. But a man of moderate means must mortgage those means to the hilt, buy what he does not need, use factory goods that he might have made for himself, in order to enable the manufacturer to give him a job.

Of course it is a fallacy. If more opportunity were given to those who wish it (and would benefit by it), to build and make for themselves, there would still be buyers enough for reasonable goods. If private thrift were permitted and encouraged in the people, they would be strengthened to return to their old position of genuine "consumers." As it is, we are acting like a child with a mechanical toy, who wants the wheels to go faster and faster until the toy breaks and is thrown away.

J. E. PERRINS.

EMIGRATION TO CANADA.

Sir,—On the morning of the 8th inst. I read your article on "Wednesday's Children," and the following quotation from a letter I received the same day from North West Canada may not only interest your readers, but give point to the need for grave consideration of the Emigration question generally in relation to our own unemployed.

"I hope you will never see the misery and poverty in England we see here among these poor foreigners lured here by dividend lusting steamship and railroad companies. Right here, in a land of plenty where no man need starve these folks are up against it. . . This Canada, rich as few countries are, in everything that makes life worth living, has thousands of unemployed, and thousands of destitute farmers."

Incidentally, the writer of the above, Mr. Harold Baldwin, is the author of "Pelicans in the Sky," a new first novel shortly to be published.

B. M. DRAPER.

League Meetings

CENTRAL BRANCH
Public meetings at the Devereux, Devereux Court, Strand, London, W.C.2, on Fridays at 7.30 p.m. Speakers:—
March 16. Special Meeting. Members only.
March 23. "The Sanctity of Private Property," by Anthony M. Ludovici.
Non-members particularly invited to meetings.

BIRMINGHAM BRANCH
The following programme has been arranged for the early part of 1934. Meetings will be held at Queen's College, Paradise Street, and will commence at 7.30 p.m.
Friday, March 23. "The Distributist Reply."

Another Handicraft Exhibition will be held on May 11 and 12 in Birmingham and craftsmen are invited to send exhibits. Full information may be obtained from Mr. C. O'Brien Donaghey, 49, Hillaries Road, Gravelly Hill, Birmingham, who will notify intending exhibitors of the conditions to be fulfilled and the place to which goods should be sent.

GLASGOW CENTRAL BRANCH
The Branch now meets on alternate Mondays in the Central Halls, Bath Street, C.1, at 8 p.m. Hon. Sec., Mr. J. J. Lynch, 122, Quarrybrae Street, Parkhead, Glasgow, E.1.

LADIES' AUXILIARY TO THE GLASGOW CENTRAL BRANCH
Meetings are held every Wednesday at 7 p.m., at 69, Carlton Place, C.5.
Secretary : Eleanor Gillan, 58, Queen's Drive, Glasgow.

CLYDESDALE BRANCH
The office at 33 Granville Street, Glasgow, is now open for meetings, addresses and discussions. Regular meeting every Wednesday, 7.30 p.m. All enquiries to Hon Sec., at above address.

SOUTHAMPTON BRANCH
Meetings are held every fortnight at 128, Warren Avenue. Write to the Secretary for particulars.

BOURNEMOUTH BRANCH
Readers of **G.K.'s Weekly** living at or near Bournemouth who are interested in the work of the Distributist League are invited to write to Mr. R. H. McCausland, 43, St. Luke's Road, Bournemouth, with a view to increasing membership of the Branch and planning future activities.

BRADFORD BRANCH
The following meetings will be held in St. Cuthbert's Guild Rooms, Wilmer Road, Heaton, commencing at 8 p.m. prompt. All interested are invited.
April 5th, Mr. M. White, "Guilds in the Middle Ages."

HIGH WYCOMBE BRANCH
Fortnightly meetings are held at 28, Crendon Street, High Wycombe, unless branch members are notified re alternate meeting-place.

MID-SUSSEX BRANCH
Hon. Sec.: Mr. Gerard T. Meynell, Laine End, Ditchling.

DUBLIN
A proposal has been made for the formation of a branch in Dublin. Will those interested write to the Hon. Secretary, 2, Little Essex Street, London, W.C.2.

The Distributist League
2, Little Essex Street, London, W.C.2.

BOOKS.

"THE FOREIGN POLICY OF THE LABOUR PARTY," by J. Ramsay MacDonald. 50 Pages, Stiff Covers. 1/- net for 6d. post free. "THE GREAT UNBORN." The problem of the age, by Edwin Pugh. 200 pp., 8vo. 2/6 net for 9d. post free. "A NEW POLICY FOR LABOUR." 110 pages, 8vo., Full Cloth Boards. 5/- net for 1/2 post free. "GUILD POLITICS." A practical programme, by G. R. Stirling Taylor. 136 Pages, Paper Boards. Pub. 3/6 net, for 1/-. Four authoritative books. 3/- post free the four.—Manager, G.K.'s Weekly.

LITERARY.

STELLA MARIS, a Catholic Magazine, contains interesting Religious Articles for all who want Certainty—Father Lester's Answers to genuine questions—Stories—Verses. By post 2½d.; 12 months, 2/6.—MANRESA PRESS, Roehampton, London, S.W.15.

LYRIC WRITERS' verses set to music. Composers' MSS. revised for publication. Piano accompaniments added to melodies. Advice free.—Carrington Briggs, Composer, Leven, Hull, Yorks.

£50 CASH IS OFFERED IN PRIZES FOR POEMS. Fiction also specially required for prompt publication. Advice and Current Catalogue free. Stockwell, Ltd., 29, Ludgate Hill, London. Established 1898.

NEW WITNESS.

Bound Volumes, No's. 1, 3, 4, 5, 6, 7, 8, 19, 20, 21, For Sale. together or separately. Any reasonable offer considered.—Apply Box 453.

TYPEWRITING, Etc.

TYPEWRITING, Literary, Scientific, Thesis, undertaken by Experienced Typist. Excellent Refs. 10d. 1,000 words, carbons 2d. 1,000.—Miss Doreen Chatterley, 204, Wellington Road. Bury, Lancs.

FOR SALE OR TO LET.

TO be sold or would let; beautifully furnished, most attractive, old-world, 6-roomed cottage; 8 miles from Dublin, close to railway. Electricity, gas, hot and cold water in bath and bedrooms; vitaglass windows; telephone; beautiful scenery; private sea bathing.—Apply: O'Connor, Solicitor, 1, Dame Street, Dublin.

FOR SALE. Pre-War House, Muswell Hill. On 2 Floors; 4 Beds., 2 Rec., Kitchen, separate Scullery. Bath and usual offices. Long garden, with fruit trees. Semi-detached. About 70 years' lease. G.R. £7/7/0. Bargain £800.—Apply, Box No. 1534.

HOME TO LET; furnished, July 30th to September 1st. 6 rooms (2 bedrooms). and bathroom. Elec. light. Garden. Some vegs., fruit and eggs. 6 gns. a week.—Rev. A. R. Webb. 163. Canterbury Road. Folkestone.

WHERE TO STAY.

SPRING HOLIDAYS. Board Residence in isolated Tudor farmhouse on the Weald. 35/- weekly, inclusive. Own produce. Lovely country.—Moat Farm House. Chart Sutton. Maidstone.

LONDON Visitors: Westminster Bridge; central; bed-breakfast, 3/6 per night, £1 1s. 0d. weekly.—Powell, 75, Lambeth Palace Road, S.E.1.

TOSSA BY THE MEDITERRANEAN SEA. The place for your holidays. Mountains, forests, sand-beach, quietness, and simplicity. Cheap travel by special-arrangement. Full board at Pesetas 12.—(6/-) day, in German-Swiss house. Information, catalogue at Guest-house of Foreigners.—CASA STEYER, Tossa de Mar (Gerona), Spain.

MISCELLANEOUS.

DELANEY
40, Brooke Street. E.C.1.,
Tel. No.: Holborn 0691.
and
65, Bishop's Road, W.2.,
Tel. No.: Bayswater 2589.
Hand-made Chocolates, Cakes & Sweets. Chocolates packed in boxes from 2/-.
Fancy boxes containing
Cream Truffles,
Cherry Brandies,
Almonds,
Muscatel & Walnut, etc.
5/-, 7/6, 10/-, 15/-, 21/-.
Cakes—
Cornish 1/3
Almond 1/-
Dundee 1/6
Plum Cake 2/6
No Powders. No Substitutes.
Luncheons and Teas.

A West Country Farmer sends CLOTTED CREAM at farm prices : ½lb. 1s. 6d., 1lb. 2s. 10d., post paid. Perfect delivery guaranteed.—BEVINGTON, Trenoweth Farm (G), Connor Downs, Hayle, Cornwall.

HOME MADE SWEETS. Boxes of mixed Fudge—Toffees. Peppermint Lumps. etc.—sent for 2/6 lb. box. Carriage paid from Mrs. Sparrow, Talybont-on-Usk.

HEPPEL BROS. & FELLS build very nice houses at very reasonable prices. Architects' and Clients' references. Estimates free.—3, Upper Park Road, Bromley. Kent.

EGGS straight from the farm. Three dozen upwards sent by rail at local market price plus carriage charges.—Moat Farm House. Chart Sutton. Maidstone.

OLD SILVER, CHINA, FURNITURE, Etc. —A. Abbey, late Art Expert to Christies, will advise you how to obtain their full value. Consultations Free.—Abbey and Co., Ltd., 1c, King Street, St. James', London, S.W.1.

CLOTHES OF CHARACTER.—Lounge Suits from 4 gns. Dress Wear from 5 gns. Overcoats from 4 gns. All hand finished.—S. G. Hunt, Monument Chambers, Eastcheap, E.C.4. 1st Floor. Adjoining Monument Station.

CHOICE Shamrock sprays; generous boxes, 1/-, 2/-, 3/-, 5/-, 10/-, 15/-, £1 each, emblems 4d. post paid.—Molly O'Donoghue, Convent Road House, Rosscarbery, Cork.

MEMBERS of the Manchester Branch are advised that Mr. Lockhart, a craftsman, produces all kinds of knitted woollen goods on his own knitting machine. Jumpers, pullovers, men's socks, boys' stockings, cardigan jackets, etc. Support your own local craftsman. Send a postcard to Mr. W. L. Lockhart, 34, Broadlea Road, Kingsway, Burnage, when requiring any of the articles mentioned.

Published by the Proprietors, G.K.'s WEEKLY, LTD., 2, Little Essex Street, Strand, London, W.C.2. (incorporating THE NEW WITNESS). Telephone: Temple Bar, 1978. Printed by THE NUNEATON NEWSPAPERS, LTD., Bond Gate, Nuneaton. Sole Agents for Australasia: Gordon & Gotch (Australasia, Ltd.). Sole Agents for South Africa: Central News Agency, Ltd. (London Agents: Gordon & Gotch, Ltd.).

GK's WEEKLY

EDITED BY G.K. CHESTERTON

APRIL 26 - - - 1934

VOL. XIX.   No. 476

Registered as a Newspaper   SIXPENCE.

THIS WEEK

HARD TIMES

NOT a single piece of useful or reasoned criticism of the Budget has appeared in any of the daily newspapers, save the London *Evening Standard*, least likely source of an attack on " big business." But it was a "big business" Budget, in spite of all the window-dressing in Mr. Chamberlain's best shop-walker style; and Low, the cartoonist, rose to the occasion magnificently. His cartoon was devastating; it said more than we can here put into words of the immeasurable abyss that now separates the governors from the governed and despised. It was in direct contradiction to whatever printed comment appeared in the same journal; or rather, it said what elsewhere was left unsaid. But we can afford to thank the *Evening Standard* for it, and to assure its proprietor that the cartoon was understanded of the people. It expressed what most of them think but are grown too inarticulate to translate into words.

We cannot afford in this paper to bandy words with those whose purpose is to seek occasion for compliments to the Chancellor. The Budget was what we might have expected of the present Government—an instrument of vulgar, bourgeois, industrial greed. If there be any of hearts so innocent as to enquire—but, what about all the concessions, to the unemployed, to the hard-hit civil servants to the tax-payer; are these of no account?—we would reply : the Budget is a deliberate exploitation of those whom it outwardly claims to benefit.

The one justifiable item—and the least costly in terms of finance—is the restoration of the dole cuts in full; but it is not enough; it is a mere silencer of feelings that have grown exacerbated. Out of a surplus of twenty-nine million pounds, the unemployed get rather more than four and a half millions. We are not concerned with the argument that they are a proportionately small section of the community. Their sacrifice, both in terms of the late lamented crisis, and the broader stringency of the times, is far beyond that of the rest of us. They are the totally dispossessed; the off-casts of industrialism; deprived of livelihood, of estate, of the social status that is their due, of any possibility of making future provision for their children.

We state deliberately, as we have stated before, that society under the existing regime, has no moral right to appropriate to itself riches that are corporate property until remedial provision has been made for those pathetic people. By that we mean a provision that will be lasting; upon which can be built a sound edifice of social well-being; which will act as a bulwark against further deprivation of this kind.

Only a week before the Budget was introduced the House of Commons debated the so-called derelict areas; so it had the urgency of the matter in full detail in mind. Members and the more responsible organs of the press took occasion to indicate agricultural development as a salvation. What assistance has the Chancellor afforded in this direction? With the connivance of the House and the industrialists he has ignored the whole problem for yet another year —the major problem of our times; and the money that would have provided so substantial a start along the right path has been frittered in other ways. The pious appointment of investigators to report what is already common knowledge is nothing less than a face-saving, time-marking, shifty expedient.

We have no bias against the high calling of the teacher nor any lack of appreciation of the sacrifice which civil servants and others have made when we say that fundamentals should have come first in the Government's survey of its available resources. These are State servants in the existing regime and their moral right to any particular scale of remuneration should be determined in relation to the well-being of those who are their real employers. The restoration of one half of the cuts imposed in 1931 is costing five and a half million pounds: a sum that, added to the lesser amount accounted for by dole restoration, might do much towards permanent alleviation of distress in derelict areas.

But even this is a small matter seen against those twin disgraces of the Budget, the sixpenny income-tax reduction and the motor-car horse-power tax. Here is the command of the industrialists, without mistake. Their voice has never resounded more strongly in Parliament. For the sixpenny bribe will mean little or nothing to three-quarters of the population; and to the rest in proportion as their means approach that level which cannot be justified in existing circumstances. The Chancellor's plea was that in addition to the real, hard-cash value of the reduction, it would have a psychological effect to be measured in industry's increased resources. Where will that new-found wealth go? Not in plans to find employment for more men, we fear;—in any case such plans, without deeper digging, would be futile—but rather in increased dividends and reserve funds.

Those who will benefit least are the fathers of families who would have benefited most, and most justly, by a full and proper restoration of the original scale of allowances. The cutting of that scale was an unjustifiable attack—even in the circumstances—upon the rights of the individual and the institution of the family. It remains.

As to the twenty-five per cent. reduction in the horse-power tax—described by the Chancellor as not trespassing for any practical purpose on his surplus—it can best be described as a gesture of hope to the booming motor industry; but the hope will fail. There are private advices that the boom, fanned by the same, senseless over-production as precipitated the acute depression of 1931, is already starting to contract. What strikes the man-in-the-street about this gesture is the way in which it conflicts with the Government's avowed policy of safety on the roads. With one hand the Government encourages not only

an increase of motor-cars before there is room for them, but also an increase of high-powered cars; with the other it professes to tackle the "problem" of over-crowded, murderous roads.

Summing up, the Budget is one that will go down to history as reflecting admirably the muddle-headed, hypocritical, pagan callousness of the industrialist regime in its waning days. With the whole nation clamant for rational reconstruction, it rode rough-shod over them all.

NOTES

Monday, April 23.

Trotsky's description of Spain as the Russia of the West has given a significance of its own to the history of the last few years in the peninsula. The King is in exile. Many churches and convents have been destroyed. Atheism has enjoyed official patronage. Posters of Lenin have adorned the streets of Madrid. The estates of nobles have been confiscated and many of the nobles themselves have suffered the rigours of African imprisonment. But the small group of Liberals with all the resources and opportunities at their command—resources ranging from a Diplomatic Corps of novelists to incendiarist gangs of gunmen, and opportunities ranging from control of the Cortes to unrestricted propaganda among the workers—have not strengthened their hold over the real Spain. On ground considered favourable by a great tactician, Communism suffers a severe reverse. Forces of the Right now control the Cortes, but their real strength is undisclosed because their policy is to seize power at a moment chosen by themselves; and the principles put forward by the vigorous Accion Popular are of a kind to appeal far more strongly than Leninism to a traditionalist and patriotic people. Despite labour troubles and attempts at sabotage, 20,000 delegates of the youth movement of the Accion Popular—the J.A.P.—met at the Escorial on Sunday, making their public profession: "Before all, Spain, and above Spain, God." Because one of their points was, "Down with Parliamentarianism, down with dictatorship, up with the people incorporated with the State organically, and by heroic rather than degenerate democracy," the comment is made that the congress was Fascist. That overworked word has lost its meaning in our language. It is applied to many countries where profoundly different political processes are developing. In Spain the inspiration is plainly the Encyclical *Quadragesimo Anno*, which amplifies the nineteenth century *Rerum Novarum* and criticises some aspects of Italian Fascism.

*   *   *   *

Communism is usually the peril against which the various schools of "Fascists" seek to arm the people, but Capitalism is the real enemy. Communism is a parasite upon Capitalism, and the exploitation of the people by Communism is more terrible only in degree. Roosevelt and de Valera are the real innovators because they have set their faces against a century of Capitalist disorder; it will be noticed that their opponents, who have the support of Big Business, accuse them of Communism. Mussolini, who leans upon international Capitalism, has a genius and justice of his own. He balances his Budget but he cuts down rents by decree. His work in Rome, on the Pontine marshes and in Sicily would alone make his regime one of civilised order. So far as Capitalism is concerned, the National Government in Great Britain and the Doumergue Government in France, may be called "Fascist" in the sense of "reactionary," for they have the faults of Mussolini without his virtues. The real cry of the revolution to-day is the cry for Social Justice, which no doubt carries with it a need for discipline. We wonder whether Sir Oswald Mosley, whose meeting at the Albert Hall attracted some attention this week, is the Capitalist Fascist or the revolutionary of Social Justice; for he springs out of the Capitalist country *par excellence*, where the need for Social Justice is more pressing than all the Budgets in the world. Are Big Business and the City with him or against him?

*   *   *   *

A protest in *The Times* by Dr. L. P. Jacks, against jerrybuilding on the new housing estates around London, brought an interesting reply from Mr. Geoffrey Faber, who denies the charge after eleven years' experience of administration on a housing estate between Kensal Green and Edgware. Mr. Faber, regarding the growth of London as inevitable, argues that the house-buying public is too shrewd and competition among speculative builders too keen, to allow the jerrybuilder any success; nevertheless, we think that most dwellers on housing estates have tales to tell of green wood, thin paint, flimsy walls and delusive gadgets. But the interesting point is that Mr. Faber deprecates what is after all the redeeming feature of the business from the point of view of the mortgagees themselves:

"No one can deny that, even upon the best and newest of these estates, there is a certain monotony... But the genius has not yet declared himself who can cover a landscape with small houses and avoid some monotony in the result. Huge, architecturally satisfying blocks of flats grouped in wide open spaces would be more pleasing to the educated eye. The unsophisticated wage-earner, for whom these new houses are built, does not, however, care a rap for that eye. He and his wife wish to have a little house of their own with a little garden where the baby can be put out in the pram, and the washing can be aired, and the proud proprietor can potter in the evenings round his sweet peas or his runner beans. Against a mass-demand of that kind the steel-and-concrete architects labour but in vain."

Surely this is defeatism. An Act of Parliament or two would soon stop the unsophisticated wage-earner from pottering round his runner beans. In a steel-and-concrete flat he might even acquire an educated eye, but we hope not.

*   *   *   *

Reflections on the League of Nations defence conference in London recently incline one to a sincere prayer that the League may be preserved against its defenders. At the meetings the leaven of those who do not normally appear on the League of Nations Union platform was reassuring, but the majority of the speeches and certainly the press accounts once again struck the dull note of academics when they were not pitched in a sanctimonious whine. However much members devoted to the League and an idealist solution of war problems may have been disappointed by the attitude of statesmen who attended, the average citizen will welcome the hardening of British political opinion, which has at last turned its back upon any futile pandering to extreme pacifists. Only by a firm decision to deal with the facts as they are, and not as we would like them to be, will any solution be found to the gravest problem that threatens civilisation.

*   *   *   *

From a letter in the *New Statesman*:—

"Unfortunately the limited liability company has replaced the individual employer and is devoid of his benevolence to a very large degree, and the number of 'bad' employers has accordingly increased in recent years.

"The reasons are easily understood. A company is only floated after all the cream of the proposition has been carefully removed—the public being given the skimmed milk liberally diluted with water. To make the proposition pay a dividend every device for cheapening labour and driving hard bargains is employed, and a director is valued for his skill and cunning in making profits at the expense of labour."

The writer of the letter was, till recently, a director of a manufacturing company. He incurred grave dislike because he "tried (1) to get a fair rate of wages for certain piece workers (2) to abolish unpaid overtime of clerical staff (3) to resist cuts in wages."

Economics in the Middle Ages
By C. Featherstone Hammond
(Concluded from page 101)

There was one further factor which was of equal, if not greater importance. It will be seen that there was no possible advantage to anyone to hoard this kind of money, for it depreciated on keeping. The quantity in active circulation was therefore free from the danger which would arise from large quantities going out of circulation into private hoards and therefore not only becoming sterile but having an effect upon the average price level, with all the disorganisation and injustice which alteration of the price level inevitably brings about. The intrinsic value of the Silver Plate from which it was minted was so low, the weight being practically negligible, that there was little fear of the coinage being melted down on account of its commodity value as metal.

If the proportion of money in circulation to services or commodities available varied, owing to unusually good or unusually bad harvests, or to any other cause, it was easily detected by the effect it had upon the general price level. The discrepancy was therefore equally simple to adjust by the issue of additional currency, or by the reverse operation, as the case demanded.

It is very interesting to read, in 'The Travels of Marco Polo,' that the Tartar Princes (circa 1200-1300), were using a similar system of Token Coinage. Both the Great Mogul Emperors, Jengis Khan and Kubla Khan, issued and controlled a kind of papier-maché token coinage made of the bark of a tree, and by similar means to those already described main-

tained a uniform price level and a stable purchasing power for their currency units. It may fairly be claimed for this paper token currency that it was in advance of the Bracteat coinage, for its intrinsic value was less and therefore it removed the possibility of its acquiring a commodity value which might militate against its merit as an ideal medium for exchange.

That this danger was a very real one may be seen from the fact that the supply of silver ultimately proved inadequate for the increasing needs of coinage as international trade increased. We shall come to this point in a moment, but it speaks volumes for the efficiency with which government was conducted by the Great Mogul Emperors, that the Minting Fee or Seignorage was as low as 2% at times and does not seem ever to have exceeded 5%, while the frequency of Minting was very much less than was the case in any part of Europe. It reflects badly upon the mentality of later historians that even this small taxation has often been referred to as a 'gross extortion.'

The mediæval economic system seems to have favoured a flourishing international trade, with no check upon the production of any commodity which the community was fitted to produce. After, as a whole nation, adequately provided for, there was still a surplus of real wealth which could be, and was, exchanged for luxury imports from all over the world. In 1270 the wool produced in England was said to be equal to half the value of the land in the country and much of this was exported to Flanders, to be re-imported as cloth. The same may be said of the foreign trade enjoyed by the Mogul Empire which seems to have been of a very extensive character. It was in no sense stifled by the currency system in use, though all foreign transactions had to be ratified by the Emperor's Exchequer.

Well before the middle of the 12th century, this system was largely adopted throughout Europe, both by the ecclesiastical and by the secular Princes. A quaint innovation was the marking of the silver pennies with dividing lines, across which the coin could be broken to provide the requirements of 'small change.'

Let us examine for a moment the apparent causes of the breakdown of this system. It is not at all clear that the system ever did break down of itself. It was, in fact, destroyed. During the three centuries and more in which the mediæval currency circulated, a constant and ever increasing agitation was maintained among the ignorant by those who had battened upon that ignorance in the past, and by their successors, an agitation for the restoration of a money which could be hoarded. A reversion to the possibility of hoarding would relegate the people to a condition under which borrowing at Usury was once more forced upon them by necessity. With the advent of the printing press at the close of the 14th century, and with the immense increase in propaganda which was made possible by this invention, this agitation attained formidable dimensions; and a lack of intelligent appreciation of the origin of the great improvement in the welfare and general prosperity inherent in the old system brought it to an end. The right of Seignorage vested in the King on behalf of his people finally disappeared from the Statute Book in the year 1666.

Here some comment may be excusable on the effect which a deviation from the Mosaic Law has had upon human thought and reasoning in so far as this applies to the Economics (or Housekeeping) of the nation at the present time. We have been regaled in recent months by accounts in the press of the great 'success' of the so-called ' Thrift ' movement which the whole country is asked to applaud. The whole power of the press has been invoked to make the Thrift movement the success that it is claimed to be. How a nation may be said to Thrive by burying the tokens of its exchange in the back yard, so to speak, it is hard to see.

We are now beginning to realise that the true function of money is to assist in the interchange of goods and services between those who have produced them, and to provide a means of distributing the surplus to the rest of the human family; and goodness knows there is enough and to spare for all. How are we to reconcile this great fact with this other great fact, which we are being told with great pride, that the working man and small trader have to their credit no less a sum than one thousand two hundred millions of pounds hoarded? There is nothing so true as that my expenditure is the other man's income, and his expenditure is my income. Does it not appear therefore that £1,220,000,000 of the Nation's means for exchange of goods and services has gone into cold storage, to become utterly sterile? Is this not the very way to have brought about the terrific fall in the average level of commodity prices which our City of London pretends to deplore? It must be remembered that the only source of interest upon this gigantic sum is ultimately by taxation, and it is not the kind of taxation to stimulate the circulation of the currency, as was the case with Seignorage. It tends by its nature to do the very reverse.

Yet another piece of propaganda which needs to be examined in the new light is the tremendous activity of the great Insurance Companies. Their recently published figures show that in the twelve months of the last business year the amount of annuities purchased marked an increase over any previous year by ten millions. This again seems to indicate that a quantity of money which might have been available to Industry has gone into the monastic seclusion of Usury and thereby become sterile; for the great Insurance Companies may not risk their funds in normal Industrial business, which might be regarded as speculative. Their income can only come from sources which are little more than taxation, but here also, a form of taxation which does nothing to stimulate the circulation or distribution of goods and services.

In conclusion, there does not appear to be any one factor which, in the Middle Ages, received more attention than the maintenance of the General Price Level. Under such conditions, by the issue of a sufficiency of currency to prevent price levels from falling and by ensuring that, whatever the system of securing revenue, it had not the effect of reducing the quantity of currency in effective circulation, the consumption capacity of the people was kept level with the capacity of the people to produce; and the Commonweal of the nation has never stood at a higher average level.

Scot *versus* Irish
(A Letter to a Scottish Friend)
By W. R. Titterton
(Concluded from page 106)

The greatest painter of our time in this country is Augustus John. He is a Welsh gypsy. As well known, perhaps, though not as great, was Sir William Orpen, an Irishman (he gave my wife her first lesson in drawing). Our most successful sculptors are Jacob Epstein, an American Jew, and Eric Gill, an Englishman.

The only world-famous British composer of the past twenty years was Sir Edward Elgar, an Englishman. Before him came Sir Arthur Sullivan, an Irishman. Frederick Delius is a Yorkshireman. Our one great conductor is Sir Thomas Beecham, an Englishman. Our second greatest is Albert Coates, born of English parents in Russia. Our greatest singer is John McCormack, an Irishman. Melba was an Australian.

The most popular dramatist of the moment is Noel Coward, an Englishman. But the most famous dramatists of the past thirty years were Shaw (Irish), Galsworthy (English), and Barrie (Scot). Other notable playwrights have been H. M. Harwood (Eng.) Clemence Dane (Eng.), Monckton Hoffe (Irish), Reginald Berkeley (Eng.), John Hastings Turner (Eng.), Walter Hackett (American). This is so far as the English theatre is concerned. But the Irish have had a splendid theatre of their own, with one world-dramatist—Synge—and several first-rate ones like Lady Gregory, W. B. Yeats, Lennox Robinson, and St. John Ervine. Even the lesser known men wrote with matchless sincerity and had a quite distinctive flavour. In England we had some fine odds and ends, but this was a theatre.

I hoped at one time that Scotland might evolve a national theatre comparable with the Irish, but though the actors were there the plays weren't. I don't think that the Scots are patriotic. When they wander they don't remember Zion, like the Jews and the Irish. They sport their nationality in their button-hole as a sign of racial superiority. As for the actors, we have all contributed our quota. The English theatres of to-day are controlled or owned mainly by Jews. Where the Scot occurs it is as business-manager.

So far I speak with knowledge. What comes next is guesswork, or at best deduction. But, arguing from the known to the unknown, I assume that the Irish have the better of the Scots in the Army, the Navy, and the learned professions as they have in the arts.

It is true that the best soldier that these islands ever produced was an Englishman—that dirty traitor Marlborough. And the second best was a Welshman —that other dirty traitor Cromwell (Williams). But the Scots have Montrose, the darling. The Irish have (among many others) Sir John Moore and Wellington. The two most prominent British generals during the great war were French and Haig. French, who had the hardest job of the lot, is thought by many to have failed. Everybody knows that Haig was a catastrophe. There were a number of good English generals like Allenby and Plumer, and one brilliant Irish general, Sir Henry Wilson.

But I admit that the war was won by the common British soldiers, ninety odd per cent of them English.

The Scots have never done much in the Navy, and in the great war their contribution to it was negligible. Beatty (Irish), Jellicoe (English), Kennedy (Irish), Keyes (English) runs the roll of the great war, though in earlier days the Navy was almost an English preserve.

The four most notable barristers of the past thirty years have been Carson (Irish), F. E. Smith (English), Simon (Jew), and Marshall-Hall (English). I don't know of any good Scots judges, but probably they are kept for home consumption.

The few surgeons whose names I know are English —Lister, Berkeley, the Fenwicks, Bland-Sutton— except Moynihan, an Irishman, though born in Malta. Oh, and then there's the ear-nose-and-throat man Gav French, an Irishman, though born in India. I don't know anything about physicians.

As for the Church, there is no fair standard of comparison. Even before I became a Catholic I thought that the wisest, most human, and most devoted British clerics I knew were the Catholic priests, most of whom were Irish.

I know nothing of architects, except that I am told that jobs are got less by compasses than by company manners. However, there is no doubt that Sir Giles Scott is a great architect, and, though apparently English, he comes of Scottish descent.

I know less about engineering than architecture, but I gather than since the egregious Watt and Stephenson commercialised Roger Bacon's steam-engine and so prepared the way for the present industrial slump, the Scot has been busy with machines. This is natural enough, since as a rule he is a Calvinist. But I am not prepared to damn a nation out of hand, and I fear that English, Irish, and Welsh have had a hand in the invention and commercial exploitation of those engines which through weakness of will we have allowed to destroy us.

Using the word machine in a figurative sense, we find the Scot very busy in the industrial and commercial machine—and highly successful. C'est son metier. But as a rule the chief exploiter is not a Scot. Salmon and Gluckstein (Lyons) are Jews, so was Lord Melchett, Lipton was Irish, Ashfield is American. Hugo Hirst is a German, Joseph (of Bovis) is a Jew. Leverhulme was an Englishman. To exploit even the machine fully you need imagination, which the Scotsman lacks.

It is the same in pure finance (I use the word pure in its technical sense). The Scot is an able second-in-command, he is seldom the principal. He is *ne plus ultra* at tots; but it breaks his heart to see good money cast upon the waters, even as bait that conceals a hook.

Now as to education. It is supposed that in this regard Scotland leads the way. I think that she can no longer do so. We agree that education is of two sorts (a) that which fits a man to be a good citizen of this world and the next, and (b) that which fits him for a career. My own idea is that the education of the schools should be confined to (a) and that (b) should be taught in a workshop or its equivalent.

Elementary schools in England are busy turning out boys and girls without any of (a) and, as for (b) fitted only for that most menial and degrading of jobs: clerking.

It is possible that Scotland still understands the importance of (a) but I doubt it, for the typical modern Scot is quite uncivilised. Perhaps it is unfair to compare him with the Irishman, for the latter has the Catholic philosophy. But it is a fact that the Irishman is civilised. In fact, so far as these islands are concerned, Ireland is the last refuge of civilisation.

I do not know if de Valera will succeed in his attempt to make Ireland a self-supporting nation of small-farmers and craftsmen, but he has a good chance of success. a much better chance than he would have in England, Scotland, or Wales. The Irish have not lost the tradition of freedom. They still believe in the family as the unit of the state. They have been taught by their Church the value of distributed ownership, and they know by experience that a family which owns home and the means of livelihood is buttressed in its freedom. As for (b) which with them grows. as it should, out of (a) the Irish small-farmer is the most competent husbandman in these islands. This I found out when, for nine months, I edited an agricultural weekly. But it is true, I must admit, of the Protestant farmer of Ulster quite as much as of the Catholic farmer of the Free State. Skilled observers in the North and South put it down to the magic of small-ownership. But I think that we must not ignore the existence of a tradition of husbandry transmitted from father to son. Perhaps *this* is what you mean by manual labour.

I suspect that you were pulling my leg. If so I am not sorry that the leg has shown this reflex action. For long I have wanted to tackle this fable of Scottish superiority. And now I have tackled it.

In conclusion let me say that I do not believe that the Irishman as an individual is superior to the Scot or the Englishman as an individual. We are all as God made us, and only He has the right foot rule. I believe in equality. I have two predelictions which amount to passions; one is for England, my nation; the other is for Ireland, which gave me my wife. But my admiration for the civilisation of Ireland is of the intellect. My one hope as a student of economics is that we shall learn the lesson that Ireland has to teach us before it is too late.

Straws in the Wind

THE MASTERLESS MAN
By G. K. CHESTERTON

SOME time ago I read a newspaper article, which contained a rather arresting phrase, which is just exactly not one of the nine to thirteen phrases which, arranged in various ways, make up the whole of most newspaper articles. It had about it a smack of history, even if it was not altogether good history; a hint of the possibility of philosophy, even if it was here used in the interest of a false philosophy. Nor, indeed, was it without other merits. The writer was contributing an article to an Organ of Democracy, one of those great Radical sheets that are the flags of the people clamouring for freedom; but, to do him justice, he did not devote the whole article to hopes of the return of Capitalism with all its monopolies and money power vested in the few; it was not from end to end a song of praise for the epoch of the employers and the unemployed, like a real democratic speech by Mr. Thomas, or a real democratic article in the Liberal press. The writer had some consciousness of the horror of the crisis that has come; and of which even its apologists admit that it may come again. He had the sense and courage to say something about the abominable recent treatment of the Unemployed; and even about the possibility of the peril becoming much more than a passing warning. But before he made any of these comparatively sane admissions, he went through a curious ritual, which I notice is now practised regularly *de rigeur*.

Before a free and unfettered Radical journalist is allowed to say that the present position is bad, he is morally forced to go through a form of saying (almost in the same words in every case) that, of course, the past was very much worse. Keep an eye on this opening, for its recurrence and regularity is very amusing. By this the journalist formally purges himself of heresy; one might well say, of history. He is allowed to hint that things are worse than they ought to be; so long as he makes first a solemn legal affirmation that they are better than they were. It is a sort of Oath of Abjuration to preserve the Protestant, or Progressive, succession. The better sort of Liberal writers, like Mr. Spender, accompany it with sad admissions of our modern futility; but, when all allowance is made for these, I cannot work myself into a heat of admiration for this new form of Christian humility. Somehow I do not care very much for the Christian who says in his general confession; " I confess most humbly that I am a miserable sinner; but you must admit that I am not such a disgusting old rip as my grandfather; I really am a good, sound, virtuous fellow, compared with my Uncle Marmaduke; and you will not deny that I am at least a much finer fellow than my father; and that I have done something to balance, by sheer conscientiousness and unselfish public spirit, the more revolting characteristics of my mother."

I repeat that this formula for repentance does not in itself attract me; but it is a formula universally demanded of all Progressives, before they are allowed to admit that modern things are sometimes a little tragic; that a good many men died in the latest and most modern war, or that a good many men were sacked in the latest and most modern Slump. The writer here in question, however, doubtless to relieve the monotony of repeating this ritual preface, strikes out one phrase which is not often used by journalists; and does really involve a number of interesting ideas, both on one side and the other. He said that crises like that of Unemployment often occurred in history; and that it was an even more tragic fate to be a Masterless Man in the Middle Ages.

Even the abuses of the Middle Ages are bright and breezy enough to bring something like a breath of fresh air into the filthy fog of the respectabilities and social virtues of the present day. And the phrase does suggest some very interesting speculations. To begin with, it is quite true that in the very early Middle Ages (that is in the converted Roman Empire partly recovering from the barbarian invasion) the Feudal System was so fixed that a man might have been unhappy through being a Masterless Man. Very few men were masterless, except the Pope and the Emperor; and even there there were complications. I am well aware, needless to say, that no man is really a masterless man. But those who complain of my articles being theological, will at least excuse me for not dwelling on the point here. It is enough to say that even the worst of the Popes had a curious tendency to believe; and that some of the worst of the Emperors had very adequate reasons to believe and tremble.

But the real point of interest is this; that since the Peasant progress, later in the Middle Ages, has expanded into the vast peasant communities spreading over all Europe to-day, a number of questions have been answered. The most important answer concerns the last question; since peasants are everywhere the prop of religious tradition, it is proved that a man may be more inclined to accept his real Master, because he has not any earthly master. But what such writers evidently do not know, is that the Masterless Man is even possible; let alone that he is universal. Now that is what is really meant by narrowness. Why are we annoyed by the crank; the really dull crank? I submit the reply that he is a man who is always solving what is solved already. He is like the cracked inventor who invents an existing invention. A civilised man's irritation with Prohibition, say, can be expressed in many ways; as that he merely dislikes what is uncivilised. But the true reason is this; he is irritated by imagining all the millions voting (at one time) for Prohibition, without knowing that in the centres of civilisation the problem has been solved without Prohibition. In the lands where most men drink wine, very few men drink too much wine. In the same way, we are irritated by the Bolshevist, who would abolish all property like wine, because we feel he does not know that property can be well divided;

and, in the old civilisation, often is well divided. The Socialist cannot imagine anything but the Trusts; just as the teetotaller cannot imagine anything but the Trade. They do not know that in an older culture, both problems have long been solved. The writer in the Liberal paper was simply ignorant of the fact that the small farmer is a very large factor. He did not know that, if there is one figure now bestriding all Europe like a giant, it is the Masterless Man. He did know, but he did not think (for such men know many things they never think of) that modern England is in so utterly unhuman and unnatural a state, that (except for a millionaire or two) there is practically no Englishman who can boast of being a Masterless Man.

Charles and Samuel
By J. P. Collins

WE are somewhere in the Elysian Fields. There is a quaint odour of the 18th century, not un-mixed with fumes or reminiscences of hot lemonade, tobacco, and gin toddy.

In the dimness we descry two interesting but ill-assorted figures. One is ponderous in his gait, bulky in form, and burly in his manner. He handles an ash cudgel, which is stout like himself, and thumps it into the ground as if he were planting the flag of King George afresh in one of those rascally American colonies.

Restlessness is his foible, rather than energy. His eyes blink as if he were refusing to see some awkward argument; his fingers keep twitching as though trying to wring the neck of some detested Whig. Even his breath is laboured, for he whistles it in and grunts it out. But he prides himself on never wasting it, for he rarely speaks unless to the purpose, either in smashing a fallacy or demolishing an opponent.

His companion is slighter, smaller, and not unprepossessing in his own peculiar way. His figure seems to dwindle away as you look at it, and to leave the impression of a noble head supported by an immaterial torso. He is flat-footed and springless in his walk, and skims his feet along the ground. He has a dark and penetrating eye and a smile that is half-whimsical, half-quizzical. The contrast between the pair is so complete that if you only added a look of wistful dismay to the one and a Yankee accent to the other, you might be reminded of those two modern celebrities—Laurel and Hardy.

They meet and bow rather stiffly; it is evidently a first encounter. Let us call them Charles and Samuel.

* * * *

C.—Dr. Johnson, I presume.

J.—Sir, you may, but on what grounds.

C.—There is,—or was,—a d-d-dictionary that would serve as c-c-credentials for any man to stand on. I r-r-remember st-t-tanding on it as a ch-ch-child at my f-f-father's table.

S.—Sir, let us leave the subject. There are no dictionaries here, and all publishers are mercifully consigned elsewhere.

C.—P-p-poor devils.

S.—Why this officious pity?

C.—Please, do not mistake me. I was th-th-thinking of the unhappy beings who have to attend on them. Fortunately they, poor devils, are no longer ob-b-bliged to accept their t-t-terms.

S.—Sir, I perceive you are an author. What have you written?

C.—(amused) Oh, a few trifles merely,—fugitive essays, certain poems, and a play or two. They beguiled my leisure and pleased my friends.

S.—Sir, there is a modesty in what you say that at our age is rare. I used to hear my friend Dr. Goldsmith dismiss inquiries in this airy manner, but his humility was insincere. The rogue was prouder of his performances than I was of mine.

C.—(slily) Incredible!

S.—(noting the sarcasm) I am not instituting comparisons, and here we can be frank. There is an atmosphere about this place which alters our standards of judgment, and those masterpieces of ours have shrunk considerably in the course of our journey.

C.—Yet there was a b-b-barbarian called Boswell, I believe. Is he here, or is there a sp-p-pecial p-p-place reserved for Sc-c-cotsmen?

S.—Sir, Master Boswell visits me once a week for an hour at a time.

C.—(to himself) Part of his expiation, I suppose.

S.—He is very deaf, and I am silent, for fear any of our deliberations might shock politer neighbours, or escape to the printers down below. He had a weakness for taking notes, which is a nuisance, but has its serviceable uses, and when I wrote my " Lives of the Poets " I regretted I had not done the same.

C.—I have always m-m-marvelled, Sir, that you went so far north for your chronicler.

S.—Sir, the rogue came and pestered me until I allowed him access, and (this complacently) a tolerably good use he made of it, by what the critics say. Have you read his book about me, Sir?

C.—My friend Coleridge has quoted it to me ad infinitum, and he complains that it lacks philosophic synthesis or metaphysic unity,—whatever that may mean.

S.—Sir, I apprehend his meaning. Your friend has insight,—possibly a scholar, though I never heard of him. As for my friend Boswell and his book (flourishing his stick) I am persuaded that I could have made a better thing of it myself.

C.—Bigger, perhaps.

S.—Sir! (This with a disconcerting frown).

C.—L-l-let us say a greater. But seriously, Sir, have you no regrets or qualms that the capital of letters is so invaded nowadays by north Britons, Switzers, Dutchmen, Hebrews, and the rest of the cosmogony?

S.—Sir, this is a difficulty of long standing. The Scriptures have something to say upon the habits of vultures and their search for prey. We have drawn upon France and Germany and Portugal for our monarchs and their consorts; and these have brought odd creatures in their train. But we must also remember the Georges came from Hanover, the Stuarts from Scotland, and the Tudors from Wales. Indeed, Sir, the further we go back, the worse we fare.

C.—(*mischievously*) You have forgotten, Sir, that Jack Cade came from Kent, and Titus Oates from——

S.—Sir, let us leave these categories to clerks——

C.—And amateur auctioneers?

S.—Sir, you are pleased to be facetious without being diverting. When I acted that part at poor Thrale's brewery, it was at the instance of friendship and not for a fee. I believe I acquitted myself with fair success,—for a novice; and I am never likely to take up the hammer again.

C.—'Twas a great episode, and you made it greater by your eloquence. (*Johnson unbends*). Indeed, the surroundings alone would have excused enthusiasm. It is not every orator who finds a rostrum in a brewery, or gets away with his m-m-emory unclouded.

S.—(*loftily*) Sir, you are trifling with my recollections of what was a perfectly sober undertaking. I gave up your kind of potation years ago.

C.—Indeed, it was a g-g-grievous loss to a worthy industry. T-t-tea is a sociable kind of plant—for women in the afternoon; but it palls on men with a legitimate thirst. By the way, did Mrs. Thrale ever suffer from a tired wrist in handling that three-quart teapot for your benefit?

S.—(*haughtily*) Sir, oblige me by respecting my friends and their regard for the laws of hospitality. Mistress Thrale would have scorned to complain of any inconveniences thus incurred. (*severely*) Your levity is odious and ill-timed, Sir,—ill-timed.

C.—Doctor, pray do not mistake me,—though for my part I could never see why gravity should be a virtue and levity a failing. I was tilting, not at the lady's forbearance, but your own capacity. It was a matter of 24 cups, I think, at a sitting. Barring the choice of the beverage, it was a massive achievement. Pray, Sir, what had Mr. Burke to say?

S.—(*pettishly*) Sir, let us call a truce to this tea-table prattle. (*He turns the fire on his interlocutor*). You were something of a practised navigator, I should fancy, in these seas of refreshment, if I mistake not by your aroma. Was it malt or punch or brandy?

C.—If you are in earnest, you may c-c-call for a double dose of gin, and just a shade of sugar and hot water.

S.—(*trenchantly*) Sir, do not seek to make me a confederate in your orgies. Bacchus and Momus and I have long been strangers. I should think it beneath my self-respect to call at any tavern for what Master Shakespeare calls so leperous a distilment.

C.—(*laughing*) Indeed, the boot is on the other foot, and you have turned my weapon against myself. Oblige me, Sir, by allowing me to call for whatever it is you most prefer, and we shall see what is meant by " standing Sam."

S.—(*wrathful at last*) Sir, pray observe the decencies of ordinary civility. I have already informed you that this kind of pot-house potation appeals to me no longer. Finding I could not be sure of moderation, I renounced the habit years ago.

C.—Sir, your pardon. As for myself and my habits, I respect your strictures, though I commiserate the critic. Even now, Sir, you must remember from experience how much the magic spell of conviviality banishes the gloom of memory and most of our fears for the morrow.

S.—(*relenting*) Sir, at last you are eminently in the right. Years ago when bereavement derived me of the best of wives, I found recourse and relief in this way, and it did no one any harm. Perhaps you also have suffered.

C.—(*dreamily*) Who—I? Ah, the best of death is that it happens only once. There are times, even now, when I lose my guardian angel, my p-p-patron saint, and when she is away, for m-m-months at a time, no man could be more lonely. Then I am apt to steep my senses in forgetfulness, as the poet says, and on those occasions the cup of cordial cheers a man like warming oneself at a neighbour's fire. If I console myself a whit too freely in her absence, she is disposed to overlook it, as a rule; but on her return home, if she is pleased to chide me, I listen attentively, and vote her voice the sweetest music in the world. Then I fly perhaps to old Burton—

S.—Sir, you said a few moments ago that malt was quite outside your potentialities.

C.—No, I meant old Burton of the " Anatomy."

S.—Sir, you have me there. The man who loves that kind of Burton is a kindred soul. Come, Sir, let us walk together along the Strand, and dilate upon his merits (*Exeunt, arm-in-arm*).

Setting Sail for Melbourne

WHEN the Centenary Celebrations of the State of Victoria (capital city, Melbourne), take place next year, there will still be in residence there many descendants of the original pioneering families, possessing among them a wealth of letters, diaries and oral traditions which give a fascinating picture of the colony as it was in those early days.

What sublime confidence they must have had, those hardy folk who set sail from England for the unknown, taking with them their children, their household goods, even their pets. In a sailing ship the voyage took from four to five months, and emigrants lived mainly on salted pork and ship's biscuits so hard and unpalateable that the vigorous had to chew these to a pap in order to enable the very young children and the aged to have any food at all. Yet the rigours of the long sea voyage were but a foretaste of the hardships to come. There were, of course, no roads, no houses and very little food. You lived in a tent, but you, or your women folk, had first to make it out of any cloth you might have happened to bring out with you and, during dense rains, many of them proved leaky and shifting habitations.

The country round the Yarra, the river upon which Melbourne stands, was extremely picturesque from the point of view of scenery, but the Ti-scrub, which represented a large part of the vegetation was almost as impenetrable as a jungle, and it would take a bullock team weeks to drag a settler and his family and household chattels a distance of sixty miles. Ten miles a week was considered admirable progress, and many disconsolate women, who had left comfortable English homes, sat on the quayside, surrounded by their baggage, and wept to see it put up for auction, for what it would fetch. With flour at £7 a bag, ready cash was more use than an ormolu clock.

The gold fever was in men's blood and, in the mad scramble after the precious gold metal, many families had emigrated in haste, not in the least providing themselves with the kinds of goods which were likely to be serviceable in a new country and, even if they had capital, which most of these early settlers had not, the distance from England and the uncertainty of the arrivals of the mails precluded the immediate possibility of obtaining from home what had been overlooked in the hasty departure.

Probably the young children were the only people who enjoyed the new life at the start. Life in a new country they found to be almost perfect; there were no schools yet, and a hundred thousand interesting happenings to share. With the men busy at the gold diggings and the women coping with housekeeping where there was no house, no ordinary food and no regular water supply, the children had, from an early age, to lend a hand all round. Chopping wood, cleaning out the stables, milking goats, nothing came amiss to the child pioneer, who would spend any leisure time earning money by manufacturing pokers and coal scuttles, for which there was a very ready sale, once tents began to be replaced by primitive houses, most of them bark or turf huts, containing a kitchen-living room and rough sleeping accommodation.

A boy of seven looked upon himself as a man, and was known to all the diggers, for what could lure a human boy more than the Shallow Diggings, where at any moment a man might find a fortune. Whenever there was a 'find,' everyone stopped work to celebrate, chiefly with grog, and at least one small boy had to be carried home dead to the world, after sharing cups with all his digger friends. The fact that he was flogged for it by his own father, when he had slept off his potations, must have seemed to him the last straw.

In time brick-built houses arose here and there, and a plethora of shoemakers sprang up, if other tradesmen were scarce. The cobblers did a roaring trade, for the muddy gulleys which were later to be transformed into streets, dealt destruction to footwear; and pioneers have to be active on their feet, seeing that transport is often denied them.

The first policeman, appointed guardian of law and order in Melbourne in 1836, held office for only four months, at the end of which period he was 'disbanded' for behaving too officiously and for not having enough to do. The Force was, however, in evidence again three years later and the first official chief of police, nicknamed affectionately *The Tulip*, must have been a grand sight, clad in his green cloth coat and cabbage tree hat. Bull-necked and purple-faced, he was equal to crook, bushranger or any other enemy to peace. In 1840 one chief of police and eight constables sufficed for the whole colony; handcuffs fixed to belts, and bludgeons, were their sign of office. It is easy to see, from the small strength of the police force in those days, that Victoria was not a dumping ground for convicts, even in early days.

The first Post Office was a small bark hut, hidden among dense Ti-tree scrub. The salary of the Post Master was fixed by the sum received for mails, and ran to about £150 a year. The Post Office was open four hours a day. Letters to Sydney cost 1/3d. The first mail ever dispatched to England went on the first wool ship, the Thomas Laurie, which left Port Phillip in 1839. The mail took six to seven weeks to reach Sydney, where nowadays it takes barely 36 hours.

For the first few years there was no regulated time in Melbourne. Then a watchmaker brought over a large clock from England and offered it for sale for £65. The Port Phillip people bought it for their market place, but had nowhere to fix it, except against a gum tree; this was not very satisfactory; the constant wind jarred the mechanism and stopped the pendulum. It was relegated to the police station, where it stayed until 1843, when it was mounted in triumph above the first brick-built post office Port Phillip ever possessed.

The native name for Melbourne was Dootigala. Records show that in 1836 it consisted of eight turf huts and five other buildings, the population five years later being 11,000, most of them sheep squatters. To-day the city population is well over 68,000, while greater Melbourne houses roughly 500,000 persons.

G.H.

Books

The Supremacy

ENGLAND UNDER QUEEN ANNE. *Vol. III. THE PEACE AND THE PROTESTANT SUCCESSION. By George Macaulay Trevelyan. Longmans. 21s.*

MR. G. M. TREVELYAN, a great upholder of the Whig Tradition in history, brings to an end in this volume his account of the transition period which was the reign of Queen Anne. It is always difficult to remember that Queen Anne was a Stuart, that she succeeded a King who belonged by marriage to the Stuart group. She was succeeded by a King who, although indeed he traced Stuart blood back to James I, was something entirely new in the English scene. He was a German Prince, fifty-four years of age, without internal or external policies to propose for the country of his rule. He became, very sensibly, the creature of the triumphant Whigs, who remained in office for forty years, reinforced less by the achievement of the Hanoverian succession than by the continued existence of Jacobite Pretenders, and during that period consolidated the English Constitution. "It has been calculated," writes Mr. Trevelyan, "that there were about seventy 'great Whig families,' who, under the early Hanoverian Kings, formed the Government and led the Opposition. Each of these great families usually had its titular head snugly in the Upper House, while its heirs and cadets sat for family boroughs and made their reputations in the faction fighting in St. Stephen's Chapel." This was the Venetian Oligarchy of Disraeli's phrase. "But," as Mr. Trevelyan proceeds, " the 'Whig Oligarchy' was submissive to the rule of law, and the English laws gave to the Executive no powers to suppress speech or writing that attacked the Government. Unless the Law Court found a critic of Government guilty of sedition, Ministers could do nothing to silence him. The Law Court, not the Government, decided what was libel, blasphemy or sedition. And the Judges were independent of the Executive, and the Juries were often hostile.''

It is no wonder that this constitutional theory attracted the admiration of other peoples during the nineteenth century. No wonder either that in the twentieth they have turned away from it, for the theory was evolved out of a definite national temper and out of particular historical facts. In England the Oligarchy which supplanted the Monarchy had interests shared by Whig and Tory; and the Oligarchy could always count on the patriotism of the people in circumstances where conflict between Haves and Have-nots might in other countries have led to civil war. Also, owing to the Industrial Revolution, the Oligarchy gave way quietly to the Plutocracy, leaving the constitutional theory intact. During the eighteenth century, rule in England was based on large landed estates. Subsequently it was based on urban industrial wealth, and quite recently it has been based on less tangible international resources. It is with the decline of the Plutocracy that the constitutional theory must now face the necessities of change; and recent events confirm the doubt whether the Whig rule of law ever was much more than a theory, or whether the Whig triumph really was a benefit to England. Members of the Oligarchy, who believed in the reign of law, were not in danger from the Press Gang; they were not turned off their land by the Squire; they were not within the jurisdiction of the Overseer of the Poor; and they were not finally gathered into the slums.

Mr. Trevelyan treats the last five years of Anne's life, when the dominant events were the end of the War of the Spanish Succession, from Malplaquet to the Treaty of Utrecht, and the invitation to George of Hanover. His verdict is that "the Tories served their country well in making Peace, and the Whigs in securing the Succession.'' But the canvas is a crowded one, for the five years were years of intrigue, and neither Whigs nor Tories appear with honour. Whatever authority Queen Anne had exercised was slipping from her grasp. The Monarchy was going down rapidly to defeat; the famous death-bed scene when she gave the White Staff to Shrewsbury is represented now as a vindication of "English liberty, religion and law,'' but there was something like a Jacobite majority in the Commons, and there was little public sympathy anywhere for Hanoverian George. The Whigs were prepared for a *coup d'état*. But the man who more straightforwardly secured the Protestant Succession was the Old Pretender himself, who refused to change his religion at the request of the Tory Ministers, although the crown would have been his for the asking. That, reinforced by a national feeling, for France was the Catholic enemy, just as Spain had been the Catholic enemy under Elizabeth. On the other hand, insistence upon the Catholic enemy was always very much a matter of pamphleteering, and Mr. Trevelyan is perhaps too much inclined to read history through the eyes of successful pamphleteers. The Old Pretender did not show himself to be divided from his subjects '' by a hedge of confessors and priests ''; certainly no more than George I was divided from his subjects by a haze of German ideas. The Protestant

persecution in Ireland under Queen Anne was, on Mr. Trevelyan's own demonstration, worse than any Catholic persecution ever attempted in England. Nor does a reading of *The Jesuit Relations* support the points that the Jesuits among the Red Indians converted numbers of them '' to a kind of Christianity''; that the Jesuits sent Indian tribes "to murder and scalp along the English frontier''; or that "the christianised tribes under Jesuit control were let loose upon the English frontier to perpetrate the most loathsome cruelties.''

On the other hand, what the Whigs possessed as a more important asset than a love of law and liberty, was the financial backing of the City of London. In 1934 it is possible to imagine that the Bank of England was a greater menace than any Stuart to the liberties of the country. The Whig supremacy was the supremacy of Debt, and of this Mr. Trevelyan gives an interesting illustration. '' It was while the Bank Election was coming on, that Addison wrote one of his rare political numbers of the *Spectator*, to point out the economic consequences of a Jacobite Restoration. He saw in his vision the fair lady, ' Publick Credit,' seated amid a heap of money-bags in the Bank, when there entered

> A young man of about twenty-two years of age, whose name I could not learn. He had a sword in his right hand, which in the dance he often brandished at the Act of Settlement; and a citizen, who stood by me, whispered that he had a sponge in his hand.

'' Credit faints, and the money-bags shrink like pricked balloons.

> Whilst I was lamenting this sudden desolation that had been made before me, the whole scene vanished. In the room of the frightful spectres, there now entered a second dance of Apparitions very agreeably matched together and made up of agreeable Phantoms. The first pair was Liberty with Monarchy at her right hand; the second was Moderation leading in Religion; and the third a person whom I had never seen, with the genius of Great Britain.

'' With the entrance of the Hanoverian heir ' the bags swell'd to their former bulk, and the heaps of paper changed into pyramids of guineas.' This was no poetic fancy of Addison's. The most solid men in the City believed that the Restoration of James III would mean the repudiation of government debts contracted since the Revolution, and it was not a little this fear that kept the members of the Bank of England faithful to the Whig cause in the hour of its deepest depression.''

At that time the Bank of England was only aged a score of years and its proceedings were still sufficiently novel to arouse interest. Addison was one of the pamphleteers persuaded to battle on its behalf; what he wrote there was a kind of newspaper cartoon in words; and one of the most popular figures of all cartoonists, John Bull, came out of the pamphlets of the same period. At the end of the process, we have lived through recent times when the money-bags shrank again like pricked balloons, and again the forces of propaganda were set in motion. To-day, however, the debt is very much larger and the issues are much more grave. Only last Budget Day, the very retiring Mr. Montagu Norman was quietly re-elected Governor of the Bank of England. And by that time, John Bull had turned into the Little Man, welcoming the Budget with servile joy. The accession of a Stuart who repudiated the Whig Debt—would that have been a disaster in 1714?   GREGORY MACDONALD,

A Book To Read

THIS PROGRESS: THE TRAGEDY OF EVOLUTION. *By Bernard Acworth. Rich & Cowan. 6s.*

IT is painfully evident that Captain Acworth is one of those "backward" people whom Professor Huxley has blamed for raking up the old controversy about evolution. The word backward is the Professor's, and one glance at this impudent book is enough to make the reader understand what he means. For instance, the writer is perpetually dragging in the names of European scientists, and quoting books written by foreigners. It is true that he quotes also from the Encyclopædia Britannica, but, apparently, only that he may question the dogmas of those who compiled that learned work. Since, unfortunately, nothing whatever has been proved by scientists with regard to the origin of life on this earth, it only complicates matters for the scientists, if we are to have a crowd of laymen asking preposterous questions, and insisting that a hypothesis is a hypothesis, and a wild guess a wild guess. The honest layman often admits that he does not understand the language of the scientist; how then, can he expect to understand his meaning?

I myself have never had any difficulty with the scientist's meaning. After such involved statements as: Credo in unum Deum, Patrem omnipotentem, factorem coeli et terrae, visibilium omnium et invisibilium, it is like a breath of reality to come to: "Living matter or life itself in all probability arose from non-living matter in the first stage of this evolutionary process. The only doubt which remains concerns the exact steps in the process, and the nature and relative importance of the various factors which have contributed to it." As Comte said to the laundress of Passy, "If we knew all about it, we should know all about it."

How far behind the best contemporary thought Captain Acworth has remained may be gathered from the fact that he has some obscure objection to taking false premises for granted; that he can bring himself to criticise Mr. H. G. Wells and Bishop Barnes; and that he has the bad taste to quote things said or written by his opponents which make them look foolish. And the worst of it is that there is no censorship in this country to prevent him from undermining the faith of little scientists.

Things being as they are, I must confine myself to recommending this book to those innocent, golden-haired, blue-eyed people who still believe that something can come out of nothing; to those whose lonely vigil among the rocks has been rewarded with a vision of fossils invisible to the sceptical eye; to the pioneer who settled, to his own satisfaction, and by sheer, strong, unwearying thought, the great matter of how the first egg laid itself. I recommend it to those who hold that the giraffe and Darwin, the cactus and the kingfisher are the fine flowers of a piece of mud that slowly discovered the lost secret of spontaneous generation. I recommend it to those who, having pitched a poet and a seagull overboard in the Bay of Biscay, proved conclusively that the seagull was the survivor, and therefore the fitter of the two; to those who claim that the traces of legs in snakes prove that snakes were once men and women, and that the shape of the neck of an embryonic ant resembles the shape of the neck of an embryonic rhinoceros, though it is much smaller. I recommend it to the painstaking people who are tabulating in black notebooks the structural changes in the reindeer since the days when his picture was scratched on the cave-walls, and to the professor who taught a whiting to live on land, grew eyebrows on it, and finally lost it when it fell off the pier at Worthing, and, being by now unaccustomed to water, was drowned. Heartily I recommend it, and with all the power of my pen, to those who know exactly how long the earth was cooling before the moment came when the Original Protoplasm shook itself, and said, in the patois, "I feel myself becoming cyanogenous. I shall soon be a proteid molecule, thanks to my incandescent heat and my nitrogenous compounds."

VINDEX.

Cervantes

THE LIFE AND MISADVENTURES OF MIGUEL DE CERVANTES. *By Mariano Tomás. G. Allen and Unwin. 10s. 6d.*

ONE of the most concise criticisms ever made of Cervantes was that of a comparatively unknown Spanish writer, Garcia de Villavejas, to the effect that there was "no satire to compare with the adventures of the Knight of La Mancha, unless indeed we consider the misadventures of his creator, Miguel de Cervantes Saavedra."

The justice of that criticism,—or, if you prefer it, that appreciation,—is amply shown in Sr. Tomás' excellent and beautifully composed work.

Oddly enough, though possibly because he was always humble and poor at the height of his fame, Cervantes is one of the few great literary men of his age about whom we know absolutely everything. But there are always lunatics in this world to supply entertainment for those who care to find it and consequently there have been quite a number of people who have maintained (a) that Cervantes never lived, (b) that he did not write don Quixote, (c) that don Quixote was not written in Castillian but in our own rough island dialect by a man called Smith, later being translated at the older University and sent out for the instruction of the dons as part of Drake's raid in 1587, and (d) which I have actually heard in argument, "A latin could not write a book of such subtlety and certainly not a Spaniard of the 16th century." A halter is best prescribed for such people, who have no place here, and I only mention them to emphasise one side of Sr. Tomás' work. Its particular delight is its complete freedom from the convulsions of the crank, being exactly what it sets out to be, as might well be expected from the pen of so well known an authority on the history of his country's literature.

But from the fact that we know all about Cervantes, —where he lived at various times, what his troubles were, the extent of his genius, and so forth,—it does not follow that there is no more to be said about him and no fresh point of view to take. There are plenty of aspects and critical studies yet to be made, and this one is certainly the best of recent years.

Sr. Tomás has a very powerful feeling both for the writings of Cervantes and for the sufferings and misadventures which befell the man himself. Being a writer of brilliance he distils this feeling from his veins on to every page till one feels that the dedication of the book might read like that magnificent and anonymous epitaph to Cervantes which runs:

" Wayfarer: the pilgrim
Cervantes here lies buried.
Earth takes back his body;
His name lives on divine.
His race at length is run
But for his fame and for his works
There is no death. And so it was
That passing from this life
Into the life beyond
He went frank-countenanced."

There is no aspect nor matter of importance in Cervantes' life which has been neglected. We meet him first in Italy as a soldier beginning to turn towards letters as a pastime. Later at Lepanto where he won the distinction which was to be his undoing. For it was on his return to Spain from Italy by sea after being at Tunis, with a letter of commendation from Don John himself, that he and the remainder of the ship's company were captured by Corsairs and taken to Algiers. Had it not been for the possession of that fateful letter Cervantes might have crossed the Mediterranean to the Christian side in a few months' time. But a letter signed by Don John commending the bearer for skill and bravery and the loss of the use of his left arm, recommending him to the command of an important company—this young man was an important person, with the consequence that his ransom was trebled beyond the hope of payment and while still under thirty, Miguel, a soldier, a budding genius who had been as free as the wind all his life, was constrained to spend seven years in heathen captivity and four times to be foiled in escape.

From that moment his misfortunes grow and his greatness begins, neither of them ever decreasing. To list these would be too long and make dull reading from my pen when you can have them adorned with beauty from the pen of Sr. Tomás. That Cervantes should have received work as a tax collector is in itself remarkable but it explains his wide knowledge of Spain in don Quixote. His marriage was almost a failure, certainly unsatisfactory to both parties, until almost the end. He is again gaoled when money he is sending to Madrid miscarries, and from then onwards he is never free for very long from the attentions of His Majesty's Accountant, rather like a man persecuted by Income Tax Collectors to-day. But it was in gaol in Seville that don Quixote was conceived.

It has been maintained, and it has been denied with equal vigour, that Cervantes meant to portray himself as don Quixote. No doubt the point will continue to be argued among Cervantesque students until we at last meet that gentle figure in Elysian meadows, and one of us screws up the courage to ask him the answer. Looking at us with his gentle eyes and the superb dignity which attended him throughout life and during death, it is Sr. Tomás' opinion that Cervantes will answer us something after this manner: " I loved my wife, Doña Catalina, and I have ever been sensitive upon points which touched my honour. Doña Catalina, *la chica* loved me and was saddened by my leaving her, not understanding the true cause. And the cause of my leaving her was the treatment I received at the hands of her relatives—not least among them the squireling Alonso Quijada. When I went to prison in Seville on a question of *maravedis* and *neales* it was she who sought to free me. But I was still indignant at the treatment I had received at the hands of her relatives. In my leisure time in gaol, having always had a feeling towards letters, I decided to Lampoon my in-laws, and having once already been in conflict with the Church on the matter of tax collection, decided to choose, not the clerical don Francisco de Palacios, my wife's brother, but rather don Alonso Quijada. I gave to him the name "Quijote" and linked my lampooning with my experiences and my views. Naturally, the discourse on Arms and Letters is myself speaking and likewise in the matter of the captive's narrative in chapters 39-41."

Thus is the manner in which Sr. Tomás would expect Cervantes to speak and of his poems and his plays he would speak differently.

The authorship of the spurious Second Part of Don Quixote is touched on by Sr. Tomás and forms one of the most interesting sections of the work. He is of opinion that Alonso Fernandez de Avellaneda, Licenciate, and a native of the town of Tordesillas, alleged author of the Second Part, was in reality no less a person than the great Lope de Vega himself or at any rate some person "put up" by Lope to do the job. Unfortunately, however, the evidence he supplies in force of his argument is insufficient to prove conclusive.

There are many stories told of and about Cervantes. The best of all comes from the memoirs of the Licentiate Marquez de Torres, chaplain (among others) to the illustrious Cardinal Archbishop of Toledo, Sr. don Bernardo Sandival y Rojas. On the 25th February, 1615, His Excellency called on the French Ambassador, one of whose gentlemen asked Marquez de Torres which of recent Spanish books made the best reading. Marquez de Torres, who was at the time censoring the Second Part of don Quixote, mentioned Cervantes' name. The French already knew it in connection with *Galatea*, and anxiously asked de Torres for a description of "this genius." Marquez de Torres replied, " He is old, a soldier, a gentleman and poor."

That in itself is historically beautiful, but scarcely had he said the words than one of the gentlemen enquired " Are not such men maintained in comfort out of the private funds?" and another diplomat cut in "If it has been necessity which has compelled him to write, please God that he may never have abundance, so that, poor himself, he may continue to enrich the world with his works "—which gives both sides of the same question. Told of the affair later, Cervantes, as you may well believe, was thoroughly amused!

PETER QUINCE.

Music

THE concert by Heinz Unger and the London Philharmonic Orchestra introduced us to a German conductor who seemed in every way typical of his kind and period: precise, earnest, extremely efficient and lacking in all the finer and deeper subtleties of expression, losing the whole in the insistence on the particular. The concert was welcome for a further opportunity of hearing Mahler's first symphony and the performance of this was easily the best thing of the evening. Strauss' *Till Eulenspiegel* and Beethoven's Pianoforte Concerto No. 4, with Franz Osborn as soloist, were played with mere technical proficiency and without inspiration.

The B.B.C. Concert on Wednesday—the last of the series—included William Walton's solemnly serious Viola Concerto. Such a work could hardly be otherwise, as the viola, even in the hands of a genius like Lionel Tertis, does not lend itself to brilliancy or cheerfulness. It is a sad instrument. On this occasion the genius was absent, his place being taken at short notice by Mr. Bernard Shore. It says a lot for the fine musicianship of this artist that we consciously lost little of the thoughtful reading and beautiful phrasing which Mr. Tertis—as the creator of the part, so to speak—had led us to expect. Dr. Boult conducted and secured, also, an average performance of the "Unfinished" Symphony and a really excellent performance of Brahms' Symphony No. 1.

Berlioz's *Te Deum* conducted by Beecham is enough to put the fear of God into anyone, and if there was one who came away from last Thursday's performance without at least the beginnings of wisdom, such a one is more hardly atheistic than I think probable. It was not, of course, an ideal performance; that is to say, it was not exactly as Berlioz conceived it. But as Berlioz demands that impressarios should have for the performances of his work not only enormous sums of money at their disposal but portable cathedrals and hundreds of highly trained choir boys and other such elaborate " props," he must occasionally rest content with the genius of Beecham working on such excellent material as this hard-up age can afford. At any rate, wherever he is now he cannot but have been pleased with the quite amazing enthusiasm—exceptional even for a Beecham concert—which the work evoked from the Philharmonic audience. It was truly a memorable occasion, and one which I did not dilute by waiting for the Hadyn symphony and the Borodin dances which followed.

The Alexandra Choral and Orchestral Society deserve strong commendation for the enterprising programmes it is giving at the Northern Polytechnic Hall. Not content only with the established masterpieces of Bach, Handel or Mendelssohn it has given the four greatest of the Elgar oratorios, Vaughan Williams' *Sea Symphony*, George Dyson's *The Canterbury Pilgrims* (last Saturday), and is including in the coming season Arthur Bliss' *Morning Heroes* and Charles Proctor's *A Song of England*. The performance last Saturday was more than adequate to impress us again with the musical worth of Mr. Dyson's setting of Chaucer's immortal poem. So far as I know the work has not been heard in London since the performance

a year or so ago by the Philharmonic Choir. While possibly not a masterpiece it is quite certainly in the best tradition of English choral writing and fills no unworthy place in that tradition. The soloists were Mabel Ritchie, Percy Manchester and John Morel; the conductor, Charles Proctor, who now directs the Society's rehearsals and concerts.

Mention of the Philharmonic Choir reminds me that on Tuesday next an interesting programme at the Queen's Hall will contain the first performance for many years in England of Graun's *Der Tod Jesu*—a work which holds in Germany almost the place that Handel's *Messiah* does over here,—also Vaughan Williams' *Magnificat* and Arnold Bax' *Fatherland*. Charles Kennedy Scott will, as usual, be the conductor.

V.N.L.

The Cockpit.

[Letters should not exceed 300 words in length and must bear the names and addresses, not necessarily for publication, of their authors.

The Editor can accept no responsibility for opinions expressed by correspondents.]

MONEY.

Sir,—If I remember rightly, Mr. Belloc's definition of Usury depends on the use made of the money by the borrower, on which loans lending for house-building could hardly be usury.

That of Mr. C. O'Brien Donaghey—to whom I owe my thanks—depends on the lender being able to prove that he has suffered a loss by depriving himself of the use of the amount of the loan. The generally accepted view is, I think, that usury consists in taking advantage of the troubles of the borrower in order to increase them to one's own benefit.

As things are no lender would have the smallest difficulty in showing that he was suffering loss by lending his money free of interest and Mr. C. O'Brien Donaghey's dictum appears to be applicable to another form of society—presumably a distributist one. It reminds me of a statement of your own, Sir, that in a distributive society it would be unnecessary for farming to pay.

The connection between the two in my mind is that they both leave me wondering whether on the one hand I am so concerned with the raising and selling of potatoes, etc., that I am unable to visualise your ideal state or whether on the other hand, your party is so little concerned with such things that they cannot always see the practical difficulties.

The peasant would have to buy some things—including *G.K.'s Weekly* surely—and if he sold a surplus cow and lent the money to his neighbour to build a barn, he would be as much entitled to interest as if he had lent him the cow and wanted paying for the milk; even if he had been so successful lately as to need only a second copy of *G.K.'s* so that his wife could read it without waiting for him to finish.

ARTHUR EMPSON.

PARLIAMENT AND THE PEOPLE.

Sir,—From the general tone of your paper, I gather that you at least hope against hope that the Government will ultimately be forced to see the necessity of returning to normal justice in the matter of land tenure and development.

You call the said government stupid; you express surprise at its inanities; you speak of its blunders. At the same time you state as a fact (and truly) the idea that the real government of this country lies in the hands of those in whom are centralized all wealth, all property, all power; namely, the plutocracy.

You teach, in essence, that the government exists and is maintained to exist, as the tool of the plutocrats, wherewith to rule, by the illusion of parliamentary procedure, the economic life of the country.

How do you suppose the government (so-called) to be

stupid, when it is the mere logical working of extremely intelligent manoeuvring? The government exists to deceive, to conceal, to tell half-truths, or lies, to pass laws just or unjust as the little combine of authority may think fit. In short, the government is sustained as the means, together with the press and the microphone, of covering the activities of the small number of men who are becoming, by this process, the masters of the servile state. Why not be honest? To hate all this corruption is right, but why deny the intelligence thereof? Why call the government stupid when it works so efficiently and perfectly towards the end for which it exists?

I am definitely anti-revolutionary, but I do not approve of hoping where there is no hope, namely for the M.P.s to turn honest and independent all of a sudden or even gradually. Logically, there are no grounds for such a hope. What is wanted is the *forcing* of the individual M.P. to be answerable to his constituency. After all the thousands of people who put a man in, expect him to work for them. He is the employee and they are the boss. What does a boss do if his employee doesn't satisfy? He watches him until he gets real evidence of his inefficiency then sacks him.

An espionage system should be adopted whereby the activities of the individual M.P. can be reported daily or at least weekly to his constituency and published therein. A Control of Parliament Board say, could be established to publish the evidence which could be obtained in large measure by unemployed men in London or the places where the M.P.s may be. The continual watching and shadowing of his activities and the publication thereof weekly, might have the effect of making the M.P. realize that there is another power, beside the two front benches, watching him, and that, the power that put him in.

Let the League undertake this work, establishing an information bureau in every district, and providing the public with weekly information. Incidentally, it would bring public attention to bear upon us. Anybody that undertakes to reduce the M.P.s to their real position of paid servants to the constituencies is bound to attract attention.

F. G. CORFE.

LUNACY LAW.

Sir,—We are glad to note your surprise " that the public do not start a spontaneous clamour to ensure their own safety "—in view of the lax state of lunacy administration in this country.

It is to be hoped that the public conscience will be awakened in this matter in much the same way that it has become alive to the slum evil. There are already welcome signs of a quickening demand for radical reform of the lunacy laws.

This Society is constantly coming into contact with cases where hasty certification has played havoc with the lives of those who merely required ordinary medical treatment.

As things are, it is far too easy for relieving officers to set in motion a machine, from whose toils it is almost impossible to extricate oneself. The lunacy machine is itself a danger to the community!

FRANCIS J. WHITE.
Secretary, National Society for
Lunacy Law Reform.

Published by the Proprietors, G.K.'s WEEKLY, LTD., 2, Little Essex Street, Strand, London, W.C.2. (incorporating THE NEW WITNESS). Telephone: Temple Bar, 1978. Printed by THE NUNEATON NEWSPAPERS, LTD., Bond Gate, Nuneaton. Sole Agents for Australasia: Gordon & Gotch (Australasia, Ltd.). Sole Agents for South Africa, Central News Agency, Ltd. (London Agents: Gordon & Gotch, Ltd.).

GK's WEEKLY

EDITED BY G.K. CHESTERTON

JANUARY 3 - 1935
VOL. XX.   No. 512

Registered as a Newspaper   SIXPENCE.

The Family

SOMETHING startling has happened. A public man had said, not merely something vital, but *the* vital thing about public affairs, which every public man should be saying every day, and which no other public man of our time has hinted at. We are not surprised that it is our King who has said it.

An enthusiastic gentleman praised His Majesty for the elegant delivery of his speech to his people which was broadcast on Christmas Day. And it is true that he spoke with a certain noble simplicity. But our great satisfaction is that the matter was worthy of the manner.

The matter provided the subject of a good many leading articles, some of which displayed the Keyword of the King's speech as their title. But all of them missed the significance of the Keyword.

That Keyword, which unlocks the doors of all politics and all economy, is Family.

The King began by reminding his hearers, his people, that Christmas Day is the festival of the Family. It was plain that he meant that primarily it was the Festival of one particular Family, and of one particular Mother and Child.

It is astounding and yet it is certain that some of his hearers needed to be reminded of this central fact of the world. It is almost equally astounding and yet as certain that far more of them failed to understand him when he went on to speak of his people "all you who are listening to me, all the peoples of the realm and empire" as "bound to me and to each other by the spirit of one great family." There was the Crib of Bethlehem, and here was this great family of British people. It was the King's urgent desire and hope that the spirit of the One should become the spirit of the other.

"We have still our own anxieties to face," he went on, "but I am convinced that if we meet them in the spirit of one family we shall overcome them."

That Keyword runs through the speech. The King speaks as a father to his children. And he speaks, says he, "as I sit in my own home."

It is plain enough that he sees the one big British family as a collection of families—not merely families of nations, but millions of individual families listening to him, family by family, each in its own separate home.

We will not take His Majesty farther along the road to Distributism than the words of his speech carry him. But we find it significant when politicians delight in talking of international factors and Weltpolitik (if the recognition of the origin of that second phrase has not made it a trifle unpopular) our King talks of nothing but those homely realities: the family and the home.

The recognition of the family as the unit of the State is the kernel of Distributism. The insistence on ownership to protect its liberty is the shell.

We that are Christians believe that the family has a divine sanction. But any reasonable pagan, if he will work it out, will discover that the family existed before the State and has prior rights; that the State exists only as a collection of families, and that its sole function is to safeguard the rights of each and all of them.

Once admit that the nation is itself one big family with its King as its father, and taking its pattern from one little simple Family, and the step to the central Distributist position seems to us inevitable. The small family is the reality which the King relies upon to give force to his splendid and tremendous figure of speech. He regards his Empire as a League of Families, a League of very little nations.

We do not regard it as remarkable that our King should speak in this familiar homely way which a dictator, still less an expert sociologist, can never hope to reach. There are good republicans among our readers. Yet even they will admit that it is a good thing to have an ordinary man as your chief ruler, since ordinary things are the important ones, and that you are far more likely to get an ordinary man as your King than as your dictator or your Prime Minister.

We need not stress the fact that, as no other secular ruler, a King is dedicated. The thing that springs to the eye is that, when all our politicians and sociologists are losing themselves in big phrases about efficient organisation, our King utters the magical word *family*.

It is as a father of a family that he talks of those unlucky children of his who are dispossessed. He asks that they may be treated in the spirit of their Elder Brother,—as brothers, and not as sociological phenomena.

It is as the father of a family that he speaks of the clash of interests among those more fortunate, or at least more powerful. And what he says admits of easy paraphrase into a call for the spirit of charity, unity, and brotherly love.

We imagine that some of his Ministers smiled when they heard his speech, and murmured: "Good, old-fashioned stuff." And of course they are right. It is good, and it is old-fashioned: as old fashioned as man, as man in a garden.

And we imagine that others of his Ministers rubbed their hands, and said: "That's the stuff to give 'em." Again they are right. Only they happen to mistake for dope what is doctrine.

At this moment when from all sides the rights of the family are threatened with invasion, and when men and women—and children—of our nation tend to be treated, not as members of separate families, not as brothers and sisters in one great family, but as cyphers, some of them insignificant, or even superfluous cyphers, in a financial statement, it comes with the force of a new revelation that our King has spoken this old-fashioned, homely, familiar, human word.

NOTES

Monday, December 31.

From an appreciation of the late Sir Albert Spicer, published in the *Times* on Saturday we quote the following:—

"The Marconi Inquiry, of which he was chairman, distressed him very much. He had been appointed chairman by the Liberal Government. But he complained that he did not get the support from the Prime Minister to which he believed he was entitled. So much was this the case that he more than once offered his resignation of the chairmanship to Mr. Asquith. This Mr. Asquith refused to accept. He complained that he was hampered in this inquiry by some of his Liberal colleagues upon it; and he went so far as to say to some of his friends that political interests rather than the interests of truth had too much to do with the opposition which he encountered when attempting to get at the evidence."

*   *   *   *

The Ministry of Transport's regulations, involving the marking of special crossings and the erection by the thousand of Belisha beacons, demonstrated their worth during the week before Christmas when 43 persons were killed and 1,221 were injured in the Metropolitan area alone. These are shocking figures, made worse by the fact that in the rest of Great Britain there were 117 fatal accidents and cases of injury to the number of 3,084. Surveying statistics for a period of forty-one weeks, the *Times* points out that the number of deaths on the roads has been "180% greater than all the deaths caused by industrial accidents in a twelvemonth," while reminding its readers that in the City of London during the week before Christmas no one was killed and only 11 were injured. Thus the explanation that the congestion of the streets increased the danger to motorist and pedestrian would seem to be negatived; for the City streets were very seriously congested and few vehicles could travel at more than the pace of a cart-horse. A study of the figures, indeed, makes this conclusion inevitable; that the menace to life and limb lies not in the presence of crowds but in fast driving. As Mr. Hore-Belisha's experiments have failed the need for the imposition of new speed limits—not by a Government Department but by Parliament—becomes imperative.

*   *   *   *

Another aspect of the current regulations was shown on Friday when Sir Rollo Graham-Campbell dismissed at Bow Street a summons against a lady who was accused of leaving a tram without having paid her fare. He held that the regulation under which the summons was taken was *ultra vires* as being repugnant to the law of the land and unreasonable, and with that decision most people will readily concur. "No act or omission," he said, "could be a crime unless *mens rea* was present, or there was express statutory provision that the act or omission was a crime without any criminal intent, or it could be clearly inferred from the terms of the statute that the mere act or omission was in itself an offence."
As a blow struck against the increasing tendency

of Government Departments to take over, with Parliamentary connivance, the duties of Parliament, this decision is a valuable one. The regulation was issued by the Board of Trade in 1920, but since the formation of the London Passenger Transport Board similar regulations have been framed with regard to omnibuses. We wonder now if they will be re-drafted or if the Board will test their applicability by further prosecutions.

*   *   *   *

The various investigations put on foot by President Roosevelt continue to bring interesting facts to the light of day: the best safeguard for his policies, because the machinations of his enemies are frustrated, the common people up and down the world find out the truth about their governing, and the executives of other countries are forced to take action. England, in one way or another, and France as well, promise soon to have an inquiry into the armaments racket. The latest disclosure, that Wall Street planned to raise an army of 500,000 and dispossess Roosevelt by force (though with every appearance of popular revolt) does not strike us as improbable. It was known last year, when the real measures were taken against the financiers, that heavily financed propaganda was on foot against Roosevelt, and the form of an armed revolt was to be expected.

*   *   *   *

To-day it is odd to notice that Roosevelt is widely credited with having won out in his fight for American prosperity, though his enactments are none the less regarded as inimical to Wall Street. We are glad to see that he still prefers public works to an idle dole. In this country, where every form of public works cries out for attention, the argument that they *cost* more than measures for demoralisation has captured the intelligent public. This is a supreme example of the hold which money has over minds.

Words and Rumours of Words

WHEN a Fundamentalist says he believes the Bible statement that Adam ate an apple or Jonah was swallowed by a whale, we duly note that he has never read the Bible. When an Evolutionist says he disbelieves the Bible, with the same statements, we know he has never read what he disbelieves. It is a small and trivial test; it is almost a trick; but it proves that both men take their views from the tradition and not from the text. There is not a word about a whale, there is not a word about an apple, even in the rather recent English translation of the ancient and mysterious Hebrew Scriptures. So much is obvious enough. The Bible-worshipper and the Bible-smasher have, neither of them, read the Bible. But at least the Bible is there to be read. Many of them, I believe, even possess Bibles. The Higher Critic, after ransacking his library, can discover the volume he criticises. The Fundamentalist may find the Family Bible after a few hours' search. But since men turned from the authority of Scripture to the authority of Science, they have been forced to look for Science in scraps and secondhand snippets, mostly scattered through the newspapers. I fancy there are thousands of Darwinians who have never read Darwin. But any-how, they could not read the thousand books written about Darwin. They may make a selection; but (to use Darwinian language) it can hardly be a natural selection.

I have been trying to find out what was actually said by certain great scientists at the recent meetings of the British Association. I can only lay my hand on fuller or scrappier newspaper reports, and all seem to be rather scrappy than full. Science is exactitude; and everything depends on the exact words; on words as definite as 'whale' or 'apple.' The reports tell me that Professor Julian Huxley said irresponsible people deny Darwinism. He may have said that some irresponsible people deny Darwinism. He surely cannot have said that only irresponsible people deny Darwinism. Professor Dwight of Harvard is not an irresponsible person; the great French biologist Vialleton is not an irresponsible person. Professor D'Arcy Thompson is not an irresponsible person; and he seems to have denied that groups can have grown from each other; and added that we know less than we did seventy years ago. Here again there may be verbal distinctions. It may not be exactly what he said; it is not exactly what he meant. He did not mean that a brick fell on an astronomer so that he forgot the Nebula of Andromeda or that a biologist lost his memory of marsupials. He meant that seventy years ago they thought they knew much more than they did. I merely give these examples to show the need of exactitude; and the prevalence of inexactitude. Another speaker was announced as saying that ' Evolution is finished.' And, I gather, some thought it meant that Evolutionism is exploded and others that it meant (as it probably did) that Evolution will evolve no further. It is the difference between my saying, ' I am fifty and have stopped growing,' and ' I was always this size and never grew.' Now the world is full of these echoes and rumours and reports and misreports of Science. And it is odd that in all the quarrels about the quarrel of Science and Scripture, nobody pointed out that practical difference. I mean the fact that Scripture is there; and that Science is anywhere. It is very hard even for scientists to follow Science; it is impossible for the normal newspaper reader who only finds it in the newspapers.

The Bosworth Guild

By K. L. Kenrick

AFTER years of patient research, a plan has at last been evolved for the resettlement of agricultural England. It is a scheme which will bear the most careful scrutiny and the most searching criticism. As it is important that this scheme should obtain at once the widest possible publicity, it must be given a short, distinctive, and easily remembered title. The scheme was first worked out, in a sufficiency of practical detail, for a projected settlement near Market Bosworth, Leicestershire. The title here suggested for it is "The Bosworth Guild Scheme." Whether the projected settlement will actually take place remains to be seen, but in any case the outstanding merits of the scheme as a model must immediately win the approval of all who are interested in or responsible for the restoration of English agriculture and the re-settlement of rural England.

A hasty outline of the scheme has already appeared in the columns of *G.K.'s Weekly*. It had long been clear that the only sane reconstruction of modern society must be on the basis of the two institutions of the family and the guild. In spite of all assaults upon it, the family still remained a sufficiently well-defined institution for everyone to realise exactly what it meant. But the guild had become vague and shadowy. The most determined efforts of those who believed in it failed to reconstruct it even in imagination. That reconstruction has now become a possibility.

The primary unit of the scheme is the family settled on a 20-25 acre farm, established in ownership of its land, house and building, live and dead stock, and thus equipped for straight family-subsistence farming. The secondary unit is the Guild, a co-operative association of the 50-100 families occupying 1,000-2,000 acres of land. The size of the Guild is determined by two considerations—it must be large enough to take full advantage of co-operative methods, and small enough for all its members to be within walking distance of its centre and to be personally acquainted with each other. A circle of a mile radius has an approximate area of 2,000 acres.

The Bosworth Guild is a development of the "Birmingham Scheme" adopted by the Distributist League a few years ago. That scheme was mainly concerned with a possible method of settling individual holders on the land. The necessity of community life was mentioned by its authors, but at that time they had no clear vision as to how the community might be brought into existence. They felt—probably more acutely than their critics—the apparent cruelty of putting families in isolation to scrape a bare living from the soil under conditions so utterly opposed to the whole trend of modern civilisation. Further they were profoundly disturbed by the apparent impossibility of making agriculture "pay" except by putting up prices against the industrial population. How could distributists, among whom sympathy with the industrial population is almost a morbid obsession, possibly advocate a return to agriculture? A further

objection frequently made to the Birmingham Scheme was that it would need special legislation.

It may be claimed that the Bosworth Guild goes a long way towards meeting all of these objections. No special legislation will be needed—the Minister of Agriculture might bring into existence the first Bosworth Guild almost without mentioning his intention to Parliament. There must be a number of wealthy people who would be glad to find the money to start any agricultural scheme which showed the least sign of promise. The sense of loneliness and of isolation in a hostile world which is one of the greatest afflictions of the English farmer of to-day is reduced by the Guild to a minimum. And finally, the power of the Guild to make subsistence-farming a real possibility and not a mere dream will largely do away with the necessity of high prices against the industrial population.

A wider consideration of the merits of the scheme demands its comparison with rival schemes—of which there are three. The first is the proposal that English agriculture be abandoned to its fate. The climate of this country is such as to make competition with foreign produce impossible. Its soil is exhausted by 2,000 years of incessant cultivation—it has no River Nile and no virgin prairie. Its inhabitants could not possibly submit to the low standard of living and the degree of monotonous never-ceasing toil which are necessary to produce an appreciable margin on the right side between output and expenses. The development of transport and the growth of the international spirit in trade, are an abundant guarantee that we need never fail of a bountiful supply of every kind of food from the very ends of the earth. Nothing is easier than to develop such statements as these into volumes of glib eloquence. But it is doubtful whether anyone ever remains more than half-convinced by them. They are the minor facets of a gratuitous assumption that human evolution of necessity means the imperial and economic unification of the human race, an assumption which can be entertained only by those who shut their eyes as tightly as possible to the history of past times and the geography of the present day. It would be just as tenable a hypothesis to maintain that human evolution means a struggle of ever-increasing harshness between peoples of different cultures.

The second proposal is that English farming must be done by machinery on the largest possible scale. This proposal again is dead against the facts. It is perfectly clear from the Cambridge reports on East Anglian farming that in 1931 it was the large farmers employing little labour who were going bankrupt, whereas the small farmers employing two or three times as much labour were keeping their heads above water. Just as the foolish belief in shipping as a substitute for agriculture necessitated a ship-building subsidy, so our foolish belief in large farming as against small farming demanded a wheat subsidy. We call ourselves a hard-headed people when really what we mean is that we have thick skulls.

The third and latest proposal goes to the other extreme. It is suggested that the unit for the next attempt at land settlement should be four acres. It is true that market-gardening can produce a large money-value per acre. An acre under glass can produce a much larger value. Pigs and poultry, fed on imported grain, do not require a very large area of land in proportion to the total value of produce. Even cattle have been kept on a smaller acreage than the usual English practice demands. All of these enterprises require an exceptional degree of skill, experience and commercial keenness. Their success depends entirely on ability to take advantage of market-prices. In every case practically the whole of the produce must be sold. The adoption of such schemes on a scale of any magnitude would produce such a disturbance of local and national markets as to require the constant and harassing interference of marketing-scheme officials. In no sense whatever can the four-acre unit be regarded as deserving the name of Land Settlement.

The Bosworth Guild combines the advantages of the 1,000-acre unit and the four-acre unit without their disadvantages. It will be free to adopt such large-scale labour-saving devices as do not involve rural depopulation. It will also be free to include a small number of specialised holdings of smaller acreage. The one object it will always keep in view will be to reduce commercial transactions and the need for money to a minimum, and so to raise the possibility of subsistence farming to a maximum.

Statecraft in Mexico
By Floyd Anderson

THERE is no peace for Catholic Mexicans in Mexico. The National Revolutionary Party dominates the Government, and one of its principal aims and purposes is to deprive the Mexicans of the Catholic Church.

Archbishop Diaz, in an interview in the New York Times on November 8, enumerated some of the difficulties under which the Church is labouring:

" Priests are not allowed to say Mass, baptise, confess, give Holy Communion, preach or perform the regular functions, contrary to the guarantees established by Articles IV, VI, XXIV, and CXXX of the Constitution of the Republic.

" The Government has seized more than 150 churches within a little more than a year and has expelled from their dioceses the Bishops of Tabasco, Vera Cruz, Campeche, Aguas Calientes, Oaxaca, Chiapas, Chilapa, Zacatecas, Chihuahua, and Teziutlan, as well as every priest in those dioceses.

" In Quéretaro every church has been closed by the State Government, as well as in Sonora. The Bishop of Quéretaro was compelled to remain hidden, while the Bishop of Sonora was exiled to the United States.

" In some States only one priest is allowed for each 100,000 Catholics, and it is physically impossible to serve them. During the last few days the daily press has made known that the Senate is studying a new law to leave only two priests for the whole Federal District, within which is the capital of the nation; two priests to attend to the spiritual needs of more than a million people."

A new President was inaugurated in Mexico on November 30. From the make-up of his Cabinet, it appears certain there will be no cessation of Catholic persecution. Here are two of them;

Narciso Bassols was named Finance Minister. Señor Bassols is the man who was responsible for the infamous sexual-education plan, against which students and parents revolted all over the country. Students went on strike in grade schools, high schools, colleges, and universities, and the protests grew to such an extent that it was deemed wise for Señor Bassols to resign from the Ministry of Education. Now, however, he is back in the Government.

Thomas Garrido Canabal was named Minister of Agriculture. Señor Canabal is an avowed Communist, was Governor of Tabasco (and according to America "made a good thing out of it"); who reported that the Catholic problem in his State had been solved, that it " has assumed some degree of violence but that has been necessary and efficacious for wiping out influences that are indestructible by other means."

General Lazaro Cárdenas is the new President, and the story of his election is an interesting one. Maurice Halperin, in the November issue of Current History, gives an interesting note on it:

" When on July 1, 1934, General Lazaro Cárdenas, candidate of the P.N.R. (Partido Nacional Revolucionario) . . became President-elect of the Republic, no one was surprised. In fact, everyone knew six months earlier, at the time of the P.N.R. convention, who the next President would be; nevertheless, the Government insisted on the elaborate pretence of a free election. Opposition parties were permitted to come into the open; anti-government papers denounced ' Callismo '; candidates toured the country, and the leading Mexico City papers kept reminding the citizens that this time everything was aboveboard. Then, the morning after the election, General Cárdenas was declared the winner with over 1,000,000 votes, while the combined total of his three opponents was announced as less than one-thirtieth of that figure, though it was curious how with the present facilities for communication so many votes could have been counted and recorded so quickly."

Incidentally, Antonio Villarreal, candidate of the Revolutionary Confederation of Independent Parties, who was recorded as having some 17,000 votes (the closest one to Cárdenas), has fled the country.

In his inauguration address on November 30, President Cárdenas referred to the new education programme, which is to be on a Socialistic basis:

" Children must understand human activities from a scientific, liberal viewpoint. My government will encourage Socialistic education with the purpose that all children shall understand the aspirations of the proletariat."

To understand the purpose of the Socialistic education plan, a reading of the amended Article 3 of the Constitution is necessary. It says:

" Article 3. Education imparted by the State shall be Socialist, and, in addition, shall exclude every religious doctrine, shall combat fanaticism and prejudice, and to this end the school will organise its teaching and activities so as to permit the creation in the young of a rational and exact concept of the universe and of social life.

" Only the State—Federation, States, Municipalities —shall impart primary, secondary or normal education. Private persons who desire to impart education in any of these three grades may be authorised to do so provided, in each case, that the following rules be complied with:

"I. The activities and teaching of the private establishment, without any exception, must be adjusted to the precepts of the initial paragraph of this article, and shall be in charge of persons who, in the opinion of the State, have sufficient professional preparation, acceptable morality, and ideology in harmony with these precepts. Under this provision, religious corporations, ministers of any religion, stock companies whose activities are exclusively or chiefly educational, and associations or societies directly or indirectly affiliated with the propagation of any religious creed, shall not in any manner intervene in primary, secondary or normal schools, nor give them economic support.

"II. The formation of plans, curricula and methods of teaching is in every case an affair of the State.

"III. Private establishments cannot function unless they have obtained, in each case before beginning to function, the express authorisation of the Public Power.

"IV. The State can revoke, at any time, any authorisation granted. Against such revocation there shall be no recourse or court action whatever.

"These same rules apply to education of every type or grade imparted to labourers or peasants.

"Primary education shall be compulsory, and imparted gratuitously by the State.

"The State, at its discretion, can withdraw at any time official recognition of validity granted to studies made in private establishments.

"The Congress of the Union, for the purpose of unifying and co-ordinating education throughout the Republic, shall promulgate laws that may be necessary—to distribute the social function of education among the Federation, the States and the Municipalities; to fix the economic contributions corresponding to this public service, and to prescribe penalties for functionaries who themselves do not comply or who fail to compel others to comply with provisions binding on them, as well as for any one who disobey such provisions."

This amendment to the Constitution has aroused widespread indignation among the mothers of the nation. In Mexico City, an organisation of 2,500 Catholic mothers are actively urging that children be kept from schools when they open on January 6. These mothers have subscribed money to pay fines they expect to be assessed against some of the mothers who keep their children from school. Many mothers work at trades, and this organisation is making plans to care for the children during the usual school hours.

In Guadalajara, Jalisco, on December 3, an active protest against the Socialistic-education programme was made. The schools opened there that day, and thirty per cent. of them remained away from the schools, as their parents defied the national law. Guadalajara is the second largest city in Mexico. Its State University was closed in October because the students refused to admit the right of the government to prescribe the governmental theories to be taught.

Meanwhile, in the United States, protests have been mounting against the persecutions. And Catholics are not alone in this. On November 15, hundreds of college students picketed the Mexican Consulate in New York, protesting against the Mexican atrocities. They have had a few pickets there every day since.

Newspapers in the larger cities have protested, such as the New York *Times* and New York *Post*, the Pittsburg *Post-Gazette*, the St. Louis *Globe-Democrat*, the Philadelphia *Record*, the Detroit *News*, and many more. Forty or fifty Jewish papers, from the Atlantic Coast to the Pacific, carried editorials denouncing the Mexican Government's actions. *The Living Church*, the *Christian Century*, and many other church magazines have vigorously protested.

The Hierarchy of the Catholic Church in the United States made a public protest on November 16. They said that " we need not repeat that we protest with our whole heart and soul against this anti-Christian tyranny, and again call upon all the faithful in our country to pray that such a reign may cease, and to do everything in their power by word and by act to make the fact of such tyranny known."

Further in the statement, the Bishops pointed out that " it is not without significance that in the present turmoil of the world and distress of nations the basic truths of religion from which has sprung the stability of nations are flouted and denied by those who seek absolutism in government."

As the Bishops said, the Catholic Church in Mexico is not only fighting for its own cause, " but the cause of human freedom and of human liberty for all the nations of the world."

Pacifists and Pacifists
BY G. K. CHESTERTON

IN our correspondence columns lately, Mr. Leo Collier asked in a very clear and pointed manner for an explanation upon some points which I am only too glad of the opportunity to explain. For I think the points at issue are the pivotal points of the peril and safety both of Europe and of England. If I may begin first with a trivial and parenthetical point, Mr. Collier queried a remark of mine to the effect that the Cecils are always patriots, and never more than when they appear to be practically Pacifists. He seems to think that he can inflame my fanatical religious passions, as a notorious inquisitor and persecutor, by asking whether this applies to the famous founder of the house. I should answer that it probably did. I am no admirer of the moral type of William Cecil; but I think nothing more misleading, touching history and politics just now, than the use of historical facts as matters of praise or blame; or of matters of praise or blame as mere partisan triumphs or defeats. I fancy William Cecil cared more for his country-seat than for his country; but I think it probable that he did care for his country. As his country-seat was almost certainly the direct or indirect loot of a monastery, he naturally thought nothing of exterminating such a trifle as the historical Christianity of his country, in the interests of that estate. But I should think it quite likely that he did feel in some vague fashion, like Elizabeth and Cromwell, the new and narrow second-best; the great *pis aller* of patriotism. It was a common feeling to fall back upon, among the adventurers and politicians after the Great Pillage. Of men like the great William Cecil the dictum of Dr. Johnson was true enough; and patriotism was very frequently the last refuge of a scoundrel.

What is perhaps most interesting in this minor matter of the Cecils, not without its bearing on the major matter of the place of England in Europe, is the way in which the patriotism of the family ranges from the most stubborn diehard tradition to the most delicate diplomatic internationalism. The one type is so nationalist that it thinks it necessary to be impossibly imperialist; but the other is none the less national for being international. The present Lord Salisbury, for instance, is a very sincere and straightforward man and far from being a fool; but it is amusing to note how desperately he takes his stand as a diehard. He said one thing in the recent party meeting about India, which showed how queerly the old Victorian and German type of imperialism persists. He actually asked people, at this time of day, to invoke the sacred memory of Bismarck! He said scornfully that Bismarck would not have asked Gandhi to tea; a horrid crime which apparently defiles the dark record of Lord Irwin. It is perhaps about as unfortunate a parallel as any Tory could take. Lord Irwin is a supremely successful statesman compared with Bismarck, who was simply a flat and flabby failure, on this particular question of dealing with a people divided on religion. When Bismarck tried to treat the Catholic culture as Lord Salisbury would have him treat the Hindoo culture, he came a cropper which was simply a complete collapse. He certainly did not ask Windthorst to tea; it was Windthorst who asked Bismarck to a banquet of humble pie at Canossa; and Bismarck partook of it very humbly indeed. That is how Bismarckian imperialism fares when it is facing real facts like the great religions of the world.

But I only take this case of a Cecil blundering through honourable but unbalanced excess of patriotism, to insist again that it is exactly the same patriotism which takes a more patient and farseeing form in the international intellectualism of Lord Robert and his brother Hugh. They are patriots who perceive, truly enough, that the present interest of England is peace. They would probably ask Hitler and Stalin and anybody else to tea, to preserve that English interest. But what I said about them is proved true by the very incident that I noted; that one of them did openly avow, after prolonged and conscientious labours for peace, and even Pacifism, that it is all nonsense to say that England can absolutely and in the abstract abdicate from all appeal to arms; and that if the war he has worked so hard to avoid should break out, he would certainly not be a Conchie in time of war, in however true a sense he may have been practically a Pacifist in time of peace.

That is enough to separate such people from the people with whom I was more particularly arguing. They are divided in turn into two groups; those who seem inclined to relieve their feelings by rash vows about what they would do in all sorts of quite unforeseen circumstances; and those who seem to think that a vow to preserve the British Empire, and to take no human interest in any other human thing, will in some way preserve them from war as completely as a theoretical renunciation of war in itself. With the second group, with which Mr. Collier more specially identifies himself, I will deal in more respectful detail in a second article. Touching the first, I can only say that what I have said I have said; and I am only too glad that there is anywhere an organ in which I can say it. I think the present mere panic of Pacifism, the repudiation of all social relations, which is really involved in the repudiation of all loyalties, the wild promise not to fight for anything however just, in any position, however perilous, under any provocation however abominable, is a moral attitude which cannot be described as anything but contemptible. The recklessness and rashness of Jingoism is dangerous enough for any nation; but at least it is in some vulgar way an exaggeration of courage. It is left for idealists and moralists to express, in a way quite as vulgar, an extravagant exaggeration of their own cowardice. No man knows the future; but if one thing is certain, it is that Englishmen who have felt that fever will someday look back on it with shame.

A Fragment of Old Chelsea This Side of the Moon!

By Mary and William Titterton

ARCHIE Boyd was not an artist, but an art critic, which accounts for his being so unobservant.

He worked for one of the *heavies*, and made a good thing of it, so that he was always a welcome guest at a bottle party, and his own do's were beyond reproach.

They were celebrated of course in that scrumptious studio of his on Cheyne Walk, which he lent to any poor devil of an artist who hadn't a north light. And that was really the cause of the tragedy.

One of us had an urgent tinkle on the 'phone, and Archie asked her to take a spot of lunch with him at the Radnor. He said it was desperately urgent, so she went.

"But mind, Archie," she said, "if you accuse anybody there of being a German, I shall walk out on you."

Archie promised to be good.

The reason for this proviso was that Archie had been born with a hatred for the Hun. That was the odder in that he had a portrait of Queen Victoria over his bed; but Archie was no genealogist. And he'd borne Her Gracious Majesty's commission during the Boer War.

Hate the Hun he did with fury. Long before the war it was a prime delight of his, when run down, to visit a certain Soho restaurant frequented by Germans, and goad them to hostilities.

He'd learnt a few insulting phrases in the Hun lingo, and he used to fire them at the Germans in the restaurant until they rose and charged.

He had some gorgeous fights, and the total cost of the fines was not more than a tenner, "No more than it costs to be a *Savage*," as Archie said.

That by the way; the other of us met Archie at the Radnor. And, as soon as he'd congratulated her on her looks and said how glad he was to see her (Archie was always the little gentleman), he poured out the tale of his woes.

It appeared that Archie had gone back to his studio unexpectedly, and found the door locked, so he knew that one of his pals was at work. He was going to turn away and nip up to the domestic hangar which goes with these posh studios, when the door of the studio opened, and a girl passed out.

Archie took off his hat, and she smiled at him. Just a downcast, sideways glint, and she was gone.

"Doc.," he said, "it really was a lovely smile. A bonny face, all dimpled with fun, and an eye—a beautiful blue eye all sparkling with roguery."

When he came to himself he had rushed into the studio, and found Harry Low putting a few last touches to a canvas.

"Harry!" said Archie, "who's that girl?"

"Model," said Harry, stepping back to survey his work.

Which was a costume-piece—in profile. And when Archie had shaken him up a bit, Harry told him that the girl who'd just left had sat for it, and her name was Pansy Beam.

You'd have thought that name would have put Archie clean off. But not it! He was fair gone on her.

The long and short of it was that he was there at the same time the next day, and Harry made Pansy and him known to each other.

"And that's where I blame Harry," he said. "He might have warned me! He might have warned me."

The courtship was brief. Archie took the girl to tea at the Cri., and one or two things like that, and then proposed.

"It was only then that, in the heat of the moment," said Archie desperately, "as she said 'Yes!' that she turned full-face to me, and I knew the worst."

"What do you mean?" asked the Doc.

"My dear Doc., she has a dreadful squint in the right eye."

"And do you mean to say you hadn't seen it before?"

"No, never! The girl was clever, and she'd told me she was a trifle deaf in her right ear. As you know Doc., my left lug has been useless ever since Maggersfontein. So that suited me perfectly. I always walked and sat on her left side."

"But, my dear Archie, when you met and—well—saluted."

"Oh, she was coy, and always half turned away her head. By Jove, though, she must be clever,—the way she manœuvred—always showing me her good profile. Just like the—the——."

"Like the moon?"

"That's it. Like the moon. And I bet the other side of the moon squints like blazes. But now what the deuce am I to do?"

Why go on? The Doc knew the sort of man Archie was, and that, having given his word to the girl, he'd keep it. So she consoled him with the fact that you have no need to look at your wife once you've married her.

But Archie said, through clenched teeth: "Doc., when I tackle a job, I tackle it. I'm going to learn to like that squint. I think I'll trot round to the Vicarage and see George about the banns."

They were married in the Spring of 1914. And as soon as the honeymoon was over, they went off to South Africa, where Archie had bought some vineyards. Then the war came, and before the Declaration Archie was on his way home to join up.

That wasn't unfaithfulness. Archie had to be in a fight. And he *did* hate the Hun.

But about fights: During the Suffragist riots Archie had gone to Parliament Square because he'd heard that trouble was expected there. And when he saw some of the girls being hauled along and one of them biting a policeman, he cried, "Bravo, lassie!" and was about to fling himself into the fray when a sergeant put his hand on Archie's shoulder, and said, "You go home, sir, or you'll get your pockets picked."

That brought Archie up short, for he is instinctively on the side of law, if not of order. So he cursed the police roundly for a lot of something bullies, and went to his paper and wrote a stinging notice of Epstein's new show.

To return to our muttons,—Archie joined up, and his Boer War record got him a commission at once and his company before he went out.

The only incident while he was in camp on Salisbury Plain was that of the Praying Mat.

Archie was a regular churchgoer, but he felt compelled to dodge the Church Parade because he had no sword—funds hadn't run to it.

So on his first Sunday morning in camp he put a mat outside his tent, and lay down inside the tent for a smoke.

As the battalion passed by, on the way to Church, the O.C.'s horse shied at the Praying Mat, and the O.C. asked what the devil was that loathsome object. He was told it was Captain Boyd's Praying Mat.

"Praying mat?" roared the old man. "Take it away, and request Capt. Boyd to report to me what he means by it."

Accordingly Archie sent a chit by his batman to say that he'd become a "Muscleman." And the O.C. roared again, and told them to fetch Capt. Boyd at once.

"Capt. Boyd," said the old man, while Archie was getting his breath. "The Moslem religion is a dam good one. I know. I've served in the East. If you haven't the sense to be a Christian, it's the only religion for a gentleman! But . . ."—and then he looked as if he was going to roar for a Court Martial— "Dam it all, man, you can't even spell it."

Archie grinned, but the old man's face didn't twitch.

"Tell me," said the O.C., "Have you in fact a religion?"

"I'm a Quaker," said Archie, solemnly. And then the old man did roar, though whether with anger or joy no man knoweth.

"You will be on Church Parade next Sunday," he said quietly. And Archie was. He sold an article on "Humours of Camp Life" to pay for the sword.

There was another half an incident.

As soon as Archie came down to the Plain he spotted a German in the ranks. A private soldier, obviously a foreigner, tubby and fat-faced, who walked like a walrus. In fact, to Archie's mind, a typical Hun.

So Archie kept his eye on the fellow. And he noticed that he seemed to dodge parades—not Church Parades, as anybody might—but ordinary ones. Obviously he wanted to go snooping around gathering information on the disposition of the troops, which, during the rains and the floods, was unruly.

Finally Archie saw the Hun hanging round the officers' quarters. With a wild cry he leapt after him. The man cast one horrified glance at Archie's face, and then ran for it.

Considering his weight the Hun was a good sprinter, and he'd almost reached the horse-lines (somehow Archie knew he'd make for the horses) before Archie caught him up.

Then, on the sound old principle of Jeddart justice, Archie lambasted him before hearing the evidence. The Hun was in a bad way when he was rescued.

"Hang it all," said the O.C., "he's the regimental cook."

Archie looked on the Hun in deepest horror, and from that moment he dined in the canteen.

Oh, by the bye, just before Archie's bunch went out, he came to town on his last leave, and met the Doc., who was on leave from the front.

He was beaming with delight.

"Doc.," he said, "I'm a father. Just had a cable. It's a boy."

Then his face fell. He seized the Doc.'s hands.

"Doc., tell me," he pleaded. And there was a pathetic tremble in his voice: "Is a squint hereditary?"

"Poll of the People"
By J. Desmond Gleeson

MOST people are aware that a *questionaire* is at present being sent out, asking for answers to about five queries with reference to peace, disarmament, the League of Nations and so on. Folk are, in fact, being asked to vote upon questions that have already been decided and on which propaganda has been running wild for months and months. The point is, however, that in this Ballot you are expected to say if you are in favour of this or that, to write "Yes" or "No" only. The questions have been framed so good-naturedly that you are not required to give any reasons for your views. You are asked "If," but there is sufficient tact among the examiners not to press for a "Why?" Now among the thousands who have heard of this Ballot is Mr. A. P. Herbert, one of the few respectable names still associated with journalism. Somehow Mr. Herbert seems to feel that this simple Ballot is hardly adequate in itself, that it scarcely covers all the points that matter in the modern world, that the richness of our common citizenship should express itself in fuller, finer manner. He has, therefore, supplemented the questions with a series of his own, no less than 56 of them, ranging widely and even a little wildly, over the whole course of human life. These questions appear in the current issue of *Punch*—current to me, of course; I cannot say what it will be to you. It is quite obvious that such a set of questions cannot be left where they stand. An attempt must be made to answer them, nor shall I be deterred therefrom on account of their great number and the fact that many are sub-divided into a, b, c, d, etc.; or even that A.P.H., not content with asking his searching questions, every now and then pulls the student up with a sinister " Why?"

* * * *

The series starts (strangely enough) (1) Do you like Mr. Lloyd George?

Answer. No, but Lloyd George does.

(2) Do you walk under ladders?

A. Having at one time in my picturesque career been a window-cleaner I have walked up and down ladders, and people who so use them are very little concerned about whether they walk under them. There may be a moral here.

(3) Would you like to have your time over again?

A. Which time? Life is made up of times outside, as well as inside, prison, bits of all right and hard times, and some would bear repetition, some wouldn't. But anyway, A.P.H. can't give me my time over again whether I want it or not.

(4) How often do you write to the papers?

A. I must interpose here with a loud " Oy! " This is hardly a question for A.P.H. to ask anyone. Let the guy who is innocent of writing for papers cast the first stone. My collection of rejection slips is a sacred matter.

(5) Were your schooldays the happiest days of your life?

A. Not on your life; window-cleaning was infinitely preferable.

(6) Do you ever have a queer sensation that what is happening to you has happened before?

A. I swear by the nine gods of Lars Porsena that I have never answered these 56 questions before, in any age, under any sun, moon or stars.

(7) Has it? Give examples.

A. Pub with strange sign: What's yours? Same again; s'luck!

(8) Have you made the smallest attempt to understand the Gold Standard?

A. Yes, exactly; the smallest attempt, and refuse to repeat it.

(9) Do you read leading articles?

A. No, but I am quite prepared to write them, my boy.

(10) Have you (a) a sense of humour? (b) a broad mind? (c) a will of your own? (d) sound ideas about most things?

A. In short, do I read the leading advertisements? No, and don't even write them.

(11) Have you ever seen a lord drunk?

A. It was once my proud privilege to help to make

a lord drunk. The process improved him out of all knowledge.

(12) How will you vote at the General Election?

A. Not at all.

(13) Are you married?

A. What the hell's that got to do with you?

(14) Why?

A. Same as Answer 13, but with greater emphasis.

(15) In your experience, which of the following is true:—

(a) "Absence makes the heart grow fonder"? (b) "Out of sight is out of mind"?

A. Even when out of sight I rarely go out of my mind and my heart behaves itself under most circumstances. I think, though, that these quotations are but expressions of one mood, which fancies that if each of us keeps to his own side of the street, we shall not fall out. Shakespeare expressed it thus: a plague on both your houses.

(16) Do you feel that if you were Dictator for one year you could put most things right?

A. One year? After answering all these questions I could do anything or anybody in less than a month.

(17) How would you begin?

A. By making another small attempt to understand the Gold Standard.

(18) Can you make (a) a pie, (b) a bowline, (c) a speech, (d) money, (e) friends, (f) love?

A. For answers to a, c, and e, you must consult my victims. A bowline is only just beyond my capabilities. Love? Why, ladies vary so much that I am bound to confess that whereas I have made love, I have also failed to make love. As to money, should I be spending my time with these questions if I have anything else to spend?

(19) Have you ever served on a jury?

A. No, sir, I have not.

(20) Did you enjoy it?

A. Yes, I think I enjoyed not serving on a jury.

(More next week, children.)

When Florence Copied London
By Barbara Barclay Carter

BELISHA Beacons and decorative crossings and all the turmoil their first appearance caused, recall the day when the City of Florence first learned the meaning of Traffic Control.

Till then, there was at least one city where the rights of pedestrians were sacred and pre-eminent. Motorists who had mown their way across Tuscany, in Florence were brought up short by a solid mass of people, strolling, standing, gesticulating, who remained unmoved amid the shouts of cabbies, the screech of horns, and the continuous clang of trambells. In Florence the streets were still used for the purposes for which, in wiser days, they were designed —to be walked in.

And then in one night, all was changed. In the morning, posted up at every corner, appeared an edict signed by the Mayor. Maybe he had been studying English in the English papers; or perhaps some friend had returned still aglow with the reverent enthusiasm that London policemen on point duty arouse in foreign visitors, and had stirred him to emulation. Should England, the land of *laissez faire* show more order than a land where Discipline had become a watchword? Never! Let traffic in Florence be as strictly regulated as traffic in London—with the natural improvements that would suggest themselves to the logical Latin mind.

And when the next day dawned there were one way streets, and streets sacred to motors, and streets where motors were forbidden, and a limited number of places where cabs might stop, and at every crossroad gendarmes with batons specially distributed (it being recognised that the revolvers they usually carried did not entirely meet the case). And the Via Tornabuoni was as Piccadilly, and the whole city one vast Trafalgar Square.

But here comes the innovation. What boots it to have regulated traffic with an unregulated pedestrian? Florence anticipated London. Latin legislation in general has small sympathy for the pedestrian, considering him an untidy, inchoate mass, rather like the Irishman's pig that could not be counted because it ran about too much. In France, as is well-known, if run over he can be fined for obstructing the traffic. In Florence it was thought sufficient to keep him in his place, i.e., the pavement, by rigorous fines.

In this measure, one thing was forgotten. That the average width of a Florentine pavement is a bare two feet—when it exists at all.

" To the pavement! To the pavement!" vociferated the gendarme on point duty, waving his baton.

And from a plump citizen rose a wail of exasperation:

" But how can one walk on the pavement when there isn't one?"

Neither was the gendarme as reminiscent of London as he liked to be thought. At the passage of an Englishman he would swell out his chest and flash his baton in the most professional manner. But at other times his face was crumpled up in the anguish of making his meaning plain to a crowd to whom a policeman on point duty seemed an amusing and bewildering novelty. At his feverish beckoning a bluebloused peasant, pushing a barrow, stopped dead, and gaped at him with wide blue eyes, wondering, evidently, whether he was beckoning to his sweetheart, or doing callisthenics, or out of his wits; never dreaming he was signing to *him*.

Nor did the new regulations make for the happiness of the cab-drivers. No longer could they be hired for the whole morning and ordered to drive from shop to shop or from gallery to gallery, but the moment their fare had set foot on the ground the ubiquitous gendarme would be signing for them to whip up their horses. There was a lady out driving with her niece who told the cabby to drive to a shop where she could buy some soap. So following a basic Italian instinct, he took her to a tobacconist's that had a side-line in soap, sweets and coffee. But no sooner had the niece disappeared into the shop than the gendarme was waving him forward. The lady protested; the cabby, with much tact, engaged the gendarme in a long and sympathetic conversation, and only thus was the situation saved.

Meanwhile, driven desperate by gyratory orders, motor-buses wandered unhappily down streets where no motor-buses should have been. I forget how many hundred people appeared at the police-station to pay the fines incurred on that memorable day. The papers on the morrow were a tale of woe, and, Fascist though they were, one and all pleaded for milder measures. Perhaps they realised that the City of Flowers could not, in a single night, become as London or New York.

Books

The Mind of Napoleon

THE MIND OF NAPOLEON.   *By R. McNair Wilson.*
Routledge.   10s. 6d.

MR. WILSON'S books rank with those of **Mr.** Belloc as obligatory textbooks of Distributism, and in reviewing one of them in *G.K.'s* one is entitled to assume that those who read the review have a previous acquaintance with the author's point of view. Those who have read " Monarchy and Money-power " will recognise the present volume as a " close up " of what was really the central episode in the earlier work. Napoleon was the first leader to fight the newly-risen Money-power on equal terms. After his defeat, the thing was never seriously challenged until to-day; when the battle has been renewed on a vaster scale, and under strangely different leadership. For Roosevelt is the completest possible antithesis to Napoleon in every respect save one: his hold on the love and trust of his people that no enemy can loosen.

It is unjust to say that English historians always belittle England's enemies. On the contrary, they have slavered over Washington and sentimentalised over St. Joan. But with Napoleon, dead or alive, they hold no truce. And the reason is that he was the enemy of a bigger thing than England—of a Power which during the Nineteenth Century nobody dared to question. In the present volume that Power is represented primarily under the guise of International Finance: but that is only one of his aspects. Taken as a whole, it represents the growing stream of hostility not merely to Christianity, but to the European tradition which was old before Christianity came into the world. Certain picturesque—not to say sensational—writers trace the growth of this Power back to the builders of Solomon's Temple: a conscious and organised Diabolist conspiracy in which Hiram of Tyre, the Old Man of the Mountains, Jacques de Molay, Anachaisis Cloatz, Weisshaupt, Lenin, and (probably) Mrs. Naomi Mitcheson, all play their allotted parts. But, without accepting the Protocols of Zion as an altogether authentic document, we are justified in believing the allegory it conveys. If so, Napoleon, though a doubtful Christian, ranks as one of the greatest champions of Christendom.

On its economic side, this secular contest is summed up in the word Usury; and the issue was joined when Usury returned to the world with the break-up of the mediæval economy. When a community passes from the static to the progressive stage, the capitalist becomes a " Venturer." He is thus subject to a twofold risk—the failure of his venture, or the failure of the market for the goods that the venture produces. But if he can persuade the working partner to pay him not a fixed proportion of the profits of the venture but a fixed sum of money, he avoids both these risks: he thus ceases to be a venturer and becomes a usurer. If, in addition to this, he is able to advance capital which he does not possess, he becomes a banker. And if, furthermore, he is able to manipulate price-levels so that the value of the money payable to him under the contract is greater than when the contract was made, he becomes a financier.

But the Financiers whom Napoleon was up against had even further strengthened their position by concealing it. The private money-lender can never be a popular figure, and is liable to be swept away on a wave of public indignation. But the Neckers and Barings lent their money to the State, and thus made the Tax-gatherers their debt-collectors. Thus public odium was diverted from the real offenders to the State and its agents, and (more justifiably) to the privileged classes who escaped their fair share of the tax-burden. Meanwhile the real offenders, by subsidising the propagation of the new Liberal economic doctrines, were able to pose as public benefactors and apostles of enlightenment. It is this alliance of the Usurer and the Highbrow which is the fundamental principle of Modernist strategy.

The one force which can oppose the Usurer is the State. But if the State is a merely materialistic organisation, it will inevitably be captured by the enemy. It is Dr. Wilson's view that the only alternative to a materialistic State is the sacramental conception of Monarchy—the mediæval synthesis of the barbarian War-Chief and the Oriental Priest-King which found its highest development in the descendants of Hugh Capet. Even in post-mediæval days and under progressive connditions this system continued to justify itself: the great constructive Statesmen of France—men like Sully and Colbert—were essentially King's servants. But by 1789 it had degenerated perhaps more than Dr. Wilson would admit. Nor perhaps, in his advocacy of Monarchy does he do full justice either to the ideals of the Republicans nor to their actual achievements. Doubtless the Financiers intended to capture the *petit bourgeois* who were the backbone of the Revolution: but somehow in the welter of the Terror, their plans went wrong: and at the end we have the small men of the Towns in firm alliance with a firmly established Peasantry. That alliance has never been broken; and thus there has never been in France that united *Bourgeois* front which has prevented all real popular reform in England. Here the middle-class hate the poor: in France (and in these other European nations where Revolutionary ideas spread) they hate the rich. Probably it was an obscure realisation of this fact which made Wellington say that Napoleon was no gentleman.

Another popular misconception is that he was an " adventurer." On the contrary, no leader ever dedicated himself more completely to a single public

purpose. As a lawgiver and as a soldier he stands out at every point as the champion of the people against that plutocracy which had its headquarters in Lombard Street. That England should have been his adversary in this fight, is one of the great tragedies of history. Yet God forbid that in these days when so many make a cult of dishonour, that we should say a word to belittle England's heroic hour or the glory of those men who

" Lay in living ruins, facing and fearing not
     The strange fierce face of the Frenchmen who
        knew for what they fought."

Napoleon, as Dr. Wilson says, waged war on English trade not because he hated England, but because it was the only way to hit the Financiers. The reasons why he failed are well known. Dr. Wilson would apparently have us believe that all his most fatal decisions were necessary to his policy: but this is the least convincing part of his book. To outrage Catholic feelings throughout the world in order to stop a minor leak in his already leaky Continental system; to invade Russia with a half-tamed Europe behind him; to treat the subjugation of Spain as a side-line—such miscalculations as these can only be explained as the lapses of a tired man. And how could he not be tired, with always the blunders of a Junot or a Lefebvre to retrieve, or the treacheries of a Talleyrand or a Bernadotte to parry? For the men who should have been his servants—men like Carnot and Condorcet—were dead or exiled. No great man ever had smaller men to serve him. And in this there is a ray of hope for us. If Roosevelt is destined to be the Napoleon of the coming revolution, he has this great advantage that he has come before the Terror, not after it. The gentlemen most competent to help him still carry their heads on their necks.

C.E.B.

The Reviewer's Dilemma
By Peter Quince

WE live in an age of canning; yet if you were to tell the mildest of mankind in a public place and among his friends, to " can it," meaning in vulgar terms either to cease or change the conversation, he would show justifiable anger at your manner of address.

It should of course be a compliment. Music, literature, and even conversation is canned quite regularly these days. A man will tell you all about Mr. Big Hit and you will bow humbly as though in the presence of one who served about the feet of this idol. But to the simple question, " Have you seen him lately?" you will hear the reply " Oh, I've never met him. I hear his broadcast talks sometimes,"—and there you are. Next time you meet Mr. Big Hit or someone like him tell him his conversation is worth " canning " and see what he has to say!

In journalism, likewise, this canning business does not only affect the cinema and wireless correspondents. It further affects the interests of their usually elder but poorer brother the literary critic, especially in this matter of Omnibus Editions.

Now omnibus editions are excellent things. They serve a purpose and that purpose is to give a handy book of reference on the particular subject dealt with. But they are not to be used for the purpose of arriving at a criterion about a certain man's work, and hence they are a bugbear to the unfortunate reviewer. Let me illustrate.

Mr. Rafael Sabatini—I know not exactly with what qualifications—has edited a most excellent omnibus called " A Century of Sea Stories " (Hutchinson, 3s. 6d.), but if the reviewer is to do his duty he is to contrast the work of Mr. W. W. Jacobs, with that of Mark Twain; the work of Conrad with that of Clark Russell, and, most difficult of all, the work of people like Capt. Alexander Bone, who is a practical sailing ship master, with the work of men who have only encountered salt water in the brine baths at Droitwich. Such work is possible but would run into volumes.

The value of an omnibus is solely as a book of reference full of enjoyable things to those who are interested in those particular matters dealt with. It is an encyclopædia of one's favourite subject if you like, and as such it would be hard to find a better example than that offered to the public by Messrs. Hutchinson and Mr. Rafael Sabatini. Forty-seven authors and over a thousand pages of nautical yarns and adventure are worth anybody's 3/6, but do not, I implore you, sit down and read it straight through as a friend of mine once did with six different books on the same subject and remained for the rest of his life hopelessly confused as to who had written which. And, secondly, do not set up as an authority upon a man's work because you have read a short story by him in an omnibus. Select your tools for the work or pleasure to be undertaken, and use them only for their right purpose.

SKIN AND BONE. *By Edwin Greenwood. Stanley Paul. 7s. 6d.*

The Engleton family owed its rise to the peerage and its wealth to the spoliation of the monasteries. But time brought at least one revenge. Although the parvenu had become by the twentieth century, the aristocrat, the family fortunes had so far declined that Engleton Priory was heavily mortgaged and Lord Engleton, a minor, was allowed a strictly limited sum of pocket-money.

Mr. Greenwood's story concerns a desperate attempt by Arabella, Lady Engleton, dowager and matriarch, to re-create wealth. Her ancestor had robbed the church of land; she would rob her relatives of money, property and life. She began by summoning a family conference.

The idea was unfolded. Lord Engleton would come of age in a short time. Why not give him at least some expectation of an income? She proposed that the other members of the family should insure their lives for varying sums to be paid to Lord Engleton after they had died. And as she had her way in most things, the insurances were duly effected; except in the case of Fr. Reginald, who had offended Arabella by becoming a Catholic and a priest.

Then began a series of coldly calculated murders. A senile clergyman was given a hot-water bottle that leaked. A major was killed " by accident " in the gun room, liniment was poured into the near-whisky distilled by two spinsters; and a lady who threatened to interfere with Arabella's plans, was offered poisoned sandwiches. Fr. Reginald averted the last catastrophe, and Arabella died as a result of taking some of her own medicine.

That humour should spring from a plot such as this would seem unlikely, but Mr. Greenwood has followed an old tradition by making the reader laugh over some of his most startling situations, which display a lively imagination and follow one another so quickly that the reader forgets to question their practical absurdity. But some of the laughter might well be checked. Arabella is an unpleasant maniac, and the victories scored over an acidulated spinster were hardly worthy of description. Moreover hero and heroine deliver accepted judgment against themselves when they call each other prigs. Indeed among all characters what sympathy can be offered goes out first to the broken daughter of a profiteer, frank in her immorality, victim of wealth, whose heart is genuinely stirred for the first time by the hero and who finally departs to complete the wrecking of her life. She is a tragic figure.

An unusual plot, the expression of anger through farce and melodrama, and the considerable skill shown in characterisation make " Skin and Bone " a novel that cannot be placed in any particular category. By some it will be regarded as being definitely unpleasant. Others will find it entertaining, even where it goes too far. Its originality cannot be questioned.   E.J.M.

The Cockpit.

[*No letter should exceed 300 words in length. The Editor does not accept responsibility for the views expressed by Correspondents.*]

Sir,—Reasons not unconnected with pressure of other work have kept me from replying to Mr. Cargill's letter of November 15.

While admitting the quotation from Bishop Lesley, I should like to draw attention to the following points.

(1) Bishop Lesley was acquainted with public affairs only after 1560, and there is no evidence that his statement about pre-Reformation Scotland is statistical, or other than an opinion.

(2) These lands were not ' owned ' in the modern sense. There is a similar statement that the Church held one tenth of the land in England at the time of the Reformation. The economist Savine has investigated this and shown it is absurd as a *modern* statement: the Church possessed in most cases only rights to small fees and jurisdictional rights which were popularly described as ownership.

(3) Much the same system was prevalent in Scotland. All the Church got was the customary rent or service. It had not full rights as in modern ownership. Also, although these lands were often held in commendam by the King and nobility; in documents they would be entered as Church lands, and it is the case that the Church often had to borrow money to pay taxation on them.

We can sum up this part of the problem by saying that, in the sense of modern heritable ownership carrying full power of development, the Church *owned* nothing like one half of the lands of Scotland.

With regard to Mr. Cargill's second point, it is obvious that since there was little chance of freedom of ownership for the small man until late in the Middle Ages, it was better that the Church should hold the land and till it efficiently and with due regard for their tenants than that it should be entirely in the hands of a marauding nobility.

Mr. Cargill denies that there is any evidence for the existence of a universal right to education before the Reformation. I have already indicated where that evidence is to be found. I can do no more.

If by "justly and fairly" Mr. Cargill means complete tolerance of any philosophy or creed, i.e., its theory *and* practice, most people are unjust and unfair as well as the clerics. Anyway, surely it was the impoverishment of the Church of Scotland by the rapacious nobility that tied its hands with regard to Education, not the nature of the cleric.

With all due respect to Mr. Cargill I do not think I am " off the rails " with regard to the teaching of English in Scottish schools. If any of the acts of the pre-Reformation Church could have been criticised it might have been its acquiescence (powerless, no doubt, in most cases) in the Court policy of favouring English as against Gaelic. The same political hostility between two sections of the country almost shipwrecked the Faith in Ireland at the Reformation. It was up to the Reformers to point the way and unite the country in one language as well as one Faith. It is noteworthy that they failed to improve on their predecessors.   A. BOYLE.

Sir,—I read with interest in your issue of Monday, December 3rd, a note concerning the Report of the Joint Select Committee for Indian Constitutional Reform.

Knowing as I do for how long Mr. Chesterton has stood for Right, and the security of the weak and oppressed, I trust that your journal will give a lead to the large number of intelligent and thoughtful people who subscribe to it, on this vital question. It requires little thought to realise that these " Reforms" will serve to bring about a situation repugnant to every idea of justice or the fulfilment of solemn pledges.

I am a fervent believer in the advancement of India towards responsible government, but I am not a believer in the creation of an oligarchy maintained in power by an electorate divided into narrow communal groups, and based upon educational and property owning qualifications which will leave the destinies of India in the hands of urban interests, to the utter ruin and neglect of the inhabitants of the five hundred thousand villages of India, towards whom our chief duty lies.

Moreover, the orthodox Hindu, who is not invariably the cruel and sex-obsessed tyrant portrayed by too many Western writers on India, regards with the greatest dismay the prospect of the reduction of the peoples of India to the cigarette-smoking, machine-worshipping, " cinema fans " who make up the servile populations of England and the United States. Their view (and since it is the view of men who are regarded with veneration by 210 millions of Indians it is worth respecting) is made very clear in a remarkable book entitled " India's Higher Call " by Mr. Acharya, who gave evidence before the Joint Select Committee—evidence which repays study, and which appears to have escaped the notice of all but the Conservative minority members of the Committee, who make some reference to it in their independent report.

If the present proposals pass into law, as they seem only too likely to do, a death blow will have been struck to the cause of true civilisation, and India must inevitably, in a comparatively brief period historically speaking, sink into the chaotic condition which now prevails in China, where, as is revealed in to-day's newspapers, 13,000 soldiers have only recently been killed in a series of minor actions on the borders of the Kwangsi and Hunan provinces.

DAVID WOODFORD.

Sir,—All systems of economics rely on systems of philosophy. F.K.C.'s Distributism rests on a philosophy, though he may not be aware of the fact. My own Distributism rests on premises drawn from the Aristotelian-Thomistic philosophy, and, for the sake of intellectual clarity, it was necessary to indicate this.

As for the list of passages deemed controversial, it was not possible to offer complete logical proof for them in an Outline, nor, I am afraid, is it possible in a letter. Still, if the Editor and F.K.C. are willing to stand it, I can write a series of articles for *G.K.'s* using each of the controverted passages as a text.

I was afraid my remark about slavery would cause a disturbance, and apparently it has. But if F.K.C. is going to hold that slavery is unnatural and immoral, he must follow out the logical consequences of his assertion, and hold that St. Paul and St. Thomas Aquinas (who both accepted it) taught immoral things. The Servile form of society has been so widespread that it is impossible to regard it as against man's nature. We may dislike it, and regard as highly imperfect, and do our level best to prevent its return, but we must recognise it for what it is.

W. P. WITCUTT.

Sir,—In his article on the Land Schemes Mr. Kenrick seems rather too sweeping when he states that those inaugurated up to the present " have been more or less complete failures.'' Under the various schemes from 1908 up to 1926, about 26,000 men were put on holdings of their own. Of these over 19,000 holdings were still in existence up to a few years ago and I don't think there is any evidence of many of these being given up.

Surely a percentage of 73 per cent. cannot be described as a failure.

With the rest of the article one cannot but agree; it forms a distinct step forward in the consideration of the only principles on which land settlement can be successful. Incidentally the schemes above referred to were of course subsidised by the Government, and it was only with the ending of that subsidy in 1926 that the movement came to a standstill.

ELSMERE HARRIS.

Sir,—Since I gather from your paper that many of its contributors are students of Jacobite history, I would be very grateful if any of them would lend me information on the following points:

Is (or was) there not a paper devoted to that idea?

What are (or where can I procure) the original Jacobite words of the National Anthem?

CHARLES SCHWARZENBERG.

Sir,—With nearly everything Mr. Kenrick says about " The Land Schemes " I am in agreement; but when he suggests, as he seems to in his last paragraph, that any scheme starting with less capital than £50,000 unencumbered is doomed to failure from its commencement, I differ. Certainly, to have such capital available would be a tremendous advantage; but the progress made by the Marydown scheme in its first year with only a mere fraction of that capital shows that a good deal can be done on far less. Started only a year ago on land that had been derelict for years and under every sort of adverse condition, the Marydown farmers have already come within sight of being self-supporting; and the little capital but much faith of the first Marydowners, coupled with unlimited grit and capacity for hard work, has produced something which can offer both inspiration and hope for the future. If we are to wait for £50,000 we shall, I am afraid, wait a very, very long time. But if there are any wealthy sympathisers with the land movement willing to put up that sum Marydown has the waiting-list, the experience, and the plan to use it to the best advantage.

T. W. C. CURD.

CHARMING BOOK GIFTS

G. K. CHESTERTON'S "Ballad of St. Barbara." Last few copies. 1st Edition special ¼ leather binding. Pub. 7/6, offered 3/6. 2nd Edition, cloth boards, Pub. 5/-, offered 2/3.

G. K. CHESTERTON'S "Ballad of the White Horse." Beautiful edition, with Austin's wood cuts; bound full cloth gilt. Pub. 12/6, offered at 7/6.

CLIFFORD BAX'S PLAYS: "Rose and Cross," "Prelude and Fugue," and "The Cloak," in one De Luxe Volume. Illustrated in colour. Limited, numbered and signed by both Author and Artist. A sumptuous gift for lovers of the good drama. Published at £2 2s. net. Offered at 5/6 post free.—Manager, G.K.'s Weekly, 2, Little Essex Street, W.C.2.

CHRISTMAS. A poem by B. H. Johnson. Printed by Ditchling Press. Woodcut frontispiece of The Madonna. 1/-.—Magnani and Son, Ltd., 6, Maiden Lane, Strand.

"TWO SIDES OF A PENNY," by Man and Wife; T. A. and Brenda Murray Draper. "Distinctly original . . . striking thought, summed up with wit, force and humour." Unique gift book. Published 1/6 net (Boards 2/6 net).—Alex Moring, Ltd., 2a, Cork Street, Bond Street, W.1.

LITERARY

AUTHORS invited forward MSS. all kinds for publication. (Fiction specially required.) £50 cash for Poems. £5 5s. 0d. monthly for short Story. Particulars free.—Stockwell Ltd., 29, Ludgate Hill, London.

"PROSPERITY"

A MONTHLY SOCIAL CREDIT JOURNAL.

A Call to Action for Everyone.

Read: "Campaign from the Rhondda Valley," the Nation versus High Finance. Women actively interested in the abolition of poverty should read the Women's Supplement, now featuring. Order now. **Prosperity Office, Paynes Lane, Coventry.** Annual subscription, 2/6. Single copies, 2½d., post free.

NEW WITNESS

Bound Volumes, No's. 1, 3, 4, 5, 6, 7, 8, 19, 20, 21, For Sale, together or separately. Any reasonable offer considered.—Apply Box 453.

Advertise in G.K.'s Weekly

The paper that stands for and appeals to the small and independent craftsman, trader and shopkeeper.

"You will be interested to hear that G.K.'s Weekly pulled more business than £30 spent by a well-known firm of advertising agents in magazines they recommended."

"We find that our advertisements in your paper attract the sort of public we want."

"During the 12 months in which I have used your back page orders have come from nearly every county in England, and from Scotland, Ireland, Egypt, Palestine, Canada, United States, Nova Scotia, Australia, Spain, etc."

The charge for prepaid advertisements on this page is one penny per word; minimum 2s. Special discount rates are allowed, as follows:
Thick type in all cases is 20 per cent. extra.

4 insertions at 2s. per insertion costs	....	7/6
9 insertions at 2s. per insertion costs	....	15/-
15 insertions at 2s. per insertion costs	....	£1/2/6

Space is charged for at the rate of 5s. per inch.

Advertisements not paid for in advance cost 25 per cent. extra to above charges.

THE NEW OPERATIC ACADEMY

Musical Director:
HERMANN GRUNEBAUM
(Royal Opera, Covent Garden, etc.).
Stage Director:
LEIGHTON LUCAS
(late Diaghilef Russian Ballet and Birmingham Repertory Co.).
Now at THE CENTURY THEATRE, Archer-street, Westbourne-grove, W.11.
Telephone No. Park 6870.
SPRING TERM begins Monday, JAN. 21st.
Prospectus on application.

WHERE TO STAY

LEAMINGTON SPA. Splendid furnished flat to let. Sleep five. Or paying guests from £2/2/0. Reduction for two sharing, and to readers of "G.K.'s Weekly."—Alpha, 151, Leam Terrace.

LONDON Visitors; Westminster Bridge; central; bed-breakfast, 3/6 per night, £1 1s. 0d. weekly.—Powell, 75, Lambeth Palace Road, S.E.1.

DELANEY,

65, Bishop's Road, Bayswater, W.2.
Telephone: Bayswater 2589.

HOME MADE CAKES and BREAD.
No Powders. No Substitutes.

PURE SWEETS FOR THE CHILDREN.
Price 2/6 per lb.

HAND-MADE CHOCOLATES
Price 4/- per lb.
Postage 6d. extra.

MISCELLANEOUS

A WEST Country Farmer sends CLOTTED CREAM at farm prices: ½lb. 1s. 6d., 1lb. 2s. 10d., post paid. Perfect delivery guaranteed.—BEVINGTON, Trenoweth Farm (G), Connor Downs, Hayle, Cornwall.

EGGS straight from the farm. Three dozen upwards sent by rail at local market price plus carriage charges.—Moat Farm House, Chart Sutton, Maidstone.

CLOTHES OF CHARACTER.—Lounge Suits from 4 gns. Dress Wear from 5 gns. Overcoats from 4 gns. All hand finished.—S. G. Hunt, Monument Chambers, Eastcheap E.C.4. 1st Floor. Adjoining Monument Station.

STELLA AGENCY, 88a, George Street, Edinburgh. First class Employment Agency, for the Supply of Men and Women Servants, Private Houses, Hotels, Schools, Institutions.

MEMBERS of the Manchester Branch are advised that Mr. Lockhart, a craftsman, produces all kinds of knitted woollen goods on his own knitting machine. Jumpers, pullovers, men's socks, boys' stockings, cardigan jackets, etc. Support your own local craftsman. Send a postcard to Mr. W. L. Lockhart, 34, Broadlea Road, Kingsway, Burnage, when requiring any of the articles mentioned.

TYPEWRITING

TYPEWRITING beautifully executed on good paper and returned quickly. Each MS. quoted for as cheaply as possible.—John Stanley, 31, Warkworth Road, London N.17.

Published by the Proprietors, G.K.'s WEEKLY, LTD., 2, Little Essex Street, Strand, London, W.C.2 (Incorporating THE NEW WITNESS). Telephone: Temple Bar, 1978. Printed by THE NUNEATON NEWSPAPERS, LTD., Bond Gate, Nuneaton. Sole Agents for Australasia: Gordon & Gotch (Australasia, Ltd.). Sole Agents for South Africa: Central News Agency, Ltd. (London Agents: Gordon & Gotch, Ltd.).

GK's WEEKLY

EDITED BY G.K. CHESTERTON

MARCH 21 - - 1935
VOL. XXI.   No. 523

Registered as a Newspaper.   SIXPENCE

The 10th BIRTHDAY

GK's WEEKLY

Every Thursday   Sixpence.
SUBSCRIPTION RATES
One Year   ... £1 - 8 - 0   ($7.00)
Six Months   ...   14 - 0   ($3.50)
Three months ...   7 - 0   ($1.75)
                post free.
2, LITTLE ESSEX ST., STRAND,
            LONDON W.C.2.
        Temple Bar 1978.

Ten Years Ago

[*Extracts from the leading article in the first number of G.K.'s* WEEKLY, *March 21, 1925.*]

IT is all very well to repeat distractedly, "What are we coming to with all this Bolshevism?" It is as relevant to add, "What are we coming to even without Bolshevism?" The answer is: Monopoly. It is certainly not private enterprise. The American Trust is not private enterprise. It would be truer to call the Spanish Inquisition private judgment. Monopoly is neither private nor enterprising. It exists to prevent private enterprise. And that is the present goal of our progress, if there were not a Bolshevist in the world. This paper exists to demand that we fight Bolshevism with something better than plutocracy. But anyhow we must get something better than silence about plutocracy . . .

Aristocracy became powerful, much too powerful, because it did not consist of individuals but had a name like a nation. Democracy will never become powerful unless every family is a great family. Perhaps it would have been better if the French Revolution had extended and not extinguished heraldry; if stormers of the Bastille, having undoubtedly borne arms, had borne armorial bearings.

Anyhow the State will always defeat the individual; if the citizen is to rule he must be more than an individual. But do we want him to rule? Bolshevism does not; and Bolshevism is not alone in that. It is absolutely certain that democracy will not be democratic unless it is domestic. . . .

In short, these sages, rightly or wrongly, cannot trust the normal man to rule in the home; and certainly do not want him to rule in the State. They do not really want to give him any political power. They are willing to give him a vote; because they have long discovered that it need not give him any power. They are not willing to give him a house, or a wife, or a child, or a dog, or a cow, or a piece of land; because these things really do give him power.

Now we wish it to be understood at the start that our policy is to give him these things . . . We alone . . . have the right to call ourselves democratic. A republic used to be called a nation of kings; and in our republic the kings really have kingdoms. All modern governments, Prussian or Russian, all modern movements, Capitalist or Socialist are taking away that kingdom from that king. . .

It is a sad conclusion of the modern scientific advance that it leaves us with a choice between the impossible and the intolerable. For if we cannot go back, it hardly seems worth while to go forward. There is nothing in front but a flat wilderness of standardisation, either by Bolshevism or Big Business. And it is strange that we at least have seen sanity, if only in a vision, while they go forward chained eternally to enlargement without liberty and progress without hope.

To-Day

TEN years have brought few changes. In 1925 the attitude of G.K.'s WEEKLY was shown to a slightly sceptical world. To-day only this difference need be noted; that, whereas ten years ago our contributors were accused of being alarmists, they now run the risk of being platitudinous.

On our tenth birthday we publish a number of contributions by artists and writers, all of whom have their own points of view, with some of whom the staff of G.K.'s WEEKLY might sharply disagree. But all have something to say and know why they say it. In a sense this issue is presented as an extension of one feature—the Cockpit, the contributors to which are offered our warmest thanks.

Next week the Editor will offer encouragement to readers, by touching on one or two of the arguments that affect the distributist movement, as well as his personal position in politics and letters.

Straws in the Wind

Our Birthday

BY G. K. CHESTERTON

AS this is a Birthday Number, I propose to write about birthdays in a futile and irresponsible manner, as befits a festive occasion; and to leave for a later issue some of the serious questions that are raised in this one. I remember that long ago, in one of my countless controversies with Mr. Bernard Shaw, I commented on a scornful remark of his that he did not keep his own birthday and would not be bothered with anybody else's; and I argued that this exactly illustrates the one point upon which he is really wrong; and that if he had only kept his birthday, he might have kept many other things along with it. It will be noted that, with the magnificent magnanimity in which he has never failed, especially in dealing with me and my romantic delusions, he has contributed to this special number an article dealing with very vital matters. I hope to answer that article, in greater detail, in due course; here I will only give a very general reply upon the particular aspect which is excellently and exactly represented by Birthdays.

For one happy hour, in talking about Birthdays, I shall not stoop to talk about Birth-Control. But when Mr. Shaw asks why I doubt that he and I, not to mention Mr. H. G. Wells and Mr. Bertrand Russell, can form a committee to produce a creed, not to say a cosmos—my general answer is that the difference begins with the very birth of the conception. A Birthday embodies certain implicit ideas; with some of which he agrees and is right; with others of which he disagrees and is wrong. In some matters the difference between us seems to amount to this: that I very respectfully recognise that he disagrees with me; but he will not even allow me to disagree with him. But there is one fundamental truth in which I have never for a moment disagreed with him. Whatever else he is, he has never been a pessimist; or in spiritual matters a defeatist. He is at least on the side of Life, and in that sense of Birth. When the Sons of God shout for joy, merely because the creation is in being, Mr. Shaw's splendid Wagnerian shout or bellow will be mingled with my less musical but equally mystical song of praise. I am aware that in the same poem the patriarch Job, under the stress of incidental irritations, actually curses the day he was born; prays that the stars of its twilight be dark and that it be not numbered among the days of the year; but I am sure that G.B.S. will not carry his contempt for birthday celebrations to that length. The first fact about the celebration of a birthday is

that it is a way of affirming defiantly, and even flamboyantly, that it is a good thing to be alive. On that matter, and it is a basic matter, there really is a basis of agreement; and Mr. Shaw and I, giving our performance as morning stars that sing together, will sing in perfect harmony if hardly with equal technique.

But there is a second fact about Birthdays, and the birth-song of all creation, a fact which really follows on this; but which, as it seems to me, the other school of thought almost refuses to recognise. The point of that fact is simply that it is a fact. In being glad about my Birthday, I am being glad about something which I did not myself bring about. In being grateful for my birth, I am grateful for something which has already happened; which happened, sad as it may seem to some, quite a long time ago. Now it seems to me that Mr. Shaw and his school start almost everything in the spirit of people who are saying, " I shall myself select the 17th of October as the date of my birth. I propose to be born at Market Harborough; I have selected for my father a very capable and humane dentist, while my mother will be trained as a high-class headmistress for the tremendous honour and responsibility of her position; before that, I think I shall send her to Girton. The house I have selected to be born in faces a handsome ornamental park, etc., etc.'' In other words, it seems to me that modern thinkers of this kind have simply no philosophy or poetry or possible attitude at all, towards the things which they *receive* from the real world that exists already; from the past; from the parent; from the patriotic tradition or the moral philosophy of mankind. They only talk about making things; as if they could make themselves as well as everything else. They are always talking about making a religion; and cannot get into their heads the very notion of receiving a revelation. They are always talking about making a creed; without seeing that it involves making a cosmos. But even then, we could not possibly make the cosmos that has made us. Now nobody who knows anything about my little tastes and prejudices will say that I am not in sympathy with the notion of making things. I believe in making thousands of things; making jokes, making pictures, making (as distinct from faking) goods, making books, and even articles (of which, as the reader will sadly perceive, there is no end), making toys, making tools, making farms, making homes, making churches, making sacred images; and, incidentally also, making war on people who would prevent me from doing these things. But the workshop, vast as it is, is only one half of the world. There is a whole problem of the human mind, which is necessarily concerned with the things that it did not make; with the things that it could not make; including itself. And I say it is a narrow view of life, which leaves out the whole of that aspect of life; all receptivity, all gratitude, all inheritance, all worship. Unless a philosopher has a philosophy, which can make tolerable and tenable his attitude towards all the actualities that are around him and before him and behind him—then he has only half a philosophy; and, though he is the wittiest man in the world, he is in that sense half-witted.

Mr. Bernard Shaw is certainly one of the wittiest men in the world, and about whole huge aspects of life, one of the wisest. But if I am to sit down with him at a committee of evolutionists, to draw up a creed for humanity, I fancy I foresee that this is the line along which I shall eventually come to issue my Minority Report. I shall find myself the representative, and I suspect the only representative, of *all* the implications of my Birthday. I do not even mind calling it the pride of birth, which of course has nothing to do with the pride of rank; so long as it involves the humility of birth also.

Now We Are Ten
By Maurice B. Reckitt

THE writers most characteristic of our time are prone to warn us against ' living in the past ' and exhort us to dwell rather upon the future. This is regarded, for some reason, as a courageous attitude, calling for an exceptional degree of resolution and independence, but I have never been quite clear why. It is not exactly obvious for what reasons the men of this century should be tempted to revel in the only part the majority of them have known, abandoned to blissful contemplation of bureaucratic legislation and its servile consequences, Marconi scandals, shelling, machine-gun fire, air-raids, high prices, low wages, no wages, malnutrition and social despair. One would imagine that after thirty-five years of this, the man of the twentieth century would prefer to look in some other direction. If history knows anything of a law of averages, even a silver jubilee may have a silver lining—we are scarcely likely, it may be imagined, to be called on to endure another quarter of a century like the last. It is more consoling as our left-ward sociologists suggest, to write about ''the next ten years'' than about the last ten. It is also easier, neither chilling the imagination nor cramping the style.

It might be easier for us, too, now that we are ten, to concentrate on the future rather than the past, to dwell upon the dazzlingly brilliant numbers that we are going to issue, the colossal circulation by which we are going to eclipse all the records of Fleet Street, the vast influence which we shall wield, and the transformation of England which will come about as a result thereof. This would all be in the very best contemporary manner, which is so singularly ready to postulate the rapid development of men like gods out of social philosophies which would appear rather to demand men like ants. Yet I cannot believe that this is really the most fruitful way of celebrating a birthday. I will leave to others the fascinating task of interpreting 1945 before it arrives, and content myself with a few words about 1925 before its memory is lost to us.

1925 will be memorable—if we except the birth of this journal—for three things, Locarno, Gold and Coal. In regard to the first, the opinions of readers of this paper may, quite naturally and justifiably, be divided. My own, indeed, are divided, for I never thought very much of the ' Locarno spirit,' but I did think a good deal of the Locarno fact. It is suggestive that while we heard a great deal about the spirit, it evaporated in a few weeks, but that very little was said about the fact, which is one of the few really salient and, as I think, salutary facts of the post-war world. For the essence of that fact was the acknowledgment of this country's responsibility to the continent from which her culture sprang. It was a fact to which our more strident imperialists never reconciled themselves, and it is significant that our ' dominions,' very justifiably from their point of view, flatly refused to accept any obligations in connection therewith. Locarno involved the assertion by England of a partnership in something more important, because more fundamental, than either the Empire or the

League of Nations—a partnership in the affairs of Europe, sanction for which is to be found rather in the atlas and the history book than in the contemporary press, which never appears to consult either. This policy is one which seems to me clearly in line with the best traditions of this paper, and after ten years we ought still to rejoice that our country took those risks for a peace which has not yet broken down.

In 1925 Winston Churchill restored the gold standard at the instance of the Bank of England. The pound looked the dollar in the face; simultaneously our export trade began to look ruin in the face. After six years of " the economic consequences of Mr. Churchill," our political life had to be—or at any rate was—violently interrupted, again at the instance of finance, to produce a government to keep us on the gold standard at all costs. Within a month it took us off. This is not the place to interpret those events, or to analyse the meaning of what we were told was 'crisis' and what we are now (still more dubiously) told is ' recovery.' But I think the inescapable lesson of the last ten years is that there is a power at work in our modern communities which reduces political sovereignty to a mockery and subordinates human happiness to the rules of an inhuman game. I am aware that my incursions into these pages must have been rendered even more tiresome than might inevitably have been the case by my insistence on this fact. That something will have to be done about money-power, and done *first*, is however a conviction among Distributists in which I am by no means so lonely as in 1925.

In 1925 came the ' crisis ' in the coal industry, a crisis from which not even economists have been able to declare a ' recovery,' a crisis which, more completely than any other factor, has produced those ' depressed areas ' now accepted as a normal feature of our industrial civilisation. " Our civilisation is built upon coal," a certain famous triolet proclaimed, in the light of which statement the essential soundness and impregnability of that civilisation is now, of course, plain to all. The administration of such a national asset by plutocratic interests has doubtless been as reckless and incompetent as every impartial inquiry into the subject has declared it to be. But fundamentally the collapse of coal is only the most inescapable of many pieces of evidence that the whole economic theory of industrialism, based on overseas investment and forced export, is crashing to the ground. Very few were ready to draw that deduction in 1925, but it is implicit in the Distributist analysis, and with ten years of converging evidence to help us we might perhaps make it more explicit than we do.

There was another revelation to come out of the coal crisis, the full force of which was discernible, if not everywhere discerned, in its first consequence, the so-called 'general' strike of 1926. This revelation was the explosion of the century-old myth of the omnipotent proletariat. Ever since William Benbow had projected his scheme for a general holiday in the eighteen-thirties, Labour had inclined to believe that at a pinch it had the last trick up its sleeve. The defeat of the general strike was the extinction of a legend, the romantic legend that the workers had but to unveil their silent might and the citadel of capitalism would crumble away. How much heart went out of the masses of our people with the explosion of this vitalising myth we shall never know. It is difficult, however, to believe that faith in the power of a General Strike can have been placidly transferred to faith in the power of a General Election. If so, perhaps 1936 will complete the disillusion which 1926 so shatteringly began. But out of disillusion may come enlightenment—or despair.

A final point occurs to me when I consider the progress of these ten years. In one of the first articles I wrote for *G.K.'s* I sought to draw a moral from the complaint of a group of the unemployed that a ' mechanical navvy,' by doing a job infinitely more quickly and effectively than they could, was robbing them of that goal of human order, employment. I am not concerned now, however, with my old moral but with a new fact. For at the end of our decade the validity of this essentially proletarian contention has been accepted in one great centre of industrialism. A town council in Lancashire has decided to scrap the labour-saving devices by which its street scavenging and repairs were done and allows 'the workers' to enter once more into their great inheritance of toil. This time I will attempt no moral. I will not even speculate upon whether, at the end of another ten years, the public mind will perceive any distinction between the fantastic facts of employment and the authentic realities of work. But perhaps if we lived a little less in the future and thought a little more in the present, our civilisation, while it might fail to breed men like gods, might give itself the chance to exhibit men like men.

Harbinger's Gland

By J. B. Morton

I UNDERSTAND from the newspaper that the Ministry of Health has been conducting investigations of the highest importance. Carefully compiled statistics prove to all but the most captious that the standard of health among the destitute is lower than that among well-to-do. And it is thought that this may be due, in part, to the fact that the destitute get less to eat. The cure for this state of affairs is said to be an intensification of organised physical drill But the discovery of Harbinger's Gland, by a young scientist in the employment of the National Sociological League, will probably modify this official decision. For Harbinger has proved that the reason why the poor are in such a mess is because they lack this gland, which is a determining factor in building character. The actual spot in which the gland is situated has not been discovered. It may be above Bundle's ligament, or below the *adductor longus*, or between that and Helps' triangle. But, with frank generosity, Harbinger vouches for its existence, and its effects have already been tabulated.

In the course of his experiments Harbinger questioned large numbers of unemployed men and women, and at the end of a week he was able to distinguish those who had been out of work for years from their more fortunate fellows by a marked listlessness, a disinclination to undergo a long oral examination and a woeful lack of interest in the forthcoming general election. These characteristics, according to Harbinger, are exactly those which one would expect to find in people without the new gland. The Sociological League, therefore, is forced to consider whether it is really worth while doing anything for such people since, without the gland, they cannot become efficient members of any modern society. The impartial observer has only to study the photographs collected by the Statistical department of the League to be struck at once by the obvious truth of Harbinger's observations. Nobody could confuse the full, healthy faces of those who, possessing the gland, have made a comfortable position for themselves, with the thin, drawn faces of those whom Harbinger himself has called, in a forceful phrase, unproductive drones. The young scientist draws attention, in the case of the latter, to the narrow ilio-tibial band, the wasting of the *fascia lata*, the comparative absence of saphenous muscles, the low inner condyle, and all the other signs which the absence of the new gland would pre-suppose. One turns with relief from such parasites to the honest, laughing, confident face of the banker (Folio 6, page 39: " Creative Genius and Constructive Ability ").

Referring to Harbinger's work last week, the President of the League said, " Fortunate indeed is the country whose employed are the cream of the nation, and whose unemployed can be proved to be lacking in that one gland which is a *sine qua non* in every walk of life. And I have no doubt that, as the figures of the unemployed rise, month by month, science will have little difficulty in showing that such people never should have been employed at all. Thus will things find their own level."

It is significant, and no fact emerges more clearly from the report of the Sociological League on Harbinger's work, that the proportion of persons possessing the gland varies according to localities. In areas of chronic unemployment the proportion is staggeringly low, and the subjects whom Harbinger examined and questioned were, in almost every case, apathetic and hopeless. In the case of families kept under observation by the police, for purposes of classification, regimentation and broad-scale planning, it was noticed that the absence of the gland produced a nervous irritability and an unstable mentality. The men showed symptoms of nerve-lesion, and in some cases, of advanced physiological deterioration. The women were, as a general rule, hypochondriacal, morbid, acutely loquacious and, often neurasthenic. The children, as one would expect in the offspring of parents neither of whom possessed Harbinger's gland, appear to be fractious, stunted, pallid and ill-nourished. And Harbinger, in a long appendix to the report, asks, pertinently enough, how long a civilised country will allow this haphazard breeding among those whose dependence on charity debars them from any place in the civic scheme of the future world-state. In one northern town Harbinger recorded a state of melancholy, depression and mental rumination, sometimes amounting to self-centred introspection and psychasthenia, in more than three-quarters of the male population.

To the suggestion that it might be possible to graft the gland on to those who do not possess it, Harbinger returns the commonsense, realistic reply that it will be necessary, first, to find the gland itself; to locate it in the human body.

Meanwhile the Society for Eliminating the Inessential has put forward a suggestion which merits consideration and discussion. Broadly, the proposal is to husband the resources of the State in so far as they are required for the glandless. The new discovery has led to a modification of former ideas on the subject of food and clothing for the unsuccessful. Harbinger has established the important fact that the juices secreted by those who have not the gland, set up a fermentation in the digestive canals which takes the place of the nutritive properties in food-matter. They thus need less to eat, the mechanism underlying the chemical distribution through the alimentary channels of whatever is liberated by the Pylorus, being adjusted to the retarded blood-stream. Experiments made on the stomach of a cat show this to be beyond dispute. And a reflex secretion co-operating with the nerve-centres, counteracts the normal reaction to torn or threadbare clothing, by setting up, throughout the entire body, a form of anæmia which provides the mind with unconscious resistance to self-criticism in the matter of covering for the body. This is called the Higher Anæsthesia. By acting on this principle, and introducing food and clothing cuts, the Government should be able, at last to give relief in the Budget to the long-suffering and patient motorist by lowering the petrol tax, and to the hard-ridden financier by reducing the super-tax.

It is perhaps not too much to say that the discovery of Harbinger's Gland will revolutionise the attitude of the State to the poor.

"Alas! poor Shakespeare"

—WILL DYSON

Provocations

BY BERNARD SHAW

"I WONDER that you will still be talking: nobody marks you." Thus one of Shakespear's merry ladies three centuries ago. Any of the melancholy ladies of to-day might very well make the same remark to Mr. Chesterton or Mr. Wells or to myself. In the nineteenth century Queen Victoria might have said it to Dickens if any sort of contact between their minds had been possible.

My own reply would be "I also wonder." My works are a Bible in which men can find bases, or jumping off places, for the solutions of all the problems they are roaring about like beasts in a Zoo when an earthquake shakes them. The works of G.K.C. and H.G.W. are full of wisdoms and warnings that, if heeded, would have abolished war, epidemics, gangsterism, and all the horrors of capitalistic civilization long ago. We three roar louder, and over wider circulations, and much more amusingly than Ruskin, Marx, or Henry George. But nobody marks us.

We do not even mark one another, except in the sense in which men mark one another with tomahawks. And that sort of mark leaves no scar; for in our lonely stand *contra mundum* we dare not slay one another. To do ourselves justice we dont want to; but anyhow we have no *esprit de corps*. G.K.C. and H.G.W. have, I am convinced, as much personal affection for me as I am capable of inspiring; yet you would never gather from the allusions in our published works that we had ever learnt anything from one another or that we were agreed up to 98%. G.K.C. treats me as if I were incapable of positive dogmatic belief, because he has an inaccurate recollection of an occasion upon which I cornered him on the subject of miracles. I admit and even insist on miracles, not only as strange and occasional marvels, but as so intimate and omnipresent a part of our daily routine that every moment is a moment of creation and every creation a miracle. The question I raised was why, under these miraculous circumstances, there were so many alleged miracles at which we unaccountably jib, refusing flatly to believe in them whilst we are ready to stake our lives on the truth of much more miraculous events.

The truth is, I am a mystic, and have a mystic's eye for facts and an insatiable interest in them. In Wells's Science of Life, which future generations of children will devour under its proper title of Gip's Fairy Tales, I am described as a sentimental ignoramus who knows nothing about somatic cells and germ cells, or about hormones and chromosomes and genes. But at least I am biologist enough to know that the first problem of biology (and perhaps the last) is, what is the difference between a dead body and a live one? The account given by the authors of the Book of Genesis is not now sufficiently matter-of-fact; but they got a long way ahead of *fin de siècle* South Kensington through their perception that there is such a question.

Now why do not we three get together; fill up the gaps in one another's culture and knowledge; and present a united front to the Philistines? Well, look at our ages. I am, by the calendar, eighteen years older than Chesterton and ten years older than Wells. I am, for life insurance purposes, in my 79th year. But this figure is grossly misleading. I was born in Dublin in 1856, which may be taken as 1756 by London reckoning. I was contemporary with Swift and Johnson, and even with Samuel Pepys; for the smoke of battle from the Boyne had not cleared away from my landscape, nor the glorious pious and immortal memory of Dutch William faded from my consciousness, when my sense of history was formed. My classics were Handel, Haydn, Mozart and Beethoven, my light literature Schubert, Weber and Mendelssohn; and I was up to the larynx in the most romantic of all the romances: the Italian operas of Rossini, Bellini, Donizetti, Verdi and Meyerbeer. Ultra-modernity to me meant being a Wagnerian. Established religion had no hold on me: the Roman Church was struggling with a great mass of Irish poverty and vulgarity both in the priesthood and the laity; and the Protestant Episcopal Church, of which I was a baptised but unconfirmed member, was a flagrant organization of snobbery, jobbery, and robbery. Neither of them had sufficient spiritual energy to shed the mass of Bedouin superstition, Red Indian militarism, and tribal magic with which they were encrusted. I knew all about Wells's South Kensington stuff and about the Materialism of Tyndall and the Fatalism (now called Determinism) that sterilized poor George Eliot before the infant H. G. knew that such a thing as Science existed. When I landed in England (this earth-shaking event occurred in 1876. when Wells was ten and G.K.C. two) and wrote those dreadful old novels of mine, I found, when I had finished the second, that I could not get a step further with this equipment, and had to throw over Materialism and Determinism as hopeless no-thoroughfares before I could write a third. After that, I needed no conversion by Butler or Bergson to make me a confirmed Neo-Vitalist and Creative-Evolutionist. By 1880 (H.G. a blushing 17: G.K.C. 9), having discovered Sidney Webb and turned to economics and assimilated Henry George and Marx, I was ripe for the development of the Fabian Society in 1884. I had added Ibsen and Wagner (as prose writer) to my equipment, and had learnt my analytic business as a critic in letters, pictures, music, and the theatre (two thousand words a week for my bread and butter) before Wells suddenly arrived with his Time Machine. Evidently a recruit for the pioneers, and sure at his zenith to be a star of the first magnitude. Shortly after the turn of the century came the amazing Chesterton with vine leaves in his hair: a sort of Anacreontic Liberal, completely ignorant of the commonest facts of hygiene, and full of a boyish delight in Berserker battles which he could gratify only on paper; for when real war came single combat went into the air; and no aeroplane with G.K.C. on board could conceivably have left the ground, so exuberant were his proportions. He also was a gorgeous recruit to the vanguard. There were others, notably Bertrand Russell, two years older than Chesterton, but, as mathematician and academic philosopher, known only to a very select audience whilst Chesterton was bombinating all over the *Daily News* and Wells pouring out a torrent of popular stories of extreme readability. Him also I counted as a recruit because, like the other two, he was really revolutionary, and had extraordinary mental powers with practically unlimited command of literary self-expression.

Naturally people ask why, if we are revolutionaries, we do not collaborate and make a revolution? The short reply is that it is not our profession. We are authors, playwrights, journalists, prophets and sages; and our jobs as such are whole time jobs. Revolution is also both a profession and a whole time job. Marx was the first modern professional revolutionist. Trotsky, when he left school and had to choose a profession or business, quite deliberately chose the profession of revolutionist just as he might have chosen the profession of dentist or the business of stockbroking. Lenin did the same. It is not a profession to be approved by respectable parents as " a life not bad for a hardy lad." Its emoluments are persecutions, imprisonments, and martyrdoms, to say nothing of chronic and desperate pecuniary straits. The professional revolutionist has to " go underground," and sometimes stays there after an interview with the hangman or the firing squad. Nevertheless the call is strong enough to enlist recruits. Stalin, brought up to be a priest, felt he must be a Bolshevist instead.

The professional revolutionists provide a good deal of their own literature; but they are made self-conscious of their destiny by reading some book. That was how Marx, who spent his life in the reading room of the British Museum, turned the moral sense of his readers completely against Capitalism by the overwhelming mass of evidence he brought forward in a book to prove that capital in pursuit of profit is the most entirely and pitilessly wicked of all social forces. The change from the exultant Capitalist Meliorism of the Ricardian Benthamites and the pursepride of the millionaires to the Marxist conviction of sin was enormous. Nothing like it had occurred since the Reformation let the Bible loose. It produced the temper of Lenin, who, though a very amiable man, was prepared to kill "exploiters" of human labor as ruthlessly as cobras are killed in India. Except for Marx's mass of evidence, which was presently horribly increased by the Congo Rubber atrocities, it was not new. It was implicit in Goldsmith's Deserted Village and Bunyan's Life and Death of Mr. Badman; but it was the massed evidence that did the trick. Nobody could read through Marx's Capital and come out as he came out from reading Macaulay's History of England.

Hear Wells half a century later. " There can be no real social stability, nor any general human happiness, while large areas of the world and large classes of people are in a phase of civilisation different from the prevailing mass. It is impossible now to have great blocks of population misunderstanding the generally accepted social purpose or at an economic disadvantage to the rest. The peasant, the field worker, and all barbaric cultivators are at an economic

disadvantage to the more mobile and educated classes; and the logic of the situation involves the supersession of this stratum by a more efficient organisation of production. It involves the progressive establishment throughout the world of a modern stratum in agriculture: a stratum giving the full advantages of a civilised life to every agricultural workman." The Class War view, already dramatized by Wells in Tono Bungay and other fictions, here finds unequivocal academic expression.

Three years later the Russian Bolsheviks came into political power and soon found out the truth of Wells's teaching. They formed a very high opinion of Wells and looked forward with interest and high expectation to visits from him, so that they might shew him in full operation just this process which he foretold. Stalin arranged to meet him and to have his oracles carefully reported and preserved.

Alas! Stalin and the Russian Wellsites did not know that an Englishman's capacity for uttering inspired truths is accompanied by an equal capacity for totally forgetting them five minutes later. This, which was Morris's criticism of Ruskin, provoked Inge's despairing contrast of the English with the Irish as " a people that never remembers and a people that never forgets." When Wells arrived in Russia, and all the bells rang for joy, he flatly refused to contemplate any of the practical results of his own teaching, and informed Stalin that the Class War postulate of Socialism is vulgar spiteful rot, and Marx an economic Stiggins. The Russians gasped, and cried " This is not Wells. By some horrible magic he has become transformed into his own Mr. Parham." Wells told Stalin that what is needed is a world State, and that all the other desiderata are red herrings drawn across the trail of this great purpose by silly people who do not know their own silly business. Whereat Stalin must have said to himself " This is not Wells: this is the ghost of Anacharsis Klootz, Orator of the Human Race."

When the report of the interview appeared I had to throw bricks at Wells to reassure the Russians as to the sanity of the British intelligentsia. Wells returned the bricks vigorously and hated me for fully half an hour. But the Russian Intellectual Proletariat breathed again; and quiet reigns on the Eastern front pending the next disparagement of Russian Communism by some Englishman who has been preaching Communism all his life.

Now as to G.K.C. He has by nature the grand manner, and under whatever pressure of contradiction always behaves so perfectly in debate, that when he went to Rome and met the Pope, with whom I should say he differs on nine out of ten of all the points on which it is possible for sane men to differ, the Pope was so pleased with him that he made him a starred Knight Commander of the Order of St. Gregory the Great. Now G.K.C., though president of an ultra-Communist body called the Distributist League (for the political quintessence of Communism is recognition of distribution as the first task of organized society, and therefore of the consumer as the true democratic unit instead of the producer or the proprietor, as the capitalists hold) has always been a champion of the peasant proprietor and of what the arch-Communist Morris sang as " the little house on the hill.'' Mr. Palme Dutt, the editor of The Labour Monthly, has rashly defined Communism as '' the merging of the individual in the community.'' Only an Indian could have made such a tactical mistake. For the Englishman's and every other man's instant reaction to that is '' The community be damned! *Io son io.* I absolutely refuse any such merger.'' Mr. Rudyard Kipling's vision of the Englishman's future is one in which no man can see the smoke from his neighbour's chimney, and in which he is safe from the hated intrusion of any other Englishman. The need for privacy, for a house of one's own, a bedroom all to one's self and so forth, is so strong that until Communism is presented as the only effective means of securing them it will never conciliate our inveterate anarchism. Has not the Soviet Government decreed that the worker on the collective farm must have three acres and a cow all to himself? The late Jesse Collins may yet have his statue in the Red Square in Moscow.

One would suppose that G.K.C. would immediately fall into the arms of Stalin with a triumphant cry of '' I told you so. Distributists of all lands, unite.'' But not a bit of it. Not a single civility has reached Stalin from G.K.C.'s Weekly to clear its editor of the suspicion that attaches to all publicly articulate Englishmen of swallowing the anti-Russian bugaboo of *The Times* Riga correspondent as credulously as the Duchess of Atholl. G.K.C. rages against capitalists and financiers like any Russian Octobrist, and is evidently sincere in his revolt against the moral foundations of Capitalism as well as against its phenomenal horrors; but when people who entirely agree with him on that point, and who have attained to political power, proceed to liquidate Capitalism, he has not a good word for them, and leaves it to be inferred that a political situation under which citizens are not free to become capitalists is a slave constitution.

At this point Hilaire Belloc comes in. An ex-parliamentary reporter, one Charles Dickens, pointed out three quarters of a century ago that Parliament is not a palladium of British liberty but an unrivalled instrument for finding out, when the people want the Government to do something, how not to do it. The impression produced by Dickens on our governing classes was that of a street boy cocking snooks at an august institution, the greatness of which he, a mere middle class inkslinger, was incapable of understanding. So Parliament went on illustrating the exactitude of Dickens's observation until Belloc, by what misrepresentations of his outlook on life I know not, got himself elected to the House of Commons, smelt it, and walked out again. Then with the late Cecil Chesterton he started a weekly paper called variously *The Eye Witness*, *The New Witness*, and finally (Cecil having been induced to throw away his life on false pretences) *G.K.'s Weekly*. Our parliamentary system was held up to utter scorn in Witness and Weekly long before it collapsed in Ireland, Italy, Spain, Germany, Russia, Turkey, Jugo Slavia, and in short wherever it became urgently necessary to get a move on, and where there was a political adventurer hardy enough to kick it into the gutter. Every one of these collapses was a triumph for Mr. Belloc. But

Mr. Belloc did not gather Michael Collins, Lenin, Mussolini, Kemal, Hitler and the rest to his bosom as having taken him at his word concerning parliament and proved his case for him. Every *coup d'état* was one up for Mr. Belloc; but instead of scoring his successes he declared for a Roman Catholic real monarchy, and appealed to history to shew that the only stable governments the world has known have been those of Catholic Kings even when they were usurping adventurers, and that such monarchies are the only real alternatives to Protestant (meaning Anarchist) plutocracy. Now Russia has shot ahead of all the Powers in combining an intense public activity with an extension of popular initiative and individual freedom beyond the power of workers under Liberal Capitalism even to conceive, and this too, mere nomenclature apart, on catholic lines corrected up to date; but if Stalin were to ask me whether I have any evidence that Mr. Belloc's attitude towards the U.S.S.R. differs materially from that of Mr. Winston Churchill I am afraid I could not satisfy him.

Take my own case. Fortunately for England I am not an Englishman. I am an Irishman, with a keen analytical faculty, a sensitive intellectual conscience, and a vindictively retentive political memory. In short, I have political qualifications which, as Milton pointed out, will not grow in the English climate. Evidently, I am the foreigner desiderated by Milton for high politics. The Englishman proceeds not by analysis and logic, but by casual emotional observation and association of ideas, with the result that his mind resembles a pawnbroker's shop window. He can never make up his mind whether intellect is the lever of Archimedes or a burglar's jemmy, but mistrusts it equally both ways. As to political memory he has for all practical purposes none. Milton knew him through and through.

It is this confounded association of ideas as opposed to my analytical method that gets me into trouble in England. If I say (as I did) that the Fascist government of Italy really governed, and in some respects governed very efficiently, where the Italian parliament had governed either very inefficiently or not at all, and that the conception of the Corporate State is an evident advance towards Socialism and away from *Laissez-faire*, I am immediately accused of having, in effect, murdered Matteotti and exiled Salvemini. When I said that on the question of the Versailles Treaty versus Hitler every German, including every persecuted German Jew, Social-Democrat, or Communist, must vote for Hitler, it was obvious to the English mind that I was advocating the total suppression of any and every sort of liberty; that I am an anti-Semite; that I have repudiated Socialism and Democracy; and that I am a dupe of the bogus Nordic ethnology of Houston Chamberlain. When I point out that the dogma of the infallibility of the Pope is just as necessary as, and much more picturesque and plausible than, our dogma of the infallibility of the Judicial Committee of the House of Lords (''the King can do no wrong''), I am taken to be affirming a fanatical belief in transubstantiation and auricular confession. When I demonstrate that an Inquisition, with powers of life and death, is a necessity in every organized community where its functions are not performed arbitrarily, amateurishly, and often disastrously by every employer, I am accused of trying to relight the fires of Smithfield and justifying the atrocities of the pious anti-Semite maniac Torquemada.

I do not know whether Mr. Wells has anything more to do with the Society called The Open Conspiracy than Browning had to do with The Browning Society; but there is such a Society, which you can join for five shillings. On being invited to join I proposed a test question for postulants as follows. On what provocation are you prepared to kill your next door neighbor in addition to the recognized provocations of the D.O.R.A. and of the Capitalist criminal code? Dead silence. And yet that is the fundamental social question. The Englishman has never made up his mind about it nor associated it with any ideas whatever. He can therefore infer nothing. I press my question by making it more precise. Are you prepared to kill and risk being killed rather than have the children who are to be the future citizens of the community brought up in our public schools to this or that state of morals and conscience, or rather than exempt them from being educated to such and such contrary states? If so, specify the states. We will then know whether your subscription of five shillings to The Distributist League or The Open Conspiracy or The Fabian Society or what not really means anything except the satisfaction of a go-to-meeting and listen-to-speeches habit which leaves England just where it was. In Ireland the Protestant north got its way by the simple formula "We wont have it," the "it" being precisely defined. None of the English societies or parties seems capable of saying either "We wont have it" or "We will have it." They never really define their "it." A Primrose Leaguer will applaud a speaker who shouts that Britons never never will be Communists (or perhaps Catholics). But ask him what, precisely, a Communist or Catholic believes—!!!

At that I must leave it for the present. I think that though I and my fellow-geniuses, being, as such, incorrigible vagabonds mentally, will not co-operate with one another, we might at least give an encouraging pat on the back to any statesman who manages by fluke or crook to make a step in our direction. And we should pay much more attention to the Churches. All the Churches should institute a good spring cleaning every year as to their doctrines and rituals, with a vigorous Reformation at least once every twenty years. They should never forget my doctrine that the law of change (discovered by Ibsen) is the law of God. If you wish to classify me denominationally I am something of a Quaker and a good deal of a Jain; but both sects are so cluttered up with obsolete rubbish that I could not make myself acceptable to them nor lend them my countenance without compromising my intellectual integrity. Islam has wandered as far from Mahomet as Christendom from Christ. The Roman Catholic Church will not repudiate the Bedouin Jehovah nor substitute electric light for smoky candles nor cremation for earth burial. The Anglican Catholic Church is bound by a set of hopelessly contradictory articles which, as one of its greatest men has observed, can be sub-

scribed only by fools, bigots, or liars. Besides, it worships the Father but not the Mother, a shocking omission. The other sects are all over the shop intellectually. Can we not help them to clean up a little, and move a step nearer to an up-to-date religion? What else are we for?

G.B.S.

A Metrical Psalm
By C. E. Baines

When God smites Sodom once again,
　No useless fires shall fall;
No fumes of brimstone spread in vain
　Their ineffective pall.
This time His anger shall a more
　Conclusive sentence pass:
The Dead Sea shall not whelm her o'er
　But a living sea of grass.

Then shall that be that was foretold:
　For in these streets of green
Our cattle shall bear fiftyfold
　O'er mouldering shames unseen:
Unseen, and long forgot; save where
　Some mattock masterful
Shall lay a usurer's carcase bare
　Or split a pervert's skull.

But we, delivered from the den
　That housed their stricken seed—
Where barren were the lusts of men
　And only gold could breed—
For freedom armed—for service shod
　Shall stand that men may see
(After how many years!) what God
　Meant Englishmen to be.

As in the Temple's inner shrine
　The polished corners glow,
Shall be the daughters of our line:
　Our sons like saplings grow,
Shall grow like timber tall and straight,
　Stronger than strength of kings,
And speak to foemen at the gate
　Unanswerable things.

Surely in those green streets of ours
　Shall no complaining be,
No homage to unholy Powers
　And no captivity.
And, surely, hushed will be our boasts
　When at His throne we bow—
The dread Almighty Lord of Hosts,
　The God who speeds the Plough!

"Cornucopia of Trash"

—POWYS EVANS.

The Untameable
By W. J. Blyton

A HUNDRED years ago died William Cobbett, after performing the life-cycle: plough-boy, soldier, farmer, editor-publicist, agitator, economist, Parliament-man. Often in the last few months, living near to Normandy Farm which he worked, I have walked into the market town, Farnham, on private pilgrimages. And when at market with other farmers I have called at the house where he was born, The Jolly Farmer, I have noticed that Cobbett's name is as conspicuous within doors as if it were that of a brewers' firm. This hardly argues that his " works," if you can call the sprightly runnings of his mother-wit by that name, are books of reference thereabouts. But it does imply pride in his nativity there, among the knowing ones.

That my own land marches alongside some of Cobbett's territory has deepened an interest already lively in his ways and prejudices. That Cobbett, a century and a half ago, put hounds off their scent at my present farm gate, gives me a genuine if irrational pleasure; and one of my further fields is not less interesting to me because as a boy he bird-nested there. True, if he strode my little domain to-day, dogmatising at the top of his voice, he would pepper his praise of my reclaiming one of those " abominable sandy heaths " with some rich insults regarding my use of nitro-chalk and potash salts: " Isn't honest farmyard dung good enough for you, man?" It is fairly certain that, back in the flesh, his visit would leave some of us, his admirers, considerably ruffled, unready with our defensive retorts until he had gone again. Wonderful to read, he was " ill to live wi'." (We may say things about him now which we should hesitate to say if he were here.) He passed beyond the reach of our criticism three years before Queen Victoria was crowned, but, as Mr. Chesterton says, " the empty chair of Cobbett is more significant and striking than the throne. With him died the sort of democracy that *was* a return to Nature, and which only poets and mobs can understand. After him Radicalism is urban—and Toryism suburban. From the time when the first shout went up for Wilkes to the time when the last Luddite fires were quenched in a cold rain of rationalism, the spirit of Cobbett, of rural republicanism, of English and patriotic democracy, burned like a beacon." He means doubtless candours like this:—

" Lord Carnarvon told a man in 1820 that he did not like my politics. But what did he mean by my *politics*? I have no politics but such as he *ought* to like. To be sure I labour most assiduously to destroy a system of distress and misery: but is that any reason why a *lord* should dislike my politics? However, dislike them or like them, to them, to those very politics, the lords themselves *must come at last*."

By the heroic note of such headstrong sentences we petty men, who argue and qualify, are exhilarated and achieve vicarious release. " Undoubtedly," said W. H. Hudson, " he talked like that . . . the glorious demagogue in his tantrums," and Mr. Leonard Woolf, with a like enthusiasm, asserts that among literary styles, of Cobbett's we say: " But this *is* English," and that when we are really civilised more and more of us will write like him. All this and more is in Hazlitt's character of Cobbett: " He is one of the best writers in the language. He speaks and thinks plain, broad, downright English. He might be said to have the clearness of Swift, the naturalness of Defoe, and the picturesque satirical description of Mandeville. He can never tire us, even of himself, and never runs to lees, but is always setting out afresh on his journey, clearing away some old nuisance and turning up new mould . . . He is not wedded to his notions, not he. He has not one Mrs. Cobbett among all his opinions. The art of prophesying does not suit Mr. Cobbett's style—he has a knack of fixing times and places."

There was something of Cobbett in Hazlitt, that he dared to speak thus. Few however know Heine's piquant impression of the popular tribune, whom he met at " that uproarious dinner at the Crown and Anchor tavern, with his scolding red face "—" a Philistine with six fingers on each hand, and the staff of his spear like a weaver's beam." There speaks the fastidious artist. " Because of the incessantness of his barking he cannot get listened to even when he barks at a real thief. Therefore the distinguished thieves who plunder England do not think it necessary to throw the growling Cobbett a bone to stop his mouth. Poor old Cobbett! England's dog!" But England's dog followed his nose like the setter or retriever, going by his instinctive likes and dislikes, with a knack of turning out right. The Englishman taking himself wilfully often does this in politics: Piers Plowman, John Ball, Ben Jonson, Milton, the Puritans, Wilkes, Fox, Canning, Carlyle, Hazlitt, Landor, Cobden, Campbell-Bannerman, and between them they went far, although the route lay over aristocratic corns and venerable abuses. It is amusing to note how the sedentary reformer reacts against his intuitive open-air brother. Thus, said Bentham: " Cobbett is a man filled with *odium humani generis*. His malevolence and lying are beyond anything." It is impossible to move in this world without galling somebody's kibe, and this peevish plaint reminds one of Mr. Shaw's disclosure: " I constantly receive the most frantic letters from people who feel that they cannot stand me any longer."

The title chosen by Cobbett for his projected autobiography, which he never wrote, was " The Progress of a Plough-Boy to a Seat in Parliament, as exemplified in the History of the Life of William Cobbett, Member for Oldham." The double allusion to Westminster implies that he felt the importance of representing the constituency. The election followed the passing of the Reform Bill. He was never successful as a public speaker. The confrontation to-day of Member and electoral division would be piquant. His agricultural *obiter dicta* might there fall from the platform into an unresisting void or into a non-committal silence. The scope for Rural Rides would be restricted; and his sensible " Cottage Economy " would require substantial revisions. Oldham to-day might not be so hard on his inconsistencies. But his idiom would be as well understood as ever:—

" How many well-meaning persons have exclaimed: ' It is a pity Cobbett is so *violent*.' Such persons never asked themselves whether they would think a man too violent who should knock down a ruffian. This has been my state: when I began to write, I was as modest as a maid and dealt in qualifications, and modifications, and mitigations to the best of my poor powers in the line of palavering; but when I was unprovokedly assaulted, I instantly resolved to proceed in the same way, giving three, four or ten blows for one."

And he would assuredly be hearkened to with approval in this vein:—

" There never yet was, and never will be, a nation permanently great, consisting, for the greater part, of wretched and miserable families. I lay it down as a maxim, that for a family to be happy, they must be well supplied with food and raiment. The doctrines which fanaticism preaches, and which teach men to be content with poverty, have a very pernicious tendency and are calculated to favour tyrants by giving them passive slaves. In spite of all refinements of sickly minds, it is *abundant living* amongst the people at large, which is the great test of good government and the surest basis of national greatness and security. If the labourer have his fair wages; if there be no false weights and measures whether of money or of goods, by which he is defrauded; if the laws be equal in their effect upon all men, if he be called upon for no more than his due share of the expenses necessary to support the government and defend the country, he has no reason to complain. But the basis of good to man is steady and skilful labour. Poverty leads to all sorts of evil consequences. Want, horrid want, is the great parent of crime. Competence is the foundation of happiness and of exertion."

Thus he tirelessly wrote in " Cottage Economy " and " Cobbett's Poor Man's Friend." It is of the earth, earthy; but he held to the primaries with the tenacity of a mastiff. His imprisonment in 1810 for the article on the Local Militia and German Legion ruined his Botley Farm; his children sent letters and bluebells to the King's Bench and kept " a journal of labours" for him; one or two of them were always with him in the prison, and by means of their letters and drawings their education was advanced. He lived on, untameable and useful, for another quarter of a century; and moved again into Normandy Farm, near Ash, Farnham and Aldershot, which he "did" exceedingly well until his death.

As full of practical detailed advice, of grotesque prejudice, of love of nature, and of choler as a chestnut is full of meat, it is impossible not to love this oaken Liberal. When he writes that the trade of shoemaker " numbers more men of sense and public spirit than any other in the Kingdam "; that the height of liberty is to snare one's food in the wild " and never to see the hang-dog face of a taxgatherer "; that London's growth is polyp-like; that the potato is a " villainous root," leading to lazy domestic economy, and tea a costly siren—we may not agree; but we know what he means, and feel a little glow of pleasure.

How Much Progress?
BY CHRISTOPHER HOLLIS

THE rulers of most men's minds are not facts nor statistics but general impressions, and, like other rulers, general impressions are only with the greatest difficulty deposed. The tenth birthday of *G.K.'s Weekly* is an occasion appropriate for the asking of the question, What is the general impression in the public mind that is the most powerful obstacle to the spread of the ideas of the paper?

I think that there is no doubt of the answer.

It is not difficult to get people to agree that there are many disadvantages in the noise, the rush, the complexity of modern life, nor to agree that in modern society there is still much miserable poverty which must be eliminated in the future. Yet, thinks the modern man, for all that, there is no doubt that things are much better than they were. If the noise and the rush and the complexity are prices to be paid, yet they are prices that we have paid for solid advantages, and, if there is still poverty, at least there is much less poverty than there used to be. What survives survives as a relic of an evil past.

Such is a perfectly respectable and intelligible position. It is the position occupied by the vast majority of those who have not studied the facts. It seems to be confirmed by the old among us who can tell perfectly truthful tales of the condition of the poor as they remember it in their young days. But what are the facts?

The extraordinarily interesting and important articles concerning mediæval conditions which appeared recently in *G.K.'s Weekly* from the pen of Mr. Featherstone Hammond must surely have raised doubts in any minds in which they were not already present concerning this easy progressive theory of history, nor are the facts really at all doubtful. In the 1870's the Professorship of Political Economy at Oxford was held by Thorold Rogers. Thorold Rogers occupied his time in going round the country and collecting exhaustive statistics of the prices and wages current at the various places in England and at the various dates in English history. The results of his inquiries are available to the world in his monumental *History of Agriculture and Prices* and *Six Centuries of Work and Wages*.

Suppose, said Rogers, that a labourer's family requires for its year's provision three quarters of wheat, three of malt and two of oatmeal. Let us take the wages current and the prices current at the various dates in English history and see how many weeks' work it would take him to earn that supply. He starts off in 1495, when the agricultural labourer's wage was 2/- a week. He gives all the prices—you can find the calculation in his *History of Work and Wages*—and he concludes that the labourer could earn the supply by 15 weeks' work. By 1564 wages had risen to 3/6 a week, but prices had risen a great deal more. He could only earn his supply then by 40 weeks' work. By 1610 prices had risen still further, and the labourer's whole year's labour would have been insufficient to earn him his supply by 24/9½.

In 1651 things are a little better and he could earn it by 40 weeks' work. In 1684 they are worse again, and his whole year's labour would have been just insufficient to earn him the supply. By 1725, when earnings were from £13 to £15 a year and the cost of the supply £16 2s. 3d., they would have been plainly insufficient. In 1866, the date at which Rogers was carrying out his investigations, the agricultural labourer's wage was 13/- a week. In Henry VII's time it had been, as we have said, 2/-. Between the two dates prices had multiplied by 12. Therefore in terms of real goods the agricultural labourer of Queen Victoria's time got about half what the labourer of Henry VII's time got. A worker in the building trade in Henry VII's time got 3/4, which, multiplied by 12 makes 40/-; in Thorold Rogers' time he got 42/9, but, whereas rent was one of the heaviest items in the budget of Thorold Rogers' builder, it was a negligible factor in that of Henry VII's or of any poor man before the Statute of Frauds of Charles II's reign. Therefore, so far from seeing there a record of steady improvement, Rogers' summary of English history was ' I contend that from 1563 to 1824 a conspiracy, concocted by the law and carried out by parties interested in its success, was entered into to cheat the English workman of his wages, to tie him to the soil, to deprive him of hope and to degrade him into irremediable poverty. . . For more than two centuries and a half, the English law and those who administered the law were engaged in grinding the English workman down to the lowest pittance, in stamping out every expression or act which indicated any organised discontent and in multiplying penalties on him when he thought of his natural rights.'

If then there has been improvement since the middle of the nineteenth century, the reason is not that improvement is the natural law of society but rather that there was so enormous a room for improvement precisely because there had been no improvement at all for the previous three hundred years. Now what are the facts for the years since Thorold Rogers? Statistics are abundant. Perhaps the most easily available are those in the *Encyclopædia Britannica* under the articles Wages and Prices.

Anyone who looks up those statistics can see that through the 1850's there were indeed oscillations both in wages and in prices but that they were such as to leave the condition of the working man just about the same as it had been before. With the 1860's a definite and steady, though perhaps slow, improvement sets in and continues up to the end of the century. Wages in 1858 were 55 to 1913's 100. Wholesale prices were 109 to 1913's 100. By 1899 prices were down to 80 and wages up to 90—a very considerable improvement. But,—and here is the vital point of which no one must be allowed to remain in ignorance,—between 1899 and 1914, between the Boer War and the European War, there was no further improvement. Indeed things slipped back somewhat. Prices rose from 80 to 100 while wages only rose from 90 to 100. It is a truism that the old financial system is to-day in ruins, but it is often said that it was the war that smashed it. It is not so. The war was the result of the fact that the system was already breaking down.

I have said nothing in this article of the reasons why wages rose when they rose and fell when they fell, for I want to concentrate the reader's attention on the facts without for the moment distracting it with the reasons for the facts. For it is important to understand the facts in order not to fall a victim to a psychological trick. 'The true test of a civilisation,' said Dr. Johnson, 'is a decent provision for the poor.' On that test it is clear that, during the four hundred years since Progress began, there have been only forty during which things have been getting better. The general rule has been that things have been getting worse. But it so happens that those forty years were the years in which those to whom we rightly look up as persons of experience were growing to manhood. There is thus a great danger that the last forty years of the nineteenth century, which were in fact a highly abnormal period, will be looked on as a normal period and that we shall slip into thinking that all the past was like that—which it wasn't.

The Quicksilver Standard
By Gregory Macdonald

IN the midst of all the hubbub, an economist who did not know when he had had enough proposed the Quicksilver Standard. His thoughtful essay attracted immediate attention, especially and most usefully among readers of *The Times*, nor could any expert object to the advantages enumerated for the new medium of exchange. "Quicksilver," wrote the economist in a passage of haunting beauty, "is a metallic element of constant fineness, with known deposits in a small number of countries. It possesses utility. It is highly medicinal. It is compact, transportable, bright and shiny, easily cornered, volatile and globular, and it amuses the kids. Quicksilver cannot be counterfeited, nor can it be clipped. It vaporizes at 360°, which is more than gold does at 360%; and when frozen can be cut with a knife."

The idea commended itself to the highest authorities everywhere. Without delay the Gold Bloc dropped off gold and began to wobble about less steadily than ever on a basis of quicksilver. There was an immediate boom in the price of the commodity, which was soon quoted at the fantastic figure of 149s. an ounce, and from all sides people brought out their thermometers—even heirloom thermometers of baroque pattern—for sale at the jewellers, who were themselves bothered by the problem of making quicksilver eternity rings for Society brides. In the first rush of enthusiasm the *London Mercury* amalgamated with the *Financial Times*.

Wise statesmanship dictated that the people should be accustomed to the use of this substitute for gold by allowing it to pass into circulation, though not for too long a period. Confidence is a prime necessity of the financial system. Under the new dispensation a certain degree of confusion was apparent. There was the man who tried to pay his 'bus fare with his fingers instead of with a spoon. There was the traditional miser who came to grief because he kept his wealth in a stocking. Bank clerks were inclined to slosh the stuff about with their shovels, but the eager customers who attempted to chase it into corners and gather it up with pieces of blotting paper discovered that quicksilver was not so easily cornered after all, except by men of experience. A salutary lesson. Bank counters were thereafter fitted out, at immense cost to depositors, with equipment which made them appear something between a kitchen sink and a public bar; and by the time that the people had settled down to easy familiarity with the new form of currency, nicknamed "swipes," it was quietly withdrawn from circulation, to be replaced by paper, for which quicksilver would be payable on demand. Soon afterwards a law was passed that only paper would be payable for the paper. The price of quicksilver rose sharply. The banks, at immense cost to depositors, were fitted out with flat counters, ink-pots and blotters.

Meanwhile the economic structure of the world began to disintegrate and change under the influence of the new monetary standard. The rise in the price of quicksilver brought marginal mines into operation. Particularly rich deposits were discovered in Illyria. With loud whoops of joy Illyria balanced her budget and grew to all outward appearances an extremely wealthy country, although the Illyrians themselves remained as poor as ever—unless they deserted agriculture or industry for finance, as some of them were able to do. In Germany Dr. Schacht and Herr Hitler established two forms of currency, Centigrade for foreign exchange and Fahrenheit for internal circulation. The riches of Spain in quicksilver attracted the *conquistadores* of Panama, whose treasure fleets passed and re-passed across the Atlantic. In London the whole available supply was cornered by the British Medical Association, which succeeded the Bank of England as the bankers' bank. Its prescriptions took the place of the old cheque system, though no further changes were thought to be necessary; and in the same way Walter Bagehot's *Lombard Street* was re-issued as *Harley Street* with simply an erratum slip: "For 'gold' read 'quicksilver' *passim*."

Yet there was one remarkable economic advantage of quicksilver quite unforeseen when the change over from gold was made, nor was its operation immediately noticed. Observant economists discovered from statistics and graphs that there seemed to be more money about in the summer than in the winter. The big shops were empty at Christmas time, but the holiday resorts were crowded from May to September. The thesis of a young don seemed to show that this phenomenon was caused by sunspots. The half-yearly trade-cycle was accepted as part of the order of nature. Then reports came through that the Iceland Loan had shrunk. There was drastic deflation among the Esquimaux. At the same time the Bush Pygmies of Central Africa began to enjoy a boom period of unbounded prosperity. Soon industry was moving south by leaps and bounds; and before anybody knew what had happened it was spread out in a ribbon development along the equatorial line, with patches of Black Country in the great deserts, the Sahara, the Gobi and the Karoo. A number of dispossessed

Bedouin started an agitation, with Back to the Sand as their slogan, but not much came of it, for by this time the industrial revolution was an accomplished fact. Raw materials were transported at great pains from Lancashire and Durham to be worked up in Timbuctoo. Families rooted for centuries in the English counties discovered in themselves the spirit of the pioneers, and having sold all that they possessed at knock-down prices, set out to secure the higher wages and the dividends of Cayenne.

Economists were delighted by these vindications, for labour was indeed fluid and capital mobile. Moreover, all the earlier statistics had to be scrapped, so that there was work for every graduate of the L.S.E. Books, essays, controversial pamphlets poured from their pens, advancing the most various hypotheses to account for what had happened, but it was the President of the B.M.A., Dr. Clarence Skinner, M.D., who hit upon the true solution. He proved by experiment that quicksilver contracts when cold and expands when warm—a result to which he came by pondering upon his own sensation of always feeling richer in a tube train. It was not difficult for him to utilise this discovery. By establishing refrigerators in the desert and equatorial banks he contracted the purchasing power available in the new markets and brought about a highly successful economic blizzard. Whatever else was proved or disproved, the advantages of a Quicksilver Standard were incontestable, for it responded to every demand made upon it, and the property of the people could from that time onward be most finely measured and controlled.

A Stave

By Walter de la Mare

O my dear one,
Do not repine
Their rose hath left
Those cheeks of thine.
In memory hid
Blooms yet, how clear,
Past fading now,
Its beauty, dear.

Yet—fallen a little
In time, soon gone,
Is the heart that yearned
Their fragrance on;
And much is quenched
Of that wild fire
That did from dust
To thee aspire.

It is our fate.
Like tapers, we
Life's pure wax waste
Unheedingly.
Till Love, grown weary
Of its light,
Frowns, puffs his cheek,
And so—good night.

The Strange Fisherman
BY ALFRED NOYES

SCENE: *The Botanical Gardens, Regent's Park, London, known to Billikins, aged four, as the " Tangling gardens."*

When Billikins walked by the pool in the tangling
   gardens
   Where Chinese ducks and the red-beaked moor-
      fowl swim,
He came on an old man, angling, under a willow;
   And Billikins thought " That's luck! I must talk
      to *him*!''

For the old man's beard and hair were as white as a
   may-bush,
   And the moons of his big horn spectacles looked
      so wise,
That he couldn't have caught much less than a roach
   for his dinner,
   Or a fine fat carp, or a perch of a pretty good size.

And Billikins thought he might lift up the lid of his
   basket
   And discover a pike, perhaps, or a red-speckled
      trout;
And watch, if he kept quite still, till the float bobbed
   under,
   And the rod doubled up like a whip, and the reel
      ran out.

So Billikins tip-toed near, and remarked politely
   " I s'pose you've caught some very fine fish to-
      day?''
And the old man stared at him over his goblin
   glasses,
   And then replied in this very peculiar way:

" *I am fishing merely for microscopical objects,*
   Which are quite invisible to the naked eye.
They have never been offered for sale in the Billings-
   gate market,
   But you'll probably swallow large numbers before
      you die.''

Then Billikins saw that, instead of a fisherman's
   basket,
   A casket of queer little bottles reposed on the
      grass;
While, instead of a hook, at the end of the line, in
   the water,
   There dangled a curious phial of shimmering glass.

And the old man remarked " *If you look at one drop*
   from that phial,
   Through a good pocket lens (which I'll lend you,
      but treat it with care!)
You'll observe a strange Beast, with a wheel that
   revolves on its top-knot,
   At very high speeds. It is known as the large
      Ro-ti-fer!''

Then he waggled his shaggy white eye-brows over
   his glasses
   And said " The Rotifera tribe is the finest I
      know '';
And Billikins stared at the big round moons in the
   may-bush
   And replied in a wise little word of one syllable—
      " *Oh!''*

THE GOLDEN ROLLER SKATES
BY DOUGLAS WOODRUFF

PUBLIC audiences at the Vatican take a great deal of the Pope's time and are a burden to a man nearing eighty and full of business. So the faithful of the diocese of Missouri, U.S.A., have come forward with the offer of a gift designed to combine dignity with that up-to-date efficiency on which the new world has for so long prided itself. They have proffered, with great respect and from a sincere desire to be helpful, a pair of golden roller-skates, on which public audiences could be, they venture to think, expeditiously and yet graciously performed. The suggestion can be made to a pontiff who was a mountaineer of some note in his earlier life, where it could hardly have been made to less athletic and well-balanced dignitaries.

To Americans, to whom it is a confession of failure to have to walk anywhere and on any occasion, any mechanical adjunct is better than none, and they can point out that it is not long since Cardinals in Rome had to maintain their dignity by never being seen on foot in the streets. In a humbler sphere, archidiaconal gaiters are not worn for the dignity they confer, but are, or were, severely practical, the dress of men who were constantly in the saddle, going their rounds. The accoutrements of the past, if they paid some attention to dignity—and to be made of gold is to be dignified enough— were pre-eminently practical, and have acquired venerableness to-day largely because their origin has been forgotten.   The pity is that modern amenities are so commonly lacking in dignity. The offer of roller skates follows on the presentation to the Pope of a golden telephone; but it has affinities also to the substitution of electric light for candles at various shrines; it is somehow a different gesture of honour to light a candle and to provide current for half an hour.

It has always been well understood that for high offices the manner of doing things, if less important than what is done, is of great moment. The great Khan of the Mongols preserved his dignity by never speaking directly to anyone. He uttered his remarks in a low voice, and special officers stood near him to catch and repeat them. He thus escaped any risk of addressing himself to unattentive ears, or of seeming to enter into any, however temporary, equality such as the idea of conversation involves. If he were here to-day, it can be taken for granted that his telephoning would always be done for him.

Even the extreme democratic tradition, as it established itself in America with the election of Andrew Jackson, and the firm insistence on the right of every citizen to grip the President in a manly and sustained handclasp has had to retreat before the terrifying developments of the new mechanical aids to intimacy. President Roosevelt's fireside broadcasts are intimate enough, but they are carefully spaced out and are substitutes for the right of every citizen to ring up the President and find out how the country is doing. Faced with the growth of populations and travelling and the multiplication of active bodies which would like patronage, Kings and Queens and Presidents had to learn in the last century to raise the height of their protective hedges. The Papal audiences, which are so frequently taken advantage of by visitors to Rome whose sole motive is curiosity and a desire to see all the sights for the purpose of subsequent description, are now the only surviving example of a custom that was once widespread. Everyone, as readers of Arthur Young's Travels will recollect, could at pleasure watch the royal family of France at their main meal. In days of organised tourism the great ones of the world may well be thankful that they some time since abolished the customs which made them habitual sights; and thankful for the inventions like television and movietone interviews which enable vivid personal contact with great numbers of people to be maintained with a minimum of physical fatigue. But whatever inventions may come, seeing Kings, actually and in the flesh, will always be a privilege valued by the run of ordinary cats.

A Happy Return
By W. R. Titterton

IT is infelicitous to wish a news or views-paper *many happy returns*. For the copies return, and not even the would-be vendor, I presume, is happy.

But I may properly congratulate the Sixpenny Siren on looking so well on her tenth birthday. Which reminds me. . . But anon, sir, anon!

Among other approximations to the joys of eternity, old age has this: that years are gone like a day. We stare incredulously at that young slow-coach, the calendar.

You may remember that *The Times*, in one of its rare moments of frivolity, wishing to scourge the House of Commons for its waste of time, made the following remarkable statement: " If we were asked

what *passed* between 6 p.m. and 6 a.m., we should say twenty-four hours." And I, if I am asked what has happened between March, 1925, and March, 1935, should be inclined to hazard a similar and probably as inaccurate a computation.

Yet no doubt things have happened, and, what is far more important, things have changed—much to the annoyance and even dismay of those who believe in progress.

The *Sixpenny Siren* is still with us—though in between whiles she went in for slimming, and nevertheless, strange to say, tucked out her Tuppenny. But some of her old friends and enemies are under the daisies.

The *Westminster Gazette* died as a *Morning* less than 10 years ago. I wrote its elegy for the *Siren*. It ran thus:

> The *Daily News*, which fought the *Gazette*, has caught the *Gazette*, and bought the *Gazette*. The poor *Gazette*, caught in a net, has died in a manner afflicting. And the *Daily News* is, free to confess, free to confess, but it won't confess, though it can't abide the Octopus Press, it's a dab at boa-constricting.
>
> Four hundred gentlemen marching along, great-hearted gentlemen singing this song: " At half-past four the world went wrong, and they gave us our blasted tickets. But the eel is full of Vitamin B. On a moonless night it's a sight to see. Yes, the eel is full of Vitamin B., which is known as a cure for rickets.
>
> Day by day our chance grows less—freedom fades, and our chance grows less, of getting a job on the Combine Press as comp. or sub. or reporter. Freedom fades, and our hope grows less. Are we disheartened? Well, frankly, yes. But the eel is full of Vitamin B., and so is a pint of porter.

And then it was the turn of the *Daily Chronicle*. And round about the same time the *Daily Graphic*, too, was assimilated. Oh, yes, there have been changes.

But March, 1925, at least remembers and I think actually knew something else in the way of newspapers. We won't haggle over dates, will we?—especially in a birthday number. But round about 1925 the *Westminster* deserted the afternoon, and not long before that the *Pall Mall* was murdered by Sir John Leigh, and not so long before that the *Globe* suddenly expired.

We who are old can remember the *Echo* and the *Sun*. But 1925 marks for me the period when, with some unhappy dispatch, the number of London Evenings was cut down to three. And those that died were the ones I liked best.

They had a common character. They were leisurely, they were conversational, and, as a consequence, they loved letters. Think of that! How possibly could any newspaper pay which had a weakness for literature?

Perhaps nowadays it would not pay. Yes, I think it wouldn't. Apart from the plain fact that there are fewer papers than there were and those in fewer hands, I think that the disappearance of the literary Evenings indicates a change in public tastes.

The Combine Press knows nothing about what the public wants, though something about what, stimulated by gifts such as the works of Shakespeare and Dickens and similar unmarketable produce, they will stand. But it has a shrewd idea about what the public will not have at any price. They will not have literature. For you see conversation bores them, and leisure makes them afraid.

The gentlemen who used to take in the *Westminster*, yes, even those who used to send in things to Miss Naomi Royde-Smith for her Saturday Competition, the gentlemen who used to love the *Turnover* in the *Globe*, and the ladies and gentlemen who used to read me in the *Pall Mall*, are either happily dead, and so beyond the power of dissolution, or they are playing bridge and/or golf and/or listening to the B.B.C. and/or manslaughtering His Majesty's lieges on the highroad.

All but a few, who, vaguely remembering that this English language is after all heroic, engage in battle every Sunday afternoon with Torquemada's cross-word puzzle! But you can't build a circulation up on them!

(By the bye, what *is* it sells the *Observer*? I will tell you. It is Professor Thingammy's cure for drunkenness. But this is an aside.)

You may say that there are still several literary weeklies. If so, which are they? And everybody knows that the heavy Sundays have scooped all the literary weeklies' advertisements by giving away copious book-reviews as an extra, and avoiding literature like the devil.

Even when we come to the Sixpenny Siren—well, it's not as fond of letters (I don't mean those of the Cockpit kind) as it was. I wouldn't say that it is more serious, but it is a thought more solemn. I fear that it goes to bed thinking about Distributism. Mind you, it's a better paper than ever it was, better put together, better informed, better worth sixpence —yes, even better worth sixpence than it was when it was tuppence. Yet, being old and in my second childhood, I miss the careless rapture of its youth when it prized the casual essay and the vagrant fragrant pome.

That is not the fault of the Siren. The whole world's in a damned hurry to finish its ultimate canter. And the age of leisure and letters has gone by.

Only G.K.C. stays put, like the shadow of a great rock in a dry and hustling land. Belloc has weakened of course. His contributions to the Siren are all thoughtful and weighty. And that makes some of our younger humorists ashamed of cutting their capers.

Nevertheless the Siren remains more literary than all the other reviews put together (if we think so, why shouldn't I say so?) and I seem to discern a tendency on the part of some of its essayists to feel once more the fun of writing as well as the fine fury of the fight.

And the Siren's public, which is not dwindling, evidently enjoys the fun. So that either our public is quite unlike the general public, which I am loth to believe, or the general public is getting tired— very, very gradually—of bridge and/or golf and/or the B.B.C. and/or manslaughtering pedestrians.

In any case it's a sign that *we* have gotten our second wind. For a while we were so breathless with the beauty of Distributism that we had no breath left for anything else. We were, I think, in danger of adopting the queer heresy of the ladies and gentlemen who so misconstrue the word *leisure* that they crave more of it in order to improve their minds.

Had I to choose between that and bridge, I should plump for bridge, especially if the bridge were accompanied, as in the case quoted by Mr. Belloc in an unpublished ballade, by boose.

But frankly, apart from the Siren and one or two places where they sing, there seems little liking in this mad age for leisure. The wheels go round faster and faster, more and more motor-cars hoot and roar, and every year in yet another thousand or two haunts of sin they play their mechanised contract half-listening to Professor Jeans on the cubic measurements of the spiritual universe, or the Banana Band in their immeasurable unvarying cacophany. Things have got much worse during these last ten years.

When at the worst will things mend? Let's hope so. Though the odds are that much else will end catastrophically with the sudden silencing of this unholy rush and clamour.

It's a nightmare we have had while under anesthetics against the natural pangs of life. I think we are coming to. I feel myself rising to the surface amid the bubble and roar. But my word shan't we be sick when we return to reason!

Little Man
By G. C. Heseltine

ON the 21st February in this year of grace there appeared in nearly all the London newspapers, the news of the discovery of " Fossil remains of a human race, only 15 inches tall," at Vadnagar, Mehsana district in Baroda State. The news item in my newspaper the *Daily Telegraph* is headed " Bombay, Wednesday." " The remains include," we are told, " those of a 15 inch pygmy man, an 18 inch pygmy cow and a 10 inch walking stick " (presumably also " pygmy ").

" Experts believe," says the news story, " that a fresh field has been thrown open now to investigation of an extinct race of pygmies, more diminutive than the Obongo, Akka and Batwa pygmies of Central Africa, who measure between 4 and 5 ft."

" This latest find," the report concludes, " recalls the Homeric reference to pygmies 13½ inches high, to which the present specimens approximate." And finally, as the source of the report—" Reuter."

Now whoever is the author of this news story—Mr. Reuter or someone who told Mr. Reuter or took his name, it appears as quoted in a most reputable and reliable newspaper (so far as newspapers go), one which may be fairly taken to represent the highest standard amongst newspapers the world over. It is read, as a source of information and opinion, by the most enlightened people in this country. Let us examine it, either as Reuter's whence it came or as the *Daily Telegraph's* which repeats it, but in any case to see what sort of informants we have.

In the first place note how the one 15 inch man becomes " fossil remains of a human *race*," at the outset. Like the odd bits of bone of the Piltdown man, the Neanderthaler, and our old friend Pithecanthropus Erectus, there is no suspicion in the modern mind of our informant that the odd item may be the only one there ever was, and therefore no evidence at all of a race or genus. It is always supposed that if we find one of anything, it must be one of many of the same kind. That began when the craze for making human daisy-chains was at its height. The theory of organic evolution required evidence of whole races of creatures to support it. Such evidence being extremely hard to find in bulk, it had to be deduced from such scanty fragments of jawbone or wristbone as might be found in each case. And since even these were rare, it was obvious that we could not afford to waste several on demonstrating the evidence of one or two races of men. As far as possible each discovery must be made to show the past existence of a distinct race. Only so could we get evidence of anything like enough races to fill in the gaps in the evolutionary daisy-chain. Even now the chain is most famous for its missing links.

The real author of the 15 inch man story knew very well the mind of his fellows. He knew that if they doubted the 15 inch man, their doubts would be dispelled with the additional evidence of a 18 inch cow to give him milk. He knew that there would be very few to suspect the inevitability of the evolutionary pygmy cow of 18 inches synchronising with the even more pygmy man of 15 inches. And so, laughing quietly to himself, he threw in the 10 inch walking stick, with the challenge " Now, doubt *that!*"

Everybody knows that if he does doubt it, if he doubts any of these discoveries of fossil remains and their instantly assumed importance to the world of knowledge, he is branded as a reactionary, an unprogressive, superstitious, priest-ridden moron—the very opposite in short, of Messrs. H. G. Wells, Julian Huxley, J. B. S. Haldane, and Uncle Bert Einstein and all.

A moment's thought will suggest to morons like myself that the proportions are all wrong—an 18 inch cow (and especially her spouse) would have been a tough problem for a 15 inch man, unless she were incredibly docile—which she should not be if the cow of to-day descends from a wilder cow. And a ten inch walking stick must have been made for a giant amongst the pygmies, the equivalent to the 15 inch man of a 9-foot man to us.

Observe how " experts believe " that a new field has been thrown open, etc. We are not told which experts. It is sufficient to-day for somebody, anybody, to say " Experts believe, experts say " and we all believe and we all say. And how naively we are told that the new race to be studied of pygmies of 15 inches high is *more diminutive* than races of *4 to 5 feet!*

It is fair to say that the *Daily Telegraph*, after the Reuter news-story adds a note " Experts Doubtful." London anthropologists doubt whether the discoveries are those of a pygmy race. But they are ready to believe that " the fossil " may be that of a child, an ape, or a monkey.

So some experts believe and some are doubtful; none, so far as we are told, are frankly incredulous as they should be at such a story. For the story is not only fantastic but uncircumstantial, and the first normal commonsense reaction to it is to regard it as nonsense—which it was. For despite the verisimilitude lent by the positive phrasing " Fossil remains *have* been discovered," " the remains include," " experts believe," " this latest find recalls," and the authority of Reuter, the bare idea of 15 inch men is no more reasonable or credible than six-foot fox terriers; and although we may be wrong occasionally if we reject the apparently absurd and incredible, such as we might when we are told of wireless telephony for the first time, the occasions will be so rare that no great harm will be done than cannot be quickly remedied.

This is one of the chief achievements of the " Age of Science." So many surprising things have been discovered that no one is any longer surprised. Everybody is blasé and absurdly credulous. This credulous frame of mind has permeated the whole of modern life, that is why it pays to advertise. Any rumour, however wild, gains wide credence. Any tale told by an idiot is listened to and believed. That is how the hard-headed American comes to buy Gold Bricks from a stranger in the Strand, that is how the poor come to believe in the Communists' promise of a land flowing with milk and honey, all wages and no work.

Great scientists believed in the Hespero-pithecus, the man who left his tooth in the Nebraska Pliocene. At least in the text books of the experts he became a man, but in fact they now admit his tooth to be false, borrowed from a bear. And since the tooth is all they know about him, they know *nothing* more about him than that he was the man who had a bear's tooth, it has dawned on even the most credulous that possibly it was a bear that had the bear's tooth and there never was any such man.

Now the end of the little man with the big cow and the bigger walking stick is that news of him came via America (though the story is headed " Bombay "), and it went to America from India started by a native, in all probability one of those who are not fit to be trusted with a vote. They are only fit to pull the legs of the enlightened and enfranchised "experts" who " believe."

For the benefit of the Cretins who will deduce from the foregoing that I am " opposed to Science," " scoffing at the well demonstrated facts of evolution," and so forth, I must add that I am not here doing any such thing. I am dealing with the *sort* of evidence which is relied upon to support the materialist conception of evolution. It is of no use to answer that the " pygmy " paragraph is soon shown to be nonsense and forgotten—the parallel case of the Hespero-pithecus was " scientic " evidence for years and still stands as such in the text-books, to make the authors blush. Here is a test: Follow up the next such discovery announced and see exactly what happens to it.

The Chancellor's Jest
By K. C. Macdonald

[*It was a favourite saying of Sir Thomas More that " a man may easily lose his head and come to no harm."*]

The crookback city hemmed about
  Great More, who stooped to die;
It vanished, and the fields without
  Rolled endless to the sky;—
Oh heavy sky, where he lay dead!—
But here, a sunny space instead.
A man may haply lose his head
  And take no harm thereby.

A sunny ground for summer sport
  The meadows stretched away,
Along the Thames, by Hampton Court,
  Where Henry sat at play;
But More, now moving heavenward,
  Knew well what heavy thing
Was lightly left to him to guard:—
  The conscience of the King.

The King, who glibly talked of Grace,
  And never grace could keep,
Whose greed was written on his face,
  Whose tears were quick and cheap,—
Who stripped the very roofs of lead
  To fill his melting-pot;
Who ate, nor ever lacked for bread,

And loved to crown a lovely head,
  But when it fell, forgot.

Who soon forgot the head of More,
  (How light he let it fall!)
Nor missed his treasure, now before
  The highest King of all.
For More, who saw the Royal Will
  So wanton on the wing,
His Chancellorship would yet fulfil,
Gave up the Seal, but treasured still
  The conscience of the King.

And loyal to his Kingly place
  Did naught of his deny,—
Withstood great Harry to his face,
  Then smiling turned to die.
" For Kings have much to do," said More,
  " Their conscience to maintain,
To curb the rich, to guard the poor
  From wicked loss and pain,—
To hold a crack of heaven's door
  Against the love of gain.
So I, if Henry slugs a-bed,
  Myself must rise and arm;
Though having other deaths in dread,
  In mine be no alarm;
A man may lightly lose his head
  And come to little harm."

One moment jesting on the block,
  The next, on country grass;
And Fisher from the Ageless Rock
  Is calling him to Mass:—
Eternal Mass in rainbow light,
  And still, beyond the sun,
No other than with humble rite
  In Chelsea Church was done.
Now More the Water and the Wine
  Has brought to Fisher's Cup,
And sorrow and delight combine
Like woven jewels to enshrine
  The gift he offers up:—

The gift of all that England lost
  While Tudors sat at play.
All on the hazard Henry tossed
  More took with him away;
And still he guards for us at home
  The once so lovely thing
That flashed a sword in Christendom,
  The faith of folk and King.—
For many a man would keep his head,—
  He gave them little blame.
The road was clear that he must tread
  Before the question came;—
And many a man would eat his bread
  Without a choice of ill:

" The loss be mine alone," he said.
  " I'll keep this conscience still.
And still in heaven be at my post
  When Kings are good and kind
And love the poorer people most
  And have their wealth in mind."
" Now merrily shall I live," he said,
  Who merry went to die;
A man may quickly lose his head
  And take no harm thereby."

The Decline of Courtesy in Architecture

A VOICE on the telephone asked me to submit some impressions on the development of architecture during the last ten years for the tenth birthday number of this Journal. Without committing myself I asked for the date of this important occasion and was told **March 21.**

On thinking the matter over I became aware of the important significance of the date and confirmed my hazardous guess that it was St. Benedict's Day. What has that to do with the last ten years of architecture? At the time of the inception of *G.K.'s Weekly* the violence of "modernism" was making a serious intrusion into England from the continent. Post-war students of architecture had completed their span of study at the architectural schools and with the prevailing spirit of unrest prevalent at the time were seeking " something new."

Their vacations were spent touring Austria, Germany and Sweden, and their training had not endowed them with the necessary inoculation against " modernism."

A misleading and a very false term is the word " modernism." It is evident from the examples of it in all arts that it is nothing more than a craze for shunning anything the worthiness of which has been proved by centuries. Any great work of art is, as Lethaby said, " Ten thousand men thick." This abandonment of beauty started in this country to a serious extent just ten years ago as far as architecture is concerned. Literature, drama, music, sculpture, painting and all other arts including the art of decent behaviour had already led the way and it was perhaps inevitable that architecture should suffer with them.

The young architects of the time, when striving to find something new, fell back on dispensing with anything which had been used before without reason or excuse apart from the fact that someone else had used it even for centuries. When talking in this strain one is reminded of Pope's lines, "We think our fathers fools, so wise we grow. Our wiser sons will, no doubt, think us so." There is probably more truth in that to-day than when it was written and doubtless our sons, in the fullness of time, will think likewise.

And what has St. Benedict to do with all this? Only, I think, that he more than anyone whose name comes to my mind stood out for the preservation and conservation of all that was beautiful, noble and worthy of permanence in the traditions of Greece and Rome. The mention of classical forms to the young artist of to-day produces either a contemptuous guffaw or a discourteous sneer. It is this manner (or lack of good manners) which leads one to serious doubt as to whether the achievements of modernists is an indication of their behaviour to their fellow men. This is particularly so in architecture; in other arts the fellow men can avoid the annoyance caused by their presence. He need not read a disgusting novel, he is not compelled to witness a vulgar stage perform- ance, a bad painting can be avoided, but a building is ever before him. Wherever he goes architecture thrusts itself upon him, and whether the man in the street realises it or not there is bound to be some reaction as a result of his environments. That is why I am so suspicious of the modern architect's outlook to his fellow beings when he so persistently and angrily kicks away the past.

Recent happenings in Germany have sent quite a number of these modernists to this country, but I hope, and indeed firmly believe, that the epidemic is now on the wane. People may have been amused when they were told day after day that a new building in Fleet Street was designed to look like a liner, but they would prefer liners to be kept in their place and Fleet Street to be lined with something which looks like a building. Reaction and a return to decency is inevitable. Traditional style and methods of design will reappear and that is why I think there is such a happy significance in the fact that this Journal's Birthday coincides with St. Benedict's Day.

J.D.K.

Land Settlement
By K. L. Kenrick

IN spite of appearances to the contrary, it cannot yet be said that the rulers of England, either actual or would-be, have proclaimed their belief in the major importance of a sane land policy either for peace or for war. When any such policy is put before them they assent to it as admirable but refuse to recognise it as vital. A few fanatics think that agriculture ought to be left to perish. A few more think that the land should now be finally depopu- lated and worked by prairie-machinery and seasonal labour-gangs from the slums. But to the majority of sensible people the picture of a vigorous and in- dependent rural population cultivating the soil and living on its produce is still a picture of great attraction.

The outcome of all is a compromise. Our effete agricultural system pursues its weary way helped on by fantastic bounties and grotesque marketing- schemes. Before he can make contact with the land, the farmer must still pay an impossible rent to a landlord, and impossible wages to labourers. To get the money, he is compelled by law to thread his way through a tangle of Government documents. Even under natural conditions. agriculture is admit- tedly the most exacting and arduous of all occupa- tions. The way in which England helps the man who is engaged in it is to give him a landlord, labourers, and now a Civil Service to carry on his

back. It is no exaggeration to say that the life of the English farmer at the present moment is a little hell-upon-earth. What keeps him going at all is the moral virtue emanating from the soil. A towns- man set in the midst of the farmer's perplexities would break his heart.

These columns have been kept in existence for ten years to protest against the economic lunacy of these modern times. They have never failed to convey the twofold message that agriculture cannot be left to perish and that agriculture cannot carry the burdens it is expected to carry. Everything that has happened in the interval has proved that mes- sage to be an authentic message.

The statesman's strongest card is that there is no popular clamour for land-settlement. There is no clamour even for agricultural reform. Hence the necessity for voluntary organisations. The most effective clamour that these associations can raise is to present statesmen with the accomplished fact of settled land.

In reviewing a decade's history of land settlement it would be futile to go back to the Small-Holdings Act of 1926. That is now ancient history. The pre- sent position is that there are two schools of thought in the proposals for land settlement. The one school envisages a community or guild of fifty families, each family settled on a 25-acre unit, producing mainly for subsistence and only alternatively for sale. The advocates of this school calculate that the maximum gross value of standard English agricultural methods is £10 an acre at present prices, and that the neces- sary expenses cannot be brought below £6 per acre. The other school has adopted the 5-acre unit as its ideal, with production almost exclusively for sale as its main purpose. It must show a profit of £20 per acre. No figures are available for showing how this is to be done.

Production for sale is entirely at the mercy of world-prices. At present prices, eggs, poultry, pigs, and market-garden produce in England would show calamitous losses. Hence the necessity for bounties and marketing-schemes. It is quite conceivable, though not probable, that a Labour Government would abolish all these in a night. What would be- come of the 5-acre farmer, dependent entirely on artificial prices?

It is admitted that spade-husbandry gives two-and-a-half times the fertility given by the plough. Who is going to dig 5 acres of land? Have those who suggest it ever dug half-an-acre? It is also admitted that on exceptionally fertile land, with an abundant market in close proximity, and with artificially adjusted prices, a limited number of five acre holdings might be made to pay. But the person who assumes a net profit of twenty pounds an acre at present prices as a basis for land settlement in England at once puts himself out of court.

The 25-acre unit is a compromise arrived at from the answers to three questions. What is the largest area a man can be expected to work for himself without going outside his own family for help? What is the smallest area that can give subsistence to a family? What kind of farming gives the maximum of elasticity for the alternatives of sale and consumption? The answer to the third question is that standard "straight" farming as understood in England produces wheat, barley, oats, beans, milk, butter, cheese, beef, with mutton as an alternative on certain kinds of land, pork, bacon, eggs, poultry, potatoes, fruit, and vegetables. The 5-acre unit excludes the major half of this produce. The 25-acre unit includes all.

A farmer of exceptional skill and exceptional physique might manage a larger area than 25 acres if it included but little arable land. But a careful calculation of the number of hours per day required for the care of live stock, together with the area of land which can be cultivated in a week of the finest spring weather, shows that 25 acres of land will tax the average man to his utmost capacity.

What produce can be expected from a farm of 25 acres? Four acres of wheat yield 72cwts., of which 9cwts. must be kept for seed for the following year. Two acres of oats yield 30cwts., of which 4½cwts. must be kept for seed. Two acres of beans yield 28cwts., of which 4cwts. must be kept for seed. Two acres of barley yield 32cwts., of which 4cwts. must be kept for seed. The total of grain grown is 162cwts., of which 22cwts. must be retained for seed. Of this grain each horse and cow will consume about 15cwts., a breeding-sow and her litters about 57cwts., and 12 head of poultry with chicks about a ton. The balance of the grain is for sale or human consumption.

It is not claimed for a moment that this type of farming can be established immediately and can become immediately self-supporting. What is claimed is that the money at present spent in bolstering up the most socially inefficient type of farming in existence should be diverted with all practicable speed to the settlement of land on the basis of co-operative guilds built up of 25 acre units.

Practical Aid for the Master Builder

By J. Desmond Gleeson

EDUCATION is, unfortunately, a word which has got mixed up with a State Department and gone rather astray. It concerns itself more with the luxuries of life than with the essentials. It provides ultimately for the leisure of the individual, but hardly for his working hours; still less for the kind of work he does. Consequently the work itself is all going wrong. What we need very seriously to-day is an extension of Education which will cover business men and workers of various trades, who have forgotten the very elements of their craft. What traditions lingered on into the early days of this century seem rapidly to be vanishing, where they have not already vanished.

Take building to-day. I mean the erection of ordinary houses for ordinary folk. Now the building of houses was obviously among the very first trades that men taught themselves. They learned by experiment and disaster, and by further experiment to avoid the disaster. They discovered, and no doubt to their real surprise, that if you wish to raise a building above the ground you must first be at pains to put in a satisfactory foundation. If it is a solid home you desire and not a jolly leaning tower, like the famous one at Pisa, you must have a firm basis. That would seem obvious enough to the ordinary person, but not so to the ordinary builder. He has somehow got it into his silly head that any sort of grounding is sufficient upon which to build his walls. And, acting on this new principle, he lifts his houses on the new estates, contrives to get the building societies to stock them with live stock, and then runs away with the utmost speed before anything happens. Unfortunately, the live stock cannot run away. They are chained to their pens with legal documents and it is their unhappy fate to stay and see what happens when you build without sure foundation.

It seldom happens that they have long to wait. While they are enjoying themselves in normal ways, slinging pots and pans at one another, pushing one another's heads into the gas oven and practising many further jolly modern pranks, a silent revolution is going on beneath the floor boards. Stealthily, with infinite caution, something is sinking. It usually starts at the front, underneath the bays. The frontage of the subtly built house alters its angle by a few degrees. The bricks break in a jagged line. The owner then has two choices. He can stick a piece of paper over the inside crack and see how long (or how short) it is before the paper tears, showing that the gap is widening; or he can drink a glass of Guinness and give the wall a push, thus getting the business over altogether and, Samson-like, bringing the house down upon his own head. Most new householders (so named because they are compelled to hold up their new houses) however are teetotallers perforce. They feel they must prop up their sinking dwellings. They therefore hire workmen to put in

I am now ten years old.

a new foundation at the emperilled part. The workmen erect a scaffolding, dig a hole down below, throw in an amount of cement, more or less cover up their traces and retire, happy in the assurance that they have under-pinned the threatened structure. The householder then goes out to look at the back, to see if that sinking sensation has yet started there.

There are some houses, however, which defy the builder's lack of foundation. They do not sink according to plan. Some unsuspected hardness discovered below holds them upright after they have been sold. Builders, heavily disguised, returning to see what nature has done to destroy the work of man, are amazed to see the dwellings still standing as they stood a month ago. They stroke their beards, to the danger of those loosely attached appendages, and wonder if they may believe their own eyes. They walk moodily away. Yet even though the foundation be safe, all is not well with these houses. There are other things to consider—the stuff they put between the bricks to keep them together, for example. And I call it "stuff" because it cannot reasonably be given a more accurate name. A long while ago the Romans, who had picked up a few tips here and there in connection with building, were also faced with this difficulty of what to put between the bricks in order that their building should stand firm and secure. They found that cement answered this purpose reasonably well. It was a pink-coloured cement that they used and it was a substance that grew harder with time, so that the bricks and it became one with the passing of the years. Indeed you may see it still clinging so tightly to the old garden wall. But the modern builder has not yet reached that point at which the Roman builder stopped. He does not realise that what he puts between the bricks should bind them together to form one surface. He seems to think that bricks should be put into a sort of mud-bath, more mud piled on top and then another brick until he reaches the top. The consequence is that when the work is finished and the builder has made his lightning-swift departure, the rain comes and the wind. The rain washes away and the wind blows away the carefully placed mud and, behold, cracks and holes appear on the new wall. It is really true that in a very few years wind and rain, but especially wind, can wear away the crumbling plaster, which by no means hardens with time, and the householder is faced with a new problem. In order to make his home damp-proof some one must crawl like a fly round the brickwork pushing cement in between the bricks. This fascinating pastime is termed "re-pointing" and costs very heavily, either in hours or dough.

There is, again, the question of the wood-work of the house. A student who had made a study of materials would suggest that great care should be taken as to the choice of wood that should be used. But the enthusiasm of the builder does not allow him time in which to make his choice. So great is his delight in designing windows and doors that he will take the first material that comes to hand without pausing to consider its suitability. The wood protests. If he listened to it he would hear it say that it was never grown for that purpose. It would insist that it could never stand the strain. And it

would be right. When the strain becomes intolerable, it wrinkles and twists in agony. But a wrinkled window will not open, or shut, and a twisted door is hardly worthy of an Englishman's castle. The door must fit in the doorway not once, but permanently. Not only should the householder be able to close it firmly against the tax-gatherer, but against the draught likewise.

Many more instances might be given showing how in the building of houses experience should be the guide, rather than experiment. Builders should have got over that experimental feeling by now and consider themselves mature and even sober citizens. A pack of well-meaning and almost too energetic men, they have been a shade impatient in the mastering of the elements of their trade. They want to race before they have learned to toddle. Therefore I say that education should be rescued from the state department and given to the people. Builders, to their unbounded astonishment, should be taught how to build—especially now when great Housing Schemes are about to be undertaken.

Plenty Always Plentiful
By Hugh de Blacam

OUR Douglasite friends make much, in their arguments, of the enormous productive power of machinery. They call this " the age of plenty " and say that we need no more than a new system of book-keeping to give everybody " purchasing power," with a consequent full share of the new plenty, the machine-made wealth of goods.

To my thinking, they are wrong about this being *the* age of plenty; they ought to say *an* age of plenty. What we see around us is not new, except in the nature of the goods that are plentiful. There have been ages of scarcity, it is true—ages that were afflicted by pestilence or immensely destructive wars, as when St. Patrick as a fugitive landed in Gaul and travelled for weeks through a war-harried desert. Such times, such conditions, are happily rare in history. In all normal times, there is plenty, thanks to the bounty of Nature.

I would have every Douglasite to cultivate a vegetable and fruit garden. Then would he see how amazingly fruitful is the earth, offering to the hands of men such lavish gifts of pure and pleasant food that it is strange that any human creatures are left hungry. Ah!—but how many city dwellers ever taste fruit and vegetables direct from the soil, fresh eggs, pure milk? Is not country food, in this mechanical age, actually a luxury?

We all know that it is. The machines have multiplied toys, ornaments, pretty fabrics, but they have left it harder than it ever was before to get at Nature's incomparable good things. However, Nature has not lost her fruitfulness. The real age of plenty is not far from us, if we sought it.

Are we not told that a mediæval labourer earned enough in one day's work to get food for a week? There was no top-heavy, unproductive population to be supported by those who lived on the land. Almost everybody, except scholars and rulers, took a share in the productive life. That left abundant leisure,

leisure which was used in the great works of popular, mediæval art, the building and beautifying of churches, the embellishment of homes, the making of laces and tapestries, the ornamenting of swords, saddles, furniture.

I suggest that the differences between the plenty of the machine age and the plenty of other times are these (i) the nature of the plentiful goods, and (ii) the use that is made of the leisure which plenty yields.

Plenty under the decadent civilisation of the ancient world was produced by slaves, instead of by machines, but it was equally real. There were free games to occupy the idle hours, which a mediæval worker would have used in some wholesome, joyous pursuit.

Production always was easy. The difficult thing was, is and will be, to see that its benefits are distributed justly and well.

The slave system and the machine system have this in common: that they ignore the desire of the man and the family to be owners. I do not doubt that the Douglas system of book-keeping would give common people a bigger share of wireless sets and more time to spend in the cinema; but it is not proved, and it is mightily unlikely, that it would give them a bigger share of the wholesome things of Nature, or would bring back that happy union of work with play which marked the middle ages and lingers in the peasant lands, still.

Whether machines are good or bad is a theme on which much breath, much ink, have been spent. Manifestly, if man can conquer the air, it is good for him to conquer the air. If a man can save his soul as an engine-driver, not less than as a farmer, his calling is not evil. What matters, however, is that the most valuable things are not multiplied by machinery, and that the recovery of those things is the task before us. In short, machinery is a side issue. Douglasism, which offers us the products of machinery, is completely beside the point. It is simply an adjustment of the present servile, machine-ruled civilisation, to make it more tolerable for the sufferers. It cannot create a real plenty; plenty comes from God and is all around us, and always was.

First things first. Lacking "purchasing power," but sharing access to Nature's bounty, our ancestors were strong, happy and free. When a penny bought what a shilling cannot buy now, the common man got a bigger share of good things, not because of the penny's power, but by reason of his right, as an owner of a piece of Nature, to Nature's fruits. The business of "purchasing power" simply was to distribute things of secondary importance, luxuries, wares from overseas.

Give us back ownership. Give us access, all of us, to Nature. Then, in our abundant and healthy leisure, we will make good use of the marvels of man's inventive power. We will take the aeroplane and fly to Rome, as a holy visit; but we will not ask the machines to give us milk, salads, apples, honey, music and art,—we will gain those with our hands, for ourselves.

William Barnes
By Rev. H. E. G. Rope, M.A.

AMONG the most attractive of Victorian poets, whose eclipse will pass with to-day's "best sellers," is the many-sided William Barnes whose life (1800-86) nearly covered the nineteenth century. To this generation a mere name, he was warmly praised by Coventry Patmore, Tennyson, Thomas Hardy, and Edmund Gosse. He restored from oblivion the Dorset dialect, the descendant of King Alfred's speech, and gave us perhaps the best and truest English pastoral poetry. As a philologist he was a pioneer of whom Dr. Furnivall and the Philological Society thought highly; as a linguist he was far wider in reach and sounder in attainment than Borrow. By persevering diligence he had educated himself; only at 47 did he enter Cambridge University; altogether he was a many-sided man who deserved well of the England he loved.

Born in Dorset of a long-settled yeoman family, he spent his life in his native Wessex, and grieved intensely to see the old rural England decline. Thankful to have been born

"Far off from town where splendour tries
To draw the looks of gather'd eyes,"

he knew better than almost any other how much of England's history was preserved in the West Country speech, a "dialect" only by geographical accident.

"I have done some little to preserve the speech of our forefathers, but I fear a time will come when it will be scarcely remembered, and none will be found who can speak it with the purity I have heard it spoken in my youth."

From Suffolk, Edmond Fitzgerald wrote to Frederick Tennyson in 1844: "London melts away all individuality into a common lump of cleverness. I am amazed at the humour and worth and noble feeling in the country, however much railroads have mixed us up with metropolitan civilisation. I can still find the heart of England beating healthily down here though no one will believe it."

From Cornwall the same testimony was borne by Hawker, from Devon by Blackmore and others, from Wessex by Barnes' friend and admirer, Hardy, from the northern Midlands by William Howitt. Run over the names of England's writers of the time that live and you will find few if any that do not bear testimony to the countryside as the living heart and strength of England. Even Londoners like Lamb and Dickens yield their testimony. Their roots are in the country. Many a born Londoner, Thomas More, has been glad to transplant his life away from the city.

The true and typical English mind has loved the things that endure, the things that do not change with whim or fashion. As Constance Holme expresses it:

"They were well on towards Watters by now, and the rhythmic dance of the light had broken over one of the gaps, catching a sudden reflection from clean steel. They stopped to look. It was only a plough, flung on its side in the hedge, waiting the morrow and the renewal of toil. The bright share told that it had been in use that day, and Lanty knew that, near it in the dark, the long, clean furrow curved up over the hill. It seemed a small inadequate tool for its great work; simple, too, as are all enduring things, yet it had the whole of history behind it." (*The Lonely Plough*, 1914, ch. xvii.) Somewhat better surely, than a "radio drive" against "illiteracy"!

In 1858 Barnes published a set of lectures called "*Views of Labour and Gold*," in which the Manchester dogmas were not applauded; with Ruskin he upheld a Christian economy. Without home life, and time to live it, he insists, man grows imbruted. "If it is not healthy to work for ever at a business in which, for example, the thumb and fingers shall gain skill while the rest of the body shall wither from inaction, so neither is it good for the man of soul and body to be holden too long in work in which the body only is in action, while the soul and mind are left in a dullness almost below rationality. Man goes forth to his work until the evening, . . but . . . in some parts of England . . the stern calls of toil leave him no evening, but keep him from the peace of his solace and rest almost till the dead of night. Cheerless to him are both the going forth and the coming home. A day's toil should be sweetened by the foretaste of the evening of freedom that looms from behind it; and the week's labour should be like a walk through the nave of a cathedral, bright from the light at the end of it, and not like a cave leading only from deep to deeper darkness."

Barnes was a parson of a fine type, now nearly vanished, a true friend of the poor among whom he was born, one who spoke their own tongue, a man rich in practical sympathy and friendly counsel, a character of sterling simplicity. Years gave him a patriarchal appearance and dignity. His friends included Catholics like Patmore, unbelievers like Gosse and Hardy. His courtesy endeared him to all.

In later years, his daughter tells us, "the increase of ready-made articles and of contrivances to save trouble did not commend themselves to him. He said it destroyed invention and self-reliance in childhood, weakened the sense of responsibility in later life, and reduced all things to a standard of mere money cheapness, which he thought involved cheapness of character too. I remember his saying: 'When I was a little chap if I wanted a toy or a whistle I must make it; but now ever so smart a one can be got for a halfpenny, and it is easier to ask 'mother' for the money than to make a whistle. It distressed him that the cottage women no longer baked, and the farmers no longer brewed. 'You can't take pride in a thing which you don't make,' he said."

The nineteenth century retained and in some cases fostered many good things which only fools and barbarians despise, and among them the "refined rusticity" of which the Dorset poet was so worthy an example. From the jungle debauch of these days it is pleasant to look back upon an England we Victorians can still remember, an England in which so many gifted and honourable men bore witness against the tyranny of Mammon. Among these we may give a high place to William Barnes.

[To meet the requirements of this special number our usual features have been held over. They will appear again next week, with the Cockpit.]

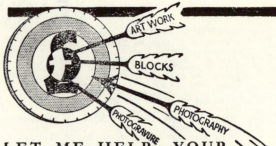

LEAGUE MEETINGS

SCOTTISH EXECUTIVE

An Interim Scottish Executive has been set up by the three Scottish Branches for the purpose of drafting a Constitution for the permanent Executive to be elected at a General Meeting of Scottish members in April, 1935. Until then, the office bearers are:—
President: Mr. Lyons, of Clydesdale Branch.
Vice-President: Mr. J. Bayne, of University Branch.
Sec. and Treas.: Mr. J. Ryan, of Glasgow Central Branch.
The Secretary's address is: 50, St. George's Road, Charing Cross, Glasgow, C.3.

CENTRAL BRANCH

Meetings are held on Fridays, at 7.30 p.m., at the Devereux, Devereux Court, Strand, W.C.2.
March 29.—Mr. E. W. Wilton: "Distributism and Education."
The Central Branch Headquarters are now at 7-8, Rolls Passage, Chancery Lane, London, E.C.4.

BIRMINGHAM BRANCH

Hon. Sec., K. L. Kenrick, 7, Soho Road, Birmingham, 21.
The Meetings for 1935 will be held at **Crown Buildings, 87, James Watt Street,** and are as follows:—
Friday, March 29, at 7.30 p.m. "Life in Norway," by Mr. B. Vogt.
Friday, April 12, at 7.30 p.m. "Herb-gardens," by Mr. F. Dukes.

GLASGOW CENTRAL BRANCH

The Branch now meets on Tuesday evenings at 8 p.m., at 69, Carlton Place.
Hon. Sec., H. Noars, 7, Howat Street, Glasgow, S.W.1.

LADIES' AUXILIARY TO THE GLASGOW CENTRAL BRANCH

Meetings will be held on alternate Wednesdays at 7.30 in 69, Carlton Place, Glasgow, C.5.
Hon. Secretary: Eleanor Gillan, 100, Dixon Avenue, Glasgow, S.2.

CLYDESDALE BRANCH

Meetings are held every Wednesday at the office, 33, Granville Street, Glasgow, at 7.30 p.m. Addresses and discussions every week. All enquiries to Hon. Sec. at above address.

SOUTHAMPTON BRANCH

Meetings are held every fortnight at 123, Warren Avenue. Write to the Secretary for particulars.

CAMBRIDGE

Will those interested in the formation of a Branch in Cambridge kindly communicate with Mr. R. E. S. Willison, 28 Stretton Avenue, Cambridge.

The Distributist League
7-8 Rolls Passage, Chancery Lane, E.C.4.

LITERARY

"TWO SIDES OF A PENNY," by T. A. and Brenda Murray Draper. "Delightful little brochure . . . genial originality." Archdeacon Lonsdale Ragg, D.D., in "The Tree Lover." Published 1/6 net. (Boards 2/6 net).—Alex. Moring, Ltd., 2a, Cork Street, Bond Street, London, W.1.

AUTHORS. MSS. of all descriptions invited for prompt publication by firm of 36 years' standing. Fiction and Poems specially required. Advice free.—Stockwell, Ltd., Dept. 3C, 29, Ludgate Hill, London.

FREE. Three lessons in Journalism, absolutely genuine. Send stamps for particulars, Victoria Institute, 145, Queen Victoria Street, E.C.4.

TYPEWRITING

TYPEWRITING beautifully executed on good paper and returned quickly. Each MS. quoted for as cheaply as possible. John Stanley, 31, Warkworth Road, London N.17.

TYPEWRITING, 6d. 1,000 words. Expert typists; new machines; personal checking.—Duplicating Bureau, 75, Dulwich Road, Birmingham.

FOR SALE

RETAIL Fruiterer's and Greengrocer's, North London District, Certified Takings over £140 per week. Price £1,000 including Stock, Lease, Fixtures, etc.—Apply Box 213.

Advertise in G.K.'s Weekly

The paper that stands for and appeals to the small and independent craftsman, trader and shopkeeper.

"You will be interested to hear that G.K.'s Weekly pulled more business than £30 spent by a well-known firm of advertising agents in magazines they recommended."

"We find that our advertisements in your paper attract the sort of public we want."

"During the 12 months in which I have used your back page orders have come from nearly every county in England, and from Scotland, Ireland, Egypt, Palestine, Canada, United States, Nova Scotia, Australia, Spain, etc."

The charge for prepaid advertisements on this page is one penny per word; minimum 2s. Special discount rates are allowed, as follows: Thick type in all cases is 20 per cent. extra.

4 insertions at 2s. per insertion costs	7/6
9 insertions at 2s. per insertion costs	15/-
15 insertions at 2s. per insertion costs	£1/2/6

Space is charged for at the rate of 5s. per inch.

Advertisements not paid for in advance cost 25 per cent. extra to above charges.

DELANEY,
65, Bishop's Road, Bayswater, W.2.
Telephone: Bayswater 2589.

HOME MADE CAKES and BREAD. No Powders. No Substitutes.

PURE SWEETS FOR THE CHILDREN.
Price 2/6 per lb.

HAND-MADE CHOCOLATES
Price 4/- per lb.
Postage 6d. extra.

MISCELLANEOUS

A WEST Country Farmer sends CLOTTED CREAM at farm prices: ½lb. 1s. 6d., 1lb. 2s. 10d., post paid. Perfect delivery guaranteed.—BEVINGTON, Trenoweth Farm (G), Connor Downs, Hayle, Cornwall.

EGGS straight from the farm. Three dozen upwards sent by rail at local market price plus carriage charges.—Moat Farm House, Chart Sutton, Maidstone.

CLOTHES OF CHARACTER.—Lounge Suits from 4 gns. Dress Wear from 5 gns. Overcoats from 4 gns. All hand finished.—S. G. Hunt, Monument Chambers, Eastcheap E.C.4. 1st Floor. Adjoining Monument Station.

HOLIDAYS

CROMER, Norfolk.—East coast resort, easy reach Norwich, the Broads, Walsingham. Moderate terms.—Write to Mrs. McManus, "Holmlee," 28, Mill Road, Cromer, Norfolk.

2,000 Miles GRAND CONDUCTED TOURS GERMANY and BALTIC COAST, July 27th—August 10th. 2nd rail. 15 days, £17/10/0.—97, Orford Road, Walthamstow, E.17.

Published by the Proprietors, G.K.'s WEEKLY, LTD., 2, Little Essex Street, Strand, London, W.C.2. (incorporating THE NEW WITNESS). Telephone: Temple Bar, 1978. Printed by THE NUNEATON NEWSPAPERS, LTD., Bond Gate, Nuneaton. Sole Agents for Australasia: Gordon & Gotch (Australasia, Ltd.). Sole Agents for South Africa: Central News Agency, Ltd. (London Agents: Gordon & Gotch, Ltd.).

GK's WEEKLY

EDITED BY G.K. CHESTERTON

JANUARY 23 - 1936
VOL. XXII. No. 567

Registered as a Newspaper. SIXPENCE

KING GEORGE V.

TO-DAY we salute sadly, but not only in sadness, a good man who was called to a great office. It is perhaps the heaviest criticism on our current culture, that ten thousand commentators will write as if the words "good" and "great" naturally go together. In truth, they are immortal antagonists. It is not easy for a man to be a good man: an echo of the empty modern cynicism can be awakened, in its hollow caves of mere derision and despair, even by saying that he was a good husband or a good father. But it grows more difficult with every inch of enlargement: and to have an Empire to survey, and still be a good man, was perceived even by Marcus Aurelius to be a paradox. But degenerate Christianity has produced a decay in the perception of common things which was to Paganism impossible: and even death and tragedy can now at last be vulgarised.

It is the returning might in the idea of Monarchy, that it presents in a single image that human simplicity which was attempted in the high vision of Democracy; and there betrayed by confusion and corruption. The perfect political vision is to envisage simultaneously all the families of the commonwealth: but often, and notably now, that perfect vision is a counsel of perfection. But at least the democratic idealist was never so completely wrong as the reactionary realist. Nothing was ever quite so false as the mere contempt for the common people. Where Democracy fails, it fails as something too high and not too low for politics. In practise, for whatever reason, it is certain at least at present, that Monarchy in its weakness can do what "Popular Government" could not do in its strength. It can be popular.

We never in fact come nearer to a vision of all those human families than in knowing, as every man of experience knows, that a vast mass of them have been thinking for days past of the tragedy of one family. And they were thinking of it as of an ordinary family. This is the abrupt and abysmal split between Monarchy and Aristocracy—let alone the Plutocracy into which the latter has decayed. This is the vital distinction, between families thinking of a family, and their thinking of " the best families." A ruling family, when thus isolated, is no longer merely ruling, let alone rich. A tragedy of monarchy can be pitied like a tragedy of poverty. It can be followed in misfortune: but a mere class of ruling families can only be a crowd of the fortunate.

King George the Fifth stood for many things normal to the nation and all normal humanity: especially those which sophists question and politicians sell. He had a very virile contempt for the garish novelties of luxury and laxity: and he was in private very candid in the expression of that contempt. He accepted, of course, in public affairs the conditions of the Constitutional office which had so long been the function of his family, that any departure from them would have been almost a breach of contract. But he certainly left the Monarchy stronger than he found it. It is supremely characteristic of the strange and topsy-turvy state of our affairs, that he owed much of this success to his genuine personal aptitude for the use of an entirely new popular instrument, much more modern than either the Press or the Parliament. As a Broadcaster he roused the admiration of an old revolutionist like Bernard Shaw, who said that this was indeed The King's English: and he gave an entirely fresh and human meaning to the odd old Parliamentary title of The King's Speech. He did not spare himself and now he may be spared many things, including speeches: for he leaves many lessons that are most fruitful in silence.

Every Thursday　　　　　　　Sixpence
SUBSCRIPTION RATES
One Year　　...　£1 - 8 - 0　($7.00)
Six Months　　　　14 - 0　($3.50)
Three Months ...　　7 - 0　($1.75)
post free.
7-8, ROLL'S PASSAGE,
BREAM'S BUILDINGS, E.C.4.
Temple Bar 1978.

Looking On

January 20, 1936

The death of Mr. Rudyard Kipling will be lamented by all: but the public lamentations almost inevitably say everything about him, except the things which really marked him as a man of genius. He is to be called the Laureate of Empire, though he despised official things like Laureateships: and his view of Empire, though alien to our own ethics, was something almost humanly alive and kicking, compared with the Imperialism of the modern monopolist press: which tries to combine the old boast of kicking everybody with a practical readiness to be kicked. His real merits cannot be seized, unless we realise that he was from the first, and certainly at the best, not only a journalist but by instinct a free-lance journalist. In his first and best sketches and rhymes about India, he was anything but an official optimist. In that juvenile volume "Departmental Ditties," said to have been published when he was twenty-one, he guys the whole governing system of the Indian Empire: and cannot have been popular with pukkha Sahibs. He describes them under the title of The Little Tin Gods: exactly the Little Tin Gods who are now praising him in funeral orations with their metallic lips. Or again, to take another example from the end of his career, we wonder how many of such eulogists are now eulogising the thing he had almost come to put first, in his political efforts: his great sense of the moral grandeur and heroic virtue of France. Kipling was sometimes a cynic; and the cynical man sometimes is tempted to be brutal: but he was not a snob: and the fashion of the hour will not praise him for the points upon which he defied it.

* * * *

Forecasting the settlement of disputes in the coal-fields, on the railways and in the shipyards the *Daily Express* reviewed the Ministry of Labour Gazette this morning in a spirit of complete optimism. Wage increases and cuts move in cycles. The past year "broke a twelve year record for increases." The "national spending power" (splendid phrase) is now higher by £9,000,000. From which it follows of course that the miners' just claims will be met, the railwaymen will be listened to sympathetically and the nation's shopkeepers will congratulate themselves on the trend of events. There is no need to point out that increases do not follow cuts unless cuts have been imposed. But one very important point has been ignored by the *Daily Express*. X may be receiving more in wages now than he received a year ago; at the same time he is paying more for food. For one reason or another the prices of coal and vegetables, butter and other foodstuffs have risen so considerably that the warming of rooms and the feeding of families offers as urgent a problem as ever. The *Daily Express* advertises winter sales; it does not advertise the fluctuations in retail prices.

* * * *

We believe and have said from the beginning that a strike will be averted in the coal-fields. No doubt the small improvement made in the miner's lot will be hailed months later as a sign of returning prosperity, a proof that increases in wages have been made all round. The truth of the matter is that the miners are being kept waiting for a promise that should have been offered weeks ago by the owners. There has been a serious delay, despite the fact that the average miner is unable adequately to support his family. Need a further appeal be made for haste in the reaching of an inevitable decision? Manœuvring becomes objectionable when families are on the fringe of starvation.

* * * *

A despatch from New York to the City pages of *The Times* to-day discusses some of the most important aspects of the economic situation in America. "Recovery," we read, "is gathering increasing momentum with the replenishing by merchants of their depleted stocks of goods and with the revival of industrial activity after a period of repair-making and inventory-taking. Barring unforeseen developments it is likely to continue unchecked for some time, for apart from the return of ordinary demand to markets it will have a continuous infusion of emergency expenditure money from the government. The Dun and Bradstreet Review reports heavy wholesale buying, with retailers reporting that their stocks by the end of the month will be the lowest for this season in six years." This recovery, following the Roosevelt policy of restoring the agricultural community to the market, with a stable price-level, an unbalanced Budget and huge government expenditure, does not please the financial experts, who have nevertheless to admit its solid character. The government's credit ought, therefore, to be seriously affected, for that credit, officially, is not the estimation of the people but the estimation of a group of anonymous money-lenders. According to the full-blooded orthodoxy of finance, if these gentlemen do not like what a government is doing, then the national credit suffers a sharp decline.

* * * *

In America, however, it appears that the present position is no test of government's credit; which means, in truth, that the credit of the country no longer rests with the money-lenders. For "it is difficult to explain satisfactorily the calm which the country is showing in face of the further threat to the nation's financial stability contained in the Bonus legislation and to explain, too, the firmness of the government bond market. No doubt they are in part due to an inability to realise yet the extent of the additional burden that is being put on the government's finances. But they are not less due to a feeling that the business recovery has now got such a strong start that it can stand almost anything. Thanks to the artificial character of the market for the government's securities, with the banks the holders of a huge part of the national debt, there is no real test anywhere of the government's credit. It was different when a goodly proportion of the securities were regularly sold to the public. And probably there will be no test again of the national credit until further recovery causes commercial borrowing from the banks to expand to something like its old time dimensions and the banks have to turn some of their ' governments ' into cash. That time is still fairly distant.''

* * * *

In other words, there is a real recovery; there is hardly any commercial borrowing; the government is borrowing heavily and giving securities as I.O.U.s; the banks hold the I.O.U.s and dare not sell them because if they did the value of the I.O.U.s would fall; therefore they cannot attack the government's credit. Meanwhile the people are buying and selling with the money put into the market by the government, and as long as there are goods in the market to meet the money there is no fear whatever of inflation. The continued industrial expansion shows that the goods are coming satisfactorily into the market, but debts decrease and rates of interest fall to near vanishing point. When the Secretary of the Treasury was asked by the Senate Finance Committee what would happen if he was unable to raise the huge sum required for next year's expenditure, he replied, " The minute I cannot raise the sum required to finance the government, that minute you will have complete chaos.'' Why? Because the banks will have refused the money, and by that act will have destroyed the value of the I.O.U.s which they hold—the government's credit. By that act also, the banks will have collapsed, self-confessed bankrupts. It is obvious, therefore, that the Secretary of the Treasury will be able to raise all the money he wants, and at the moment when the banks do confess their inability to continue the debt-system further, the Treasury will guarantee the deposits of government money put into the bank from the profits of the people, by buying back the I.O.U.s and wiping out the debt. These are the realities of the situation, by long odds more important than all the talk of choosing a Republican candidate to oppose President Roosevelt. Undoubtedly in 1940 the American people will insist on the next President, whoever he is, continuing the Roosevelt policy. It is permanent. And its success, the success of revolutionary commonsense, of a return to " the ancient truths,'' makes our own penurious heavy industries boom look silly.

* * * *

By common and well-informed consent the oil embargo has been tactfully shelved, we hope for good and all. Not even Mr. Eden appears now to advocate it, if we may judge by his speech at Leamington. Yet it seems not impossible that the sanctions-making Committee of Eighteen will ventilate the subject again, for

the Prime Minister has been meeting the Defence Committee, oil shares are falling noticeably, and Sweden (the great country for the oil-tanker business) has come out with a loud official voice on behalf of continued sanctions. Considerable attention has been paid to Swedish opinion since the beginning of the League policy, and the sympathies of the Socialist Government are with Geneva. If the oil embargo is proceeded with, it can only have the effect of bringing back the bad old days in the Mediterranean, perhaps of goading Italy into the extension of a violent policy, and what the end of that will be nobody knows: certainly the end of it will not be the settlement of the Abyssinian War, which is the real point at issue. However, if Italy sits tight and says nothing, despite an oil embargo, it may prove not so drastic after all. Certainly the League Council shows no disposition to promote a settlement, and the condition of international affairs, with every stress laid upon disputes and upon armaments, instead of upon positive and radical measures for economic, financial and political appeasement, shows every sign of worsening.

* * * *

The question to ask is, where is the real heart of the conflict? The heart of the conflict may seem at the moment to have moved to Germany, for the dispute in Danzig (not this time a Polish-German dispute, but of course involving Polish and German interests), the threat to the demilitarised Rhineland Zone, and the renewal of an Austrian tension, all seem to mean that Germany is breaking loose again. This may be true (as the *Financial News* suggests to-day), for "to many who are convinced that Signor Mussolini's Abyssinian adventure is only his specific brand of a New Deal to escape the suffocating grips of deflation, the chance of Germany one day seeking refuge from internal troubles in a ' diversion ' is causing acute uneasiness.'' Note that the City of London, which rearmed Germany, and the Government, which recognised the German submarine navy, have little reason now to confront us with a German menace. Yet it does not seem likely that Germany can move just yet, because her internal position is not consolidated; the present sabre-rattling is to prove that she is not quiescent, and the Soviets are the people who fear the sabre-rattling most, because the Franco-Soviet Pact has not been ratified. But Russia fears attack because her intentions are directed against Japan. The Far East must still be considered, the chief object of high policy. Our own main objection to Mussolini is that he is pinning the Fleet down in the Mediterranean while the silver policy is preventing the deflation of China and while the Japanese military authorities are preventing both Russia and ourselves from moving in that area. The Bolsheviks have been rightly described as the best and most expert deflationists in the world. Consequently the policy of both Capitalists and Communists (united at Geneva, with the highest ideals of civilised men as their support) is to get the Italian affair liquidated quickly by the destruction of Italy, and then to move into the Far East. It is difficult to say how far these policies are consciously watched by European Governments, but Dr. Goebbels' latest blood and thunder speech had a curious note: " We are paupers while the rest of the world is swimming in wealth. . . We must live a hard life. We are confronted with difficulties which we cannot master from within, because a higher Power stands above us.'' For ourselves, we repeat that a full settlement of economic, financial and political question is urgently needed. The Abyssinian war is the by-product of a more universal conflict.

*   *   *   *

It is not so obvious now that the Radical Socialists are making things hard for M. Laval as that he is making things hard for the Radical Socialists. Their chief aim at the moment is to avoid taking power. They would have to ratify the Franco-Soviet Pact, which might land France in a war with Germany, or else go back on their principles. They would also have to take the odium of devaluation—which is actually desirable and safe for France to adopt at last, but made unpopular by past difficulties—and at the end of it all M. Laval would come back with the support of the Right. It seems, in fact, that whether he resigns or not this week he has the situation in his hands.

*   *   *   *

The best editorial stunt devised so far by the *Daily Express* has as its purpose a lessening of the appalling dangers of traffic on the King's Highway. With photographs, descriptive articles and slogans, readers are being urged to stop and stare (a curious choice of word, this) before they step off the pavement; and no doubt if the next official returns show that fewer accidents have occurred, the result will be hailed as a tribute to the persuasive powers of the *Daily Express*. Conditions are now so desperate that we welcome any effort whatever to deal with them. Even the orange globes to which motorists no longer pay the slightest attention were a proof of good intentions. But why do all these measures tackle the problem from the wrong end? It may be that many pedestrians are careless. Nevertheless they have definite rights with regard to the road; they can claim without qualification that whereas the machine has the right of way on the railway, the walking man has the right of way on the road, and it is the duty not of the walker to avoid the car but of the car to avoid the walker.

*   *   *   *

This point of view is seldom expressed in the newspapers. If five people are killed in a wreck we read about their fate on the posters. Small headlines, on the other hand, are large enough for reports of street accidents. It may be that advertisers interested in the car industry would not look favourably on any prominence in editorial display that would tend to bring motorists into disrepute. It may be that editors think merely that the pedestrian is a person who ought to keep out of the way of fast traffic. Whatever the view we wish it would change. A special prize might be awarded to the first daily newspaper that proposes the compulsory limitation of the *potential* speed of cars to twenty, or perhaps as a special concession, to thirty miles an hour.

*   *   *   *

Mr. A. P. Herbert's lively crusade against the misuse of words has not prevented people interested in the sale of wood from saying that they want to make the public '' timber-conscious ''; an aim in which success would hardly follow a phrase like that unless the public were wooden-headed. Now a worse campaign is to begin. We are to be asked by ad-

vertisements and editorial propaganda to be '' can-conscious '' whenever we buy beer. It has often been said that beer tastes best when it comes from a can, but usually by people who referred to a pewter pot. The new idea is to abolish the bottle in favour of a tin can in which the beer will be sealed as if it were synthetic soup. No doubt there are important commercial advantages to be considered; no doubt the quality of the drink supplied over the counter will not be affected by the substitution of tin for glass. But it will take some time for the average person to recover from the change. It may induce some to sigh for the neglected pleasures of the barrel.

*   *   *   *

Our reference to the timber trade, however, must not be taken slightingly. The words may be wrong, but the idea is good; for we can welcome any scheme devised to persuade people that wood has its victories no less renowned than steel. An article in this issue draws attention to the grave results that follow the neglect of trees and we feel sure that equally grave results in a different sphere may follow the neglect of the wood-worker. Quite apart from the effect on the eye and on general comfort of sound beams and good panelling and skilfully fashioned furniture, of the log on the fire, and the worthy page in a book it must be remembered that craftsmanship is most likely to flourish where wood is widely used, to decline where metal substitutes are accepted from the factories. True the craftsman suffers in competition with the mass-producer, whatever the medium. But encourage us to think more of the use of wood and we may begin to think more of the value of good timber, well seasoned. That at least would be a step in the right direction.

*   *   *   *

Histories of the aeroplane by writers yet unborn will attend more to personal achievements than to the speeds coaxed from the machines. Brief mention will be made of record flights. Bleriot's success over the Channel will be found more interesting than the centenary race to Melbourne and it may be that the Schneider Cup will have been forgotten. Few writers, however, will be able to resist the dramatic rescue of Hawker in mid-Atlantic, or the safe return from isolation of Lincoln Ellsworth and Hollick Kenyon after hope of their being alive had practically been abandoned. That they were the first to fly across Antarctica matters less than that they were thought to have perished on the ice. They have said nothing as yet adequate to describe their hardships, which one of them has passed over with the remark that he had a slight cold. The adventure was undertaken by men not by engines, and few have stopped to think about their aeroplane. As a matter of fact the inanimate hero was a sledge.

The Poet of Empire

Jungle and swamp and mirage-ridden sands—
  How much he showed: how little he revealed!
Till, homing from those endless empty lands,
  He found his Little England in the Weald.

C.E.B.

The Antiquity of Modern Plays

ANOTHER combination of competition with culture has appeared in the form of a request to numerous citizens of the United States to state what is the best modern play. I have the same difficulty as in the case of other competitions; that I find it very difficult to compare *Peer Gynt* with *Mrs. Warren's Profession*. But I am quite certain of one thing, in connection with the best modern play, that it is probably the play that is the least modern.

Mr. H. L. Mencken and other distinguished critics decline to criticise the plays they have not seen; a bold departure from the habit of many critics, who continue to criticise anything so long as they have not seen it. But in any case, while not confining myself to either form of criticism, I repeat that modern criticism will probably be right if it is not modern criticism; and that plays will have a future so long as they are not modern. The best of Mr. Bernard Shaw's plays is *Caesar and Cleopatra*; precisely because it deals with antiquity and therefore cannot be antiquated. The worst of Mr. Bernard Shaw's plays are those like *The Philanderer* (witty as it is in its way) precisely because it was once a modern play—about thirty years ago. The whole point of it is, not that the characters are members of an Ibsen Club, but that an Ibsen Club is the very latest thing. When the sprightly young people talk about " Ibsen's way—our way," we only feel that those young people must already have white whiskers like Ibsen. But Caesar had no whiskers, and none are growing on him; even his baldness, like the baldness of realism, had its advantages. For instance, the extreme pacifism which dislikes punishment as well as war may be an error, but it is an eternal error. Any number of Greek or Indian sages might have expressed it. A Modern play will express it by talking of disarmament and poison gas and peace conferences, and all sorts of entirely temporary forms of gas and poison. But Shaw's Caesar does speak as Caesar might have spoken; " Until the gods are sick of blood and create a race that can understand."

I wish to court the derision of the cultured by associating myself with those critics who have praised *Cyrano de Bergerac*. Those who dismiss it as romantic make the deadly mistake of supposing that French wit is shallow because it is clear. Cyrano is not romantic, but realistic. He is described under the conventions of romanticism, as Racine's heroes under the conventions of classicism. But the hero is heroic because he knows he is ugly; a good title for a popular play, " He Knows His Nose." He is also heroic because he tells the truth; the one great ideal of the French. Nobody understands it who does not understand the supreme play of all French drama: *Le Misanthrope*. The French ideal is intellectual courage; and until that is understood, nothing is understood; and certainly not the play of *Cyrano de Bergerac*.

G.K.C.

Rent and Royalties
By C. Featherstone Hammond

THE right to demand Rent and the right to levy Royalties are synonymous terms, for—in principle—both are the equivalent of the exercise of the right of taxation. This will be the more apparent if we penetrate the fog of misunderstanding in which most of us are enveloped when we speak of wealth and income and, while we do so, retain a mental picture of these in terms of ' money.'

Writing in the *Economist*, Sir Henry Strakosch, G.B.E., drew attention to the illusory condition of the public mind in which Money is mistaken for Wealth, the shadow for the substance. He said:— " Money itself—whether made of a precious metal or of paper—is incapable of satisfying our daily needs; we can neither eat, drink, nor clothe our bodies with it. Its ' Value ' resides in the fact that it confers on the holder of it a title, exercisable either now or later, to exchange it for the things we need for our sustenance and for our comfort. It is the production of these things which provides incomes for the community in the form of *real wealth*."

Money incomes, therefore, should be strictly related to the availability of real wealth in the only form in which it can exist for the consumer, which Sir Henry now joins in defining as " that which is capable of satisfying our daily needs." Money, then, not only serves as a means of distribution and exchange, but should also function as a means of accounting the actual production and consumption of a people. The criterion by which we may judge as to whether or no money is honestly performing this function is by its ' stability,' for let it be remembered that we are using money to keep us informed (1) as to the availability of commodities, freely offered, and (2) whether these commodities, being available, have been distributed.

Money can do these things only if its mechanism is understood and as long as we avoid the mistake of associating 'value' with money—the shadow—instead of with the substance—commodities—which the shadow should only indicate. Since commodities are, for the most part and in varying degrees, not only consumable but also perishable if not consumed forthwith, it follows that money, if it is to be the true reflection of those commodities, must exhibit the same characteristics of depreciation and of extinction with the consumption and extinction of the commodities. As we have said, it will do so only if its mechanism is understood properly, and if the operation of that mechanism is protected from interference.

We have studied already the question and nature of those synonymous abstractions ' Value ' and ' Worth,'* which we have seen to arise out of the numerical ratio of the ' contemporary exchange relationships ' which commodities bear to one another. These, in their turn, are made evident by ' prices,' which are the numerical relationships of the ' votes polled,' as it were, by the different commodities. Money units being used as votes, and being regarded

---

* See ' Value or Worth,' available as a reprint, from
G.K.'s Weekly.

in this light, we find that prices are the records of past transactions, as they arise only as a record of transactions completed. In-so-far as they are records of the relative importance in which the various commodities were held in the estimation of the community at the time that the distribution and consumption of those commodities took place, such prices may be a *guide* to the probable ratio in which those votes will be cast again, but they can and must be nothing more. Here let us reiterate the statement ' The demand for consumption should determine the direction in which energy will be expended in production '† and, remembering that demand is made manifest by a voting mechanism provided by 'money units' we shall appreciate the necessity of avoiding any perpetuation of systems entailing the arbitrary ' fixing ' of prices of individual commodities, for such fixation predetermines the number of votes which the public shall register. Seeing so many instances of the existence of ' Cartels ' and ' Combines ' upon all sides, all of which exist for the sole purpose of artificial maintenance of prices, can it be wondered at that a free and natural growth of the ' Body Politic ' upon Christian ideals has become increasingly difficult when such misconceived practices are accepted without any effective protest?

In constructing an ' Average Index of Commodity Prices ' we have seen that this is arrived at from statistics compiled by the constituted authority—a department of The Bureau of Labour Statistics, in the U.S.A., the Board of Trade in Great Britain, the Statistical Department of the Riksbank, in Sweden—in which the total distribution in the markets at the various prices (that is the ' contemporary exchange relationships ' existing between commodities) is set against a common denominator consisting of the total claims that have been registered ' in the markets.' By comparison with a previously ascertained ratio between total prices and total purchasing power, this equation should always result in ' unity.' If the equation is less than unity the error in hundredths of unity will indicate the percentage rise in the commodity price index; if greater than unity, the error in hundredths of unity will indicate the percentage fall which has occurred in the price index.

In simpler terms, any fall in the commodity price index is evidence of the fact that there have been too few ' votes ' cast to distribute all the commodities without some of those commodities having to go short; any rise in the ' average index ' shows that there have been more ' votes cast,' or money tokens spent in the markets than there were commodities to go round. It is the business of government to insure that —in distributing money or titles to commodities—when that money has done service in transferring or distributing real income to those to whom it has paid this money—the money is then retired or ' taxed back ' now that the commodities have been consumed. This ' taxing back ' of money to the source of its issue is the operation necessary to the maintenance of 'Revenue'—from the French verb *revenir*, and meaning 'that which returns to the source of its issue'—and is the only means whereby currency can remain ' current.' So far we have carried out the provision

† See ' The Nature of Wealth.'

that, to reflect the depreciation or consumption and extinction of commodities, money must be extinguished with the consumption of the commodities which it reflects. Taxation, therefore, is the means by which this extinction of money takes place. However, it will be appreciated that production and consumption are continuous processes which can only be reflected by something which is equally continuous, that is by currency which is kept current. We can now carry the ' reflective function of money ' a step further, for with the *replacement* of the commodities, currency must be re-issued or re-spent in the markets in reflection of the physical fact of this replacement.

When we have a mental picture of this process, and visualising the physical facts of wealth and income as applying not to money, but to the things for which money is exchanged—we shall see that all the outcry against the injustices of the ' tithe ' should properly be directed against the ' debt ' system, which is interfering with the proper function of money, to which the ' tithe ' in its original and fundamental sense bears no relationship whatever. Since all money spent—and therefore circulated—by the government is only, by its very nature, a quasi ' tax ' upon the increase resulting from industry, it is equivalent in every sense to the ' tithe.' Such money has no proper place, and therefore must not be allowed to have any effect upon the purely ' barter ' relationship existing between one functionally specialised group and another in the industrial organism of the community. Instead, its function, and one which it is actually performing, is to ' tithe,' and therefore to distribute, some of the *increase* of industry. (Such real increase being something over and above that production which the producer himself must consume, directly or indirectly, in order to maintain himself and his family in a decent standard of life.)

If it were not for the ' revenue ' brought about by taxation, such money as the government spend—and in spending, provide a very large proportion of our population with both useful occupation and with claims to subsistence (or the right to eat)—such money would do one of two things. Either it would enter the circulatory system which exists in reflection of the purely ' barter ' transactions which are continuously taking place between the various specialised groups representing our industrial population, in which case it would effect an indefinite inflation of the ' price level ' (but only if the Banks were able to operate a credit inflation upon this redundant money); or, having reached the industrial community via the markets, it might remain in the Banks as an ever growing hoard of unusable money until the vaults, and every cubic foot of the Bank premises, were full to bursting point.

Let us, on the other hand, examine the converse of this proposition in which we will suppose that instead of expenditure without taxation, we have *taxation without expenditure*—or with much reduced expenditure. Devoid of the means by which goods surplus to the producer's own consumption needs are reflected in the money mechanism as *real profit* (How can it ' profit ' anyone for commodities to remain unconsumed?), the industrialist, or husbandman, is now under compulsion to pay his taxes in terms of money which does not exist, for the ' currency ' is no longer ' current.' We have here the exact conditions which arise when Landlords absent themselves. They tax the community by levying rents, but the tax is of the nature of ' one way traffic,' for there is no equivalent expenditure.

Despite the fact that judicious expenditure within his own economic boundaries would enable the landlord to claim a ' tithe of the increase ' of his tenants, the absentee landlord is deliberately shirking his responsibilities, his duty to his fellow man, for his only justification for any claim to the rank of ' Lordship ' is recognition of his duties and responsibilities as ' Little Father ' of his people, in which position he may justly be entitled to maintenance out of ' a tithe of the increase ' (or a fraction of the real profit) resulting from the fact that there has been ' an increment of association ' resulting, in turn, from his co-ordinating effort in bringing his people together in association for mutual aid.

We need only trace back the history of ' mineral rights ' to appreciate that here again, the claim to ' royalties ' has arisen out of the social order which recognised the essentially ' corporate ' nature of civilisation, and, recognising the advantage of a system of life co-ordinated under an elected head, who entered into solemn undertakings to regard all members of the community as members of his own family, doing justice to all, showing favour to none—it was obviously no burden to provide income (and therefore sustenance) for their elected head by dedicating or setting aside a ' tithe of the increase ' or fraction of the profit after all had secured sufficient for their own sustenance.

The commutation of these tithes, either agricultural or mineral, for a fixed payment in terms of an inadequate currency, was an attempt to ' buy off ' the responsibility which ' landlordship ' entailed. It is, perhaps, one of the most insidious forms which usury now takes, but it is usury none the less. It is even more than usury, however, for it is, in effect, the delegation of the duties and rights of government into private hands—the delegation of the rights of levying taxes—without any appreciation of the duties attaching to the position. Yet, under such conditions as will inevitably arise as the result of a popular demand for a ' stabilised currency,' even this condition—in which an otherwise honest and for the most part inherently Christian section of the community find themselves occupying a position which is fundamentally parasitic—will gradually, and by a process of evolution, transforms itself into one in which ' ownership ' becomes synonymous with 'trusteeship.'

Under such a fiscal system as results inevitably from the stabilisation of the Currency, the private ownership of anything in the nature of ' Capital Wealth,' whether it is in Land, Workshop, or Factory, together with their ancillary capital equipment (farm implements, tools, machinery, etc.), such proprietary rights are but in the nature of a sacred trust. Unless that ' private ownership ' is accompanied by a productive use, which in its turn is able to secure an ' income ' for the owner (which of itself only arises out of the receipt of the ' votes ' of the owner's fellow men, polled by him and appearing as ' demand ' for the commodity which he is able to offer as a result of his proper use of his property), he will soon be deprived of his ownership. Unable to secure any income from the ownership of the land, workshop, or factory, he would be forced to sell his title to its possession in exchange for the means of subsistence, and it would become the ' property ' of another better fitted to use it in the interest of his fellow man.

Coal

" Who could have dream't,"
     The Poet asked,
" That times should come like these,
     When monstrous Poverty with ugly head,
     And suffering and disease,
     Afflict the poor,
     And strike their hearts with dread."

" Who could have dream't,"
     The Miner said,
" That toil could earn so little bread,
     That men commanding wealth and land,
     And Christian men not less,
     For Selfishness,
     Deny their fellow-men a gen'rous hand."

" Who could have dream't,"
     An Angel cried,
" That Christ in agony had died
     In grief too terrible for tears
     For men like these,
     Who, at their ease
     Withhold the fruits of mankind's sweated
          years."

F. O'ROURKE.

Straws in the Wind

AND SO TO BED

BY G. K. CHESTERTON

I WILL not say that the Englishman is the most subtle of all the beasts of the field; for he is obviously not a beast, still less a snake, and least of all a devil. But it is true that he is in many ways the most complex type in Christendom. He is never so complex as when he is not entirely conscious; and especially when the last twist of his labyrinthine complexity takes the form of claiming to be simple; to be rough and tough and bluff like Major Bagstock. And one of the weirdest things about him is the subconscious or semi-conscious art and skill, with which he arranges history and human facts so as to soothe and satisfy himself, without quite clearly realising what he is doing or why he is doing it. In truth, the Englishman is the one man really made for psychoanalysis. He really does instinctively erect screens and scenery, half symbolic and half secretive, to protect a hidden thought. All these things filtered through my mind in reading Mr. Arthur Bryant's excellent last volume on Pepys: *Samuel Pepys; The Years of Peril.*

Nine men out of ten in this country, above the most unlettered class, could tell you with some confidence who Pepys was. He was a funny fellow who kept a Diary. He was a roguish fellow; and the fun of his Diary consists chiefly in his confessions of infidelity to a wife, or flirtations with a chambermaid. He wrote in quaint short sentences, often parodied in the newspapers; and he ended as many entries as possible with the phrase, " and so to bed." Now it is a very queer thing that this should be so universally known, and that nothing else about the same man should be known at all. For this mildly scandalous journal was only kept for a short time, comparatively early in his life; and even so the proportion of scandal is exaggerated. There were not many men in England then, or possibly now, whose sincere confessions in youth would be very different. Meanwhile, the rest of his life was a public life of practical usefulness and profound importance. He, with about one other man, made modern England a great naval power. The reply, it will be generally supposed, is that the public heard of the Diary first, long ago, while curious scholars have lately dug up the details about the permanent official. But in mere common sense, the case is exactly the other way. The Diary was kept in a close cipher, apparently impenetrable and long unpenetrated. But the political life of Pepys had been no more private than the public life of Cromwell or Cardinal Wolsey. Political foes tried to impeach him as openly as Warren Hastings in Westminster Hall; that he might be executed as openly as Charles I at Whitehall. In the famous phrase of the Regicide, this thing was not done in a corner. His foes were the first men of the age, like Shaftesbury and Halifax; and they filled the streets with mobs of the Brisk Boys with the Green Ribbons, roaring for the blood of such servants of the Crown. And the roguish little fellow of the Diary stood up under that storm and steered like a ship the policy that has launched the ships of England. He fought for a fighting fleet, more or less of the modern model, exactly as Cobden fought for Free Trade or Gladstone for Home Rule. And he did not write anything corresponding to "and so to bed" till he had seen those ships make their harbour. Now why is that most exciting passage in patriotic history practically left out of our rather too patriotic histories? Why is the hero of it known only as a buffoon winking at a maidservant? There is no reason that can be called simple, in the sense of superficial. Pepys was a very normal national man; Protestant like any other and as insular as most. Englishmen, especially English historians, are excessively devoted to what is national and very particularly to what is naval. And it is hardly exaggerative to say he could have written " Samuel Pepys," like the signature of a craftsman or architect, under the word " Victory " where it shone upon the ship of Nelson.

There is only one explanation. There can be no other; and it is simply this. You cannot praise the patriotism of Pepys without also praising the patriotism of James II, then James, Duke of York. You cannot tell the story at all, without letting it stand out with startling clearness that Samuel Pepys the Protestant might never have started work, and would certainly never have done the work, without the devoted practical support, and even prompting, of James Stuart the Papist. And *his* story has to be told so as to enforce only one moral; that Papistry was the enemy of Patriotism. In plain words, you have to admit that the prince, who did more than any other to enable Britannia to rule the waves, was the same prince who was driven across the same waves into exile, simply and solely because he was a Roman Catholic. And that was more than the English historians dared to admit; merely to do justice to the patriotism of a poor little Government official. That single catastrophe, in the way of letting the Catholic cat out of the Protestant bag, would have turned upside-down the whole orthodox official academic History of England.

But the point is, as I have said, that the thing is almost unthinkably subtle, often semi-conscious; and at once collective and secretive. It is a sort of vague but repeated gesture (like that of somebody stroking the cat) which has gradually put all this lively part of history to sleep; and moulded the story so as to soothe the successful side. There is no veto on studying the period; no overt official command to take a certain line; there was simply an instinct to take the line of least resistance. The main facts of the time were seldom even contradicted; they were only neglected. And I can imagine with what a stare of simple wonder I should be regarded, by the man in the tram or tube, who is quite willing to talk to me about

Pepys, if I said there was a sort of conspiracy to connect Pepys only with his Diary. Is not the Diary a very amusing book? Yes. Was not Pepys a Protestant? Yes. Do we not generally praise patriots, especially Protestant patriots? Yes. But if Pitt or Palmerston or Disraeli had written a very amusing Diary, people would discuss each statesman with reference to his statesmanship; and *then* say, "I always think he is most delightful in his Diary. Have you read his Diary?"

By this vast vague corporate craft or silent strategy, there has been built up in this country a quite abnormal condition of mental and moral Comfort. And we know, because Mr. Winston Churchill tells us in the *Strand Magazine*, that we have a noble Parliament and more freedom than any foreigners; and a poor man has as much chance as a rich man in our courts of law. And so to bed.

Afforestation
By A. Mason

THE problem of afforestation is an integral part of any land policy. Agriculture and forestry cannot be separated. Combined they form the whole problem of the development of the soil. When, therefore, Distributism advances detailed land settlement proposals, its policy of afforestation must be considered as their complement. Together the policies of land settlement and afforestation provide one complete policy for the fullest development of our natural resources in land.

Our agriculture is in decay, and our forests and woodlands are as bad, if not worse. Like arable land they have been exploited by a capitalist society which has permitted the wholesale felling of standing timber, and has failed to impose any conditions for replanting it.

This country, which was once famous for its forests, is now becoming known for its prairies. A literature abounding in references to forests in all parts of the country still survives. It has survived the forests which have disappeared under the axe of the commercial vandals, to remind us of yet another loss which the Industrial Revolution has inflicted upon us.

In certain ways the loss of our woodlands is more serious than the decay of our agriculture. With hard work and good feeding the soil can be brought into good heart for the production of crops within the course of a year or two. But, as with good wine, maturity plays an important part in the production of good timber. It take a life-time for soft-woods to reach that condition. In the case of hard-woods, which must be recognised as a much more important asset to the natural wealth of the country, it often requires the span of several life-times before it is ready for the woodman's axe.

The cause of our present insufficiency of woodlands is to be found within the evils attendant upon an industrial civilisation. The old aristocracy which was possessed of the true traditions of the soil has been extinguished. Where it has not degenerated by inter-marriage with the vulgar plutocracy, it has been almost completely dispossessed by the same class. That class, recognising that timber can never be expected to return its annual five per cent. on invested capital, has chosen to sink its money in factory and foundry, stocks and shares, where an immediate gain is promised. Personal gain is the be-all and end-all of existence to them. Their patriotism is measured by the excess of their dividends over the normal return of invested capital during any given period. And for posterity they care nothing. Standing forests represented an opportunity for so much immediate personal gain, and that gain was speedily realised. To-day we are suffering for that greed of gain.

As far back as 1914 home-grown timber accounted for less than 10 per cent. of our total annual consumption. The war found us with less than 4,500,000 acres of woodlands and much of that was scrub and of little value. So serious was the shortage that it became necessary to contract for the whole supplies of timber for the forces in France during the war from French forests. And it is interesting to remember that much of the timber supplied under that contract came from the Landes, where 2,000,000 acres of soil which was almost desert was effectively afforested by the French.

This serious shortage of home-grown timber was in no small measure responsible for the appointment of the Acland Commission, which in 1917 reported that at least 2,000,000 acres more should be under woodlands. That this acreage represents the minimum is apparent. For the Royal Commission on Coast Erosion, Afforestation, etc., placed the area very much higher, and suggested that our minimum requirements could only be met if 7,500,000 acres were under forests.

We not only have a smaller proportion of land under timber, but a larger proportion of wholly unused land than any country comparable in size and situation. And yet in the whole of the Island, Scotland included, there are only about 3,500,000 acres of land above the 1,500 feet level, below which all land is potential woodland. The same state of hopeless insecurity for food supplies in which it is now generally agreed that we live, pertains also to our timber supplies.

In the past, under the old aristocracy, a landowner felt it to be a duty incumbent upon him to plant woodlands as an investment for his descendants. The forests were an endowment for his children's children, and he invested in them in the same way as the new plutocracy invests in an insurance policy to meet death-duties.

The discovery and exploitation of the vast virgin forests of the new continents played a considerable part also in the neglect of our afforestation. That new and seemingly inexhaustible supply of timber offered an added advantage to the commercial classes by increasing the opportunities for overseas trade, and every factor was then present under industrial conditions for the continued and aggravated neglect of home supplies.

Now when our insecurity for supplies of home-grown timber has become acute, official recognition is being given to the problem.

During the period of neglect, the character of the problem has, however, completely changed. It is now recognised that the shortage is so acute that it cannot be dealt with by individual landowners alone. It has become a matter for the State to deal with on a National basis, but though the Forestry Commission has done its best with the limited grants at its disposal it confesses that " it is more than doubtful whether any real progress has been made in maintaining the existing woodlands on even the relatively low pre-war standards."

One consequence of this report may be found in the recent offer of the government to make grants to landowners planting timber of £2 per acre for softwoods and £4 per acre for hard-woods.

The dangers which result from the failure to preserve standing woodlands is well exemplified to-day in the Middle West of the United States of America, where the rich virgin lands of the States of Arkansas and Nebraska are rapidly being converted into an American Sahara. Had the virgin woodlands in that vast area not been felled to facilitate large-scale farming, the windstorms which sweep across that once fertile plain would not be carrying the rich top-soil before it across the Continent, until it actually darkens the skies of New York.

In the same way as soil is impaired by the absence of woodlands, their proximity improves it. They improve climatic conditions and prevent the rapid evaporation of soil moisture by acting as condensors. They are invaluable improvers of poor soil, and excellent for holding land which has been reclaimed or is threatened by erosion. Thus they help to bring back disused land into cultivation. Furthermore they provide a fair demand for skilled arboricultural labour, while at the same time providing alternative employ-

ment for small-holders, which in some districts, characterised by poorer soil, is just sufficient to make the holdings economic.

On every count therefore, afforestation is a national investment. It can increase the available arable area, and improves the existing acreage. It would remove the country's insecurity in timber supplies; and by increasing the rural population help to restore the balance between town and country.

But the methods of future afforestation policy must differ from those practised by the Forestry Commission during the past fifteen years. During that period only 7 per cent. of the acreage planted by the Commission was in hardwoods. The other 93 per cent. was in conifers. Yet the hardwoods are indigenous to the country, while it is generally admitted that conifers grown here are never of the same standard of quality as those produced in Scandinavia and America. The respective areas planted by the Commission during the 15 years under review was conifers 233,800 acres and hardwoods 16,490 acres.

The prime reason for the preference for conifers is the industrial demand for them as pit-props; and this consideration, coupled with their comparatively rapid maturity, has tended to lure the Commission into a false policy. The conifer, being rapid in growth, has a real place in forestry as a protection for the slower growing hardwood saplings, but to specialise in its production is disastrous. The proportions of planting should be reversed.

Moreover the rate of planting must be accelerated. With even a minimum increase of forest lands, a further 3,000,000 acres must be planted with the maximum expedition. And it should be the national policy to overtake this work at the rate of 150,000 acres a year, while at the same time maintaining and improving the existing woodlands.

It has been estimated that full time employment is provided by each 100 acres of forest for one man. So that the pursuit of the policy recommended would provide for the settlement of 30,000 foresters and their families on the new forest lands, while many thousands more would be given settlement under the scheme for the improvement and maintenance of existing woodlands. At the same time the small-holders and farmers on the fringes of the new forests would be provided with alternative work during the winter months when not fully employed on their holdings. Felling, trimming, sawing and hauling could not be undertaken by the forest population alone without outside assistance. Man and beast would both be required, thus giving the beast also an opportunity to pay for his keep at the season when it is usually eating its head off and consuming its summer earnings.

The growing use of mechanised methods in farming is inimical to a forestry policy. The machines demand large expanses of unobstructed land for their proper functioning. Thus there is no doubt that if the ownership of land was more widely distributed, much more timber would be grown.

The subsistence farmer on his holding would plant trees for the protection of his mixed crops and the preservation of soil moisture. His trees would be not only an endowment to his descendants, but a store upon which the local village craftsmen, the cartwright, wheelwright, joiner, etc., could draw to the continuous benefit of each village community, by their restoration to their natural places as indispensable members of society. But in the meantime the problem is too urgent to await a natural solution such as this.

It must be undertaken as a national policy to meet a national emergency. With afforestation developed along national lines by the State, and agriculture by methods outlined by the Distributist policy we may look for the way out from the present economic impasse. Between these two policies, and the natural rehabilitation of village crafts which would follow in the wake of a prospering rural population, a million families could be settled on the soil within the next twenty years.

A Call To Arms
By W. P. Witcutt

THE recent flood of semi-official pamphlets on the question of land settlement shows clearly the attitude which the Government has taken up. It is that of leaving agriculture to its fate; allowing the old traditional England to sink into decay. The arguments by which they support their action are, from a short-sighted point of view, sound enough, viz., that any increase in food-production would result in a dislocation of the export trade, since foreigners have to pay for our goods chiefly in food; and, what one suspects is more important, they have to pay by the same means the interest and dividends on our loans and investments abroad, the chief part of our so-called " invisible exports." Is this the finish? Are we to acquiesce in the continuance of this system which we hate?

By now we are generally agreed on the outline of the new society we wish to build up—that of the chain of more or less self-sufficient communities of small agricultural owners and craftsmen using but not mastered by the machine.

Sir John Russell, the great agricultural authority, has given his benediction to this scheme. It has been given its classical expression by Mr. Penty in his " Post-Industrialism." It would not interfere with exports—visible or invisible, since the new settlers would not produce for the industrial towns but for themselves.

We must set about building up a new society in the teeth of the combined opposition of the industrial and financial interests. We must build a new England apart.

The number of influential men, chiefly writers, who oppose Industrialism, is something astonishing. Penty, Montague Fordham, H. J. Massingham, Aldous Huxley, J. B. Priestley, to name only a few; but they are all working independently, in the void, so to speak. What we want is an organisation for action. A true His Majesty's Opposition. A gathering together of all men of good will who reject and despise the present system. These leaders who have to the present stood outside the Distributist movement, though in sympathy with it, could be asked to become part of this committee for agrarian action. The sectional land associations whose work is now held up could become part and parcel of this new organisation.

The two principles upon which this new " Opposition " would unite are (i) The principle of the self-sufficient community, the organic unit of the new England apart. Those who do not hold this principle by conviction must be with us on the grounds that in no other way is the re-colonisation of rural England possible. (ii) The restoration of that union between man and nature which the industrial revolution so rudely broke, the ancient agricultural ritual and rhythm upon which man's happiness has depended since time immemorial, the repair of " that disintegration of the ancient pact between man and nature which is one of the tragedies of our age," as H. J. Massingham puts it.

We must take charge. We must be masters of our own destinies, and make some effort to control the mad sweep of society towards that end which we foresee and fear.

Rudyard Kipling

By W. R. Titterton

R.D.B., writing in the *Daily Express*, said of Kipling that he was always a journalist. This is an exaggeration, but it is illuminating criticism. Kipling tended to be captured by the momentary appearance, the news value, of things, and to ignore their eternal values. And often at his best he was the rootless wanderer, commenting acutely and with relish on things and persons in which and whom he had only the interest of the connoisseur in effects.

Thus I don't think he knew anything about the ordinary British soldier in India, but he got some damn fine copy out of three British soldiers. He knew more about the zeal and tribulations of Anglo-Indian officials, but his Simla satires are merely superb gossip-mongering.

His visits to the Bazaar, which annoyed his fellow-Indians so much, resulted in great journalism—no more. It is a marvel how he creates the illusion of reality, yet he never persuades me that he got inside the skin of one Hindoo—not even Puran Baghat. And the Baghat comes in one of Kipling's real books.

The Jungle Books stand by themselves. I mean of course the Mowgli stories. These are sincere, simple, afire with visionary imagination. Kipling got inside the skins of all his jungle characters. But, though they are animal skins, there are human beings inside.

They are heathen warriors of the Viking sort. And this is natural enough, for spiritually Kipling was a heathen Norseman who had somehow entirely escaped the infection of Latin culture. It is splendid stuff, the Saga of Mowgli; and the perfect incidental poems have all the magic of the Northman's dauntless hate.

And so we come to the poems. Kipling was a first-rate prose writer, he gave us some of the finest short-stories in English (perhaps the best short-stories tend to be inhuman, for if you love your characters you can't let them go) and he gave us Mowgli, Baghera, Kaa, Baloo, and the Seeoonee pack. But some of his verses are better than all that.

I am not thinking now of his Empire stuff. Kipling the poet is at his best in intimate personal stuff.

What's the use of grieving
When the mother that bore you
(Mary pity women!)
Knew it all before you? . . .

So it's knock out your pipes, and follow me,
And it's finish off your swipes, and follow me.
(Passing the love of women.)
Follow me, follow me home . . .

There's a whisper down the field
Where the year has shot her yield,
And the ricks stand grey in the sun.
And it's over, come over,
For the bee has quit the clover,
And your English summer's done . . .

There is that great love-song " Mandalay," there are a score of other Barrack Room Ballads, and there are numberless delicate and delicious interludes to the stirring and sometimes almost passionate bombast of his imperialistic and wide-open-spaces work.

He has another attractive note—the riotous defiance of things or tyrants by rootless wanderers.

Once we saw, between the squalls, lying head to swell,
Mad with work and weariness, wishing they was we,
Some damned liner's lights go by, like a grand hotel.
Cheered her from the Bolivar, sinking in the sea!

Then this, from the Song of the Banjo:

My bray ye may not alter nor mistake
When I stand to jeer the fatted soul of things,
And the song of lost endeavour that I make,
Is it hidden in the twanging of the strings?
With my Tara-rara-rara-rara-rup'
Is it naught to you that hear and pass me by?
For the word, the word is mine,
When my squadrons lead the line,
And the lean locked ranks go roaring down to die.

Again, there's this, from the poem that cost Kipling the laureateship:

Take hold of the wings of the morning.
And flop round the earth till you're dead,
And you won't get away from the tune that they play
To that blooming old rag overhead.
(Poor beggars, it's 'ot overhead.)

It will be noted that Kipling's rootless wanderers are in lean locked ranks, and subjected to stern discipline. It is assumed that, for all the protest, they like it; and anyhow it's good for them. Kipling loved the Empire, first of all as a fine hunting-ground for rootless wanderers, and secondly as a fine machine. Is there a contradiction here? I think not. The two things are complementary. As soon as there are a number of rootless wanderers in one place the need for discipline becomes plain. To the heathen the only imaginable discipline is the mechanical sort. And in the end the heathen always falls down and worships the machine.

But Kipling recanted. Recanted his devotion to rootlessness, or Imperialism. Recanted to a large extent his love of the machine; yes, though he *had* sung McAndrew's Hymn, and though he is claimed by R.D.B. as a journalist mainly because he loved the machinery of the Press.

Kipling was born and bred under an unkindly star. As an Englishman born in India, he was an exile without a home. The settled things around him were all alien, though they interested him enormously, and got a taint of the inhuman detachment of the East. The people of his own race around him were fellow-exiles not anxious to meet this fellow. The only household god he had to chat with was Pax Britannica, who had little of Britain in her, thank heaven, and scarcely anything of Pax.

Naturally his admiration was all for bold exiles without a home (though ready enough to spout about the Old Grey Mother) who went out to die in the process of spreading the worship of Pax Britannica thick over the Great Open Spaces.

He had nothing but contempt for Englishmen who stayed rooted in England. What did they know who only England knew? "Beefy face and grubby 'and! Lor, what do they understand? I've a neater sweeter maiden in a greener cleaner land."

And then he came home. And found that it *was* home. And he recanted. Much to the annoyance of Wilfred Scawen Blount, he acquired half the shares (Belloc had the other half) in Sussex by the Sea. And he discovered the English peasant. Who was England. Who had been England for a thousand years. Bone of her bone, flesh of her flesh, the great gnarled roots striking deep down.

As in some other cases, he did not write so well after his conversion. He had discovered a truth, and that cramps your style. Besides, he was an old man. But I think he was a happy old man. It is a great and glorious thing for a lifelong exile to come home.

Books

READY REFUSALS. *Compiled by Nicholas Bentley* "*who drew the pictures.*" Methuen. 5s.

With a very pleasing disregard for accuracy, Mr. Bentley calls this the "White Liar's Engagement Book." A large number of the quotations he has selected for use by those who do not want to accept invitations, suggests that the user will have no desire whatever to dissimulate. "Give me excuse, good Madam, I will obey you in everything hereafter" is a most courteous white lie, but there is a steady descent in the book to blunt refusal, from James Montgomery's "There is no union here of hearts," to Thackeray's emphatic "I would rather go to the Black Hole of Calcutta."

Still it must be said that the title, if not the sub-title, is very fully expressed in Mr. Bentley's work. For each day of the year he has an apt quotation; for each month three diverting illustrations. And for each type of reader he has the suitable excuse. The polite will thank Tennyson for "My needful seeming harshness pardon it," without emulating the gentleman in the picture who is treading on his prospective hostess; the "plain-speaker" will recoil, with the hero of another illustration, at the thought of gushing visitors—"Old friendships are like meats served up repeatedly, cold, comfortless and distasteful. The stomach turns against them." I hope, however, that none will sunder relationships by too slavish a following of "Ready Refusals." Mr. Bentley offers some terrible temptations and illustrates them persuasively. In other words this is a book to buy and enjoy but one from which it would be dangerous to learn lessons.

Music

DURING the war a major in the English army, actively engaged in the immediate problem of defending culture and civilisation by force of arms, found sufficient time and hope for the future to tell Sir Walford Davies that if he (the major) came out alive he would want to know what music is all about. Since the war Sir Walford Davies has been most actively and gallantly engaged in the more complicated task of saving culture and civilisation in the respite of peace. But he did not forget the major's question, and "The Pursuit of Music" (Nelson and Sons, 7s. 6d.) is his attempt "to face the issues raised."

It should be unnecessary to state that no better person could be asked to face so onerous a task. It is certain that no other could better have succeeded in so short a space as one book. The real virtue of the book is that it can be read with ease and with pleasure by anyone however remotely interested in music or however indifferent a lover of the art. Music may have charms to soothe savage breasts but talking about music appears to have raised—especially of late—the most extraordinary savage instincts in the breasts of persons otherwise most generous and worthy citizens. To such I can heartily recommend this book with confidence that they will not even be driven to gnashing of teeth. No savage instincts could be aroused by an exposition so lucid, so balanced, so sane, by a master of his craft.

Naturally, of course, those of us already initiated into the mysteries of the cult will find deeper pleasure and interest in the book. Though the author definitely disclaims that it can be regarded as a text book or as a musical history the knowledge and experience gathered in a long life strenuously devoted to one subject cannot be hid and there is instruction here and matter for much thought for the greatest master of the musical profession. Part 5, "Music in Double Harness," in particular, is an extremely valuable addition to the matter now so debated of the relation of music to poetry, to drama and to the other mobile arts. Perhaps the hall mark of the vulgarity of our utilitarian age is that art, if considered at all, is considered only as entertainment or, at the best, as decoration, very inferior in social value to scientific discovery or mechanical invention. Those few, those unhappy few, who have any artistic values and appreciation left can lighten their sorrow a little with a book such as this. Is it too much to hope that it may a little lighten the darkness of others?

V.N.L.

The Cockpit

Sir,—This title of Mr. Hilaire Belloc's article would surely be more applicable to Signor Mussolini.

Speaking at Rome on December 30th, 1930, the Duce said:—"How can it be thought that I consider without horror the eventuality of a War? To-day a War, even if it broke out between two nations only, would become fatally universal and the whole of civilisation would be in danger. Italy will never take the initiative in a War. She needs Peace. Fascism seeks to assure the Italian people, in co-operation with other peoples, a future of Prosperity and Peace."

In opposition to that policy of five years ago, we have Mussolini's initiation of a war in Abyssinia to-day.

In spite of that, however, Mr. Belloc does not hesitate to try to suggest that it is our duty to ignore all the present actions in favour of concentration on Mussolini's excuses for having instituted that action.

I place little emphasis on the question as to whether Italian airmen have or have not deliberately bombed Red Cross units in Abyssinia. I contend that the point that matters is that they have no right to be bombing in Abyssinia at all. If a poacher were arrested for shooting pheasants in a preserved wood, no magistrate would acquit him merely because he swore that he was aiming at partridges.

Worst of all in my opinion, is Mr. Belloc's attempt to suggest that the recent actions on the North West Frontier are comparable with Mussolini's aggression. In the British case, the facts were that the Haji of Turangazi, a tribesman, and his three sons were raiding loyal natives round Peshawar on British territory. In defence of those natives, we were compelled to take local action to round up the raiders, which was done without mobilising Britain and without attacking a fellow-member of the League of Nations. . . .

It is painfully apparent, however, that Mr. Belloc is not perturbed by Mussolini's decision to "initiate a war that would place the whole of civilisation in danger" but is merely anxious to protest against any attempt on the part of civilisation to terminate that action.

C. CLAXTON TURNER,
Late D.C.L.I.

Sir,—In reply to Mr. Angold I merely wished to stress the point that Cobbett, in common with so many economists who have written on that period, ascribed the entire rise of prices to the "infamy" of the Bank in issuing paper money in excess of its gold supply.

Of greater importance is the assertion made by Mr. Angold, together with the majority of both the Douglas and the Soddy schools, that the banker in some way cheats the community by creating money. Now we both agree that the growing industry of the country needs a constant stream of fresh money. If the government creates the money, a fresh Civil Service is required, with rules and regulations for the issue. A private banker creates money in proportion to the demand at a rate which must compete with other banks. In proportion as he is a capable business man he can make loans with a smaller gold reserve, and give cheaper terms. His customers know that if they all demand gold together, they cannot get it; but they rarely need gold, and most of them need cheap credit. I admit that there is little competition among banks to-day; but it is surely sounder politics to press for the abolition of the laws that prevent competition in banking than to give the government a monopoly of banking. Competition will tend to reduce the banks' interest to the mere cost of valuing averagely safe security, and I repeat that there is no evidence that the State can perform this operation as efficiently and cheaply as can competing private banks.

HENRY MEULEN.

Sir,—Two lines in my quotation from Hawker's "Quest of the Sangraal" were marred by misprints. As Hawker's poetry is not well-known I hope you can find space to print the correct reading which is as follows:

'Ho! for the Sangraal, vanished vase of heaven!
That held, like Christ's own heart, an hin of blood!'

It may interest some of your readers to know that Mr. Edward Walters, of 36a, Oppidans Road, N.W.3, has in preparation an edition of "The Quest of the Sangraal" to be printed by hand on hand-made paper and embellished with wood-engravings by Mr. Philip Hagreen.

M. G. S. SEWELL.

On The Future

A lecture on "Distributism" was delivered to the Men's Fellowship at the village of New Marske, Yorkshire, by Dr. C. Northcote Parkinson, on January 6th. The lecturer began by describing an imaginary industrial town called Mudborough and an imaginary firm, doing business there, called Blenkinsop's. After a description of the ill-built premises, vulgar advertisement, shoddy work, and petty tyranny over the employees, which are the chief characteristics of the firm, he proceeded to make an excursion into the future. Giving some account of the great Socialist Revolution of 1945, he then drew a fresh picture of the same business in 1950, showing how little it had altered in essentials. Moving still further into the future, the lecturer described the Distributist Revolution of 1965, and its effect both on Mudborough and on Blenkinsop's; which involved the entire destruction of both.

Assuming a general agreement with the desirability of doing away with our industrial system, Dr. Parkinson went on to show that its abolition is practicable. Further, he pointed out that the system would, before very long, collapse of itself, whether we liked it or not; as it had already collapsed in New Marske. Whether or not this final collapse should be hastened by war, industrial disputes or financial crisis, he showed that the collapse would come. The imported foodstuff on which this Country had come to depend would fail as the population increased in the lands from which it came; and the means of paying for it would fail even sooner as industry developed in the colonies. He drew the conclusion that a village such as New Marske could only survive by making itself as far as possible self-supporting.

THE DISTRIBUTIST LEAGUE

Below is re-printed a list of books, some directly concerned with Distributist policy, some of general interest to Distributists. They may be ordered from the offices of the League.

Two of our own publications explain briefly why the League was formed, what it is doing and plans to do, and why it feels entitled to ask for your support.

WHAT DISTRIBUTISM MEANS
By J. Desmond Gleeson
2d. net.

In this pamphlet Mr. Gleeson sums up the circumstances that made necessary the Distributist campaign for the restoration of liberty by the encouragement of small ownership and the defence of the family. If you are a member of the League already, give copies to your friends and thus persuade them to become members. If you are not a member, "What Distributism Means" will make you one.

THE DISTRIBUTIST PROGRAMME
1s. net.

A statement of practical policies by the introduction of which large scale capitalism and its twin brother Communism could be replaced by a Distributist State.

Order "What Distributism Means" and "The Distributist Programme" from The Distributist League, 7/8, Rolls Passage, London, E.C.4.

BOOKS TO READ

Two books everyone must read:—

The Outline of Sanity. G. K. Chesterton. 3s. 6d.

The Servile State. Hilaire Belloc. 4s. 6d.

Some League Publications.

The Distributist Programme. 1s.
What Distributism Means. J. D. Gleeson. 2d.
The Problem of Machinery. 6d.
Some Arguments for the Dedistribution of Property. 8d.
The Drink Problem. H. S. D. Went. 1d.
War on the Weak. K. L. Kenrick. 2d.

On Land Settlement.

Flee to the Fields. A Symposium with Introduction by Hilaire Belloc. 5s.
Town to Country. G. C. Heseltine. 1s. 6d.
New Maryland. Rev. Vincent Baker. 1s.

On Agriculture.
The Agricultural Problem. F. N. Blundell. 6d.
William Cobbett.
Rural Rides. 2 vols. 4s.
Cottage Economy. 1s. 6d.
Advice to Young Men. 1s. 6d.
Progress of a Ploughboy.

On Economics.

Analysis of Usury. Jeffrey Mark. 6s.
The Two Nations. Christopher Hollis. 10s. 6d.
The Defeat of Debt. R. McNair Wilson. 6s.
Young Man's Money. R. McNair Wilson. 3s. 6d.
Promise to Pay. R. McNair Wilson. 3s. 6d.
Monarchy or Money Power. R. McNair Wilson. 3s. 6d.
Economics in the Middle Ages. C. Featherstone Hammond. 1s.
The Breakdown of Money. Christopher Hollis. 4s. 6d.

Miscellaneous.

Francis Thompson and Other Essays. Vincent McNabb, O.P. 5s.
The Well and the Shallows. G. K. Chesterton. 7s. 6d.
The Devil's Devices. H. D. C. Pepler. 5s.
G.K.'s Miscellany. 7s. 6d.

Send your order with remittance to the Distributist League and the books will be despatched promptly.

THE DISTRIBUTIST LEAGUE,
7/8, Rolls Passage, London, E.C.4.

THE SCOTTISH DISTRIBUTIST LEAGUE,
50, St. George's Road, Charing Cross, Glasgow.

Do You Value Your G.K.'s Weekly?

If so, will you not help us to get new readers?

◉

We will send free for one month a copy to anyone whom you may think would be interested in the Paper and the views it expresses.

◉

Just send us the name on a postcard.

◉

Subscription rates are as follows:
1 Year, 28s.; 6 months, 14s.;
3 months, 7s.

◉

Write to The Manager,
G.K.'s Weekly,
7-8 Rolls Passage,
London, E.C.4.

◉

WHERE TO STAY

LONDON Visitors; Westminster Bridge; central; bed-breakfast, 3/6 per night; £1 1s. 0d. weekly.—Powell, 75, Lambeth Palace Road, S.E.1.

TUITION

BACKWARD Children coached privately. —Box 1912, G.K.'s Weekly.

LITERARY

AUTHORS. MSS. of all descriptions invited for prompt publication by firm of 36 years' standing. Fiction specially required. £50 cash for Poems; particulars free.—Stockwell, Ltd., 29, Ludgate Hill, London.

NEW WITNESS

Bound Volumes, Nos. 1, 3, 4, 5, 6, 7, 8, 19, 20, 21, For Sale, together or separately. Any reasonable offer considered.—Apply Box 453.

The Notice Board
The Distributist League

CENTRAL BRANCH
Meetings are held on Fridays at the Devereux, Devereux Court, Strand, London, W.C.2., at 7.30. The first meeting of the year is announced below:—
JAN. 24.—MEETING CANCELLED.
Jan. 31.—Mr. C. M. R. Bonacina: "Humanism and the Future."
Feb. 7.—Mr. Anthony M. Ludovici: "Liberty."
Feb. 14.—Mr. Hugh Kingsmill: "What They Said at the Time."

BIRMINGHAM BRANCH
Hon Sec.: K. L. Kenrick, 7, Soho Road, Birmingham, 21.
Meetings at Crown Buildings, James Watt Street, at 7.30 p.m.

EDINBURGH
A Branch of the League is now being formed in Edinburgh. All interested are asked to write to Mr. O'Rorke, 47, Balgreen Road, Edinburgh.

PORT GLASGOW
A branch of the League has been formed in Port Glasgow. All interested are asked to write to the Secretary, Frank Brady, 11, Glenburn Street, Port Glasgow, Renfrewshire.

Advertise in G.K.'s Weekly

The paper that stands for and appeals to the small and independent craftsman, trader and shopkeeper.

"You will be interested to hear that G.K.'s Weekly pulled more business than £30 spent by a well-known firm of advertising agents in magazines they recommended."

"We find that our advertisements in your paper attract the sort of public we want."

"During the 12 months in which I have used your back page orders have come from nearly every county in England, and from Scotland, Ireland, Egypt, Palestine, Canada, United States, Nova Scotia, Australia, Spain, etc."

The charge for prepaid advertisements on this page is one penny per word; minimum 2s. Special discount rates are allowed, as follows: Thick type in all cases is 20 per cent. extra.

4 insertions at 2s. per insertion costs 7/6
9 insertions at 2s. per insertion costs 15/-
15 insertions at 2s. per insertion costs £1/2/6

Space is charged for at the rate of 5s. per inch.

Advertisements not paid for in advance cost 25 per cent. extra to above charges.

DELANEY,
65, Bishop's Road, Bayswater, W.2.
Telephone: Bayswater 2589.

HOME MADE CAKES and BREAD.
No Powders. No Substitutes.

PURE SWEETS FOR THE CHILDREN.
Price 2/6 per lb.

HAND-MADE CHOCOLATES
Price 4/- per lb.
Postage 6d. extra.

POULTRY

WELL-REARED tender young roasting birds dressed ready for oven. Live weight approximately 5 lbs. Post Free, 5/9. Few larger, 6/9. State requirements early.—Jos. Wilchinsky, "Southlands Smallholding," Tushmore Lane, Crawley, Sussex. ('Phone: Crawley, Sussex, 401.)

MISCELLANEOUS

BOOKBINDING of all kinds executed by pupil of Mr. Douglas Cockerell. Leather bound books re-backed and repaired.—L. A. Corsbie, 8, Green Lane, Letchworth, Herts.

POSTERS, etc. Artist undertakes figure, animal or portrait subjects, also line work for blocks.—A. Jules Debenham, Beechcroft, Langton Road, Norton Matton, Yorks.

CLOTHES OF CHARACTER.—Lounge Suits from 4 gns. Flannel Trousers from 1 gn. Raincoats from 37/6. All hand finished.—S. G. Hunt, Monument Chambers, Eastcheap, E.C.4. 1st Floor, Adjoining Monument Station.

TYPEWRITING

TYPEWRITING beautifully executed on good paper and returned quickly. Each MS. quoted for as cheaply as possible. —John Stanley, 31, Warkworth Road, London, N.17.

EXPERT and accurate TYPIST undertakes any kind of work at short notice, own typewriter.—Write P.S., 295, Seven Sisters Road, London, N.4.

Published by the Proprietors, G.K.'s WEEKLY, LTD., 7/8, Rolls Passage, London, E.C.4. (incorporating THE NEW WITNESS). Telephone: Holborn 8538. Printed by THE NUNEATON NEWSPAPERS, LTD., Bond Gate, Nuneaton. Sole Agents for Australasia: Gordon & Gotch (Australasia, Ltd.). Sole Agents for South Africa: Central News Agency, Ltd. (London Agency: Gordon & Gotch, Ltd.).

G K's WEEKLY

EDITED BY G.K. CHESTERTON

JANUARY 30 - 1936
VOL. XXII. **No. 568**

Registered as a Newspaper. SIXPENCE

THE NEW REIGN

By G. K. CHESTERTON

ONLY once I have had the honour of speaking with the man who is now my Sovereign: at the Literary Fund Dinner; a charity for struggling writers. And I feel like a very struggling writer in striving to suggest a sense of something new in society; the new casualness and candour he symbolised even then. He had just spoken to the effect that his father, his grandfather, and his great-grandfather, had all spoken for the same Fund; and he added, equally gravely, " It is also true that they all made the same speech." And that is symbolic in two ways. First, that this modern monarchy is continuous in action or (what is often more important) inaction. And second, that the monarchy nevertheless mirrors the mood of every generation. For I can hardly fancy Prince Albert making that joke about his father; George the Fifth might have done it in private; but somehow, I think, not in public. A grave and graceful flippancy was of the new world. The new King has always been, and even looked, very much a young man of his period. But he is also of his nation; and it is a curious nation; which the more you love, the less you understand.

In domestic affairs, the problem facing a public-spirited prince stands somewhat thus. In various countries, for various reasons, politicians are unpopular. The difference is that in England politics are unpopular. By a paradox, the politicians are a shade more popular than they would be if politics were popular. They are regarded by a sporting nation as toffs pursuing one obscure sport, like drawing badgers; but the natural leaders are those in the national sports; and politics is not national and hardly normal. The King is the leader of the social world; and with us, the social eclipses the political. The late King was very largely influential because he was a very good shot. The second fact is that England, more than most people understand, is ruled by the Permanent Officials. It is our way of balancing the difficulties of government by assembly; balanced in America by the Presidential initiative or Supreme Court. The King is the first Permanent Official. His Ministers are supposed to advise him; but he very often advises them, like the other officials; being very permanent. Those two functions represent what Royalty really does in England; and both mean that the influence is deliberately indirect. He can have a policy in private which takes effect in public. For instance, the late King had a very strong policy, as a social leader, of resisting the modern looseness in manners. Only what makes the present problem is this. With King George it was a conviction, but it was also a tradition; and it was *one* tradition; the one ideal that had once been common. The new King faces a world with widely different ideals, apart from the wild and bewildering realities. We do not know which of several branching paths of progress he will follow; however unobtrusively. It is not his national office to start a public movement, like the American President; but it will make a monstrous difference where he wishes us to move. And this is equally true in domestic and foreign policy.

The old English Party System is much more dead than the American. We used to chaff the French about the Group System; but we ourselves have now got nothing but a Group System. This is as obvious in England as elsewhere, touching ethical and economic problems. It is not only no longer a choice between Toryism and Liberalism, or Toryism and Labour. It is no longer a choice between Socialism and Capitalism. The very word Socialist has come very near to meaning merely Sentimentalist. It means a man not bold and logical enough to call himself a Communist. The real difference is in the history and philosophy of the Slump. Did the Slump mean that modern finance, industrialism and the wage system are showing the cracks of catastrophe, and a new social life must be built on ruins; or was the Slump only a Slump, no more final than a snowstorm? I try to put the question fairly; though I happen to be firmly of the first opinion. But the new social life is not necessarily Socialism; and hardly anybody in England wants it to be Communism. But a very vast number of people in England feel caught in a mechanical trap of Trusts and Banks and an unnatural dependence; but they would mostly break out in different directions; the Douglas Scheme or Distributism or what is called Functionalism. These are new words now; but in twenty years they may be the main political divisions; and be much affected even by the private preference of a popular King.

It is the same in international policy. There is a Group for British Isolation; generally trying to identify it with American Isolation. I think myself that it misses on both sides what can be discovered on a map; that England is in Europe. American Isolation has a meaning manifest on the map; and I think my countrymen have hardly realised that the natural desire not to be bothered with Europe includes not being bothered with England. But anyhow, it is a Group; it corresponds to no Party. There is a Group so sincerely hopeful of the League of Nations that it is willing to wage another War to establish a Peace. There is a Group that would fight Italy as an imperial rival; a Group that would fight Germany; there are even some anti-militarists who have heard of Japan. There are some who swear never to fight anybody; but find it difficult to keep it up. But the point is that all these things can be called Ideals; there is no longer a party of idealists. And those who have to choose between ideals have the horrid task of thinking about ideas.

It is, therefore, in a new sense that we say we have a New King. He is new to new things; not to be simplified by any political placards. Here he has an advantage, in that very differentiation of father and son that has become an historical joke about his House. He knows the young; he has heard of all these things; he approaches them without any tangle of fictitious loyalties. But on him is put a heavier burden than the old burden of doing his best; the burden of deciding what is best. One thing I believe; if ever he *did* quarrel with the Constitution where it means merely the commercial oligarchy, as Roosevelt has done, it would not now be possible to slander Monarchy again. For under all the oligarchic stratification, sunk in the subconsciousness are certain words written by a great defeated man : " The Parliament is the Parliament of a class. The King is the King of the whole people."

Looking On

Monday, January 27, 1936

Nothing has been more striking during the past week of sad and majestic events than the contrast between the dry dignity with which constitutional theorists would endow the Throne and the very human sympathy which it arouses among the people. The contrast was perhaps unintentionally accented by M. André Maurois, when he wrote for the *Evening Standard* an article on " British Monarchy," a compound of the very best of Bagehot and his kind, but distant by a century from the facts of to-day. Unreality reached its height in a paragraph which cast illumination on legal habits of thought, but certainly not on the Monarchy. " Sir Maurice Amos," we read, " explaining this function of the Sovereign [namely, the right to be consulted, the right to encourage, the right to warn; 'and no wise King will ever desire more'] compares the country to a limited liability company administered by Parliament as its board of directors. The King might then be compared to the former owner of the business, who has retained his seat as chairman of the board. Having surrendered nearly all his holding of shares he can no longer vote; but his advice still commands most respect, and everything is done in his name." A moment's reflection shows that a living nation of deep roots and of immemorial traditions (as the ceremonies of the past week remind the world) cannot be compared at all with a private association for profit, a modern and transitional instrument of commerce. Even if the comparison were theoretically apt, nobody after Jubilee Day could continue sensibly to speak of the King of England as a former owner of the business who had surrendered nearly all his holding. Clearly, this is not the opinion of the shareholders but a fiction of the company lawyers.

*   *   *   *

These fictions have, however, made their mark upon the commentators, whose reflections are curiously restrained and pessimistic in contrast with the awakened confidence of the people. All the commentators recognise the popular affection for the Throne, but in their search for historical parallels they seem to dwell upon the difficulties rather than upon the positive qualities of Kingship. Mr. Baldwin, in the House of Commons on Accession Day, reverted to the memory of Simon de Montfort, quoting George Trevelyan, and from there went on to praise the remark of Bolingbroke two centuries ago, that it was far easier to fasten the advantages of a republic upon a monarchy than to fasten the advantages of a monarchy on a republic. Some days later, *The Times*, in a moving passage on Westminster Hall, evoked its royal associations: " King William Rufus, who built the Hall, died execrated by all men in the New Forest; King Richard of Bordeaux, who renewed it, was thrust down from his throne by civil mutiny; when King Charles faced his judges there the Crown had been trampled in the blood and mire of internal strife; while the fourth George, holding his coronation banquet, came there triumphant over his own Queen after the last unseemly episode of a long public brawl."

The national tradition will surely recognise in a different form the royal associations with Westminster Hall of Henry I, Edward I, Richard II, Charles I and Charles II, and see them supported by the Chancellors, Judges, Bishops, Common Lawyers and Lieges, who within those walls served both the Commons and the King with works which still uphold the Constitution. The flexibility of the Constitution is so constantly the boast of lawyers that we would be loath to-day to put upon it any narrow legalistic interpretation. The feelings and the traditions of the country favour instead the conception of a voluntary association like a family, where rights are governed by a common loyalty. And the events of the past week indicate one thing more. It is a current phrase that the King stands above the meanness of Party strife, but in the full tide of affairs the highest virtue ascribed to some politician is that he puts the Party first. Let the meanness of Party strife be admitted as a normal condemnation, so as to make easier the task of the King.

*   *   *   *

Every effort has been made during recent weeks to convince the newspaper reader that President Roosevelt is in great difficulties, what with the passing of the Bonus Bill so soon after the Supreme Court decision, the rapid fall in the dollar, the talk of inflation and the talk of devaluation: the angry speech made by Mr. Al. Smith at the dinner of the Liberty League was likely to confirm that impression. We see no grounds for thinking that the President's power is at all shaken. For reasons which we explained last week, he is in no danger of a money shortage. The suggestion was made at the last meeting of the American Bankers' Convention that the banks should restrict their purchases of Government securities—but if they do, they go bankrupt. The appropriation for the Bonus Bill may be vicious as a precedent, but it is forced over Roosevelt's head. It appears certain enough that the money will meet goods in a stable market. The only precautionary measure taken by the Administration was to prevent an inflationary boom in the stock markets, by raising the maximum margin requirement on stocks from 45 per cent. to 55 per cent. This comes into effect on February 1, on which day, also, all the Federal Reserve Board Governors, except Mr. Eccles, will be replaced, so that a consistent Treasury policy will be assured. The omissions indicated by this programme are as important as the actions taken. President Roosevelt has not accepted the challenge to fight on the constitutional issue. He has not disclosed his intentions with regard to gold and silver: with the whole world whispering about devaluation, he has neither devalued nor publicly committed himself against that policy. Inspired opinion is now beginning to whisper about revaluation, and in a sense the fall in the dollar is just such a policy.

*   *   *   *

As Roosevelt's opponents have not in fact forced him into inflation, and as he retains control of gold, silver and internal prices, we conclude that the fall of the dollar is at his own initiative. Why was that policy adopted? The events of last week in Europe continued the attempt to free Russia for action in the Far East (as against Japan and to control the Chinese market) with the Danzig question used before the League tribunal to engage Germany. At the same time it was hoped that a Government of the Left in France, or a succession of such Governments, would both put through the ratification of the Franco-Soviet Pact and cause a drain of gold as one crisis followed another. Unfortunately for that plan, M. Laval stepped aside without fear of consequences, for the Government which succeeded him, under M. Sarraut, is still too far to the Right to touch the Franco-Soviet Pact, while the presence of M. Flandin (who had M. Laval as Foreign Minister in his own day) expressly guarantees continuity in external affairs. Meanwhile, the Danzig affair was composed outside the League by Germany, Danzig and Poland. There was, admittedly, a fall in the franc: but the dollar took the strain off that by coming down with it, almost to the point of gold leaving New York for Paris. Probably the chief loser in the end was our own Exchange Equalisation Fund, for it had to buy francs with sterling to prevent the downward tendency, which was robbing us of our advantage in the export trade. That is to say, the fall of the dollar and the fall of the franc together, was exactly what Roosevelt would want to happen, with stabilisation in view, and exactly what the City of London would at all costs avoid.

*   *   *   *

Accurate prediction of a poll is particularly difficult when it is conducted by post, but we imagine that Mr. Ramsay MacDonald will have trouble in the Combined Scottish Universities. Not only is the "Machine" helping him in a very bungling fashion, but the bungling itself is being trumpeted about for all the world to know. The fact that highly undemocratic methods are being used on his behalf is made as clear as daylight to everybody concerned: as a rule the same methods are used with considerable discretion. We are not concerned whether Mr. Ramsay MacDonald is elected or not—Scottish Nationalism is in fact more to our way of thinking—but we feel that there has been something weird and wonderful about his recent adventures in the constituencies.

*   *   *   *

The reports of the Bank chairmen continue to cover a position disquieting for them with a thin veil of optimism. Thus, it appears that the loans made by the Big Five are up by 3 per cent.; but this figure is only by 7 per cent. (or £46.1 millions) above the lowest point of the slump, in comparison with a decline by 25 per cent. (or £219.6) between 1929 and 1933. On the other hand, deposits have reached a new high record, a year's advance by 5.5 per cent. bringing the total to £1,850.4 millions. Meanwhile, Treasury bill holdings are up from £232.5 to £277.3 millions, and the investment portfolio stands at a new high record of £520.5 millions, accounting for no less than 28 per cent. of the deposits. In sum, the Banks are in a position of difficulty should depositors demand their money back, for the investments could not be sold to meet the demand; and the *Financial News* is anxious to postpone " a re-stabilisation until such time as the internal banking situation has returned to something much nearer normality than it is at present." One of the most striking disclosures was made by Barclay's Bank in an analysis of advances, for it showed that no less than 35.7 per cent. of the loans were made to " Professional and private individuals " (an average of £448 each among 123,764 persons), whereas loans to all the productive industries together amounted to no more than 24.8 per cent. of the total. Which appears to mean that the search for " credit-worthy borrowers " has ended up with the granting of overdrafts to clergymen, doctors, lawyers, and others whose professional or public status is accepted as a sufficient security. We doubt whether these overdrafts would have been considered ten years ago. A Roman collar or a doctor's practice, even when attached to a life insurance policy, is a form of collateral less easily negotiated than a boot-factory.

*   *   *   *

We commented last May upon a Distributist address given by Mr. Ogden L. Mills, a former Secretary of the U.S. Treasury, at Bowdoin College, under the title, " The Proprietary State." It was an appeal for " the ideal state contemplated by our fathers where freedom will be combined with security, through the distribution of ownership of property, among so large a proportion of the families of the country as to fix the character of society, making it neither Communist nor Fascist but proprietary." The aim could hardly have been better expressed, but even when Mr. Hoffman Nickerson appealed to the same speech as proof that the Distributist leaders of America were among the conservative and cultured (or monied) elements of America we wondered uneasily whether Mr. Ogden L. Mills had ever been heard to express those same sentiments before the New Deal began; or was he adroitly stealing the thunders to come? Now we find him reported in a different key, in the *Financial News*:

> Mr. Ogden Mills, a former Secretary of the Treasury, a close associate of Mr. Hoover, and a person high in the councils of the Republican party, to-day demanded the repeal of the whole body of " new deal " banking and currency legislation, thus taking up the challenge issued by President Roosevelt in his recent Message to Congress on the state of the Union.
>
> Mr. Mills called for the restoration of the old non-partisan character of the Reserve System, the withdrawal of the powers granted to the Secretary of the Treasury to manipulate the Money market, the return of the gold standard, the abandonment of the silver programme, the ending of the President's power of issuing " green-backs," and the balancing of the Budget.
>
> Mr. Mills asserted that the Government had " acquired complete direction of the economic life of the nation," and demanded the restoration of the free action of the individual to earn what he can wherever possible.
>
> The statement is significant as showing, at least, that the inclination of part of the Republicans to take up certain " new deal " vagaries will not go unopposed.

There seems now to be an echo of the Manchester School—of rugged individualism—in the doctrine preached by Mr. Mills; and it is difficult to see how he reconciles Distributism with Mr. Hoover.

*   *   *   *

A suitable destination for the gate-money collected at football matches on Saturday would be King George's Jubilee Trust Fund.

As we feared, the miners have had to accept a settlement that meets their claim halfway. Increases are promised as from February (with a retrospective adjustment) but these are to be paid for not by the owners and royalty holders but by the general public; for as coal prices have risen, so will the cost of other fuels and of various commodities. Attention has been drawn already to the fact that the middlemen began to charge more for the coal supplied to householders immediately after the beginning of negotiations; and the increase, which was accompanied by no sort of guarantee, will cause real hardship in very many homes. We do not suggest that the money will go wholly to the owners. When the middleman has taken his percentage there may be barely enough to cover the miners' extra wages, leaving no profit on the terms of the settlement. It would be interesting to hear what owners of the better sort think of their colleagues.

Differential Rents
By F. H. O'Donnell

THE following formal letter was till recently familiar to many Leeds families applying for Corporation houses—" I regret that accommodation cannot be offered you at present. Your family is unsuited to a two-bedroomed flat and there is nothing within your means that can be offered."

The general explanation of this letter was that although the Corporation might build new houses, prospective tenants could not afford the new rents.

This state of affairs has now been changed and to-day Leeds has the most complete system of differential renting in the country. All the Council's houses are included (Addison, Wheatley and Greenwood) and tenants pay the rent they can afford and no more.

In connection with the Housing Act, 1930 (Slum Clearance) the Government rent subsidy to a municipality for a period of 40 years is a sum of money ascertained by multiplying the sum of two pounds, five shillings per year by the number of persons displaced from unhealthy areas for whom new housing accommodation has been rendered available. The Municipality's rent subsidy, which is a contribution from the rates, must be three pounds, fifteen shillings per house per year for 40 years.

The value of the Government Grant and the municipal contribution together must be used (as in the case of the 1924 subsidy) to reduce the Municipal (based on cost) rent, i.e. it must be passed on in its entirety to benefit the tenants. The Local Authority, however, need not distribute this subsidy on a per house basis, and in Leeds it is given on a family basis according to need. In brief, a displaced tenant may be called upon to pay the full Municipal Economic rent, or, being in poor circumstances, he may be allowed to live rent free. This system, of course, involves a means test and the following is, broadly, what happens:—

Tenants wishing to receive rent relief apply for it by filling up forms declaring the income and special expenditure of their family. The Corporation Housing Sub-Committee dealing with the matter then proceeds to assess rent relief (if any). It does so after consultation of a 'subsistence scale' and "graduated tables." The subsistence scale shows the amount of income that is allowed to be retained by the tenant before any rent at all is chargeable by the Corporation. The "graduated tables" show the amount of rent (exclusive of rates) to be charged according to the surplus of tenant's income over his subsistence allowance.

The subsistence scale per week is as follows:—

	s. d.
Man living alone	11 0
Woman living alone	10
Persons over 65 years of age	9 0
Man and Wife	19 0
Children under ten years of age	4 0
Persons over 10 and under 14 years of age	5 6
Persons 14 years of age and over living in family	8 0

In addition, five shillings per week of the income of every person aged 16 or over who is in work is not to be taken into account.

The operation of the scheme will, I hope, be clear from the details of the following cases, in which it will be noticed that the Leeds Means Test works on the opposite principle to that employed by the means test for ordinary Public Assistance, and in connection with the Unemployment Assistance Board where, after a certain amount has been allowed for subsistence, every penny is regarded as available for the common purposes of the family.

CASE (A) Father and Mother, one child under 10 occupying a 3-bedroomed house, the full rent and rates of which is 13/7d. (rent 9/-, rates 4/7d.).

The Father's average wages are £2 10s. net. The subsistence scale for this family is 19/- for man and wife, plus 4/- for the child; 5/- of the father's earnings are not to be taken into account. The total subsistence allowance therefore is 28/- and the man has a surplus of 22/-.

The graduated tables show that a man with a wife and one child in a 3-bedroomed house and a 22/- margin must pay a rent of 5/9d. (exclusive of rates) or, in other words, a rent relief of 3/3 a week is granted.

CASE (B) A slightly complicated case, there being a child at work.

Man, wife, girl 15 and one child under ten, living in a 3-bedroomed house, the full rent and rates of which are 13/8d. (rent 9/-, rates 4/8d.). The father's earnings are £2 6s. net; girl's earnings 15/- net.

Taking first the liability of the head of the family, the subsistence scale is 19/- for man and wife, plus 4/- for the child. Five shillings of his earnings are not to be taken into account. The total subsistence allowance, therefore, is 28/- and the man has a surplus of 18/.

In all cases of mixed earnings in a family of over three persons with two children or less the liability of the head of the family is determined upon the man, wife and two children table. This for the family in question shows amount of rent payable (exclusive of rates) to be 4/9d.

There is then to be considered what contribution is to be added to this as from the girl. The girl obviously has a bedroom to herself, but at 15/- per week there can be very little "profit" on her, and 6d. only has been added, making a total payment of 5/3d. rent plus rates, or a rent relief of 3/9d. per week.

CASE (C) is a little more complicated. Father and mother, father earning £3 net; lad 19 earning £1 10s. net; lad 14 earning 15/- net; and 4 other children, two over and two under 10 years of age.

Taking first the liability of the head of the family, the subsistence scale for man and wife is 19/-; 2 children under 10, 8/-; 2 children between 10 and 13, 11/-; total 38/-. Five shillings of the father's earnings is not to be taken into account. The subsistence allowance, therefore, is 43/- and his surplus is 17/-. This family are living in a 3 bedroomed flat, the full rent and rates of which are 10/6d. per week (rent 7/- rates 3/6d.).

The man, wife and four dependent, table for the three bedroomed flat shows that at a margin of 17/-, 4/- rent exclusive of rates is payable.

Considering then the appropriate contribution from the two sons who are at work, it is obvious that this flat is really overcrowded and that the accommodation the sons occupy cannot be very spacious; in the circumstances the Committee have adjudged that a contribution of 2/6d. from them together is sufficient; making a total payment of 6/6d. per week plus rates, or a rent relief of 6d. per week.

(This is a case where the application for rent relief has revealed unreported overcrowding and the family has been noted for transfer to a 4 bedroomed house.)

CASE (D) is a simple one of father, mother and one

child aged 12 and 2 children under 10, living in a 3 bedroomed flat; full rent and rates 10/6d. (rent 7/- rates 3/6d.). The father's net average earnings are £1 18s. 0d. per week.

The subsistence scale for this family is father and mother 19/-; child 12, 5/6d.; 2 children under 10, 8/-; total 32/6d. Five shillings of the father's earnings are not to be taken into account. There is a subsistence allowance, therefore, of 37/6d. and a surplus of 1/4d. only. In this case a total rent relief is given leaving the tenant with only the rates to pay.

The figures from the latest Quarterly Return (dated 25th November, 1935) issued by the Leeds City Council show that out of 11,010 tenants occupying Municipal houses, 4,460 are paying the full economic (based on cost) rent and 6,550 are receiving rent relief, of amounts ranging from one penny to eleven shillings per week. Of these 6,550 cases, 5,315 are receiving partial rent relief and the remaining 1,235 are receiving total rent relief or, in other words, are living rent free.

The approximate value of the Rent Subsidy pool per week is £1,697. The total weekly relief granted is £1,582.

The application of the Leeds Differential Rents Scheme has caused the bitterest Municipal controversy in recent years, but so far nobody has suggested a reasonable alternative.

Scientific Distributism
By W. P. Witcutt

UP to the present we have designed our ideal Distributist State with a romantic bias. Your Distributist is a medievalistic, jovial, and beer-extolling person. We can hardly imagine him in any other guise. It comes as a shock, therefore, to find our familiar Distributism metamorphosed into something as hard and cold as Russian Communism. But that is what Dr. Carrel—of the Rockefeller Institute and a former Nobel prize-winner—has done, in his "Man the Unknown."

All the familiar schemata are there—the diffusion of property, the general reappearance of the peasant and the craftsman, the subordination of machinery to handicrafts, the assertion of the rights of the family, even guilds. And all viewed from an entirely different angle. Not from our familiar literary and historical point of view, but from the viewpoint of a scientist—physician and psychologist. The thing is intensely interesting.

First of all Dr. Carrel—quite cold-bloodedly—has passed sentence of death upon Industrial civilization. It simply is not suited to man's nature. "Men cannot follow modern civilization along its present course, because they are degenerating." He speaks of "the necessity. . . . of the overthrow of industrial civilization."

"To-day, the principles of industrial civilization should be fought with the same relentless vigour as was the ancient regime by the encyclopedists." Ecrasez l'infame! But here is no fury. We are reminded of a judge putting on his black cap and coldly pronouncing sentence of death.

The great cities and the numberless machines must go. Put out of the way, as a criminal is put out of the way by an executioner. Why? Dr. Carrel tells us why throughout the whole book. It is hard to select particular passages, because they are so many. Modern civilization is unnatural. Its product is degenerate and defective. The modern man is "soft, sentimental, lascivious and violent." "The inhabitants of the new cities show great uniformity in their mental and moral weakness"—it must be borne in mind that Dr. Carrel appears to be a psychologist of great standing. "Despite the marvels of scientific civilization, human personality tends to dissolve." "Man does not stand, without damage, the mode of existence and the uniform and stupid work imposed on factory and office workers." One could multiply quotations indefinitely. And the accumulated evidence is conclusive and damning.

The Leisure State? One has an uneasy feeling that in Dr. Carrel's ideal society the advocates of the Leisure State would be—humanely and painlessly—liquidated. "In the poor, as in the rich, leisure engenders degeneration." Dr. Carrel's remedy is the exact opposite of the Leisure State. It is the restoration of a society where hard work and difficulty of attainment are necessary conditions of existence. The young are to be subjected to an almost Spartan training. The masses are to be deliberately returned to pre-Industrial conditions. "It is a primary datum of observation that man does not progress in complete poverty, in prosperity, in peace, in too large a community, or in isolation. He would probably reach his optimum development in the psychological atmosphere created by a moderate amount of economic security, leisure, privation and struggle."

The Distributist State (though he does not call it that) must be constructed. "In order to reconstruct personality, we must break the frame of the school, factory and office, and reject the very principles of technological civilization." Dr. Carrel would put the entire Distributist programme into operation.

"There have been, in the past, industrial organizations which enabled the workman to own a house and land, to work at home when and as they willed, to use their intelligence, to manufacture entire objects, to have the joy of creation." These must be restored. "The peasant owning his land," "the fisherman owning his boat" must be the norm. "It seems that modern business organization and mass-production are incompatible with the full development of the human self. If such is the case, then industrial civilization, and not civilized man, must go." The great cities must go too. "Men would live in small communities instead of in immense droves. Each would preserve his human value within his group." A committee of scientists would watch jealously the introduction of new inventions and ensure the prohibition of those that would change man's natural environment. Education would be restored primarily to the family. The population would be trained in a rigid and stern morality. It is typical of this grim scientific Distributism of the future that, prisons being abolished, only two punishments are prescribed—the whip for minor crimes and capital punishment for greater. This new Distributism of the scientists will stand no nonsense.

It is strange how fast events are moving.

A KING'S LAST COURT

BY CLEMENT PAUL

HOW pitifully still he lay after his triumphs, under that weight of jewelled crown, orb and sceptre. He was utterly alone, remote even from his marbled guard, in the middle of the great hall of Westminster. We had remembered him—we who filed so silently by: his humble commoners—as a not very tall or majestic man; a man of quiet ways rather than loud deeds; a lover of privacy and an upholder of the dignities that his day was apt to overlook: a man who approximated very nearly to our English ideal of citizenship. No King before him had ever spoken into our homes, no King for centuries had so strived to win an individual response from our hearts.

We pondered his words of a few months ago in this very hall—his last visit to it:

" Here is the anvil whereon our common law was forged. . . . Beneath these rafters of medieval oak, the silent witnesses of historic tragedies and pageants, we celebrate the present under the spell of the past."

And now he himself had stolen into the past and his words were become stuff for a history primer; and his deeds, too. A few paces from where he lay his proud predecessor, Charles I was sentenced to execution; and Cromwell was proclaimed Lord Protector; and on the roof above him Cromwell's head was left to rot. Thus was Kingship vindicated in England and every Sovereign since the Restoration has dined, supped, spoken or lain in State in this hall. They have been a varied and diverse line, even within the thongs that bound them to acceptance of an ill-defined Constitution. But who shall say that any of them so dignified the Office or so worthily strove to remember every moment of the day of their solemn anointing, as he whose body now lay beneath the pall?

It was hard, even in this deathly presence, to think of him as gone. It would have been less hard had he posed for all these years, impersonal, on a pedestal. But his proudest name was " Father " and if there were some in the land who would have preferred that the Court should be more brilliant and its Monarch more diamond-hard, at least we, his commoners, loved him the more for it. When he came to this Palace of St. Stephen's, attired in robes and this very crown, to open his successive Parliaments we discerned in him at least, among all the assembled votaries of the place, a friend; one who being above the people, was yet of the people. The clipped formalities of those printed speeches he delivered made unexciting reading; we saw in them the hand of the politician; but we never doubted that the King was watchful. We never doubted either his power or his courage to say behind the gilded scene what Constitutional practice forebade

to be written in the parchment. Some of the things he said—perhaps in our defence, when the bureaucratic mind tried to match its hardness against his sympathy—may yet come to light. We liked to think so as we filed past his corpse. We never felt so sure that he had well tilled the soil for the Prince who has succeeded him.

Here in the presence of a dead King we, his commoners, saw in a flash how difficult was his path and how in his " modest stillness and humility," he has done much to rehabilitate Kingship in a dark day for kings. Above the tall catafalque and its Royal regalia we thought we perceived—God grant it was no mirage —the re-emergence of chivalry and nobility and God-guided Leadership; and therein we found much comfort. If this flower of his planting, this slowly unfolding sympathy between Sovereign and subject, may be tended with understanding and watered with spiritual affinity, not even the scheming of all the shadier politicians nor the greed of the oppressors of the poor shall prevail.

With such thoughts in mind, like starved town children seeking light and air, we saw in the six tall candles about the bier something more than the Christian salute of tradition to a departed soul; and in the immobile guard of honour a salute to an ideal as well as to a King. Between those flickering points of light, so infinitesimally small in so vast a chamber, there burned something brighter; it may be the dawn of a new era, the pure first-flame of a new Kingly courtesy that shall join the hearts of the commoners in a truer democracy. May those medieval roof-bearing angels of Westminster Hall, carved by craftsmen in an age of faith, watch jealously over this emerging spirit that it be protected from taint and held high when the candles have burned out and the King's body is gone to burial.

We commoners go seldom to Westminster; we sometimes feel that we are strangers there—intruders, even. But not one, not the lowliest of us, of all the thousands who went uninvited to the King's last court, felt an intruder in that presence. We shall treasure the memory of a reverie but two minutes long that seemed poised on the edge of eternity. It was a reverie that took us—even the hack writers among us—away from the awesome, serene, beautiful scene we had come to try and describe. Of that, an impression remains of a Cathedral-like interior; of a vast window set only half glowing in January sunlight; of carved beams of oak as old as Christianity in England; of a tiny focal point, bathed in pale light; of a Queen's cross of flowers, softening the Imperial jewels; of Guardsmen like altar-figures; yeomen like statues; and a double file of pitying humanity stealing in ghostly silence and a field of shadowy grey towards some inevitable exit,

COAL

By C. Featherstone Hammond

I.

THERE is much confusion of thought when the question of coal is in the public mind. On the one hand, there is the very great social problem of the people engaged in the coal industry, which is, unfortunately, invariably confined to the restricted view including only those occupied in raising the coal to the surface. Surely this limited outlook is responsible for a great measure of social injustice. It is the writer's view, that the only way to regard industry, is to visualise it as embracing all stages in the process of winning something from the natural resources of the earth, and converting this to man's use. Looked at in this way, it is obvious that every stage in the process of coal to the ultimate form in which it is used by the public, whether this be as electricity, gas, water, etc., is part of one industry in which all units engaged in that industry are interdependent. Not one single unit can live unto itself alone; every unit is ultimately and entirely dependent upon its basic raw material; coal.

Now what should we say if, in the management of an industry having its own supply of raw material, that management singled out the people engaged upon the initial operations of handling the raw material, and, out of the total distribution of income represented by the distribution of the industry's total production, gave these a totally inadequate claim upon their own product, and, to others in the organisation, claims greatly in excess of their possible consumption needs? And yet we have a close analogy in the case before us. The utility services enumerated above are paying a price for their raw material which provides a totally inadequate standard of living to the miner, while they distribute the means to a reasonably good standard of living to the humblest member of their own organisation, and a much more than adequate standard to their highest executives. Indeed, so much in excess of requirement is the distribution of claims to real income—as represented by the commodity income that those claims represent—that a very large proportion of these claims are hoarded by investment in debt, in the hope of still more income as interest upon these debt investments, out of which still further investment will be made in further ' debt,' in the form of Stocks and Bonds, ad infinitum.

Few of these people realise that they are sterilising claims to real wealth when their income is used in this way. It comes as a shock to many when they begin to realise that, in many cases, their income is someone else's expenditure, and that, without that expenditure, they would be deprived of an income. When regarded in this way, realisation gradually dawns upon them that they may be responsible for denying to some of their fellow human beings the right to live at all. Indeed, so far have people neglected to hold themselves personally responsible for the troubles of their fellows, that it has been necessary for the Government, through taxation, to undertake the responsibility for them.

Statesmanship can rise to the occasion and deal with this problem by tackling it in its broadest aspect, but it takes a Roosevelt to apply the vision necessary to its appreciation and solution on the national scale. The 'Processing Taxes' were designed to meet just these conditions. In the vast farm surpluses which were America's problem we have the parallel problem of the vast potential surplus of coal with which we are faced in Great Britain. With the artificially depressed standard of living imposed upon the American Farm community by the existence of farm produce vastly in excess of the home market's capacity to consume, we have our own parallel in the depressed standard of living now being meted out to the miners. But President Roosevelt saw two broad issues. In the first place the Farm industry had been organised to supply a world market, which (owing to the fact that countries which did not produce their own supply before the war had now encouraged their own people to produce all and even more than their own consumption needs) had gone for ever. In the second place he saw that, faced with this surplus production, the American farmer had been forced to accept a standard of living bordering on the starvation line, whilst Industries which processed the farm products were making claim not only to a very much higher standard of living, but were demanding money-incomes which were not being used to claim their equivalent commodity-income but instead, were being distributed to those who sterilised these by 'investing' them in stocks and bonds—that is to say, in the acquisition of claims to debt.

By the application of ' Processing Taxes,' as well as by the broadest measure of ' economic planning ' (not to be confused with our own example of this, which is directed toward crushing industry into an inadequate financial mould) by cutting down wheat acreage and by 'feeding back' misused or unused purchasing power from the financial end of the whole organism into the farmer's or raw material end, the President not only has restored the Farming community to a decent standard of living, but has brought prosperity to the Factory community as well. This is not to be wondered at, for the Farm community provide the market for the produce of the Factories, just as the Factory community provide the markets for the Farmer; the two are interdependent, but, on a final analysis, all are dependent upon the capacity of the earth to grow food.

Can the parallel be lost upon us? There are few who would expect to see the restoration of our world market for coal which is surplus to our own home consumption needs. In the first place, this market, while we had it, was of artificial value and was only rendered possible while we lent other nations the money with which to 'buy' our goods. The bare bones of the situation are explained by the fact that, in the last 50 years, out of a so-called 'favourable trade balance' of upwards of 8,000 million pounds worth of very excellent British commodities, of which coal must have been a very large proportion, 4,000 million pounds worth have been exchanged for what has proved to be bad paper, for this has been repudiated altogether. In other words, Great Britain has been the 'milch cow' in a scheme of financial imperialism directed to the extension of the 'debt system' of usury for its own sake. This is euphemistically referred to as the 'Credit' system, though why credit facilities—which are facilities which are extended to all and sundry to get themselves into irredeemable debt—should have so bemused the British people as to get them to acquiesce in a system which depresses their own standard of living by the amount by which foreigners are allowed to help themselves to produce which they have done nothing towards producing—is one of the wonders of the age in which we live.

Whether we shall even continue to receive the interest upon the remaining foreign 'investments' is doubtful; that we shall ever be able or willing to receive the principal in re-payment, even if it were offered to us, is, beyond question, quite unthinkable.

In a world in which economic sanity is restored, we may look forward, however, to a greatly increased trade in surpluses of all kinds, but this trade will necessarily be a balance of commodities for commodities and not in exchange for debt. Rather than that, in fact, it would have paid us to have given commodities away, particularly in those cases where we had a monopoly of raw materials, it would have avoided war in more than one instance, and the result has been the same inasmuch as we shall never receive any equivalent commodities for those which nation after nation have been persuaded by the 'City' to borrow the money to buy.

Our mining industry is capable of something of the order of two to five times the output necessary to satisfy our own consumption needs if every miner and every mechanical device were put to work at capacity. Yet such countries as Italy are without coal resources. This is not to suggest that Italy could use anything but a fraction of our surplus productive capacity. Indeed it must be patent to everyone that there are other countries, all of whom have their eyes upon Italy as a potential market for their own surplus production of coal. How much of the present world chaos is bound up with the same basic economic problem?

(To be continued.)

Christian History

THE TWO NATIONS. *By Christopher Hollis. Routledge. 10s. 6d.*

THIS book, *The Two Nations*, is no doubt handicapped by its description as " a financial history of England from the standpoint of a monetary reformer." There are many people, trained or amateur historians, active and politically-minded citizens, who will shy away from it at once with the remark that ' Finance, and all that sort of thing, is above my head'; and a careful tradition, not unfortified by painful experience, makes of the monetary reformer a simple crank. The social order which was precariously (we may now add, temporarily) erected on the divisions of Christendom taught men either to devote themselves entirely to finance, to the orthodox monetary theory, or else to leave the unholy mysteries alone. So there exists a small priestly caste, adept in a lore which the masses of the people are not expected to understand. Unfortunately for the masses of the people, however, the point and purpose of the sacred writings is to establish the domination of the priesthood over the people, by giving to the few an absolute control over the life-blood of the community:

over the means of exchange in trade and commerce, over the means and instruments of production, over natural resources and landed property. The priesthood holds the common wealth, so that in every country the teeming masses of the labouring poor are subjected to the policies of a smaller group, of whose habits and thoughts they are as ignorant as they would be if belonging to separate races or to separate nations. The two nations, in Disraeli's phrase, are the rich and the poor. The poor are deprived of property: the rich abuse it.

The upshot is that every objection urged against the old priests in the sixteenth century, and afterwards, is writ large in the nature of the new priests who sapped away the property and the liberty of the people. The group of enriched men who destroyed the old priests were very soon after to kill the King and to sequestrate the yeoman's land. A reviving Monarchy was again checked, strictly limited in its functions, held in jeopardy by a long period of disputed succession, while the system entirely new to England of estimating wealth as debt was fastened upon the people, and engraved in the popular mind, by every ingenious artifice of class education, class legislation, constitutional arrangement and mass suggestion—its powerful sanctions being the control of debt, and therefore of the use of wealth, and therefore of prices in the market, so that whether men rebelled against the system, or whether the system failed by its inherent falsity, the widespread consequences would be bankruptcy and ruin. It was always possible to rally a frightened people in defence of debt; the thing bore every appearance of popularity. But see how contemporary facts answer the charges laid against the priests of Christendom. Do not the new priests threaten the recalcitrant with economic death and damnation? Do they not excommunicate at will, and lay defaulting countries under interdict? Do they not perpetuate in their doctrines a meaningless hocus-pocus, a mingle-mangle of superstition? The theory of trade-cycles is only one obvious example. Do they not acquire vast estates and live in luxury, deluding the people with pretended miracles?—for it is a miracle when out of nothing they create the credit (or debt) that makes wool grow on the backs of sheep; and a profitable miracle when they demand repayment with interest in the goods and servitude of others. Do they not require pilgrimage to their shrines (all except that really rowdy and popular pilgrimage, a run on the bank)? If it is the status of saints that you abhor, have a look at Cobden in Mornington Crescent, or at Alexander Hamilton in the New York Stock Exchange. And on the pediment of our own Royal Exchange there is carved, more blasphemous than the Rood of Boxley, the hypocritical device, " The earth is the Lord's, and the fulness thereof." Under this very text, the new priests are propagating the doctrine that the figure of 2,000,000 unemployed—2,000,000 deprived of the fulness of the Lord's earth—is a normal and expected figure for Great Britain alone.

The system, then, stripped of Whig history and of a farrago of technical terms, is simply the greed of a few. An elaborate social philosophy has been woven around the sins of defrauding labourers, of oppressing the widow and the orphan. Consequently Mr. Hollis and those who think with him—he would mention the

Editor of this paper, Mr. Belloc, Dr. R. McNair Wilson and Mr. C. F. Hammond among many living writers who have inspired this book—are not financial historians or monetary reformers, but Christians, urging a return to Christian principles. The distinction is important. True, every one of these writers has to watch the tricks of the heathen, exposing their methods and bringing to light the suppressed truths of past and present history, but not one of them wants to be preoccupied with the unrealities of economics and finance as taught to our generation.

The Two Nations, far from being a negative criticism of finance, or the elaboration of a formula whereby materialists may be comforted with the shared out fruits of mass-production, is a social history which strikes back to the ancient truths of the organic and corporate life of Christendom. " It is said that the younger Pitt once greeted Adam Smith with the remark, ' We are all your pupils here.' It was the tragic truth. No one who reads the strong pages of the *Wealth of Nations* can fail to be captured with delight at their powerful reasoning. The faults of that book are not in its reasoning, but in its premises—in its unproved assumption that a society must necessarily consist of a few capitalists and the propertyless proletariat, who can get a living only by working for the capitalists for a subsistence wage. To St. Thomas Aquinas property existed to promote the well-being of society, but to Adam Smith society existed to defend the rights of the owners of property " (p.87). " It is clear then that the battle between capitalism and communism, so far from being the eternal struggle of our race, was in reality little more than a family quarrel between two Jews for the divine right to deceive mankind—between the Dutch Jew Ricardo and the German Jew Marx. And before the menace of a real challenge to the system—the challenge that has come in our day from President Roosevelt—even the family quarrel is forgotten, and the finance-ridden Western European countries and communist Moscow come easily together . . . Now every tradition of our race stands in opposition to the whole insolent plan for rearranging the poor and refuses to take sides either with Ricardo and his claim that the capitalist shall not be interfered with by the commissar, or with Marx and his claim that the commissar shall not be interfered with by the capitalist " (p.131). " Now if it was two Jews, their minds confused with bogus Whig history, who were most largely responsible for imposing this dessication upon mankind, it was a third Jew who saw most clearly the folly of it. Disraeli . . . saw, too, that the gulf between these two nations could be abridged only by some great force utterly challenging the liberal laws of political economy and the communist doctrine of the class war. That great force was the gigantic, explosive force of real Christian faith " (p.136). For such men as Sadler and Shaftesbury, " a Christian world could not be a world of the two nations; it was a world in which ' barbarian and Scythian, bond and free ' were united in the transcendant unity of Christ and, if political economy knew nothing of such a world, so much, they said, with all simplicity and all humility, the worse for political economy " (p.139). President Roosevelt's inaugural address " was the deliberate repudiation of a heresy that has cursed and warped the story of mankind for

five hundred years—the gigantic heresy that Man is sufficient to himself and that it is possible to organise a human society apart from God. In Dante's great vision of Hell, among the false gods that have deceived mankind to none is there given a more shameful place than to Plutus. He is the most cowardly of them all. He alone is dumb, for greed dare not honestly preach its gospel, since it is a gospel that can be accepted only when it is misunderstood. Before the words of a brave man it collapses, Dante tells us, ' as the sails swollen with the wind fall when the mast breaks.' So it proved six hundred years after Dante died " (p.245).

Perhaps these extracts show best the central argument put forward by Mr. Hollis with a humanism foreign to modern essays in the dismal science. Here the science is no longer dismal because it is no longer based upon that ridiculous abstraction (common to Manchester and to Moscow), the Economic Man. The book should convince anyone ordinarily well-read that he can follow a straightforward argument in a territory which he has hitherto avoided, because the object of the Whigs is to confuse the issue and the object of Mr. Hollis is to clarify it. A favourite method of the Whigs is to suppress, or to minimise the importance of, various writings which give the whole game away. Mr. Hollis's method is to uncover that lost tradition. His earlier chapters on the control of the price-level by the old Monarchy, and on the misfortunes of England when the price-level suffered interference, are based upon the famous but seldom-quoted research of Professor Thorold Rogers, who lost his Professorship for his pains. It was Thorold Rogers who came to the conclusion that " from 1563 to 1824, a conspiracy, concocted by the law and carried out by parties interested in its success, was entered into to cheat the English workman of his wages, to tie him to the soil, to deprive him of hope and to degrade him into irremediable poverty." It was Rogers who wrote in 1867 that " the condition of the peasant is now lower than it was even in Cobbett's time." Cobbett, than whom there is no better witness on the social history of his times, was penalised in a more savage fashion, but he upholds the lost tradition and the verdict which Mr. Hollis passes: " If you had asked the Englishman of Henry VIII's time, he would have repudiated with horror the notion that the poor would ever be forced to live as they were forced to live in Cromwell's England, the Cromwellian Puritan would never have dreamed of the degradations of Charles II's England, the nobleman of 1688, little as were his illusions about the gloriousness of his revolution, at least was not so cynical as to believe that the conditions of the early factory system would come to its inevitable results."

The clamp that was fixed upon England, after the first attacks against the Church and against the Monarchy, was the credit system of ' Dutch Finance,' expressed by the foundation of the Bank of England and accompanied by the limitation of the Monarchy, so that the politicians (drawn from the banking families and their auxiliaries) stood between the King and the people. Here again there is the witness for the old tradition: Bishop Berkeley, whose financial writings, nearly suppressed altogether, explain in uncanny detail every fallacy in the credit (or debt) system and every reason why it must break down whenever a strain is put upon it. But Bishop Berkeley, ignored in his own day, was soon lost entirely because his chance readers could no longer understand him. The Whigs, who used Burnet to poison the springs of history, took possession of the whole educational system of the country, and brought up the gentlemen of the public schools and universities to forget the first principles of the old social order. Mr. Hollis does nothing better than his description of Townshend's educational schemes. He explains how it was that some (not all) of the worst injustices committed against England and Ireland—he might have added a chapter on Scotland—were committed as though traditionally and benevolently; how it was that a would-be Christian society could stomach the doctrines preached by Malthus, Lord Althorp and Ricardo; how it was that some of the mightiest revolts came from men like Lingard, Cobbett, and the Irish poor, who had never been " properly " educated.

Space forbids the possibility of following Mr. Hollis in his survey (which is particularly valuable in its extension to American history), as the debt system fastened itself upon the world, inevitably driving down conditions of living in one country after another; inevitably spreading wars and rumours of wars, because all countries were interested primarily in export; and inevitably producing, not only the cycle of booms and slumps, but also an increasing devastation with each collapse. Fortunately he is able to trace as well the mitigation of disaster with the counter-attacks of men inspired by Christian principles—for Christian principles, not mere " monetary reform," define the issue in our civilisation—and fortunately he is able to see at this moment the probability of their success. Perhaps these remarks will persuade people who avoid " finance " to read *The Two Nations*, for it is both straightforward and comprehensive: an eye-opener for anyone educated by the Whigs. It will be interesting to observe its effects upon the Oxford History Schools, whence come many of the historical writers of the future.

GREGORY MACDONALD.

Eternal Numbers

THE NEW BOOK OF ENGLISH VERSE. *Edited by Charles Williams.* Gollancz. 7s. 6d.

TO begin by saying, in accordance with its own mild advertisement of itself, that this book is designed as a companion to the *Oxford Book* and Palgrave's *Treasury*, anthologies so long left unchallenged in their comprehensive field, would be in a sense to perpetuate a wrong impression. For it is something quite different. True, the deliberate decision to be complementary and not redundant of necessity harnesses *The New Book* with the two great collections of English verse, if it is to be allowed to be sufficiently representative for general taste. But it also forces a modification which is important. There is a natural tendency in anthology-making to prefer the lyric. Had Mr. Williams done so, he would have had to make many disappointing second choices. In widening his scope, he offers something of immense service to the large appreciative public that must accept the dictum of the anthology-maker, if it has

not the time or the experience to range the great poetic English field. The choice delights, the omissions intrigue, and the reader is at once aware that he must not be satisfied with this fine selection from the writers of epic and drama, satire and dissertation, but must himself explore further. Nor will he suffer the disappointment that might be his, if he only sought to hear again the lovely first song of the lark. Many will find this book an encouragement to a serious study of poets whom they have long loved in a few great poems only—or whom they have set aside as having nothing for themselves. Others will find themselves meditating on yet another Book of English Verse, made up of personally-loved omissions and many suggested possibilities. There might be several such and yet no overlapping. Personal taste must enter into these matters, there is no reason why personal prejudices and interests should not do so, that the book may have reality and form.

This one certainly has it: it is catholic, but it bears the stamp of a mind. The editor confesses that many inclusions and omissions have been made against advice, and in his Introduction and final notes he admits to principles guiding his choice.

One, that every inclusion should be poetically important: examination quickly proves that there is no hard division between major and minor poet in the editor's mind. His touchstone is sincerity, or as he says in the Introduction, an avoidance of *Cant*: this, of course, applies to the form as well as the content. Regarded from this viewpoint, there is very little wastage.

Two, his own predilection for poetry that criticises poetry has been allowed to direct many choices. This betrays the genuine student of poetry: it is not too obvious in the selection, which is, however, sufficiently academic.

The third suggested principle implies a curious limitation. For here, an anthology which begins with the freshness of Canute and the monks of Ely and ends with the dying sonnet of Gerard Manley Hopkins is claimed to express the rounding-off of an era.

" It is the moment of the close of the myths. English verse had carried in its tradition a continual use of the myths—of Achilles, Alexander, Arthur, of the fables and the religions, especially of the greatest of the myths (whatever energy of morals or statement of fact it justly carries, it must necessarily be a myth in poetry), Christianity. In the Nineties there were two poets of importance, Mr. Kipling and Mr. Yeats; one tended to turn from the myths, the other to translate them into his own parables. Social and philosophical changes accentuated a change in the imagination. Where Tennyson and even Hardy had occasionally been a little sad about their loss of simple faith, the newer poets much more healthily forgot it. The wistful atheist disappeared. Christianity became to every poet either a necessity or a nuisance, and the lesser myths in general became more and more merely a nuisance. Flecker and Francis Thompson picturesquely delayed them a little; Mr. Eliot for a moment recovered Agamemnon; Mr. Chesterton made them ceremonial with apocalypse. But in general, in public, they were done, and it was time. Hector and Solomon, Helios and Odin, had had a long day, and it may be that still some poet may find them necessary; if so, it will be private compulsion rather than public habit. Pan is dead."

But Pan was dead, nearly two thousand years ago, when the voices were heard lamenting from the shore. Does Mr. Williams actually look on the fine anthology that he has made with the eye of an antiquary? Keats is dead also. Is he dust? Has he no part with us?

> By all the echoes that about thee ring,
>   Hear us, O Satyr King!
>
> O Hearkener to the loud clapping shears
> While ever and anon to his shorn peers
> A ram goes bleating: Winder of the horn!

There is an elusiveness at this point in the Introduction amounting to obscurity, and it is necessary to avoid misunderstanding. I think that the Editor is voicing artistic standards and not ideas. "Gerard Hopkins was the last notable poet of the myths" does not mean that that was a myth by which Hopkins lived and died.

> Nay in all that toil, that coil, since (seems)
>   I kissed the rod,
> Hand rather, my heart lo! lapped strength,
>   stole joy, would laugh, chéer.
> Cheer whom though? the hero whose
>   heaven-handling flung me, fóot tród
> Me? or me that fought him? O which one?
>   is it each one? That night, that year
> Of now done darkness I wretch lay
>   wrestling with (my God!) My God.

These lines, with which the collection ends, seem indeed a powerful ending to an epoch. They sound rather in our ears like a trumpet call, a new rousing and waking. What a contrast to *The Last Word* of Matthew Arnold, or Thomas Hardy's *He Abjures Love*. These are quoted just before, and might in a different spirit mark an ending.

> —I speak as one who plumbs
>   Life's dim profound,
> One who at length can sound
>   Clear views and certain.
> But—after love what comes?
>   A scene that lours,
> A few sad vacant hours,
>   And then, the Curtain—

Mr. Williams did not choose to make an end at this point. He chose to make an end with a vigorous and not a failing thing, and thereby refuted his own argument.   K.C.M.

Delius

FREDERICK DELIUS. *By Clare Delius. Ivor Nicholson and Watson. 15s.*

AMONG the many interesting facts revealed in this study of the great composer by his sister is that Delius retained to the end an appreciation and an occasional use of the Yorkshire idiom:—" He never forgot their broad speech and used to employ it frequently." For Delius is a problem to the modern age. What was he? Yorkshire, English, German, French? "A good European" he declared himself; and perhaps that best explains him to all who understand that Europe is more than a geographical conglomeration of nationalities: that behind all the divisions, the cults, the sects and the denominations, there is a thing we instinctively appreciate as European, something more than Latin, Slav, Teutonic, Celtic, Anglo-Saxon or Nordic.

It, therefore, may not be entirely surprising if Delius, despite an influence wider on modern music than any contemporary composer, with the possible exception of Sibelius, still remains a problem to a nationalistic and systematised generation. He cannot be conveniently registered, docketted and pigeon-holed. In law we can claim him. He was born, of naturalised German parents, in Bradford, in Plantaganet England, in 1862. In 1884 he left England for Florida, from whence he departed after a short stay for Germany and later to his eventual home in Northern France. But for occasional visits, mostly during the war when driven from his adopted home by German invasion, he remained an exile from England until he found this last resting place in the quiet graveyard at Limpsfield in 1935.

Yet he is recognisable as peculiarly and essentially English. "He was born in a part of the world," said Sir Thomas Beecham, "which was particularly odious to him. It was the arid north, the business, the hard north. He grew up a rebel and a dissentient. He strove to escape and he did escape. . . War broke out and something strange happened. . . this country turned its back on the idols of the market place and the country house and embarked on the greatest adventure of idealism the world has perhaps ever known. From that moment the eyes of this great musician turned inquiringly and wonderingly towards the shore of his native land. Also . . . his music, which I venture to say, is extraordinarily redolent of the soil of this country and characteristic of the finer elements of the national spirit, had become known. . . So far as it is possible to foresee, if there is any music that will remain honoured and immortal in the memory of the people of any one country, it is the music of this composer."

With this tribute let us leave it. This book makes no pretence to discuss Delius as a composer. It is a record of impressions remembered of him as a man and as a brother. The early chapters, in particular, are interesting, dealing as they do with the period of his life shared in the family. The description of the Delius household is very vividly portrayed, as, too, are the early struggles against parental discipline and the divided loyalty of his duty to his father's ambitions and the growing consciousness of creative genius. The book is clearly printed and the few illustrations are excellent.   V.N.L.

Craftsmanship

By Montague Weekley

HAVING lunched with Lady Algernon Carew-Grenville at 16, Carlton Street, Mr. Oliver Edrington, Director of the Crawford Museum, walked back to Bute Square.

His appearance suggested a clever magazine illustrator's conception of a polished diplomat. Dark, with fine, expressive eyes and a clear-cut profile, he was tall, slender and beautifully groomed.

Discrimination was reflected in every detail of his dress. His black, soft hat, of a kind associated with Diplomacy or High Finance, became him well and did infinite credit to the maker. A double-breasted, pin-stripe suit of inspired cut and a choice shade of grey, bespoke the sartorial accomplishment of Messrs. Poulton and Briggs, undisputed sovereigns of Savile Row. He was shod to perfection by Clegg, and a Sparkes umbrella, exquisitely rolled, dangled from his arm. The grey and black silk tie alone expressed a measure of artistic licence. It was obviously French.

From Winchester and New College Mr. Edrington had passed through an architect's office to the editorship of "The Art Review" and a special interest in furniture. If you study the subject and can afford expensive books, you must know his two volumes on "English Walnut Furniture of the Seventeenth and Eighteenth Centuries," Camford University Press, six guineas net.

When Sir Jabez Crawford bequeathed to the nation his magnificent Adam house in Bute Square, his famous collection of English furniture, and a lavish endowment providing for a curator, additional purchases and running expenses, Mr. Edrington had been invited to take charge of the new museum.

As his salary was reinforced by private means and he was unmarried, the Director was in a position to satisfy his fastidious inclinations. He moved in an elegant orbit—chambers in Albany and week-ends at the country houses of aristocratic and wealthy amateurs; holidays at Biarritz or by the Italian lakes; private and exclusive cruises in Mediterranean waters. Health and grace were preserved by fencing and tennis at "Queen's."

Entering the museum, he graciously acknowledged the salute of a much be-medalled custodian and crossed the splendid hall to his room. The Director's office, a small, but very fine Adam interior, had been furnished with discreet taste.

He pressed the bell on his ponderous Empire desk of mahogany with brass inlay. A deferential tap on the door was followed by the appearance of a uniformed attendant.

" Yes, sir? "

" Oh Salter, I want to see the marquetry chest-of-drawers from Lord Bracebridge—in here, please."

The human machine expressed prompt obedience and departed. In a few moments four attendants carried in the chest-of-drawers. It was placed in the middle of the room, facing the wide, arched windows. Mr. Edrington stepped across to examine it. The

pale-gold autumn light played on the glowing brown of walnut and the sombre, yet warm yellow of the sycamore marquetry panels. Here at last was a piece that would fill a disturbing gap in an otherwise representative collection of English furniture. Mr. Edrington had long been looking for a fine and characteristically English specimen of marquetry belonging to the borderline of the 17th and 18th Centuries.

Having indulged in an intensely satisfying contemplation of its delightful proportions, he studied the marquetry, the engraved escutcheons and drop-handles of brass. The veneer was very slightly swollen and cracked, inevitable marks of Time's unrelenting hand. Essentially, however, a dealer would have described this piece of furniture as being " in mint condition."

Mr. Edrington decided that the marquetry bureau-bookcase in the Long Gallery, an ill-proportioned affair, surmounted by flamboyant, gilt figures, was more than ever detestable. The chest-of-drawers would provide a really worthy specimen of the same period.

He moved back to his desk and summoned by telephone his technical assistant, Gold. The incomparable Gold, a wonderfully skilled joiner and doctor of woodwork, who could also draw with accuracy details of ornament and mouldings for museum catalogues. As Mr. Edrington wittily observed to the Duke of Berkshire, Chairman of the museum trustees : " I'm afraid we shall never get another Technician up to the Gold Standard."

The Technician, an elderly, white-haired, fresh-faced man, had a curious habit of putting on a grey Trilby hat whenever he left the workshop for another part of the building. He now stood, hat in hand, before the Director's desk.

" Ah, there you are Gold," said the Director pleasantly. " I wanted you to see the chest-of-drawers over there. It's on approval for purchase from Lord Bracebridge. You know he's selling Netherton Hall and he's very kindly given us the first refusal."

Gold went round to the window and made a very cursory inspection. He seemed ill at ease when he came back to the desk, twisting his hat nervously between his hands.

" Well," said Mr. Edrington, gently nettled, " you don't seem to be much interested. I think it's an enchantingly lovely piece of marquetry."

" It's a pretty good job, sir," Gold admitted. " But if I may say so, sir, I hope you won't buy it."

Mr. Edrington was surprised to see that Gold, usually so self-possessed, continued to twist his hat with nervous fingers.

" You think it's wrong? "

" I'm afraid it is, sir."

" Of course Gold, you know that I have the highest opinion of your knowledge and always consult you about new acquisitions, but this time you do seem to have made up your mind in rather a hurry. What's the matter with it? "

The Technician appeared to be overwhelmed by an agonizing embarrassment, while Mr. Edrington's velvet composure was in danger of becoming ruffled.

" The fact—er is, sir," Gold stammered at last, " I —er made it myself, when I was working for Mr. Weinberger."

The Cockpit

Sir,—With regard to the article in your issue of
January 16th, entitled The Two Policies and commencing with the words ' The strength of England's
position in her efforts to destroy the new Italy.'

Will Mr. Belloc kindly produce the proofs that
this is the case. The ' proof to a demonstration '
would appear to be necessary if one is to be considered scrupulous.

To assert in bald words the intention of any country,
even one's own, to destroy a fellow nation stands in
need of exact substantiation.

                        R. R. D. Paton.

Sir,—As one who stands to gain very considerably
financially by a rise in miners' wages, may I point
out the discrepancy between miners' and agricultural
wages. In my village there are many colliers, who
are earning fifteen shillings and more for a seven
hours shift. In the same village, with the same cost
of living and the same rent to pay there are agricultural labourers receiving seven shillings for a nine
hours day.

Must we always have propaganda, can we never
have truth and justice ?   Reg Micklethwait.

Sir,—Some time ago we read in the Press of the
country that the Electrical Undertakings, Gas companies, Imperial Chemical Industries, etc., etc., had
all very generously agreed to pay 1/- per ton more
for their coal in order to help the poor miners.

Whilst full of sympathy for the latter, I had a feeling of apprehension when I read this information.
Something told me there was a catch in it somewhere.

A few days ago my Gas Company informed me that
all their fuels would be advanced 1d. per cwt., i.e.,
1/8 per ton.

Need I say any more.   M. J. Corr.

Sir,—I may be wrong, but it seems to me that Mr.
Turner was right merely because he did not go far
enough. Granted that Great Britain was provoked
when she bombed the tribesmen on the North-West
frontier, but has not Mussolini claimed that Abyssinian slave traders invaded Italian Territory ? In
any case, what assurance have we that Great Britain's
explanation was not, in fact, an excuse,—But I may
be wrong.   W. Lyon.

Sir,—It seems that the coal question has been
settled for the present. A more dishonourable settlement it would be difficult to imagine. In a hole and
corner fashion the burden has been put on to the
consumer, a burden, which in any normal country,
might well prove the last straw. It is a recognised
fact that the unemployed and the workers have barely
enough to live upon, and now the price of coal and
consequently of everything else is to be raised. There
must of course be a corresponding rise in unemployment pay and wages. The Government seem to be
acting under the impression that the people are so
devoid of initiative and such slaves to their masters
that they will settle down under a system of inequality
which, in modern parlance, is a blot on our civilisation.   Margaret French.

THE DISTRIBUTIST LEAGUE

The Necessity for Readjustment

At the annual meeting of Barclays Bank, Mr. Tuke, the Chairman, made one point of particular interest. He calculated that although the output of manufacturers in this country in the first three quarters of 1935 was 15 per cent. more than in the same period of 1930, the volume of exports of manufacturers was 10 per cent. inferior to the corresponding period in 1930. He referred without much amplification to the " very great adjustments " in social life.

An admission from such a source that a fall in foreign trade is at least as likely as an increase is significant. Distributists have emphasised the danger of living on foreign trade long before the immense fall took place as a consequence of the imposition of tariffs. The position now seems to be that home industry, which has expanded to meet home demand for goods previously imported will soon become stationary, except so far as increase in the population or increased spending power enable it to expand; while exports will remain stationary or decrease. In other words, we shall reach a state of stabilisation, but it will be stabilisation at a low level of industrial wealth.

The alternatives which can be adopted to solve the difficulty of permanent unemployment are to decrease working hours and spread the amount of employment available over a larger number, with an inevitable decrease in wages, or to provide an alternative means of livelihood. The only way in which the latter alternative can be achieved is by the production of consumable wealth. And the only source of that production which is available and undeveloped is the land. We can no longer pay two million people to live idle when a great part of the country is uncultivated.

The Government must provide facilities for all people able and willing to do so to provide their own food. If necessary this will be only on terms that the production is for subsistence and not for sale. If necessary sufficient of the unemployment benefit to provide clothing and fuel must be continued. The essential is that the appalling waste of idle men and idle land should be put an end to.

HAVE YOU READ

The Notice Board
The Distributist League

CENTRAL BRANCH

Meetings are held on Fridays at the Devereux, Devereux Court, Strand, London, W.C.2., at 7.30.
JAN. 31.—MR. C. M. R. BONACINA: "HUMANISM AND THE FUTURE."

Feb. 7.—Mr. Anthony M. Ludovici: "Liberty."
Feb. 14.—Mr. Hugh Kingsmill: "What They Said at the Time."

BIRMINGHAM BRANCH

Hon Sec.: K. L. Kenrick, 7, Soho Road, Birmingham, 21.
Meetings at Crown Buildings, James Watt Street, at 7.30 p.m.

EDINBURGH

A Branch of the League is now being formed in Edinburgh. All interested are asked to write to Mr. O'Rorke, 47, Balgreen Road, Edinburgh.

PORT GLASGOW

A branch of the League has been formed in Port Glasgow. All interested are asked to write to the Secretary, Frank Brady, 11, Glenburn Street, Port Glasgow, Renfrewshire.

Published by the Proprietors, G.K.'s WEEKLY, LTD., 7/8, Rolls Passage, London, E.C.4. (incorporating THE NEW WITNESS). Telephone: Holborn 8538. Printed by THE NUNEATON NEWSPAPERS, LTD., Bond Gate, Nuneaton. Sole Agents for Australasia: Gordon & Gotch (Australasia, Ltd.). Sole Agents for South Africa: Central News Agency, Ltd. (London Agency: Gordon & Gotch, Ltd.).

IN REPLY TO CRITICS

BY G. K. CHESTERTON

IN thanking my friends and fellow Distributists, who signed the protest published in this paper last week, for the very just and moderate and reasonable tone of their criticism, I have also two preliminary remarks to make; one of which is merely an apology and only the other in any sense an apologia. I must ask them to forgive me if, owing to purely personal circumstances, I only deal with one half of the real question they raise in this issue; for there are other aspects of it that deserve a more close consideration than I can manage to give at this moment. The second general and preliminary remark is this: that, in the case at least of a great many critics who have criticised this paper upon this point, their criticism would really be more cogent if it were true that I ever made myself a champion, or even a defender, of the recent military policy of Italy; either about gas or bombing or about anything else.

Now there may have been respected and responsible writers on this paper who might, without any extravagant stretch of language, be defined as defenders of the Italian policy itself; but just as I am glad to permit them to express their differences from me, so I have never failed to state that I have quite definite differences from them. Distributists are not in any danger of calling themselves by the old pedantic title of Individualists; which, as Mr. Belloc points out in his recent admirable summary on the Restoration of Property, was really a word with no meaning; and largely adopted, I may add, as a label for people with no morals. We are not individualists, but we are individuals; and we most of us have a certain healthy human pleasure in figuring on fitting occasions as irritating individuals. There have been disagreements among the strongest contributors of our staff, which are very much wider than any

which divide the signatories of the protest from me, or even from those who are much more purely pro-Italian than myself. In the article called "Apologia," of which the particular complaint is made, I summed up my view both of the admitted policy and the alleged military method in a sentence like this: "I am ready at any moment to condemn any Imperialism that can be shown to have used it; as I have again and again condemned any Imperialism for which it could be used." That is, I definitely expressed disapproval both of the action considered in itself, and of the cause considered in itself. I cannot see why it should be supposed that, having damned both these things as separate and disconnected things, I should be supposed to be excusing one of them because it is also a breach of an agreement.

There are, of course, some incidental distinctions to be made. I did not in fact say very much, or really say anything at all, about the question of poison gas; because I was not at the time certain of the details and the facts in relation to the highly hostile and irresponsible reports. I confined myself practically to the question of bombing from the air; that is, of bombing open towns or peaceful populations of non-combatants; or bombing under conditions in which it is practically impossible to avoid doing these things. I thoroughly approve of a provision against this being made; and I should most certainly disapprove of its being disregarded when it is made; but I can hardly feel confident, as a matter of commonsense or common information, that this has been provided against quite so precisely or prohibitively as is suggested in the line of the argument. The very reply made to Mr. Belloc, when he alleged similar action by our own authorities on the northern borders of India, did not really amount to a complete denial of the fact, but to a contrast in the degree; and other defences have urged that conditions and warnings alter the nature of the operation. The value of different Imperial propagandist explanations is not quite so rapidly and easily to be resolved. And if I have an uncomfortable suspicion that modern war may tend generally to relapse into the evil ways of the Great War, in spite of some honourable attempts to reassert the standards of chivalry, I can hardly think I am altogether alone in that impression. In fact, it seems to me the impression now imposed on the imagination of the whole world, by almost every form of fact and fiction, publicity and propaganda; but quite especially, oddly enough, by the propaganda of the extreme humanitarians. For if all such things have been finally renounced, what is the meaning of the universal wail about the War That Will End Everything; why do Mr. Wells and the prophets of Apocalypse die daily; why do nine-tenths of the writers and speakers of our time tell us at the top of their voices, all the time, that under the next expansion of aviation in action our civilisation itself will die?

But all these things, though I have treated them first, are in a manner matters of degree or impression or proportion; and I willingly admit that I may be wrong in my guesses about what will or may occur; so long as there is no mistake or misrepresentation about my view of what ought to occur. I have never set up to be a prophet; and I am only concerned touching the things I defend, such as Distributism, with maintaining that they should exist, and not at any time that they must exist or will exist. But when I come to the remarks made by my friends and critics about my views about keeping promises, and respecting established compacts, and especially to their impressions of my meaning in the discussion about " drawing the line," or the advisability of poisoning foreign generals—then I am confronted with so complete and almost colossal a misunderstanding of my meaning, that I can only devote another complete article to dealing with it.

NOTE—

Monday, June 8, 1936.

So Unlike Foreigners

With the return of M.P.s to Westminster after the recess the findings of the Budget Enquiry Tribunal come once more into prominence. There will have to be a debate but neither Government nor Opposition wants to open it. Nor does there seem to be any desire for a discussion on the culpability or innocence of the people involved. Mr. Thomas has resigned from the Government, it is said, and as the matter was probed promptly and thoroughly by the Tribunal we should be content now to erect new safeguards against future leakages or political gambling. At the same time as the American is claiming that there have been other unauthorised disclosures in the recent past, the whole question of official secrecy should be thrashed out. There is, alas, one temptation that few of the politicians who speak will feel able to resist: one and all will talk about the general blamelessness of men in public life, the rarity of scandals and their prompt investigations. Indeed the debate may degenerate into an orgy of back-patting.

On Low Wages

The world did not need to be told by the International Labour Office at Geneva that " low wages or lack of purchasing power is the root cause of undernourishment." But that is hailed by a newspaper as the outstanding statement in its recent report on " Workers Nutrition and Social Policy." When a man is forced into the position of a wage-slave, or must maintain a family on the dole, unless he is paid well obviously he cannot scrape together enough money to buy food. And precious little can he grow on his own little plot of land if he happens to have one. There are, however, other findings in the report that justify its publication. One is that large numbers of workers " even in the most advanced industrial countries " are inadequately nourished, which means that they are underpaid, which means also that their employers are profiting from sweated labour. And it is suggested that in order to lower the cost of foodstuffs, production and marketing costs should be reduced and trade barriers removed. Certainly much could be done by the removal of restrictions which enable the middlemen to make fortunes, and much could be done were shorter routes to be found between producer and consumer. An obvious check on exploitation, though difficult to apply, would be to make illegal the payment of dividends by any firm the employees of which did not receive a living wage.

Starvation Outside Slums

I have been reading passages from a book "Poverty and Public Health," written by a medical officer and a sanitary inspector, and published to-day (6s.) by Gollancz. The picture it draws of life on a housing estate, to which people were "transferred" from a slum in Stockton-on-Tees is so horrible that one hopes either that the authors are mistaken, or that this particular estate is unique. Their method of examination was to study the weekly budgets of 28 families on the new estate and of 27 families in the old slum; then to collect all the information they could from 144 families earning between 35s. and £4. And they found that the removal from the slum, by doubling the rent to be paid and necessitating other extra expenses forced the families to put the buying of food last on their lists. Some families were found to have 2s. 10½d. a week per man for food; and even the notorious estimate of the British Medical Association was much higher than that. Remember that the B.M.A. report was issued in 1932. Since then the cost of food has risen.

High Death-Rate

Everyone in the families in receipt of less than £4 was short of the amount of food needed for a healthy life. In the slums they were a little better-nourished, because despite the evil conditions there, less had to be put aside for rent. As for the fortunate who happen to be employed, it seems that they cannot possibly devote as much as 45 per cent. of their incomes to the purchase of food. No wonder that the chart showing the relation of wages to mortality rates shows a death-rate of the earners of low wages more than double that of the earners of £4 a week.

Cecil Houses

The annual report of the Cecil Houses Committee avoids the cold impersonality of a formal statement by recounting experiences and quoting from letters. They show how warmly the facilities offered by the five Houses are appreciated and how much good can be done by the supporters of an admirable fund. One House has had to be closed for re-building, but will re-open early in 1937. Readers of G.K.'s WEEKLY are urged to contribute gifts of clothing as well as subscriptions and donations. All are badly needed, for the number in London of public lodging houses of suitable character, available for women is very small indeed and a minimum of £7,000 has to be found before a new Cecil House can be opened. Letters should be addressed to the offices of Cecil Houses, Incorporated, 11, Golden Square, W.1.

Unemployment Down

To-day's figures from the Ministry of Labour are more encouraging than any issued in recent months. It was known that the Government's re-armament scheme would have an effect on unemployment, but it does not account by any means for the general improvement noted. The total of all classes this month is some 120,000 less than in the previous month and 339,710 less than in May last year. This does not afford more than partial satisfaction, however, for we do not know how many of the men and women who have been able to take their names off the registers have found economic freedom. The totals may continue to drop, but particular names may be disappearing and re-appearing. The report notes that 24 per cent. of the people on the registers have been unemployed for 12 months or more.

Interviewer and Interviewee

The *Newspaper World* protests against camera interviews which consist of a strip of photographs under each of which is a " snippet of inept dialogue." It adds:—"The modern interviewing style which always reveals more of the personality and sweet aspirations of the reporter than the interviewee, is bad enough, but it does occasionally go wrong and allow the interview to tell a few facts about the subject. But this holding of stories in camera. . . ! Perhaps it is due

to the present frenzied lust for novelty, which is rapidly making news and art editors excellent copies of the proprietors of penny fun fairs."

The New Enclosures

Mr. Gillie Potter has written to the *Star* to protest against " the increasing closure of the countryside to country people." Recently he visited the pocket borough of a nobleman whom he calls Lord Marshmallow, and found barbed wire and notices warning against trespassing " along paths deeply scored by the feet of thousands." And " the notices are in themselves explanations of the new situation which has arisen: they are signed, not as are older notices on the same estate, ' Lord Marshmallow's Estate Office,' but ' By Order of the Hogsnorton Estate Company Ltd.' " In short, " with the flotation of private estates as companies for the evasion of taxation has come the company promoting itch for further unscrupulous exploitation."

Parliament and the People

Mr. William Mabane, M.P., discussing the work of Mr. Winston Churchill and others in Parliament tells us that they have no desire to rebel against the Government. " They are fighting for House of Commons control. It is in this way that the struggle between democracy and dictatorship is proceeding at home under our very noses, and democracy depends on the restoration of direct responsibility to Parliament." Yes, but to whom or what is Parliament responsible? Since M.P.s cannot be elected without sufficient financial backing to cover election expenses and the initial deposit, and are very seldom elected without the political backing of the parties Mr. Mabane might be asked to define democracy.

" Green and Pleasant Land "

The effect of progress on the countryside is aptly described in *News-Review*:—

" On August 20, 1935, a farmer and a sheepdog walked into a well-nibbled meadow hard by the railway station of Denham and drove the sheep from one of the juiciest stretches of pasture in Buckinghamshire. Three days later two walrus-moustached men on a motor-cycle clattered over the bumpy-field path, cast a wistful eye at the cool winding river, dumped a ball of string and began pegging out the land.

" It was the beginning of England's million-pound Hollywood. . . ."

I read this after returning home from a sale of plants and trees at a nursery soon to be replaced by a super-cinema.

" All Sorts of King "

Addressing its two million readers editorially, the *Daily Express* last week deplored the victimisation of the small man by the trusts and combines. No doubt the article was read with grim amusement by the proprietors of independent daily newspapers in the Midlands and the North of England. But it need not be supposed that this glimpse of sanity will influence to any great extent the policy of the paper. Indeed the *Sunday Express*, unwittingly no doubt, supplied an antidote by retailing the biography of

513

South Africa's " 5ft. Napoleon," Mr. I. W. Schlesinger. " Penniless forty years ago," I read, he " lived ' on tick.' " Now he is " insurance king, cinema king, property king, orange and lemon king, all sorts of ' king.' " His latest exploit has been to found a newspaper in Johannesburg and name it the " Sunday Express."

Cobley

Looking On
By Gregory Macdonald

The Wall Street correspondent of the *Sunday Times* reported last week-end that he had called on one of the best-known international bankers in the Street, one with the best connections in London and Paris, in an effort to get a line on what was likely to happen in France. " This banker said he and his partners and other bankers, as far as he knew, were entirely confused over the position." The discussion then turned on the American election, where the banker was more sure of his ground: " It is not what you or I think that is going to decide the November election. What the average voter in the interior thinks is what is going to count. I am afraid that too many are getting, or hoping to get, something for nothing from the New Dealers." The oracle is worth pondering. It is probably quite true that the international bankers are confused over the French situation, because what is happening is outside the rules of the old game. Secondly, it is an excellent point that what Wall Street thinks is not going to decide the November election.

*   *   *   *

Most illuminating of all the angry accusation of a banker that the New Deal gives something for nothing. By creating money and demanding interest on it, bankers have been getting something for nothing all these years. What harm now if, to some degree, the mediæval idea of largesse is revived: we have suffered too long from the notions that all things (and all men) have their price, or that the State is only a tax-collector and judge of default. That mediæval ideas are indeed returning, the banking system has to observe. " Not since the later Middle Ages," writes Mr. D. Graham Hutton in *Lloyds Bank Monthly Review* for June, " have nations deliberately set out, as they do to-day, to be as economically self-sufficing as possible. For in the seventeenth and eighteenth, and most of the nineteenth centuries, the importance of the balance of payments as opposed to the balance of trade, and of the balance of trade as opposed to the mere securing of bullion and coin for a ' war-chest,' was fully realised. It has been reserved for the neo-Mercantilists of our uncertain age to rummage in mediæval *bric-à-brac*, and to deck out the old bullion Mercantilism with ' Just so ' stories about the national nature of modern productive technique." The passage is interesting, if not for its exact analysis at least for its pained appreciation of the truth.

There are many items of news to suggest that the best-known international bankers are entirely confused over the position. They have suffered one reverse after another—most of them major defeats —and things are being said and done nowadays that in their palmy days the bankers would never have allowed. The Japanese Government, for example, announces a continued policy of expansion at declining rates of interest. The Rexistes in Belgium—declared foes of political finance—improve by the poll for the Provincial Councils the victory won at the general elections. In Alberta, Mr. Aberhart forces upon bondholders a compulsory reduction in interest rates, relieving the burden of the people by £1,600 a day, while the Provincial Secretary, Mr. Manning, makes what *The Times* calls a curious prediction, that " this step completes the programme necessary to make Alberta self-contained so far as finances are concerned, and therefore marks a turning-point in the history of the Province. It means no more borrowing, a gradual liquidation of the Province's indebtedness, and an ultimate rise to the summit of economic security and independence, wages and money finally being par wages for goods and services." In America, most new security offerings are for the repayment of past loans, and the Treasury offerings of $1,000,000,000 of new securities at the record low rates for such bonds, of 2¾ and 1⅜ per cent., were over-subscribed sevenfold in one day. At the same time Senator Byrd is complaining that in the fiscal year beginning on July 1, the Government will spend for ordinary purposes and relief $600,000,000 more than in the current year, nearly $1,000,000,000 more than last year, and about $3,000,000,000 more than three years ago. Yet the price index-figure has not risen: new money has been put into the market to meet goods in the market.

*   *   *   *

These reverses, great and small—perhaps the most notable of them were the *coup d'état* in Tokyo, the occupation of the Rhineland and the collapse of the League of Nations policy—mean that the old international power can no longer exert its secret pressure upon national states, so that everywhere a victory has been won by the nationalists; not that in every country the change has been understood or that the politicians have emancipated themselves from the mentality of the debt system. But where the victory has been understood it has been followed up. There is no doubt at all that the events of the past week have been confused, but an interpretation is possible; and the interpretation (at least to be watched) is that in Moscow the Russian elements of the Bolshevik system have at last turned upon the international elements. Not only are there renewed overtures of friendship between Russia and Japan; not only did the broadcast delivered by President Benes on Friday contain cordial references to Germany; but perhaps most remarkable, the projected reforms of the Soviet Constitution, which would continue the anonymous rule under the cloak of an electoral system, to befuddle revolutionary democrats abroad, were suddenly deferred to a meeting of the All-Union Congress of Soviets, which may mean a delay of one or two years. At the same time the talk of a Russian loan died out in the City of London. And at the time of writing the attempt from Canton to cause either a civil war in China, or a war of China and Russia against Japan, looks remarkably like a damp squib. Canton is not receiving the necessary backing, and General Chiang-Kai-shek of Nanking, while appealing neither to Moscow or to Tokyo for assistance, is not treating the crisis as one of desperate urgency.

*   *   *   *

Now all this has its bearing upon the turn of events in France. It will be remembered that the Communists and M. Blum have, as exponents of the financial policy, long stood for the devaluation of the franc. It was presumed that when M. Blum came into office he would devalue the franc. Instead, his assumption of power synchronised with a concerted wave of stay-in-strikes (partly communist in origin and partly, as they spread, a kind of spontaneous national revolution) with demands which, if granted, would make devaluation impossible—for it is no use granting wage increases if the increases are to be wiped out by devaluation (the British devaluation was accompanied by a fall in primary products, so that the decline in real wages was offset). But the alternative to devaluation is a much more terrible prospect for the international monetary power, namely, an embargo on the export of gold. This will be tantamount to the confiscation of £100,000,000 of the City of London's gold earmarked in the Bank of France. The prospect of that embargo provides a powerful bargaining counter against the City of London, which is now caught between two fires. When the embargo is applied, either the sterling price of gold will drop below the hundred shilling line, to the ruination of the people who have hoarded by gold and gold shares, or else the City of London will have to appeal to Washington and accept Washington's terms for stabilisation; an agreement between London and Washington is already hinted at and denied. A fall in the price of gold will also hit hard the gold-producing countries, especially South Africa, Russia and Australia. If the interpretation is wrong, that Russia has gone nationalist, it is difficult to see how other events have been allowed to happen; if Russia has gone nationalist, the fall in the price of gold can be remedied in its effects by currency management. It may confirm the view of some change having taken place in Russia to observe that a note of unusual criticism of Russian shipping policy and other matters has crept into our inspired Press.

*   *   *   *

Whatever the exact genesis of France's stay-in strikes, whatever the mood in which M. Blum capitulated to them, it cannot be said that the strikers' demands were exorbitant or that the outcome was a Communist regime—unless it be argued that the Communist tactics are to propose what is reasonable, as against the old regime, and

then to whip up revolution when what is reasonable is not granted. So some argue that M. Blum will proceed to attack the church to obtain funds for financing his expansionist policy. But by his own declaration he can obtain all the money he wants, just as other Governments obtain it, by Treasury borrowing, with a stable price level. The new programme is in general a good one, cutting the Gordian Knot of deflation, and at the same time bringing under control both the big industrialists and the Bank of France. It would be a happier event if anybody other than M. Blum had achieved it, but even so the present M. Blum is not the old advocate of devaluation and the champion of encirclement. In his speech on Saturday he spoke positively for peace and for a cessation of the armaments race. It is an interesting point that the *Financial News* is far from gratified by the turn of events. The actual development of affairs must now be carefully watched. Events in France will certainly have their repercussions in this country.

*   *   *

In America the point has been reached where President Roosevelt stands unopposed for the presidency. That is to say, he is the one man who matters politically and, in the words of *The Times*, " the coming election will not be a contest between the differing philosophies of government represented coherently by the Republican and Democratic parties so much as an enlistment of all the forces available to defeat one man—President Roosevelt —with another man." But the other man is far to seek. He will not be found in Hoover, Borah, Landon or Vandenberg, while for policy the Republicans must either come East for sound finance or go West for a full-throated endorsement of President Roosevelt's own programme. Meanwhile he continues his way with an unexpectedly favourable verdict upon the Tax Bill from the Senate and with a present from the Supreme Court of a decision upon minimum wages which sweeps away the novel Republican argument that the contest is one between States' rights and Federal rights, by declaring against States' rights themselves. The Constitutional issue is now common ground for both parties, and President Roosevelt should have four more years—and quieter years— in which to handle it successfully.

REARMAMENTS AND ALLIANCE
BY HILAIRE BELLOC

IT has been said universally in this country and very widely on the Continent, that the heavy loss of power recently suffered through the failure of the challenge to Italy was due to the insufficient armament of Great Britain. Therefore (it is argued) the remedy is obvious and easy. We have but to increase our armament and all will be back again in the old situation.

That proposition is, I say, universally accepted in this country, and the universal acceptation of it is doing us an injury which, if it be not easily repaired, may prove finally irreparable.

The loss of control over the Mediterranean, the *subsequent* hasty decision to call in the League of Nations on our side, and the lamentable fiasco that followed was not due to insufficient British armament. It was due to the revolution in strategic conditions following on the advent of the Fourth Arm: aircraft.

No matter how heavily the general armament of Great Britain be enforced, the old conditions of complete security can never be restored.

The whole tradition of British foreign policy for at least two long lifetimes from 1794 to 1914 reposed upon an absolute foundation. That foundation was composed of two elements, the political unity of the country, which grew firmer and firmer as class-government grew more and more accepted, and an invincible fleet. My readers may well be weary of hearing such truths repeated, but they are still so imperfectly understood, obvious though they should be, that most part of educated conversation and writing to-day still ignores them. You may differ as to the cause of England's astonishing unity, but no man can question the existence of that unique fact. You may even discuss the causes of naval supremacy as it existed from Howe's great victory of the 1st of June till the first sinking of our Men of War in home waters twenty-two years ago. You may ascribe the old British supremacy by sea to something inherent in the race—a flattering and therefore a popular theory. You may ascribe it to the fact that England is an island. You may ascribe it to an ever-maturing tradition and habit in the Senior Service. You may ascribe it to voluntary recruitment. You may even, if you are very foolish, ascribe it to luck; or if you are still more foolish you may ascribe it to a star. But no one can deny the fact that it was there. England, from the time when Napoleon was a youth of twenty-four to the time when the great grandsons of Napoleon's Marshals appeared on French Amy Lists in the opening of the Great War, could act in complete independence of any other power, and could impose her will through command of the sea with no fear of the consequences, so long as what she willed was reasonably and skilfully planned, nor ever pushed to that extreme in which it would have provoked a general coalition against her.

This situation had two effects: it bred in Englishmen of every class but in particular of the governing class a certitude of security, and it produced a conception of war as being necessarily and primarily conditioned by sea power.

The invention and development of aircraft progressively changed all that, but, as always happens, the formed and mature habit of mind permeating the whole of so singularly united a society, long survived the conditions in which that habit of mind had arisen. It survived so tenaciously that it brought us a few months ago within an ace of irremediable disaster. Even now (as we pointed out in these columns a fortnight ago) the name Pantelleria means nothing to our press.

As things now are rearmament in aircraft will provide powers of retaliation: it will not and cannot undo the loss of insularity, the loss of surface control over any sea passage less than three hundred miles wide; it will not restore the immunity of the trade routes on which the wealth and therefore the power of Great Britain depends.

That heavy increase of armament, especially in aircraft is necessary few will deny and soon, I think, none. That the expense incurred will strain our top-heavy fiscal system to near breaking point will be less easily accepted, but the most essential point of all which is most difficult to get accepted is the truth that such measure of security as we obtain will now inevitably depend upon an alliance. The decision must be taken and taken rapidly as to where that alliance is to be found.

The Peace of Vron

By C. W. Empson

VRON is four days' march from London on the road to Paris—four days, that is, if you take a great curve to avoid the suburbs and main roads near London, and use the old ferry from Dover to Calais, so that you take a full week to walk to Paris. Easter Monday in France is a *jour de ferie*, which is French for bank holiday; it was marked by a cold north wind, with frequent showers of snow and rain, and after dark one would not have gone beyond Nampont if the inhabitants of that town had not refused harbourage. At first Vron was equally unaccommodating, though much more civil; they directed me to the last café on the left, not easily identified in pitch darkness, and there at last I was admitted by an old lady.

I had gone to France to look for an old lady. Sick of the perpetual complaint against France and the French I had gone over to ease my mind. I did not mind so much about the men; Frenchmen have ten times the intelligence of Englishmen of my class, and would probably make allowances. French girls—what comrades they were, twenty years ago!—why, girls do not judge men by their politics; it was not the possible ill opinion of French girls that worried me. But the old ladies of France—who can know them without love and admiration? Madame *la patronne* does all the work of the cafe; first up in the morning and last to bed at night; infinitely capable, infinitely kind, behind perpetual grumbling. She complains about her poor feet but never rests. She produces a meal out of nothing and cooks anything at any time. She clutches the *sous* and gives extraordinary value for them. She is a mass of sense and sensibility without a trace of sentimentality. She is the soul and strength of France, and that she might be thinking ill of such as me was more than I could bear.

The *patronne* of Vron was exactly as I had known her like all over the north of France. She had the usual warm kitchen with immense stove, the usual mixture of a family with no possibility of finding out who was the father, husband, wife or child of whom. There was the familiar promise of a little something before bed, the little something that turns into an excellent dinner as one unexpected delicacy follows another. When at last we clinked coffee-cups after the ritual replacement of the first two sips by *eau-de-vie*, I was aglow with physical and spiritual comfort. Not many good things are stable in this age of transition and it gives a very deep pleasure to find one good thing unchanged.

Yet I felt a shadow darkening the friendly atmosphere. In the morning it was more obvious. I, remembering my mission, tackled Madame over my coffee; " It seems, Madame, that the French and the English are not always such good friends as they used to be?"

" They say, Monsieur, that the English will march against us with the Boche," and Madame looked sideways with pain at the thought of that disloyalty.

" Think ill of us, Madame, but not so ill as that. We are an unimaginative and ignorant people, we may not see the perils that you see, we may not think with you that the Boche is always the Boche, we might not march with you, but I believe it impossible that we should ever march against you, and I think the notion that we could do so is the invention of mischievous people who do not speak for the heart of England at all."

" Monsieur."

" It is indeed true that there is much criticism of French people and the French attitude. Maybe the criticism is just, maybe unjust, but you agree that criticism is not disloyalty?"

" Monsieur."

" One of our misfortunes is that we started the war with a volunteer army, which contained the best available men, and followed with a conscript army which inevitably was below average. A result was that there was not the good fellowship at the end of the war that there was at the beginning. Our men criticised you for being grasping; even if it were true, they asked for it. Then our aristocracy was destroyed by the war and replaced by a plutocracy; the former had far more French culture and sympathy than the latter. It seems to suit some people to make bad blood between us. Possibly a majority would say that they have as much sympathy with the Boche as with you; I believe a majority of the middle class (the most ignorant and stupid of us all) would say so.''

" Monsieur.''

" But these things are not decided by majorities. A small body with intense feeling will sway a country far more than a loose majority. There is no body with intense pro-German feeling; there is a body, perhaps small, with intense pro-French feeling, and that body is the heart of England.. It contains all the people who still think the war was just, and who have never regarded themselves as disillusioned. All outside that body have changed their opinions, if not their loyalty; that body is constant. I have no idea how large it is; I only suggest that it is decisive. War of any sort is terrible to us, but war with you would break the heart of the only steadfast people in England, and I think that heart is too steadfast to submit to be broken so.''

" Monsieur.''   Each acknowledgment was a little happier than before, till the sound was perfectly contented. With a handshake we settled the Peace of Vron, and however unlikely it is that a single Englishman tramping across France could remove bad blood and improve international relations to any decisive extent yet I walked on to Paris as happily as if I had done my country a service.

A Midsummer Night's Dream
By K. C. Macdonald

I.

AT Ricote, in that lingering summer of 1592, the September day draws to its close—a day of excitement in the village, for the Queen herself has come to the wedding of Sir John Norris and his Irish bride. The people of Ricote approve of the Queen; for she loves the place, and she has given it her protection in times of trouble.

Now for a while there is a pause in the festivities. There is to be a play to-night in the garden of the manor, and the villagers are waiting to be admitted. Before the low Tudor house, the clipped yews make strange long shadows across the flawless lawn. The sunset sky reflects the vivid colours of the dahlias in the formal beds. The walls are heavy with fruit, and sprayed with creepers already crimson: full-throated summer, deep-breasted autumn, walk arm-in-arm in Lady Norris' Oxfordshire garden. And arm in arm with her black-browed hostess, her dear Crow, the Queen walks slowly and admires the flowers. She is snatching a few minutes of peace in the company of an old friend, before returning to the business of the day—compliments to a strange young bride, always a difficult thing to the secretly embittered Elizabeth—and recognition to a bride of yesterday, who has just now arrived at Ricote. That is a far more difficult task, for Frances Walsingham has for the second time snatched a courtier and favourite from her envious hands,—and this time it is Essex.

Yet she has publicly forgiven Essex at Greenwich in the spring, and now, in late summer, consented to see and forgive his fellow-culprit. In this house, the house she knew and loved when she was herself but a girl in disgrace, troubler of her sister Mary's rest, she cannot be anything but kind. And she has no ill will at all for the blue-eyed Amazon that the brave young Norris has brought back as spoil of his Irish campaigns.

(The brave young Norris, she notes, even now treats Frances Walsingham with chivalrous respect. He was with her in the Netherlands when Philip Sidney died. Inconsiderate, rash fool, thinks Elizabeth, who in her heart cares little for deeds of knightly valour. Handsome and talented young noblemen should never be so careless of their lives. Nor should they leave mousey, pathetic widows behind them to steal the hearts of susceptible hero-worshippers—like Essex.)

But the Countess of Pembroke is here too, Sidney's sister. The bride of Essex is under her protection, and no one, not even Queen Elizabeth, would willingly give pain to Mary Sidney.

The Queen returns to her throne on the summer lawn. She is gracious to them all. She kisses the young Countess and offers her tardy good wishes. She discourses on the failings of Essex, on the recent festivities at Oxford, on the virtues of Lord Buckhurst, whom she has just now installed as Chancellor of Oxford in disappointment of the hopes of Essex—and then abruptly she turns away and insists that the rest of the company be presented to her.

It is a varied company, and almost every one is known to her. She has the memory for names and faces that is part of royal greatness. The neighbouring gentry, the notables who have followed her from Oxford, the household;—Mistress Shakespeare? Our poet's mother? Has she not been presented to us before?—Long ago?

Yes, she has: but Mary Shakespeare is not worldly-wise, except in the caution that her many difficulties have taught her. It does not occur to her to take advantage of the passing interest of the Queen. She assents, and lets it pass; whether in fact Elizabeth remembers it or not, it was at Kenilworth, seventeen years ago. But she has not come from Stratford for any personal honour, only to bring Hamlet her grandson to play in his father's play. For Will's sake, she prefers to avoid questions that might lead to the disclosure of the name of Arden.

The Queen is looking forward to this play of Shakespeare's, which is new. There is a lightness and surety in his touch that she has not found in English playwrights, since ' old Heywood with his mad merry wit ' withdrew from the Court with his Jesuit sons.

It is September twilight. All over the garden gay coloured lanterns are springing to life. The long green bank, backed by a wooded knoll that a few months since was carpeted with wild flowers, is now cleared and lit and prepared for action. The guests are seated and expectant. Lord Norris is beside Elizabeth, the boy-Earl of Pembroke on a stool at her feet. Mary Sidney, seated between her one-time sister and her dead brother's friend, John Norris, watches the Queen and wonders if her plotting with Master Shakespeare will be fruitful.

She is so easily moved by memories, the strange Queen, especially if they are connected with triumphs and friendships (and grudges, too) that are altogether hers. The beetle-browed Lady Norris, the fair, pale Countess of Pembroke have put their handsome heads together to make use of these.

Lady Norris can tell you why Jasper Heywood the Jesuit was released from his chains and sent abroad, though his fellow-prisoners were condemned. He was once Elizabeth's page. She could also tell you, if she chose, why Babington's execution was so merciless. For he had been page to Mary Stuart; Elizabeth's kindness did not stretch so far. But there had been another child favourite not quite so long ago. Mary Sidney could tell you that, for she remembered his quick-witted impudence, and the delight he gave the Queen. She had remembered his name, and recognised him when she saw him playing the courtier in his own play, —the first that was seen by the Court. It was the pert imp Moth gave her the clue when she wanted

it. Will Shakespeare, of course, the merry little singer at Kenilworth! They had called him *Moth*, because he was small for his age, and quick as a flash with his answers. The Queen had noticed the resemblance and other gay allusions to old days, and for that reason approved of *Love's Labour's Lost*. But she did not then connect the playwright's name.

Would she connect it now? Her friends have deliberately planned to invoke those happier memories. They have called the playwright into their counsels, and found him as tactful as he is witty. He has to be so. Almost from childhood he has trod a dangerous path between his popularity with the wealthy and his affectionate loyalty to his own.

But he has understood their need. A play to please the Queen—a marriage hymn that will not offend her; a reminder of past pleasures that will not rouse regrets; another Moth, small replica of his childish self, to recall her contest with Leicester for possession of a singing-boy, seventeen years ago: happy, confident hours in her spoiled life, before the net had quite closed around her, before she had realised her loss of power in her unwilling forfeiture of youth.

(*To be continued.*)

ON A PARAGRAPH

I WAS some time ago respectfully mystified by a paragraph in an American paper about Mr. Erle Stanley Gardner; who, it was stated, is rapidly becoming known as the American Edgar Wallace. He follows his prototype in the promise of writing a number of books; and " is also under agreement to turn out several hundred thousand words a year for the pulps." I have not the presumption to set myself up as the English Erle Stanley Gardner; but it constantly seems to me that I am writing hundreds of thousands of words; a depressing thought, which is brought to a close by the grand and gloomy certainty that I am undoubtedly writing them for the pulps. But the American Edgar Wallace appears, by this account, to move through life in a much more dazzling manner than I do, and one more appropriate to the romances of his fore-runner. He " has just left for the Orient with three secretaries, an electric typewriter and his wife." I quote the statement exactly as it is stated and I apologise to Mr. Gardner if this Oriental romance originated with the newspaper and not with the novelist. And, as stated, it seems stimulating and mysterious; there are so many aspects of it. Can the journalist have intended to insinuate that the author who travelled in the Occident with three secretaries and one wife, would eventually travel in the Orient with three wives and one secretary? In that case, the journalist was a very bad and unscrupulous man; which is almost unknown among

journalists. But there are other peculiar things in the statement, even as stated. The social precedence, or moral order, in which the things are mentioned, seems a little peculiar. It is very right perhaps that the secretaries should march in front; but hardly that the wife should be so completely left behind. The interposition of an electric typewriter between the two may have technical conveniences with which I am unacquainted; but then, there are so many things with which I am unacquainted. I shall doubtless expose the most grovelling ignorance, but what *is* an electric typewriter? I have read romances of science and invention, according to which a typewriter could do all the work of a typist. I have also read romances of earnest and ethical reform, according to which a typist could be a complete substitute for a wife. But I do not altogether understand where electricity comes in; unless indeed the just anger of heaven should blast all the blasted fools in such fiction with an all-destroying thunderbolt. Now so far as I know, and for all I know so far as anybody knows, Mr. Erle Stanley Gardner is a perfectly sane and reasonable citizen, who happens to make his living (as I do myself) by writing an intolerable number of articles for newspapers or tales for magazines. It is very natural that he should go travelling with his wife, and take his secretaries, and add an electric typewriter to his luggage if he feels inclined. But mine seems to me the more natural order of these objects; and I wonder whether poor, miserable, downtrodden literary men really like to be advertised in the papers in this way.

G.K.C.

Stormy's Back Again

By Peter Quince

FOR at least two hours old Joe and I had been leaning over the parapet of Gravesend landing stage, each of us enjoying himself—as only sailors can—by just looking at a familiar and well loved scene which the world, which is so largely directed by motives of human folly, and the necessity of gaining a livelihood by travelling immense distances over salt water, had deprived us.

Joe had returned on a British India boat after a rather "confused" trip which seemed to have had its starting place in Singapore and its itinerary Indian ports, West Africa, then back to the Gulf and finally Calcutta and home. Nothing would induce him to talk of it in any detail! I myself had returned direct from the Plate on a meat boat and by that strange law of coincidence which has appeared in our joint lives before we had docked next to each other on the same day. We had taken the Woolwich ferry and here we were.

With that strange telepathy which runs between understanding minds, neither of us felt the least need of conversation. Though it was nearly a year since we had met and we each of us had a packet of lies to tell the other we had a strange feeling that it could all keep! Stranger still, we could with ease have thrown a heaving line into the bar of The Three Daws which, of all sailor pubs. is the pub. *par excellence*. Neither of us had had a smell of beer but even that could wait, too. All we wanted to do was to stare and stare and stare up and down the London River, feasting our eyes on that loveliness of home, filling our hearts with memories which only grey water sailors understand, for they, of all this human world, best know the pith and marrow of utter loneliness.

When the heaven of this June evening had been smothered in darkness, when the sounds we knew so well occurred at longer and longer intervals, when the cluster lights at Tilbury Dock over against us twinkled, winked and laughed at the midget stevedores who ran, pushed and swore in the great innards of the big P. and O. there discharging, then would be the right time for beer and a yarn.

As I turned from the Lower Hope to gaze upstream it seemed to me that the texture of the light was that of very deep purple velvet fading by an infinity of degrees to deepest black above me and the lightest possible primrose still lingering like a strip of ribbon along the horizon to westward. Against this palest of colours, which had nothing of gold or of fire in it, the derricks and luffing cranes of the Royal Docks stood out silhouetted like the up-turned, grabbing limbs of giant spiders.

A sailing barge with a following breeze was coming down stream and a voice—a fine baritone voice—was singing. As she approached I was better able to pick out the air which I knew at once for a deep water chanty of a vanished age. Then I got the words :

"Poor old Stormy's dead and gone.—To me way —hé—hé—Mr. Stormalong!

"We lowered his coffin on chains of silver— Fare e well, Mr. Stormalong!"

"There goes one o' the old un's," was Joe's only comment; "toes like fingers. and fingers like fishhooks." He spat and turned towards the shore where lights were already burning . . . .

But now I tell you that from that gay celestial tavern where sailors bang their pots and tell each other stories that not even the narrators themselves believe, Mr. Stormalong has returned to give us his memoirs in the shape of Capt. J. R. Murphy, whose book "Storm Along," published by Blackie at 7/6d., I have no hesitation in saying is the best book of its kind that has come my way and I have not missed the written memoirs of a square rigged sailor for the last ten years.

Critics will say "We have had too many of these books. They are all the same. When you have read one you have read all." But critics can go and burn themselves—except that most of them are too wet to take fire.

The author tells a plain straightforward tale which is equally interesting to landsmen and sailors even if it only be considered by the standards of the excellence of its writing. On the other hand, considered as a life story it is more remarkable than the life of many an eminent field marshall through which I have often had to cut my way with a jungle knife.

When sailors were craftsmen instead of scientists and mechanics, they laughed as hard as they worked and that is saying a lot! How many sailors to-day under fifty can do sword-matting and fancy work? How many would like to come down a back-stay "just to save time"? Who put red-lead in the bos'un's snuff?

Only one technical error. "Lake Sincoe," facing pp. 32, is described as a barque. Unless I am a candidate for the Horse Marines she is a barquentine by her rig.

If every square rigged sailor wrote his life story there would still be room for more without repetition, but they would have to be very good indeed to come up to " Storm Along."

Ships and Sealing Wax

LORD INCHCAPE. *By Hector Bolitho. John Murray.* 15s. *net.*

"MANY people remember the first Lord Inchcape as a brilliant financier and as the doyen of ship-owners. In India, where he made his fortune, he was known as the ' Napoleon of Finance.' His Scottish phlegm and reserve hid the other side of him from public appreciation and this biography, written by Hector Bolitho, will be a surprise to those who know nothing of Lord Inchcape's secret influence in politics, in the Foreign Office and in the India Office."

The publishers themselves produce Lord Inchcape proudly as a brilliant financier, as a Napoleon of Finance, as a rich man exerting a secret influence in politics. By custom when a book of this sort comes out, references to Lord Inchcape run through the Press, and a general impression is given that here was a noble character, a builder and a preserver of Empire. Mr. Hector Bolitho—Napoleon of Victorian Biographers—much more carefully tries to avoid the expected note of adulation. To quote the publisher once more : " Mr. Bolitho's biography of Lord Inchcape is more critical than complimentary; he has not asked us to believe in a hero. Rather has he shown the balance between faults and virtues in a man who succeeded as inevitably as he breathed." It stands to reason that Lord Inchcape did not breathe inevitably, that he did not succeed inevitably, if at all, and that the kindness of a very rich man for his personal friends and dependents does not necessarily balance out against the evil that lives after him.

James Lyle Mackay was born at Arbroath in 1852, the son of a Scots sea captain. He died, eighty years after, as Lord Inchcape, one of the richest men in Great Britain, after a career which had been notably associated with Indian trade and finance, with the trustification of the P. and O., with the amalgamation of English banking, with the sale of ex-enemy ships after the Great War, with the Geddes economies and with a raging tearing campaign for *laissez faire* economics which had one expression in a series of revealing letters to *The Times*.

The point is, and Mr. Bolitho makes it clear, that the best of James Mackay was a sailor like his father. He might have made a success of life if he had owned and navigated one ship. Initiation into the workings of the financial system gave him a considerable measure of power over other men, and he was lucky to have his best days in the palmy period of the nineteenth century; but it took him from contact with the sea and gave him in the end the rage and fear of a rich man clinging feverishly to his possessions, when time and the march of history seemed bent upon taking them away from him.

So we have all his angry letters against high taxation; his loud cries that Government must not interfere with business men; his fulsome letters to politicians, including those wild Socialists, Ramsay MacDonald and J. H. Thomas, both of whom he was determined to flatter. At the same time his very riches possessed him and conformed him to type. First, he was fanatically tidy and efficient: at home the sharp eye saw that not a rug was crooked. Secondly : " In great issues Lord Inchcape was always guided by . . [a] broad and unmiserly conception of wealth. He once offered to endow the office of the Prime Minister with one hundred thousand pounds, to augment the state salary and to guarantee a pension . . He was splendid in the way he distributed his pounds, but he was awfu' canny in guarding pennies— which were not his own, but for the spending of

which he considered himself responsible. His office economies were sometimes almost eccentric. At the end of the war he wrote to his agent in Colombo : ' Your people use a great deal of sealing-wax on my letters. I think we might do without it nowadays.' When he was travelling on the steamers of his fleet he would nose into every cranny to devise ways of saving money. He once asked the steward to find out what had happened to an unused roll of butter which he had left on his early-morning tea-tray." The same fanaticism he carried with him into national affairs, and as a member of the Geddes Committee he directed the great deflationary drive which was imposed upon the country after the Great War.

Mr. Bolitho gives as many details as possible from the life of a man who left few letters and whose biggest deals were carried out by telephone or by personal negotiation. Mr. Bolitho does not, however, assess the real meaning, or the importance, of some of his facts. He mentions " an amusing tribute to . . [Lord Inchcape's] impartiality as a judge," for when there was a public scare over the amalgamation of banks and the dangers of the great ' money trusts,' Lord Inchcape was appointed chairman of the Government's Committee of Inquiry, although he had engineered some of the big amalgamations which were being criticised.

Again, at the end of 1917, " Lord Inchcape subscribed, through his company, his friends and from his own fortune, the sum of £9,279,330 to the National War Loan, a gesture which Mr. Bonar Law described in a letter to him as the ' high-water mark of public spirit and patriotism.' " The National War Loan is now known to have been a ramp, and at the end of 1917 the interest rate had once more risen; and the high-water mark of patriotism was at that moment to be seen elsewhere —in France.

But Lord Inchcape's activities were on the world-wide scale even before the war. Amalgamation, and the Geddes' Axe campaign were of lesser importance than the work he undertook in divorcing India from silver. In 1936, when the restoration of the East by the remonetisation of silver is a play of world policy, Lord Inchcape's share in demonetising silver has a significant interest : the policy is euphemistically described as one of placing India on the Gold Standard. Sir James Mackay was sent from India to give evidence before the Herschell Committee on a measure about which (as Sir Arthur Godley wrote) " the public knew little and cared less, but which was nevertheless of the utmost importance not only to India but in a less degree to the world at large. It is difficult now (1916) when the advocates of the gold standard have apparently triumphed in all parts of the world, to realise how strong and bitter was the opposition which they had to encounter in 1893, when the struggle began."

After his success, Sir James was sent to negotiate a commercial treaty with China, following the Boxer Rising; this time to increase foreign trade with China by abolishing the inland customs

barriers. The treaty was successfully negotiated after long conversations (though it never came into operation because the other Powers opposed it), and Lord George Hamilton wrote in congratulation from the India Office: " This is the first treaty of its kind which has not been negotiated with shotted guns behind the British negotiators."

Another incident, which may be regarded now as of some importance, is described by Mr. Bolitho as something like a family joke in the Inchcape household: in 1921 Lord Inchcape was requested to accept the Kingship of Albania. Very sensibly he refused. But the letter of invitation announced that " feelings towards Great Britain are very friendly, the Tobacco Monopoly is on the point of being sold to a British group, and an Anglo-Persian group are negotiating for the Oil Concessions. . . In any case if you turn it down entirely perhaps you would feel called upon to suggest the name of some wealthy Englishman or American with administrative power who would care to take up the cudgels on Albania's behalf, thereby securing an honourable position as Albania's King."

It would have been an odd piece of history to have a shipping magnate crowned king by a tobacco monopoly and by an Anglo-Persian group of oil concessionaires. Yet this letter is an interesting sidelight upon the internationalism of the rugged individuals who often control national policies. It is much to be regretted that Lord Inchcape negotiated so many of his deals over the telephone, or by conversation. No doubt his words are still reverberating somewhere in space, but the archives of the twentieth century will be incomplete.   G.M.

Correction

Owing to a typographical error, which we regret, Dr. David Mathew's " Catholicism in England " (Longmans, 9s.) was ascribed in a review last week to Dr. David Mather. Our readers, of course, will have had no difficulty in perceiving the mistake at the time.

Gramophone Notes

AS June has not brought us much so far in the way of summer we can console ourselves in the chilly evenings with the excellent and varied entertainment which the gramophone companies have provided us. There are many recordings this month of first-class interest. If I put first the Columbia recording of Sibelius' *Festivo*, played by Sir Thomas Beecham and the L.P.O. (LX501) it is because one must start somewhere. This work is not the greatest Sibelius but there is fine stuff in it and the orchestral writing is distinctly individual. It consists of two suites dating from 1879 and 1912 respectively and though the material is original it reflects the very national idiom which Sibelius generally adopted. The playing is magnificent and the recording excellent. Beethoven interpreted by Weingartner and the Vienna Philharmonic Orchestra is always an event of major importance. The recording by

the Columbia Company of the Seventh Symphony will appeal to all who value great music finely performed (LX484-8). So too will the playing by Egon Petri of the great piano sonata in C minor (op. 111). The quality of pianoforte recording has improved enormously in recent years and this is representative of the finest technical achievement. Mr. Petri is in his best form and that is very high (LX491-3). Another fine pianoforte recording is issued by the H.M.V. Company of Moriz Rosenthal playing his popular encore item, the *Carneval de Vienne* on themes by Johann Strauss (DB2836), an astonishing display of virtuosity. Debussy's lovely *La Cathédral Engloistic* is played by Gieseking with fine poetic understanding. An excellent example of modern pianoforte recording and is issued by the Columbia Company (LB30).

Bronislaw Huberman's fluent technique is quite equal to the task of Mozart's Violin Concerto in G major (K216). This work, with its beautiful second movement, is in many ways the finest as well as the most difficult of the Violin Concertos and despite its brightness there is more than a hint of the tragic Mozart of the later days. The recording is good without being outstanding (Col., LX 494-6). The same may be said of the Decca Company's recording of Mozart's Piano Variations in B flat, played by Borowsky (CA8237). The Decca Company's finest achievement is the recording of Vaughan Williams' London Symphony, still, probably the composer's best known work. The recording is in album form and the discs, five twelve inch, are not sold separately. Complete with album and descriptive leaflet it costs 25/-.

An outstanding violin recording is provided by H.M.V. with Dvorak's Concerto in A minor played by Menuhin and the Conservatoire Orchestra conducted by Georges Enesco (DB2838-41). This is the kind of music which best suits this young violinist's brilliant genius and a performance such as this makes one wonder at the comparative neglect which this work receives. Few works provide such grateful music for the violin. Vocal records include two more by Mme. Kirsten Flagstad, singing Elizabeth's Prayer from *Tannhauser* (DB2747) and Dich teure Halle (*Tannhauser*) and Elsa's Dream (Lohengrin) (DB2748). The recording is better than those issued of this fine singer last month but they are not yet adequate to show the real beauty of the singer, as we have experienced it at Covent Garden this year.

V.N.L.

The Cockpit

Sir,—Mr. Field seemed to invite a reply from me in his interesting letter on foreign affairs. I cannot recapitulate what I have written in G.K.'s WEEKLY already, with many quotations and factual references, but the point is something like this. Sir George Paish was reported in *The Times* as having said on October 11, at Malvern, that " it was vital that Great Britain should resume the position she held before the War as the world's banker." That is a national, or international, aim which not many Distributists would support. But the revival of international lending is desired by our politicians and by the City of London, which has certainly been in the past an aggressive imperialist menace to national freedom and independence.

My argument is that policy during the past years, and especially the past months, has had the objective of restoring London to the position of the world's banker. The objective has been thwarted in various fashions by various nations. It is true that their nationalism is distorted by reaction. Mr. Field, as an old reader of this paper, will know that I have myself written against Prussia. But the indications now are that Prussia is not in control of Germany: notice how the money and propaganda that once helped Prussia against Poland are now turned upon exaggerating the importance of German paganism. Distorted and rigid though nationalism may be in Germany and Italy, many people in this country would gladly welcome an equal force of national regeneration. Distributism should assist in making it an undistorted regeneration. The tradition of St. Edward the Confessor or of Dr. Johnson or of Cobbett should not require a Hitler or a Mussolini; but these latter will become more rigid in their nationalism while they are under pressure.

Finally, I do not agree that European affairs can now be discussed as though isolated from affairs in America and the Far East. I am convinced that Russia, with its explicit atheism, has been associated with the implicit atheism of Money. Also, Hitler and Mussolini *may yet* be the peace-makers of Europe; the internationalist statesmen have not much furthered the cause of peace.

GREGORY MACDONALD.

Sir,—May I ask Mr. Field to follow the argument I tried to develop, no doubt very imperfectly, in my letter, and not to attach more meaning to isolated phrases in it than they were intended to bear as part of that argument?

Perhaps he will then accept my statement that I did not intend to " belittle the misdeeds of the Prussian "; in fact I think that had the criminals in Germany who started the last war been properly punished, militarist maniacs like Mussolini and Hitler might have thought twice before imitating them, and the world to-day have been a better place for decent people to live in. But to punish an international lawbreaker it is necessary to have an international tribunal recognised and supported by an international "police force," and this would require a closer federation of nations than that of the present League—in fact an approximation to a United States of Europe. Surely

to work towards this end is the best way to show that we are " good Europeans."

I cannot agree with Mr. Field that the Nazi neopagans are worse enemies of Christianity than the Russian atheists and communists. The former, by reason of their peculiar racial ideas, so well described by Mr. Chesterton and Mr. Wilson, necessarily confine their doctrine to their own country; while the latter carry on unceasing propaganda in other countries, notably at the moment in Spain and France. Both, as Mr. Belloc pointed out on April 23, may desire war in Europe—the Germans as an instrument of conquest and domination, and the Russians (or Jewish-Communists) as a pre-condition for the spreading of communism. (Mr. Belloc also stated that the Moscow Government did not desire to start war themselves; but this fact, I think, does not affect the argument of my previous letter.)

I did not accuse G.K.'s WEEKLY of excessively blaming Germany; but had in mind rather Mr. Chesterton's own apparent application to current foreign affairs of Mr. Belloc's well-known phrase regarding Europe and the Faith which made him seem to blame Germany more than Italy for their respective latest offences.

May I say that I quite agree with Mr. Field's concluding sentences?　　　　　　LEO COLLIER.

Sir,—Can Mr. Field answer the following points:

1. How, without throwing logic overboard, can he visualise England and Russia leading a crusade against Imperialism?

2. Does he not fail to appreciate that the German situation is still undecided and obscure? Is it to be Hitler or Schacht, or " the neo-pagan diabolism of von Schirach," or Berlin, or Munich, or Vienna?

3. Is it true that there exists an English propaganda as well as that which comes from Italy and Germany?

4. On what grounds is Stalin excluded from the dictatorial bunch? Do not the activities of Communism in Eastern Asia, as well as in Paris and Madrid qualify Russia for a leading place among the " aggressive imperialist menaces "?

5. As to Mr. Field's proposed Russo-Franco-English racket, would not such an alliance produce precisely that situation which was so largely responsible for the last war?

Finally—talking of morality, why is an alliance with " atheist communism " a wise retort to " neopagan diabolism "?　　　　　J. McDONAUGH.

T. CHARLES EDWARDS.

Sir,—Excuse me, but what is your paper for? I always understood that it existed to print important views that would not otherwise get into print so that the reader might turn from the popular clamour and hear the other side. I did not understand that the views must necessarily be yours, Sir, or those of distributists or of any other particular body; only that they must be suggestive, worthy of consideration. I ask because I notice a tendency of critics not merely to challenge views expressed, which is presumably what the Cockpit is for, but to complain of the printing of those views. I for one should be very sorry if you ceased to print things with which I can disagree.　　　　　C. W. EMPSON.

Sir,—With reference to your music critic's review of "The Robber Symphony," the producers cannot and surely would not claim that music has been specially written for the film for the first time in the history of the cinema.   Several silent films had specially composed accompaniments including, I think, "A Woman of Paris" and, of course, all Chaplin's later pictures were not only written and produced by him but given his own music.

What Mr. Feher has done is to make music and action interdependent—plot, settings, characterisation and music were planned or "composed" together; so one might say that the original musical score included parts for the actors and for the camera.

"Composed film" is an awkward phrase, but it does suggest Mr. Feher's intention and will not I hope keep people away from one of the most entertaining films of recent years.

EDWARD J. MACDONALD.

[V.N.L. replies:—"Composed film" may or may not be an awkward phrase as I still do not know what it means. How can a musical score include parts for an actor and a camera? I hope, with Mr. Macdonald, that nothing keeps people away from an entertainment which, I was careful to point out, gave me great delight. But when the description of symphony is applied it generally means—and ought to mean—a certain musical form. I failed to gather what was symphonic in Mr. Feher's production and do not appreciate his claim that this production is the first "composed" film. Surely Mr. Macdonald does not mean that the specially composed accompaniments— as he terms it—for Chaplin's later films were independent of the film. I very much dislike the practice of adapting for the purpose of a dramatic plot music composed for something quite different; and I am pleased to notice that recently film producers are asking for special music composed for the exigencies, emotional and otherwise, of their plots. Except, as I mentioned in my review, for an occasional use of *leit-motif*, I am unable to see where Mr. Feher is in any way pioneering. It is possibly my fault.]

Sir,—Mr. V. N. Lucas seems to imply in his letter of this week that Germany used poison gas for the first time in 1916. I should like to inform him that I myself was in a gas attack on May 5th, 1915, at "Hill 60." And that was not the first time Germany used poison gas. It may also be well to remember in this discussion, that when Germany attacked with poison gas for the first few times, we had no protection whatever against it; and the Germans knew it: whereas, the Abyssinians were well supplied with the most efficient gas-masks (by those who are a greater menace to civilisation than even Prussianised Germany is); and the Italians knew it.

CHARLES C. LAVIN.

Sir,—Is it a fact that the use of tear gas by the British authorities in Palestine and by the police in the United States constitutes an infringement of the Geneva Agreement of 1925 which pledged its signatories to abandon the use of gas?

Is it a fact that bombing raids have been carried out in Palestine?

Is it a fact that bombing raids occur on the North West Frontier, not with the object of destroying villages, but in order to burst dams and thus flood the fields, ruin the crops and cut off domestic supplies of water?

PETER JOHNSON.

Sir,—I must admit that I am to blame for Mr. Lucas's misunderstanding of my position. But it was none the less a misunderstanding. When mention was made of the incidental sins and mistakes of Italy, I meant not that they are incidental to Italians but to the larger issue of preserving the true European tradition, the sole basis of our resistance to the Servile State. It is to be supposed that even non-Christian distributists believe in the existence of such a tradition which has been the life of the European family for nearly 2,000 years. They cannot think that the distributist affirmations about human personality began with the distributist movement or with what is called liberalism.

But if one admits that tradition it can hardly be denied that of the larger nations Italy, apart from her universities, is the least infected by the sceptical philosophy that denies it. Moreover her university life has now an antidote in the new university at Milan so finely led by Dr. Gemelli. In regard to an organic union with Italy and other distributist elements on the Continent I was thinking more of an intellectual union, though I would also welcome a political one. Surely Mr. Lucas has not joined the isolationist camp commanded by the doughty Lord Beaverbrook.

Europe is a unity even more important than the nation and unless the more or less healthy elements in that unity combine, the nations will certainly perish. As Dr. Gurian says in his latest book "The future of Bolshevism depends upon the answer to the question whether Europe still possesses sufficient *moral* forces to resist it." Now because Italy goaded almost to desperation by the League of Nations has decided that the use of poison gas was the lesser of two evils in her campaign in Abyssinia that is no reason for refusing her help, her decisive help, in the present crisis. The other nations have decided that they will be driven to the use of the same dreadful weapon as can be seen from the fact that they too are making detailed preparation to use it.

GERALD FLANAGAN.

Sir,—The long-suffering indulgence with which you have treated correspondents who seem to mistake the Cockpit for a Bearpit has recently been particularly obvious. This excellent part of G.K.'s WEEKLY has usually been a debating ground for the theoretical and applied principles of Distributism and I think it is a pity that it has degenerated into a clearing-house for grousers who take a gruesome delight in mauling over the indigestible after-effects of a very unpleasant international orgy.

Such letters—however wise, or other-wise—would be more at home in the Popular Press. But, of course, the editors of the Popular Press are neither indulgent nor long-suffering.

NORMAN DAWSON.

The Notice Board

THE DISTRIBUTIST LEAGUE

CENTRAL BRANCH

Informal meetings are held at the League Office, 7/8, Rolls Passage, Chancery Lane, every Friday evening, at 7.0.

BIRMINGHAM BRANCH

Hon. Sec.: K. L. Kenrick, 7, Soho Road, Birmingham, 21.

Meetings at 6, Greenfield Crescent, Birmingham, on the first Friday of the month, at 7 p.m.

Committee meetings: third Friday in the month at 6 p.m. at 7, Soho Road.

PORT GLASGOW

A branch of the League has been formed in Port Glasgow. All interested are asked to write to the Secretary, Frank Brady, 11, Glenburn Street, Port Glasgow, Renfrewshire.

EDINBURGH

A Branch of the League is now being formed in Edinburgh. All interested are asked to write to Mr. O'Rorke, 47, Balgreen Road, Edinburgh.

The Distributist League

PRESIDENT : G. K. CHESTERTON.   VICE-PRESIDENT : H. BELLOC.

The Secretary Writes:—

Mr. Chesterton's article, printed on this page last week, under the title "Future Plans," may be summarized under the heading

Restoration of Property

This is not merely an affair of the publication of a book by our Vice-President, but a reminder of the basis of our distributive constitution. We are on the side of property. The first property being the land it is natural that we should be interested in Land Settlement, even though there be no farmer at present on the executive and we still are entertained by Derrick's cartoon of our President milking a cow.

During the past week the office has been visited by several sympathisers who complain that the League has done nothing. We are so much accustomed to Company meetings reporting increase and decrease in trade, to societies whose turn-over is registered in activities ultimately related to balance sheets, to newspapers taking pride in their circulations, that the spectacle of a League which has neither badge nor banner and is unable to boast of a daily good deed gives the impression of death. Because we cannot at the moment rise and shine, because we are not "news," because we are horribly involved in a system which we distrust and dislike, we are not necessarily defunct. Is there any group in the world with a president and a vice-president to compare with ours? Are they idle? Are they to be despised because they do not supply us with coloured shirts and a dictatorship? Let consciences be stirred and subscriptions paid so that we may at least be in being before facing the problem of doing.   H.D.C.P.

P.S.—Subscriptions (5/-) for 1936-7 are now due; and much labour is helpfully saved if members accept this intimation and do not wait for reminders by post. Distributists are encouraged to ask for "The Restoration of Property" from local libraries and booksellers.

Mr. Belloc's Book

AN ESSAY ON THE RESTORATION OF PROPERTY. *By Hilaire Belloc. Distributist League* 1s.

Mr. E. S. P. Haynes wrote in G.K.'s WEEKLY :—

"I much hope that this little volume, which is equally full of commonsense and good English, will be widely read and have its effect."

Welcoming the book "most heartily," the *Universe* said that it "sets forward with the precision of a mathematical statement the possibilities of restoring property in England."

"Hundreds have taken up the battle cry since the days when Mr. Belloc first uttered it and defended it with his own arguments in the *Eye-Witness*. But it is he who has provided the original thought and inevitable logic. A shilling does not seem a large sum to pay for this vital and creative product of a master mind."

According to the *Law Times*, however it may convince it will interest a large number more, while *Current Literature* :—

"The merit of this book lies in its calm lucidity and its positive attitude against acquiescence in monopolies."

Having quoted from a few reviews we leave you to read the book. But do so because it is an important book, not because a London letter writer has said that it may acquire scarcity value.

LAND SETTLEMENT COLONISATION. *By C. Duvale Bishop. The Distributist League* 6d.

Mr. Bishop describes how people can remain within the system, buy their own houses and practise part-time subsistence farming. His pamphlet concentrates on advice for a practical man and is illustrated by plans. The Press has praised it and you will not be thoroughly well-informed until you have read it.

WHAT DISTRIBUTISM MEANS. *By J. Desmond Gleeson. The Distributist League* 2d.

An essay on Distributism is here reprinted from G.K.'s WEEKLY, as it explains simply the purpose of the Distributist Movement. Mr. Gleeson's popularity as an essayist and as the author of "The Tragedy of the Stuarts" has attracted attention to "What Distributism Means" for which further orders should be sent without delay.

Meanwhile do not forget that *The Distributist Programme* (1s.) describes Distributist policy and the opportunities it can sieze for a return to Distributist life in England.

THE DISTRIBUTIST LEAGUE,
7/8, Rolls Passage, London, E.C.4.

THE SCOTTISH DISTRIBUTIST LEAGUE,
50, St. George's Road, Charing Cross, Glasgow

Published by the Proprietors, G.K.'s WEEKLY, LTD., 7/8, Rolls Passage, London, E.C.4 (incorporating THE NEW WITNESS). Telephone: Holborn 8588. Printed by THE NUNEATON NEWSPAPERS, LTD., Bond Gate, Nuneaton. Sole Agents for Australasia: Gordon & Gotch (Australasia, Ltd.) Sole Agents for South Africa: Central News Agency, Ltd. (London Agency: Gordon & Gotch, Ltd.)

G K's WEEKLY

EDITED BY G.K CHESTERTON

JUNE 18 - - - 1936
VOL. XXIII.   No. 588

Registered as a Newspaper.   SIXPENCE

Every word in the following tributes emphasises the grievous loss sustained by those who served Gilbert Keith Chesterton on the staff of " G.K.'s Weekly," and who have had the task of preparing this issue. The opportunity must be taken to express gratitude for the many messages that have been received and which cannot yet be acknowledged individually.

Future plans will be announced at a later date. Meanwhile his staff, his colleagues, his friends and adherents to the great crusade he led, desire as his monument the completion of the work to which he was devoted. They hope to carry on without his genius but with the inspiration of his greatness and the knowledge of his aim.

*   *   *   *

" We have lost a man, a big man of unique strength, a man of courage and conviction.

" G.K., as he was everywhere known, was an ardent Catholic, a lover of liberty, a sound philosopher, an apologist of highest value, a keen, clean humourist. He will be sadly missed in days when men of the mould of St. Thomas More are rare.

" Those who share our heritage of English speech may well owe a great debt to G. K. Chesterton for his work as a master artist. Some will certainly repay him with the meed of many words. But his friends and comrades in the ranks of the Church militant will remember chiefly that he staunchly fought the good fight and upheld the faith. To them words without prayers will seem a scant and empty requital of his unswerving loyalty."

✠ ARTHUR,
Archbishop of Westminster.

*   *   *   *

MR. ROBERT LYND in the " News Chronicle " :

The truth is, he never ceased to be a poet even when he was writing prose. How fine a poet he was at his best everyone who has read the " Ballad of the White Horse " knows. Some of his verse might be described as a riot of rhetoric, but the rhetoric is the genuine expression of a riotous and exuberant imagination.

The novels, too, were riots—some of them glorious riots, with little imps of nonsense tumbling head-over-heels among apocalyptic visions.

There are writers who hold that Chesterton squandered his genius and endangered his literary immortality by his indifference to form. He was certainly of a squandering temperament, but in his case it was not a common spendthrift but a millionaire who did the squandering.

He once said that if he were a millionaire he would like just to " chuck his money about "—not to deserving people, but " just to chuck it about."

In literature and journalism he may be said to have chucked his genius about. It seems to me likely that we shall still for many generations to come be collecting the gold pieces that he has strewn with such magnificent recklessness.

*   *   *   *

MR. E. C. BENTLEY, during a broadcast tribute on Sunday said :

" Gilbert Keith Chesterton was not only one of the most greatly gifted, but one of the most beloved men of his time. . . .

" His intellectual powers were amazing. Included in their range were some of the noblest of modern poems and some of the most sparkling of light verse.

" Mr. Chesterton had in him the stuff of a great artist in the commonly accepted sense of the word. There was nothing he could not do with a pencil or, by preference, what, in our boyhood, we called a box of chalks. He honoured simplicity and kindness. As he once put it in an unforgettable lyric line—' Kindness which is God's last word.' "

"GILBERT"

By HILAIRE BELLOC

THE death of our Editor is an event of such national magnitude that it is impossible to set down in a brief word the meaning of it and the meaning of the man who has gone. Yet the word must be brief because it is written just as the paper over which he presided for so long goes to press.

I have known him, and still know him, not only as a most intimate friend from the days when I first came up to London from Oxford nearly 40 years ago, still more as one in whose expression of thought I continually lived. His was the one expression of thought in England which could convey to his fellow-citizens those things they most need to know and from which they are most debarred, and therefore men such as I, for whom those things are vital, sought the expression of them continually as hungry men seek for food. During all those years—it is the whole of an active lifetime—there was no other pen writing thus and no other voice speaking thus. And the first movement of the mind provoked by the hearing of such news is a question—and an unanswered one—" Will that great effort bear fruit?"

That it should do so in any society not moribund is self-evident; that it should bear ample fruit in any society not sterilised is a thing with which all men of culture throughout Europe will agree. But what fruit it will bear, even whether it will bear fruit, is something veiled from us. It is customary, I know, to take for granted the success of energy directed towards those objects which we most desire. It is thought, through some confusion of mind, an actual duty to prophesy success. But indeed there is no duty in these matters save that of telling the truth—and the truth is that we do not know.

The effect of Gilbert Chesterton's focussed and exact appreciation of reality, of his vivid untiring stream of exposition, will certainly be great in the United States. It will more slowly be felt, but certainly be felt, in Europe; every patriot will hope that it may be sufficiently felt also at last here. The special character of his work was a triumph in journalism; and he was the first to welcome that despised word and to give it its full and real value. He was proud to say, " I am a journalist", and he was indubitably the chief of that trade: our trade. He was not only the chief of that trade but the most complete representative of it; for the journalist is the man who discovers the truth about important happenings affecting his country in the world, even as they happen, and who, having discovered the truth, proclaims it in such fashion that his fellows shall know it too. Now the journalist to act thus must be a free man. No one working under the orders of another is fully free in that sense. Gilbert Chesterton remained free of his own will and through his own action, all his life. That is even a greater thing to say of such a man than to say how great his genius was.

Not so long ago in England we had some dozens of such men, not of his stature indeed, but free. The capital which furnished the printing of their words, which for that matter paid them their salaries, was commonly the capital of others, but they were not the servants of those others. To-day they are nearly all of them servants. What they say is not of themselves, they are not telling truths that they have discovered, they do not make personal comment upon affairs vitally affecting their fellow citizens, rather do they write what a master pays them to write and omit what that master desires to have omitted. So that it is often said abroad and increasingly said that here in England we have no true journalism left.

But in Gilbert Chesterton England had such a man. It is the fullest commentary I know on the condition into which we have fallen, the social and intellectual level to which we have sunk, that such a man should not have been seen at his full stature and should not have been acclaimed upon the level of what he was. One other free man in his own profession, the late Mr. Orage, said of him as exactly true a thing as was said anywhere; he said it many years ago, before the War, and the truth of it stands out enormously to-day. He said that Gilbert Chesterton was the most typically English man in England: not Englishman, but English man. He was for our generation what Dr. Johnson was for his. But Dr. Johnson telling some truth was heard by all the England of his time, all the England which counted, in the sense of that word "heard" when we use it to mean understood and taken for what he was in full. We have no longer the social machinery for such appreciation.

" The Times," which men still talk of as though it were particularly national, published upon hearing the news an obituary so utterly beneath the level of its subject as to be negligible, and I take that pronouncement to be typical of that tragic truth which I am announcing here.

A great Englishman has left England, and that English-man who was most English. By the knowledge of his fellow Englishmen may have of such a truth, by the measure with which they measure that truth, they may be politically judged.

IN MEMORIAM

By VINCENT McNABB, O.P.

GILBERT CHESTERTON IS DEAD.

I keep on moaning this to myself. If I did not believe the things he believed, his death would be almost the death of hope. I should despair of everyone; and of myself most of all.

For how could I again trust my judgment when it once misled me into hailing as one of the great men and major prophets of her country a man whose death has been announced amidst a thousand trivialities, with the banalities of praise?

Yet in this hour of temptation to despair I re-enkindle hope by recalling how often I have said that sometimes even greater than the gift of prophecy is the gift of recognizing the prophet! In the night-hour of Chesterton's death despair seems treason for me as for all the group who knew the time of their visitation because they knew that in giving him to them God had visited His people.

* * * *

I looked upon this child of London Town as one of the greatest sons born to England for four centuries. Londoners at their best like More and Chesterton do not look down on England; they look round on England and see its central place in Europe and the world. Their London River (as the seamen call it) after its long quiet sauntering through England's smiling meadow-land welcomes with a smile all nations of the earth.

Londoner of Londoners. English of the English Gilbert Chesterton towered shoulder high above his contemporaries. His massive body, crowned with a massive head, struck me as being only the well-proportioned outward visible sign of the massive intellectual, spiritual reality within. And this inward reality was in the sphere of memory, mind and heart.

His memory was not just beyond the average, but far beyond the average. Had it not been balanced by equal powers of mind it would have been, as in lesser minds, a danger or even a disease. But Gilbert Chesterton's memory was a storehouse of such ordered facts that from it, almost at will and always at need, he could bring forth things old and new.

In control of this vast, densely filled memory was a mind of more than average power. It was not just a power of reason—though few could reason better;—it was an unusual power of instant intuition; which, the philosophers say, is to be found only in a few men; and, as the theologians say, is found in all the angels.

One of his books he called *An Outline of Sanity*. The title was the man. His was the sane healthy mind that recognizes in the outline the first necessary line of thought received or thought expressed.

His thought about things was always the deep philosophical recognition not of resemblance but of differences. Unconsciously he acted on the principle that "a philosopher is one who knows how to divide."

His rapidly moving intelligence recognised in one principle a hundred conclusions; and in one phenomenon of nature or one fact of history recognised a hundred principles. This made him the best of listeners. But whilst he listened even to something he had already heard and perhaps knew better than the speaker knew, his giant mind was tracing within the accurate outline of the subject an elaborate diaper of thought.

The myriad epigrams of his style were not carefully designed effects. But they were the irrepressible and spontaneous results of a clear mind always set with philosophic instinct on discerning differences.

* * * *

It is terrifying to think what this extraordinary gift of memory and intelligence might have been and done had it been the supreme quality of his soul. Lesser intelligences amongst his contemporaries have risen from wealth to wealth or from power to power to a wealth and power that meant the impoverishment or enslavement of their fellow men. But God's greatest gift to Gilbert Chesterton was a heart that could seek neither wealth nor power, so deeply did he love the people. Even those who knew him least—say, by the books he wrote and they read—were conscious that his heart was no little part of his manifest greatness. But those who knew him best and marvelled at his gifts of mind, knew that his still greater gifts of heart were needed and used to keep the balance of his soul.

His was a richly furnished memory controlled by a brilliantly clear mind; but above all a noble chivalrous heroic heart in full control of memory and mind.

I remember that once his instant chuckle of laughter showed how he understood the humour in the Preface of the Mass when the Priest says to the people : " Lift up your hearts," and the people reply almost testily : " We have lifted them up."

Gilbert Chesterton's heart was never otherwise than " lifted up." He sought only the highest aims for himself, and for the England that he loved, and for his fellow men whom he loved, if that were possible, more than his England.

A long life of battling came to an end last Sunday at Top Meadow, Beaconsfield. We might well ask was his aim ever lower than towards the topmost? And in this knighty quest of the highest at all costs except the cost of honour, was his life and work ever less than a great beacon of light to England and the world?

Here and there in the heavy harvest of his writings his pen becomes one of the angriest, sharpest swords in Europe. But you will search this angry sword-battling without finding that the swordsman was ever defending himself. A laugh was usually self-defence enough for him. But behind his angry swordsmanship you will find some of the most defenceless or destitute beings of the world—the poor, the persecuted, the unfit—or some of the greatest principles, like loyalty, or wedded love or the homestead or liberty.

Once upon a time I called a book of his poems " Bugle-Music." Now I know there is in truth no Bugle-music, but only Bugle-calls. Every word that came from Gilbert Chesterton's pen-hand (which I kissed in his unconsciousness last Saturday) was like a Bugle-call to some of those tops of human aim to which from boyhood he had never been disloyal. But

GILBERT CHESTERTON IS DEAD.

His great heart gave way. Our Beacon is burned out. And what was left of this great Beacon we have buried in God's field. But in our memory there is something of him that will never burn out, till our ashes are as his.

THE G.K.C. OF FLEET STREET

By MRS. CECIL CHESTERTON

THE news that G.K.C. is dead must come as a hurt to his fellow men of all sorts and conditions, to thousands whom he could not have known but who learnt to regard him with intimate affection and admiration.

There are those who must mourn him as a great poet, as a famous writer, but how many are there who, apart from his fame, will miss him as an infinitely understanding, kindly friend, as ready to unloose his matchless imagination for the diversion of a little child or an inconsiderable acquaintance as the entertainment of a waiting universe.

His voice on the air, full and deep and rounded, with that incomparable chuckle which circled the world with laughter, was always the signal for a family gathering. He never lectured or talked down to people, he was at one with them in a marvellous sort of fireside intimacy—an intimacy which radiated from his unequalled fantasies, his satire, essays and unexpected novels.

There are so many small people—small, that is to say, in the sense that they have no public life—who owe a great deal to his marvellous capacity for bringing out the best in them. His greatness never overshadowed the individuality of anyone, but was rather the kindly warmth that draws from hidden sources a sudden burgeoning of confidence.

His associates and those who worked for and with him had a sense of happiness in their relationship. Charmingly and outrageously absent-minded, with an incorrigible habit of mislaying things G.K. was amazedly grateful when resourceful secretaries came to the rescue. I remember those devoted competent young people—Kathleen Cheshire, Bunny Dunham, and, lastly, Dorothy Collins who, perhaps, more than all of them understood and ministered to his genius and tactfully enforced his literary commitments.

But though I know and appreciate all these different sides, I think of Gilbert more intimately and clearly as a Fleet Street journalist who, like me, knew the adventures, the disappointments, the thrills and joy of companionship that go to its make-up.

I see G.K. in his favourite wine bar with polished barrels and oak tables, turning out reams of copy in that decorative caligraphy reminiscent of a mediaeval missal. Over a glass of Burgundy he would look up with a sudden gleam and give out sparkling gems like my favourite lines :—

" I don't care where the water goes,
If it doesn't get into the wine."

He had the inborn capacity of the true journalist and could write anywhere and everywhere, on an omnibus, in an A.B.C. shop or at an office table.

I recall the picturesque figure, with flowing cape and swordstick, hailing a taxi with a spacious gesture—to take him possibly just across the road. He might want the *Daily Telegraph*, the Cheshire Cheese, or the *Daily News*—and what were taxis for but to convey him thither. Time and distance were inconsiderable items to the G.K.C. of those days, and of time as of money he was always lavish. The veriest penny-a-liner could always go to him for copy and get it, red hot, with the incomparable sense of news that is the birthright of the journalist.

And when, alas, Fleet Street knew him less often in the flesh, his absence did not rid him of his pensioners. Broken-down pressmen, the erstwhile newspaper seller and the man who said he had been "told by Mr. Chesterton to call" still trailed their way knowing they would not leave empty-handed " the night they went to Beaconsfield by way of Bethnal Green."

I see him again as I first met him, at a meeting of The Moderns—his splendid leonine head flung back, his voice pealing through the small back room in a Fleet Street alley, in a brilliant paradox, a scintillating epigram. We were a Debating Society and met to hammer at each other on the problems of the day, the possibilities of the morrow.

It was a mixed lot who gathered at these discussions—there was Cecil, the antithesis of his brother, politically speaking, with his keen brain and relentless logic; Conrad Noel the red and revolutionary padre, Louis McQuilland, Bill Titterton, my brother Charles Sheridan Jones, and others of the glorious company of the *New Witness*.

His zest for life, I think, made him such a good companion. A hard worker, he entered into schoolboy games with that serious delight which animates his unforgettable ballads of the Simple Life.

I love to think of Gilbert in one of his bursts of high spirits, sitting at a Mock Trial in Judge's wig and gown, and laying down the law with a quick wit that never overlaid his perceptiton of the part.

A great man of letters, yes, but an incomparable playboy whose very zest sharpened his sense of the serious issues of life and his never ending campaign for justice, sincerity and truth.

His exit to me rings down the curtain on an era of bright spirits, full of gallantry and comradeship —Cecil, the man who would not know fear; his old friend and controversial sparring partner Clifford Sharp; Stacey Aumonier, the beloved vagabond; C. K. Scott Moncrieff, soldier and satirist; Tommy Pope, round faced and full of fun; and Thomas Seccombe, kindliest of critics.

All, all are gone, the old familiar faces. And yet they still are with me, glad ghosts who haunt the Fleet Street we all loved.

SOME MEMORIES

By W. R. TITTERTON

WHAT shall we do without him? You who knew him as I did, and had for him as deep an affection, are bewildered by our loss. As a family when their father dies, so we are stricken.

No need to tell you what he had done, or what he stood for. All that's in our blood. Nor can I describe him. He is too big, and too near; as well as too simple. The best I can do is to try to recall some memories of him.

The last memory is of him sitting beside me on the platform at the Essex Hall. He was too crippled with arthritis to stand up when he spoke; yet when I had my head turned from him I got the illusion that he was on his feet, fighting with the old vehement gaiety. Well his spirit never grew old.

Not long before that, when I went down to Beaconsfield to get him to talk for the papers, ever and again his head went up, and out came that deep-throated laugh that was like the challenge of a trumpet.

But there was a time, not so long ago either, when his rising converted the dullest debate into a festival, his very entry into a room was like sunburst. You see him, don't you, towering suddenly beside the chairman, his big jolly face lit with laughter and loving kindness, as he tosses his boyish curls—Don John of Austria, with the brave locks curled—and falls on with lusty joy!

Don John? Oh well, I always saw Gilbert Chesterton as a Knight. God knows that he seemed like the last Knight in England taking weapons from the wall.

" The last and lingering troubadour to whom the bird has sung
   That once went singing southward when all the world was young."

When he came into the office, big soft hat on head, huge cloak flapping round him, I always imagined a sword by his side.

He was all compact of chivalry. If he had a weakness in polemic, it was that he hated to hurt. Yet in a good cause, the good old cause, he could, against the urge of his heart, be ruthless. But he had to be roused.

Chivalrous, and one of the few instinctive democrats that I have known! The mystical doctrine of the equality of man was to him a self-evident fact like granite. Yet, though he felt superior to no man, he was the humblest of them all. And the simplest. Stranger still in a democrat, it was the simple people he liked best and respected most.

Of course he loved children, being a child. When he used to dawn on me in the office, the wraith of a cigarette sprouting from beneath his fierce moustache, and the pince-nez perpetually tumbling from before those wise, bold, innocent eyes, and the big cloak trailing, I knew that here was a child upon whom " the shades of the prison-house " had never closed, who trailed his clouds of glory still.

Prison-house! You can imagine what the wise child would have had to say about that vile slander on God's world.

I think it was his humility and simplicity that led the mandarins to under-rate his verse. The usual poet dramatizes himself—writes in a toga with a laurel wreath cocked over one eye. But G.K.C. wrote poetry as he drank wine or ate bread-and-cheese, and had as much zest for a squib as for an epic. And so, if you please, the author of *The Ballad of the White Horse*, and *Lepanto* and twenty more of the major poems in English literature was not a "dedicated poet" like the solemn Johnnies who . . . but never mind!

All this talk doesn't account for him—a child who was a very wise man, a gay companion who was profoundly serious, a simple soul who gloried in tumultuous decoration. But the Gothic he loved gives us a hint. The surface of his work is often a riot of decoration. Yet the outline is sane and simple, the bulk of it is majestic, and inside it is a shrine.

And this may be added: We may say of his work what Walt Whitman said of *The Leaves of Grass*: " Comrade this is no book. Who touches this touches a man,"

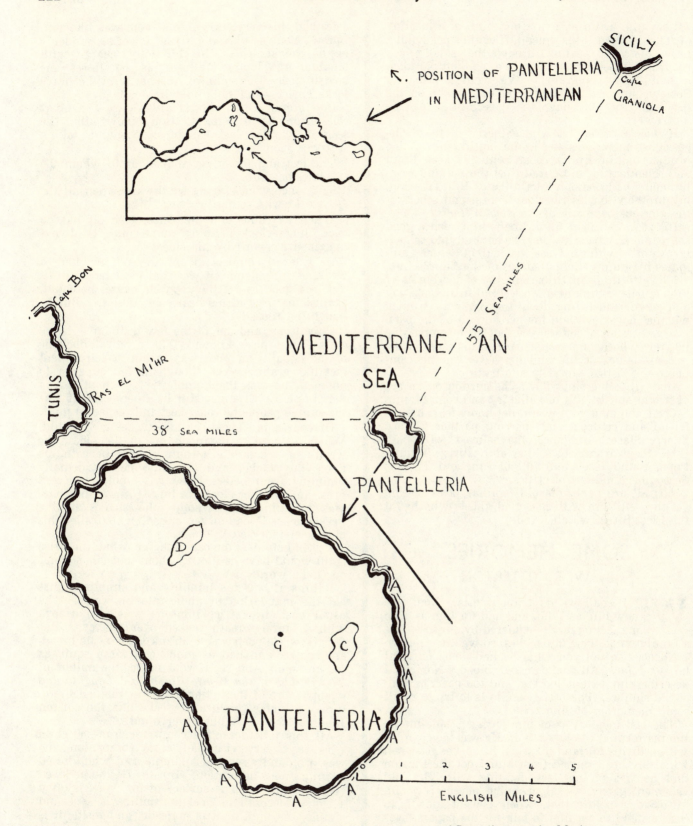

Sketch Maps by Michael Lindsey Clark showing *(a)* the position of Pantelleria in the Mediterranean *(b)* distances between Tunis and Sicily and *(c)* the configuration of the Island,

PANTELLERIA
BY HILAIRE BELLOC

THE first mention of Pantelleria in our official Press was made a fortnight after its description in these columns. It is noteworthy that a misprint in our original note—Pantellaria, for Pantelleria was reproduced in this mention. The official Press does well to follow our instruction even belatedly, but it should, in common honesty give a reference to the source of its information.

The Island of Pantelleria is to-day potentially the most important strategic point in the world.

Let me justify that statement. I say "potentially" because it has not yet been fully established whether the island can be sufficiently used for the purposes of armed flying craft and submarines, nor even whether it could be permanently safely used by large surface craft provided with a large fortified harbour. But if it is capable of these three functions, it commands the Mediterranean.

Why does Pantelleria command the Mediterranean? Because it divides that great inland sea into two basins; surface craft, armed or commercial, cannot pass from the eastern to the western basin or *vice versa* if the masters of Pantelleria forbid their passage.

How far hostile aircraft prevents the use of narrows may be disputed; we may say that a stretch of water even three hundred miles broad can be so threatened by powerful air bases upon even one shore thereof as to make passage through it impossible to hostile commerce; or we may put the limits much lower, saying that straits two hundred miles as still usable; but no one can deny that narrows of approximately fifty miles or less in width are absolutely closed by powerful hostile air bases on either side. Now Pantelleria is only just over fifty sea miles from the Sicilian coast and is under forty sea miles from the African coast. Any surface craft proposing to pass from the eastern to the western Mediterranean or *vice versa* must either go through the Straits of Messina, which are the width of a river and commanded by one government on either shore, or between Pantelleria and Sicily, which are under one government, or between Pantelleria and the coast of Tunis, the latter being under an alien government. Though the possession by one government of both sides of a strait makes the control of that strait doubly secure, yet the possession of only one side of the strait is sufficient if the narrows are sufficiently

limited. A strait fifty miles broad, each shore of which is controlled by the same government, is equivalent strategically to one of half that width for aircraft from either shore dominate the half width opposite their bases. Even if the further shore be in alien hands, aircraft working from the home shore can dominate the strait, if it be sufficiently narrow. Now in the case of Pantelleria surface craft attempting to pass between that island and Sicily to the north and east are running the gauntlet at the range of under 27 miles upon the one side or the other. And even if they attempt the passage between Pantelleria and the Tunisian coast they are running the gauntlet at the range of 39 miles or rather less. These figures are enough to show why Pantelleria locks the door between the eastern and western Mediterranean.

But next it will be asked whether the Mediterranean is essential to domination in the modern world, and, if so, why? The control of it does not apparently affect the vast oceanic world outside, the Indian Ocean and the Pacific on the one side the Atlantic on the other. The Mediterranean can, it may be objected, be neglected by a power sufficiently superior on the main oceans.

The error of this criticism lies in its misapprehension of three points, two of them political, the third mechanical or strategic. The two political points are these: First, the control of the Mediterranean means the control of main communications between all the southern part of the ancient world, N. Africa, the southern parts of Russia, and the Levant. Mastery in the Mediterranean involves supremacy in the old world of Europe, which still is and will presumably remain the chief centre of human action. Secondly, it is in the Mediterranean, and particularly in the eastern Mediterranean, that Islam and Christendom, the two cultures of Europe and the Near East and all that is effective in Africa meet. When those in control of the Mediterranean, and particularly the eastern Mediterranean, lose that control, they have lost half or more than half their hold upon the world of Islam.

The third point, mechanical or strategic, consists in this: that he who holds the Mediterranean commands as against the ocean routes what are called "interior lines"; that is, the power of choice in the direction of attack and greater rapidity in the delivery of attack. If you are working within the arc of a circle, for instance, against forces which have to work from without that arc, you can strike left or right, transferring your forces at will, while your opponent outside must cover much greater distances and suffer corresponding delay in meeting your thrusts.

On this account it is even now being debated (and has not been decided) whether the full and final policy of this country should envisage abandonment of the eastern Mediterranean or no. If it be ultimately abandoned the political effects must be very great indeed; the loss of status for this country so considerable as to be, perhaps, catastrophic. On the other hand, it can only be held in the long run it would seem (in the present state of our knowledge and in the present preponderance of air power and in the present lack of defence against the same) by action based upon India, and working northwards through the Red Sea and the Suez Canal, or, if the Suez Canal be forbidden, then by land from the Red Sea through Palestine. That is why it is proposed to fortify Akabah. Whether it will be possible for a European power to work from a base so distant as India against any power working from a base near at hand is the crux of the problem.

But can Pantelleria be used effectively by the submarine, surface craft, and aircraft?

Even if Pantelleria did not exist the passage between Italy and Tunis being well under a hundred miles is certainly dominated by aircraft working from Sicily. What Pantelleria can do is to make that certitude doubly sure. The main difficulties in the military utilisation of Pantelleria lie in its volcanic character and its uneven surface coupled with its restricted dimensions. The volcanic character of the soil might make any works upon it impermanent, and the fact that it is one mass of mountain might prohibit its use by aircraft; it is a mass of volcanic hills rising everywhere somewhat steeply from the coast line to about 2,500 feet (at G on the sketch map appended). As for elbow room it has not (or had not) any port save the very small and shallow one at the point marked P on the N.W. of the island, a mere fishing port with from 8 to 10 feet of water and impossible for ships of any size. The whole island is barely nine miles long and at its greatest width barely 5 miles across, but the sea is not very deep just outside the old port, it would be easy to construct there a sufficient harbour of refuge. The coast is almost inaccessible along the western end, rocky and has steep cliffs along the edge marked A.A.A. on the sketch, but it is approachable everywhere else, and there is good holding ground along all the north-western end. Of land available for the landing and departure of aircraft there are two main flats marked C and D on the sketch. C is rather marshy, but could be drained. D is rather larger. Each of them is a mile or a little over a mile in length and could be extended by artificially levelling. How far the potentialities of Pantelleria are what are here suggested can only be determined by experts after work upon the spot, but there is every indication that the island can be and will be fully used.

Looking On
By Gregory Macdonald

The Chancellor of the Exchequer's calculated indiscretion at the 1900 club was backed up by the calculated indiscretion of an ex-Chancellor, Sir Robert Horne. The joint declaration entailed either the end of sanctions or a change of administration as though after a Carlton Club meeting. An immediate and open split was avoided after clumsy attempts on the part of *The Times* to explain the speeches away, and after an attempt by Mr. Baldwin in the House of Commons to joke it off, had plainly indicated to observers at home and abroad that the ruling group was split from end to end. Until the Government regains cohesion it is useless to hope for a firm policy in foreign affairs, and there is no likelihood that the coming debate in Parliament will establish a policy that will unite the nation. Yet foreign affairs once more become the pressing problem. Whatever reply Berlin makes to the famous questionnaire, it will not now be conciliatory: the demands may take any form. On the one hand there is the demand for colonies, backed up by internal propaganda in the mandated territories. If this demand is pressed to the point of inconvenience, the Government may choose to allow Germany a free hand in Eastern Europe, where indeed her commercial and political influence is already growing. The next question, of equal magnitude, is that of Italy. At present the proposal is that the British Government will embark upon a policy of collaboration with Rome: a *volte face* which will be resented by the "fifty nations" of the sanctions front, however eagerly they may wish to be discharged from their obligations—and the collaboration with Rome will not now be achieved except in so far as Italy is satisfactorily accommodated.

*   *   *   *

It is improbable that the Democratic Convention for the renomination of President Roosevelt will admit defeat to the Republican Convention at Cleveland in the matter of ballyhoo, but at least it has already found a candidate, and in the candidate a programme. President Roosevelt's pledges are in operation, with all the time to run until November for their fulfilment. The recent behaviour of the price index has shown how carefully the Administration's policy is carried out. During the past few weeks the stable figure of 80 to the 100 of 1926 has been allowed to drop a point or two, for the outpouring of the Veteran's Bonus (by which its original sponsors hoped to produce an inflationary rise in prices) will undoubtedly have the effect of causing a suddenly increased demand for goods, and the Administration wants to have the index well in hand. But too much increase of the money in the market will not be allowed: hence the Tax Bill, which should soon be ready for the President's approval. Congress cannot, however, hope to fix any figure below the President's requirements, because the Tax Bill is in substitution for taxes ruled invalid by the Supreme

Court, and to take up the slack of expenditure forced upon him by Congress. In one way or another, Congress will have to vote him the money necessary for the balancing of the ordinary current Budget, and can hardly take on itself the responsibility for unbalancing it. The President may insist on the Tax Bill he wants before adjournment, or he may insist upon Congress imposing indirect taxation for which the members of Congress would not be thanked by their electors.

*   *   *   *

Despite the apparent unanimity of Governor Landon's nomination, the Republican Party is left with as many problems as it can comfortably handle. Not only is there a quarrel between the Old Guard and the insurgents, but, as *The Times* remarks, the programme adopted at Cleveland is "so thoroughly Mid-Western in some of its planks as to be extremely disheartening to those who believe that the greatest single obstacle to world recovery—including the recovery of the United States—is economic nationalism." In other words, the "safe" Eastern States have lost the Republican Party under the pressure of New Deal policies, and the universal forces which stand for the restoration of international trade based on international loans have lost it as well. The Cleveland programme is a bundle of impossible contradictions to which Landon himself adds a proposed amendment of the Constitution, to ensure minimum wages, and a return to the gold standard. The former addition destroys the Republican championship of the Constitution, for though amendments have been added before, the Constitutional issue has now quite a special significance. The latter addition alienates Senator Borah, and with him a body of "progressive" voters who would have been very useful. Governor Landon has been carefully coached for some months past by a group of bankers and economists who must pin all their hopes on him, but Wall Street itself has little expectation that he will enter the White House.

*   *   *   *

An obscure situation continues in France, and it may be that M. Auriol's declaration on the financial position this Thursday will precipitate a crisis. The City of London columns are monotonously repeating a demand for the devaluation of the franc, with every now and then the real fear emerging that instead of devaluation they will be faced with a gold embargo. One writer solemnly advised the British Government last week to have all the Bank of England's gold, earmarked at the Bank of France, shipped over to London at once by Imperial Airways. While M. Blum's ultimate policy remains in doubt there must be hesitation to endorse fully what he has already done; and the situation in Russia has not been clarified by the publication of the new Constitution, which is significantly labelled " Stalin's Constitution " instead of being given an impersonal title. On the Russian side of events there is this also to notice, that no great Russian aid was given to whip up Canton against Nanking: any powerful forces at work could have made that affair something much more like a civil

war. On the French side of the question, devaluation can be carried out only by an open betrayal of the workers. On the other hand, the franc must be defended, and a gold embargo is the obvious method. Certainly the British authorities are already negotiating with Washington for joint action in either case: so far, however, no agreement has been reached, though the prospects favour "a temporary arrangement rather than a permanent stabilisation gesture." There is no such thing as a permanent gesture: it means that true stabilisation is still refused by the City. The first sensational move may come from another direction. It is reported, for instance, that Signor Suvich is likely to be appointed to Washington, where, according to the Daily Telegraph, "he is esteemed in American financial circles." The only American financial circles are in Washington. If the appointment is made, it may presage a currency agreement.

*   *   *   *

The sharp rise in the average rate of discount for Treasury Bills to 18s. 1d. marks the highest point reached for two years. The reason is a narrowing of the market. The banks themselves have had to withdraw from tendering because, owing to the continuation of a stable price-level and a consequent rise of deposits, they must keep their resources for demands over the counter instead of investing them in securities. The same necessity for keeping cash on hand is driving them to call in loans already out.

Banks, Profits and Pay

By J. L. Benvenisti

THERE is a mystery in England, for which I have long been seeking a reasonable explanation. It concerns a group of men, whose qualifications are generally recognised as valuable, whose work is well done, and who are expected to possess, and do possess in a high degree, qualities of integrity, courtesy, tact and shrewd judgment. I refer to the managers and staffs of the Great Banks.

Whatever may be the future character and function of these institutions (and I for one hope it will be vastly different from what it is now), men such as these will be an asset to any community. If any men should be well paid, these men should be well paid. They are not well paid. They are very badly paid. I do not say that there is any instance on record of a bank clerk fainting over his ledger from lack of food. But by any decent standard and in proportion to the responsibility which they bear, I say that these men are very badly paid. They are paid on a scale, which could only be excused, if their employers were on the verge of bankruptcy.

That is very far from being the case. The profits of bank shareholders are notorious. Two of the big five, for instance, distribute annually dividends on their issued capital varying between ten and eighteen per cent. The sum of money actually distributed averages roughly three and a half million pounds a year. These two banks together employ about thirty thousand people. A reduction of the dividend by one and a half millions would allow every one of these men an average increase in salary of £50 a year, and still leave the shareholders a profit, of which, by ordinary commercial standards, they would have no right to complain.

All this does not take into account the sums placed annually to the hidden or 'internal' reserves. Sir Reginald McKenna (that very able man) for once appeared to let the cat out of the bag rather badly when discussing the annual report for 1934. For he pointed out that the declared dividend (16% if I remember rightly) represented little more than the scale of profit of depositors in the Post Office Savings Bank, if the shareholders real capital, that is to say the issued capital plus the published and internal reserves, were taken into consideration. The inference as to the size of the sums placed annually to the 'internal reserves' is pretty staggering.

However my argument will stand up without that. Let us judge this matter on the published figures alone. I say that on the strength of these, bank managers and staffs should get more money. Now the argument advanced against giving them more money is this: that the shares are at a premium, and consequently shareholders are getting a much smaller return on their capital, than is indicated by the amount of the dividend.

This argument, which is repeatedly brought forward on public occasions is, of course, nonsense. It would, if referring to any other institution, immediately be recognised as nonsense. If a big combine, or any other organisation, whose shares changed hands well above parity value, were known to underpay their staff, and if a demand for human conditions were resisted on the ground that shareholders were not receiving the excessive dividend they appeared to be receiving, because the shares were at a premium, such an argument would immediately be killed by a burst of nationwide spontaneous ridicule.

And rightly so. People would, most justifiably, say as follows: " You have bought shares in an enterprise which made inflated profits out of sweating. Because of these inflated profits, you bought the shares at an inflated price. If the sweating ceases, and if in consequence the profits decline, and with them the value of the shares, that is your funeral. You should, before buying the shares, have satisfied yourself that the profits were justly earned."

Now why is that reply never given to the Banks? It is a mystery. I cannot probe it. But I think the answer lies in that unjust priority and privilege to which the holder of money is assumed to be entitled as against the physical producer. It is a line of thought related to that which insists on absolute security for savings, without realising that savings forfeit their claim to such security in the moment they demand to be made fruitful. It is part of the special blindness and special idolatry of our age, in which (and, may I say it, nowhere more than in England) the usurer is sacrosanct.

A Midsummer Night's Dream
By K. C. Macdonald

II.

ON the turf-carpeted, lantern-lit summer stage, Theseus invokes the tardy moon, and speaks the prologue to the play; Shakespeare himself, grave, courteous and kingly, plays his part, and declares the revels open.

Young Lady Norris, already a little tired with the day's formalities, a little chilled by the company, a little choked by starched ruff and whalebone and stiff jewelled stomacher, is roused to a fresh awareness by the music of his words.

Hippolyta, I woo'd thee with my sword,
And won thy love, doing thee injuries;
But I will wed thee in another key,
With pomp, with triumph, and with revelling—

The brave young Norris smiles at her, recalling their first meeting; and she returns it, waveringly, since for her the memory has perplexities. She is here in Ricote becauses he loves him, after all. But it is a long way from the woods of Lismore, where she slept under the stars, and hunted with her brothers, and cursed with unction the name of Raleigh, to this scene of English exquisiteness and courtly fashion, where the hated names of Raleigh and Spenser and Sidney are extolled on every side. How she had despised and flouted Norris at that first meeting, when she stood beside her father at the parley in the meadows! Yet, though she had been quick enough to rail at her family's wrongs, had she really felt them? Had she not been secretly glad that her schooldays were to be prolonged, that she might run wild in the heather still, and avoid the household tasks and ladylike accomplishments, the threatened visit to her aunt in Dublin, that she had always dreaded? Perhaps if she had been older when it all happened, her loyalties might not have dissolved in such confusion at the test of Norris's love.

Separated now from her disappointed father, her hurt and angry brothers, divided from them by her affection for her husband and the kindness of his people, she understands their loss and their betrayal as she never did while she was with them.

*   *   *   *

Theseus invokes the moon: always the moon: Elizabeth has grown used to these poetic comparisons. When she was younger she enjoyed them: Cynthia, the chaste goddess, Diana the white huntress: the waters of virtue that quench the lover's ardour: one wearies of it a little as the years go on: though she finds it difficult to admit, even now, that she has always been in two minds about it, and never accepted the role entirely through her own choice.

Chanting faint hymns to the cold fruitless moon— This Shakespeare strikes a truer note: he leaves you with no sugary sense of flattery. Periodically, Elizabeth feels vehemently that she hates flattery above all things. And his gentle voice goes on. For a moment he seems to speak directly to her, to touch her thoughts and memories, to soothe and justify even *her* lengthy indecision.

> Thrice-blessed they that master so their blood,
> To undergo such maiden pilgrimage;
> But earthlier happy is the rose distill'd,
> Than that which, withering on the virgin
>   thorn,
> Grows, lives, and dies, in single blessedness.

Within the circle of her monstrous, spangled ruff, the white face of the Virgin Queen stares up at the poet through the gathering gloom. Poor Cynthia, poor mortal moon, he thinks: so seldom among friends, so seldom mistress of her own desires. For a space he stands royally above her, and gives counsel. The mantle of Heywood, of Tarleton and his kind, has fallen upon him. By his peculiar genius he is heir to the privileges of the dispossessed jester; but his words are winged with healing, and do not wound. Hermia in a moment will declare her right to choose not where her soul consents not. Hippolyta's sympathy will be proclaimed by silence. The tyranny of circumstance, assisted by the tyranny of thoughtlessness, of desire, of self-righteousness, of selfishness, will receive the spoken and unspoken comment of the women. Indeed, this play might have been written by a woman, thinks old Lady Norris, and she glances suspiciously at the strong, calm profile of Mary Sidney. But the Queen accepts the kind shrewdness of the poet, as she accepted the sharper thrusts of the jester long ago. And she sees her life reflected in his speeches.

Even at the beginning, was it possible for her to make a choice? For Hermia, the prohibition is plain: for her, a web of warnings, admonishments, intrigues, all built around her own uncertainties. Love and ambition, personal preference and policy, swayed her from one side to the other. Which course would best content her? Which course would best secure her throne? Were these aims incompatible? Perhaps Mary was right, when she maintained that she would better preserve her sovereignty as a monarch by yielding her sovereignty as a woman. But what had Mary accomplished? And what had she? Had her advisers or her own instincts deceived her most? Was she not yielding, year by year, her protective rights of sovereignty in England?

She had hesitated so often. There was Leicester:

> The course of true love never did run smooth;
> But either it was different in blood—
> O cross! too high to be enthrall'd to low—

The young princes of France:

> Or else misgraffèd in respect of years;
> O spite! too old to be engaged to young—
> Or else, it stood upon the choice of friends;
> O hell, to choose love by another's eyes!

Mary Sidney, who is aware that this lover's colloquy comes rather close, displays a touch of uneasiness at this point. But the Queen shows no sign of displeasure. It is all true, and that is how she felt about it, twenty years ago, when she eased her anger against Leicester, against her own ministers, against Henry III of France, by playing with

Alençon. Even in those days of bitterness, she had believed that it was still in her power to conquer circumstance, to rebuild that old structure of Kingship that she had been trained from childhood to believe was divinely ordered, the bulwark against greed and oppression. After all she was in the prime of life, still vigorous and handsome, still confident of her abilities—if only Burleigh would give over reminding her that her title was insecure: if only Leicester would not tease her by alternate pressure and withdrawal; if only the people would conform to her perpetually offered compromises—

The Countess of Essex stirs and sighs, drawing the Queen's attention. She, too, is held by memories; in spite of herself, Elizabeth is impelled to sympathy—though there is a touch of triumph in it, for she cannot be *other* than herself. No doubt the girl is thinking of Philip Sidney as she listens to the lines that follow—and Essex is at the wars in France.

> Or, if there were a sympathy in choice,
> War, death, or sickness did lay siege to it,
> Making it momentary as a sound,
> Swift, as a shadow; short, as any dream;
> Brief, as the lightning in the collied night;
> So quick bright things come to confusion.

(To be concluded.)

Battle to Rheims

SAINT JOAN OF ARC. *By V. Sackville-West. Cobden-Sanderson.* 10s.

IN this carefully historical, very vivid book, Miss Sackville-West has endeavoured to solve the problem of Joan of Arc, and admits that she cannot solve it, though she submits it to every test permitted by modern thought. For the amazing career of St. Joan of Arc is no national or poetic legend that has grown with time, and may be dissolved at a scientific touch. It is a generally-known, well documented story to which nobody has ever added a tittle of legendary matter fit to be taken seriously, except Mr. Bernard Shaw. As Miss Sackville-West has said, " We know practically every detail of her passive existence as a child and, as to the few months of her active career, they are so thoroughly documented that we know exactly where she spent each day, and in whose company; what she wore, what horse she rode, what arms she bore, what she ate and drank; and, more importantly still, what words she uttered. Scores of her friends, neighbours, followers, and companions-in-arms have left vivid testimony as to her appearance, manners, habits, character, and speech. The idea that there is any paucity of material for reconstructing her life and personality is fallacious in the last degree."

Yet it is difficult to bridge a gap of five hundred years. The medieval mind, the medieval background must be added to the personal history of this medieval genius. She is better understood in our age, she means more to our future and our development, than she meant to the "liberal" ideas of a hundred years ago. We may even go so far as to say that her own character is easier to estimate in an era of active womanhood than at a time when the blight of Puritanism was still heavy on feminine enterprise of every kind. But the unified philosophy and belief of the fifteenth century are not ours in Europe to-day; we must see and accept them as they really were before we can attempt an explanation of St. Joan.

Miss Sackville-West does see and accept them as far as history presents them, though she does not accept their findings in all things, nor is she at one with their beliefs. For example, she admits the possibility that Joan held converse with the souls of the dead—with St. Catherine and St. Margaret, learned Roman and Scottish Queen; psychical research has once again brought this idea into prominence: but she cannot bring herself to accept the Archangels Gabriel and Michael, since she has been accustomed to consider them as fictions. Yet may not Joan's testimony be accepted on this point as on the other? This is not the only documentary evidence for the manifestation of angels.

However, that is not the main point to be noted here. What must be noted is that Miss Sackville-West has contributed a very valuable and very interesting study to the problem of Joan of Arc,—straightforward and uncompromising in its regard for evidence, acute in its estimation of character:

ranking with that of Andrew Lang for sympathy and accuracy, surpassing it in her regard for feminine reactions and her willingness to accept phenomena that cannot be explained rationally,—because the evidence is there. Her picture of the dark-haired, direct, healthy-minded little peasant-girl, loyal and ardent but plain-spoken, and very clear as to what was essential and what was not essential in her actions, accords with history. It is a genuine picture of a practical idealist; there are no suggestions of hysteria, no " complexes," no fuzzy mediumistic edges. But there are also the "Voices" by which this clear-headed child was directed to take on a task quite out of her sphere, and which she did take on and did accomplish—a soldier's and statesman's task, which every one, looking back on it across the centuries, must declare to have been well done. Her biographer does not minimise the part played by the Voices in the achievement of Joan of Arc. She finds it impossible to dismiss them as subjective; ' witchcraft ' is not in her vocabulary, even if it were possible in St. Joan's case to reiterate that ancient calumny; and therefore she accepts the fact, with some reservations of her own, that the peasant-girl of Domrémy had exterior supernatural guidance when she became the saviour and rebuilder of France. She suggests that as our scientific knowledge increases we may understand how such things occur. And she leaves the problem otherwise unanswered.

It is necessary to add that to the mind and faith of which St. Joan was part, there is no problem. Her contemporaries, when they doubted and questioned her, did not doubt that such things were possible: they merely demanded proof of their authenticity in her case. They were believing, but not credulous. We, who venerate her, have that proof. To us, who accept the great Mystery of the Incarnation of God in the world as the focus of all world-history, it is not difficult to contemplate this interaction of temporal and eternal. We may see Time itself as a support for our feet in this brief period of our pilgrimage, but as no barrier of distance between one soul and another. Five hundred years cannot separate us by one second from Joan of Arc, nor Joan from Margaret of Scotland, nor Margaret from Catherine of Alexandria; nor æons of geological time from Gabriel, who announces the Incarnation to the world of men, or Michael who upholds it before the angels.

Yet we must have our physical being in time and space; we know that this spiritual breaking-through, especially this purposive and proven breaking-through, as in the case of St. Joan of Arc, or of St. Bernadette of Lourdes, is rare and precious. We know that in those early years of the fifteenth century history was being hopelessly mismanaged, and the great medieval civilisation was threatened with destruction. That it was not destroyed, though the shell of it still stands, battered and broken but capable of rebuilding, as the Cathedral of Rheims after many an attack on itself and the principle it stands for, is due in part to the vision and sacrifice of Joan of Arc.   K.C.M.

Roughly Speaking

Letters to Peter—V.
By Charles Williams

My dear Peter,

"Faults have you, child of Adam's stem," and I should be the last person to say that only heaven knew of them. Heaven has communicated its knowledge with an almost indecent publicity. But I will say that, so far, I had not reckoned grab or hold-fast among them. I had almost allowed a flicker of cheerfulness to break in when I contemplated your young generosity, your willingness to hold things in common. Hope hesitatingly suggested that you might not be keen on accumulation, on things, on, in short, property. And now Mr. Belloc* has shown me that that is all wrong. He has made me feel that not to want to own a house and three acres—to say nothing of the cow—is so cretinous as to be depraved, or so depraved as to be cretinous. You and I, Peter, are the kind of person among whom normal human instincts are lost. I have tried—how feebly!—not to want to own anything, and here I am helping to re-establish slavery. Who was it said that the virtues always betray each other? "Nobody; I myself." It is true, all the same. In this life we cannot happily endure the mere complexity of the Good.

We must try, however. It seems you had better desire as a social fact what you must not seek for personal gain. You must possess altruistically. You must own your proper house on behalf of a doctrine, and cultivate (O Peter can I see you doing it?) your proper garden lest your neighbour should lose his job. The recovery of property, Mr. Belloc teaches us, is the only way—if it is still possible—by which we can economically become free men. I think he is entirely right. But I never assented to a doctrine with less personal enthusiasm. I have been very fortunate; the yoke of wage-slavery has pressed very lightly on me, owing to the tradition of an English University and the illustrious good-will of my own Cæsar. But I have never forgotten the edge of the abyss and how near it might be; my head swims to look into it and see the skulls and bones at the bottom.

Besides one must have the idea, the possibility, of property, in order to be free from it. There are times when the right hand ought to know what the left is doing in order to counteract it. Nehemiah (the Tirshatha—admirable title!) made his people work at the building of their City with one hand while carrying arms for the same City in the other. It is perhaps a more difficult thing (though that must have been a little awkward) to build up ownership without while destroying ownership within, to own something and possess nothing, to be free economically and spiritually. Could one indeed poise on such a pinnacle? It is our old problem—can the saint and the citizen be one? Yes, certainly, or we deny that there is rule

*"*An Essay on the Restoration of Property*"
   by Hilaire Belloc

in unity itself. (It is no use blaming me Peter; he did say everything as Keats said he did. Who? Oh go away!)

With a passionate desire to make useful suggestions, and with one eye on your future (the dropping, not the auspicious eye), it occurred to me to wonder whether there are not in existence two sets of men engaged in two trades who might form the subjects of practical consideration. I am less than a baby in these things, but I know by accident that publishers and booksellers exist. I know also that they quarrel as men do, over discounts, charges, sales. The associations on both sides allude to he other as consisting of catamounts, catalepts, and......catalects. But they make free agreements and keep them. Both associations—publishers and booksellers—are so far free, speaking generally, from domination by inclusive companies and chain-shops. Both encourage the smaller men, and both desire a kind of guild independence for their members. In so far as, on the publishers' side, you have larger bodies behind—societies or institutions—the tendency will be, ever so little, in favour of freedom from eternal control. Two strong guilds of this kind, supported perhaps by the authors, might form a very useful body, both as an example of working property, and *e.g.* in legal affairs—they might help to remedy the law of libel. I suggest that the idea of charters for them might be discussed; licences, as Mr. Belloc suggests, might be necessary for the sale of books by a vendor of other things, and the squeezing out of both publisher and bookseller by some million-armed milliner or fishmonger prevented. But this is far from you at present, Peter, and I doubt if you will ever effectively be either. Besides, this morning what heart have we, but by duty, for these things? I do not know what name will be most on your tongue in the next ten years, or what mind will be a banner of music to you. But I know very well when I was a little older than you how one summer evening on the pier at Southend I read for the first time " The Napoleon of Notting Hill," and immediately turned back and re-read it; and all the Saturdays when the *Daily News* was the most important thing in the universe. I have never been convinced that the best of those articles were saved—the most militant were reprinted, but not the most superb. For he was a poet, and a very fine poet: he was I have always thought, one of the greatest of the moderns. " The Ballad of the White Horse " had a metropolitan energy in it; it was of the stuff of greatness. And so was he.

Peter, there are only your generation left about me. The last of my lords is dead.

Always,

C.W.

Music

MR. PEPLER'S interesting article on opera and action which appeared in the paper a week or two ago, reminds me of a story among many stories told of a certain operatic impressario whom it is unnecessary to mention. A prima donna complained that her tenor hero staged a death too suddenly to allow her to make full dramatic use of it; to which she received the reply that no operatic artist ever dies too soon. Mr. Pepler might almost claim to be the saviour of operatic artists; he would have all the deaths and drama by mimes and puppets, while the melody lingers on off stage.

Admittedly, opera is a complicated problem. The drama requires appropriate music, the music requires appropriate drama and the performance requires artists who can sing, look and act the parts written for them. But it is not quite true that the ideal performer, if and when discovered, is required to sacrifice the music to the exigencies of the drama (not true, that is, if the composer knows his job—as did Wagner or Puccini) and despite its merciful expediency, I am not entirely happy about Mr. Pepler's proposed solution. He is obviously right to suggest that discord of movement weakens the musical unity. There are certain situations where the use of mime or of ballet is advantageous. He mentions, for example, the flower maidens in "Parsifal." There are also the Rhine Maidens, or the Queen of the Night's ladies in Mozart's " Magic Flute." In such situations where unity and rhythmic movement is of primary importance and difficult to obtain in conjunction with unity of sound, Mr. Pepler's proposal might be an excellent solution for the difficulty. But it will be, nevertheless, a compromise and if applied to the problem of Kundry or of Isoldi or of Sarastro I fear that the effect of separating the acting from the singing could only be one of painful artificiality; for, as it is true that to play Isoldi as Wagner intended, requires for the singing a dramatic sense,

so it is true that to act the part as it should be acted, the actor must sing. In other words, Isoldi is an operatic character and was created as such. Perhaps the ideal is found in our generation in Chaliapine's "Boris." No one could equal the acting of that great drama if he did not sing it as does Chaliapine or conversely. Incidentally, rhythm is a far more subtle quality than metric accuracy.

Despite the earnest endeavour of those responsible for entertainment notices which almost invariably lump opera and ballet under one head, the two things are not similar. The problem which faced—for example—Tchaikowsky when he essayed Eugene Onegin was not the same as that which he had to solve with The Swan Lake. Ballet as an art form is one of symmetry of movement and of grouping to achieve a desired effect whether it be one of pure geometrical form or for the more dramatic effect of comedy or of romance—as *Les Sylphides*. The introduction of mime has given to modern ballet more dramatic opportunities; there is a world of difference between *Carnival* and *Choreartium*. But it is a difference inside the problem of expressing an emotion by movement. It is a different problem from that which confronts the producer of *Hamlet* and again different from the problem of producing *Parisfal*.

The fact is that we do not know what will be the future development of Opera; whether, indeed, it has any future. Possibly all that it is capable of as an art form has been achieved. I do not think this is the actuality, but the possibility must be admitted. We are living in a curiously traditional period, a period in which little great art, in any form, is being produced. Demand secures supply, and as there is only a limited field for opera to-day —and that more in reproduction than in creation— there is a scarcity of operatic performers of the first rank. If the supply gets less it is quite probable that for any kind of adequate performance such a compromise as Mr. Pepler suggests may become necessary. But the present existence of a Frieda Leider, a Kirsten Flagstad, a Chaliapine, or a Boekelmann rather disproves his theory as an ultimate solution.

V.N.L.

WANTED

WHERE TO STAY

The Notice Board

THE DISTRIBUTIST LEAGUE

CENTRAL BRANCH

Informal meetings are held at the League Office, 7/8, Rolls Passage, Chancery Lane, every Friday evening, at 7.0.

BIRMINGHAM BRANCH

Hon. Sec.: K. L. Kenrick, 7, Soho Road, Birmingham, 21.

Meetings at 6, Greenfield Crescent, Birmingham, on the first Friday of the month, at 7 p.m.

Committee meetings: third Friday in the month at 6 p.m. at 7, Soho Road.

PORT GLASGOW

A branch of the League has been formed in Port Glasgow. All interested are asked to write to the Secretary, Frank Brady, 11, Glenburn Street, Port Glasgow, Renfrewshire.

EDINBURGH

A Branch of the League is now being formed in Edinburgh.　All interested are asked to write to Mr. O'Rorke, 47, Balgreen Road, Edinburgh.

MISCELLANEOUS

TYPEWRITING

NEW WITNESS

The Distributist League

Critics say—

An Essay on the Restoration of Property. *By Hilaire Belloc.*

The Distributist League. 1s. net.

"I much hope that this little volume, which is equally full of common-sense and good English, will be widely read and have its effect."

E. S. P. HAYNES IN G.K.'S WEEKLY.

"This is a deeply pessimistic little book. It sounds the knell of property, and shows how its evanescence is almost inevitable. There is little of the tactful, bedside manner of a fashionable and popular physician about its author. May we not, therefore, fasten on to his faint, meagre, cautious words of hope all the more confidently?"

**ANTHONY M. LUDOVICI
in the New English Weekly.**

"The merit of this book lies in its calm lucidity and its positive attitude against acquiescence in monopolies."

Current Literature.

"... sets forth with the precision of a mathematical statement the possibilities of restoring property in England... Hundreds have taken up the battle cry, since the days when Mr. Belloc first uttered it and defended it with his own arguments in the *Eye-Witness*. But it is he who has provided the original thought and inevitable logic. A shilling does not seem a large sum to pay for this vital and creative product of a master mind."

The Universe.

"Mr. Belloc's *Essay on the Restoration of Property* shares with Herr Gurian's book [*The Future of Bolshevism*, published by Messrs. Sheed and Ward] the great merit of focusing the attention of the reader on the social philosophy which lies behind the social order... Mr. Belloc certainly cannot be accused of optimism in his view of the possibility of the restoration of property; in fact, his chapter on taxation and his contemptuous remarks about parliamentary government make one wonder whether he really believes it can ever come about at all. But in matters like this it is certainly unwise to belittle the difficulties which lie in the path of any root and branch change for the better."

**LEWIS WATT, S.J.,
in the Clergy Review.**

WHAT DISTRIBUTISM MEANS
By J. DESMOND GLEESON
2d. net.

In this pamphlet Mr. Gleeson sums up the circumstances that made necessary the Distributist campaign for the restoration of liberty by the encouragement of small ownership and the defence of the family. If you are a member of the League already, give copies to your friends and thus persuade them to become members. If you are not a member, "What Distributism Means" will make you one.

THE DISTRIBUTIST PROGRAMME
1s. net.

A statement of practical policies by the introduction of which large scale capitalism and its twin brother Communism could be replaced by a Distributist State.

Order "What Distributism Means" and "The Distributist Programme" from The Distributist League, 7/8, Rolls Passage, London, E.C.4.

The Agricultural Problem
By F. N. BLUNDELL

As a practical farmer, a County Councillor and member of a Small Holdings Committee, formerly in Parliament, a member of important Commissions, and vice-chairman of the Liverpool Catholic Land Association, Mr. Blundell has been able to write with unique authority on all aspects of Agricultural organisation, and his views will be studied with interest by all Distributists. He writes from the Conservative rather than the Distributist standpoint; he "favours evolutionary rather than revolutionary methods"; but Distributists will find more to agree with than to dispute in his book. The book includes a brief outline of some salient points in the history of Agriculture; a detailed study of post-war legislation and its effect; and some interesting deductions and a hint of the future.

"The Agricultural Problem" was published by Messrs. Sheed and Ward. We are in a position now to offer copies at a special price.

Cr. 8vo., 90 pp. Price 6d.; 8d. post free.

**THE DISTRIBUTIST LEAGUE,
7/8, Rolls Passage, London, E.C.4.**

**THE SCOTTISH DISTRIBUTIST LEAGUE,
50, St. George's Road, Charing Cross, Glasgow**

Published by the Proprietors, G.K.'s WEEKLY, LTD., 7/8, Rolls Passage, London, E.C.4 (incorporating THE NEW WITNESS). Telephone: Holborn 8538. Printed by THE NUNEATON NEWSPAPERS, LTD., Bond Gate, Nuneaton. Sole Agents for Australasia: Gordon & Gotch (Australasia, Ltd.). Sole Agents for South Africa: Central News Agency, Ltd. (London Agency: Gordon & Gotch, Ltd.).

INDEX

Index

A

Aberhart, William, 514
Abyssinia, 193
Abyssinian War, 481, 482, 492, 524
Accion Popular, 416
Acharya, Mr., 444ᐧ
Acland, B. D., 129
Acrostics, 25
Acworth, Capt. Bernard, 411, 426
Adam and Eve, 58-60
Adams, Bridges, 145
Addison, Christopher, 385
Addison, Joseph, 373
Administrative law, 307-8
Advertising, 85-86, 147
Aeroplanes, 390-91, 411-412, 482, 516
Agricultural Marketing Act, 385
Agriculture, 120, 129, 155, 174, 185, 241, 276, 304, 434-35, 460-62
Air Force, 411. *See also* Aeroplanes
Aitkin, Max, 306
Alberta, Canada, 514
Alcala-Zamora, Don, 370
Allen, Arabella, 321
Allenby, Gen. Edmund, 420
America, 143, 164, 192, 203, 209, 248-49, 277, 284, 341, 351-53, 433, 480-81, 514, 515, 534-35
Americanism, 98
Amery, L. S., 31, 322
Amos, Sir Maurice, 496
Anderson, Floyd, 435-36
Annuities, 348-49
Anschluss, 307
Antarctica, 50, 272
Anti-clericalism, 54
Anti-Semitism, 13. *See also* Jews; Semitism
Anti-Socialism, 98
Anti-Vice Society, 167
Aquinas, Thomas, 7
Architecture, 470-71
Arianism, 211
Aristocracy, 21, 448
Arles, Council of, 192
Arnold, Matthew, 143, 389
Ashfield, Lord, 224, 231, 420
Ashley, Kenneth H., 131
Ashley, Oliver, 134
Askwith, Lady, 167
Asquith, Mr., 150, 432
Astor, Lady Waldorf, 273
Atheism, 386, 387, 416
Atta, Sir Ofori, 240
Aubry, Octave, 376
Augold, Mr., 492
Aumonier, Stacey, 531
Auriol, M., 535
Austin, Alfred, 390
Austin, Sir Herbert, 384-85
Australia, 78, 97, 324, 423-24
Austria, 367, 401-2, 405, 407

Austro-Hungarian politic-economic association, 401
Autobiography (Chesterton), 6, 8
Automobiles, 2, 147. *See also*
Pedestrians; Roads and highways

B

Babbinotti, Signor, 61
Babilon, Lucent, 226
Bacon, Francis, 377
Bacon, Roger, 420
Bagshot, Walter, 274
Baines, C. E., 348, 457
Balderdash, 311
Baldwin, Harold, 23, 144, 150, 163, 164, 202, 208, 212, 215, 217, 262, 291, 305, 322, 336, 368, 401, 413, 496, 534
Balfour, Lord Arthur, 73, 150, 170
Ballad of the White Horse, 7
Bancroft, Sir Squire, 31
Bank Holidays, 100
Banking, 351-53, 396, 492, 497-98, 514-15, 535-36
Bank of England, 322, 451
Baptism, 123
Baring, Maurice, 13, 31, 128
Barker, Sir Herbert, 124
Barnes, Bishop William, 155, 476
Barrie, J. M., 390-91, 419
Bartex, 337
Bartlett, Vernon, 272
Bassols, Narciso, 435
Bastille, storming of, 21
Bates, G. H., 132
Baty, T., 193
Baylis, Lilian, 145
B.B.C., 64, 272, 275, 322
Beatty, David, 420
Beaverbrook, Lord, 31, 210, 288, 399-400, 524
Bedaux system, 370-71
Beecham, Sir Thomas, 419
Beerbohm, Max, 31
Beevers, John L., 316
Begehot, Walter, 288
Belgium, 23, 271
Belloc, Hilaire, 9-10, 13, 29-30, 55-56, 77, 79-80, 99, 112, 179, 211, 248-49, 284, 306, 323-24, 332, 337-39, 355-56, 380-81, 385-86, 396, 456, 491, 492, 508, 512, 516, 523, 528-29, 533-34
Benbow, William, 451
Benes, President Edvard, 514
Benevideo, 347-48
Bennet, Henry, 377
Bennett, Arnold, 100, 132
Benson, E. C., 349
Benson, Sir Frank, 145
Bentham, Jeremy, 26
Bentley, E. C., 527
Benvenisti, J. L., 535-36

Bergerac, Cyrano, 54
Berkeley, 420
Besant, Annie, 386-87
Bessarabia, 50
Bethwin, John, 364
Bettany, Mr., 28
Betting clubs, 370
Bibilon, Lucent, 226
Biddulph, Geoffrey, 193
Big Business, 22, 23, 150, 415-16, 448
Bilke, 126
Binks, A., 146
Birrell, Augustine, 99
Birth control, 2, 51-52, 97, 122, 124, 316, 325, 386, 387, 406-7, 449
Birth rate, 343-44, 368
Bismarck, 437
Blacam, Hugh de, 474-75
Blackfriars journal, 15
Black, Joseph, 178
Blake, William, 101
Bland-Sutton, 420
Blavatsky, Madame, 386
Bliss, William, 284
Blomfield, S. Reginald, 290
Bloomsbury Group, 3
Blount, Wilfred Seawen, 491
Blücher, Gebhard, 26
Blum, M., 515, 534-35
Blundell, F. N., 174, 358-59
Blunt, Wilfrid Scawen, 193
Blyton, W. J., 459-60
Boak, John, 396
Boer War, 215, 255
Bogue, K., 409-10
Bolshevism, 13, 21-22, 23, 32, 49-50, 53, 144, 146, 172, 208, 223, 293, 405, 412, 421-22, 448, 514, 524
Bonacina, Conrad, 411-12
Bonus Act, 480-81, 497
Book of Common Prayer, 2
Book reviews, 38-39, 41, 43, 66-68, 90-93, 114-16, 137-41, 158-62, 180-81, 196-98, 200, 206, 213, 221, 232-33, 246, 264-65, 280-81, 296-97, 313-14, 328-30, 344-46, 361-63, 375-77, 391-94, 410, 424-27, 441-43, 491, 503-6, 520-22, 538-40
Borah, Senator William Edgar, 164, 192, 535
Boswell, James, 404
Bosworth Guild, 434-35
Bourchier, Arthur, 165
Bowden, Mr., 349
Boyd, Archie, 438-39
Boyd, Ian, 9, 10
Boyle, A., 444
Bradley, Dennis, 74, 123
Braintree, John, 134-35, 204
Brass, Sir Henry, 228
Brémond, Abbé, 240
Brémond, M. Henri, 240
Brenner Guard, 193

Index

Man Who Was Thursday, 7

Index

DEMCO